ATHLETICS ANNUAL 1985

PETER MATTHEWS

ASSOCIATION OF TRACK & FIELD STATISTICIANS

Current World Lists
Current World Junior Lists
World All-time Lists
World and Continental Records
Top Athletes' Profiles
National Champions 1984
Review of Athletics Year
Major Events of 1985

Published by Sports World Publications Ltd, a division of London & International Publishers Ltd.

Copyright for all statistical material: Association of Track and Field Statisticians.
Copyright for all other material: London & International Publishers Ltd.
All rights reserved. No part of this publication may be reproduced or transmitted in any form or by any means, including photocopying and recording, without the written permission of the publishers. Such written permission must also be obtained before any part of the publication is stored in any retrieval sytem of any nature.

This publication incorporates the ATFS Annual.

Photographs provided by Mark Shearman.

Cover designed by Martin Bronkhorst.

Typeset by J. C. Tomlinson, Cambridge in association with Goodfellow & Egan, Cambridge.

Printed by William Clowes Ltd., Beccles, Suffolk.

ISBN 0 948208 023 (Paperback)

CONTENTS

Forward
List of ATFS Members 7
Introduction 10
Metric/Imperial Conversion Tables 11
Notes from the Editor 12

Review of 1984 17
  Athlete of the Year: Carl Lewis 17
  Athletes of 1984 17
  Junior Athletes of 1984:
Danny Harris and Zola Budd 38
  Diary of the Year 41
  Olympic Games: Review and leading Results 53
  Other Major Meetings 60
  European Indoor Championships 61
  Cross Country – National Champions 1984 63
  Balkan Games 64
  Eight Nations Meeting 64
  Obituaries 66

1985 Preview – Review of Major Meetings 71
  IAAF/Mobil Grand Prix 71
  IAAF World Race Walking Cup 74
  European Cup Competitions 74

Other Major Championships 1986–90 76

Special Features 77
  Alberto Juantorena 77
  800 Metres Review 78
  The Olympians 79
  Olympic Track and Field Events 83

Wallis and the Javelin 85
Modern Marathon Trends 87
C. B. Fry 88
What is Tactical Running? 90
Jim Thorpe at the 1912 Olympics 91

Corrections to the 1984 Annual 95

National Championships and Biographies 98

Introduction to World Lists and Index 164

World and Continental Records 169

Men's Lists 182
  All-time World Lists 182
  1984 World Lists 221
  Junior All-time Lists 310
  1984 World Junior Lists 322

Women's Lists 333
  All-time World Lists 333
  1984 World Lists 361
  Junior All-time Lists 431
  1984 World Junior Lists 439

International Marathon Winners 1984 446

Men's Index 453
Women's Index 499

Early 1985 Results 531
World Indoor Games 1985 534

International Amateur Athletic Federation
(Fédération Internationale d'Athlétisme Amateur)

3 Hans Crescent, Knightsbridge
London SW1X 0LN, England

Telephone: 01 (London) 581 8771/2/3/4
Telex: .... 296859 IAAF HQ
Cables: .... Marathon, London S.W.1

1985-6 PUBLICATIONS AVAILABLE

I.A.A.F. Handbook 1985/6 (English)	£3.00
I.A.A.F. Handbook 1985/6 (French)	£3.00
I.A.A.F. Bulletin (4 times per Year) English/French. Surface Mail	£4.00
World Cup Reports — 1981 or 1979	£1.00
I.A.A.F. World Record List (with yearly supplements)	£1.50
I.A.A.F./ATFS Statistics Almanac	£6.00
I.A.A.F. Directory of Addresses	£1.50
I.A.A.F. Scoring Tables (1985 Edition)	£2.00
I.A.A.F. 70 Golden Years Book	£12.50
I.A.A.F. World Championships Report	£20.00

Development Programme Publications

Book 1 — A Basic Coaching Manual (English)	£2.50
Book 2 — Athletes Officiating (English/French)	£2.00
Book 3 — Running (English)	£2.00
Book 4 — Guidelines for the Conduct of Road Racing	£2.00

Coaching Posters — with explanatory leaflet in English/French
General or Specific Warm Up Programme £2.00 each
Sprint Start, Sprint Run, Long Distance, Long Jump,
High Jump, Javelin, Discus, Pole Vault,
Hammer Throw, Shot Put (Orthodox Technique)
100m Hurdles, Shot Put (Rotational Technique) £1.50 each

Track Designs

13b Athletic Arena — Standard Layout	£1.75
15b Track Markings and Staggered Starts	£1.75
23b Steeplechase Courses, 1500, 2000, 3000	£1.75
25 Field Events Constructional Details	£1.75
International Colour Markings for 400m All Weather Athletic Tracks	£2.00

Please add 40p per item for 2nd class Surface Mail
Air Mail rates available upon request

When ordering please send payment with order, either by — Cheque drawn on a Bank in the UNITED KINGDOM by INTERNATIONAL MONEY ORDER or by POSTAL ORDER.

FOREWORD

The 1985 A.T.F.S. Annual is greatly enhanced compared with previous editions, as a result of the inclusion of a new section covering records, championship results and biographical details for all major countries. For this change we have to thank our new colleagues, London & International Publishers, and in particular Klaus Boehm and Shaie Selzer, whose foresight and enthusiasm have been chiefly instrumental in enabling us to produce this mass of extra material.

The Annual has been published privately for the last 6 years, thanks to the personal efforts of our Treasurer, Palle Lassen. The book has grown steadily in size from his initial offering of 190 pages in 1979 to the 1984 edition of amost 400 pages. All those interested in extensive statistical documentation of our ever more complex sport are deeply indebted to Palle for his years of labour on this task, and also to our chief compilers – Nejat Kok, Jan Popper, Richard Hymans, Pino Mappa, Roberto Quercetani and many others who have helped in these enterprises. For the new edition, we were fortunate in that Peter Matthews became available to act as General Editor and to compile the bulk of the new sections.

In returning to the embraces of a commercial publisher, we are naturally hopeful that we shall be able to benefit from the opportunities for sponsorship now arising through the increasing world-wide interest in athletics. Perhaps more importantly, we are always eager to extend the distribution of our work to the widest possible readership, an aim made more possible with our new partnership.

We are delighted that co-operation with the I.A.A.F. continues at a high level. The I.A.A.F./A.T.F.S. Statistics Handbook, published in time for the Olympic Games, was another significant landmark in these ventures. We should also congratulate Nejat Kok and Rich Perelman for their notable contributions to the media information systems established in Los Angeles.

Mention of the Olympic Games, however, brings to mind the sad intrusion of politics once more, with a major boycott being staged for the third successive occasion. We can only sympathise with all those who were prevented from competing in the Games, and conjecture what further marvellous results might have been recorded there had the politicians left sport to conduct its own affairs in peace.

Bob Sparks

Alberto Juantorena, double Olympic champion in 1976, who announced his retirement in 1984.

ATFS/ASSOCIATION OF TRACK & FIELD STATISTICIANS

HONORARY MEMBERS
J.B. Holt (U.K.)
N.D. McWhirter (U.K.)
L. Mengoni (ITA)
S.L. Nilsson (SWE)
F. Regli (SUI)
F. Steinmetz (GFR)
B.J. Weckman (FIN)

EXECUTIVE COMMITTEE (1984–88)
President: R. Sparks (UK)
General Secretary:
  A. Huxtable (UK)
Treasurer: P. Lassen (DEN)

OTHER MEMBERS OF THE EXECUTIVE COMMITTEE
R.G. Ashenheim (JAM)
S.S. Davis (USA)
R. Hymans (UK)
N. Kök (TUR)
R. Magnusson (SWE)
V.A. Otkalenko (USSR)
Y. Pinaud (FRA)
J. Popper (CS)
D.H. Potts (USA)
R.L. Quercetani (ITA)
H. Vogel (GFR)

MEMBERS (1st February 1985)

Argentina
Gerardo Bönnhoff
Luis R. Vinker

Australia
Bernie Cecins
Paul Jenes
Fletcher McEwen
Michael J. McLaughlin
Ian R. Smith

Austria
Erich Kamper

Belgium
Willy Bouvier
André de Hooghe
Bienvenu Lams

Bolivia
Juan Coronel Quitoga

Brazil
José C. Gonçalves

British Virgin Is
Reynold O'Neal

Bulgaria
Grigor Christov
Georgi Kaburov

Canada
Doug Clement
Paul F. Houde
Dave Lach
Tom MacWilliam
Ted Radcliffe
Cecil Smith

Chile
J. Francisco Baraona Urzúa

Colombia
Jaime Ortiz Alvear

Cuba
Prof Jesus Argüelles
Basilio Fuentes

Cyprus
Antonios Dracos

Czechoslovakia
Svatopluk Dubský
Luděk Follprecht
Jiří Havlín
Jiri Hetfleiš
Milan Hlaváček
Stanislav Hrnčíř
Zdeněk Jebavý
Alfons Juck
Zdeněk Kašlík
Václav Klvaňa
Ceněk Kohlmann
Ladislav Krnáč
Otto Kudelka
Karel Míšek
Miroslav Ondruška
Jan Popper
Milan Skočovský
Milan Urban
Vladimír Višek
Josef Zdychynec

Denmark
Hans A. Larsen
Palle Lassen
Valborg Lassen
Emanuel Rose

Dominican Republic
Dante Toribio

Ecuador
Ramiro Almeida Rothenbach

Finland
Kaj Böstrom
Matti Hannus
Juhani Jalava
Esa Laitinen
Torsten Lindqvist
Kauko Niemelä
Björn-Johan Weckman

France
Alain Bouillé
Jacques Carmelli
J.L. Absin de Cassière
Jean Gilbert-Touzeau
Guy Kerfant
Michel Nazé
Robert Parienté
Jean Claude Patinaud
Yves Pinaud
Daniel Urien

German Dem. Rep
Werner Gessner
Dieter Huhn
Werner Kurtze

Federal Rep. Germany
Walter Abmayr
Klaus Amrhein
Max Heilrath
Raymund Herdt
Winifred Kramer
Rolf von der Laage
Ekkehard zur Megede
Fritz Steinmetz
Otto Verhoeven
Heinz Vogel

Gibraltar
Mark Sanchez

Greece
Angelos Cocconis
G. Constantopoulos
John A. Kyriacos
Leandros J. Slavis

Hong Kong
Ian Buchanan

Hungary
Andrew Kahlich
Jozsef von Képessy
György Lévai
Zoltán Subert
Gabriel Szabo
Dr István Zahumenszky

Iceland
Örn Eidsson
Brynjolfur Ingólfsson

India
Ranjit Bhatia
Ramesh G. Kharkar

R. Murali Krishnan
Norris Pritam Marquis
Jal D. Pardivala
Lokesh Sharma

Iran

Fred Sahebjam

Ireland

Fionnbar Callanan
Liam Hennessy
John Murray
Tony O'Donoghue

Israel

Elchanan Bar-Lev
Arieh Cooks
David Eiger
Uri Goldbourt

Italy

Ottavio Castellini
Gastone Dannecker
Gianni Galeotti
Silvio Garavaglia
Vincenzo Guglielmelli
Raul Leoni
Giorgio Malisani
Gabriele Manfredini
Giuseppe Mappa
Salvatore Massara
Luigi Mengoni
Pino Montagna
Dr Roberto L. Quercetani
Carlo Santi
Raffaele Tummolo

Jamaica

Richard G. Ashenheim

Japan

Atsushi Hoshino
Wakaki Maeda

Luxembourg

Gérard Rasquin

Malaysia

Balwant Singh Kler

Gurbaksh Singh Kler
Loong Teck Chew

Mexico

Jorge Molina Celis

Netherlands

Jacobus Koumans
Nic Lemmens

New Zealand

Barry S. Hunt

Nicaragua

Istvan Hidvegi

Norway

Hans T. Halvorsen
Tore Johansen
Jan-Jørgen Moe
Ingmund Ofstad
Einar Otto Øren
Ole Petter Sandvig
Bernt A. Solaas
Magne Teigen

Panama

Luis Rossi

Philippines

Col Romulo A Constantino
Sy Yinchow

Poland

Zbigniew Dobrowolny
Wojciech Gaczkowski
Zygmunt Guszek
Daniel Grinberg
Zbigniew Ojewski
Stefan J.K. Pietkiewicz
Jozsef Pliszkiewicz
Lesaw Skinder
Edward Szatkowski
Jerzy Szymonek
Tadeusz Woejko

Portugal

Luis O.H. Lopes

Puerto Rico

Fernando Rodil-Vivas

Romania

Adrian Ionescu
Nicolae Marasescu
Romeo Vilara
Tudor Vornicu

R.S.A.

Harry N. Beinart
André Brink
Riël Hauman
Arrie A. Joubert
Harry Lombaard
Quintus van Rooyen
Gert J.J. le Roux
Joe Stutzen

Spain

José Corominas
Pedro Escamilla
José Maria Garcia

Sweden

Owe Froberg
A. Lennart Julin
Ove Karlsson
Rooney Magnusson
Stig L. Nilsson
Reino Sepp
Nils Tangen
Ture Widlund

Switzerland

Alberto Bordoli
Antonin Heyda
Gabor Kobzos
Fulvio Regli

Syria

Fouad Habash

Taiwan

Liao Han-shui

Trinidad & Tobago

Bernard Linley

Jed Brickner
Frank Candida
Pete Cava
Scott S. Davis
Wally Donovan
James O. Dunaway
Tom Feuer
Edward C. Gordon
Bob Hersh
Garry Hill
David Johnson

Michael Kennedy
Frank Litsky
Steve McPeek
Bill Mallon
Dr. David E. Martin
Alan Mazursky
Walt Murphy
Albert D. Nelson
Cordner B. Nelson
Rich Perelman
Martin A. Post

Dr. Donald H. Potts
Dr. J. Gerry Purdy
S.F. Vince Reel
Mike Renfro
Stan Saplin
J. Larry Story
Carol R. Swenson
Michael Takaha
Bruce Tenen
H.D. Thoreau
Howard Willman

Frank Zarnowski

Yugoslavia

Olga Acić
Mladen Delić
Ozren Karamata

Zambia

Matthew Mulwanda

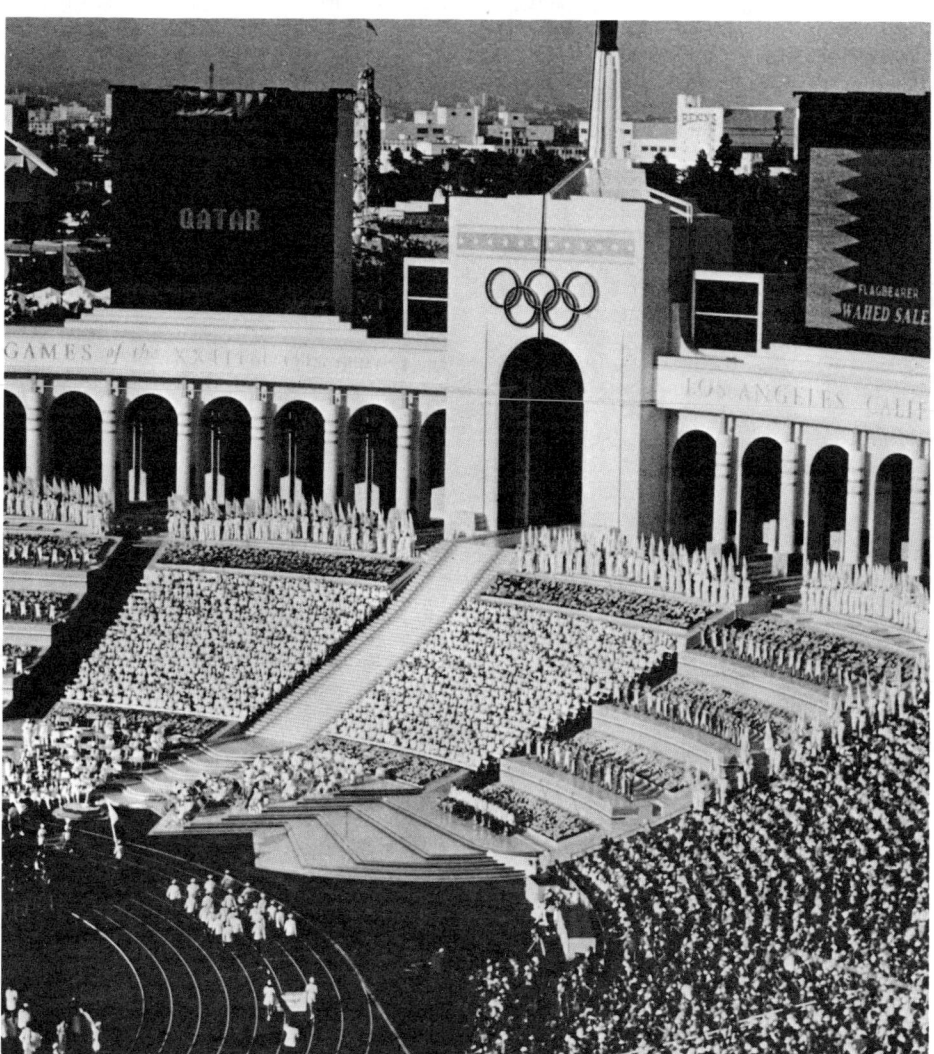

The opening ceremony of the 1984 Olympic Games in Los Angeles.

9

INTRODUCTION

The first annual compiled by the Association of Track and Field Statisticians (ATFS) was published in Switzerland in 1951. It was a slim, pocket-sized booklet of 126 pages covering the 1950 season and the general editors were Roberto Quercetani and Fulvio Regli, who had previously compiled and published the 50 best European Track and Field Performances of 1949. In association with Don Potts, Roberto Quercetani had also produced *A Handbook on Olympic Games Track and Field Athletics* in 1948, which contained deep all-time lists, world lists for 1947 and lists of Olympic medallists.

The world of athletics and the work of the ATFS has advanced considerably since those days. The Potts and Quercetani world lists for 1950 published in that first annual included 25 performers per event. 100 deep has been the norm for many years, and indeed in this book we publish full details for the top 100 and go on to much deeper levels in summarised form. The standards have of course improved enormously, so that many of the world's best performances in 1950 do not approach the level needed to make the best 200 in the world today. The table below shows the world best and 25th best for 1950.

As can be seen from the membership list, the ATFS is a truly international body. Its members supply details about athletics from all parts of the world, so that the lists included in this book are compiled to the highest standards of accuracy and completeness.

That first ATFS Annual did not contain women's lists and indeed women's participation in athletics was then far from widespread. Nor did it contain junior lists or all-time lists, all of which are regular features now and are included in this book. However it did contain national records and results of national championships, subjects which have not been included in ATFS Annuals in recent years.

This year the ATFS Annual is published for the first time by London & International Publishers, under their Sportsworld imprint. We have taken the extensive lists compiled by the ATFS and have added feature material, a review of 1984, a preview of 1985 and an extensive biographical section so as to make this the definitive annual for our great sport. We have reintroduced lists of national champions for leading countries and hope in future years to expand this section further. We will welcome contributions from ATFS members and others around the world so as to further extend the authoritative coverage that we give to international athletics.

Any suggestions or comments on this book which can be helpful for our plans for future editions would be gratefully received. Amendments or additions to the lists would also be welcomed. Please send these to me or to the ATFS compilers.

Peter Matthews, 6 Broadfields, Goffs Oak, Waltham Cross, Herts EN7 5JU, England.

WORLD MEN'S BEST PERFORMANCES 1950

		BEST	25th BEST
100m	10.1	Lloyd La Beach (Panama)	10.6
200m	20.7	Lloyd La Beach (Panama)	21.5
400m	45.8	George Rhoden (Jamaica)	47.6
800m	1:48.5*	Malvin Whitfield (USA)	1:51.4
1500m	3:46.6	Gaston Reiff (Belgium)	3:52.2
1 mile	4:06.2	Gaston Reiff (Belgium)	4:12.2
5000m	14:03.0	Emil Zatopek (Czechoslovakia)	14:35.6
10000m	29:02.6	Emil Zatopek (Czechoslovakia)	30:58.0
110mh	13.5	Richard Attlesey (USA)	14.5
400mh	51.5	Charles Moore (USA)	54.0
3000mSt	9:00.0	Curt Söderberg (Sweden)	—
High jump	2.05	Robert Walters (USA)	1.97
Pole vault	4.56	Robert Richards (USA)	4.21
Long jump	7.85	James Holland (USA)	7.37
Triple jump	16.00	Adhemar Ferreira da Silva (Brazil)	14.76
Shot	17.95	James Fuchs (USA)	15.66
Discus	55.47	Adolfo Consolini (Italy)	49.18
Hammer	59.88	Imre Nemeth (Hungary)	53.56
Javelin	73.93	Ragnar Ericzon (Sweden)	67.56

Zatopek's times may look ordinary now, but they were extraordinary then, for the second best man at 5000m ran 14:20.2 and at 10000m 30:07.0.

METRIC – IMPERIAL CONVERSION TABLES

Throughout this book measurements are given in the metric system. For those readers who are more familiar with imperial units we give a basic conversion table which specifically covers those distances achieved by top class athletes in the field events. This will be hope provide a useful cross check for those wishing to convert.

1.70m. – 5ft 7in	5.60m. – 18ft 4½in	17.50m. – 57ft 5in	66.00m. – 216ft 6in
1.75m. – 5ft 8¾in	5.80m. – 18ft 0¼in	18.00m. – 59ft 0¾in	68.00m. – 223ft 1in
1.80m. – 5ft 10¾in	6.00m. – 19ft 8¼in	18.50m. – 60ft 8½in	70.00m. – 229ft 8in
1.85m. – 6ft 0¾in	6.25m. – 20ft 6¼in	19.00m. – 62ft 4in	72.00m. – 236ft 3in
1.90m. – 6ft 2¾in	6.50m. – 21ft 4in	19.50m. – 63ft 11¾in	74.00m. – 242ft 9in
1.95m. – 6ft 4¾in	6.75m. – 22ft 1¾in	20.00m. – 65ft 7½in	76.00m. – 249ft 4in
2.00m. – 6ft 6¾in	7.00m. – 22ft 11¾in	20.50m. – 67ft 3¼in	78.00m. – 255ft 11in
2.05m. – 6ft 8¾in	7.25m. – 23ft 9½in	21.00m. – 68ft 10¾in	80.00m. – 262ft 5in
2.10m. – 6ft 10¾in	7.50m. – 24ft 7¼in	21.50m. – 70ft 6½in	82.00m. – 269ft 0in
2.15m. – 7ft 0½in	7.75m. – 25ft 5¼	22.00m. – 72ft 2¼in	84.00m. – 275ft 7in
2.20m. – 7ft 2½in	8.00m. – 26ft 3in	22.50m. – 73ft 10in	86.00m. – 282ft 2in
2.25m. – 7ft 4½in	8.25m. – 27ft 0¾in	23.00m. – 75ft 5½in	88.00m. – 288ft 8in
2.30m. – 7ft 6½in	8.50m. – 27ft 10¾in	50.00m. – 164ft 0in	90.00m. – 295ft 3in
2.35m. – 7ft 8½in	8.75m. – 28ft 8½in	52.00m. – 170ft 7in	92.00m. – 301ft 10in
2.40m. – 7ft 10½in	9.00m. – 29ft 6½in	54.00m. – 177ft 2in	94.00m. – 308ft 5in
4.60m. – 15ft 1in	15.00m. – 49ft 2½in	56.00m. – 183ft 9in	96.00m. – 314ft 11in
4.80m. – 15ft 9in	15.50m. – 50ft 10¼in	58.00m. – 190ft 3in	98.00m. – 321ft 6in
5.00m. – 16ft 4¾in	16.00m. – 52ft 6in	60.00m. – 196ft 10in	100.00m. – 328ft 1in
5.20m. – 17ft 0¾in	16.50m. – 54ft 1¾in	62.00m. – 203ft 5in	102.00m. – 334ft 8in
5.40m. – 17ft 8½in	17.00m. – 55ft 9¼in	64.00m. – 210ft 0in	104.00m. – 341ft 2in

In the biographies section athletes' weights are given in kilograms, the following guide will help those who are more familiar with weights in pounds:

50kg. – 110lbs.	80kg. – 176lbs.	110kg. – 243lbs.	130kg. – 287lbs.
60kg. – 132lbs.	90kg. – 198lbs.	120kg. – 265lbs.	140kg. – 309lbs.
70kg. – 154lbs.	100kg – 220lbs.		

The World cross-country championships 1984. Pat Porter (USA) leads from Steve Jones (Wales), Carlos Lopes (Portugal) and Tim Hutchings (England).

11

NOTES FROM THE EDITOR

The booming sport
There can be no question that athletics is at a peak of interest worldwide. Such interest, however, can exacerbate the sport's susceptibility to external pressures, given also that athletics is the most widespread of all sports and that the Olympic Games, the highest aspiration for all athletes, is the biggest international get-together of any human activity. No wonder then that, with the intense media spotlight on the Games, politicians have found it convenient to use athletes for political propaganda.

The World Championships in Helsinki in 1983 were an enormous success. Although the depth of competition was not as good, so too were the 1984 Olympic Games in Los Angeles. We missed the Eastern Bloc athletes, they too missed the opportunity to compete in this the ultimate athletics test, but the Games went on in marvellous weather, with fine organisation and produced much magnificent athletics.

Television brought the Olympics to millions around the world and popular support of athletics, intensified by the Games, is readily maintained by the profusion of international meetings, especially in Europe. Indeed such profusion may be a danger to the sport, if the top athletes are expected at each and every meeting. However the interest in the sport has fuelled considerable support from sponsors, from governments and from the public.

The best athletes can now earn substantial sums, and this has been a significant factor in more talented men and women remaining in competition. Particularly in the USA, many used to retire from the sport after finishing University, often before reaching their peak, in order to concentrate on pursuing careers. Now the rewards that can be earned from their sporting success can be enough for them to at least delay a move in other directions. Of course athletes from the Eastern bloc are not rewarded in the same way, but they are given every encouragement to achieve success.

In 1985 the European circuit meetings, as well as other leading events from around the world, are being brought together into the IAAF/Mobil Grand Prix. This will provide some extra purpose to these fixtures, although no doubt world record attempts will continue to be the means by which promoters will attract public interest.

With such rapid evolution, there will need to be sure handling of events by the sport's governing bodies. They must ensure that they balance commercialism and the needs of athletes at all levels. So far, however, the moves by the IAAF to initiate new competitions, such as the Grand Prix and World Championships, indoors and out and for juniors, and to find ways of bringing money into the sport and to the benefit of athletes, have been far-seeing and highly progressive.

Amateurs and professionals
While much has been done to recognise the changing conditions of modern sport and to keep athletics in tune with commercial realities, there remain many problem areas in determining where to draw the line. Disadvantaged, for instance, have been those American athletes who became fully acknowledged professional sportsmen. Some of the athletes who joined the International Track Association (ITA) in the early 1970s have been partially readmitted to track and field competition, but Brian Oldfield, who achieved the most notable success in the ITA ranks and who set a US shot record in 1984, was not permitted to compete in the US Olympic Trials and thus return to the Olympic arena. He lost a lawsuit against the IOC, TAC and IAAF in April 1984 and his petition to compete in the Trials was turned down by a federal judge on the day before the competition.

Renaldo Nehemiah and Willie Gault as pro footballers have also been denied the opportunity to return to 'amateur' athletics and compete against the highly paid stars who have not gone 'professional' in name.

Drugs and Doping
The greatest menace to our sport is that posed by the usage of drugs and by such unnatural practices as "blood boosting". There has however been some progress during the past year towards more widespread drug testing. All major international championships must have drug-testing procedures and since December 1983, the IAAF have required that all world record claims must be accompanied by a certificate of testing. At long last some positive progress has been made in the USA, with testing introduced at a number of meetings and by the NCAA, as well, of course, as at the US Olympic Trials and at the Games themselves.

Nonetheless equivocal attitudes persist far too widely. Too often the cry goes up of "how can we compete unless we take them too". I also feel that the practice by several nations of having advisory testing at trials meetings, to warn and screen out those who have been caught, but not penalise them, is a further sign of weakness.

The IAAF, at its Congress in Canberra, announced the names of six athletes who were to be suspended: Tatyana Kazankina (USSR), who refused to take a test in Paris; Anna Verouli (Gre), Martti Vainio (Fin), Cleanthos Ierissiotis and Dimitris Delifolis (Gre) found to have taking illegal substances at the Olympic Games, and Al Schotermann (USA) from the US Olympic Trials. It was subsequently revealed that Vainio had also failed an earlier test at the Rotterdam Marathon in April. The admittance of "blood boosting' by members of the US cycling team at the Olympics was a reminder that this practice, too, which may not be detectable, is also cheating and is another threat.

The practice of reinstating after 18 months, athletes who have been banned for life can be deplored, but then can we really insist on a hard line if we know that those detected are only the tip of the iceberg. Random testing of athletes at any time may be the answer, but this may be very difficult to police adequately or sufficiently comprehensively throughout the world.

The President of the European AA, Sir Arthur Gold, has been a prominent crusader in the battle against drugs. It is to be hoped that his fight will be fully supported so that success at athletics is not just a question of who's laboratories can best keep ahead of drug detection. Above all what is needed is a concerted effort to ensure that artificial stimuli are universally regarded as unethical and not to be tolerated within the sport.

Goodbye to great champions

Although athletes stay in the sport longer than they used, we have to reconcile ourselves to the departure from competon of great favourites at the end of every season. This year such athletes as Ulrike Meyfarth, Lucyna Kalek and Waldemar Cierpinski announced their retirements. Two particulary outstanding track champions of the 1976 Olympic Games have also had their last race in major competition. Alberto Juantorena is the subject of a profile by Bob Phillips elsewhere in this annual, and Don Quarrie has also called it a day.

Don Quarrie has amassed a tremendous haul of medals, yet none pleased him more than the silver medal he won in Los Angeles as a member of Jamaica's sprint relay team. A graduate of the

Don QUARRIE – born Kingston, Jamaica 25 Feb 1951
Progression and championship record

Year	100m	200m	Championship
1968	10.3	21.1*	
1969	10.4	21.1	
1970	10.3/10.24w	20.56/20.48w/20.4w	CG: 1st 100m, 200m & 4×100mR
1971	10.29/10.14w/10.1	19.86	PAm: 1st 100m, 200m & 4×100mR
1972	10.1/9.9w	20.43/20.3*	OG: sf 200m
1973	10.2/9.3y/9.1yw	20.1*	
1974	10.38/10.0	20.06/20.0*w	CG: 1st 100m & 200m, 4th 4×100mR
1975	10.16/10.0	20.12/19.8	
1976	10.07/9.9	20.23/19.8	OG: 1st 200m, 2nd 100m
1977	10.12	20.11/20.1	
1978	10.22/10.03w/10.2	20.35/20.2	CG: 1st 100m, sf 200m
1979	10.27/10.26w	20.50	
1980	10.29	20.29	OG: 3rd 200m, sf 100m
1981	10.42	20.47/20.42w	WCp: 4th 200m
1982	10.38	20.39	CG: sf 100m & 200m
1983	10.35	20.77/20.5w	
1984	10.40/10.31w	20.48/20.41w	OG: 2nd 4×100mR, sf 200m

Won AAU titles at 100m 1975 and 1977; at 200m 1971, 1974 and 1975
Won AAA titles at 100m 1976; at 200m 1976, 1978 and 1982
World records

University of Southern California, he now lives in Los Angeles and the staging of the Games in that city had provided the motivation that he needed to stay in training. He had won Olympic gold at 200m and silver at 100m in 1976 and completed his set with bronze at 200m in 1980. He was at his peak in the early to mid-seventies, but pulled a muscle in the 1972 Olympic 200m semi-finals. 1984 was thus the fourth Games at which he competed, although he was selected also for 1968, but then was unable to compete due to a muscle pull in training in Mexico City.

He first came to worldwide attention with a sprint treble, 100m, 200m and relay, at the 1970 Commonwealth Games in Edinburgh. With three more successes – at 100m and 200m in 1974 and at 100m in 1978 – he has a record number of Commonwealth gold medals by a man. He set four world records: at 100 metres, a 9.9 at Modesto in 1976, and at 200 metres, three times of 19.8. The first, also auto-timed at 19.86, was when he won the Pan-American title at the high altitude of Cali, Columbia in 1971. Then he twice ran 19.8 at Eugene in June 1975. The latter was when he won the third of his AAU 200m titles (he also won two at 100m), and in both those 1975 races he beat Steve Williams, whom he considered his greatest sprint rival.

His long career is unparalleled, being challenged only by Pietro Mennea among sprinters. He has been a superb runner, a great sportsman and a inspiration to his countrymen, his colleagues and to spectators around the world.

The super veterans

Particular pleasure has been given to athletics enthusiasts by those athletes who have remained in the sport for many years and by those who have come back to be able to compete at the highest level after years absent.

The oldest athletics competitor at the 1984 Olympic Games was Joyce Smith (UK), who at the age of 46 placed 11th in the women's maarthon in a world best time for her age group of 2:32:48. She first competed internationally at cross-country in 1957, a decade before the youngest 1984 Olympians were born. Although the era of women's long distance running has come very late in her career, she has nonetheless achieved considerable success since her marathon debut at the age of 41, including six British records. Her LA teammate Priscilla Welch only started running at the age of 34, but five years on set a world's veterans best of 2:28:54 for sixth in the Olympic marathon.

The US hammer thrower Ed Burke competed in the Olympic Games of 1964 and 1968, when he retired at the age of 28, holder of the US record at 71.92m. He returned in 1980 after twelve years out of competition and soon exceeded his previous best, as he reached 73.72m in 1982 and improved further to 74.10 in 1983. In 1984 at the age of 44 he improved yet again to 74.34m and achieved his ambition by qualifying for the Olympics, even if he then failed to make the finals.

Another man who had contested those 1964 and 1968 Games and of course those of 1956 and 1960 was the incomparable quadruple gold medallist, Al Oerter. Injury denied him the chance to have a shot at achieving the greatest return in the history of sport, but he was still able to throw with the best. He had a 1984 season's best of 63.92m and placed sixth in the US discus championships – not bad for a 47-year-old!

The greatest gathering of veterans in 1984 took place in the South of England, where two sites, Brighton and Crawley, were needed to accommodate the six-day European Veterans Championships. This catered for such youngsters as the women's 35–39 group right up to the over-85s, as more than 3000 athletes took part. Former internationals were matched against men and women who took up the sport later in life to provide a great experience for all concerned.

Women's Distance Running

There was continued progress in 1984 towards a full programme of women's distance running events being included in major meetings. The marathon was run by women for the first time in the Olympic Games, although legal efforts by the 'International Runners' Committee' to get the 5000m and 10000m added to the Los Angeles programme failed to get through US courts. The case was fought on the grounds of discrimination against women. The last minute addition of these distances may have been impractical in 1984, but the 10000m is to be run in the 1985 World Cup and in major championships thereafter, including Commonwealth and Olympic Games and the World Championships. As from 1985 the IAAF have added the 1000m, 2000m, 20km, 25km, 30km and 1 hour events to the list of events at which world records can be recognised, thus bringing women's running events into line with the men's. The 10000 metres walk has also been added to the programme of the 1987 World Championships.

It is salutary to reflect that the 1500m was first included in a major international championships as recently as 1969, the 3000m in 1974 and the marathon in 1982. Such has been the progress as prejudices against women running long distance have been exposed and swept away.

One Governing Body for UK Athletics

The plethora of administrative bodies of athletics in Britain must amaze outsiders. While recognising that the interests of athletes in the separate nations that constitute the United Kingdom need to be catered for, there has, for many years, been pressure within the sport to bring the various bodies together in a more coordinated manner. It was encouraging, therefore, to note that the largest of these bodies, the Amateur Athletic Association, catering for men's athletics in England and Wales, formally put in hand plans to work towards a unified body.

Sponsorship of British Athletics

The Amateur Athletic Association and the British Amateur Athletic Board appointed, in late 1984, Alan Pascoe Associates as agents to assemble a sponsorship package for British athletics. At the time of writing these notes the company, headed by the 1974 European and Commonwealth 400mh gold medallist, had already announced the details of sponsorship by three major companies – Pearl Assurance, Peugeot Talbot and Kodak. The latter was the biggest of all with a deal worth £2 million over five years and included the prestigious annual AAA Championships.

These major infusions of support into British athletics were preceded by news of the transfer of the contract for televising BAAB and AAA meetings from the BBC to Independant Television for the first time. The new TV contract, worth £10.5 million runs for five years from 1 April 1985. However other companies withdrew from sponsorship, including U-Bix Copiers and Coca-Cola Bottlers. The latter had supported each year since 1968 the meeting, staged by the International Athletes Club, which had become established as Britain's most popular meeting.

New Decathlon scoring tables

New scoring tables have been accepted by the IAAF for scoring multi-event competitions, especially the decathlon and heptathlon, for use from 1 April 1985. These update the previous tables, introduced in 1964 (men) and (1971) women. Rather confusingly the resulting points scores for world-class performances are similar to those on the old tables, and while some anomalies have been corrected, many statisticians are unhappy about many aspects of the new tables. Much rescoring of old competitions is now underway, but in this annual we show decathlon and heptathlon scores as calculated on the old tables, i.e. those that were in use up to 1984.

Under the new tables Daley Thompson replaces Jürgen Hingsen as decathlon world record holder with 8846 points to 8831.

New javelin from 1986?

The IAAF Congress in Los Angeles announced that the specification of the men's javelin would change in 1986. The weight would remain the same at 800 grams, but the regulations regarding centre of gravity would alter so as to change the flight characteristics of the javelin and considerably reduce the distances thrown.

The age of the 100-metre throw ushered in by Uwe Hohn means that there are problems in catering for the event within the restricted areas inside stadiums. However much concern has been expressed by leading javelin throwers about the change, which will dramatically alter the nature of the event. The fact that the javelin would not 'fly' as before would not only be less aesthetically satisfying, but would make the event much more a test of strength rather than skill, thus encouraging athletes to bulk, with the attendant drugs related possibliities.

New York Marathon

The possible rewards available for athletes continue to hit new peaks. The 1985 New York Marathon offers $1 million to any runner who breaks 2 hours 7 minutes. That rather unlikely occurence, taking 65 seconds off the record set by Steve Jones at Chicago in 1984, is being underwritten by Lloyd's of London.

In 1981 Alberto Salazar ran the world's fastest for a marathon with a time of 2:08:13. Grete Waitz set women's world bests at New York in 1978, 1979 and 1980. World marathon statistics have now been thrown into confusion with the news that the 1981 course has been accurately remeasured and found to be 170 yards (155m) short of the full marathon distance. That is equivalent to about 30 seconds at marathon running pace. At the time of writing it is uncertain whether the 1981 course was identical to that used in other years. The all-time lists and biographies in this book include New York times, but the position will have to be sorted out for future lists.

One must of course bear in mind that all road racing times should be assesssed with care as conditions of terrain and atmosphere can vary considerably.

Record IAAF membership
Bhutan, Cyprus and Monaco were accepted into membership of the IAAF in 1984. This brought the total membership to 173 federations, the highest for any sport, or indeed any international body. 116 of these nations were represented in track and field events at the 1984 Olympic Games, compared to 151 at the 1983 World Championships.

Suspended after failing drug test
Juan de la Cruz (Dom), 1983
Dimitrios Delifotis (Gre), 1984
Ronald Desruelles (Bel), 1980
Naser Fahemy (Irn), 1983
Knut Hjeltnes (Nor), 1977
Seppo Hovinen (Fin), 1977
Kleanthis Ierisotis (Gre), 1984
Dariusz Juzyszyn (Pol), 1983
Jerzy Kaduskiewicz (Pol), 1982
Lars-Erik Källström (Swe), 1983
Hans-Joachim Krug (FRG), 1978
Yevgeniy Mironov (SU), 1978
Hein-Direck Neu (FRG), 1978
Juan Núñez (Dom), 1983
Arne Pedersen (Nor), 1982
Asko Pesonen (Fin), 1977
Ben Plucknett (USA), 1981
Elisio Rios (Por), 1983
Walter Schmidt (FRG), 1977
Al Schoterman (USA), 1984
Vladimir Shaloshik (SU), 1974
László Szabó (Hun), 1981
Markku Tuokko (Fin), 1977
Martti Vainio (Fin), 1984

Velko Velev (Bul), 1975
Vasiliy Yershov (SU), 1978

(Women)
Nunu Abashidze (SU), 1981
Maria-Christina Betancourt (Cub) 1983
Ilona Briesenick – see Slupianek
Valentina Cioltan (Rum), 1975
Rosa Colarado (Spa), 1980
Rosa Fernández (Cub), 1983
Yekaterina Gordienko (SU), 1978
Linda Haglund (Swe), 1981
Ágnes Herczeg (Hun), 1983
Karoline Käfer (Aut), 1981
Yelena Kovalyova (SU), 1979
Nadya Kudryavtseva (SU), 1979
Evelyn Lendl (Aut), 1981
Natalia Maraşescu/Betini (Rum), 1979
Gael Mulhall/Martin (Aus), 1981
Alexis Paul MacDonald (Can), 1981
Totka Petrova (Bul), 1979
Danuta Rosani (Pol), 1976
Ileana Silai (Rum), 1979
Ilona Slupianek/Briesenik (GDR), 1977
Elena Stoyanova (Bul), 1978 & 1982
Daniela Teneva (Bul), 1979
Nadyezhda Tkachenko (SU), 1978
Vera Tsapkalenko (SU), 1977
Anna Verouli (Gre), 1984
Sanda Vlad (Rum), 1979
Joan Wenzel (Can), 1975
Anna Włodarczyk (Pol), 1982

Suspended for refusing drug test
Colin Sutherland (UK), 1978
Dave Voorhees (USA), 1978
Tatyana Kazankina (SU), 1984
Maria Lambrou (Gre/Cyp), 1982

Two British athletes, Jeff Teale (1974) and Barry Williams (1977), were suspended by the B.A.A.B. following newspaper allegations. Williams appealed against his suspension and, after investigations into the case, he was reinstated in April 1978.

WORLD ATHLETE OF 1984 – CARL LEWIS

TOM FEUER

'Preparation and competition.' Those were the primary elements which the world's greatest athlete, Carl Lewis, credits for contributing to his unparalleled successes in 1984. Four gold medals in the summer Olympic Games in Los Angeles, his third consecutive undefeated season in the long jump, three victories and three meet records at the U.S. Final Olympic Trials, undefeated campaigns at 100 and 200 meters, a world indoor long jump record, an Olympic record at 200 meters, and a world record in the 400 meter relay, these were the highlights of an incredible season. Yet Carl Lewis did fail in one respect. He set no new personal bests in 1984. But then again he had to save something for 1985 and beyond, when he will no doubt solidify his position as the greatest track and field athlete of all-time.

'I think the reason why 1984 was so successful was that I prepared individually for each meet as it appeared on the schedule instead of concentrating my whole season on just the Olympics. It really took the pressure off,' Lewis said. 'It also helped that I came into the season confident. I knew I had a lot of talent and I had no injuries holding me back. I was also better prepared in my own mind than anyone else because I believe I have the best coach in the world in Tom Tellez.'

Much of Lewis' confidence coming into 1984 was the result of a brilliant season in 1983. The highlight was reached in Helsinki, Finland where he won three gold medals in the inaugural World Athletics Championships, including a world record in the 400 meter relay. However, throughout 1983 Lewis made what previously appeared impossible commonplace. He captured the 100, 200 and long jump in the American championships in a span of two days, setting low altitude world bests in the latter two events. Earlier in the season he had already tagged the sea level best at the 100. Indoors he broke the 60 yard dash world best. '1983 may have been more spectacular,' Lewis said, 'but in 1984 I did more events and the quality of performance in each event was higher than in '83.' Nowhere was this more evident than in the long jump where he competed a total of eight times with his worst distance measuring 8.54, a mark that only three other athletes have ever achieved even once.

Three times in eight finals, all at low altitude, Lewis ran 9.99 for 100 meters. His slowest clocking all season was a 10.13. In four 200 meter finals, all again at sea level, Lewis broke 20 seconds twice and his slowest was a 20.21. He even broke 20 seconds (19.84) in a preliminary round of the U.S. Final Olympic Trials in a race that seemed more like a country stroll.

The reason why Lewis did not break any records in 1984, personal or otherwise, was more the result of bad luck rather than a deterioration of skills. For instance, he ran a pair of 200 meters into negative winds at the Final Olympic Trials (19.86) and the Olympic Games (19.80) that were without a doubt intrinsically superior to Pietro Mennea's world record set at altitude of 19.72. 'I have never had good timing when it comes to records,' Carl states. 'An example of everything going just right is Calvin's (Smith) 100 record. He had both a tailwind and altitude.' Lewis' lack of 'world' marks does not disturb him. 'I'm real patient and I think eventually my time will come.'

Why has Lewis remained on top of the dash heap longer than any American sprinter in history? 'I don't think athletes concentrate enough on the basics,' Carl said. 'In the sprints the keys are acceleration, relaxation, patience and not overcompeting.' It is the latter category that has proven to be the Achilles heel for most athletes, especially sprinters. Lewis avoids that pitfall by letting his personal manager Joe Douglas handle the off the track minutiae.

Douglas, the head coach of the Santa Monica Track Club, for whom Lewis competes, filters through the myriad requests from the media, meet promoters, and others. It was Douglas' idea to limit Lewis' appearances after he stopped competing for his Houston University team in 1981. Before Lewis broke precedent, it was fashionable for most American dashmen to compete from 40–60 times in a season, including relays. With such a gruelling schedule it wasn't a surprise that no American sprinter before Lewis could stay on top for more than a year or two at a time.

His infrequent competitive appearances mean that quality and not quantity is the Lewis trademark. He may not compete often but he always competes well. A classic example was the Millrose Indoor Games, in

Review of 1984

Kirk Baptiste smashes the world best for 300 metres, and the great Carl Lewis.

Review of 1984

Carl LEWIS in 1984

Date	Venue/meeting	Event	Place	Mark
Indoors				
16 Jan	Osaka	60m	2	6.69 (1. P. Narracott)
27 Jan	N.York – Millrose G	LJ	1	8.79 World best
4 Feb	Dallas	60y	1h	6.18
		60y	2	6.07 (1. R. Brown)
11 Feb	E. Rutherford	LJ	1	8.55
17 Feb	San Diego	50m	2	5.72 (1. R. Brown)
		60y	2	6.12 (1. R. Brown)
24 Feb	New York – TAC	LJ	1	8.50
Outdoors				
7 Apr	Tempe – Sun Angel	4×100mR	(2	38.98)
	for S. Monica TC	Sp. MedR	–	19.6 for 200m in (3:11.72)
29 Apr	Walnut – Mt SAC	100m	1	10.06
	for S. Monica TC	4×100mR	(2	39.25)
6 May	Houston	100m	1	9.99
	for S. Monica TC	4×400mR	–	46.4 in (3:04.41)
13 May	Los Angeles – Pepsi	LJ	1	8.71
26 May	San Jose – Jenner	100m	1	10.00w
		200m	1	20.01w
16 Jun	Los Angeles – O. Trials	100m	1h	10.29w
		100m	1qf	10.14
17 Jun		100m	1sf	10.15
		100m	1	10.06
18 Jun		LJ	q	8.39
19 Jun		LJ	1	8.71
		200m	1h	20.53
		200m	1qf	19.84
21 Jun		200m	1sf	20.09
		200m	1	19.86
21 Jul	Sacramento	LJ	1	8.56w
3 Aug	Los Angeles –	100m	1h	10.32w
	Olympic Games	100m	1qf	10.04
4 Aug		100m	1sf	10.14
		100m	1	9.99
5 Aug		LJ	q	8.30w
6 Aug		LJ	1	8.54
		200m	1h	21.02
		200m	1qf	20.48
8 Aug		200m	1sf	20.27
		200m	1	19.80
10 Aug	for USA	4×10mR	1h	38.89
11 Aug	for USA	4×100mR	1sf	38.44
	for USA	4×100mR	1	37.83 World record
18 Aug	London – Nike	300m	4	32.18 (1. K. Baptiste)
20 Aug	Budapest GP	100m	1	10.05
22 Aug	Zurich – Weltklasse	100m	1	9.99
24 Aug	Brussels – van Damme	LJ	1	8.65
26 Aug	Koln	200m	1	20.21
	for USA	4×100mR	1	38.58
14 Sep	Tokyo – 8 Nations	100m	1	10.13

19

Review of 1984

New York City, January, 1984. Down to his sixth and final attempt in the long jump and trailing Larry Myricks, Lewis responded by blasting an indoor world best 8.79, equalling his own global low altitude world best, with a performance that may very well have been the greatest in any event in indoor history.

Lewis' limited competition schedule infuriated many meet promoters, who knew that if they had the 23 year old 'wunderkind,' they had guaranteed box office. Yet, in terms of frustration, meet promoters were a distant runner-up to reporters who were angered when their requests for interviews were denied. Douglas received on the average 15 calls a day from members of the press seeking to gain access to Lewis. If Douglas had granted even a small percentage of those requests, Lewis' Olympic preparations would have been seriously disrupted. While the Lewis/Douglas strategy was more than vindicated by the extraordinary results on the track, both athlete and manager were unfairly villified in print by snubbed reporters anxious for revenge. 'I found out the definition of aloof and arrogant,' Douglas said. 'Both mean denying an interview to a reporter.'

While reporters for whatever reason refuse to give Lewis the accolades he deserves it is clear by now to the insiders of the sport that Lewis is in a class by himself. It is Lewis that the ghosts of Owens and Beamon should be chasing. After all Owens never enjoyed the level of superiority that Lewis currently commands over his rivals in an era where the quality of competition is so much greater than in the 1930's. As far as Beamon is concerned, two meters of maximum wind at the high altitude in Mexico City tell the entire story.

Is there anyone around who could challenge Carl Lewis in the near future? 'I think Kirk Baptiste, Henry Thomas and Roy Martin Jr. would be the top sprinters if I were to retire. How good Roy and Henry become will really depend on which college they attend.'

What of Carl Lewis' future? One of the most interesting prospects is a potential change of event. 'If I do hang around until 1988 I may drop the 100 for the 400. Guys running the 400 now don't have the basic speed. I believe that if you are fast then you can compensate for anything. I think I proved that in the 200 this year.' Lewis cautioned, however, that he may not be around in '88 if he does not perform to his satisfaction. 'I don't want to deteriorate. If I can improve through 1987 I will compete in '88. But if I can't compete at the high level I have already established then I'll just forget it.'

His immediate plans include 'maybe one or two 400's'.

Experimentation in the triple jump is out for now but 'I may try the high hurdles in '86.' For the time being though record breaking will receive the most emphasis from Lewis in '85, and he would like all of his world marks to fall in the United States. 'I respect the European crowds and I've especially always enjoyed Zürich but I really feel more comfortable at home.' Lewis even has a plan for his assault on the record books. 'Ideally, I would like the long jump record to go in my home town of Houston on the first weekend in May. Then I will go after the 200 record in Los Angeles the week before the nationals (in early June), and I'd like the 100 record at the TAC's in Indianapolis.' Since Carl Lewis has always accomplished that which he has set out to do, record revisions seem inevitable in 1985.

SAID AOUITA

Before 1984 the only Olympic medal ever won for Morocco had been a silver by Rhadi Ben Abdesselem in the 1960 marathon. In Los Angeles two Moroccans won gold medals. First Nawal El Moutawakil sprung a delightful surprise to win the women's 400 metres hurdles and then Said Aouita won the 5000 metres. Aouita's feat was rather more expected, following his Helsinki bronze at 1500m in 1983 and the tremendous form he had displayed in 1984, but the manner of his victory was deeply impressive. After fast early pace from Canario of Portugal, Aouita strode away majestically with a 55 second last lap to win comfortably.

Before 1984 Aouita's best time for 5000 metres was a mere 13:39.0. After a 13:34.8 in May, he brought his best down by 30 seconds in Firenze (Florence) with the second fastest time ever. That and the ease of his Olympic victory point to his ability to break Dave Moorcroft's world record of 13:00.41, and indeed the super-confident Aouita's target for 1985 is a time in the 12:50–12:51 range.

There was much speculation prior to the Olympics as to which event, 1500m or 5000m, Aouita would choose to run in Los Angeles. At the last minute he opted for the easier victory prospect at the longer event, but he would surely have given even the magnificently resurgent Seb Coe a hard fight at the 1500m. Aouita headed the 1984 lists at 1500m, 3000m and 5000m (and at 1 mile), the first time that one man has done this since Sandor Iharos of Hungary in 1955, and, as can be seen from his list of races, compiled a perfect season's record.

Born in Kenitra on the Moroccan coast, Aouita was originally a soccer player, but his promise at middle distance running has been evident since he was a

Said AOUITA in 1984

Date	Venue/meeting	Event	Place	Mark	
13 May	Livorno	5000m	1	13:34.8	NR
2 Jun	Turin	800m	1	1:46.81	
3 Jun	Turin	1500m	1	3:36.31	
13 Jun	Firenze	5000m	1	13:04.78	AR
6 Jul	Hengelo	1500m	1	3:31.54	AR
10 Jul	Lausanne	5000m	1	13:12.51	
14 Jul	Rabat – African Champs	1500m	1	3:38.18	
18 Jul	Grosseto	1500m	1	3:34.82	
8 Aug	Los Angeles –	5000m	4h	13:45.66	
9 Aug	Olympic Games	5000m	1sf	13:28.39	
11 Aug		5000m	1	13:05.59	
22 Aug	Zurich – Weltklasse	800m	1	3:49.54	NR
24 Aug	Brussels – van Damme	3000m	1	7:33.3	NR
29 Aug	Koblenz	1500m	1	3:34.10	
4 Sep	Paris	1500m	1	3:34.13	
7 Sep	London – Coke	1 mile	1	3:55.43	

Review of 1984

teenager. In his first major international appearance he won the 1981 World Student Games 1500m title. After that he moved to Europe, first to France and then to Italy, where he is now advised by Enrico Disnisi.

Apart from the Coke mile, in which Steve Cram fell, Aouita was denied the opportunity of meeting the great British middle distance trio of Coe, Cram and Ovett in 1984, but he will be gunning for them and their records in the future. Seb Coe is moving up to 5000m and a race between these two beautiful runners would indeed be a treat for athletics enthusiasts.

LYUDMILA ANDONOVA

Since two metres was first jumped by a woman, by Rosemarie Ackermann at Berlin in 1977, the world record has moved steadily upwards at the hands of Sara Simeoni, Ulrike Meyfarth and Tamara Bykova. It was no surprise when Bykova added a centimetre in clearing 2.05m at Kiev in June, but the next improvement was certainly a major shock. Lyudmila Andonova came to the Olympic Day meeting in East Berlin on 20 July with recent Bulgarian records at 1.96m and 1.99m to her credit, but here she successively cleared 2.00m, 2.02m and 2.07m, as Bykova was second at 1.98m.

Lyudmila ANDONOVA – high jump competitions in 1984

Date	Venue/meeting	Place	Mark	
Indoors:				
14 Jan	Vilnius	3	1.93	(1. M.Doronina)
28 Jan	Vienna	2	1.86	(1. T.Malesev)
2 Feb	Vienna	1	1.91	
12 Feb	Sofia	1	1.84	
19 Feb	Sofia – Bulgarian Ch.	2	1.84	(1. S.Kostadinova)
Outdoors:				
6 May	Sofia	1	1.89	
13 May	Sofia	1	1.89	
19 May	Sofia – Narodna Ml.	1	1.96	NR
30 May	Schwechat	1	1.90	
2 Jun	Sofia – Bulgarian Ch.	1	1.91	
9 Jun	Worrstadt	1	1.99	NR
16 Jun	Sofia – Bul v Rom v GDR	3	1.92	(1. S.Kostadinova)
29 Jun	Le-Chaux-de-Fonds, Bern	1	1.95	
20 Jul	East Berlin – Olympic D	1	2.07	WR
5 Aug	Sofia	1	2.00	
17 Aug	Prague – Friendship G	1	1.96	
20 Aug	Budapest GP	2	1.94	(1. S.Costa)
25 Aug	Sofia	2	1.82	(1. S.Kostadinova)
29 Aug	Rovareto	1	2.00	
31 Aug	Rome – Golden Gala	1	2.02	
2 Sep	Rieti	1	2.03	
4 Sep	Paris	1	1.98	
9 Sep	Athens – Balkan Games	1	1.97	

Lyudmila Zhecheva was born in the Soviet Union, very near to Rostov-on-Don, coincidentally the birthplace of her great rival Tamara Bykova. Her Bulgarian father was working there at the time and married a Russian, Tatyana. The family returned to Bulgaria a month after Lyudmila's birth.

She showed early promise in rhythmic gymnastics before joining her local athletics club in Stara Zagora. Taking up high jumping, she cleared 1.70m in her first year at the event in 1977 when she was 17. She then joined the Akademik club in Sofia, where she is coached by Raicho Tsonev (7.87m long jump in 1964). She broke through into international class in 1980 and 1981, and in the latter year succeeded in taking the national record, held by the former world record holder Yordanka Blagoyeva (1.94m in 1972). That year too she married Atanas Andonov, the Bulgarian decathlon record holder.

She missed the 1983 season as she gave birth to daughter Jana on 18 August. A month later she was back in training, and in 1984 moved steadily up to and beyond her previous best. After her record she maintained great form with further victories over Bykova and in the major meetings.

EVELYN ASHFORD

Evelyn Ashford first competed in the Olympic Games in 1976, when as a 19-year-old she placed fifth in the 100 metres final. She was then in her first year at UCLA, which was to be used as one of the Olympic villages eight years later. From then she dedicated herself to Olympic success, unabashedly seeking fame and fortune. Her hopes were dashed in 1980 through the US boycott, but in any case she got injured. Before 1984 her best years had been in 1979 and 1981 when she twice won victory at both 100m

Evelyn ASHFORD in 1984

Date	Venue/meeting	Event	Place	Mark	
14 Jan	Los Angeles	800m	2	2:15.2	
27 Jan	Santa Monica	800m	3	2:13.07	
10 Mar	Los Angeles	400m	1	52.55	
24 Mar	Los Angeles	4x400mR	1st leg	(3:40:18)	for P&ETC
14 Apr	Santa Monica	100m	1	11.16	
		200m	2	22.75	
29 Apr	Walnut – Mt SAC	100m	1	10.88w	
		400m	2	52.11	(1. C.Cheeseborough)
12 May	Modesto – Cal.R.	100m	1	10.78w	world fastest
19 May	Los Gatos	800m	5	2:20.34	
17 Jun	Los Angeles – O.Trials	100m	1h	11.29	
		100m	1qf	11.24	
18 Jun		100m	3sf	11.43	
		100m	1	11.18	
21 Jun		200m	–h	dnf	
25 Jul	Walnut-for USA	4x100mR	1	42.15	
4 Aug	Los Angeles –	100m	1h	11.06	
	Olympic Games	100m	1qf	11.21	
5 Aug		100m	1sf 11.03		
		100m	1	10.97	
11 Aug	for USA	4x100mR	1h	42.59	
	for USA	4x100mR	1	41.65	
18 Aug	Berlin – ISTAF	100m	1h	10.92	
		100m		10.94	
22 Aug	Zurich – Weltklasse	100m	1	10.76	World record
26 Aug	Koln	200m	1	22.76	
31 Aug	Rome – Golden Gala	100m	1	10.93	

23

Review of 1984

Ashford achieved her first goal with the world record for 100m when she ran 10.79 at the high altitude of Colorado Springs in the summer of 1983. The previous mark had been 10.81 by her great rival Marlies Göhr. She was thus set for 1984 and trained very hard under the guidance of coach Pat Connolly for the Olympic Games in her hometown.

Her smooth action was in perfect order and unlike in the World Championships the previous year she was unbeaten by injury as she dominated the short sprint and went on to win a second gold with the US sprint relay team in LA.

and 200m in the World Cup. In 1978 she married basketball player Ray Washington, but she continued to run under her maiden name.

Göhr, of course, was not at the Olympics, so Ashford's triumphant year was completed in the best possible way when they met at Zürich and Ashford swept to victory and the world record of 10.76.

JOAN BENOIT

Right from the start of the first women's Olympic marathon Joan Benoit, a slim grey-clad figure, wearing a white peaked hat, pulled away from the talented field. Padding rhythmically along Ocean Avenue and onto Santa Monica freeway she just kept stretching her lead until soon after halfway she was nearly two minutes up on the rest of the field. Grete Waitz, the greatest name in women's distance running, closed that gap, but nothing could disturb the iron will of this remarkable lady, who came into the Coliseum to a rapturous reception from the morning crowd. Just 1.60m tall and 47.5kg in weight she must be the smallest ever Olympic athletics champion.

Benoit, who lives and trains in the seclusion of Maine, ran her first marathon on a last-minute whim in Bermuda in January 1979. She had been until then a moderate track runner, but after being sidelined with glandular fever in 1978, had given notice of her ability at longer distances when she set a US road record for 10km, 33:15, in October of that year.

Joan BENOIT in 1984

Date	Venue/meeting	Event	Place	Mark	
22 Jan	Boston (indoors)	1 mile	1	4:45.1	
27 Jan	New York (indoors)	1 mile	5	4:44.91	
11 Feb	E.Rutherford (indoors)	3000m	2	9:06.99	
10 Mar	Mobile – road race	10km	1	31:57	
12 May	Olympia – US Trials	Mar	1	2:31:04	
17 Jun	Los Angeles	10000m	1	32:07.41	
5 Aug	Los Angeles – Olympics	Mar	1	2:24:52	
6 Sep	Philadelphia	Half marathon	1	1:08:34	US record

Her Bermuda marathon time of 2:50:54 was drastically reduced less than three months later when she won the prestigious Boston marathon in 2:35:15, a US record. Further improvements followed, 2:31:23 at Auckland in 1980 and 2:30:16 at Boston in 1981, although Patti Catalano had taken her US record. This, however, she regained at Eugene in September 1982 with 2:26:11. In April 1983 she produced her greatest feat. In winning her second Boston marathon, she set out at a tremendous pace, passing halfway in 1:08:23, and holding on to a world best time of 2:22:43.

Despite her considerable success she has been plagued by problems with her Achilles tendons ever since that first marathon, and has had operations on both of them. Even worse was to come, for her Olympic build-up was shattered by a right knee injury in March 1984. With the US Trials, her only hope for selection, looming she was forced to undergo arthroscopic surgery on the knee. Dr Stan James operated on 25 April by cutting through inflamed tissue behind the lining of the knee joint. The operation was a complete success and Benoit's season was crowned with success, but it took a very special athlete to persevere and win, overcoming such adversity.

SERGEY BUBKA

World records have been set in the pole vault more frequently than in any other event. This is perhaps not surprising when one considers the nature of the activity. From the first world record to be set with a fibre-glass pole, 4.83m by George Davies in 1962, there were, to the end of the 1983 season, 47 performances from 20 men in the lists of pole vault world records broken or equalled. In 1984 Sergey Bubka became the 21st as he added four more records to that list. He had also set three world indoor bests, for which successes he had been voted the *Track & Field News* Indoor Athlete of the Year.

Bubka had a disappointing start to his international career with seventh place in the 1981 European Indoor Championships, but his talent was well regarded in the Soviet Union. Nonetheless his selection for the 1983 World Championships was a surprise, but one that was amply rewarded when he won the gold medal. In 1984 he showed clearly that he was the world's number one vaulter. Towards the end of the season he lost a couple of times to his main Soviet rivals, but by then he had compiled a formidable record. Working carefully with his coach, Nikanorov Petrov, he contested a limited number of

Sergey Bubka – pole vault competitions in 1984

Date	Venue/meeting	Place	Mark	
Indoors:				
15 Jan	Vilnius	1	5.81	WB
22 Jan	Leningrad	1	5.70	
1 Feb	Milan	1	5.82	WB
10 Feb	Inglewood – LA Times	1	5.83	WB
11 Feb	East Rutherford	1	5.70	
19 Feb	Richfield	nh	–	(1. Bell 5.60)
24 Feb	New York – TAC	1	5.64	
Outdoors:				
23 May	Ostrava	1	5.65	
26 May	Bratislava	1	5.85	WR
2 Jun	St Denis	1	5.88	WR
4 Jul	Kiev	1	5.70	
13 Jul	London – P-Talbot G	1	5.90	WR
17 Aug	Moscow – Friendship G	2	5.70	(1. Volkov 5.80)
31 Aug	Rome – Golden Gala	1	5.94	WR
2 Sep	Rieti	2	5.65	(1. Krupskiy 5.65)
8 Sep	Donyetsk – USSR Champs	1	5.80	

Review of 1984

competitions with the aim of reaching his peak in early August to coincide with the Olympics. Of course he was denied that opportunity, but showed just what form he was in with world records on either side of that period, the latter in his epic duel with Thierry Vigneron in Rome, when, for the first time since Bill Sefton and Earle Meadows in 1937, two men set world records in one competition. Vigneron set his fifth world record in five years at 5.91m only for Bubka to display his great competitive ability less than ten minutes later in clearing 5.94m.

Bubka's technique has greatly impressed his rivals. He is very fast and very strong and above all has shown that he can control the pole from a higher grip than anyone else. Using a 5.10m pole his top hand is very near the top, at about 5.03m. This ability gives him the opportunity to jump higher than his rivals, and on his form in 1984 and the way he sailed over 5.90 plus, he must be the favourite to attain six metres in the very near future.

SEBASTIAN COE

From 1979 to 1981 Seb Coe set new standards in middle distance running. He ended the latter year as world record holder at 800m and 1000m and in his last three races set two world records for the 1 mile and won the World Cup 800m. Despite the wealth of running talent around the world, all three of those world records still stand as 1985 gets underway.

As an 800 metre runner Coe had everything, the speed to be able to run a 45.5 relay leg for Britain's 4x400m relay team, and the endurance to set world records at 1500m or 1 mile in his infrequent essays at four laps. Above all he possessed the ability to kick again off an already fast pace. Yet this seemingly complete runner did not win a major championship at

Sebastian Coe in 1984

Date	Venue/meeting	Event	Place	Mark	
31 Mar	Cranford – road relay	3.75M	–	16:16	fastest leg
7 Apr	Wimbledon – road relay	3.5M	–	15:07	fastest leg
21 Apr	S. Coldfield – rd rly	3.1M	–	14:00	second fastest leg
12 May	Wolverhampton –	400m	–	46.8	relay leg
19 May	Enfield – Middlesex Ch.	800m	1h	1:53.0	
19 May		800m	1	1:45.2	
1 Jun	London (CP) –	1500m	1h	3:46.06	
	Southern Champs.	1500m	1	3:43.11	
23 Jun	London (CP) –	1500m	1h	3:43.40	
24 Jun	AAA Champs.	1500m	2	3:39.79	(1. P.Elliott)
28 Jun	Olso – Bislett G	800m	1	1:43.84	
4 Jul	Haringey	1 mile	1	3:54.6	
3 Aug	Los Angeles –	800m	1h	1:45.71	
4 Aug	Olympic Games	800m	3qf	1:46.75	
5 Aug		800m	1sf	1:45.51	
6 Aug		800m	2	1:43.64	
9 Aug		1500m	2h	3:45.30	
10 Aug		1500m	3sf	3:35.81	
11 Aug		1500m	1	3:32.53	
19 Aug	Haringey	1500m	1	3:45.2	

Review of 1984

800m. He set a fast pace in Prague in the 1978 Europeans, only to be passed by Steve Ovett, and then the amazing Olaf Beyer, on his day of days, swept past them both. That, however, was Coe's first taste of major senior championships, and in 1980 he was an obvious, clear favourite to win the Olympic title. He ran an appalling race tactically and lost to arch-rival Ovett. However then he showed his extraordinary talent and above all his character to come back to win the 1500 metres. In 1982 he was again favourite for the European 800m, but his preparation had been hampered by a stress fracture of the shin and he could not produce his usual response when challenged by Hans-Peter Ferner in the finishing straight.

Then we discovered that he was suffering from swollen glands and he ended his season and withdrew from the Commonwealth Games. In early 1983 he was back and set world indoor bests at 800m and 1000m. However this promising start was not maintained for in his mid-season build-up to the World Championships he suffered four defeats. After the last of these, an 800m at Gateshead in which he finished fourth, his worst placing at the event since 1977, he had hospital tests. Eventually it was discovered that he was suffering from a disease, the lymphatic form of acquired toxoplasmosis. As a result he was unable to do any running for five months, so that it wasn't until early 1984 that he could begin the long build up to an Olympic comeback.

There must have been many who doubted his ability to return to his best form, many who would say 'They never come back'. That he did, in triumph at Los Angeles, was wonderful to behold. He lost to Cruz at 800 metres, but, in contrast to Moscow, did everything right in setting his best time since his world record three years earlier, losing to a younger and faster man, who was now a truly great athlete. Coe's fitness and ability to handle the challenging programme of seven tough races in nine days carried him ultimately to his greatest triumph with his resounding victory in the 1500 metres. That set the seal on the greatest comeback in athletics history.

Now Coe looks towards the longer distances and perhaps the 5000 metres in the championships of 1986.

JOAQUIM CRUZ

Joaquim Cruz won the 1984 Olympic 800 metres with a new Olympic record of 1:43.00. It seemed fitting that the previous record holder was Alberto Juantorena, for Cruz's immense, seemingly tireless stride was so reminiscent of the giant Cuban. Since Juantorena ran 1:43.44 in 1977 only Seb Coe had bettered that time, smashing through with 1:42.33 and 1:41.73. Yet after Los Angeles Cruz embarked on a brilliant European tour and within a week, missing Coe's record by just a fraction, ran three of the six fastest times ever at 800m as well as the fourth best ever at 1000m. All three 800m races were run at a similar pace, with a first lap in 49.7–49.9, whereas in the Olympic final Cruz had splits of 51.16 and 51.84.

27

Review of 1984

Cruz came to the USA from Brazil in 1982 with Luiz de Oliveira, who had been his coach from the age of eleven. After he had struggled to learn to speak English, Cruz joined his coach at the University of Oregon and in that distance running environment sharpened the talent which had earlier been evidenced by his 1:44.3 world junior record in 1981. He carried the yellow and gold colours of his University to double victory in the 1984 NCAA Championships. This 800m/1500m double had previously been achieved only by Ron Delany in 1958 and Don Paige in 1979.

In Brazil he is now a hero, although Brazilian officials seem to have resented his move away from his home near Brazilia in Taguatinga, where his mother and elder sisters still live. One was even reported to have said that by withdrawing from the Olympic 1500m – with a bad cold and perhaps the effects of victory and four hard races at 800m – he was disgracing his country.

Cruz's only defeat in 1984 came by just one hundredth of a second by Steve Scott, but 3:53.00 was nonetheless a pretty sensational debut at 1 mile. It is perhaps at the longer distances of 1000m, 1500m and 1 mile, at which he is comparatively inexperienced, that he may make the greatest impact in the future, although for now he has undoubtedly succeeded Seb Coe as the king at two laps.

Joaquim CRUZ in 1984

Date	Venue/meeting	Event	Place	Mark	
24 Mar	Sacramento	1500m	1	3:39.4	NR
31 Mar	Eugene	1500m	1	3:38.43	NR
7 Apr	Eugene	800m	1	1:47.21	
	for Oregon at	4x440yR	1	46.9 leg in 3:12.72	
21 Apr	Berkeley	1500m	1	3:37.72	NR
13 May	Los Angeles – Pepsi	1 mile	2	3:53.00	NR (1. S.Scott)
		(1500m	–	3:38.4)	
19 May	Pullman – Pac 10	800m	1h	1:47.47	
		800m	1	1:45.12	
30 May	Eugene – NCAA Champs	800m	1h	1:46.34	
31 May		1500m	2h	3:41.80	
1 Jun		800m	1	1:45.10	
2 Jun		1500m	1	3:36.48	NR
17 Jun	Ibirapuera	1500m	1	3:38.98	
21 Jul	Eugene	1000m	1	2:14.54	NR
3 Aug	Los Angeles –	800m	1h	1:45.66	
4 Aug	Olympic Games	800m	1qf	1:44.84	
5 Aug		800m	1sf	1:43.82	NR
6 Aug		800m	1	1:43.00	NR
20 Aug	Nice – Nikaia	1000m	1	2:14.09	NR
22 Aug	Zurich – Weltklasse	800m	1	1:42.34	NR
24 Aug	Brussels – van Damme	800m	1	1:42.41	
26 Aug	Koln	800m	1	1:41.77	NR

HEIKE DRECHSLER

Anisoara Cusmir (now Stanciu) of Romania had added an astonishing 22cm to her own world long jump record when she cleared 7.43 at Bucharest in June 1983. By the end of the year her previous best of 7.21m remained the second best legal jump ever, although Cusmir had been beaten in the World Championships in Helsinki by the 18-year-old East German, Heike Daute, who with a following wind jumped 7.27m.

In 1984 Heike Daute compiled a flawless season's record, and although she did not quite match the world record, her series of performances established her on easily the highest level ever for a woman long jumper. She started with a world indoor best in her national championships, and in her very first outdoor meeting added 15cm to her GDR record. In that competition she had four jumps over the 7 metre mark, a level she maintained throughout the year as she added two further national records. Two days after her 7.40m she married the Wismut Gera soccer player Andreas Drechsler, the son of high jump coach Erich Drechsler.

She has studied as a precision tool maker, but now wants to become a nursery school teacher. As she emerges from teenage years there is no reason to suppose that she has yet tapped all her potential. She will work with her coach, Peter Hein, whom she regards as a fine motivator, in refining her technique and building strength, and looks set to follow as a record breaker and champion in the footsteps of other members of her famous club, SC Motor Jena, such as Marlies Göhr and Bärbel Wöckel.

Heike DRECHSLER – long jump competitions in 1984

Date	Venue/meeting	Place	Mark	
Indoors:				
21 Jan	Senftenberg – GDR Ch.	1	6.99	WB
1 Feb	Cosford – GDR v UK	1	6.78	
13 May	Jena	1	7.29	NR
19 May	Dresden	1	7.34	NR
25 May	Potsdam	1	7.18	
2 Jun	Erfurt – GDR Champs	1	7.00	
9 Jun	East Berlin	1	7.09	
15 Jul	East Berlin	1	7.18	
20 Jul	East Berlin – Olympic D	1	7.32	
26 Jul	Dresden	1	7.40	NR
16 Aug	Prague – Friendship G	q	6.80	
17 Aug		1	7.15	

Review of 1984

UWE HOHN

The first 100-metre javelin throw. As a barrier breaking achievement that must rate with the first sub 10-second 100 metres or the first sub four-minute mile. On 20 Jul 1984 at the Olympic Day meeting in East Berlin Uwe Hohn sent his javelin sailing out over the 100-metre line to hit the ground 104.80 metres away. Not only a world record but also, by adding 5.08m to Tom Petranoff's 1983 mark, the biggest ever improvement in the world record. The previous biggest had been the 4.70m added by Terje Pedersen (Nor) when he became the first ever 90-metre thrower in 1964.

Uwe Hohn has for several years been regarded as the man most likely to reach the top in javelin throwing. He had shown potential when he threw a leather ball 35m in his first year of school at the age of six. This talent was nurtured by Hartmut Wolter at the Child and Youth Sport School in Brandenburg so that Hohn progressed to win the GDR Spartakiad in 1977. He set a European Junior record in 1981 to win the European Junior title in Utrecht and moved into the senior ranks with the gold medal, and again a personal best, at the 1982 European Championships.

Such success, however, was achieved despite a catalogue of setbacks – a motorcycle accident in 1981, and operations, in 1982 for a torn ligament and in 1983 to remove a cartilage, which caused him to miss the entire season. Working hard with his respected coach, Wolfgang Skibba (a 71.90m hammer thrower in 1975) he was back, stronger than ever in 1984 and as the table shows compiled a faultless season's record. In December he was voted GDR Sportsman of the Year.

Actually he already had a 100-metre throw to his credit, though not with the javelin. He had thrown a 600 gram practice hand grenade 100.02m in 1982!

His throw has certainly exacerbated the problem of maintaining javelin throws within existing stadia. It was thus not surprising that the IAAF have now determined to change the javelin from 1986. However, in common with other leading throwers, Hohn is unhappy about the proposed changes as they affect the flight characteristics. He would prefer that the weight should be increased from 800 to 1000 grams rather than the changes which will not permit the javelin to 'fly', and which seem likely to diminish the aesthetic attractions of the event. However the same javelins will be in use for a final year in 1985, and as Hohn expects to continue to improve, he may well mark the 650th anniversary celebrations of his hometown, Rheinsberg, with an unassailable mark.

Uwe HOHN – Javelin competitions in 1984

Date	Venue/meeting	Place	Mark	
6 May	Potsdam	1	86.46	
13 May	Jena	1	94.82	
25 May	Potsdam	1	99.52	European record
2 Jun	Erfurt – GDR Champs	1	93.80	
15 Jul	East Berlin	1	97.12	
20 Jul	East Berlin – Olympic Day	1	104.80	World record
26 Jul	Dresden	1	91.24	
17 Aug	Moscow – Friendship G	1	94.44	
20 Aug	Budapest GP	1	93.16	
22 Aug	Zurich – Weltklasse	1	87.48	

MARITA KOCH

Marita Koch must be the prime choice for the athlete of the past decade. She has three times headed the annual Woman Athlete of the Year poll in *Track & Field News* – in 1978, 1979 and 1982, and was ranked second to Evelyn Ashford in 1984. During this time she has set 15 world records, ten individual and five in relays and her medal haul in major championships reads: twelve gold, four silver, one bronze.

From her loss to Irina Szewinska in the 1977 World Cup, Marita Koch was supreme at 400 metres until challenged by Jarmila Kratochvilova, who beat her twice in 1981. However in 1982 Koch came back to set her sixth world record at the event and beat Kratochvilova in the European Championships. 1983 was Kratochvilova's year at both 400 metres and 800 metres, while Koch concentrated on the sprints, winning the world title at 200m and picking up a silver at 100m, as well as adding two more golds to her total with the GDR 4x100m and 4x400m relay teams.

Koch returned to 400 metres running in 1984 and reached, in her own estimation, her best ever form, with a very high level throughout the year. She was undefeated at 200m and 400m and equalled her best times, the former the world record and the latter the

Marita KOCH in 1984

Date	Venue/meeting	Event	Place	Mark	
5 May	Potsdam	100m	2	11.13	(1. M.Göhr)
13 May	Jena	200m	1	22.17	
19 May	Dresden	100m	2	11.53	(1. M.Göhr)
20 May	Karl-Marx-Stadt	200m	1	22.13	
	for national team	4x100mR	1	42.21	
25 May	Potsdam	400m	1	49.44	
1 Jun	Erfurt – GDR Champs	400m	1h	49.96	
2 Jun		400m	1	48.86	
3 Jun	for national team	4x400mR	1	47.7	leg in 3:15.92 WR
9 Jun	East Berlin	100m	2	11.19	(1. M.Göhr)
	for national team	4x100mR	1	42.62	
15 Jul	East Berlin	400m	1	48.89	
	for national team	4x100mR	1	42.23	
21 Jul	Potsdam – Olympic Day	200m	1	21.71	= world record
	for national team	4x100mR	1	41.69	
26 Jul	Dresden	400m	1	48.26	
16 Aug	Prague – Friendship G	400m	2h	50.29	
		400m	1	48.16	= GDR record
22 Aug	Zurich – Weltklasse	200m	1	21.87	
	for national team	4x100mR	1	41.85	
14 Sep	Tokyo – 8 Nations	200m	1	22.20	

On all the 4x100m relays she ran the second leg.

Review of 1984

GDR record, for Kratochvilova had improved the world record to 47.99 in 1983. However Koch considered that her 48.26 run in Dresden at the end of July was her best performance, for there was an adverse wind of 4.6 m/s in the straight and a wet track. She thought that to be worth 47.6–47.7.

Marita Koch plans to marry her coach, Wolfgang Meier, at the conclusion of her career and her aim is to seal it with a world record for 400m in the 1985 World Cup. It would indeed be a fitting end to a wonderful career and a true reward for her hard work over the years. However she may yet go on to further triumphs in 1986 at Stuttgart.

CARLOS LOPES

1956 when Alain Mimoun of France at the age of 35 won the International cross-country title and went to Olympic victory in his first marathon.

For Lopes, Olympic victory came in his third marathon. He had failed to finish the 1982 New York marathon, pulling out at 21 miles, but at Rotterdam in April 1983, in losing by just two seconds to Rob de Castella, he set a European best of 2:08:39.

Carlos Alberto Sousa Lopes started work in a steel factory at the age of twelve, and only started training for athletics when he was eighteen. He first came to prominence at cross-country with his third place in the national junior championships in 1966, which he followed with 25th place in the International junior race. Since then he has been coached by Mario Moniz Pereira. Progress was steady, although unspectacular in the years that followed. He set his first national record at 10000m in 1971, but in the European

At the age of 37 Carlos Lopes showed clearly in 1984 that he had lost none of his zest or ability. Indeed he reached new heights in achieving the first double of world cross-country championship and Olympic gold medal since Mohammed Gammoudi in 1968. For a close parallel to his achievement one has to go back to

Carlos LOPES in 1984

Date	Venue/meeting	Event	Place	Mark	
7 Jan	Albufeira – Road race	7km	1	19:20	
15 Jan	Funchal – Road race	10.5km	1	29:47	
5 Feb	Acoteias – E.Club X-C	10.2km	3	29:20	
12 Feb	Le Trembley – X-C	9.9km	1	27:44	
19 Feb	Sintra – Lisbon X-C	11km	1	31:31	
4 Mar	Viseu – Portuguese X-C	12km	1	34:26	
11 Mar	Paco de Arcos Road relay	6.9km	–	19:16	
25 Mar	E.Rutherford – World X–C	12km	1	33:25	
14 Apr	Rotterdam	Mar	–	dnf	
3 Jun	Lisbon	5000m	5	13:35.8	(1. F.Mamede)
10 Jun	Viseu – Road race	17km	1	51:08	
17 Jun	Lisbon – Westathletic	10000m	1	28:05.40	
28 Jun	Oslo – Bislett G	5000m	3	13:16.38	(1. F.Mamede)
2 Jul	Stockholm – DNG	10000m	2	27:17.48	(1. F.Mamede)
12 Aug	Los Angeles – Olympics	Mar	1	2:09:21	
7 Oct	Denver – road race	10km	2	29:10	(1. S.Kigen)
13 Oct	El Paso – road race	15km	1	43:20	
21 Oct	Chicago	Mar	2	2:09:06	(1. S.Jones)

Review of 1984

Championships that year went out in his heat in the steeplechase and came in 33rd and last in the 10000 metres, in 30:05.6 nearly two laps behind the winner.

His major breakthrough came in 1976 when he won the world cross-country title and later the Olympic silver medal at 10000 metres. Such a move into world-class was undoubtedly helped by the assistance of a government scheme whereby he was found a job, in the personnel department of a bank, tailored around his training schedules. Then Achilles tendon trouble held him back and as his early 30s passed and his times slowed many would have written him off as a contender for major titles. However in 1982 he came back better than ever, smashing the European 10000 metres record and even bringing his 1500m best down three seconds to 3:41.4.

In 1983 he was second in both the world cross-country championships and in the Rotterdam marathon, but may have regretted his decision to contest only the 10000m in the World Championships in Helsinki. After a slow early pace he was outkicked and came in sixth. That must have steeled his resolve to commit himself to the marathon and he followed a carefully planned schedule of limited racing in 1984.

Lopes had won Portugal's first ever athletics medal in 1976, and in convincing style in Los Angeles went one better with his nation's first ever gold. Where he has led others have followed, for Rosa Mota and Antonio Leitao also won distance medals, even though the most talented Portuguese runner of all, Fernando Mamede, again failed in a major championship.

Married for ten years to Teresa, with two sons Nuno (9) and Pedro (3), Lopes lives in Lisbon and sees no reason for contemplating retirement from the sport. He started 1985 in fine style with a win in the traditional New Years Eve midnight race in Sao Paulo.

EDWIN MOSES

The enormous respect in which Edwin Moses is held in the world of athletics was shown when he was chosen at the end of 1984 as one of the three representatives of the USA to the IAAF. He thus became the first active athlete to take on this responsibility. Perhaps too that high regard had been enhanced when he fluffed his words when taking the Olympic Oath on behalf of the competitors at the Opening Ceremony in Los Angeles. For it could be argued that it showed him to be human after all! His brilliant year was further emphasised by his selection

Edwin MOSES – 400m hurdles competitions in 1984

Date	Venue/meeting	Place	Mark
13 May	Los Angeles – Pepsi	1	48.79
7 Jun	San Jose – TAC	1h	49.61
8 Jun		1sf	48.25
16 Jun	Los Angeles –	1h	48.83
17 Jun	US Olympic Trials	1sf	47.58
18 Jun		1	47.76
3 Aug	Los Angeles –	1h	49.33
4 Aug	Olympic Games	1sf	48.51
5 Aug		1	47.75
17 Aug	Berlin – ISTAF	1	48.49
26 Aug	Koln	1	47.95
29 Aug	Koblenz	1	47.32
31 Aug	Rome – Golden Gala	1	48.01

Review of 1984

by *Sports Illustrated* as their Sportsman of the Year.

USA Today has estimated that he (or his trust fund) had the highest earnings of any track and field athlete in 1983, his $457,500 coming from sponsorship, appearance money, shoe and clothing contracts. The figure would surely have been even higher in 1984. This highly intelligent, supremely dedicated man has dominated his event in a way unparallelled for years. One has to go back to Emil Zatopek at 10000 metres in the early 1950s or "Dutch' Warmerdam at pole vault in the early 1940s to find anything comparable.

He came into athletics comparatively late. Having achieved nothing of note at high school, he blossomed when he enrolled as an engineering student at Morehouse College in Georgia. In his first year, 1975, he ran one race at 440y hurdles, running the event in 52.0. The next year, however, he was sensational. He ran 50.1 in his first race at 400mh and stormed on to win the US Olympic Trials and then the Olympic title in his first world record of 47.63. He lost only three finals that year and had compiled a sequence of 18 successive victories up to his last competition of 1977. That race, at the ISTAF meeting in Berlin, goes down in history for Harald Schmid won, 49.07 to 49.29. Since then Moses has compiled his fabulous win streak. To the end of 1984 he had won 94 successive competitions, 109 if we include heats, and why should we not since he always runs to win?

No track athlete in the history of the sport has got anywhere this figure. He took one year off from competition, 1982, in which year he married Myrella, but returned to improve his world record to 47.02 in 1983. Now a resident of Laguna Hills in California, he hopes to further reduce that time and although there is much talent around, at 400 metres hurdles Edwin Moses is quite simply the King. Long may he continue to reign.

SABINE PAETZ

Since the heptathlon replaced the pentathlon as the multi-events competition for women, it has been dominated by GDR athletes. Ramona Neubert led the way with four successive world records and the 1982 European and 1983 World titles. Behind her Sabine Paetz won silver medals at both competitions and in 1983 Anke Vater completed a clean sweep for the GDR with the bronze medal.

In 1984, however, Paetz came through, setting first two world indoor pentathlon bests and then, at Potsdam in May, adding 31 points to Neubert's world record for heptathlon. She hoped to improve further at the Olympic Day meeting in July, but fell behind her target with a 6.58 long jump and poor javelin throw. Her talent and success in 1984 was underlined by her success at the individual disciplines of 100m hurdles and long jump, in both of which events she ranked in the world's top five.

Sabine Mobius (she was married in 1983) showed early talent at the pentathlon by winning the GDR schools event at the age of 13 in 1971 followed by the youth Spartakiad in 1972. She concentrated on the hurdles for the next few years, before again taking up the pentathlon in 1978. Since then she has made steady progress to the top, working closely with her coach Jorg Graf since 1980.

The new scoring tables being introduced in 1985 will add about 100 points to her totals and this helps to make 7000 points an attainable target for her. However so it is also for Ramona Neubert, who is nearly a year younger, and who will be hoping to regain the world lead from her teammate, after a year in which injury held back her training.

Review of 1984

Sabine PAETZ in 1984

Date	Venue/meeting	Event	Place	Mark	
Indoors					
6/7 Jan	Senftenberg – GDR Ch. (8.12, 14.84, 1.74, 6.53, 2:14.4)	Pen	1	4717	world best
14 Jan	East Berlin	60mh	1h	8.08	
		60mh	3	8.12	(1. C.Riefstahl)
21 Jan	Senftenberg – GDR Ch.	LJ	2	6.82	(1. H.Daute)
22 Jan		60mh	2	7.95	(1. C.Riefstahl)
26/27 Jan	Senftenberg – GDR v USSR (8.03, 15.28, 1.77, 6.65, 2:13.0)	Pen	1	4862	world best
Outdoors					
5/6 May	Potsdam (12.64, 1.80, 15.37, 23.37, 6.86, 44.62, 2:08.93)	Hep	1	6867	world record
12 May	Erfurt	100mh	1h	12.91	
		100mh	1	12.86	
13 May	Jena	200m	1	22.17	
19 May	Dresden	LJ	2	7.12	(1. H.Daute)
13 Jul	Leipzig	100m	1	11.46	
		100mh	1	12.80	
15 Jul	East Berlin	100mh	1h	12.74	
		100mh	1	12.54	
21 Jul	Potsdam (12.71, 1.74, 16.16, 23.23, 6.58, 41.94, 2:07.03)	Hep	1	6758	
26 Jul	Dresden	LJ	5	6.74	(1. H.Daute)
27 Jul	Dresden	100mh	1	12.58w	
16 Aug	Prague – Friendship G	100mh	1h	12.67	
		100mh	2	12.60	(1. Y.Donkova)
22 Aug	Zurich – Weltklasse	100mh	2	12.68	(1. L.Kalek)
28 Aug	Prague	100mh	1h	13.07	
		100mh	1	12.98	
14 Sep	Tokyo – 8 Nations	100mh	1	12.72	

YURIY SEDYKH

Even before last season started there could be little doubt as to Yuriy Sedykh's status as the greatest hammer thrower of all time. Despite not being able to win his third Olympic gold medal, as he surely would but for the Soviet boycott, his performances in 1984 reached new heights. His throwing was amazingly consistent and, as can be seen from the table, his standard tremendous, bearing in mind that the world record at the start of the year was Sergey Litvinov's 84.14. He beat that 13 times in his final six competitions of the year.

Both Sedykh's Olympic golds were at the head of Soviet 1-2-3s. His first came at the age of 21 in 1976,

Review of 1984

with the defending champion, his coach Anatoliy Bondarchuk third. While others have threatened his position, he has consistently come through to win the major titles, the European in 1978 and 1982 and the Olympics in 1980. The latter best demonstrated his ability. He started the year with two world records, but his 80.64m was passed by Litvinov a week later with 81.66m. Juri Tamm was also over 80 metres, but Sedykh as always rose to the occasion and with the very first throw of the Olympic final sent his hammer out to a new record of 81.80m, a mark his rivals were unable to match.

Sedykh has been a great innovator in hammer technique. His hallmark has been a finely grooved technique accentuated with great speed in the circle. His post-graduate dissertation was on 'The effectiveness of powerbuilding means in hammer throw training', and he certainly seems to have found the secret. In 1983 he had been surpassed by Sergey Litvinov, not only with the world record but also by the latter's victory over Sedykh in the World Championships. However in 1984 Sedykh once again reigned supreme.

Yuriy SEDYKH – hammer competitions in 1984

Date	Venue/meeting	Place	Mark	
25 Feb	Sochi	3	77.06	
2 Jun	Turin – USSR Int	1	81.52	
	(78.58, 81.52, 79.12, N, N, N)			
9 Jun	Sochi – Znamenskiy M	1	81.34	
	(80.94, 81.34, N, 80.52, 80.70, 80.78)			
20 Jun	Kiev – Izvestia Cup	q	79.86	
21 Jun		1	82.60	
	(81.70, 81.82, 82.52, 81.66, 82.60, 81.80)			
3 Jul	Cork	1	86.34	WR
	(86.34, 86.00, 85.20, 81.66, 82.60, 81.80)			
13 Jul	London – P-Talbot G	1	85.60	
	(85.04, 85.60, 85.52, N, N, 82.96)			
17 Aug	Moscow – Friendship G	1	85.60	
	(84.44, 83.10, 83.38, 85.60, 83.88, 84.84)			
20 Aug	Budapest GP	1	85.02	
	(N, 83.06, 83.86, 83.52, 82.96, 85.02)			
31 Aug	Rome – Golden Gala	1	83.90	
	(83.90, 83.90, 83.82, 83.20, 83.44, 83.50)			
14 Sep	Tokyo – 8 Nations	1	84.60	
	(84.58, 84.48, 84.60NN 81.72)			

DALEY THOMPSON

When he stepped into the discus circle for his final throw in Los Angeles, Daley Thompson had lost the overall lead in the Olympic decathlon. A record first-day score of 4633 had left him 114 points clear of his great rival, the world record holder Jürgen Hingsen. The latter had gained a mere six points in the opening event of the second day, the 110m hurdles, but the discus gave him his big chance and he proved his worth with fine throws of 49.80m and a personal best 50.82. Thompson responded with a terrible 37.90 and a mediocre 41.24, for a score 176 points worse than Hingsen's, who did not improve with his third effort of 47.18.

Daley Thompson then showed just why he has compiled such a tremendous record in this most taxing of all events, for, concentrating hard, he threw 46.56m and the crisis was over. He retained the decathlon lead although Hingsen had narrowed the gap to 32 points. Stomach trouble hindered Hingsen in the pole vault as he could clear only 4.50m, but when Thompson vaulted 4.90 on his third attempt he knew that the competition was all but won and celebrated with a magnificent back somersault off the landing area. He went on to clear 5.00m and the javelin and 1500m seemed almost formalities.

Review of 1984

Yet again he had won a major title and held off the challenge of Hingsen. Since his silver medal in the 1978 European Championships Daley Thompson has won every major decathlon title open to him and is now looking to repeat his victory cycle leading up to the next Olympic Games. His gold medal haul to date reads two Olympic, two Commonwealth, and one each at World, European and European Junior Championships.

Daley Thompson is a highly competent performer at many disciplines, indeed he is easily Britain's best long jumper, and ranks in the national top ten at sprints, hurdles and pole vault. He competes regularly for his club, Newham and Essex Beagles, in league fixtures at a variety of events and scores handfuls of points, yet then his relaxed attitude is so very different from that which he brings to his carefully chosen decathlon efforts. Before a decathlon he is unapproachable, as his usual happy-go-lucky nature is cast aside by a fierce determination and concentration on every move. The result is a record that compares more than favourably with any decathlete in history.

The great decathletes – in alphabetical order

	No.	Wins	8000+	WR	Championships won (places in brackets)
Nikolay Avilov	29	10	11	1	OG '72 (3rd '76, 4th '68); WSG '70
Jim Bausch	5	4	–	1	OG '32
Milton Campbell	5	2	–	–	OG '56 (2nd '52)
Jürgen Hingsen	22	6	14	3	(OG 2nd '84, WCh 2nd '83, ECh 2nd '82)
Bruce Jenner	29	16	10	3	OG '76; PAm '75
Rafer Johnson	11	9	2	3	OG '60 (2nd '56); PAm '55
Guido Kratschmer	40	15	18	1	(OG 2nd '76, 4th '84; ECh '74 3rd)
Vas. Kuznyetsov	40	29	–	2	ECh '54, '58, '62; (OG 3rd '56, '60)
Bob Mathias	10	10	–	3	OG '48, '52
Glenn Morris	3	3	–	2	OG '36
Daley Thompson	25	16	13	3	OG '80, '84; WCh '83; ECh '82; CG '78, '82 (ECh 2nd '78)
Bill Toomey	38	22	13	2	OG '68; PAm '77
C.K.Yang	17	12	1	1	(OG 2nd '60)
Paavo Yrjola	14	10	–	4	OG '28

Columns give respectively: number of decathlons contested, number won, number of scores over 8000 on the 1962 tables, and number of world records.

Review of 1984

WORLD JUNIOR MALE ATHLETE 1984 – DANNY HARRIS

It would have taken remarkable judgement for anybody to have selected Danny Harris as an Olympic medallist at the start of 1984. His mighty progress at the 400 metres hurdles, often referred to as the man-killer of track and field, culminated in his Olympic silver medal behind the incomparable Edwin Moses, yet he had never run the event until just five months earlier.

His achievements closely paralleled those of the Texan Eddie Southern in 1956. Southern had run 440 yards hurdles in 53.4 in 1955 and then came storming through in 1956 to run 400m hurdles in 49.7 and take the Olympic silver medal behind Glenn Davis at the age of 18 years and 325 days. He is still the youngest

Date	Venue/meeting	Event	Place	Mark	
	Indoors at other events:				
11 Feb	Lincoln	440y	1	46.98	
25 Feb	Lincoln – Big 8	300y	1h	30.20	
		300y	1	30.09	
9 Mar	Syracuse – NCAA	400m	1h	47.81	
		400m	4	46.81	(1. A.McKay)
	Outdoors at other events				
11 May	Lincoln – Big 8	400m	1h	45.79	

Danny HARRIS – 400m hurdles competitions in 1984

Date	Venue/meeting	Place	Mark	
17 Mar	Long Beach	1	51.3	
23 Mar	Baton Rouge	1h	50.77	
24 Mar		1	49.55	WJR
6 Apr	Austin – Texas Relays	1h	51.01	
		1	49.44	WJR
27 Apr	Des Moines – Drake R	1h	51.84	
		1	49.4	
11 May	Lincoln – Big 8	1h	51.06	
12 May		1	49.16	WJR
18 May	Knoxville – Gatorade	1h	50.64	
19 May		1	49.20	
30 May	Eugene – NCAA Champs	1h	50.62	
1 Jun		1	48.81	WJR
16 Jun	Los Angeles –	1h	49.18	
17 Jun	US Olympic Trials	2sf	48.02	WJR
18 Jun		2	48.11	
14 Jul	Villanova – Elliott	1	50.00	
3 Aug	Los Angeles –	1h	49.81	
4 Aug	Olympic Games	1sf	48.92	
5 Aug		2	48.13	

WJR = world junior record

ever 400mh medallist, for Harris won his silver at just eight days older!

As a 17-year-old in 1983 Harris won the California state title at 300 metres over 2ft 6in (76cm) low hurdles in a US high school record time of 35.52. He represented Perris High School, from which he went at the end of the year to the University of Iowa with the aim of playing football (he is a defensive back) as well as taking part in track and field. His 300m hurdling was good training for the longer event and the higher hurdles, but to move so rapidly from novice to world class at the taxing 400mh event was extraordinary.

Virtually all his track experiences in 1984 were novel. He competed indoors for the first time, and won the Big 8 300 yards flat title, before placing a respectable fourth in the NCAA 400 metres. As the table shows, his first 400mh race was on 17th March in an all-comers meeting at Long Beach. Such is his talent that he broke the world junior record, which had been improved from Southern's 1956 mark of 49.7 to 49.61 by Harald Schmid back in 1976, in only his third race at the distance. This first record came in the Paper-Tiger Invitational at Baton Rouge, Louisiana, despite him hitting the sixth and ninth hurdles. Further improvements followed rapidly, all the way down to 48.02 in the US Olympic Trials, at which he, and another, if slightly older, newcomer to the event Tranel Hawkins smashed a talented field in filling the runner-ups spots to the inevitable Edwin Moses.

Moses goes on compiling the greatest winning sequence in track history, but if Danny Harris improves further, and indeed his technique is as yet still very raw, then it might be a matter of time before a new master takes over the event.

WORLD JUNIOR WOMAN ATHLETE – ZOLA BUDD

Zola Budd had for long idolised Mary Decker, so their clash in Los Angeles, which ruined the medal hopes of both was especially ironic. Not since Mary Decker herself had run so brilliantly as a tiny figure against the Soviets at the age of 14 and 15 had a teenage woman runner so captured the public imagination as this elfin youngster.

Born and raised in the healthy climate and pure air of Bloemfontein in the Orange Free State at an altitude of some 1400m above sea-level, she started running seriously at the age of 14. She won her first South African titles and set her first national record in 1982 and her 5000m debut in January 1983 resulted in her first world junior best time. Since then she has run faster than any junior woman at distances from 1500m to 5000m.

Her 1984 season started dramatically as she smashed Decker's world best for 5000m at Stellenbosch. A highly successful South African season followed with a series of records leading up to her 1500m record on 21 March. Then the full glare of media publicity turned on her as she was brought to Britain to claim the UK citizenship which would enable her to run internationally and escape the isolation imposed on South Africa due to that nation's Apartheid policies.

Zola's grandfather had been born in London in 1886 and emigrated to South Africa in his twenties. Her father was thus enabled to claim British citizenship and this enabled Zola in turn to claim this right; as a minor (under 18) she would not need to undergo a period of naturalisation. Her application was rushed through with extraordinary speed, which aroused considerable controversy, and indeed if this had been submitted after her 18th birthday on 26th May she woud have had to serve a five-year residency qualification.

She arrived in Britain on 24th March with her family and coach Peter Labuschagne and her citizenship papers were issued on 6th April. Under contract to the London newspaper, the *Daily Mail*, her attendant progress towards her Olympic dream was celebrated in the full blaze of publicity.

39

Review of 1984

The shy figure was whisked onto and off the running tracks of Britain, heavily 'minded' by her newspaper guardians and she was given little chance of meeting her competitors. From her first race at Dartford it quickly became apparent that she was a prodigious talent and she impressed more and more in each ensuing race. She had been so used to running virtually solo time trials that we may have doubted her ability to cope with good opposition, but she firmly dispelled such speculation with a fine debut against the world's best (Kristiansen and Waitz) in the Oslo road race, and victory over Boxer and Benning in her final pre-Olympic race at Crystal Palace, when she set a world's best for 2000 metres.

Nevertheless thoughts about a gold medal were surely premature and her coach wisely conselled that 1987 or 1988 would be the likely time for her to reach the top. Tragically it all went wrong in Los Angeles, when Mary Decker tripped over her. Budd returned to South Africa and there was considerable speculation as to her future. The conflicting interests of athletics and her family were it seems reconciled with her return to Europe at the end of the year, but there would undoubtedly be much concern if she continued to be based in South Africa. Whatever the political considerations however she is a wonderful athlete with still unrealised potential.

Zola BUDD in 1984

Date	Venue/meeting	Event	Place	Mark	
5 Jan	Stellenbosch	5000m	1	15:01.83	World best
25 Jan	Potchefstroom	3000m	1	9:07.42	
30 Jan	Bloemfontein	1 mile	1	4:37.52	
6 Feb	Bloemfontein	2000m	1	5:44.4	SAR
15 Feb	Stellenbosch	3000m	1	9:03.8	
20 Feb	Bloemfontein	1500m	1	4:05.81	WJB
25 Feb	Pretoria	3000m	1	9:05.9	
29 Feb	Stellenbosch	3000m	1	8:37.5	WJB
5 Mar	Germiston	3000m	1	8:52.84	
7 Mar	Port Elizabeth	5000m	1	15:09.86	
16 Mar	Kroonstad	800m	1	2:00.9	
21 Mar	Port Elizabeth	1500m	1	4:01.81	WJB
		3000m	1	8:54.7	
14 Apr	Dartford	3000m	1	9:02.6	UKJR
25 Apr	London	1500m	1	4:10.82	UKJR
6 May	Oslo – road race	10km	3	31:42	(1. I.Kristiansen)
27 May	Cwmbran – UK Champs	1500m	1h	4:16.27	
28 May		1500m	1	4:04.39	EJR
6 Jun	London – Olympic Trials	3000m	1	8:40.22	EJR
19 Jun	Belfast	3000m	1	8:51.99	
23 Jun	Birmingham – Eng. Int.	1500m	1	4:14.22	
13 Jul	London – P-Talbot G	2000m	1	5:33.15	World best
		(1 mile	–	4:30.7	UKJR)
8 Aug	Los Angeles – Olympic Games	3000m	3h	8:44.62	
		3000m	7	8:48.80	(1. M.Puica)
30 Dec	Zürich – road race	8km	1	26:26.7	

WJB = World junior best (all also South African records)

SAR = South African record

UKJR = UK Junior Record

EJR = European Junior Record

40

DIARY 1984

JANUARY 5	Stellenbosch, South Africa. The phenomenal 17-year-old Zola Budd ran 5000 metres in 15:01.83. However it could not be ratified as a world record (held by Mary Decker at 15:08.26) as South Africa are no longer members of the IAAF. Despite windy conditions Budd led from the start and finished a lap and a half in front of runner-up Sonja Laxton (16:49.19).
15	Houston marathon, USA. $8000 was decided by a hair's breadth as Charlie Spedding (UK) in his first marathon was adjudged the winner from Massimo Magnani (Ita), both men being timed in 2:11:54. The winner's prize fund benefitted by $20,000 to $12,000 for the runner-up. $20,000 was also the reward for the women's winner, in 2:27:51, Ingrid Kristiansen (Nor). She had also won the previous year, but in between had given birth to a daughter in August 1983.
16	Osaka, Japan. Paul Narracott (Aus) scored an upset win at 60m over Carl Lewis, 6.62 to 6.68. Lewis's sister Carol set a US indoor long jump record of 6.67m.
21–22	GDR Indoor Championships at Senftenberg. World indoor bests were set by Heike Daute, women's long jump 6.99m, and Thomas Schroder a time of 9.50 for the rarely contested 100 yards. The latter equalled the time he had run at the same venue two weeks earlier.
26–27	GDR v USSR Multi-events at Senftenberg. Sabine Paetz set a world indoor pentathlon best with 4862 points. The GDR won the women's match and the USSR the men's seven-eventer.
27	Millrose Games at Madison Square Garden, New York, USA. Carl Lewis set a world indoor long jump best of 8.79 to equal his outdoor best. This jump came in the final round with Lewis facing defeat as he was behind Larry Myricks 8.30m to 8.38m. He hit the board absolutely perfectly. As usual the meeting had the largest attendance of the indoor season – 18,210.
FEBRUARY 1	Milan, Italy. Italy beat the USSR and Spain in a men's indoor international. In the women's match the USSR beat Italy. Three world indoor bests were set: Igor Paklin (USSR) high jumped 2.36m, Giuliana Salce (Ita) walked 3000m in 13:08.09 and Sergey Bubka (USSR) set his second record of the winter as he pole vaulted 5.82m. He had cleared 5.81m in Vilnius, Lithuania on 15 January.
10	Los Angeles Times Games at Inglewood, Los Angeles. Sergey Bubka improved his world pole vault best to 5.83m, and for the first time ever two vaulters cleared over 19ft in the same competition. Bubka's jump was one and a half inches over that height and, in setting an American indoor record of 5.80m, Billy Olson had a quarter of an inch to spare.
10–11	West German Indoor Championships at Stuttgart. Ralf Lübke twice improved the world indoor best for 200m, running 20.67 in his semi-final and 20.57 in the final. Brigitte Kraus won her 50th German national title with her win in the 1500m in 4:08.15; her first was as a junior in 1971.

Review of 1984

11 **Gainesville**, Florida, USA. Antonio McKay produced a major surprise with a world indoor 400m best of 45.79. He had run 45.9 outdoors in 1982 but had then had surgery on a torn cartilage in his right knee and had missed the 1983 season.

11 **Gasparilla Classic** 15km road race at Tampa, Florida, USA. Grete Waitz won the women's race in a world best time for the distance of 47:52 from Wendy Sly (UK) 48:42. Mike McLeod (UK) won the men's race in 42:55 from Mike Musyoki (Ken) and John Treacy (Ire), both 42:57. All five went on to win Olympic medals.

17–19 **USSR Indoor Championships** at Moscow. Sergey Kasnauskas set a European indoor shot best of 21.46m.

24 **USA Indoor Championships** at New York. This was the first meeting in the United States ever to have formal drug testing, as it was required of all athletes who accepted nomination to the national team to compete against England on 10 March. Carl and Carol Lewis, who did not want the trip, nonetheless submitted urine samples to prove that they also did not use drugs. All the athletes tested passed the tests. Jim Heiring set an indoor world best for 2 miles walk with 12:11.21. Leading winning marks included: Carl Lewis LJ – 8.50, Greg Foster 60yh – 6.95, Tamara Bykova (USSR) HJ – 2.00m.

24 **West Berlin**. Carlo Thränhardt, who had a record 15 meetings at 2.30m or better in 1983, maintained his consistency with a world indoor high jump best of 2.37m.

26 **Women's Ekiden Renown Cup**, Japan. The women's international road relay race over the marathon distance was won by England's team of Shireen Samy, Carole Bradford, Marina Samy, Julie-Ann Laughton, Mary Cotton and Carol Haigh. They clocked 2:20:54 ahead of Australia 2:23:50 and USSR 2:25:24.

MARCH
3 The **English National cross-country championships** at Newark set new records for a national championship. The senior race had a record 1862 starters of whom 1723 finished the race won by Eamonn Martin. There were also 490 finishers from 575 in the junior race and 556 from 579 in the youths.

3–4 **European Indoor Championships** at Göteborg, Sweden. The world pole vault record holder outdoors, Thierry Vigneron (Fra), with 5.85m regained the world indoor best and also this title, both of which he had held in 1981. Helena Fibingerova (Cs) won the women's shot for the seventh time, which equalled the most at one event set by Valeriy Borzov (USSR) in the men's sprints between 1970 and 1977. In Olympic year the Championships presented generally rather weak fields. (see p. 61 for medallists).

9–10 **NCAA Indoor Championships** at Syracuse, USA. Held for the first time on an 8-lane unbanked synthetic track. Leading team results: MEN – 1. Arkansas 38, 2. Iowa State 36, 3. Washington State 28; WOMEN – 1. Nebraska 59, 2. Tennessee 48, 3. Villanova. Shot putter Mike Carter of Southern Methodist University won his fourth indoor title at the same event to equal the record held by Suleiman Nyambui (at 1 mile 1979–82).

16–18 **Montauban**, France. Ramon Zabalo (Fra) smashed the world best for 48 hours on the track. In this time he ran 420 kilometres, also setting bests at 300km – 32:13:20 and 200 miles – 34:56:41. Eleanor Adams (UK) set a women's record woth 325.158km.

25 **World Cross-country Championships** at the Meadowlands Racecourse, East Rutherford, New Jersey, USA. Two outstanding champions, now well into their 30s, regained their titles. Carlos Lopes (Por) had won previously in 1976 and Maricica Puica (Rom) in 1982. The Championships were staged by the New York Road Runners Club and a crowd of 17,418 attended the track, usually used for horse racing. Ethiopia have contested this event only four times, but for the fourth successive year they won the men's team title and for the third successive year won the junior men's title. The USA won their sixth women's title. Leading results: MEN (12km):1. Carlos Lopes (Por) 33:25, 2. Tim Hutchings (Eng) 33:30, 3. Steve Jones (Wal) 33:32, 4. Pat Porter (USA) 33:34, 5. Wilson Waigwa (Ken) 33:41, 6. Ed Eyestone (USA) 33:46, 7. Pierre Levesier (Fra) 33:51, 8. Bekele Debele (Eth) 33:52, 9. Adugna Lema (Eth) 33:52, 10. Francesco Panetta (Ita) 33:54, 11. Alberto Cova (Ita), 12. Christoph Herle (GFR), 13. John Treacy (Ire), 14. Niels Kim Hjorth (Den), 15. Martti Vainio (Fin), 16. Mohammed Kedir (Eth), 17. Craig Virgin (USA), 18. Stijn Jaspers (Hol), 19. Paul Kipkoech (Ken), 20. Rex Wilson (NZ). 238 finished. Team:1. Ethiopia 134, 2. USA 161, 3. Portugal 223, 4. Kenya 233, 5. Italy 258, 6. England 269, 7. Spain 270, 8. New Zealand 276, 9. France 371, 10. Ireland 388. 28 teams (of six) finished. JUNIOR MEN (8km):1. Pedro Casacuberta (Spa) 21:34, 2. Doju Tessema (Eth) 21:34, 3. Giovanni Castellano (Can) 21:37. 94 finished. Team: 1. Ethiopia 21, 2. Spain 34, 3. England 68, 4. USA 72. 15 teams (of four) finished. WOMEN (5km):1. Maricica Puica (Rom) 15:56, 2. Galina Zakharova (USSR) 15:58, 3. Grete Waitz (Nor) 15:58, 4. Ingrid Kristiansen (Nor) 16:04, 5. Jane Furniss (Eng) 16:10, 6. Christine Benning (Eng) 16:15, 7. Midde Hamrin (Swe) 16:16, 8. Angela Tooby (Wal) 16:18, 9. Betty Springs (USA) 16:20, 10. Cathy Branta (USA) 16:21, 11. Eva Ernström (Swe), 12. Francine Peeters (Bel), 13. Zhanna Tursunova (USSR), 14. Dianne Rodger (USA), 15. Ruth Smeeth (Eng), 16. Sabrina Dornhoefer (USA), 17. Cathy Twomey (USA), 18. Lynn Williams (Can), 19. Mary O'Connor (NZ), 20. Tina Krebs (Den). 108 finished. Team:1. USA 52, 2. England 65, 3. New Zealand 91, 4. Ireland 105, 5. Sweden 122, 6. Romania 127, 7. Belgium 136, 8. Norway 154, 9. Portugal 156, 10. Canada 177. 17 teams (of four) finished.

APRIL 1 **New Orleans, USA.** Mark Nenow (USA) ran the fastest ever 10km on the road. His time was 27:22 for the certified point-to-point course. Behind him Mike Musyoki (Ken) 27:29 and Nick Rose (UK) 27:34 were also inside the previous world best.

6 **Zola Budd granted UK citizenship.** As a South African the immensely talented 17-year-old, holder of world junior best times for 1500m and 3000m and the world best for 5000m, was ineligible to run internationally. However her grandfather had been British and because of this her father had been able to claim British nationality. Zola, as she was under 18, was able to follow suit. She had arrived in Britain with her family on 24 March under contract to the London newspaper the *Daily Mail* and her citizenship papers were rushed through with extraordinary speed. Her subsequent career was attended with enormous media interest throughout the summer as her track form led to Olympic selection and the trauma in Los Angeles.

16 **Boston Marathon.** The 88th running of this, much the oldest of annual marathon races, resulted in men's and women's victories for Geoff Smith (UK) 2:10:34 and Lorraine Moller (NZ) 2:29:28.

Review of 1984

MAY
5
Softeland Grand Prix at Fana, Norway. This annual festival of walking produced world track records for Ernesto Canto (Mex) at 20km – 1:18:39.9 and for Yan Hong (Chn) at women's 5km – 21:40.2. Behind Canto, Erling Andersen (Nor) set a European record of 1:20:36.7 and two other women, Xu Yongju (Chn) 21:41.0 and Natalya Serbinyenko (USSR) 21:59.0, were also under the previous world record. On the following day at Softeland, Serbinyenko walked the fastest 3km ever on the road by a woman in 12:32.

5–6
Potsdam, GDR. Sabine Paetz set a world women's heptathlon record with a score of 6867 points, adding 31 to the record of teammate Ramona Neubert.

8
The Soviet Union announced that it would boycott the Olympic Games in Los Angeles. This decision followed intensive propaganda against the Games. Cited had been the failure of the Los Angeles Organising Committee to follow the Olympic Charter, the heat and smog of Los Angeles and the refusal by the United States to grant entry visas to certain Soviet personnel. The principal reason then given for the boycott was the problem of security for Soviet athletes participating in the Games. The Soviet decision was followed by nearly all the Eastern Bloc nations, the one exception being Romania, who eventually competed in Los Angeles with considerable success. So for the third successive Olympics the Games were marred by a significant boycott, this being the most serious in terms of overall standards although more nations had followed the US-inspired boycott of Moscow in 1980.

13
London Marathon. This race again set new records for the most competitors in a marathon. 21,337 entries were accepted. The total number of starters was 16,992 of whom 15,649 completed the distance. These figures compared to 19,735, 16,581 and 15,776 the previous year. In windy conditions 56 men ran under 2 hrs 20 mins, compared to the record 93 the previous year. The men's winner was Charlie Spedding (UK) in 2:09:57 and the women's Ingrid Kristiansen (Nor) in 2:24:26, the second fastest ever run.

13
KIFs Jubilaeumsmarch, Copenhagen, Denmark. Yan Hong (Chn) set a world record of 45:39.5 to win the women's 10km walk. Ernesto Canto won the men's race in 39:34.2.

19–20
Götzis, Austria. Winners in this major annual multi-events competition: Decathlon – Grigoriy Degtyarov (USSR) 8579, a Soviet record; Heptathlon – Nadezhda Vinogradova (USSR) 6319.

26
Bratislava, Czechoslovakia. Sergey Bubka, following his great indoor season, set his first outdoor world pole vault record at a height of 5.85m.

26
Bruce Jenner Classic at San Jose, California, USA. Brian Oldfield, who had put a world best as a professional in 1975, came within 3cm of the world shot record with a US record 22.19m. Despite lawsuits, as a reinstated amateur he was not allowed to compete in the US Olympic Trials.

27
Sochi, USSR. Natalya Lisovskaya returned the women's shot record to the USSR after ten years in other Eastern European hands when she put 22.53m. Her best in 1983 had been 20.85m and she improved to 21.75m on 20 May.

Review of 1984

27 European Women's Club Cup at Madrid, Spain. First three teams: 1. Bayer Leverkusen (GFR) 166, 2. Sisport Fiat Iveco (Ita) 153, 3. Borough of Hounslow (UK) 118.5.

28–2 June NCAA Championships at Eugene, Oregon, USA. This was the 63rd edition of these championships and the third in succession to be held at Hayward Field, Eugene, where the spectators are the most enthusiastic and best informed in the USA. Leading team results: MEN – 1. Oregon 113, 2. Washington State 94.5, 3. Arkansas 85; WOMEN – 1. Florida State 145, 2. Tennessee 124, 3. Stanford 71. Oregon were led by the Brazilian Joachim Cruz, who won both 800m and 1500m events in 1:45.10 and 3:36.48 respectively, the latter a South American record. Florida State similarly benefited from a sprint double by Randy Givens, 100m in 11.06w and 200m in 22.87. She also ran on both their winning relay teams, at 4x100m and 4x440y. Other double winners were Mike Conley (Arkansas) LJ – 8.23w and TJ – 17.36, and John Brenner (UCLA) SP – 21.92 and DT – 63.44. Conley had also won both events at the NCAA indoor championships and so completed the first ever such double-double in the horizontal jumps. Brenner's Collegiate record pushed Mike Carter into second place at 21.76m; Carter had never previously lost in an NCAA title meet, having won three outdoor and four indoor titles. Danny Harris (Iowa State) won the 400mh in 48.81, his fourth world junior record of the season. History was made by the inclusion of the women's triple jump, the first time that the event had been held in any major championship; the winner was Terri Turner of Texas with a wind-assisted 13.52m, the best ever by a woman.

JUNE 1 Comrades Marathon, Pietermaritzburg to Durban, South Africa. Bruce Fordyce won his fourth successive victory in this famous 88km race with a record time of 5:27:18.

1–3 GDR Championships at Erfurt. The National Team of Gesine Walther, Sabine Busch, Dagmar Rübsam and Marita Koch improved the world record for 4x400m by 3.12 seconds. Koch rounded off this superlative effort with a 47.70 anchor leg, a time bettered only by the 47.6 run by Jarmila Kratochvilova on the last leg for Czechoslovakia in the 1982 European Championships. Marlies Göhr ran the second fastest ever 200m to beat Bärbel Wöckel 21.74 to 22.19, and also won her eighth successive 100m title in 10.89. The men's 4x400m team set a European record of 3:00.07.

2 Saint-Denis, Paris, France. Sergey Bubka set his second outdoor world pole vault record with a clearance at 5.88m. In this competition he beat three previous world record holders: Vladimir Polyakov, Thierry Vigneron and Wladyslaw Kozakiewicz.

2–3 Neubrandenburg, GDR. USSR beat GDR in both men's and women's multi-event competitions. Individual winners were: Decathlon – Aleksandr Apaychev (USSR) 8643 from Uwe Freimuth (GDR) 8553, both national records; Heptathlon – Anke Vater (GDR) 6566. Apaychev's score featured the highest ever second day tally of 4352 points.

4 Dublin, Ireland. There was a record field in a women's only race, as over 9000 runners competed in a 10km road race won by Regina Joyce in 32:34.

45

Review of 1984

7–9 **TAC Championships** at San Jose, California. The prospect of the imminent US Olympic Trials may have reduced participation at the national championships, but there was nonetheless still a high standard, headed by American records from Earl Bell, 5.80m pole vault, Valerie Brisco-Hooks, 49.83 for 400m, and Judi Brown, 54.99 for 400m hurdles. The team winners were Bud Light Track America (men) and Puma & Energizer TC (women). (See US section for winners).

8–9 Mannheim, F.R. Germany. Jürgen Hingsen set his third world decathlon record as he improved his previous mark by 19 points to 8798 as he won his national Olympic trial, which was combined with an international in which the GFR beat Poland.

9–10 European Men's Club Cup at Milan, Italy. First three teams: 1. Pro Patria Pierrel (Ita) 301, 2. Fiamme Oro Padova (Ita), 3. Futbol Club Barcelona (Spa) 256.

10 Eberstadt, F.R.Germany. The annual high jump competition here has become established as a high-class one. Jacek Wszola (Pol) had set a world record of 2.35m at the meeting, a one event affair, in 1980. This year's contest set new standards throughout, with a record five men over 2.30m and eleven men at 2.24m or higher. The winner, Zhu Jianhua (Chn) cleared 2.39m for a new world record, and in second and third places the West Germans Carlo Thränhardt and Dietmar Mögenburg equalled the European record of 2.36m.

16–24 **US Olympic Trials** at Los Angeles. The strict US selection methods, decreeing that the Olympic team is selected only on the basis of the Trials always ensures a meeting of the highest quality and highest tension. Unusually for this four-yearly bonanza no world records were set but there were six US records. These came from four men: Earl Jones and Johnny Gray, 800m in 1:43.74, Dwight Stones, HJ 2.34m, Mike Tully, PV 5.81m, and three women: Chandra Cheeseborough, 400m 49.28, Judi Brown, 400mh 54.93 and Jackie Joyner, Heptathlon 6520 points. Carl Lewis maintained his emulation of Jesse Owens by winning at 100m, 200m and long jump. Discus thrower John Powell won his event to qualify for his fourth US Olympic team, while seven men and three women qualified for the third time. Included in this number was the 44-year-old hammer thrower Ed Burke, who had placed seventh in the 1964 Olympics and twelfth in 1968, when he retired. He came back to competition in 1980 and by 1982 had comfortably exceeded his old US record of 71.90m set back in 1967. The biggest shock was the defeat of Mary Decker in the women's 1500m by Ruth Wysocki, Decker's first loss to a US athlete on the track since 1980. Decker did however qualify for both 1500m and 3000m, but notable athletes to miss the first three and Olympic selection included Mel Lattany, James Robinson, Billy Olson, Jane Frederick and Stephanie Hightower. The latter was undoubtedly the unluckiest. She had won the Trials in 1980, only to lose the chance to compete at the Olympics through the US boycott of the Moscow Games. This time she was fourth at 100m hurdles but her time of 13.13 was the same as that given to second and third and just 1/100th of a second behind the winner, Kim Turner.

20–24 **Izvestia Cup** at Kiev, USSR. This was the highest quality Soviet meeting during the year. Three women's world records were set: Margarita Ponomaryeva ran the 400mh in 53.58 just three days after her 21st birthday, Olga Bondarenko ran 10000m in 31:13.78 and Tamara Bykova added a centimetre to her high jump record with 2.05m. Soviet records were also set by Vasiliy Matveyev at 800m 1:44.25, by Olga Vladykina women's 400m 48.98, and by the multi-events winners

Review of 1984

of the Soviet Championships: Grigoriy Degtyarev, Dec 8652, and Natalya Shubenkova, Hep 6799.

23–24   **AAA Championships** at Crystal Palace, London, UK. Peter Elliott defeated Sebastian Coe at 1500m, 3:39.66 to 3:39.77, for the latter's first loss to a UK athlete at the distance since 1976.

28   **Bislett Games** at Oslo, Norway. Ingrid Kristiansen stepped down from the marathon to run the first sub-15 minute 5000m by a woman, with a time of 14:58.89. Seb Coe and Steve Ovett showed their return to fitness with wins at 800m in 1:43.84 and 1500m in 3:34.50 respectively. Fernando Mamede (Por) led seven men under 13:20 to win the 5000m in 13:12.83. Krystof Wesolowski (Pol) set a world best in the 2000m steeplechase with 5:20.00.

JULY
2   **DN Galan** at Stockholm, Sweden. The Portuguese 10000m runners Fernando Mamede and Carlos Lopes smashed Henry Rono's six-year-old world record of 27:22.5. They passed 5000m in 13:45.40 before stepping up the pace. Mamede kicked with two laps to go, running the final 400m in 57.5 for an overall time of 27:13.81, which meant that he had run his second 5000m in 13:28.41. Lopes was second in 27:17.48.

2–8   **Randall's Island, New York**, USA. The 6-day record of 623.75 miles (1003.83km) set by George Littlewood (UK) which had remained unapproached since 1888 was bettered by Yiannis Kouros (Gre). He ran successive daily mileages of 164, 84, 111, 90, 94 and 92 to total 635 miles 1023 yards (1022.87km). Eleanor Adams set a women's best of 462 miles 278 yards (743.77km).

3   **Cork City International**, Ireland. Two Soviet world record setters in the hammer came to Cork in prime form, for both Yuriy Sedykh and Sergey Litvinov had thrown 82.60m in Kiev on 21 June. They produced the greatest display of hammer throwing ever as they smashed Litvinov's 1983 world record of 84.14m. Litvinov had the following series: N, 85.20, 84.84, 83.74, N, N, but he was well beaten for Sedykh regained the record with his first throw and maintained fantastic form as is shown by his series: 86.34, 86.00, 85.20, 84.16, 83.30, N.

12–15   **African Championships** at Rabat, Morocco. The Kenyans did not include their Olympic representatives, and there were no competitors from such strong nations as Ethiopia and Tanzania. Nonetheless 29 nations took part. Winners: MEN 100m: Chidi Imo (Nig) 10.40, 200m: Innocent Egbunike (Nig) 20.66, 400m: Gabriel Tiacoh (IvC) 45.52, 800m: Sammy Koskei (Ken) 1:45.17, 1500m: Said Aouita (Mor) 3:38.18, 5000m: Abderrazak Bounour (Alg) 13:41.94, 10000m: Kipsubai Koskei (Ken) 28:11.7, 3000mSt: Joshua Kipkemboi (Ken) 8:27.88, 110mh: Philip Sang (Ken) 14.15, 400mh: Amadou Dia Ba (Sen) 49.30, HJ: Mohamed Aghlal (Mor) 2.17, PV: Mohamed Bouihiri (Mor) 4:60, LJ: Paul Emordi (Nig) 7.90, TJ: Joseph Taiwo (Nig) 17.19, SP: Ahmed Mohamed Achouche (Egypt) 18.45, DT: Mohamed Naguib (Egypt) 58.62, HT: Hakim Toumi (Alg) 68.64, JT: Tarek Chaabani (Tun) 77.40, Dec: Moured Mahour Bacha (Alg) 7024, 20kmW: Abdelwahab Ferguene (Alg) 1:30:02; 4x100mR: Nigeria 39.49, 4x400mR: Senegal 3:04.76
WOMEN 100m: Doris Wiredu (Ghana) 11.88, 200m/400mh: Nawal el Moutawakil (Mor) 23.93/56.01, 400m: Ruth Atuti (Ken) 54.05, 800m/1500m: Justina Chepchirchir (Ken) 2:04.52/4:18.45, 3000m: Mary Chepkemboi (Ken) 9:19.05, 100mh: Maria Usifo (Nig) 13.42, HJ: Awa Dioum-Ndiaye (Sen) 1.76, LJ: Marianne

Review of 1984

Mendoza (Sen) 5.93, SP: Odette Mistoul (Gabon) 15.51, DT: Zoubida Laayouni (Mor) 52.70, JT: Tenin Camara (IvC) 45.48, Hep: Cherifa Meskaoui (Mor) 5448, 4x100mR/4x400mR: Kenya 46.18/3:37.76

13 **Peugeot-Talbot Games** at Crystal Palace, London, UK. Sergey Bubka set his third world pole vault record of the year when he cleared 5.90m by a huge margin on his first attempt. After a long delay while the height was checked, he tried again at 5.92m, but couldn't manage it. He had actually asked for 6.00m, but the standards would go no higher than 5.92m. In an event which had not yet attained world record status, Zola Budd showed that she could handle good opposition as she ran the fastest ever women's 2000m in 5:33.15 ahead of Christina Boxer and Christine Benning. Yuriy Sedykh again displayed tremendous hammer throwing with his first three throws of 85.04, 85.60 and 85.52m.

20 **Olympische Tag in East Berlin**, GDR. Lyudmila Andonova (Bul) had returned to high jumping after giving birth to a daughter in October 1983. She improved to 1.99m in early June but here she astonished everyone by adding a further eight centimetres, as she cleared 2.00m, 2.02m and finally a world record height of 2.07m. No less sensational was the world's first 100m javelin throw by another athlete to have missed the 1983 season, Uwe Hohn (GDR), whose 104.80m added 5.08m to the world record, its largest ever improvement.

21 **Olympische Tag in Potsdam**, GDR. In another very high quality meeting in East Germany, Marita Koch equalled her five-year old 200m record of 21.71 ahead of Bärbel Wöckel 21.85 and Marlies Göhr 22.22.

21 **Prefontaine Classic** at Eugene, Oregon, USA. Top performances were a US pole vault record of 5.82m by Mike Tully and a South American 1000m record of 2:14.54 by Joaquim Cruz (Bra).

AUGUST
3 **Eugene**, Oregon, USA. Mary Decker (USA) improved the world women's best for 2000m to 5:32.7.

3–12 **Olympic Games** in Los Angeles (see separate section).

5–6 **Moscow City Championships**, USSR. Tatyana Kazankina made a further improvement on the women's 2000m best, clocking 5:28.72. More world records came from the quartet of Nadyezhda Olizarenko, Lyubov Gurina, Lyudmila Borisova and Irina Podyalovsakya with their time of 7:50.17 for the 4 x 800m relay, and from Natalya Artyemova in the mile at 4:15.8.

16–18 **Friendship Games in Prague**, Czechoslovakia. Most of the best women from the Eastern bloc nations competed in this meeting, although there were a few notable absentees from the GDR. One world record was set, Irina Meszynski (GDR) throwing the discus 73.36m. Other winners: 100m: Marlies Göhr (GDR) 10.95, 200m: Bärbel Wöckel (GDR) 22.15, 400m: Marita Koch (GDR) 48.16, 800m: Irina Podyalovskaya (USSR) 1:57.31, 1500m: Nadyezhda Ralldugina (USSR) 3:56.63, 3000m: Tatyana Kazankina (USSR) 8:33.01, Mar: Zoya Ivanova (USSR) 2:33:44, 100mh: Yordanka Donkova (Bul) 12.55, 400mh: Marina Stepanova (USSR) 53.67, HJ: Lyudmila Andonova (Bul) 1.96, LJ: Heike Drechsler (GDR) 7.15, SP: Natalya Lisovskaya (USSR) 21.96, JT: Petra Felke (GDR) 73.30, Hep: Natalya Grachova (USSR) 6477, 4x100mR: Bulgaria 42.62, 4x400mR: USSR 3:19.12.

Review of 1984

17-18 **Friendship Games in Moscow**, USSR. As with the women in Prague so most of the best Eastern bloc men competed here. No world records were set, and the standards were generally highest in the field events. Winners: 100m: Osvaldo Lara (Cuba) 10.17, 200m: Vladimir Muravyev (USSR) 20.34, 400m: Viktor Markin (USSR) 44.78, 800m: Ryszard Ostrowski (Pol) 1:45.68, 1500m: Andreas Busse (GDR) 3:36.65, 5000m: Evgeni Ignatov (Bul) 13:26.35, 10000m: Valeriy Abramov (USSR) 27:55.17, Mar: Dereje Nedi (Eth) 2:10:32, 3000mSt: Boguslaw Maminski (Pol) 8:27.15, 110mh: György Bakos (Hun) 13.52, 400mh: Aleksandr Vasilyev (USSR) 48.63, HJ: Valeriy Sereda (USSR) 2.25, PV: Konstantin Volkov (USSR) 5.80, LJ: Konstantin Semykin (USSR) 8.38, TJ: Oleg Protsenko (USSR) 17.46, SP: Sergey Kasnauskas (USSR) 21.64, DT: Yuriy Dumchev (USSR) 66.70, HT: Yuriy Sedykh (USSR) 85.60, JT: Uwe Hohn (GDR) 94.44, Dec: Grigoriy Degtyarev (USSR) 8523, 4x100mR/4x400mR: USSR 38.32/3:00.16, 20kmW: Sergey Protsishin (USSR) 1:21:57, 50kmW: Andrey Perlov (USSR) 3:43:06.

17 **ISTAF** in West Berlin, GFR. In the first major post-Olympic meeting in Western Europe, Greg Foster (USA) reversed places with his Olympic conqueror, Roger Kingdom, with 13.16 to 13.17 for 110mh.

18 **Nike Classic** at Crystal Palace, London, UK. Kirk Baptiste (USA), the Olympic silver medallist for 200m, smashed the world best for 300m as he ran the distance in 31.70 secs, compared to the previous best of 32.16 in 1983. He also scored a major upset by defeating Carl Lewis, who lead around the bend, but who faded badly in the last 50 metres to place fourth in 32.18. Todd Bennett (UK) also broke the previous best with 32.14 and Walter McCoy (USA) was third in 32.16. In the women's races there were UK and Commonwealth bests for Kathy Cook (UK) at 300m, 35.46 and Wendy Sly, 1 mile, 4:28.07.

20 **NIKAIA** at Nice, France. Joaquim Cruz embarked upon his barnstorming European tour with a further improvement on his best for 1000m, 2:14.09, the fourth fastest ever run.

20 **Budapest Grand Prix**, Hungary. Yuriy Sedykh maintained his brilliant hammer throwing form. His win at 85.02m was his fourth successive meeting over 85 metres. Carl Lewis won the 100m in 10.05 and Steve Cram, though failing in a record bid, won the 1500m in 3:33.13. Tatana Kocembova (Cs) confirmed her ascendency over Jarmila Kratochvilova by beating her at 400m, 49.23 to 49.35.

20-25 **European Veterans Championships** at Brighton and Crawley, UK. More than 3,000 athletes competed at the various age ranges.

22 **Weltklasse at Zürich**, Switzerland. As usual this meeting attracted the best field of any of the IAAF permit meetings. A host of top-class performances were headed by a world record that came not in a paced race, but in a classic head-to-head confrontation. Evelyn Ashford (USA) sealed her status as world's premier 100m sprinter by adding the world record to her Olympic crown and by beating her arch-rival Marlies Göhr (GDR) 10.76 to 10.84. Other Olympic champions to run even faster than in Los Angeles were Carl Lewis who won the 100m in 9.99, Joachim Cruz, the 800m in 1:42.34 and Sebastian Coe, the 1500m in 3:32.39. World champions from 1983 who showed how they were missed in LA included women's winners Marita Koch, 200m in 21.87 and Jarmila Kratochvilova, 800m in 1:57.68. Fernando Mamede again showed his ability to race well in all but major

Review of 1984

championships (he had dropped out in the Olympic 10000m final) as he beat the Olympic 2-3-4 with 13:20.61 for 5000m.

24 **Ivo Van Damme Memorial** in Brussels, Belgium. Joseph Mahmoud (Fra), the Olympic silver medallist, ran the second fastest 3000m steeplechase ever, a European record 8:07.62 to beat the top Olympic absentee in this event, Boguslaw Maminski (Pol) 8:09.18. Joachim Cruz followed his Zurich win, the third fastest ever 800m, with the fourth fastest – 1:42.41. Fourth fastest ever also was the 7:33.3 run by Said Aouita (Mor) for 3000m. In the long jump Carl Lewis remained supreme with a win at 8.65m, but behind him Larry Myricks produced the best ever non-winning mark of 8.45m.

26 **Weltklasse at Köln**, GFR. Joachim Cruz won the 800m in 1:41.77, just four hundredths of a second off Seb Coe's world record, which had been measured by photocells. Cruz followed the pacemaker through 400m in 49.6, before taking control of the race and going through 600m in 1:16.1. Behind him were the best ever times for second, third and fourth – Sammy Koskei (Kenya), not selected for the Olympics, an African record 1:42.28, Johnny Gray, who equalled his two-day-old US record of 1:43.28, and Agberto Guimares (Bra) 1:43.91.

26 **Leningrad City Championships**, USSR Tatyana Kazankina (USSR) set a world 3000m record of 8:22.62. This made her the first woman ever to have set world marks at 800m, 1500m and 3000m.

26 **Nitra**, Czechoslovakia. Zdenka Silhava improved the women's discus world record to 74.56m with her first throw of the competition.

29 **Sportfest at Koblenz**, GFR. Ed Moses (USA) ran the fastest 400mh of the year, 47.32 to stay well clear of his perennial runner-up Harald Schmid (GFR) 48.04. This was Moses's 93rd successive victory in a final and 27th sub-48 second time. Without Cruz to contend with, Johnny Gray improved his US 800m record to 1:42.96, and Steve Cram (UK) and John Walker (NZ) both broke 3:50 for the mile.

31 **Golden Gala** in Rome. A magnificent pole vault competition was climaxed by two men breaking the world record for the first time in this event since the unratified marks of 5.59m by both Kjell Isaksson (Swe) and Bob Seagren (USA) at El Paso in 1972. First Thierry Vigneron (Fra) added a centimetre to Sergey Bubka's world record for his fifth world mark since 1980, while Bubka himself failed at this height. Then Bubka had the bar moved up to 5.94m and sailed clear, for the first time that the record had been raised twice in the history of pole vaulting. Vigneron eventually failed at 5.97m and Bubka at 6.00m. In her final race of the season Evelyn Ashford won the 100m in 10.93, her fifth successive sub-11 second time. There was a clear comparison of form between East and West in the women's 800m, as the Olympic 1-2-3 were respectively 5th, 7th and 9th in a race won by Jarmila Kratochvilova from three Soviet runners.

SEPTEMBER 1–2 **Finland v Sweden** at Helsinki. International dual matches have become somewhat outmoded these days, but this is the major exception, as it remains vitally important for these two great rivals. Finland won both matches, the men by 216 points to 193 and the women by 155 to 145.

2 **Rieti**, Italy. Two days after the pole vaulting dual in Rome, two high jumpers battled

in this Northern Italian town. Valeriy Sereda (USSR), on his first jump, and Carlo Thränhardt (GFR) on his third, cleared 2.37m for the European record. Both then failed at 2.40m. In a similar occurance to the 800m in Rome, Gabriella Dorio, the Olympic champion, was well beaten at 1500m by three Soviet women led by Yekaterina Podkopayeva who ran 3:56.65 to Dorio's seasonal best of 4:01.96.

4 **Paris, France.** Tatyana Kazankina won the 5000m easily in 15:23.12, but afterwards, seemingly on the advice of her team manager, refused to take a drug test. This led to her suspension first by her national federation and then by the IAAF. Said Aouita maintained his season's unbeaten record with a 3:34.13 1500m victory over Olympic bronze medallist José Abascal (Spa).

7 **IAC/Coca-Cola meeting** at Crystal Palace, London. The major race billed was the 1 mile confrontation between Said Aouita and Steve Cram. After a slow pace there might have been a thrilling finish but Cram tripped and fell at the start of the back straight and Aouita came home unchallenged to win in 3:55.43. In the women's mile Christina Boxer set a UK and Commonwealth record of 4:22.64 behind Ruth Wysocki (US) 4:21.78.

8–9 **USSR Championships** at Donyetsk. There were several upsets in this meeting, which lacked some quality, due to the Soviet tour of Italy and the forthcoming 8-nations meeting, and also perhaps because of its late season date. Most notable marks were the Soviet women's discus record of 73.28m by Galina Savinkova, and world junior records by Olga Turchak, who won the women's high jump with 1.96m and Rodion Gataullin, second to Sergey Bubka (5.80m) with 5.65m in the pole vault. Turchak at age 17 became the youngest ever Soviet champion.

14 **8 Nations meeting** in Tokyo, Japan. The USA in particular was well below full strength for this meeting. Team result: 1. GDR 183, 2. USSR 171, 3. Great Britain 149, 4. USA 121.5, 5. Hungary 113, 6. Italy 93.5, 7. Japan 92, 8. Asia 75. Carl Lewis was the crowd's favourite and he won the 100m in 10.13. Perhaps the best marks came from Yuriy Sedykh, 84.60m in a hammer competition outside the match, and from GDR javelin thrower Petra Felke, who sealed a brilliant season with a win at 72.86m.

22 **New York's Fifth Avenue Mile** was won by John Walker (NZ) in 3:53.62. The women's race was won by Maricica Puica (Rom) in 4:24.35. Street miles have become popular in recent years in many cities, but this remains the best known.

23 **Avon Women's Marathon** at Paris, France. Lorraine Moller (NZ) won her third victory in this prestigious annual race which is held at varying locations around the world. Her victory was worth $15,000 for her prize fund.

29–30 **Spartathlon** from Athens to Sparta, Greece. This race, in commemoration of the great run by Pheidippides in 490BC, over a mountainous 250km course was won, as in 1983, by Yiannis Kouros. His time of 20 hours 25 mins was over four hours better than the runner-up.

OCTOBER
21 **Chicago marathon**, USA. Steve Jones (UK) had failed to finish this race in 1983, his only previous attempt at a marathon, but he proved that a fast 10000 metres runner can succeed at the highest level in marathon running without specific racing

Review of 1984

experience by overcoming a very high class field to run a world best time of 2:08:05, eight seconds better than Alberto Salazar had run at New York three years earlier. His tremendous pace over the closing miles (he ran the 26th mile in 4:45) proved too much for the Olympic and World champions who followed him home – Carlos Lopes second in 2:09:06 and Rob de Castella third in 2:09:09. Jones's trust fund benefitted by some $97,500, including a $50,000 bonus for the world best time. The women's race was won by Rosa Mota (Por) in the fastest women's time ever for a loop course, 2:26:01. The course was re-measured later and found to be 65m over distance.

28 **New York marathon**, USA. Record high temperature and humidity severely affected runners in a race which had also been adversely affected in quality by the fact that so many top marathoners had raced at Chicago. The first prize for both men and women was $25,000 and a Mercedes car – Orlando Pizzolato (Ita) won in 2:14:53. Grete Waitz, in 2:29:30, won the women's race for the sixth time in seven years. 16,315 runners started the race of whom 14,590 (12,195 men and 2395 women) finished.

NOVEMBER
7–8 **Sri Chinmoy 24 Hours Road Race** – at Flushing Meadow, New York. Yiannis Kouros aagin surpassed in an ultra-distance event. He ran a world road bests for 200km, 15:11:48 and for 24 hours, 177 miles (284.853km).

11 **Women's World Championship – 10km Road Race** – at Madrid, Spain. Leading placings: 1. Aurora Cunha (Por) 33:04, 2. Rosa Mota (Por) 33:18, 3. Carole Bradford (UK) 33:25, 4. Debbie Peel (UK) 33:51, 5. Ann-Marie Malone (Can) 34:01, 6. Sally Pierson (Aus) 34:05, 7. Carol Haigh (UK) 34:08, 8. Monica Joyce (Ire) 34.09. Leading teams (11 placed): 1. UK 1:41:24, 2. Portugal 1:42:33, 3. USA 1:43:11, 4. Italy 1:45:19, 5. Spain 1:45:25. 6. Ireland 1:46:34.

DECEMBER
31 **Sao Silvestre race at Sao Paulo**, Brazil. The Portuguese pair of Carlos Lopes and Rosa Mota sealed their highly successful year with wins in the men's and women's races at this famous midnight New Year race. Their times for the 12.6km course: Lopes 36:43.79, Mota 43:35.57.

Opening ceremony in Los Angeles.

OLYMPIC GAMES 1984

The Games of the XXIIIrd Olympiad were staged in Los Angeles, USA from 28 July to 12 August 1984. In all sports a record 140 countries and about 7400 competitors took part. Unquestionably the Games were a great success, with record spectator attendance, television coverage, and profit, for the Los Angeles Organising Committee declared after the Games that the estimated surplus would be about $162 million from an income of $619 million. That money would be used to benefit youth activities, particularly in Southern California, but some would also be offered to the IOC for development of sport in deprived parts of the world.

The financial success was in sharp contrast to the excess expenditure incurred in, for instance, Montreal in 1976, but sadly the Games were again struck by political considerations. Just as in 1976 and at Moscow in 1980 a significant number of nations boycotted the Games, each time with a growing effect

ANALYSIS OF PLACES 1–8 BY NATION

Nation	1st	2nd	3rd	4th	5th	6th	7th	8th
USA	16	15	9	9	7	8	5	5
F.R. of Germany	4	2	5	3	5	5	3	–
United Kingdom	3	7	6	4	6	3	6	5
Romania	3	3	4	–	–	–	–	1
Italy	3	1	3	4	5	2	2	–
Finland	2	1	1	3	1	–	2	–
Mexico	2	1	–	–	–	–	–	–
Morocco	2	–	–	–	–	–	–	–
France	1	1	2	2	1	4	1	2
Australia	1	1	1	2	2	3	2	1
Portugal	1	–	2	–	–	1	–	1
Kenya	1	–	1	2	1	3	2	1
Brazil	1	–	–	1	–	–	–	1
Netherlands	1	–	–	–	–	–	1	1
Canada	–	2	3	3	1	2	2	7
Sweden	–	2	1	1	1	–	1	1
Jamaica	–	1	2	–	3	1	–	2
Norway	–	1	–	2	1	–	–	1
Switzerland	–	1	–	–	2	1	1	–
Ireland	–	1	–	–	–	–	–	1
Ivory Coast	–	1	–	–	–	–	–	–
China	–	–	1	1	2	–	2	1
Spain	–	–	1	–	–	2	3	1
Nigeria	–	–	1	–	–	1	2	1
Japan	–	–	–	1	1	–	2	–
India	–	–	–	1	–	–	1	–
New Zealand	–	–	–	–	1	–	–	–
Senegal	–	–	–	–	1	–	–	–
Bahamas	–	–	–	–	–	2	–	1
Barbados	–	–	–	–	–	1	–	–
Iceland	–	–	–	–	–	1	–	–
Tanzania	–	–	–	–	–	1	–	–
Belgium	–	–	–	–	–	–	1	1

One seventh place: Trinidad & Tobago, Uganda
One eighth place: Djibouti, Sudan, South Korea

Review of 1984

on the standards in track and field events. 1984 absentees were Afghanistan, Albania, Angola, Bulgaria, Cuba, Czechoslovakia, Ethiopia, GDR, Hungary, Iran, Korean PR, Laos, Mongolia, Poland, USSR, Vietnam, Yemen. Undoubtedly athletes from these nations, particularly from the GDR and USSR, would have made a major impact if they had been in Los Angeles. By contrast, however the team from the People's Republic of China was warmly welcomed back for their first appearance since 1948.

The great star of the athletics events was Carl Lewis, who succeeded in his quest to emulate the feat of Jesse Owens in 1936 by winning four gold medals. He won every event easily, displaying majestic form, but his triumphs were perhaps over-anticipated and thus did not excite as much as soon of the other great deeds in Los Angeles. The US team was by far the most successful and also provided the other leading multi-medallists, their women sprinters Valerie Brisco-Hooks with three gold, Chandra Cheeseborough, two gold and a silver, and Evelyn Ashford, two gold. Joan Benoit was their most acclaimed star for her runaway marathon victory, fearlessly ignoring great rivals and overcoming the fact that she had had arthroscopic surgery on her knee earlier in the year.

The men's middle distance races produced an unprecedented standard as each final up to 5000 metres was run at a fast pace. Joaquim Cruz and Said Aouita displayed awe-inspiring talent and Seb Coe returned in triumph after severe illness to again win gold and silver as he had in Moscow. Daley Thompson, at the decathlon, joined his teammate Coe as the only athletes to retain their Olympic titles from 1980. Ed Moses, prevented from competing in 1980, won as he had in 1976, as he continued to reign supreme at 400m hurdles, and Ulrike Meyfarth matched the longest span of Olympic success ever as she regained the women's high jump title that she had won in 1972.

Marathon victor Carlos Lopes, at 37, was the oldest gold medallist and the youngest was Lillie Leatherwood (women's 4x400m relay) at 20. Olympic history was set as the Joyners became the most successful brother and sister ever, although Jackie narrowly missed making it double family gold.

Just one world record was set, in the men's sprint relay. Standards were, however, high at the top. It was in the depth of performance that the Eastern bloc boycott was most felt, and this was particularly apparent in the women's events.

A record Olympic attendance of 1,129,465 paid to see the track and field events in the 15 sessions. The peak crowd was 90,861 on Saturday, 11 August for the late afternoon session. This was the largest crowd ever to watch athletics in the USA. The Closing Ceremony the following day attracted even more, 91,432, and that included the marathon finish. The peak morning attendance was 77,083 on Sunday, 5 August, a session which included the finish of the women's marathon.

Great American athletes featured in the Opening Ceremony as Edwin Moses took the Olympic oath on behalf of all the competitors and Rafer Johnson lit the Olympic flame after receiving the torch from Gina Hemphill, the grand-daughter of Jesse Owens, quadruple gold medallist in 1936. Rafer Johnson had set three world records at the decathlon, at which event he had won the Olympic silver medal in 1956 and gold in 1960.

EVENTS SURVEY

Listed are the first eight in each event together with brief comments. For each event the number of contestants is shown in brackets in the heading, followed by a letter indicating the date of the final and, where relevent, the wind speed in the final.

Dates of finals: 3 Aug = (a), 4 Aug = (b), 5 Aug = (c), 6 Aug = (d), 8 Aug = (e), 9 Aug = (f), 10 Aug = (g), 11 Aug = (h), 12 Aug = (i)

MEN
100 Metres (82) (b) (wind +0.2m/s)
Carl Lewis won all four races clearly; his victory margin of 0.20 was the largest in Olympic 100m history on auto-timing. His 10.04 quarter final and 9.99 in the final were Olympic bests at sea-level. Defending champion Allan Wells (UK) went out in the semi-finals.

1. Carl Lewis (USA)   9.99
2. Sam Graddy (USA)   10.19
3. Ben Johnson (Can)   10.22
4. Ron Brown (USA)   10.26
5. Mike McFarlane (UK)   10.27
6. Ray Stewart (Jam)   10.29
7. Donovan Reid (UK)   10.33
8. Tony Sharpe (Can)   10.35

54

Review of 1984

200 Metres (76) (e) (−0.9m/s)
Carl Lewis again won all four races clearly and set an Olympic record to win the final. His 100m splits were 10.23 and 9.57, as Baptiste finished fastest with 9.55 for the second half. The US medal sweep was their fifth at this event. Pietro Mennea became the first track athlete ever to run in four finals at one event; from 1972 he has placed 3rd, 4th, 1st, 7th. Defending champion Don Quarrie (Jam) went out in the semi-finals.
1. Carl Lewis (USA)   19.80
2. Kirk Baptiste (USA)   19.96
3. Thomas Jefferson (USA)   20.26
4. Joao Batista da Silva (Bra)   20.30
5. Ralf Lübke (GFR)   20.51
6. Jean-Jacques Boussemart (Fra)   20.55
7. Pietro Mennea (Ita)   20.55
8. Ade Mafe (UK)   20.85

400 Metres (80) (e)
All but one (Clark) of the finalists were US Collegians. Bert Cameron was forced to scratch through injury following a tremendous run in his semi-final, when he qualified despite stopping with cramp and losing about ten metres. Babers's winning time was just 0.01 short of Alberto Juantorena's low altitude world best. Darren Clark led up to 300 metres, which he reached in 32.3. Tiacoh won the Ivory Coast's first Olympic medal.
1. Alonzo Babers (USA)   44.27
2. Gabriel Tiacoh (IvC)   44.54
3. Antonio McKay (USA)   44.71
4. Darren Clark (Aus)   44.75
5. Sunder Nix (USA)   44.75
6. Sunday Uti (Nig)   44.93
7. Innocent Egbunike (Nig)   45.35
Bert Cameron (Jam) scratched

800 Metres (63) (d)
There was a tremendous standard in this event, with a total of 33 sub 1:46 times recorded in qualifying rounds and final; the previous Olympic best had been 11 in 1976. Cruz's 400m splits in the final were 51.16 and 51.84, as he broke Juantorena's Olympic record set in 1976. Koech led through 200m, 24.02, 400m, 51.07 and 600m, 1:17.20. Cruz's preliminary times were 1.45.66, 1:44.84 and 1:43.82.
1. Joaquim Cruz (Bra)   1:43.00
2. Sebastian Coe (UK)   1:43.64
3. Earl Jones (USA)   1:43.83
4. Billy Konchellah (Ken)   1:44.03
5. Donato Sabia (Ita)   1:44.53
6. Edwin Koech (Ken)   1:44.86
7. Johnny Gray (USA)   1:47.89
8. Steve Ovett (UK)   1:52.28

1500 Metres (59) (h)
Seb Coe improved Kip Keino's 1968 Olympic record as he retained the 1500m title; the only other man ever to have done that being James Lightbody (USA), if one includes the 1906 Games. Steve Ovett was forced to drop out when well placed in the final due to bronchial problems which had affected him throughout the Games. Joaquim Cruz decided to withdraw from his semi-final due to a cold. 400m pace in the final: Khalifa 58.85, Steve Scott 1:56.81, Abascal and Coe 2:53.3. Coe's last lap was 53.25. The 1–2 by the UK was their first since 1920. Steve Scott faded to 10th in 3:39.86.
1. Sebastian Coe (UK)   3:32.53
2. Steve Cram (UK)   3:33.40
3. José Abascal (Spa)   3:34.30
4. Joseph Cheshire (Ken)   3:34.52
5. Jim Spivey (USA)   3:36.07
6. Peter Wirz (Swi)   3:36.97
7. Andres Vera (Spa)   3:37.02
8. Omer Khalifa (Sud)   3:37.11

5000 Metres (56) (h)
Said Aouita set a new Olympic record in running the third-fastest 5000m ever. He ran the last 400m in 55.08 and the last 800m in 1:55.2. Times for places 2–3–4–5 were the fastest ever run. Ezequiel Canario (Por) set a fast pace, 2:37.22 for 1000m, picked up by Leitao, 2000m in 5:17.77, 3000m in 7:59.24, and 4000m in 10:38.76. World record holder Dave Moorcroft was in severe pain from a pelvic injury and unable to do more than run around to finish 14th and last in 14:16.61.
1. Said Aouita (Mor)   13:05.59
2. Markus Ryffel (Swi)   13:07.54
3. Antonio Leitao (Por)   13:09.20
4. Tim Hutchings (UK)   13:11.50
5. Paul Kipkoech (Ken)   13:14.40
6. Charles Cheruiyot (Ken)   13:18.41
7. Doug Padilla (USA)   13:23.56
8. John Walker (NZ)   13:24.76

10,000 Metres (45) (d)
The early pace in the final was slow, as 5000m was passed in 14:19.84. Nick Rose (UK) made a break, which only Cova and Vainio followed. Rose soon dropped back (he finished 12th in 28:31.73), and Cova produced a tremendous finish, running 27.7 for the last 200m; his second 5000m took 13:27.0! World

Review of 1984

record holder Fernando Mamede (Por) won his heat in fine style but succumbed to his big race nerves and ran off the track just after half-way in the final.
1. Alberto Cova (Ita) 27:47.54
2. Mike McLeod (UK) 28:06.22
3. Mike Musyoki (Ken) 28:06.46
4. Salvatore Antibo (Ita) 28:06.50
5. Christoph Herle (GFR) 28:08.21
6. Sosthenes Bitok (Ken) 28:09.01
7. Yutaka Kanai (Jap) 28:27.06
8. Steve Jones (UK) 28:28.08
Martti Vainio finished second in 27:51.10 but was subsequently disqualified for drug usage.

Marathon (103 of whom 78 finished) (i)
Carlos Lopes set an Olympic record and won Portugal's first ever Olympic gold medal. It was his third marathon, Treacy's first and Spedding's third. 14th and 15th were two of the favourites, Toshihiko Seko (Jap) and Alberto Salazar (USA)
1. Carlos Lopes (Por) 2:09:21
2. John Treacy (Ire) 2:09:56
3. Charlie Spedding (UK) 2:09:58
4. Takeshi Soh (Jap) 2:10:55
5. Rob de Castella (Aus) 2:11:09
6. Juma Ikangaa (Tan) 2:11:10
7. Joseph Nzau (Ken) 2:11:28
8. Djama Robleh (Djibouti) 2:11:39

3000m Steeplechase (35) (f)
Korir's win followed in the footsteps of Kenyans Amos Biwott (1968) and Kip Keino (1972) and he improved his personal best by 5.6 secs. Peter Renner (NZ), who finished 11th in 8:29.81, led at 1km – 2:47.40 and 2km – 5:32.51.
1. Julius Korir (Ken) 8:11.80
2. Joseph Mahmoud (Fra) 8:13.31
3. Brian Diemer (USA) 8:14.06
4. Henry Marsh (USA) 8:14.25
5. Colin Reitz (UK) 8:15.48
6. Domingo Ramon (Spa) 8:17.27
7. Julius Kariuki (Ken) 8:17.47
8. Pascal Debacker (Fra) 8:21.51

110m Hurdles (26) (d) (wind −0.4m/s)
Before Kingdom improved it in the final, the old Olympic record of 13.24 was equalled three times: by Foster in his heat and by first Kingdom and then Foster in winning the semi-finals. The US 1–2 was the twelth at this event in Olympic history, but the first since 1968.
1. Roger Kingdom (USA) 13.20

2. Greg Foster (USA) 13.23
3. Arto Bryggare (Fin) 13.40
4. Mark McCoy (Can) 13.45
5. Tonie Campbell (USA) 13.55
6. Stéphane Caristan (Fra) 13.71
7. Carlos Sala (Spa) 13.80
8. Jeff Glass (Can) 14.15

400m Hurdles (45) (c)
Edwin Moses regained the title that he had been unable to defend in 1976, in winning his 90th successive final and in his 28th sub-48 second time.
1. Edwin Moses (USA) 47.75
2. Danny Harris (USA) 48.13
3. Harald Schmid (GFR) 48.19
4. Sven Nylander (Swe) 48.97
5. Amadou Dia Ba (Sen) 49.28
6. Tranel Hawkins (USA) 49.42
7. Michel Zimmerman (Bel) 50.69
8. Henry Amike (Nig) (fell) 53.78

High Jump (30) (h)
Mogenburg cleared each of the six heights he attempted up to 2.35m first time, before failing at 2.40m. World record holder Zhu Jianhua was disappointed with his third place, nevertheless he won China's first ever Olympic athletics medal.
1. Dietmar Mögenburg (GFR) 2.35
2. Patrik Sjöberg (Swe) 2.33
3. Zha Jianhua (Chn) 2.31
4. Dwight Stones (USA) 2.31
5. Doug Nordquist (USA) 2.29
6. Milt Ottey (Can) 2.29
7. Liu Yunpeng (Chi) 2.29
8. Cai Shu (Chn) 2.27

Pole Vault (19) (e)
The pole vault has become by far France's best athletics event in recent years. Their gold and bronze were most welcome; the only previous French medal was Fernand Gonder's win at 3.50m in 1906.
1. Pierre Quinon (Fra) 5.75
2. Mike Tully (USA) 5.65
3. Earl Bell (USA) 5.60
4. Thierry Vigneron (Fra) 5.60
5. Kimmo Pallonen (Fin) 5.45
6. Doug Lytle (USA) 5.40
7. Felix Böhni (Swi) 5.30
8. Mauro Barella (Ita) 5.30

Long Jump (31) (d)
Carl Lewis needed just three jumps to win the event,

his qualifying leap of 8.30w, 8.54 in the first round and then a foul in the second round of the final. He passed his remaining jumps, as the other medallists' bests came as the first two jumps of the final round. Honey won the silver with a second best of 8.18 to 8.09 for Evangelisti.
1. Carl Lewis (USA)   8.54
2. Gary Honey (Aus)   8.24
3. Giovanni Evangelisti (Ita)   8.24
4. Larry Myricks (USA)   8.16
5. Liu Yuhuang (Chn)   7.99
6. Joey Wells (Bah)   7.97
7. Junichi Usui (Jap)   7.87
8. Kim Jong-Il (Korea)   7.81

Triple Jump (28) (b)
These were the first US gold and silver medals at this event since 1904. Joyner's series was 17.26w (+2.1m/s), 17.04, 16.83, N, 16.94, 17.04. Mike Conley produced the best jump with 17.36 in qualifying, but sprained his ankle on his first jump, 16.91, in the final. He aggravated this later, with his best coming in the third round. His final jump was a huge one of 17.50 plus, but a no jump by a few centimetres.
1. Al Joyner (USA)   17.26w
2. Mike Conley (USA)   17.18
3. Keith Connor (UK)   16.87
4. Zou Zhenxian (Chn)   16.83
5. Peter Bouschen (GFR)   16.77
6. Willie Banks (USA)   16.75
7. Ajayi Agebebaku (Nig)   16.67
8. Eric McCalla (UK)   16.66

Shot (19) (h)
Andrei's series was 20.41, 20.97, 21.26, 20.55, 20.92, 20.96. Carter led in the first round with 20.63 and set his best in the third. The bests of Laut and Wolf were in the final round.
1. Alessandro Andrei (Ita)   21.26
2. Michael Carter (USA)   21.09
3. Dave Laut (USA)   20.97
4. Augie Wolf (USA)   20.93
5. Werner Günthor (Swi)   20.28
6. Marco Montelatici (Ita)   19.98
7. Soren Tallhem (Swe)   19.81
8. Erik de Bruin (Hol)   19.65

Discus (20) (g)
Danneberg was perhaps the most surprising athletics gold medallist of 1984, as the favourites Wilkins and Powell, both medallists in 1976, fell short.

Review of 1984

Danneberg's series: 64.74, N, 63.64, 66.60, N, 66.22.
1. Rolf Danneberg (GFR)   66.60
2. Mac Wilkins (USA)   66.30
3. John Powell (USA)   65.46
4. Knut Hjeltnes (Nor)   65.28
5. Art Burns (USA)   64.98
6. Alwin Wagner (GFR)   64.72
7. Luciano Zerbini (Ita)   63.50
8. Stefan Fernholm (Swe)   63.22

Hammer (23) (d)
Tiainen beat Riehm by just ten centimetres, as both their best throws came in the third round. Tiainen's series: 70.56, 72.64, 78.08, 74.54, 75.26, 75.82.
1. Juha Tiainen (Fin)   78.08
2. Karl-Hans Riehm (GFR)   77.98
3. Klaus Ploghaus (GFR)   76.68
4. Giampaolo Urlando (Ita)   75.96
5. Orlando Bianchini (Ita)   75.94
6. Bill Green (USA)   75.60
7. Harri Huhtala (Fin)   75.28
8. Walter Ciofani (Fra)   73.46

Javelin (28) (c)
On his 29th birthday David Ottley led for three rounds, before Harkonen – series N, 78.74, 84.34, 86.76, N, N – produced his best. There were six 90-metre men in the final, but most could not cope with the tricky wind conditions of the Coliseum. Ex-world record holder Tom Petranoff (USA) was tenth with 78.40m.
1. Arto Harkonen (Fin)   86.76
2. David Ottley (UK)   85.74
3. Kenth Eldebrink (Swe)   83.72
4. Wolfram Gambke (GFR)   82.46
5. Masami Yoshida (Jap)   81.98
6. Einar Vilhjalmsson (Ice)   81.58
7. Roald Bradstock (UK)   81.22
8. Laslo Babits (Can)   80.68

Decathlon (26) (e&f)
Daley Thompson led throughout and again showed superb competitive ability to retain his title, and thus emulate Bob Mathias (Olympic champion 1948 and 1952). His performances: 100m: 10.44, LJ: 8.01, SP: 15.72, HJ: 2.03, 400m: 46.97, 110mh: 14.34, DT: 46.56, PV: 5.00, JT: 65.24, 1500m: 4:35.00. His first day score was a best ever at 4633, and he ended with an Olympic record, but just one point short of Hingsen's world record. The first three placings were the same as in the 1983 world championships.
1. Daley Thompson (UK)   8797
2. Jürgen Hingsen (GFR)   8673

57

Review of 1984

3. Siegfried Wentz (GFR)   8412
4. Guido Kratschmer (GFR)   8326
5. William Motti (Fra)   8266
6. John Crist (USA)   8130
7. Jim Wooding (USA)   8091
8. Dave Steen (Can)   8047

20km Walk (38) (a)
Both Mexico's two previous Olympic athletics medals have been in walking events, and this tradition was brilliantly upheld. The first three bettered Damilano's old Olympic record. Remarkably and uniquely no walkers were disqualified.
1. Ernesto Canto (Mex)   1:23:13
2. Raul Gonzales (Mex)   1:23:20
3. Maurizio Damilano (Ita)   1:23:26
4. Guillaume Leblanc (Can)   1:24:29
5. Carlo Mattioli (Ita)   1:25:07
6. José Marin (Spa)   1:25:32
7. Marco Evoniuk (USA)   1:25:42
8. Erling Andersen (Nor)   1:25:54

50km Walk (31, of whom 17 finished and 5 were disqualified) (h)
Gonzales led throughout with an impeccable display, going clear from 35km, and set an Olympic record. He became the first Olympic walker to win medals at both 20km and 50km at the same Games. His 10km splits showed very level pace: 46:02, 45:10, 45:12, 45:26 and 45:36.
1. Raul Gonzales (Mex)   3:47:26
2. Bo Gustafsson (Swe)   3:53:19
3. Sandro Bellucci (Ita)   3:53:45
4. Reima Salonen (Fin)   3:58:30
5. Raffaello Ducceschi (Ita)   3:59:26
6. Carl Schueler (USA)   3:59:46
7. Jorge Llopart (Spa)   4:03:09
8. Jose Pinto (Por)   4:04:42

4 x 100m Relay (20) (g)
The US team of Sam Graddy, Ron Brown, Calvin Smith and Carl Lewis set the only athletics world record of the Games. 100-metre splits were given for them as 10.29, 9.19, 9.41 and 8.94. This was the 13th US win in 16 Olympic Games. Don Quarrie ran the third leg for Jamaica, thus gaining his fourth Olympic medal at his fourth Games.
1. USA   37.83
2. Jamaica   38.62
3. Canada   38.70
4. Italy   38.87
5. GFR   38.99

6. France   39.10
7. UK   39.13
8. Brazil   39.40

4 x 400m Relay (25) (g)
Splits for the winning US team: Sunder Nix 45.59, Ray Armstead 43.97, Alonzo Babers 43.75, Antonio McKay 44.60. Their total was the second fastest ever run and the world sea-level best. Continental records were set by the first four teams. The second fastest leg was 43.96 by Darren Clark (Aus) on the second leg. The fastest anchor leg was 44.35 by Phil Brown (UK)
1. USA   2:57.91
2. UK   2:59.13
3. Nigeria   2:59.32
4. Australia   2:59.70
5. Italy   3:01.44
6. Barbados   3:01.60
7. Uganda   3:02.09
8. Canada   3:02.82

WOMEN

100 Metres (46) (c) (wind −1.2m/s)
Evelyn Ashford won all four rounds by clear margins, running an Olympic record in the final.
1. Evelyn Ashford (USA)   10.97
2. Alice Brown (USA)   11.13
3. Merlene Ottey-Page (Jam)   11.16
4. Jeanette Bolden (USA)   11.25
5. Grace Jackson (Jam)   11.39
6. Angela Bailey (Can)   11.40
7. Heather Oakes (UK)   11.43
8. Angella Taylor (Can)   11.62

200 Metres (37) (f) (wind −0.1m/s)
Valerie Brisco-Hooks completed the first ever Olympic 200m–400m double with an Olympic record. Her 100m splits were 11.20 (behind Griffith's 11.17) and 10.61.
1. Valerie Brisco-Hooks (USA)   21.81
2. Florence Griffith (USA)   22.04
3. Merlene Ottey-Page (Jam)   22.09
4. Kathy Cook (UK)   22.10
5. Grace Jackson (Jam)   22.20
6. Randy Givens (USA)   22.36
7. Rose-Aimée Bacoul (Fra)   22.78
8. Liliane Gaschet (Fra)   22.86

400 Metres (28) (d)
Brisco-Hooks ran 200m splits of 23.5 and 25.4 for an

Review of 1984

Olympic record, as the USA won their first ever gold and silver medals at the event. Cook led at 200m in 23.4.
1. Valerie Brisco-Hooks (USA) 48.83
2. Chandra Cheeseborough (USA) 49.05
3. Kathy Cook (UK) 49.42
4. Marita Payne (Can) 49.91
5. Lillie Leatherwood (USA) 50.25
6. Ute Thimm (GFR) 50.37
7. Charmaine Crooks (Can) 50.45
8. Ruth Waithera (Ken) 51.56

800 Metres (25) (d)
Dorio led at 200m (27.68) and 400m (57.28). Melinte took the lead with 250m to go, passing 600m in 1:27.85.
1. Doina Melinte (Rom) 1:57.60
2. Kim Gallagher (USA) 1:58.63
3. Fita Lovin (Rom) 1:58.83
4. Gabriella Dorio (Ita) 1:59.05
5. Lorraine Baker (UK) 2:00.03
6. Ruth Wysocki (USA) 2:00.34
7. Margrit Klinger (GFR) 2:00.65
8. Caroline O'Shea (Ire) 2:00.77

1500 Metres (22) (h)
Gabrielle Dorio, a consistent placer over a decade of major championships, triumphed to win her first gold with a final lap in 61.46. Boxer had led through 400m in 66.14 and 800m in 2:14.61. At 1200m Dorio led with 3:16.91.
1. Gabriella Dorio (Ita) 4:03.25
2. Doina Melinte (Rom) 4:03.76
3. Maricica Puica (Rom) 4:04.15
4. Roswitha Gerdes (GFR) 4:04.41
5. Christine Benning (UK) 4:04.70
6. Christina Boxer (UK) 4:05.53
7. Brit McRoberts (Can) 4:05.98
8. Ruth Wysocki (USA) 4:08.92

3000 Metres (31) (g)
This most eagerly awaited final was marred by the incident at 1730m when Mary Decker ran too close to the leading Zola Budd, tripped and fell, her hopes dashed, into the infield. Decker had led at 1000m in 2:50.43. At 2000m Budd led at 5:44.09 but she slipped back as Sly led at the bell in 7:30.41 from Puica, who produced a 31.8 last 200m to win.
1. Maricica Puica (Rom) 8:35.96
2. Wendy Sly (UK) 8:39.47
3. Lynn Williams (Can) 8:42.14
4. Cindy Bremser (USA) 8:42.78
5. Cornelia Burki (Swi) 8:45.20
6. Aurora Cunha (Por) 8:46.37
7. Zola Budd (UK) 8:48.80
8. Joan Hansen (USA) 8:51.53

Marathon (50, of whom 44 finished) (c)
Joan Benoit ran away from the field from the start as the remaining leading runners were unprepared to match her pace. She passed halfway in 1:11:54 and at 30km led by 1min 50sec. At this point Grete Waitz set off in pursuit, but although she gained ground, Benoit's lead was unassailable. She came in to a rapturous reception and the first Olympic women's marathon title. Priscilla Welch (age 39) set a world veterans best, and Joyce Smith (age 46) in running 2:32:48 for 11th place ran a world best for her age group.
1. Joan Benoit (USA) 2:24:52
2. Grete Waitz (Nor) 2:26:18
3. Rosa Mota (Por) 2:26:57
4. Ingrid Kristiansen (Nor) 2:27:34
5. Lorraine Moller (NZ) 2:28:34
6. Priscilla Welch (UK) 2:28:54
7. Lisa Martin (Aus) 2:29:03
8. Sylvie Ruegger (Can) 2:29:09

100m Hurdles (22) (g) (wind −0.7m/s)
The most remarkable aspect of the race was the long debate over the bronze medal. Originally ruled a tie between Turner and Chardonnet, that judgement was protested by the French, only for the Jury of Appeal to award third to Turner and fourth to Chardonnet. A further French protest was disregarded, but eventually, months after the Games, the original tie verdict was reinstated.
1. Benita Fitzgerald-Brown (USA) 12.84
2. Shirley Strong (UK) 12.88
3. Kim Turner (USA) 13.06
3. Michele Chardonnet (Fra) 13.06
5. Glynis Nunn (Aus) 13.20
6. Marie-Noëlle Savigny (Fra) 13.28
7. Ulrike Denk (GFR) 13.32
8. Pamela Page (USA) 13.40

400m Hurdles (26)(e)
A new Olympic event, the Olympic record progressed as follows: 1st round – Judi Brown 55.97, Ann-Louise Skoglund 55.75, Semis – Skoglund 55.17, Final – El Moutawakil, who won Morocco's first ever Olympic gold medal, as she reduced her African record by 0.76. Usha set a Commonwealth record in recording

59

Review of 1984

much the best international result ever by an Indian woman.
1. Nawal el Moutawakil (Mor)   54.61
2. Judie Brown (USA)   55.20
3. Cristina Cojacaru (Rom)   55.41
4. P.T.Usha (Ind)   55.42
5. Ann-Louise Skoglund (Swe)   55.43
6. Debbie Flintoff (Aus)   56.21
7. Tuija Helander (Fin)   56.55
8. Sandra Farmer (Jam)   57.15

High Jump (29) (g)
Meyfarth regained the title she had won as a 16-year-old in Munich in 1972, thus, in an achievement without parallel in Olympic history, becoming both the youngest and the oldest to win the event. Simeoni's 1980 Olympic record of 1.97 was equalled three times, then improved twice at 2.00m before Meyfarth won with a first-time clearance at 2.02. Simeoni became only the second woman to contest four Olympic finals at one event (the other was Lia Manoliu in the discus 1952–68), as she won her third medal (two silvers and a gold).
1. Ulrike Meyfarth (GFR)   2.02
2. Sara Simeoni (Ita)   2.00
3. Joni Huntley (USA)   1.97
4. Maryse Ewanje-Epée (Fra)   1.94
5. Debbie Brill (Can)   1.94
6. Vanessa Browne (Aus)   1.94
7. Zheng Dazheng (Chi)   1.91
8. Louise Ritter (USA)   1.91

Long Jump (23) (f)
Stanciu's series was 6.80, 6.68, N, 6.96, 6.89, N. Nunn made her third final, as this followed the hepathlon and 100m hurdles.
1. Anisoara Stanciu (Rom)   6.96
2. Vali Ionescu (Rom)   6.81
3. Susan Hearnshaw (UK)   6.80w
4. Angela Thacker (USA)   6.78w
5. Jackie Joyner (USA)   6.77
6. Robyn Lorraway (Aus)   6.67
7. Glynis Nunn (Aus)   6.53w
8. Shonel Ferguson (Bah)   6.44

Shot (13) (a)
Held as a straight final, the competition was a close one between Losch – 19.97, 20.31, 19.33, 20.06, 19.96, 20.48 and Loghin – 19.67, 19.73, 19.95, 20.47, 20.25, 20.09. The winning margin was the smallest ever for an Olympic women's throwing event.
1. Claudia Losch (GFR)   20.48

2. Mihaela Loghin (Rom)   20.47
3. Gael Martin (Aus)   19.19
4. Judith Oakes (UK)   18.14
5. Li Meisu (Chn)   17.96
6. Venissa Head (UK)   17.90
7. Carol Cady (USA)   17.23
8. Florenta Craciunescu (Rom)   17.23

Discus (17) (h)
Stalman led from the first round to the fifth when passed by Deniz, but won with her final throw. Her series: 64.50, 61.16, 63.70, 64.28, 63.64, 65.36.
1. Ria Stalman (Hol)   65.36
2. Leslie Deniz (USA)   64.86
3. Florenta Craciunescu (Rom)   63.64
4. Ulla Lundholm (Fin)   62.84
5. Meg Ritchie (UK)   62.58
6. Ingra Manecke (GFR)   58.56
7. Venissa Head (UK)   58.18
8. Gael Martin (Aus)   55.88

Javelin (24) (d)
Sanderson's winning throw came in the first round, her series: 69.56, 66.56, 63.68, 64.84, 66.86, 64.10. Lillak threw her best in the second round but then was forced to withdraw because of an ankle injury. No British woman had ever won an Olympic throwing medal before Sanderson and Whitbread's double success.
1. Tessa Sanderson (UK)   69.56
2. Tiina Lillak (Fin)   69.00
3. Fatima Whitbread (UK)   67.14
4. Tuula Laaksalo (Fin)   66.40
5. Trine Solberg (Nor)   64.52
6. Ingrid Thyssen (GFR)   63.26
7. Beate Peters (GFR)   62.34
8. Karin Smith (USA)   62.06

Heptathlon (23) (a & b)
Glynis Nunn produced a consistent series of marks to win the inaugural heptathlon title: 13.02, 1.80, 12.82, 24.06, 6.66, 35.58, 2:10.57. Simpson led at the end of the first day with 3759 to 3739 for Joyner and 3731 for Nunn. Joyner would surely have won but for the fact that two no jumps in the long jump forced her to take a 'safety' leap of 6.11, way below her best. A further 3cm would have given her the gold.
1. Glynis Nunn (Aus)   6390
2. Jackie Joyner (USA)   6385
3. Sabine Everts (GFR)   6363
4. Cindy Greiner (USA)   6281
5. Judy Simpson (UK)   6280

6. Sabine Braun (GFR)   6236
7. Tineke Hidding (Hol)   6147
8. Kim Hagger (UK)   6127

4 x 100m Relay (11) (h)
The US team of Alice Brown, Jeanette Bolden, Chandra Cheeseborough and Evelyn Ashford won by the biggest ever margin for the event. Their splits were 11.38, 10.18, 10.32 and an astonishing 9.77 for Ashford, as the next best anchor leg was 10.36 by Heather Oakes (UK).
1. USA   41.65
2. Canada   42.77
3. UK   43.11
4. France   43.15
5. GFR   43.57
6. Bahamas   44.18
7. Trinidad & Tobago   44.23
8. Jamaica   53.54

4 x 400m Relay (10) (h)   The US victory completed their clean sweep of the relay gold medals for the first time in Olympic history. Their team set a new Olympic record with splits – Lillie Leatherwood 50.50, Sherri Howard 48.83, Valerie Brisco-Hooks 49.23, Chandra Cheeseborough 49.73. The next fastest leg was 50.07 by Marita Payne for Canada on the final leg.
1. USA   3:18.29
2. Canada   3:21.21
3. GFR   3:22.98
4. UK   3:25.51
5. Jamaica   3:27.51
6. Italy   3:30.82
7. 3:32.49
Puerto Rico scratched

EUROPEAN INDOOR CHAMPIONSHIPS

GÖTEBORG, SWEDEN 3–4 MARCH 1984

RESULTS OF FINALS – MEN

60 Metres
1. Christian Haas (GFR)   6.68
2. Antonio Ullo (Ita)   6.68
3. Ronald Desruelles (Bel)   6.69
4. Antoine Richard (Fra)   6.70
5. José Arques (Spa)   6.72
6. Bruno Marie-Rose (Fra)   6.73
7. Jean-Jacques Boussemart (Fra)   6.73
8. Jozef Lomicky (Cs)   6.77

200 Metres
1. Aleksandr Yevgenyev (USSR)   20.98
2. Ade Mafe (UK)   21.34
3. Giovanni Bongiorni (Ita)   21.48
4. Roland Jokl (Aut)   21.78

400 Metres
1. Sergey Lovachev (USSR)   46.72
2. Roberto Tozzi (Ita)   47.01
3. Didier Dubois (Fra)   47.29
4. Thomas Futterknecht (Aut)   47.29

800 Metres
1. Donato Sabia (Ita)   1:48.05
2. André Lavie (Fra)   1:48.35
3. Phil Norgate (UK)   1:48.39
4. Ikem Billy (UK)   1:48.41
5. Ronny Olsson (Swe)   1:48.75
6. Pyotr Piekarski (Pol)   1:51.98

1500 Metres
1. Peter Wirz (Swi)   3:41.35
2. Riccardo Materazzi (Ita)   3:41.57
3. Thomas Wessinghage (GFR)   3:41.75
4. Anti Loikkanen (Fin)   3:42.42
5. Grzegorz Basiak (Pol)   3:42.71
6. Robert Nemeth (Aut)   3:43.28

3000 Metres
1. Lubomir Tesacek (Cs)   7:53.16
2. Markus Ryffel (Swi)   7:53.61
3. Karl Fleschen (GFR)   7:54.45
4. Uwe Mönkemeyer (GF   7:55.78
5. Czeslaw Mojzysz (Pol)   7:56.20
6. Patriz Ilg (GFR)   8:01.06
7. Spyros Andriopoulos (Gre)   8:04.98
8. Rune Lochting (Nor)   8:09.57

60m Hurdles
1. Romuald Giegiel (Pol)   7.62
2. György Bakos (Hun)   7.75
3. Jiri Hudec (Cs)   7.77
4. Javier Moracho (Spa)   7.78
5. Daniele Fontecchio (Ita)   7.81

Review of 1984

6. Wojciech Zawila (Pol)   7.88
7. Jürgen Schoch (GFR)   8.02
8. Reijo Byman (Fin)   8.03

High Jump
1. Dietmar Mögenburg (GFR)   2.33
2= Carlo Thränhardt (GFR)   2.30
2= Roland Dalhäuser (Swi)   2.30
4. Valeriy Sereda (USSR)   2.27
5= Hrvoje Fizuleto (Yug)   2.24
5= Miroslaw Wlodarczyk (Pol)   2.24
7. Patrik Sjöberg (Swe)   2.24
8. Igor Paklin (USSR)   2.20

Pole Vault
1. Thierry Vigneron (Fra)   5.85
2. Pierre Quinon (Fra)   5.75
3. Aleksandr Krupskiy (USSR)   5.60
4. Gerhard Schmidt (GFR)   5.55
5. Peter Volmer (GFR)   5.50
6. Marian Kolasa (Pol)   5.50
7. Mariusz Klimczyk (Pol)   5.40
8= Three men at 5.30

Long Jump
1. Jan Leitner (Cs)   7.96
2. Matthias Koch (GDR)   7.91
3. Robert Emmiyan (USSR)   7.89
4. Marco Piochi (Ita)   7.85
5. Giovanni Evangelisti (Ita)   7.82
6. Zdenek Hanacek (Cs)   7.78
7. Markus Kessler (GFR)   7.59
8. Anders Hoffström (Swe)   7.56

Triple Jump
1. Grigory Yemets (USSR)   17.33
2. Vlastimil Marinec (Cs)   17.16
3. Bela Bakosi (Hun)   17.15
4. Jan Cado (Cs)   16.93
5. Khristo Markov (Bul)   16.89
6. John Herbert (UK)   16.70
7. Ralf Jaros (FRG)   16.48
8. Dario Badinelli (Ita)   16.43

Shot
1. Janis Bojars (USSR)   20.84
2. Werner Günthör (Swi)   20.33
3. Alessandro Andrei (Ita)   20.32
4. Remigius Machura (Cs)   20.11
5. Josef Kubes (Cs)   20.01
6. Jovan Lazarevic (Yug)   20.01
7. Janusz Gassowski (Pol)   19.99

8. Helmut Krieger (Pol)   19.76

WOMEN

60 Metres
1. Beverly Kinch (UK)   7.16
2. Anelie Nuneva (Bul)   7.23
3. Nellie Cooman (Hol)   7.23
4. Jayne Christian (UK)   7.30
5. Eva Murkova (Cs)   7.35
6. Edith Oker (GFR)   7.42
7. Lena Möller (Swe)   7.42
Els Vader (Hol) scratched

200 Metres
1. Jarmila Kratochvilova (Cs)   23.02
2. Marie-Christine Cazier (Fra)   23.68
3. Olga Antonova (USSR)   23.80
Els Vader (Hol) scratched

400 Metres
1. Tatana Kocembova (Cs)   49.97
2. Erika Rossi (Ita)   52.37
3. Rositsa Stamenova (Bul)   52.41
4. Regine Berg (Bel)   53.41

800 Metres
1. Milena Matejkovicova (Cs)   1:59.52
2. Doina Melinte (Rom)   1:59.81
3. Cristina Cojocaru (Rom)   2:01.24
4. Jill McCabe (Swe)   2:02.88
5. Petra Kleinbrahm (GFR)   2:03.46
6. Zuzana Moravcikova (Cs)   2:03.72

1500 Metres
1. Fita Lovin (Rom)   4:10.03
2. Elly Van Hulst (Hol)   4:11.09
3. Sandra Gasser (Swi)   4:11.70
4. Vanya Gospodinova (Bul)   4:11.79
5. Gloria Palle (Spa)   4:15.88
6. Roswitha Gerdes (GFR)   4:16.34
7. Maria Radu (Rom)   4:20.84
8. Gabriella Dorio (Ita)   4:23.76

3000 Metres
1. Brigitte Kraus (GFR)   9:12.07
2. Tatyana Pozdnyakova (USSR)   9:15.04
3. Ivana Kleinova (Cs)   9:15.71
4. Monika Schäfer (GFR)   9:16.61
5. Agnese Possamai (Ita)   9:17.90
6. Brigitta Wahlin (Swe)   9:26.80

Review of 1984

60m Hurdles
1. Lucyna Kalek (Pol)   7.96
2. Vera Akimova (USSR)   7.99
3. Yordanka Donkova (Bul)   8.09
4. Edith Oker (GFR)   8.14
5. Ulrike Denk (GFR)   8.14
6. Marjan Olijslager (Hol)   8.21
7. Jana Tesarkova (Cs)   8.39
8. Anne Piquereau (Fra)   8.76

High Jump
1. Ulrike Meyfarth (GFR)   1.95
2. Maryse Ewanje-Epée (Fra)   1.95
3. Danuta Bulkowska (Pol)   1.95
4. Christine Soetewey (Bel)   1.92
5. Tamara Malesev (Yug)   1.92
6. Brigitte Holzapfel (GFR)   1.92
7. Jolanta Komsa (Pol)   1.92

8. Marina Doronina (USSR)   1.85

Long Jump
1. Susan Hearnshaw (UK)   6.70
2. Eva Murkova (Cs)   6.55
3. Stefania Lazzaroni (Ita)   6.08
4. Pia Sandberg (Swe)   5.93
5. Siv Christensen (Nor)   5.68

Shot
1. Helena Fibingerova (Cs)   20.34
2. Claudia Losch (GFR)   20.23
3. Heidi Krieger (GDR)   20.18
4. Nunu Abashidze (USSR)   20.03
5. Mihaela Loghin (Rom)   19.76
6. Heike Dittrich (GDR)   19.50
7. Birgit Petsch (GFR)   17.41
8. Simone Creantor (Fra)   16.29

CROSS-COUNTRY – NATIONAL CHAMPIONS 1984

	MEN	WOMEN
Austria	Gerhard Hartmann	Anni Muller
Belgium	Vincent Rousseau	Francine Peeters
England	Eamonn Martin	Jane Furniss
Finland	Martti Vainio	Tuija Toivonen
France	Pierre Levisse	Joëlle Debrouwer
GDR	Werner Schildhauer	Ulrike Bruns
F.R.Germany	Hans-Jürgen Orthmann	Monika Lovenich
Ireland	Jerry Kiernan	Roisin Smith
Italy	Alberto Cova	Agnese Possamai
Kenya	Paul Kipkoech	Esther Kiplangat
New Zealand	Rex Wilson	Gail Rear
Northern Ireland	Deon McNeilly	
Norway	Stig Roar Husby	Ingrid Kristiansen
Portugal	Carlos Lopes	Rosa Mota
Romania	György Marko	Maricica Puica
Scotland	Nat Muir	Elise Lyon
South Africa	Matthews Temane	Tanya Peckham
Spain	Antonio Prieto	Ana Isabel Alonso
USA (Nov)	Pat Porter	Cathy Branta
Wales	Steve Jones	Angela Tooby
Yugoslavia	Stanislav Rozman	Marica Mrsic
Balkans	György Marko (Rom)	Maricica Puica (Rom)
European Club Cup	Alberto Cova (Ita)	Angela Tooby (Wal)
Maghreb (N.Africa)	Arbi El Mouadhen (Mor)	Hasnia Drami (Mor)
World Students	Michael Scheytt (GFR)	Asuncion Sinovas (Spa)

Where countries have national championships over more than one distance I have listed the winners of the longer event.

43RD BALKAN GAMES

AT ATHENS, GREECE 7-9 SEPTEMBER

WINNERS
MEN

100m/200m: Mladen Nikolic (Yug) 10.34/20.74, 400m: Athanassios Kaloyiannis (Gre) 45.90; 800m/1500m: Petru Dragoescu (Rom) 1:48.72/3:40.28, 5000m: Evgeni Ignatov (Bul) 14:01.6/28:37.15, Mar: Mehmet Terzi (Turkey) 2:21:30 3000mSt: Panayiot Kachanov (Bul) 8:36.72, 110mh: Plamen Krastev (Bul) 13.73, 400mh: Toma Tomov (Bul) 49.54, HJ: Constantin Militaru (Rom) 2.26, PV: Ivo Yanchev (Bul) 5.50, LJ: Atanas Atanasov (Bul) 7.77, TJ: Stoitsa Iliev (Bul) 16.64, SP: Georgi Todorov (Bul) 19.42, DT: Kamen Dimitrov (Bul) 62.66, HT: Emanuil Dyulgerov (Bul) 77.52, JT: Antonios Papadimitriou (Gre) 80.74, Dec: Cecko Mitrakiev (Bul) 7614, 20kmW: Lyubomir Ivanov (Bul) 1:29:42, 4x100mR/4x400mR: Bulgaria 39.42/3:07.00

WOMEN

100m: Anelia Nuneva (Bul) 11.14, 200m: Nadezhda Georgieva (Bul) 22.66, 400m: Rositsa Stamenova (Bul) 52.01, 800m: Fita Lovin (Rom) 2:05.09, 1500m: Doina Melinte (Rom) 4:17.74, 3000m: Maricica Puica (Rom) 8:46.19, 100mh: Yordanka Donkova (Bul) 12.92, 400mh: Nicoleta Vornicou (Rom) 56.12, HJ: Lyudmila Andonova (Bul) 1.97, LJ: Valeria Ionescu (Rom) 6.82, SP: Mihaela Loghin (Rom) 19.61, DT: Tsvetanka Khristova (Bul) 66.90, JT: Antoaneta Todorova (Bul) 62.24, Hep: Corina Tifrea (Rom) 6066, 4x400mR: Romania 3:30.77

EIGHT NATIONS MEETING

TOKYO 14 SEPTEMBER 1984

First four at each event:
MEN

100 Metres (wind +0.2m/s)
1. Carl Lewis (USA)   10.13
2. Thomas Schröder (GDR)   10.27
3. Stefano Tilli (Ita)   10.29
4. Mike McFarlane (UK)   10.30

200 Metres (wind +1.5m/s)
1. Kirk Baptiste (USA)   20.47
2. Ade Mafe (UK)   20.57
3. Attila Kovacs (Hun)   20.70
4. Purnomo (Asi/Indonesia)   21.02

400 Metres
1. Susumu Takano (Jap)   45.69
2. Todd Bennett (UK)   45.72
3. Jens Carlowitz (GDR)   45.81
4. Gusztav Menczer (Hun)   46.26

800 Metres
1. Viktor Kalinkin (USSR)   1:46.21
2. Andreas Hauck (GDR)   1:47.25
3. Robert Harrison (UK)   1:47.80
4. Stefano Cecchini (Ita)   1:48.52

1500 Metres
1. Steve Cram (UK)   3:47.12
2. Andreas Busse (GDR)   3:47.51
3. Igor Lotarev (USSR)   3:47.90
4. Claudio Patrignani (Ita)   3:48.29

5000 Metres
1. Tim Hutchings (UK)   13:40.20
2. Dmitriy Dmitriyev (USSR)   13:41.22
3. Werner Schildhauer (GDR)   13:50.03
4. Masami Ohtsuka (Jap)   13:50.04

10,000 Metres
1. Valeriy Abramov (USSR)   30:14.37
2. Werner Schildhauer (GDR)   30:14.87
3. Masanari Shintaku (Jap)   30:14.64
4. Karl Harrison (UK)   30:15.93
race won by non-scorer Yutaka Kanai (Jap) in 30:13.79

3000m Steeplechase
1. Hagen Melzer (GDR)   8:35.87
2. Graeme Fell (UK)   8:38.17
3. Franco Boffi (Ita)   8:44.62
4. Don Clary (USA)   8:48.97

64

Review of 1984

110m Hurdles(wind +1.4m/s)
1. Tonie Campbell (USA)   13.30
2. Gyorgy Bakos (Hun)   13.45
3. Thomas Munkelt (GDR)   13.78
4. Sergey Usov (USSR)   13.78

400m Hurdles
1. Bart Williams (USA)   49.64
2. Joszef Szalai (Hun)   50.05
3. Ryoichi Yoshida (Jap)   50.63
4. Ahmed Hamada (Asi/Bahrain)   50.92

High Jump
1. Gennadiy Avdeyenko (USSR)   2.30
2. Takao Sakamoto (Jap)   2.30
3. Andreas Sam (GDR)   2.27
4. Liu Yunpeng (Asi/Chn)   2.24

Pole Vault
1. Konstantin Volkov (USSR)   5.55
2. Andreas Kramss (GDR)   5.50
3. Mauro Barella (Ita)   5.30
4. Ji Zebiao (Asi/Chn)   5.30

Long Jump
1. Lutz Dombrowski (GDR)   8.25
2. Larry Myricks (USA)   8.23
3. Sergey Layevskiy (USSR)   7.97
4. Gyula Paloczi (Hun)   7.86

Triple Jump
1. Aleksandr Yakovlev (USSR)   17.20
2. Willie Banks (USA)   17.17
3. Volker Mai (GDR)   17.02
4. Keith Connor (UK)   16.46

Shot
1. Ulf Timmermann (GDR)   20.73
2. Augie Wolf (USA)   20.50
3. Sergey Kasnauskas (USSR)   20.01
4. Laszlo Szabo (Hun)   18.92

Javelin
1. Uwe Hohn (GDR)   92.76
2. Duncan Attwood (USA)   85.44
3. DDavid Ottley (UK)   82.62
4. Masami Yoshida (Jap)   82.34

4 x 100m Relay
1. USSR   38.70
2. United Kingdom   39.23
3. Hungary   39.38
4. USA   39.63

4 x 400m Relay
1. GDR   3:01.95
2. United Kingdom   3:02.20
3. Hungary   3:05.76
4. USSR   3:06.93

WOMEN

100 Metres(wind −0.8m/s)
1. Marlies Göhr (GDR)   10.97
2. Lyudmila Kondratyeva (USSR)   11.06
3. Jeanette Bolden (USA)   11.35
4. Heather Oakes (UK)   11.51

200 Metres(wind +0.8m/s)
1. Marita Koch (GDR)   22.22
2. Svetlana Zhizdrikova (USSR)   22.89
3. Joan Baptiste (UK)   23.25
4. Carla Mercurio (Ita)   24.00

400 METRES
1. Olga Vladykina (USSR)   50.22
2. Dagmar Rubsam (GDR)   50.78
3. Michelle Scutt (UK)   52.72
4. P.T.Usha (Asi/Ind)   52.90

800 Metres
1. Irina Podyalovskaya (USSR)   2:00.45
2. Hildegard Ullrich (GDR)   2:01.20
3. Katalin Szalai (Hun)   2:01.57
4. Lorraine Baker (UK)   2:03.16

10,000 Metres
1. Ulrike Bruns (GDR)   32:46.08
2. Olga Bondarenko (USSR)   32:48.50
3. Angela Tooby (UK)   32:58.07
4. Karolin Szabo (Hun)   34:24.29

100m Hurdles(wind +1.0m/s)
1. Sabine Paetz (GDR)   12.72
2. Vera Akimova (USSR)   12.90
3. Xenia Siska (Hun)   13.19
4. Kim Turner (USA)   13.70

High Jump
1. Lyudmila Butuzova (USSR)   1.95
2. Diana Elliott (UK)   1.92
3. Andreas Bienias (GDR)   1.92
4. Zheng Dazheng (Asi/Chn)   1.86

Review of 1984

Long Jump
1. Heike Daute/Dreschsler (GDR)   6.95
2. Niole Medvedyeva (USSR)   6.93
3. Susan Hearnshaw/Telfer (UK)   6.71
4. Zsuzsa Vanyek (Hun)   6.21

Javelin
1. Petra Felke (GDR)   72.86
2. Karin Smith (USA)   64.68
3. Natalya Kalenchukova (USSR)   63.54
4. Emi Matsui (Jap)   58.50

4 x 100m Relay
1. GDR   42.44
2. USSR   43.50
3. United Kingdom   43.65
4. USA   45.44

Combined Results: 1. GDR 183; 2. USSR 171; 3. UK 149; 4. USA 121 1/2; 5. HUNGARY 113; 6. ITALY 93; JAPAN 92; ASIA 75

OBITUARIES 1984

Deaths were reported of the following notable athletes and officials in 1984:

Dick ATTLESEY (USA) (b.10 May 1929) on 14 October. Set three world records at 110mh/120yh: 13.5y, 13.6 and 13.5 in 1950. AAU champion in 1950 and 1951 and NCAA champion while at USC in 1950.

Chris BRATHWAITE (Tri) (b.12 Aug 1948) on 13 November – shot dead by a teenage sniper in a football stadium in Eugene, Oregon, USA. Sprint relay silver medallist at the 1978 Commonwealth Games, when he was also seventh at 100m.

Lord (Frank) BYERS (UK) (b.24 Jul 1915) on 6 February. Liberal leader in the House of Lords from 1967, and Member of Parliament 1940–5. He was British Universities 400mh champion in 1937 and gave his name to the report of the Committee of Enquiry into British Athletics, which he chaired in 1968.

Ken CARPENTER (USA) (b.19 Apr 1913) on 15 March. Won the 1936 Olympic discus title. AAU champion in 1935 and 1936 with a pb of 53.08m in 1936.

Herman ENGELHARD (GFR) (b.21 Jun 1903) on 6 January. In his best year, 1928, he won a silver medal at 4x400mR and bronze at 800m at the Olympic Games, won the German 800m title, set a German 400m record of 47.6 and an 800m pb of 1:51.8.

Janos FARAGO (Hun) (b.8 Jul 1946). Threw the discus over 60 metres each year from 1970 to 1981 with a best of 65.84m in 1976.

Jim FIXX (USA) (b.1932) while jogging in Vermont in July. Author of the phenomenally successful 'The Complete Book of Running'.

Fred GABY (UK) (b.1895) on 7 April. Set three UK 120yh records 1923–6 and had a pb of 14.9 for 110mh in 1928 when he was sixth in the Olympics. Won a bronze medal at 120yh' in the 1930 Commonwealth Games and won five AAA titles between 1922 and 1927.

Stijn JASPERS (Hol) (b.3 Jun 1961) on 18 October of a heart attack at Clemson University, USA. Just two months earlier he had been eliminated in the heats of the Olympic 5000m. Best time of 13:24.46 for 5000m in 1984.

Gary KNOKE (Aus) (b.5 Feb 1942) in July. Fourth at 400mh in the 1964 Olympics. Finallist at 400mh at four Commonwealth Games: 1962 – 4th, 1966 – 5th, 1970 – 8th, 1974 – 7th. Best time of 49.3 in 1972.

Juri LOSSMAN (Estonia) (b.4 Feb 1891) on 1 May. Silver medallist in the 1920 Olympic marathon, when he lost by 13 sec, the smallest ever winning margin in this race. His time of 2:32:48.6 stood as an Estonian record for 35 years.

Toivo LOUKOLA (Fin) (b.2 Oct 1902) in January. He won the 3000m steeplechase at the 1928 Olympics in a world best of 9:21.8.

Helge LOVLAND (Nor) (b.11 May 1890). 1920 Olympic decathlon champion. General Secretary of the Norwegian Sports federation.

Bert NELSON (USA) on 15 April. Had best high jump in the world in 1932 of 2.03m.

Karl NECKERMANN (GFR) (b.14 Mar 1911) on 14 March. Won European gold medal at 4x100mR in 1938. Equalled European 100m record with 10.3 in 1939. German champion at 100m 1939, 200m 1935.

Onni NISKANEN (Fin) (b.31 Aug 1910) in Sweden on 20 March. Particularly renowned for his work as Ethiopian national coach.

Donald PAIN (UK) (b.14 Sep 1905) on 12 September. Technical Manager at the 1948 Olympic Games in London, he went on to be Hon.Secretary/Treasurer of the IAAF from 1953 to 1970.

Sten PETTERSSON (Swe) (b.11 Sep 1902) on 1 June. Bronze medallist at 110mh in the 1924 Olympics. pbs of 14.8 for 110mh in 1927 and 52.4 for 400mh in 1928, both European records. Won 22 Swedish titles: seven at 400mh, six at 110mh, three at 200m and HJ, two at 100m and one at 400m between 1923 and 1933.

Martin STOKKEN (Nor) (16 Jan 1923). Won a record 20 Norwegian titles: six at 10000m and cross-country, four at 5000m and 3000m St, and set 17 Norwegian records. Fourth in the 1948 Olympic 10000m and 1950 European 3000mSt. Won an Olympic silver medal in the cross-country relay at skiing in 1952.

Dr Ernst VAN AAKEN (GFR) (b.16 May 1910) on 2 April. Great German distance running coach, particularly instrumental in popularising women's marathon running.

Laurie WEATHERILL (UK) (b.1904) on 9 April. In the Empire Games he was sixth at 3 miles and fifth at 6 miles in 1938

Squire YARROW (UK) (b.28 Jul 1905) on 11 April. In the European Championships marathon he was 2nd in 1928 and 7th in 1946, in which year he won the AAA title. pb 2:37:50 in 1939. President of the AAA 1978–84.

THE I.A.A.F. WORLD CUP

The Fourth World Cup is to be staged in Canberra, the capital of Australia on the 5th, 6th and 7th October 1985. The idea of having a competition between teams representing the continents and top athletics nations was first conceived in 1975 and the first World Cup was staged in Dusseldorf in the Federal Republic of Germany on 2–4 September 1977.

The combination of national and continental teams was admitted by the then President of the IAAF, Adriaan Paulen, to be a somewhat artificial formula but with each event thus a straight final, magnificent athletics ensued. The aggregate attendance was over 135,000 and, with television fees, a profit of over 1.2 million Deutschmarks was reported. Undoubtedly the fourfold aims of the IAAF were achieved. These were to provide a great athletics meeting, to offer additional world–class competition for the sport's elite, to stimulate the continental areas not only in the World Cup competition itself but also by the staging of trial meetings to determine the teams, and not least to provide additional revenue for the development of athletics throughout the world.

The second World Cup was contested in the Montreal Olympic Stadium, Canada from 24–26 August 1979. On this occasion, however, a loss of some 50,000 Canadian dollars was made as the total three–day attendance was only just over 54,000. The World Cup returned to Europe and to large crowds with its third running in the Olympic Stadium in Rome, Italy on 4–6 September 1981 in front of a combined attendance of 185,000.

The World Cup is contested by the following teams – both men and women:
Africa
America (excluding USA)

Review of 1984

POSITIONS AND POINTS IN WORLD CUP COMPETITIONS

Men

Team	1977	1979	1981
Africa	6th– 78	6th– 84	7th– 66
Americas	5th– 92	5th– 98	5th– 95
Asia	8th– 44	8th– 36	9th– 59
Europe	4th– 111	2nd– 112	1st– 147
GDR	1st– 127	3rd– 108	2nd– 130
GFR	3rd– 112	–	–
Italy	–	–	6th– 93
Oceania	7th– 48	7th– 58	8th– 61
USA	2nd– 120	1st– 119	3rd– 127
USSR	–	4th– 102	4th– 118

Women

Team	1977	1979	1981
Africa	7th– 32	7th– 30	9th– 26
Americas	5th– 56	5th– 68	5th– 72
Asia	8th– 30	8th– 26	8th– 32
Europe	1st– 109	3rd– 88	2nd– 110
GDR	2nd– 93	1st– 106	1st– 120.5
GFR	–	–	–
Italy	–	–	6th– 68.5
Oceania	6th– 46	6th– 47	7th– 58
USA	4th– 60	4th– 76	4th– 89
USSR	3rd– 90	2nd– 98	3rd– 98

Evelyn Ashford(r) beats Maries Göhr(l) in Montreal at the 1979 World Cup.

Asia
Europe – the top two men's and women's teams from the preceding European Cup
– the rest of Europe
Oceania
USA

In 1981 an additional, ninth, team was permitted. This was the host nation, Italy, taking advantage of the addition of a ninth lane to the track in Rome.

Individual event winners – MEN
100 metres: 1977 Steve Williams (USA) 10.13; 1979 James Sanford (USA) 10.17; 1981 Allan Wells (Eur/UK) 10.20
200 metres: 1977 Clancy Edwards (USA) 20.17; 1979 Silvio Leonard (Ame/Cub) 20.34; 1981 Mel Lattany (USA) 20.21
400 metres: 1977 Alberto Juantorena (Ame/Cub) 45.36; 1979 Hassan El Kashief (Afr/Sud) 45.39; 1981 Cliff Wiley (USA) 44.88
800 metres: 1977 Alberto Juantorena (Ame/Cub) 1:44.04; 1979 James Maina (Afr/Ken) 1:47.69; 1981 Sebastian Coe (Eur/UK) 1:46.16
1500 metres: 1977 Steve Ovett (Eur/UK) 3:34.45; 1979 Thomas Wessinghage (Eur/GFR) 3:46.00; 1981 Steve Ovett (Eur/UK) 3:34.95
5000 metres: 1977 Miruts Yifter (Afr/Eth) 13:13.82; 1979 Miruts Yifter (Afr/Eth) 13:35.9; 1981 Eamonn Coghlan (Eur/Ire) 14:08.39
10000 metres: 1977 Miruts Yifter (Afr/Eth) 28:32.3; 1979 Miruts Yifter (Afr/Eth) 27:53.07; 1981 Werner Schildhauer (GDR) 27:38.43
3000 metres steeplechase: 1977 Michael Karst (GFR) 8:21.6; 1979 Kiprotich Rono (Afr/Ken) 8:25.97; 1981 Boguslaw Maminski (Eur/Pol) 8:19.89
110 metres hurdles: 1977 Thomas Munkelt (GDR) 13.41; 1979 Renaldo Nehemiah (USA) 13.39; 1981 Greg Foster (USA) 13.32
400 metres hurdles: 1977 Ed Moses (USA) 47.58; 1979 Ed Moses (USA) 47.53; 1981 Ed Moses (USA) 47.37
High jump: 1977 Rolf Beilschmidt (GDR) 2.30; 1979 Franklin Jacobs (USA) 2.27; 1981 Tyke Peacock (USA) 2.28
Pole vault: 1977 Mike Tully (USA) 5.60; 1979 Mike Tully (USA) 5.45; 1981 Konstantin Volkov (USSR) 5.70
Long Jump: 1977 Arnie Robinson (USA) 8.19; 1979 Larry Myricks (USA) 8.52; 1981 Carl Lewis (USA) 8.15
Triple Jump: 1977 Joao de Oliveira (Ame/Bra) 16.68; 1979 Joao de Oliveira (Ame/Bra) 17.02; 1981 Joao de Oliveira (Ame/Bra) 17.37

Review of 1984
Shot: 1977 Udo Beyer (GDR) 21.74; 1979 Udo Beyer (GDR) 20.45; 1981 Udo Beyer (GDR) 21.40
Discus: 1977 Wolfgang Schmidt (GDR) 67.14; 1979 Wolfgang Schmidt (GDR) 66.02; 1981 Armin Lemme (GDR) 66.38
Hammer: 1977 Karl–Hans Riehm (GFR) 75.64; 1979 Sergey Litvinov (USSR) 78.70; 1981 Yuriy Sedykh (USSR) 77.42
Javelin: 1977 Michael Wessing (GFR) 87.46; 1979 Wolfgang Hanisch (GDR) 86.48; 1981 Dainis Kula (USSR) 89.74
4 x 100 metres relay: 1977 USA 38.03; 1979 Americas 38.70; 1981 Europe 38.73
4 x 400 metres relay: 1977 F.R.Germany 3:01.34; 1979 USA 3:00.70; 1981 USA 2:59.12

Individual event winners – WOMEN
100 metres: 1977 Marlies Oelsner (GDR) 11.16; 1979 Evelyn Ashford (USA) 11.06; 1981 Evelyn Ashford (USA) 11.02
200 metres: 1977 Irena Szewinska (Eur/Pol) 22.72; 1979 Evelyn Ashford (USA) 21.83; 1981 Evelyn Ashford (USA) 22.18
400 metres: 1977 Irena Szewinska (Eur/Pol) 49.52; 1979 Marita Koch (GDR) 48.97; 1981 Jarmila Kratochvilova (Eur/Cze) 48.61
800 metres: 1977 Totka Petrova (Eur/Bul) 1:59.20; 1979 Nikolina Shtereva (Eur/Bul) 2:00.52; 1981 Lyudmila Veselkova (USSR) 1:57.48
1500 metres: 1977 Tatyana Kazankina (USSR) 4:12.7; 1979 Totka Petrova (Eur/Bul) won in 4:06.46 but was subsequently disqualified for infringing the doping regulations; 1981 Tamara Sorokina (USSR) 4:03.33
3000 metres: 1977 Grete Waitz (Eur/Nor) 8:43.5; 1979 Svyetlana Ulmasova (USSR) 8:36.32; 1981 Angelika Zauber (GDR) 8:54.89
100 metres hurdles: 1977 Grazyna Rabsztyn (Eur/Pol) 12.70; 1979 Grazyna Rabsztyn (Eur/Pol) 12.67; 1981 Tatyana Anisimova (USSR) 12.85
400 metres hurdles: 1977 not held; 1979 Barbara Klepp (GDR) 55.83; 1981 Ellen Neumann (GDR) 54.82
High jump: 1977 Rosemarie Ackermann (GDR) 1.98; 1979 Debbie Brill (Ame/Can) 1.96; 1981 Ulrike Meyfarth (Eur/GFR) 1.96
Long jump: 1977 Lynette Jacenko (Oce/Aus) 6.54; 1979 Anita Stukane (USSR) 6.64; 1981 Sigrid Ulbricht (GDR) 6.80
Shot: 1977 Ilona Slupianek (GDR) 20.93; 1979 Ilona Slupianek (GDR) 20.98; 1981 Ilona Slupianek (GDR) 20.60
Discus: 1977 Faina Melnik (USSR) 68.10; 1979 Evelin Jahl (GDR) 65.18; 1981 Evelin Jahl (GDR) 66.70

Review of 1984

Javelin: 1977 Ruth Fuchs (GDR) 62.36; 1979 Ruth Fuchs (GDR) 66.10; 1981 Antoaneta Todorova (Eur/Bul) 70.08
4 x 100 metres relay: 1977 Europe 42.51; 1979 Europe 42.19; 1981 GDR 42.22
4 x 400 metres relay: 1977 GDR 3:24.04; 1979 GDR 3:20.38; 1981 GDR 3:20.62

The women's 10000 metres has been added to the programme for 1985.

Most individual event wins: 4 Evelyn Ashford and Miruts Yifter, who each won double doubles, Ashford at women's 100m and 200m in 1979 and 1981 and Yifter at 5000m and 10000m in 1977 and 1979.
Three wins at one event: Ed Moses (USA) 400mh, Joao de Oliveira (Bra) TJ, Udo Beyer (GDR) SP, Ilona Slupianek (GDR) women's SP.

Just one world record has been set in World Cup competition: the 38.03 4 x 100 metres relay time by the US team of Bill Collins, Steve Riddick, Cliff Wiley and Steve Williams in 1977. However World Cup competition has produced a feast of track and field athletics of ther highest class. There have, for instance, been several performances which were at the time the second best ever achieved.

Included amongst these second best evers were the epic women's 400 metres duels in 1977 and 1981, in both of which Marita Koch (GDR) came second. In betweeen these two races Koch was supreme at the event winning all her 18 races. In 1977 the 20-year-old Koch set off at a blazing pace, passing 200m in 23.1 and 300m in 35.4, when she still had a three metres lead over the European women's team captain Irena Szewinska of Poland. The latter, eleven years older than Koch, had for long graced women's athletics and had an unrivalled collection of major titles and world records. She had only turned to 400 metres for the first time in 1973, but the following year became the first woman to break the 50 seconds barrier and went on to win the 1976 Olympic title in the world record time of 49.29. In the World Cup her coolness and determination enabled her to close the gap on her young rival and her long legs took her to a 2 metre victory, 49.52 to 49.76. After 1977, however Szewinska had to pass her mantle as world's number one to Koch. They met again three times at 400 metres, Koch winning with Szewinska third on each occasion: 1978 European Championships, 1979 European Cup Final, 1979 World Cup Final. The latter was won by Marita Koch with her accustomed ease, 48.97 to 50.60 for the runner-up Maria Kulchunova (USSR).

In 1981 another star, Jarmila Kratochvilova of Czechoslovakia, had emerged to challenge the East German. Kratochvilova's first competitive 400 metres had been at the age of 20 in 1971, when she ran 60.2. Over the years she improved but by 1977 was only down to 53.3. Intensive hard work resulted in an improvement to the edge of world class in 1978 when her best was 51.09. In 1980 she ran 49.46 to gain the Olympic silver medal behind Koch's 48.88, and improved thrice more the following year with times of 49.23, 49.17 and 49.01 prior to the World Cup. Marita Koch had run three sub-50 sec times and won the European Cup so the stage was set for a classic confronation. The pair were level for most of the race but in the finishing straight the Czech's power proved irresistible and her stormed away to win with 48.61, just 0.01 off the world record, to 49.27 for Koch.

Edwin Moses has twice run times second only to his own world records. Indeed he has completely dominated this event in the World Cup, as of course he has throughout this period while remaining undefeated. His margins of victory have been: 1977 - 1.25 secs over Volker Beck (GDR), 1979 - 1.18 secs over Harald Schmid (GFR), 1981 - 1.79 secs over Beck. In 1979 he was rivalled as athlete of the meeting by Evelyn Ashford, who completed the first of her World Cup sprint double successes, by Miruts Yifter with his second distance double triumph and by Larry Myricks in the long jump.

Myricks had come to Montreal in 1976 for the Olympic Games, but during the warm-up for the final cracked his ankle, which injury was to put him out of long jumping for 19 months. His victory in the same stadium in 1979 was thus all the sweeter, not least for the fact that he produced the greatest ever jump at sea-level, 8.52m, just half an inch short of the 28-foot barrier, which, and 29 feet, had been so amazingly swept past by Bob Beamon at altitude in Mexico City in 1968 with his prodigious 8.90m.

In 1981 the favoured US men's team had a depressing competition, not managing to produce a competitor in the discus, with Henry Marsh disqualified in the steeplechase, and losing valuable points in the 100 metres of all events when Carl Lewis, of all people, could only trail in last in 10.96! Lewis had not been able to train properly for a month, but still won the long jump. Olympic champions Allan Wells, Sebastian Coe and Steve Ovett were British winners for the winning European team. The women's competition resulted in a clear win for the GDR, with shot putter Ilona Slupianek winning her event for the third time.

Continental teams to have had no individual winners, with their highest placings:
Men
Asia: 2nd Zou Zhenxian (Chi) TJ 1981
Oceania: 2nd Mike O'Rourke (NZ) JT 1979, John Walker (NZ) 1981, Gary Honey (Aus) LJ 1981

Women
Africa: 5th Sakina Boutamine (Alg) 1500m 1979
Asia: 4th Esther Rot (Isr) 100mh 1977

Canberra
Canberra, the capital of Australia since 1927, has a population of about 250,000. The stadium at which the competition will take place was first used to stage the third Pacific Conference Games in 1977, and it forms part of the National Sports Centre, situated in the northern Canberra suburb of Bruce. The Organising Committee is chaired by the President of the Australian AAU, Mr.A.W.McDonald. The Deputy Chairman is Mr.John F.Treloar, who won gold medals at 100 yards, 220 yards and sprint relay in the 1950 Commonwealth Games. The General Manager is Mr.John H.Marshall.

IAAF/MOBIL GRAND PRIX 1985

In 1983 and 1984 various major invitational meetings around the world had been given the status of IAAF Permit meetings. In 1985 a coherent competitive structure has been given to these fixtures by bringing them together, with major sponsorship from Mobil Oil, into the IAAF/Mobil Grand Prix. Fifteen competitions have been scheduled leading to a grand final in Rome on 7 September.

Events included in 1985 are: MEN – 200m, 400m, 1500m, 5000m, 110mh, PV, TJ, DT, JT; WOMEN – 100m, 800m, 3000m, 400mh, HJ, LJ, SP. The remaining standard Olympic events will be the events included in the 1986 Grand Prix. Athletes score points on a 9–7–6–5–4–3–2–1 basis, with an extra six points for breaking a world record or three for tying one. The top eight athletes in each event, based on scoring from their best five meetings will be invited to compete in the Grand Prix Final in Rome, where the points scored will be doubled. The top six individuals in each event earn prizes to be paid into their trust funds, administered by their national federations, of $10,000, $7000, $4000, $3000, $2000 and $1000. In addition the top four men and top four women over all events receive bonuses of $25,000, $15,000, $10,000 and $5000.

Athletes eligible to compete will be those who have in 1984 or 1985 equalled or bettered outdoors, under legal conditions, the 50th best mark in the world in 1984.

IAAF/MOBIL GRAND PRIX MEETINGS 1985

25 May 'Bruce Jenner Classic' – San Jose, California, USA
Named after the US decathlete who won the Olympic title in 1976, when he set his third world decathlon record with a score of 8617 points. The Jenner Classic was held annually in mid-April from 1979, when Renaldo Nehemiah ran 13.16 for the world record for 110mh, to 1982, succeeeding the San Jose Invitational meeting. From 1983 the meeting has moved to the last weekend in May, and a high class meeting has been staged.

1 Jun 'Prefontaine Classic' – Eugene, Oregon, USA
Named after the great distance runner, who was tragically killed in a car accident on 30 May 1975 at the age of 24. Steve Prefontaine had placed fourth at 5000m in the 1972 Olympics and held US records at each distance from 2000m to 10000m. He was undoubtedly the most popular US athlete, and there was a growing industry in 'Go Pre' sloganed T-shirts. The meeting was first held on 7 Jun 1975, when Don

1985 Preview – Review of Major Meetings

Quarrie and Steve Williams ran 19.9 hand-timed for 220 yards (19.8 at 200m), the fastest ever. Since then it has usually been held close to the anniversary of Prefontaine's death, although in 1984 it was held in late July. Over the past three seasons the overall standard has been impressive, but the distance events have always been strong, and Mary Decker set a world record for 5000m in 1982 at 15:08.26.

8 Jun 'Znamenskiy Memorial' – Moscow, USSR
This meeting was first held in 1949 in memory of Serafim and Georgiy Znamenskiy, the Soviet distance running stars who had been killed in the war. Between them they had won eleven USSR titles: Serafim at 1500m in 1934, 5000m in 1934, 1936–38 and 1940, 10000m in 1934, 1936 and 1938; Georgiy at 5000m and 10000m in 1939. At these three distances they had set 18 Soviet records, with Serafim leading the way with bests at 5000m of 14:37.0 and 10000m of 30:44.8 and Georgiy at 1500m with 3:57.9. The meeting has been predominantly a Soviet rather than an international meeting, with world records in the past decade from Faina Melnik, DT 70.50m in 1976, Tatyana Kazankina, 1500m 3:55.0 in 1980, and Anna Ambraziene, 400mh 54.02 in 1983.

22 Jun 'Rosicky Memorial' – Prague, Czechoslovakia
This meeting was first held in 1947 in memory of Evzen Rosicky, the middle-distance runner killed in the war. He had won Czechoslovak 800m titles each year from 1933 to 1937. His best 800m time was 1:54.6 in 1935. The Stadium, used for the European Championships in 1978, was renamed the Evzen Rosicky Stadium in 1975.

2 Jul DN Galen' – Stockholm, Sweden
First held (as the Stockholm Games) in 1966, at which meeting Ron Clarke smashed the world record for 5000m with his time of 13:16.6. Other world records at the meeting have been set by Anders Garderud, 8:09.70 for 3000m steeplechase in 1975, by Dick Quax, 13:12.86 for 5000m in 1977, and by Fernando Mamede, 27:13.81 for 10000m in 1984. The meeting is organised by 'Stadionklubbarna', made up of the 12 major athletics clubs in Stockholm. DN stands for Dagens Nyheter, the leading Swedish morning newspaper. Staged at the 1912 Olympic Stadium, at which more than 60 officially approved world records have been set.

4 Jul 'World Games' – Helsinki, Finland
The 'Maailmankisat' has been held since 1961, originally biennially, in the Olympic Stadium, which was opened in 1938. Four world records have been set: Judy Pollock (Aus), 2:01.0 for women's 800m in 1967, Ben Jipcho (Ken), 8:13.91 for 3000m steeplechase in 1973, Samson Kimobwa, 27:30.47 for 10000m in 1977 and Tiina Lillak's 72.40 world javelin record in 1982. The latter was especially ecstatically received as it was the first world record ever thrown by a Finnish woman at the event the Finns love above all others.

16 Jul 'NIKAIA' – Nice, France
Held annually since 1976 at the Parc des Sports de l'Ouest. Joaquim Cruz starred in 1984 with 2:14.09 for 1000 metres. The IAAF Golden pole vault competition was staged in 1980 and the vault has been a major feature each year; Pierre Quinon set a meeting record of 5.80m in 1984.

19 Jul 'Peugeot-Talbot' Games – Crystal Palce, London, UK
Held annually under sponsorship from the Talbot Motor Company since 1980. Highlights have included the UK All-Comers 100m record of 10.06 by Mel Lattany (USA) in pouring rain in 1981 and in 1984 two world records, from Sergey Bubka (USSR) with his 5.90m pole vault and Zola Budd, who ran 5:33.15 for the women's 2000 metres, a distance that had yet to be accepted as an official distance by the IAAF (it has now been so recognised).

17 Jul 'Bislett Games' – Oslo, Norway
Held annually in the famous Bislett stadium, which was opened in 1922 and used for the 1946 European Championships. Over 40 world records have been set on the track including many of the most famous in history, from such pre-war performances as Jack Torrance (USA) 17.40m shot in 1934 and Forrest Towns (USA) 13.7 for 110mh in 1936, to Roger Moens (Bel) 1:45.7 800m 1955, the first 90m javelin throw by Terje Pedersen (Nor), 91.72m in 1964, Ron Clarke (Aus) 27:39.4 10000m 1965, and to the more recent running exploits of the British trio of Seb Coe, Steve Ovett and Dave Moorcroft. Coe has led the way with four world records on this track, including two at the Bislett Games – his 1:42.33 for 800m in 1979 and 2:13.40 for 1000m in 1980, when Steve Ovett set the mile mark at 3:48.8. Other world records in the past decade at the Bislett Games: 1976 John Walker 2000m in 4:51.4, 1978 Henry Rono 3000m in 7:32.1,

1985 Preview – Review of Major Meetings

1984 Ingrid Kristiansen 5000m in 14:58.89.

2 Aug 'IAC Meeting' – Crystal Palace, London
Organised by the International Athletes Club and sponsored by the British Bottlers of Coca-Cola annually since 1968, when Ron Clarke (Aus) set a world two miles record of 8:19.6.

4 Aug 'Grand Prix' – Budapest, Hungary
First held in 1978. This has become a major meeting point for athletes from the Eastern bloc and from the West. Standards have been high, but as yet no world records have been set. The venue, the Nepstadion, was opened in 1953 and was the site of the World Student Games in 1965 and the European Championships in 1966.

21 Aug 'Weltklasse' – Zürich, Switzerland
First held in 1962, originally as the Züricher International. The Letzigrund stadium in Zürich has hosted, under the organisation of the Leichtathletik Club Zürich, the most consistently high-class meeting on the international circuit in recent years. The President of the organising committee is Andreas Brügger. Eight world records have been set over the past twelve years: 1973 Rod Milburn 110mh 13.1, 1975 Faina Melnik DT 70.20, 1979 Seb Coe 1500m 3:32.03, 1980 Tatyana Kazankina 1500m 3:52.47, 1981 Seb Coe 1M 3:48.53 and Renaldo Nehemiah 110mh 12.93, 1983 Calvin Smith 100m 9.97, 1984 Evelyn Ashford 100m 10.76.

23 Aug 'ISTAF' – Berlin, F.R. Germany
This is the one meeting on the Grand Prix circuit which originates from pre-war days. The Internationales Stadionfest (ISTAF) was first held in 1921 in the 1916 Olympic stadium in Berlin and was revived in the 1936 Olympic stadium in 1937, when Luz Long set a European long jump record of 7.90m. The first world record at the meeting was the 6.12m women's long jump by Christel Schulz in 1939. The standard has been consistently top-class, although the last world records set at the meeting were in 1978 by Krzystyna Kacperczyk, 55.40 at 400mh, and in 1977 by Rosemarie Ackermann (GDR), when she became the first woman ever to clear two metres in the high jump.

25 Aug 'ASV-Sportfest der Weltklasse' – Köln, F.R. Germany
Organised by the club ASV Köln in the Kolner Stadion, Müngersdorf. In 1984 Joaquim Cruz missed Seb Coe's world record for 800m by just 0.04 sec., and in the previous year's meeting two world records had been set, Sydney Maree, 3:31.24 for 1500m and Pierre Quinon, 5.82m pole vault.

30 Aug 'Ivo van Damme Memorial' – Brussels, Belgium
Held annually since 1977 in the Heizel Stadium in memory of the great Belgian middle distance runner Ivo van Damme. He was killed in a car crash on 29 December 1976 at the age of 22, just a few months after winning Olympic silver medals at both 800m and 1500m. World records have been set at the meeting by Steve Ovett, 1500m 3:32.11 in 1979, and by Seb Coe, 3:47.33 to win the IAAF Golden Mile in 1981. Manager of the organising committee is Wilfried Meert.

7 Sep Grand Prix Final – Rome, Italy
The Olympic stadium in Rome will host the Grand Prix finals. This is sure to be an outstanding meeting in a setting which since the 1960 Olympic Games has also hosted the 1974 European Championships and the 1981 World Cup. The results from the Golden Gala meeting in Rome over the past two years have been headed by world pole vault records: Thierry Vigneron clearing 5.83m in 1983 and 5.91m in 1984, only to be outjumped by Sergey Bubka at 5.94m.

OTHER MAJOR FIXTURES IN 1985

In addition to the fifteen IAAF/Mobil Grand Priz meetings athletes will be able to receive participation money at the following IAAF permit meetings:
21 Mar – Melbourne, Australia; 6 May – Sponichi International at Tokyo, Japan; 10 Jun – Sears Ultraccec at Sao Paulo, Brazil; 14/15 Jun – Pravda Televizia Slovnaft at Bratislava, Czechoslovakia; 18 Jun – Harry Jerome Classic at Vancouver, Canada; 27 Jun – Oslo Games, Norway; 10 Jul – Lausanne, Switzerland; 12 Jul – Paris, France; 23 Jul – Edinburgh Games, UK; 7 Aug – Citta di Viareggio, Italy; 28 Aug – Abendsportfest Koblenz, GFR; 4 Sep – Rieti, Italy; 14 Sep – Nanjing, China; 15 Sep – Seoul, Korea

WORLD UNIVERSITY GAMES

These Games, run by the Fédération Internationale du Sport Universiaire (FISU), will be held in Kobe, Japan from 29 August to 4 September 1985.

The Games have been held bienially on a fully international basis since 1963, although international university games were first held in Warsaw in 1924.

1985 Preview – Review of Major Meetings

AFRICAN CHAMPIONSHIPS

– to be held in Alexandria, Egypt on 15–18 August 1985. The first African Championships (as distinct from the quadriennial multi-sport African Games) were held in Dakar, Senegal in 1981.

IAAF WORLD RACE WALKING CUP

The finals of the biennial contests for the Lugano Trophy (men) and Eschborn Cup (women) will be held at Douglas, Isle of Man, UK on 28–29 September 1985. The following teams will compete: LUGANO – Algeria, Australia, Canada, China, India, Italy, Kenya, Mexico, UK, USA, USSR; ESCHBORN – Australia, Canada, China, Mexico, UK, USA, USSR; and in each the first two teams from each of the three European Qualifying matches, to be held at Boras, Sweden on 15/16 June, St Aubin, France and Russe, Bulgaria on 22/23 June.

The Lugano Trophy is contested by men's national teams walking over 20km and 50km. Previous winners have been:
1961 United Kingdom, 1963 United Kingdom, 1965 GDR, 1967 GDR, 1970 GDR, 1973 GDR, 1975 USSR, 1977 Mexico, 1979 Mexico, 1981 Italy, 1983 USSR.

The individual winners at Bergen, Norway in 1983 were Josef Pribilinec (CS) at 20km in 1:19:30 and Raul Gonzales (Mex) at 50km in 3:45:37. The leading six nations were: 1. USSR 231, 2. ITA 189, 3. MEX 146, 4. CS 138, 5. UK 137, 6. SPA 135.

The Eschborn Cup is contested by women's teams walking over 10km. Previous winners have been (over 5km in 1979 and 1981): 1979 UK, 1981 USSR, 1983 Chinese PR.

The individual winner in 1983 was Xu Yongju (Chi) in 45:13.4. The leading six nations: 1. CHI 132, 2. USSR 130, 3. AUS 16, 4. SWE 118, 5. ITA 88, 6. NOR 86.

EUROPEAN CUP

The European Cup is contested biennially by European nations, with each team entering one athlete per event and one team in each relay. The Cup is dedicated to the memory of Dr Bruno Zauli, the former President of the European Committee of the IAAF, who died suddenly in 1963 soon after the decision

Year	Venue	MEN			WOMEN		
1965	Stuttgart (men)	1. USSR	2. GDR	3. POL			
	Kassel (women)				1. USSR	2. GDR	3. POL
1967	Kiev	1. USSR	2. GDR	3. GFR	1. USSR	2. GDR	3. GFR
1970	Stockholm (men)	1. GDR	2. USSR	3. GFR			
	Budapest (women)				1. GDR	2. GFR	3. USSR
1973	Edinburgh	1. USSR	2. GDR	3. GFR	1. GDR	2. USSR	3. BUL
1975	Nice	1. GDR	2. USSR	3. POL	1. GDR	2. USSR	3. GFR
1977	Helsinki	1. GDR	2. GFR	3. USSR	1. GDR	2. USSR	3. UK
1979	Turin	1. GDR	2. USSR	3. GFR	1. GDR	2. USSR	3. BUL
1981	Zagreb	1. GDR	2. USSR	3. UK	1. GDR	2. USSR	3. GFR
1983	London	1. GDR	2. USSR	3. GFR	1. GDR	2. USSR	3. CS

1985 Preview – Review of Major Meetings

had been made to start this competition.

From 1965 until 1981 the competition was staged with a qualifying round, semi-finals and final, but from 1983 the nations have been arranged into groups according to strength, with eight men's and eight women's teams in both 'A' and 'B' groups.

In 1985 the 'A' group finals for men and women will be staged in Moscow on 17/18 August. The 'B' Group final will be staged in Budapest, Hungary, the 'C1' Group in Schwechat, Austria and the 'C2' Group in Reykjavik, Iceland – all on 10/11 August. There will be one up and one down promotion and relegation between A and B, and two up and two down between B and C.

The full 1983 finals result:
Men: 1. GDR 117, 2. USSR 106, 3. FRG 102, 4. UK 94.5, 5. POL 86.5, 6. ITA 81.5, 7. FRA 70, 8. HUN 60.5
Women: 1. GDR 107, 2. USSR 85, 3. CS 77, 4. UK 77, 5. GFR 58, 6. BUL 58, 7. POL 43, 8. HUN 34

Individual records
Most wins: 8 Marlies Göhr (GDR) – 1st at women's 100m and 4x100mR each year from 1977 to 1983; 7 Renate Stecher (GDR) – 1st at women's 100m, 200m and 4x100mR 1973 and 1975, and at 200m 1970.

Most wins at one event: 4 Ruth Fuchs (GDR) – 1st women's javelin each final from 1970 to 1977. She was also 2nd in 1979 and 3rd in 1967; and by Göhr (above) at 100m.

EUROPEAN COMBINED EVENTS CUP

The 1985 finals for Decathlon (men) and Heptathlon (women) will be held on 7/8 September. The 'A' Group finals will be staged at Krefeld, GFR, the 'B' Group at Arles, France, the 'C1' Group at Copenhagen, Denmark and the 'C2' Group at Brunico, Italy.

This competition has been held bienially since 1973. The first three nations in previous Cup Finals have been:

Year	Venue	MEN – Decathlon			WOMEN – Heptathlon		
1973	Bonn	1. POL	2. USSR	3. GDR	1. GDR	2. USSR	3. BUL
1975	Bydgoszcz	1. USSR	2. POL	3. SWE	1. GDR	2. USSR	3. GFR
1977	Lille	1. USSR	2. GFR	3. GDR	1. USSR	2. GFR	3. FRA
1979	Dresden	1. GDR	2. GFR	3. USSR	1. GDR	2. USSR	3. GFR
1981	Birmingham	1. GFR	2. GDR	3. POL	1. GDR	2. GFR	3. USSR
1983	Sofia	1. GFR	2. GDR	3. USSR	1. GDR	2. USSR	3. BUL

The full 1983 finals result:
Men: 1. GFR 24609, 2. GDR 24359, 3. USSR 24208, 4. SWI 23800, 5. POL 23482, 6. BUL 23093
Women: 1. GDR 19242, 2. USSR 18698, 3. BUL 18666, 4. GFR 17842, 5. UK 17710, 6. HUN 16469

Individual records
Athletes to have won two finals: Burglinde Pollak (GDR) won the women's pentathlon in 1973 and 1975, Ramona Neubert (GDR) won the women's heptathlon in 1981 and 1983.

Most finals: 6 Guido Kratschmer (FRG) – decathlon each year from 1975 to 1983, with a best placing of second in 1979.

Cup records: Decathlon – 8501 Uwe Freimuth (GDR) 1983 Heptathlon – 6722 Ramona Neubert (GDR) 1983

Other Major Championships 1986-90

EUROPEAN MARATHON CUP

The European Marathon Cup will be contested at Rome on 15 September 1985. This event was first staged in 1981 at Agen in France, when the men's team competition was won by Italy from USSR and Poland. The individual winner was Massimo Magnani (Ita) in 2:13:29. The women's race was won by Zoya Ivanova (USSR) in 2:38:58, but there was no women's team competition.

The 1983 event was run at Laredo, Spain. Thirteen nations contested the men's race. The first six: 1. GDR 22, 3. ITA 28, 3. SPA 45, 4. GFR 70, 5. BEL 103, 6. UK 111. Individual winner was Waldemar Cierpinski (GDR) in 2:12:26. The women's race was won by Nadyezhda Gumerova (USSR) in 2:38:36.

EUROPEAN JUNIOR CHAMPIONSHIPS

The European Junior Championships will be staged at Cottbus, GDR on 22-25 August 1985.

This event was first held as an unofficial competition at Warsaw in 1964. It was officially recognised as the European Junior Games in 1966 and 1968, and has been the European Championships for Juniors in 1970 and biennially since 1973. One new event added in 1985 is the women's 5000m track walk.

Juniors in 1985 are: MEN – those born in 1966 or later; WOMEN – those born in 1967 or later.

EUROPEAN CLUBS CUP

This competition is contested by the champion clubs of European nations. The men's event will be at Haringey, London, UK on 8-9 June and the women's at Zürich, Switzerland on 2 June.

Previous winning clubs:
Men: 1975 – Wattenscheid (GFR), 1976 – Alco Rieti (Ita), 1977 – Wattenscheid (GFR), 1978 – Wattenscheid (GFR), 1979 – Iveco Fiat (Ita), 1980 – Iveco Fiat (Ita), 1981 – Dukla Praha (CS), 1982 – Fiamma D'Oro (Ita), 1983 – Fiamma D'Oro (Ita), 1984 – Pro Patria Pierrel (Ita)
Women: 1981 – Bayer Leverkusen (GFR), 1982 – Bayer Leverkusen (GFR), 1983 – Bayer Leverkusen (GFR), 1984 – Bayer Leverkusen (GFR)

MAJOR CHAMPIONSHIPS 1986-90

1986
European Indoor Championships – Madrid, Spain (27-28 February)
World Cross-Country Championships – Neuchatel, Switzerland
World Junior Championships – Athens, Greece
Commonwealth Games – Edinburgh, Scotland (24 July – 2 August)
European Championships – Stuttgart, GFR (26-31 August)
Asian Games – Seoul, Korea (20 September-5 October)
1987
European Indoor Championships – Lievin, France (14-15 February)
World Indoor Games
World Cross-Country Championships – Warsaw, Poland
Pan-American Games – Indianapolis, USA (17 July-2 August)
World University Games – Zagreb, Yugoslavia
World Championships – Rome, Italy (29 August-6 September)
1998
Olympic Games – Seoul, Korea
1990
Commonwealth Games – Auckland, New Zealand

ALBERTO JUANTORENA

BOB PHILLIPS

I remember many years ago seeing a newspaper photograph of a 7ft-tall US schoolboy who according to the imaginative caption had run 440 yards in 49 secs and now intended to break the World record. The gawky lad was depicted wearing canvas boots and knee-length stocks, striding out like young Superman and gazing disdainfully at the camera.

As it happened, he never did run any faster. His name was Wilt Chamberlain, and he grew up to be a universally-renowned professional basketball player. But the idle fancy of one generation sometimes has a curious habit of becoming the inexorable fact of the next: so maybe it was not so surprising that Alberto Juantorena should for a time in the 1970s have been the best 800 metres runner in history, and that he can still justifiably claim in the wake of his recently-announced retirement to be the greatest-ever exponent of the 400/800 combination of events.

Juantorena, too, was a basketball player at 19, but maybe he thought that even at 1.89 metres in height he did not have the physique for the game because he apparently took it upon himself to try athletics as an alternative. In 1971 he moved from provincial Cuba to the capital, Havana, where he met up with a Polish coach, Zygmunt Zabierzowski, and within a few months had run 48.2 for 400 metres.

The following year Juantorena performed with great credit in the Munich Olympic 400 metres, placing fifth in the semi-finals. A year later he was World University Games champion, and in 1974 his time of 44.7 led the World rankings. He had also already dabbled at 800 metres, recording a respectable 1:49.8.

In April and May of 1976 he tackled two laps rather more seriously, setting times of 1:46.9 and 1:46.1 in Cuba then a startling 1:45.2 in Italy with precisely equal laps of 52.6. The news of that achievement must have caused some sleepless nights for 800 metres specialists like Rick Wohlhuter, and his worst forebodings were duly realised a couple of months later.

At the Montreal Olympics Juantorena simply ran away from the field at 600 metres to win the gold and break Marcello Fiasconaro's three-year-old World record for good measure with a time of 1:43.50. It was only the 11th 800 metres race of the Cuban's career, and a subsequent second gold medal at 400 metres, with a 44.26 which represented the best-ever low-altitude performance, established him beyond doubt as one of the greatest athletes in the full panoply of the sport.

The 1977 season was equally spectacular as Juantorena marginally improved on his World record to 1:43.44 in the World University Games in Sofia, followed by a 1:43.64 win in Zürich after a 49.65 first lap, and a monumental victory over Mike Boit in the World Cup (1:44.04), all within the space of 12 days. At 25 he was at the height of his powers, and it seemed just a matter of time before he ran 1:42 and then turned his attentions to the 1,500 metres and brought his 20.7 200 metres speed to bear on revolutionising that event, too. The era of the sprinter-miler was surely about to dawn.

Yet Juantorena was never quite the same man again. True, in 1978 he ran 1:44.38 to still rate fourth in the World behind Beyer, Coe and Ovett, but the following year he could only manage 1:46.4 for 23rd ranking, and in the 1980 Olympics he opted simply to defend his 400 metres title, finishing fourth in 45.09. Injuries, and maybe waning enthusiasm, were curtailing his competitive appearances, and Sebastian Coe was about to take 800 metres running on to an altogether higher plane.

In the interests of the honour of Cuba, Juantorena soldiered on, and to some good effect because he produced an unexpected 1:45.15 in 1982 and an even more exciting 1:44.06 on the eve of the inaugural World Championships the next year. Unhappily, he stepped on the trackside kerb as he qualified in his first-round 800 metres heat in Helsinki and was carried off on a stretcher, face grimaced in pain and fists beating the air in frustration.

It was a dismal but not altogether out-of character end to his major international career. There has always been something distinctly eccentric about this hulking man with the fuzzy halo haircut and the Desperate Dan jawline, casually ambling away from the starting-line

Special Features

and giving everyone else 10 metres leeway as if he felt that it would not be an entertaining enough race without his having to make up lost ground in the comic-strip manner of some Afro-Cuban white-clad Wilson of the Wizard. Like Wilt the Stilt in that yellowing press cutting, long white socks added to the incongruity of it all.

His final efforts in 1984, even though they still featured a best of 1:44.88, served merely to show that the magic had finally gone. The galloping stride had become a languid lope and the opposition no longer succumbed abjectly on perfect dramatic cue. Like so many great athletes before him – Snell and Clarke most readily recalled – Juantorena had run just one season too many.

But no one thinks any the less in hindsight of Snell and Clarke for that; nor of Juantorena, either. The art of 400 and 800 metres running has never been more majestically demonstrated than by Castro's Cuban Caballero.

Progression and championships record

Year	400m best	800m best	Championships
1971	48.2		
1972	45.94		OG: sf 400m
1973	45.36	1:49.8	WSG: 1st at 400m
1974	44.7	1:50.9	CAC: 1st at 400m and 4x400mR
1975	44.80	–	PAm: 2nd at 400m and 4x400m relay
1976	44.26	1:43.50	OG: 1st at 400m and 800m
1977	44.65	1:43.44	WSG: 1st at 800m; WCp: 1st at 400m and 800m
1978	44.27	1:44.38	CAC: 1st at 400m and 800m
1979	45.24	1:46.4	PAm: 2nd at 400m and 800m
1980	45.09	–	OG: 4th at 400m
1981	46.55	1:46.0	
1982	45.51	1:45.15	CAC: 1st at 800m and 4x400m relay
1983	–	1:45.04	WCh: sf at 800m
1984	45.69	1:44.88	

(CAC = Central American and Caribbean)
World records at 800m: 1:43.50 at Montreal on 25 Jul 1976, 1:43.44 at Sofia on 21 Aug 1977.
World low-altitude best for 400m: 44.26 at Montreal on 29 Jul 1976.

800 METRES – SPEED AND STAMINA

BOB PHILLIPS

Basic speed has long been regarded as the prerequisite for success in every track event. Thus the popular belief has been established that the best 400m runners, for example, will be those who have converted from 100m and 200m; the best 800m runners will be ex-400m runners; and so on.

Of course, there are plenty of individual examples at 400m to prove the case, and not a single leading exponent of the event has not also been a sprinter of at least international class. This has led many experts to argue that if you could find someone who runs 400m faster than the 800m specialists, and then give him sufficient stamina training, he would become champion at the latter distance.

It sounds perfectly logical, and the recent retirement of Alberto Juantorena, Olympic champion at both 400

and 800m, reminds us of the maxim. Furthermore, Juantorena succeeded as World record-holder for 800m another outstanding 400m man, Marcello Fiasconaro.

Yet these two are very much the exceptions rather than the rule. Contrary to expectation, the 800m remains the preserve of the endurance runner. They outnumber speed-orientated runners by a 2:1 ratio among the 142 men who have beaten 1:46.00 for the distance – broadly regarded as the criterion for international class.

What is more, the most recent developments in the event suggest that the trend will continue. The 1984 Olympic champion, Joaquim Cruz, is no more than a respectable 400m runner with a best of 47.17 to his credit but has achieved 3:36.48 for 1,500m and

Special Features

3:53.00 for the mile. Sebastian Coe (46.87/3:31.95) shows a similar balance of capabilities, and even the newest American star, Earl Jones, gained his first successes as a 1,500m runner.

Apart from Juantorena and Fiasconaro, only Tom Courtney, George Kerr and Harald Schmid of the sub-1:46.00 runners have also been World-class performers at 400m. In contrast, the list of endurance types who have beaten 1:46.00 also includes Steve Ovett, Said Aouita, Jim Ryun, Rick Wohlhuter, Mike Boit, Peter Snell, Dave Wottle, Pekka Vasala, John Walker, Steve Scott and Filbert Bayi.

Of the 142 sub-1:46.00 men, 76 can be definitely classified as endurance types according to their best times for 1,500m or one mile; 42 are sprinter types on the basis of their 400m times; and the evidence for the remaining 24 remains inconclusive.

Only 11 of those 142 have recorded 46.00 or better for 400m. Exactly twice as many have achieved times in the 46.00–46.99 range. More than twice as many again (47 in all) have run 47.00 or slower. No 400m times have been traced for the remainder which indicates (but does not conclusively prove) that they would probably fall into the 47.00-plus category.

As a further comparison, it is worth noting that 34 of the ranked 800m runners have achieved 3:37.80 or better for 1,500m, which is roughly equivalent in World all-time ranking terms to 46.00 or better for 400m.

There is still every likelihood that other great 400m runners will move up to 800m successfully. Yet even of the most promising young 800m runners around at present only two – Billy Konchellah (45.38) and Donato Sabia (45.73) – have achieved anything of real note at 400m. The overwhelming strength of evidence indicates that future gold-medallists and record-breakers at 800m will be capable of no more than internationally-respectable 400m times (in the 46.00–46.30 range) but will be able to run at least 3:34.00 for 1,500m.

THE OLYMPIANS: FROM TEEN-AGED TO MIDDLE AGED

STAN GREENBERG, BILL MALLON AND PETER MATTHEWS

At the end of each Olympic Games, the President of the IOC in his closing remarks, always '... calls upon the youth of the world to assemble in four more years at the Games of the – Olympiad in the city of –––––.' It is in keeping with the wish of Baron Pierre de Coubertin that the Olympics be a chance for the youth of the world to assemble and meet in friendly combat. But how old are these youths – especially in the premier sport of the Games, track & field athletics?

The following is a brief analysis of the ages of the gold and other medallists in track & field at all Olympic Games. It can be seen that while many of the athletes are youths, for others youth is but an evanescent memory.

First, we present the top tens (performers and performances) for youngest and oldest, by sex, and type of medal won. It must be remembered that this is the best information known. In the cases of the earliest Games, some of the medal winners' birthdates have never been found.

OLDEST AND YOUNGEST MEDALLISTS BY EVENT

Men Youngest

	Medal	Years/Days			Oldest Years/Days	Name/Country/Date
100m	G	19–128	Reggie Walker (SAF) 1908		28–83	Allan Wells (UK) 1980
	M	18–234	Donald Lippincott (USA) 1912		31–226	McDonald Bailey (UK) 1952
200m	G	20–47	Percy Williams (CAN) 1928		28–30	Pietro Mennea (ITA) 1980
	M	17–287	Dwayne Evans (USA) 1976		30–170	Barney Ewell (USA) 1948
400m	G	21–98	Archie Williams (USA) 1936		30–323	Mike Larrabee (USA) 1964
	M	20–193	Antonio McKay (USA) 1984		30–323	Mike Larrabee (USA) 1964
800m	G	20–237	Ted Meredith (USA) 1912		31–147	Albert Hill (UK) 1920
	M	20–025	Earl Jones (USA) 1984		32–58	Arthur Wint (JAM) 1952
1500m	G	21–96	Arnold Jackson (UK) 1912		31–149	Albert Hill (UK) 1920
	M	21–96	Arnold Jackson (UK) 1912		31–149	Albert Hill (UK) 1920
5000m	G	20–321	Joseph Guillemot (FRA) 1920		36–78	Miruts Yifter (ETH) 1980

79

Special Features

Youngest

Event	Medal	Years/Days	Name/Country/Date
10 000m	M	20–321	Joseph Guillemot (FRA) 1920
	G	22–212	Hannes Kolehmainen (FIN) 1912
Marathon	M	20–324	Joseph Guillemot (FRA) 1920
	G	20–301	Juan Zabala (ARG) 1932
	M	19–178	Ernst Fast (SWE) 1900
3000m Steeplechase	G	21–37	Amos Biwott (KEN) 1968
	M	21–37	Amos Biwott (KEN) 1968
110m Hurdles	G	20–304	Fred Kelly (USA) 1912
	M	20–304	Fred Kelly (USA) 1912
400m Hurdles	G	20–329	Ed Moses (USA) 1976
	M	18–325	Eddie Southern (USA) 1956
4 x 100m	G	18–118	Johnny Jones (USA) 1976
	M	17–229	Ture Persson (SWE) 1912
4 x 400m	G	19–100	Edgar Ablowich (USA) 1932
	M	17–+	Pal Simon (HUN) 1908
20 km Walk	G	23–109	Maurizio Damilano (ITA) 1980
	M	21–253	Noel Freeman (AUS) 1960
50 km Walk	G	25–103	Norman Read (NZ) 1956
High Jump	M	25–26	Antal Roka (HUN) 1952
	G	19–214	Jacek Wszola (POL) 1976
	M	18–140	Valeriy Brumel (USSR) 1960
Pole Vault	G	17–360	Lee Barnes (USA) 1924
	M	17–360	Lee Barnes (USA) 1924
Long Jump	G	19–17	Randy Williams (USA) 1972
	M	19–17	Randy Williams (USA) 1972
Triple Jump	G	20–225	Gustaf Lindblom (SWE) 1912
	M	20–38	Arnoldo Devonish (VEN) 1952
Shot	G	19–166	Ralph Rose (USA) 1904
	M	19–166	Ralph Rose (USA) 1904
Discus	G	20–69	Al Oerter (USA) 1956
	M	20–69	Al Oerter (USA) 1956
Hammer	G	20–161	Jozsef Csermak (HUN) 1952
	M	19–187	Uwe Beyer (GER) 1964
Javelin	G	20–34	Erik Lundkvist (SWE) 1928
	M	20–34	Erik Lundkvist (SWE) 1928
Decathlon	G	17–263	Bob Mathias (USA) 1948
	M	17–263	Bob Mathias (USA) 1948

G = Gold Medallist M = Medallist

Oldest

Years/Days	Name/Country/Date
36–78	Miruts Yifter (ETH) 1980
36–73	Miruts Yifter (ETH) 1980
36–73	Miruts Yifter (ETH) 1980
37–176	Carlos Lopes (POR) 1984
40–90	Mamo Wolde (ETH) 1972
32–211	Kip Keino (KEN) 1972
32–211	Kip Keino (KEN) 1972
29–16	Harrison Dillard (USA) 1952
33–50	Willie Davenport (USA) 1976
29–207	Roy Cochran (USA) 1948
33–133	Leonard Tremeer (UK) 1908
30–355	Mel Pender (USA) 1968
33–292	Jocelyn Delecour (FRA) 1968
32–62	Arthur Wint (JAM) 1952
32–62	Arthur Wint (JAM) 1952
33–110	Peter Frenkel (GDR) 1972
37–71	Peter Frenkel (GDR) 1976
38–128	Thomas Green (UK) 1932
48–115	Tebbs Lloyd Johnson (UK) 1948
30–3	Con Leahy (UK/IRE) 1906
32–85	Con Leahy (UK/IRE) 1908
30–280	Bob Richards (USA) 1956
30–280	Bob Richards (USA) 1956
28–113	Arnie Robinson (USA) 1976
31–192	Peter O'Connor (UK/IRE) 1906
31–195	Peter O'Connor (UK/IRE) 1906
34–296	Viktor Saneyev (USSR) 1980
32–151	Wladyslaw Komar (POL) 1972
37–59	Denis Horgan (UK/IRE) 1908
35–240	Ludvik Danek (CS) 1972
37–46	John Powell (USA) 1984
35–187	John Flanagan (USA) 1908
45–205	Matt McGrath (USA) 1924
33–149	Tapio Rautavaara (FIN) 1948
38–332	Jozsef Varszegi (HUN) 1948
30–102 s1	Helge Lovland (NOR) 1920
30–102	Helge Lovland (NOR) 1920

s1 Thomas Kiely (GBR) won the all round title in 1904 aged 34 years 314 days.

Women Youngest

Event	Medal	Years/Days	Name/Country/Date
100m	G	16–343	Elizabeth Robinson (USA) 1928
	M	16–343	Elizabeth Robinson (USA) 1928
200m	G	18–254	Betty Cuthbert (AUS) 1956
	M	17–116	Raelene Boyle (AUS) 1968
400m	G	19–340	Monika Zehrt (GDR) 1972
	M	18–152	Christina Brehmer (GDR) 1976
800m	G	20–251	Madeline Manning (USA) 1968
	M	20–100	Inge Gentzel (SWE) 1928
1500m	G	24–226	Tatyana Kazankina (URS) 1976
	M	22–256	Ulrike Klapezynski (GDR) 1976
80/100m Hurdles	G	17–19	Maureen Caird (AUS) 1968
	M	17–19	Maureen Caird (AUS) 1968
4 x 100	G	15–123	Pearl Jones (USA) 1952
	M	15–123	Pearl Jones (USA) 1952
4 x 400	G	18–154	Christina Brehmer (GDR) 1976
	M	17–236	Mable Fergerson (USA) 1972
High Jump	G	16–123	Ulrike Meyfarth (GFR) 1972
	M	16–115	Dorothy Odam (UK) 1936
Long Jump	G	20–256	Tatyana Kolpakova (USSR) 1980

Oldest

Years/Days	Name/Country/Date
30–98	Fanny Blankers-Koen (HOL) 1948
30–98	Fanny Blankers-Koen (HOL) 1948
30–102	Fanny Blankers-Koen (HOL) 1948
30–102	Fanny Blankers-Koen (HOL) 1948
30–66	Irena Szewinska (POL) 1976
30–66	Irena Szewinska (POL) 1976
27–223	Doina Melinte (ROM) 1984
33–205	Fita Lovin (ROM) 1984
34–013	Maricica Puica (ROM) 1984
33–24	Gunhild Hoffmeister (GDR) 1976
31–133	Shirley Strickland (AUS) 1956
34–95	Karin Balzer (GDR) 1972
31–136	Shirley Strickland (AUS) 1956
32–313	Marga Petersen (GER) 1952
28–78	Nina Zuskova (USSR) 1980
28–78	Nina Zuskova (USSR) 1980
28–98	Ulrike Meyfarth (GFR) 1984
31–113	Sara Simeoni (ITA) 1984

Special Features

Shot	M	17–332	Willye White (USA) 1956	29–67	Viorica Viscopoleanu (ROM) 1968
	G	21–186	Galina Zybina (USSR) 1952	30–365	Tatyana Talysheva (USSR) 1968
	M	21–186	Galina Zybina (USSR) 1952	34–255	Ivanka Khristova (BUL) 1976
Discus	G	20–121	Evelin Schlaak (GDR) 1976	34–255	Ivanka Khristova (BUL) 1976
	M	20–100	Ruth Osburn (USA) 1932	36–176	Lia Manoliu (ROM) 1968
Javelin	G	17–86	Mihaela Penes (ROM) 1964	36–176	Lia Manoliu (ROM) 1968
	M	17–86	Mihaela Penes (ROM) 1964	33–190	Herma Bauma (AUT) 1948
Penthahlon	G	21–271	Sigrun Siegl (GDR) 1976	37–348	Dana Zatopkova (CS) 1960
	M	21–85	Burglinde Pollak (GDR) 1972	33–59	Mary Peters (UK) 1972
				33–59	Mary Peters (UK) 1972

G = Gold Medallist M = Medallist

Oldest, Men, Gold Medal
42–023	Pat McDonald (USA) 1920., 56lbwt
38–234	John Mikaelsson (SWE) 1952, 10kmw
38–128	Thomas Green (UK) 1932, 50kmw
37–176	Carlos Lopes (POR) 1984, Mar
36–130	Mamo Wolde (ETH) 1968, Mar
36–078	Miruts Yifter (ETH) 1980, 5000
36–073	Yifter (ETH) 1980, 10,000
36–058	Werner Järvinen (FIN) 1906, DTg
35–335	Alain Mimoun (FRA) 1956, Mar
35–240	Ludvik Danek (CS) 1972, DT
35–187	John Flanagan (USA) 1908, HT

Oldest, Women, Gold Medal
36–176	Lia Manoliu (ROM) 1968, DT
34–255	Ivanka Khristova (BUL) 1976, SP
34–012	Maricica Puica (ROM) 1984, 3000
33–190	Herma Bauma (AUT) 1948, JT
33–059	Mary Peters (UK) 1972, Pen
32–313	Marga Petersen (GER) 1952, 4x100R
32–243	Ria Stalman (HOL) 1984, DT
31–309	Nadyezda Tkachenko (USSR) 1980, Pen
31–136	Shirley de la Hunty (AUS) 1956, 4x100R
31–133	de la Hunty (AUS) 1956, 80h
31–131	Nina Ponomaryeva (USSR) 1960, DT

Oldest, Men, Medal
48–115	Tebbs Lloyd-Johnson (UK) 1948, 50kmW
45–205	Matt McGrath (USA) 1924, HT
42–034	Yevgeni Ivchenko (USSR) 1980, 50kmW
42–023	Pat McDonald (USA) 1920, 56lbWt
40–363	John Ljunggren (SWE) 1960, 50kmW
40–215	James Mitchel (USA) 1904, 56lbWt
40–090	Mamo Wolde (ETH) 1972, Mar
39–336	Arthur Schwab (SUI) 1936, 50kmW
39–196c	Ernest Webb (UK) 1912, 3500mW
39–193c	Webb (UK) 1912, 10kmW
39–038	Ossian Skiöld (SWE) 1928, HT

Note: It is known that Ernest Webb was born in 1872. The above estimates are his minimum ages on the days of the events. He could have been as much as 40–195 which would move him up several places. His exact birthdate is unknown.

Oldest, Women, Medal
37–348	Dana Zatopkova (CS) 1960, JT
36–176	Lia Manoliu (ROM) 1968, DT
34–255	Ivanka Khristova (BUL) 1976, SP
34–095	Karin Balzer (GDR) 1972, 80h
34–013	Maricica Puica (ROM) 1984, 1500
34–012	Puica (ROM) 1984, 3000
33–272	Galina Zybina (USSR) 1964, SP

33–241	Kaisa Parviainen (FIN) 1948, JT
33–205	Fita Lovin (ROM) 1984, 800
33–190	Herma Bauma (AUT) 1948, JT
33–059	Mary Peters (UK) 1972, Pen

Youngest, Men, Gold Medal
17–263	Bob Mathias (USA) 1948, Dec
17–360	Lee Barnes (USA) 1924, PV
18–118	Johnny Jones (USA) 1976, 4x100R
18–237	Ugo Frigerio (ITA) 1920, 10kmW
18–240	Frigerio (ITA) 1920, 3500mW
18–280	Frank Wykoff (USA) 1928, 4x100R
18–347	Charles Dumas (USA) 1956, HJ
19–017	Randy Williams (USA) 1972, LJ
19–100	Edgar Ablowich (USA) 1932, 4x100R
19–125	Harvey Glance (USA) 1976, 4x100R
19–128	Reggie Walker (SAF) 1908, 100

Youngest, Women, Gold Medal
15–123	Pearl Jones (USA) 1952, 4x100R
16–123	Ulrike Meyfarth (GFR) 1972, HJ
16–343	Elizabeth Robinson (USA) 1928, 100
17–019	Maureen Caird (AUS) 1968, 80h
17–086	Mihaela Penes (ROM) 1964, JT
17–271	Margaret Bailes (USA) 1968, 4x100R
18–020	Eva Klobukowska (POL) 1964, 4x100R
18–035	Babe Didrikson (USA) 1932, JT
18–039	Didrikson (USA) 1932, 80h
18–087	Miloslava Rezkova (CS) 1968, HJ
18–095	Ethel Catherwood (CAN) 1928, HJ

Youngest, Men, Medal
17–206c	Pal Simon (HUN) 1908, 1600 medley relay
17–229	Ture Persson (SWE) 1912, 4x100R
17–263	Bob Mathias (USA) 1948, Dec
17–287	Dwayne Evans (USA) 1976, 200
17–360	Lee Barnes (USA) 1924, PV
18–011	Michail Dorizas (GRE) 1906, Stone Throw
18–110	Valeri Brumel (USSR) 1960, HJ
18–118	Johnny Jones (USA) 1976, 4x100R
18–232c	Frank Waller (USA) 1904, 400
18–234c	Waller (USA) 1904, 400h
18–234	Donald Lippincott (USA) 1912, 100

Note: The exact dates of birth for Simon and Waller are not known, only their years of birth. The above estimates are "worst cases", i.e., Simon was born in 1891; if it was 01 JAN 1891, he would have been 17–206 on the day of the relay. He could have been much younger. As Simon is then unquestionably the youngest male to have won an Olympic track & field medal, this should stand as a challenge to Hungarian ATFS members to find his exact birthdate.

81

Special Features

Youngest, Women, Medal

15–123	Pearl Jones (USA) 1952, 4x100R
16–115	Dorothy Odam (UK) 1936, HJ
16–123	Ulrike Meyfarth (GFR) 1972, HJ
16–161	Wilma Rudolph (USA) 1956, 4x100R
16–169	Linsey MacDonald (UK) 1980, 4x400R
16–332	Willye White (USA) 1956, LJ
16–343	Elizabeth Robinson (USA) 1928, 100
17–019	Maureen Caird (AUS) 1968, 80h
17–086	Mihaela Penes (ROM) 1964, JT

Finally we make a guess as to the youngest and oldest competitors ever in track & field at the Olympics. It must be stated that prior to 1936, the ages of all the competitors are not well documented, and so we could be in error. But as far as is known, the oldest and youngest competitors are as follows:

Men, Oldest	49–074	John Deni (USA, 1952, 50kmW)
Women, Oldest	46–282	Joyce Smith (UK, 1984, Mar)
Men, Youngest	16–061	Farhad Navab (IRAN, 1972, 100)
Women, Youngest	15–056	Deborah Wells (AUS, 1976, 100)

As can be seen, many youths have assembled to contest Olympic track & field athletics. And probably those no longer young chronologically are kept that way psychologically by the great benefits of the sport itself.

Ulrike Meyfarth – the youngest and the oldest Olympic women's high jump champion.
Don Quarrie(l) and Tietros Manea(r) tied for supremacy at 200 metres for well over a decade.

OLYMPIC TRACK & FIELD: LOST DREAMS. MISSING ATHLETES

BILL MALLON

The talk at the 1980 and 1984 Olympic Games has been as much about the athletes not in attendance as those who were actually there. But in reality, this is far from a new occurrence.

Though the athletes were absent in greater numbers than usual at the last two Olympics, due to injury, ineligibility, and politics, many of our greatest athletes have been forced to sit on the sidelines while their Olympic dreams whisked by.

The first Olympics in 1896 featured almost none of the greatest athletes in the world. The top sprinter in the world was Bernie Wefers; the top milers were Tom Conneff, George Orton and Fred Bacon; the top hurdlers were Godfrey Shaw and Stephen Chase. But these races were won by people named Burke, Flack and Curtis, none in the class of the above named. Of the dominant American team, only Tom Burke was a national champion, having won the 400 title the year before.

The 1900 Olympics was similar although the field was a bit better. But the world's top jumper was Mike Sweeney and he was ineligible because he had turned professional. In 1904 the Olympics degenerated into an American club contest as almost none of the great European athletes could afford the journey across the sea. James Lightbody won the 1500 but one wondered how he would have fared versus Alfred Shrubb. Pole vault record holder Fernand Gonder failed to show, as did Denis Horgan of Ireland, which prevented a great shot battle with Ralph Rose.

The years from 1908 through 1928 were much better. The Games had become more international in scope and all the great athletes wanted to be in attendance. In addition, they had not yet been transmogrified into a political ogre which would eventually hinder participation. Still some great athletes missed out on their chances. Norway's Charles Hoff was one of the great vaulters of all time yet he competed in the 1924 Olympics only in the 800, due to injury. Before the next Games, he was declared ineligible as a professional. And several countries were not yet fully into the Olympics. Japan did not compete in 1908, depriving Minoru Fuji, the great sprinter/pole vaulter his chance, although he would have likely been declared a professional. And certainly the Soviet Union had great athletes in the twenties, after the revolution, but they were not heard from.

In 1932, the world again came to America, in greater force than 1904, but still not as it could have been. With one exception it can be stated that the world's top track & field athletes were present in Los Angeles. But the depression and the long, expensive journey prevented European countries from fielding large teams. Thus, if you were not at the very top in your event you were not sent. This led to strong fields, but not deep ones, and there was scant chance for a Billy Mills to emerge from the pack. And the exception was in the marathon, where we were deprived of seeing Paavo Nurmi run, the IOC 'gods' having ruled him a professional shortly before the Games. He watched from the stands.

Berlin 1936 and Jesse Owens are synonymous to most, but where was Eulace Peacock, his conqueror in both the sprints and long jump in 1935? Peacock was injured and never competed in an Olympic Games. Other athletes also missed Berlin. Surely there were some German Jews capable of representing that country. They were titularly allowed at the national trials but none made the team. And there were isolated instances of athletes not going to Germany in protest of Hitler's policies, but none among the truly great.

The madness that was Hitler prevented the next two celebrations and the world's athletes lost their stage. Can there be a sadder omission from the Olympic pantheon than that of Cornelius 'Dutch' Warmerdam, the greatest pole vaulter ever, but one who never saw the Olympian fields, or even those of the U.S. Final Trials? If there is, it is that Sweden's Gunder Hägg and Arne Anderson missed what should have been the 1944 Olympics and then were declared professionals as they were setting their sights on 1948.

In 1948, the athletes of Germany, Italy and Japan were not allowed to compete, presumably as punishment for the world-wide conflagration, as if the athletes had caused it and it were not enough punishment by itself. And the Soviet Union still did not wish to compete, although by now their athletes were setting numerous European and world records.

83

Special Features

The years 1952 through 1964 stand out as a beacon in Olympic track & field history. It is difficult to find the missing in those years. There were an isolated few – Laszlo Tabori missed the 1956 Games due to the Hungarian Uprising; Jim Golliday was probably the top sprinter in 1952, but was injured at the US Trials and Lindy Remigino won sprint gold; George Brown was the top long jumper that year but failed miserably at the Olympic mark; and Jim Peters, who after 1952 became one of the greatest marathoners ever, retired before Melbourne, victim of heatstroke at the 1954 Commonwealth Games. The only major country not to appear in these years was the Republic of China. Though it harbored almost one-fourth of the world population, at that time its athletes were not prominent and no great names were absent.

In 1968 the Games were held at Mexico City and most of the world's greatest athletes were there, but only in a sense. In place of the great Ron Clarke, we saw only an ashen-grey, hypoxic Australian, done in by the altitude. A similar fate could be attributed to Jim Ryun, who lost in his best shot at Olympic gold, although one wonders if Kip Keino was beatable on that day.

At Munich in 1972, most of the greats were present but after the events of 5 September, the will of some was gone, and only the bodies remained. But even as we speak of 1968 and 1972 as being Olympics at which the world's best were present, our thoughts can turn to athletes from non-IAAF countries, like Ni Chih-Chin of China, Shin Keum-Dan of North Korea, and some great South Africans like John Van Reenan and Danie Malan. They never competed in an Olympic Games.

Montreal was the beginning of the large-scale boycotts. Most of Africa stayed home, and we missed Filbert Bayi to run against John Walker and Mike Boit to contend with Alberto Juantorena. It was the prelude to the silliness that became Moscow and Los Angeles.

Looking at all this, one wonders if, in 776 B.C., whether Coroebus, the Elysian cook who won the first Olympic title, was actually the greatest sprinter, or whether there existed a Spartan, or Athenian, who did not compete.

But who are the losers here and who have been the winners? Certainly the track fans of the world have been deprived of great duels. Certainly the athletes have been deprived their chance to prove their greatness on the greatest battlefield of all. And the governments of the world have proved nothing in their political attempts to control the Olympics. Russian insurrection in Afghanistan goes on. U.S. foreign policy has changed not a whit.

It can probably be stated that there have been no winners. You can argue that the fans of the sport have suffered the greatest loss. But I say the biggest loser has been our society as a whole, which has lost the chance to meet and find out about our neighbours, however different their ideologies may be. The Olympics, you see, are actually more than all the above great duels that were missed. They are a chance for the world's people to meet, and intermingle. The chance for a Russian white and an American black to meet and say, 'I like you. We are more alike than we are different.' It is the chance for Hal and Olga to meet and marry, no matter the future course of events. It is where Luz Long and Jesse Owens can become the best of friends. It is the chance to break down barriers and discover that we are all merely Homo sapiens, all wishing for peace and happiness in some way. In that sense, the great contests we have missed as track fans become incidental. But the contests we have missed as humans become oh, so painful, indeed.

WALLIS AND THE JAVELIN

TONY ISAACS

Tucked away in the remoteness of the Pacific Ocean is an unexpected source (almost a production line) of top-class javelin throwers. The Wallis and Futuna Islands are an isolated French possession lying Northeast of Fiji and West of Samoa which, with the help of a French coaching project called 'Operation Javelot', has produced a succession of French champions and 80 metre throwers. The appearance of these Polynesian throwers on the international javelin scene has gone largely unnoticed outside of France and yet it ranks as one of the most spectacular successes in bringing together natural ability and top-class coaching.

Wallis Island is named after Samuel Wallis who found the little island in HMS Dolphin in 1767 – though the Wallisians claim to have discovered the island before him! Futuna Island lies some 230km from Wallis Island and was found by the Dutch navigators even earlier in 1616. Together these tiny specks of land in a vast expanse of ocean became a French protectorate in 1886–7 and, at the wish of their inhabitants, were made a French Overseas Territory in 1961. There are only 6,000 people on Wallis, some 3,000 on Futuna, but another 10,000 migrants live and work in Noumea, New Caledonia. It is from these 19,000 Wallisians that such fantastic talent has emerged. Physically the Wallisians are huge and with the skills of spear-fishing in their cultural background they are built and naturally-gifted for javelin throwing. The French coach Didier Poppe, based in Noumea, and the former French champion Lolesio Tuita, based on Wallis, have got their 'production line' into top gear and new throwers with 80m potential now seem to appear regularly.

It all began in 1963 when three Wallisians were chosen to represent New Caledonia at the first South Pacific Games in Suva, Fiji. Penissio Muanoa, Petelo Wakalina and Maleto Toruafe placed 2nd, 4th and 5th respectively and, since then, the Wallis group has produced six French champions, three International Military champions, won every South Pacific title since 1963, and even gained eleventh and twelfth places at the Olympic Games. The fantastic achievements of these Wallisian throwers is best told by looking at the records of the five men who so far have beaten the 80m barrier and thus reached world-class standard.

One of the three Wallisians at the 1963 South Pacific Games, Petelo Wakalina, made the first breakthrough. Wakalina (born at Futuna on 3 April 1933) moved to France for military service and in 1966 he became a triple champion by winning the javelin at the French Championships (74.08m), the International Military Championships (80.16m) and the 2nd South Pacific Games (69.14m). He also competed for France in the 1966 European Championships but was eliminated in the qualifying round (74.12m). Wakalina took the French title again in 1968 (74.38m) and during his athletics career represented France 15 times. He died in 1982.

Lolesio Tuita was born on Wallis on 15 July 1943 but took up athletics when serving with the French Army in Martinique in 1967. Again, a move to France brought a rapid improvement and he won the French title in 1970 (79.00m), 1972 (77.44m) and 1973 (78.48m). He also replaced Wakalina as South Pacific Games champion in 1969 (72.76m) and retained this title in 1971 (71.10m), 1975 (73.20m), 1976 (74.54m) and 1978 (68.06m). He won the International Military Championship in 1973 (76.54m) and represented France at the 1972 Olympic Games placing eleventh (76.34m) and also at the 1974 European Championships where he was eliminated in the qualifying round (68.86m). In all, he competed for France 19 times before returning to Wallis in 1975. His best throw of 81.70m was set at the European Cup Semi-Final at Nice in 1973.

The next Wallisian to appear on the European scene was Penitio Lutui, a protege of Tuita. Born on Wallis on 16 October 1951, Lutui won the silver medal behind Tuita at the 1975 South Pacific Games, then moved to France in 1976 and very quickly established himself as the top French javelin thrower. He won the French title in 1977 (76.64m), 1978 (77.10m), 1979 (82.08m) and 1981 (72.10m but 80.00m in the qualifying round). He also won the International Military title in 1979 (82.22m), was Mediterranean Games champion in the same year (81.08m) and is still competing at top level in France. His best throw of 83.46m came at the 1979 European Cup Semi-Final in Geneva.

The 1979 South Pacific Games was won by a young Wallisian Jean-Paul Lakafia, who was born in Noumea, New Caledonia on 29 June 1961. His winning throw of 64.44m was set in appalling rainy

Special Features

conditions and later in 1979 he threw 72.22m in Noumea. With an eye on his potential, Didier Poppe took him to New Zealand in late 1980 where he really came good with a new French record of 83.56m in Auckland. In 1981 and 1982 he came to France for the national championships but only made 4th place each time. However 1983 was success year with the French title (80.82m) and another French record of 84.74m when winning the South Pacific Games in Apia, Western Samoa in September. In 1984 Lakafia travelled the world with the international athletics circuit. He retained his French title with a new personal best throw of 85.08m and placed 12th for France at the Los Angeles Olympics with 70.86m, a big disappointment after throwing 80.52m in the qualifying round. In the final, one of his throws landed at around 85m but was ruled a foul, hotly disputed by the French and others because, had it been allowed, it would have taken the bronze-medal. Other 80m plus throws in 1984 came at international meets in Hamilton, New Zealand (82.24m), Kobe, Japan (81.54m), Luxembourg (80.92m), Munich (82.40m) and Nice (81.76m). Lakafia will probably be back in Europe in 1985 and, still only 23, he could produce further surprises this year.

The fifth 80m thrower, Peta Tauhavili, is the same age as Lakafia, having been born on Wallis on 16 February 1961. After throwing 72.56m in Noumea in October 1981, Poppe took him and another Wallisian, Soane-Malia Tuugahala, to New Zealand for the International Tour meetings in early 1982. With a best throw of only 70.40m in Auckland, Tauhavili gave no indication of what was to come at the 1982 French Championships where he beat both Lutui and Lakafia to win with 80.76m. He placed second behind Lakafia at the 1983 South Pacific Games with 77.68m but, despite other trips overseas to New Zealand and France in 1984, he did not throw over 80m again.

Finally, a mention of the first Wallisian woman to break into the top-rank of French throwers. In 1979, 14 year-old Monika Fiafialoto (born on Wallis on 1 March 1965) placed third in the South Pacific Games with 43.96m. Since then she has progressed through the French age groups winning the Cadettees (Under 16) title in 1981 (49.68m), placing second in both the Junior (53.06m) and Senior (52.74m) events in 1982 and taking the Senior title in 1983 with 57.10m, a new French record. In 1984 she finished in fifth place with another Wallisian, Evelyne Filikesa, third with 51.10m

Poppe and Tuita have a large squad of other throwers straining to achieve selection for competition overseas so the Wallisian javelin revolution is far from finished. Watch for even more Polynesian-sounding names in the world rankings above 80m in the years ahead.

ALL TIME BEST PERFORMANCES (to 31 December 1984)

Jean-Paul	LAKAFIA	85.08	Villeneuve d'Asq	1. 7.84
Penitio	LUTUI	83.46	Geneva	1. 7.75
Lolesio	TUITA	81.70	Nice	5. 8.73
Peta	TAUHAVILI	80.76	Colombes, France	8. 8.82
Petelo	WAKALINA	80.16	Coruna, Spain	2. 7.66
Fabiano	FAKATAULAVELUA	78.26	Villeneuve d'Asq	1. 7.84
Tomasi	ULUTUIPALELEI	77.80	Utufoa, Wallis	18. 7.82
Kepeliele	TAUOTA	77.50	Utufoa, Wallis	18. 7.82
Sloane-Patita	SISELO	76.76	Noumea, New Caledonia	7. 1.84
Folotini	MULILOTO	76.64	Anthony, France	13. 6.81
Henri	SIAKI	76.38	Creteil, France	23. 6.84
Soane-Malia	TUUGAHALA	76.20	Mata Utu, Wallis	14.10.82
Sui	HEAFALA	75.10	Mata Utu, Wallis	14.10.82
Maleto	TORUAFE	73.08	Noumea, New Cal.	16. 4.66
Silipetato	LAKALAKA	72.38	St. Denis, France	1. 6.84
Vito	PUAKA	70.70	Bourail, New Cal.	19. 9.81

MODERN MARATHON TRENDS

ROGER GYNN

It is now a regular occurrence to find major performances at an international level over 42.195km being attained in the early stages of a runner's *marathon* career, almost irrespective of age, particularly with regard to Olympic success. This was no better demonstrated than in 1984 when the three Los Angeles medallists had completed no more than three marathons (in five attempts) between them prior to the Olympic show-down. Yet this is not an entirely new trend. Indeed since the War the average number of competitive marathons run by the gold medallists (in the case of Abebe Bikila and Waldemar Cierpinski at the time of their first success) prior to their Olympic wins has been just three!

Post-War Olympic Champions, age at time of win and number of prior marathons

1948	Delfo Cabrera (Arg) 29	None
1952	Emil Zatopek (Cs) 29	None
1956	Alain Mimoun (Fra) 35	None
1960	Abebe Bikila (Eth) 28	2
1964	Bikila	9
1968	Mamo Wolde (Eth) 36	8
1972	Frank Shorter (USA) 24	5
1976	Waldemar Cierpinski (GDR) 26	4
1980	Cierpinski	14
1984	Carlos Lopes (Por) 37	3

Before the War the average (on available records and including 1906) was only slightly higher (at four) but that included the two most experienced winners, apart from Cierpinski in 1980, in Hannes Kolehmainen (1920) and Kitei Son (1936) who had both taken part in ten marathons before their victories at Antwerp and Berlin respectively.

This trend does not stop at Olympic level. Of the most recent World record breakers Steve Jones and Alberto Salazar had each only run the distance once before (in the case of Jones not even that as he dropped out of his first marathon attempt) whilst the first to break 2:10, Derek Clayton, ran 2:09:36.4 in his fifth. The runner who started the sub 2:20 ball rolling back in 1953, Jim Peters, set World records in his third, fifth, eighth and tenth marathons, and recent European record holders Carlos Lopes and Gerard Nijboer had only run one and two marathons respectively before achieving their records.

Of the All-Time sub 2:09 runners a table showing marathons run before their ranked performance has, with two exceptions, a familiar ring about it.

2:08:05	Steve Jones (UK) 29	1
2:08:13*	Alberto Salazar (USA) 23	1
2:08:18	Rob de Castella (Aus) 24	5
2:08:34	Derek Clayton (Aus) 26	8
2:08:38	Toshihiko Seko (Jap) 26	8
2:08:39	Carlos Lopes (Por) 36	1
2:08:53	Dick Beardsley (USA) 26	15
2:08:55	Takeshi Soh (Jap) 30	20
2:08:55	Juma Ikangaa (Tan) 26	6
2:08:59	Rod Dixon (NZ) 33	2

Of the top British runners, Geoff Smith ran the fastest ever debut marathon in 2:09:08, Ian Thompson, a European and Commonwealth record of 2:09:12 in his second race – and incidentally has since run a further 48 without coming close to that time, and Charlie Spedding 2:09:57 in his second, followed by an Olympic bronze 2:09:58 in his third.

There are of course exceptions to every rule but of the 32 current members of the sub 2:10 club only Ron Hill (2:09:28 in his 18th marathon), Ron Tabb (2:09:32 – 21st), Bill Rodgers (2:09:27 – 23rd) and Benji Durden (2:09:58 – 25th) exceed Beardsley and Takeshi Soh as late developers whilst 24 of the elite have achieved their personal best in their first ten marathons contested.

* In New York marathon, course found on re-measurement in 1985 to be 170 yards (155 metres) short.

C.B. FRY: LONG JUMPER EXTRAORDINARY

ANDREW HUXTABLE

Ninety years ago, on 3 July 1895, the athletics career of Charles Burgess Fry came to an end, when he finished second in the long jump for Oxford v Cambridge at Queen's Club, West Kensington, London. The 'sports', as the annual track and field clash, inaugurated in 1864, was popularly known, had been postponed from March, owing to frost. (In fact, never before, or since, has the contest been held so late in the year.)

A fine biography of Fry, entitled simply 'C.B.', by Clive Ellis was published recently (Dent, 1984). Rather revealingly, the front cover shows Fry, 'the master batsman', padded-up in July 1903. Even though Fry was co-world record holder for the long jump and an international soccer player (one appearance for England v Ireland in 1901), he was best known for his cricketing prowess, making 26 Test match appearances for England between 1895 and 1912 (18 v Australia, 8 v South Africa), and ranking as one of the greatest batsmen of that era.

Fry was born at Croydon on 25 April 1872, the eldest son of Lewis Fry, who was employed by the Civil Service, and Constance White. The family moved from Surrey to Kent, and after attending two preparatory schools, Charles was sent to Repton, a public school near Derby. In his autobiography, 'Life Worth Living' (Eyre & Spottiswoode, 1939), Fry recalled that he had first realised his long jumping talents in escaping from the family's pet dog, which he feared was suffering from rabies! At Repton, he competed in athletics from 1886 until 1891 and there received the only coaching of his career from his housemaster, Rev. Arthur Forman: 'One afternoon he happened to be crossing the school paddock when I was practising the long jump on the rough turf into an elementary pit. He stopped for a few minutes, told me I did not jump high enough, took off his black mackintosh and made a heap of it between the take-off and the pit. The mackintosh frightened me into jumping much higher. It is rather interesting that up at Oxford when I jumped over 23 feet (7.01m) and did a world's record in the long jump, I used to be well over 5 feet (1.52m) in the air in a human ball at the peak of my parabola. No doubt I saw a ghostly mackintosh and remembered Mr Forman's vibrant voice. Nowadays, they have invented a new technique, called the hitch-kick, with which performers such as Jesse Owens cover some 26 feet (7.92m). At the peak of his jump Jesse Owens is by no means a black ball in the air. He figures rather like an angel sprinting up into the clouds, with his legs repeating his previous strides along the level. In fact, rather like running up Jacob's ladder.'

Fry went up to Wadham College, Oxford, in 1891 and immediately made an impact, winning the 100y, 120yH, HJ and LJ in the Freshmen's Sports in November; later that month, in the College sports, he took the 100y, 440y, 120yH, HJ, LJ and HT! His performances for Oxford v Cambridge in the long jump from 1892 to 1895 are given in the appended list. Additionally, Fry competed for Oxford in 100y in 1893 (equal 1st) and 1894 (4th) and HJ in 1892 (4th). The mark of 7.14m exceeded the previous English record of 22'10 (6.97m) by Jenner Davies in 1874 and the British record of 23'3" (7.08m) by John Purcell in 1886, and was probably the one referred to by Fry in his autobiography: 'The best long jump from toe mark to heel I made was 24 feet 2 inches (7.36m), but I took off 9 inches (23cm) before the board. In those days the taking-off board in the long jump was fixed with the breadth of the board vertical and the upper edge flush with the track. There was a sheer drop into a little trench about 5 inches (12cm) deep on the far side of the take-off; so if one overstepped by a couple of inches (5cm) one took a severe header into the pit. Nowadays, the whitewashed taking-off board, which is twice as broad as it was, is flush with the surface on both sides, so that a jumper, though his jump does not count if he oversteps the mark, has nothing to fear in the way of an accident.'

Fry obviously regretted ceasing to compete in track and field after leaving Oxford, 'because I should probably have improved during the next four years'.

If Fry (on form), John Mooney, Matthew Roseingrave and William Newburn had competed in Athens on 26 March 1896, it is unlikely that the first modern Olympic long jump title would have been won with such a modest leap as 20'10" (6.35m).

Interestingly, Fry wrote: '...the event I really fancied myself at was the 120 yards hurdles. My first two years we had several very good hurdlers, and I was not allowed to develop my ambition. Afterwards I was wanted for the long jump and the sprint, and could not take on the third event. Why is it that one always wants

88

Special Features

to do something else? I did once run against Godfrey Shaw, the amateur champion hurdler of the time [best of 15.6 in 1892]. He beat me, but to mitigate my defeat told me that he was sure that if I took up hurdling seriously I might win the championship.'

And he speculated on the improvements which took place in the succeeding 45 years: 'The standard performances in every kind of track athletics has in recent years gone up amazingly. No one has settled the question whether the individual men are superior or whether the improvement is due to improved technique and more specialised training.'

Athletics was, however, much less important to him than cricket, at which his Test match career overlapped with two legendary figures: Dr W G (William Gilbert) Grace (1848–1915) and Jack (Sir John Berry) Hobbs (1882–1963). Fry's unavailability for several overseas tours restricted his Test appearances, but his final game in first-class cricket came in India during the 1921–22 season, when he was nearly 50.

After leaving Oxford with a 1st class Mods Hons degree in Literae Humaniores, Fry taught for two years at Charterhouse School (1896–98), became editor of Fry's Magazine in 1904 (it ceased publication 10 years later on the outbreak of World War I), before taking over as Honorary Director of Training Ship 'Mercury' based at Hamble, Hampshire in 1908 on the death of Charles Hoare. Fry made this his life's work and remained in this position until 1950.

He achieved international prominence outside sport when he became assistant to Kumar Shri Ranjitsinhji, Jam Sahib of Nawanagar (with whom he had played cricket for Sussex and England) at the League of Nations on its formation in 1920. He entered the domestic political arena, standing as Liberal candidate in the 1922 (Brighton), 1923 (Banbury) and 1924 (Oxford) General Elections, each time unsuccessfully, though he failed to win by only 224 votes in 1923.

He had married Beatrice Holme Sumner in 1898; they had three children: Charis, Stephen and Faith. Holme Sumner was, in fact, assisting Hoare on TS 'Mercury' and had borne two (illegitimate) children, Robin and Sybil Hoare. (Hoare was a Roman Catholic, and thus unable to divorce his wife). Fry died at his Hampstead, London home on 7 September 1956 from kidney failure.

As a footnote, it is interesting to recall that Harold Abrahams, Honorary President of the ATFS from its foundation in 1950 until his death in 1978, followed Fry at Repton School and succeeded him as English record holder with 23'7¼" (7.19m) and 23'8¾" (7.23m) in 1923 and 24'2½" (7.38m) in 1924.

Charles Burgess FRY height: 5'10½ (1.79); weight: 175lb (79.5)Annual progress at long jump: 1888 – 5.31; 1889 – 6.04; 1891 – 6.53; 1892 – 7.14; 1893 – 7.17; 1894 – 7.02; 1895 – 6.63.

Best long jump marks:

23'6½"/7.17	(1)	4 Mar 93	Oxford	(OUAC Sports)
23'5"/7.14	(1)	8 Apr 92	West Kensington	(OUAC v CUAC)
23'0½"/7.02	(1)	23 Mar 93	West Kensington	(OUAC v CUAC)
23'0½"/7.02	(1)	28 Feb 94	Oxford	(OUAC Sports)
22'7½"/6.89	(1)	26 Mar 92	Oxford	(OUAC Sports)
22'4"/6.81	(1)	17 Mar 94	West Kensington	(OUAC v CUAC)
22'0¾"/6.72	(3)	16 Jul 94	West Kensington	(OUAC v Yale)
21'9½"/6.64	(1)	9 Apr 92	West Kensington	(Corinthians v Barbarians)
21'9"/6.63	(2)	3 Jul 95	West Kensington	(OUAC v CUAC)

Best marks at other events:
100y – 10.2 (1893), 220y – 24.6 (1889), 400y – 56.8 (1891), 120yh – 17.6 (1889 and 1894), HJ – 1.74m (1893), SP – 7.59m (1892), HT – 17.83m (1891).

With acknowledgements to W.B. Downing, Clive Ellis, Peter Lovesey and Dave Terry.

WHAT IS 'TACTICAL' RUNNING?

A. LENNART JULIN

A frequently used expression in the running vocabulary is *tactical*. The 1500m finals in most recent international championship meets have been so billed by many observers. Those races have been characterised by a (very) slow early part and by an all-decisive sprint finish over the last lap.

However, to use *tactical* as synonymous with 'slow start – sprint finish', is not only a euphemism, but is surely incorrect as that kind of race really should be called *atactical* (= the opposite of tactical)! If the description *tactical* is to be meaningful, it should express a thoroughly considered plan by one runner or a group of runners to develop the race into the pattern that suits him/them better than the other competitors!

But if there is anything that is typical of the normal so-called *tactical* race it is that it is totally devoid of anything resembling the execution of a plan by any of the runners! Rather it is a perfect demonstration of collective paralysation: everybody expects someone else to take care of the pace-setting and has no alternative when nobody does.

The runner possessing the best finishing speed is of course not doing anything wrong – he will get his victory without wasting too much energy. Observers however have often wondered why so many runners act as if they truly believed they had the ability to win in a sprint finish. The answer is that the runners *act* as if they were confident, but if you analyse the situation a little bit further the passive attitude is really due to lack of confidence in their own ability – especially for the closing stages of the race!

The runners are afraid of being at a disadvantage at the end of the race if they have been unable to save maximum energy for the final sprint: 'If I take the lead now I will get tired while everyone else will be able to rest. Thereby I will lose whatever small chance I have to be in the top six!'

But if the *'slow'* races are *atactical* – what races are the truly *tactical* ones? The answer – at least in world-class competition – is the *'fast'* races where runners intentionally force or vary the pace! Although thereby they are 'hurting' themselves they are doing it with the objective of hurting the other runners even more.

When Filbert Bayi burst on the scene some ten years ago, running the first 800m of a 1500m/1 mile race in 1:51–1:52, he was criticised for his lack of 'tactical sense' and told that he had to learn how such races 'should' be run. But it was not Bayi that was wrong! He did not possess a sprint finish that could match, for example, John Walker's and thus Bayi's chance of winning was to force a pace that would kill the kick of Walker and others. And Bayi was quite successful with his intelligent tactics, getting world records and many important victories.

Thus we can define true *tactical* running: To make the race pattern suit you better than your opponents even if it is tough and demanding also on yourself! One other good example of that was Brendan Foster's sustained one-lap drives in his major 5000m races. The key-word here is 'sustained'. Short bursts of speed – like Dave Bedford used – tend to hurt the one who surges more than the others if they are running sensibly. But Foster's 60-second mid-race lap was long enough to give him a margin that was big enough to make the others disillusioned as to their chances of ever catching up.

Another well-known representative of the 'hurt yourself but the others even more' -philosophy was Herb Elliott. His third-lap move in the 1500m final at the 1960 Olympics was perhaps not 'necessary' but it meant that he totally eliminated the chances of the runners who were hoping for a race decided solely by sprinting ability.

Despite these examples of tactical winners it should be noted that a victory is not necessarily synonymous with a supreme *tactical* performance. Instead the best *tactical* moves are often performed by runners placing second or third – behind a physically clearly superior winner but ahead of competitors of similar or slightly superior ability. A good illustration of this was provided by the 5000m final in the Los Angeles Olympics. Said Aouita was by far the best runner in all aspects – both speed and endurance – and did not have to do anything more than keep in touch with the leader until the last lap – a sufficient but not very complicated or demanding *tactical* behaviour. For Antonio Leitao the situation was quite different as he had the endurance to survive a fast pace but lacked a sprint finish to match the freshly converted middle-distance runners

Special Features

in the race. So Leitao – together with countryman Ezequiel Canario – set a very stiff pace that put the 'speed runners' so far back when it came to the finish of the race that their superior speed was to no avail. That was a beautifully executed tactical plan, which brought Leitao a bronze medal that he would never have got in a slow-pace race!

Said Aouita did not have to use any active tactical moves to win – and the same was true in the 1980 Olympics for Miruts Yifter, who also was a very superior runner who could have won any kind of race. Obviously he was not quite aware of that and the races were complicated by unnecessary – and for themselves, especially in the 5000m, disastrous – numerous bursts of speed by his fellow countrymen. A 'hurt the other runners but yourself even more' - version of tactical running!

Thinking back to the most recent Olympic Games there are more runners than Leitao who should get recognised for their tactics, like José Abascal and Joaquim Cruz. Abascal's third lap 'killed' everyone but Coe and Cram and earned him a bronze medal. And Cruz should now be relieved of an undeserved reputation as a runner who needed to learn to conserve his energy in a better way. By running fast also in the preliminary rounds he forces everyone else to run fast and they suffer more from the fast pace than Cruz does – thus Cruz demonstrates a very sound and tactical way of running the preliminaries!

A dissertation on tactical running is not complete without mentioning the man who was perhaps the greatest tactical genius – Lasse Viren. But his long career contains so many examples of intelligent tactical moves – even in races he did not have the physical capacity to win – that it is worth a separate feature article!

JIM THORPE AT THE 1912 OLYMPIC GAMES

The official restoration of Jim Thorpe to his rightful place amongst the pantheon of Olympic heroes was one of the more pleasing decisions ratified by the I.O.C. and I.A.A.F. in 1984. The story of Thorpe's triumphs in the Pentathlon and Decathlon at the 1912 Olympic Games, and his subsequent disqualification for 'professionalism' (including the erasure of his name from all official results and record lists), is too well known to need repetition here. However, preparation of the Official Report must have been too well advanced by the time the disqualification was announced, since Thorpe's performances are recounted throughout the text, giving the whole section an oddly unbalanced appearance. It seems appropriate now to complete the rehabilitation by restoring the results section to its true original state.

Thorpe earned his selection for the Games by winning a Pentathlon trial held at Central Park, New York, on 18 May. The Decathlon trial, due to be held the following weekend, was cancelled as only two entries (Thorpe and Klage) were received. Despite this apparent lack of interest, six Americans eventually lined up for the inaugural Olympic contest. The hosts, meanwhile, had been working diligently on their preparations for the new competitions, establishing the rules and experimenting with scoring systems. For one thing, they were keen to have 'both-hand' competitions for the throws (as already established in their national championships initiated in 1909), but this proved unpopular with other associations so the concept was dropped.

The first Swedish trial with the eventual schedule of events took place on 15 Oct 1911 and was won by Hugo Wieslander (the 1909 champion) with 6138.33 points, scored on a linear-based system. Attempts to produce a progressive (non-linear) method were not successful, so the linear model was finally retained, with the Olympic records (up to 1908) as basis for 1000 points. This system was used in two final Swedish trials held in June 1912, both won by Wieslander from Gösta Holmér and Charles Lomberg, the first by the slender margin of 7099.845 to 7049.24 (the previous year's inaugural record, incidentally, converted to 6903.92), the second by a more decisive 300+ points in improving the record to 7244.10.

Thus it was that Wieslander, Holmér and Lomberg led the Swedish contingent in both Pentathlon and Decathlon events, the former commencing only 17 days after the second Decathlon trial. Pentathlon scoring was by position in each of the 5 events – thus 1 point for 1st place, 2 points for 2nd, etc., although the Decathlon Tables were to be used to split ties. Thorpe quickly established his superiority in the Long

91

Special Features

Jump, followed by Ferdinand Bie (Norway) and James Donahue (USA). Wieslander finished this first event well down in 14th place, but the Swedish squad improved its position in the Javelin with Wieslander and Oscar Lemming securing the first two places. That was their final fling, however, as the American Indian proceeded to win the remaining three events to secure an overwhelming victory with 7 points – just two above the minimum possible. Wieslander was the only Swede to feature in the final reckoning, Scandinavian pride being salvaged by Bie's silver medal in a competition otherwise dominated by North Americans.

Here is a summary of performances and positions in the competition. Note that only the best 12 were permitted to continue after 3 events, while for the 1500m the best 6 were retained (in fact, 7 ran in the final event, there being a tie for 6th after the Discus). Points were reallocated after 3 events (i.e. eliminating the non-qualifiers), as shown in the summary below.

Thorpe warmed up for the Decathlon, which started six days later, by competing in the High Jump on 8 July (he finished 4th with 1.85) and the Long Jump on the following day (finishing 7th with 6.89). The Decathlon was originally intended to be completed in two days; because of the large number of entries, however, it was extended to three days. The 29 starters were divided into 10 heats for the 100m, Gösta Holmer winning the first in 11.4 from his team-mate, Wieslander. It was another Swede, Jacobsson, and Mercer (USA) who achieved the fastest time of 11.0, while Thorpe won his heat in 11.2 for third best overall. Charles Lomberg provided further encouragement for the hosts by leading the Long Jump with 6.87, but Mercer (6.84) went into the lead after two events and Thorpe's relatively modest 6.79 was enough to move him up to second. The Pentathlon champion had the best Shot mark at 12.89 and closed the first day over 240 points ahead, as Mercer (9.76) slipped back to third place behind Lomberg.

Olympic Pentathlon Championship, 7 Jul 1912

Long Jump		Javelin		Leaders after 2 events	
1. Thorpe	7.07	1. Wieslander	49.56	1. Thorpe	4 pts.
2. Bie	6.85	2. Lemming	49.51	2. Bie	6
3. Donahue	6.83	3. Thorpe	46.71	3. Lemming	7
4. Brundage	6.58	4. Bie	46.45	4. Brundage	13
5. Lemming	6.55	5. Holmer	45.46	5. Wieslander	15
6. Lomberg	6.52	6. ?		6. Donahue	18

200 metres		Leaders after 3 events		(Adjusted scores)	
1. Thorpe	22.9	1. Thorpe	5 pts	1. Thorpe	5 pts
2. Donahue &		2. Bie	13	2. Bie	11
Menaul	23.0	3. Donahue	20	3. Donahue	12
4. Eller	23.1	4. Lemming	21	4. Lemming	19
5. Failliot &		5. Brundage	26	5. Lukeman &	
Lukeman	23.2	6. Wieslander	27	Wieslander	21

Discus		Leaders after 4 events		1500 metres	
1. Thorpe	35.57	1. Thorpe	6 pts	1. Thorpe	4:44.8
2. Brundage	34.72	2. Bie	15	2. Menaul	4:49.6
3. Lukeman	33.76	3. Lukeman &		3. Donahue	4:51.0
4. Bie	31.79	Brundage	24	4. Wieslander	4:53.1
5. Holmer	31.78	5. Donahue	26	5. Lukeman	5:00.2
6. Menaul	31.38	6. Menaul &		6. Bie	5:07.8
7. Wieslander	30.74	Wieslander	28	7. Brundage	n.t.

Final Positions		LJ	JT	200m	DT	1/00m	pts	score
1.	James Thorpe (USA)	7.07	46.71	22.9	35.57	4:44.8	7	4041.53
2.	Ferdinand Bie (Nor)	6.85	46.45	23.5	31.79	5:07.8	21	3623.84
3.	James Donahue (USA)	6.83	38.28	23.0	29.64	4:51.0	29	3475.865
4.	Frank Lukeman (Can)	6.45	36.02	23.2	33.76	5:00.2	29	3396.975
5.	James Menaul (USA)	6.40	35.85	23.0	31.38	4:49.6	30	3378.21
6.	Avery Brundage (USA)	6.58	42.85	24.2	34.72	–	31	–
7.	Hugo Wieslander (Swe)	6.27	49.56	24.1	30.74	4:51.1	32	3552.565

Special Features

Six of the starters failed to report for the High Jump at 9 a.m. the following day. Thorpe extended his lead considerably in this event (1.87), although Lomberg (1.80) stayed in contention, while Wieslander (1.75) moved up to third place overall. Mercer's 1.65 left him back in 5th, but he rebounded with an excellent 400m in 49.9, nearly two seconds clear of the next best. Lomberg could manage no better than 55.0, but clung to second place somewhat remotely behind Thorpe and only just ahead of Mercer and Wieslander. Next came the Discus, which was dominated by G.W.Philbrook, another of the U.S. contingent, whose 41.56 was the first (and only) performance to exceed the 1000-point ceiling (and confused the scorers, who credited him with 1038 points instead of 1003.8). This moved him up to 2nd overall, but almost 500 points behind Thorpe. The real cruncher, however, was the hurdles, 'Thorpe's running in the fifth heat being quite a surprise', according to the Official Report. His time of 15.6 left him with a massive 613 points lead over Philbrook, whose 16.8 kept him almost 100 points clear of Lomberg and Wieslander at the end of the second day. Incidentally, Thorpe underlined his potential in this event a week later when defeating the Olympic Champion, Fred Kelly, and equalling Smithson's World record of 15.0 at a meeting in France.

The final day's proceedings commenced at the Pole Vault pit, with 16 of the 29 starters reporting for duty. Mercer emerged a clear leader with 3.60, 20cm ahead of Donahue, while Thorpe maintained his inexorable progress by clearing 3.25. Philbrook could manage no more than 2.50 and dropped back to 5th place overall, with Lomberg back in second place ahead of Wieslander. The latter's best event was the Javelin, and he excelled this time with a cast of 50.40, moving ahead of Lomberg for the first time. By now, however, his World record had already been surpassed, for Thorpe's 45.70 took his total after 9 events to 7633.155.

Lukeman and Brundage retired after the Vault, to be joined by Bie (runner-up in the Pentathlon) and Philbrook after the Javelin, leaving 12 men to contest the 1500m. The first of the three races was a close affair won by Holmer in 4:41.9, while Wieslander closed his account with 4:45.0 to regain (temporarily) his record with a total of 7724.495. Thorpe ran most of the final heat in splendid isolation, coming home in 4:40.1 to win the title by almost 700 pts. Lomberg was content to bring up the rear, knowing his position in third place ahead of Holmer was secure. The three Swedes all improved their personal bests by several hundred points, but were totally eclipsed by the phenomenon from Oklahoma.

Event-by event Summary
(First day, 13 July 1912)

100 metres		Long Jump		Leaders (2 events)	
1. Mercer	11.0 (952.4)	1. Lomberg	6.87 (850.55)	1. Mercer	1795.60
2. Jacobsson	11.0 (952.4)	2. Mercer	6.84 (843.20)	2. Thorpe	1735.75
3. Lukeman	11.2 (904.8)	3. Thorpe	6.79 (830.95)	3. Jacobsson	1702.50
4. Thorpe	11.2 (904.8)	4. Bie	6.69 (806.45)	4. Röhr	1623.75
5. Failliot	11.3 (881.0)	5. Donahue	6.48 (755.00)	5. Lomberg	1612.55
6. Röhr	11.3 (881.0)	6. Wieslander	6.42 (740.30)	6. Bie	1592.25

Shot Putt		Leading positions after 3 events			
1. Thorpe	12.89 (809)	1. Thorpe	2544.75	7. Philbrook	2138.90
2. Nilsson	12.83 (803)	2. Lomberg	2299.55	8. Bie	2132.25
3. Philbrook	12.79 (799)	3. Mercer	2291.60	9. Röhr	2124.75
4. Wieslander	12.14 (734)	4. Wieslander	2236.30	10. Holmer	2107.70
5. Lomberg	11.67 (687)	5. Nilsson	2205.20	11. Failliot	2104.65
6. Schafer	11.50 (670)	6. Jacobsson	2157.50	12. Wickholm	2087.55

(Second day, 14 July 1912)

High Jump		Leading positions after 4 events			
1. Thorpe	1.87 (958)	1. Thorpe	3502.75	7. Röhr	2844.75
2. Lomberg &		2. Lomberg	3159.55	8. Holmer	2827.70
Philbrook	1.80 (860)	3. Wieslander	3026.30	9. Lukeman	2815.50
4. Andre,		4. Philbrook	2998.90	10. Brundage	2754.20
Lukeman &		5. Mercer	2941.60	11. Wickholm	2667.55
Wieslander	1.75 (790)	6. Nilsson	2925.20	12. Jacobsson	2667.50

Special Features

400 metres		Leading positions after 5 events			
1. Mercer	49.9 (943.60)	1. Thorpe	4359.87	7. Holmer	3647.22
2. Donahue	51.6 (879.68)	2. Lomberg	3911.39	8. Bie	3601.77
3. Lukeman	52.1 (860.88)	3. Mercer	3885.20	9. Donahue	3533.68
4. Thorpe	52.2 (857.12)	4. Wieslander	3830.78	10. Wickholm	3520.91
5. Wickholm	52.3 (853.36)	5. Philbrook	3686.82	11. Brundage	3498.52
6. Bie & Holmer	53.2 (819.52)	6. Lukeman	3676.38	12. von Halt	3481.52

Discus		Leading positions after 6 events			
1. Philbrook	41.56 (1003.80)	1. Thorpe	5189.63	7. von Halt	4253.52
2. Schäfer	37.14 (835.84)	2. Philbrook	4690.62	8. Bie	4228.99
3. Thorpe	36.98 (829.76)	3. Lomberg	4679.21	9. Brundage	4217.70
4. Wieslander	36.29 (803.54)	4. Wieslander	4634.32	10. Mercer	4143.82
5. von Halt	35.46 (772.00)	5. Holmer	4279.38	11. Donahue	4096.30
6. Lomberg	35.35 (767.82)	6. Lukeman	4260.66	12. Wickholm	4077.07

110 metres Hurdles		Leading positions after 7 events			
1. Thorpe	15.6 (943.0)	1. Thorpe	6132.63	7. Holmer	5089.38
2. Donahue	16.2 (886.0)	2. Philbrook	5519.62	8. Brundage	5018.20
3. Lukeman	16.3 (876.5)	3. Lomberg	5432.21	9. Mercer	5010.88
4. Andre,		4. Wieslander	5425.32	10. von Halt	4997.02
Bie &		5. Lukeman	5147.16	11. Donahue	4982.30
Mercer	16.4 (867.0)	6. Bie	5095.99	12. Wickholm	4887.07

(Third day, 15 July 1912)

Pole Vault		Leading positions after 8 events			
1. Mercer	3.60 (940.6)	1. Thorpe	6884.23	7. Holmer	5813.98
2. Donahue	3.40 (832.6)	2. Lomberg	6183.81	8. Bie	5658.59
3. Lomberg,		3. Wieslander	6095.92	9. Wickholm	5638.67
Schäfer,		4. Mercer	5951.42	10. Lukeman	5591.76
Thorpe &		5. Philbrook	5866.22	11. Brundage	5580.80
Wickholm	3.25 (751.6)	6. Donahue	5814.90	12. von Halt	5451.62

Javelin		Leading positions after 9 events			
1. Wieslander	50.40 (878.175)	1. Thorpe	7633.155	7. Donahue	6327.050
2. Bie	48.52 (826.475)	2. Wieslander	6974.095	8. Mercer	6332.395
3. Holmer	46.28 (764.875)	3. Lomberg	6826.310	9. Wickholm	6301.795
4. Thorpe	45.70 (748.925)	4. Holmer	6578.855	10. von Halt	6038.845
5. Kugelberg	45.67 (748.100)	5. Philbrook	6504.320	11. Kugelberg	5999.380
6. Wickholm	42.58 (663.125)	6. Bie	6485.065	12. Schäfer	5939.985

1500 metres					
(Race 1)		(Race 2)		(Race 3)	
1. Holmer	4:41.9 (769.0)	1. Kugelberg	4:43.5 (759.4)	1. Thorpe	4:40.1 (779.8)
2. Wickholm	4:43.9 (757.0)	2. Mercer	4:46.3 (742.6)	2. von Halt	5:02.8 (643.6)
3. Donahue	4:44.0 (756.4)	3. Schultz	4:46.4 (742.0)	3. Schäfer	5:05.3 (628.6)
4. Wieslander	4:45.0 (750.4)	4. Alsleben	5:08.6 (608.8)	4. Lomberg	5:12.2 (587.2)

Decathlon Result, 13/14/15 July 1912

		Score	100m	LJ	SP	HJ	400m	DT	110H	PV	JT	1500m
1.	J.R.Thorpe (USA)	8412.955	11.2	679	1289	187	52.2	3698	15.6	325	4570	4:40.1
2.	H.Wieslander (Swe)	7724.495	11.8	642	1214	175	53.6	3629	17.2	310	5040	4:45.0
3.	C.Lomberg (Swe)	7413.510	11.8	687	1167	180	55.0	3535	17.6	325	4183	5:12.2
4.	G.Holmér (Swe)	7347.855	11.4	598	1098	170	53.2	3178	17.0	320	4628	4:41.9
5.	J.J.Donahue (USA)	7083.450	11.8	648	967	165	51.6	2995	16.2	340	3709	4:44.0
6.	E.R.L.Mercer (USA)	7074.995	11.0	684	976	165	49.9	2195	16.4	360	3232	4:46.3
7.	W.Wickholm (Fin)	7058.795	11.5	595	1109	160	52.3	2978	17.0	325	4258	4:43.9
8.	E.Kugelberg (Swe)	6758.780	12.3	620	998	165	55.7	3148	17.2	300	4567	4:43.5
9.	K.von Halt (Ger)	6682.445	12.1	608	1112	170	54.2	3546	17.7	270	3982	5:02.8
10.	J.Schäfer (Aut)	6568.585	12.3	604	1150	155	58.2	3714	18.9	325	4106	5:05.3
11.	A.Schultz (Rus)	6134.470	12.3	575	1008	155	54.6	3134	17.8	270	3899	4:46.4
12.	A.Alsleben (Rus)	5294.615	12.2	627	848	170	59.0	2921	19.5	0	3734	5:08.6

(Non-finishers)

G.W.Philbrook (USA)	12.4	634	1279	180	56.7	4156	16.8	250	4167	–
F.R.Bie (Nor)	11.7	669	1020	165	53.2	3165	16.4	290	4852	–
F.L.Lukeman (Can)	11.2	614	929	175	52.1	3052	16.3	270	–	
A.Brundage (USA)	12.2	640	1112	170	55.2	3407	17.1	290	–	
G.I.André (Fra)	11.6	560	990	175	54.5	2537	16.4	–		
A.Pagani (Ita)	12.4	583	967	165	56.1	3020	17.2	–		
E.Nilsson (Swe)	11.5	572	1283	170	–					
O.Röhr (Ger)	11.3	643	981	170	–					
S.Jacobsson (Swe)	11.0	646	935	155	–					
G.Ronström (Swe)	12.3	599	1069	160	–					
A.Abraham (Ger)	12.0	552	1129	150	–					
P.Failliot (Fra)	11.3	605	1054	–						
H.S.Babcock (USA)	11.6	629	1016	–						
S.Langkjaer (Den)	12.0	589	986	–						
W.Hackberg (Swe)	12.5	564	1030	–						
M.Legat (Ita)	12.1	556	823	–						
M.Megherian (Tur)	13.3	543	1105	–						

CORRECTIONS TO 1984 ANNUAL

(From Pino Mappa, Milan Skocovsky, Francisco Baraona, Garry Hill, Mike Renfro, Jean Gilbert-Touzeau)

Page No.
29/50 Clarke 27:39.4m, not 27:39.89 (Auto-timing not in operation)
36 Delete-Ockerman 10.14w (manual timing)
37 Norman 20.06A
41 Coe 1:41.73e (Photo-electric cell time)
77 Delete-Vashchenko 8087 (see 8124e)
90 Jackson 10.28 (2), not (1)
92 Petrov 10.35w (2)h, not (1)h
94 Boussemart 20.54 (1)h4, not h2.
95 Lomba 20.78 on 15 May
98 Myburgh 45.32A in h2. Tomko 45.64 at Rosicky Memorial.
100 Cannon 45.72 on 25 Jun
103 Härkönen 1:46.39 on 7 Aug
106 Monkemeyer 3:38.71 not 3:38.64
108 Scott 3:51.56, and Coe 3:52.93 at AAA
112 Spivey 13:19.24 at Bisl
113 Zdravkovic 13:35.83 vHUN. Matthew, not Matthews Temane 13:36.92
116 Toomas Turb at 28:21.27
118 Jensen 8:22.54 at FBK Hengelo 12 Jul. Add:- Peter Daenens BEL 60 8:23.11 (2) VD Bruxelles 26 Aug
127 Pienaar 49.96, not 49.56
128 Add:- Thränhardt 2.30 (2) Recke 17 Jun
133 Reverse:- Vannuesluoma at Lappeenranta, Rodion Gataullin (not Radion Gitaulin) at Schwechat. Salbert 5.50i v GDR.
134 Kolasa and Radzikowski 5.50i at NC

137 Wodars 7.96 on 12 Jun
139 Leitner 7.96w v AUT,HUN
140 Lorraway 17.35, and Conley 17.23i on 12 Mar
141 Lisichonuk (not Lisochonuk) SU (not US) 16.92. Markov 16.88 at Nar, Abramov 16.59 (6), not (5). Add:- Gennadiy Kachno SU 64 16.49 ( ) Stavropol 7 Aug.
142 Johnson 16.19 BAH, not USA
145 Andrei 20.19 on 14(not 19) Jul
146 Montelatici- delete 19.17, see 19.36
148 Wilkins 68.26 on 12 (not 13) Jun
151 Kwasny 80.18 on 21 Aug
154 Barnett 90.34, not 90.36
155 Ivanov 83.90 (1)e2. Makarov 83.70 (3)
156 Thomas, not Viktor Schäffner
188 1500m Add:- Lorenzo Hidalgo SPA 65 3:44.65 (5) La Coruna 17 Aug
189 5000m   Add:- Jose M. Albentosa SPA 64 13:56.18 (1) Granollers 18 Jun
Delete:- Mayfat 13:58.0 born 1963.
Add:- Peter K. Rono KEN 65 14:09.4 (1) Nakuru 9 Jul
Pedro del Arco SPA 64 14:12.0 (3) Toledo 25 Jun
Alfonso Alvarez SPA 64 14:13.54 ( ) Vigo 6 Jul Erdina Shabanov BUL 64
2000m St Dmitriy Archipov 64 at 5:39.85
190 110mH   Add:- Elvis Cederic VEN 64 14.29 ( ) San Juan 26 Jun
191 400mH   Add:- Ettiene de Villiers RSA 64 A51.5 (1) Johannesburg 21 Oct

Corrections to the 1984 Annual

192 PV   Correct spelling:- Rodion Gataullin 5.55
193 TJ   Amend:- Kachno from 16.17 to 16.49 ( )
Stavropol 7 Aug
194 SP   Amend:- Klejza from 17.42 to 18.23 ( )
Volgograd 25 May
Mikhail Karasev at 17.68
Amend:- Pachin from 18.38 to 17.62 ( )
Dnepropetrovsk 25 Sep
Add:- Vasiliy Falvorochniy SU 64 17.17 ( )
Togliatti 22 May
195 HT Add:- Aleksandr Gomorev SU 64 68.94 ( )
Pyatigorsk 24 Aug
Amend:- from 66.72, Pavel Repnikov 68.60 ( )
Rovno 6 May
Add:- Fedor Makovskiy SU 65 68.10 ( )
Togliatti 22 May,
Aleksey Ipatov SU 65 68.06 ( ) Alushta 16 Feb,
Vladimir Glubokov SU 64 67.10 ( ) Tashkent 20 Sep,
Vladimir Voropayev SU 65 66.50 ( )
Krasnodar 23 Apr
JT   Grinchenko 75.86 at Gorlovka 27 Aug
Add:- Oleg Bazhutkin SU 64 75.50 ( ) Adler 28 Apr
196 Dec Amend:- Medved from 7509 to 7572 (1) Kiev 4 Sep
(11.30 7.05 13.09 1.97 50.47 15.20 44.56 4.50 48.80 4:32.09)
Amend:- Mironov from 7393 to 7575m (1) Kharkov 22 Aug
(11.2 7.41 12.86 1.90 50.6 16.2 38.40 4.80 57.04 4:28.6)
Amend:- Kushnir from 7534m to 7540m (4) Donyetsk 8 May
Differing marks:- SP 12.70, DT 43.48, JT 57.68, 1500 4:42.1
Add:- Mikhail Ivanov SU 64 7536m (1) Minsk 30 Jun
(11.2 6.96 13.49 1.94 52.4 15.1 42.16 4.30 61.60 4:38.2)
Yevgeniy Bogdashin SU 64 7522m (2) Karaganda 22 Jul
(11.6 6.99 13.30 1.99 51.5 15.2 46.22 4.00 62.86 4:38.8)
Amend:- Michalchenko from 7298 to 7419 (10) Krasnodar 26 May
(11.25 6.96 13.74 1.89 51.35 15.70 42.58 4.40 61.22 4:53.23)
Add:- Igor Davydov SU 64 7514m (2) Minsk 30 Jun

(11.0 6.90 13.90 1.91 50.4 15.6 44.40 3.80 55.98 4:28.5)
Nikolay Savko SU 64 7510m (1) Alushta 8 May
(10.8 7.09 13.40 2.05 51.5 15.6 38.32 4.00 53.14 4:33.0)

204 W100 Göhr 10.91 at Berlin on 31 Jul 83 ;
Ferrell-Edmondson 11.12
not 11.11; Haglund 11.16 not 11.17.
206 W200   Wind on Helten's 22.68 0.0.
212 WMile   Tabb 4:21.46 Bisl on 26 Jun 82 ;
Maracescu 4:22.09 not 4:22.1
McRoberts 4:29.90 at Pepsi. Monica not Monika Joyce.
Waitz 8:32.1 at Bisl
213 W3k   Olofsson 8:42.3 and Merrill 8:42.6 at Bisl. Sadreydinova move up from 8:44.10 to 8:41.05 (9) Leningrad 27 Jul 83.
221 WLJ   Alyoshina (not Alyeshina) 6.84 in 1983 not 1981
224 WSP   Shcherbanos 19.41 on 10 Jun 83.
Savinkova 73.26 on 21 May 83
WDT   Meg Ritchie not Ritshie.
231 EP 4*400 on 21 Aug 83.
235 W100   Delete :- Olsen 11.48 (Only 11.97); Pomoshnikova (1) h3 not (2)
250 W1500   Mishkel 4:08.4 not Mishel.
265 W400h   Add: Anita Lauvensteine SU 63 58.7
277 WDT   Akhrimenko 64.14 not 64.16
357 Akhrimenko DT 64.14 64.60 –80.
361 Creantor born 2 Jun 48
364 Gaschet 23.03, not 23.05
370 Levesque previous best 2:39:29 –80, and nee Fouache.
377 Rougeron born 14 Jun 61
381 Truwant born 17 Sep 65
386 Soboleva (58.96–DT) nee Yerokha.

96

NATIONAL CHAMPIONSHIPS AND BIOGRAPHIES

Potted biographies are given for nearly 600 of the world's top athletes, listed by nation. The information includes:
Name – date and place of birth – height – weight.
Previous name(s) for married women – club or university – occupation.
Major championships record – all placings in such events as the Olympic Games (OG), World Championships (WCh), European Championships (ECh), Commonwealth Games (CG), World Cup (WCp) and European Cup Final (ECp); leading placings in the European Junior Championships and other Continental Championships; and first three in European Indoors (EI) or World Student Games (WSG).
National titles won or successes in other major events.
Records set – world, continental and national; indoor world bests.
Progression of best marks over the years at major event.
Personal best performances at other events.
Other comments.

    Details are to the end of 1984, with the addition of some performances made in January 1985, including performances at the first World Indoor Games.

    I am most grateful to various ATFS members who have helped check these details. Additional information or corrections would be welcomed for next year's Annual. We also hope to expand the number of countries for which national champions are listed.

Peter Matthews
6 Broadfields,
Goffs Oak, Waltham Cross,
Herts EN7 5JU
England

National Championships

AUSTRALIA

Governing body: Amateur Athletic Union of Australia, Grandstand, Olympic Park Athletic Track, Swan Street, Melbourne, Victoria 3002. Founded 1897.
National Championships first held in 1893 (men), 1930 (women)
1984 Champions: MEN
100m: Paul Narracott 10.62, 200m: Peter van Miltenberg 21.17, 400m: Bruce Frayne 45.96, 800m: Peter Bourke 1:47.42, 1500m: Mike Hillardt 3:36.26, 5000m/10000m: Zephaniah Ncube (Tan) 13:51.52/28:31.08, 3000mSt: Gary Zeuner 8:34.52, 110mh: Don Wright 13.87, 400mh: Dale Horrobin 51.00, HJ: John Atkinson 2.28, PV: Rob Chisholm 4.90, LJ: Gary Honey 8.15, TJ: Ken Lorraway 16.59, SP: Ray Rigby 17.92, DT: Paul Nandapi 56.50, HT: Hans Lotz 66.86, JT: David Dixon 73.82, Dec: Peter Hadfield 7692, 5000mW: David Smith 19:31.53, 50kmW: Andrew Jackno 4:01:02
WOMEN
100m/200m: Debbie Wells 11.60/23.25, 400m: Kim Robertson (NZ) 52.54, 800m: Heather Barralet 2:01.78, 1500m: Anne McKenzie (NZ) 4:17.90, 3000m: Donna Gould 9:15.11, 10000m: Sally Pierson 33:33.66, 100mh/Hep: Glynis Nunn 13.81/6273, 400mh: Debbie Flintoff 56.88, HJ: Vanessa Browne 1.90, LJ: Robyn Lorraway 6.68, SP/DT: Gael Martin 17.64/55.98, JT: Petra Rivers 62.66, 5000mW: Susan Cook 22:04.42

Darren CLARK
b.6 Sep 1965 Sydney 1.79m 76kg
Club: Ryde-Hornsby. Salesman.
Ch. record at 400m: OG: '84 – 4; WCh: '83 – sf. Won AAA 400m '83 – 4. Two Australian 400m records in 1984.
Progression at 400m: 1982 – 46.62, 1983 – 45.05, 1984 – 44.75
pbs: 100m: 10.47/10.3 '83; 200m: 20.49 '83

Robert de CASTELLA
b.27 Feb 1957 Melbourne 1.80m 65kg
Club: Old Xaverians, Glenhuntly. Biophysicist with the Australian Institute of Sport, Canberra. Married to Gayelene Clews, also a marathon runner and Australian cross-country international.
Ch. record at marathon: OG: '80 – 10, '84 – 5; WCh: '83 – 1; CG: '82 – 1. Australian marathon champion 1979. World cross-country best placing 6th in 1981 and 1983. Pacific Conference 10000m champion 1977. Set Commonwealth records at 20km: 58:37.2 and 1 hour: 20516m in 1982 amd marathon best 1981.
Progression at Mar: 1979 – 2:13:23, 1980 – 2:10:44, 1981 – 2:08:18, 1982 – 2:09:18, 1983 – 2:08:37, 1984 – 2:09:09
pbs: 1500m: 3:50.0 '76, 3000m: 8:04.9 '79, 5000m: 13:34.28 '81, 10000m: 28:02.73 '83.
'Deke' was the Olympic favourite after winning four successive major marathons, including World and Commonwealth titles, but had to settle for fifth. Has run eleven marathons in all, four sub 2:10 and all sub 2:15, winning six of them. Very strong runner, who has stayed clear of injuries. His brother Nick ran a 2:15:04 marathon in 1983.

Michael HILLARDT
b.24 Jan 1961 Brisbane 1.80m 68kg
Club: Toowong Harriers. Was at University of Queensland.
Ch. record at 1500m: OG: '84 – sf; CG: '82 – 5; WIG: '85 – 1. At 800m: WCh: '83 – sf, WCp: '81 – 4. Australian champion at 800m 1981, 1500m 1980, 1982 and 1984. Set Australian records at 1000m (three 1982 – 4) and 1500m (two 1984).
Progression at 1500m/1M: 1978 – 3:46.0, 1979 – 4:01.6M, 1980 – 3:39.67, 1981 – 3:41.74/3:56.6, 1982 – 3:38.04/3:53.33, 1983 – 3:41.51/3:57.09, 1984 – 3:34.20/3:52.34.
pbs: 800m: 1:45.74 '83, 1000m: 2:18.0 '84, 3000m: 7:52.17 '84, 5000m: 14:01.1 '83.

Gary HONEY
b.26 Jul 1959 Thomastown, Melbourne 1.83km 70kg
Club: Keon Park. Teacher of physical education.
Ch. record at LJ: OG: '80 – dnq, '84 – 2; WCh: '83 – 6; CG: '82 – 1; WCp: '79 – 5, '81 – 2. Australian champion 1979, 1981 – 4. Five Australian long jump records 1981 – 4 including Commonwealth record 1984. **Progression at LJ:** 1977 – 7.32, 1978 – 7.64, 1979 – 7.97/8.09w, 1980 – 7.98/8.10w, 1981 – 8.11/8.13w, 1982 – 8.13, 1983 – 8.12, 1984 – 8.27/8.39w
pbs: 100m: 10.5 '81, 400m: 46.9, TJ: 16.08 '81

Ken LORRAWAY
b.6 Feb 1956 Wagga Wagga 1.80m 72kg
Bank clerk. Married to Robyn (qv).
Ch. record at TJ: OG: '80 – 8, '84 – dnq; CG: '78 – 4 (8 at LJ), '82 – 2; WCp: '81 – 6. Australian champion 1980 – 4, AAA 1982. Set Australian triple jump records in 1981 and 1982.
Progression at TJ: 1973 – 15.47, 1974 – 15.37, 1975 – 15.94, 1976 – 16.15, 1977 – 16.03, 1978 – 16.50, 1979 – 16.83, 1980 – 16.98/17.35w, 1981 – 17.12, 1982 – 17.46/17.54w, 1983 – 17.35, 1984 – 16.81i/17.07w
pbs: 100m 10.4 '78, 10.0w '82, 200m: 21.0/20.8w '79, LJ: 7.91 '82.
Injuries caused him to miss the 1983 world championships and have prevented him from regaining his 1982 form when he had a tremendous battle with Keith Connor for the Commonwealth title.

Paul NARRACOTT
b.8 Oct 1959 Brisbane 1.82km 72kg
Club: Toowong H. Graduate of University of Queensland.
Ch. record at 100m/200m: OG: '84 – qf/h; WCh: '83 – 7/qf; CG: '78 – 6/4, '82 – 4/4; WCp: '77 – 8 at 100m. Australian 100m champion 1977 – 9, '82 – 4, and record holder at 10.26.
Progression at 100m, 200m: 1975 – 10.76 – 10.1w/10.3, 20.6; 1977 – 10.2/10.43, 20.5; 1978 – 10.0/10.35, 20.6/20.71w; 1979 – 10.2, 20.4; 1980 – 10.3, 20.8; 1981 – 10.2, 20.8; 1982 – 10.31/10.09w/9.9w, 20.65; 1983 – 10.33, 20.97/20.81w; 1984 – 10.26/9.9, 20.7/20.3w
Handed Carl Lewis a very rare defeat at 60m indoors in Tokyo in January 1984.

WOMEN
Susan COOK
b.23 Apr 1958 1.77m 57kg née Orr. Clerk.
Ch. record at 10kmW: WCp: '83 – 3. Since 1980 has set numerous world bests at walking distances from 1500m to 30km including official world record at 10km in 1983. Won first Australian championship in 1977. Won WAAA 5000mW 1982.
Track walk pbs: 1500m: 6:10.8 '84, 1M: 6:47.9 '81, 3000m: 12:56.5 '82, 5000m: 22:04.42 '84, 10000m: 45:47.0 '83, 1 hour: 12036m '84. Road walk pbs: 10km: 45:26.4 '83, 15km: 1:12:10 '82, 20km: 1:36:36 '82, 30km: 2:45:52 '82.

National Championships

Debbie FLINTOFF
b.20 Apr 1960 Melbourne 1.71m 53kg
Club: Glenhuntly. Clerk.
Ch. record at 400mh: OG: '84– 6; WCh: '83– sf; CG: '82– 1 (2 at 4x400mR). Australian champion 1982–4. Set three Australian, including one Commonwealth, 400mh records 1982.
Progression at 400mh: 1980 – 59.34, 1981 – 57.94, 1982 – 55.89, 1983 – 56.22, 1984 – 56.02
pbs: 100m: 11.7 '83, 200m: 23.7 '82, 400m: 52.49 '82, 800m: 2:09.1 '83, 100mh: 14.2w '79, HJ: 1.69 '79

Robyn LORRAWAY
b.20 Jul 1961 1.70m 56kg née Strong. Married to Ken (qv). Part-time receptionist.
Ch. record at LJ: OG: '84– 6; WCh: '83– 8; CG: '82– 2. Australian champion 1983–4, WAAA 1982. Set three Australian long jump records 1982–4.
Progression at LJ: 1979 – 6.10, 1980 – 6.28, 1981 – 6.41/6.48w, 1982 – 6.72/6.88w, 1983 – 6.74, 1984 – 6.75/6.90w
pbs: 100m: 11.4w '79; 100mh: 13.60/13.5 '80, 13.58w '81

Gael MARTIN
b.27 Aug 1956 Melbourne 1.73m 88kg née Mulhall. Married to weightlifter Nigel Martin. Club: Glenroy.
Ch. record at SP/DT: OG: '80 – 12/dnq, '84 – 3/8; WCh: '83 – 11/–; CG: '74 – 10/9, '78 – 1/2, '82 – 2/2; WCp: at DT – '77 – 6, '79 – 5. Australian champion – SP: 1976 – 81, '83 – 4; DT: 1977 – 81, '83 – 4. Set 13 Commonwealth shot records 1978 – 84, Australian shot and discus record holder since 1977.
Progression at SP: 1972 – 13.68, 1973 – 13.93, 1974 – 13.61, 1975 – 12.90, 1976 – 13.92, 1977 – 16.48, 1978 – 18.16, 1979 – 18.17, 1980 – 18.55, 1981 – 18.37, 1982 – 18.85, 1983 – 18.98, 1984 – 19.74. pb DT: 63.08 '79
World powerlifting record holder for 90kg and 90+kg classes. Suspended for drugs abuse 1981.

Lisa MARTIN
b.12 May 1960 1.65m 50kg née O'Dea. In the USA, member of Nike TC, was at University of Oregon. Married to US steeplechaser Kenny Martin (pb 8:20.97 '80, won 1981 AAA title); he moved up to the marathon in 1984 and won the US title in 2:11:24.
Ch. record at Mar: OG: '84– 7 Australian records at marathon (3) and 10000 (2) 1983–4.
Progression at Mar: 1983 – 2:32:22, 1984 – 2:27:40
pbs: 1500m: 4:21.2 '83, 3000m: 9:14.88 '83, 5000m: 15:43.21 '84, 10000m: 32:50.6 '84, 400mh: 60.73 '79

Won first two marathons, then set Australian records in the Olympics and when second at Chicago 1984.

Glynis NUNN
b.4 Dec 1960 Toowoomba 1.68m 58kg née Saunders. Married to Christopher Nunn (7208 decathlon '82). Physical education teacher.
Ch. record at 100mh/Hep: OG: '84 – 5/1 (7 at LJ); WCh: '83 – sf/7; CG: '78 – dnf, '82 – 6/1 (7 at LJ). Australian champion: 100mh: 1982 – 4, Pen/Hep: 1978, '80 – 2, '84. Set Commonwealth heptathlon record to win Olympic title '84, Australian record holder since 1980.
Progression at Pen (p) /Hep: 1975 – 3538p, 1976 – 3897p, 1977 – 4180p, 1978 – 4006p, 1979 – 3963p, 1980 – 4251p, 1981 – 5834w, 1982 – 6282, 1983 – 6195, 1984 – 6390
pbs: 200m: 24.02 '83, 800m: 2:10.57 '84, 100mh: 13.02 '84, 400m: 57.23 '83, HJ: 1.80 '84, LJ: 6.66 '84, SP: 13.93 '82, JT: 35.30 '82
Uniquely a finalist at three events in both Commonwealth and Olympic Games.

Sally PIERSON
b.10 Mar 1963 1.60m 39kg
Club: Doncaster. Physiotherapist.
Ch. record at 10kmW: WCp: '83 – 4. At 10km running won Australian title and 6th World road championship 1984. Set two world track walking bests at 3000m and a Commonwealth record at 5000m in 1982–3.
Track walk pbs: 1500m: 6:27.0 '82, 3000m: 12:45.5 '83, 5000m: 22:24.0 '83, 10000m: 49:45 '83. Road walk pbs: 10km: 45:39.4 '83, 15km: 1:15:29 '83, 20km: 1:39:06 '83. Running: 3000m: 9:32.0 '84, 10000m: 33:28.1 '84.
Has successfully combined both running and walking.

Christine STANTON
b.12 Dec 1959 Cottesloe, WA 1.83m 68kg née Annison. Club: Karrinyup. Secretary.
Ch. record at HJ: OG: '80– 6=, '84– 11=; WCh: '83– dnq; CG: '82– 2; WCp: '77– 6, '81– 4. Australian champion at high jump 1976–7, '80–1, '83 and long jump 1981. Set thee Australian high jump records in 1984 and Commonwealth heptathlon record in 1981.
Progression at HJ: 1974 – 1.69, 1975 – 1.79, 1976 – 1.83, 1977 – 1.88, 1978 – 1.88, 1980 – 1.91, 1981 – 1.92, 1982 – 1.88, 1983 – 1.92, 1984 – 1.95
pbs: LJ: 6.40/6.45w '81, Hep: 5724w '81

AUSTRIA

Governing body: Osterreichischer Leichtathletik Verband, Vienna 1040, Prinz Eugenstrasse 12. Founded 1900.
National Championships first held in 1911 (men), 1918 (women)

1984 Champions: MEN
100m/200m: Andreas Berger 10.62/21.45, 400m/400mh: Thomas Futterknecht 48.41/50.28, 800m: Herwig Tavernaro 1:48.59, 1500m: Robert Nemeth 3:42.19, 5000m/10000m: Dietmar Millonig 13:46.27/29:10.33, Mar: Gerhard Hartmann 2:18:54, 110mh: Herbert Kreiner 14.43, HJ: Wolfgang Tschirk 2.15, PV: Herman Fehringer 5.40, LJ/TJ: Alfred Stummer 7.46/15.83, SP: Erwin Weitzl 19.86, DT: Arno Rupp 55.38, HT:

Johann Lindner 73.20, JT/Dec: Georg Werthner 71.42/8061, 20kmW: Martin Toporek 1:27:13, 50kmW: Wilfried Siegele 4:17:49

WOMEN
100m/100mh/LJ: Sabine Seitl 11.80/13.77/6.37, 200m: Grace Pardy 24.49, 400m/400mh: Gerda Haas 54.28/58.17, 800m: Karoline Kafer 2:03.53, 1500m/3000m/5000m: Anni Muller 4:18.94/9:29.94/17:09.94; Mar: Monika Naskau 2:54.58, HJ: Silvia Kirchmann 1.87, SP: Ursula Weber 13.91, DT: Maria Schramseis 53.16, JT: Veronika Langle 57.52, Hep: Beate Osterer 5754

99

National Championships

Wolfgang KONRAD
b.22 Dec 1958 1.84m 65kg
Ch. record at 3kmSt: OG: '80– h; ECh: '78– h, '82– 5.
Progression at 3kmSt: 1976 – 9:08.0, 1977 – 9:18.3, 1978 – 8:32.6, 1979 – 8:22.8, 1980 – 8:24.92, 1981 – 8:50.36, 1982 – 8:17.22, 1984 – 8:40.64
pbs: 800m: 1:49.73 '81, 1000m: 2:18.94 '82, 1500m: 3:39.56i '80, 1M: 4:00.4 '79, 2000m: 5:06.48 '81, 3000m: 7:52.5 '80, 5000m: 13:48.43 '82, 10000m: 29:51.04 '82.
Handicapped by injuries in recent years.

Dietmar MILLONIG
b.1 Jun 1955 1.69m 56kg
Ch. record at 5000m: OG: '80– 6; WCh: '83– 8; ECh: '78– h (& h at 1500m), '82– 5; EJ: '73– 5.
Progression at 5000m: 1972 – 14:45.8, 1973 – 14:25.0, 1974 – 14:15.0, 1975 – 14:06.6, 1976 – 14:34.46, 1977 – 13:47.59, 1978 – 13:40.4, 1979 – 13:31.4, 1980 – 13:23.25, 1981 – 13:22.68, 1982 – 13:15.31, 1983 – 13:27.01, 1984 – 13:27.13
pbs: 800m: 1:49.72 '81, 1000m: 2:21.3 '78, 1500m: 3:38.38 '82, 1M: 3:57.7 '79, 10000m: 27:42.98 '82, 15000m: 44:54.0 '82, 1 hour: 19898m '82, 20km: 1:00:19.5 '82. Austrian records at all distances from 3000m to 20000m.

Robert NEMETH
b.5 Jun 1958 1.89m 70kg
Ch. record at 1500m: OG: '80– sf; WCh: '83– sf; ECh: '78– h, '82– 4, EJ: '77– 8. Austrian record holder at 1000m, 1500m, 1M, 2000m.
Progression at 1500m: 1975 – 3:58.0, 1976 – 3:49.2, 1977 – 3:47.1, 1978 – 3:40.1, 1979 – 3:39.9, 1980 – 3:38.14, 1981 – 3:35.8, 1982 – 3:37.81, 1983 – 3:38.97, 1984 – 3:35.80
pbs: 800m: 1:48.65 '83, 1000m: 2:18.20 '82, 1M: 3:52.42 '81, 2000m: 4:59.56 '84, 3000m: 7:44.08 '84; 5000m: 13:35.90 '84, 10000m: 29:01.2 '82, 3000mSt: 8:42.98 '81

Georg WERTHNER
b.7 Apr 1956 1.90m 87kg
Ch. record at Dec: OG: '76– 16, '80– 4, '84– 9; ECh: '78– dnf, '82– 5; EJ: '75– 2; WSG: '81– 3, '83– 3
Progression at Dec: 1973 – 6407, 1974 – 6554, 1975 – 7468, 1976 – 7728, 1977 – 7728, 1978 – 7814, 1979 – 7824, 1980 – 8050, 1981 – 7825, 1982 – 8229, 1983 – 7905, 1984 – 8061
pbs: 100m: 11.04 '82, 400m: 48.64 '82, 1500m: 4:14.89 '82, 110mh: 14.81 '82, HJ: 2.07 '82, PV: 4.85 '80, LJ: 7.43 '82, TJ: 15.66 '77, 15.86w '82, SP: 14.84 '82, DT: 43.04 '84, JT: 76.96 '84

BAHAMAS

Governing body: Bahamas Amateur Athletic Association, P.O.Box S.S.5517, Nassau.

WOMEN

Shonel FERGUSON
b.5 Nov 1957 1.70m 52kg
Club: Bahamas Pioneers. Graduate of University of Florida, USA.
Ch. record at LJ: OG: '76– dnq (h at 100m), '84– 8; WCh: '83– 14; CG: '78– 5, '82– 1; PAm: '79– 6; WCp: '77– 8, '81– 5. TAC champion 1984.
Progression at LJ: 1975 – 5.69, 1977 – 6.41, 1978 – 6.41, 1979 – 6.12, 1980 – 6.50, 1981 – 6.50/6.69w, 1982 – 6.80/6.91w, 1983 – 6.65/6.85w, 1984 – 6.71
pb 100m: 11.62 '83, 100mh: 13.85 '82.

BELGIUM

Governing bodies: VAL – Vlaamse Atletiek Liga; LBFA – Ligue Belge Francophone d'Athlétisme. Original governing body founded 1889.
National Championships first held in 1889 (men), 1921 (women)
1984 Champions: MEN
100m/LJ: Ronald Desruelles 10.30/7.85, 200m: Jacques Borlee 21.41, 400m: Danny Roelandt 46.84, 800m: Marnix Maebe 1:52.72, 1500m: Rudi De Wijngaert 3:51.57, 5000m: Vincent Rousseau 13:56.19, 10000m: Alex Hagelsteens 28:53.60, Mar: Johan Geirnaert 2:12:16, 3000mSt: Peter Daenens 8:39.36, 110mh: Rik Folens 14.39, 400mh: Michel Zimmerman 49.64, HJ: Marc Borra 2.02, PV: Patrick Desruelles 5.30, TJ: Didier Falise 16.24, SP: Noel Legros 16.35, DT: Robert van Schoor 50.04, HT: Marnix Verhegge 64.48, JT: Jean-Paul Schlatter 73.08, 20kmW: Eric Ledune 1:35:31
WOMEN
100m: Ingrid Verbruggen 11.67, 200m: Karin Verguts 23.73, 400m: Regine Berg 52.41, 800m: Isabelle De Bruycker 2:05.76, 1500m: Betty Vansteenbroek 4:19.00, 3000m: Corine Debaets 9:24.26, Mar: Marie-Christine Deurbroeck 2:32:32, 100mh: Christa Van der Cruyssen 13.84, 400mh: Jacqueline Hautenauve 58.71, HJ: Christine Soetewey 1.90, LJ: Myriam Duchateau 6.12, SP: Brigitte Deleeuw 14.37, DT:Ingrid Engelen 49.34, JT: Gaby Labeau 45.04, 5kmW: Claudine Hoogstoel 26:35.1

National Championships

Eddy ANNYS
b.15 Dec 1958 Wilrijk 1.87m 66kg
Club: Vlierzele Sportief. In Army.
Ch. record at HJ: OG: '84– dnq; WCh: '83– 14; WSG: '83– 2. Belgian high jump record holder since 1981. Belgian champion 1983.
Progression at HJ: 1972 – 1.45, 1973 – 1.70, 1976 – 1.90, 1977 – 2.15, 1978 – 2.20, 1979 – 2.21, 1980 – 2.18, 1981 – 2.25, 1982 – 2.24i, 1983 – 2.34, 1984 – 2.32. pb LJ: 6.78 '82.

Ronald DESRUELLES
b.14 Feb 1955 1.87m 81kg
Club: Vlierzele Sportief.
Ch. record at LJ: OG: '76– dnq; ECh: '78 & '82 – dnq; EI: '78 – 2. Won AAA '79. At 100m: OG: '84– qf; ECh: '78– h. At 60m: WIG: '85– 3. Set Belgian records at 100m (twice) and 200m in 1984, and five at long jump 1976–80. Belgian champion at LJ 1975–9, '81–4 and 100m 1978–9, '82, '84.

Progression at 100m: 1971 – 11.4, 1972 – 11.0, 1973 – 10.7, 1974 – 10.6, 1975 – 10.5, 1976 – 10.4, 1977 – 10.2, 1978 – 9.9/10.43, 1979 – 10.2/10.42, 1980 – 10.5, 1981 – 10.3, 1982 – 10.47, 1983 – 10.2, 1984 – 10.25.
pbs: 200m: 20.66 '84, PV: 4.10 '74, Dec: 6514 '74.
After winning 1980 European Indoor LJ title was disqualified on a positive drugs test. Is now concentrating on sprints rather than long jump. His brother Patrick is Belgian pole vault record holder (5.60m in 1981).

Armand PARMENTIER
b.15 Feb 1954 Waregem 1.75m 64kg
Club: AV Wingene. Mathematics teacher.
Ch. record at marathon: OG: '84– 30; WCh: '83– 6; ECh: '82– 2 Set Belgian marathon record in 1983.
Progression at Mar: 1982 – 2:15:51, 1983 – 2:09:57, 1984 – 2:14:16
pbs: 800m: 1:50.5 '78, 1000m: 2:24.3 '77, 1500m: 3:41.8 '78, 3000m: 7:57.4 '78, 5000m: 13:43.7 '80, 10000m: 28:36.5 '80

BRAZIL

Governing body: CBAT – Confederação Brasileira de Atletismo – CBAt, Av. Graca Aranha, 81 – Conj 808/811, 20 030 Rio de Janeiro. Founded 1914.
National Championships are held bienially, none in 1984.

João BATISTA da SILVA
b.22 Aug 1963 Joao Pessoa 1.78m 74kg
Ch. record at 200m: OG: '84– 4; WCh: '83– 8; PAm: '83– 6; WIG: '85– 3. South American 200m record in 1984.
Progression at 200m: 1981 – 20.7, 1982 – 20.95, 1983 – 20.51, 1984 – 20.30
pb 100m: 10.40 '83

Joaquim CRUZ
b.12 Mar 1963 Taguatinga, Brasilia 1.88m 77kg. Student at Oregon University (won NCAA 800m 1983–4, 1500m 1984).
Ch. record at 800m: OG: '84– 1 (sf at 1500m); WCh: '83– 3; WCp: '81– 6. South American record holder at 800m, 1000m,

1500m and 1 mile. Set world junior record for 800m of 1:44.3 in 1981.
Progression at 800m: 1978 – 1:51.4, 1979 – 1:49.8, 1980 – 1:47.85, 1981 – 1:44.3, 1982 – 1:46.95, 1983 – 1:44.04, 1984 – 1:41.77
pbs: 400m: 47.4 '80, 1000m: 2:14.09 '84; 1500m: 3:36.48 '84; 1 mile: 3:53.00 '84
Ran four of the six fastest times ever at 800m, all in August 1984, starting with his Olympic 800m triumph. Ran best ever debut mile (3:53.00).

Agberto GUIMARÃES
b.18 Aug 1957 Belém 1.75m 57kg
Ch. record at 800m (1500m in brackets): OG: '80– 4, '84– sf(sf); WCh: '83– 6; PAm: '79– 3(3), '83– 1(1); WCp: '79– 5; SACh: '75– 3, '77– 1; WSG: '77– 4.
Progression at 800m: 1976 – 1:49.4, 1977 – 1:46.0, 1978 – 1:47.7, 1979 – 1:45.94, 1980 – 1:46.20, 1981 – 1:47.52, 1982 – 1:45.13, 1983 – 1:45.15, 1984 – 1:43.63
pbs: 400m: 46.34 '80, 1000m: 2:15.81 '83, 1500m: 3:39.9 '84, 1M: 4:00.0 '84

BULGARIA

Governing body: Bulgarian Athletics Federation, 18 Tolboukhine Bd, Sofia. Founded 1924
National Championships first held in 1926 (men), 1938 (women)
1984 Champions: MEN
100m/200m: Bogomil Karadimov 10.38/21.18, 400m: Krasimir Demirev 46.69, 800m: Binko Kolev 1:49.25, 1500m: Mestafa Mustafov 3:45.03, 5000m: Zdrawies Todorov 14:08.74, 10000m: Rumen Mechandshiski 29:31.56, Mar: Vasil Lechev 2:17:42, 3000mSt: Panayot Kachanov 8:40.05, 110mh: Plamen Krastev 13.66, 400mh: Toma Tomov 49.97, HJ: Georgi Gadshev 2.18, PV: Atanas Tarev 5.72, LJ: Ivan Tuparov 8.07, TJ: Khristo Markov 17.19, SP: Nikolai Gemishev 20.20, DT: Velko Velev 64.70, HT: Ivan Tanev 75.24, JT: Raicho Dimitrov

78.54, Dec: Cecko Mitrakiev 7829, 10kmW/20kmW: Lyubomir Ivanov 40:27.0/1:22:19, 50kmW: Ravil Ibriamov 4:41:53
WOMEN
100m/200m: Nadezhda Georgieva 11.32/22.51, 400m: Rositsa Stamenova 50.99, 800m: Svobodka Damyanova 2:03.62, 1500m: Vanya Stoyanova 4:10.12, 3000m: Radka Naplatanova 9:06.81, 10000m: Nedyalka Bakalova 39:15.63, Mar: Nedyalka Bakalova 3:08:41, 100mh: Yordanka Donkova 12.62, 400mh: Nadezhda Assenova 56.59, HJ: Lyudmila Andonova 1.91, LJ: Lyudmila Ninova 6.78, SP: Svetla Mitkova 18.58, DT: Maria Petkova 66.60, JT: Antoaneta Todorova 60.82, Hep: Emilia Pencheva 6050, 5000mW: P.Bogdanova 28:34.48

National Championships

Atanas ATANASOV
b.7 Oct 1956 1.85m 76kg
Club: Lokomotiv Plovdiv
Ch. record at LJ: ECh: '82– 8. Set Bulgarian LJ record in 1984.
Progression at LJ: 1973 – 6.96, 1974 – 7.35, 1975 – 7.45, 1976 – 7.30, 1977 – 7.18, 1978 – 7.28, 1979 – 7.46, 1980 –7.72, 1981 – 8.11, 1982 – 8.09, 1983 – 8.16, 1984 – 8.31. pb TJ: 15.77 '80.

Emanuil DYULGEROV
b.7 Feb 1955 Razgrad 1.78m 95kg
Club: Levski Spartak
Ch. record at HT: WCh: '83– 8; OG: '80– 6; ECh: '78– 14, '82– dnq; WSG: '77– 1. Bulgarian hammer champion 1977–8, '80, '83, and has set 13 Bulgarian records 1977–84.
Progression at HT: 1972 – 56.04, 1973 – 59.50, 1974 – 62.08, 1975 – 67.38, 1976 – 70.76, 1977 – 74.50, 1978 – 74.60, 1979 – 73.80, 1980 – 75.74, 1981 – 75.84, 1982 – 77.40, 1983 – 77.98, 1984 – 80.64

Evgeni IGNATOV
b.25 Jun 1959 Ruse 1.83m 66kg
Club: ACSP Lokomotif
Ch. record at 5000m: ECh: '82– 4. Bulgarian records (1980–4): 1 at 1500m and 2000m, 2 at 3000m, 3 at 5000m.
Progression at 5000m: 1978 – 14:18.4, 1979 – 13:58.9, 1980 – 13:48.4, 1981 – 13:30.82, 1982 – 13:27.78, 1983 – 14:03.9, 1984 – 13:26.35
pbs: 800m: 1:51.43 '82, 1500m: 3:39.53 '82, 2000m: 5:07.7 '82, 3000m: 7:47.74 '84, 10000m: 28:24.73 '84

Plamen KRASTEV
b.18 Nov 1958 1.87m 76kg
Club: ZSKA Sofia.
Ch. record at 110mh: OG: '80– sf; EJ: '77– 7. At 60mh: EI: '82– 2. Bulgarian 110mh champion 1978, '80–2, '84 and five Bulgarian records 1979–84.
Progression at 110mh: 1975 – 15.5, 1976 – 14.6, 1977 – 14.18, 1978 – 14.12, 1979 – 13.92, 1980 – 13.86, 1981 – 13.68/13.5, 1982 – 13.82, 1983 – 13.75, 1984 – 13.46/13.4

Christo MARKOV
b.27 Jan 1965 Dimitrovgrad 1.85m 75kg
Club: Lokomotiv, Ruse.
Ch. record at TJ: WCh: '83– dnq; EJ: '83–1; WIG: '85– 1. Set one World and five European Junior triple jump records in 1983–4.
Progression at TJ: 1981 – 15.72, 1983 – 16.88, 1984 – 17.42. pb LJ: 7.95 '84.

Atanas TAREV
b.31 Jan 1958 Boliatzi, Plovdiv 1.80m 65kg
Club: Trakja, Plovdiv
Ch. record at PV: WCh: '83– 3; OG: '80– dnq; ECh: '82– 3; EJ: '77– 3 15 Bulgarian pole vault records from 5.07m in 1977. Bulgarian champion 1976–84.
Progression at PV: 1975 – 4.50, 1976 – 4.90, 1977 – 5.15, 1978 – 5.22, 1979 – 5.40, 1980 – 5.44, 1981 – 5.51, 1982 – 5.70, 1983 – 5.71, 1984 – 5.75

Toma TOMOV
b.6 May 1958 Jambol 1.79m 68kg
Club: Akademik. Physical education student.
Ch. record at 400mh: WCh: '83– sf; ECh: '82– 8. Bulgarian records at 400mh (4) and 400m (1). Balkan and Bulgarian 400mh champion 1984.
Progression at 400mh: 1981 – 51.81, 1982 – 49.74, 1983 – 49.24, 1984 – 48.99
pb 400m: 45.86 '84.

WOMEN

Lyudmila ANDONOVA
b.6 May 1960 Novocherkassk, USSR 1.77m 58kg née Zhecheva. Married to Atanas Andonov (Bulgarian decathlon record holder – 8220 '82). Club: Akademik Sofia.
Ch. record at HJ: ECh: '82– 6=; WSG: '81– 2; ECp: '81– 2. Balkan Games champion 1981 and 1984. World high jump record of 2.07m in 1984. Five Bulgarian records 1981–4.
Progression at HJ: 1977 – 1.70, 1978 – 1.73, 1979 – 1.70, 1980 – 1.84, 1981 – 1.95, 1982 – 1.94, 1983 – 1.85i, 1984 – 2.07
Gave birth to daughter, Jana in 1983, then soared 30cm over her own head to a new world record record a year later. Has a Bulgarian father and Soviet mother.

Yordanka DONKOVA
b.28 Sep 1961 Dolni Bogrov 1.75m 67kg
Club: Levski Spartak
Ch. record at 100mh: OG: '80– sf; ECh: '82– 2; EJ: '79– 8; ECp: '81– 5. At Hep: ECp: '83– 7; At 60mh: EI: '82– 3, '84– 3. Bulgarian 100mh champion 1984, four Bulgarian records in 1982.
Progression at 100mh: 1977 – 14.84, 1978 – 13.91, 1979 – 13.57, 1980 – 13.24, 1981 – 13.39/12.9, 1982 – 12.44, 1983 – 12.65, 1984 – 12.50
pbs: 100m: 11.27 '82, 200m: 22.95 '82, HJ: 1.78 '82, LJ: 6.39 '82, Hep: 6240 '83

Nadezhda GEORGIEVA
b.2 Sep 1961 Ruse 1.58m 48kg
Club: Akademik, Sofia.
Ch. record at 100m/200m (R – 4x100m relay): WCh: '83– sf/sf (4R); ECh: '82– 7/– (4R). Balkan 200m champion 1984. Bulgarian 100m and 200m champion 1983–4. Bulgarian records at 100m and 200m in 1983.
Progression at 100m/200m: 1977 – –/25.99, 1978 – 12.20/25.02, 1979 – 12.37/24.91, 1980 – 11.97/24.21, 1981 – 11.52/23.51/23.40w, 1982 – 11.33/22.90, 1983 – 11.09/22.42, 1984 – 11.21/22.51

Tsvetanka KHRISTOVA
b.14 Mar 1962 Kazanlak 1.75m 80kg
Club: Rozova dolina, Kazanlak
Ch. record at DT: WCh: '83– 4; ECh: '82– 1; EJ: '79– 3. Balkan champion 1984.
Progression at DT: 1977 – 46.90, 1978 – 48.84, 1979 – 54.76, 1980 – 58.44, 1981 – 64.38, 1982 – 70.64, 1983 – 66.88, 1984 – 68.34

Stefka KOSTADINOVA
b.5 Mar 1965 Plovdiv 1.80m 60kg
Club: Tralija Plovdiv.
Ch. record at HJ: WIG: '85– 1.
Progression at HJ: 1977 – 1.45, 1978 – 1.66, 1979 – 1.75, 1980 – 1.84, 1981 – 1.86, 1982 – 1.90, 1983 – 1.83i, 1984 – 2.00
Runner–up to Andonova in 1984 Bulgarian Championships and Balkan Games.

Anelia (Vechernikova) NUNEVA
b.30 Jun 1962 Bjala 1.67m 57kg
Club: Lokomotif, Ruse.
Ch. record at 100m/200m: WCh: '83– sf/6; ECh: '82– 4/6; ECp: '83– 2/4. At 60m: EI: '84– 2. Balkan 100m champion 1984. Two Bulgarian 100m records 1982–3.

National Championships

Progression at 100m/200m: 1978 – 12.23/25.60, 1979 – 12.10/25.90, 1981 – 11.34/11.31w/23.58, 1982 – 11.14/22.93, 1983 – 11.07/22.58, 1984 – 11.10/22.67

Maria PETKOVA
b.3 Nov 1950 Plovdiv 1.82m 105kg née VERGOVA. Club: Levski Spartak. Sports instructor.
Ch. record at DT: OG: '76– 2, '80– 2; WCh: '83– 3; ECh: '74– 4, '82– 2; WSG: '73– 4, '75– 1, '77– 1; WCp: '81– 2; ECp: '75– 4, '81– 1, '83– 3. Set world discus record of 71.80m in 1980, seven Bulgarian records 1974–80.
Progression at DT: 1968 – 35.60, 1969 – 38.90, 1970 – 42.60, 1971 – 50.40, 1972 – 53.20, 1973 – 60.72, 1974 – 68.48, 1975 – 66.98, 1976 – 68.62, 1977 – 68.20, 1979 – 65.02, 1980 – 71.80, 1981 – 71.30, 1982 – 71.20, 1983 – 70.74, 1984 – 71.22. pb SP: 17.56 '81.
Gave birth to son in 1978.

Radostina SHTEREVA (Dimitrova)
b.6 Aug 1966 1.63m 78kg
Club: Spartak, Varna.
Ch. record at 400mh: EJ: '83– 1 Set two world and three European junior records at 400mh 1983–4, also two Bulgarian records.

Progression at 400mh: 1982 – 58.46, 1983 – 56.01, 1984 – 55.53
pb 400m: 52.77 '83, 100m: 13.59 '83

Antoaneta TODOROVA
b.8 Jun 1963 Sanovodene 1.70m 74kg
Ch. record at JT: OG: '80– 10; EJ: '79– 3, '81– 1; WCp: '81– 1; ECp: '81– 1, '83– 6. Bulgarian champion 1983–4, Balkan champion 1980– 1. Set four world junior javelin records in 1980–1, the last also a world record.
Progression at JT: 1978 – 47.86, 1979 – 57.76, 1980 – 66.40, 1981 – 71.88, 1982 – 66.96, 1983 – 64.00, 1984 – 65.40. pb SP: 14.96 '81.

Ginka ZAGORCHEVA
b.12 Apr 1958 Plovdiv 1.72m 53kg
Club: Levski Spartak
Ch. record at 100mh: WCh: '83– 3; ECh: '82– 8; ECp: '83– 3 Bulgarian 100mh champion 1983.
Progression at 100mh: 1975 – 13.9, 1977 – 13.90, 1978 – 13.39, 1979 – 13.22, 1981 – 13.74, 1982 – 12.73, 1983 – 12.49, 1984 – 12.62.
pb 100m: 11.38 '83

CANADA

Governing body: Canadian Track and Field Association, 333 River Road, Ottawa, Ontario K1L 8H9. Formed as the Canadian AAU in 1884.
National Championship first held in 1884 (men), 1925 (women).
1984 champions: MEN
100m: Ben Johnson 10.01w, 200m: Tony Sharpe 20.56w, 400m: Doug Hinds 46.52, 800m: Bruce Roberts 1:47.52, 1500m/5000m: Paul Williams 3:49.14/14:02.6, 10000m: Alain Bordeleau 28:53.77, 3kmSt: Greg Duhaime 8:35.4, 110mh: Mark McKoy 13.34w, 400mh: Lloyd Guss 50.86, HJ: Milt Ottey 2.26, PV: Mark Bradley 5.18, LJ: Richard Rock 7.82, TJ: George Wright 15.81, SP: Luby Chambul 18.45, DT: Rob Gray 60.54, HT: Harold Willers 63.50, JT: Laslo Babits 77.00, Dec: Milan Popadich 7540w, 20km walk: Marcel Jobin 1:27:28
WOMEN
100m/200m: Angella Taylor 11.13w/22.61w, 400m: Marita Payne 51.07, 800m: Camille Cato 2:04.49, 1500m: Debbie Scott 4:13.32, 3000m: Lynn Williams 9:02.69, 10000m: Colette Desrosiers 36:19.53, 100mh: Sylvia Forgrave 13.29w, 400mh: Andrea Page 57.26, HJ: Debbie Brill 1.94, LJ: Carol Galloway 6.54w, SP: Rosemary Hauch 16.12, DT: Carmen Ionescu 51.82, JT: Cindy Crapper 54.34, Hep: Jill Ross-Giffen 5913, 5000m walk: Ann Peel 23:36.27

Ben JOHNSON
b.30 Dec 1961 Jamaica 1.80m 75kg
Club: York Optimists. Student at Seneca College.
Ch. record at 100m: (4x100m relay in brackets): OG: '84– 3 (3R), WCh: '83– sf; CG: '82– 2 (2R); PAm: '83– 6; WSG: '83– 5 (2R). Member 1980 Olympic team. At 60m: WIG: '85– 1. Set two Canadian 100m records 1984. At 60m indoors set Commonwealth best of 6.56 in 1985.
Progression at 100m: 1978 – 10.79/10.4, 1979 – 10.66, 1980 – 10.62/10.38w, 1981 – 10.25, 1982 – 10.30/10.05w, 1983 – 10.19, 1984 – 10.12/10.01w.

pb 200m: 21.00 '83, 20.37w '82.
First Canadian to win an Olympic medal since 1964.

Guillaume LEBLANC
b.14 Apr 1982 Sept–Iles 1.84m 75kg Club d'Athletisme de Sept–Isles
Ch. record at 20kmW: OG: '84– 4 (dnf 50kmW); WCh: '83– 8; WSG: '83– 1; CG: '82– 3 at 30kmW. Member 1980 Olympic team.
Progression at 20kmW: 1979 – 1:33:35, 1981 – 1:26:32, 1982 – 1:24:28, 1983 – 1:22.04, 1984 – 1:24:29. pb 50kmW: 3:58:33 '83

Mark McKOY
b.10 Dec 1961 Georgetown, Guyana 1.81m 70kg
Club: York Optimists. Student at York University, formerly at Clemson University, USA.
Ch. record at 110mh: OG: '84– 4; WCh: '83– 4; CG: '82– 1 (2 at 4x100mR); WSG: '83– 3; PAm: '83– 6. Member 1980 Olympic team. Set seven Canadian, including three Commonwealth 110mh records 1982–4.
Progression at 110mh: 1979 – 14.19, 1980 – 14.02, 1981 – 13.97, 1982 – 13.37, 1983 – 13.53/13.51w, 1984 – 13.27/13.16w
pbs: 100m: 10.44 '81; 200m: 21.09, 20.96w '84, 400mh: 53.75 '77

Milt OTTEY
b.29 Dec 1959 May Pen, Jamaica 1.78m 66kg
Club: York Optimists and Pacific Coast Club, USA. Moved to Canada at age of ten. Was at University of Texas at El Paso.
Ch. record at HJ: OG: '84– 6; WCh: '83– 9; CG: '82– 1; PAm: '79– 3; WCp: '79– 5, '81– 5. Won TAC and NCAA 1982. Member 1980 Olympic team. Set Commonwealth high jump records at 2.30m and 2.32m in 1982.
Progression at HJ: 1977 – 1.95, 1978 – 2.11, 1979 – 2.19, 1980 – 2.20i, 1981 – 2.24, 1982 – 2.32, 1983 – 2.30, 1984 – 2.29

Tony SHARPE
b.26 Jun 1981 Jamaica 1.78m 73kg
Club: York Optimists.

National Championships

Ch. record at 100m/200m (4x 100m relay): OG: '84 – 8/qf (3R); WCh: '83 – sf 100m; CG: '82 – 6/6 (2R); WSG: '82 – 2R; PAm: '83 – 7 200m. Member 1980 Olympic team. Set Canadian 200m record in 1982.
Progression at 100m/200m: 1978 – 10.53/21.62, 1979 – 10.56/21.29, 1980 – 10.46/21.33, 1981 – 10.49/21.29, 1982 – 10.19/10.11w/20.22, 1983 – 10.31/20.79, 1984 – 10.33/10.09w/20.64/20.56w.
pb 400m: 48.0 '81

Dave STEEN
b.14 Nov 1959 New Westminster, BC 1.85m 80kg University of Toronto Track Club. Student at the Univerity of Toronto.
Ch. record at Dec: OG: '84 – 8; CG: '82 – 2; WSG: '81 – 5, '83 – 1; PAm: '83 – 1. Member 1980 Olympic team.
Progression at Dec: 1977 – 6917, 1978 – 6860, 1979 – 7647, 1980 – 7778, 1981 – 7924, 1982 – 8019, 1983 – 8205, 1984 – 8292
pbs: 100m: 11.03, 400m: 47.71 '83, 1500m: 4:14.10 '83, 110mh: 14.81 '83, HJ: 2.15i '83, PV: 5.18 '84, LJ: 7.67 '81, SP: 14.36 '84, DT: 51.58 '83, JT: 67.20 '82.
Uncle Dave won Commonwealth shot title in 1966 and 1970, father Don was Canadian decathlon champion in 1956.

Desai WILLIAMS
b.12 Jun 1959 Basseterre, St.Kitts 1.75m 66kg
Club: York Optimists. Student at York University.
Ch. record at 100m/200m (4x100m relay): OG: '84 – sf/sf (3R); WCh: '83 – 8/sf; CG: '78 – 4R, '82 – 8/8 (2R); PAm: '79 – 8/6; WSG: '83 – 2 100m (2R). Member 1980 Olympic team. Canadian champion at 100m and 200m 1983. Set Canadian records: three at 200m 1978–81 and one at 100m 1983, and Commonwealth indoor 200m best at 21.14 in 1982.
Progression at 100m, 200m: 1976 – 10.7; 1977 – 10.55/10.54w, 21.2; 1978 – 10.31, 20.68; 1979 – 10.43, 20.70; 1980 – 10.26/10.12w, 20.71/20.35w; 1981 – 10.32, 20.60; 1982 – 10.30/10.17w, 20.54; 1983 – 10.17, 20.29; 1984 – 10.27/10.19w, 20.45/20.40w. pb 400m: 45.92 '84

WOMEN

Angela BAILEY
b.28 Feb 1962 Coventry, UK 1.57m 52kg Student at University of Toronto
Ch. record at 100m/200m (4x100m relay): OG: '84 – 6/sf (2R); WCh: '83 – 5/7; CG: '78 – sf/h (2R), '82 – 4/8 (2R). Member 1980 Olympic team.
Progression at 100m, 200m: 1976 – 11.8, 24.7; 1977 – 11.66, 24.2; 1978 – 11.52, 23.91; 1979 – 11.49, 24.12; 1980 – 11.44/11.27w, 23.42/23.19w; 1981 – 11.21, 22.86; 1982 – 11.23, 23.44/22.75w; 1983 – 11.17, 22.64; 1984 – 11.25, 22.75. pb 400m: 51.96 '83

Debbie BRILL
b.10 Mar 1953 Mission, BC 1.77m 60kg
Club: Vancouver Olympic Club
Ch. record at HJ: OG: '72 – 8, '76 – dnq, '84 – 5; WCh: '83 – 6; CG: '70 – 1, '78 – 2, '82 – 1; PAm: '71 – 1, '75 – 4, '79 – 3; WCp: '77 – 3, '79 – 1; WSG: '77 – 2. Member 1980 Olympic team. Won US HJ 1979 & 1982. Has taken the Commonwealth high jump record from 1.84m in 1970 to 1.98m in 1984 as well as the indoor best of 1.99 in 1982.
Progression at HJ: 1966 – 1.41, 1967 – 1.63, 1968 – 1.71, 1969 – 1.76, 1970 – 1.84, 1971 – 1.85, 1972 – 1.86, 1974 – 1.87, 1975 – 1.89, 1976 – 1.90, 1977 – 1.91, 1978 – 1.92i/1.91, 1979 – 1.96, 1980 – 1.97, 1982 – 1.99i/1.95, 1983 – 1.95, 1984 – 1.98

First woman to use flop style effectively as she pioneered the 'Brill bend' in the late 1960s. Youngest ever Commonwealth champion in 1970 at 17 years 137 days in 1970, and won again in 1982. Gave birth to son, Neil in 1981 and returned to set world indoor best at 1.99m in 1982.

Charmaine CROOKS
b.8 Aug 1961 Mandeville, Jamaica 1.70m 60kg
Club: York Optimists. University of Texas at El Paso.
Ch. record at 400m (4x400m relay): OG: '84 – 7 (2R); WCh: '83–sf (4R); CG: '82 – 7 (1R); PAm: '83 – 1; WSG: '83 – 4 (2R); WCp: '81 – 3R
Progression at 400m: 1979 – 53.12, 1980 – 52.33, 1981 – 52.32, 1982 – 52.01, 1983 – 51.49, 1984 – 50.45. pb 200m: 23.30 '83

Jacqueline GAREAU
b.10 Mar 1953 Conte Labell, Quebec 1.57m 45kg Owns her own business.
Ch. record at Mar: OG: '84 – dnf; WCh: '83 – 5 Won Los Angeles marathon 1984, won Boston 1980 and 2nd 1982 and 1983. Set two Commonwealth marathon bests in 1980.
Progression at Mar: 1977 – 3:44:00, 1978 – 2:55:00, 1979 – 2:39:06, 1980 – 2:30:58, 1981 – 2:31:26, 1982 – 2:36:09, 1983 – 2:29:27, 1984 – 2:31:57, 1985 – 2:29:32. pb 3000m: 9:38.5 '79.
Has won six of 20 marathons to second place at Houston 1985.

Marita PAYNE
b.7 Oct 1960 Barbados 1.72m 57kg Came to Canada as 9-year-old.
Club: York Optimists. Florida State University – won NCAA 400m 1984.
Ch. record at 400m: OG: '84 – 4 (2 at 4x100mR, 4 x400mR); WCh: '83 – 5; CG: '82 – sf (2 at 4x100mR); PAm: '79 – 7; WCp: '79 – 4, '81 – 3 at 4x400mR; WSG: '83 – 2 at 200m, 4x100mR and 4x400mR. Member 1980 Olympic team. Set former Commonwealth 400m record at 1983 World champs.
Progression: 1979 – 53.01, 1981 – 52.01, 1982 – 51.99, 1983 – 50.06, 1984 – 49.91. pbs: 100m: 11.43, 11.34w '83; 200m: 22.62 '83

Sylvia RUEGGER
b.23 Feb 1961 Oshawa, Ontario 1.68m 55kg Student at University of Guelph.
Ch. record at marathon: OG: '84 – 8. Canadian cross-country champion 1980. Ran fastest ever first marathon, 2:30:37 to win Canadian trials 1984. Improved to Canadian records: 2:29:09 in Olympic Games 1984 and 2:28:36 to win Houston marathon 1985. 7th World 10km road 1983.
pbs: 1500m: 4:24.7 '80, 3000m: 9:25.6 '80

Angella TAYLOR
b.28 Sep 1958 Jamaica. 1.65m 61kg
Club: York Optimists
Ch. record at 100m/200m (4x100mR): OG: '84 – 8 at 200m (2R); WCh: '83 – 7 at 100m; CG: '78 – ht 200m, '82 – 1/3 (2R, and 1 at 4x400mR); PAm: '79 – 3/2; WCp: '79 – 5/5, '81 – 4/4; WSG: '83 – 3/4 (2R). Member 1980 Olympic team. Set Commonwealth record of 11.00 at 100m to win 1982 Commonwealth title, and world indoor 300m best of 36.91 in 1980. Canadian records: four at 100m and seven at 200m 1979–82.
Progression at 100m, 200m: 1977 – 12.4; 1978 – 12.07, 23.87; 1979 – 11.20, 22.80/22.74w; 1980 – 11.23/11.03w, 22.61; 1981 – 11.12, 22.55/22.46w; 1982 – 11.00/10.92w, 22.25/22.19w; 1983 – 11.22/11.17w, 22.81; 1984 – 11.16/11.09w, 22.61/22.44w. pb 400m: 51.81 '81

Lynn WILLIAMS
b.11 Jul 1960 Regina, Saskatoon 1.52m 48kg
Club: Valley Royals. née Kanuka, married to Paul Williams

National Championships

(Canadian 10km record holder). Graduate of San Diego State University, USA.
Ch. record at 3000m: OG: '84 – 3; WCh: '83 – 10; WSG: '83 – 3
Progression at 3000m: 1979 – 9:47.0, 1980 – 9:21.1, 1981 – 9:13.13, 1982 – 9:13.1, 1983 – 8:50.20, 1984 – 8:42.14
pbs: 800m: 2:03.7 '83, 1500m: 4:06.09 '84, 5000m: 15:53.78 '84

CHINA

Governing body: Athletic Association of the People's Republic of China, 9 Tiyuguan Road, Beijing
National championships first held in 1910 (men), 1959 (women)
1984 Champions: MEN
100m: Zheng Cheng 10.64, 200m: Li Feng 21.25, 400m: Wang Yonghua 46.86, 800m: Huang Luotao 1:51.01, 1500m: Zhang Shouting 4:00.03, 5000m/10000m: Zhang Guowei 14:03.41/28:52.73, 3000mSt: Li Yuanming 8:48.18, 110mh: Yu Zhicheng 14.06, 400mh: Wang Guihua 50.99, HJ: Liu Yunpeng 2.21, PV: Liang Xuereng 5.30, LJ: Liu Yuhuang 7.48, TJ: Mai Guoqiang 16.16, SP: Ding Zhinian 17.24, DT: Zhang Nan 55.72, HT: Jin Yonggao 66.54, JT: Pei Xueliang 76.60, Dec: Xi Xiashun 7598
WOMEN
100m/200m: Wu Liping 11.82/24.04, 400m/400mh: Chen Dongmei 55.68/58.83, 800m: Ni Xiuping 2:08.69, 1500m: Geng Xiujuan 4:18.93, 3000m: Zhang Xiuyun 9:16.90, 5000m/10000m: Luo Yuxiu 16:05.38/33:52.84, 100mh: Liu Huajin 13.45, HJ: Zheng Dazheng 1.89, LJ: Liao Wenfen 6.24, SP: Cong Yuzheng 17.80, DT: Jiao Yunxiang 56.82, JT: Wang Jing 59.44, Hep: Yang Qifen 5464.

LIU YUHUANG
b.25 Jul 1959 Fujian 1.76m 70kg
Ch. record at LJ: OG: '84 – 5; WCh: '83 – 16; WSG: '81 – 2; WCp: '81 – 4; AsG: '78 – 5, '82 – 2; AsCh: '79 – 4, '81 – 1, '83 – 1. Set two Asian long jump records 1981–2.
Progression at LJ: 1978 – 7.70, 1979 – 7.86, 1980 – 7.95, 1981 – 8.11/8.22w, 1982 – 8.14, 1983 – 8.07, 1984 – 7.99

ZHU JIANHUA
b.29 May 1963 Shanghai 1.96m 74kg Physical education student
Ch. record at HJ: OG: '84 – 3; WCh: '83 – 3; WSG: '81 – 2; AsG: '82 – 1; AsCh: '81 – 1, '83 – 1; WCp: '81 – 9. Three world high jump records: 2.37m and 2.38m in 1983, 2.39m in 1984. Seven Chinese records since 1981.

Progression at HJ: 1975 – 1.51, 1976 – 1.69, 1977 – 1.83, 1978 – 1.95, 1979 – 2.13, 1980 – 2.25, 1981 – 2.30, 1982 – 2.33, 1983 – 2.38, 1984 – 2.39

ZOU ZHENXIAN
b.10 Nov 1955 Liaoning b.10 Nov 1955 1.84m 72kg
Ch. record at TJ: OG: '84 – 4; WCh: '83 – 16; WSG: '81 – 1; WCp: '79 – 4, '81 – 2; AsG: '78 – 2, '82 – 1; AsCh: '79 – 1, '81 – 1 Set four Asian triple jump records 1979–81.
Progression at TJ: 1977 – 16.60, 1978 – 16.90, 1979 – 17.02, 1980 – 16.90/17.04w, 1981 – 17.34, 1982 – 16.93, 1983 – 16.46, 1984 – 16.83
pb LJ: 7.75 '79

WOMEN
LI MEISU
b.17 Apr 1959 Hebei 1.76m 80kg
Ch. record at SP: OG: '84 – 5; WCh: '83 – dnq; AsG: '82 – 1. Set Asian shot record in 1984.
Progression at SP: 1979 – 16.33, 1980 – 16.33, 1981 – 16.95, 1982 – 17.88, 1983 – 17.97, 1984 – 18.47

YAN HONG
b.23 Oct 1966 Liaoning 1.54m 44kg. Set world records at 5000m walk – 21:40.3 and 10000m walk – 45:39.5 in 1984.
In 1983 finished first in the IAAF World Cup 10km, but was disqualified. Second WIG 3000m (13:05.56) 1985.

XU YONGJU
b.29 Oct 1964 Liaoning 1.58m 46kg. Won IAAF World Cup road 10km walk in 45:13.4 in 1983.
Track pbs: 5000mW: 21:42.0 '84, 10000mW: 46:52.0 '84

ZHENG DA-ZHEN
b.22 Sep 1959 Xiamen 1.75m 60kg Physical education student
Ch. record at HJ: OG: '84 – 7; WCh: '83 – 18; WCp: '79 – 7; AsG: '78 – 1, '82 – 1; AsCh: '79 – 1, '81 – 2, '83 – 1. Set three Asian high jump records 1980–2.
Progression at HJ: 1972 – 1.34, 1973 – 1.48, 1974 – 1.52, 1975 – 1.69, 1976 – 1.76, 1977 – 1.78, 1978 – 1.88, 1979 – 1.89, 1980 – 1.92, 1981 – 1.91, 1982 – 1.93, 1983 – 1.90, 1984 – 1.91

CUBA

Governing body: Federacion Cubana de Atletismo, Calle 13 No.601, Zona Postale 4, Vedado, Ciudad de la Habana. Founded 1922

Lazaro BETANCOURT
b.18 Mar 1963 Havana 1.89m 83kg Sports student.
Ch. record at TJ: PAm: '83 – 2, CAmG: '82 – 2; WIG: '85 – 2. Won AAA title '84. Set three Cuban triple jump records and won Cuban

championship 1983–4.
Progression at TJ: 1979 – 14.96, 1980 – 15.56/15.78w, 1981 – 16.11, 1982 – 16.64, 1983 – 17.40/17.50w, 1984 – 17.45, 1975 – 17.30i.
pb LJ: 7.48 '83

Alejandro CASANAS
b.29 Jan 1954 Havana 1.88m 79kg
Ch. record at 110mh (R – 4x100m relay): OG: '72 – h, '76 – 2, '80 – 2; WCh: '83 – sf; PAm: '75 – 1 (2R), '79 – 2 (2R), '83 – 2; WCp: '77 – 2, '79 – 3, '81 – 2; WSG: '77 – 1; CAmG: '74 – 1, '78 –

105

National Championships

1, '82 – 1.
Progression at 110mh: 1969 – 15.9, 1970 – 14.6, 1971 – 13.9, 1972 – 13.3, 1974 – 13.64/13.3, 1975 – 13.44/13.2, 1976 – 13.33, 1977 – 13.21/13.0w, 1978 – 13.55, 1979 – 13.23, 1980 – 13.40, 1981 – 13.36, 1982 – 13.36, 1983 – 13.51, 1984 – 13.53/13.40w.
pbs: 100m: 10.1 '76, 200m: 20.81/20.6 '74
Double Olympic silver medallist, with a long and distinguished record.

Luis Mariano DELIS
b.6 Dec 1957 Guantanamo 1.85m 106kg
Ch. record at DT: OG: '80 – 3; WCh: '83 – 2; PAm: '79 – 3, '83 – 1 (1 at SP); WCp: '79 – 3, '81 – 2; WSG: '83 – 1; CAmG: '78 – 1, '82 – 1 (1 at SP). Won US title '82. Cuban discus champion 1978–83.
Progression at DT: 1973 – 43.54, 1974 – 49.02, 1975 – 50.70, 1976 – 56.82, 1977 – 61.02, 1978 – 62.14, 1979 – 66.52, 1980 – 68.04, 1981 – 67.28, 1982 – 70.58, 1983 – 71.06, 1984 – 69.74.
pb SP: 19.89 '82.

Jaime JEFFERSON
b.17 Jan 1962 Guantanamo 1.89m 78kg
Ch. record at LJ: PAm: '83 – 1. Set three Cuban long jump records 1984.
Progression at LJ: 1981 – 7.25, 1982 – 7.50, 1983 – 8.05, 1984 – 8.37

Osvaldo LARA
b.13 Jul 1955 1.71m 72kg Sports student.
Ch. record at 100m (R – 4x100m relay): OG: '80 – 5 (8 at 200m); WCh: '83 – sf; PAm: '79 – 6 (7 at 200m, 2R), '83 – 4 (2R); CAmG: '78 – 2, '82 – 2; WSG: '77 – 3
Progression at 100m: 1976 – 10.43/10.0, 1977 – 10.20/10.1/10.0w, 1978 – 10.11, 1979 – 10.27/10.23w, 1980 – 10.21/10.1, 1981 – 10.1/10.29w, 1982 – 10.26/9.7w/10.2, 1983 – 10.21, 1984 – 10.14/10.0.
pb 200m: 20.6 '82, 20.77 '77

Juan MARTINEZ
b.17 May 1958 1.86m 122kg
Ch. record at DT: WCh: '83 – 7; PAm: '79 – 4, '83 – 3
Progression at DT: 1976 – 53.98, 1977 – 57.24, 1978 – 60.34, 1979 – 64.88, 1980 – 66.46, 1982 – 63.70, 1983 – 70.00, 1984 – 67.32

Leandro PEÑALVER
b.23 May 1961 1.75m 71kg

Ch. record at 100m/200m: WCh: '83 – sf/ –; PAm: '83 – 1/2 (2 at 4x100mR); CAmG: '82 – 1/1
Progression at 100m: 1981 – 10.55/10.24w/10.4, 1982 – 10.16/10.1, 1983 – 10.06, 1984 – 10.14.
pb 200m: 20.42/20.3 '82

Javier SOTOMAYOR
b.13 Oct 1967 Limonar 1.96m 76kg
Ch. record at HJ: WIG: '85 – 2. Cuban champion and record holder 1984.
Progression at HJ: 1982 – 2.00, 1983 – 2.17, 1984 – 2.33
Teenager who has made sensational progress.

WOMEN

Maria Caridad COLON
b.25 Mar 1958 Baracoa 1.75m 70kg
Ch. record at JT: OG: '80 – 1; WCh: '83 – 8; PAm: '79 – 1, '83 – 1; CAmG: '78 – 1, '82 – 1; WCp: '79 – 3. Six times Cuban javelin champion.
Progression at JT: 1974 – 42.24, 1975 – 43.62, 1976 – 49.74, 1977 – 54.32, 1978 – 63.50, 1979 – 64.38, 1980 – 68.40, 1982 – 62.80, 1983 – 65.70, 1984 – 69.96.
Has steadily regained the form that won her the Olympic javelin gold medal in 1980. Married to her coach Angel Salcedo. Missed 1981 season, when she had a baby.

Silvia COSTA
b.4 May 1961 1.79m 60kg
Ch. record at HJ: WCh: '83 – 10=; PAm: '83 – 2; WSG: '83 – 5; CAmG: '82 – 1 Cuban high jump record holder since 1980;WIG-3=.
Progression at HJ: 1977 – 1.57, 1978 – 1.64, 1979 – 1.82, 1980 – 1.90, 1981 – 1.88, 1982 – 1.95, 1983 – 1.98, 1984 – 1.99.
pb 100mh: 14.52 '80

Maria Elena SARRIA
b.14 Sep 1954 1.84m 104kg
Ch. record at SP: OG: '76 – 11, '80 – 9; WCh: '83 – 8; PAm: '75 – 1, '79 – 1, '83 – 1; WCp: '79 – 5, '81 – 3; CAmG: '74 – 1, '82 – 1.
Won TAC title 1982
Progression at SP: 1973 – 13.97, 1974 – 14.70, 1975 – 18.03, 1976 – 19.18, 1977 – 18.80, 1979 – 19.52, 1980 – 20.40, 1981 – 19.21, 1982 – 20.61, 1983 – 20.36, 1984 – 20.25

Mayra VILA b.5 Jun 1960 1.67m 64kg
Ch. record at JT: WCh: '83 – 12; WSG: '79 – 3, '81 – 3, '83 – 3; WCp: '81 – 5. Set Cuban javelin record 1983.
Progression at JT: 1978 – 52.40, 1979 – 60.98, 1980 – 59.90, 1981 – 63.88, 1982 – 63.22, 1983 – 68.76, 1984 – 66.02

CZECHOSLOVAKIA

Governing body: Ceskoslovensky atleticky svaz, Na Porici 12, 115 30 Praha. Founded 1897 (AAU of Bohemia)
National Championships first held in 1907 (Bohemia), 1919 (Czechoslovakia)
1984 Champions: MEN
100m: František Ptacnik 10.41, 200m: Frantisek Brecka 20.84, 400m: Ján Tomko 46.09, 800m: Ladislav Subrt 1:49.13, 1500m: Josef Vedra 3:41.76, 5000m/10000m: Martin Vrabel 13:55.30/28:45.34, 3000mSt: Vaclav Patek 8:35.24, 110mh: Jiri Hudec 13.87, 400mh: Stanislav Navesnak 50.65, HJ: Lubomir Rosko 2.18, PV: František Jansa 5.35, LJ: Jan Leitner 7.90, TJ: Vlastimil Mařnec 16.97, SP: Remigius Machura 20.30, DT: Imrich Bugár 67.98, HT: Zdeněk Bednar 68.78, JT: Zdeněk Adamec 84.88, Dec: Martin Machura 7561, 20kmW: Jozef pribilinec 1:25:07, 50kmW: Jozef Hudak 4:00:51
WOMEN
100m: Štěpánka Sokolová 11.89, 200m: Taťána Kocembová 22.62, 400m: Jarmila Kratochvílová 49.47, 800m: Zuzana Moravčíková 2:03.18, 1500m: Ivana Kleinová 4:16.49, 3000m/10000m: Ludmila Melicherova 9:26.19/34:06.99, 100mh: Helena Otáhalová 13.75, 400mh: Anna Filičková 57.55, HJ: Ivana Jobbova 1.90, LJ: Jarmila Ştrejčková 6.48, SP: Helena Fibingerová 20.57, DT: Zdeňka Šilhavá 67.62, JT: Elena Burgárová 66.12, Hep: Marcela Koblasova 6044, 10kmW: Dana Vavracova 48:45

National Championships

Zdeněk ADAMEC
b.9 Jan 1956 Mělník 1.81m 93kg
Club: LIAZ Jablonec. Electrician.
Ch. record at JT: WCh: '83– 7. Czechoslovak javelin champion 1980, 1983–4 and six records 1983–4.
Progression at JT: 1973 – 65.56, 1974 – 70.54, 1975 – 69.24, 1976 – 76.40, 1977 – 75.94, 1978 – 80.14, 1979 – 79.96, 1980 – 80.84, 1981 – 81.88, 1982 – 82.82, 1983 – 85.76, 1984 – 91.12

Pavol BLAŽEK
b.9 Jul 1958 Trnava 1.68m 57kg
Club: Dukla B.Bystrica. Toolmaker.
Ch. record at 20kmW/50kmW: OG: '80– 14/10; WCh: '83– 6/17; ECh: '78– 14/–; '82– 3/dnf; LT: '83– 9/–. Czechoslovak 20kmW champion 1981.
Progression at 20kmW: 1977 – 1:33:34, 1978 – 1:27:50, 1979 – 1:25:14, 1980 – 1:25:00t, 1981 – 1:24:07, 1982 – 1:23:59, 1983 – 1:21:37, 1984 – 1:21:24t
pb 50kmW: 4:03:22 '83

Imrich BUGÁR
b.14 Apr 1955 Dunajska Streda 1.95m 120kg
Club: Dukla Praha. Civil servant.
Ch. record at DT: OG: '80– 2; WCh: '83– 1; ECh: '78– 3, '82– 1; WCp: '81– 3. Czechoslovak champion 1978–84 and five discus records 1981–3.
Progression at DT: 1972 – 44.42, 1973 – 48.22, 1974 – 51.38, 1975 – 53.88, 1976 – 57.52, 1977 – 62.54, 1978 – 65.96, 1979 – 64.88, 1980 – 66.38, 1981 – 67.48, 1982 – 68.60, 1983 – 70.72, 1984 – 70.26.
pb SP: 15.19 '82
World and European discus champion who competes often and throws consistently well. He was a handball prospect at school, but learned to throw the discus in a few weeks at the age of 17 in 1972.

Jan CADO
b.7 May 1963 Trstena 1.82m 75kg
Club: Slavia Praha IPS. Student.
Ch. record at TJ: WCh: '83– 6; EI: '83– 4, '84– 4. Set Czechoslovak triple jump record 1984.
Progression at TJ: 1979 – 14.14, 1980 – 14.85, 1981 – 15.40, 1982 – 16.31/16.66w, 1983 – 17.06, 1984 – 17.34.
pbs: 100m: 10.60 '84, LJ: 8.09 '84

Jan LEITNER
b.14 Sep 1953 Znojmo 1.86m 87kg
Club: Dukla Praha. Civil servant.
Ch. record at LJ: OG: '80– dnq; WCh: '83– 10; ECh: '78– 11, '82– 3; EI: '84– 1; WIG: '85– 1. Czechoslovak champion 1975, '77–82, '84, and set four records 1977–82.
Progression at LJ: 1970 – 6.22, 1971 – 6.45, 1972 – 7.13, 1973 – 7.25, 1974 – 7.61, 1975 – 7.74/7.88w, 1976 – 7.76/7.90w, 1977 – 7.95/8.04w, 1978 – 8.03, 1979 – 7.78/7.86w, 1980 – 7.95, 1981 – 8.07, 1982 – 8.10, 1983 – 7.94/7.96w, 1984 – 8.10.
pb TJ: 16.21 '82.

Remigius MACHURA
b.3 Jul 1960 Rychnov n.Kneznou 1.87m 111kg
Club: VŠ Praha. Student.
Ch. record at SP: WCh: '83– 3; ECh: '82– 3; EI: '82– 2; EJ: '79– 1 (5 at DT); WIG: '85– 1. Czechoslovak champion 1983–4 and record holder (1982).
Progression at SP: 1976 – 14.50, 1977 – 16.61, 1978 – 17.46, 1979 – 18.64, 1980 – 19.23, 1981 – 19.22i, 1982 – 21.74, 1983 – 21.41, 1984 – 21.52.
pb DT: 60.30 '82.

His brother Martin is the Czechoslovak decathlon record holder (7974 '83).

Vlastimil MAŘINEC
b.9 Jan 1957 Pacov 1.84m 76kg
Club: Slavia Praha IPS. Agricultural engineer.
Ch. record at TJ: WCh: '83– 5; EI: '84– 2. Czechoslovak champion at TJ 1980–1, '83–4, LJ 1983, and triple jump record in 1983.
Progression at TJ: 1975 – 14.19, 1976 – 14.91, 1977 – 14.83, 1978 – 15.56, 1979 – 15.46, 1980 – 16.35, 1981 – 16.60, 1982 – 16.18, 1983 – 17.21, 1984 – 17.16i.
pb LJ: 7.99 '83

Jozef PRIBILINEC
b.6 Jul 1960 Kremnica 1.68m 66kg
Club: Dukla B.Bystrica. Sports instructor.
Ch. record at 20kmW: OG: '80– 20; WCh: '83– 2; ECh: '82– 2; LT: '83– 1; EJ: '79– 1 at 10kmW. Czechoslovak 20kmW champion 1979, '82–4. World track best for 5000m walk: 18:51.2 '81, world junior record for 3000m walk: 11:13.2 '79. World road best for 20kmW in 1983.
Progression at 20kmW: 1978 – 1:33:07, 1979 – 1:22:44, 1980 – 1:21:40, 1981 – 1:21:56, 1982 – 1:22:27, 1983 – 1:19:30, 1984 – 1:25:07.
pb 50kmW: 4:16:41 '84

Pavol SZIKORA
b.26 Mar 1952 Lučenec 1.76m 65kg
Club: Dukla Banska Bystrica. Mechanic.
Ch. record at 50kmW: WCh: '83– 11. Czechoslovak champion 1983.
Progression at 50kmW: 1980 – 4:01:03, 1981 – 4:19:46, 1982 – 4:02:42, 1983 – 3:56:14, 1984 – 3:45:53.
pb 20kmW: 1:24:29 '81.

Lubomir TESÁČEK
b.9 Feb 1957 Brno 1.71m 54kg
Club: Dukla Praha. Sports instructor. Won EI 3000m 1984. Czechoslovak 5000m champion 1980 and 1983, and 3000m records 1981 and 1983.
Progression at 5000m: 1975 – 15:00.2, 1976 – 14:59.8, 1977 – 14:05.6, 1978 – 13:58.9, 1979 – 13:49.83, 1980 – 13:39.6, 1981 – 13:49.16, 1982 – 13:41.36, 1983 – 13:30.42, 1984 – 13:30.88
pbs: 1500m: 3:42.2 '79, 2000m: 5:08.46 '84, 3000m: 7:46.99 '83

Gejza VALENT
b.3 Oct 1953 Praha 1.96m 120kg
Club: Vítkovice. Technician.
Ch. record at DT: WCh: '83– 3; ECh: '82– 6.
Progression at DT: 1970 – 44.76, 1971 – 46.38, 1972 – 49.44, 1973 – 49.94, 1974 – 54.00, 1975 – 54.96, 1976 – 56.64, 1977 – 56.10, 1978 – 53.04, 1979 – 55.56, 1980 – 58.64, 1981 – 65.42, 1982 – 61.58, 1983 – 67.26, 1984 – 69.70
pb SP: 15.98 '81
Leapt into world class in the 1980s after a decade of little progress. His father, Gejza, had a personal best discus mark of 53.84m in 1956, which ranked him 16th in the world.

WOMEN

Elena BURGÁROVÁ
b.13 Nov 1952 Liptovsky Mikulas 1.68m 65kg née Kubanova. **Club:** Sparta Praha. Textile designer.
Ch. record at JT: WCh: '83– dnq; ECh: '78– 11, '82– 11 Czechoslovak javelin champion 1977, '80–4 and eight javelin records 1977–84.
Progression at JT: 1969 – 37.74, 1970 – 37.28, 1971 – 40.20,

107

National Championships

1972 – 46.76, 1973 – 50.62, 1974 – 51.56, 1975 – 52.46, 1976 – 54.68, 1977 – 59.08, 1978 – 58.54, 1979 – 48.94, 1980 – 57.38, 1981 – 63.90, 1982 – 64.54, 1983 – 65.56, 1984 – 66.56

Helena FIBINGEROVÁ
b.13 Jul 1949 Víceměřice 1.79m 99kg
Club: Vítkovice. Married (1977) Jaroslav Smíd (18.82m shot in 1970).
Ch. record at SP: OG: '72– 7, '76– 3; WCh: '83– 1; ECh: '69– 10, '71– 12, '74– 3, '78– 2, '82– 2; EI: 1st '73–4, '77–8, '80, '83–4, 2nd '75, '81–2. WCp: '77– 2, '79– 2, '81– 2; ECp: '83– 1. Czechoslovak champion 1970–9, '81–4. Set world records at 21.99m in 1976 and 22.32m in 1977 as well four world indoor bests, headed by 22.50m in 1977. Czechoslovak record holder since 1970.
Progression at SP: 1966 – 13.61, 1967 – 14.60, 1968 – 15.29, 1969 – 16.01, 1970 – 16.77, 1971 – 16.57, 1972 – 19.18, 1973 – 20.80, 1974 – 21.57, 1975 – 21.43, 1976 – 21.99, 1977 – 22.32/22.50i, 1978 – 21.87, 1979 – 21.18, 1980 – 21.53, 1981 – 21.57, 1982 – 21.55, 1983 – 21.46, 1984 – 21.60
pb DT: 50.28 '73
She scored an emotional triumph in Helsinki in 1983, for it was her first win outdoors in a long major championships career. Indoors she ties the record for the most European titles.

Taťána KOCEMBOVÁ
b.2 May 1962 Ostrava–Vítkovice 1.69m 55kg
Club: Vítkovice. Clerk.
Ch. record at 400m (R – 4x400m relay): WCh: '83– 2 (2R); ECh: '82– 3 (2R); EI: '84– 1; EJ: '79– 8; ECp: '83– 1 (1R, 4 at 100m). Czechoslovak champion at 200m 1983–4, 400m 1981.
Progression at 200m/400m: 1977 – 26.2/60.4, 1978 – 25.64/59.0, 1979 – 25.12/54.02, 1980 – 55.99, 1981 – 23.95/52.41, 1982 – 23.10/50.41, 1983 – 22.50/48.59, 1984 – 22.47/48.73.
pb 100m: 11.31 '83, 500m: 65.9 '84
In 1984 ran a 47.84 relay last leg and had her first success over Kratochvilova at 400m, beating her three times.

Jarmila KRATOCHVÍLOVÁ
b.26 Jan 1951 Golčuv Jeníkov 1.70m 64kg
Club: VS Praha. Researcher.
Ch. record at 400m (R = 4x400m relay): OG: '80– 2; WCh: '83– 1 (2R, 1 at 800m); ECh: '78– sf, '82– 2 (2R); EI: '79– 2, '81– 1, '82– 1, '83– 1, ('84– 1 at 200m); WCp: '79– 4R, '81– 1 (2 at 200m); ECp: '83– 1R, 1 at 200m, 800m. World records at 400m and 800m in 1983. Set indoor world bests at 200m – 23.19 in 1979 and 22.76 in 1981, 300m – 36.14 in 1981, 400m – 51.02 and 49.64 in 1981 and 49.59 in 1982, 800m – 1:58.33 (oversized track) in 1983.

Czechoslovak records: 100m (3), 200m (11), 400m (9), 800m (2) 1978–83.
Progression at 200m, 400m/800m: 1971 – 60.2; 1972 – 24.8, 55.0; 1973 – 25.3, 56.0/2:13.8; 1974 – 24.7, 55.5/2:13.7; 1975 – 57.4/2:11.4; 1976 – 23.6, 53.1; 1977 – 24.35/24.24w, 53.3; 1978 – 23.50, 51.09; 1979 – 23.19i, 51.47; 1980 – 22.53, 49.46; 1981 – 21.97, 48.61; 1982 – 22.36, 48.85/1:56.59; 1983 – 22.40, 47.99/1:53.28; 1984 – 22.57, 49.02/1:57.68.
pb 100m: 11.09 '81.
Broke Czechoslovak junior 400m record in 1972 but was slowed by injuries and did not set her first national record until the age of 27 in 1978. She won the first women's 400m/800m double in a major championships when she starred in Helsinki in 1983 and ran the fastest ever 400m relay leg, 47.6, at the 1982 European Championships.

Eva MURKOVÁ
b.29 May 1962 Bojnica 1.68m 56kg
Club: Slávia PF B.Bystrica. Student.
Ch. record at LJ: WCh: '83– 7; ECh: '82– dnq; EI: '83– 1, '84– 2; ECp: '83– 2. Czechoslovak 100m and LJ champion 1983, three Czechoslovak long jump records 1983–4.
Progression at LJ: 1977 – 5.14, 1978 – 5.13, 1979 – 5.76, 1980 – 6.10, 1981 – 6.42, 1982 – 6.74, 1983 – 6.92, 1984 – 7.17w/7.01
pb 100m: 11.43 '83, 11.4 '84; 200m: 24.21 '83.

Zdeňka ŠILHAVÁ
b.15 Jun 1954 Krnov 1.78m 85kg. Formerly Kusá and Bartoňová, now married to Josef Šilhavý (64.90m discus 1975)
Club: RH Praha. Civil Servant.
Ch. record at SP/DT: OG: '80– 10/11; WCh: '83– 9/6; ECh: '78– 9/–, '82– 9/13; ECp: '83– –/4. Czechoslovak champion SP 1980, DT 1980–4. World record discus at 74.56m in 1984. Ten Czechoslovak discus records 1980–4.
Progression at SP/DT: 1970 – 11.96, 1971 – 12.30, 1972 – 12.51, 1973 – 13.07/39.84, 1974 – 14.28/42.88, 1975 – 16.82/49.08, 1976 – 17.40/49.02, 1977 – 18.42i/53.22, 1978 – 19.42/56.70, 1979 – 18.70/56.30, 1980 – 20.00/64.50, 1981 – 19.54/65.74, 1982 – 20.55/68.66, 1983 – 21.05/70.00, 1984 – 20.12/74.56

Milena STRNADOVA
b.23 May 1961 Ústí n.Laben 1.61m 53kg née Majějkovičová. Club: VS Praha. Student.
Ch. record at 800m (R – 4x400m relay): WCh: '83– 7 (2R); ECh: '82– 2R; EI: '84– 1.
Progression at 800m: 1981 – 2:07.17, 1982 – 2:05.14, 1983 – 1:57.28, 1984 – 1:59.43i.
pb 400m: 51.88 '83

DENMARK

Governing body: Dansk Athletik Forbund, Idraettens Hus, Brondby Stadion 20, DK-2600 Glostrup.
National Championships first held in 1894
1984 Champions: MEN
100m: Lars Pedersen 10.60, 200m: Peter Regli 21.49, 400m: Jesper Carlsen 47.47, 800m: Hans Christian Jensen 1:48.88, 1500m: Mogens Guldberg 3:48.4, 5000m: Kjeld Johnsen 14:09.50, 10000m: Ole Hansen 29:27.8, 3000mSt: Flemmimg Jensen 8:42.82, 110mh: Tommy Jensen 14.40w, 400mh: Jørgen Troest 52.60, HJ: Rene Tyranski Nielsen 2.09, PV: Carsten Lange 5.00, LJ: Carl Emil Falbe Hansen 7.18w, TJ: Niels Geil 14.80, SP: Michael Henningsen 16.33, DT: Peter Jarl Hansen 53.78, HT: Peter Christensen 61.88, JT: Jørgen Jelstrøm 78.07, Dec: Jesper Tegenwaldt 7543
WOMEN
100m/100mh: Dorthe Rasmussen 11.81/13.45, 200m: Berit Danielsen 24.35, 400m/400mh: Helle Sichlau 54.90/58.15, 800m: Heidi Christiansen 2:07.98, 1500m: Annette B»low 4:27.84, 3000m: Dorthe Rasmussen 9:19.59, HJ/LJ: Lene Demsitz 1.80/6.31, SP: Vivian Krafft 13.48, DT: Lise Lotte Hansen 50.29, JT: Simone Frandsen 55.98, Hep: Bettina Poulsen 5031

National Championships

ETHIOPIA

Governing body: National Ethiopian Athletic Federation, Addis Ababa Stadium, PO Box 3241, Addis Ababa

Kebede BALCHA
b.7 Sep 1951 1.66m 49kg
Ch. record at Mar: WCh: '83– 2; OG: '80– dnf; AfCh: '82– dnf
Major marathon wins: Athens 1977, Montreal 1979, 1981 & 1983. 4th London 1983.
Progression at Mar: 1977 – 2:14:41, 1979 – 2:11:35, 1981 – 2:11:11, 1983 – 2:10:04, 1984 – 2:11:40, 1985 – 2:12:01.
pb 10000m: 30:30.7 '82.
Has won four of his 14 marathons.

Wodajo BULTI
b.11 Mar 1957 1.85m 60kg
Ch. record at 5000m: WCh: '83– 7; AfCh: '82– 1 (3 at 1500m)
Progression at 5000m: 1981 – 13:40.20, 1982 – 13:07.29, 1983 – 13:22.32, 1984 – 13:10.08
pbs: 1500m: 3:40.08 '82, 3000m: 7:40.64 '83; 10000m: 27:58.24 '84

Bekele DEBELE
b.12 Mar 1963 1.70m 55kg
Ch. record at 10000m: WCh: '83– 10. World cross-country champion 1983 and 8th 1984.
pbs: 5000m: 13:33.74 '84, 10000m: 27:49.30 '83

Mohammed KEDIR
b.6 Sep 1953 1.66m 45kg
Ch. record at 10000m: OG: '80– 3 (12 at 5000m); WCh: '83– 9; WCp: '81– 2; AfG: '78– 3; AfCh: '79– 2, '82– 1. World cross-country: '81– 2, '82– 1. Set world best for half-marathon, 1:01:02, in 1982.
Progression at 10000m: 1974 – 30:26.4, 1975 – 29:40.0, 1976 – 28:11.4, 1977 – 28:04.8, 1978 – 28:42.0, 1979 – 28:18.9, 1980 – 27:44.64, 1981 – 27:39.44, 1982 – 28:25.8, 1983 – 28:07.16, 1984 – 27:57.09
pbs: 3000m: 7:55.3 '79, 5000m: 13:17.5 '80

Dereje NEDI
b.10 Oct 1955 1.75m 55kg
Ch. record at Mar: OG: '80– 7; WCh: '83– dnf; AfCh: '79– dnf, '82– dnf. Set Ethiopian marathon records in 1983 and 1984.
Progression at Mar: 1976 – 2:17:07, 1977 – 2:14:49, 1978 – 2:23:08, 1979 – 2:22:13, 1980 – 2:12:44, 1981 – 2:12:14, 1982 – 2:13:25, 1983 – 2:10:39, 1984 – 2:10:32, 1985 – 2:12:48
First major international marathon wins – at Frankfurt and Moscow, in 1984.

FINLAND

Governing body: Suomen Urheiluliitto ry, Box 25202, 00250 Helsinki 25. Founded 1907.
National Championships first held in 1907 (men), 1913 (women)
1984 Champions: MEN
100m/200m: Kimmo Saaristo 10.44/20.83, 400m: Hannu Mykrä 46.54, 800m: Jorma Härkönen 1:48.38, 1500m: Timo Lehto 3:42.08, 5000m/10000m: Martti Vainio 13:24.99/28:06.89*, 3000mSt: Tommy Ekblom 8:29.43, 110mh: Arto Bryggare 13.64, 400mh: Tapio Kallio 51.75, HJ: Erkki Niemi 2.28, PV: Kimmo Pallonen 5.50, LJ: Jarmo Kärnä 7.86, TJ: Esa Viitasalo 16.53w, SP: Aulis Akonniemi 19.72, DT: Juhani Tuomola 60.40, HT: Juha Tiainen 79.72, JT: Tero Saviniemi 86.78, Dec: Harri Sundell 7781, 20kmW: Matti Katila 1:32:35, 50kmW: Reima Salonen 3:57:42
WOMEN
100m/200m: Helinä Marjamaa 11.37/23.15, 400m: Riitta Vesanen 54.60, 800m: Kaisa Ylimäki 2:06.98, 1500m: Irene Marttila 4:16.88, 3000m/10000m: Tuija Toivonen 9:09.86/32:39.25, 100mh: Ritva Valkeinen 14.33, 400mh: Tuija Helander 57.12; HJ: Niina Ranta 1.88, LJ: Anna-Maija Bryggare 6.05, SP: Asta Hovi 16.18, DT: Ulla Lundholm 63.14, JT: Tuula Laaksalo 64.58, 5000mW: Sirkka Oikarinen 23:38.03

*At the end of the year, after positive drug tests, Martti Vainio was stripped of his Finnish titles won in 1984 – the second placed runners were: 5000m: Hannu Okkola 13:51.08, 10000m: Seppo Liuttu 28:46.77.

Arto BRYGGARE
b.26 May 1958 Kouvola 1.94m 82kg
Club: Lappeenrannan Urheilu-Miehet. Economics student.
Ch. record at 110mh: OG: '80– 6, '84– 3; WCh: '83– 2; ECh: '78– 3, '82– 3; EJ: '75– 7, '77– 1; ECp: '77– 4. At 50mh/60mh: EI: '77– 3, '79– 2, '81– 1, '83– 2. Finnish 110mh champion 1977–84. 11 Finnish 110mh records 1976–84. Set European junior 110mh record in 1977 and world indoor best of 13.58 in 1983.
Progression at 110mh: 1975 – 14.46, 1976 – 14.04, 1977 – 13.66, 1978 – 13.56, 1979 – 13.81, 1980 – 13.76, 1981 – 13.77, 1982 – 13.57, 1983 – 13.44, 1984 – 13.35. pbs: 100m: 10.5/10.60 '77, 200m: 21.3 '77, 200m: 23.1 '78.
Very consistent hurdler in the major events.

Tommy EKBLOM
b.20 Sep 1959 Porvoo 1.76m 62kg
Club: Porvoon Urheilijat. Sports instructor.
Ch. record at 3kmSt: OG: '80– 12, '84– 9; WCh: '83– 12; ECh: '82– 8; WSG: '81– 2. Finnish champion at 3kmSt 1979, '81–2, '84 and 5000m 1983.
Progression at 3kmSt: 1976 – 9:29.4, 1977 – 9:11.8, 1978 – 8:39.8, 1979 – 8:37.31, 1980 – 8:20.20, 1981 – 8:21.93, 1982 – 8:21.4, 1983 – 8:19.40, 1984 – 8:20.54
pbs: 1500m: 3:44.82 ''81, 3000m: 7:49.59 '83, 5000m: 13:37.19 '81, 10000m: 28:30.14 '81.

Arto HARKONEN
b.13 Jan 1959 Helsinki 1.90m 92kg
Club: Helsingin Kisa-Veikot. Commercial student.
Ch. record at JT: OG: '84– 1; WCh: '83– 14; ECh: '82– 5; EJ: '77– 2; WSG: '79– 2. Won IAAF 'Golden Javelin' 1979. Finnish champion 1982. Set European junior record in 1978 and in 1979 became the youngest ever 90m thrower.
Progression at JT: 1975 – 66.54, 1976 – 75.88, 1977 – 82.98, 1978 – 85.70, 1979 – 90.18, 1980 – 90.26, 1981 – 91.04, 1982 – 88.14, 1983 – 87.80, 1984 – 92.40

Harri HUHTALA
b.13 Aug 1952 Paattinen 1.87m 110kg

109

National Championships

Club: Tampereen Pyrinto. Policeman
Ch. record at HT: OG: '80– 9, '84– 6; WCh: '83– 10; ECh: '78– 11, '82– 5; ECp: '75– 5. Finnish champion 1975–6, '80, '82–3. Set six Finnish hammer records 1978–83.
Progression at HT: 1968 – 44.98, 1969 – 49.22, 1970 – 55.92, 1971 – 59.12, 1972 – 60.30, 1973 – 66.04, 1974 – 69.10, 1975 – 71.04, 1976 – 71.40, 1977 – 72.68, 1978 – 73.66, 1979 – 74.22, 1980 – 75.94, 1981 – 76.76, 1982 – 77.02, 1983 – 78.68, 1984 – 78.74. Has improved for 17 successive years.

Reima SALONEN
b.19 Nov 1955 Taivassalo 1.77m 70kg
Club: Turun Weikot. Fireman.
Ch. record at 50kmW (20kmW): OG: '80– dnf (9), '84– 4; WCh: '76– 3, '83– 4 (12); ECh: '82– 1 (8). EJ: '73– 13 at 10kmW. Finnish champion 11 successive years 1973–83 at 20kmW, 8 times at 50kmW 1974–82, 1984.
Progression at 50kmW: 1974 – 4:35:48, 1975 – 4:37:47, 1976 – 3:58:53, 1977 – 4:12:28, 1978 – 3:51:38, 1979 – 3:49:52, 1981 – 4:03:23, 1982 – 3:49:47, 1983 – 3:52:53, 1984 – 3:48:36.
pb 20kmW: 1:19:35 '80
Undefeated by a Finnish walker since 1973; disqualified only once in career.

Juha TIAINEN
b.5 Dec 1955 Uukuniemi 1.82m 107kg
Club: Lappeenrannan Urheilu-Miehet. Policeman.
Ch. record at HT: OG: '80– 10, '84– 1; WCh: '83– 9; ECh: '82– 12; ECp: '77– 6. Finnish hammer champion 1977,'79,'81,'84, set eight Finnish records 1976–84.
Progression at HT: 1972 – 40.94, 1973 – 49.62, 1974 – 51.64, 1975 – 65.12, 1976 – 71.80, 1977 – 72.62, 1978 – 71.08, 1979 – 74.42, 1980 – 75.88, 1981 – 76.64, 1982 – 78.34, 1983 – 81.02, 1984 – 81.52.
pb SP: 15.14 '76
Finland's first ever Olympic champion at the hammer.

Martti VAINIO
b.30 Dec 1950 Vehkalahti 1.90m 74kg
Club: Lapuan Virkia. Businessman.
Ch. record at 10000m (5000m): OG: '76– h, '80– 13 (11), '84– dq; WCh: '83– 4 (3); ECh: '78– 1 (6), '82– 3 (8); WCp: '81– 5; ECp: '77– 4. Finnish champion at 5000m: '78, '80–2, '84 and 10000m 1977–8, '80–4. Finnish records at 5000m in 1984, 10000m in 1978.
Progression at 5000m/10000m: 1973 – 14:55.6, 1974 – 13:55.6/29:09.6, 1975 – 13:47.4/29:00.0, 1976 – 13:35.26/28:07.43, 1977 – 13:40.6/28:07.23, 1978 – 13:28.03/27:30.99, 1979 – 13:21.85/28:04.24, 1980 – 13:29.54/28:00.64, 1981 – 13:28.79/27:45.50, 1982 – 13:24.89/27:42.51, 1983 – 13:20.07/28:01.37, 1984 – 13:16.02/27:41.75
pbs: 1500m: 3:41.09 '83, 2000m: 5:17.5 '80 3000m: 7:44.42 '84, Mar: 2:13:05 '84, 3000mSt: 8:55.0 '75
Did not start athletics until 21 years old. Failed drugs test after finishing second in the 1984 Olympic 10000m.

WOMEN

Tuula LAAKSALO
b.21 Apr 1953 Rovaniemi 1.70m 66kg née Hyytiäinen. **Club:** Virtain Urheilijat. Bank officer.
Ch. record at JT: OG: '84– 4; WCh: '83– 6; ECh: '82– 12. Finnish champion 1982 and 1984.
Progression at JT: 1978 – 49.26, 1979 – 54.12, 1980 – 56.34, 1981 – 63.82, 1982 – 64.48, 1983 – 67.40, 1984 – 67.38

Tiina LILLAK
b.15 Apr 1961 Helsinki 1.80m 73kg
Club: Esbo IF. Student.
Ch. record at JT: OG: '80– dnq, '84– 2; WCh: '83– 1; ECh: '82– 4; EJ: '79– 14. Finnish champion 1980–1, 1983. Ten Finnish records 1980–3, including two world records (72.40m and 74.76m) in 1983, the first ever set by a Finnish woman thrower.
Progression at JT: 1976 – 44.94, 1977 – 47.92, 1978 – 51.60, 1979 – 56.36, 1980 – 61.02 , 1981 – 66.34, 1982 – 72.40, 1983 – 74.76, 1984 – 74.24
pb SP: 14.31 '83
Full name Ilse Kristiina Lillak. Her win on the final throw in Helsinki in 1983, and the attendant roar of the crowd will long be remembered as one of the great moments in athletics history. In 1984 she was held back by a broken bone in her foot, but still managed to gain the Olympic silver medal. Her coach, Kalevi Härkönen is the father of the 1984 Olympic men's gold medallist, Arto Härkönen.

Ulla LUNDHOLM
b.21 Jan 1957 Helsinki 1.74m 70kg
Club: Viipurin Urheilijat. Telephone official.
Ch. record at DT: OG: '84– 4; WCh: '83– 13; ECh: '82– 11. Finnish champion 1980–1, 1983–4. Set eight Finnish discus records 1980–2.
Progression at DT: 1972 – 30.30, 1973 – 33.58, 1974 – 34.06, 1975 – 40.54, 1976 – 47.64, 1977 – 50.52, 1978 – 54.38, 1979 – 53.04, 1980 – 64.60, 1981 – 64.68, 1982 – 64.04, 1983 – 67.02, 1984 – 66.02.
pb SP: 15.71 '83
Retired from athletics after 1984 season.

FRANCE

Governing body: Fédération Française d'Athlétisme, 10 rue du Faubourg Poissonnière, 75010 Paris. Founded 1920.
National Championships first held in 1888 (men), 1918 (women)
1984 Champions: MEN
100m: Bruno Marie-Rose 10.29, 200m: Jean-Jacques Boussemart 20.46, 400m: Vann Quentrec 46.25 (1. Gabriel Tiacoh –IVC–45.51), 800m: Philippe Dupont 1:49.02, 1500m: Pascal Thiebault 3:39.05, 5000m: Francis Gonzalez 13:51.07, 10000m: Philippe Legrand 28:45.98, Mar: Patrick Joannès 2:12:36, 3kmSt: Joseph Mahmoud 8:23.66, 110mh: Stéphane Caristan 13.63w, 400mh: Gérard Brunel 50.11, HJ: Franck Verzy 2.26, PV: Pierre Quinon 5.70, LJ: Claude Morinière 7.78, TJ: Alain René-Corail 16.52, SP: Luc Viudes 17.70, DT: René-Jean Coquin 59.42, HT: Walter Ciofani 75.16, JT: Jean Paul Lakafia 85.08, Dec: Frédéric Sacco 7751, 20kmW: Gérard Lélièvre 1:24:13.7, 50kmW: Dominique Guebey 4:04:45
WOMEN
100m: Marie France Loval 11.25w, 200m: Liliane Gaschet 22.95w, 400m: Raymonde Naigre 52.61, 800m: Florence Giolitti 2:03.98, 1500m/3000m: Annette Sergent 4:11.27/9:02.05, 100mh: Laurence Elloy 12.72w, 400mh: Dominique Le Disses 57.65, HJ: Maryse Ewanje-Epée 1.90, LJ: Géraldine Bonnin 6.38, SP: Léone Bertimon 16.87, DT: Catherine Beauvais 55.76, JT: Nadine Schoellkopf 56.30, Hep: Chantal Beaugeant 6089, 5kmW: Suzanne Griesbach 23:55.60

National Championships

Patrick ABADA
b.20 Mar 1954 Colombes 1.89m 80kg
Club: Racing Club de France. Commercial director.
Ch. record at PV: OG: '76– 4; WCh: '83– 6; ECh: '74– 9, '78– 9; EI: '80– 3, '83– 3; WCp: '79– 2; ECp: '75– 4, '79– 2, '83– 1; WSG: '79– 3. French champion 1975. Set French pole vault record at 5.65m in 1979.
Progression at PV: 1971 – 4.55, 1972 – 5.05i, 1973 – 5.20, 1974 – 5.20, 1975 – 5.35, 1976 – 5.45, 1977 – 5.30, 1978 – 5.40, 1979 – 5.65, 1980 – 5.55i, 1982 – 5.60, 1983 – 5.70, 1984 – 5.53i/5.50
A good competitive record, although his team-mates now vault much higher.

Jean-Jacques BOUSSEMART
b.11 Apr 1963 Lourdes 1.80m 68kg
Club: Bordeaux. Physical education student.
Ch. record at 200m: OG: '84– 6; WCh: '83– sf; EJ: '81– 4; ECp: '83– 4. French champion 1983–4.
Progression at 200m: 1980 – 21.33/21.2, 1981 – 20.88, 1982 – 20.81/20.73w, 1983 – 20.54/20.41w, 1984 – 20.41.
pb 100m: 10.33 '84.

Stéphane CARISTAN
b.31 May 1964 Créteil 1.87m 75kg
Club: AC Paris. Student.
Ch. record at 110mh: OG: '84– 6; WCh: '83– h. French champion 1983–4. At 60mh: WIG: '85– 1.
Progression at 110mh: 1981 – 14.95, 1982 – 14.35, 1983 – 13.86, 1984 – 13.43
pbs: 100m: 10.51 '84, PV: 5.00 '83, LJ: 7.79i '84

Gérard LELIEVRE
b.13 Nov 1949 Laval 1.66m 58kg
Club: ALCL Grand-Quevilly. National Walking trainer.
Ch. record at 20kmW: OG: '76– 9, '84– 15; WCh: '83– 5; ECh: '74– dnf, '78– 11, '82– 4; LT: '75– 14, '77– 5; WSG: '73– 2, '77– 1. At 50kmW: OG: '80– dnf, '84– dnf; WCh: '83– dnf; LT: '81– 9, '83– 5; WSG: '73– 7, '77– 2. At 3kmW: WIG: '85– 1. Set world record for 20km walk at 1:22:19.4 in 1979 and world best for 100kmW, 8:58:12 in 1984 when winning his 34th French walking title (he won his first in 1972). He is French record holder at all standard walking distances.
Progression at 20kmW/50kmW: 1969 – 1:45:01, 1970 – 1:39:39, 1971 – 1:39:27, 1972 – 1:36:24/4:22:25, 1973 – 1:28:51/4:23:47, 1974 – 1:30:47/4:12:15, 1975 – 1:30:51/4:05:48, 1976 – 1:31:35/4:09:40, 1977 – 1:32:52/4:19:26, 1978 – 1:24:35/4:21:06, 1979 – 1:22:20/3:57:52, 1980 – 1:27:09/3:58:16, 1981 – 1:24:49/3:57:35, 1982 – 1:22:53/4:13:14, 1983 – 1:25:52/3:53:57, 1984 – 1:22:14
Track walk pbs: 5km: 19:06.22i '85, 10km: 39:51.34 '84, 1Hr: 15094m '84.
Retired after winning World Indoor Games title to concentrate on his job as French national walking coach.

Joseph MAHMOUD
b.13 Dec 1955 Safi, Morocco 1.74m 65kg
Club: CMS Marignane. Sports teacher.
Ch. record at 3kmSt: OG: '84– 2; WCh: '83– 4; ECh: '82– h; ECp: '81– 6, '83– 3. French champion 1980–4. Five French steeplechase records 1982–4, including European record in 1984.
Progression at 3kmSt: 1975 – 9:00.0, 1976 – 8:43.4, 1977 – 8:43.5, 1978 – 8:40.3, 1979 – 8:32.88, 1980 – 8:30.78, 1981 – 8:24.75, 1982 – 8:20.54, 1983 – 8:15.59, 1984 – 8:07.62
pbs: 1500m: 3:38.39 '84, 3000m: 7:47.58 '84, 5000m: 13:48.19 '84

William MOTTI
b.25 Jul 1964 Bondy 1.99m 92kg. Student at Mt.St Mary's College, USA.
Ch. record at Dec: OG: '84– 5; EJ: '81– 2 at HJ, '83– dnf Dec. Set French decathlon record in 1984 Olympics.
Progression at Dec: 1982 – 7745, 1983 – 7371, 1984 – 8266
pbs: 100m: 11.05 '82, 400m: 48.01 '84, 1500m: 4:35.15 '84, 110mh: 14.67 '84, HJ: 2.22i '82, PV: 4.60 '84, LJ: 7.45 '84, SP: 14.90i '85, DT: 50.92 '84, JT: 70.38 '82

Pierre QUINON
b.20 Feb 1962 Lyon 1.80m 74kg
Club: Racing Club de France. Business student.
Ch. record at PV: OG: '84– 1; WCh: '83– nh; ECh: '82– 12=; EI: '84– 2; EJ: '81– 2. French champion 1982-4. Set world pole vault record at 5.82m in 1983.
Progression at PV: 1976 – 3.40, 1977 – 3.90, 1978 – 4.50, 1979 – 5.00, 1980 – 5.10i, 1981 – 5.50, 1982 – 5.70, 1983 – 5.82, 1984 – 5.80.
Competed much less frequently than his pole vault rivals in 1984, but jumped consistently well and triumph in Los Angeles.

Thierry VIGNERON
b.9 Mar 1960 Gennevilliers, Paris 1.81m 73kg
Club: Racing Club de France. Physical education student.
Ch. record at PV: OG: '80– 7, '84– 3=; WCh: '83– 8=; ECh: '82– 5=; EI: '81– 1, '84– 1; EJ: '77– 8, '79– 3; WSG: '81– 4, '83– 2; WIG: '85– 2. French champion 1980. Has set five world pole vault records: 5.75m twice in 1980, 5.80m (world's first 19ft vault) in 1981, 5.83m in 1983 and 5.91m in 1984. Has also set three world indoor bests: 5.70m twice in 1981 and 5.85m in 1984, and three world junior records: 5.45m, 5.52m and 5.61m in 1979.
Progression at PV: 1974 – 3.70, 1975 – 4.20, 1976 – 4.95i, 1977 – 5.10, 1978 – 5.30, 1979 – 5.61, 1980 – 5.75, 1981 – 5.80, 1982 – 5.71, 1983 – 5.83, 1984 – 5.91.
A prolific vaulter, who has set many records, but until recently did not have the championship results to match. His latest world record lasted just ten minutes for it came in his epic duel with Sergey Bubka in Rome.

WOMEN

Rose Aimée BACOUL
b.9 Jan 1952 Francoise, Martinique 1.60m 56kg. Physical education instructor.
Ch. record at 100m (R = 4x100mR): OG: '84 – sf (4R and 7 at 200m); WCh: '83–sf; ECh: '82– 3 (3R). French 100m and 200m champion 1981-3. Three French 200m records 1983–4.
Progression at 100m/200m: 1970 – 12.3, 1971 – 12.1/25.0; 1972 – –/24.9, 1973 – 12.0/–, 1974 – 11.8/24.3, 1975 – 11.6/23.9, 1976 – 11.75/–, 1977 – 12.0/–, 1978 – 11.7/24.32, 1979 – 11.84/24.20, 1980 – 11.62/11.2w/23.3, 1981 – 11.39/11.24w/23.37, 1982 – 11.23/22.90/22.8; 1983 – 11.16/22.59, 1984 – 11.34/11.30w/22.53

Michèle CHARDONNET
b.27 Oct 1956 Toulon 1.70m 60kg
Club: Racing Club de France. Student.
Ch. record at 100mh: OG: '84– 3=; WCh: '83– sf; EC: '82– h; WSG: '81– 5. French champion 1981 and 1983.
Progression at 100mh: 1973 – 14.4, 1974 – 14.2, 1975 – 13.8, 1976 – 13.5, 1977 – 13.98, 1978 – 13.85, 1979 – 13.48, 1980 – 13.7, 1981 – 13.10/13.07w, 1982 – 12.97, 1983 – 13.02, 1984 – 13.06/12.91w.
pbs: 100m: 11.6 '74, 200m: 24.02 '75
At first placed third equal at Los Angeles, but led off in tears after jury

111

National Championships

decided that she was fourth. However in November the IOC restored her medal by awarding her third equal place.

Laurence ELLOY
b.3 Dec 1959 Rouen 1.68m 57kg née Machabey.
Club: Stade Francais. Secretary.
Ch. record at 100mh: OG: '80– sf, '84– h; WCh: '83– sf; ECh: '78– h, '82– sf; EJ: '77– 4. French champion 1979, '82, '84. At 60mh: WIG: '85– 2. Two French 100mh records in 1982.
Progression at 100mh: 1976 – 14.9, 1977 – 13.82, 1978 – 13.47, 1979 – 13.33, 1980 – 13.13, 1981 – 13.19, 1982 – 12.90/12.81w, 1983 – 12.95, 1984 – 12.94/12.72w
pb 100m: 11.94 '82.

Maryse EWANJE-EPEE
b.4 Sep 1964 Poitiers 1.76m 62kg
Club: Montpellier UC. Student of literature and drama.
Ch. record at HJ: OG: '84– 4; WCh: '83– 12=; ECh: '82– 10; EI: '83– 3, '84– 2; WSG: '83– 3; EJ: '81– 6 at Hep. French high jump champion 1982–4. Three French high jump records 1983.
Progression at HJ: 1977 – 1.52, 1978 – 1.61, 1979 – 1.69, 1980 – 1.76, 1981 – 1.87, 1982 – 1.89, 1983 – 1.95, 1984 – 1.95i/1.94
pbs: Hep: 5648 '83, 100mh: 13.82 '82, 13.6 '84

GERMAN DEMOCRATIC REPUBLIC

Governing body: Deutscher Verband für Leichtathletik der DDR, 1005 Berlin, Storkower Strasse 118. Founded 1950.
National Championships first held in 1950.
1984 Champions: MEN
100m: Thomas Schröder 10.27, 200m: Frank Emmelmann 20.48, 400m: Thomas Schönlebe 45.13, 800m: Detlef Wagenknecht 1:45.62, 1500m: Andreas Busse 3:36.03, 5000m/10000m: Hansjörg Kunze 13:47.31/27:33.10, 3kmSt: Rainer Wachenbrunner 8:39.47, 110mh: Thomas Munkelt 13.51, 400mh: Manfred Konow 49.78, HJ: Gerd Wessig 2.27, PV: Andreas Kramss 5.40, LJ: Lutz Dombrowski 8.28, TJ: Volker Mai 16.94, SP: Udo Beyer 21.72, DT: Jürgen Schult 65.40, HT: Ralf Haber 78.04, JT: Uwe Hohn 93.80, 20kmW: Ronald Weigel 1:22:16, 50kmW: Axel Noack 4:00:41
WOMEN
100m/200m: Marlies Göhr 10.89/21.74, 400m: Marita Koch 48.86, 800m: Hildegard Ullrich 1:58.31, 1500m/3000m: Ulrike Bruns 4:01.38/8:42.81, 100mh: Cornelia Riefstahl 12.64, 400mh: Birgit Uibel 54.90, HJ: Andrea Bienias 1.94, J. Heike Daute 7.00, SP: Ilona Briesenick 21.20, DT: Gisela Beyer 70.32, JT: Petra Felke 65.90.

Udo BEYER
b.9 Aug 1955 Eisenhüttenstadt 1.94m 135kg
Club: ASK Vorwärts Potsdam. Sports student.
Ch. record at SP: OG: '76– 1, '80– 3; WCh: '83– 6; ECh: '74– 8, '78– 1, '82– 1; EJ: '73– 1; WSG: '79– 1; WCp and ECp: '77– 1, '79– 1, '81– 1; WIG: '85– 2. GDR champion 1977–84. Five GDR shot records, the last two also made records in 1978 and 1983, and five European junior records in 1973–4.
Progression at SP: 1971 – 15.71, 1972 – 17.08, 1973 – 19.65, 1974 – 20.20, 1975 – 20.97, 1976 – 21.12, 1977 – 21.74, 1978 – 22.15, 1979 – 21.74, 1980 – 21.98, 1981 – 21.69, 1982 – 21.94, 1983 – 22.22, 1984 – 22.04
pbs: DT: 56.42 '74, HT: 66.84 '73.
Established for years as the world's number one shot putter since winning the 1976 Olympic title at the age of 20, losing only a handful of times in the past decade. A pulled back muscle cost him the chance of winning the 1980 Olympic title.

Andreas BUSSE
b.6 May 1959 Dresden 1.85m 69kg
Club: SC Einheit Dresden. Fitter.
Ch. record at 1500m: OG: '80– 4; WCh: '83– 7; ECh: '82– 11; ECp: '83– 2. At 800m: OG: '80– 5; ECh: '78– 6; EJ: '75– 4, '77– 1. GDR 1500m champion 1983–4. Set world junior records at 1000m in 1977 and 800m in 1978, and GDR 1000m record in 1983.
Progression at 1500m: 1975 – 3:51.1, 1978 – 3:40.9, 1979 –

3:38.6, 1980 – 3:38.6, 1981 – 3:42.51, 1982 – 3:38.92, 1983 – 3:37.19, 1984 – 3:34.10
pbs: 400m: 47.95 '80, 800m: 1:44.72 '80, 1000m: 2:15.25 '83

Jens CARLOWITZ
b.8 Aug 1964 Karl-Marx-Stadt 1.85m 75kg
Club: SC Karl-Marx-Stadt. Electrician.
Ch. record at 400m: EJ: '81– 2 (1R), '83– 2 (1R)
Progression at 400m: 1978 – 55.9, 1979 – 51.81, 1980 – 48.5, 1981 – 46.58, 1982 – 47.13, 1983 – 45.72, 1984 – 44.95

Waldemar CIERPINSKI
b.3 Aug 1950 Neugattersleben 1.70m 59kg
Club: SC Chemie Halle. Sports instructor.
Ch. record at Mar: OG: '76– 1, '80– 1; WCh: '83– 3; ECh: '78– 4 (19 at 10000m); ECp: '81– 2, '83– 1. At 3000mSt: ECp: '73– 6. GDR champion at 3000mSt 1972, 10000m 1979–80, marathon 1976 and 1982.
Progression at Mar: 1974 – 2:20:29, 1975 – 2:17:31, 1976 – 2:09:55, 1977 – 2:16:01, 1978 – 2:12:20, 1979 – 2:15:50, 1980 – 2:10:24, 1981 – 2:15:44, 1982 – 2:13:59, 1983 – 2:10:37, 1984 – 2:12:00
pbs: 1500m: 3:42.2 '74, 3000m: 7:56.2 '74, 5000m: 13:36.6 '75, 10000m: 28:28.2 '75, 3000mSt: 8:32.4 '74
Followed in the footsteps of Abebe Bikila by winning two Olympic marathon gold medals. Ran 27 marathons 1974–84, winning 11 of them. Announced retirement from major competition at the end of the 1984 season.

Lutz DOMBROWSKI
b.25 Jun 1959 Karl-Marx-Stadt 1.87m 87kg
Club: SC Karl-Marx-Stadt. Machine fitter.
Ch. record at LJ: OG: '80– 1, '84– sf; ECh: '82– 1; WCp: '79– 2; ECp: '79– 1. GDR champion 1979 and 1984. At TJ: EJ: '77– 4; WCp: '81– 7; ECp: '81– 5. Set two European long jump records in 1980.
Progression at LJ: 1971 – 5.25, 1972 – 5.46, 1873 – 6.41, 1974 – 6.35, 1975 – 7.13, 1976 – 7.49, 1977 – 7.80i, 1978 – 8.31, 1980 – 8.54, 1982 – 8.30/8.41w, 1984 – 8.50.
pbs: 100m: 10.4; TJ: 16.61i '77 (European junior best).
Won the 1980 Olympic title with the world's first 28ft long jump (Beamon of course had jumped over 29ft). His father Helmut was German youth 100m champion in 1939.

Frank EMMELMANN
b.15 Sep 1961 Schneidlingen 1.85m 76kg
Club: SC Magdeburg. Fitter. Married Kirsten Siemon (Gold at 4x400m relay in the 1982 European Champs) in 1984.
Ch. record at 100m/200m (R – 4x100m relay): WCh: '83– sf/5; ECh: '82– 1/3 (2R); WCp: '81– 3/3 (2R); ECp: '81– 2/1, '83– 1/–.

National Championships

GDR champion at 100m 1981-2, 200m 1981 and 1984. GDR records at 100m in 1984 and 200m in 1981.
Progression at 100m, 200m: 1977 – 10.9; 1978 – 10.70, 22.00; 1979 – 10.42/10.2, 20.90; 1980 – 10.39; 1981 – 10.19/10.15w, 20.33/20.23w; 1982 – 10.20/10.11w, 20.47; 1983 – 10.18, 20.55; 1984 – 10.11, 20.46
Has compiled a fine championships record in the sprints.

Uwe FREIMUTH
b. 10 Sep 1961 Rathenow 1.91m 90kg
Club: ASK Vorwärts Potsdam. Student.
Ch. record at Dec: WCh: '83 – 4; ECp: '81 – 3, '83 – 1 Four GDR decathlon records 1983-4.
Progression at Dec: 1978 – 7221, 1979 – 7573, 1980 – 7772, 1981 – 8213, 1982 – 8034, 1983 – 8501, 1984 – 8704
pbs: 100m: 11.01 '81, 400m: 48.17 '83, 1500m: 4:23.25 '83, 110mh: 14.54 '83, HJ: 2.15 '81, PV: 5.15 '84, LJ: 7.79 '83, SP: 16.42 '84, DT: 51.54 '84, JT: 73.02 '84

Hartwig GAUDER
b. 10 Nov 1954 Vaihingen, GFR 1.86m 70kg
Club: SC Turbine Erfurt. Architectural student.
Ch. record at 50kmW: OG: '80 – 1; ECh: '82 – 4; LT: '81 – 2. At 20kmW: ECh: '78 – 7; LT: '79 – 7. At 10kmW: EJ: '73 – 1. GDR champion at 20kmW 1975-6, 50kmW 1979 and 1982
Progression at 50kmW: 1979 – 4:01:20, 1980 – 3:48:15, 1981 – 3:46:57, 1982 – 3:49:44, 1983 – 3:43:23, 1984 – 3:41:24.
pbs: Track – 3kmW: 11:23.8i '81, 5kmW: 19:08.59i '81, 10kmW: 39:50.9i '84; Road – 20kmW: 1:21:33 '83
Family moved from West Germany when he was aged five.

Detlef GERSTENBERG
b. 5 Mar 1957 Eisenhüttenstadt 1.86m 115kg
Club: SC Dynamo Berlin. Cook.
Ch. record at HT: OG: '80 – 5; ECh: '78 – 4, '82 – 6; EJ: '75 – 1 Set two GDR hammer records in 1984.
Progression at HT: 1974 – 61.58, 1975 – 70.58, 1976 – 71.74, 1977 – 75.28, 1978 – 76.94, 1979 – 77.82, 1980 – 78.94, 1982 – 77.02, 1983 – 76.50, 1984 – 80.50

Ralf HABER
b. 18 Aug 1962 Altenburg-1.89m 110kg
Club: SC Karl-Marx-Stadt. Sports student.
Ch. record at HT: EJ: '81 – 4. GDR hammer champion 1984 and GDR record in 1983.
Progression at HT: 1979 – 52.18, 1980 – 66.44, 1981 – 70.88, 1982 – 76.42, 1983 – 79.02, 1984 – 79.38

Uwe HOHN
b. 16 Jul 1962 Rheinsberg 1.98m 112kg
Club: ASK Potsdam. Student
Ch. record at JT: ECh: '82 – 1; EJ: '81 – 1 First man to throw the javelin over 100 metres, with 104.80m in East Berlin on 20 Jul 1984. This, at 5.08m, was the biggest ever improvement on a world javelin record. Two months earlier he set a European record of 99.52m. Set European Junior record in 1981.
Progression at JT: 1975 – 41.92, 1976 – 54.38, 1977 – 63.52, 1978 – 72.76, 1979 – 74.06, 1980 – 85.32, 1981 – 86.56, 1982 – 91.34, 1984 – 104.80
pb DT: 54.50 '81.
Missed 1983 season through injury.

Ralf KOWALSKY
b. 22 Mar 1962 Elgersburg 1.83m 64kg
Club: TSC Berlin. Student.
Ch. record at 20kmW: WCh: '83 – 14. GDR champion 1981 and 1983. At 10kmW: EJ: '81 – 1. Set two world junior records at both 10km and 20km track walks in 1980-1, and world records at 2 hours (28358m) and 30km (2:06:54) track walks in 1982.
Progression at 20kmW: 1978 – 1:32:34, 1979 – 1:29:30, 1980 – 1:24:08i, 1981 – 1:21:39.1t, 1982 – 1:22:52, 1983 – 1:21:52, 1984 – 1:20:35
Track pbs: 5kmW: 18:42.66 (world best) '84, 10kmW: 38:54.75 '81

Hansjörg KUNZE
b. 28 Dec 1959 Rostock 1.79m 63kg
Club: SC Empor Rostock. Medical student.
Ch. record at 10000m: WCh: '83 – 3. At 5000m: OG: '80 – sf; ECh: '82 – 9; WCp: '79 – 4, '81 – 2; ECp: '79 – 1, '81 – 3, '83 – 4. At 3000m: EJ: '73 – 3. World cross-country: '82 – 4. GDR champion at 5000m 1981, '83-4, 10000m 1984. European 5000m record in 1981 and world indoor 5000m best of 13:13.3 in 1983.
Progression at 5000m/10000m: 1974 – 15:14.6, 1975 – 14:20.4, 1978 – 13:42.2/29:57.9, 1979 – 13:27.7, 1980 – 13:26.4/28:00.73, 1981 – 13:10.40/28:12.25, 1982 – 13:12.53, 1983 – 13:13.3i/27:30.69, 1984 – 13:33.90i/27:33.10.
pbs: 1500m: 3:40.04 '79, 3000m: 7:44.05 '83 (GDR record)

Detlef MICHEL
b. 13 Oct 1955 Berlin 1.88m 97kg
Club: TSC Berlin. Water and gas installer.
Ch. record at JT: OG: '80 – dnq; WCh: '83 – 1; ECh: '78 – 4, '82 – 3; WCp: '81 – 2; ECp: '75 – 2, '81 – 1, '83 – 1. GDR champion 1975, '79–80, '82–3. Five GDR javelin records 1981-3, the last equalled the European record at 96.72m.
Progression at JT: 1970 – 64.08, 1971 – 67.96, 1972 – 75.80, 1973 – 72.48, 1974 – 76.70, 1975 – 84.58, 1976 – 84.72, 1977 – 82.44, 1978 – 86.12, 1979 – 89.74, 1980 – 90.98, 1981 – 92.48, 1982 – 94.52, 1983 – 96.72, 1984 – 93.68
pb LJ: 7.20 '77.
A strong and most consistent thrower.

Thomas MUNKELT
b. 3 Aug 1952 Zedtlitz 1.85m 78kg
Club: SC DHfK Leipzig. Student.
Ch. record at 110mh: OG: '76 – 5, '80 – 1; WCh: '83 – 5; ECh: '74 – 4, '78 – 1, '82 – 1 (2 at 4x100mR); WSG: '73 – 3, '79 – 2; WCp: '77 – 1, '79 – 2; ECp: '73 – 2, '75 – 2, '77 – 1, '79 – 1, '83 – 1. EI: at 60mh – '73 – 3, '77 – 1, '78 – 1, '79 – 1, '83 – 1. GDR champion 1975-80, '82-4. Three world indoor bests at 60m hurdles: 7.62 in 1977, 7.59 in 1979, 7.48 in 1983. Set two GDR 110mh records in 1975-6.
Progression at 110mh: 1971 – 14.5, 1972 – 14.0, 1973 – 13.5, 1974 – 13.5, 1975 – 13.45, 1976 – 13.44, 1977 – 13.37, 1978 – 13.50, 1979 – 13.42, 1980 – 13.39, 1981 – 13.65, 1982 – 13.41, 1983 – 13.48, 1984 – 13.51
pbs: 100m: 10.37/10.29w '80, 200m: 21.25 '75

Jörg PETER
b. 23 Oct 1955 Dresden 1.76m 66kg
Club: SC Einheit Dresden.
Ch. record at 10km: OG: '80 – 6; WCp: '77 – 2; ECp: '77 – 1. At 5000m: ECh: '78 – 12. At 3000m: '78 – 3. GDR champion at 5000m 1976-8, 1980 and 10000m 1977.
Progression at marathon: 1980 – 2:12:56, 1983 – 2:15:34, 1984 – 2:09:14
pbs: 800m: 1:49.86 '76, 1500m: 3:39.2 '76, 3000m: 7:50.1i '78, 5000m: 13:23.5 '79, 10000m: 27:55.50 '77
Set GDR marathon best after earlier placing second in the 1984 Tokyo marathon. Has won two of his six marathons 1980-4.

Gunther RODEHAU
b. 6 Jul 1959 Meissen 1.79m 116kg

113

National Championships

Club: SC Einheit Dresden. Vehicle mechanic.
Ch. record at HT: WCh: '83– 5; ECp: '83– 3 Set GDR hammer record in 1984.
Progression at HT: 1977 – 49.94, 1978 – 60.84, 1979 – 68.90, 1980 – 74.02, 1981 – 74.42, 1982 – 72.18, 1983 – 78.14, 1984 – 80.20

Werner SCHILDHAUER
b.5 Jun 1959 Dessau 1.82m 65kg
Ch. record at 10000m (5000m): OG: '80– 7; WCh: '83– 2/2; ECh: '82– 2/2; WCp: '79– 6, '81– 1; ECp: '79– 4, '81– 1, '83– 1; EJ: '77– 2 at 3000m. World cross-country: '82– 8. Three GDR 10000m records 1981–3. GDR champion at 5000m 1982, 10000m 1981–3.
Progression at 5000m/10000m: 1978 – 13:54.0, 1979 – 13:30.1/28:23.6, 1980 – 13:30.2/27:53.51, 1981 – 13:31.59/27:38.43, 1982 – 13:12.54/27:33.66, 1983 – 13:26.36/27:24.95, 1984 – 13:26.23/28:09.05
pbs: 1500m: 3:38.57 '82, 2000m: 5:06.18 '81, 3000m: 7:46.5i '82, Mar: 2:17:20 '80. Also GDR records at 15km: 43:50.2, 20km: 58:30.2, 1 hour: 20,536m in 1983.

Thomas SCHONLEBE
b.6 Aug 1965 Frauenstein 1.85m 72kg
Club: SC Karl-Marx-Stadt. Student.
Ch. record at 400m: WCh: '83– 6; EJ: '83– 1 (1R), ECp: '83– 2; WIG: '85– 1. GDR champion 1983–4. Set three European Junior 400m records 1983–4 and world indoor best of 45.60 in 1985.
Progression at 400m: 1981 – 47.50, 1982 – 46.71, 1983 – 45.29, 1984 – 45.01
pb 200m: 21.19 '83

Thomas SCHRODER
b.23 Aug 1962 Waren 1.78m 75kg
Club: SC Neubrandenburg. Law student.
Ch. record at 100m (200m, R – 4x100m relay): WCh: '83– sf (4R); ECh: '82– sf; EJ: '79– 1 (2), '81– 1 (1, 2R). GDR 100m champion 1983–4. Set world indoor best for 100 yards at 9.50 twice in 1984.
Progression at 100m: 1977 – 11.15/10.9, 1978 – 10.89, 1979 – 10.41, 1980 – 10.42, 1981 – 10.35/10.14w, 1982 – 10.39/10.38w, 1983 – 10.22, 1984 – 10.27
pb 200m: 20.56 '84

Jürgen SCHULT
b.11 May 1960 Neuhaus, Krs. Hagenow 1.93m 110kg
Club: SC Traktor Schwerin. Machine fitter.
Ch. record at DT: WCh: '83– 5; EJ: '79– 1; ECp: '83– 1. GDR champion 1983–4.
Progression at DT: 1978 – 51.82, 1979 – 57.22, 1980 – 61.26, 1981 – 61.56, 1982 – 63.18, 1983 – 66.78, 1984 – 68.82.
pb SP: 18.59 '84.

Ulf TIMMERMANN
b.1 Nov 1962 Berlin 1.94m 118kg
Club: TSC Berlin. Mechanical engineering student.
Ch. record at SP: WCh: '83– 2; EJ: '81– 2 (9 at DT); ECp: '83– 2 European indoor shot best 1985.
Progression at SP: 1979 – 16.23, 1981 – 19.00, 1982 – 20.22, 1983 – 21.36, 1984 – 21.75, 1985 – 21.87i.
pb DT: 52.68 '81

Torsten VOSS
b.24 Mar 1963 Gustrow 1.86m 88kg
Club: SC Traktor Schwerin. Mechanic.
Ch. record at Dec: WCh: '83– 7; ECh: '82– dnf; EJ: '81– 2. GDR champion 1982–3. Set world junior decathlon record in 1982.
Progression at Dec: 1977 – 5083, 1978 – 6325, 1979 – 7318,

1980 – 7571, 1981 – 8044, 1982 – 8387, 1983 – 8335, 1984 – 8535
pbs: 100m: 10.54 '84, 400m: 47.50 '84, 1500m: 4:17.00 '81, 110mh: 14.09 '84, HJ: 2.11 '81, PV: 5.10 '84, LJ: 8.02 '84, SP: 15.39 '84, DT: 44.74 '84, JT: 62.90 '82
Highly consistent with five scores in the range 8428–8535 in 1984.

Detlef WAGENKNECHT
b.3 Jan 1959 Berlin 1.93m 74kg
Club: SC Dynamo Berlin. Marketing student.
Ch. record at 800m: OG: '80– 6; WCh: '83– sf; ECh: '78– sf, '82– 6; EJ: '77– 2 (1 at 4x400mR); WCp: '81– 3; ECp: '83– 2. GDR 800m champion 1978, 1980, 1982–4.
Progression at 800m: 1974 – 1:57.5, 1975 – 1:51.6, 1976 – 1:50.0, 1977 – 1:47.4, 1978 – 1:45.84, 1979 – 1:46.5, 1980 – 1:45.89, 1981 – 1:44.81, 1982 – 1:45.02, 1983 – 1:45.13, 1984 – 1:45.44
pbs: 400m: 47.04 '80, 1000m: 2:16.7 '82, 1500m: 3:40.28 '82

Ronald WEIGEL
b.8 Aug 1959 Hildburghausen 1.76m 61kg
Club: ASK Vorwärts Potsdam. Student of journalism.
Ch. record: WCh: '83– 1 at 50kmW; EJ: '77– 2 at 10kmW. GDR champion at 20kmW 1984, 50kmW 1983. European 20km track walk record at 1:20:54.9 in 1983, and indoor best of 1:20:40 in 1980. Set world's fastest 50km road walk (3:38:31) and GDR road bests at 30km (2:12:41) and 35km (2:34:40) in 1984.
Progression at 20kmW/50kmw: 1975 – 1:40:56, 1976 – 1:30:49, 1977 – 1:27:51, 1978 – 1:27:00, 1979 – 1:25:00, 1980 – 1:20:40i/1:22:50, 1981 – 1:22:40/3:49:53, 1982 – 1:29:36/3:44:20, 1983 – 1:20:55/3:41:31, 1984 – 1:19:56/3:38:31.
Track pbs: 5kmW: 18:53.38 '84, 10kmW: 38:35.5i '80.
Unbeaten in 1984.

Gerd WESSIG
b.16 Jul 1959 Lubz 2.01m 84kg
Club: SC Traktor Schwerin. Cook/ gastronomic student.
Ch. record at HJ: OG: '80– 1. GDR champion 1980, 1984. Set world record at 2.36m to win 1980 Olympic high jump title.
Progression at HJ: 1976 – 2.06, 1977 – 2.13, 1978 – 2.19, 1979 – 2.23i, 1980 – 2.36, 1982 – 2.26, 1983 – 2.21, 1984 – 2.30
pbs Dec: 8015 '83, 100m: 10.77 '83, 110mh: 14.96 '83, PV: 4.60 '83, LJ: 7.24 '83, 7.31w '82, DT: 45.70 '83
Held back by complications following a foot operation after winning the 1980 Olympic high jump title.

Roland WIESER
b.6 May 1956 Zschopau 1.87m 71kg
Club: SC Dynamo Berlin. Vehicle mechanic.
Ch. record at 20kmW: OG: '80– 3; WCh: '83– 10; ECh: '78– 1, '82– 8; LT: '77– 7, '79– 9, '81– 2; EJ: '75– 1 at 10kmW. GDR champion at 20kmW and 50kmW 1978. For 10km track walk set world outdoor best at 38:54.3 in 1980, and European junior record at 41:46.8 in 1975.
Progression at 20kmW: 1973 – 1:33:24, 1974 – 1:30:15, 1975 – 1:31:12, 1976 – 1:27:28, 1977 – 1:26:41, 1978 – 1:23:12, 1979 – 1:21:22, 1980 – 1:22:18, 1981 – 1:22:12, 1982 – 1:24:21, 1983 – 1:22:43, 1984 – 1:22:33.
pb 50kmW: 4:07:40 '78.

WOMEN

Ingrid AUERSWALD
b.2 Sep 1957 Jena 1.68m 59kg née Brestrich. **Club:** SC Motor Jena. Sports student.
Ch. record at 100m (R – 4x100m relay): OG: '80– 3 (1R); WCh: '83– 1R; ECp: '77– 1R, '79– 1R, '83– 1R. Ran on six world record

National Championships

4x100m teams 1979-83.
Progression at 100m: 1975 – 11.9, 1976 – 11.71, 1977 – 11.29, 1978 – 11.36, 1979 – 11.28, 1980 – 11.08/10.93w, 1981 – 11.34, 1982 – 11.77, 1983 – 11.17, 1984 – 11.04.
pb 200m: 22.60 '80

Gisela BEYER
b.16 Jul 1960 Eisenhüttenstadt 1.80m 94kg (Reissmüller).
Club: ASK Vorwärts Potsdam. Shop assistant.
Ch. record at DT: OG: '80– 4; WCh: '83– 5; ECh: '82– 4; EJ: '77– 2. GDR champion 1983–4. GDR discus record at 73.10m in 1984.
Progression at DT: 1974 – 34.06, 1975 – 47.78, 1976 – 52.82, 1977 – 54.56, 1978 – 55.18, 1979 – 62.28, 1980 – 67.44, 1981 – 68.76, 1982 – 69.76, 1983 – 70.96, 1984 – 73.10.
pb SP: 18.02 '82
Sister of Udo Beyer (qv)

Andrea BIENIAS
b.11 Nov 1959 Leipzig 1.80m 68kg née Reichstein. Club: SC DHfK Leipzig. Sports student.
Ch. record at HJ: OG: '80– 6=; WCh: '83– 10=; ECh: '82– 6=; EI: '82– 2; EJ: '77– 6; ECp: '81– 5=. GDR champion 1981–2, '84. Set European indoor high jump best at 1.99m in 1982.
Progression at HJ: 1972 – 1.43, 1973 – 1.53, 1974 – 1.65, 1975 – 1.70i, 1976 – 1.83, 1977 – 1.90, 1978 – 1.85, 1979 – 1.86, 1980 – 1.94, 1981 – 1.95, 1982 – 1.99i, 1983 – 1.97, 1984 – 1.96

Ilona BRIESENICK
b.24 Sep 1956 Demmin 1.80m 94kg née Schoknecht, formerly Slupianek. Married to Hartmut Briesenick, European shot champion 1971 and 1974.
Club: SC Dynamo Berlin.
Ch. record at SP: OG: '76– 5, '80– 1; WCh: '83– 3; ECh: '78– 1, '82– 1; EI: '76– 3, '77– 2, '79– 1, '81– 1; WCp: '77– 1, '79– 1, '81– 1; ECp: '77– disq (1), '79– 1, '81– 1; EJ: '73– 1 (2 at DT). GDR shot champion 1977, '79–84. Seven GDR shot records, the last two world records, 22.36m and 22.45m in 1980. Set 11 world junior records 1973–4.
Progression at SP: 1970 – 12.50, 1971 – 13.32, 1972 – 14.40, 1973 – 17.05, 1974 – 19.23, 1975 – 20.12, 1976 – 21.30, 1977 – 21.79, 1978 – 22.06, 1979 – 22.04, 1980 – 22.45, 1981 – 21.61, 1982 – 21.80, 1983 – 22.40, 1984 – 21.85
pb DT: 64.40 '77
Suspended for a year for use of drugs at the 1977 European Cup Final.

Ulrike BRUNS
b.17 Nov 1953 Cottbus 1.70m 58kg née Klapezynski.
Club: ASK Vorwärts Potsdam. Medical student.
Ch. record at 1500m: OG: '76– 2, '80– 5; ECh: '74– 6, '78– 7 (7 at 800m), '82– 5; WCp: '77– 3 (4 at 3000m), '81– 3; ECp: '75– 2 at 800m, '77– 2, '81– 2, '83– 2 at 3000m; EI: '78– 1 at 800m. GDR champion: 1500m 1978, '82, '84; 3000m 1976, '81, '84 GDR records: 800m (1) in 1976, 1500m (1) 1976, 3000m (5) 1976–84.
Progression at 1500m/3000m: 1968 – 4:59.0, 1969 – 4:43.4, 1970 – 4:28.0, 1971 – 4:28.8, 1972 – 4:25.1, 1973 – 4:16.3, 1974 – 4:09.9, 1975 – 4:08.8, 1976 – 3:59.9/8:55.6, 1977 – 4:04.52/8:49.2, 1978 – 4:01.95, 1980 – 4:00.62, 1981 – 4:01.44/8:49.67, 1982 – 4:00.78/8:54.09, 1983 – 4:04.25/8:44.88, 1984 – 4:01.38/8:36.38
pbs: 400m: 54.77, 800m: 1:57.06 '76, 1000m: 2:31.95 '78, 10000m: 32:46.08 '84.
Long and distinguished career, has gradually moved up in distances run. Unbeaten in 1984. Gave birth to a daughter in 1979.

Sabine BUSCH
b.21 Nov 1962 Erfurt 1.77m 65kg

Club: SC Turbine Erfurt. Student.
Ch. record at 400m (R – 4x400m relay): WCh: '83– sf (1R); ECh: '82– 4 (1R); ECp: '83– 4. GDR champion 1983. Ran on 4x400m world record team 1984.
Progression at 400m: 1978 – 62.4, 1979 – 53.97, 1980 – 51.41/51.0, 1981 – 52.03, 1982 – 50.57, 1983 – 50.26, 1984 – 49.24
pbs: 100m: 11.80 '82, 200m: 22.83 '83

Katrin DORRE
b.6 Oct 1961 1.70m 55kg
Club: SC DHfK Leipzig. She has run six and won five marathons 1982–4, setting GDR records on each occasion. Won at Osaka and Tokyo in 1984.
Progression at Mar: 1982 – 2:43:19, 1983 – 2:37:41, 1984 – 2:26:52
pbs: 1500m: 4:32.6 '82, 3000m: 9:04.01 '84, 10000m: 33:00.0 '84

Heike DRECHSLER
b.16 Dec 1964 Gora 1.81m 70kg née Daute. Married Andreas Drechsler 28 July 1984.
Club: SC Motor Jena. Instrument maker.
Ch. record at LJ: WCh: '83– 1; ECh: '82– 4; EI: '83– 3; EJ: '81– 1; ECp: '83– 1. GDR champion 1981, 1983–4. Four GDR long jump records 1983–4. World indoor bests of 6.88m in 1983 and 6.99m in 1984 and 1985. World junior records in 1981 and 1982 and at heptathlon in 1981.
Progression at LJ: 1977 – 4.46, 1978 – 5.69, 1979 – 5.90, 1980 – 6.64/6.70w, 1981 – 6.91/7.01w, 1982 – 6.98, 1983 – 7.14/7.27w, 1984 – 7.40
pbs: 100m: 11.75 '81, 100mh: 14.12 '80, HJ: 1.80 '81, Hep: 5891 '81
The youngest gold medallist of the 1983 world championships. She recorded the best four long jump marks, has 31 jumps in all over 7 metres and was unbeaten in 1984.

Petra FELKE
b.30 Jul 1959 Saalfeld 1.72m 64kg
Club: SC Motor Jena. Sports student.
Ch. record at JT: WCh: '83– 9; ECh: '82– 7; EJ: '77– 2; WSG: '81– 1; WCp: '81– 2. GDR champion and record holder 1984.
Progression at JT: 1973 – 36.07, 1974 – 42.10, 1975 – 50.40, 1976 – 49.32, 1977 – 61.24, 1978 – 61.90, 1979 – 61.38, 1980 – 62.10, 1981 – 66.60, 1982 – 65.56, 1983 – 69.02, 1984 – 74.72
Had seven of the best ten javelin marks in the world in 1984.

Ellen FIELDER
b.10 Nov 1958 Demmin 1.74m 65kg née Neumann.
Club: SC Dynamo Berlin. Agricultural student.
Ch. record at 400mh: WCh: '80– 2, '83– 3; WCp: '81– 1; ECp: '81– 1, '83– 1. GDR 400mh champion 1981-3 and record in 1983.
Progression at 400mh: 1978 – 58.12, 1980 – 54.56, 1981 – 54.79, 1982 – 54.96, 1983 – 54.20, 1984 – 55.40
pbs: 200m: 23.58/23.44w '81, 400m: 52.13 '83, 100mh: 13.4 '75

Silke GLADISCH
b.20 Jun 1964 Stralsund 1.68m 59kg
Club: SC Empor Rostock. Student.
Ch. record at 100m (R – 4x100m relay): WCh: '83– sf (1R); ECp: '83– 1R; EJ: '81– 1R. At 60m: EI: '83– 2; WIG: '85– 1. Ran on world record 4x100m team 1983.
Progression at 100m: 1978 – 12.6, 1979 – 12.39, 1980 – 11.8, 1981 – 11.63, 1982 – 11.54/11.33w, 1983 – 11.03, 1984 – 11.10.
pb 200m: 22.70 '84

Marlies GOHR
b.21 Mar 1958 Gera 1.65m 55kg née Oelsner.

115

National Championships

Club: SC Motor Jena. Psychology student.
Ch. record at 100m: (R – 4x100m relay): OG: '76– 8 (1R), 80– 2 (1R); WCh: '83– 1 (1R); ECh: '78– 1 (3R, 2 at 200m), '82– 1 (1R); EJ: '75– 2 (1R); WSG: '79– 1; WCp: '77– 1, '79– 2 (2R), '81 – 3 (1R); ECp: '77, '79, '81, '83 – all 1 (1R). El 60m: 1st '77–9, '82–3. GDR champion – 100m: 1977–84, 200m: 1978, '81, '84. Set three world 100m records 1977–83, and ran on eight world 4x100m and one 4x200m world relay records. Set world indoor bests at 60m (7.12 in 1978 and 7.10 in 1980), 100y (10.41 1978, 10.35 1979, 10.29 in 1980 and 1983) and 100m (11.37 1977, 11.29 1979 and 11.16 in 1980). European junior 100m record 1976.
Progression at 100m/200m: 1971 – 12.8, 1972 – 12.1/24.8, 1973 – 11.8/24.5, 1974 – 11.6/11.81/24.3, 1975 – 11.54/11.42w/23.8, 1976 – 11.17/23.26, 1977 – 10.88/23.23, 1978 – 10.94/22.38, 1979 – 10.97/22.36, 1980 – 10.93/10.79w/22.45, 1981 – 11.09, 1982 – 10.88/22.78, 1983 – 10.81, 1984 – 10.84/21.74
Her outstanding sprinting career includes a record number of European Cup Final victories. The first woman to run a sub 11-second 100 metres, to the end of 1984 she had run a record 22 such times, including one mark with excess wind assistance. Lost to Evelyn Ashford's world record, but ran the next five fastest 100m races in the world in 1984.

Grit HAUPT
b.4 Jun 1966 1.80m 90kg
Club: SC Motor Jena. Child care student. Set world junior records at shot (two) and discus in 1984.
Progression at SP/DT: 1980 – 14.32/34.78, 1981 – 13.23/43.36, 1982 – 14.56/50.36, 1983 – 16.68/56.64, 1984 – 19.57/65.96

Bettina JAHN
b.3 Aug 1958 Karl-Marx-Stadt 1.70m 60kg née Gärtz.
Club: SC Karl-Marx-Stadt. Student of textiles industry.
Ch. record at 100mh: OG: '80– 7; WCh: '83– 1; ECh: '82– 4; ECp: '83– 1; El at 60mh: '82– 2, '83– 1. GDR champion 1982–3. Set world indoor best for 60mh at 7.75 in 1983. GDR 100mh record 1983.
Progression at 100mh: 1975 – 14.8, 1976 – 14.12, 1977 – 13.63/13.52w, 1979 – 13.43, 1980 – 12.67, 1981 – 13.16, 1982 – 12.55, 1983 – 12.42/12.35w, 1984 – 12.53.
pb 100m: 11.69 '82

Helma KNORSCHEIDT
b.31 Dec 1956 Nauendorf 1.76m 90kg
Club: SC Chemie Halle. Language student.
Ch. record at SP: WCh: '83– 2; ECh: '82– 6; El: '81– 3, '83– 2; WSG: '77– 3, '79– 2; ECp: '83– 2
Progression at SP: 1971 – 11.81, 1972 – 13.25, 1973 – 15.18, 1974 – 16.96, 1975 – 18.58, 1976 – 18.78, 1977 – 20.24, 1978 – 20.99, 1979 – 20.63, 1980 – 20.46, 1981 – 21.01, 1982 – 21.12, 1983 – 20.70, 1984 – 21.19

Marita KOCH
b.18 Feb 1957 Wismar 1.71m 64kg
Club: SC Empor Rostock. Student of pediatric medicine.
Ch. record at 400m (R = 4 x 400m relay): OG: '76– sf, '80– 1 (2R); ECh: '78– 1 (1R), '82– 1 (1R); El: '77– 1; EJ: '75– 2 (1R); WCp: '77– 2 (1R), '79– 1 (1R), '81– 2 (1R); ECp: '77– 1 (1R), '79– 1 (1R), '81– 1 (1R), '83– 2R. WCh '83: 1 at 200m, 4x100mR, 4x400mR, 2 at 100m. At 200m: El: '83– 1; WSG: '79– 1, WCp: '79– 2; ECp: '83– 2; WIG: '85– 1. At 50m/60m: El: '79– 2, '81– 3. GDR champion at 200m 1979, '82–3; at 400m 1977–8, '80– 1, '84. 15 world records: 4 at 200m (1978–84), 6 at 400m (1978–82), 2 at 4x100mR (1979 and 1983), 1 at 4x200mR (1980), 2 at 4x400mR (1982 and 1984). World indoor bests at 50m (6.11 in 1980), 60m (7.08 in 1983), 100m (11.15 in 1980), 200m (22.39 in 1983), 400m (51.80, 51.57 and 51.14 in 1977).
Progression at 200m/400m: 1972 – 25.5/60.3, 1973 – 24.5, 1974 – 24.2/55.5, 1975 – 23.92/23.7/51.60, 1976 – 22.0/50.19, 1977 – 22.38/49.53, 1978 – 22.06/48.94, 1979 – 21.71/48.60, 1980 – 22.34/48.88, 1981 – 49.27, 1982 – 21.76/48.16, 1983 – 21.82, 1984 – 21.71/48.16.
pb 100m: 10.83 '83.
A career of unparallelled brilliance has brought her every major honour. She was only the second woman to break 50 seconds for 400m and to the end of 1984 had run 30 sub-50 sec. times. She lost in the 1977 World Cup to Irena Szewinska, but since then has been beaten at the distance only twice – by Jarmila Kratochvilova in 1981 and by Bärbel Wöckel in 1982. Her record at the shorter sprints is markedly less tremendous. Ran 47.70 anchor leg for world record 4 x 400m in 1984. Unbeaten at 200m and 400m in 1984.

Hildegard KORNER
b.20 Dec 1959 Urnshausen 1.70m 54kg née Ulrich.
Club: SC Turbine Erfurt. Sports student.
Ch. record at 800m: OG: '80– 5; ECh: '78– 5, '82– 5; EJ: '75– 1 at 4x400mR, '77– 2; El: '81– 1. GDR champion 1980 and 1984. Set world junior best for 1000m at 2:36.8 in 1977.
Progression at 800m: 1972 – 2:26.4, 1973 – 2:16.3, 1974 – 2:09.4, 1975 – 2:04.3, 1976 – 2:04.7, 1977 – 2:01.9, 1978 – 1:57.45, 1979 – 1:58.8, 1980 – 1:57.20, 1981 – 1:57.56, 1982 – 1:58.19, 1984 – 1:57.77
pbs: 400m: 54.15 '79, 1000m: 2:34.8 '84, 1500m: 4:06.5 '80, 3000m: 9:36.2 '81, 400mh: 56.47 '78

Gloria KOVARIK
b.13 Jan 1964 1.72m 54kg
Club: SC Cottbus.
Ch. record at 100mh: EJ: '81– 2
Progression at 100mh: 1979 – 14.29, 1981 – 13.26, 1983 – 13.00, 1984 – 12.79
pbs: 100m: 11.60/11.46w '84, 200m: 24.34 '81

Heidi KRIEGER
b.20 Jul 1965 1.87m 100kg
Club: SC Dynamo Berlin
Ch. record at SP: El: '84– 3; EJ: '83– 1 (1 at DT)
Progression at SP: 1981 – 14.05, 1982 – 16.82, 1983 – 19.03i, 1984 – 20.51i/20.24.
pb DT: 61.98 '83

Irina MESZYNSKI
b.24 Mar 1962 Berlin 1.75m 97kg
Club: TSC Berlin. Law student.
Ch. record at DT: ECh: '82– 8; EJ: '79– 1. GDR champion 1982. Set world discus record in 1984 and two world junior records in 1980.
Progression at DT: 1975 – 44.12, 1976 – 45.00, 1977 – 48.48, 1978 – 50.54, 1979 – 62.42, 1980 – 64.86, 1981 – 67.38, 1982 – 71.40, 1984 – 73.36
pb SP: 17.33 '81
Her world discus record at the Friendship Games in 1984 followed a year out of competition when she had a knee operation.

Ines MULLER
b.2 Jan 1959 Grimmen 1.82m 94kg née Reichenbach.
Club: SC Empor Rostock. Sports student.
Ch. record at SP: OG: '80– 8; WIG: '85– 2. At DT: EJ: '77– 1.
Progression at SP: 1975 – 13.03, 1976 – 13.07, 1977 – 17.30, 1978 – 18.24, 1979 – 20.81, 1980 – 21.00, 1981 – 21.14, 1982 – 20.93, 1983 – 20.54, 1984 – 21.32
pb DT: 65.04 '82

National Championships

Dagmar NEUBAUER
b.3 Jun 1962 Suhl 1.72m 58kg née Rübsam.
Club: SC Turbine Erfurt. Student.
Ch. record at 400m (R – 4x400m relay): WCh: '83– 7 (1R); ECh: '82– 6 (1R); EI: '82– 2; EJ: '79– 1 (1R); WCp: '81– 1R; ECp: '81– 1R. GDR champion 1982. Ran on two world record 4x400m teams, 1982 and 1984.
Progression at 400m: 1977 – 58.6, 1979 – 51.55, 1980 – 51.01, 1981 – 50.98, 1982 – 50.52, 1983 – 50.48, 1984 – 49.58
pbs: 100m: 11.73 '80, 200m: 22.87 '84, 800m: 1:58.36 '84

Ramona NEUBERT
b.26 Jul 1958 Pirna 1.74m 65kg née Göhler.
Club: SC Einheit Dresden. Student.
Ch. record at Pen/Hep: OG: '80– 4; WCh: '83– 1; ECh: '78– 8, '82– 1; ECp: '79– 3, '81– 1, '83– 1. GDR champion at heptathlon 1981, long jump 1982. Has set four world heptathlon records: 6621 and 6716 in 1981, 6772 in 1982 and 6836 in 1983.
Progression at LJ/Pen (p) or Hep: 1973 – 5.55/3538p, 1974 – 5.93/3808p, 1975 – 6.20/4166p, 1976 – 6.42/4299p, 1977 – 6.30/4295p, 1978 – 6.59/4565p, 1979 – 6.73/4602p, 1980 – 6.72/6.83w/4718p, 1981 – 6.90/7.00w/6716, 1982 – 6.88/6772, 1983 – 6.79/6836, 1984 – 6.71/6740
pbs: 100m: 11.5 '81, 200m: 23.14 '82, 400m: 53.41i '82, 800m: 2:04.73 '84, 100mh: 13.13 '83, HJ: 1.86 '81, SP: 15.44 '82, JT: 49.94 '83

Martina OPITZ
b.12 Dec 1960 Leipzig 1.78m 85kg
Club: SC DHfK Leipzig. Sociology student.
Ch. record at DT: WCh: '83– 1; ECh: '83– 1 Held GDR discus record for a week in 1984.
Progression at DT: 1974 – 34.67, 1975 – 41.42, 1976 – 44.92, 1977 – 55.00, 1978 – 57.82, 1979 – 64.50, 1980 – 64.32, 1981 – 52.12, 1982 – 64.32, 1983 – 70.26, 1984 – 72.32.
pb SP: 17.10 '78
After little progress for some years came through strongly to become world champion in 1983.

Cornelia OSCHKENAT
b.29 Oct 1961 Neubrandenburg 1.78m 65kg née Riefstahl. Married Andreas Oschkenat (2nd EJ 110mh 1981, pb 13.50 '83) in 1984.
Club: SC Dynamo Berlin. Agricultural student.
Ch. record at 100mh: WCh: '83– 7; ECh: '82– h. GDR champion 1984.
Progression at 100mh: 1978 – 14.36, 1979 – 14.36, 1980 – 13.78/13.73w, 1981 – 13.25/13.09w, 1982 – 12.90, 1983 – 12.72, 1984 – 12.57
pbs: 100m: 11.34/11.10w '84, 200m: 23.15 '84

Sabine PAETZ
b.16 Oct 1957 Dobeln 1.74m 67kg née Mobius.
Club: DHfK Leipzig. Sports student.
Ch. record at Pen/Hep: WCh: '83– 2; ECh: '82– 2; ECp: '79– 4, '81– 4 GDR pentathlon record 1979, world heptathlon record 1984. Set world indoor pentathlon best, 4862 points in 1984.
Progression at 100mh/pentathlon (p) – heptathlon: 1972 – 14.8, 1973 – 14.5, 1974 – 14.1, 1975 – 14.4, 1976 – 13.9, 1977 – 13.50, 1978 – 13.40/4154p, 1979 – 13.41/4619p, 1980 – 13.21/4627p, 1981 – 13.36/6210, 1982 – 12.83/6594, 1983 – 13.06/6662, 1984 – 12.54/6867
pbs: 100m: 11.46 '84, 200m: 23.23w/23.37 '84, 800m: 2:07.03 '84, HJ: 1.83 '82, LJ: 7.12 '84, SP: 16.16 '84, JT: 44.62 '84
In 1984 emerged from status as perennial runner-up to Neubert with world indoor pentathlon best (4862), a world record for the heptathlon (including record first day score of 4001) and individual

event success at 100m hurdles with wins in the Friendship Games and 8-nations meeting. Ranks in world all-time top ten at 100m hurdles and long jump.

Petra PFAFF
b.16 Oct 1960 Hoyerswerda 1.72m 58kg
Club: SC Cottbus. Sports student.
Ch. record at 400mh: WCh: '80– 3, '83– 4; ECh: '82– 2. GDR champion 1980.
Progression at 400mh: 1978 – 59.56, 1979 – 56.46, 1980 – 55.60, 1981 – 55.54, 1982 – 56.21, 1983 – 54.64, 1984 – 55.63.
pbs: 200m: 23.11 '84, 400m: 52.1i '84

Margitta PUFE
b.10 Sep 1952 Gera 1.80m 90kg née Ludewig, then Droese.
Club: SC Motor Jena.
Ch. record at SP (DT): OG: '76 – 6, '80– 3 (5); ECh: '78– 3 (2); EI: '78– 2; EJ: '70– 3 (6). GDR champion 1978.
Progression at SP: 1966 – 10.61, 1967 – 12.30, 1968 – 13.55, 1969 – 14.78, 1970 – 16.01, 1971 – 16.08, 1973 – 16.40, 1974 – 17.30, 1975 – 19.71, 1976 – 21.23, 1977 – 21.29, 1978 – 21.58, 1979 – 21.45, 1980 – 21.22, 1981 – 21.08, 1982 – 20.77, 1984 – 21.01.
pb DT: 68.64 '79.

Helga RADTKE
b.16 May 1962 Sanitz 1.71m 65kg
Club: SC Empor Rostock. Student.
Ch. record at LJ: WCh: '83– 12; EI: '83– 2; EJ: '79– 1; WIG: '85– 1
Progression at LJ: 1977 – 5.68, 1978 – 5.74, 1979 – 6.63, 1980 – 6.71, 1982 – 6.83, 1983 – 6.83, 1984 – 7.21.
pbs: 100mh: 14.67 '79, HJ: 1.75 '82

Sybille THIELE
b.6 Mar 1965 1.78m 72kg
Club: SC Dynamo Berlin
Ch. record at Hep: EJ: '83– 1; ECp: '83– 9. Set three world junior records for heptathlon in 1982-3.
Progression at Hep: 1980 – 5435, 1981 – 5800, 1982 – 6063, 1983 – 6421, 1984 – 6359
pbs: 200m: 24.07 '83, 800m: 2:14.47 '83, 100mh: 13.49 '83, HJ: 1.90 '83, LJ: 6.69 '84, SP: 14.63 '83, JT: 37.22 '84

Birgit UIBEL
b.30 Oct 1961 Belten 1.66m 54kg née Sonntag.
Club: SC Cottbus
Ch. record at 400mh: ECh: '82– 6; WSG: '81– 2. GDR champion 1984.
Progression at 400mh: 1978 – 59.36, 1980 – 57.75, 1981 – 55.90, 1982 – 55.70, 1983 – 56.03, 1984 – 54.68
pbs: 200m: 23.72 '84, 400m: 51.27i '84, 100mh: 14.21 '81

Anke VATER
b.5 Jun 1961 1.74m 63kg
Ch. record at Heptathlon: WCh: '83– 3; ECh: '82– 4; ECp: '81– 5; EJ: '79– 3 (Pen). GDR champion 1983.
Progression at Pen (p)/Hep: 1977 – 3648p, 1978 – 4114p, 1979 – 4321p, 1980 – 5890, 1981 – 6259, 1982 – 6389, 1983 – 6532, 1984 – 6722
pbs: 200m: 23.20w/23.26 '84, 800m: 2:03.76 '84, 100m: 13.30 '84, HJ: 1.86 '80, LJ: 6.84 '84, SP: 15.26 '82, JT: 38.70 '82

Gesine WALTHER
b.6 Oct 1962 Weissenfels 1.76m 65kg
Club: SC Turbine Erfurt. Student
Ch. record at 200m (R – 4x100m relay): ECh: '82– 4 (1R, 5 at 100m); EI: '82– 1; WCp: '81– 1R; ECp: '81– 1R. Ran on world

117

National Championships

record 4x400m team 1984. Set world indoor 200m best of 22.64 in 1982.
Progression at 200m/400m: 1978 – 25.01, 1979 – 24.9, 1980 – 22.55, 1981 – 22.42, 1982 – 22.24/51.10, 1984 – 22.32/50.03.
pb 100m: 11.13 '82, 10.97w '80

Bärbel WOCKEL
b.21 Mar 1955 Leipzig 1.74m 62kg née Eckert.
Club: SC Motor Jena. Student of education.
Ch. record at 200m (100m, R – 4x100m relay): OG: '76– 1 (1R), '80– 1 (1R); ECh: '74– 7 at 100m (1R), '82– 1 (2, 1R); EJ: '73– 1 (1 at 100mh, R); WCp: '77– 2, '81– 3 (1 at 4x100mR and 4x400mR); ECp: '77– 3, '81– 1 (1 at both relays). GDR champion 1976-7, '80-1. Set three world records at 4x100m and one at 4x200m relay in 1980. GDR 200m record in 1976 and European junior records at 200m (twice) and 100mh in 1973.
Progression at 200m: 1970 – 25.3, 1971 – 24.9, 1972 – 24.2, 1973 – 22.85, 1976 – 22.37, 1977 – 22.66, 1978 – 23.30, 1979 – 23.12w, 1980 – 22.01, 1981 – 22.07/21.9, 1982 – 22.04/21.85w, 1983 – 22.42, 1984 – 21.85

pbs: 100m: 10.95 '82, 10.92w '80, 400m: 49.56 '82, 100mh: 13.50 '74, 13.14w/13.1 '73.

Katrin WUHN
b.19 Nov 1965 1.73m 57kg
Club: SC Chemie Halle.
Ch. record at 800m: EJ: '83– 1
Progression at 800m: 1982 – 2:08.4, 1983 – 2:00.18, 1984 – 1:57.86
pbs: 400m: 54.24 '83, 1000m: 2:35.4 '84, 1500m: 4:10.22 '84

Antje ZOLKAU
b.23 Jun 1963 Saalfeld 1.72m 69kg née Kempe.
Club: SC Motor Jena. Student.
Ch. record at JT: WCh: '83– 11; ECh: '82– 2; EJ: '81– 2; ECp: '83– 2. GDR javelin champion and record 1983.
Progression at JT: 1976 – 38.24, 1977 – 44.58, 1978 – 49.66, 1979 – 55.54, 1980 – 53.92, 1981 – 64.62, 1982 – 68.38, 1983 – 71.00, 1984 – 72.16

FEDERAL REPUBLIC OF GERMANY

Governing body: DLV – Deutscher Leichtathletik-Verband, Rheinstrasse 20a, 6100 Darmstadt. Founded in 1898.
National Championships
first held in 1891.
1984 champions: MEN
100m/200m: Ralf Lübke 10.42/20.87, 400m: Erwin Skamrahl 46.27, 800m: Axel Harries 1:46.87, 1500m: Uwe Becker 3:38.32, 5000m: Karl Fleschen 13:55.34, 10000m: Christoph Herle 28:41.83, Mar: Ralf Salzmann 2:14:25, 3000mSt: Torsten Tiller 8:36.32, 110mh: Peter Scholz 13.99, 400mh: Harald Schmid 48.92, HJ: Dietmar Mögenburg 2.26, PV: Günther Lohre 5.30, LJ: Joachim Busse 7.92, TJ: Ralf Jaros 16.81, SP: Karsten Stolz 19.73, DT: Alwin Wagner 65.28, HT: Karl-Hans Riehm 78.20, JT: Klaus Tafelmeier 90.10, Dec: (unfinished) Jens Schulze leading with 5797, 20kmW: Alfons Schwarz 1:26:00, 50kmW: Walter Schwoche 3:57:26
WOMEN 100m/200m: Heide-Elke Gaugel 11.26/23.02, 400m: Ute Thimm 51.35, 800m/1500m: Margrit Klinger 2:00.61/4:08.81, 3000m: Brigitte Kraus 8:58.71, 10000m: Charlotte Teske 33:29.76, Mar: Susanne Riermeier 2:38:13, 100mh: Ulrike Denk 13.12, 400mh: Marlies Harnes 57.99, HJ: Heike Redetzky 1.91, LJ: Anke Weigt 6.43, SP: Claudia Losch 19.67, DT: Ingra Manecke 63.08, JT: Ingrid Thyssen 65.00, Hep: Anke Köninger 5725, 5kmW: Ingrid Adam 24:12.1

Peter BOUSCHEN
b.16 May 1960 Düsseldorf 1.81m 78kg
Club: DJK LG Düsseldorf/Neuss. Student.
Ch. record at TJ: OG: '84– 5; WCh: '83– 9; EJ: '79– 5; ECp: '81– 6, '83– 1. GFR champion 1981, 1983. GFR triple jump record 1983.
Progression at TJ: 1976 – 12.67, 1977 – 14.20, 1978 – 14.97, 1979 – 16.06, 1980 – 15.99, 1981 – 16.97i, 1982 – 16.69, 1983 – 17.33, 1984 – 17.20.
pb LJ: 7.43 '84

Rolf DANNEBERG
b.1 Mar 1953 Hamburg 1.98m 112kg
Club: LG Wedel/Pinneberg. Teacher.
Ch. record at DT: OG: '84– 1; ECh: '82– dnq. GFR champion 1980.

Progression at DT: 1974 – 50.56, 1975 – 55.30, 1976 – 55.96, 1977 – 56.02, 1978 – 61.12, 1979 – 61.02, 1980 – 62.86, 1981 – 62.50, 1982 – 63.74, 1983 – 62.84, 1984 – 67.40
Caused major upset to win Olympic discus title.

Hans-Peter FERNER
b.6 Jun 1956 Neuburg 1.76m 72kg
Club: MTV Ingolstadt. Engineer.
Ch. record at 800m: OG: '84– sf; WCh: '83– 7; ECh: '78– sf, '82– 1; WSG: '79– 3
Progression at 800m: 1976 – 1:53.7, 1978 – 1:47.04, 1979 – 1:45.6, 1980 – 1:45.7, 1981 – 1:46.72, 1982 – 1:45.27, 1983 – 1:44.93, 1984 – 1:45.11
pbs: 400m: 46.98 '79, 1000m: 2:17.3 '81, 1500m: 3:47.32 '84
Scored surprise victory over Seb Coe to win 1982 European title.

Christian HAAS
b.22 Aug 1958 Nuremberg 1.81m 76kg
Club: LAC Quelle Fürth. Merchant.
Ch. record at 100m (R at 4x100m relay): OG: '84– sf; WCh: '83– 6; ECh: '82– sf (3R); ECp: '81– 6, '83– 5. At 60m: EI: '80– 2, '83– 2, '84– 1. GFR champion at 100m 1980–3, 2000m 1980. Set GFR 100m records in 1981 and 1983, and European indoor 60m best of 6.55 in 1980 and 1984.
Progression at 100m: 1976 – 11.0, 1977 – 10.90, 1978 – 10.79, 1979 – 10.45, 1980 – 10.25/10.12w, 1981 – 10.23, 1982 – 10.27, 1983 – 10.16, 1984 – 10.20
pbs: 200m: 20.46 '83; LJ: 7.38 '79
His father, Karl-Friedrich (in 1954 and 1958) and mother Maria (in 1954) both won European Championships medals. Karl-Friedrich Haas was also fourth in the 1956 Olympic 400m.

Christoph HERLE
b.19 Nov 1955 Königstein 1.83m 68kg
Club: LAC Quelle Fürth. Architect.
Ch. record at 10000m: OG: '84– 6 (sf 5000m); WCh: '83– 8; ECp: '83– 4. At 5000m: ECh: '78– 14, '82– 13. At 3000m – EI: '79– 2. GFR 10000m champion 1983–4. Set GFR marathon record in 1983.
Progression at 10000m: 1978 – 28:15.36, 1979 – 28:44.5, 1980 – 28:14.68, 1981 – 28:27.01, 1982 – 28:03.25, 1983 – 28:04.13, 1984 – 28:05.0

National Championships

Other pbs: 1500m: 3:40.17 '78, 2000m: 5:03.9 '80, 3000m: 7:45.44i '79, 5000m: 13:21.31 '83, Mar: 2:12:14 '83.

Jürgen HINGSEN
b.25 Jan 1958 Duisburg 2.00m 100kg
Club: LAV Bayer Uerdingen/Dormagen. Physical education student.
Ch. record at Dec: OG: '84– 2; WCh: '83– 2; ECh: '78– 13, '82– 2; WSG: '79– 2; ECp: '79– 10, '81– 2. GFR champion at decathlon 1982 and long jump 1983. Three decathlon world records: one each year 1982–3–4.
Progression at Dec: 1977 – 7524, 1978 – 7966, 1979 – 8240, 1980 – 8407, 1981 – 8168, 1982 – 8723, 1983 – 8779, 1984 – 8798
pbs: 100m: 10.70w '84/10.74 '82, 200m: 21.66 '82, 400m: 47.65 '82, 1500m: 4:12.3 '79, 110mh: 14.07/13.84w '84, 13.8w '83, HJ: 2.18 '78, PV: 5.10 '84, LJ: 8.04 '82, SP: 16.42 '83, DT: 50.82 '84, JT: 67.42 '83.
Great decathlete who is perennial runner-up to Daley Thompson, who has beaten him on all seven occasions on which they have met.

Patriz ILG
b.5 Dec 1957 Aalen-Oberalfingen 1.73m 63kg
Club: LAC Quelle Fürth. Physical education and crafts teacher.
Ch. record at 3000mSt: WCh: '83– 1; ECh: '78– 2, '82– 1; ECp: '81– 3. At 3000m: El: '82– 1; EJ: '75– 2. GFR steeplechase champion 1978, 1980–2.
Progression at 3000mSt: 1977 – 8:40.4, 1978 – 8:16.92, 1980 – 8:25.89, 1981 – 8:21.13, 1982 – 8:17.04, 1983 – 8:15.06, 1984 – 8:40.53.
pbs: 1500m: 3:40.53 '83, 3000m: 7:45.06 '78, 5000m: 13:24.4 '83, 10000m: 28:47.6 '78.
Injuries caused the World and European steeplechase champion to miss most of the 1984 season, as they had in 1979. A great finisher who has yet to run all out for fast times.

Guido KRATSCHMER
b.10 Jan 1953 Grossheubach 1.86m 94kg
Club: USC Mainz. Physical education teacher.
Ch. record at Dec: OG: '76– 2, '84– 4; WCh: '83– 9; ECh: '74– 3, '78– dnf, '82– 9; ECp: 75– 9, '77– 3, '79– 2, '81– 5, '83– 11. GFR champion at decathlon 1975–80, and 110m 1978. World decathlon record of 8649 in 1980, European record 8498 in 1978 and two more GFR records in 1976.
Progression at Dec: 1972 – 7550, 1973 – 7488, 1974 – 8129, 1975 – 8005, 1976 – 8411, 1977 – 8088, 1978 – 8498, 1979 – 8484, 1980 – 8649, 1981 – 8095, 1982 – 8215, 1983 – 8456, 1984 – 8420
pbs: 100m: 10.54/10.4w '79, 200m: 21.58 '84, 21.4 '81; 400m: 47.64 '78, 1500m: 4:21.3 '80, 110m: 13.85/13.6 '78, HJ: 2.03 '76, PV: 4.90 '84, LJ: 7.84 '78, SP: 16.67 '84, DT: 49.74 '78, JT: 69.40 '84

Ralf LUBKE
b.17 Jun 1965 Mulheim/Ruhr 1.92m 81kg
Club: LG Bayer Leverkusen. Student.
Ch. record at 200m: OG: '84– 5; ECj: '83– 2 (1 at 4 x 100m relay). GFR 100m and 200m champion 1984. Set world indoor bests for 200m at 20.98 and 20.77 in 1983, and 20.67 and 20.57 in 1984.
Progression at 200m: 1980 – 22.04, 1981 – 21.43, 1982 – 21.04, 1983 – 20.50, 1984 – 20.51. pb 100m: 10.42/10.40w '84

Dietmar MOGENBURG
b.15 Aug 1961 Leverkusen 2.01m 78kg
Club: ASV Köln. Architectural student.
Ch. record at HJ: OG: '84– 1; WCh: '83– 4; ECh: '82– 1; El: '80– 1, '81– 2=, '82– 1, '84– 1; EJ: '79– 1, '83– 3. GFR champion 1980–4. Has set six GFR high jump records, including a world, and world junior, record 2.35m in 1980 and two European records at 2.36m in 1983.
Progression at HJ: 1972 – 1.41, 1973 – 1.67, 1974 – 1.74, 1975 – 1.90, 1976 – 2.05, 1977 – 2.10, 1978 – 2.23, 1979 – 2.32, 1980 – 2.35, 1981 – 2.30, 1982 – 2.34i/2.30, 1983 – 2.32, 1984 – 2.36.
pb LJ: 7.76 '80.
A supreme competitor, who has made a habit of winning the important competitions, since his first major success when he won the 1979 European Cup Final high jump at the age of 17 in 1979.

Klaus PLOGHAUS
b.31 Jan 1956 Gelnhausen 1.86m 110kg
Club: Bayer Leverkusen. Physical education student.
Ch. record at HT: OG: '84– 3; WCh: '83– 6; ECh: '78– 12, '82– 8; EJ: '73– 4, '75– 2; WSG: '79– 1, '81– 1. GFR champion in 1982.
Progression at HT: 1973 – 59.72, 1974 – 65.40, 1975 – 69.30, 1976 – 71.62, 1977 – 71.88, 1978 – 73.14, 1979 – 76.76, 1980 – 77.60, 1981 – 80.56, 1982 – 77.44, 1983 – 80.04, 1984 – 79.36

Karl-Hans RIEHM
b.31 May 1951 Konz 1.87m 107kg
Club: TV Wattenscheid. Interior designer.
Ch. record at HT: OG: '76– 10, '76– 4, '84– 2; WCh: '83– 7; ECh: '78– 3; EJ: '70– 4; WCp: '77– 1, '79– 2, '81– 2; ECp: '75– 1, '77– 1, '79– 1, '81– 2, '83– 4. GFR hammer champion 1973, '75–81, '83–4. Set three world records at Rehlingen on 19 May 1975 – 76.70m, 77.56m and 78.50m, when he achieved the unique feat of having all six throws exceed the previous world record. Subsequently improved the GFR record twice more, in 1978 and 1980.
Progression at HT: 1968 – 57.01, 1969 – 60.38, 1970 – 64.51, 1971 – 70.23, 1972 – 73.92, 1973 – 73.98, 1974 – 71.10, 1975 – 78.50, 1976 – 78.52, 1977 – 77.60, 1978 – 80.32, 1979 – 78.66, 1980 – 80.80, 1981 – 78.72, 1982 – 79.48, 1983 – 80.26, 1984 – 79.44.

Harald SCHMID
b.29 Sep 1957 Hanau 1.87m 82kg
Club: TV Gelnhausen. Physical education student. Married to Elzbieta Rabsztyn (7th European 100mh for Poland).
Ch. record at 400mh (R = 4 x 400m relay): OG: '76– sf (3R), '84– 3; WCh: '83– 2 2R); ECh: '78– 1 (1R), '82– 1 (1R); WCp: '77– 3 (1R), '79– 2; ECp: '77– 2, '79– 1, '81– 2, 83– 1. At 400m: EJ: '75– 7 (2R); ECp: '79– 1 (1R). GFR champion at 400mh 1977-8, '80-4 and at 400m 1979. Four GFR 400m records, including European records at 47.85 in 1979, 47.48 in 1982. European junior record in 1976.
Progression at 400mh: 1974 – 54.9, 1975 – 51.8, 1976 – 49.81, 1977 – 48.85, 1978 – 48.43, 1979 – 47.85, 1980 – 48.05, 1981 – 48.64, 1982 – 47.48, 1983 – 48.49, 1984 – 47.69
pbs: 100m: 10.3 '78, 200m: 20.69 '80, 400m: 44.92 '79, 800m: 1:44.84 '79, 110mh: 14.7 '78.
He is the last man to have defeated Edwin Moses at 400mh (at the ISTAF meeting in 1977) and has been consistently number two in the world to Moses since then.

Erwin SKAMRAHL
b.8 Mar 1958 Oberg 1.78m 67kg
Club: SV Union Gross Ilsede. Policeman.
Ch. record at 400m (R at 4 x 400m relay): OG: '84– qf; WCh: '83– 4 (2R); ECh: '82– 1R. At 200m: ECh: '82– 4; El: '82– 1; ECp: '81– 3, '83– 3. GFR champion at 200m 1981–3, 400m 1980, 1982, 1984. European 400m record at 44.50 in 1983 and world indoor 200m best at 20.99 in 1982.
Progression at 400m: 1974 – 52.3, 1975 – 48.3, 1976 – 47.05, 1977 – 47.2, 1978 – 46.75, 1979 – 45.84, 1980 – 45.80, 1981 –

National Championships

45.3, 1982 – 45.09, 1983 – 44.50, 1984 – 45.74.
pbs: 100m: 10.47 '83, 200m: 20.44 '83, 20.25w '81

Klaus TAFELMEIER
b.12 Apr 1958 Singen 1.90m 87kg
Club: Bayer Leverkusen. Physical Education student.
Ch. record at JT: OG: '84– dnq; WCh: '83– 8; ECh: '82– 13; EJ: '75– 6, '77– 1; ECp: '81– 4, '83– 3. GFR champion 1982-4.
Progression at JT: 1974 – 62.46, 1975 – 77.82, 1976 – 82.12, 1977 – 84.14, 1978 – 86.00, 1979 – 89.78, 1980 – 88.34, 1981 – 88.48, 1982 – 87.30, 1983 – 91.44, 1984 – 90.10.
Many long throws, but he has failed to place well in major events since his European Junior win in 1977.

Carlo THRANHARDT
b.5 Jul 1957 Bad Lauchstädt 1.99m 85kg
Club: ASV Köln. Student of journalism.
Ch. record at HJ: OG: '84– 10; WCh: '83– 7; ECh: '78– 5; EI: '81– 2=, '83– 1, '84– 2=; WCp: '77– 4; ECp: '77– 5. Won AAA title 1980. Seven GFR high jump records 1977-84, including European records at 2.36m and 2.37m in 1984. Set world indoor best at 2.37m in 1984.
Progression at HJ: 1975 – 2.09, 1976 – 2.15, 1977 – 2.25, 1978 – 2.26i, 1979 – 2.30, 1980 – 2.31, 1981 – 2.28i, 1982 – 2.30, 1983 – 2.34, 1984 – 2.37

Alwin WAGNER
b.11 Aug 1950 Melsungen 1.96m 122kg
Club: USC Mainz. Policeman.
Ch. record at DT: OG: '84– 6; WCh: '83– 16; ECh: '78– 6, '82– 10; ECp: '79– 2, '81– 3, '83– 2. GFR champion 1981-4.
Progression at DT: 1967 – 42.00, 1970 – 50.28, 1971 – 56.00, 1972 – 58.40, 1973 – 60.14, 1974 – 60.96, 1975 – 60.10, 1976 – 61.88, 1977 – 66.52, 1978 – 64.40, 1979 – 63.74, 1980 – 66.30, 1981 – 65.58, 1982 – 67.10, 1983 – 65.40, 1984 – 66.58.
pb SP: 17.71 '74

Hartmut WEBER
b.17 Oct 1960 Kamen 1.86m 70kg
Club: VfL Kamen. Administrative clerk.
Ch. record at 400m (R = 4 x 400m relay): WCh: '83– 5 (2R); ECh: '82– 1 (1R); EJ: '79– 1 (1R); WCp: '81– 4 (2R); ECp: '79– 1R, '81– 1, '83– 1. GFR champion 1981, 1983. European indoor 400m best at 45.96 in 1981.
Progression at 400m: 1976 – 48.9, 1977 – 47.80, 1978 – 46.60, 1979 – 45.77, 1980 – 45.87, 1981 – 45.27, 1982 – 44.72, 1983 – 45.12, 1984 – 45.97i/45.99
pbs: 100m: 10.52 '82, 10.4 '81, 200m: 20.75 '82, 500m: 1:00.32 '83 (former world best), 400mh: 49.10 '82
Injuries spoiled 1984 season.

Siegfried WENTZ
b.7 Mar 1960 Röthenbach 1.92m 87kg
Club: USC Mainz. Medical student.
Ch. record at Dec: OG: '84– 3; WCh: '83– 3; ECh: '82– 20; EJ: '79– 1; ECp: '81– 4, '83– 3
Progression at Dec: 1977 – 6994, 1978 – 7541, 1979 – 7821, 1980 – 7902, 1981 – 8191, 1982 – 8313, 1983 – 8718, 1984 – 8482
pbs: 100m: 10.85w '84/10.89 '83, 400m: 47.38 '83, 1500m: 4:19.78 '82, 110mh: 13.94 '83, HJ: 2.09 '83, PV: 4.80 '83, LJ: 7.50 '83, SP: 15.87 '84, DT: 49.82 '83, JT: 75.08 '83

Thomas WESSINGHAGE
b.22 Feb 1952 Hagen 1.83m 69kg
Club: ASV Köln. Doctor of medicine.
Ch. record at 1500m: OG: '72–sf, '76– sf (sf at 800m); ECh: '74– 3, '78– 4; EI: 1st in '75, '80, '81, 2nd in '74, '76, '78, '79; EJ: '70– 8; WCp: '77– 2, '79– 1; ECp: '75– 1, '77– 2, '79– 2; WSG: '75– 1. At 5000m: WCh: '83– 6; ECh: '82– 1; ECp: '81– 5, '83– 1. GFR champion at 1500m 1975, '77–82 and 5000m 1982. GFR records at 1500m (5), 1 mile, 3000m, 5000m (2). Set European records at 1 mile: 3:53.10 in 1976 and 3:52.50 in 1978, and at 2000m in 1982.
Progression at 1500m/5000m: 1969 – 3:58.2, 1970 – 3:47.6, 1971 – 3:42.2, 1972 – 3:40.5, 1973 – 3:39.47, 1974 – 3:39.30, 1975 – 3:36.37, 1976 – 3:34.78, 1977 – 3:36.0, 1978 – 3:37.19/13:37.30, 1979 – 3:34.77/13:19.87, 1980 – 3:31.58/13:19.76, 1981 – 3:33.49/13:13.47, 1982 – 3:32.85/13:12.78, 1983 – 3:34.72/13:18.86, 1984 – 3:38.61/13:53.09
pbs: 800m: 1:46.56 '76, 1000m: 2:16.4 '77, 1 mile: 3:49.98 '83, 2000m: 4:52.20 '82, 3000m: 7:36.75 '81.
European 5000m champion had to miss 1984 Olympics through injury.

Willi WULBECK
b.18 Dec 1954 Oberhausen 1.86m 70kg
Club: TV Wattenscheid. Student.
Ch. record at 800m: OG: '76– 4; WCh: '83– 1; ECh: '74– 8, '82– 8; EJ: '73– 2; WCp: '77– 3, '79– 3; ECp: '77– 1, '79– 3, '81– 2, '83– 1. GFR champion at 800m for record ten successive years 1974-83. GFR records: two each at 800m, 1979 and 1983, and 1000m, 1977 and 1984.
Progression at 800m: 1970 – 2:01.9, 1971 – 1:54.3, 1972 – 1:52.64, 1973 – 1:47.57, 1974 – 1:46.31, 1975 – 1:45.44, 1976 – 1:45.26, 1977 – 1:45.46, 1978 – 1:45.12, 1979 – 1:44.66, 1980 – 1:44.96, 1981 – 1:44.96, 1982 – 1:45.34, 1983 – 1:43.65
pbs: 400m: 47.83 '78; 1000m: 2:14.53 '80; 1500m: 3:33.74 '80; 1 mile: 3:56.38 '79, 2000m: 5:04.86 '81; 3000m: 8:00.3 '79
The 1983 world champion had to miss the 1984 season because of injury.

WOMEN

Sabine BRAUN
b.19 Jun 1965 Essen 1.72m 60kg
Club: LAV Düsseldorf. High school student.
Ch. record at Hep: OG: '84– 6; EJ: '83– 2
Progression at Hep: 1982 – 5627, 1983 – 6273, 1984 – 6442
pbs: 200m: 23.88 '84, 800m: 2:09.46 '84, 100mh: 13.55 '83, HJ: 1.81 '83, LJ: 6.24 '83, SP: 13.09 '84, JT: 52.14 '84.

Gabriele BUSSMANN
b.8 Oct 1959 Haltern/Westfalia 1.70m 55kg
Club: SC Eintracht Hamm. Student of psychology.
Ch. record at 400m (R = 4 x 400m relay): OG: '84– sf (3R); WCh: '83– 4; ECh: '78– sf, '82– 7; EI: '82– 3; EJ: '77– 1 (1R); ECp: '81– 2, '83– 3. GFR 400m champion 1978, '80, '82-3. Five GFR 400m records 1981-3.
Progression at 400m: 1975 – 55.4, 1976 – 53.31, 1977 – 52.33, 1978 – 51.74, 1979 – 51.77, 1980 – 51.10, 1981 – 50.83, 1982 – 50.64, 1983 – 49.75, 1984 – 50.98
pbs: 100m: 11.65 '81, 11.4 '83; 200m: 23.15 '83; 800m: 1:59.39 '83

Sabine EVERTS
b.4 Mar 1961 Düsseldorf 1.69m 55kg
Club: LAV Düsseldorf, Student of physical education and philology.
Ch. record at Pen/Hep: OG: '84– 3; WCh: '83– 4; ECh: '82– 3; EJ: '79– 1; ECp: '79– 7, '81– 3. At LJ: ECh: '82– 6; EI: '82– 1; ECp: '83– 5 (and 5 at 400mh). GFR titles at Pen/Hep 1980-3 and LJ 1979-80, '82. Five GFR heptathlon records 1981-2.

National Championships

Progression at LJ/Pen (p) or Hep: 1974 – 5.26, 1975 – 5.38, 1976 – 6.20, 1977 – 6.28/4225p, 1978 – 6.21/4366p, 1979 – 6.57, 6.69w/4627p, 1980 – 6.64i/4657p, 1981 – 6.66/6357, 1982 – 6.77/6484, 1983 – 6.66/6398, 1984 – 6.77/6363
pbs: 100m: 11.81/11.72w '82, 11.5 '80; 200m: 23.43 '82; 400m: 52.35i '81; 800m: 2:06.17 '83; 100mh: 13.17 '82; 400mh: 56.70 '83; HJ: 1.89 '82; SP: 12.86 '81; JT: 38.70

Margrit KLINGER
b.22 Jun 1960 Hönebach/Hessen 1.65m 55kg
Club: TV Obersuhl. Administrative clerk.
Ch. record at 800m: OG: '84– 7; WCh: '83– 4; ECh: '82– 3; ECp: '81– 4, '83– 3. GFR champion at 800m 1980–82, 800m and 1500m 1984. GFR 800m record 1982.
Progression at 800m: 1973 – 2:16.9, 1974 – 2:15.1, 1975 – 2:13.1, 1976 – 2:11.3, 1977 – 2:06.7, 1978 – 2:02.6, 1979 – 1:59.48, 1980 – 1:59.20, 1981 – 1:59.54, 1982 – 1:57.22, 1983 – 1:58.01, 1984 – 2:00.00
pbs: 400m: 53.4 '80, 1000m: 2:34.94 '83, 1500m: 4:02.66 '83

Brigitte KRAUS
b.12 Aug 1956 Bensberg 1.80m 57kg
Club: ASV Köln. Draughtswoman.
Ch. record at 3000m: OG: '84– dnf; WCh: '83– 2; ECh: '82– 7; El '84– 1; ECp: '77– 5. At 1500m: OG: '76– sf; ECh: '78– sf; El: '76– 1, '78– 3, '82– 2, '83– 1; ECp: '79– 6, '81– 4. At 800m: ECp '75– 7. Has won a record 51 GFR junior and senior titles indoors and out. Senior outdoor titles: 800m 1976; 1500m 1976, '78–9, '81, '83; 3000m 1976–7, '79, '83–4. GFR records at 1000m (3 – 1976–9), 1500m (3 – 1976–8) and 3000m (5 – 1976–83). Set world indoor 1000m best of 2:34.8 in 1978.
Progression at 1500m/3000m: 1971 – 4:38.4, 1972 – 4:22.97, 1973 – 4:24.0, 1974 – 4:17.4, 1975 – 4:13.91, 1976 – 4:04.21/9:05.6, 1977 – 4:08.7/9:01.29, 1978 – 4:01.54/9:29.7, 1979 – 4:04.8/8:54.4, 1980 – 4:06.62/9:26.2, 1981 – 4:05.47/9:16.6, 1982 – 4:04.22i/8:44.43, 1983 – 4:02.42/8:35.11, 1984 – 4:06.00/8:40.90
pbs: 400m: 55.6 '78, 800m: 1:59.28 '83, 1000m: 2:33.44 '79, 1 mile: 4:25.93 '82

Claudia LOSCH
b.10 Jan 1960 Wanne-Eickel 1.81m 84kg
Club: LAC Quelle Fürth. Optician.
Ch. record at SP: OG: '84– 1; WCh: '83– 7; El: '84– 2; WSG: '83– 2. GFR champion 1982–4.
Progression at SP: 1975 – 12.58, 1976 – 13.14, 1977 – 13.71, 1978 – 14.14, 1979 – 15.00, 1980 – 15.85, 1981 – 15.50, 1982 – 18.51, 1983 – 20.08, 1984 – 20.55.
pb DT: 55.22 '83
Rapid progress to the status of top Western shot-putter.

Ingra MANECKE
b.31 Mar 1956 Göttingen 1.83m 80kg
Club: LAC Quelle Fürth. Medical student.
Ch. record at DT: OG: '84– 6; ECh: '78– 12, '82– 10; ECp: '77– 7, '79– 6, '81– 4. GFR champion eight successive years 1977–84. GFR discus record 1982.
Progression at DT: 1974 – 40.22, 1975 – 46.16, 1976 – 50.10, 1977 – 57.20, 1978 – 59.68, 1979 – 59.50, 1980 – 63.28, 1981 – 63.10, 1982 – 67.06, 1983 – 65.10, 1984 – 66.68

Ulrike MEYFARTH
b.4 May 1956 Frankfurt 1.88m 71kg
Club: LG Bayer Leverkusen. Physical Education student.
Ch. record at HJ: OG: '72– 1, '76– dnq, '84– 1; WCh: '83– 2; ECh: '71– dnq, '74– 7, '78– 5, '82– 1; El: '76– 2, '79– 3, '84– 1; EJ: '73– 2=; WSG: '79– 2; WCp: '81– 1; ECp: '75– 2, '81– 1, '83– 1. GFR champion 1973, '75, '79–83. Set world (and world junior) high jump record at 1.92m when she won the 1972 Olympic title in Munich at the age of 16 years 123 days, the youngest ever Olympic champion at an individual event. Regained world record 10 years and 4 days later when she won the 1982 European title in Athens. Set a third world record when she won the 1983 European Cup final. Set European indoor best at 1.99m in 1982. 16 GFR high jump records 1972–83.
Progression at HJ: 1969 – 1.57, 1970 – 1.68, 1971 – 1.80, 1972 – 1.92, 1973 – 1.83, 1974 – 1.85, 1975 – 1.92, 1976 – 1.90, 1977 – 1.83, 1978 – 1.95, 1979 – 1.93i, 1980 – 1.94, 1981 – 1.96, 1982 – 2.02, 1983 – 2.03, 1984 – 2.02
Announced her retirement at the end of the 1984 season, having sealed her career in triumph by regaining her Olympic title after the longest ever gap between gold medals. GFR Sportswoman of the Year 1982, 1983 and 1984.

Ute THIMM
b.10 Jul 1958 Bochum 1.66m 53kg. née Finger.
Club: ASV Köln. Student of sociology.
Ch. record at 400m (R = 4 x 400m relay): OG: '84– 6 (3R); WCh: '83– 6R (qf 200m); ECh: '82– 4R. GFR champion 1981, 1984.
Progression at 400m: 1977 – 55.4, 1980 – 54.6, 1981 – 52.32, 1982 – 51.47, 1983 – 50.78, 1984 – 50.37.
pbs: 100m: 11.52 '84, 200m: 22.95 '84

Ingrid THYSSEN
b.9 Jan 1956 Aachen. 1.70m 70kg
Club: LG Bayer Leverkusen. Physical education student.
Ch. record at JT: OG: '84– 6; WCh: '83– 14; ECh: '78– 7, '82– 9; WSG: '82– 4; ECp: '81– 3. GFR champion for seven successive years 1978–84. GFR javelin record 1982.
Progression at JT: 1970 – 35.50, 1971 – 39.66, 1972 – 46.08, 1973 – 49.38, 1974 – 51.90, 1975 – 55.72, 1976 – 60.00, 1977 – 57.14, 1978 – 60.42, 1979 – 60.40, 1980 – 64.04, 1981 – 65.56, 1982 – 68.10, 1983 – 65.80, 1984 – 66.12

National Championships

GREECE

Governing body: SEGAS – Hellenic Amateur Athletic Association, 137 Syngrou Avenue, Athens 404. Founded 1896.
National Championships first held in 1895.
1984 Champions: MEN
100m/200m: Theodoros Gatzios 10.69/21.36, 400m: Angelos Soultanis 48.23, 800m: Panayotis Stefanapoulos 1:51.62, 1500m/3000mSt: Fotios Kourtis 3:45.28/8:52.38, 5000m: Emmanouil; Hantzos 14:04.54, 1000m: Spiridoy Andripoulos 28:40.70, Mar: Mihail Koussis 2:16:40, 110mh: Yeorgios Tsiantas 14.53, 400mh: Yeorgios Vamkakas 51.16, HJ: Dimitrios Kattis 2.21, PV: Andreas Tsonis 5.00, LJ: Mihail Filandarakis 7.81w, TJ: Dimitrios Mihas 16.27, SP: Vassilios Manganas 17.12, DT: Koystantinos Yeorgakopoulos 58.72, HT: Panayotis Kremastiotis 69.74, JT: Antonios Papadimitriou 77.50, Dec: Ioannis Mavrikis 7364, 20kmW: Hristos Karayorgos 1:29:16.
WOMEN
100m/200m: Yeorgia Drakopoulou 12.43/25.71, 400m: Artemis Vassilikopoulou 56.11, 800m: Klaudia Tsakelidou 2:15.42, 1500m: Aspassia Potou 4:37.38, 3000m: Ekaterini Dori 9:58.18, Mar: Yeorgia Papanastassiou 2:58:25, 100mh: Hionati Kapeti 15.07, 400mh: Hrissanthi Giroussi 61.30, HJ: Niki Gavera 1.74, LJ: Sofia Mavromati 5.71, SP: Soultana Saroudi 16.85, DT: Vassiliki Panayotopoulou 46.68, JT: Anna Verouli 72.64, Hep: Despina Pakou 5065.

WOMEN

Sofia SAKORAFA
b.29 Apr 1957 Trilaka 1.77m 73kg Student. Married her coach Dimitrios Kostavelis in 1982.
Ch. record at JT: OG: '76– dnq, '80– dnq; ECh: '78– dnq, '82– 3; EJ: '75– 5. Set a world javelin record at 74.20m in 1982, having set her first Greek record in 1975.
Progression at JT: 1972 – 41.32, 1973 – 49.70, 1974 – 51.94, 1975 – 56.04, 1976 – 57.40, 1977 – 55.74, 1978 – 59.76, 1979 – 58.92, 1980 – 59.34, 1981 – 63.46, 1982 – 74.20, 1983 – 72.28.
pb SP: 14.60 '82.
Missed both World Championships and Olympic Games due to injuries.

Anna VEROULI
b.13 Nov 1956 Saloniki 1.66m 75kg Physical education teacher.
Ch. record at JT: OG: '84– dnq; WCh: '83– 3; ECh: '82– 1. Set her first Greek javelin record in 1981.
Progression at JT: 1971 – 34.90, 1972 – 40.96, 1973 – 45.50, 1974 – 48.94, 1975 – 50.22, 1976 – 54.24, 1977 – 49.94, 1978 – 48.42, 1979 – 53.62, 1980 – 57.70, 1981 – 61.86, 1982 – 70.02, 1983 – 70.90, 1984 – 72.70.
pb SP: 15.24 '82. There were emotional scenes in 1982 in her home-town of Athens, where she won the party ever gold medal by a Greek woman in the European Championships. She was disqualified at the 1984 Olympics for illegal drug use.

HUNGARY

Governing body: Magyar Atletikai Szovetség, 1143 Budapest, Dozsa Gyorgy utca 1–3. Founded 1897.
National Championships first held in 1896 (men), 1932 (women)
1984 Champions: MEN
100m/200m: Attila Kovacs 10.37/20.51w, 400m: Gusztáv Menczer 46.40, 800m: Zsolt Szabó 1:47.58, 1500m: Bucsuhazi 3:45.01, 5000m/3000mSt: Gabór Markó 14:00.15/8:33.09, 10000m: Jozsef Majer 29:09.50, Mar: Zoltan Kiss 2:15:04, 110mh: Gyorgy Bakos 13.80, 400mh: Jozsef Szalai 50.59, HJ: István Gibicsár 2.20, PV: Ferenc Salbert 5.50, LJ: Gyula Paloczi 8.22, TJ: Béla Bakosi 16.83, SP: Laszló Szabó 18.96, DT: Ferenc Tegla 60.92, HT: Imre Szitás 77.16, JT: András Temesi 81.74, Dec: Jozsef Hoffer 7611, 20kmW: Janos Szalas 1:26:00, 50kmW: Laszlo Sator 3:56:16
WOMEN
100m/100mh: Xénia Siska 12.11/13.22, 200m/400m: Ibolya Petrika 23.75w/52.60, 800m/1500m/3000m: Katalin Szalai 2:05.07/4:17.4/9:07.23, 10000m: Karolina Szabó 32:38.5, Mar: Antónia Ladányi 2:40:10, 400mh: Erika Szopori 58.21, HJ: Olga Juha 1.84, LJ: Klára Novobáczky 6.69, SP: Hajnal Voros-Herth 16.72, DT: Márta Kripli 60.94, JT: Katalin Hartai 58.74, 10kmW: Dana Vavracova (Cze) 49:15

Gyorgy BAKOS
b.6 Jul 1960 Zalaegerszeg 1.88m 77kg
Ch. record at 110mh: WCh: '83– 6; ECh: '82– sf; EI: '84– 2; EJ: '79– 2. Hungarian champion 1980, 1983–4. Seven Hungarian 110mh records 1981–4.

Progression at 110mh: 1979 – 14.21, 1980 – 14.12, 1981 – 13.77/13.5w, 1982 – 13.80, 1983 – 13.49, 1984 – 13.45
pbs: 100m: 10.69 '81, 200m: 21.21 '83, 400m: 48.11 '78, 400mh: 52.25 '79

Béla BAKOSI
b.18 Jun 1957 Kemecs 1.80m 67kg
Club: Nyiregyhaza Club.
Ch. record at TJ: WCh: '83– 7; OG: '80– 7; ECh: '78– 15, '82– 3; EI: '80– 1, '82– 1, '83– 3, '84– 3; WSG: '81– 5; WCp: '81– 5; ECp: '83– 3. Hungarian champion: TJ 1979–82 and 1984, LJ 1979. Three Hungarian triple jump records 1979–82.
Progression at TJ: 1975 – 15.25, 1976 – 15.74, 1977 – 16.04, 1978 – 16.45, 1979 – 16.90, 1980 – 16.88, 1981 – 17.13/17.21w, 1982 – 17.20/17.29w, 1983 – 17.13, 1984 – 17.15i.
pb LJ: 7.88 '79

László SZALMA
b.21 Oct 1957 Nagymaros 1.90m 80kg
Ch. record at LJ: OG: '80– 4; WCh: '83– 4; ECh: '78– dnq, '82– 11; EI: '78– 1, '83– 1; WSG: '81– 1; WCp: '81– 7. Hungarian champion 1978, 1980–3. Seven Hungarian long jump records 1977–84.
Progression at LJ: 1975 – 7.50, 1976 – 7.81, 1977 – 7.97, 1978 – 8.00i, 1979 – 7.82i, 1980 – 8.13/8.25w, 1981 – 8.12/8.23w, 1982 – 8.20, 1983 – 8.24, 1984 – 8.27.
pb 100m: 10.4 '80, 10.59 '82.

122

WOMEN
Xénia SISKA
b.3 Nov 1957 1.74m 57kg
Ch. record at 100mh: OG: '80– sf; WCh: '83– sf; ECh: '78– sf; EJ: '75– 3; ECp: '81– 7, '83– 7. At 60mh: WIG: '85– 1. Set nine Hungarian 100mh records 1978–84.

National Championships
Progression at 100mh: 1974 – 14.3, 1975 – 13.78, 1976 – 13.7, 1977 – 13.95, 1978 – 13.36/13.2, 1979 – 13.57/13.44w/13.3, 1980 – 13.17, 1981 – 13.50, 1982 – 13.37/13.05w, 1983 – 13.16, 1984 – 12.76
pbs: 100m: 11.88/11.85w/11.6 '78, 200m: 24.2 '78, 400mh: 59.83 '80, LJ: 6.10 '75.

ICELAND

Governing body: Frjalsiprottasamband Islands, P.O.Box 1099, Iprottamidstodinni Laugardal, Reykjavik. Founded in 1947.
National Championships first held in 1927
1984 Champions: MEN
100m/LJ: Stefansson 11.11/6.82, 200m: Gunnarsson 23.87, 400m/400mh: Adalsteinn Bernhardsson 48.48/55.8, 800m: Gunnar Joakimsson 1:56.66, 1500m: Magnus Haraldsson 4:05.26, 5000m/3kmSt: Hafstein Oskarsson 15:09.5/9:31.8, 110mh: Gisli Sigurdsson 15.03, HJ: Unnar Vilhjalmsson 2.07, PV: Kristjan Gissurarson 4.40, TJ: Fridrik Oskarsson 14.21, SP/DT/HT: Eggert Bogasson 16.53/54.02/51.50, JT: Unnar Vilhjalmsson 65.58
WOMEN
100m: Svanhildur Kristjansdottir 12.25, 200m: Oddny Arnadottir 25.31, 400m/800m: Unnur Stefansdottir 57.61/2:17.03, 1500m: Lilly Vidarsdottir 4:58.02, 100mh/400mh: Helga Hallsdottir 14.89/63.1, HJ/LJ: Bryndis Holm 1.70/5.81, SP: Soffia Gestsdottir 13.33, DT: Margret Oskarsdottir 39.46, JT: Birgitta Gudjonsdottir 41.94

Einar VILHJALMSSON
b.1.6.60 1.88m 97kg Student at University of Texas, USA – won NCAA JT 1983 and 1984.
Ch. record at JT: OG: '84– 6; WCh: '83– 13; ECh: '82– dnq; WSG: '83– 4. Icelandic record holder at javelin since 1980. Set US collegiate record 1984.
Progression at JT: 1980 – 76.76, 1981 – 81.22, 1982 – 80.74, 1983 – 90.66, 1984 – 92.42
His father, Vilhjalmur Einarsson, won Iceland's only Olympic medal when second in the 1956 triple jump.

INDIA

Governing body: Amateur Athletic Federation of India, Room N.0028, "A" Block, Jawaharlal Nehru Stadium, Lodi Road, New Delhi 110003. Founded 1946.
National Championships first held as Indian Games in 1924.
1984 Champions: MEN
100m: Adille Sumariwala 10.6, 200m: Amitabh Rai 21.9, 400m: Pavittar Singh 47.5, 800m/1500m: Bagicha Singh 1:51.0/3:51.0, 5000m: Raj Kumar 14:02.9, 10000m: V.K.Pokhriyal 30:09.4, 3000mSt: Gopal Saini 9:02.2, 110mh: Parveen Jolly 14.5, 400mh: Basant Singh 53.2, HJ: Nalluswami Annavi 2.10, PV: Sunder Singh Tanwar 4.45, LJ: Balwinder Singh 7.13, TJ: Subhash George 15.47, SP: Balwinder Singh 17.78, DT: Ajmer Singh 55.88, HT: Satnam Singh 56.92, JT: Gurtej Singh 72.84, Dec; P.K.Sharma 5954
WOMEN
100m/200m/400m: P.T.Usha 11.7/23.7/52.6, 800m: Shiny Abraham 2:04.9, 1500m/3000m: Suman Rawat 4:33.2/9:48.2, 100mh/400mh: M.D.Valsamma 14.3/58.9, HJ: Priyatha Menon 1.57, LJ: P.M.Rosely 5.54, SP/DT: Vijayamala Dutta 12.55/38.76, JT: Razia A.Sheikh 41.14, Hep: Reeth Abraham 4957

P.T.USHA
b.20 May 1964 Payyoli 1.70m 57kg
Ch.record at 400mh: OG: '84– 4. AsG: '82– 2 at 100m, 200m; AsCh: '83– 1 at 400m, 2 at 200m. Set three Commonwealth and four Asian 400mh records in 1984.
pbs (all are Indian records): 400mh: 55.42 '84; 100m: 11.4 '84, 11.95 '82; 200m: 23.0 '84; 400m: 52.6 '84.
Ran 57.8 in first ever 400mh in May 1984 and went on to attain greatest success of any Indian woman athlete. P.T. stands for Pilavullakandi Thekeparampil after names of her family-title and her house, as is the practice in her home state of Kerala.

123

National Championships

IRELAND

Governing body: BLE – Bord Luthchleas Na h'Eireann, 11 Prospect Road, Glasnevin, Dublin 9. Founded in 1967. Original Irish AAA founded in 1885.
National Championships first held in 1873.
1984 champions: MEN
100m/200m: Derek O'Connor 10.67/21.06, 400m: Gerry Delaney 46.92, 800m: Ian Marron 1:49.10, 1500m: Marcus O'Sullivan 3:43.91, 5000m: John Treacy 13:33.59, 10000m: John Woods 29:02.90, Mar: Dick Hooper 2:14:39, 3kmSt: Liam O'Brien, 110mh: Ciaran McDunphy 14.92, 400mh: John J.Barry 51.56, HJ: Richard Garvey 2.11, PV: Frank Evers 4.53, LJ: Hugo Duggan 6.81, TJ: Seamus Costelloe 14.41, SP: Paul Quirke 16.86, DT: Denis McSweeney 45.66, HT: Sean Egan 69.12, JT: Terry McHugh 68.82, 3kmW: Jimmy McDonald 13:25.95
WOMEN
100m: Michelle Walsh 11.98, 200m: Patricia Amond 23.88, 400m: Caroline O'Shea 54.41, 800m: Mary McKenna 2:06.01, 1500m: Roisin Smith 4:20.30, 3000m: Louise McGrillen 9:10.20, Mar: Christine Kennedy 2:49:46, 100mh: Olive Burke 14.28, 400mh: Mary Parr 58.74, HJ: Bridget Corrigan 1.77, LJ: Mary Coogan 5.83, SP: Marita Walton 16.15, DT: Patricia Walsh 57.60, JT: Kay McGovern 45.62, 3kmW: Mary Hennessy 15:58.9.

The winners in the national marathon championships races were Gerry Kiernan 2:14:30 and Deidre Nagel 2:48:26, but both were disqualified for wearing unacceptable advertising logos. In the men's 400 metres hurdles Barry's time was a new national record, breaking the previous record set by Robert Tisdall at 51.66, when he won the 1932 Olympic title in Los Angeles.

Eamonn COGHLAN
b.21 Nov 1952 Dublin 1.77m 63kg Graduate of Villanova University, USA.
Ch. record at 1500m: OG: '76– 4; ECh: '78– 2; EI: '79– 1. Won AAU '76, AAA '77. At 5000m: OG: '80– 4; WCh: '83– 1; ECh: '74– ht; WCp: '81– 1. Won AAA '79, '81. Won first Irish title at 800m in 1974. Won four NCAA 1500m/1 mile titles indoors and out in 1975–6. Irish record holder at 1500m, 1 mile, 2000m and 3000m. Set European 1 mile record in 1975. Indoors has set world bests at 1500m: 3:35.6 in 1981, and four times at 1 mile: 3:55.0 and 3:52.6 in 1979, 3:50.6 in 1981 and 3:49.78 in 1983. The latter made him the first sub 3:50 miler indoors.
Progression at 1500m/1 mile(M), 5000m (y = 3 miles): 1970 – 4:26.0M; 1971 – 4:19.0M, 14:28.0; 1972 – 4:10.0M, 13:58.0y; 1973 – 4:03.9iM, 13:45.0y; 1974 – 3:41.9/4:00.9i, 13:26.6y; 1975 – 3:43.9i/3:53.3, 13:35.0y; 1976 – 3:37.01/3:55.07; 1977 – 3:38.95/3:53.4; 1978 – 3:36.57/3:56.0i, 13:26.6; 1979 – 3:37.4, 3:52.45, 13:23.54; 1980 – 3:38.58/3:52.9, 13:20.99; 1981 – 3:35.6i/3:50.6i, 13:19.13; 1983 – 3:36.2/3:49.78i/3:51.59, 13:23.53; 1984 – 13:38.37. Missed 1982 season and much of 1984 through injury.
Other pbs: 800m: 1:47.8 '77, 1000m: 2:20.2 '77, 2000m: 4:57.66 '83, 3000m: 7:37.60 '80
After years of placing well in major races, but winning mainly indoors, he won the world 5000 metres championships in devastating style in 1983. Had a stress fracture of the tibia bone in his right leg early in 1984. Returned at end of year to place sixth in the TAC cross-country and was back at his best with a series of wins indoors in early 1985.

Ray FLYNN
b.22 Jan 1957 Longford Town 1.82m 65kg Now lives in Johnson City, Tennessee, USA. Graduate of East Tennessee State University.
Ch. record at 1500m: OG: '80– h; WCh: '83– sf; ECh: '78– h, '82– 8; EI: '80– 2. At 5000m: OG: '84– 11. Won AAA 5000m 1984.
Progression at 1500m/1 mile: 1976 – 3:41.5, 1977 – 3:40.9/3:55.3, 1978 – 3:37.66, 1979 – 3:38.61/3:55.7, 1980 – 3:37.59/3:55.7, 1981 – 3:36.38/3:52.95, 1982 – 3:33.5/3:49.77, 1983 – 3:37.03/3:51.20i, 1984 – 3:35.06/3:52.79. At 5000m: 1982 – 13:34.7, 1983 – 13:49.52, 1984 – 13:19.52
pbs: 800m: 1:48.30 '80, 1000m: 2:18.96 '81, 2000m: 4:59.40 '82, 3000m: 7:41.60 '84
Many fast times in recent years at 1500m and 1 mile, but did not win major races until 1984 when moved up to 3000m and 5000m.

John TREACY
b.4.6.57 Villierstown, Waterford 1.75m 59kg
Graduate of Providence University, USA
Ch. record at 5000m: OG: '80– 7; ECh: '78– 4; EJ: '75– 2. At 10000m: OG: '80– ht, '84– 10; WCh: '83– h; ECh: '78– 11. Won AAA 10km 1979. At marathon: OG: '84– 2. World cross-country champion 1978 and 1979 (13th 1984, 3rd Junior 1974 and 1975). Irish record holder at 5km and 10km and ran 2:09:56 for Olympic silver medal in first ever marathon.
Progression at 5000m/10000m: 1975 – 14:04.6, 1976 – 28:04.8 (6 miles), 1977 – 13:39.8/28:41.37, 1978 – 13:26.5/27:55.2, 1979 – 13:32.1/28:12.10, 1980 – 13:21.93/27:48.7, 1981 – 13:28.45/28:41.65, 1982 – 13:34.96i, 1983 – 13:35.02/28:35.58, 1984 – 13:16.81/28:01.3.
pbs: 1500m: 3:44.2 '79, 3000m: 7:45.22 '80.

National Championships

ITALY

Governing body: FIDAL (Federazione Italiana di Atletica Leggera, viale Tiziano 70–00196, Roma, Italy. Constituted 1926. First governing body formed 1896.
National Championships first held in 1906 (men), 1927 (women).
1984 champions: MEN
100m: Stefano Tilli 10.21, 200m: Pietro Mennea 20.35, 400m/800m: Donato Sabia 45.97/1:48.19, 1500m: Claudio Patrignani 3:45.43, 5000m: Stefano Mei 13:48.27, 10000m: Gianni De Madonna 28:55.67, 3kSt: Franco Boffi 8:35.51, Mar: Gianni Poli 2:11:05, 110mh: Daniele Fontecchio 13.75, 400mh: Stefano Bizzaglia 51.40, HJ: Paolo Borghi 2.21, PV: Mauro Barella 5.50, LJ: Claudio Cherubini 7.64, TJ: Dario Badenelli 16.25, SP: Alessandro Andrei 21.50, DT: Marco Bucci 64.04, HT: Lucio Serrani 74.72, JT: Agostino Ghessini 76.84, Dec: Moreno Martini 7502, 10kmW/20kmW: Maurizio Damilano 40:51.53/1:20:09, 50kmW: Raffaello Ducceschi 3:43:02 (short)
WOMEN
100m: Marisa Masullo 11.49, 200m: Carla Mercurio 23.83, 400m: Erica Rossi 53.65, 800m: Nicoletta Tozzi 2:08.39, 1500m: Gabriella Dorio 4:07.19, 3000m: Agnese Possamai 9:05.91, 10000m: Rita Marchisio 33:29.58, Mar: Paola Moro 2:33:00, 100mh: Laura Rosati 13.66, 400mh: Giuseppina Cirulli 58.23, HJ: Sandra Dini 1.80, LJ: Antonella Capriotti 6.17, SP: Assunta Chiumariello 16.00, DT: Renata Scaglia 51.14, JT: Fausta Quintavalla 62.68, Hep: Esmeralda Pecchio 5606, 5kmW: Giuliana Salce 23:45.58

Alessandro ANDREI
b.3 Jan 1959 Firenze 1.91m 118kg
Club: Fiamme Oro, Padova. Policeman.
Ch. record at SP: OG: '84– 1; WCh: '83– 7; ECh: '82– 10; EI: '84– 1; EJ: '77– 9; ECp: '83– 4; WCp: '81– 7. Italian champion 1983–4. Ten Italian shot records 1982–4.
Progression: 1976 – 15.32, 1977 – 17.46, 1978 – 17.32, 1979 – 18.41, 1980 – 19.58, 1981 – 19.92, 1982 – 20.35, 1983 – 20.19, 1984 – 21.50.
pb DT: 47.54 '79.

Salvatore ANTIBO
b.7 Feb 1962 1.70m 60kg
Club: Fiamme Oro. Policeman.
Ch. record at 10000m: OG: '84– 5; ECh: '82– 6. At 5000m: OG: '84– sf; WCh: '83– 13; ECh: '82– h; EJ: '81– 2.
Progression at 10000m: 1981 – 30:16.4, 1982 – 28:16.25, 1983 – 29:32.47, 1984 – 27:48.02.
pb 5000m: 13:31.84 '82.

Alessandro BELLUCCI
b.21 Feb 1955 Lanuvio, Roma 1.70m 55kg
Club: Fiamme Gialle. Accountant.
Ch. record at 50kmW: OG: '84– 3; WCh: '83– 7; ECh: '78– 7, '82– dq (also '74– 7 at 20kmW); LT: '81– 3
Progression at 50kmW: 1976 – 4:21:02, 1977 – 4:15:53, 1978 – 3:58:26, 1979 – 3:51:20, 1980 – 3:56:48, 1981 – 3:54:57, 1982 – 3:54:52, 1983 – 3:55:38, 1984 – 3:53:45.
pb 20kmW: 1:23:16 '82

Orlando BIANCHINI
b.4 Jun 1955 Montecelio di Guidonia 1.93m 130kg
Club: Fiamme Gialle. Accountant.

Ch. record at HT: OG: '84– 5; ECh: '78– dnq, '82– dnq; WSG: '83– 4. Set Italian hammer records at 75.84m in 1980 and 77.94m in 1984.
Progression at HT: 1973 – 56.94, 1974 – 62.48, 1975 – 67.68, 1976 – 72.14, 1977 – 70.26, 1978 – 73.44, 1979 – 75.00, 1980 – 77.02, 1981 – 72.56, 1982 – 75.44, 1983 – 76.88, 1984 – 77.94

Alberto COVA
b.1 Dec 1958 Inverigo, Como 1.76m 58kg
Club: Pro Patria Pierrel.
Ch. record: at 10km: OG: '84– 1; WCh: '83– 1; ECh: '82– 1; ECp: '83– 2. At 5km: ECh: '82– dq; ECp: '81– 6, '83– 2; EJ: '77– 6. At 3km: EI: '82– 2 World X-C: '82– 7, '83– 10, '84– 13. Five Italian championships: 5000m 1980, '82–3, 10000m 1981–2. Italian record at 5000m 1982.
Progression at 5km/10km: 1976 – 14:38.4, 1977 – 14:04.0, 1978 – 14:07.4, 1979 – 13:58.2, 1980 – 13:40.4/29:20.5, 1981 – 13:27.20/28:19.12, 1982 – 13:13.71/27:41.03, 1983 – 13:38.13/27:37.59, 1984 – 13:18.24/27:47.54
pbs: 800m: 1:53.2 '78, 1500m: 3:40.97 '83; 3000m: 7:46.40 '83, 3000mSt: 8:37.2 '80
Blistering finish has brought him the major 10km title in each of the last three years.

Maurizio DAMILANO
b.6 Apr 1957 Scarnafigi 1.83m 70kg
Club: Iveco Torino.
Ch. record at 20kmW: OG: '80– 1, '84– 3 (dnf 50kmW); WCh: '83– 2; ECh: '78– 6, '82– dq (dq 50kmW); WSG: '81– 1, '83– 2; LT: '77– 4, '81– 6, '83– 4. At 10kmW: EJ: '75– 4. At 3kmW: WIG: '85– 2. 10 Italian championships (5 each at 10kmW, 20kmW), 1978–84. Set three Italian records at 20kmW.
Progression at 20kmW: 1976 – 1:29:15, 1977 – 1:25:33, 1978 – 1:24:58, 1979 – 1:22:59.1t, 1980 – 1:21:47.8t, 1981 – 1:22:26, 1982 – 1:22:06, 1983 – 1:20:10, 1984 – 1:20:09.
pb 50kmW: 4:04:55 '83. Track pbs: 3kmW: 11:07.75 '81 (world outdoor best), 5kmW: 19:07.96i '84, 10kmW: 39:21.92 '81, 30kmW: 2:11:14.8 '83, 1 hour: 14932m '84.
When he won the 1980 Olympic 20km walk title, his twin brother Giorgio was 11th.

Raffaello DUCCESCHI
b.25 Feb 1962 Sesto San Giovanni 1.83m 65kg
Club: Fiamme Oro, Padova. Architectural student.
Ch. record at 50kmW: OG: '84– 5. Italian champion 1983 and 1984 (short course 3:43:02).
Progression at 50kmW: 1983 – 3:58:28, 1984 – 3:59:26
pbs: 10kmW (track): 42:27.4 '84, 20kmW: 1:27:26 '84.

Giovanni EVANGELISTI
b.11 Sep 1961 Rimini 1.79m 60kg
Club: P.P.Pierrel.
Ch. record at LJ: OG: '84– 3; WCh: '83– 19; ECh: '82– 6; EI: '82– 3; WCp: '81– 6; ECp: '81– 8, '83– 6; WIG: '85– 3. Italian champion 1981–2. Five Italian long jump records 1982–4.
Progression at LJ: 1976 – 5.40, 1977 – 6.10, 1978 – 6.68, 1979 – 7.30, 1980 – 7.84, 1981 – 7.94, 1982 – 8.10i/8.07/8.21w, 1983 – 8.09/8.11w, 1984 – 8.24
pbs: 100m: 10.4 '81, TJ: 16.30 '80

125

National Championships

Carlo MATTIOLI
b.23 Oct 1954 Pergola 1.78m 68kg
Club: GS Caribinieri. Soldier
Ch. record at 20kmW: OG: '84– 5; WCh: '83–18; ECh: '82– 6; LT: '83– 7; WSG: '81– 2. Set world indoor bests at 3kmW and 5kmW (twice) in 1980.
Progression at 20kmW: 1978 – 1:30:45, 1979: 1:24:56, 1980 – 1:24:53, 1981 – 1:23:54, 1982 – 1:22:34, 1983 – 1:21:11, 1984 – 1:22:07
Track pbs: 3kmW: 10:54.6i '80, 5kmW: 18:59.2i '80, 10kmW: 40:05.80 '84

Pietro MENNEA
b.28 Jun 1952 Barletta 1.78m 68kg
Club: Athletic Club Bergamo.
Ch. record at 200m: OG: '72– 3, '76– 4, '80– 1, '84– 7; WCh: '83– 3; ECh: '71– 6, '74– 1, '78– 1; EJ: '70– 5; WSG: '73– 1, '75– 1, '79– 1; WCp: '77– 2; ECp: '75– 1, '79– 2, '83– 2. At 400m: EI: '78– 1; OG: '80– 3 at 4x400mR; ECh: '82– 6 at 4x400mR. At 100m or 4x100m relay (= R): WCh: '83–2R; ECh: '71– 3R, '74– 2 (2R), '78– 1; WSG: '73– 3 (3R), '75– 1, '79– 1R; WCp: '77– 4; ECp: '75– 2, '77– 2, '79– 1, '83– 1R. Italian champion 100m (3): 1974, '78, '80; 200m (11): 1971–4, '76–8, '80, '83–4. Set World 200m record at 19.72 and European 100m at 10.01 in 1979 World Student Games. At 300m set world indoor best at 32.84 in 1978 and outdoor best 32.23 in 1979. Italian records: 6 at 100m, 8 at 200m 1971–9. 50 internationals.
Progression at 100m, 200m: 1969 – 10.8; 1970 – 10.5, 21.5; 1971 – 10.2, 20.88/20.5w; 1972 – 10.0, 20.30; 1973 – 10.2, 20.56; 1974 – 10.29, 20.53; 1975 – 10.0/10.20, 20.1/20.23; 1976 – 10.2/10.35, 20.1/20.23; 1977 – 10.25, 20.11; 1978 – 10.19/9.99w, 20.16; 1979 – 10.01, 19.72; 1980 – 10.19, 19.96; 1982 – 20.68; 1983 – 10.30, 20.22; 1984 – 10.28, 20.07.
pb 400m: 45.87 '77
Won ten major championships gold medals in a sprint career rivalled only by Don Quarrie. Retired after 1980 season, when he became the oldest man ever to win Olympic 200m title, but returned to top class three years later. In 1984 he became the first athlete ever to contest a track final at four Olympic Games. Retired again at the end of 1984 in protest against "the growing use of drugs by athletes".

Pier Francesco PAVONI
b.21 Feb 1963 Roma 1.82m 70kg
Club: P.P.Pierrel. Engineering student.
Ch. record at 100m: OG: '84– ht; WCh: '83– qf (2R); ECh: '82– 2; EJ: '81– 3; WCp: '81– 6; ECp: '81– 7. Italian champion 1982–3. Set European junior 100m record in 1982.
Progression at 100m: 1979 – 11.0, 1980 – 10.58, 1981 – 10.36/10.35w, 1982 – 10.25, 1983 – 10.24. Injured in 1984.
pb 200m: 20.49 '83

Donato SABIA
b.11 Sep 1963 Potenza 1.80m 70kg
Club: Athletic Club Bergamo. Policeman.
Ch. record at 800m: OG: '84– 5; WCh: '83– h; ECh: '82– h; EI: '84– 1; ECp: '83– 4. Italian champion 1983–4 (also won 400m on same day in 1984). World best for 500m at 1:00.08 and world indoor best for 600m at 1:15.77 in 1984.
Progression at 800m: 1979 – 1:58.0, 1980 – 1:50.6, 1981 – 1:49.19, 1982 – 1:47.29, 1983 – 1:46.62, 1984 – 1:43.88
pbs: 400m: 45.73 '84, 600m: 1:15.33 '84

Stefano TILLI
b.22 Aug 1962 Orvieto 1.75m 65kg
Club: Cus Roma. Student.
Ch. record (R– 4x100mR): OG: '84– sf at 100m & 200m (4R);

WCh: '83– 2R; ECp: '83– 1R; EI: '83– 1 at 60m. Italian 100m champion 1984.
Progression at 100m/200m: 1980 – 10.7, 1981 – 10.89/22.4, 1982 – 10.82, 1983 – 10.28/10.06w/20.54, 1984 – 10.16/20.40

Gian Paolo URLANDO
b.7 Jan 1945 Padova 1.78m 100kg
Club: Snia Milano. Instructor.
Ch. record at HT: OG: '76– dnq, '80– 7, '84– 4; WCh: '83– 13; ECh: '78– 8, '82– 11; WCp: '81– 3; ECp: '75– 8, '777– 5, '79– 4, '81– 4, '83– 6. US hammer champion 1980. Ten Italian titles and eight Italian records 1967–84.
Progression at HT: 1965 – 55.25, 1966 – 61.64, 1967 – 62.90, 1968 – 64.82, 1970 – 60.46, 1971 – 60.02, 1972 – 55.66, 1974 – 63.82, 1975 – 68.32, 1976 – 71.70, 1977 – 77.22, 1978 – 75.64, 1979 – 73.76, 1980 – 77.84, 1981 – 75.56, 1982 – 77.92, 1983 – 77.78, 1984 – 78.16.
pb SP: 15.50 '80.

WOMEN

Gabriella DORIO
b.27 Jun 1957 Veggiano 1.67m 55kg
Club: Iveco Torino. Physical Education instructor.
Ch. record at 1500m (800m in brackets): OG: '76– 6(sf), '80– 4(8), '84– 1(4); WCh: '83– 7; ECh: '74– 9, '78– 6(sf), '82– 3; EI: '82– –/1; EJ: '73– 8 at 800m, '75– 3; WSG: '79– 5(4), '81– 1(2), '83– 1; WCp: '81– 2(4); ECp: '79– 7. World cross-country: '75– 4, '76– 3. 17 Italian championships (7 at 800m, 10 at 1500m) 1973–84, 60 internationals. Italian records: 4 at 800m, 4 at 1500m, 1 at 1 mile, 1 at 3000m 1976–82.
Progression at 800m/1500m/3000m: 1972 – 2:10.8; 1973 – 2:05.9/4:27.6, 1974 – 2:07.5/4:12.1, 1975 – 2:04.5/4:07.27, 1976 – 2:01.63/4:07.27, 1977 – 2:05.5/4:10.84, 1978 – 2:00.43/4:01.25/9:13.3, 1979 – 2:00.8/4:06.03/9:05.4, 1980 – 1:57.66/3:59.82/8:49.96, 1981 – 1:58.82/4:03.27/8:48.65, 1982 – 1:59.13/3:58.65/9:30.22, 1983 – 2:00.05/4:02.43/9:04.96, 1984 – 1:59.05/4:01.96
pb 400m: 54.9 '80, 1000m: 2:33.18 '82, 1 mile: 4:23.29 '80

Laura FOGLI
b.5 Oct 1959 Commachio 1.68m 50kg
Club: Snia Milano. Housewife.
Ch. record at Mar: OG: '84– 9; WCh: '83– 6; ECh: '82– 2; ECp: '81– 5. New York marathon: 4th 1981–2, 3rd 1983–4. Won Rome marathon 1982.
Progression at Mar: 1981 – 2:34:48, 1982 – 2:33:01/2:31:08 short, 1983 – 2:31:49, 1984 – 2:29:28
pbs: 800m: 2:11.4 '79, 1500m – 4:19.8 '80, 3000m – 9:17.3 '78, 10000m: 33:39.04 '84
Very consistent racer, with three Italian bests 1981–4, although she has only won one of her ten marathons.

Giuliana SALCE
b.16 Jun 1955 Roma 1.69m 52kg
Club: Coop 2001 Roma. Third WIG 3000m 1985. World records at 5km walk in 1983 and 3km walk in 1984. Three world indoor bests: 3000mW – 13:08.09 and 12:56.70 in 1984, 5000m – 23:31.47 in 1983.
Progression at 3kmW/5kmW: 1979 – 25:55.1, 1980 – 14:12.5, 1981 – 14:45.0i, 1982 – 13:42.6/23:59.1, 1983 – 13:03.83/21:51.85, 1984 – 12:42.33/22:28.3
Track walk pbs: 1 mile: 6:53.2 '83, 10000m: 47:45.3 '83, 1 hour: 12456m '84.

Sara SIMEONI
b.19.4.53 Verona 1.78m 60kg
Club: Francesco Francia Bologna. Physical education instructor.
Ch. record at HJ: OG: '72– 6, '76– 2, '80– 1, '84– 2; WCh: '83– dnq; ECh: '71– 9, '74– 3, '78– 1, '82– 3; EI: '77– 1, '78– 1, '80– 1, '81– 1; EJ: '70– 5; WSG: '73– 3, '75– 2, '77– 1, '79– 3, '81– 1; WCp: '77– 2, '79– 2; ECp: '79– 2. 13 Italian HJ titles (1970–80, 1982–3). Set two world high jump records at 2.01m in 1978. Set 21 National Championships
Italian records, the most for any event, from her first at 1.71m in 1970. 62 internationals.
Progression at HJ: 1966 – 1.45, 1967 – 1.48, 1968 – 1.55, 1969 – 1.65, 1970 – 1.75, 1971 – 1.80, 1972 – 1.85, 1973 – 1.86, 1974 – 1.90, 1975 – 1.89, 1976 – 1.91, 1977 – 1.93, 1978 – 2.01, 1979 – 1.98, 1980 – 1.98, 1981 – 1.97i, 1982 – 1.98, 1983 – 1.93, 1984 – 2.00 – 1.97i, 1982 – 1.98, 1983 – 1.93, 1984 – 2.00

IVORY COAST

Governing body: Fédération Ivoirienne d'Athlétisme, Boulevard Lagunaire, BP 2844, Abidjan 10. Founded in 1960.

Gabriel TIACOH
b. 10 Sep 1963 1.80m 75kg Student at Washington State University, USA.
Ch. record at 400m: OG: '84– 2; WCh: '83– qf; AfCh: '84– 1. Won French 400m title 1984. Set African 400m record in 1984.
Progression at 400m: 1981 – 48.79, 1982 – 46.94, 1983 – 45.86, 1984 – 44.54
pb 200m: 20.71 '84
Won first ever Olympic medal for the Ivory Coast.

JAMAICA

Governing body: Jamaica Amateur Athletic Association, PO Box 272, Kingston 5. Founded 1932.
1984 Champions: MEN
100m: Ray Stewart 10.37, 200m: Gus Young 20.47, 400m: Bert Cameron 45.07, 800m: Owen Hamilton 1:47.93, 1500m: Gawain Guy 3:47.40, 5000m: Derrick Adamson 14:45.92, 10000m: Joseph Cross 31:13.58, 110mh: Andrew Parker 14.3, 400mh: Ken Gray 50.3, HJ: Desmond Morris 2.21, LJ: Steven Keys 7.48, TJ: Locksley Walters 15.30, SP/DT: Calvin Stamp 15.23/43.84
WOMEN
100m/200m: Grace Jackson 11.40/22.53, 400m: Cathy Rattray 52.90, 800m: Reva Knight 2:09.6, 1500m: Joy Bryson 4:48.2, 100mh: Sophia Hunter 13.92, 400mh: Overill Dwyer-Brown 59.57, HJ: Lindy McCurdy (Can) 1.73, LJ: Dorothy Scott 6.43, DT: Marlene Lewis 53.32

Bert CAMERON
b.16 Nov 1959 Spanish Town 1.88m 79kg
Graduate of University of Texas at El Paso.
Ch. record at 400m (R – 4x400m relay): OG: '80– qf, '84 – dns; WCh: '83– 1; CG: '78– qf (2R), '82– 1; PAm: '79– 4 (2R); WCp: '81– 3 (3R); CAmG: '82– 1. NCAA champion 1980–1, '83 (also indoors 1980–1). Set Commonwealth 400m record 1981.
Progression at 400m: 1978 – 47.20, 1979 – 45.97, 1980 – 45.23, 1981 – 44.58, 1982 – 44.69, 1983 – 44.62, 1984 – 45.07.
pb 200m: 20.74 '83
The World and Commonwealth champion produced a devastating burst of speed to qualify for the Olympic 400m final after pulling up with a suspected injury in his semi-final. Alas the inury was sustained and he could not run the final.

Ray STEWART
b.18 Mar 1965 1.78m 73kg
Ch. record at 100m (R – 4x100m relay): OG: '84– 6 (2R), WCh: '83– sf; PAm: '83– 5. Jamaican 100m champion 1984.
Progression at 100m: 1982 – 10.73, 1983 – 10.22, 1984 – 10.19
Promising sprinter, who was the youngest man in the 1984 Olympic 100m final.

WOMEN

Grace JACKSON
b.14 Jun 1961 St.Ann 1.78m 59kg
Club: Atoms Track Club, USA
Ch. record at 100m/200m (R – 4x100m relay): OG: '84– 5/5; WCh: '83: –/5; CG: '82– sf/7 (3R); WSG: '83– 6/3. CAmG: '78– 2 at HJ.
Progression at 100m, 200m: 1981 – 11.86/11.81w; 1982 – 11.68/11.45w, 22.92; 1983 – 11.27/11.22w, 22.46; 1984 – 11.24, 22.20.
pb 400m: 51.69 '83

Merlene OTTEY
b.10 May 1960 Jamaica 1.73m 59kg
Graduate of Nebraska University, USA. Married US high jumper Nat Page (2.28i '81 and 1979 NCAA champion) on 3 Feb 1984.
Ch. record at 100m/200m (R – 4x100m relay): OG: '80– –/3, '84– 3/3; WCh: '83– 4/2 (3R); CG: '82– 2/1 (3R); PAm: '79– –/3. Won NCAA 100m '82–3, 200m '83, TAC 100m '84, 200m '82 and '84. Has set four Commonwealth records at 200m and two at 100m, 1980–4. Holds world indoor bests for 300y (32.63 '82) and 300m (35.83 '81).
Progression at 100m, 200m: 1975 – ,25.9; 1976 – 12.0, 24.7; 1977 – 12.2, 25.1; 1978 – 12.6, 24.5; 1979 – 11.59/11.4, 23.10/22.79w, 1980 – 11.36/11.0, 22.20; 1981 – 11.07/10.94w, 22.35; 1982 – 11.03/10.97w, 22.17; 1983 – 11.07/10.98w, 22.19/22.11w, 1984 – 11.01, 22.09.
pb 400m: 51.12 '83
Graceful sprinter, who has been consistently in the medals in recent major championships.

127

National Championships

JAPAN

Governing body: Nippon Rikujo-Kyogi Renmei, 1–1–1, Jinnan, Shibuya-Ku, Tokyo 150. Founded 1911.
National Championships first held in 1914 (men), 1925 (women)
1984 Champions: MEN
100m: Kaoru Matsubara 10.28w, 200m/400m: Hiromi Kawasumi 21.31/47.52, 800m/1500m: Yutaka Hirai 1:49.35/3:48.11, 500m: Kenji Ide 14:07.94, 10000m: Masanari Shintaku 27:59.79, 3000mSt: Hajime Nagasato 8:45.83, 110mh: Masuhiko Mizuno 14.19, 400mh: Ryoichi Yoshida 49.75, HJ: Takao Sakamoto 2.21, PV: Takumi Takahashi 5.20, LJ: Junichi Usui 7.76, TJ: Kiyoshi Ueda 16.08, SP: Yoshiro Ito 16.93, DT: Yuji Takahashi 53.86, HT: Nobuyaki Ifuku 63.00, JT: Masami Yoshida 85.52, 20kmW: Tadahiro Kosaka 1:33:47.
WOMEN
100m: Emiko Konishi 11.97, 200m: Hiromi Isozaki 24.42, 400m: Junko Yoshida 55.54, 800m: Fumiko Arai 2:07.73, 1500m/3000m: Kazue Kojima 4:39.72/9:39.33, 10000m: Hisano Yokosuka 33:58.04, 100mh: Teruyo Yamazaki 13.83, 400mh: Yoko Sato 48.84, HJ: Hisayo Fukumitsu 1.90, LJ: Satomi Takase 6.19, SP: Miyuki Sasaki 14,92, DT: Ikuko Kitamori 52.22, JT: Emi Matsui 59.42.

Toshihiko SEKO
b.15 Jul 1956 Yokkaiichi City 1.70m 62kg Graduate of Waseda University, works for SB Foods.
Ch. record at Mar: OG: '84– 14. Won Fukuoka marathon 1978–80, 1983, Boston 1981, Tokyo 1983. Has run four Asian marathon bests 1979–83. World records for 25km, 1:13:55.8 and 30km, 1:29:18.8 in 1981. Asian record for 10,000 metres 1980.
Progression at Mar: 1977 – 2:15:01, 1978 – 2:10:21, 1979 – 2:10:12, 1980 – 2:09:45, 1981 – 2:09:26, 1983 – 2:08:38, 1984 – 2:14:13
pbs: 5000m: 13:30.94 '80, 10000m: 27:43.44 '80, 20km: 58:18.1 '83
Disappointed in Los Angeles after single-minded preparation and five successive marathon wins since 1979. In all has won six of his eleven marathons.

Shigeru and Takeshi SOH
Twins b.9 Jan 1953 Oita 1.78m 61/59kg
Ch. record at Mar: Shigeru – OG: '76– 20, '84– 17. Takeshi – OG: '84– 4.
Progression at Mar: Shigeru/Takeshi 1973 – 2:17:29/2:17:47, 1974 – 2:18:32/2:16:38, 1975 – 2:15:50/2:12:52, 1976 – 2:14:59/–, 1977 – –/2:17:35, 1978 – 2:09:56/2:12:49, 1979 – 2:10:37/2:10:40, 1980 – 2:10:23/2:09:49, 1981 – 2:10:19/2:11:29, 1983 – 2:09:11/2:08:55, 1984 – 2:14:38/2:10:55
pbs: Shigeru: 5000m: 13:40.8 '78, 10000m: 28:17.6 '78; Takeshi: 5000m: 13:42.3 '79, 10000m: 27:59.3 '78
Takeshi arrived five minutes before Shigeru. Shigeru has beaten Takeshi 11–9 in the twenty marathons they have contested together. Shigeru won the Tokyo marathon in February 1985 in 2:10:32.

Junichi USUI
b.5 Oct 1957 Miyagi 1.78m 70kg Graduate of Juntendo University.
Ch. record at LJ: OG: '84– 7; AsG: '78– 2; AsCh: '79– 1; WSG: '79– 2; WCp: '77– 6. Won AAA title 1982. Set Asian long jump record in 1979.
Progression at LJ: 1976 – 7.70, 1977 – 7.92, 1978 – 7.80, 1979 – 8.10, 1980 – 8.04, 1981 – 7.75, 1982 – 8.06, 1983 – 7.93, 1984 – 8.02/8.03w
pb 100m: 10.54 '79

KENYA

Governing body: Kenya Amateur Athletic Association, Gill House, Government Road, PO Box 46722, Nairobi. Founded 1951.
National Championships
1984 Champions: MEN
100m: Peter Wekesa 10.6, 200m: Kipkemboi 21.3, 400m: David Kitur 45.1, 800m: Juma Ndiwa 1:46.5, 1500m: Kipkoech Cheruiyot 3:43.6, 5000m: Paul Kipkoech 13:42.2, 10000m: Jackson Ruto 28:35.0, 3000mSt: Kiprotich Rono 8:29.4, 110mh: Philip Sang 14.2, 400mh: Meshak Munyoro 49.9, HJ: N.Rotich 2.05, PV: Japhet Kiplimo 4.00, LJ: Moses Kiyai 7.62, TJ: Solomon Kaptich 15.53, SP: Wesely Moso 14.72, DT: Joseph Onkware 45.85, HT: Cornelius Kemboi 49.04, JT: George Odera 74.72
WOMEN
100m/200m/400m: Ruth Waithera 11.6/23.5/53.3, 800m: Justina Chepchirchir 2:05.8, 1500m: Mary Chepkemboi 4:18.6, 3000m: Helen Kimaiyo 9:23.1, 100mh: Frida Kiptala 15.3, 400mh: Rose Tata 58.0, HJ: R.Chepkoech 1.58, LJ: Pemina Akama 5.57, SP: Herina Malit 11.29, DT: Phillis Macharia 36.68, JT: Milka Johnson 43.87

Sosthenes BITOK
b.23 Mar 1957 1.88m 68kg
Club: Roos., USA. Was at Richmond University.
Ch. record at 10000m: OG: '84– 7
Progression at 10000m: 1982 – 29:30.24, 1983 – 28:29.12, 1984 – 27:50.0
pbs: 1000m: 2:19.58i '83, 1500m: 3:39.06 '82, 1M: 3:56.1 '83, 3000m: 7:56.63 '83, 2M: 8:29.5 '82, 5000m: 13:29.02i '83

Charles CHERUIYOT
b.2 Dec 1964 1.63m 57kg
Ch. record at 5000m: OG: '84– 6. Kenyan champion at 3000mSt 1981, 5000m 1983. Set world junior record for 5000m and African junior record for 3000m in 1983.
Progression at 5000m: 1982 – 14:01.5, 1983 – 13:25.33, 1984 – 13:18.41
pbs: 800m: 1:50.4 '82, 1500m: 3:41.83 '83, 3000m: 7:47.47 '83, 10000m: 28:34.74 '84, 3000mSt: 8:51.6 '80
Twin brother Kipkoech Cheruiyot was the 1982 African 1500m champion and set the world junior record for 1500m at 3:34.92 in 1983.

128

National Championships

Joseph CHESHIRE
b.12 Nov 1957 1.70m 60kg
Ch. record at 1500m: OG: '84– 4; WIG: '85– 3.
Progression at 1500m: 1984 – 3:34.52.
pb 800m: 1:47.1 '84
Talented newcomer, who made his first mark with 2nd at 1500m and 4th at 800m in 1984 Kenyan Championships.

Julius KARIUKI
b.12 Apr 1961 1.81m 62kg Civil servant.
Ch. record at 3000mSt: OG: '84– 7
Progression at 3000mSt: 1981 – 9:34.5, 1984 – 8:17.47.
pbs: 1500m: 3:42.28 '84, 3000m: 7:52.87 '84
Made tremendous progress in 1984, his best recorded mark in 1983 was a 3:52.8 1500m!

Simeon KIGEN
b.1961 1.70m 63kg
Club: Team Nike, USA. Was at Mississippi State University.
Progression at Mar: 1983 – 2:10:52, 1984 – 2:10:18
pbs: 1500m: 3:43.68 '82, 5000m: 14:03.92 '81, 10000m: 27:57.68 '84, 3000m St: 8:35.93 '81.
Won San Francisco marathon 1984.

Paul KIPKOECH
b.6 Jan 1962 1.73m 58kg Soldier.
Ch. record at 5000m: OG: '84– 5; WCh: '83– 9; AfCh: '82– 4 (5 at 10000m). Kenyan champion at 10000m 1983 and 5000m 1984.
Progression at 5000m: 1982 – 13:51.03, 1983 – 13:25.08, 1984 – 13:14.40
pbs: 3000m: 7:46.18 '83, 10000m: 28:05.4 '84, 3000mSt: 8:56.4 '83

Edwin KOECH
b.23 Jul 1961 1.74m 64kg
Ch. record at 800m: OG: '84– 6
Progression at 800m: 1982 – 1:47.2, 1983 – 1:48.59, 1984 – 1:44.12
pbs 100m/200m/400m: 10.9/22.0/47.7 '80, 1500m: 3:49.8 '84.
Great new talent, second in 1984 Kenyan Championships. Showed front running abilities at the Olympics.'

Billy KONCHELLAH
b.20 Oct 1961 1.88m 74kg
Ch. record at 800m: OG: '84– 4. Set African junior record for 800m in 1980.
Progression at 800m: 1980 – 1:46.79, 1981 – 1:49.79, 1982 – 1:51.3, 1984 – 1:44.03.
pbs: 200m: 21.2/21.20w '80, 400m: 45.38 '79, 600m: 1:17.4 '82

Julius KORIR
b.21 Apr 1960 1.73m 62kg Student at Washington State University, USA – won NCAA 5000m '84.
Ch. record at 3000mSt: OG: '84– 1; WCh: '83– 7; CG: '82– 1;
AfCh: '82– 2. Kenyan steeplechase champion 1982.
Progression at 3000mSt: 1981 – 8:44.0, 1982 – 8:23.94, 1983 – 8:20.02, 1984 – 8:11.80.
pbs: 800m: 1:48.42 '84, 1500m: 3:40.31 '83, 3000m: 7:54.77 '83, 5000m: 13:38.7 '82
While his Commonwealth victory was a surprise, he confirmed his status with a clear Olympic win.

Sammy KOSKEI
b.14 May 1961 1.83m 66kg Was at Southern Methodist University, then North Texas University, USA.
Ch. record at 800m: WCh: '83– sf; CG: '82– 9; AfCh: '84– 1. Won NCAA '81. Set two African records at 800m 1984.
Progression at 800m: 1980 – 1:46.90, 1981 – 1:45.32, 1982 – 1:44.93, 1983 – 1:46.40, 1984 – 1:42.28
pbs: 1000m: 2:16.58 '83, 1500m: 3:40.83 '84, 1M: 3:56.79 '82
Missed out on Kenyan Olympic selection, but won African title and went on to run an African record for 800m.

Mike MUSYOKI
b.28 May 1956 1.68m 54kg
Ch. record at 10000m (5000m): OG: '84– 3; CG: '78– 2 (2); AfG: '78– 2 (2). Won NCAA 10000m '78 while at the University of Texas at El Paso. Set African junior 10000m record in 1975.
Progression at 5000m/10000m: 1975 – 29:05.2, 1976 – 13:35.0/28:40.0, 1977 – 13:35.08/27:41.92, 1978 – 13:24.89/28:05.2, 1979 – 13:54.6/28:03.35, 1980 – 13:51.1/28:20.5, 1981 – 13:38.5/28:34.43, 1982 – 28:13.86, 1983 – 13:56.55/28:06.7, 1984 – 27:46.0
Great success in US road running, including 42:27.55 world best for 15km in 1983.

Joseph NZAU
b.14 Apr 1950 1.73m 64kg
Ch. record: OG: '84: 15 at 10000m, 7 at marathon
Progression at marathon: 1982 – 2:11:40, 1983 – 2:09:45, 1984 – 2:10:40
pbs: 3000m: 8:00.1 '84, 5000m: 14:02.38 '81, 10000m: 28:06.63 '84, 3000mSt: 8:43.8 '79
Has achieved major success on the US road running circuit. Won Chicago marathon 1983.

Wilson WAIGWA
b.15 Feb 1949 1.72m 64kg Graduate of University of Texas at El Paso
Ch. record at 5000m: OG: '84– 10; CG: '82– 13. Won AAA '82. At 1500m: CG: '78– 5, '82– 9; AfrG: '78– 2. Won NCAA '77. 5th world cross-country 1984.
Progression at 5000m: 1976 – 13:48.29, 1977 – 14:02.4, 1978 – 13:24.43, 1979 – 13:42.1, 1980 – 13:20.36, 1981 – 13:57.14, 1982 – 13:29.32, 1983 – 13:21.98, 1984 – 13:27.34
pbs: 800m: 1:49.1 '77, 1500m: 3:35.0 '83, 1 mile: 3:50.7 '83, 2000m: 5:05.41 '82, 3000m: 7:40.52 '83

National Championships

MEXICO

Governing body: Federacion Mexicana de Atletismo, Avenida del Conscripto y Anillo Periferico, Lomas de Sotelo, Mexico 10, D.F. Founded 1933

Martin BERMUDEZ
b.19 Jul 1958 1.74m 74kg
Ch. record at 50kmW: OG: '80– dnf, '84– disq; WCh: '83– disq; PAm: '79– 2, '83– 2; LT: '79– 1, '81– 6
Progression at 50kmW: 1977 – 4:19:07, 1978 – 3:58:48, 1979 – 3:43:36, 1980 – 3:48:22, 1981 – 3:53:10, 1982 – 3:53:00, 1983 – 3:50:43, 1984 – 3:48:03
pbs: Track – 3kmW: 11:51.0 '83, 20kmW: 1:24:54 '79. Road – 20kmW: 1:22:22 '80

Ernesto CANTO
b.18 Oct 1959 1.70m 58kg
Ch. record at 20kmW: OG: '84– 1 (10 at 50kmW); WCh: '83– 1; PAm: '83– 2; LT: '79– 6, '81– 1, '83– 2; CAmG: '82– 1. Set world walking records at 20km – 1:18:39,9 and 1 hour – 15,253m in 1984.
Progression at 20kmW: 1979 – 1:21:12, 1980 – 1:19:02, 1981 – 1:23:08, 1982 – 1:23:13, 1983 – 1:19:41, 1984 – 1:18:40t

pbs: Track – 3kmW: 11:50.0 '83, 10kmW: 39:29.2 '84. Road: 50kmW: 3:51:10 '82

Marcellino COLIN
b.2 Jun 1961 1.65m 48kg 6th in the 1983 World Cup 20kmW in 1:20:40. pb 3kmW: 11:22.0 '83.

Raul GONZALES
b.29 Feb 1952 1.75m 64kg
Ch. record at 50kmW (20kmW): OG: '72– 20, '76– (5), '80– dnf (6), '84– 1 (2); WCh: '83– 5 (9); PAm: '79– 1, '83– 1 (2); LT: '77– 1, '79– 4, '81– 1, '83– 1; CAmG: '74– (1), '78– (2), '82– 2 (2). Set world track records at 30kmW (2:11:53.4 in 1979) and twice at 50kmW (3:52:23.5 in 1978, 3:41:38.4 in 1979), and world road bests at 30kmW (2:07:29 '79) and twice at 50kmW in 1978.
Progression at 20kmW/50kmW: 1972 – 4:26:14, 1973 – 1:30:00, 1974 – 1:27:53, 1975 – 1:27:51/4:07:18, 1976 – 1:24:19, 1977 – 1:24:08t/4:04:16, 1978 – 1:24:36t/3:41:20, 1979 – 1:24:05/3:41:39, 1980 – 1:23:03/3:43:43, 1981 – 1:22:51/3:47:16, 1982 – 1:20:44/3:45:23, 1983 – 1:22:06/3:45:37, 1984 – 1:21:49t/3:46:41
pbs: Track – 3kmW: 11:43.8i '82, 10kmW: 40:16.8 '82, 1hrW: 14486m '79

MOROCCO

Governing body: Fédération Royale Marocaine d'Athlétisme, Centre National des Sports, Bellevue Avenue, Ibn sina Agdal, Rabat. Founded 1957.

Said AOUITA
b.2 Nov 1960 Kenitra 1.75m 58kg
Ch.record: OG: '84– 1 at 5km; WCh: '83– 3 at 1500m; WSG: '83– 1 at 1500m; AfCh: '79– 9 at 1500m, '82– 3 at 800m, 2 at 1500m; '84– 1 at 1500m.
Progression at 1500m/5000m: 1978 – –/14:10.0, 1979 – 3:42.3/13:48.5, 1980 – 3:37.08, 1981 – 3:37.69/13:39.0?, 1982 – 3:37.37/14:05.7, 1983 – 3:32.54, 1984 – 3:31.54/13:04.78
Other pbs: 800m: 1:44.38 '83, 1000m: 2:15.71 '83, 1M: 3:49.54 '84, 2000m: 5:02.44 '82, 3000m: 7:33.3 '84, 3000mSt: 8:40.2 '79
Moved from Morocco to Marignane, near Marseille, France in 1982, then to Florence, Italy 1983. Unbeaten in 1984, when he set African records at 1500m and 5000m.

NAWAL EL MOUTAWAKIL
b.15 Apr 1962 Casablanca 1.62m 50kg Physical education student at Iowa State University – won NCAA 400mh 1984.
Ch.record at 400mh: OG: '84– 1; WCh: '83– sf; AfCh: '82– 1 (1 at 100mh, 2 at 100m), '84– 1 (1 at 200m); WCp: '81– 8 at 100m. Four African records at 400mh 1983–4 and one at 400m 1984. Set African junior record for 100m at 11.89 in 1979.
Progression at 400mh: 1981 – 60.1, 1982 – 58.3, 1983 – 56.23, 1984 – 54.61
Other pbs: 100m: 11.4 '83, 11.2w '84, 11.86 '81; 200m: 23.84 '83, 23.7 '84; 400m: 51.84 '84; 100mh: 13.4 '83 (all national records)
First Moroccan and first African woman, apart from South Africans, to win an Olympic gold medal. Second smallest ever Olympic champion. Underwent operation on right knee at end of 1984.

National Championships

NETHERLANDS

Governing body: KNAU: Koninklijke Nederlandse Atletiek-Unie Nachtegaalstraat, P.O.Box 14444, Utrecht, 3508 SM. Founded 1901.
National Championships first held in 1910 (men), 1921 (women)
1984 Champions: MEN
100m: Peter v.d.Heyden 10.54, 200m: Ahmed de Kom 21.32, 400m: Allan Ellsworth 46.65, 800m/1500m: Rob Druppers 1:49.15/3:45.08, 5000m: Martin ten Kate 13:49.83, 10000m: Klaas Lok 29:20.31, Mar: Gerard Nijboer 2:14:28, 3000mSt: Hans Koeleman 8:29.24, 110mh: Ysbrand Visser 14.40, 400mh: Harry Schulting 50.72, HJ: Marco Schmidt 2.12, PV: Chris Leeuwenburgh 5.20, LJ: Emiel Mellaard 7.84, TJ: Anne-Jan v.d.Veen 15.80w, SP/DT: Erik de Bruin 19.29/60.98, HT: Peter van Noort 62.58, JT: Bert Smit 72.64, Dec: Robert de Wit 7443, 20kmW: Frank van Ravensberg 1:29:37.5
WOMEN
100m/200m: Els Vader 11.25w/22.90, 400m: Desiree de Leeuw 53.49, 800m/1500m/3000m/5000m/10000m: Elly van Hulst 2:04.29/4:22.11/9:12.35/15:50.11/34:45.98, Mar: Eefje van Wissen 2:43:51, 100mh/LJ/Hep: Tineke Hidding 13.75/6.47/6038, 400mh: Olga Commander 58.26, HJ: Marjon Wijnsma 1.84, SP/DT: Debby Dunant 15.87/50.10, JT: Lida Berkhout 51.64

Elly Van Hulst won a unique clean sweep of five track titles from 800m to 10000m. She also won the national road title at 10km (35:35.4).

Rob DRUPPERS
b.29 Apr 1962 1.86m 70kg
Ch. record at 800m: WCh: '83– 2; ECh: '82– 5; EJ: '81– h. Three Dutch records at 800m and two at 1000m 1982-4.

Progression at 800m: 1976 – 2:10.5, 1977 – 2:03.9, 1978 – 1:59.1, 1979 – 1:52.6, 1980 – 1:48.8, 1981 – 1:46.88, 1982 – 1:44.54, 1983 – 1:44.20, 1984 – 1.44.60.
pbs: 400m: 47.1 '83; 1000m: 2:17.07 '84; 1500m: 3:39.3 '84.
After a very consistent record in 1982 and 1983 injuries prevented him appearing often in 1984.

Gerard NIJBOER
b.18 Aug 1955 Uffelte 1.82m 70kg
Ch. record at Mar: OG: '80– 2, '84– dnf; WCh: '83– 29; ECh: '82– 1
Progression at Mar: 1979 – 2:16:48, 1980 – 2:09:01, 1982 – 2:15:16, 1983 – 2:16:59, 1984 – 2:10:53
pbs: 3000m: 8:05.6 '79, 5000m: 13:56.2 '79, 10000m: 28:49.2 '80
Ran twelve marathons, 1979–84, winning three, including a European best at Amsterdam in 1980. Has been troubled by knee injuries.

WOMEN

Ria STALMAN
b.11 Dec 1952 1.80m 98kg
Club: Sparta. Attended US universities: UTEP and Arizona State
Ch. record at DT: OG: '84– 1; WCh: '83– 7; ECh: '82– 12. US champion at discus 1982 and 1984, shot 1984. Has set 16 Dutch discus records 1974–84 and one at shot in 1984.
Progression at DT: 1968 – 36.32, 1969 – 37.45, 1970 – 43.52, 1971 – 46.82, 1972 – 48.58, 1973 – 51.40, 1974 – 54.14, 1975 – 57.42, 1976 – 58.18, 1977 – 54.30, 1978 – 55.62, 1979 – 56.36, 1980 – 57.66, 1981 – 62.34, 1982 – 66.58, 1983 – 67.20, 1984 – 71.22.
pb SP: 18.02 '84.

NIGERIA

Governing body: Amateur Athletic Association of Nigeria, P.O.Box 211, Lagos. Founded 1944.

Ajayi AGBEBAKU
b.6 Dec 1955 1.85m 80kg Was at Missouri University, USA
Ch. record at TJ: OG: '84– 7; WCh: '83– 3; WSG: '83– 1; AfCh: '79– 1 (1 at LJ), '84– 2; WCp: '79– 7, '81– 8. Set five African triple jump records 1981-3.
Ch. record at TJ: 1974 – 14.66, 1975 – 15.14, 1976 – 14.98i, 1977 – 16.10, 1978 – 16.60i, 1979 – 16.57/16.82w, 1980 – 16.48i, 1981 – 16.88, 1982 – 17.00i, 1983 – 17.26, 1984 – 16.96.
pb LJ: 7.94 '79

Innocent EGBUNIKE
b.30 Nov 1961 1.74m 68kg Azusa Pacific College, USA

Ch. record at 400m: OG: '84– 7 (3 at 4x400mR). At 200m: WCh: '83– 7 (qf at 100m); WSG: '83– 1; AfCh: '84– 1. Set African records at 200m in 1983 and at 100m in 1984. Ran a Commonwealth indoor 300m best of 33.35 in 1983.
Progression at 400m: 1982 – 47.99, 1984 – 44.81
pbs: 100m: 10.15/10.12w '84; 200m: 20.42/20.4 '83, 20.23w '84

Sunday UTI
b.23 Oct 1962 1.75m 68kg Iowa State University, USA
Ch. record at 400m (R – 4x400m relay): OG: '80– h, '84– 6 (3R); WCh: '83– h (disq); WSG: '83– 1; AfCh: '84– 2
Progression at 400m: 1979 – 48.6, 1981 – 45.9, 1982 – 45.84, 1983 – 44.96, 1984 – 44.83. pb 200m: 20.94/20.6 '84

National Championships

NORWAY

Governing body: Norges Fri-Idrettsforbund, Tollbugt. 11, 0152 Oslo 1. Founded 1896.
National Championships first held in 1897 (men), 1947 (women).
1984 Champions: MEN
100m: Tore Bergan 10.83, 200m: Einar Sagli 21.40, 400m: Sindre Ryan 47.88, 800m: Espen Borge 1:48.48, 1500m: Torstein 3:43.34, 5000m: Peder Arne Sylte 14:02.46, 10000m: Are Nakkim 29:44.18, Mar: Jan Erik Viholmen 2:16:18, 3000mSt: Steinar Gresslos 8:45.48, 110mh: Robert Ekpete 14.15, 400mh: Petter Hesselberg 51.87, HJ: Terje Totland 2.19, PV: Bertil Reppen 4.80, LJ: Tomm Wisloff 7.71, TJ: Birger Nielsen 15.92, SP/DT: Knut Hjeltnes 18.32/64.44, HT: Tore Johnsen 64.56, JT: Per Erling Olsen 84.76; Dec: Robert Ekpete 7519, 50kmW: Erling Andersen 3:58:44
WOMEN
100m/200m/400m: Mona Evjen 11.82/23.65/54.94, 800m: Marit Eriksen 2:07.05, 1500m: Jorun Flaten 4:18.94, 3000m: Ingrid Kristiansen 9:01.90, 5000m: Mona Kleppe 16:37.51, Mar: Oddrun Hovsengen 2:46:47, 100mh: Heidi Benserud 14.00, 400mh: Berit Marstein 59.71, HJ: Kristin Gran 6.20w, SP: Stine Lerdahl 15.36, DT: Mette Bergmann 53.10, JT: Trine Solberg 61.60, Hep: Heidi Benserud 5584, 10kmW: Frøydis Hilsen 49:04

Erling ANDERSEN
b.22 Sep 1960 Bergen 1.82m 66kg
Ch. record at 20kmW: OG: '84– 8; WCh: '83– 21; ECh: '78– 23. At 50kmW: disq OG '84 and WCh '83; ECh: '82– dnf. At 10kmW: EJ: '75– 10, '77– 11, '79– 2. Set European 20km walk records in 1980 and 1984. Set world junior records at 5kmW, 19:56.9 and 10kmW, 40:50.0 in 1979.
Progression at 20kmW: 1978 – 1:27:47, 1979 – 1:23:59, 1980 – 1:20:57t, 1981 – 1:23:47, 1982 – 1:23:54, 1983 – 1:23:50t, 1984 – 1:20:36.7t
pbs: Track – 3kmW: 11:11.2 '81, 5kmW: 19:16.5 '82, 10kmW: 39:53.4 '84, 1 hrW: 14957m '84; Road – 50kmW: 3:54:00 '83.

Knut HJELTNES
b.8 Dec 1951 Ulvik 1.92m 120kg
Club: IL Gular. Was at Western Maryland and Penn State Universities, USA.
Ch. record at DT: OG: '76– 7, '84– 4; WCh: '83– 9; ECh: '78– 5, '82– 12; WCp: '79– 4. Norwegian champion at DT: 1975–6, '79–84 and SP 1975–6, '78–84. Norwegian shot and discus record holder since 1975.
Progression at DT: 1968 – 41.90, 1969 – 49.00, 1970 – 51.52, 1971 – 50.68, 1972 – 58.96, 1973 – 58.92, 1974 – 56.70, 1975 – 61.52, 1976 – 64.64, 1977 – 65.66, 1978 – 65.44, 1979 – 69.50, 1980 – 67.66, 1981 – 67.64, 1982 – 64.24, 1983 – 66.74, 1984 – 67.30.
pb SP: 20.55 '80, JT: 77.86 '76.
Suspended for drugs abuse in 1977.

Per Erling OLSEN
b.30 Mar 1958 1.90m 75kg
Club: SK Vidar.
Ch. record at JT: OG: '84– 9; WCh: '83– 5; ECh: '82– 10. Norwegian champion 1979, 1981–4.
Progression at JT: 1975 – 62.66, 1977 – 72.70, 1978 – 74.00, 1979 – 79.98, 1980 – 86.36, 1981 – 88.02, 1982 – 84.30, 1983 – 90.30, 1984 – 84.76

WOMEN

Ingrid KRISTIANSEN
b.21 Mar 1956 Trondheim 1.69m 58kg née Christensen.
Club: IL Skjalg. Medical researcher.
Ch. record at Mar: OG: '84– 4; ECh: '82– 3. At 3000m: WCh: '80– 3; ECh: '78– 10, '82– 8. World cross-country: '82– 6, '84– 4. Major marathon wins: Stockholm 1980–2, Houston 1983–4, London 1984 (in European best time). Set world 5000m records in 1981 (15:28.43) and 1984 (14:58.89).
Progression at Mar: 1977 – 2:45:15, 1980 – 2:34:25, 1981 – 2:30:09, 1982 – 2:33:26, 1983 – 2:33:27, 1984 – 2:24:26.
pbs: 800m: 2:09.7 '81, 1500m: 4:13.27 '84, 3000m: 8:39.56 '84, 5000m: 14:58.89 '84
Won Houston marathon just five months after giving birth to son in 1983. Has won 7/14 marathons to the end of 1984. At cross-country skiing was 15th in the 1978 world championships.

Trine SOLBERG
b.18 Apr 1966 1.72m 65kg
Club: Ski IL. Student.
Ch. record at JT: OG: '84– 5; ECh: '82– dnq. EJ: '81– 5, '83– 2.
Progression at JT: 1978 – 31.04, 1979 – 44.08, 1980 – 49.54, 1981 – 56.06, 1982 – 58.02, 1983 – 61.58, 1984 – 65.02
Full name Else Katrine Solberg. She was the top goalscorer in Norwegian second division handball in 1984, and but for her interest in the javelin would have been a candidate for the national team.

Grete WAITZ
b.1 Oct 1953 Oslo. 1.72m 54kg née Andersen, she married Jack Nilsen, who is now her coach, and together they took the name Waitz.
Club: SK Vidar. Teacher.
Ch. record at marathon: OG: '84– 2; WCh: '83– 1. At 3000m: ECh: '78– 3; WCp: '77– 1, '79– 2. At 1500m: OG: '72– h, '76– sf; ECh: '71– h (h at 800m), '74– 3, '78– 5. World cross-country: record five wins – 1978–81 and 1983, third in 1982 and 1984. Set two world records at 3000m: 8:46.6 in 1975 and 8:45.4 in 1976, European 5000m record: 15:08.80 in 1982, and European junior 1500m record: 4:17.0 in 1971. Has set four world bests for the marathon. The first three came each year from 1978 to 1980 when in her first three marathons she won in New York, and the fourth when she won the 1983 London marathon. She won the New York marathon again in 1982, 1983 and 1984. Of her eleven marathons she has won eight, was second in Los Angeles and did not finish twice. She holds world road bests for 10km: 30:59.8 in 1980, 15km: 47:52 in 1984, 10 miles: 53:05 in 1979, half marathon: 1:07:50 in 1982 and 20 miles: 1:51:23 in 1980.
Progression at marathon: 1978 – 2:32:30, 1979 – 2:27:33, 1980 – 2:25:41, 1982 – 2:27:14, 1983 – 2:25:29, 1984 – 2:26:18
pbs: 800m: 2:03.1 '75, 1500m: 4:00.55 '78, 1 mile: 4:26.90 '79, 3000m: 8:31.75 '79, 5000m: 15:08.80 '82
Waitz was unbeaten for twelve years in cross-country races and her first ever loss on the road was to Maricica Puica in 1981. A statue of her was erected outside the Bislett Stadium in Oslo in 1984.

132

National Championships

NEW ZEALAND

Governing body: New Zealand Amateur Athletic Association, PO Box 741, Wellington.
National Championships first held in 1888 (men), 1926 (women)
1984 Champions: MEN
100m: Joe Leota 10.91, 200m: Shane Downey 21.62, 400m: Murray Gutry 47.03, 800m: Chris Rogers 1:51.46, 1500m: Peter O'Donoghue 3:45.76, 5000m/3000mSt: Peter Renner 13:46.52/8:33.49, 10000m: Yutaka Kanai (Jap) 28:46.42, Mar: Barry Thompson 2:19:03, 110mh: Tim Soper 14.80, 400mh: Wayne Paul 51.55, HJ: Roger TePuni 2.15, PV: Keiran McKee 4.60, LJ: Steven Walsh 7.55, TJ: Kevin Todd 14.88, SP/DT: Henry Smith 16.52/53.70, HT: Murray Cheater 54.92, JT: John Staplyton-Smith 80.34, Dec: Simon Poelman 7330, 5000mW: Shane Donnelly 21:40.98
WOMEN
100m: Andrea Wade 12.16, 200m/400m: Kim Robertson 23.61/52.55, 800m: Jolanta Janucta (Pol) 2:04.78, 1500m: Anne McKenzie 4:17.95, 3000m: Christine Hughes 9:09.54, Mar: Mary Belsey 2:41:39, 100mh/400mh: Lynn Massey 14.04/58.11, HJ: Trudy Painter 1.81, LJ: Jayne Mitchell 6.33, SP: Glenda Hughes 15.78, DT: Heather Marsters 46.04, JT: A.Tulitau (New Caledonia) 46.48, Hep: Karen Forbes 5481

Rod DIXON
b.13 Jul 1950 Nelson 1.86m 70kg Promotions executive.
Ch. record at Mar: OG: '84– 10. At 1500m: OG: '72– 3; CG: '74– 4, '78– 8. Won AAU and French titles 1974. At 5000m: OG: '76– 4; CG: '78– 8. World cross-country: '71– 10, '73– 3, '82– 3. NZ champion at 5000m 1978–81, 10000m 1981.
Progression at Mar: 1982 – 2:11.21, 1983 – 2:08:59, 1984 – 2:12:57
pbs: 800m: 1:47.6 '73, 1000m: 2:17.2 '74, 1500m: 3:33.89 '74, 1 mile: 3:53.62 '75, 2000m: 5:01.67 '75, 3000m: 7:41.0 '74, 2 miles: 8:14.32 '74, 5000m: 13:17.27 '76, 10000m: 29:16.7 '80
After a great track career, now concentrates on road running. In five serious marathons to date he ran the short course at Auckland in 1977, won at Auckland in 1982 and at New York in 1983 (first non-American winner), before his Olympic 10th place. He dropped out of the 1984 New York race.

Peter RENNER
b.27 Oct 1959 Mosgiel, near Dunedin 1.86m 75kg
Club: New Brighton. Bushman.
Ch. record at 3000mSt: OG: '84– 11; WCh: '83– sf; CG: '82– 5 (8 at 5000m); WCp: '81– 9 at 5000m. NZ champion at 3000mSt 1982–4, 5000m 1984. Two NZ steeplechase records 1984.
Progression at 3000mSt: 1980 – 8:36.6, 1981 – 8:37.63, 1982 – 8:28.4, 1983 – 8:23.38, 1984 – 8:14.05.
pb 5000m: 13:46.52 '84.

John WALKER
b.12 Jan 1952 Papukura 1.83m 74kg Sports co-ordinator.

Ch. record at 1500m: OG: '76– 1 (h at 800m); WCh: '83– 9; CG: '74– 2 (3 at 800m), '82– 2 (4 at 800m); WCp: '77– dnf, '81– 2. At 5000m: OG: '84– 8. World cross-country: '75– 4. NZ champion 800m 1972–3, '77, '80–2; 1500m 1974, '79–83. World records at 1 mile, 3:49.4 in 1975 and 2000m, 4:51.4 in 1976.
Progression at 1500m/1 mile: 1970 – 3:52.4, 1972 – 3:46.4, 1973 – 3:38.0/3:58.8, 1974 – 3:32.52/3:54.9, 1975 – 3:32.4/3:49.4, 1976 – 3:34.19/3:53.07, 1977 – 3:32.72/3:52.0, 1978 – 3:40.3/3:56.4, 1979 –3:37.0/3:52.85, 1980 – 3:33.31/3:52.7, 1981 – 3:34.5/3:50.12, 1982 – 3:33.7/3:49.08, 1983 – 3:33.84/3:49.73, 1984 – 3:35.93/3:49.73. At 5000m: 1981 – 13:20.89, 1984 – 13:24.46.
pbs: 400m: 48.9 '73, 800m: 1:44.94 '74, 1000m: 2:16.57 '80, 2000m: 4:51.4 '76, 3000m: 7:37.49 '82, 2 miles: 8:20.57 '75.
The first sub 3:50 miler ran his 100th four-minute mile on 17th Feb. 1985. Although no longer the world's number one that he was in the mid-70s, Walker remains a top class runner.

WOMEN

Anne AUDAIN
b.1 Nov 1955 Auckland 1.68m 53kg née Garrett.
Club: Otahuhu.
Ch. record at Mar: OG: '84– dnf. At 3000m: CG: '82– 1. At 1500m: OG: '76– h (at 800m); CG: '74– 6. NZ champion 800m 1979; 1500m 1976, '79–80; 3000m 1982. Set Commonwealth 3000m record and world 5000m record in 1982. Has set NZ records from 1500m to 10000m since 1976.
Progression at 3000m/Mar: 1975 – 9:14.9, 1980 – 8:59.8, 1982 – 8:45.53, 1983 – 2:32:14, 1984 – 2:32:07
pbs: 800m: 2:04.4 '76, 1500m: 4:10.68 '76, 5000m: 15:13.22 '82, 10000m: 32:21.47 '83
Has had considerable success in recent years on the US road running circuit. Ran the then fastest debut marathon for fourth at Chicago in 1983, and was second in the 1984 Los Angeles marathon.

Lorraine MOLLER
b.1 Jun 1955 Putaruru 1.74m 58kg Housewife, former school teacher. Graduate of University of Otago. Married marathoner Ron Daws in 1981.
Ch. record: OG: '84– 5 Mar; WCh: '83– 14 at 3000m; CG: '74– 5 at 800m, '82– 3 at 1500m and 3000m. Marathon wins: Avon 1980, 1982 and Boston 1984. Set Commonwealth marathon best in 1980.
Progression at Mar: 1979 – 2:37:37, 1980 – 2:31:42, 1981 – 2:29:36, 1982 – 2:36:13, 1984 – 2:28:34
pbs: 1500m: 4:12.67 '82, 1 mile: 4:38.16 '81, 3000m: 8:51.78 '83, 5000m: 15:40.23 '82•
Won her first eight marathons, before second to Joyce Smith at London in 1982; record is now 11 wins out of 15.

133

National Championships

POLAND

Governing body: PZLA – Polski Zwiazek Lekkiej Atletyki, 00–372 Warszawa, ul.Foksal 19. Founded 1919.
National Championships first held in 1920 (men), 1922 (women)
1984 Champions: MEN
100m/200m: Leszek Dunecki 10.26/20.62, 400m: Andrzej Stepien 46.40, 800m: Ryszard Ostrowski 1:46.39, 1500: Miroslaw Zerkowski 3:41.16, 5000m/10000m: Antoni Niemczak 13:41.16/29:04.70, Mar: Wojciech Ratkowski 2:12:49, 3000mSt: Henryk Jankowski 8:36.76, 110mh: Romuald Giegiel 13.69, 400mh: Ryszard Szparak 49.81, HJ: Jacek Wszola 2.28, PV: Wladyslaw Kozakiewicz 5.65, LJ: Stanislaw Jaskulka 7.92, TJ: Zdzislaw Hoffmann 17.28w, SP: Janusz Gassowski 20.59, DT: Stanislaw Grabowski 58.44, HT: Mariusz Tomaszewski 79.42, JT: Stanislaw Witek 82.04, Dec: Wojciech Podsiadlo 8017, 20kmW/50kmW: Jan Klos 1:24:17/4:00:19
WOMEN
100m: Elzbieta Tomczak 11.18, 200m: Ewa Kasprzyk 22.50w, 400m: Genowefa Blaszak 51.82, 800m: Brygida Bak 2:02.61, 1500m: Danuta Piotrowska 4:16.06, 3000m: Wanda Panfil 9:13.98, 5000m/10000m: Renata Kokowska 16:39.8/34:04.66, Mar: Gabriela Gorzynska 2:39:21, 100mh: Lucyna Kalek 12.68w, 400mh: Jolanta Stalmach 59.40, HJ: Danuta Bulkowska 1.94, LJ: Anna Wlodarczyk 6.96, SP: Bogumila Suska 15.45, DT: Ewa Siepsiak 55.16, JT: Genowefa Olejarz 61.22, Hep: Malgorzata Nowak 6256, 5kmW/10kmW (Rd): Beata Baczyk 24:21.02/50:01

Romuald GIEGIEL
b.8 May 1957 Warszawa 1.86m 76kg
Club: AZS Warszawa
Ch. record at 110mh: ECh: '78– 7, '82– 6; ECp: '81– 3, '83– 3. At 60mh: EI: '80– 2, '84– 1. Polish 110mh champion 1978, 1984–1.
Progression at 110mh: 1974 – 15.20, 1975 – 14.48, 1976 – 14.29, 1977 – 13.94, 1978 – 13.71, 1979 – 13.99, 1980 – 14.01, 1981 – 13.68, 1982 – 13.57, 1983 – 13.65/13.54w, 1984 – 13.69/13.64w

Zdzislaw HOFFMANN
b. 27 Aug 1959 Swiebodzin 1.91m 85kg
Club: Slask Wroclaw
Ch. record at TJ: OG: '80– dnq; WCh: '83– 1; ECp: '81– 7, '83– 2. Polish champion 1981, '83–4. Set four Polish triple jump records in 1983.
Progression at TJ: 1974 – 13.32, 1975 – 13.60, 1976 – 14.50, 1977 – 15.80, 1978 – 15.84, 1979 – 16.40, 1980 – 16.48, 1981 – 16.58, 1982 – 16.49, 1983 – 17.42, 1984 – 17.34/17.55w.
pb LJ: 8.09 '83.

Wladyslaw KOZAKIEWICZ
b.8 Dec 1953 Wilno, Lithuania 1.87m 86kg
Club: Baltyk Gdynia
Ch. record at PV: OG: '76– 11, '80– 1; WCh: '83– 8=; ECh: '74– 2, '78– 4; EI: '75– 3, '77– 1, '79– 1, '82– 3; WSG: '77 – 1, '79– 1; WCp: '77– 2; ECp: '75– 1, '77– 1, '79– 3, '81– nh. Polish champion 1973, '76–79, '81, '84. Set seven Polish pole vault records 1973–80, of which four were European records 1975–7 and then two world records in 1980 – 5.72m and 5.78m, the latter when he won the Olympic title.
Progression at PV: 1968 – 2.95, 1969 – 3.85, 1970 – 4.26, 1971

– 4.65, 1972 – 5.02, 1973 – 5.35i, 1974 – 5.38, 1975 – 5.60, 1976 – 5.62, 1977 – 5.66, 1978 – 5.62, 1979 – 5.61, 1980 – 5.78, 1981 –'5.62, 1982 – 5.60, 1983 – 5.62, 1984 – 5.75.
pb Dec: 7683 '77.
He was suspended for six months at the end of the 1984 season by the Polish federation for competing internationally without authorization. Brother Eduard had a decathlon pb of 7764 points in 1974.

Zdzislaw KWASNY
b.6 Nov 1960 Kwilicz 1.94m 104kg
Club: Olimpia Poznan
Ch. record at HT: WCh: '83– 3; ECp: '83– 2; EJ: '79– 9. Polish champion and three Polish hammer records in 1983
Progression at HT: 1977 – 50.55, 1978 – 60.04, 1979 – 65.40, 1980 – 66.24, 1981 – 70.12, 1982 – 72.82, 1983 – 80.18, 1984 – 73.76
Burst through to world class in 1983. In the world championships he had to settle for bronze rather than silver when his final throw (81.54m) was readjudged to be a foul.

Boguslaw MAMINSKI
b.18 Dec 1955 Kamien Pomorski 1.81m 68kg
Club: Legia Warszawa
Ch. record at 3000mSt: OG: '80– 7; WCh: '83– 2; ECh: '82– 2; WCp: '81– 1; ECp: '81– 2, '83– 1 ('79– 6 at 1500m). Polish champion 3000mSt 1979, 5000m 1983. Set Polish 2000m record in 1982.
Progression at 3000mSt: 1978 – 8:34.8, 1979 – 8:23.0, 1980 – 8:18.78, 1981 – 8:16.66, 1982 – 8:17.41, 1983 – 8:12.62, 1984 – 8:09.18
pbs: 1000m: 2:20.8 '78, 1500m: 3:38.93 '80, 2000m: 5:02.12 '82, 3000m: 7:51.06 '83, 5000m: 13:26.09 '80
Has compiled a great competitive record in recent years.

Edward SARUL
b.16 Nov 1958 Nowy Kosciol 1.95m 117kg
Club: Gornik Zabrze. Miner.
Ch. record at SP: WCh: '83– 1; ECh: '82– 11; ECp: '83– 1.Polish champion 1979–80, '82–3. Two Polish shot records in 1983
Progression at SP: 1975 – 13.20, 1976 – 14.93, 1977 – 16.74, 1978 – 18.24, 1979 – 19.06, 1980 – 19.80, 1981 – 18.44, 1982 – 20.64, 1983 – 21.68, 1984 – 20.89

Mariusz TOMASZEWSKI
b.23 Apr 1956 Poznan 1.91m 113kg
Club: AZS Poznan.
Ch. record at HT: WCh: '83– 18; ECh: '82– 10; ECp: '81– 5. Polish champion 1981 and 1984. Polish hammer records in 1981 and 1982(2).
Progression at HT: 1974 – 51.50, 1975 – 60.10, 1976 – 60.30, 1977 – 62.88, 1978 – 67.22, 1979 – 70.10, 1980 – 73.76, 1981 – 77.14, 1982 – 78.38, 1983 – 78.40, 1984 – 79.46

Krzysztof WESOLOWSKI
b.9 Dec 1956 Walbrzych 1.79m 64kg
Club: Slask Wroclaw
Ch. record at 3000mSt: OG: '80– sf; WCh: '83– sf; ECh: '78– 11, '82– h; ECp: '77– 7, '79– 4. Polish champion 1981, 1983. Set a world 2000m steeplechase best of 5:20.00 in 1984.
Progression at 3000mSt: 1976 – 8:49.8, 1977 – 8:34.0, 1978 – 8:19.53, 1979 – 8:27.0, 1980 – 8:23.0, 1981 – 8:25.03, 1982 – 8:22.65, 1983 – 8:20.10, 1984 – 8:15.28

pbs: 1500m: 3:40.44 '80, 3000m: 7:53.16 '84, 5000m: 13:44.8 '78

Marian WORONIN
b.13 Aug 1956 Grodzisk Mazowiecki 1.87m 82kg
Club: Legia Warszawa. Sports student.
Ch. record at 100m (200m) (R – 4x100m relay): OG: '76– sf (4R), '80– 7 (7, 2R); WCh: '83– qf; ECh: '74– h (h), '78– sf (1R), '82– 3; EJ: '75– 3; WCp: '79– 3, '81– 1R; ECp: '77– 8, '79– 2 (3, 1R), '81– 4 (1R). EI: (at 50m/60m): '77– 3, '79– 1, '80– 1, '81– 1, '82– 1. Polish champion 100m 1978–83, 200m 1983. European 100m record in 1984. Polish records: 4 at 100m 1979–84, 2 at 200m 1978–79.
Progression at 100m/200m: 1972 – 11.2, 1973 – 10.7, 21.8, 1974 – 10.47/10.3, 21.29/21.1, 1975 – 10.55/10.3, 21.4/21.56, 1976 – 10.38/10.2, 20.8/20.73w, 1977 – 10.61, 21.48, 1978 – 10.25, 20.77/20.73w, 1979 – 10.16, 20.50/20.43w, 1980 – 10.19/10.13w, 20.49, 1981 – 10.28/10.15w, 20.55, 1982 – 10.17, 20.83, 1983 – 10.23/10.10w, 20.64; 1984 – 10.00, 20.78

Jacek WSZOLA
b.30 Dec 1956 Warszawa 1.94m 75kg
Club: AZS Warszawa
Ch. record at HJ: OG: '76– 1, '80– 2; WCh: '83– 13; ECh: '74– 5, '78– 6, '82– dnc; EJ: '75– 1; EI: '77– 1, '80– 2; WSG: '77– 1, '79– 4; WCp: '77– 3, '79– 2; ECp: '75– 5, '77– 2, '83– 5=. Polish champion 1974–80, '82, '84 (he was the youngest ever in 1974 at the age of 17). Ten Polish high jump records 1974–80, including a European record at 2.29m in 1976 and a world record at 2.35m in 1980.
Progression at HJ: 1971 – 1.60, 1972 – 1.80, 1973 – 2.08, 1974 – 2.20, 1975 – 2.23, 1976 – 2.29, 1977 – 2.30, 1978 – 2.24, 1979 – 2.29, 1980 – 2.35, 1981 – 2.28i, 1982 – 2.28, 1983 – 2.28, 1984 – 2.31

WOMEN

Genowefa BLASZAK
b.2 Aug 1957 1.66m 62kg née Mowaczyk.
Club: Örkan Poznan.
Ch. record at 400mh: ECh: '78– 8 (3 at 4x400mR), '82– 8; WCp: '81– 2; ECp: '81– 3, '83– 8. Set two Polish 400mh records 1984.

Progression at 400mh: 1975 – 58.8, 1976 – 59.59, 1978 – 56.67, 1981 – 55.78, 1982 – 55.76, 1983 – 55.97, 1984 – 54.78
pbs: 100m: 12.19 '81, 200m: 23.22 '84, 400m: 51.21 '84

Danuta BULKOWSKA
b.31 Jan 1959 1.78m 60kg
Club: AZS Wroclaw.
Ch. record at HJ: OG: '80– dnq; EI: '84– 3. Polish high jump record 1984.
Progression at HJ: 1976 – 1.73, 1977 – 1.86, 1978 – 1.87, 1979 – 1.86i, 1980 – 1.90, 1981 – 1.88i, 1982 – 1.85, 1983 – 1.91, 1984 – 1.97

Lucyna KALEK
b.9 Jan 1956 Tychy 1.67m 54kg née Langer.
Club: GKS Tychy.
Ch. record at 100mh: OG: '80– 3; ECh: '78– 5, '82– 1; WSG: '79– 1; WCp: '81– 3; ECp: '81– 3, '83– 2; EI: '84– 1 at 60mh. Polish 100mh champion 1982–4.
Progression at 100mh: 1974 – 14.7, 1975 – 14.28/14.2, 1976 – 13.82/13.6, 1977 – 13.27, 1978 – 12.89, 1979 – 12.62, 1980 – 12.44, 1981 – 12.97/12.91w, 1982 – 12.45, 1983 – 12.73, 1984 – 12.43.
pbs: 100m: 11.44 '82, 200m: 23.38 '82.
The European 100mh champion announced her retirement at the end of the 1984 season.

Anna WLODARCZYK
b.24 Mar 1951 Zielona Gora 1.74m 63kg
Club: AZS-AWF Warszawa. Doctor of sports.
Ch. record at LJ: OG: '80– 4; ECh: '82– disq (5); EI: '80– 1; WCp: '81– 3; ECp: 775– 7, '77– 7, '81– 2. Polish champion 1979, '81, '84. Four Polish long jump records 1980–4.
Progression at LJ: 1972 – 6.09, 1973 – 6.39, 1974 – 6,40, 1975 – 6.44, 1976 – 6.20, 1977 – 6.51, 1978 – 6.58, 1979 – 6.54, 1980 – 6.95, 1981 – 6.88, 1982 – 6.69, 1984 – 6.97w/6.96.
pb 100m: 11.62 '80, 100mh: 14.00 '79, Pen: 4093 '79.
Disqualified for use of anabolic steroids at 1982 European Championships.

PORTUGAL

Governing body: Federacao Portuguesa de Atletismo, Av.Infante Santo, 68 – E-F, 1300 Lisboa. Founded 1921.
National Championships first held in 1910 (men), 1937 (women)
1984 Champions: MEN
100m/200m: Luís Barroso 10.77/20.95, 400m: Alberto Jorge Ferreira 47.87, 800m: Mario Silva 1:49.34, 1500m: Joao Campos 3:41.7, 5000m: Guilherme Alves 13:49.9, 10000m: Luis Horta 28:52.2, Mar: Manuel Oliveira 2:17:20, 3000mSt: Jose Regalo 8:44.90, 110mh: Joao Lima 14.5, 400mh: Alvaro Silva 53.18, HJ: Jose Lima 2.05, PV: Manuel Miguel 4.85, LJ: Adriano Ribeiro 7.36, TJ: Luis Azevedo 15.69, SP: Mario Pinto 15.25, DT: Paulo Santos 44.34, HT: Jose Pedroso 59.40, JT: Paulo Santos 70.26, 20kmW: Jose Pinto 1:27:24, Dec: Pedro Albuquerque 6799
WOMEN
100m/LJ: Vera Lisa 12.48/5.77, 200m: Maria Joao Maia 25.04, 400m: Marta Cristina Moreira 57.79, 800m: Alice Silva 2:12.71, 1500m/3000m/5000m: Aurora Cunha 4:17.37/9:10.55/15:21.0, Mar: Maria Conceição Ferreira 2:44:46, 100mh: Ana Isabel Oliveira 14.4, 400mh: Helena Teixeira 62.65, HJ/Hep: Graca Borges 1.68/4838, SP/DT: Adilia Silverio 13.50/45.50, JT: Fatima Pinto 42.54, 5000mW: Paula Gracioso 25:29.9

António LEITÃO
b.22 Jul 1960 Espinho 1.76m 68kg Student.
Ch. record at 5000m: OG: '84– 3; WCh: '83– 10; ECh: '82– h; EJ: '79– 3. Has won two national titles, one each at 5000m and 3000mSt. Set Portugese records at 5000m in 1982, 3000m in 1983 and 3000m St in 1984.

Progression at 5000m: 1977 – 14:14.3, 1978 – 14:12.6, 1979 – 13:54.83, 1980 – 13:52.1, 1981 – 13:42.5, 1982 – 13:07.70, 1983 – 13:14.13, 1984 – 13:09.20
pbs: 800m: 1:53.7 '81, 1500m: 3:38.2 '82, 3000m: 7:39.69 '83, 2M: 8:20.86 '84, 10000m: 29:22.9 '80, 3000mSt: 8:26.19 '84
Had posted several fast times but little major success until the

National Championships

Olympics, when he ensured that the pace was fast in the final, and reaped his reward with a bronze medal.

Carlos LOPES
b.18 Feb 1947 Viseu 1.67m 56kg
Club: Sporting Club of Lisbon. Bank employee.
Ch. record at Mar: OG: '84– 1. At 10000m: OG: '72– h (h – 5000m), '76– 2; WCh: '83– 6; ECh: '71– 33 (h– 3000mSt), '74– dnf, '82– 4. World cross-country: '76– 1, '77– 2, '83– 3, '84– 1. Portuguese titles: 2 at 5000m and 10000m, 1 at 3000mSt, 9 at cross-country. Set European 10000m record in 1982 and marathon best in 1983. Portuguese records (1976–83): 2 at 3000m, 9 at 5000m, 8 at 10000m, 1 each at 2M, 15km, 20km, 1 hour, also the marathon best.
Progression at 10000m/Mar: 1967 – 30:52.0, 1968 – 30:45.6, 1969 – 30:40.6, 1970 – 30:26.6, 1971 – 29:28.0, 1972 – 28:53.6, 1973 – 28:37.0, 1974 – 28:38.8, 1975 – 28:30.6, 1976 – 27:42.65, 1977 – 28:44.6, 1978 – 28:05.0, 1979 – 28:44.3, 1981 – 27:47.8, 1982 – 27:24.39, 1983 – 27:23.44/2:08:39, 1984 – 27:17.48/2:09:06
pbs: 1500m: 3:41.4 '82, 3000m: 7:48.8 '76, 5000m: 13:16.38 '84, 3000mSt: 8:39.6 '73
Triumphed in 1984 at the age of 37 by winning the world cross-country and Olympic marathon titles. The latter was just his second completed marathon, his first was his second place to Rob de Castella in Rotterdam in 1983. He had failed to finish at New York in 1982. He went on to place second to Steve Jones at Chicago in 1984.

Fernando MAMEDE
b.1 Nov 1951 Beja 1.75m 59kg
Club: Sporting Club of Lisbon. Bank employee.
Ch. record at 10000m: OG: '84– dnf; WCh: '83– 14. At 5000m: ECh: '78– 15. At 800m/1500m: OG: '72– h/h, '76– h/sf; ECh: '71– h/h, '74– sf/h; EJ: '70– h at 800m. World cross-country: '81– 3. Portuguese titles: 800m– 1, 1500m– 4, 10000m– 2, cross-country– 3. At 10000m set world record in 1984, and European records in 1981 and 1982. Portuguese records: 7 at 1500m, 5 at 800m, 4 at 10000m, 2 each at 1000m, 3000m and 5000m, 1 at 1 mile and 2000m.
Progression at 5000m/10000m: 1973 – 14:24.8, 1974 – 13:55.2, 1975 – 14:19.8, 1976 – 13:49.4, 1977 – 13:38.7/29:10.6, 1978 – 13:17.76/28:39.6, 1979 – 13:26.0/28:16.4, 1980 – 13:20.0/27:37.88, 1981 – 13:19.2/27:27.7, 1982 – 13:14.6/27:22.95, 1983 – 13:08.54/27:25.13, 1984 – 13:12.83/27:13.81

pbs: 400m: 48.2 '71, 800m: 1:47.47 '74, 1500m: 3:37.98 '76, 2000m: 5:00.8 '84, 3000m: 7:43.94 '83
A great distance runner but sadly he has totally failed to produce his form in major track finals. Ran off the track in the 1984 Olympic final, unable to control his nerves.

WOMEN

Aurora CUNHA
b.31 May 1959 Ronfe, near Guimañaes 1.55m 48kg
Club: FC Oporto. Textiles worker.
Ch. record at Mar: OG: '84– 6; WCh: '83– 9; ECh: '82– 10 (10 at 1500m). Won 1984 IAAF World 10km road championship. Won 18 Portuguese titles: 1500m– 6, 3000m– 6, 5000m– 3, cross-country– 3. Has set 39 Portuguese records (1976–84): 15 at 3000m, 12 at 1500m, 5 at 5000m, 3 at 2000m, 2 at 1000m, 1 at 800m and 10000m.
Progression at 3000m/5000m: 1976 – 9:54.0, 1977 – 9:42.35, 1978 – 9:28.4, 1979 – 9:16.7, 1980 – 9:04.7/16:41.6, 1981 – 9:30.2, 1982 – 8:54.5/15:35.2, 1983 – 8:50.20/15:31.7, 1984 – 8:46.37/15:09.07
pbs: 800m: 2:05.4 '82, 1000m: 2:45.8 '82, 1500m: 4:09.31 '83, 2000m: 5:54.0 '82, 10000m: 31:52.85 '83

Rosa MOTA
b.29 Jun 1958 Foz do Douro 1.57m 45kg
Ch. record at Mar: OG: '84– 3; WCh: '83– 4; ECh: '82– 1 (12 at 3000m). World 10km road: '84– 2. Portuguese titles: 800m– 1, 1500m– 3, 3000m– 2, 5000m– 1, cross-country– 6. Portuguese records (1974–84): 6 at 1500m, 5 at 3000m, 2 at 5000m, 1 each at 1000m, 15km, 20km, 1 hour. Also six marathon bests.
Progression at Mar: 1982 – 2:36:04, 1983 – 2:31:12, 1984 – 2:26:01
pbs: 800m: 2:12.3 '81, 1500m: 4:19.53 '83, 3000m: 8:53.84 '84, 5000m: 15:30.63 '84, 10000m: 32:46.78 '83, 20km: 1:06:55.5 '83 (world best), 1 hour: 18027m '83.
Won the European title in 1982 in her first attempt at the marathon, and has improved her best in each of the five marathons that she has run subsequently, including in the world and Olympic championships. In the latter she won the first ever Olympic medal by a Portuguese woman. She won her other three marathons, at Rotterdam in 1983 and at Chicago in 1983 and 1984. In the latter she set a world best for a loop course.

ROMANIA

Governing body: Federation Romana de Atletism, Str. Vasile Conta 16, 70139, Bucaresti. Founded in 1912.
National Championships first held in 1921 (men), 1925 (women)
1984 Champions: MEN
100m: Paul Stanciu 10.74, 200m: Cornel Hapaianu 21.53, 400m/400mh: Horia Toboc 46.90/50.02, 800m: Costel Ene 1:47.41, 1500m: Constantin Rosu 3:45.63, 5000m/10000m: Gyrgy Marko 13:59.32/29:17.70, Mar: Alexandru Chiran 2:20:43, 3000mSt: Vasile Bichea 8:31.09, 110mh: Ion Oltean 14.05, HJ: Sorin Matei 2.30, PV: Dan Glanea 5.00, LJ: Laurentiu Budur 7.87, TJ: Bedros Bedrosian 16.79, SP: Sorin Tirichita 18.31, DT: Ion Zamfirache 63.26, HT: Stan Tudor 73.02, JT: Dumitru Negoita 81.76, Dec: Ion Buliga 7788, 20kmW: Costel Sofran 1:29:51, 50kmW: Grigore Toader 4:21:49
WOMEN
100m: Lucia Militaru 11.58, 200m: Maria Samungi 23.44, 400m: Niculina Lazarciuc 51.68, 800m/1500m: Doina Melinte 1:56.53/3:58.26, 3000m: Maricica Puica 8:33.57, Mar: Adriana Mustata 2:53:38, 100mh/Hep: Liliana Nastase 13.34/6160, 400mh: Cristina Cojocaru 55.45, HJ: Niculina Vasile 1.95, LJ: Anisoara Stanciu 7.14, SP: Mihaela Loghin 20.24, DT: Florenta Craciunescu 64.32, JT: Mihaela Stanescu 58.76, 5000mW: Liliana Dragan 24:16.6, 10kmW (Road): Mia Gologan 50:20.8

National Championships

WOMEN

Cristina COJOCARU
b.2 Jan 1962 1.71m 61kg
Ch. record at 400mh: OG: '84– 3; WCh: '83– 8; ECh: '82– h. At 800m: EI: '84– 3; WIG: '85– 1. At 1500m: EJ: '79– 3. Seven Romanian 400mh records 1982–4.
Progression at 400mh: 1977 – 61.59, 1978 – 61.3, 1979 – 62.39, 1981 – 57.67, 1982 – 56.50, 1983 – 56.26, 1984 – 55.24
pbs: 400m: 52.11 '83, 800m: 2:00.76 '84, 1500m: 4:12.2 '79, 3000m: 9:28.4 '79

Florenta CRACIUNESCU
b.7 May 1955 Craiova 1.81m 92kg née Ionescu. Formerly Tacu.
Ch. record at DT: OG: '80– 6, '84– 3 (8 at SP); WCh: '83– 9; ECh: '82– 7; WSG: '79– 3, '81– 1, '83– 1; ECp: '79– 4. Set Romanian discus record in 1981.
Progression at DT: 1971 – 36.50, 1972 – 47.70, 1973 – 50.82, 1974 – 56.70, 1975 – 59.26, 1976 – 60.10, 1977 – 57.28, 1978 – 58.34, 1979 – 65.06, 1980 – 67.02, 1981 – 68.98, 1982 – 68.24, 1983 – 67.74, 1984 – 66.08.
pb SP: 17.71i '80.

Valeria 'Vali' IONESCU
b.21 Aug 1960 Turnu Magurele 1.73m 58kg
Ch. record at LJ: OG: '84– 2; WCh: '83– 9; ECh: '82– 1; EI: '82– 3; WSG: '81– 3, '83– 3. Romanian champion 1980-3. Balkan Games champion 1984. Set world record at 7.20m in 1982.
Progression at LJ: 1976 – 5.52, 1977 – 5.49, 1978 – 5.58, 1979 – 6.07, 1980 – 6.54, 1981 – 6.75, 1982 – 7.20, 1983 – 6.92, 1984 – 7.11

Miheala LOGHIN
b.1 Jun 1952 Roman 1.70m 75kg Physical Training instructor.
Ch. record at SP: OG: '84– 2; WCh: '83– 6; ECh: '78– 8, '82– 8; WSG: '75– 2, '79– 3; ECp: '79– 5. 12 Romanian shot records 1975–84.
Progression at SP: 1968 – 12.94, 1969 – 13.70, 1970 – 14.61, 1971 – 16.11, 1972 – 16.07, 1973 – 15.94, 1974 – 16.77, 1975 – 19.15, 1976 – 19.02, 1977 – 18.63, 1978 – 19.13, 1979 – 19.41, 1980 – 19.55, 1981 – 19.92, 1982 – 19.98, 1983 – 20.95, 1984 – 21.00.
pb JT: 51.20 '76.

Fita LOVIN
b.14 Jan 1951 1.65m 54kg née Rafira
Ch. record at 800m: OG: '80– sf, '84– 3; ECh: '78– 5; EI: '79– 3; WSG: '77– 4, '79– 3 ECp: '79– 5. At 1500m: OG: '84– 9; EI: '84– 1; WIG: '85– 2. World X–C: '82– 2, '83– 8.
Progression at 800m/1500m: 1968 – 2:12.8, 1969 – 2:07.7/4:29.7, 1970 – 2:06.2/4:27.5, 1971 – 2:04.8, 1972 – 2:04.0/4:24.8, 1973 – 2:06.6/4:35.4, 1974 – 2:03.27/4:25.4, 1975 – 2:04.8, 4:13.0, 1976 – 2:02.2/4:15.1, 1977 – 1:59.0/4:09.6, 1978 – 1:58.81/4:08.42, 1979 – 1:57.4/4:05.4, 1980 – 1:56.67/4:03.7, 1981 – 1:57.42/4:01.67, 1982 – 2:00.74i/4:06.92i, 1983 – 2:00.19/4:00.12, 1984 – 1:58.83/4:01.43
pbs: 400m: 53.4 '80, 1 mile: 4:21.40 '81, 3000m: 9:06.2 '83

Doina MELINTE
b.27 Dec 1956 Hudesti 1.77m 56kg née Besliu
Ch. record at 800m/1500m: OG: '80– sf 800m, '84– 1/2; WCh: '83– 6/6; ECh: '82– 6/9; WSG: '81– 1/2, '83– 3/2; EI at 800m: '82– 1, '84– 2. Set Romanian 800m record in 1982.
Progression at 800m/1500m: 1976 – 2:13.4/4:43.4, 1977 – 2:11.8/4:38.4, 1978 – 2:06.1, 1979 – 2:04.4/4:18.6, 1980 – 2:00.5/4:00.68, 1981 – 1:57.81/4:03.70, 1982 – 1:55.05/4:01.40, 1983 – 1:57.06/4:01.49, 1984 – 1:56.53/3:58.1
pb 400m: 52.80 '82

Maricica PUICA
b.29 Jul 1950 Bucharest 1.68m 55kg née Luca, married to trainer Ion Puica.
Ch. record at 3000m (1500m): OG: '76– (h), '80– (7), '84– 1 (3); ECh: '78– 4 (11), '82– 2 (4); EI: '82– 2; WSG: '77– (3); WCp: '81– 2; ECp: '77– 2, '79– 2. World cross-country: 1st '82, '84; 3rd '78. At 1 mile set European record in 1981 and world record in 1982.
Progression at 1500m/3000m: 1969 – 4:35.8, 1970 – 4:34.1, 1971 – 4:28.8, 1972 – 4:28.7, 1973 – 4:22.6/9:33.0, 1974 – 4:18.2/9:19.0, 1975 – 4:12.8, 1976 – 4:06.1/9:18.4, 1977 – 4:05.1/8:46.44, 1978 – 4:03.18/8:40.94, 1979 – 3:59.8/8:49.1, 1980 – 3:59.3/9:00.2, 1981 – 3:58.29/8:34.30, 1982 – 3:57.48/8:31.67, 1983 – 4:10.91/9:04.20, 1984 – 3:57.22/8:33.57
pbs: 800m: 1:57.8 '79, 1000m: 2:35.7 '84, 1 mile: 4:17.44 '82.
First woman to beat Grete Waitz in a road race, she followed her cross-country successes with a convincing win in Los Angeles. Missed most of the 1983 season through injury.

Anisoara STANCIU
b.28 Jun 1962 Braila 1.73m 65kg née Cusmir. Married to Paul Stanciu, who set a Romanian 100m record at 10.41 in 1983. Draughtswoman.
Ch. record at LJ: OG: '84– 1; WCh: '83– 3; ECh: '82– 2; WSG: '81– 2, '83– 1. She has set four world long jump records: 7.15m in 1982, 7.21m, 7.27m and 7.43m in 1983, the latter represented the biggest ever improvement. Also set two world indoor bests (6.92m and 6.94m) in 1983.
Progression at LJ: 1974 – 4.25, 1975 – 4.83, 1976 – 5.02, 1977 – 5.56, 1978 – 5.98, 1979 – 5.99, 1980 – 6.53/6.55w, 1981 – 6.91, 1982 – 7.15, 1983 – 7.43, 1984 – 7.27.
pb 100m: 11.69 '82

SENEGAL

Governing body: Fédération Sénégalaise d'Athlétisme, B.P.1737, Dakar

Amadou Dia BA
b.22 Aug 1958 1.90m 82kg
Ch. record at 400mh: OG: '84– 5; WCh: '83– 7; WSG: '83– 2; AfG: '78– 3 at HJ, '82– 1 (1 at 400m); AfCh: '84– 1; WCp: '81– 7 at HJ
Progression at 400mh: 1982 – 49.55, 1983 – 49.03, 1984 – 48.73
pb 400m: 45.8 '82, HJ: 2.18 '81
Switched from high jump to 400m hurdles with immediate success in 1981.

137

National Championships

SOUTH AFRICA

Governing body: South African Amateur Athletic Union, P.O. Box 1261, Pretoria 0001. Founded 1894. Membership of the IAAF terminated in 1976.
National Championships first held in 1894 (men), 1929 (women)
1984 Champions: MEN
100m/200m: Wessel Oosthuizen 10.54/20.80, 400m: Edwin Modibedi 45.57, 800m/1500m: Johan Fourie 1:47.56/3:37.48, 5000m/10000m: Steve Morake 13:54.31/28:42.79, Mar: Ernest Seleke 2:09:41, 3000mSt: Daniel Prinsloo 8:39.37, 110mh: Jurie van der Walt 14.58, 400mh: Hannes Pienaar 49.97, HJ: Edwin Ludick 2.18, PV: Andrré Franken 5.05, LJ: Francois Fouch 7.77, TJ: Michael O'Hare 15.52, SP/DT: Sakkie Kotzé 16.22/57.02, HT: Charlie Koen 60.82, JT: Herman Potgieter 80.56, Dec: Joepie Loots 7591, 20kmW: Willie Vermeulen 1:31:53
WOMEN
100m/200m: Evette de Klerk 11.76/23.36, 400m/400mh: Myrtle Simpson 52.0/56.25, 800m: Helga van Wermerskerken 2:01.92, 1500m: Eranee van Zyl 4:15.22, 3000m: Tanya Peckham 9:10.8, Mar: Adaleen Joubert 2:48:46, 100mh: Ina van Rensburg 13.34, HJ: Desiree du Plessis 1.87, LJ: Maryna van Niekerk 6.38, SP: Janeene Swart 13.09, DT: Sandra Willms 63.76, JT: Susan Lion-Cachet 56.76, Hep: Heidi de Kock 5674

Johan FOURIE
b.2 Dec 1959 Springs 1.80m 70kg Sergeant in South African Police, Pretoria. South African champion at 1500m 1979–84, 800m 1984 South African records at 1500m (3), 1 mile (2), 2000m (2), 3000m.
Progression at 1500m/1 mile: 1982 – 3:37.02/3:53.29, 1983 – 3:35.2/3:52.31, 1984 – 3:34.3/3:51.23
pbs: 800m: 1:47.5 '79, 1000m: 2:17.34 '83, 2000m: 4:56.5 '84, 3000m: 7:46.20 '83, 5000m: 13:51.8 '81

SPAIN

Governing body: Real Federacion Española de Atletismo, Calle Miguel Angel 16, Madrid–10. Founded 1918.
National Championships first held in 1917 (men), 1931 (women)
1984 Champions: MEN
100m: José Javier Arqués 10.60, 200m: Antonio Sanchez 20.73w, 400m: Juan José Prado 46.80, 800m: Colomán Trabado 1:49.10, 1500m: José Abascal 3:39.31, 5000m: José Albentosa 13:54.21, 10000m: Antonio Prieto 28:46.6, Mar: Eleuterio Antón 2:13:28, 3000mSt: Domingo Ramón 8:29.91, 110mh: Javier Moracho 13.57, 400mh: José Alonso 50.72, HJ: Roberto Cabrejas 2.18, PV: Alberto Ruiz 5.55, LJ: Antonio Corgos 8.02w, TJ: Juan Ambrosio Gonzalez 16.28, SP: Martín Vara 17.82, DT: Sinesio Garrachón 55.98, HT: Raul Jimeno 71.42, JT: Antonio Lago 69.00, Dec: Gerardo Trujillano 7233, 20kmW: Manuel Alcalde 1:29:05, 50kmW: José Marin 3:50:12
WOMEN
100m/200m: Teresa Rione 11.54/23.59, 400m: Esther Lahoz 55.75, 800m: Rosa Colorado 2:06.48, 1500m: Mercedes Calleja 4:19.89, 3000m: Asunción Sinovas 9:27.28, 5000m: Ana Isabel Alonso 16:38.4, 10000m: Amelia Lorza 35:50.9, Mar: Consuelo Alonso 2:50:54, 100mh: Maria José Martinez 13.68w, 400mh: Yolanda Dolz 59.26, HJ: Isabel Mozun 1.86, LJ: Olga Dalmau 6.05, SP: Enriqueta Díaz 13.15, DT: Encarnación Gambús 46.74, JT: Aurora Moreno 54.52, Hep: Ana Perez 5332, 5000mW/10km road W: Maria Cruz Diaz 24:18.0/48:51

José Manuel ABASCAL
b.17 Mar 1958 Alceda 1.82m 67kg
Club: FC Barcelona.
Ch. record at 1500m: OG: '80– h, '84– 3; WCh: '83– 5; ECh: '78– h, '82– 3; EI: '82– 2, '83– 2; EJ: '75– 8, '77– 1 at 3000m. Spanish 1500m champion 1978, '81–2, '84. Three Spanish 1500m records 1977–82 and Spanish 2000m record in 1984.
Progression at 1500m: 1975 – 3:48.8, 1976 – 3:47.7, 1977 – 3:38.2, 1978 – 3:40.0, 1979 – 3:37.93, 1980 – 3:37.4, 1981 – 3:36.6, 1982 – 3:33.12, 1983 – 3:33.18, 1984 – 3:33.69
pb 800m: 1:49.4 '81, 1000m: 2:19.57 '81, 1 mile: 3:51.71 '83, 2000m: 5:01.1 '84, 3000m: 7:54.56 '84, 5000m: 13:39.27 '84, 3000mSt: 8:38.8 '81

Antonio CORGOS
b.10 Mar 1960 Barcelona 1.83m 76kg
Club: FC Barcelona
Ch. record at LJ: OG: '80– 7, '84– 10; WCh: '83– 7; ECh: '82– 2; EI: '81– 2; EJ: '77– 9. Spanish champion 1980, '82–4. Four Spanish long jump records 1978–80 and European junior records in 1978 and 1979.
Progression at LJ: 1976 – 6.87, 1977 – 7.30/7.35w, 1978 – 8.01, 1979 – 8.09, 1980 – 8.23, 1981 – 7.97i, 1982 – 8.19, 1983 – 8.06, 1984 – 8.02
pb 100m: 10.62/10.57w '83, 10.4/10.2w '84'; HJ: 2.08 '78; TJ: 16.33i '80

José-Luis GONZALEZ
b.8 Dec 1957 Villaluenca de la Sagra, Toledo 1.80m 61kg
Ch. record at 1500m: OG: '80– sf, '84– h; WCh: '83– sf; EI: '82– 1; WIG: '85– 2. EJ: '75– 3 at 3000m.

138

Progression at 1500m: 1975 – 3:46.1, 1976 – 3:45.8, 1977 – 3:49.1, 1978 – 3:43.4, 1979 – 3:36.34, 1980 – 3:35.1, 1981 – 3:34.41, 1982 – 3:38.70i, 1983 – 3:33.44, 1984 – 3:34.61
pbs: 800m: 1:46.6 '83, 1 mile: 3:49.67 '81 (Spanish record), 3000m: 7:45.44 '84 (Spanish record), 5000m: 13:38.0 '80, 10000m: 29:03.5 '80
In Paris in 1983 became the first man to beat Seb Coe in a 1500m or 1 mile final for seven years.

Jorge LLOPART
b.5 May 1952 El Prat de Llobregat, Barcelona 1.69m 59kg
Club: GCR La Seda
Ch. record at 50kmW: OG: '80– 2, '84– 7; WCh: '83– dnf (28 at 20kmW); ECh: '78– 1, '82– 6; LT: '83– 4. Spanish champion 1978-9, '81
Progression at 50kmW: 1975 – 4:30:11, 1976 – 4:22:43, 1978 – 3:53:30, 1979 – 3:44:33, 1980 – 3:45:55, 1981 – 3:48:17, 1982 – 3:51:12, 1983 – 3:47:48, 1984 – 4:03:09.
pb 20kmW: 1:25:20 '80. Track pb: 10kmW: 41:30.4 '80.

José MARIN
b.21 Jan 1950 El Prat de Llobregat 1.64m 60kg
Club: CN Barcelona.

Ch. record at 20kmW/50kmW: OG: '80– 5/6, '84– 6/–; WCh: '83– 4/2; ECh: '78– 5/dnf, '82– 1/2; LT: '79– 7 at 50kW, '81– 5 at 20kW. Spanish champion at 20kmW: '74–5, '77, '79, '81; 50kmW: '80, '82–4. Set world records at 2 hours (28165m) and 30km (2:07:59.8) in 1979.
Progression at 20kmW/50kmW: 1975 – 1:31:17t, 1976 – 1:29:16t/4:13:43, 1977 – 1:33:24t, 1978 – 1:24:39/4:10:48, 1979 – 1:24:18/3:49:46, 1980 – 1:23:52/3:43:35, 1981 – 1:23:54/3:55:37, 1982 – 1:23:27/3:49:08, 1983 – 1:20:00/3:40:46, 1984 – 1:25:17/3:50:12
Track pbs: 3kmW: 11:40.1i '79, 5kmW: 19:24.5 '80, 10kmW: 40:18.7 '81

Domingo RAMON
b.10 Mar 1958 Crevillente, Alicante 1.62m 57kg
Club: Hercules-Benacantil.
Ch. record at 3000mSt: OG: '80– 4, '84– 6; WCh: '83– 10; ECh: '78– h, '82– 3; EJ: '77– 2 at 2000mSt. Won AAA 3000mSt 1984. Spanish champion 1980–2, '84. Spanish steeplechase record 1980.
Progression at 3000mSt: 1976 – 9:09.0, 1977 – 8:44.8, 1978– 8:29.17, 1979 – 8:25.75, 1980 – 8:15.74, 1981 – 8:21.09, 1982 – 8:20.48, 1983 – 8:19.60, 1984 – 8:17.27. pbs: 1500m: 3:49.8, 5000m: 13:44.56 '82

SUDAN

Governing body: Sudan Amateur Athletic Association, P.O.Box 1938, Khartoum. Founded 1959.

OMER KHALIFA
b.1953? 1.77m 63kg Formerly at Loughborough University, England.
Ch. record at 800m/1500m: OG: '84– sf/8; WCh: '83– h/h; AfrG: '78– 8/6; AfrCh: '79– 2/4, '82– 5/4, '84– 3/2; WCp: '81– 5 at 800m. Won AAA 800m 1980.

SWEDEN

Governing body: Svenska Fri-Idrottsförbundet, Sofiatornet, Stadion, S–114 33, Stockholm. Founded 1895.
National Championships first held in 1896 (men), 1927 (women)
1984 Champions: MEN
100m/200m/400m: Tommy Johansson 10.52/21.26/46.19, 800m: Ronny Olsson 1:47.84, 1500m: Johnny Kroon 3:45.64, 5000m/10000m: Mats Erixon 13:53.33/28:40.37, Mar: Tommy Persson 2:15:00, 3000mSt: Jan Hagelbrand 8:45.85, 110mh: Christer Gullstrand 14.45, 400mh: Thomas Nyberg 50.47, HJ: Patrik Sjöberg 2.25, PV: Kasimir Zalar 5.30, LJ: Åke Fransson 7.53, TJ: Thomas Eriksson 16.51w, SP: Anders Jönsson 18.89, DT: Stefan Fernholm 62.76, HT: Kjell Bystedt 65.60, JT: Kenth Eldebrink 83.28, Dec: Staffan Blomstrand 7628, 10kmW/20kmW: Bo Gustafsson 42:15.5/1:26:49.3, 50kmW: Bengt Simonsen 3:59:17
WOMEN
100m: Maria Fernstrom 11.71, 200m/100mh: Ann-Louise Skoglund 23.85/13.88, 400m: Monica Strand 54.38, 800m: Annika Ericson 2:05.97, 1500m: Anette Westerberg 4:21.49, 3000m: Marie-Louise Hamrin 9:08.21, 5000m/Mar: Evy Palm 16:08.13/2:39:38, 400mh: Christina Wennberg 58.66, HJ: Susanne Lorentzon 1.93, LJ: Lena Wallin 6.46w, SP: Caroline Isgren 14.54, DT: Anna Östenberg 47.52, JT: Karin Bergdahl 57.82, Hep: Annette Tånnander 5972, 3kmW/5kmW: Ann Jansson 13:15.9/23:12.9, 10kmW: Siw Vera-Ibañez 47:35.6

Rickard BRUCH
b. 2 Jul 1946 Göteborg 1.98m 130kg
Club: Malmo AI. Disc jockey/ author/ actor etc.
Ch. record at DT: OG: '68– 8, '72– 3, '76– dnq; WCh: '83– dnq; ECh: '69– 2, '71– 9, '74– 3; ECp: '70– 1. At SP: El: '71– 3. Swedish champion at discus: 1967, '69–70, '72–8, '83; shot 1970 and 1972.

Set world discus record at 68.40m in 1972, following a European record 68.06m in 1969. Swedish records: five at shot 1968–73, 15 at discus 1968–84.
Progression at DT: 1964 – 52.36, 1965 – 53.73, 1966 – 56.26, 1967 – 59.34, 1968 – 61.98, 1969 – 68.06, 1970 – 67.14, 1971 – 68.32, 1972 – 68.58, 1973 – 67.58, 1974 – 68.16, 1975 – 66.88,

139

National Championships

1976 – 63.64, 1977 – 63.60, 1978 – 60.78, 1979 – 56.30, 1980 – 56.90, 1981 – 64.50, 1982 – 63.44, 1983 – 67.08, 1984 – 71.26.
pbs: SP: 20.28 '73, HT: 61.08 '71.
Made a remarkable return to achieve his first 70m throw at the age of 38, setting Swedish records of 70.48, 71.00 and 71.26 in late 1984.

Kenth ELDEBRINK
b.14 May 1955 Morjärv 1.90m 95kg
Club: Södertalje IF. Teacher.
Ch. record at JT: OG: '84– 3; WCh: '83– 6; ECh: '78– dnq, '82– 11. Swedish champion 1977, '79, '82, '84. Two Swedish javelin records 1981–3.
Progression at JT: 1972 – 44.40, 1973 – 63.74, 1974 – 73.96, 1975 – 73.00, 1976 – 84.58, 1977 – 81.68, 1978 – 82.26, 1979 – 88.24, 1980 – 86.26, 1981 – 90.00, 1982 – 87.96, 1983 – 91.14, 1984 – 87.08.
pbs: SP:15.91 '82, DT: 50.00 '77

Bo GUSTAFSSON
b.29 Sep 1954 Stromstad 1.75m 64kg
Club: Enhorna.
Ch. record at 50kmW: OG: '80– dnf (dq 20kmW), '84– 2; WCh: '83– dnf; ECh: '78– 10 at 20kmW, '82– 3 (dq 20kmW).
Progression at 50kmW: 1979 – 4:14:57, 1981 – 4:03:55, 1982 – 3:53:22, 1983 – 3:51:49, 1984 – 3:53:19.
pb 20kmW: 1:21:38 '83

Sven NYLANDER
b.1 Jan 1962 Varberg 1.92m 80kg
Club: IF Göta. Southern Methodist University, USA (won NCAA 400mh '83)

Ch. record at 400mh: OG: '84– 4; WCh: '83– 4; ECh: '82– 7; EJ: '79– 6 at 110mh. Swedish champion at 400mh 1982, 110mh 1979 and 1983. Two Swedish 400mh records 1982–3.
Progression at 400mh: 1978 – 54.8, 1979 – 52.62, 1981 – 51.58, 1982 – 49.64, 1983 – 48.88, 1984 – 48.97.
pb 400m: 47.8i '81, 48.10 '82; 110mh: 14.07 '83.

Patrik SJÖBERG
b.5 Jan 1965 Göteborg 2.00m 78kg
Club: Örgryte IS.
Ch. record at HJ: OG: '84– 2; WCh: '83– 11; ECh: '82– 10=; EJ: '81– 8, '83– 3; WIG: '85– 1. Swedish champion 1981–4. Eight Swedish high jump records 1982–4.
Progression at HJ: 1976 – 1.40, 1977 – 1.59, 1978 – 1.80, 1979 – 1.91, 1980 – 2.07, 1981 – 2.21, 1982 – 2.26, 1983 – 2.33, 1984 – 2.33
pb LJ: 7.21 '82, TJ: 15.87 '83.

WOMEN

Ann-Louise SKOGLUND
b.28 Jun 1962 Karlstad 1.74m 58kg
Club: IF Göta. Clerk.
Ch. record at 400m: OG: '84– 5; WCh: '83– 6; ECh: '82– 1. At 400m: OG: '80– ht, EJ: '79– 6. Swedish champion at 100m 1980, 200m 1982–4, 400m 1980–1, 100mh 1981 and 1984, 400mh 1978, '80. Swedish records: four at 400m 1980–3, nine at 400mh 1978–82.
Progression at 400mh: 1977 – 62.6, 1978 – 57.58, 1979 – 57.87, 1980 – 56.68, 1981 – 56.00, 1982 – 54.57, 1983 – 54.80, 1984 – 55.17.
pbs: 100m: 11.87 '82, 11.7 '78, 11.5w '77; 200m: 23.47 '82, 400m: 51.78 '83, 100mh: 13.46 '81, 13.26w '82; LJ: 5.59 '82.

SWITZERLAND

Governing body: SALV (Schweizerischer Leichtathletikverband), Case Postale 2233, CH 3001, Berne. Formed in 1905 as the Athletischer Ausschuss des Schweizerischen Fussball-Verbandes.
National Championships first held in 1906 (men), 1934 (women).

1984 Champions: MEN
100m/200m/LJ: René Gloor 10.40w?/21.01/8.11w, 400m: Marcel Arnold 45.37, 800m: Peter Wirz 1:48.56, 1500m: Markus Ryffel 3:41.40, 5000m/10000m: Kurt Hürst 14:29.35/29:53.76, 3kmSt: Roland Hertner 8:47.09, Mar: Michael Longthorn (UK) 2:17:23, 110mh: Jean-Marc Muster 13.98, 400mh: Franz Meier 49.77, HJ: Roland Dalhäuser 2.26, PV: Daniel Forter 4.80, TJ: Roland Steinemann 15.28, SP: Werner Gunthor 20.31, DT: Theo Wyss 51.48, HT: Michele Obrist 65.34, JT: Alfred Grossenbacher 78.54, Dec: Michele Rüfenacht 7920
WOMEN
100m/200m: Vroni Werthmuller 11.33w?/23.50, 400m: Elisabeth Hofstetter 53.84, 800m/1500m/3000m: Cornelia Bürki 2:07.21/4:18.20/9:36.10, Mar: Margrit Isenegger 2:47:26, 100mh/LJ: Rita Heggli 13.50/6.27, 400mh: Caroline Plüss 58.57, HJ: Kathrin Lindenthal 1.80, SP: Ursula Staheli 15.67, DT: Claudia Elsener 49.14, JT: Regula Egger 60.02.

Felix BOHNI
b.14 Feb 1958 1.89m 82kg
Club: LC Zürich. Student at San Jose State University, USA.
Ch. record at PV: OG: '80– dnq, '84– 7; WCh: '83– 10=; ECh: '82– 9; EJ: '75– 2, '77– 2. Won NCAA 1983. Swiss champion 1976–9, 1981, 1983. Twelve Swiss pole vault records 1976–83
Progression at PV: 1973 – 4.40, 1974 – 4.69, 1975 – 4.87, 1976 – 5.25, 1977 – 5.30i/5.20, 1978 – 5.30, 1979 – 5.30, 1980 – 5.55, 1981 – 5.40, 1982 – 5.52, 1983 – 5.71, 1984 – 5.60

Roland DALHAUSER
b.12 Apr 1958 1.91m 86kg
Club: LC Zürich. Caretaker.
Ch. record at HJ: OG: '80– 5, '84– nh; WCh: '83– dnq; ECh: '82– 7; EI: '81– 1, '82– 3, '84– 2=. Swiss champion 1979–80, 1982–3. Nine Swiss high jump records 1976–81.
Progression at HJ: 1973 – 1.44, 1974 – 1.85, 1975 – 2.00, 1976 – 2.18, 1977 – 2.21, 1978 – 2.19, 1979 – 2.22, 1980 – 2.26i/2.25, 1981 – 2.31, 1982 – 2.32i/2.30, 1983 – 2.30, 1984 – 2.30

Pierre DELEZE
b.25 Sep 1958 Nendaz 1.75m 62kg
Club: CA Sion. Arts graduate.
Ch. record at 1500m: OG: '80– ht, '84– ht; WCh: '83– 6; ECh: '78– h, '82– 1; EI: '80– 3; EJ: '77– 3; WSG: '79– 2. Swiss 1500m champion 1978–81. Swiss record holder 1000m, 1500m, 1M, 2000m.

National Championships

Progression at 1500m: 1974 – 4:01.82, 1975 – 3:49.84, 1976 – 3:49.8, 1977 – 3:41.8, 1978 – 3:39.82, 1979 – 3:36.7, 1980 – 3:33.80, 1981 – 3:36.90, 1982 – 3:34.40, 1983 – 3:32.97, 1984 – 3:33.64
Other pbs: 800m: 1:48.92 '82, 1000m: 2:16.87 '83, 1M: 3:50.38 '82, 2000m: 4:56.51 '83, 3000m: 7:44.08 '80, 5000m: 13:28.77 '82

Werner GUNTHOR
b.1 Jun 1961 2.00m 124kg
Club: ST Bern. Commercial student.
Ch. record at SP: OG: '84– 5; WCh: '83– dnq; El: '84– 2. Swiss champion 1981–4. Three Swiss shot records in 1984.
Progression at SP: 1978 – 13.60, 1979 – 15.08, 1980 – 16.42, 1981 – 16.65, 1982 – 17.51i, 1983 – 20.01, 1984 – 20.80.
pbs: DT: 51.72 '84, JT: 74.88 '81

Franz MEIER
b.16 Sep 1956 1.76m 67kg
Club: LV Wettingen-Baden. Construction engineer.
Ch. record at 400mh: OG: '80– 7, '84– sf; WCh: '83– sf; ECh: '78– 4, '82– sf; EJ: '75– 7. Swiss champion 1978–9, 1981, 1983–4. Three Swiss 400mh records 1978–84
Progression at 400mh: 1975 – 51.85, 1976 – 51.35, 1977 – 50.5, 1978 – 49.84, 1979 – 50.48, 1980 – 50.00, 1981 – 50.07, 1982 – 50.31, 1983 – 49.53, 1984 – 49.42.
pbs: 400m: 47.95 '84, 110mh: 14.33 '78

Stephan NIKLAUS
b.17 Apr 1958 1.89m 90kg
Club: LC Basel. Draughtsman.
Ch. record at Dec: OG: '80– 12; WCh: '83– 5; ECh: '82– dnf; ECp: '83– 2. Swiss champion 1981–3. Four Swiss decathlon records 1981–3.
Progression at Dec: 1976 – 6345, 1977 – 7070, 1978 – 7375, 1979 – 7242, 1980 – 7766, 1981 – 8118, 1982 – 8176, 1983 – 8337, 1984 – 8036.
pbs: 100m: 10.64 '81, 10.59w '83, 400m: 47.41 '82, 1500m: 4:37.7, 110mh: 14.47 '81, HJ: 2.07 '8., PV: 4.50 '82, LJ: 7.48 '83, SP: 15.77 '83, DT: 49.56 '83, JT: 73.96 '82.

Markus RYFFEL
b.5 Feb 1955 1.67m 55kg

Club: ST Bern. Shop-keeper, formerly a typographer.
Ch. record at 5000m: OG: '76– ht, '80– 5 (dnf 10km), '84– 2; WCh: '83– 12 (dnf 10km); ECh: '78– 2=, '82– 10; EJ: '73– 7. At 3000m: El: '77– 3, '78– 1, '79– 1, '84– 2. Has won 13 Swiss senior titles at various distances. Swiss record holder at 3000m, 5000m and 10000m – first record in 1976.
Progression at 5000m/10000m: 1972 – 15:15.8, 1973 – 14:03.1, 1974 – 14:08.8/30:21.8, 1975 – 13:50.8/28:54.04, 1976 – 13:32.65/28:05.37, 1977 – 13:23.93 28:36.0, 1978 – 13:19.97/28:21.55, 1979 – 13:13.32/28:41.7, 1980 – 13:23.03/28:47.8, 1981 – 13:19.74/27:54.99, 1982 – 13:17.80/28:19.9, 1983 – 13:19.38/27:54.88, 1984 – 13:07.54/29:05.89
pbs: 1500m: 3:38.6 '79, 1M: 3:58.05 '84, 2000m: 4:59.54 '78, 3000m: 7:41.00 '79, Mar: 2:16:40 '83
Fast finisher, returned to best in 1984.

Peter WIRZ
b.29 Jul 1960 1.81m 68kg
Club: ST Bern. Operations planner.
Ch. record at 1500m: OG: '84– 6; WCh: '83– h; El: '84– 1; EJ: '79– 3. Swiss 800m champion 1983–4.
Progression at 1500m: 1979 – 3:42.7, 1980 – 3:45.00, 1982 – 3:40.61, 1983 – 3:36.81, 1984 – 3:35.83
Other pbs: 800m: 1:47.98 '84, 1000m: 2:18.37 '83; 1M: 3:57.74 '83; 2000m: 4:58.29 '84, 3000m: 7:55.68 '83

WOMEN

Cornelia BURKI
b.3 Oct 1953 South Africa 1.60m 53kg. Swiss national by marriage.
Ch. record: At 1500m: OG: '80– h; WCh: '83– 11; ECh: '78– 8. At 3000m: OG: '84– 5; WCh: '83– 11; ECh: '78– 6, '82– 11. 5th World cross-country 1978. Swiss record holder at 800m, 1500m, 1 mile and 3000m – first record in 1976.
Progression at 1500m/3000m: 1974: 4:32.20/–, 1975 – 4:14.5/9:15.4, 1976 – 4:09.9/9:33.8, 1977 – 4:12.14/9:07.56, 1978 – 4:04.60/8:46.13, 1979 – 4:06.3/–, 1980 – 4:04.39/8:53.76, 1981 – 4:09.65/9:16.02, 1982 – 4:07.88/8:55.67, 1983 – 4:07.85/8:46.94, 1984 – 4:05.67/8:45.20
pbs: 800m: 2:01.14 '79, 1M: 4:31.75 '84, Mar: 2:42:33 '84

TANZANIA

Governing body: Tanzania Amateur Athletic Association, PO Box 2172, Dar-es-Salaam. Founded 1954.

Zakariah BARIE
b.29 May 1953 1.74m 56kg
Ch. record at 10000m (5000m): OG: '80– dnf (sf), '84– 14; WCh: '83– h; CG: '82– 2 (4)
Progression at 10000m: 1980 – 28:29.9?, 1981 – 28:54.19, 1982 – 27:38.6, 1983 – 28:02.2, 1984 – 28:03.17
pbs: 3000m: 7:51.46i '84, 5000m: 13:29.47 '80, Mar: 2:11:47 '84
Ran road 10km best of 27:43 and was second in the Rotterdam marathon in 1984.

Juma IKANGAA
b.19 Jul 1957 Dodoma 1.63m 58kg
Ch. record at Mar: OG: '84– 6; WCh: '83– 15; CG: '82– 2; AfrCh: '82– 1
Progression at Mar: 1982 – 2:09:30, 1983 : 2:08:55, 1984 – 2:10:49

pbs: 5000m: 14:17.6 '81, 10000m: 28:23.29 '84
First African to better 2hrs 10min for marathon, when second to de Castella in epic Commonwealth duel in 1982. Improved his African best when second at Fukuoka in 1983. Won Tokyo and Melbourne marathons and sixth in London in 1984.

Gidamis SHAHANGA
b.3 Sep 1957 Katesh 1.80m 57kg University of Texas at El Paso, USA
Ch. record at Mar: OG: '80– 15, '84– 22 (h 10000m); CG: '78– 1, '82– 6 (1 at 10000m); AfrG: '78– 1; AfrCh: '79–2; WCh: '83– 5 at 10000m. Won NCAA 5000m and 10000m 1983.
Progression at 10000m/Mar: 1978 – 2:15:40, 1979 – 30:15.0/2:18:50, 1980 – 2:16:47, 1981 – 28:12.6, 1982 – 27:38.1/2:14:25, 1983 – 27:46.93/2:11:05, 1984 – 28:03.24/2:10:19.
pbs: 3000m: 7:48.26 '83, 5000m: 13:34.18 '83
Shahanga was the first African ever to win the Commonwealth title and also the youngest ever medallist at the event when he scored a major upset in 1978. Won a second Commonwealth gold at 10000m in 1982. Won marathons at Los Angeles and Rotterdam in 1984.

141

National Championships

UNITED KINGDOM

Governing body: British Amateur Athletic Board, Francis House, Francis Street, London SW1P 1DL. Founded 1932. The Amateur Athletic Association was founded in 1880 and the Women's Amateur Athletic Association in 1922.
UK National Championships first held in 1977.
1984 Champions: MEN
100m: Mike McFarlane 10.08w, 200m: Todd Bennett 20.36, 400m: Kriss Akabusi 46.10, 800m: Peter Elliott 1:46.08, 1500m: Alan Salter 3:43.31, 5000m: Eamonn Martin 13:32.11, 10000m: Nick Rose 28:00.70, 3000mSt: Paul Davies-Hale 8:33.16, 110mh: Hugh Teape 13.98w, 400mh: Martin Briggs 50.97, HJ: Alex Kruger 2.15, PV: Keith Stock 5.35, LJ: Derrick Brown 7.71w, TJ: Aston Moore 16.80, SP: Billy Cole 17.57, DT: Paul Mardle 59.70, HT: David Smith 72.34, JT: Peter Yates 82.54, Dec: Brad McStravick 7975w, 10000mW: Phil Vesty 40:53.60
WOMEN
100m/200m: Heather Oakes 11.08w/23.00w, 400m: Jane Parry 53.46, 800m: Christina Boxer 2:01.64, 1500m: Zola Budd 4:04.39, 3000m: Christine Benning 8:56.79, 5000m: Angela Tooby 15:27.56, 100mh: Pat Rollo 13.12w, 400mh: Gladys Taylor 58.2, HJ: Diana Elliott 1.90, LJ: Susan Hearnshaw 7.00w, SP: Judy Oakes 17.94, DT: Venissa Head 57.44, JT: Fatima Whitbread 65.44, Hep: Kim Hagger 6100, 5000mW: Jill Barrett 23:53.13

National Road Walk Champions: MEN – 20kmW: Ian McCombie 1:25:34, 50kmW: Paul Blagg 4:20:31. WOMEN – 5kmW: Jill Barrett 23:38, 10kmW: Virginia Birch 50:25.

AAA Championships first held in 1880. 1984 Champions: 100m: Donovan Reid 10.42, 200m: Todd Bennett 20.79w, 400m: Darren Clark (Aus) 45.66, 800m: Steve Cram 1:46.84, 1500m: Peter Elliott 3:39.66, 5000m: Ray Flynn (Ire) 13:19.52, 10000m: Steve Jones 28:09.97, Mar: Charlie Spedding 2:09:57, 3000mSt: Domingo Ramon (Spa) 8:23.12, 110mh: Nigel Walker 13.78, 400mh: Martin Gillingham 50.24, HJ: Francisco Centelles (Cub) 2.30, PV: Jeff Gutteridge 5.40, LJ: Fred Salle 7.59, TJ: Lazaro Betancourt (Cub) 16.93, SP: Mike Winch 18.39, DT: Robert Weir 62.50, HT: David Smith 72.40, JT: David Ottley 81.34, Dec: Kevin Atkinson (Ire) 7451, 3000mW: Phil Vesty 11:42.94, 10000mW: Ian McCombie 41:33.0

WAAA Championships first held in 1922. 1984 Champions: 100m/200m: Kathy Cook 11.44/22.77, 400m: Tracy Lawton 52.74, 800m: Heather Barralet (Aus) 2:02.37, 1500m: Christine Benning 4:07.27, 3000m: Debbie Peel 9:15.0, 5000m: Shireen Samy 16:10.10, Mar: Priscilla Welch 2:30:06, 100mh: Shirley Strong 12.96, 400mh: Gladys Taylor 56.78, HJ: Diana Elliott 1.86, LJ: Susan Hearnshaw 6.79w, SP: Judy Oakes 18.01, DT: Lynda Whiteley 57.32, JT: Fatima Whitbread 65.76, Hep: Sarah Owen 5150, 5000mW: Jill Barrett 23:51.63

Todd BENNETT
b.6 Jul 1962 Southampton 1.70m 66kg
Club: Southampton & Eastleigh. Clerical officer.
Ch. record at 400m (R – 4x400m relay): OG: '84– qf (2R); WCh: '83– sf (3R); ECh: '82– sf (2R); CG: '82– 5 (1R); EJ: '81– 1 (2R); ECp: '83– 1R; WIG: '85– 2. At 200m won UK and AAA titles 1984. Set Commonwealth bests at 300m in 1984 and 400m indoors (45.97) in 1985.
Progression at 400m: 1978 – 50.9, 1979 – 48.8, 1980 – 47.54, 1981 – 46.6, 1982 – 45.89, 1983 – 45.58, 1984 – 45.45.
pbs: 100m: 10.6 '82, 10.5w '81; 200m: 20.36 '84, 300m: 32.14 '84, 400mh: 52.6 '83, LJ: 7.01 '82.

Ikem BILLY
b.25 Jan 1964 Oxton, Birkenhead 1.81m 62kg
Club: Wirral. Student at Loughborough.
Ch. record at 800m: EJ: '83– 1; EI: '84– 4; WIG: '85– 3.
Progression at 800m: 1977 – 2:18.0, 1978 – 2:11.5, 1979 – 2:04.1, 1981 – 1:55.0, 1982 – 1:50.8, 1983 – 1:47.0, 1984 – 1:44.65
pbs: 400m: 47.4 '84, 1500m: 3:43.3 '84, 1M: 4:03.89 '84.

Sebastian COE
b.29 Sep 1956 Chiswick, London 1.77m 54kg
Club: Haringey. Graduate of Loughborough University.
Ch. record at 800m: OG: '80– 2, '84– 2; ECh: '78– 3, '82– 2; EI: '77– 1; WCp: '81– 1; ECp: '77– 4, '79– 1, '81– 1. At 1500m: OG: '80– 1, '84– 1; EJ: '75– 3. UK 800m champion 1978. Won AAA 800m 1981. Britain's most prolific world record setter: 800m (2), 1000m (2), 1500m (1), 1M (3), 4x800mR (1) 1979–82. Set world indoor records at 800m: 1:46.0 in 1981 and 1:44.91 in 1983 and 1000m: 2:18.58 in 1983. UK records: 800m (5), 1000m (2), 1500m (2), 1M (3) in 1977–81.
Progression at 800m, 1500m/1M: 1970: –, 4:31.8; 1971 – 2:08.4, 4:18.0; 1972 – 1:59.9, 4:05.9; 1973 – 1:56.0, 3:55.0; 1975 – 1:53.8, 3:45.2; 1976 – 1:47.7, 3:42.67/3:58.35; 1977 – 1:44.95, –/3:57.67; 1978 – 1:43.97, –/4:02.17; 1979 – 1:42.33, 3:32.03/3:48.95; 1980 – 1:44.7, 3:32.19; 1981 – 1:41.73, 3:31.95/3:47.33; 1982 – 1:44.48, 3:39.1/3:59.5; 1983 – 1:43.80, 3:35.17/3:52.93; 1984 – 1:43.64, 3:32.39/3:54.6.
pbs: 400m: 46.87 '79, 600m: 1:14.1 '78, 1000m: 2:12.18 '81, 2000m: 4:58.84 '82, 3000m: 7:55.2i '81, 5000m: 14:06.2 '80
Made wonderful recovery from serious illness in 1983 to retain Olympic 1500m title. Was undefeated in a 1500m or 1 mile final from 14 Sep 1976 to 24 Jun 1983.

Keith CONNOR
b.16 Sep 1957 Anguilla, West Indies 1.86m 78kg
Club: Windsor, Slough & Eton. Graduate of Southern Methodist University, USA
Ch. record at TJ: OG: '80– 4, '84– 3; WCh: '83– 15; ECh: '78– 6, '82– 1; CG: '78– 1, '82– 1; EI: '78– 2; WSG: '81– 3; ECp: '77– 4, '83– 4. UK champion 1978 and 1980. Won AAA 1979, NCAA 1982–3. Set world indoor triple jump best at 17.31m to win NCAA title in 1981. Three UK, including two Commonwealth, records 1978–82.
Progression at TJ: 1974 – 14.25, 1975 – 14.78, 1976 – 15.95, 1977 – 16.33, 1978 – 16.76/17.21w, 1979 – 16.48i, 1980 – 17.16, 1981 – 17.31i, 1982 – 17.57/17.81w, 1983 – 17.26/17.48w, 1984 – 16.87.
pbs: 100m: 10.81/10.69w '79, 200m: 21.9 '79, 400m: 49.4 '76, LJ: 7.71i '81

Garry COOK
b.10 Jan 1958 Wednesbury, W.Midlands 1.83m 72kg
Club: Wolverhampton & Bilston. Manager Alexander Stadium, Birmingham. Married to Kathy Cook (qv).
Ch. record at 800m (R– 4x400m relay): OG: 84– 2R; WCh: '83–

142

National Championships

sf (3R); ECh: '82– 4 (2R); CG: '78– 5, '82– sf (1R); EJ: '77– 4; WSG: '79– 2; ECp: '83– 1R Ran on world record 4 x 800m relay team 1982.
Progression at 800m: 1974 – 1:54.4, 1975 – 1:51.4, 1976 – 1:50.9, 1977 – 1:47.75, 1978 – 1:45.84, 1979 – 1:46.28, 1980 – 1:46.85, 1981 – 1:45.42, 1982 – 1:44.71, 1983 – 1:44.96, 1984 – 1:44.55
pbs: 200m: 21.7 '81, 400m: 46.18 '80/ 46.0 '81, 600m: 1:15.4 '84, 1000m: 2:18.28 '81, 1500m: 3:49.7 '78, 400mh: 52.31 '80

Steve CRAM
b.14 Oct 1960 Gateshead 1.86m 69kg
Club: Jarrow & Hebburn.
Ch. record at 1500m: OG: '80– 8, '84– 2; WCh: '83– 1; CG: '78– h, '82– 1; ECh: '82– 1; ECp: '81– 3, '83– 1. At 3000m: EJ: '79– 1. AAA champion at 1500m 1981–3, 800m 1984. Ran on world record 4 x 800m relay team 1982.
Progression at 1500m/1 mile: 1973 – 4:31.5, 1974 – 4:22.3, 1975 – 4:13.9, 1976 – 4:07.1, 1977 – 3:47.7, 1978 – 3:40.09/3:57.43, 1979 – 3:42.5/3:57.03, 1980 – 3:34.74/3:53.8, 1981 – 3:34.81/3:49.95, 1982 – 3:33.66/3:49.90, 1983 – 3:31.66/3:52.56, 1984 – 3:33.13/3:49.65
pbs: 400m: 49.1 '82, 600m: 1:16.79 '83, 800m: 1:43.61 '83, 1000m: 2:15.98 '84, 3000m: 7:43.1 '83, 2 miles: 8:14.9 '83, 5000m: 14:13.5 '79.
Set world age 17 mile best in 1978. Despite severe injury problems completed a major championship hat trick in 1983 and went on to gain Olympic silver in 1984.

Peter ELLIOTT
b.Rawmarsh, Rotherham 1.81m 67kg
Club: Rotherham. Joiner with British Steel.
Ch. record at 800m: OG: '84– sf; WCh: '83– 4; EI: '83– 2; EJ: '81– 4; ECp: '83– 3. UK 800m champion 1983–4. Won AAA 800m 1982, 1500m 1984. Ran on world record 4 x 800m team 1982.
Progression at 800m: 1975 – 2:20.8, 1976 – 2:05.9, 1977 – 2:01.9, 1978 – 1:52.05, 1979 – 1:50.7, 1980 – 1:51.3, 1981 – 1:47.35, 1982 – 1:45.61, 1983 – 1:43.98, 1984 – 1:45.49.
pbs: 400m: 48.2 '84, 600m: 1:16.6 '83, 1000m: 2:17.65 '83, 1500m: 3:36.97 '84, 1M: 3:55.71 '84.
In 1984 became the first British runner to beat Seb Coe at 1500m since 1976.

Roger HACKNEY
b.2 Sep 1957 Swansea 1.83m 74kg
Club: Aldershot, Farnham & District. Doctor in the Royal Air Force. Graduate of Birmingham University.
Ch. record at 3kmSt: OG: '80– sf, '84– 10; WCh: '83– 5; ECh: '82– h; CG: '82– 4 (11 at 5000m); ECp: '81– 7. UK champion 1982, AAA champion 1980 and 1982.
Progression at 3000mSt: 1977 – 9:10.0, 1978 – 8:47.60, 1979 – 8:32.97, 1980 – 8:27.12, 1981 – 8:29.71, 1982 – 8:21.41, 1983 – 8:19.38, 1984 – 8:20.16
pbs: 1500m: 3:43.65 '82, 1M: 4:03.3 '83, 2000m: 5:07.99 '83, 3000m: 7:49.47 '84, 5000m: 13:48.17 '80, 2000mSt: 5:23.6 '82 (UK best), 400mh: 56.8 '81
Wife Gillian is a useful sprinter (54.9 for 400m).

Tim HUTCHINGS
b.4 Dec 1958 London 1.83m 71kg
Club: Crawley. Graduate of Loughborough University.
Ch. record at 5000m: OG: '84– 2; WCh: '82– 7; CG: '82– 14. At 1500m CG: '78– 10. UK champion 1982. World cross-country: '84– 2. English National X–C champion 1983.
Progression at 5000m: 1979 – 14:06.76, 1981 – 14:18.4, 1982 – 13:25.08, 1983 – 13:24.10, 1984 – 13:11.50

Hugh JONES
b.1 Nov 1955 North London 1.79m 60kg
Club: Ranelagh H. Graduate of Liverpool University.
Ch. record at Mar: OG: '84– 12; WCh: '83– 8; ECp: '81– 5.
Progression at Mar: 1978 – 2:25:13, 1979 – 2:20:28, 1980 – 2:18:56, 1981 – 2:11:00, 1982 – 2:09:24, 1983 – 2:09:45, 1984 – 2:11:54.
pbs: 5000m: 14:04.2 '78, 10000m: 28:49.51 '78.
Has run 14 marathons, winning five including AAA 1981 and London 1982. Much troubled by Achilles tendon injuries.

Steve JONES
b.4 Aug 1955 Tredegar, Gwent 1.78m 61kg
Club: Newport H. Corporal in the Royal Air Force (technician).
Ch. record at 10000m: OG: '84– 8; WCh: '83– 12; ECh: '82– 7; CG: '82– 11; ECp: '83– 5. At 5000m: CG: '78– 11. World cross-country: '79– 7, '80– 9, '84– 3. Won AAA 10000m titles both on track and road in 1984. Set world marathon best of 2:08:05 in 1984.
Progression at 10000m: 1980 – 28:13.25, 1981 – 28:00.58, 1982 – 28:05.74, 1983 – 27:39.14, 1984 – 27:58.64.
pbs: 1500m: 3:42.3 '82, 1M: 4:00.6" '80, 3000m: 7:49.80 '84, 2M: 8:26.71 '80, 5000m: 13:18.6 '82, 3000mSt: 8:32.00 '80.
After placing worthily, though a little disappointingly in all the major 10000m championships over the past three seasons, he moved sensationally into the limelight by winning the 1984 Chicago marathon in the world's best time. His only previous attempt at the event had resulted in him dropping out of Chicago in 1983.

Mike McFARLANE
b.2 May 1960 London 1.78m 76kg
Club: Haringey.
Ch. record (R– 4x100m relay): OG: '80– qf 200m (4R), '84– 5 100m; CG: '78– 5 100m/sf 200m, '82– 5 100m/ 1= 200m; EJ: '79– 3 100m/ 1 200m (2R). UK champion at 100m 1984, 200m 1982.
Progression at 100m: 1975 – 10.9/10.8w, 1976 – 10.69, 1977 – 10.61, 1978 – 10.32/10.29w, 1979 – 10.43, 1980 – 10.59/10.32w, 1981 – 10.49/10.35w/10.3, 1982 – 10.37/10.11w, 1983 – 10.42/10.20w, 1984 – 10.27/10.08w.
pbs: 200m: 20.43 '82, 300m: 34.2 '83

Mike McLEOD
b.25 Jan 1952 Dilston, Northumberland 1.81m 63kg
Club: Elswick H. Travel consultant.
Ch. record at 10000m: OG: '80– 12, '84– 2; ECh: '78– 14; CG: '78– 3, '82– 9. At 5000m: ECh: '82– 12; CG: '78– 4. Won IAAF 'Golden 10km' 1979 and 1981. UK 5000m champion 1978. World cross-country: '82– 5. English National X–C champion 1979.
Progression at 10000m: 1977 – 28:10.23, 1978 – 28:04.21, 1979 – 27:39.76, 1980 – 28:40.78, 1981 – 27:59.42, 1982 – 28:46.97, 1983 – 28:49.65, 1984 – 28:06.22
pbs: 800m: 1:53.7 '75, 1500m: 3:45.3 '78, 1M: 3:56.38 '79, 3000m: 7:48.18 '78, 2M: 8:25.6 '80, 5000m: 13:23.36 '80, Mar: 2:20:50 '83.
Moved up from bronze to silver after Vainio's disqualification from the Olympic 10000m. Had outstanding road running season in 1984.

Ade MAFE
b.12 Nov 1966 Isleworth, Middlesex 1.85m 77kg
Club: London Irish. Student.
Ch. record at 200m: OG: '84– 8; EJ: '83– 5; EI: '84– 2; WIG: '85– 2. Commonwealth indoor 200m bests of 21.13 and 20.96 in 1985.

143

National Championships

Progression at 200m: 1978 – 26.1, 1979 – 24.1, 1980 – 23.3, 1981 – 22.4, 1982 – 21.6, 1983 – 20.92, 1984 – 20.57/20.55w
pbs: 100m: 10.58 '84 (in 200m!), 300m: 32.85 '84, 400m: 49.8i '83.
Set UK junior 200m record to reach Olympic final, at 17 Britain's youngest ever male Olympic finalist.

David MOORCROFT
b.10 Apr 1953 Coventry 1.80m 68kg
Club: Coventry Godiva. Director of community sports project. Was at Loughborough.
Ch. record at 5000m: OG: '80– sf, '84– 14; ECh: '82– 3; CG: '82– 1; ECp: '81– 1. At 1500m: OG: '76– 7; ECh: '78– 3; CG: '78– 1. AAA 1500m champion 1978, UK champion at 1500m and 5000m 1980. Set world 5000m record and UK record in 1982.
Progression at 5000m: 1973 – 14:31.0, 1974 – 14:04.8, 1975 – 14:06.8, 1976 – 13:58.4, 1979 – 13:30.33, 1980 – 13:29.1, 1981 – 13:20.51, 1982 – 13:00.41, 1984 – 13:28.44
pbs: 800m: 1:46.64 '82, 1000m: 2:18.95 '76, 1500m: 3:33.79 '82, 1M: 3:49.34 '82, 2000m: 5:02.89 '82, 3000m: 7:32.79 '82, 2M: 8:16.75 '82
Sadly illness and injuries caused him to miss nearly all the 1983 season, and although he made the 1984 Olympic final, he could do no more than trail around in last place, a pale reflection of the great athlete of his 'annus mirabilis' in 1982.

David OTTLEY
b.5 Aug 1955 Thurrock 1.88m 95kg
Club: Telford. Youth Training Scheme supervisor, former school teacher. Was at Borough Road College.
Ch. record at JT: OG: '80– dnq, '84– 2; ECh: '82– 12; CG: '78– 5, '82– 7; WSG: '77– 2; ECp: '79– 4, '81– 5, '83– 4. UK champion 1978–82 and won AAA 1977, '82, '84. UK javelin record in 1980.
Progression at JT: 1970 – 54.94, 1971 – 62.20, 1972 – 66.34, 1973 – 66.52, 1974 – 72.10, 1975 – 74.74, 1976 – 80.08, 1977 – 81.50, 1978 – 79.20, 1979 – 80.82, 1980 – 85.52, 1981 – 84.40, 1982 – 85.36, 1983 – 84.76, 1984 – 85.86.
pb SP: 14.49 '81.
Achieved greatest success with Olympic silver on his 29th birthday.

Steve OVETT
b.9 Oct 1955 Brighton 1.83m 70kg
Club: Phoenix, Brighton.
Ch. record at 800m: OG: '76– 5, '80– 1, '84– 8; ECh: '74– 2, '78– 2; EJ: '73– 1; ECp: '75– 1. At 1500m: OG: '76– sf, '80– 3, '84– dnf; WCh: '83– 4; ECh: '78– 1; WCp: '77– 1, '81– 1; ECp: '77– 1. UK 1500m champion 1977 and 1981. Won AAA 800m 1974–6, 1500m 1979–80. Set first world record at 3:32.09 for 1500m in 1980, followed by two more at 1500m 1980 and 1983 and two at 1 mile 1980 and 1981. Set world 2 miles best in 1978. UK records: 800m (1), 1000m (1), 1500m (4), (4), 2000m (2) 1977–83. European junior 800m record in 1974.
Progression at 800m, 1500m/1M: 1970 – 2:00.0, 4:10.7; 1971 – 1:55.3; 1972 – 1:52.5, 4:01.5; 1973 – 1:47.34, 3:44.8/4:00.0; 1974 – 1:45.76, 3:46.2/3:59.4; 1975 – 1:46.09, 3:39.5/3:57.00; 1976 – 1:45.44, 3:37.89; 1977 – 1:48.31, 3:34.45/3:54.69; 1978 – 1:44.09, 3:35.59/3:52.8; 1979 – 1:44.91, 3:32.11/3:49.57; 1980 – 1:45.40, 3:31.36/3:48.8; 1981 – 1:46.40, 3:31.57/3:48.40; 1982 – 1:46.08, 3:38.48; 1983 – 1:45.25, 3:30.77/3:50.49; 1984 – 1:44.81, 3:34.50.
pbs: 400m: 47.5 '74, 600m: 1:16.0 '79, 1000m: 2:15.91 '79, 2000m: 4:57.71 '82, 3000m: 7:41.3 '77, 2M: 8:13.51 '78, 5000m: 13:25.0 '77.
Started his championship success at 400m with the English Schools Junior title in 1970 and AAA Youth titles in 1971 and 1972. Bravely failed to overcome bronchial problems at the 1984 Olympics. Won 45 successive races at 1500m or 1 mile 1977–80.

Colin REITZ
b.6 Apr 1960 Clapton, London 1.86m 73kg
Club: Newham & Essex Beagles.
Ch. record at 3000mSt: OG: '80– sf, '84– 5; WCh: '83– 3; ECh: '82– 9; CG: '82– 8 (6 at 1500m); EJ: '79– 2 at 2000mSt. AAA 3000mSt champion 1983. Set three UK steeplechase records 1982–4.
Progression at 3000mSt: 1975 – 9:43.8, 1976 – 9:16.6, 1977 – 9:03.27, 1978 – 9:01.54, 1979 – 8:42.75, 1980 – 8:29.75, 1981 – 8:29.31, 1982 – 8:18.80, 1983 – 8:17.75, 1984 – 8:13.78.
pbs: 800m: 1:50.0 '80, 1500m: 3:38.86 '84, 1M: 3:55.41 '82, 2000m: 5:04.86 '82, 3000m: 7:44.40 '83, 2000mSt: 5:23.87 '84

Nick ROSE
b.30 Dec 1951 Bristol 1.75m 59kg
Club: Bristol. Graduate of Western Kentucky University, USA.
Ch. record at 10000m: OG: '84– 12; WCh: '83– 7. At 5000m: OG: '80– sf; ECh: '78– 7; CG: '78– 12, '82– 2; WCp: '77– 4; ECp: '77– 1. UK champion at 5000m 1977, 10000m 1984. Won AAA 10000m 1980. World cross-country: '80– 3 and won junior race in 1971. Won English National X–C in 1980 and US X–C in 1977.
Progression at 10000m: 1977 – 28:49.0, 1979 – 29:59.4, 1980 – 28:11.98, 1981 – 27:59.68, 1982 – 28:17.71, 1983 – 27:31.19, 1984 – 28:00.70.
pbs: 800m: 1:51.0 '73, 1500m: 3:40.41 '80, 1M: 3:57.49 '80, 2000m: 4:59.57 '78, 3000m: 7:40.4 '78, 2M: 8:23.04 '76, 5000m: 13:18.91 '84.

Geoff SMITH
b.24 Oct 1953 Liverpool 1.73m 61kg
Club: Liverpool H. Providence University, USA. Former fireman.
Ch. record: OG: '80– h 10000m, '84– dnf Mar. 2nd IAAF Golden 10km 1981. Set UK marathon best when 2nd in first marathon at New York 1983. Won Boston marathon 1984. Set UK half-marathon best of 1:01:39 in 1983.
Progression at Mar: 1983 – 2:09:08, 1984 – 2:10:34.
pbs: 800m: 1:51.5 '80, 1500m: 3:42.6 '81, 1M: 3:55.8 '81, 2000m: 5:04.56 '83, 3000m: 7:52.68 '81, 2M: 8:22.98 '80, 5000m: 13:22.17i '82, 10000m: 27:43.76 '81.

Charlie SPEDDING
b.19 May 1952 Bishop Auckland, Co.Durham 1.74m 63kg
Club: Gateshead H. Product services manager for Nike. Qualified as pharmacist.
Ch. record at Mar: OG: '84– 3. At 10000m: ECh: '82– 8; CG: '82– 4. AAA champion at 10000m 1983, marathon 1984. Made his marathon debut in January 1984, winning at Houston in 2:11:54. He went on to win London with 2:09:57 and place third in Olympics with 2:09:58.
pbs: 1500m: 3:45.36 '73, 1M: 4:03.5 '76, 2000m: 5:12.02 '82, 3000m: 7:54.0 '75, 2M: 8:26.87 '76, 5000m: 13:28.7 '78, 10000m: 28:08.12 '83.
Major success since the age of 30, but he has had a long career, placing second in the 1971 English Schools 1500m, but had many injuries in the 1970s.

Daley THOMPSON
b.30 Jul 1958 Notting Hill, London 1.84m 88kg
Club: Newham & Essex Beagles.
Ch. record at Dec: OG: '76– 18, '80– 1, '84– 1; WCh: '83– 1; ECh: '78– 2, '82– 1; CG: '78– 1, '82– 1; EJ: '77– 1 (5 at LJ). UK long jump champion 1979. Won AAA decathlon 1976 and LJ 1977. At decathlon has set three world records (8622 in 1980, 8704 and 8743 in 1982), two world junior records in 1977, and eight UK and Commonwealth records.

National Championships

Progression at Dec: 1975 – 7100, 1976 – 7905, 1977 – 8190, 1978 – 8467w, 1979 – 6954dnf, 1980 – 8622, 1981 – 7936, 1982 – 8743, 1983 – 8666, 1984 – 8797.
pbs: 100m: 10.36/10.28w '84, 200m: 20.88 '79, 300m: 33.94 '81, 400m: 46.86 '82, 1500m: 4:20.3 '76, 110mh: 14.26 '84, 400mh: 52.6 '77, HJ: 2.14i '82, PV: 5.20 '81, LJ: 8.01 '84, 8.11w '78, SP: 16.10 '84, DT: 47.68 '84, JT: 65.38 '80.
His supreme competitive ability has brought him unparalleled decathlon success. In his career, from 1975 to 1984, he has won 16 of the 25 decathlons that he has contested. He did not finish two decathlons, one in 1979 and one in 1984, but has otherwise won nine in succession from his European second place in 1978. Has never contested a decathlon in England!

Allan WELLS
b.3 May 1952 Edinburgh 1.83m 83kg
Club: Edinburgh Southern H. Laboratory assistant, qualified as a marine engineer.
Ch. record at 100m/200m (R– 4x400m relay): OG: '80– 1/2 (4R), '84– sf 100m; WCh: '83– 4/4; ECh: '78– 6 100m; CG: '78– 2/1 (1R), '82– 1/1= (3R); WCp: '81– 1/2; ECp: '79– 3/1, '81– 1/2, '83– 2/1.
Won IAAF Golden Sprints 1981. Set UK records at 100m (3) and 200m (5) 1978–80.
Progression at 100m, 200m: 1971 – 11.1; 1972 – 10.9w, 22.1w; 1973 – 11.1, 22.4; 1975 – 11.0, 22.2w; 1976 – 10.55/10.4w, 21.42/21.2w; 1977 – 10.62/10.52w, 21.10/20.9/20.7w; 1978 – 10.15/10.07w, 20.61/20.12w; 1979 – 10.19/10.0w, 20.42/20.19w; 1980 – 10.11/10.05w, 20.21/20.11w; 1981 – 10.17/10.15w, 20.26/20.15w; 1982 – 10.20/10.02w, 20.43; 1983 – 10.15, 20.52; 1984 – 10.18, 20.62/20.55w. **pbs:** 400m: 49.1 '75, LJ: 7.32 '72.
Only took up sprinting seriously at the age of 24.

WOMEN

Lorraine BAKER
b.9 Apr 1964 Ipswich 1.60m 47kg
Club: Coventry Godiva. Clerk.
Ch. record at 800m: OG: '84– 5; CG: '82– 6; EJ: '81– 5.
Progression at 800m: 1977 – 2:12.6, 1978 – 2:09.77, 1979 – 2:09.31, 1980 – 2:03.72, 1981– 2:03.21, 1982 – 2:01.66, 1983 – 2:01.71, 1984 – 2:00.03
pbs: 400m: 54.31 '84, 600m: 1:27.33 '80, 1500m: 4:32.4 '83
Her uncle, Joe Baker played soccer for England and her father, Gerry also played in the First Division. Her elder sister Karen is a British 400m international with a pb of 54.36.

Christine BENNING
b.30 Mar 1955 Urmston, Manchester 1.60m 50kg née Tranter.
Club: Southampton & Eastleigh. Teacher.
Ch. record at 1500m: OG: '84– 5; ECh: '78– 12; CG: '78– 2; ECp: '79– 5. At 3000m: WCh: '83– 13. Won UK 3000m 1984, WAAA 800m 1979, 1500m 1984, 3000m 1978. World cross-country: '84– 6. Won National cross-country 1983. UK & Commonwealth records: two at 1500m in 1979, one at 3000m (8:52.33) in 1978.
Progression at 1500m: 1970 – 4:45.9, 1971 – 4:52.5, 1973 – 4:25.2, 1974 – 4:22.81, 1975 – 4:17.55, 1976 – 4:22.03, 1977 – 4:09.7, 1978 – 4:07.53, 1979 – 4:01.53, 1980 – 4:04.2.3 (1M), 1981 – 4:09.57, 1982 – 4:14.82, 1983 – 4:13.70, 1984 – 4:01.83
pbs: 800m: 2:01.24 '79, 1000m: 2:40.52 '81, 1M: 4:24.57 '84, 2000m: 5:37.00 '84, 3000m: 8:44.26 '84

Christina BOXER
b.25 Mar 1957 Northolt, Middlesex 1.63m 51kg
Club: Aldershot, Farnham & District. Promotions manageress, sports goods.

Ch. record at 1500m: OG: '84– 6; WCh: '83– 9; CG: '78– 11, '82– 1. At 800m: OG: '80– sf; ECp: '79– 6, '81– 5. Won UK 800m 1979–80, 1984; WAAA 800m 1977–8, 1500m 1982. Commonwealth records at 1500m and 1 mile in 1984, and UK records at 800m and 1 mile in 1979.
Progression at 1500m: 1970 – 4:44.1, 1971 – 4:39.1, 1972 – 4:29.0, 1977 – 4:20.7, 1978 – 4:10.0, 1979 – 4:07.06, 1980 – 4:09.15, 1981 – 4:10.22, 1982 – 4:04.48, 1983 – 4:06.74, 1984 – 4:00.57
pbs: 400m: 55.14 '79, 800m: 1:59.05 '79, 1000m: 2:35.62 '82, 1M: 4:22.64 '84, 2000m: 5:33.85 '84, 3000m: 8:56.09 '83.
Won National junior cross-country title in 1971.

Zola BUDD
b.Bloemfontein, South Africa 26 May 1966 1.61m 43kg
British citizenship by parentage obtained 6 April 1984.
Club: Aldershot, Farnham & District.
Ch. record at 3000m: OG: '84– 7. While in South Africa set world 5000m best of 15:01.83 in 1984 and world junior bests at 1500m (2), 1 mile (1), 2000m (2), 3000m (3) and 5000m (4). Since taking up British citizenship has set world best at 2000m, world junior best at 1 mile, European junior records at 1500m (4:04.39) and 3000m (8:40.22). Commonwealth indoor 3000m record of 8:56.13 in 1985. South African champion at 1500m and 3000m 1982 and 1983. Won UK 1500m 1984.
Progression at 1500m/3000m/5000m: 1980 – 4:24.3/10:06.5, 1981 – 4:19.0, 1982 – 4:09.1/8:59.2, 1983 – 4:06.87/8:39.00/15:10.65, 1984 – 4:01.81/8:37.5/15:01.83
pbs: 800m: 2:00.9 '84, 1M: 4:30.7 '84, 2000m: 5:33.15 '84

Kathy COOK
b.3 May 1960 Winchester 1.80m 67kg
Club: Wolverhampton & Bilston. née Smallwood. Married to Garry Cook (qv). Bank liaison officer. Graduate of Borough Road College.
Ch. record at 400m: OG: '84– 3. At 200m (100m, R– 4 x 100m relay): OG: '80– 5 (6, 2R), 84– 4 (3R); WCh: '83– 3 (2R); ECh: '78– sf(2R), '82– 2 (2R); CG: '78– 5 (1R), '82– 2(1R); EJ: '77– 3 (3, 3R); WSG: '79– 2 (2, 2R), '81– 1 (2R); WCp: '81– 2 at 100m; ECp: '79– 4 (3R), '81– 2 (2, 2R), '83– 3 (3, 3R). UK & Commonwealth 400m records in 1982 and 1984, UK 100m record in 1981, and four UK 200m records 1979–84, including a Commonwealth record in 1982. Set world 300m best in 1984.
Progression at 200m, 400m: 1974 – 25.1; 1975 – 24.46; 1976 – 24.57/24.3; 1977 – 23.22/23.1w, 56.0; 1978 – 22.99/22.73w; 1979 – 22.70, 54.5; 1980 – 22.31, 54.3; 1981 – 22.58/22.57w, 51.08; 1982 – 22.13, 50.46; 1983 – 22.26, 50.95; 1984 – 22.10, 49.42.
pbs: 100m: 11.10 '81, 11.08w '83; 300m: 35.46 '84; HJ: 1.63 '75.
By far Britain's biggest medal winner ever at major Games, she has never failed to win a sprint relay medal at any championships.

Venissa HEAD
b.1 Sep 1956 Merthyr Tydfil 1.87m 97kg
Club: Cardiff.
Ch. record at SP (DT): OG: '84– 6 (7); WCh: '83– 10 (dnq); CG: '78– 6 (8), '82– (6); ECp: '81– 6, '83– 4. UK champion at shot 1977, '81, '83, discus 1981, '83–4. Four UK shot records 1981–2.
Progression at SP: 1974 – 13.01, 1975 – 14.36, 1976 – 15.39, 1977 – 15.72, 1978 – 15.52, 1979 – 16.35, 1980 – 17.05, 1981 – 17.84, 1982 – 17.93, 1983 – 18.41, 1984 – 19.06i/18.93. pb DT: 64.68 '83.

Beverly KINCH
b.14 Jan 1964 Ipswich 1.69m 55kg
Club: Hounslow.
Ch. record at LJ: WCh: '83– 5; CG: '82– 3; WSG: '83 – 4 (1 at

145

National Championships

100m). At 60m – EI: '83– 4, '84– 1. UK champion 1983. UK & Commonwealth long jump record 1983.
Progression at LJ: 1977 – 5.37, 1978 – 5.53, 1979 – 5.86, 1980 – 6.14/6.28w, 1981 – 6.21, 1982 – 6.49/6.78w, 1983 – 6.90/6.93w, 1984 – 6.79
pbs: 100m: 11.30/11.13w '83, 200m: 25.1 '82, 100mh: 14.6 '83

Heather OAKES
b.14 Aug 1959 London 1.66m 63kg née Hunte. Married to Gary Oakes (3rd Olympic 400mh 1980 in 49.11).
Club: Haringey. Clerical officer
Ch. record at 100m (R– 4x100m relay): OG: '80– 8 (3R), '84– 7 (3R); WCh: '83– sf; CG: '82– 7; EJ: '77– 4 (3R); WCp: '79– 1R; ECp: '79– 4 (3R). At 60m: WIG: '85– 2. UK champion 100m 1979–80, '82, '84 and 200m 1979, '84. Won WAAA 100m 1979.
Progression at 100m: 1972 – 12.5, 1973 – 12.5/12.3w, 1974 – 12.0w, 1975 – 12.02/11.8/11.7w, 1976 – 11.79/11.6, 1977 – 11.58, 1978 – 11.60/11.3, 1979 – 11.30/11.26w, 1980 – 11.20/11.01w/11.1, 1981 – 12.2, 1982 – 11.36/11.32w, 1983 – 11.37/11.35w, 1984 – 11.27/11.08w.
pb 200m: 23.06/22.9 '80, 23.00w '84.

Judy OAKES
b.14 Feb 1958 Lewisham, London 1.63m 81kg
Club: Croydon H. Gymnasium assistant.
Ch. record at SP: OG: 84– 4; WCh: '83– 12; CG: '78– 3, '82– 1; EI: '79– 3; ECp: '77– 7. UK champion 1978, '82, '84. Won WAAA 1979–80, '82–4. Three UK shot records 1979–82.
Progression at SP: 1973 – 11.73, 1974 – 12.50, 1975 – 14.22, 1976 – 15.94, 1977 – 16.24i, 1978 – 16.74i, 1979 – 16.72, 1980 – 17.20, 1981 – 16.88, 1982 – 17.92, 1983 – 18.28, 1984 – 18.35i/18.28.
pbs: DT: 49.96 '84, JT: 44.24 '84.
Won world powerlifting titles at 75kg in 1981 and 82kg in 1982.

Margaret RITCHIE
b.6 Jul 1952 Kirkcaldy, Fife 1.78m 104kg
Club: Edinburgh Southern H. University of Arizona, USA.
Ch. record at DT (SP): OG: '80– 9, '84– 5; WCh: '83– 8 (16); ECh: '78– 13; CG: '74– 6, '78– 4 (8), '82– 1 (7); ECp: '75– 7, '77– 8, '79– 5, '81–7, '83– 5. UK discus champion 1977–80. Won WAAA 1975, '77, '81 and NCAA shot and discus 1982. Set ten UK, including five Commonwealth, discus records 1977–81; also six UK, and one Commonwealth (unratified), shot records 1978–83.
Progression at DT: 1971 – 36.60, 1972 – 43.38, 1973 – 50.54, 1974 – 52.18, 1975 – 55.94, 1976 – 54.10, 1977 – 59.88, 1978 – 60.80, 1979 – 58.62, 1980 – 65.96, 1981 – 67.48, 1982 – 66.04, 1983 – 67.44, 1984 – 65.02.
pb SP: 18.99 '83.

Tessa SANDERSON
b.St.Elizabeth, Jamaica 14 Mar 1956 1.68m 72kg
Club: Wolverhampton & Bilston. Sports promotion assistant in Leeds.
Ch. record at JT: OG: '76– 9, '80– dnq, '84– 1; WCh: '83– 4; ECh: '74– 13, '78– 2; CG: '74– 5, '78– 1; EJ: '73– 12; WCp: '77– 2; ECp: '75– 7, '79– 2, '81– 3. UK champion 1977–78 and won WAAA 1975–7, '79–80. Set ten UK, including five Commonwealth javelin records 1976–83; also two UK & Commonwealth heptathlon records in 1981.
Progression at JT: 1970 – 31.86, 1971 – 42.02, 1972 – 43.06, 1973 – 51.34, 1974 – 55.04, 1975 – 54.40, 1976 – 57.20, 1977 – 67.20, 1978 – 64.00, 1979 – 65.34, 1980 – 69.70, 1981 – 68.86, 1982 – 66.00, 1983 – 73.58, 1984 – 69.56
pbs: 200m: 24.89 '81, 400m: 57.3 '72, 800m: 2:26.20 '81, 100mh: 13.46 '81, 400mh: 60.46 '77, HJ: 1.69 '73, LJ: 5.97 '81, SP: 13.27 '81, Hep: 6110 '81

Judy SIMPSON
b.Kingston, Jamaica 14 Nov 1960 1.82m 72kg née Livermore. Married to Robin Simpson (4.60m PV). Club: Birchfield H. Student at Birmingham Polytechnic.
Ch. record at Pen/Hep: OG: '80– 13, '84– 5 (dnq HJ); WCh: '83– dnf (sf 100mh); ECh: '82– 7; CG: '82– 2 (5 at 100mh); WSG: '81– 4, '83– 3; ECp: '83– 5. WAAA heptathlon champion 1982-3. Set Commonwealth heptathlon records in 1981, 1982 and 1983.
Progression at Hep (p – Pen): 1977 – 3870p, 1978 – 4028wp, 1979 – 5163/4090p, 1980 – 4357p, 1981 – 5962, 1982 – 6286, 1983 – 6353, 1984 – 6280
pbs: 200m: 24.75 '83, 400m: 53.76 '81, 800m: 2:11.49 '82, 100mh: 13.07 '84, HJ: 1.92 '83, LJ: 6.40 '84, SP: 14.59 '84, JT: 39.18 '83.
Former UK champion at Tae Kwan Do.

Wendy SLY
b.5 Nov 1959 Hampton, Middlesex 1.66m 51kg née Smith. Married to Chris Sly (2nd European Junior 1500m 1977).
Club: Hounslow and Brooks Racing Team, USA.
Ch. record at 3000m: OG: '84– 2; WCh: '80– dnf, '83– 5; CG: '82– 2. At 1500m: WCh: '83– 5; ECp: '83– 4; EJ: '77– 11; WSG: '81– 6. Won IAAF world road 10km title 1984. UK 3000m champion 1983. Won English national X–C 1981. UK & Commonwealth records at 3000m 1982 and 1983, 1 mile 1984.
Progression at 3000m: 1977 – 9:32.0, 1978 – 9:21.8, 1980 – 8:53.78, 1981 – 8:56.7i, 1982 – 8:46.01, 1983 – 8:37.06, 1984 – 8:39.47
pbs: 400m: 57.9 '78, 800m: 2:02.89 '83, 1000m: 2:39.94 '80, 1500m: 4:04.14 '83, 1M: 4:28.07 '84, 2000m: 5:42.15 '82. UK road bests: 10km: 31:29 '83, 15km: 48:18 '83
Has fared successfully at road running in the USA.

Shirley STRONG
b.Northwich, Cheshire 18 Nov 1958 1.70m 66kg
Club: Stretford.
Ch. record at 100mh: OG: '80– sf, '84– 2; WCh: '83– 5; CG: '78– 2, '82– 1; ECp: '81– 4, '83– 5. Won UK title 1979–80, '83 and WAAA 1979–84.
Progression at 100mh: 1974 – 16.0, 1975 – 14.7, 1976 – 14.52/14.28w, 1977 – 13.76/13.55w, 1978 – 13.41/13.08w, 1979 – 13.21, 1980 – 13.06, 1981 – 13.14/12.83w, 1982 – 13.13/12.78w, 1983 – 12.87/12.78w, 1984 – 12.88/12.86w
pbs: 100m: 11.69w '81, 11.8 '78; 200m: 24.57 '79, 24.4w '80; 800m: 2:11.7 '79; 400mh: 63.6 '82, LJ: 5.58 '77

Susan TELFER
b.Liversedge, Yorkshire 26 May 1961 1.80m 67kg née Hearnshaw. Club: Hull Spartan.
Ch. record at LJ: OG: '80– 9, '84– 3; ECh: '78– dnq; CG: '78– 3, '82– 5; EI: '84– 1; EJ: '77– 12, '79– 3; WSG: '81– 5 (2 at 4x100mR). ECp: '81– 6. UK champion 1980 and 1984. Won WAAA 1979 and 1984.
Progression at LJ: 1973 – 4.50, 1974 – 5.27/5.61w, 1975 – 5.75, 1976 – 6.07, 1977 – 6.25/6.41w, 1978 – 6.40/6.59w, 1979 – 6.68, 1980 – 6.66, 1981 – 6.53, 1982 – 6.47/6.50w, 1983 – 6.48, 1984 – 6.83/7.00w
pbs: 100m: 11.66/11.56w '84; 200m: 23.43 '84; 100mh: 14.5 '83, 14.3w '84; Hep: 4874 '84.
Her fine consistent 1984 season was marked by sharply improved sprinting speed. Mother, Muriel Pletts, ran in the 1948 Olympics – 4th at 4x100m relay.

Angela TOOBY
b.24 Oct 1960 Woolhope, Hereford 1.66m 51kg
Club: Cardiff. Teacher. UK champion at 5000m 1984. World X–C: '84– 8.

Progression at 3000m/5000m: 1983 – 9:23.3, 1984 – 8:52.59/15:22.50
pbs: 1500m: 4:23.0 '84, 10000m: 32:58.07 '84, Mar: 3:29 '81
Twin sister Susan has pbs of 3000m: 8:57.17 and 5000m: 15:35.40 in 1984.

Priscilla WELCH
b.22 Nov 1944 Bedford 1.65m 50kg
Club: Nuneaton H. Housewife.
Ch. record at Mar: OG: '84– 6. British marathon champion 1984, when 2nd London. 3rd New York 1983. Set UK and world veterans marathon best at Olympics 1984.
Progression at Mar: 1979 – 3:26, 1981 – 2:55:15, 1982 – 2:46:58, 1983 – 2:32:31, 1984 – 2:28:54.
Track pb: 10000m: 33:34.7 '84.

Only started running at the age of 34. Has won five of her 19 marathons to her victory at Columbus in 1984.

Fatima WHITBREAD
b.Hackney, London 3 Mar 1961 1.67m 77kg
Club: Thurrock H. Born of Greek Cypriot parents and adopted by Margaret Whitbread, UK javelin coach and ex-international (45.18m in 1959).
Ch. record at JT: OG: '80– dnq, '84– 3; WCh: '83– 2; ECh: '82– 8; CG: '78– 6, '82– 3; EJ: '79– 1; ECp: '83– 1
Progression at JT: 1975 – 34.94, 1976 – 41.20, 1977 – 48.34, 1978 – 53.88, 1979 – 58.20, 1980 – 60.14, 1981 – 65.82, 1982 – 66.98, 1983 – 69.54, 1984 – 71.86.
pbs: 200m: 24.38 '84, SP: 15.41 '84.
Has made continuous improvement for ten successive seasons.

USA

Governing body: TAC – The Athletics Congress of the United States, 155 West Washington Street, Indianapolis, Indiana. Founded 1979, when it replaced the AAU (founded 1888) as the governing body.
National Championships first held in 1876 (men), 1923 (women)
1984 Champions: MEN
100m: Sam Graddy 10.28, 200m: Brady Crain 20.09w, 400m: Mark Rowe 45.34, 800m: James Robinson 1:47.46, 1500m: Jim Spivey 3:40.54, 5000m: Sydney Maree 13:51.31, 10000m: Jon Sinclair 28:42.54, Mar: Ken Martin 2:11:24, 3000mSt: Henry Marsh 8:26.7, 110mh: Tonie Campbell 13.26, 400mh: David Patrick 49.08, HJ: Jimmy Howard 2.32, PV: Earl Bell 5.80, LJ: Mike McRae 8.27, TJ: Al Joyner 16.92, SP: Augie Wolf 21.48, DT: John Powell 71.42, HT: Jud Logan 73.30, JT: Curt Ransford 84.40, 20kmW: Raymond Funkhouser 1:31:48
WOMEN
100m/200m: Merlene Ottey (Jam) 11.12/22.20, 400m: Valerie Brisco-Hooks 49.83, 800m/1500m: Kim Gallagher 1:59.87/4:08.08, 3000m: Jan Merrill 9:01.31, 5000m: Katie Ishmael 16:07.5, 10000m: Bonnie Sons 35:03.6, 100mh: Stephanie Hightower 12.99, 400mh: Judi Brown 54.99, HJ: Pam Spencer 1.93, LJ: Shonel Ferguson (Bah) 6.71, SP/DT: Ria Stalman (Hol) 18.02/67.58, JT: Karin Smith 60.62, Hep: Cindy Greiner 6154, 10kmW: Debbie Lawrence 51:00.3

Ray ARMSTEAD
b.27 May 1960 1.87m 76kg Northeast Missouri University.
Ch. record: OG: '84– 1 at 4x400mR.
Progression at 400m: 1982– 46.13, 1984 – 44.83

Duncan ATWOOD
b.11 Oct 1955 Seattle 1.88m 93kg
Club: Athletics West. Graduate of University of Washington.
Ch. record at JT: OG: '84– 11; PAm: '79– 1; WCp: '79– 8. US champion 1979–80. Won US Olympic Trials 1984 and 3rd 1980.
Progression at JT: 1973 – 71.04, 1974 – 74.02, 1976 – 80.32, 1977 – 81.00, 1978 – 85.54, 1979 – 84.32, 1980 – 87.00, 1981 – 81.54, 1982 – 86.34, 1983 – 82.24, 1984 – 93.44

Alonzo BABERS
b.31 Oct 1961 Montgomery, Alabama 1.88m 70kg Graduate of the US Air Force Academy. Second Lieutenant in the US Air Force.
Ch. record at 400m (R – 4x400m relay): OG: '84– 1 (1R); PAm: '83– 1R.

Progression at 400m: 1981 – 46.8, 1982 – 45.9, 1983 – 45.07, 1984 – 44.22
pb 200m: 20.82 '84
Ran for the US 4 x 400m team in the heats at the 1983 world championships. Has made steady improvement, culminating in a magnificent victory in the Olympics, when he also had the fastest relay leg (43.75).

Willie BANKS
b.11 Mar 1956 Travis Air Force Base, California 1.90m 77kg
Club: Athletics West. Graduate of UCLA.
Ch. record at TJ: OG: '84– 6; WCh: '83– 2; PAm: '79– 2; WCp: '79– 5, '81– 3; WSG: '77– 3, '79– 1. Won US Olympic Trials 1980. US champion 1980–1, '83. Three US records in 1981, including the world low-altitude best of 17.56m. Set world indoor best at 17.41 in 1982.
Progression at TJ: 1973 – 15.02, 1974 – 15.62, 1975 – 16.79, 1976 – 16.66/16.88w, 1977 – 16.88, 1978 – 17.05, 1979 – 17.23w/17.34, 1980 – 17.13/17.36w, 1981 – 17.56, 1982 – 17.41i, 1983 – 17.26/17.32w, 1984 – 17.39
pb LJ: 8.11 '81.
The ebullient Banks has made the triple jump into a star event by the force of his own personality, encouraging crowds to clap him down the runway to an accelerating tempo.

Kirk BAPTISTE
b.20 Jun 1963 Beaumont, Texas 1.85m 75kg
Club: Santa Monica Track Club. Houston University.
Ch. record at 200m: OG: '84– 2. 2nd US Trials and won NCAA '84. Set world best at 300m of 31.70 in 1984.
Progression at 100m, 200m: 1982 – 21.29; 1983 – 10.34, 20.38; 1984 – 10.16/10.13w, 19.96.
pb 400m: 46.38 '84.
Training companion of Carl Lewis.

147

National Championships

Earl BELL
b.25 Aug 1955 Ancon, Panama Canal Zone 1.91m 75kg
Club: Pacific Coast Club. Graduate of Arkansas State University.
Ch. record at PV: OG: '76– 6, '84–3=; PAm: '75– 1. US champion 1976 and 1984. Won NCAA '75–7, AAA '81. Set world record at 5.67m in 1976 and US record at 5.80m in 1984.
Progression at PV: 1968 – 3.22, 1969 – 3.50, 1970 – 3.85, 1971 – 4.11, 1972 – 4.40, 1973 – 4.72, 1974 – 5.09, 1975 – 5.51, 1976 – 5.67, 1977 – 5.60, 1978 – 5.50, 1979 – 5.48i, 1980 – 5.60, 1981 – 5.65, 1982 – 5.65i, 1983 – 5.65, 1984 – 5.80.
Inspired by the challenge of the Olympics, Bell regained the American pole vault record after eight years in 1984.

John BRENNER
b.4 Jan 1961 1.92m 129kg
Club: Stars & Stripes TC. Student at UCLA. Won NCAA shot and discus in 1984.
Progression at SP: 1980 – 17.10, 1981 – 18.08, 1982 – 19.71, 1983 – 20.80, 1984 – 21.92.
pbs: DT: 63.44 '84, HT: 64.34 '84, JT: 69.86 '84

Ron BROWN
b.31 Mar 1961 Los Angeles 1.82m 84kg
Club: Stars & Stripes TC. Arizona State University.
Ch. record: OG: '84: 4 at 100m, 1 at 4x100mR.
Progression at 100m: 1979 – 10.3, 1980 – 10.32/10.19w, 1981 – 10.15/10.08w, 1982 – 10.20, 1983 – 10.06, 1984 – 10.12/10.05w.
pb 200m: 20.74 '82.
Turned down a $1 million offer from the Cleveland Browns to turn pro footballer so that he could compete at the Olympics, but now plays for the Los Angeles Rams in the NFL. Only man to beat Carl Lewis at 100m in 1983 and followed that with three wins over Lewis at indoor 60s in 1984.

Art BURNS
b.19 Jul 1954 Washington, DC 1.88m 119kg
Club: Athletics West. Graduate of University of Colorado.
Ch. record at DT: OG: '84– 5; WCh: '83– 8. Third TAC and US Trials in 1984.
Progression at DT: 1975 – 55.06, 1976 – 59.28, 1977 – 63.88, 1979 – 64.44, 1980 – 66.90, 1981 – 67.86, 1982 – 68.20, 1983 – 70.36, 1984 – 70.98

James BUTLER
b.21 Jun 1960 Broken Bow, Oklahoma 1.75m 66kg
Club: Bud Light Track America. Graduate of Oklahoma State University.
Ch. record at 200m: Won US Olympic Trials 1980, NCAA 1982.
Progression at 200m: 1979 – 20.96, 1980 – 20.36/20.22w, 1981 – 20.93/20.64w/20.2w, 1982 – 20.23/20.07w, 1983 – 20.32, 1984 – 20.31
pb 100m: 10.14/10.13w – 82

Tonie CAMPBELL
b.14 Jun 1960 Los Angeles 1.88m 73kg
Club: Stars & Stripes TC. Graduate of University of Southern California.
Ch. record at 110mh: OG: '84– 5; PAm: '83– 2; WSG: '81– 4. Won TAC '84. US Olympic Trials: 3rd 1980, 2nd 1984. Set US indoor record for 60mh at 7.58 in 1984.
Progression at 110mh: 1979 – 14.31, 1980 – 13.44, 1981 – 13.44, 1982 – 13.48/13.46w, 1983 – 13.32/13.1, 1984 – 13.23/13.1.
pb 400mh: 50.28 '81

Mike CARTER
b.29 Oct 1960 Dallas 1.88m 125kg Team Adidas. Southern Methodist University.
Ch. record at SP: OG: '84– 2; WSG: '81– 1, '83– 1. Won NCAA 1980–1, 1983 (also won four NCAA indoor titles). Set world junior shot record in 1979.
Progression at SP: 1977 – 16.67, 1978 – 18.71, 1979 – 20.65, 1980 – 20.61i, 1981 – 21.25i, 1983 – 21.07, 1984 – 21.76.
pb DT: 61.94 '81.
An outstanding college footballer, who after gaining his Olympic silver medal signed to play pro football for the San Francisco 49ers. First to put the 12lb shot over 80ft with 24.78m while at Thomas Jefferson High School, Dallas in 1979.

Mike CONLEY
b.5 Oct 1962 Chicago 1.88m 77kg
Club: Bud Light Track America. University of Arkansas.
Ch. record at TJ: OG: '84– 2; WCh: '83– 4 (3 at LJ); WSG: '83– 1. Won US Trials TJ and NCAA LJ/TJ double in 1984. Won AAA TJ 1983.
Progression at LJ, TJ: 1980 – 6.84, 15.13; 1981 – 7.46/7.56w, 15.80/15.83w; 1982 – 8.19, 17.01; 1983 – 8.38w/8.28, 17.23i/17.37w; 1984 – 8.21/8.23w, 17.50
pbs: 100m: 10.39w '84, 10.6 '81, 200m: 20.37/20.0 '84.
Made very rapid progress to top world class in both horizontal jumps.

Brian DIEMER
b.10 Oct 1961 Grand Rapids, Michigan 1.76m 63kg
Club: Athletics West. Graduate of University of Michigan
Ch. record at 3000mSt: OG: '84– 3; WCh: '83– sf. Won NCAA 1983.
Progression at 3000mSt: 1981 – 8:45.48, 1982 – 8:37.96, 1983 - 8:22.13, 1984 – 8:13.16
pbs: 1M: 3:59.93i '83, 3000m: 7:56.07i '84, 2M: 8:30.49i '83, 3M: 13:14.60i '84, 5000m: 13:47.15 '82

Dwayne EVANS
b.13 Oct 1958 Phoenix, Arizona 1.86m 66kg Stars & Stripes Track Club. Was at Arizona State University.
Ch. record at 200m: OG: '76– 3. US champion 1979, won NCAA 1981. Set world junior 200m record in 1976.
Progression at 200m: 1973 – 22.5 (220y), 1974 – 21.3, 1975 – 20.9, 1976 – 20.22, 1977 – 21.04, 1979 – 20.28, 1980 – 20.68/20.62w, 1981 – 20.34/20.20w, 1982 – 20.84, 1983 – 20.76/20.74w, 1984 – 20.38/20.21w
pb 100m: 10.20/10.07w '81, 10.1 '78
With the bronze at the age of 17 in 1976, he is the youngest ever Olympic 200m medallist.

Greg FOSTER
b.4 Aug 1958 Maywood, Illinois 1.90m 85kg
Club: World Class AC. Graduate of UCLA.
Ch. record at 110mh: OG: '84– 2; WCh: '83– 1; WCp: '81– 1. Won TAC 110mh '81, '83, NCAA 110mh '78, '81 and 200m '79, US Olympic Trials '84. Set US 110mh record at 13.22 in 1978, and world indoor best of 6.35 for 50m in 1985.
Progression at 110mh: 1977 – 13.54 for 0yh, 1978 – 13.22, 1979 – 13.28/13.0, 1980 – 13.27, 1981 – 13.03, 1982 – 13.22, 1983 – 13.11, 1984 – 13.15
pbs: 100m: 10.28 '79, 200m: 20.20 '79

Michael FRANKS
b.23 Sep 1963 St Louis, Missouri 1.80m 68kg
Club: Atlantic Coast Club. Southern Illinois University.
Ch. record at 400m: WCh: '83– 2. 3rd TAC '83, 2nd NCAA '84.
Progression at 400m: 1981 – 48.7, 1983 – 44.96, 1984 – 45.20
pbs: 100m: 10.25 '84, 200m: 20.62/20.58w '83

National Championships

Harvey GLANCE
b.28 Mar 1957 Phoenix City, Alabama 1.73m 67kg
Club: SMTC. Graduate of Auburn University.
Ch. record at 100m (R – 4 x 100m relay): OG: '76– 4 (1R); PAm: '79– 2 (1R); WCp: '79– 2R. NCAA champion at 100m 1976–7, 200m 1977. US Olympic Trials at 100m: 1st 1976, 2nd 1980, 7th 1984. At 100m set two world records at 9.9, and world junior records at 10.12 and 10.11 in 1976.
Progression at 100m (y = 100 yards): 1972 – 9.9y, 1973 – 9.7y, 1974 – 9.5y, 1975 – 10.3/9.4y, 1976 – 10.11/9.9, 1977 – 10.16/9.8, 1978 – 10.15/10.07w/9.9, 1979 – 10.13, 1980 – 10.14/10.07w, 1981 – 10.20w/9.8, 1982 – 10.31, 1984 – 10.09/10.07w.
pb 200m: 20.39 '79, 20.1 '76; LJ: 7.87 '77

Sam GRADDY
b.10 Feb 1964 Gaffney, S.Carolina 1.78m 68kg
Tennessee University.
Ch. record at 100m (R = 4x100m relay): OG: '84– 2 (1R); PAm: '83– 3 (1R); WSG: '83– 3. Won NCAA and TAC, 2nd US Trials '84. At 60m: WIG: '85– 2.
Progression at 100m (y = 100 yards): 1981 – 10.23y, 1982 – 9.61y/10.4, 1983 – 10.18/10.16w, 1984 – 10.09/10.08w.
pb 200m: 20.62 '84.

Johnny GRAY
b.19 Jun 1960 Los Angeles 1.92m 76kg
Club: Santa Monica Track Club. Was at Arizona State University. Married Judy Terrel on 4 Sep 1984.
Ch. record at 800m: OG: '84– 7. 2nd US Trials '84. Set four US records at 800m in 1984.
Progression at 800m: 1977 – 2:06.0, 1978 – 1:51.8, 1979 – 1:49.39, 1980 – 1:47.06, 1982 – 1:45.41, 1983 – 1:45.50, 1984 – 1:42.96
pbs: 400m: 46.3 '83, 600m: 1:14.16 '84 (world best), 1000m: 2:17.27 '84, 1500m: 3:43.98 '84

Jason GRIMES
b.10 Sep 1959 Philadelphia 1.79m 76kg
Club: Athletics West. University of Tennessee.
Ch. record at LJ: WCh: '83– 2. 2nd TAC 1982–3, 4th US Trials '84.
Progression at LJ: 1976 – 7.12i, 1977 – 7.63, 1978 – 7.73, 1979 – 7.75i, 1980 – 8.03i, 1981 – 7.99, 1982 – 8.19/8.57w, 1983 – 8.39/8.41w, 1984 – 8.32/8.40w
pbs: 100m: 10.2 '79; 200m: 20.74 '79, 20.5w '82

Danny HARRIS
b.7 Sep 1965 1.82m 77kg. Student at Iowa State University. Made his debut at 400mh on 24 Mar 1984, set world junior records in his 3rd, 4th, 6th, 9th and 11th races at the event, taking the record from 49.55 to 48.02! Won NCAA, 2nd US Trials, 2nd Olympics.
pb 400m: 45.3 '84.
Had set US high school record at 35.52 for 300mh in 1983. Also good footballer.

Tranel HAWKINS
b.17 Sep 1963 Dayton, Ohio 1.96m 81kg. Angelo State University, Texas
Ch. record at 400mh: OG: '84– 6. 2nd NCAA and 3rd US Olympic Trials 1984.
Progression at 400mh: 1983 – 50.27, 1984 – 48.28
Recruited to Angelo State as basketball player, made remarkable progress at 400mh in a year.

Jimmy HOWARD
b.11 Sep 1959 Texas City 1.96m 80kg

Club: Pacific Coast Club. Chemical engineering graduate of Texas A&M University. US high jump champion 1984. 3rd US Olympic Trials 1980. US indoor high jump record in January 1985.
Progression at HJ: 1978 – 2.11, 1979 – 2.21i, 1980 – 2.23, 1981 – 2.26, 1982 – 2.19i, 1983 – 2.30, 1984 – 2.33, 1985 – 2.34i

Thomas JEFFERSON
b.8 Jun 1962 1.83m 75kg Kent State University.
Ch. record at 200m: OG: '84– 3. 2nd TAC and 3rd US Trials '84.
Progression at 200m: 1980 – 21.4, 1981 – 21.2, 1982 – 21.11, 1983 – 20.90, 1984 – 20.26/20.21w.
pb 100m: 10.25/10.17w/9.9w '84

Earl JONES
b.11 Jul 1964 1.81m 77kg Eastern Michigan University
Ch. record at 800m: OG: '84– 3. Won US Olympic Trials 800m in US record of 1:43.74 in 1984. 2nd NCAA 1500m in 1983.
Progression at 800m: 1982 – 1:52.3, 1983 – 1:48.6, 1984 – 1:43.74
pbs: 400m: 46.33 '84, 1500m: 3:40.64 '83; 1M: 4:01.6 '84
Exciting front runner who made tremendous breakthrough to the top in 1984.

Al JOYNER
b.10 Jan 1961 East St.Louis, Illinois 1.86m 77kg
Club: Athletics West. Graduate of Arkansas State University.
Ch. record at TJ: OG: '84– 1; WCh: '83– 8. Won TAC and 2nd US Trials '84.
Progression at TJ: 1978 – 15.30, 1979 – 15.76, 1980 – 15.80, 1981 – 16.27, 1982 – 16.78i, 1983 – 17.12/17.14w, 1984 – 17.19/17.26w
pb 110mh: 13.83/13.6 '84, 13.81w '80
Won Olympic gold while sister Jackie (qv) won silver.

Emmit KING
b.24 Mar 1959 Alabama 1.77m 78kg
Club: New Balance TC. Was at University of Alabama.
Ch. record at 100m (R – 4x100m relay): WCh: '83– 3 (1R); PAm: '79– 3. Won NCAA 1983.
Progression at 100m (y – 100 yards): 1977 – 9.5y, 1978 – 9.5y, 1979 – 10.16/10.0, 1980 – 10.30, 1981 – 10.18/10.14w, 1982 – 10.13, 1983 – 10.06/10.05w, 1984 – 10.18/10.17w.
pb 200m: 20.86 '82
Overall winner of Mobil Grand Prix series US indoor season 1984 (won TAC 60y).

Roger KINGDOM
b.26 Oct 1962 Vienna, Georgia 1.83m 84kg
Club: New Image TC. University of Pittsburgh.
Ch. record at 110mh: OG: '84– 1; PAm: '83– 1. Won NCAA '83, 2nd TAC and 3rd US Trials '84.
Progression at 110mh: 1982 – 14.07, 1983 – 13.44, 1984 – 13.16/13.1/13.00w
College footballer, who has stormed to the top over the past two years.

Mel LATTANY
b.10 Aug 1959 Brunswick, Georgia 1.75m 71kg
Club: Bud Light Track America. Graduate of University of Georgia.
Ch. record (R – 4x100m relay): WSG at 100m: '79– 7, '81– 1 (1R); WCp at 200m: '79– 5 (2R), '81– 1 (3R). Set world junior 100m record in 1978 and world 100m low altitude best of 9.96 in 1984.
Progression at 100m/200m: 1977 – 9.9 (100y), 21.7 (220y); 1978 – 10.09, 20.77; 1979 – 10.16, 20.28/19.9; 1980 – 10.14, 20.60/20.50w; 1981 – 10.04, 20.21; 1982 – 10.14/9.9, 20.45; 1983 – 10.03/9.95w, 20.22; 1984 – 9.96, 20.73/20.41w

149

National Championships

pbs: 300m: 32.15 '83 (former world best), 400m: 46.9 '78
Unluckily lost a shoe in semi-final of 1983 US trials and was injured in 1984, so has missed the major championships.

Dave LAUT
b.21 Dec 1956 Findley, Ohio 1.93m 116kg
Club: Athletics West. Graduate of UCLA.
Ch. record at SP: OG: '84– 3; WCh: '83– 4; PAm: '79– 1; WCp: '79– 4, '81– 3. US champion 1979, '81, '83. Won NCAA '78–9. Equalled US shot record in 1982.
Progression at SP: 1976 – 17.33, 1977 – 18.83, 1978 – 20.15, 1979 – 21.11, 1980 – 21.10, 1981 – 21.60, 1982 – 22.02, 1983 – 21.94, 1984 – 21.64
Uses the rotational shot technique.

Mike LEHMANN
b.11 Mar 1960 Oak Lawn, Illinois 1.85m 116kg
Club: Team Adidas. University of Illinois.
Ch. record at SP: WCh: '83–10. 3rd TAC 1983 and 1984.
Progression at SP: 1979 – 18.06, 1980 – 18.58, 1981 – 20.53i, 1982 – 21.10i, 1983 – 21.43, 1984 – 21.27

Carl LEWIS
b.1 Jul 1961 Birmingham, Alabama 1.88m 77kg
Club: Santa Monica Track Club. Was at Houston University.
Ch. record at 100m/LJ (R – 4 x100m relay): OG: '84– 1/1 (1R, and 1 at 200m); WCh: '83– 1/1 (1R); PAm: '79– –/3; WCp: '81– 9/1. Won TAC 100m 1981-3, 200m 1983, LJ 1981-3. Won NCAA 100m 1980–1, LJ 1981. Won 100m/200m/LJ treble at US Trials 1984. Two world records at 4x100mR 1983 and 1984. Low altitude world bests at 100m (3), 200m, LJ (4). World indoor bests: 60y – 6.02 in 1983, long jump: 8.49m '81, 8.56m '81, 8.79m '84. US 200m record 1983.
Progression at 100m, 200m, LJ: 1974 – 5.77 LJ; 1975 – 6.01 LJ; 1976 – 11.1y, –, 6.93; 1977 – 10.6y, –, 7.26; 1978 – 10.5/9.3yw, –, 7.57/7.85w; 1979 – 10.3, 20.9, 8.13; 1980 – 10.21/10.16w, 20.66, 8.11/8.35w; 1981 – 10.00/9.99w, 20.73, 8.62/8.73w; 1982 – 10.00, 20.27, 8.76; 1983 – 9.97/9.93w, 19.75, 8.79; 1984 – 9.99, 19.80, 8.79i/8.71.
pb 300m: 32.18 '84
Has won 40 successive long jump competitions 1981– Feb '85, and has recorded 24 of the 30 long jumps in history over 28ft (8.53m). Emulated Jesse Owens in winning four Olympic gold medals. Sullivan Award winner 1981. Numerous awards as best athlete of the year 1982-3–4.

Doug LYTLE
b.7 Aug 1962 1.85m 77kg
Club: Bud Light Track America. Kansas State University.
Ch. record at PV: OG: '84– 6. 2nd TAC and US Trials 1984.
Progression at PV: 1980 – 5.11, 1981 – 5.31, 1982 – 5.52, 1983 – 5.61, 1984 – 5.71

Walter McCOY
b.15 Nov 1958 Daytona Beach, Florida 1.75m 68kg
Club: Bud Light Track America. Graduate of Florida State University.
Ch. record at 400m (R – 4x400m relay): WSG: '79– 3 (1R), '81– 2 (2R); WCp: '81– 1R. 3rd US Olympic Trials 1980, 2nd TAC 1984.
Progression at 400m: 1976 – 47.8y, 1977 – 46.52, 1978 – 45.56, 1979 – .16, 1980 – 45.49, 1981 – 44.99, 1982 – 44.97, 1983 – 44.97, 1984 – 44.76.
pbs: 200m: 20.86 '84, 20.7w '83; 300m: 32.16 '84.
Prodigiously consistent 400m runner, who has run 93 sub-46 sec. races 1978–84.

Antonio McKAY
b.9 Feb 1964 1.83m 80kg Georgia Tech University.
Ch. record at 400m (R = 4x400m relay): OG: '84– 3 (1R). Won NCAA (indoors and out) and US Trials in 1984. Set world indoor 400m best of 45.79 in 1984.
Progression at 400m: 1981 – 47.84y, 1982 – 45.9, 1984 – 44.71
Underwent surgery on a torn cartilage in his right knee in 1982, and missed the 1983 season, but stormed through first indoors and then out in 1984.

Mike McRAE
b.9 Jul 1955 1.85m 79kg
Club: Bay Area Striders
Ch. record at LJ: OG: '84– 11. Won TAC 1984.
Progression at LJ: 1976 – 7.65, 1977 – 7.80w, 1978 – 7.67/7.91w, 1980 – 7.82/7.87w, 1981 – 8.04/8.32w, 1982 – 7.46, 1983 – 8.19, 1984 – 8.27/8.34w
pb 100m: 10.44/10.34w '84

Sydney MAREE
b.9 Sep 1956 Atteridgeville, Pretoria, S.Africa 1.80m 66kg
Club: Reebok Racing Club. Graduate of Villanova University. Left South Africa for the USA in 1978, permanent resident from 1981 and granted full US citizenship on 1 May 1984.
Ch. record at 1500m: WCh:'83– sf; WCp: '81– 5. US champion at 1500m 1981, 5000m 1984. Won NCAA 1500m 1980–1, 5000m 1979. Set world 5000m record in 1983.
Progression at 1500m/1 mile: 1976 – 3:42.0/3:57.9, 1977 – 3:41.2/3:57.2, 1978 – 3:38.87/3:56.0, 1979 – 3:38.2i/3:53.7, 1980 – 3:38.64/3:55.9, 1981 – 3:32.30/3:48.83, 1982 – 3:32.12/3:48.85, 1983 – 3:31.24/3:50.30, 1984 – 3:37.02
pbs: 800m: 1:48.11 '82, 1000m: 2:19.5 '81, 2000m: 5:01.69 '82, 3000m: 7:33.37 '82, 5000m: 13:20.63 '79, 10000m: 28:21.46 '80
Third in US Olympic 1500m Trials 1984 but had to withdraw from the Olympics due to injury.

Henry MARSH
b.15 Mar 1954 Boston, Mass. 1.78m 72kg
Club: Athletics West. Graduate of Brigham Young University.
Ch. record at 3kmSt: OG: '76– 10, '84– 4; WCh: '83– 8; PAm: '79– 1; WCp: '79– 4, '81– dq. Won six US title: '78, '79, '81–4, and US Trials in 1980 and 1984. Set three US steeplechase records, 1977, 1980 and 1984.
Progression at 3kmSt: 1973 – 9:25.0, 1975 – 9:35.0, 1976 – 8:23.99, 1977 – 8:21.55, 1978 – 8:22.5, 1979 – 8:23.51, 1980 – 8:15.68, 1981 – 8:18.58, 1982 – 8:16.17, 1983 – 8:12.37, 1984 – 8:14.25
pbs: 1M: 4:01.6 '78, 3000m: 8:02.61 '82, 2M: 8:33.90i '84, 5000m: 13:45.2 '84
Has met with ill fortune in major events: in the 1981 World Cup he ran inside a barrier and was disqualified, and in the 1983 World Championships tripped over the final barrier.

Roy MARTIN
b.25 Dec 1966 1.85m 77kg Student at Roosevelt High School, Dallas, Texas. 4th US Olympic Trials 200m 1984.
Progression at 200m: 1981 – 21.9, 1982 – 21.69/21.33w, 1983 – 21.00/20.28w, 1984 – 20.28.
pbs: 100m: 10.32/10.16w '84, 400m: 48.3 '82.

Edwin MOSES
b.31 Aug 1955 Dayton, Ohio 1.87m 77kg
Club: Team Adidas. Graduate of Morehouse College, Atlanta, Georgia; now lives at Laguna Hills, California.
Ch. record at 400mh: OG: '76– 1, '84– 1; WCh: '83– 1; WCp: '77– 1, '79– 1, '81– 1. US champion 1977, '79, '81, '83; AAA champion

National Championships

1979. Won US Trials 1976, 1980 and 1984. Has set four world records - one each in 1976, 1977, 1980 and 1983.
Progression at 400mh: 1975 – 52.0 (440y), 1976 – 47.63, 1977 – 47.45, 1978 – 47.94, 1979 – 47.53, 1980 – 47.13, 1981 – 47.14, 1982 – did not compete, 1983 – 47.02, 1984 – 47.32.
pbs: 400m: 45.60 '77, 800m: 1:48.98 '83, 100mh: 13.64/13.5 '78. Has dominated his event for nearly a decade, and has set up the greatest ever winning streak by a track athlete - 109 successive 400mh races (94 finals) since beaten by Harald Schmid in Berlin on 26 Aug 1977. His total career record at 400mh, 1975–84, is 140 wins in 145 races. Sullivan Award winner 1983.

Larry MYRICKS
b.10 Mar 1956 Clinton, Mississippi 1.86m 75kg
Club: Bud Light Track America. Was at Mississippi College.
Ch. record at LJ: OG: '76– nj, '84– 4; WCp: '79– 1. WCh: '83– ht at 200m. US long jump champion 1979–80, won NCAA 1976 and 1979, AAA 1981. Won US Olympic Trials 1980, 2nd 1976 and 1984. Set world low altitude best to win 1979 World Cup long jump.
Progression at LJ: 1974 – 7.17i, 1975 – 7.83, 1976 – 8.09i/8.26w, 1978 – 8.05, 1979 – 8.52, 1980 – 8.38i, 1981 – 8.45, 1982 – 8.56, 1983 – 8.23/8.64w, 1984 – 8.59.
pbs: 100m: 10.31 '83, 200m: 20.03 '83, 400m: 46.74 '84
Broke his leg warming up for the 1976 Olympic long jump final, but returned to Montreal to win at the 1979 World Cup with world low altitude best.

Mark NENOW
b.16 Nov 1957 Fargo, N.Dakota 1.72m 57kg
Club: Todds Road Stumblers. Accountancy degree from University of Kentucky.
Ch. record at 10000m: WCh: '83– 12; PAm: '83– 3. Ran world road 10km best of 27:22 in 1984.
Progression at 10000m: 1978 – 28:46.5, 1979 – 30:55.9, 1980 – 28:32.7, 1981 – 28:45.86, 1982 – 27:36.7, 1983 – 27:52.41, 1984 – 27:40.56
pbs: 3000m: 7:53.22 '83, 5000m: 13:18.54 '84
US fastest at 5000m and 10000m in 1984.

Sunder NIX
b.2 Dec 1961 Birmingham, Alabama 1.75m 65kg Indiana University.
Ch. record at 400m (R – 4x400m relay): OG: '84– 5 (1R); WCh: '83– 3; WSG: '83– 3 (1R). Won TAC 1983.
Progression at 400m: 1979 – 48.8, 1980 – 46.6, 1981 – 45.66, 1982 – 44.68, 1983 – 44.87, 1984 – 44.75

Doug NORDQUIST
b.20 Dec 1958 1.93m 84kg
Club: Tiger International. Graduate of Washington State University.
Ch. record at HJ: OG: '84– 5. 2nd US Olympic Trials.
Progression at HJ: 1979 – 2.19, 1980 – 2.13, 1981 – 2.24, 1982 – 2.19i, 1983 – 2.22, 1984 – 2.31

Brian OLDFIELD
b.1 Jun 1945 Elgin, Illinois 1.95m 123kg
Club: Team Adidas. Graduate of Middle Tennessee State.
Ch. record at SP: OG: '72– 6. US champion 1980. Won AAA shot and discus 1980. Set world bests as an ITA pro in 1975 with 22.11i, 22.25 and 22.86. As a reinstated amateur set two US records, 1982 and 1984.
Progression at SP: (p – professional marks): 1964 – 16.38, 1965 – 17.28, 1966 – 18.03, 1968 – 18.65, 1969 – 19.68, 1970 – 19.47i, 1971 – 18.59i, 1972 – 20.97, 1973 – 21.60ip, 1974 – 21.12p, 1975 – 22.86p, 1976 – 22.45p, 1977 – 19.95, 1979 – 21.02, 1980 – 21.82, 1981 – 22.02, 1982 – 20.71, 1983 – 21.22, 1984 – 22.19.
pb DT: 62.26 '75

His astonishing performances as a professional in 1975–6 remain unapproached but, although as a reinstated amateur he is ineligible for the Olympics, Oldfield topped the world list in 1984 at the age of 39.

Billy OLSON
b.19 Jul 1958 Abilene, Texas 1.88m 73kg
Club: Pacific Coast Club. Graduate of Abilene Christian University.
Ch. record at PV: WCh: '83– nh; WCp: '81– 3. US champion 1981 and 1982 (tie). Has set one US pole vault record outdoors (5.72m in 1982) and seven world indoor bests from 5.71m in 1982 to 5.80m in 1983.
Progression at PV: 1975 – 4.49, 1976 – 4.82, 1977 – 5.18, 1978 – 5.45, 1979 – 5.50, 1980 – 5.67, 1981 – 5.60, 1982 – 5.74i/5.72, 1983 – 5.80i/5.70, 1984 – 5.80i/5.74

Doug PADILLA
b.4 Oct 1956 Oakland, California 1.73m 64kg
Club: Athletics West. Graduate of Brigham Young University.
Ch. record at 5000m: OG: '84– 7; WCh: '83– 5; WSG: '81– 1. US 5000m champion 1983 and won US Olympic Trials 1984. US 3000m record 1983.
Progression at 5000m: 1975 – 15:14.0, 1979 – 13:43.0, 1980 – 13:36.50, 1981 – 13:33.5, 1982 – 13:20.55i, 1983 – 13:17.69, 1984 – 13:23.56
pbs: 800m: 1:49.4 '80, 1500m: 3:37.95 '83, 1M: 3:56.3i '82, 2000m: 5:03.84 '83, 3000m: 7:35.84 '83, 2M: 8:16.5i '83
Went on Mormon mission to El Salvador 1976–8.

Don PAIGE
b.31 Oct 1956 Syracuse, New York 1.86m 70kg
Club: Athletic Attic. Graduate of Villanova University.
Ch. record: PAm: '79– 1 at 800m & 1500m. Won NCAA 800m '79–80, 1500m '79, US Olympic Trials 800m '80. Set world indoor bests for 1000y: 2:04.9 in 1981 and 2:04.7 in 1982.
Progression at 800m: 1974 – 1:56.6y, 1975 – 1:51.8y, 1978 – 1:47.55, 1979 – 1:45.54, 1980 – 1:44.53, 1982 – 1:46.7, 1983 – 1:44.29, 1984 – 1:45.17
pbs: 1000m: 2:18.06 '84, 1500m: 3:37.33 '79, 1M: 3:54.19 '82

David PATRICK
b.12 Jun 1960 Centralia, Illinois 1.83m 74kg
Club: Team Adidas. Graduate of University of Tennessee.
Ch. record: WCh: '83– 8 at 800m; WSG: '81– 5 at 400mh. Won TAC 400mh 1982 and 1984, 800m 1983; NCAA 400mh 1982.
Progression at 400mh: 1979 – 54.26, 1980 – 50.90, 1981 – 49.25, 1982 – 48.44, 1983 – 48.05, 1984 – 48.80.
pb: 800m: 1:44.70 '83.

Tyke PEACOCK
b.24 Feb 1961 Urbana, Illinois 1.86m 80kg
Club: Puma & Energizer Track Club.
Ch. record at HJ: WCh: '83– 2; WCp: '81– 1. US champion 1981. Two US high jump records in 1983.
Progression at HJ: 1976 – 1.97, 1977 – 2.04, 1978 – 2.13, 1979 – 2.21, 1980 – 2.23, 1981 – 2.28, 1982 – 2.30, 1983 – 2.33, 1984 – 2.28, 1985 – 2.31.
Good basketball player. Christian names actually Charles William.

Tom PETRANOFF
b.8 Apr 1958 Aurora, Illinois 1.87m 98kg
Club: Athletics West.
Ch. record at JT: OG: '84– 10; WCh: '83– 2. Set world javelin record in 1983.
Progression at JT: 1977 – 77.48, 1978 – 79.74, 1979 – 78.18, 1980 – 85.44, 1981 – 76.04, 1982 – 88.40, 1983 – 99.72, 1984 – 89.50

National Championships

Andre PHILLIPS
b.5 Sep 1959 Milwaukee 1.88m 79kg
Club: World Class AC. Graduate of UCLA.
Ch. record at 400mh: WCh: '83– 5. NCAA champion 1981.
Progression at 400mh: 1977 – 53.41 (440yh), 1978 – 50.67, 1979 – 49.47, 1980 – 49.30, 1981 – 48.10, 1982 – 48.45, 1983 – 47.78, 1984 – 48.42
pbs 400m: 45.94 '84, 110mh: 13.95 '81
Has been the closest American challenger to Ed Moses, and is the only other US athlete to break 48 sec. for 400mh.

Ben PLUCKNETT
b.13 Apr 1954 Beatrice, Nebraska 2.01m 147kg
Club: Team Nike. Graduate of University of Missouri. Set two US discus records in 1981, both superior to world record, but not ratified due to his drugs suspension.
Ch. record at DT: Won TAC '81. 3rd US Olympic Trials 1980.
Progression at DT: 1973 – 55.55, 1974 – 52.76, 1975 – 56.24, 1976 – 61.52, 1977 – 60.60, 1978 – 62.30, 1979 – 66.12, 1980 – 68.18, 1981 – 72.34dq, 1982 – 68.50, 1983 – 71.32, 1984 – 63.16.
pb SP: 20.59 '81.
Suspended in 1981 for drug use, detected at the Pacific Conference Games.

Pat PORTER
b.31 May 1959 1.83m 62kg.
Club: Athletics West. Adams State College. Lives in Alamosa, Colorado.
Ch. record at 10000m: OG: '84– 16. 3rd US Trials '84. World X–C: '83– 9, '84– 4. US cross-country champion 1982–4.
Progression at 10000m: 1982 – 28:26.27, 1983 – 28:04.31, 1984 – 27:49.5
pb 5000m: 13:50.27i '83

John POWELL
b.25 Jun 1947 San Francisco 1.88m 107kg
Club: Bud Light Track America. Graduate of San Jose State University. Real Estate Broker, former San Jose policeman.
Ch. record at DT: OG: '72– 4, '76– 3, '84– 3; WCh: '83– dnq; PAm: '75– 1. US champion 1974–5, '83–4, AAA champion 1974, '76, '79, '81. Won US Olympic Trials 1984, 2nd 1972, '76, '80. Set world discus record at 69.08m in 1975.
Progression at DT: 1967 – 50.01, 1968 – 57.12, 1969 – 59.44, 1970 – 61.42, 1971 – 63.12, 1972 – 64.22, 1973 – 66.66, 1974 – 68.08, 1975 – 69.08, 1976 – 67.54, 1977 – 67.98, 1978 – 58.16, 1979 – 67.34, 1980 – 68.20, 1981 – 69.98, 1982 – 68.32, 1983 – 68.30, 1984 – 71.26.
pbs: SP: 17.09 '76, HT: 58.50 '84.

Elliott QUOW
b.3 Mar 1962 St. Vincent 1.85m 78kg
Club: Team Adidas. Rutgers University, New York.
Ch. record at 200m: WCh: '83– 2; PAm: '83– 1 (1 at 4x100mR); WSG: '83– 2. Won NCAA 200m 1983.
Progression at 200m: 1980 – 21.5, 1981 – 20.83/20.63w, 1982 – 20.39, 1983 – 20.16, 1984 – 20.47/20.40w.
pb 100m: 10.35 '83, 10.30w '84.

Tony RAMBO
b.30 May 1960 Atlanta 1.75m 77kg
Club: Budweiser TC. Was at South Carolina University.
Progression at 400mh: 1979 – 50.7, 1980 – 49.90, 1981 – 50.04, 1982 – 48.90, 1983 – 50.79, 1984 – 48.16

James ROBINSON
b.27 Aug 1954 Oakland, California 1.80m 67kg
Club: Inner City AC. Graduate of University of California.

Ch. record at 800m: OG: '76– sf; WCh: '83– 5; PAm: '79– 1; WCp: '79– 2, '81– 2. Won record seven US 800m titles 1976, '78–82, '84. 2nd US Olympic Trials '76, '80, 4th '84.
Progression at 800m (y – 880 yards): 1972 – 1:51.5y, 1973 – 1:49.1y, 1974 – 1:45.7, 1975 – 1:49.1y, 1976 – 1:45.86, 1977 – 1:45.90, 1978 – 1:45.47, 1979 – 1:44.70, 1980 – 1:45.47, 1981 – 1:44.63, 1982 – 1:44.72, 1983 – 1:44.32, 1984 – 1:43.92.
pbs: 400m: 46.3 '76, 600m: 1:14.84 '84, 1000m: 2:16.3 '81
Almost always hangs back off the pace, and then produces a devastating finish.

Bob ROGGY
b.6 Aug 1956 Ridgewood, New Jersey 1.94m 109kg
Club: Team Adidas. Graduate of Southern Illinois University.
Ch. record at JT: WCh: '83– 9. Won NCAA '78, TAC '82. Set three US javelin records in 1982.
Progression at JT: 1974 – 61.86, 1975 – 69.12, 1976 – 78.08, 1977 – 81.64, 1978 – 89.30, 1979 – 88.26, 1980 – 87.90, 1981 – 89.02, 1982 – 95.80, 1983 – 86.16, 1984 – 90.80.
pb HJ: 2.03 '77

Alberto SALAZAR
b.7 Aug 1958 Havana, Cuba 1.81m 64kg
Came to Florida, USA in 1960, now lives in Eugene, Oregon.
Club: Athletics West. Graduate of University of Oregon. Married to Molly Morton 34:28.0 '79).
Ch. record at Mar: OG: '84– 15. At 10000m: WCh: '83– 17; WCp: '81– 3; World X–C: '82– 2, '83– 4. Won TAC 10000m 1981 and 1983. US records at 5000m and 10000m in 1982. Won first four marathons in sub 2:10 times – 2:09:41 at New York in 1980, world best 2:08:13 to win at New York in 1981, and Boston and New York marathons in 1982. Since then four more marathons but no wins.
Progression at 10000m/Mar: 1977 – 29:03.4, 1978 – 28:46.55, 1979 – 28:06.12, 1980 – 27:49.3/2:09:41, 1981 – 27:40.69/2:08:13, 1982 – 27:25.61/2:08:51, 1983 – 28:00.36/2:09:21, 1984 – 27:45.5/2:11:44
pbs: 1500m: 3:44.56 '79, 2000m: 5:11.9i '80, 3000m: 7:43.79 '79, 5000m – 13:11.93 '82
Has a reputation of running himself all-out, but has not been as successful in past two years as previously.

Steve SCOTT
b.5 May 1956 Upland, California 1.86m 73kg
Club: Sub 4 TC. Graduate of University of California at Irvine. Now lives in Scottsdale, Arizona.
Ch. record at 1500m: OG: '84– 10; WCh: '83– 2; WCp: '77– 2, '79– 4. US champion 1977–9, '82–3. Won US Trials '80, NCAA '78 at 1500m and AAA '79 at 800m. US records at 1500m (1), 1 mile (4), 2000m (1), 3000m (1). Set world indoor best for 2000m at 4:58.6 in 1981.
Progression at 1500m/1 Mile: 1973 – 4:25.0M, 1974 – 3:56.8/4:15.0, 1975 – 3:47.5/4:08.0, 1976 – 3:40.43/4:05.5, 1977 – 3:36.13/3:55.21, 1978 – 3:36.0/3:52.93, 1979 – 3:34.6/3:51.11, 1980 – 3:33.33/3:52.7, 1981 – 3:31.96/3:49.68, 1982 – 3:32.33/3:47.69, 1983 – 3:32.71/3:49.21, 1984 – 3:33.46/3:52.99
pbs: 800m: 1:45.05 '82, 1000m: 2:16.40 '81, 2000m: 4:54.71 '82, 3000m: 7:36.69 '81, 5000m: 13:38.4 '79
America's top miler of recent years, prolific fast times, including 94 sub-four-minute miles to February 1985, and a fine competitive record, but he faded disappointingly in the Olympic final.

Calvin SMITH
b.8 Jan 1961 Bolton, Mississippi 1.78m 64kg
Club: Bud Light Track America. University of Alabama.
Ch. record at 100m/200m (R – 4 x 100m relay): OG: '84– 1R; WCh: '83– 2/1 (1R); WSG: '81– 2/– (1R). Won TAC 200m '82. Set world records at 100m in 1983 and twice at 4 x 100m relay 1983–4.

National Championships

Progression at 100m, 200m: (y – 100y/220y): 1978 – 9.6y, 21.5y; 1979 – 10.36/10.30w, 20.7; 1980 – 10.17/10.12w, 20.64; 1981 – 10.21, 21.00; 1982 – 10.05/9.91w, 20.31/20.20w; 1983 – 9.93, 19.99; 1984 – 10.11/9.94w, 20.33

Willie SMITH
b.28 Feb 1956 Rochester, Pennsylvania 1.73m 73kg Puma & Energizer Track Club. Graduate of Auburn University.
Ch. record at 400m (R – 4x400m relay): PAm: '79– 3; WCp: '79– 1R, '81– 1R; WSG: '77– 2 (1R). US champion 1979–80. 2nd 1980 US Olympic Trials.
Progression at 400m (y at 440 yards): 1976 – 46.2y, 1977 – 45.7y, 1978 – 44.73, 1979 – 45.10, 1980 – 45.33, 1981 – 45.05, 1983 – 45.19, 1984 – 45.07
pbs: 100m: 10.26/10.20w '76, 200m: 20.76 '78, 20.6y '74.
Reserve on US Olympic relay teams: 4x100m in 1976, 4x400m in 1984. A long career from being High School athlete of the year in 1974.

Jim SPIVEY
b.7 Mar 1960 Oak Park, Illinois 1.78m 61kg
Club: Athletics West. Graduate of Indiana University.
Ch. record at 1500m: OG: '84– 5; WSG: '81– 4. Won NCAA '82, TAC '84. At 5000m: WCh: '83– sf.
Progression at 1500m/1M: 1976 – 4:35.5M, 1977 – 4:18.3M, 1978 – 4:06.2, 1979 – 3:44.7, 1980 – 3:38.56/3:58.9i, 1981 – 3:37.24/3:57.0, 1982 – 3:37.34/3:55.56, 1983 – 3:36.4/3:50.59, 1984 – 3:34.19/3:53.88
pbs: 800m: 1:46.5 '82, 1000m: 2:16.54 '84, 3000m: 7:53.3 '81, 2M: 8:24.69 '81, 5000m: 13:19.24 '83
Has a renowned finishing kick, as he showed when he outsprinted Steve Scott to win the US Olympic Trials 1500m.

Milan STEWART
b.31 Oct 1960 Los Angeles 1.81m 79kg
Club: Stars & Stripes TC. Was at USC (won NCAA 110mh 1982).
Progression at 110mh: 1977 – 14.4, 1978 – 14.42, 1979 – 13.85/13.70w, 1980 – 13.72, 1981 – 13.65, 1982 – 13.46/13.44w, 1983 – 13.58, 1984 – 13.48/13.4
pb: 400mh: 51.01 '82.

Dwight STONES
b.6 Dec 1953 Irvine, California 1.96m 81kg
Club: Pacific Coast Club. Graduate of Cal State-Long Beach. TV Commentator.
Ch. record at HJ: OG: '72– 3, '76– 3, '84– 4; WCh: '83– 6; WCp: '77– 2. US champion 1973–4, '76–8, '83. Also won AAA and French titles in 1974. Three world high jump records: 2.30m in 1973, 2.31m and 2.32m in 1976, and a fourth US record at 2.34m in 1984. Set seven world indoor bests from 2.26m to 2.30m in 1975–6.
Progression at HJ: 1969 – 1.92, 1970 – 2.00, 1971 – 2.17, 1972 – 2.21, 1973 – 2.30, 1974 – 2.28, 1975 – 2.28i, 1976 – 2.32, 1977 – 2.30, 1978 – 2.30, 1980 – 2.26, 1981 – 2.31, 1982 – 2.31i, 1983 – 2.29, 1984 – 2.34
Won an Olympic bronze medal as a teenager, and has maintained his position amongst the world's best high jumpers.

Mike TULLY
b.21 Oct 1956 Long Beach, Cal. 1.90m 88 kg
Club: New York AC. Graduate of UCLA.
Ch. record at PV: OG: '84– 2; PAm: '83– 1; WCp: '77–1, '79– 1. US champion 1977 and 1979, ran NCAA 1978, AAA 1976 and 1979. Won US Olympic Trials 1984 (and 2nd= 1980). Set world junior record in 1975, unratified world pole vault best of 5.71m and indoor world bests at 5.59m and 5.62m in 1978. Set three more US records in 1984.

Progression at PV: 1972 – 3.50, 1973 – 4.31, 1974 – 5.10, 1975 – 5.43, 1976 – 5.44, 1977 – 5.60, 1978 – 5.71, 1979 – 5.56, 1980 – 5.65, 1982 – 5.60, 1983 – 5.49, 1984 – 5.82
Double World Cup winner returned to the top with the lure of Olympic competition in 1984.

Craig VIRGIN
b.2 Aug 1955 Belleville, Illinois. 1.78m 59kg
Club: Front Runner Racing Team. Graduate of University of Illinois. Runs a public relations company – Front Runner Inc.
Ch. record at 10000m: OG: '76– h, '84– h; WCp: '79– 2. US Olympic Trials: 1st 1980, 2nd 1976 and 1984. US champion 1978–9, 1982. World cross-country champion 1980 and 1981. US records at 10000m in 1979 and 1980.
Progression at 10000m (y – 6 miles): 1974 – 28:10.8y, 1975 – 27:48.8y, 1976 – 27:59.43, 1977 – 28:22.5, 1978 – 27:57.2, 1979 – 27:39.4, 1980 – 27:29.16, 1982 – 28:07.88, 1983 – 28:13.06, 1984 – 28:02.27
pbs: 1 mile: 4:03.2, 3000m: 7:48.2 '79, 2 miles: 8:22.00 '79, 5000m: 13:19.1 '80, Mar: 2:10:26 (2nd Boston) '81.
Has comeback from serious kidney problems in 1982.

Mac WILKINS
b.15 Nov 1950 Eugene, Oregon 1.93m 118kg
Club: Athletics West. Graduate of University of Oregon.
Ch. record at DT: OG: '76– 1, '84– 2; WCh: '83– 10; PAm: '79– 1; WCp: '77– 2, '79– 2. US champion 1973, '76–80. NCAA champion 1973. Won US Olympic Trials '76, '80. Four world records in 1976, three in one competition at San Jose. Also set a US record in 1980.
Progression at DT: 1968 – 44.00, 1969 – 47.24, 1970 – 49.84, 1971 – 53.64, 1972 – 59.72, 1973 – 64.77, 1974 – 65.14, 1975 – 66.79, 1976 – 70.86, 1977 – 69.18, 1978 – 70.48, 1979 – 70.66, 1980 – 70.98, 1981 – 62.88, 1982 – 68.20, 1983 – 70.36, 1984 – 70.44
pbs: SP: 21.06i '77, HT: 63.66 '77, JT: 78.44 '70

Bart WILLIAMS
b.29 Sep 1957 Vallejo 1.79m 72kg
Club: Stars & Stripes TC. Was at Cal Poly San Luis Obispo.
Ch. record at 400mh: WSG: '79– 6. 3rd= US Olympic Trials 1980.
Progression at 400mh: 1976 – 51.04, 1977 – 51.34, 1978 – 49.32, 1979 – 49.41, 1980 – 49.21, 1981 – 48.81, 1982 – 50.31, 1983 – 49.58, 1984 – 48.63
pbs: 100m: 10.5 '78, 200m: 20.5 '78, 400m: 46.1 '78

August 'Augie' WOLF
b.3 Sep 1961 Minnesota 1.99m 127kg
Club: Budweiser TC. Graduate of Princeton University. Studying German banking at the University of Bonn.
Ch. record at SP: OG: '84– 4. Won TAC, 2nd US Trials '84.
Progression at SP: 1980 – 16.43, 1981 – 19.06, 1982 – 19.63i, 1983 – 20.47, 1984 – 21.73.
pb DT: 59.98 '84.

WOMEN

Evelyn ASHFORD
b.15 Apr 1957 Shreveport, Louisiana 1.65m 52kg
Club: Puma & Energizer TC. Was at UCLA. Married to basketball player Ray Washington.
Ch. record at 100m (200m, R – 4x100m relay): OG: '76– 5, '84– 1 (1R); WCh: '83– dnf; PAm: '79– 1 (1R); WCp: '77– 5 (4), '79– 1 (1), '81– 1 (1). US champion at 100m 1977, '79, '81–3; 200m 1977–9, '81, '83. Set world records for 100m in 1983 and 1984. US records at 100m (5) and 200m (4) 1977–84. Set world indoor bests for 50

153

National Championships

yards (5.77 and 5.74) in 1983, and for 60 yards (6.54) in 1982.
Progression at 100m, 200m: 1975 – 11.5/24.2, 1976 –
11.21/23.9w, 1977 – 11.25/22.62, 1978 – 11.16/22.66, 1979 –
10.97/21.83, 1980 – 11.33, 1981 – 10.90/21.84, 1982 –
10.93/22.10, 1983 – 10.79/21.88, 1984 – 10.76/21.75
pbs: 400m: 51.08 '84, 800m: 2:13.07 '84.
Twice a double sprint World Cup winner, Ashford finally achieved Olympic success in 1984 and perhaps even more significantly followed that by beating Marlies Göhr and the world 100m record in Zurich. Since 1976 she has beaten Göhr 4–3 in 100m finals. Ran her final 100m leg in the Olympic sprint relay in 9.77 secs. Unbeaten in sprints in 1984.

Joan BENOIT
b.16 May 1957 Cape Elizabeth, Maine 1.60m 47kg
Club: Athletics West. Graduate of Bowdoin College. Married Scott Samuelson on 29 Sep 1984.
Ch. record at Mar: OG: '84– 1. At 3000m: PAm: '83– 1. World X–C: '83– 4. Has set five US records at the marathon from 1979 to 1983, the last the world best. US road bests for 10km: 31:37 '83 and half marathon: 1:08:34 '84.
Progression at Mar: 1979 – 2:35:15, 1980 – 2:31:23, 1981 – 2:30:16, 1982 – 2:26:11, 1983 – 2:22:43, 1984 – 2:24:52.
pbs: 1500m: 4:24.88 '82, 1 mile: 4:36.48i '83, 3000m: 8:53.49 '83, 5000m: 15:40.42 '82, 10000m: 32:07.41 '84.
Has won seven of her twelve marathons, climaxed by her sensational Olympic victory, made possible by winning the US Trials race just 17 days after undergoing arthroscopic surgery on her right knee.

Jeanette BOLDEN
b.26 Jan 1960 Los Angeles 1.74m 62kg
Club: Tiger World Class AC. Was at UCLA.
Ch. record at 100m (R – 4x100m relay): OG: '84– 4 (1R); WCp: '81– 1R. Set former world bests for 50y (5.80) and 60y indoors (6.60) in 1982.
Progression at 100m: 1977 – 11.68, 1980 – 11.41, 1981 – 11.18, 1982 – 11.16/11.12w, 1983 – 11.48, 1984 – 11.15
pbs: 200m: 23.49 '82, 23.02w '84; 100mh: 13.95 '84, 13.64w '84

Cindy BREMSER
b.5 May 1953 Milwaukee, Wisconsin 1.62m 51kg
Club: Wisconsin United. Graduate of the University of Wisconsin. Has taken Masters degree in pediatric nursing.
Ch. record at 3000m: OG: '84– 4; WCh: '83– h; At 1500m: PAm: '75– 4, '83– 2. Has 13 2nd or 3rd placings in US championships at 1500m and 3000m but no wins.
Progression at 3000m: 1975 – 9:13.4, 1976 – 9:27.6, 1977 – 9:03.97, 1978 – 9:04.8, 1979 – 8:59.93, 1980 – 9:16.21, 1981 – 8:55.39, 1982 – 8:51.11, 1983 – 8:55.48, 1984 – 8:38.60
pbs: 800m: 2:04.20 '83, 1500m: 4:05.76 '82, 1 mile: 4:29.21 '82, 2000m: 5:47.89 '84, 2 miles: 9:45.0i '80, 5000m: 15:41.82 '84

Valerie BRISCO-HOOKS
b.6 Jul 1960 Greenwood, Mississippi 1.69m 59kg
Club: World Class AC. Was at Long Beach City College. Married to Alvin Hooks (10.36 for 100m in 1980), with one child.
Ch. record at 400m (R – 4x400m relay): OG: '84– 1 at 200m, 400m, 4x400mR; PAm: '79– 4 at 200m, 1 at 4x100mR. US 400m champion 1984. US 200m and 400m (2) records in 1984.
Progression at 200m/400m: 1977 – 24.4/54.19, 1978 – 23.77/53.70, 1979 – 23.16/22.53w/52.08, 1981 – 23.49/52.25, 1983 – 23.10/53.61, 1984 – 21.81/48.83
pb 100m: 11.08/11.02w '84
Won three Olympic gold medals in 1984, a feat previously achieved by only three other women. Her victory celebration with coach Bob Kersee will long be remembered!

Alice BROWN
b.20 Sep 1960 Jackson, Mississippi 1.57m 56kg
Club: World Class AC. Graduate of Cal State Northridge.
Ch. record at 100m (R – 4 x 100m relay): OG: '84– 2 (1R); WCh: '83– sf; WCp: '81– 2R. Won TAC and US Trials in 1980 and 2nd at both in 1984. Set former world indoor best for 60 yards at 6.62 in 1981.
Progression at 100m: 1978 – 11.64, 1979 – 11.73/11.65w, 1980 – 11.21/11.17w, 1981 – 11.28/11.13w, 1982 – 11.37, 1983 – 11.08, 1984 – 11.13/11.07w
pb 200m: 22.41 '83

Judi BROWN
b.14 Jul 1961 Milwaukee, Wisconsin 1.80m 67kg
Club: Athletics West. Michigan State University.
Ch. record at 400mh: OG: '84– 2; WCh: '83– sf; PAm: '83– 1 (1 at 4x400m relay). Won NCAA 1983, TAC and US Trials 1984. Set two US 400mh records in 1984.
Progression at 400mh: 1980 – 59.95, 1981 – 59.49, 1982 – 57.80, 1983 – 56.03, 1984 – 54.93.
pbs: 200m: 23.53 '84, 400m: 52.63 '84.
Her uncle, Bill Brown won a silver medal at 800m and gold at 4x400m relay in the 1951 Pan-American Games.

Chandra CHEESEBOROUGH
b.10 Jan 1959 Jacksonville, Florida 1.65m 59kg
Club: Athletics West. Graduate of Tennessee State University.
Ch. record at 400m: OG: '84– 2 (1 at 4x100mR & 4x400mR). At 200m (R – 4x100m relay): OG: '76– sf (6 at 100m); PAm: '75– 1 (1R), '79– 1R. US champion at 100m 1976. Won US Olympic Trials at 200m 1980, 400m 1984. Set world junior record for 100m in 1976. Set former world best for 60y at 6.68 in 1979. US 200m record in 1975 and two US 400m records in 1984.
Progression at 200m/400m: 1975 – 22.77, 1976 – 23.18/22.64w, 1977 – 22.89, 1978 – 23.40, 1979 – 23.34/22.84w, 1980 – 22.84/22.70w, 1981 – 22.65, 1982 – 23.05, 1983 – 51.00, 1984 – 22.47/49.05
pbs: 100m: 11.13 '76 & '84, 10.99w '83, 300m: 35.46 '84 (US best)
US international since she won the 1975 Pan-American 200m gold medal at the age of 16 in 1975. Moved up most successfully to 400m in 1984.

Leslie DENIZ
b.25 May 1962 Oakland, California 1.70m 86kg
Arizona State University.
Ch. record at DT: OG: '84– 2; WCp: '81– 6. US champion 1981 and 1983. Set five US discus records 1983–4.
Progression at DT: 1977 – 43.92, 1978 – 44.00, 1979 – 53.60, 1980 – 56.06, 1981 – 55.70, 1982 – 60.88, 1983 – 64.94, 1984 – 65.20.
pb SP: 17.03i '83

Benita FITZGERALD-BROWN
b.6 Jul 1961 Warrenton, Virginia 1.78m 64kg
Club: Team Adidas. University of Tennessee – degree in industrial engineering. Married Laron Brown (45.45 for 400m in 1983) in 1984.
Ch. record at 100mh: OG: '84– 1; WCh: '83– 8; PAm: '83– 1; WSG: '83– 3. Won TAC '83, NCAA '82–3. 2nd US Trials 1980 and 1984.
Progression at 100mh: 1978 – 14.00, 1979 – 13.33, 1980 – 13.11, 1981 – 13.10, 1982 – 12.92, 1983 – 12.84, 1984 – 12.84.
pbs: 100m: 11.36/11.2/11.13w '82, 200m: 23.22 '81, 23.0 '83

Jane FREDERICK
b.7 Apr 1952 Oakland, California 1.78m 74kg
Club: Athletics West. Graduate of the University of Colorado.

154

National Championships

Ch. record at Pen/Hep: OG: '72– 21, '76– 7; WCh: '83– dnf, PAm: '79– dnf (5 at LJ); WCp: '77– 7 at LJ, WSG: '75– 1, '77– 2. US champion at Pen/Hep: '72–3, '75–6, '79, '81, '83 and 100mh: '75–6. Has set six US heptathlon records, from a world best of 6166 in 1981 to 6714 in 1984. Also set six US pentathlon records 1974–79. World indoor best (hand-timed) of 7.3 for 60y hurdles in 1977.
Progression at Pen (p)/Hep: 1972 – 4284p, 1973 – 4281p, 1974 – 4391p, 1975 – 4676p, 1976 – 4732p, 1977 – 4625p, 1978 – 4704p, 1979 – 4708p, 1981 – 6308, 1982 – 6458, 1983 – 6457, 1984 – 6714.
pbs: 200m: 23.9/24.13 '76, 800m: 2:10.25 '84, 100mh: 13.25 '78, HJ: 1.89 '83, LJ: 6.56/6.58w '78, SP: 16.18 '78, JT: 52.74 '84.
Missed 1984 Olympics due to injury at US Trials.

Kim GALLAGHER
b. Philadelphia 11 Jun 1964 1.65m 49kg
Club: Puma & Energizer TC.
Ch. record at 800m: OG: '84– 2. Won TAC 800m and 1500m and US Trials 800m in 1984.
Progression at 800m (y – 880y): 1973 – 2:33.2y, 1974 – 2:32.9y, 1975 – 2:30.7y, 1976 – 2:26.6, 1977 – 2:15.9, 1978 – 2:11.7, 1979 – 2:07.6, 1980 – 2:04.75, 1981 – 2:01.82, 1982 – 2:00.07, 1983 – 2:05.39, 1984 – 1:58.50
pbs: 1500m: 4:08.08 '84, 3000m: 9:19.67 '81, 5000m: 16:34.7 '79

Randy GIVENS
b.27 Mar 1962 Alexandra, Louisiana 1.67m 54kg
Club: Bud Light Track America. Florida State University
Ch. record at 200m (100m, R – 4x100m relay): OG: '84– 6; WCh: '83– sf; WSG: '83– 1 (2, 1R); PAm: '83– 1 (1R). Won NCAA 100m and 200m 1984.
Progression at 200m: 1978 – 25.5y, 1979 – 24.0yw, 1980 – 23.56/23.23w, 1981 – 23.57/23.35w, 1982 – 22.59/22.3, 1983 – 22.31, 1984 – 22.36
pbs: 100m: 11.27/11.06w '84, 400m: 52.80 '84

Florence GRIFFITH
b.21 Dec 1959 Los Angeles 1.68m 57kg
Club: World Class AC. Graduate of UCLA.
Ch. record at 200m: OG: '84– 2; WCh: '83– 4; WCp: '81– 2 at 4x100mR. Won NCAA 200m '82, 400m '83.
Progression at 100m, 200m: 1978 – 10.85yw, 24.4y; 1980 – 11.51, 23.55/23.02w; 1981 – 11.23, 22.81/22.61w; 1982 – 11.12, 22.39/22.23w; 1983 – 11.06/10.96w, 22.23; 1984 – 10.99, 22.04.
pb 400m: 50.94 '83.
Has four inch fingernails on her left hand!

Stephanie HIGHTOWER
b.19 Jul 1958 Fort Knox, Kentucky 1.64m 54kg
Club: Bud Light Track America. Graduate of Ohio State University.
Ch. record at 100mh: WSG: '81– 1; WCp: '81– 4. US champion 1980–2, 1984. Won US Olympic Trials 1980, 4th in 1984. Has set three world indoor bests for 60y hurdles 1980–3, best of 7.36.
Progression at 100mh: 1976 – 14.60, 1977 – 14.27w, 1978 – 13.50, 1979 – 13.09, 1980 – 12.90, 1981 – 13.03, 1982 – 12.79, 1983 – 13.00, 1984 – 12.90/12.78w
pb 100m: 11.56 '78
Missed US Olympic selection in 1984 by the narrowest of margins. Overall winner of Mobil Grand Prix series 1984 US indoor season.

Joni HUNTLEY
b.4 Aug 1956 McMinnville, Oregon 1.73m 61kg
Club: Pacific Coast Club. Was at Oregon State University and Cal State, Long Beach.
Ch. record at HJ: OG: '76– 5=, '84– 3; PAm: '75– 1, '83– 3. US champion 1974–77. Set US records in 1974 and 1975, US indoor records in 1978, 1980–1, but didn't improve outdoor pb until 1984.
Progression at HJ: 1972 – 1.67, 1973 – 1.78, 1974 – 1.85, 1975 – 1.90, 1976 – 1.89, 1977 – 1.86, 1978 – 1.93i, 1979– 1.84, 1980 – 1.94i, 1981 – 1.95i, 1982 – 1.90, 1983 – 1.90, 1984 – 1.97.
pb LJ: 6.18 '78.

Jackie JOYNER
b.3 Mar 1962 1.78m 63kg
Club: World Class AC. UCLA. Sister of triple jumper Al Joyner.
Ch. record at Heptathlon: OG: '84– 2 (5 LJ); WCh: '83– dnf. Won TAC '82, NCAA '82–3.
Progression at LJ, Hep: 1978 – 6.06; 1979 – 6.28/6.30w; 1980 – 6.34/6.40w; 1981 – 6.39/6.47w, 5827w; 1982 – 6.44/6.61w, 6126; 1983 – 6.74/6.77w, 6372; 1984 – 6.81, 6520
pbs: 200m: 23.70 '83, 800m: 2:13.03 '84, 100mh: 13.53 '84, HJ: 1.87 '83, SP: 14.39 '84, JT: 45.40 '84.

Lillie LEATHERWOOD
b.6 Jul 1964 1.67m 56kg University of Alabama.
Ch. record at 400m (R – 4x400m relay): OG: '84– 5 (1R). 2nd TAC, 3rd US Trials '84.
Progression at 400m: 1983 – 53.2, 1984 – 50.19
pbs: 100m: 11.74/11.42w '84, 200m: 23.66 '84

Carol LEWIS
b.8 Aug 1963 Birmingham, Alabama 1.78m 68kg
Club: Santa Monica Track Club. University of Houston. Sister of Carl Lewis.
Ch. record at LJ: OG: '84– 9; WCh: '83– 3. Won TAC '82–3, NCAA '83, US Trials '84 (3rd in 1980).
Progression at LJ: 1975 – 4.65, 1976 – 5.29, 1977 – 5.71, 1978 – 6.22/6.23w, 1979 – 6.37, 1980 – 6.60, 1981 – 6.59i, 1982 – 6.81, 1983 – 6.97/7.04w, 1984 – 6.97/7.03w.
pbs: 100mh: 13.46/13.45w '83; HJ: 1.80 '83, JT: 38.04 '84
Won record five Junior TAC titles.

Leslie MAXIE
b.4 Jan 1967 1.79m 61kg. Student at Mills High School, Millbrae, California. Set world junior record of 55.20 for 400mh when second in the TAC Championships in 1984, her first year of running the event.
pbs: 200m: 23.44 '83, 400m: 53.07 '84.

Louise RITTER
b.18 Feb 1958 Dallas, Texas 1.78m 60kg
Club: Pacific Coast Club. Graduate of Texas Woman's University.
Ch. record at HJ: OG: '84– 6; WCh: '83– 3; PAm: '79– 1; WCp: '77– 4, '79– 5. US champion 1978, won US Olympic Trials 1980 and 1984. Won AIAW title 1977–9. Seven US high jump records 1978–83.
Progression at HJ: 1973 – 1.74, 1974 – 1.78, 1975 – 1.80, 1976 – 1.82, 1977 – 1.86, 1978 – 1.90, 1979 – 1.93, 1980 – 1.95, 1981 – 1.94, 1982 – 1.93i, 1983 – 2.01, 1984 – 1.96i.
Switched to 'flop' in 1977, straddle best 1.82m.

Mary SLANEY
b.4 Aug 1958 Flemington, New Jersey 1.68m 51kg née Decker.
Club: Athletics West. Was at University of Colorado. Married British discus thrower Richard Slaney (pb 64.66m in 1984, 4th at SP and DT in the 1982 Commonwealth Games) on 1 January 1985. Formerly married to 2:09:32 marathon runner Ron Tabb.
Ch. record at 3000m: OG: '84– dnf; WCh: '83– 1. At 1500m: WCh: '83– 1; PAm: '79– 1. US champion at 800m '74, 1500m '82–3, 3000m '83. Won US Olympic Trials at 1500m '80, 3000m '84. Set world records for 1 mile in 1980 (4:21.7) and at 1 mile, 5000m and 10000m in 1982, and holds US records at seven distances from

National Championships

800m to 10000m. Has set scores of world indoor bests from 1974 to 1985, best times: 880y – 1:59.7 '80, 1000y – 2:23.8 '78, 1500m – 4:00.2 '80 (oversized track), 1 mile – 4:17.55 '80 (oversized track), 2000m – 5:34.52 '85, 3000m – 8:47.3 '82, 2 miles – 9:31.7 '83.
Progression at 1500m (M = 1 mile)/3000m: 1971 – 5:04.8M, 1972 – 4:35.9, 1973 – 4:37.4M, 1974 – 5:00.8M, 1978 – 4:08.9, 1979 – 4:05.0, 1980 – 3:59.43/8:38.73, 1982 – 4:01.7/8:29.71, 1983 – 3:57.12/8:34.62, 1984 – 3:59.19/8:34.91
pbs: 400m: 53.84 '73, 800m: 1:57.60 '83, 1 mile: 4:17.55i '80/ 4:18.08 '82, 2000m: 5:32.7 '84, 5000m: 15:08.26 '82, 10000m: 31:35.3 '82.
She became the youngest ever US international at 14 years 224 days when she ran 1 mile indoors against the USSR in 1973. Later that year she won at 800m v USSR, and she set a world indoor best for 880y at 2:02.3 in 1974. However for the next four years she competed rarely due to a series of injuries. She overcame these to dominate US distance running, and score double success at the 1983 world championships. Seeking to add Olympic success, she fell in the 3000m final in Los Angeles.

Angie THACKER
b.27 Jun 1964 St Louis 1.67m 59kg University of Nebraska
Ch. record at LJ: OG: '84– 4
Progression at LJ: 1981 – 5.71, 1982 – 6.02, 1983 – 6.53w/6.54, 1984 – 6.81
pbs: 100m: 11.39 '84, 11.20w '83; 200m: 23.15 '84, 23.07w '83.

Kim TURNER
b.21 Mar 1961 Lives in Detroit 1.65m 57kg
Club: Puma & Energizer TC. University of Texas at El Paso.
Ch. record at 100mh: OG: '84– 3=; PAm: '83– 2. Won NCAA and US Trials in 1984.
Progression at 100mh: 1978 – 15.4, 1979 – 13.83, 1981 – 13.38/13.17w, 1982 – 13.09/12.8, 1983 – 12.95, 1984 – 13.01/12.96w

Diane WILLIAMS
b.14 Dec 1961 Chicago, Illinois 1.62m 56kg
Club: Puma & Energizer TC. Was at Cal State University, Los Angeles
Ch. record: WCh: '83– 3 at 100m.
Progression at 100m: 1980 – 11.37/11.32w, 1982 – 11.14/11.13w, 1983 – 10.94, 1984 – 11.04.
pb 200m: 23.04/22.65w '83.
Strong finisher

Ruth WYSOCKI
b.8 Mar 1957 1.75m 61kg née Kleinsasser, formerly Caldwell. Married to Tom Wysocki (28:19.56 for 10000m in 1980).
Club: Brooks Racing Team. Was at Citrus College.
Ch. record: OG: '84– 6 at 800m, 8 at 1500m. Won 800m and 1500m double at 1984 US Olympic Trials. US 800m champion 1978.
Progression at 800m/1500m: 1975 – 2:07.6, 1976 – 2:03.9/4:16.0, 1977 – 2:05.8, 1978 – 2:01.99/4:18.0, 1980 – 2:05.28, 1984 – 1:58.65/4:00.18
pbs: 1 mile: 4:21.78 '84, 2000m: 5:40.09 '84, 3000m: 8:49.93i '85
Did not compete seriously 1980–3, but came back to become the first US woman to beat Mary Decker in a track race for four years in the Trials 1500m.

USSR

Governing body: Light Athletic Federation of the USSR, Louzhnetskaya Naberezhnay, 119270 Moscow.
National Championships first held in 1920 (men), 1922 (women)

1984 Champions: MEN
100m: Aleksandr Semonov 10.37, 200m: Mikhail Kulikov 20.91, 400m: Vladimir Krylov 46.05, 800m/1500m: Viktor Kalinkin 1:47.61/3:40.48, 5000m: Vitaliy Tishchenko 13:47.47, 10000m: Anatoliy Krakhmalyuk 28:38.78, Mar: Vladimir Nikityuk 2:13:36, 3000mSt: Ivan Konovalov 8:29.65, 110mh: Igor Kazanov 13.59, 400mh: Vladimir Budko 49.74, HJ: Viktor Malchugin 2.28, PV: Sergey Bubka 5.80, LJ: Sergey Layevskiy 8.32, TJ: Gennadiy Valyukevich 17.38, SP: Vladimir Kiselyov 21.43, DT: Dmitriy Kovtsun 64.54, HT: Igor Nikulin 78.70, JT: Viktor Yevsyukov 90.50, Dec: Grigoriy Degtyarev 8652, 20kmW: Nikolay Polozov 1:23:53, 50kmW: Andrey Perlov 3:47:20
WOMEN
100m: Irina Slyusar & Natalya Pomoschikova 11.61, 200m: Yelena Vinogradova 22.87, 400m: Olga Vladykina 50.50, 800m: Yekaterina Podkopayeva 1:59.51, 1500m: Nadezhda Ralldugina 4:04.36, 3000m: Galina Zakharova 8:37.37, Mar: Zoya Ivanova 2:31:11, 100mh: Mariya Merchuk 13.05, 400mh: Yelena Filipishina 55.02, HJ: Olga Turchak 1.96, LJ: Yelena Kokonova 7.09, SP: Nunu Abashidze 21.13, DT: Galina Savinkova 73.22, JT: Zinaida Gavrilina 67.00, Hep: Natalya Shubenkova 6799, 10kmW: Olga Krishtop 46:15.0

Aleksandr APAYCHEV
b.6 May 1961 Kirov 1.87m 90kg
Club: Trudovye Rezervy, Brovary. Sports student. Set USSR decathlon records at 8560 and 8643 in 1984.
Progression at Dec: 1978 – 7028, 1979 – 7530, 1980 – 7581, 1981 – 7966, 1982 – 8111, 1983 – 8260, 1984 – 8643
pbs: 100m: 10.87 '84, 400m: 48.40 '84, 1500m: 4:18.78 '84, 110mh: 13.93 '84, HJ: 2.00 '84, PV: 5.00i '84, LJ: 7.61 '83, SP: 16.20 '84, DT: 48.00 '84, JT: 76.52 '81.
Recorded best ever second day score for a decathlon – 4352 points at Neubrandenburg on 3 June 1984.

Gennadiy AVDEYENKO
b.4 Nov 1963 Odessa 2.02m 82kg Refrigeration mechanic.
Ch. record: WCh: '83– 1
Progression at HJ: 1980 – 2.06, 1981 – 2.21, 1982 – 2.22, 1983 – 2.32, 1984 – 2.31.
pb TJ: 15.57 '80.
Perhaps the most surprising world champion of 1983, he again displayed his big-meet ability by winning the 1984 8-nations meeting in Tokyo.

Pavel BOGATYRYOV
b.19 Mar 1961 1.94m 84kg
Progression at PV: 1979 – 5.10, 1980 – 5.30i, 1981 – 5.50, 1982 – 5.55, 1983 – 5.74, 1984 – 5.75

Janis BOJARS
b.12 May 1956 Ilukste, Latvia 1.85m 127kg Sports instructor.
Ch. record at SP: WCh: '83– 5; ECh: '82– 2; EI: '83– 1, '84– 1; ECp: '83– 3; WIG: '85– 3. USSR champion 1983.

National Championships

Progression at SP: 1973 – 13.40, 1974 – 15.20, 1975 – 16.64, 1976 – 17.07, 1977 – 17.75, 1978 – 18.84, 1979 – 19.42, 1980 – 20.02, 1981 – 20.36, 1982 – 21.31, 1983 – 21.40, 1984 – 21.74

Sergey BUBKA
b.4 Dec 1963 Voroshilovgrad, Ukraine 1.83m 80kg Student in Donetsk
Ch. record at PV: WCh: '83– 1; EJ: '81– 7 =; WIG: '85– 1. USSR champion 1984. Set four world records and three world indoor pole vault bests in 1984.
Progression at PV: 1975 – 2.70, 1976 – 3.50, 1977 – 3.60, 1978 – 4.40, 1979 – 4.80, 1980 – 5.10, 1981 – 5.40, 1982 – 5.55, 1983 – 5.72, 1984 – 5.94
The surprise world champion in 1983 has gone on to dominate the world of pole vaulting. Has the speed and strength to manage a very high hold on the pole. His elder brother Vasiliy has a PV best of 5.70m in 1984 and was third in the World Indoor Games 1985.

Vladimir BUDKO
b.4 Feb 1965 1.86m 79kg
Ch. record at 400mh: EJ: '83– 2. Set three European Junior 400mh records in 1984.
Progression at 400mh: 1982 – 51.40, 1983 – 50.05, 1984 – 48.74
pb 400m: 46.78 '84

Grigory DEGTYAROV
b.16 Jul 1958 Vorkuta 1.90m 90kg
Club: Trud, Kirov. Sports student.
Ch. record at Dec: WCh: '83– dnf; ECh: '82– 6. USSR champion 1983 and 1984. Set USSR decathlon records at 8538 in 1983, 8579 and 8652 in 1984.
Progression at Dec: 1974 – 4780, 1975 – 5000, 1976 – 6340, 1977 – 7228, 1978 – 7419, 1979 – 7360, 1980 – 7706, 1981 – 8124, 1982 – 8247, 1983 – 8538, 1984 – 8652
pbs: 100m: 10.87 '84, 400m: 49.40 '83, 1500m: 4:14.30 '81, 110mh: 14.45 '84, HJ: 2.10 '84, PV: 5.10 '84, LJ: 7.75 '83, SP: 16.03 '84, DT: 51.20 '84, JT: 67.08 '84

Dmitriy DMITRIYEV
b.3 Mar 1956 Leningrad 1.75m 65kg Serviceman
Ch. record at 5000m: WCh: '83– 4; ECh: '82– 11; ECp: '83– 2. At 1500m: EJ: '75– 2. USSR champion at 1500m 1980, 5000m 1980–3.
Progression at 5000m: 1977 – 14:07.0, 1978 – 13:55.3, 1980 – 13:39.5, 1981 – 13:24.23, 1982 – 13:19.18, 1983 – 13:21.1, 1984 – 13:17.37
pbs: 800m: 1:47.7 '82, 1500m: 3:36.60 '84, 3000m: 7:42.05 '84

Viktor DOROVSKIKH
b.19 Oct 1950 Khatanga, Krasnoyarsk 1.83m 73kg Serviceman based in Leningrad.
Ch. record at 50kmW: WCh: '83– 8; ECh: '78– 5, '82– dnf; LT: '79– 3, '83– 3. USSR champion 1979 and 1982.
Progression at 50kmW: 1978 – 3:56:47, 1979 – 3:45:51, 1980 – 3:41:02, 1981 – 3:55:14, 1982 – 3:46:54, 1983 – 3:49:47, 1984 – 3:53:53.
pb 20kmW: 1:24:53 '79

Igor DUGINYETS
b.20 May 1956 Yuzhno-Sakhalinsk 1.96m 100kg
Club: Dynamo, Odessa. Serviceman.
Ch. record at DT: OG: '80– 6; WCh: '83– 11; ECh: '78– 10, '82– 2; EJ: '75– 3; ECp: '79– 3. USSR champion 1978, 1982–3.
Progression at DT: 1972 – 39.78, 1973 – 43.70, 1974 – 48.62, 1975 – 58.58, 1976 – 59.88, 1977 – 63.00, 1978 – 64.16, 1979 – 65.30, 1980 – 65.98, 1981 – 62.00, 1982 – 68.52, 1983 – 64.28, 1984 – 66.56

Yuriy DUMCHEV
b.5 Aug 1958 Rossosh, Voronezh 2.00m 128kg
Ch. record at DT: OG: '80– 5; WCh: '83– 17; EJ: '77– 1. USSR champion 1980–1. Set world discus record in 1983. Three USSR records.
Progression at DT: 1976 – 53.57, 1977 – 58.32, 1978 – 59.28, 1979 – 61.64, 1980 – 68.16, 1981 – 66.42, 1982 – 69.16, 1983 – 71.86, 1984 – 67.42
pb SP: 18.40 '82

Rodion GATAULLIN
b.23 Nov 1965 Tashkent 1.91m 78kg
Club: Burevestnik, Tashkent. Medical student.
Ch. record at PV: EJ: '83– 1. Set world junior pole vault record when second in USSR championships 1984.
Progression at PV: 1979 – 3.80, 1980 – 4.20, 1981 – 4.80, 1982 – 5.20, 1983 – 5.55, 1984 – 5.65

Vladimir GRANYENKOV
b.1 Jun 1959 Bolshoi Lug, Irkutsk 1.94m 78kg
Club: Trudovye Rezervy, Kiev. Serviceman.
Ch. record at HJ: ECh: '82– 6.
Progression at HJ: 1978 – 2.06, 1979 – 2.18, 1980 – 2.21, 1981 – 2.30, 1982 – 2.26, 1983 – 2.28, 1984 – 2.33

Sergey KASNAUSKAS
b.20 Apr 1961 Minsk 1.92m 126kg Sports instructor.
Ch. record at SP: EJ: '79– 3. Set two European indoor bests (21.43m and 21.46m) in 1984.
Progression at SP: 1978 – 16.83, 1979 – 18.03, 1980 – 18.50i, 1982 – 18.52, 1983 – 21.17, 1984 – 21.64
A reported 22.09 in 1984 was apparently irregular.

Aleksandr KHARLOV
b.18 Mar 1958 Tashkent 1.93m 87kg Sports instructor.
Ch. record at 400mh: OG: '80– sf; WCh: '83– 3; ECh: '82– 6; ECp: '83– 2; WSG: '83– 1. USSR champion 1983.
Progression at 400mh: 1977 – 54.1, 1979 – 51.15, 1980 – 49.51, 1981 – 51.11, 1982 – 49.40, 1983 – 48.78, 1984 – 49.15.
pb 110mh: 14.0 '76.

Vladimir KISELYOV
b.1 Jan 1957 Kremenchug, Ukraine 1.86m 125kg
Club: Trud, Kremenchug. Sports instructor.
Ch. record at SP: OG: '80– 1; ECh: '82– 7; EI: '79– 3; EJ: '75– 1; WSG: '79– 4. USSR shot champion 1984.
Progression at SP: 1973 – 15.17, 1974 – 17.75, 1975 – 19.12, 1976 – 19.51, 1977 – 19.50i, 1978 – 20.07, 1979 – 20.71, 1980 – 21.35, 1982 – 21.09, 1983 – 20.77, 1984 – 21.58

Aleksandr KRUPSKIY
b.4 Jan 1960 Irkutsk 1.85m 77kg
Club: Lokomotiv, Irkutsk.
Ch. record at PV: ECh: '82– 1; EI: '81– 2, '84– 3; EJ: '79– 2; ECp: '83– 2.
Progression at PV: 1974 – 3.00, 1975 – 4.10, 1976 – 4.80, 1977 – 4.90, 1978 – 5.20, 1979 – 5.50, 1980 – 5.50, 1981 – 5.70, 1982 – 5.70, 1983 – 5.74, 1984 – 5.82

Dainis KULA
b.28 Apr 1959 Tukums, Latvia 1.89m 94kg
Ch. record at JT: OG: '80– 1; WCh: '83– 3; ECh: '82– 4; WSG: '81– 1, '83– 1; WCp: '81– 1; ECp: '81– 2. USSR champion 1981 and 1983.

157

National Championships

Progression at JT: 1974 – 52.50, 1975 – 60.03, 1976 – 61.80, 1977 – 75.42, 1978 – 80.48, 1979 – 86.04, 1980 – 92.06, 1981 – 90.54, 1982 – 90.96, 1983 – 91.88, 1984 – 88.80.
pb HJ: 2.06 '80
Won 1980 Olympic title in fine style but only after two no throws in the final and a third which looked flat to some observers.

Yuri KUTSENKO
b.5 Mar 1952 Tavrovo, Belgorod 1.90m 93kg
Club: Trud, Belgorod.
Ch. record at Dec: OG: '80– 2; ECh: '78– 5; ECp: '79– 4. USSR champion 1980.
Progression at Dec: 1976 – 7376, 1977 – 7877, 1978 – 8080, 1979 – 8086, 1980 – 8331, 1981 – 8302, 1982 – 8229, 1984 – 8512
pbs: 100m: 10.6, 400m: 48.67 '80, 1500m: 4:10.0 '82, 110mh: 14.94 '84, HJ: 2.13 '84, PV: 4.90 '80, LJ: 7.74 '80, SP: 15.14 '80, DT: 50.90 '82, JT: 68.18 '80

Sergey LAYEVSKIY
b.23 May 1959 1.78m 79kg. USSR long jump champion 1984.
Progression at LJ: 1980 – 7.59, 1981 – 7.91, 1982 – 8.13, 1983 – 7.87, 1984 – 8.32

Sergey LITVINOV
b.23 Jan 1958 Tsukarov, Krasnodar 1.80m 100kg Soviet Army officer working for physical education diploma.
Ch. record at HT: OG: '80– 2; WCh: '83– 1; ECh: '82– 3; EJ: '75– 3, '77– 2; WCp: '79– 1; ECp: '79– 2, '83– 1. USSR champion 1979 and 1983. Set three world hammer records, in 1980, 1982 and 1983, and world junior record in 1976.
Progression at HT: 1974 – 60.68, 1975 – 65.32, 1976 – 72.38, 1977 – 74.32, 1978 – 76.22, 1979 – 79.82, 1980 – 81.66, 1981 – 79.60, 1982 – 83.98, 1983 – 84.14, 1984 – 85.20

Viktor MARKIN
b.23 Feb 1957 Oktyabrski Ust-Tarskog, Novosibirsk 1.83m 73kg.
Club: Burevestnik, Novosibirsk. Physician.
Ch. record at 400m (R – 4x400m relay): OG: '80– 1 (1R); WCh: '83– sf (1R); ECh: '82– 3 (3R); WSG: '81– 1R, '83– 2; WCp: '81– 5; ECp: '81– 1R. USSR 400m champion 1981. European 400m record 1980.
Progression at 400m: 1976 – 49.5, 1977 – 49.2, 1978 – 47.4, 1979 – 47.20, 1980 – 44.60, 1981 – 45.70, 1982 – 45.30, 1983 – 45.38, 1984 – 44.78
pbs: 100m: 10.4 '80, 200m: 21.39 '80, 21.1 '77.
Ducked under 45 seconds in 1984 for the first time since winning the 1980 Olympic title in Moscow.

Vladimir MURAVYEV
b.30 Sep 1959 Karaganda 1.78m 75kg Serviceman.
Ch. record at 200m (R – 4x100mR): OG: 6 at 100m (1R); WCh: '83– sf (2R); ECh: '82– 7 (sf 100m); WSG: '81– 5 (2R), '83– 4; WCp: '81– 4R; ECp: '81– 5 at 100m (2R), '83– 6; EJ: '81– 2 at 50m; EJ: '77– 4R. USSR 200m champion 1983.
Progression at 200m: 1975 – 23.0, 1976 – 21.9, 1977 – 21.4, 1978 – 21.7, 1979 – 21.0, 1980 – 20.76, 1981 – 20.53, 1982 – 20.76/20.7w, 1983 – 20.46, 1984 – 20.34.
pb 100m: 10.23 '84.

Aleksandr NEVSKIY
b.21 Feb 1958 Severny, Tomsk 1.90m 88kg
Club: Dynamo, Kiev. Student.
Ch. record at Dec: WCh: '83– 6; ECp: '79– 3. USSR champion 1981.
Progression at Dec: 1978 – 7776, 1979 – 8057, 1980 – 8065, 1981 – 8170, 1982 – 8153, 1983 – 8412, 1984 – 8476
pbs: 100m: 10.7 '78, 400m: 48.44 '84, 1500m: 4:17.03 '83, 110mh: 14.67 '84, 14.63w '83, HJ: 2.14i '80, PV: 4.70 '84, LJ: 7.58 '83, SP: 15.57 '84, DT: 49.08 '83, JT: 69.56 '84

Igor NIKULIN
b.14 Aug 1960 Moscow 1.91m 105kg
Ch. record at HT: WCh: '83– 4; ECh: '82– 2; EJ: '79– 1; WSG: '81– 3. USSR hammer champion 1981 and 1984.
Progression at HT: 1975 – 48.50, 1976 – 58.14, 1977 – 63.40, 1978 – 71.60, 1979 – 75.20, 1980 – 80.34, 1981 – 77.50, 1982 – 83.54, 1983– 82.92, 1984 – 82.56
He became the youngest ever 80m hammer thrower in 1980. His father Yuriy was fourth in the 1964 Olympic hammer.

Igor PAKLIN
b.15 Jun 1963 Frunze, Kirghizia 1.91m 72kg
Club: Urozhai. Student at Polytechnic Institute, Frunze.
Ch. record at HJ: WCh: '83– 4 =; EJ: '81– 4; WSG: '83–1. World indoor high jump best of 2.36 in 1984
Progression at HJ: 1978 – 1.85, 1979 – 2.06, 1980 – 2.18, 1981 – 2.21, 1982 – 2.24, 1983 – 2.33, 1984 – 2.36i/2.30

Andrey PERLOV
b.12 Dec 1961. Soviet champion at 50km walk in 1983. Set world junior record at 20km track walk with 1:22:42.8 in 1980.
Progression at 50kmW: 1981 – 4:05:29, 1983 – 3:45:49, 1984 – 3:43:06
pbs: 10kmW track: 39:40.8 '83, 20kmW: 1:21:16 '80.

Nikolay POLOZOV
b.10 Oct 1951 1.83m 72kg. USSR 20km walk champion 1984.
Progression at 20kmW: 1973 – 1:29:35, 1974 – 1:29:49, 1975 – 1:28:11, 1976 – 1:26:56, 1977 – 1:25:07, 1978 – 1:24:05, 1979 – 1:23:49, 1980 – 1:20:50, 1981 – 1:22:49, 1983 – 1:24:12, 1984 – 1:22:40

Vladimir POLYAKOV
b.17 Apr 1960 Aleksin, Tula region 1.90m 75kg
Club: Spartak, Moscow.
Ch. record at PV: WCh: '83– 10=, ECh: '82– 2; EI: '80– 2, '83– 1; EJ: '79– 1; WSG: '81– 2. USSR champion 1983. Set Soviet pole vault records at 5.72m and 5.81m in 1981, the latter was a world record.
Progression at PV: 1973 – 3.00, 1974 – 3.80, 1975 – 4.50, 1976 – 4.90, 1977 – 5.00, 1978 – 5.20, 1979 – 5.40, 1980 – 5.60, 1981 – 5.81, 1982 – 5.60, 1983 – 5.73i, 1984 – 5.80

Oleg PROTSENKO
b.11 Aug 1963 1.86m 72kg
Club: Dynamo Zhukovski. Sports student.
Progression at TJ: 1979 – 15.05i, 1980 – 15.94, 1981 – 16.68, 1982 – 16.59, 1983 – 17.27, 1984 – 17.52. Friendship Games winner and world's best at triple jump in 1984.

Sergey PROTSISHIN
b.1959
Ch. record at 20kmW: LT: '83– 10.
Progression at 20kmW: 1982 – 1:23:04, 1983 – 1:22:03, 1984 – 1:21:57.
pbs: track: 5kmW: 19:34.29i '84, 10kmW: 39:42.7 '83; road: 50kmW: 4:04:58 '82.

Heino PUUSTE
b.7 Oct 1955 Lagedi, Estonia 1.88m 90kg
Club: Trud, Talinn.
Ch. record at JT: OG: '80– 4; WCh: '83– 4; ECh: '82– 2; WSG: '79– 3, '81– 3; ECp: '83– 2. USSR champion 1979.
Progression at JT: 1973 – 64.70, 1974 – 72.86, 1975 – 76.62,

National Championships

1976 – 80.54, 1977 – 82.56, 1978 – 84.06, 1979 – 84.42, 1980 – 89.32, 1981 – 87.22, 1982 – 90.72, 1983 – 94.20, 1984 – 91.86

Yuriy SEDYKH
b.11 Jun 1955 Novocherkassk 1.85m 106kg
Graduate of the Kiev Institute of Physical Culture.
Ch. record at HT: OG: '76– 1, '80– 1; WCh: '83– 2; ECh: '78– 1, '82– 1; EJ: '73–1; WSG: '75– 3, '77– 2, '79– 3; WCp: '77– 4, '81– 1; ECp: '77– 3, '81– 1. USSR hammer champion 1976, 1978, 1980. Set world junior records in 1973 and 1974, and six Soviet records, including four world records: 80.38, 80.64 and 81.80 in 1980, 86.34 in 1984.
Progression at HT: 1971 – 57.02, 1972 – 62.96, 1973 – 69.04, 1974 – 70.86, 1975 – 75.00, 1976 – 78.86, 1977 – 76.60, 1978 – 79.76, 1979 – 77.58, 1980 – 81.80, 1981 – 80.18, 1982 – 81.66, 1983 – 80.94, 1984 – 86.34.
pb 35lb Wt: 23.46 '79 (former world indoor best).
The greatest hammer thrower of all-time, who reached new peaks in 1984, throwing consistently over 85 metres. Coached by his predecessor as Olympic champion, Anatoliy Bondarchuk. Won the 1980 Olympic title by setting a new world record with the first throw of the competition.

Konstantin SEMYKIN
b.26 May 1960 Moscow 1.80m 76kg Sports student.
Progression at LJ: 1976 – 6.75, 1977 – 6.95, 1978 – 7.20, 1979 – 7.45, 1980 – 7.66, 1981 – 7.63, 1982 – 7.93, 1983 – 8.10, 1984 – 8.38
pbs: 100m: 10.6, TJ: 15.95
Made big progress in 1984 to win Friendship Games event.

Valeriy SEREDA
b.30 Jun 1959 Pyatigorsk 1.86m 73kg
Serviceman based in Leningrad.
Ch. record at HJ: WCh: '83– 8; ECh: '82– 5; WCp: '81– 4; ECp: '81– 1, '83– 2. USSR champion 1983. Set European high jump record of 2.37m in 1984.
Progression at HJ: 1972 – 1.60, 1973 – 1.80, 1974 – 1.85, 1975 – 2.00, 1976 – 2.09, 1977 – 2.15, 1978 – 2.16, 1979 – 2.20i, 1980 – 2.18, 1981 – 2.30, 1982 – 2.28i, 1983 – 2.35, 1984 – 2.37.

Igor SOBOLEVSKIY
b.4 May 1962 Dushanbe, Tadjikstan 1.80m 85kg
Serviceman based in Kiev.
Ch. record at Dec: ECp: '83– 7.
Progression at Dec: 1979 – 7110, 1980 – 7659, 1981 – 7448, 1982 – 7886, 1983 – 8234, 1984 – 8530.
pbs: 100m: 10.64 '84, 400m: 48.24 '84, 1500m: 4:27.04 '83, 110mh: 14.82 '84, HJ: 2.01 '84, PV: 4.70 '84, LJ: 7.98 '84, SP: 16.07 '84, DT: 50.54 '84, JT: 71.30 '83

Anatoly SOLOMIN
b.2 Jul 1952 Komarovka, Penza 1.80m 73kg Serviceman based in Kiev.
Ch. record at 20kmW: OG: '80– disq; ECh: '78– 3; LT: '77– 8, '79– 4, '81– 7, '83– 3. USSR champion 1977 and 1981. Set world record for 20km walk at 1:22:59.4 in 1979 and world track best for 1 hour walk, 14384m in 1977. European track walking records for 1 hour (15042m) in 1980, and 20km (1:24:29.9) in 1977.
Progression at 20kmW: 1971 – 1:32:23, 1972 – 1:30:27, 1973 – 1:27:42t, 1974 – 1:33:00, 1975 – 1:28:54, 1976 – 1:24:07, 1977 – 1:24:30t, 1978 – 1:23:30, 1979 – 1:20:13, 1980 – 1:20:35, 1981 – 1:23:36t, 1982 – 1:23:27, 1983 – 1:19:43, 1984 – 1:22:21.
Track pbs: 5kmW: 19:19.93i '83, 10kmW: 39:19.32 '81.

Valery SUNTSOV
b.10 Jul 1955 Debessy, Udmurt ASSR 1.76m 65kg

Club: Burevestnisk Izhevsk. Engineer.
Ch. record at 50kmW: ECh: '82– 7; LT: '81– 7. WSG: '81– 5 at 20kmW.
Progression at 50kmW: 1979 – 3:56:31, 1980 – 3:37:59 (?short), 1981 – 3:54:14, 1982 – 3:46:58, 1983 – 3:46:34, 1984 – 3:47:44.
pb 20kmW: 1:22:34 '80.

Juri TAMM
b.5 Feb 1957 Parnu, Estonia 1.93m 120kg
Ch. record at HT: OG: '80– 3; WSG: '81– 2, '83– 1. Set world record for hammer in 1980, only to be overtaken by Yuriy Sedykh in same competition.
Progression at HT: 1974 – 49.16, 1975 – 54.76, 1976 – 66.86, 1977 – 72.44, 1978 – 74.58, 1979 – 75.18, 1980 – 80.46, 1981 – 77.26, 1982 – 74.82, 1983 – 79.18, 1984 – 84.40

Yuriy TARASYUK
b.11 Apr 1957 Minsk 1.88m 101kg
Club: Minsk Burvestrick.
Progression at HT: 1976 – 66.82, 1977 – 71.20, 1978 – 71.74, 1979 – 75.46, 1980 – 74.78, 1981 – 74.86, 1982 – 80.72, 1983 – 81.18, 1984 – 81.44

Gennadiy VALYUKEVICH
b.1 Jun 1958 Brest Litovsk 1.82m 74kg
Ch. record at TJ: WCh: '83– 10; ECh: '78– 5, '82– 4; EI: '79– 1, '82– 2, '83– 2; EJ: '77– 1; WCp: '79– 2. USSR triple jump champion 1979 and 1984. Set world indoor bests at 17.18m and 17.29m in 1979.
Progression at TJ: 1974 – 13.65, 1975 – 14.71, 1976 – 15.68, 1977 – 16.60, 1978 – 17.02, 1979 – 17.29i, 1980 – 16.61, 1981 – 17.18, 1982 – 17.42, 1983 – 17.23, 1984 – 17.47.
pb 100m: 10.4, LJ: 7.41.

Aleksandr VASILYEV
b.26 Jul 1961 Shostka, Ukraine. 1.91m 83kg
Serviceman, based in Minsk.
Progression at 400mh: 1979 – 52.06, 1980 – 51.51, 1981 – 49.84, 1982 – 49.64/49.4, 1983 – 49.07, 1984 – 48.45

Konstantin VOLKOV
b.28 Feb 1960 Irkutsk 1.85m 79kg Serviceman based in Irkutsk
Ch. record at PV: OG: '80– 2=; WCh: '83– 2; EI: '79– 2, '80– 1, '82– 2; WSG: '81– 1, '83– 1; WCp: '79– 3, '81– 1; ECp: '79– 1, '81– 1=. USSR champion 1979. Set world junior pole vault records at 5.55m and 5.60m in 1979 and four USSR records 1980–4.
Progression at PV: 1971 – 2.80, 1972 – 3.10, 1973 – 3.20, 1974 – 3.70, 1975 – 4.40, 1976 – 4.60, 1977 – 4.90, 1978 – 5.35, 1979 – 5.60, 1980 – 5.70i, 1981 – 5.75, 1982 – 5.65i, 1983 – 5.70, 1984 – 5.85
Excellent competitor. A mark of 5.84m in 1981, in excess of the then world record, was described as an exhibition mark. His father Yuriy vaulted 5.16i in 1970.

Aleksandr YAKOVLYEV
b.8 Sep 1957 Irpensk, Kiev 1.82m 74kg
Ch. record at TJ: EI: '78– 3. Won 8-Nations TJ '84.
Progression at TJ: 1972 – 13.76, 1973 – 14.41, 1974 – 15.56, 1975 – 15.80, 1976 – 16.60, 1977 – 16.83, 1978 – 16.89, 1979 – 16.95, 1980 – 16.73, 1981 – 16.63, 1982 – 16.93, 1983 – 17.05i, 1984 – 17.50.
pb LJ: 8.10i '84

Grigory YEMETS
b.8 Oct 1957 Krivoy Rog, Ukraine 1.90m 80kg
Club: Trud, Krivoi Rog. Clerk.
Ch. record at TJ: EI: '84– 1. Set European indoor triple jump best in 1984.

National Championships

Progression at TJ: 1974 – 12.90, 1975 – 14.51, 1976 – 14.53, 1978 – 15.31, 1979 – 16.10, 1980 – 15.82, 1981 – 16.28/16.40w, 1982 – 16.68, 1983 – 17.27, 1984 – 17.33i/17.30
The European indoor triple jump champion was also second in both indoor and outdoor Soviet championships in 1984.

Aleksandr YEVGENYEV
b.10 Jul 1961 Leningrad 1.74m 72kg
Club: Dynamo, Leningrad. Student.
Ch. record at 200m: EI: '83– 1, '84– 1; WIG: '85– 1. ECh: '82– sf at 100m.
Progression at 200m: 1976 – 23.7, 1977 – 22.5, 1978 – 21.84, 1980 – 21.4, 1981 – 21.19, 1982 – 21.06, 1983 – 20.72, 1984 – 20.41.
pb 100m: 10.22 '84.

Yevgeny YEVSYUKOV
b.2 Jan 1950 Krasnoyarsk 1.74m 65kg Serviceman based in Sochi.
Ch. record at 20kmW: OG: '80– 4; WCh: '83– 3; LT: '77– 6, '81– 4, '83– 5. At 50kmW: WCh: '76– 10.
Progression at 20kmW: 1969 – 1:36:45, 1970 – 1:32:09, 1971 – 1:32:03, 1972 – 1:31:09, 1973 – 1:28:43, 1974 – 1:28:20, 1975 – 1:29:12, 1976 – 1:24:43, 1977 – 1:24:42, 1978 – 1:24:18, 1979 – 1:21:48, 1980 – 1:19:53, 1981 – 1:22:19, 1982 – 1:22:33t, 1983 – 1:20:30, 1984 – 1:24:43.
pbs – track: 3kmW: 11:31.1i '79, 5kmW: 19:41.66i '83, 10kmW: 40:15.0 '82; road – 50kmW: 3:59:44 '79

Sergey YUNG
b.10 Aug 1955 Lugovye, Ivanova region 1.78m 67kg Serviceman in Vladimir.
Ch. record at 50kmW: WCh: '83– 3; WCp: '83– 2. USSR champion 1983.
Progression at 50kmW: 1978 – 4:04:28, 1979 – 3:53:14, 1980 – 3:46:48, 1981 – 3:53:07, 1982 – 3:47:16, 1983 – 3:48:26.
pb 20kmW: 1:24:25 '80

Sergey ZASIMOVICH
b.6 Sep 1962 Karazanda, Kazakhstan 1.88m 73kg
Progression at HJ: 1976 – 1.55, 1977 – 1.75, 1978 – 1.96, 1979 – 2.03, 1980 – 2.12, 1981 – 2.28, 1982 – 2.29, 1983 – 2.28, 1984 – 2.36

WOMEN

Nunu ABASHIDZE
b.27 Mar 1955 Novo-Volyansk 1.68m 90kg
Club: Dynamo, Odessa. Sports instructor.
Ch. record at SP: OG: '80– 4; WCh: '83– 4; ECh: '82– 3; EJ: '73– 4; ECp: '79– 2, '83– 3; WIG: '85– 3. USSR champion 1979, 1982 and 1984.
Progression at SP: 1970 – 12.04, 1971 – 13.15, 1972 – 14.71, 1973 – 16.64, 1974 – 17.72, 1975 – 17.59, 1976 – 19.08, 1977 – 18.62, 1979 – 20.25, 1980 – 21.37, 1981 – 18.57i, 1982 – 21.23, 1983 – 20.94, 1984 – 21.53
Suspended for drugs use at the 1981 European Indoors.

Ravilya AGLETDINOVA
b.10 Feb 1960 Kurgan-Tyube, Tadjikstan 1.69m 57kg
Club: Urozhai, Minsk. Student.
Ch. record at 1500m: WCh: '83– 4. At 800m: ECh: '82– 4
Progression at 800m/1500m: 1974 – 2:24.8, 1975 – 2:10.8, 1976 – 2:06.01/4:21.5, 1977 – 2:04.0/4:14.42, 1978 – 2:03.6/4:16.1, 1979 – 2:04.2/4:11.5, 1980 – 2:02.0/4:06.6, 1981 – 1:58.65/4:04.40, 1982 – 1:56.1/4:07.41, 1983 – 1:57.0/3:59.31, 1984 – 1:58.08/3:58.70.
pb 1000m: 2:37.18i '84

Vera AKIMOVA
b.5 Jun 1959 Tashkent 1.68m 58kg née Yeremeryeva. Servicewoman
Ch. record: El 60mh: '84– 2.
Progression at 100mh: 1975 – 14.5, 1976 – 13.8, 1977 – 13.6, 1978 – 13.4, 1979 – 13.28/12.9, 1980 – 13.4, 1981 – 13.2, 1982 – 13.2/13.63, 1983 – 13.03/12.7/12.88w, 1984 – 12.50

Anna AMBRAZIENE
b.14 Apr 1955 Vilnius, Lithuania 1.73m 61kg née Kastetskaya.
Ch. record at 400mh: WCh: '83– 2; ECh: '82– 4; WSG: '81– 1 (1 at 4x400mR); WCp: '81– 3; ECp: '81– 2, '83– 2. USSR champion 1981 and 1983. Two USSR and one world record at 400mh in 1983.
Progression at 400mh: 1976 – 63.2, 1977 – 59.4, 1978 – 57.09, 1979 – 56.2, 1980 – 55.81/55.7, 1981 – 55.51, 1982 – 55.09, 1983 – 54.02, 1984 – 54.81
pbs: 200m: 23.2 '83, 400m: 51.96 '83, 800m: 2:01.9 '79

Natalya ARTYEMOVA
b.5 Jan 1963 Rostov-on-Don 1.65m 49kg
Ch. record at 3000m: WCh: '83– 8. USSR champion 1983. Set world 1 mile record at 4:15.8 in 1984.
Progression at 1500m/3000m: 1982 – 4:10.6, 1983 – 4:02.63/8:47.98, 1984 – 4:00.68/8:38.84.
pb 800m: 1:58.6 '84, 1000m: 2:37.45i '84

Irina BASKAKOVA
b.24 Aug 1956 Leningrad 1.76m 67kg Servicewoman.
Ch. record at 400m (R – 4x400m relay): WCh: '83– 6 (3R); ECh: '82– 5 (3R); WSG: '81– 1 (1R); ECp: '81– 2R, '83– 2R and 5 at 200m
Progression at 400m: 1974 – 58.2, 1975 – 57.3, 1976 – 55.1, 1977 – 54.8, 1979 – 51.97, 1980 – 51.55, 1981 – 51.43, 1982 – 50.54, 1983 – 50.19, 1984 – 50.45/50.4.
pbs: 100m: 11.4 '81, 200m: 22.96/22.80w '83

Yelena BISEROVA
b.24 Mar 1962 Leningrad 1.77m 63kg
Club: Lokomotiv, Leningrad. Student
Ch. record at 100mh: WCh: '83– 6; WSG: '83– 2; ECp: '83– 4. USSR champion 1983.
Progression at 100mh: 1976 – 14.6, 1977 – 14.2, 1978 – 14.0, 1979 – 13.6, 1980 – 13.90, 1981 – 13.19/13.17w, 1983 – 12.87/12.80w, 1984 – 12.66
pbs: 100m: 11.0/11.2w '83, 200m: 23.48 '83 •

Natalya BOCHINA
b.4 Jan 1962 Leningrad 1.73m 56kg
Club: Dynamo, Leningrad. Student.
Ch. record at 100m/200m (R – 4x100m relay): OG: '80– sf/2 (2R); EJ: '79– –/3= (2R); WCp: '81– 5/5 (3R); ECp: '81: –/3 (3R). El: '81– 2 at 400m. USSR 100m & 200m champion 1981. Set four world junior records for 200m in 1980.
Progression at 200m: 1978 – 23.72, 1979 – 23.22, 1980 – 22.19, 1981 – 22.90/22.5, 1984 – 22.45/22.1.
pbs: 100m: 11.22/11.0 '80, 400m: 51.47 '81

Olga BONDARENKO
b.2 Jun 1960 1.53m 41kg
née Krentser. Set world records at 10000m in 1981 and 1984.
Progression at 3000m/10000m: 1978 – 9:24.8, 1979 – 9:08.2, 1980 – 8:52.5, 1981 – 8:51.5/32:30.80, 1982 – 8:57.73i, 1983 – 8:47.02/31:35.61, 1984 – 8:36.20/31:13.78.
pbs: 1500m: 4:06.2 '84, Mar: 2:35:17 '84

National Championships

Lyudmila BORISOVA
b.1959 née Ashikhmina. World record at 4x800m relay 1984.
Progression at 800m: 1979 – 2:03.4, 1980 – 2:00.7, 1981 – 1:59.11, 1982 – 2:02.8, 1983 – 1:57.4, 1984 – 1:56.78
pbs: 400m: 51.79 '84, 1000m: 2:38.95i '83

Lyudmila BUTUZOVA
b.28 Feb 1957 1.84m 71kg
Progression at HJ: 1974 – 1.77, 1975 – 1.84, 1976 – 1.84, 1978 – 1.86i, 1979 – 1.88i, 1980 – 1.86i, 1983 – 1.91, 1984 – 1.98

Tamara BYKOVA
b.21 Dec 1958 Azov, near Rostov–on–Don 1.78m 63kg
Club: Burevestnik, Rostov–on–Don. Student of education.
Ch. record at HJ: OG: '80 – 9; WCh: '83 – 1; ECh: '82 – 2; EI: '83 – 1; WSG: '81 – 3, '83 – 1; WCp: '81 – 2, ECp: '83 – 2. USSR champion 1980, 1982 – 3. In 1983 she set world indoor high jump bests at 2.02m and 2.03m, and then world records at 2.03m and 2.04m. She set a third world record at 2.05m in 1984. Has set eight USSR records.
Progression at HJ: 1974 – 1.50, 1975 – 1.72, 1976 – 1.70, 1977 – 1.70, 1978 – 1.85, 1979 – 1.88, 1980 – 1.97, 1981 – 1.96, 1982 – 1.98, 1983 – 2.04, 1984 – 2.05

Galina CHISTYAKOVA
b.26 Jul 1962 1.74m 62kg Sports student. Set two USSR long jump records in 1984.
Progression at LJ: 1978 – 6.04, 1979 – 6.43, 1980 – 6.43, 1981 – 6.36/6.54w, 1982 – 6.43, 1984 – 7.29

Yelena FILIPISHINA
b.18 Jun 1962 Mednogorsk, Orenburg 1.76m 62kg
Club: Sports instructor.
Ch. record at 400mh: ECh: '82 – 5; WSG: '83 – 2. USSR champion 1982, 1984. Set USSR 400mh record at 54.72 in 1983.
Progression at 400mh: 1979 – 62.79, 1980 – 58.7, 1981 – 56.4, 1982 – 55.00, 1983 – 54.72, 1984 – 54.56

Natalya GRACHOVA
b.1 Jan 1952 Ingults, Dnepropetrovsk 1.78m 79kg née Prokopchenko. **Club:** Avangaard, Nikopol. Teacher.
Ch. record at pentathlon: ECp: '77 – 5. USSR heptathlon record and champion 1982.
Progression at pentathlon: 1974 – 4012, 1975 – 4255, 1976 – 4445, 1977 – 4531. At heptathlon: 1980 – 5955, 1981 – 6040, 1982 – 6611, 1984 – 6563
pbs: 200m: 23.86 '82, 800m: 2:06.59 '82, 100mh: 13.45 '84, HJ: 1.85 '77, LJ: 6.77 '84, SP: 16.60 '81, JT: 40.42 '82

Yekaterina GRUN
b.10 Aug 1958 Krasnodar 1.68m 57kg née Fesenko.
Club: Trudovye Rezervy, Krasnodar. Student.
Ch. record at 400mh: WCh: '83 – 1; ECh: '82 – 7; WSG: '83 – 1 (1 at 4x400mR). USSR champion 1980.
Progression at 400mh: 1978 – 60.4, 1979 – 57.11, 1980 – 55.66, 1981 – 57.09, 1982 – 55.42, 1983 – 54.14, 1984 – 54.34.
pb 400m: 52.26 '80

Lyubov GURINA
b.6 Aug 1957 Matyushkino, Kirov region 1.66m 54kg
Club: Trud, Kirov. Sports instructor.
Ch. record at 800m: WCh: '83 – 2. World record at 4x800m relay 1984.
Progression at 800m: 1976 – 2:15.7, 1977 – 2:08.0, 1978 – 2:04.6, 1979 – 2:00.2, 1980 – 1:59.9, 1981 – 1:58.72, 1982 – 1:57.3, 1983 – 1:56.11, 1984 – 1:56.26
pbs: 400m: 51.38 '83, 1000m: 2:37.60i '83, 1500m: 4:09.40 '81

Svetlana GUSAROVA
b.19 May 1959 Alma Ata 1.64m 56kg Servicewoman in Alma Ata.
Progression at 100mh: 1977 – 13.97, 1978 – 13.6, 1979 – 13.90, 1980 – 13.21, 1981 – 13.50, 1982 – 13.16/12.8, 1983 – 12.86, 1984 – 12.74
pbs: 100m: 11.7 '81, 200m: 23.3 '82.

Svetlana GUSKOVA
b.19 Aug 1959 Tiraspol, Moldavia 1.60m 50kg
Club: Trudovye Rezervy, Tiraspol. Sports instructor.
Ch. record: EI: '79 – 3 at 1500m; ECp: '79 – 1 at 3000m.
Progression at 3000m: 1976 – 9:14.8, 1977 – 9:12.54, 1978 – 8:47.6, 1979 – 8:46.8, 1982 – 8:29.36, 1983 – 8:35.06, 1984 – 8:29.59
pbs: 800m: 1:59.5 '78, 1500m: 3:57.05 '82

Zoya IVANOVA
b.14 Mar 1952 Zaton, North Kazakhstan. 1.64m 51kg
Club: Trud, Alma–Ata
Ch. record at Mar: WCh: '83 – 23; ECh: '82 – 8; ECp: '81 – 1. Has won all the USSR marathon titles, 1981 – 4 and has set three USSR marathon records. Won Tokyo marathon 1982.
Progression at Mar: 1980 – 2:45:02, 1981 – 2:38:58, 1982 – 2:34:26, 1983 – 2:36:31, 1984 – 2:31:11.
pb 10000m: 32:36.96 '82.
Has won seven of twelve marathons.

Tatyana KAZANKINA
b.17 Dec 1951 Petrovsk 1.62m 48kg (Kovalenko).
Club: Burevestnik, Leningrad. Sports instructor.
Ch. record at 1500m: OG: '76 – 1 (1 at 800m), '80 – 1; ECh: '74 – 4; EI: '75 – 2; WCp: '77 – 1; ECp: '75 – 3, '77 – 1. At 3000m: WCh: '83 – 3; ECp: '83 – 1. At 800m: WSG: '77 – 2. World cross–country: '76 – 2. USSR 1500m champion 1975 – 7. Won unique Olympic 800m/1500m double in 1976, setting a world record at 800m. She set three more world records at 1500m, 1976 – 80, one at 3000m in 1984, and one at 4x800m relay in 1976. Also set world 2000m best at 5:28.72 in 1984.
Progression at 800m/1500m/3000m: 1971 – –/4:19.0, 1972 – 2:05.2/4:13.6, 1973 – 2:03.5/4:14.22/9:41.2i, 1974 – 2:03.08/4:05.94, 1975 – 2:01.70/4:07.9/8:57.8, 1976 – 1:54.94/3:56.0, 1977 – 1:58.6/4:04.2, 1979 – 2:00.4/4:07.8, 1980 – 1:56.5/3:52.47, 1981 – 2:00.84/4:08.95, 1982 – 8:36.54, 1983 – 1:58.9/4:01.23/8:32.08, 1984 – 1:57.20/3:58.63/8:22.62.
pb 5000m: 15:23.12 '84.
Had babies in 1978 and 1982. Suspended in 1984 for refusing to take a drugs test in Paris.

Lyudmila KONDRATYEVA
b.11 Apr 1958 Shakhty, Rostov 1.68m 57kg
Club: Burevestnik, Rostov–on–Don. Sports instructor.
Ch. record at 100m/200m (R – 4x100m relay): OG: '80 – 1/2; ECh: '78 – 6/1 (1R), '82 – sf 100m; EJ: '75 – 4 200m; WCp: '79 – 4/3, '81 – 3R; ECp: '79 – 2/1, '81 – 3R, '83 – 3R. At 60m: EI: '80 – 3. USSR 100m & 200m champion 1979. USSR records: 100m (2), 200m (4) 1978–80.
Progression at 100m: 1970 – 13.6, 1971 – 12.4, 1972 – 12.1, 1973 – 11.5, 1974 – 11.6/11.81, 1975 – 11.6, 1976 – 11.5/11.72, 1977 – 11.5, 1978 – 11.35, 1979 – 11.15/11.0w/11.1, 1980 – 11.06/10.87?, 1981 – 11.4, 1982 – 11.28, 1983 – 11.71, 1984 – 11.02
pbs: 200m: 22.31 '80, 400m: 51.87 '80, 100mh: 13.7 '76.

Yelena KOKONOVA
b.4 Aug 1963 1.71m 64kg née Stetsura.
Progression at LJ: 1981 – 6.20, 1982 – 6.50, 1983 – 6.83, 1984 – 7.09.

161

National Championships

Nadyezhda KORSHUNOVA
b.18 May 1961 1.67m 56kg
Progression at 100mh: 1979 – 13.92, 1980 – 13.4, 1981 – 13.60/13.2, 1982 – 13.48/12.9, 1983 – 12.99/12.97w, 1984 – 12.65

Natalya LISOVSKAYA
b.16 Jul 1962 Alegazy, Bashkir ASSR 1.88m 94kg
Club: Spartak, Moscow. Student.
Ch. record at SP: WCh: '83 – 5; EI: '82 – 3; WSG: '83 – 1; WIG: '85 – 1. USSR champion 1981 and 1983. Set world shot record in 1984.
Progression at SP: 1978 – 13.22, 1979 – 14.50, 1980 – 14.91, 1981 – 18.66, 1982 – 19.84, 1983 – 20.85, 1984 – 22.53.
pb DT: 63.44 '82
Recorded nine of the best ten women's shot marks in the world in 1984.

Niole MEDVEDYEVA
b.20 Oct 1960 1.75m 61kg née Blushkyte.
Ch. record at LJ: WIG: '85 – 3.
Progression at LJ: 1978 – 6.30, 1980 – 6.50, 1982 – 6.71i, 1984 – 7.02
pb Hep: 5670 '82.

Galina MURASHOVA
b.22 Dec 1955 Vilnius, Lithuania 1.80m 92kg
Club: Dynamo, Vilnius. Student.
Ch. record at DT: OG: '80 – 7; WCh: '83 – 2; ECh: '82 – 6; ECp: '83 – 2. USSR champion 1983.
Progression at DT: 1971 – 34.00, 1972 – 42.00, 1973 – 47.64, 1974 – 50.04, 1976 – 53.56, 1977 – 57.82, 1978 – 61.80, 1979 – 63.38, 1980 – 67.52, 1981 – 62.52, 1982 – 69.06, 1983 – 68.86, 1984 – 72.14

Nadezhda OLIZARENKO
b.28 Nov 1953 Bryansk 1.65m 54kg née Mushta. Married to Sergey Olizarenko (8:24.0 for 3000m St '78). Sports instructor in Odessa.
Ch. record at 800m: OG: '80 – 1 (3 at 1500m); ECh: '78 – 2 (2 at 4x400mR); WSG: '79 – 1; WCp: '79 – 2. USSR champion 1980. Set two world records for 800m in 1980, 1:54.85 and 1:53.43, the latter in winning the Olympic title, and also ran on the world record 4x800m team 1984.
Progression at 800m: 1970 – 2:11.4, 1972 – 2:08.6, 1974 – 2:05.0, 1975 – 2:03.3, 1976 – 2:05.8, 1977 – 1:59.76, 1978 – 1:55.82, 1979 – 1:57.5, 1980 – 1:53.43, 1983 – 1:58.16, 1984 – 1:56.09
pbs: 400m: 50.96 '80, 1500m: 3:56.8 '80

Maria PINIGINA
b.9 Feb 1958 Ivanovo, Frunze, Kirghizia 1.71m 57kg née Kulchunova. Club: Spartak, Kiev. Sports instructor.
Ch. record at 400m (R – 4x400m relay): WCh: '83 – 3 (3R); ECh: '78 – 4 (2R); EJ: '75 – 4; WSG: '79 – 1, '83 – 1(1R); WCp: '79 – 2; ECp: '79 – 2 (2R), '83 – 2 (2R). USSR champion 1978 – 9 and 1983. Four USSR 400m records – 3 in 1979, 1 in 1984.
Progression at 400m: 1971 – 64.4, 1972 – 64.3, 1973 – 57.4, 1974 – 54.47, 1975 – 52.62, 1976 – 51.80, 1977 – 52.92, 1978 – 50.83, 1979 – 49.63, 1980 – 51.2/51.43, 1983 – 49.19, 1984 – 49.74
pbs: 100m: 11.4 '76, 200m: 22.80 '83, 800m: 2:08.4

Yekaterina PODKOPAYEVA
b.11 Jun 1952 Moscow 1.68m 57kg née Poryvkina.
Ch. record at 800m/1500m: WCh: '83 – 3/3; ECp: '79 – 2 at 800m. USSR 800m champion 1979 and 1984.
Progression at 800m/1500m: 1970 – 2:20.2, 1971 – 2:15.3, 1972 – 2:08.6, 1973 – 2:06.8, 1974 – 2:09.0, 1975 – 2:05.6, 1976 – 2:05.2/4:15.7, 1977 – 2:06.6/4:13.7, 1978 – 2:00.6/4:11.7, 1979 – 1:57.2, 1980 – 1:58.9/3:57.4, 1982 – 4:10.07, 1983 – 1:55.96/4:00.3, 1984 – 1:57.07/3:56.65
pbs: 1000m: 2:36.35i '84, 2000m: 5:43.30i '83 (former world indoor best)

Irina PODYALOVSKAYA
b.19 Oct 1959 Vishenka, Mogilev region 1.65m 53kg
Club: Trudovye Reservy, Moscow. Sports instructor.
Ch. record at 800m: WSG: '83 – 1. USSR champion 1983. World record at 4x800m relay 1984.
Progression at 800m: 1975 – 2:08.2, 1976 – 2:06.03, 1977 – 2:03.65, 1979 – 2:01.6, 1981 – 2:00.2, 1982 – 1:59.64, 1983 – 1:57.99, 1984 – 1:55.69
pb 400m: 51.67 '84

Margarita PONOMARYEVA
b.19 Jun 1963 1.76m 60kg
Club: Trudovye Reservy, Leningrad. Student of economics.
Ch. record at 400mh: EJ: '81 – 3 (2 at 4x400mR). Set world record for 400mh in 1984.
Progression at 400mh: 1981 – 57.45, 1983 – 56.9, 1984 – 53.58
pb 400m: 52.05 '84

Tatyana POZDNYAKOVA
b.4 Mar 1956 Sosnovo–Ozerskoye 1.64m 51kg Student
Ch. record at 3000m: ECh: '82 – 4; EI: '84 – 2; WCp: '81 – 4. USSR champion 1980. World X–C: '81 – 9, '82 – 11, '83 – 3.
Progression at 1500m/3000m: 1974 – 4:51.0, 1975 – 4:44.7/10:12.0, 1976 – 4:34.0/9:37.4, 1977 – 4:30.2/9:33.5, 1978 – 4:22.5/9:15.0, 1979 – 4:15.2/9:03.7, 1980 – 4:05.2/8:37.6, 1981 – 3:59.84/8:34.80, 1982 – 3:56.50/8:35.31, 1983 – 4:01.69/8:37.32, 1984 – 3:57.70/8:32.0
pbs: 800m: 1:57.5 '82, 1000m: 2:34.13 '82, 2000m: 5:29.64 '84, 10000m: 31:48.94 '83

Nadezhda RALLDUGINA
b.15 Nov 1957 Voikovo, Crimea 1.66m 54kg
Club: Lokomotiv, Simferopol. Sports instructor.
Ch. record at 1500m: ECp: '83 – 1. USSR champion 1984.
Progression at 1500m: 1975 – 5:01.0, 1976 – 4:33.4, 1977 – 4:19.3, 1978 – 4:19.8, 1979 – 4:14.2, 1980 – 4:09.1, 1981 – 4:05.13, 1982 – 3:58.17, 1983 – 4:01.67, 1984 – 3:56.63
pbs: 800m: 2:00.28 '84, 1000m: 2:36.07i '84, 1M: 4:28.46i '82, 3000m: 8:49.17 '83

Tatyana RODIONOVA
b.13 Jan 1956 Krasnodar 1.74m 64kg née Proskuryakova
Club: Dynamo, Krasnodar.
Ch. record at LJ: WCh: '83 – 4, WIG: '85 – 2.
Progression at LJ: 1975 – 5.83, 1976 – 6.02, 1977 – 6.32, 1978 – 6.38, 1979 – 6.44i, 1980 – 6.60, 1981 – 6.83, 1983 – 7.04, 1984 – 7.02

Galina SAVINKOVA
b.15 Jul 1953 Kemerovo 1.82m 98kg
Club: Dynamo, Moscow. Sports instructor.
Ch. record at DT: WCh: '83 – 11; ECh: '82 – 3; WCp: '81 – 3, ECp: '81 – 2. USSR champion 1984. Has set three USSR discus records 1983 – 4, including a world record in 1983.
Progression at DT: 1971 – 33.00, 1972 – 41.10, 1973 – 55.72, 1974 – 59.78, 1976 – 76.60, 1977 – 61.48, 1978 – 62.18, 1979 – 65.78, 1980 – 67.22, 1981 – 69.70, 1982 – 69.90, 1983 – 73.26, 1984 – 73.28. pb SP: 16.50 '80.

National Championships

Natalya SHUBENKOVA
b.22 Apr 1957 Srosty, Altai province. 1.72m 64kg
Club: Dynamo, Barnaul. Teacher.
Ch. record at Hep: WCh: '83– dnf; ECh: '82– 5; ECp: '81– 7.
USSR champion 1983 and 1984. USSR heptathlon record 1984.
Progression at Hep: 1980 – 5473, 1981 – 6081, 1982 – 6520, 1983 – 6526, 1984 – 6799
pbs: 200m: 23.57 '84, 800m: 2:04.60 '84, 100mh: 12.93 '84, HJ: 1.83 '84, LJ: 6.73 '84, SP: 13.84 '84, JT: 46.98 '84

Raissa SMEKHNOVA
b.16 Sep 1950 Kaltan, Kemerovo 1.66m 50kg née Katyukova.
Club: Trud, Minsk. Athletics coach.
Ch. record at Mar: WCh: '83– 3. At 1500m: OG: '76– 9. USSR 3000m champion 1975. World X–C: '79– 2, '82– 8. USSR marathon records 1983 and 1984.
Progression at Mar: 1981 – 2:37:57, 1982 – 2:37:04, 1983 – 2:31:13, 1984 – 2:29:10
pbs: 800m: 2:01.9 '79, 1500m: 3:59.8 '76, 3000m: 8:41.77 '76, 10000m: 31:59.70 '84

Marina STEPANOVA
b.1 May 1950 Myaglovo, Leningrad 1.70m 60kg née Makeyeva.
Ch. record at 400mh: ECh: '78– 6; WCp: '79– 2; ECp: '79– 1. USSR champion 1979. Set world 400mh record in 1979.
Progression at 400mh: 1976 – 60.80, 1977 – 58.75, 1978 – 56.16, 1979 – 54.78, 1980 – 55.21, 1983 – 56.03, 1984 – 53.67
pbs: 400m: 51.25 '80, 800m: 1:59.8 '80

Nadezhda VINOGRADOVA
b.1 May 1958 Ust–Barguzin 1.70m 65kg
Club: Trudovye Rezervy, Ulan–Ude. Student.
Ch. record at Hep: ECp: '83– 8; WSG: '81– 2. World best for heptathlon – 6212 in 1981.
Progression at Hep: 1979 – 5843, 1980 – 6114, 1981 – 6212, 1982 – 6228, 1983 – 6443, 1984 – 6312
pbs: 200m: 23.69 '83, 800m: 2:05.72 '83, 100mh: 13.58 '81, HJ: 1.80 '84, LJ: 6.70 '84, SP: 15.19 '84, JT: 43.72 '84

Olga VLADYKINA
b.30 Jun 1963 Krasnokamsk, Perm 1.70m 62kg

Club: Dynamo, Voroshilovgrad. Sports instructor. USSR 400m record and champion 1984.
Progression at 400m: 1977 – 63.0, 1978 – 59.8, 1979 – 57.8, 1980 – 55.19, 1981 – 54.23, 1982 – 51.89, 1983 – 50.58, 1984 – 48.98

Galina ZAKHAROVA
b.7 Sep 1956 1.62m 50kg
2nd World cross–country 1984. Set European indoor best and won USSR titles indoors and out at 3000m in 1984.
Progression at 3000m: 1979 – 9:18.6, 1980 – 9:05.0, 1981 – 8:46.0, 1982 – 8:33.40, 1983 – 8:34.60, 1984 – 8:37.37
pbs 800m: 1:57.08 '84, 1500m: 3:57.72 '84, 2000m: 5:30.92, 10000m: 31:15.00 '84

Zamira ZAYTSEVA
b.16 Feb 1953 Andizhan, Uzbekistan 1.63m 50kg née Akhtyamova.
Club: Spartak, Andizhan.
Ch. record at 1500m: WCh: '83– 2; ECh: '82– 6; EI: '79– 2. USSR champion 1983.
Progression at 1500m: 1971 – 4:44.0, 1972 – 4:34.0, 1973 – 4:20.0, 1974 – 4:14.0, 1975 – 4:17.0, 1977 – 4:10.3, 1978 – 4:04.5, 1979 – 4:03.9i, 1980 – 3:56.9, 1981 – 3:58.70, 1982 – 3:56.14, 1983 – 4:01.19, 1984 – 4:00.50
pbs: 800m: 1:56.21 '83, 1M: 4:22.5 '81, 2000m: 5:37.55 '84, 3000m: 8:53.2 '84
Well remembered for her unavailing dive at the line in Helsinki 1983.

Tatyana ZUBOVA
b.12 Dec 1958 1.65m 55kg
Ch. record at 400m: WSG: '81– 3
Progression at 400m: 1977 – 59.4, 1978 – 56.97, 1979 – 57.44/57.3, 1980 – 56.09, 1981 – 55.4/55.58, 1983 – 56.8, 1984 – 54.43

Lyubov ZVERKOVA
b.14 Jun 1955 1.80m 101kg née Krakova. Then Urakova.
Progression at DT: 1973 – 52.74, 1974 – 50.86, 1975 – 53.18, 1979 – 59.34, 1980 – 57.12, 1981 – 59.64, 1982 – 64.00, 1983 – 64.68, 1984 – 68.58

YUGOSLAVIA

Governing body: Atletski Savez Jugoslavije, Stahinica Bana 73a, 11000 Beograd. Founded in 1921.
National Championships first held in 1920
1984 champions: MEN
100m/200m: Mladen Nikolic 10.36/20.77, 400m: Zeljko Knapic 47.17, 800m: Robert Sikonja 1:50.36, 1500m/3kmSt: Vinko Pokrajcic 3:47.83/8:46.29, 5000m: Dragan Sekulic 14:10.01, 10000m: Sava Alempic 29:31.84, Mar: Tomislav Askovic 2:20:46, 110mh: Petar Vukicevic 14.18, 400mh: Rok Kopitar 51.67, HJ: Novica Canovic 2.21, PV: Zelimir Sarcevic 4.80, LJ: Dusan Sukletovik 7.51, TJ: Djordje Kozul 16.10, SP: Mladen Jegdic 17.73, DT: Zeljko Tarabaric 59.36, HT: Srecko Stiglic 69.11, JT: Sead Krdzalik 79.00, Dec: Ivan Makarovic 6705, 20kmW: Milan Balek 1:33:31
WOMEN
100m: Dijana Istvanovic 11.87, 200m/400m: Natasa Seliskar 23.80/53.23, 800m: Slobodanka Colovic 2:03.62, 1500m: Jasmina Focak 4:20.48, 3000m: Mara Micanovic 9:21.51, 100mh: Margita Papic 13.69, 400mh: Mojca Pertot 59.44, HJ: Tamara Malesev 1.85, LJ: Snezana Dancetovic 6.39, SP: Mirjana Tufegdzic 15.66, DT: Branka Bandur 47.82, JT: Ankica Sumaher 50.60, Hep: Marina Mihajlova 5096

Nenad STEKIC
b.7 Mar 1951 Beograd 1.81m 73kg
Club: Crvena zvezda, Beograd. Technical secretary of Athletic Association of Srbija. Economics graduate of University of Beograd.
Ch. record at LJ: OG: '76– 6, '80– dnq, '84– dnq; WCh: '83– 5; ECh: '69– 10, '71– dnq, '74– 2, '78– 2, '82– 5; EI: '80– 2; EJ: '70– 3; WSG: '75– 2, '77– 4; WCp: '77– 4; ECp: '79– 4, '81– 7. Balkan champion 1973–4, '76, '78–80; Yugoslav champion 1972–7 and 1983. Five Yugoslav long jump records 1969–75, including European record at 8.45m in 1975.
Progression at LJ: 1965 – 6.27, 1966 – 6.49, 1968 – 7.34, 1969 – 7.73/7.78w, 1970 – 7.71/7.75w, 1971 – 7.85, 1972 – 7.60, 1973 – 7.96/8.12w, 1974 – 8.24, 1975 – 8.45, 1976 – 8.12/8.39w, 1977 – 8.27/8.32w, 1978 – 8.32, 1979 – 8.27, 1980 – 8.11/8.19w, 1981 – 8.01, 1982 – 8.12, 1983 – 8.11, 1984 – 8.45
pbs: 100m: 10.4 '74, HJ: 1.95 '68, TJ: 14.93 '77.
Has 18 wins in 45 Internationals 1969–84, and 105 8-metre plus jumps in 47 competitions.

INTRODUCTION TO WORLD LIST AND INDEX

RECORDS
Listed are World, World Junior, Olympic, Continental and Area records. In running events up to and including 400 metres, only fully automatic times are shown. Marks given are those which are considered statistically acceptable by the ATFS, and thus will differ from official World Records where the performance was set indoors or while the athlete was a professional.

WORLD ALL-TIME AND WORLD YEARLIST
These lists are presented in the following format: First Name, Family Name, Nationality in abbreviated form, Year of birth (last two digits), Mark, Wind reading (in metres/second), Position in competition, Meeting name (if significant), Venue, Date of performance. Full details are given for the first 100 places in world lists, beyond that position, meet and venue details are omitted for reasons of space.

INDEX
These lists contain the names of all athletes ranked with full details in the 1984 yearlists. The format of the index is as follows: –
Family name, First name, Nationality, Birthdate, Height (cm) and Weight (kg), Event, 1984 best mark, Lifetime best and year of mark as at the end of 1983.

ABBREVIATIONS

Dates	The year of the first holding of the relevant meet shown in parentheses.	1984
AAA	(UK) Amateur Athletic Association Championships (1880)	23–24 Jun
AAU	(USA) Amateur Athletic Union Championships (1888)	
AfrC	African Championships (1979)	13–17 Jul
AfrG	African Games (1973)	
AIAW	Association of Intercollegiate Athletics for women championships (1969)	
AsiC	Asian Championships (1973)	
AsiG	Asian Games (1951)	
Balk	Balkan Games (1929)	7–9 Sep
Barr	(Cuba) Barrientos Memorial	19–20 May
BGP	Budapest Grand Prix (1978)	20 Aug
Bisl	Bislett Games,	28 Jun
CAC	Central American and Caribbean Championships (1967)	
CAG	Central American and Caribbean Games (1926)	
CalR	California Relays (1942)	12 May
Chn IC	Chinese International Championships	
CISM	International Military Chamionships (1946)	
Coke	Coca Cola Invitational, London (1968)	7 Sep
CommG	Commonwealth Games (1930)	
DNG	DN-Galan, Stockholm	2 Jul
DrakeR	Drake Relays (1910)	27–28 Apr
Druzba	Youth Meet of Socialist Countries	4–5 Aug
DRZ	Druzhba/Friendship Games, Moskva (men), Praha (women)	17–18 Aug
EC	European Championships (1934)	
EC–jun	European Junior Championships (1970)	
EP	European Cup (1965)	
EP/sf	European Cup Semi-final	
FlaR	Florida Relays	30–31 Mar
FOT	(USA) Final Olympic Trials (1920)	16–24 Jun

GGala	Golden Gala, Roma	31 Aug
GS	Golden Spikes, Ostrava (1969)	23 May
Hb	Hannes Braun Memorial, Munchen	
IAAF-g	IAAF Golden events	
ISTAF	International Stadionfest, Berlin (1921)	17 Aug
Izv	(USSR) Izvestia Cup	20–24 Jun
Jerome	Harry Jerome Memorial	16 Jul
KansR	Kansas Relays, Lawrence (1923)	20–21 Apr
King	Martin Luther King Games (1969)	22 Apr
Kuso	Janusz Kusocinski Memorial (1954)	9–10 Jun
Kuts	Vladimir Kuts Memorial	
LB	Liberty Bell, Philadelphia	
Man	Manley Games, Kingston	
MedG	Mediterranean Games (1951)	
Mich	Michalowicz Memorial	
MSR	Mt.San Antonio College Relays (1959)	28–29 Apr
Nar	Narodna Mladesh, Sofia (1955)	19–20 May
NC	National Championships	
NC-j	National Junior Championships	
NC-y	National Youth Championships	
NCAA	National Collegiate Athletic Association Champs. (1921)	28 May–2 Jun
Nik	Nikaia, Nice (1976)	20 Aug
OD	Olympic Day, Berlin (and Potsdam 1984)	20 Jul
OG	Olympic Games (1896)	3–12 Aug
OT	Olympic Trials	
PAG	Pan American Games (1951)	
PennR	Pennsylvania Relays (1895)	24–28 Apr
Pepsi	Pepsi Cola Invitational	13 May
PNG	Paavo Nurmi Games	26 Jun
PO	Pre Olympic Meet	
Prav	(USSR) Pravda Cup	
PTS	Pravda-Televizia Slovnaft, Bratislava (1960) 25–26 May	
Pre	Steve Prefontaine Memorial (1975)	21 Jul
Ros	Evzen Rošicky Memorial (1952)	9 Jun
RumIC	Rumanian International Championships (1948)	
SoAmC	South American Championships (1919)	
Spart	(USSR) Spartakiad (1956)	
TAC	(USA) The Athletics Congress Championships (1980)	7–9 Jun
TexR	Texas Relays (1925)	4–7 Apr
USOC	US Olympic Committee Festival	
USTFA	US Track and Field Association Championships (1978)	
USTFF	US Track and Field Federation Championships (1963)	
VD	Ivo Van Damme Memorial (1977)	24 Aug
WA	West Athletic Meet (AUT/BEL/DEN/HOL/IRL/POR/SPA/SWI)	16–17 Jun

WAAA	(UK) Women's Amateur Athletic Association Champs. (1923)	15–16 Jun
WC	World Championships (1983)	
WG	World Games, Helsinki (1961)	4 Jul
WK	Weltklasse, Zurich (1962)	22 Aug
WP	World Cup (1977)	
WPT	World Cup Trials (1977)	
WUG	World University Games (1923)	
Znam	Znamenskiy Brothers Memorial (1958)	9–10 Jun

Dual and triangular matches are indicated by 'v' (versus) followed by the name(s) of the opposing country or countries. Quadrangular and larger inter- nation matches are denoted by the relevant number and –N; viz 8–N = The 8 Nations meeting in Tokyo.

ACKNOWLEDGEMENTS

The statistical section of the 1985 ATFS Annual has been prepared very much as a team effort, with a large number of experts contributing valuable assistance. The World lists were prepared by Nejat Kok, Jiri Havlin together with Jan Popper and the CS-group, Vladimir Visek, Dr Roberto Quercetani, and Richard Hymans.

The All-Time Lists, again abbreviated to 50-deep were prepared by Pino Mappa and Nejat Kok. Both the World Lists and All-Time Lists were compiled using computerised listings.

Milan Skocovsky and Ian Hodge prepared the junior lists, and Ian Hodge also supplied many additions and corrections to the senior lists.

Nejat Kok prepared the women's index.

The records section was again prepared by ATFS president Bob Sparks, who also advised on the general organisation of the annual.

We are indebted to the following experts for vital assistance on specific sections of the annual: Vaclav Klvana(CS), Rooney Magnusson(SWE), Leo Heinla(SU) and Frank Zarnowski(USA) – Decathlon and Heptathlon ; Milan Urban(CS) – Heptathlon ; Roger Gynn(UK), Antonin Hejda(SWZ) – Marathon ; Ian Smith(AUS) – Middle and Long distance events; Luigi Mengoni(ITA) – Women's marks.

The following specialists supplied information for their respective areas and countries:
Africa – Yves Pinaud (FRA), Walter Abmayr(FRG), Mark Woodlands(UK); Asia – Rolf von der Laage; Australia – Paul Jenes; Austria – Erich Kamper; Belgium – Andre de Hooghe; Brasil – Jose Goncalves; Bulgaria – Grigor Khristov; Canada – Cecil Smith; Central America – Bernard Linley(TRI) and Francisco Baraona(CHL); Czechoslovakia – Milan Skocovsky; Cuba – Basilio Fuentes; Finland – Juhani Jalava and Matti Hannus; France – Jacques Carmelli and Jean Gilbert – Touzeau; GDR – Dieter Huhn and Werner Kurtze; FRG – Heinz Vogel; Greece – Georgios Constantopoulos and Leandros Slavis; Holland – Jacobus Koumans; Hungary – Gabriel Szabo and Gabor Kobzos(SWZ); Israel – David Eiger; Italy – Gianfranco Colasante and Roberto Quercetani; India – Murali Krishnan; Jamaica – Richard Ashenheim; Japan – Atshushi Hoshino; Norway – Ole Petter Sandvig, Jan Morgen Moe and Bernd Solaas; Poland – Tadeusz Wolejko, Wojciech Gaczkowski, Daniel Grinberg and Edward Szatkowski; Portugal – Luis Lopes; Rumania – Alexandru Ardeleanu and Vladimir Moraru; South Africa – Arrie Joubert; Soviet Union – Ants Teder, Nikolay Ivanov, Andris Stagis; Spain – Jose Maria Garcia and Jose Corominas; Sweden – Lennart Julin, Owe Froberg and Bengt Holmberg; Switzerland – Fulvio Regli and Alberto Bordoli; USA – Scott Davis, the late Stan Eales, Dave Johnson, Howard Willman, Pete Cava, Bob Hersh Fred Baer, Jack Shepard, Larry Story, and Mike Kennedy; Yugoslavia – Ozren Karamata.

Various other non-ATFS indivuals and organisations also gave valuable help, namely Ruth Laney(USA), more than 200 US colleges, and the national federations of FINLAND, the USA, CHINA, FRANCE, and the Soviet Union.

Finally we would like to thank the IAAF for its continuing cooperation and assistance.

GENERAL NOTES

ALTITUDE AID
Although there are not separate world records for altitude assisted events, it is understood by athletics experts that in all events up to 400 metres in length (with the possible exclusion of the 110m hurdles), and in horizontal jumps, marks produced at altitude are materially benefitted by the thinner atmosphere. As yet there is no scientific formula for quantifying such aid. In the meantime, all marks in the above mentioned events have been prefixed with the letter 'A'. Conversely performances at events longer than 800 metres are adversely affected by high altitude. Thus they also have this prefix, which serves to underline the quality of the relevant performance.

A supplement is included in relevant events for athletes with seasonal bests at altitude who nevertheless have low altitude marks qualifying for the main list.

AUTOMATIC TIMING
In the main lists for sprints and hurdles, only times recorded by fully automatic timing devices are included. By definition, such a timing device is one which is started automatically by the firing of the starter's gun, with the finish recorded photographically with a strip camera or a movie camera and linked back electronically to the start.

HAND TIMING
In the sprints and hurdles supplementary lists are included for races which are hand timed. Any athlete with a hand timed best 0.01 seconds or more better than his or her automatically timed best has been included. Hand timed lists have been terminated close to the differential levels considered by the IAAF to be equivalent to automatic times, i.e. 0.24 for 100m, 200m, 100mh, 110mh, and 0.14 for 400m and 400mh.

In events beyond 400m, automatically timed marks are integrated with hand timed marks, with the latter designated with the symbol ₁m'. All-time lists also include auto times in tenths of a second, where the 1/100th time is not known, but the reader can differentiate these from hand timed marks as they do not have the suffix 'm'. The 'm' marks are listed after a 1/100th auto time ending in zero, but before a 1/100th time ending with 1; i.e. 1:46.70, then 1:46.7m, then 1:46.71.

INDOOR MARKS
Indoor marks are included in the main lists for field events and straightway track events, but not for other track events. This is because there is no curb for indoor races which theoretically can enable athletes to run less than full distance, and more importantly because track sizes vary greatly in circumference and banking, while outdoor tracks are far more standardized.

Athletes whose seasonal best are indoors are shown in a supplemental list if they also have outdoor marks qualifying for the world list.

SUPPLEMENTARY FIELD EVENT MARKS
Non-winning marks in a series which, had they been winning marks, would have qualified for the top-30 performances list are included in a supplement at the end of the relevant event.

WIND ASSISTANCE
In the lists for 100m, 200m, 100mh, 110mh, long jump and triple jump, anemometer readings have been supplemented where available. The readings are shown in metres per second to one decimal place. Where the figure was given originally to two decimal places, it has been rounded to the next tenth upwards, e.g a wind reading of 2.01, beyond the IAAF legal limit of 2.0m/s is rounded to 2.1m/s.

Negative readings are similarly shown. This is partly to follow the logic as shown above, but also because wind gauges which record only to 1/10th of a metre per second automatically move on a tenth if the wind strength increases 1/100th beyond the round tenth. Thus – 1.21m/s is recorded as – 1.3m/s.

DISQUALIFICATIONS
The following athletes were disqualified in 1984 for infringing doping regulations. Athletes disqualified in previous years are listed in full in the 1984 Annual.

Men
Dimitrios Delifotis (GRE)
Kleanthis Ierissiotis (GRE)
Al Schoterman (USA)
Martti Vainio (FIN)

Women
Tatyana Kazankina (SU)
Anna Verouli (GRE)

Keen observers may spot errors in the lists. They are
invited to send corrections to the editors.

(Men)
Richard Hymans
37 Colehill Lane
Fulham
London SW6

(Women)
Nejat Kok
P.K.181
Kucukesat
Ankara
Turkey

MISCELLANEOUS ABBREVIATIONS

D – Made in decathlon competition
H – Made in heptathlon competition
e – Made in field event
h – Made in heat
i – Indoor mark

m – manual timing in events beyond 400 metres
Q – Mark made in qualifying round
q – Mark made in quarter-final

r – Denotes race number in a series of races
s – Semi-final
w – Wind-assisted
= – Tie (ex-aequo)
* – Converted time from

yards to metres:
in 200m lists * = 220 yards less 0.11 seconds
in 400m lists * = 440 yards less 0.26 seconds
in 110mh lists * = 120yh plus 0.03 seconds

NATIONS ABBREVIATIONS IN WORLD LISTS AND INDEX

ALB	Albania	EGY	Egypt	JAM	Jamaica	SUD	Sudan
ARG	Argentina	ETH	Ethiopia	JAP	Japan	SWE	Sweden
AUS	Australia	FIN	Finland	KEN	Kenya	SWZ	Switzerland
AUT	Austria	FRA	France	LUX	Luxemburg	TAI	Taiwan
BAH	Bahamas	FRG	Fed. Rep. Germany	MAL	Malaysia	TAN	Tanzania
BEL	Belgium			MEX	Mexico	THA	Thailand
BER	Bermuda	GAM	Gambia	MOR	Morocco	TRI	Trinidad
BHN	Bahrain	GDR	German D Rep.	NIG	Nigeria	TUN	Tunisia
BRA	Brazil			NKO	Korea PDR	TUR	Turkey
BUL	Bulgaria	GHA	Ghana	NOR	Norway	UGA	Uganda
CAM	Cameroon	GRE	Greece	NZ	New Zealand	UK	United Kingdom
CAN	Canada	GUY	Guyana	PAN	Panama	UPV	Upper Volta
CHL	Chile	HOL	Holland	PHI	Philippines	USA	United States of America
CHN	P.R.China	HUN	Hungary	POL	Poland		
COL	Colombia	ICE	Iceland	POR	Portugal	UVI	US Virgin Isles
CON	Congo	IND	India	PR	Puerto Rico	VEN	Venezuela
CS	Czechoslovakia	IRL	Ireland	QAT	Qatar	YUG	Yugoslavia
CUB	Cuba	IRN	Iran	RSA	South Africa	ZAM	Zambia
CYP	Cyprus	IRQ	Iraq	RUM	Romania	ZIM	Zimbabwe
DEN	Denmark	ISR	Israel	SKO	South Korea		
DJI	Djibouti	ITA	Italy	SPA	Spain		
DOM	Dominican Rep.	IVC	Ivory Coast	SU	Soviet Union		

WORLD AND CONTINENTAL RECORDS

W = World: I = I.A.A.F. (if different):   C = Commonwealth: Afr = Africa: Asi = Asia: CAC = Central America & Caribbean   E = Europe: Nam = N. America: Oce = Oceania: SAm = S. America: OG = Olympic Games: WJ = World Junior

^ = altitude over 100m: + = timing by photo-electric cell   * = awaiting ratification: = not officially ratified

100 METRES

W,NAm	9.93^	Calvin	Smith	USA	Colorado Springs	3 Jul 83
CAC	9.98^	Silvio	Leonard	Cub	Guadalajara	11 Aug 77
E	10.00	Marian	Woronin	Pol	Warszawa	9 Jun 84
C	10.04^	Lennox	Miller	Jam	Ciudad de Mexico	14 Oct 68
Afr	10.15 ?	Innocent	Egbunike	Nig	Charleston	25 May 84
	10.16	Peter	Okodogbe	Nig	Lagos	16 Jun 78
SAm	10.22^	Nelson	dos Santos	Bra	Ciudad de Mexico	8 Sep 79
Oce	10.26	Paul	Narracott	Aus	Melbourne	6 Mar 84
Asi	10.34^	Hideo	Iijima	Jap	Ciudad de Mexico	14 Oct 68
	10.34^	Mei Guh	Su	SKo	Ciudad de Mexico	8 Sep 79
	10.34	Hiroki	Fuwa	Jap	Tokyo	6 May 84
	10.34	Hiroki	Fuwa	Jap	Tokyo	2 Jun 84
	10.34	Purnomo		Ina	Taipei	8 Sep 84
OG	9.95^	Jim	Hines	USA	Ciudad de Mexico	14 Oct 68
WJ	10.07	Stanley	Floyd	USA	Austin	24 May 80

200 METRES

W,E	19.72^	Pietro	Mennea	Ita	Ciudad de Mexico	12 Sep 79
NAm	19.75	Carl	Lewis	USA	Indianapolis	19 Jun 83
C,CAC	19.86^	Donald	Quarrie	Jam	Cali	3 Aug 71
Oce	20.06	Peter	Norman	Aus	Ciudad de Mexico	16 Oct 68
SAm	20.30	Joao	da Silva	Bra	Los Angeles	8 Aug 84
Afr	20.41^	Wessel	Oosthuizen	RSA	Pretoria	16 Mar 83
Asi	20.81	Toshio	Toyota	Jap	Tokyo	11 Sep 82
OG	19.80	Carl	Lewis	USA	Los Angeles	8 Aug 84
WJ	20.22	Dwayne	Evans	USA	Eugene	22 Jun 76

400 METRES

W,NAm	43.86^	Lee	Evans	USA	Ciudad de Mexico	18 Oct 68
CAC	44.26	Alberto	Juantorena	Cub	Montreal	29 Jul 76
E	44.50	Erwin	Skamrahl	FRG	Munchen	26 Jul 83
Afr	44.54	Gabriel	Tiacoh	IvC	Los Angeles	8 Aug 84
C	44.58	Bert	Cameron	Jam	Baton Rouge	6 Jun 81
Oce	44.75	Darren	Clark	Aus	Los Angeles	8 Aug 84
SAm	45.21	Gerson	Souza	Bra	Rieti	16 Sep 82
Asi	45.57	Isidoro	Del Prado	Phi	Manila	1 Dec 84
OG	43.86^	Lee	Evans	USA	Ciudad de Mexico	18 Oct 68
WJ	44.69	Darrell	Robinson	USA	Indianapolis	24 Jul 82

800 METRES

W,C,E	1:41.73+	Sebastian	Coe	UK	Firenze	10 Jun 81
SAm	1:41.77	Joaquim	Cruz	Bra	Köln	26 Aug 84
Afr	1:42.28	Sammy	Koskei	Ken	Köln	26 Aug 84
NAm	1:42.96	Johnny	Gray	USA	Koblenz	29 Aug 84

World Records

CAC	1:43.44	Alberto	Juantorena	Cub	Sofiya	21 Aug 77
Oce	1:44.3 m	Peter	Snell	NZ	Christchurch	3 Feb 62
Asi	1:45.77	Sri Ram	Singh	Ind	Montreal	25 Jul 76
OG	1:43.00	Joaquim	Cruz	Bra	Los Angeles	6 Aug 84
WJ	1:44.9ym	Jim	Ryun	USA	Terre Haute	10 Jun 66
	1:44.3 m	Joaquim	Cruz	Bra	Rio de Janeiro	27 Jun 81

1500 METRES

W,C,E	3:30.77	Steve	Ovett	UK	Rieti	4 Sep 83
NAm	3:31.24	Sydney	Maree	USA	Köln	28 Aug 83
Afr	3:31.54	Said	Aouita	Mor	Hengelo	6 Jul 84
Oce	3:32.4 m	John	Walker	NZ	Oslo	30 Jul 75
SAm	3:36.48	Joaquim	Cruz	Bra	Eugene	2 Jun 84
Asi	3:38.24	Takashi	Ishii	Jap	Düsseldorf	3 Sep 77
CAC	3:38.85	Eduardo	Castro	Mex	Ciudad Bolívar	14 Aug 81
OG	3:32.53	Sebastian	Coe	UK	Los Angeles	11 Aug 84
WJ	3:34.92	Kipkoech	Cheruiyot	Ken	München	26 Jul 83

1 MILE

W,C,E	3:47.33	Sebastian	Coe	UK	Bruxelles	28 Aug 81
NAm	3:47.69	Steve	Scott	USA	Oslo	7 Jul 82
Oce	3:49.08	John	Walker	NZ	Oslo	7 Jul 82
Afr	3:49.45	Mike	Boit	Ken	Bruxelles	28 Aug 81
SAm	3:53.00	Joaquim	Cruz	Bra	Los Angeles	13 May 84
CAC	3:57.34	Byron	Dyce	Jam	Stockholm	1 Jul 74
Asi	3:59.7 m	Takashi	Ishii	Jap	Melbourne	10 Dec 77
WJ	3:51.3 m	Jim	Ryun	USA	Berkeley	17 Jul 66

3000 METRES

W,C,Afr	7:32.1 m	Henry	Rono	Ken	Oslo	27 Jun 78
E	7:32.79	Dave	Moorcroft	UK	London	17 Jul 82
NAm	7:33.37	Sydney	Maree	USA	London	17 Jul 82
Oce	7:37.49	John	Walker	NZ	London	17 Jul 82
CAC	7:47.44	Rodolfo	Gómez	Mex	Köln	22 Jun 77
SAm	7:53.0 m	José	da Silva	Bra	Gateshead	26 Jul 75
Asi	7:54.0 m	Takao	Nakamura	Jap	Troisdorf	11 Jul 79
WJ	7:43.20	Ari	Paunonen	Fin	Köln	22 Jun 77

5000 METRES

W,C,E	13:00.41	Dave	Moorcroft	UK	Oslo	7 Jul 82
Afr	13:04.78	Said	Aouita	Mor	Firenze	13 Jun 84
NAm	13:11.93	Alberto	Salazar	USA	Stockholm	6 Jul 82
Oce	13:12.87	Dick	Quax	NZ	Stockholm	5 Jul 77
Asi	13:24.69	Masanari	Shintaku	Jap	Tokyo	24 Sep 82
CAC	13:27.52	Rodolfo	Gómez	Mex	Lüdenscheid	30 Aug 77
SAm	13:29.67	Domingo	Tibaduiza	Col	Zürich	16 Aug 78
OG	13:05.59	Said	Aouita	Mar	Los Angeles	11 Aug 84
WJ	13:25.33	Charles	Cheruiyot	Ken	München	26 Jul 83

10000 METRES

W,E	27:13.81	Fernando	Mamede	Por	Stockholm	2 Jul 84
C,Afr	27:22.47+	Henry	Rono	Ken	Wien	11 Jun 78
NAm	27:25.61	Alberto	Salazar	USA	Oslo	26 Jun 82

World Records

Oce	27:39.89	Ron	Clarke	Aus	Oslo	14 Jul 65
Asi	27:43.44	Toshihiko	Seko	Jap	Stockholm	7 Jul 80
SAm	27:53.02+	Domingo	Tibaduiza	Col	Wien	11 Jun 78
CAC	27:56.74	José	Gómez	Mex	Eugene	4 Jun 83
OG	27:38.35	Lasse	Viren	Fin	München	3 Sep 72
WJ	28:32.7 m	Rudy	Chapa	USA	Des Moines	24 Apr 76

3000 METRES STEEPLECHASE

W,C,Afr	8:05.4 m	Henry	Rono	Ken	Seattle	13 May 78
E	8:07.62	Joseph	Mahmoud	Fra	Bruxelles	24 Aug 84
NAm	8:12.37	Henry	Marsh	USA	W.Berlin	17 Aug 83
Oce	8:14.05*	Peter	Renner	NZ	Koblenz	29 Aug 84
Asi	8:19.52	Masanari	Shintaku	Jap	Stockholm	8 Jul 80
SAm	8:28.99	Emilio	Ulloa	Chl	Los Angles	8 Aug 84
CAC	8:31.88	Carmelo	Rios	PRc	Los Angeles	8 Aug 84
OG	8:08.02	Anders	Gärderud	Swe	Montréal	28 Jul 76
WJ	8:29.50	Ralf	Pönitzsch	GDR	Warszawa	19 Aug 76

110 METRES HURDLES

W,NAm	12.93	Renaldo	Nehemiah	USA	Zürich	19 Aug 81
CAC	13.21	Alejandro	Casanas	Cub	Sofiya	21 Aug 77
C	13.27	Mark	McKoy	Can	Walnut	25 Jul 84
E	13.28	Guy	Drut	Fra	St. Etienne	29 Jun 75
Oce	13.58	Don	Wright	Aus	Brisbane	4 Oct 82
Afr	13.69	Fatwel	Kimaiyo	Ken	Christchurch	26 Jan 74
	13.69	Godwin	Obasogie	Nig	Austin	3 Apr 76
Asi	13.90	Chin-Ching	Wu	Tai	Kuwait	5 Nov 83
SAm	14.02	Wellington	Araujo	Bra	Sao Paulo	9 Jun 84
OG	13.20	Roger	Kingdom	USA	Los Angeles	6 Aug 84
WJ	13.23	Renaldo	Nehemiah	USA	Zürich	16 Aug 78

400 METRES HURDLES

W,NAm	47.02	Edwin	Moses	USA	Koblenz	31 Aug 83
E	47.48	Harald	Schmid	FRG	Athinai	8 Sep 82
C,Afr	47.82	John	Akii-Bua	Uga	München	2 Sep 72
CAC	49.17	Karl	Smith	Jam	Houston	15 May 82
Oce	49.32	Bruce	Field	Aus	Christchurch	29 Jan 74
Asi	49.43	Ahmad	Hamada	Bhn	Kuwait	7 Nov 83
SAm	49.65	Antonio	Ferreira	Bra	Sao Paulo	17 Jun 84
OG	47.63	Edwin	Moses	USA	Montreal	25 Jul 76
WJ	48.02	Danny	Harris	USA	Los Angeles	17 Jun 84

HIGH JUMP

W,Asi	2.39	Jianhua	Zhu	Chn	Eberstadt	10 Jun 84
E	2.37i	Carlo	Thränhardt	FRG	W.Berlin	24 Feb 84
	2.37	Valeriy	Sereda	Sov	Rieti	2 Sep 84
		Carlo	Thränhardt	FRG	Rieti	2 Sep 84
NAm	2.34	Dwight	Stones	USA	Los Angeles	24 Jun 84
CAC	2.33	Javier	Sotomayer	Cub	Habana	19 May 84
C	2.32	Milt	Ottey	Can	Provo	4 Jun 82
Afr	2.28	Othmane	Belfaa	Alg	Amman	20 Aug 83
Oce	2.28	John	Atkinson	Aus	Melbourne	31 Mar 84
SAm	2.25	Claudio	Freire	Bra	Rio de Janeiro	10 Oct 82
OG	2.36	Gerd	Wessig	GDR	Moskva	1 Aug 80
WJ	2.35i	Volodymyr	Yashchenko	Sov	Milano	12 Mar 78
	2.35	Dietmar	Mögenburg	FRG	Rehlingen	26 May 80

World Records

POLE VAULT

W,E	5.94	Sergey	Bubka	Sov	Roma	31 Aug 84
NAm	5.82	Mike	Tully	USA	Eugene	21 Jul 84
C	5.65	Keith	Stock	Eng	Stockholm	7 Jul 81
SAm	5.56	Tom	Hintnaus	Bra	Redondo Beach	15 Jun 84
Oce	5.53	Don	Baird	Aus	Long Beach	16 Apr 77
Asi	5.53	Tomomi	Takahashi	Jap	Tokyo	6 May 84
Afr	5.34	Lakhdar	Rahal	Alg	Paris	4 Jun 79
CAC	5.33	Roberto	More	Cub	Habana	26 Jun 76
OG	5.78	Wladyslaw	Kozakiewicz	Pol	Moskva	30 Jul 80
WJ	5.65	Rodion	Gataullin	Sov	Donetsk	8 Sep 84

LONG JUMP

W,NAm	8.90^	Bob	Beamon	USA	Ciudad de Mexico	18 Oct 68
E	8.54	Lutz	Dombrowski	GDR	Moskva	28 Jul 80
CAC	8.37	Jaime	Jefferson	Cub	Moskva	17 Aug 84
SAm	8.36	Joao Carlos	de Oliveira	Bra	Rieti	21 Jul 79
C,Oce	8.27	Gary	Honey	Aus	Budapest	20 Aug 84
Afr	8.26i	Charlton	Ehizeulen	Nig	Bloomington	7 Mar 75
	8.21	Yussuf	Alli	Nig	Edmonton	7 Jul 83
Asi	8.14	Yuhuang	Liu	Chn	Nanjing	6 Sep 82
OG	8.90^	Bob	Beamon	USA	Ciudad de Mexico	18 Oct 68
WJ	8.34	Randy	Williams	USA	München	8 Sep 72

TRIPLE JUMP

W,SAm	17.89^	Joao Carlos	de Oliveira	Bra	Ciudad de Mexico	15 Oct 75
C,E	17.57^	Keith	Connor	UK	Provo	5 Jun 82
NAm	17.56	Willie	Banks	USA	Sacramento	21 Jun 81
Oce	17.46	Ken	Lorraway	Aus	London	7 Aug 82
CAC	17.45	Lazaro	Betancourt	Cub	Köln	26 Aug 84
Asi	17.34	Zhenxian	Zou	Chn	Roma	5 Sep 81
Afr	17.26	Ajayi	Agbebaku	Nig	Edmonton	8 Jul 83
OG	17.39^	Viktor	Sanyeyev	Sov	Ciudad de Mexico	17 Oct 68
WJ	17.42	Khristo	Markov	Bul	Sofiya	19 May 84

SHOT PUT

W	22.86p	Brian	Oldfield	USA	El Paso	10 May 75
I,E	22.22	Udo	Beyer	GDR	Los Angeles	25 Jun 83
NAm	22.86p	Brian	Oldfield	USA	El Paso	10 May 75
	22.19	Brian	Oldfield	USA	San Jose	27 May 84
C	21.68	Geoff	Capes	Eng	Cwmbran	18 May 80
Afr	20.71	Nagui	Asaad	Egy	Praha	21 Jun 72
SAm	19.94	Gert	Weil	Chi	Los Angeles	11 Aug 84
CAC	19.89	Luis	Delis	Cub	Santaigo de Cuba	7 Mar 82
Oce	19.80	Les	Mills	NZ	Honolulu	3 Jul 67
Asi	18.66	Bahadur	Singh	Ind	Patiala	30 May 76
OG	21.35	Volodymyr	Kiselyov	Sov	Moskva	30 Jul 80
WJ	21.05i	Terry	Albritton	USA	New York	22 Feb 74
	20.65	Mike	Carter	USA	Boston	4 Jul 79

World Records

DISCUS

W	72.34dq	Ben	Plucknett	USA	Stockholm	7 Jul 81
I,E	71.86	Yuriy	Dumchev	Sov	Moskva	29 May 83
NAm	72.34dq	Ben	Plucknett	USA	Stockholm	7 Jul 81
	71.32	Ben	Plucknett	USA	Eugene	4 Jun 83
CAC	71.06	Luis	Delis	Cub	Habana	21 May 83
Afr	68.48	John	van Reenen	RSA	Stellenbosch	14 Mar 75
C	67.32	Rob	Gray	Can	Etobicoke	30 Apr 84
Oce	65.08	Wayne	Martin	Aus	Newcastle	3 Jan 79
Asi	61.06	Djalal-Ali	Keshmiri	Irn	Lancaster	19 May 74
SAm	55.64	Tito	Steiner	Arg	Provo	11 Jul 80
OG	68.28	Mac	Wilkins	USA	Montreal	24 Jul 76
WJ	63.64	Werner	Hartmann	FRG	Strasbourg	25 Jun 78

HAMMER

W,E	86.34	Yuriy	Sedykh	Sov	Cork	3 Jul 84
C	77.54	Martin	Girvan	NI	Wolverhampton	12 May 84
NAm	76.52	Bill	Green	USA	Walnut	15 Jul 84
Asi	75.94	Shigenobu	Murofushi	Jap	Walnut	15 Jul 84
Oce	75.90	Peter	Farmer	Aus	Vanves	14 Aug 79
CAC	74.74	Armando	Orozco	Cub	Habana	25 May 80
Afr	73.86	Adam	Barnard	RSA	Johannesburg	26 Mar 76
SAm	66.04	José	Vallejo	Arg	Bahia Blanca	8 Dec 74
OG	81.80	Yuriy	Sedykh	Sov	Moskva	31 Jul 80
WJ	78.14	Roland	Steuk	GDR	Leipzig	30 Jun 78

JAVELIN

W,E	104.80	Uwe	Hohn	GDR	E.Berlin	20 Jul 84
NAm	99.72	Tom	Petranoff	USA	Westwood	15 May 83
Afr	91.24	Koos	van der Merwe	RSA	Middelburg	5 Feb 83
C,Oce	90.58	Mike	O'Rourke	NZ	Auckland	22 Jan 83
Asi	89.14	Maomao	Shen	Chn	Philadelphia	17 Jul 80
CAC	87.90	Ramon	Gonzalez	Cub	Habana	21 May 83
SAm	79.16	Luis	Lucumi	Col	Cali	13 Nov 82
OG	94.58	Miklos	Nemeth	Hun	Montreal	26 Jul 76
WJ	87.90	Ramon	Gonzalez	Cub	Habana	21 May 83

DECATHLON (1962/1984 TABLES)

W,E	8798/8832	Jurgen	Hingsen	FRG	Mannheim	9 Jun 84
W,E,C	8798 /8847	Daley	Thompson	UK	Los Angeles	9 Aug 84
NAm	8617 /8634	Bruce	Jenner	USA	Montreal	30 Jul 76
SAm	8377m/8291	Tito	Steiner	Arg	Provo	23 Jun 83
	8124 /8105	Tito	Steiner	Arg	Austin	5 Apr 79
Oce	8090m/7991	Peter	Hadfield	Aus	Adelaide	8 Apr 84
	7886 /7855	Peter	Hadfield	Aus	Adelaide	20 Mar 81
Asi	8089m/8009	Chuan-Kuang	Yang	Tai	Walnut	28 Apr 63
Afr	8006m/7922	Ahmed	Mansour Balcha	Alg	Alger	3 Jun 82
CAC	7881m/7749	Rigoberto	Salazar	Cub	Habana	25 May 79
	7726 /7734	Douglas	Fernandez	Ven	Caracas	27 Aug 83
OG	8797 /8846	Daley	Thompson	UK	Los Angeles	9 Aug 84
WJ	8387 /8397	Torsten	Voss	GDR	Erfurt	7 Jul 82

World Records

MARATHON

W,E,C	2:08:05	Steve	Jones	Wal	Chicago	21 Oct 84
Oce	2:08:18	Rob	de Castella	Aus	Fukuoka	6 Dec 81
Asi	2:08:38	Toshihiko	Seko	Jap	Tokyo	13 Feb 83
NAm	2:08:52	Alberto	Salazar	USA	Boston	19 Apr 82
Afr	2:08:55	Juma	Ikangaa	Tan	Fukuoka	4 Dec 83
CAC	2:09:12	Rodolfo	Gomez	Mex	Tokyo	13 Feb 83
SAm	2:11:21	Domingo	Tibaduiza	Col	New York	23 Oct 83
OG	2:09:20.5	Carlos	Lopes	Por	Los Angeles	12 Aug 84
WJ	2:15:28	Paul	Gompers	USA	Huntsville	10 Dec 83

20km WALK (ROAD)

W,E	1:19:29.6	Jozef	Pribilinec	CS	Bergen	24 Sep 83
CAC	1:19:40.4	Ernesto	Canto	Mex	Bergen	24 Sep 83
C,Oce	1:20:22.7	Dave	Smith	Aus	Melbourne	18 Dec 83
NAm	1:22:04	Guillaume	Leblanc	Can	Helsinki	7 Aug 83
SAm	1:25:19	Querubin	Moreno	Col	Bucaramanga	4 Nov 84
Asi	1:25:22.8	Fuxin	Zhang	Chn	Bergen	24 Sep 83
Afr	1:27:08	Hassen	Shemzu	Eth	Moskva	17 Aug 84
OG	1:23:12.4	Ernesto	Canto	Mex	Los Angeles	3 Aug 84
WJ	1:21:39.1	Ralf	Kowalsky	GDR	Jena	7 Aug 81

20,000m WALK (TRACK)

W,CAC	1:18:40.0	Ernesto	Canto	Mex	Fana	5 May 84
E	1:20:36.7	Erling	Andersen	Nor	Fana	5 May 84
SAm	1:24:12	Hector	Moreno	Col	Santa Fe	29 Sep 83
NAm	1:24:17.0#	Marcel	Jobin	Can	Trois Rivieres	24 Sep 80
	1:24:58.8	Marcel	Jobin	Can	Quebec	12 May 84
Oce	1:26:07.8	Dave	Smith	Aus	Melbourne	27 Jun 81
Afr	1:26:39.93	Benamar	Kachkouche	Alg	Thonon-les-Bains	20 Jun 84
Asi	1:27:14.0	Shaohong	Jiang	Chn	Fana	5 May 84
WJ	1:22:42	Andrey	Perlov	Sov	Donetsk	6 Sep 80

50km WALK (ROAD)

W,E	3:38:31	Ronald	Weigel	GDR	E.Berlin	20 Jul 84
CAC	3:41:19.2	Raul	Gonzalez	Mex	Praha-Podebrady	11 Jun 78
C,Oce	3:46:34	Willi	Sawall	Aus	Adelaide	6 Apr 80
NAm	3:47:48	Marcel	Jobin	Can	Quebec	20 Jun 81
Asi	4:03:02	Fuxin	Zhang	Chn	Jiading	14 Mar 83
Afr	4:14:30	Eddie	Michaels	RSA	Cape Town	11 Mar 67
SAm	4:18:08	Ernesto	Alfaro	Col	Mixhuca	23 Mar 80
OG	3:47:25.4	Raul	Gonzalez	Mex	Los Angeles	11 Aug 84

50,000m WALK (TRACK)

W,CAC	3:41:38.4	Raul	Gonzalez	Mex	Fana	25 May 79
E	3:46:11*	Mykola	Udovenko	Sov	Uzhgorod	3 Oct 80
	3:48:59	Vladimir	Rezayev	Sov	Fana	2 May 80
C	4:05:47.3	Chris	Maddocks	Eng	Birmingham	22 Sep 84
Oce	4:06:39	Willi	Sawall	Aus	Melbourne	14 Aug 76
NAm	4:12:44.5	Dan	O'Connor	USA	Irvine	19 Nov 83
Asi	4:20:45	Kazuo	Shirai	Jap	Tokyo	9 Mar 80
Afr	4:21:44.5	Abdelwahab	Ferguene	Alg	Toulouse	25 Mar 84
SAm	4:39:13.8	Wolfgang	Kleiber	Chl	Hamburg	8 Apr 73

The graceful sprinting duo Merlene Ottey & Grace Jackson.

Anisoara Stanciu – Olympic long jump champion.

Susan Telfer – Olympic bronze and a windy 7 metre long jump in 1984.

Steve Jones leads Nick rose who beat him in this UK Championship race at 10000 metres. Jones went on to run a world marathon later in Chicago.

Alonzo Babers – supereme in the 1984 Olympic 400 metres.

Sergey Litvinov – world hammer champion in 1983.

Mary Decker leads Zola Budd and Wendy Sly in the Olympic 3000m final.

Nawal El Moutawakil made history by winning the women's 400m hurdles in Los Angeles.

Tessa Sanderson – Olympic javelin champion.

Steve Ovett has Steve Cram on his shoulder as both follow Stefano Mei (510) in the Olympic 1500m semi-final.

Kirk Baptiste smashes the world best for 300 metres, and the great Carl Lewis.

Mike Conley – probably the world's most consistently successful triple jumper in 1984, but beaten by Al Joyner at the Olympics.

Konstantin Volkov was the only man to beat Sergey Bubka in 1984.

World Records

4x100 METRES RELAY

W,NAm	37.83	USA	(Graddy, Brown, C.Smith, Lewis)	Los Angeles	11 Aug 84
E	38.26	Sov	(Muravyov,Sidorov,Aksinin,Prokofyev)	Moskva	1 Aug 80
CAC	38.39^	Jam	(Stewart, Fray, Forbes, Miller)	C.de Mexico	19 Oct 68
	38.39^	Cub	(Ramirez, Morales, Montes, Figuerola)	C.de Mexico	20 Oct 68
C	38.39^	Jam	(Stewart, Fray, Forbes, Miller)	C.de Mexico	19 Oct 68
Afr	38.73^	IvC	(Oure, Meite, Nogboum, Kablan)	C.de Mexico	13 Sep 79
SAm	38.8	Bra	(Oliveira, da Silva, Nakaya, Correia)	Sao Paulo	1 May 84
	39.02^	Bra	(de Castro, dos Santos, Pegado,Filho)	C.de Mexico	4 Sep 79
Oce	39.31	Aus	(Lewis, D'Arcy, Ratcliffe, Haskell)	Christchurch	2 Feb 74
Asi	39.54	Jap	(Y.Harada, A.Harada, Matsura, Toyota)	Canberra	3 Dec 77
OG	37.83	USA	(Graddy, Brown, C.Smith, Lewis)	Los Angeles	11 Aug 84
WJ	39.00^	USA	(Jessie, Franklin, Blalock, Mitchell)	Col.Springs	18 Jul 83

4x400 METRES RELAY

W,NAm	2:56.16^	USA	(Matthews, Freeman, James, Evans)	C.de Mexico	20 Oct 68
E,C	2:59.13	UK	(Akabusi, Cook, Bennett, Brown)	Los Angeles	11 Aug 84
Afr	2:59.32	Nig	(Uti, Ugbusie, Peters, Egbunike)	Los Angeles	11 Aug 84
Oce	2:59.70	Aus	(Frayne, Clark, Minihan, Mitchell)	Los Angeles	11 Aug 84
CAC	3:01.60	Bar	(Louis, Peltier, Edwards, Forde)	Los Angeles	11 Aug 84
SAm	3:02.79	Bra	(da Silva, Barbosa, Guimaraes, Souza)	Caracas	28 Aug 83
Asi	3:05.28	Jap	(Takano, Koike, Isobe, Asaba)	Edmonton	9 Jul 83
OG	2:56.16^	USA	(Matthews, Freeman, James, Evans)	C.de Mexico	20 Oct 68
WJ	3:02.46	USA	(Cannon, Jackson, Davis, Rolle)	New Britain	31 Jul 83

World Records

WORLD & CONTINENTAL RECORDS – WOMEN

W = World: I = I.A.A.F. (if different): C = Commonwealth: Afr = Africa: Asi = Asia: CAC = Central America & Caribbean E = Europe: NAm = N. America: Oce = Oceania: SAm = S. America: OG = Olympic Games: WJ = World Junior

^ = altitude over 100m: + = timing by photo–electric cell * = awaiting ratification: # = not officially ratified

100 METRES

W,NAm	10.76	Evelyn	Ashford	USA	Zurich	22 Aug 84
E	10.81	Marlies	Göhr	GDR	E.Berlin	8 Jun 83
C	11.00	Angella	Taylor	Can	Brisbane	4 Oct 82
CAC	11.01	Merlene	Ottey/Page	Jam	Walnut	25 Jul 84
Oce	11.20^	Raelene	Boyle	Aus	Ciudad de Mexico	15 Oct 68
Asi	11.22	Cheng	Chi	Tai	Wien	18 Jul 70
Afr	11.31	Rufina	Ubah	Nig	Brisbane	4 Oct 82
SAm	11.31	Esmeralda	Garcia	Bra	Caracas	24 Aug 83
OG	10.97	Evelyn	Ashford	USA	Los Angeles	5 Aug 84
WJ	11.13	Chandra	Cheeseborough	USA	Eugene	21 Jun 76

200 METRES

W,E	21.71	Marita	Koch	GDR	Karl-Marx-Stadt	10 Jun 79
	21.71*	Marita	Koch	GDR	Potsdam	21 Jul 84
NAm	21.81	Valerie	Brisco-Hooks	USA	Los Angeles	9 Aug 84
C,CAC	22.09	Merlene	Ottey/Page	Jam	Los Angeles	9 Aug 84
Oce	22.35	Denise	Boyd	Aus	Sydney	23 Mar 80
Asi	22.62	Cheng	Chi	Tai	Munchen	12 Jul 70
Afr	22.76^	Evette	de Klerk	RSA	Sasolburg	21 Apr 84
SAm	22.94^	Beatriz	Allocco	Arg	La Paz	11 Nov 78
OG	21.81	Valerie	Brisco-Hooks	USA	Los Angeles	9 Aug 84
WJ	22.19	Natalya	Bochina	Sov	Moskva	30 Jul 80

400 METRES

W,E	47.99	Jarmila	Kratochvilova	CS	Helsinki	10 Aug 83
NAm	48.83	Valerie	Brisco-Hooks	USA	Los Angeles	6 Aug 84
C	49.43	Kathy	Cook	UK	Los Angeles	6 Aug 84
CAC	50.56	Aurelia	Penton	Cub	Medellin	16 Jul 78
Afr	50.97	Mimmie	Snyman	RSA	Germiston	17 Mar 82
Oce	51.08	Raelene	Boyle	Aus	Brisbane	4 Sep 82
Asi	51.2 m	Keum-Dan	Shin	NKo	Pyongyang	31 Oct 64
	52.90	Usha		Ind	Tokyo	14 Sep 84
SAm	52.8 m	Tania	Miranda	Bra	Sao Paulo	1 Aug 82
	52.96	Tania	Miranda	Bra	Sao Paulo	16 Jun 84
OG	48.83	Valerie	Brisco-Hooks	USA	Los Angeles	6 Aug 84
WJ	49.77	Christina	Brehmer/Lathan	GDR	Dresden	9 May 76

800 METRES

W,E	1:53.28	Jarmila	Kratochvilova	CS	München	26 Jul 83
NAm	1:57.60	Mary	Decker/Slaney	USA	Gateshead	31 Jul 83
Asi	1:58.0 m	Keum-Dan	Shin	NKo	Pyongyang	5 Sep 64
C,Oce	1:59.0 m	Charlene	Rendina	Aus	Melbourne	28 Feb 76

World Records

Afr	1:59.39	Ilze	Venter	RSA	Stellenbosch	25 Mar 83
CAC	2:01.31	Angelita	Lind	PRc	Walnut	25 Jul 84
SAm	2:03.17	Alejandra	Ramos	Chl	Barcelona	24 Sep 83
OG	1:53.43	Nadyezhda	Olizarenko	Sov	Moskva	27 Jul 80
WJ	1:59.40	Christine	Wachtel	GDR	Los Angeles	26 Jun 83

1500 METRES

W,E	3:52.47	Tatyana	Kazankina	Sov	Zürich	13 Aug 80
NAm	3:57.12	Mary	Decker/Slaney	USA	Stockholm	26 Jul 83
C	4:00.57	Christina	Boxer	Eng	Gateshead	6 Jul 84
Afr	4:01.81	Zola	Budd	RSA	Port Elizabeth	21 Mar 84
Oce	4:08.06	Jenny	Orr	Aus	Munchen	4 Sep 72
SAm	4:13.73	Alejandra	Ramos	Chl	Helsinki	20 Jun 79
CAC	4:14.7	Charlotte	Bradley	Mex	Sofiya	23 Aug 77
Asi	4:14.8 m	Ok-Sun	Kim	NKo	Pyongyang	26 Oct 78
OG	3:56.56	Tatyana	Kazankina	Sov	Moskva	1 Aug 80
WJ	4:01.81	Zola	Budd	RSA	Port Elizabeth	21 Mar 84

1 MILE

W,E	4:15.8*	Natalya	Artyomova	Sov	Leningrad	6 Aug 84
	4:17.44	Maricica	Puica	Rum	Rieti	16 Sep 82
NAm	4:17.55i	Mary	Decker/Slaney	USA	Houston	17 Feb 80
	4:18.08	Mary	Decker/Slaney	USA	Paris	9 Jul 82
C	4:22.64	Christina	Boxer	Eng	London	7 Sep 84
Afr	4:28.4 m	Sarina	Cronje	RSA	Stellenbosch	15 Nov 80
Oce	4:33.93	Anne	Audain	NZ	Christchurch	15 Jan 83
WJ	4:30.6	Zola	Budd	RSA	Bloemfontein	30 Jan 84

3000 METRES

W,E	8:22.62	Tatyana	Kazankina	Sov	Leningrad	26 Aug 84
NAm	8:29.71	Mary	Decker/Slaney	USA	Oslo	7 Jul 82
C	8:37.06	Wendy	Sly	Eng	Helsinki	10 Aug 83
Afr	8:37.5	Zola	Budd	RSA	Stellenbosch	29 Feb 84
Oce	8:44.1	Donna	Gould	Aus	Eugene	13 Jul 84
Asi	9:05.57	Kiuyun	Zhang	Chn	Nanjing	18 Sep 84
SAm	9:22.08	Monica	Regonessi	Chl	Los Angeles	26 Jun 83
CAC	9:30.0	Genoveva	Dominguez	Mex	Nassau	24 Aug 84
OG	8:35.96	Maricica	Puica	Rom	Los Angeles	10 Aug 84
WJ	8:37.5	Zola	Budd	RSA	Stellenbosch	29 Feb 84

5000 METRES

W,E	14:58.89	Ingrid	Kristiansen	Nor	Oslo	28 Jun 84
Afr	15:01.83	Zola	Budd	RSA	Stellenbosch	5 Jan 84
NAm	15:08.26	Mary	Decker/Slaney	USA	Eugene	5 Jun 82
C,Oce	15:13.23	Anne	Audain	NZ	Auckland	17 Mar 82
Asi	15:38.29	Akemi	Masuda	Jap	Oslo	26 Jun 82
SAm	17:12.5	Margot	Vargas	Arg	Buenos Aires	9 Dec 84
CAC						
OG	–	(event not held	prior to 1988	)		
WJ	15:01.83	Zola	Budd	RSA	Stellenbosch	5 Jan 84

World Records

10000 METRES

W,E	31:13.78	Olga	Bondarenko	Sov	Kiyiw	24 Jun 84
NAm	31:35.3 m	Mary	Decker/Slaney	USA	Eugene	16 Jul 82
C,Oce	32:21.47	Anne	Audain	NZ	Auckland	17 Feb 83
Asi	32:48.1	Akemi	Masuda	Jap	Kobe	2 May 82
Afr	32:50.25	Esther	Kiplagat	Ken	Kobe	30 Apr 84
SAm	34:37.95	Eva	Guevara	Per	Cape Girardeau	23 May 84
CAC	36:06.8	Maricela	Hurtado	Mex	Ciudad de Mexico	24 Jun 84
OG	–	(event not held	prior to 1988	)		
WJ	32:48.1	Akemi	Masuda	Jap	Kobe	2 May 82

100 METRES HURDLES

W,E	12.36	Grazyna	Rabsztyn	Pol	Warszawa	13 Jun 80
NAm	12.79	Stephanie	Hightower	USA	Karl-Marx-Stadt	10 Jul 82
C	12.87	Shirley	Strong	Eng	Zürich	24 Aug 83
Asi	12.93	Cheng	Chi	Tai	München	12 Jul 70
	12.93	Esther	Rot	Isr	W.Berlin	20 Aug 76
Oce	12.93	Pam	Ryan	Aus	Munchen	4 Sep 72
Afr	13.14^	Ina	van Rensburg	RSA	Germiston	23 Apr 82
CAC	13.18	Grisel	Machado	Cub	Habana	8 Aug 82
SAm	13.45	Beatriz	Capotosto	Arg	Santiago/Chile	27 Oct 84
OG	12.56	Vera	Komisova	Sov	Moskva	28 Jul 80
WJ	12.95	Candy	Young	USA	Walnut	16 Jun 79

400 METRES HURDLES

W,E	53.58	Margarita	Ponomaryova	Sov	Kiyiw	22 Jun 84
Afr	54.61	Nawal	El Moutawakil	Mar	Los Angeles	8 Aug 84
NAm	54.93	Judi	Brown	USA	Los Angeles	21 Jun 84
C,Asi	55.42	Usha		Ind	Los Angeles	8 Aug 84
Oce	55.89	Debbie	Flintoff	Aus	Brisbane	7 Oct 82
CAC	56.05	Sandra	Farmer	Jam	Los Angeles	6 Aug 84
SAm	57.4 m	Conceicao	Geremias	Bra	Rio de Janeiro	27 Jun 81
	57.61	Conceicao	Geremias	Bra	Ciudad Bolivar	15 Aug 81
OG	54.61	Nawal	El Moutawakil	Mar	Los Angeles	8 Aug 84
WJ	55.20	Leslie	Maxie	USA	San Jose	9 Jun 84

HIGH JUMP

W,E	2.07	Lyudmila	Andonova	Bul	E.Berlin	20 Jul 84
NAm	2.01	Louise	Ritter	USA	Roma	1 Sep 83
CAC	1.99	Silvia	Costa	Cub	Turin	2 Jun 84
C	1.99i	Debbie	Brill	Can	Edmonton	23 Jan 82
	1.98	Debbie	Brill	Can	Rieti	2 Sep 84
Afr	1.96	Charmaine	Gale	RSA	Bloemfontein	4 Apr 81
Oce	1.95	Chris	Stanton	Aus	Perth	22 Apr 84
Asi	1.93	Hisayo	Fukumitsu	Jap	Tokyo	7 Jun 81
	1.93	Dazhen	Zheng	Chn	Beijing	23 Apr 82
SAm	1.90	Liliana	Arigoni	Arg	Santa Fe	5 May 84
OG	2.02	Ulrike	Meyfarth	FRG	Los Angeles	10 Aug 84
WJ	1.96	Charmaine	Gale	RSA	Bloemfontein	4 Apr 81
		Olga	Turchak	Sov	Donetsk	7 Sep 84

World Records

LONG JUMP

W,E	7.43	Anisoara	Cusmir/Stanciu	Rum	Bucuresti	4 Jun 83
NAm	7.00	Jodi	Anderson	USA	Eugene	28 Jun 80
C	6.90	Beverley	Kinch	Eng	Helsinki	14 Aug 83
CAC	6.82	Jennifer	Innis	Guy	Nice	14 Aug 82
Afr	6.77^	Maryna	van Niekerk	RSA	Bloemfontein	26 Apr 80
Oce	6.75	Robyn	Lorraway	Aus	Canberra	28 Jan 84
Asi	6.57	Wenfen	Xiao	Chn	Nanjing	7 Jun 84
SAm	6.56	Esmeralda	Garcia	Bra	Gainesville	21 Mar 81
OG	7.06	Tatyana	Kalpakova	Sov	Moskva	31 Jul 80
WJ	6.98	Heike	Daute/Dreschler	GDR	Potsdam	18 Aug 82

SHOT PUT

W,E	22.53	Natalya	Lisovskaya	Sov	Sochi	27 May 84
CAC	20.61	Maria	Sarria	Cub	Habana	22 Jul 82
NAm	19.09	Maren	Seidler	USA	Walnut	16 Jun 79
C,Oce	19.74*	Gael	Martin	Aus	Berkeley	14 Jul 84
Asi	18.47	Meisu	Li	Chn	Beijing	7 Apr 84
Afr	17.32	Mariette	van Heerden	RSA	Germiston	29 Nov 80
SAm	16.32	Maria-Nilba	Fernandes	Bra	Manaus	2 Jul 83
OG	22.41	Ilona	Briesenick	GDR	Moskva	24 Jul 80
WJ	19.57	Grit	Haupt	GDR	Gera	7 Jul 84

DISCUS

W,E	74.56	Zdenka	Silhava	CS	Nitra	26 Aug 84
CAC	69.08	Carmen	Romero	Cub	Habana	17 Apr 76
C	67.48	Meg	Ritchie	Sco	Walnut	26 Apr 81
NAm	65.20	Leslie	Deniz	USA	Tempe	7 Apr 84
Oce	63.08	Gael	Mulhall/Martin	Aus	Melbourne	11 Jan 79
Asi	61.80	Xiaohui	Li	Chn	Baoding	3 May 80
Afr	58.14	Mariette	van Heerden	RSA	Potchefstroom	1 Dec 80
SAm	53.00	Odete	Domingos	Bra	Rio de Janeiro	3 Sep 83
OG	69.96	Evelin	Jahl	GDR	Moskva	1 Aug 80
WJ	65.96	Grit	Haupt	GDR	Leipzig	13 Jul 84

JAVELIN

W,E	74.76	Tiina	Lillak	Fin	Tampere	13 Jun 83
C	73.58	Tessa	Sanderson	Eng	Edinburgh	26 Jun 83
CAC	69.96	Maria	Colon	Cub	Sofiya	17 Jun 84
NAm	69.32	Kate	Schmidt	USA	Fürth	11 Sep 77
Oce	69.28	Petra	Rivers	Aus	Brisbane	20 Mar 82
Asi	61.64	Guoli	Tang	Chn	Tokyo	7 Jun 81
Afr	61.28	Nellie	Basson	RSA	Stellenbosch	31 Oct 83
SAm	56.90	Marli	dos Santos	Bra	Nice	21 Aug 77
OG	69.56	Tessa	Sanderson	UK	Los Angeles	6 Aug 84
WJ	71.88	Antoaneta	Todorova	Bul	Zagreb	15 Aug 81

HEPTATHLON (1971/1984 TABLES)

W,E	6867/6946	Sabine	Möbius	GDR	Potsdam	6 May 84
NAm	6714/6803	Jane	Frederick	USA	Talence	16 Sep 84

World Records

C,Oce	6390/6387	Glynis	Nunn	Aus	Los Angeles	4 Aug 84
SAm	6084/6017	Conceicao	Geremias	Bra	Caracas	25 Aug 83
CAC	5973/5930	Hildelise	Despaigne	Cub	Praha	17 Aug 84
Afr	5674/5596	Heidi	de Kock	RSA	Durban	14 Apr 84
Asi	5666/5573	Lianying	Ye	Chn	Shanghai	26 Sep 83
OG	6390(6387)	Glynis	Nunn	Aus	Los Angeles	4 Aug 84
	(6363)6388	Sabine	Everts	FRG	Los Angeles	4 Aug 84
WJ	6421/6465	Sybille	Thiele	GDR	Schwechat	28 Aug 83

MARATHON

W,NAm	2:22:43	Joan	Benoit	USA	Boston	18 Apr 83
E	2:24:26	Ingrid	Kristiansen	Nor	London	13 May 84
C,Oce	2:25:28.8	Allison	Roe	NZ	New York	25 Oct 81
Asi	2:30:30	Akemi	Masuda	Jap	Eugene	11 Sep 83
SAm	2:36:17	Elisabeth	Oberli-Schuh	Ven	Frankfurt/Main	13 May 84
Afr	2:36:44	Sonja	Laxton	RSA	Cape Town	30 Jun 84
CAC	2:38:52	Maria	Trujillo	Mex	New York	23 Oct 83
OG	2:24:51.4	Joan	Benoit	USA	Los Angeles	5 Aug 84
WJ	2:34:24	Cathy	Schiro	USA	Washington	12 May 84

5000 METRES WALK (TRACK)

W,E	21:36.2	Olga	Krishtop	Sov	Penza	3 Aug 84
Asi	21:40.3	Hong	Yan	Chn	Fana	5 May 84
C,Oce	22:04.42	Sue	Cook	Aus	Melbourne	1 Apr 84
NAm	22:17.5	Ann	Peel	Can	Fana	5 May 84
Afr	26:29.5	Cheruiyot	Darmao	Ken	Nairobi	15 Jun 84
CAC	26:52.5	Estella	Rodarte	Mex	Ciudad de Mexico	20 Apr 81
WJ	21:40.3	Hong	Yan	Chn	Fana	5 May 84

10,000 METRES WALK (TRACK)

W,Asi	45:39.5	Hong	Yan	Chn	Kobenhavn	13 May 84
E	46:15.6*	Roza	Undyerova	Sov	Oryol	28 Aug 83
C,Oce	45:47.0	Sue	Cook	Aus	Leicester	14 Sep 83
NAm	50:01.91	Ann	Peel	Can	Laval	17 Jun 83
CAC	55:47.4	Maria	de la Cruz	Mex	Ciudad de Mexico	7 Apr 84
Afr	64:08.6	Alice	Okello	Ken	Kericho	28 Feb 81
WJ	45:39.5	Hong	Yan	Chn	Kobenhavn	13 May 84

10km WALK (ROAD)

W,E	44:51.6	Olga	Krishtop	Sov	Penza	5 Aug 84
Asi	45:13.4	Yongju	Xu	Chn	Bergen	24 Sep 83
C,Oce	45:26.4	Sue	Cook	Aus	Bergen	24 Sep 83
NAm	47:01.8	Ann	Peel	Can	Bergen	24 Sep 83
CAC	51:23	Maria	de la Cruz	Mex	Bucaramanga	3 Nov 84
SAm	54:27	Elsa	Abril	Col	Bucaramanga	3 Nov 84
Afr	70:18	Mercy	Nyambura	Ken	Nakura	1 Oct 83
WJ	46:38.7	Ping	Quan	Chn	Bergen	24 Sep 83

4x100 METRES RELAY

W,E	41.53	GDR	(Gladisch, Koch, Auerswald, Göhr)	E.Berlin	31 Jul 83
NAm	41.61^	USA	(Brown,Williams,Cheeseborough,Ashford)	Col.Springs	3 Jul 83

World Records

C	42.43	Eng	(Oakes, Cook, Callender, Lannaman)	Moskva	1 Aug 80
CAC	42.73	Jam	(Hodges, Pusey, Cuthbert, Ottey/Page)	Helsinki	10 Aug 83
Oce	43.18	Aus	(Wilson, Wells, Boyd, Boyle)	Montreal	31 Jul 76
Afr	44.35	Gha	(Asiedua, Ocran, Afriyie, Annum)	Christchurch	2 Feb 74
SAm	44.90^	Arg	(Fava, Godoy, Cragno, Allocco)	C.de Mexico	20 Oct 75
Asi	45.13	Jap	(Konishi, Isozaki, Akimoto, Yoshida)	New Delhi	25 Nov 82
OG	41.60	GDR	(Müller, Wöckel, Auerswald, Göhr)	Moskva	1 Aug 80
WJ	43.73^	USA	(Gilmore, Finn, Simmons, Vereen)	Col.Springs	19 Jul 83

4x400 METRES RELAY

W,E	3:15.92	GDR	(Walther, Busch, Rübsam, Koch)	Erfurt	3 Jun 84
NAm	3:18.29	USA	(Leatherwood,Howard,Brisco,Cheeseb')	Los Angeles	11 Aug 84
C	3:21.21	Can	(Crooks,Richardson,Killingbeck,Payne)	Los Angeles	11 Aug 84
Oce	3:25.56	Aus	(Canty, Burnard, Rendina, Nail)	Montreal	31 Jul 76
CAC	3:26.56	Jam	(Oliver, Green, Rattray, Jackson)	Los Angeles	10 Aug 84
Asi	3:32.49	Ind	(Valsamma, Rao, Abraham, Usha)	Los Angeles	11 Aug 84
Afr	3:34.91	Nig	(Akinyemi, Ayanlaja, Vaughan, Elumelu)	Stuttgart	11 Jul 80
SAm	3:39.3 m	Bra	(Miranda, dos Santos, Silva, Oliveira)	Sao Paulo	9 May 81
	3:39.3 m	Bra	(Miranda, dos Santos, Silva, Oliveira)	Curitiba	23 May 82
OG	3:18.29	USA	(Leatherwood,Howard,Brisco,Cheeseb')	Los Angeles	11 Aug 84
WJ	3:30.39	GDR	(Feuerbach,Witzel,Vogelgesang,Bohne)	Utrecht	23 Aug 81

ALL-TIME WORLD LISTS

100 METRES

Calvin	Smith	USA 61	A 9.93	1.4	(1)	USOC SF	Colorado Springs	3 Jul 83
Jim	Hines	USA 46	A 9.95	0.3	(1)	OG	Mexico, D.F.	14 Oct 68
Mel	Lattany	USA 59	9.96	0.1	(1)		Athens, GA	5 May 84
Carl	Lewis	USA 61	9.97	1.5	(1)R1		Modesto	14 May 83
C	Smith		9.97	1.6	(1)	WK	Zurich	24 Aug 83
Silvio	Leonard	CUB 55	9.98	0.6	(1)	WPT	Guadalakara	11 Aug 77
	Lewis		9.99	1.3	(1)		Houston	6 May 84
	Lewis		9.99	0.2	(1)	OG	Los Angeles	4 Aug 84
	Lewis		9.99	0.9	(1)	WK	Zurich	22 Aug 84
	Lewis		10.00	0.0	(1)	SWC	Dallas	16 May 81
	Lewis		10.00	1.9	(1)	CAL R.	Modesto	15 May 82
Marian	Woronin	POL 56	10.00	2.0	(1)	KUSOC	Warszana	9 Jun 84
Pietro	Mennea	ITA 52	A10.01	0.9	(1)		Mexico, D.F.	4 Sep 79
Charles	Green	USA 44	A10.02	2.0	(1)Q4	OG	Mexico, D.F.	13 Oct 68
James	Sanford	USA 57	10.02	1.0	(1)	PEPSI	Westwood	11 May 80
	Hines		10.03	0.9	(1)S1	AAU	Sacramento	20 Jun 68
	Leonard		10.03		(1)		Habana	13 Sep 77
J	Sanford		A10.03	1.6	(1)		El Paso	19 Apr 80
Stanley	Floyd	USA 61	A10.03	1.9	(1)R1	NCAA	Provo	5 Jun 82
(20/10)								
	Lattany		10.03	1.6	(2)	WK	Zurich	24 Aug 84
Lennox	Miller	JAM 46	A10.04	0.3	(2)	OG	Mexico, D.F.	14 Oct 68
Steve	Riddick	USA 51	10.05	1.2	(1)	WK	Zurich	20 Aug 75
Bob	Hayes	USA 42	10.06	1.1	(1)	OG	Tokyo	15 Oct 64
Hasely	Crawford	TRN 50	10.06	0.1	(1)	OG	Montreal	24 Jul 76
Leandro	Penalver	CUB 61	10.06	2.0	(1)	PAG	Caracas	24 Aug 83
Ron	Brown	USA 61	10.06	1.6	(3)	WK	Zurich	24 Aug 83
Emmit	King	USA 59	10.06	1.6	(4)	WK	Zurich	24 Aug 83
Valeriy	Borzov	SU 49	10.07	0.0	(1)Q3	OG	Munchen	31 Aug 72
Don	Quarrie	JAM 51	10.07	0.1	(2)	OG	Montreal	24 Jul 76
Clancy	Edwards	USA 55	10.07	1.7	(1)	NCAA	Eugene	2 Jun 78
(20)								
Eddie	Hart	USA 49	A10.07	1.8	(1)	USOC SF	Colorado Springs	30 Jul 78
Steve	Williams	USA 53	10.07	0.1	(1)	WK	Zurich	16 Aug 78
Mike	Roberson	USA 56	A10.07−	0.6	(1)S1	WUG	Mexico, D.F.	8 Sep 79
Darrell	Green	USA 60	10.08	0.1	(1)		San Angelo	13 Apr 83
Sam	Graddy	USA 64	10.09	1.4	(1)H2		Baton Rouge	12 May 84
Hermes	Ramirez	CUB 48	A10.10	0.5	(1)Q2	OG	Mexico, D.F.	13 Oct 68
Willie	Gault	USA 60	A10.10	1.9	(2)R1	NCAA	Provo	5 Jun 82
Roger	Bambuck	FRA 45	A10.11	1.6	(2)S1	OG	Mexico, D.F.	14 Oct 68
Harvey	Glance	USA 57	10.11	1.9	(1)	FOT	Eugene	20 Jun 76
Curtis	Dickey	USA 56	10.11	1.7	(2)	NCAA	Eugene	2 Jun 78
(30)								
Osvaldo	Lara	CUB 55	A10.11		(2)	CAC G	Medellin	16 Jul 78
Don	Coleman	USA 51	A10.11	1.8	(3)	USOC SF	Colorado Springs	30 Jul 78
Allan	Wells	UK 52	10.11	1.4	(1)Q1	OG	Moskva	24 Jul 80
Jeff	Phillips	USA 57	10.11	1.8	(1)S3	NCAA	Baton Rouge	5 Jun 81
Mike	Miller	USA 59	A10.11	1.9	(3)R1	NCAA	Provo	5 Jun 82
Eugen	Ray	GDR 57	10.12	0.0	(1)	EP	Helsinki	13 Aug 77
Ben	Johnson	CAN 61	10.12	0.9	(3)	WK	Zurich	22 Aug 84
Houston	McTear	USA 57	10.13	0.5	(1)		Koln	22 Jun 77
Petar	Petrov	BUL 55	10.13	1.4	(2)Q1	OG	Moskva	24 Jul 80
Ronnie Ray	Smith	USA 49	10.14	0.9	(2)S1	AAU	Sacramento	20 Jun 68
(40)								
Pablo	Montes	CUB 45	A10.14	0.6	(1)H4	OG	Mexico, D.F.	13 Oct 68
James	Butler	USA 60	A10.14	1.6	(1)R2	NCAA	Provo	5 Jun 82

All-time Lists – Men

Juan	Nunez	DOM 59	10.14*	2.0	(1)	PAG	Caracas	21 Aug 83
Mel	Pender	USA 37	10.15	0.9	(3)S1	AAU	Sacramento	20 Jun 68
Colin	Bradford	JAM 55	10.15	0.0	(1)	WPT	Ciudad Bolivar	14 Aug 81
Valentin	Atanasov	BUL 61	10.15	1.9	(1)		Sofia	14 Aug 82
Innocent	Egbunike	NIG 61	10.15		(1)		Charleston	25 May 84
Robert	Taylor	USA 48	10.16	0.0	(2)Q3	OG	Munchen	31 Aug 72
Guy	Abrahams	PAN 53	10.16	1.3	(1)S1	AAU	Westwood	8 Jun 78
Peter	Okodogbe	NIG 58	10.16		(1)		Lagos	16 Jun 78
(50)								
Christian	Haas	FRG 58	10.16	2.0	(1)S1	NC	Bremen	24 Jun 83
Stefano	Tilli	ITA 62	10.16	1.7	(1)H1	WK	Zurich	22 Aug 84
Kirk	Baptiste	USA 62	10.16	0.9	(1)	G. GALA	Roma	31 Aug 84
(53)								

* = disqualified for drug abuse
Marks made with assisting wind

William	Snoddy	USA 57	9.87	11.2	(1)		Dallas	1 Apr 78
James	Sanford	USA 57	9.88	2.3	(1)		Westwood	3 May 80
Bob	Hayes	USA 42	9.91	5.3	(1)S1	OG	Tokyo	15 Oct 64
Calvin	Smith	USA 61	9.91	2.1	(1)	V GDR	Karl-Marx-Stadt	9 Jul 82
Carl	Lewis	USA 61	9.93	2.3	(1)	MSR	Walnut	24 Apr 83
C	Smith		9.94	4.6	(1)		Sacramento	21 Jul 84
Willie	Gault	USA 60	9.95	8.9	(1)		Knoxville	2 Apr 83
Mel	Lattany	USA 59	9.95	2.4	(1)		Athens, GA.	7 May 83
C	Smith		9.97	8.9	(2)		Knoxville	2 Apr 83
Cole	Doty	CAN 55	9.98	11.2	(2)		Dallas	1 Apr 78
Pietro	Mennea	ITA 52	9.99	7.2	(1)	V GRE	Bari	13 Sep 78
	Lewis		9.99	2.6	(1)	NCAA	Baton Rouge	5 Jun 81
	Lattany		9.99	8.5	(1)		Edinburgh	26 Jun 83
C	Smith		9.99	4.1	(1)		Knoxville	14 Apr 84
J	Sanford		10.00	3.4	(1)H3	NCAA	Austin	5 Jun 80
Jeff	Phillips	USA 57	10.00	2.6	(2)	NCAA	Baton Rouge	5 Jun 81
	Lewis		10.00	2.1	(1)		San Jose	26 May 84
Ron	Brown	USA 61	10.01	2.3	(2)	MSR	Walnut	24 Apr 83
	Lattany		10.01	4.0	(1)		Modesto	12 May 84
Ben	Johnson	CAN 61	10.01	5.5	(1)	NC	Winnipeg	30 Jun 84
Allan	Wells	UK 52	10.02	5.9	(1)	CG	Brisbane	4 Oct 82
R	Brown		10.02	3.4	(1)	JENNER	San Jose	28 May 83
Don	Quarrie	JAM 51	10.03	7.6	(1)	CG	Edmonton	7 Aug 78
J	Sanford		10.03	4.2	(1)	USOC SF	Syracuse	25 Jul 81
C	Smith		10.03	2.6	(1)	V FRG AFR	Durham	26 Jun 82
	Lewis		10.03	3.4	(2)	JENNER	San Jose	28 May 83
Ray	Brooks	USA 56	10.04	11.2	(3)		Dallas	1 Apr 78
(27/15)								
Emmit	King	USA 59	10.05	2.3	(1)H1	NCAA	Houston	2 Jun 83
Jerome	Deal	USA 58	A10.06	8.8	(1)	WAC	El Paso	6 May 78
Stefano	Tilli	ITA 62	10.06	4.3	(1)		Cagliari	9 Oct 83
Harvey	Glance	USA 57	10.07	4.5	(1)H6	NCAA	Eugene	1 Jun 78
Dwayne	Evans	USA 58	10.07	3.8	(1)	CAL R	Modesto	16 May 81
Cameron	Sharp	UK 58	10.07	5.9	(3)	CG	Brisbane	4 Oct 82
Johnny	Jones	USA 58	10.08	4.0	(1)		Austin	20 May 77
Mike	Roberson	USA 56	10.08	3.4	(1)S2	NCAA	Austin	6 Jun 80
Mike	Miller	USA 59	10.08	8.3	(1)		Lexington	17 Apr 82
Sam	Graddy	USA 64	10.08	2.4	(1)		Knoxville	19 May 84
Mike	McFarlane	UK 60	10.08	4.5	(1)	NC	Cwmbran	27 May 84
Charles	Greene	USA 44	10.09	2.8	(1)H1	OG	Mexico, D.F.	13 Oct 68
Eugen	Ray	GDR 57	10.09	2.4	(1)S1	NC	Dresden	1 Jul 77
Hasely	Crawford	TRN 50	10.09	7.6	(3)	CG	Edmonton	7 Aug 78
Ellison	Portis	USA	10.09		(1)S1	NAIA	Abilene	23 May 80
(30)								

All-time Lists – Men

Rod	Richardson	USA 62	10.09	2.1	(1)		College Station	20 Mar 82
Paul	Narracott	AUS 59	10.09	5.9	(4)	CG	Brisbane	4 Oct 82
Stanley	Blalock	USA 64	10.09	4.1	(1)		Athens, GA.	19 Mar 83
Tony	Sharpe	CAN 61	10.09	5.5	(2)	NC	Winnipeg	30 Jun 84
Stanley	Floyd	USA 61	10.10	3.4	(2)S2	NCAA	Austin	6 Jun 80
Herschel	Walker	USA 62	10.10	4.8	(1)		Athens, GA.	20 Mar 82
Donovan	Reid	UK 63	10.10	8.5	(2)		Edinburgh	26 Jun 83
Bill	Collins	USA 51	10.11	4.0	(2)		Austin	20 May 77
Mike	Kelley	USA 57	10.11	11.2	(4)		Dallas	1 Apr 78
Billy	Mullins	USA 58	10.11	2.3	(2)		Westwood	3 May 80
(40)								
Drew	McMaster	UK 57	10.11	8.5	(3)		Edinburgh	26 Jun 83
Christian	Haas	FRG 58	10.12	2.8	(1)H2	OD	Berlin	28 May 80
Desai	Williams	CAN 59	10.12	3.2	(1)	NC	Sherbrooke	14 Jun 80
Jerome	Harrison	USA 62	A10.12		(1)		Colorado Springs	25 Jul 81
William	Davis	USA 60	10.12		(1)		Abilene	12 Mar 83
Innocent	Egbunike	NIG 61	10.12	3.4	(1)		Pomona	31 Mar 84
Dannie	Carter	USA 60	10.12	6.5	(1)H3		Arlington	5 May 84
Luke	Watson	UK 57	10.12	4.5	(2)	NC	Cwmbran	27 May 84
Alvin	Matthias	USA 56	10.13		(1)S3	NAIA	Abilene	23 May 80
James	Butler	USA 60	10.13	4.7	(1)H1	BIG 8	Norman	14 May 82
(50)								
Kirk	Baptiste	USA 63	10.13	4.6	(2)		Sacramento	21 Jul 84
Eric	Brown	USA 60	10.14	3.7	(2)H5	NCAA	Austin	5 Jun 80
Thomas	Schroder	GDR 62	10.14	3.6	(1)	EC-J	Utrecht	20 Aug 81
Herman	Panzo	FRA 58	10.14	2.3	(1)R1	ISTAF	Berlin	21 Aug 81
Verril	Young	USA 60	10.14	2.7	(1)		Beaumont	30 Apr 83
Roy	Martin	USA 66	10.14	4.0	(1)	TEX R.	Austin	6 Apr 84
Wieslaw	Maniak	POL	10.15	5.3	(2)S1	OG	Tokyo	15 Oct 64
Felix	Mata	VEN 51	10.15		(1)		Panama City	24 Feb 73
James	Gilkes	GUY 52	10.15	7.6	(4)	CG	Edmonton	7 Aug 78
Vassilios	Papageorgopoulos	GRE 47	10.16	2.5	(1)	AAA	London	15 Jul 72
(50)								
Dwayne	Strozier	USA 57	10.16	4.0	(1)H2	TEX R	Austin	6 Apr 78
Ron	Ingram	USA 59	10.16	4.0	(1)H1	TEX R	Austin	3 Apr 81
Herkie	Walls	USA 61	10.16	4.0	(2)		Austin	22 May 81
Wessel	Oosthuizen	RSA 61	10.16	3.8	(1)H	NC-J	Krugersdorp	10 Apr 82
Phillip	Epps	USA 58	10.16	2.3	(1)H1	SWC	Houston	14 May 82
Marty	Krulee	USA 56	10.16	2.3	(4)	MSR	Walnut	24 Apr 83
Al	Miller	USA 63	10.16		(1)H4		Walnut	5 May 83
Bruce	Davis	USA 63	10.16	3.5	(1)		Austin	12 May 84
Greg	Sholars	USA 66	10.16	4.0	(1)		Austin	12 May 84
Claude	Magee	USA 62	10.16	2.4	(2)		Knoxville	19 May 84
(70)								
Elliston	Stinson	USA 62	10.16	3.2	(1)H3	NCAA	Eugene	31 May 84

200 METRES

Pietro	Mennea	ITA 52	A19.72	1.8	(1)	WUG	Mexico, D.F.	12 Sep 79
Carl	Lewis	USA 61	19.75	1.5	(1)	TAC	Indianapolis	19 Jun 83
	Lewis		19.80	−0.9	(1)	OG	Los Angeles	8 Aug 84
Tommie	Smith	USA 44	A19.83	0.9	(1)	OG	Mexico, D.F.	16 Oct 68
	Lewis		19.84	0.2	(1)Q3	FOT	Los Angeles	19 Jun 84
Don	Quarrie	JAM 51	19.86	1.0	(1)	PAG	Cali	3 Aug 71
	Lewis		19.86	−0.2	(1)	FOT	Los Angeles	21 Jun 84
John	Carlos	USA 45	A19.92	1.9	(1)	FOT	Echo Summit	12 Sep 68
	Mennea		A19.96	0.2	(1)H9	WUG	Mexico, D.F.	10 Sep 79
	Mennea		19.96	0.0	(1)		Barletta	17 Aug 80
Kirk	Baptiste	USA 63	19.96	−0.9	(2)	OG	Los Angeles	8 Aug 84
Calvin	Smith	USA 61	19.99	0.6	(1)	WK	Zurich	24 Aug 83

184

All-time Lists – Men

Name	Surname	Nat/Club	Time	Wind	Pos	Meet	Venue	Date
Valeriy	Borzov	SU 49	20.00	0.0	(1)	OG	Munchen	4 Sep 72
	Mennea		20.01	0.0	(1)	G.GALA	Roma	5 Aug 80
Clancy	Edwards	USA 55	20.03	1.6	(1)		Westwood	29 Apr 78
	Mennea		20.03	0.4	(1)	8 NAT	Tokyo	20 Sep 80
	Mennea		20.03	−0.1	(1)		Beijing	27 Sep 80
Larry	Myricks	USA 56	20.03	1.5	(2)	TAC	Indianapolis	19 Jun 83
	Mennea		A20.04	0.0	(1)S1	WUG	Mexico, D.F.	11 Sep 79
	Mennea		20.05	0.4	(1)	VD	Bruxelles	22 Aug 80
	Baptiste		20.05	−0.2	(2)	FOT	Los Angeles	21 Jun 84

(21/10)

Peter	Norman	AUS 42	A20.06	0.9	(2)	OG	Mexico, D.F.	16 Oct 68
Silvio	Leonard	CUB 55	20.06	1.7	(1)	KUSOC	Warszawa	19 Jun 78
James	Mallard	USA 57	20.07		(1)		Tuscaloosa	20 Apr 79
Albert	Robinson	USA 64	20.07	0.3	(1)		Indianapolis	5 May 84
Lamonte	King	USA 59	20.08	0.9	(1)	TAC	Walnut	15 Jun 80
Millard	Hampton	USA 56	20.10	1.7	(1)	FOT	Eugene	22 Jun 76
James	Gilkes	GUY 52	20.14	1.8	(1)		Ingelheim	12 Sep 78
Mike	Miller	USA 59	A20.15	0.3	(1)H2	NCAA	Provo	2 Jun 82
Steve	Williams	USA 53	20.16	−0.1	(1)		Stuttgart	26 Aug 75
Elliott	Quow	USA 62	20.16	1.5	(4)	TAC	Indianapolis	19 Jun 83

(20)

Larry	Black	USA 51	20.19	0.0	(2)	OG	Munchen	4 Sep 72
James	Sanford	USA 57	20.19	0.7	(1)		Westwood	28 Apr 79
Phillip	Epps	USA 59	20.19	1.9	(1)		College Station	20 Mar 82
Greg	Foster	USA 58	20.20	0.7	(2)		Westwood	28 Apr 79
Allan	Wells	UK 52	20.21	0.9	(2)	OG	Moskva	28 Jul 80
Mel	Lattany	USA 59	20.21	0.1	(1)	WP	Roma	6 Sep 81
Dwayne	Evans	USA 58	20.22	1.7	(2)	FOT	Eugene	22 Jun 76
Tony	Sharpe	CAN 61	A20.22	0.4	(1)		Colorado Springs	20 Jul 82
James	Butler	USA 60	A20.23	0.3	(2)H2	NCAA	Provo	2 Jun 82
Leslek	Dunecki	POL 56	A20.24	1.8	(2)	WUG	Mexico, D.F.	12 Sep 79

(30)

Bernie	Jackson	USA 61	20.26	1.5	(5)	TAC	Indianapolis	19 Jun 83
Thomas	Jefferson	USA 62	20.26	−0.9	(3)	OG	Los Angeles	8 Aug 84
Wardell	Gilbreath	USA 54	20.27	0.9	(1)		Tucson	1 May 76
William	Snoddy	USA 57	A20.27	1.6	(1)	USOC SF	Colorado Springs	30 Jul 78
Jeff	Phillips	USA 57	20.27	0.2	(1)		San Jose	17 Apr 82
Larry	Questad	USA 43	A20.28	1.9	(3)	FOT	Echo Summit	12 Sep 68
Roy	Martin	USA 66	20.28	1.0	(1)Q2	FOT	Los Angeles	19 Jun 84
Jerry	Bright	USA 47	A20.29	1.9	(4)	FOT	Echo Summit	12 Sep 68
Tom	Randolph	USA 42	A20.29	1.9	(5)	FOT	Echo Summit	12 Sep 68
Desai	Williams	CAN 59	A20.29	−0.1	(1)		Provo	21 May 83

(40)

Clinton	Davis	USA 65	20.29	1.5	(1)	TAC-J	University Park	26 Jun 83
Joao Batista	Da Silva	BRA 63	20.30	−0.9	(4)	OG	Los Angeles	8 Aug 84
Steve	Riddick	USA 51	20.31+	0.5	(2)	WK	Zurich	20 Aug 75
Larry	Jackson	USA 53	20.33		(1)		Lincoln	15 May 76
Frank	Emmelmann	GDR 61	20.33	0.3	(1)	EP	Zagreb	16 Aug 81
Edwin	Roberts	TRN 41	A20.34	0.9	(4)	OG	Mexico, D.F.	16 Oct 68
Vladimir	Muravyev	SU 59	20.34	−1.2	(1)	DRZ	Moskva	18 Aug 84
Efrem	Coley	USA 59	20.35		(1)		Austin	24 May 80
Rod	Barksdale	USA 62	20.35		(1)		Tempe	21 Apr 84
Henry	Carr	USA 42	20.36	−0.8	(1)	OG	Tokyo	17 Oct 64
Lennox	Miller	JAM 46	A20.36*	0.9	(2)	NCAA	Provo	17 Jun 67

(50)

* = 220 yards time less 0.11

185

All-time Lists – Men

Marks made with assisting wind

James	Sanford	USA 57	19.94	4.0	(1)S1	NCAA	Austin	7 Jun 80
Mike	Roberson	USA 56	19.95	3.4	(1)H3	NCAA	Austin	5 Jun 80
	Roberson		19.96	2.8	(1)	NCAA	Austin	7 Jun 80
Derald	Harris	USA 58	20.01	2.5	(1)		San Jose	9 Apr 77

(5/4)

	Lewis		20.01	2.1	(1)		San Jose	26 May 84
James	Butler	USA 60	A20.07	2.1	(1)R1	NCAA	Provo	4 Jun 82
Brady	Crain	USA 56	20.09	3.7	(1)	TAC	San Jose	9 Jun 84
Allan	Wells	UK 52	20.11	3.7	(1)		Edinburgh	20 Jun 80
Dwayne	Evans	USA 58	20.20	2.5	(1)	NCAA	Baton Rouge	6 Jun 81
Thomas	Jefferson	USA 62	20.21	3.8	(1)S2	TAC	San Jose	9 Jun 84
Eric	Brown	USA 60	A20.22	2.1	(4)R1	NCAA	Provo	4 Jun 82

(10)

Dave	Smith	JAM	20.22	5.9	(1)		Bozeman	19 May 84
Frank	Emmelmann	GDR 61	20.23	3.2	(1)	V UK	Dresden	14 Jun 81
Innocent	Egbunike	NIG 61	20.23	4.5	(1)		Pomona	31 Mar 84
Reggie	Jones	USA 53	20.24*	4.1	(1)S2	NCAA	Austin	8 Jun 74
Erwin	Skamrahl	FRG 58	20.25	3.2	(1)	NC	Gelsenkirchen	19 Jul 81
Roy	Martin	USA 66	20.25*		(1)		Mesquite	5 May 84
Marshall	Dill	USA 52	A20.34	2.2	(1)S2	PAG	Cali	3 Aug 71

(17)

* = 220 yards time less 0.11

400 METRES

Lee	Evans	USA 47	A43.86		(1)	OG	Mexico, D.F.	18 Oct 68
Larry	James	USA 47	A43.97		(2)	OG	Mexico, D.F.	18 Oct 68
	Evans		A44.06		(1)	FOT	Echo Summit	14 Sep 68
	James		A44.19		(2)	FOT	Echo Summit	14 Sep 68
Alberto	Juantorena	CUB 50	44.26		(1)	OG	Montreal	29 Jul 76
	Juantorena		A44.27		(1)	CAC G	Medellin	16 Jul 78
Alonzo	Babers	USA 61	44.27		(1)	OG	Los Angeles	8 Aug 84
Fred	Newhouse	USA 48	44.40		(2)	OG	Montreal	29 Jul 76
Ron	Freeman	USA 47	A44.41		(3)	OG	Mexico, D.F.	18 Oct 68
Ronald	Ray	USA 54	A44.45		(1)	PAG	Mexico, D.F.	18 Oct 75
Erwin	Skamrahl	FRG 58	44.50		(1)R1		Munchen	26 Jul 83
Gabriel	Tiacoh	IVC 63	44.54		(2)	OG	Los Angeles	8 Aug 84
Bertland	Cameron	JAM 59	44.58		(1)	NCAA	Baton Rouge	6 Jun 81
John	Smith	USA 50	A44.60		(1)	PAG	Cali	1 Aug 71
Viktor	Markin	SU 57	44.60		(1)	OG	Moskva	30 Jul 80
	Freeman		A44.62		(3)	FOT	Echo Summit	14 Sep 68
	Cameron		44.62		(1)	NCAA	Houston	4 Jun 83
	Tiacoh		44.64		(1)S2	OG	Los Angeles	6 Aug 84
	Juantorena		44.65		(1)		Habana	13 Sep 77
Vince	Matthews	USA 47	44.66		(1)	OG	Munchen	7 Sep 72

(20/13)

Sunder	Nix	USA 61	44.68		(1)	USOC SF	Indianapolis	24 Jul 82
Darrell	Robinson	USA 63	44.69		(2)	USOC SF	Indianapolis	24 Jul 82
Karl	Honz	FRG 51	44.70		(1)	NC	Munchen	21 Jul 72
Cliff	Wiley	USA 55	44.70		(1)	TAC	Sacramento	21 Jun 81
Antonio	McKay	USA 64	44.71		(1)	FOT	Los Angeles	21 Jun 84
Hartmut	Weber	FRG 60	44.72		(1)	EC	Athinai	9 Sep 82
Willie	Smith	USA 56	44.73		(1)		Tuscaloosa	15 Apr 78

All-time Lists – Men

(20)
James	Rolle	USA 64	A44.73	(1)		USOC SF	Colorado Springs	2 Jul 83
Darren	Clark	USA 65	44.75	(4)		OG	Los Angeles	8 Aug 84
El Kashief	Hassan	SUD 56	A44.76	(1)H4		NCAA	Provo	3 Jun 82
Walter	McCoy	USA 58	44.76	(2)		WK	Zurich	22 Aug 84
Wayne	Collett	USA 49	44.80	(2)		OH	Munchen	7 Sep 72
Chris	Whitlock	USA 59	A44.80	(2)		USOC SF	Colorado Springs	2 Jul 83
Innocent	Egbunike	NIG 61	44.81	(1)		PEPSI	Westwood	13 May 84
Wendell	Mottley	TRN 41	44.99*	(1)		BCG	Kingston	11 Aug 66
Maxie	Parks	USA 51	44.82	(1)		AAU	Westwood	12 Jun 76
Sunday	Uti	NIG 62	44.83	(2)S2		OG	Los Angeles	6 Aug 84

(30)
Ray	Armstead	USA 60	44.83	(3)		WK	Zurich	22 Aaug 84
Billy	Mullins	USA 58	44.84	(1)		PEPSI	Westwood	11 May 80
Richard	Mitchell	AUS 55	44.84	(2)		OG	Moskva	30 Jul 80
Maurice	Peoples	USA 50	44.85*	(1)		NCAA	Baton Rouge	9 Jun 73
Zeke	Jefferson	USA 61	44.86	(1)		SWC	Dallas	16 May 81
Mathias	Schersing	GDR 64	44.86	(1)		OD	Potsdam	21 Jul 84
Frank	Schaffer	GDR 58	44.87	(3)		OG	Moskva	30 Jul 80
Michael	Paul	TRI 57	44.88	(2)			Koln	22 Aug 82
Leslie	Kerr	USA 58	44.90	(2)		SWC	Dallas	16 May 81
Julius	Sang	KEN 46	44.92	(3)		OG	Munchen	7 Sep 72

(40)
Harald	Schmid	FRG 57	44.92	(1)		NC	Stuttgart	11 Aug 79
Howard	Henley	USA 61	44.92	(1)		PEPSI	Westwood	10 May 81
David	Jenkins	UK 52	44.93	(1)		AAU	Eugene	21 Jun 75
Eddie	Carey	USA 60	A44.94	(3)		USOC SF	Colorado Springs	2 Jul 83
Rod	Jones	USA 64	44.94	(1)			Austin	12 May 84
Herman	Frazier	USA 54	44.95	(3)		OG	Montreal	29 Jul 76
Jens	Carlowitz	GDR 64	44.95	(2)		OD	Potsdam	21 Jul 84
Michael	Franks	USA 63	A44.96	(4)		USOC SF	Colorado Springs	2 Jul 83
Larance	Jones	USA 51	44.98*	(1)		TEX R.	Austin	13 Apr 74
Charles	Phillips	USA 82*	44.98	(1)			Arlington	7 May 83

(50)
Ken	Randle	USA 54	44.99	(1)S2		NCAA	Philadelphia	4 Jun 76

(51)

* = 440 yards time less 0.26

400 METRES

Hand Timing

								Best Auto time
Wayne	Collett	USA 49	44.1	1		FOT	Eugene	9 Jul 72	44.80
John	Smith	USA 50	44.2*	1		AAU	Eugene	26 Jun 71	A44.60
Fred	Newhouse	USA 48	44.2	1s1		FOT	Eugene	7 Jul 72	44.40
J.	Smith		44.3	2		FOT	Eugene	9 Jul 72	
Vince	Matthews	USA 47	A44.4	1			Echo Summit	31 Aug 68	44.66
Curtis	Mills	USA 48	44.4*	1		NCAA	Knoxville	21 Jun 69	
	Collett		44.4*	2		AAU	Eugene	26 Jun 71	
	Juantorena		A44.4	1			Mexico D.F.	3 Jul 76	
Tommie	Smith	USA 44	44.5#	1			San Jose	20 May 67	(45.25)
	Evans		A44.5	1			S.Lake Tahoe	12 Sep 69	
J.	Smith		44.5	1		NCAA	Eugene	3 Jun 72	

(11/8)
Adolph	Plummer	USA 38	44.6*	1			Tempe	25 May 63	

All-time Lists – Men

Benny	Brown	USA 53	44.7*	1		Westwood	5 May 73	(45.08)
Ken	Randle	USA 54	44.8*	1		Westwood	3 May 75	44.99
Warren	Edmondson	USA 50	44.8*	2	ITA	Atlanta	25 Apr 76	45.51

* = 440 Yards less 0.3 seconds. # = During 440 Yards race.

800 METRES

Sebastian	Coe	UK 56	1:41.73 &		(1)		Firenze	10 Jun 81
Joaquim	Carvalho Cruz	BRA 63	1:41.77		(1)		Koln	26 Aug 84
Sam	Koskei	KEN 61	1:42.28		(2)		Koln	26 Aug 84
	Coe		1:42.33		(1)	BISL	Oslo	5 Jul 79
	Carvalho Cruz		1:42.34		(1)	WK	Zurich	22 Aug 84
	Carvalho Cruz		1:42.41		(1)	VD	Bruxelles	24 Aug 84
Johnny	Gray	USA 60	1:42:46		(1)		Koblenz	29 Aug 84
	Carvalho Cruz		1:43.00		(1)	OG	Los Angeles	6 Aug 84
	Gray		1:43.28		(2)	VD	Bruxelles	24 Aug 84
	Gray		1:43.28		(3)		Koln	26 Aug 84
	Koskei		1:43.28		(2)		Koblenz	29 Aug 84
Alberto	Juantorena	CUB 50	1:43.44		(1)	WUG	Sofia	21 Aug 77
Rick	Wohlhuter	USA 48	1:43.5 *	m	(1)		Eugene	8 Jun 74
	Juantorena		1:43.50		(1)	OG	Montreal	25 Jul 76
	Koskei		1:43.51		(2)	WK	Zurich	22 Aug 84
Mike	Boit	KEN 49	1:43.57		(1)	ISTAF	Berlin	20 Aug 76
	Gray		1:43.59		(1)		Rieti	2 Sep 84
Steve	Cram	UK 60	1:43.61		(1)		Oslo	23 Aug 83
Agberto	Guimaraes	BRA 57	1:43.63		(3)		Koblenz	29 Aug 84
	Juantorena		1:43.64		(1)	WK	Zurich	24 Aug 77
	Coe		1:43.64		(2)	OG	Los Angeles	6 Aug 84
Willi	Wulbeck	FRG 54	1:43.65		(1)	WORLD C.	Helsinki	9 Aug 83

(22/10)

Marcello	Fiasconaro	ITA 49	1:43.7	m	(1)	V CSR	Milano	27 Jun 73
Earl	Jones	USA 64	1:43.74		(1)	FOT	Los Angeles	19 Jun 84
Olaf	Beyer	GDR 57	1:43.84		(1)	EC	Praha	31 Aug 78
John	Kipkurgat	KEN 44	1:43.85		(1)	BCG	Christchurch	29 Jan 74
Ivo	Van Damme	BEL 54	1:43.86		(2)	OG	Montreal	25 Jul 76
Donato	Sabia	ITA 63	1:43.88		(1)		Firenze	13 Jun 84
Jose	Marajo	FRA 54	1:43.9	m	(1)		Saint Maur	12 Sep 79
John	Marshall	USA 63	1:43.92		(3)	FOT	Los Angeles	19 Jun 84
James	Robinson	USA 54	1:43.92		(4)	FOT	Los Angeles	19 Jun 84
William	Wuycke	VEN 58	1:43.93		(2)		Rieti	2 Sep 84

(20)

Peter	Elliott	UK 62	1:43.98		(2)		Oslo	23 Aug 83
Billy	Konchellah	KEN 61	1:44.03		(4)	OG	Los Angeles	6 Aug 84
Luciano	Susanj	YUG 48	1:44.07		(1)	EC	Roma	4 Sep 74
Steve	Ovett	UK 55	1:44.09		(2)	EC	Praha	31 Aug 78
Edwin	Koech	KEN 61	1:44.12		(2)S1	OG	Los Angeles	5 Aug 84
Juma	N'Diwa	KEN 60	1:44.20		(1)		Munchen	6 Jul 83
Rob	Druppers	HOL 62	1:44.20		(2)	WORLD C.	Helsinki	9 Aug 83
James	Maina Boi	KEN 54	1:44.24		(1)	WK	Zurich	15 Aug 79
Vasiliy	Matveyev	SU 62	1:44.25		(1)	IZV	Kiev	22 Jun 84
Don	Paige	USA 56	1:44.29		(1)		Rieti	4 Sep 83

(30)

Peter	Snell	NZL 38	1:44.3	+m	(1)		Christchurch	3 Feb 62
Jim	Ryun	USA 47	1:44.3	*m	(1)	USTFF	Terre Haute	10 Jun 66
Dave	Wottle	USA 50	1:44.3	m	(1)	FOT	Eugene	1 Jul 72
Jose Luis	Barbosa	BRA 61	1:44.3	m	(1)	NC	Sao Paulo	26 Jun 83
Said	Aouita	MOR 60	1:44.38		(1)		Lausanne	30 Jun 83
David	Mack	USA 61	1:44.39		(1)R1		Koblenz	31 Aug 83
Ralph	Doubell	AUS 45	1:44.40		(1)	OG	Mexico, D.F.	15 Oct 68

All-time Lists – Men

Pekka	Vasala	FIN 48	1:44.5	m	(1)		V SWE	Helsinki	20 Aug 72
Danie	Malan	RSA 50	1:44.5	*m	(2)			Los Angeles	27 May 73
Garry	Cook	UK 58	1:44.55		(4)			Koblenz	29 Aug 84

(40)

Wilson	Kiprugut	KEN 38	1:44.57		(2)		OG	Mexico, D.F.	15 Oct 68
James	Mays	USA 59	1:44.62		(1)		DNG	Stockholm	2 Jul 84
Ikem	Billy	UK 64	1:44.65		(1)			Oslo	21 Jul 84
Dicky	Broberg	RSA 49	1:44.7	m	(1)			Stellenbosch	31 Mar 71
David	Patrick	USA 60	1:44.70		(1)		TAC	Indianapolis	19 Jun 83
Andreas	Busse	GDR 59	1:44.72		(1)		OT	Potsdam	10 May 80
Viktor	Kalinkin	SU 60	1:44.73		(2)		IZV	Kiev	22 Jun 84
Peter	Bourke	AUS 58	1:44.78		(1)		NC	Brisbane	20 Mar 82
Ken	Swenson	USA 48	1:44.80		(1)		V FRG	Stuttgart	16 Jul 70
Detlef	Wagenknecht	GDR 59	1:44.81		(2)		NC	Jena	8 Aug 81

(50)

* = 880 yards time less 0.6   + = made during 880 yards race   &= photo-cell time

1000 METRES

Sebastian	Coe	UK 56	2:12.18		(1)			Oslo	11 Jul 81
	Coe		2:13.40		(1)		BISL	Oslo	1 Jul 80
Rick	Wohlhuter	USA 48	2:13.9	m	(1)			Oslo	30 Jul 74
Joaquim	Carvalho Cruz	BRA 63	2:14.09		(1)		NIK	Nice	20 Aug 84
Willi	Wulbeck	FRG 54	2:14.53		(2)		BISL	Oslo	1 Jul 80
	Carvalho Cruz		2:14.54		(1)		PRE	Eugene	21 Jul 84
Steve	Cram	UK 60	2:15.12		(1)		COKE	London	17 Sep 82
Andreas	Busse	GDR 59	2:15.25		(1)			Berlin	31 Jul 83
	Carvalho Cruz		2:15.28		(1)			Bern	29 Jul 83
Mike	Boit	KEN 49	2:15.3		(1)			Wattenscheid	23 Sep 77
Ivo	Van Damme	BEL 54	2:15.5		(1)			Namur	14 Jul 76
Said	Aouita	MOR 60	2:15.75		(1)			Grosseto	18 Aug 83
Agberto	Guimaraes	BRA 57	2:15.81		(2)			Bern	29 Jul 83
	Cram		2:15.84		(1)			London	7 Aug 82
Steve	Ovett	UK 55	2:15.91		(1)			Koblenz	6 Sep 79
	Boit		2:15.98		(1)			Nice	20 Aug 78
	Cram		2:15.98		(1)			Loughborough	17 Jun 84
Danie	Malan	RSA 50	2:16.0		(1)			Munchen	24 Jun 73
Vladimir	Malozemlin	SU 56	2:16.0	m	(1)			Kiev	11 Jun 81
	Boit		2:16.03		(1)		NIK	Nice	23 Aug 81

(20/13)

Tom	Byers	USA 55	2:16.1	m	(1)			Kobenhavn	6 Aug 81
Jurgen	May	GDR 42	2:16.2		(1)			Erfurt	20 Jul 65
Franz-Josef	Kemper	FRG 45	2:16.2		(1)			Hannover	21 Sep 66
James	Maina	KEN 54	2:16.25		(3)			Koblenz	6 Sep 79
James	Robinson	USA 54	2:16.3	m	(2)			Kobenhavn	6 Aug 81
Andreas	Hauck	GDR 60	2:16.3	m	(1)			Potsdam	12 Jul 84
Thomas	Wessinghage	FRG 52	2:16.4		(3)			Wattenscheid	23 Sep 77

(20)

Nikolay	Shirokov	SU 55	2:16.4		(2)			Kiev	11 Jun 81
Steve	Scott	USA 56	2:16.40		(2)		NIK	Nice	23 Aug 81
Bodo	Tummler	FRG 43	2:16.5		(2)			Hannover	21 Sep 66
Jim	Spivey	USA 60	2:16.54	m	(2)		PRE	Eugene	21 Jul 84
William	Wuyke	VEN 58	2:16.56		(3)			Bern	29 Jul 83
John	Walker	NZL 52	2:16.57		(3)		BISL	Oslo	1 Jul 80
Sammy	Koskei	KEN 61	2:16.58		(2)			Byrkjelo	3 Jul 83
Peter	Snell	NZL 38	2:16.6		(1)			Auckland	12 Nov 64
Antonio	Paez	SPA 56	2:16.64		(4)		BISL	Oslo	1 Jul 80
Siegfried	Valentin	GDR 36	2:16.7	m	(1)			Potsdam	19 Jul 60

(30)

189

All-time Lists – Men

Detlef	Wagenknecht	GDR 59	2:16.7	m	(1)		Berlin	26 May 82
Jose'	Marajo	FRA 54	2:16.8	m	(1)		Paris	17 Jun 80
Vitaliy	Tishchenko	SU 57	2:16.8	m	(3)		Kiev	11 Jun 81
Graham	Williamson	UK 60	2:16.82		(1)		Edinburgh	17 Jul 84
Pierre	Deleze	SWZ 58	2:16.87		(4)		Bern	29 Jul 83
Francesco	Arese	ITA 44	2:16.9	m	(1)		Torino	11 Oct 70
Jurgen	Straub	GDR 53	2:16.92		(1)		Potsdam	13 Jul 80
Marcel	Philippe	FRA 51	2:17.0		(1)		Paris	28 Jun 73
Byron	Dyce	JAM 48	2:17.0	m	(2)		Kobenhavn	15 Aug 73
Lutz	Zauber	GDR 58	2:17.0	m	(2)		Berlin	26 May 82
(40)								
Rob	Druppers	HOL 62	2:17.07		(3)	PRE	Eugene	21 Jul 84
Riccardo	Materazzi	ITA 63	2:17.14		(1)		Pisa	Jun 84
Rodney	Dixon	NZL 50	2:17.2	m	(4)		Oslo	30 Jul 74
Vladimir	Sheronov	SU 55	2:17.2	m	(1)		Podolsk	30 Aug 78
Rob	Harrison	UK 59	2:17.20		(1)		London	18 Aug 84
Johnny	Gray	USA 60	2:17.27		(2)		London	18 Aug 84
Harald	Norpoth	FRG 42	2:17.3	m	(3)		Hannover	21 Sep 66
Hans-Peter	Ferner	FRG 56	2:17.3	m	(3)		Kobenhavn	6 Aug 81
Joel	Ngetich	KEN 55	2:17.34		(3)		Koln	22 Aug 82
Johan	Fourie	RSA 59	2:17.34		(1)		Pretoria	14 Mar 84
(50)								

1500 METRES

Steve	Ovett	UK 55	3:30.77		(1)		Rieti	4 Sep 83
Sydney	Maree	USA 56	3:31.24		(1)		Koln	28 Aug 83
	Ovett		3:31.36		(1)		Koblenz	27 Aug 80
Said	Aouita	MOR 60	3:31.54		(1)	FBK	Hengelo	6 Jul 84
	Ovett		3:31.57		(1)	BGP	Budapest	29 Jul 81
Thomas	Wessinghage	FRG 52	3:31.58		(2)		Koblenz	27 Aug 80
Steve	Cram	UK 60	3:31.66		(1)	VD	Bruxelles	26 Aug 83
Sebastian	Coe	UK 56	3:31.95		(1)	DNG	Stockholm	7 Jul 81
	Ovett		3:31.95		(1)		Milano	8 Jul 81
Harald	Hudak	FRG 57	3:31.96		(3)		Koblenz	27 Jul 80
Steve	Scott	USA 56	3:31.96		(1)		Koblenz	26 Aug 81
	Coe		3:32.03		(1)	WK	Zurich	15 Aug 79
	Ovett		3:32.09		(1)		Oslo	15 Jul 80
	Ovett		3:32.11		(1)	VD	Bruxelles	4 Sep 79
	Maree		3:32.12		(1)	VD	Bruxelles	27 Aug 82
Filbert	Bayi	TAN 53	3:32.16		(1)	BCG	Christchurch	2 Feb 74
	Coe		3:32.19		(1)	WK	Zurich	13 Aug 80
	Maree		3:32.30		(1)		Hamburg	12 Sep 81
	Scott		3:32.33		(1)		Lausanne	14 Jul 82
	Coe		3:32.39		(1)	WK	Zurich	22 Aug 84
(20/9)								
John	Walker	NZL 52	3:32.4	m	(1)		Oslo	30 Jul 75
Pierre	Deleze	SWZ 58	3:32.97		(2)R1	WK	Zurich	24 Aug 83
Jim	Ryun	USA 47	3:33.1	m	(1)	V BR.C	Los Angeles	8 Jul 67
Jose Manuel	Abascal	SPA 58	3:33.12		(2)	G.GALA	Roma	14 Sep 82
Ben	Jipcho	KEN 43	3:33.16		(3)	BCG	Christchurch	2 Feb 74
Jose Luis	Gonzalez	SPA 57	3:33.44		(2)	VD	Bruxelles	26 Aug 83
Ray	Flynn	IRL 57	3:33.5	+m	(2)		Oslo	7 Jul 82
Mike	Boit	KEN 49	3:33.67	+	(2)	VD	Bruxelles	28 Aug 81
Jurgen	Straub	GDR 53	3:33.68		(1)		Potsdam	31 Aug 79
Willi	Wulbeck	FRG 54	3:33.74		(4)		Koblenz	27 Aug 80
David	Moorcroft	UK 53	3:33.79		(1)		Hengelo	27 Jul 82
(20)								
John	Robson	UK 57	3:33.83		(2)	VD	Bruxelles	4 Sep 79
Rod	Dixon	NZL 50	3:33.89		(4)	BCG	Christchurch	2 Feb 74
Steve	Lacy	USA 56	3:33.99		(4)		Oslo	15 Jul 80
Todd	Harbour	USA 59	3:33.99		(2)	WK	Zurich	18 Aug 82

All-time Lists – Men

Jean	Wadoux	FRA 42	3:34.0	m	(1)		Colombes	23 Jul 70
Graham	Wiliamson	UK 60	3:34.01		(3)	BISL	Oslo	28 Jun 83
Andreas	Busse	GDR 59	3:34.10		(1)	OD	Potsdam	21 Jul 84
Omer	Khalifa	SUD 53	3:34.11		(5)		Koblenz	27 Aug 80
Jim	Spivey	USA 60	3:34.19		(5)	WK	Zurich	22 Aug 84
Mike	Hillardt	AUS 61	3:34.20		(1)		Sydney	11 March 84
(30)								
Graham	Crouch	AUS 48	3:34.22		(5)	BCG	Christchurch	2 Feb 74
Johan	Fourie	RSA 59	3:34.3	m	(1)		Port Elizabeth	21 Mar 84
Philippe	Dien	FRA 57	3:34.52		(2)		Viareggio	27 Jul 83
Joseph	Chesire	KEN 57	3:34.52		(4)	OG	Los Angeles	11 Aug 84
Chuck	Aragon	USA 59	3:34.7	+	(3)		Oslo	21 Jul 84
Uwe	Becker	FRG 55	3:34.84		(3)		Koblenz	31 Aug 83
Dragan	Zdravkovic	YUG 59	3:34.85		(2)	EP/B	Praha	20 Aug 83
Jan	Kubista	CSR 60	3:34.87		(3)	EP/B	Praha	20 Aug 83
Igor	Lotarev	SU 64	3:34.88		(2)	OD	Potsdam	21 Jul 84
Kipchoge	Keino	KEN 40	3:34.91		(1)	OG	Mexico, D.F.	20 Oct 68
(40)								
Kipkoech	Cheruiyot	KEN 64	3:34.92		(1)		Munchen	26 Jul 83
Jose	Marajo	FRA 54	3:34.93		(3)		Rieti	4 Sep 83
Wilson	Waigwa	KEN 49	3:35.0	+	(2)		Koblenz	31 Aug 83
Alex	Gonzalez	FRA 51	3:35.07		(3)	VD	Bruxelles	4 Sep 79
Steve	Crabb	UK 63	3:35.16		(4)	BISL	Oslo	28 Jun 84
Craig	Masback	USA 55	3:35.28		(3)		Lausanne	14 Jul 82
John	Gregorek	USA 60	3:35.3	+	(6)	BISL	Oslo	26 Jun 82
Vladimir	Malozemlin	SU 56	3:35.4		(1)R2		Sochi	23 May 80
Olaf	Beyer	GDR 57	3:35.58		(3)	WP	Roma	5 Sep 81
Herb	Elliott	AUS 38	3:35.6	m	(1)	OG	Roma	6 Sep 60
(50)								

+ = during 1 mile race

ONE MILE

Sebastian	Coe	UK 56	3:47.33		(1)	VD	Bruxelles	28 Aug 81
Steve	Scott	USA 56	3:47.69		(1)		Oslo	7 Jul 82
Steve	Ovett	UK 55	3:48.40		(1)		Koblenz	26 Aug 81
	Coe		3:48.53		(1)	WK	Zurich	19 Aug 81
	Scott		3:48.53		(1)	BISL	Oslo	26 Jun 82
	Ovett		3:48.8	m	(1)	BISL	Oslo	1 Jul 80
Sydney	Maree	USA 56	3:48.83		(1)		Rieti	9 Sep 81
	Maree		3:48.85		(2)	BISL	Oslo	26 Jun 82
	Coe		3:48.95		(1)		Oslo	17 Jul 79
John	Walker	NZL 52	3:49.08		(2)		Oslo	7 Jul 82
	Scott		3:49.21		(1)	ISTAF	Berlin	17 Aug 83
	Ovett		3:49.25		(1)		Oslo	11 Jul 81
David	Moorcroft	UK 53	3:49.34		(3)	BISL	Oslo	26 Jun 82
	Walker		3:49.4	m	(1)		Goteborg	12 Aug 75
	Maree		3:49.42		(1)		Cork	13 Jul 82
Mike	Boit	KEN 49	3:49.45		(2)	VD	Bruxelles	28 Aug 81
	Scott		3:49.49		(1)		Oslo	9 Jul 83
	Walker		3:49.50		(4)	BISL	Oslo	26 Jun 82
Said	Aouita	MOR 60	3:49.54		(1)	WK	Zurich	22 Aug 84
Steve	Cram	UK 60	3:49.65		(1)		Koblenz	29 Aug 84
Jose-Luis	Gonzalez	SPA 57	3:49.67		(2)		Oslo	11 Jul 81
(21/10)								
Ray	Flynn	IRL 57	3:49.77		(3)		Oslo	7 Jul 82
Thomas	Wessinghage	FRG 52	3:49.98		(3)	ISTAF	Berlin	17 Aug 83
Todd	Harbour	USA 59	3:50.34		(5)		Oslo	11 Jul 81
Pierre	Deleze	SWZ 58	3:50.38		(4)		Koblenz	25 Aug 82
Jim	Spivey	USA 60	3:50.59		(2)		Oslo	9 Jul 83

All-time Lists – Men

Graham	Williamson	UK 60	3:50.64		(4)		Cork	13 Jul 82
Wilson	Waigwa	KEN 49	3:50.73		(3)		Koblenz	31 Aug 83
Tom	Byers	USA 55	3:50.84		(6)		Koblenz	25 Aug 82
Jose	Marajo	FRA 54	3:50.98		(4)		Oslo	9 Jul 83
Filbert	Bayi	TAN 53	3:51.0	m	(1)	KING	Kingston	17 May 75
(20)								
Jim	Ryun	USA 47	3:51.1	m	(1)	AAU	Bakersfield	23 Jun 67
Johan	Fourie	RSA 59	3:51.23		(1)		Port Elizabeth	7 Mar 84
John	Gregorek	USA 60	3:51.34		(6)	BISL	Oslo	26 Jun 82
Rich	Harris	USA 59	3:51.39		(3)		Koblenz	29 Aug 84
Jack	Buckner	UK 61	3:51.57		(4)		Koblenz	29 Aug 84
Eamonn	Coghlan	IRL 52	3:51.59		(5)		Oslo	9 Jul 83
Chuck	Aragon	USA 59	3:51.62		(3)		Oslo	21 Jul 84
Jose Manuel	Abascal	SPA 58	3:51.71		(1)	G.GALA	Roma	1 Sep 83
Suleiman	Nyambui	TAN 53	3:51.94		(4)		Lausanne	14 Jul 81
Craig	Masback	USA 55	3:52.02		(3)		Oslo	17 Jul 79
(30)								
Pascal	Thiebaut	FRA 59	3:52.02		(4)		Oslo	21 Jul 84
Ben	Jipcho	KEN 43	3:52.17		(1)	DNG	Stockholm	2 Jul 73
Marty	Liquori	USA 49	3:52.2	m	(2)	KING	Kingston	17 May 75
Dragan	Zdravkovic	YUG 59	3:52.24		(5)	ISTAF	Berlin	17 Aug 83
Vittorio	Fontanella	ITA 53	3:52.31		(6)	WK	Zurich	19 Aug 81
Mike	Hillardt	AUS 61	3:52.34		(1)	JEROME	Burnaby	16 Jul 84
Uwe	Becker	FRG 55	3:52.36		(7)		Koblenz	25 Aug 82
Robert	Nemeth	AUT 58	3:52.42		(3)		Rieti	9 Sep 81
John	Robson	UK 57	3:52.44		(8)		Oslo	11 Jul 81
Frank	O'Mara	IRL 60	3:52.50		(3)		Cork	13 Jul 83
(40)								
Jozef	Plachy	CS 49	3:52.59		(2)	DNG	Stockholm	3 Jul 78
Alex	Gonzalez	FRA 51	3:52.78		(6)		Lausanne	14 Jul 81
Joaquim	Carvalho Cruz	BRA 63	3:53.00		(2)	PEPSI	Westwood	13 May 84
Francis	Gonzalez	FRA 52	3:53.02		(8)		Lausanne	14 Jul 81
Kipchoge	Keino	KEN 40	3:53.1	m	(1)	EAFR CH	Kisumu	10 Sep 67
Tony	Waldrop	USA 51	3:53.2	m	(1)	PENN R.	Philadelphia	27 Apr 74
Ian	Stewart II	UK 60	3:53.20		(8)		Koblenz	25 Aug 82
Dave	Wottle	USA 50	3:53.3	m	(1)		Eugene	20 Jun 73
Rick	Wohlhuter	USA 48	3:53.3	m	(1)	USTFF	Wichita	31 May 75
Andreas	Busse	GDR 59	3:53.55		(2)	ISTAF	Berlin	20 Aug 82
(50)								

2000 METRES

John	Walker	NZL 52	4:51.4		m(1)	BISL	Oslo	30 Jun 76
Thomas	Wessinghage	FRG 52	4:52.20		(1)		Ingelheim	31 Aug 82
Steve	Scott	USA 56	4:54.71		(2)		Ingelheim	31 Aug 82
Michel	Jazy	FRA 36	4:56.2		m(1)		Saint Maur	12 Oct 66
Johan	Fourie	RSA 59	4:56.5		m(1)		Stellenbosch	23 Apr 84
Pierre	Deleze	SWZ 58	4:56.51		(1)		Bern	3 Aug 83
	Walker		4:56.8		m(1)		Goteborg	30 Aug 75
Willy	Polleunis	BEL 47	4:57.1		m(1)		Louvain	21 Sep 78
	Fourie		4:57.2		m(1)		Stellenbosch	22 Feb 83
	Deleze		4:57.27		(1)		Lancenthal	27 Jul 84
Eamonn	Coghlan	EIR 52	4:57.66		(1)		London	29 Aug 83
Steve	Ovett	UK 55	4:57.71		(1)		Oslo	7 Jul 82
Harald	Norpoth	FRG 42	4:57.8		m(1)		Hagen	10 Sep 66
	Ovett		4:57.82		(1)		London	3 Jun 78
	Polleunis		4:58.1		m(1)		Saint Maur	27 Sep 78
Francis	Gonzalez	FRA 52	4:58.1		m(1)		Rennes	22 Jun 79
Peter	Wirz	SWZ 60	4:58.29		(2)		Lancenthal	27 Jul 84
Graham	Williamson	UK 60	4:58.38		(2)		London	29 Aug 83
	Jazy		4:58.4		m(1)		Chambery	24 Sep 66
	Wessinghage		4:58.42		(2)		Oslo	7 Jul 82
(20/13)								

All-time Lists – Men

Stefano	Mei	ITA 63	4:58.65		(1)		Viareggio	15 Aug 84
Sebastian	Coe	UK 56	4:58.84		(1)		Bordeaux	5 Jun 82
Rich	Harris	USA 59	4:59.04		(2)		Viareggio	15 Aug 84
Filbert	Bayi	TAN 53	4:59.21		(1)		Schaan	17 Sep 78
Todd	Harbour	USA 59	4:59.28		(3)	NIK	Nice	14 Aug 82
Ray	Flynn	EIR 57	4:59.40		(1)		Stuttgart	29 Aug 82
Markus	Ryffel	SWZ 55	4:59.54		(2)		Schaan	17 Sep 78
(20)								
Robert	Nemeth	AUT 58	4:59.56		(1)		Klagenfurt	8 Aug 84
Nick	Rose	UK 51	4:59.57		(2)		London	3 Jun 78
Alex	Gonzalez	FRA 51	4:59.59		(2)		Bordeaux	5 Jun 82
Jurgen	Straub	GDR 53	4:59.6		m(1)		Potsdam	5 Jul 80
Suleiman	Nyambui	TAN 53	4:59.71		(3)		Schaan	17 Sep 78
Emiel	Puttemans	BEL 47	4:59.8		m(1)		Landen	12 Aug 73
Peter	Daenens	BEL 60	4:59.8		(1)		Neerpelt	19 Aug 83
Gianni	Del Buono	ITA 43	5:00.0		m(1)		Reggio Emilia	24 Sep 72
Craig	Masback	USA 55	5:00.11		(5)		Bordeaux	5 Jun 82
John	Gregorek	USA 60	5:00.19		(3)		Oslo	7 Jul 82
(30)								
Tim	Hutchings	UK 58	5:00.37		(3)		London	29 Aug 83
Karl	Fleschen	FRG 55	5:00.4		m(2)	BISL	Oslo	30 Jun 76
Klaus-Peter	Hildenbrand	FRG 52	5:00.6		m(3)	BISL	Oslo	30 Jun 76
Fernando	Mamede	POR 51	5:00.8		m(1)		Lisboa	10 Jun 84
Joao	Campos	POR 58	5:00.8		m(2)		Lisboa	10 Jun 84
Bob	Verbeeck	BEL 60	5:00.9		(2)		Neerpelt	19 Aug 83
Dragan	Zdravkovic	YUG 59	5:01.0		m(1)		Titovo Uzice	24 Sep 82
Eamonn	Martin	UK 58	5:01.09		(1)		Belfast	19 Jun 84
Jose-Manuel	Abascal	SPA 58	5:01.1		m(1)		Santander	27 Jul 84
Josef	Odlozil	CSR 38	5:01.2		m(1)		Stara Boleslav	8 Sep 65
(40)								
Joost	Borm	HOL 56	5:01.27		(7)		Bordeaux	5 Jun 82
Steve	Foley	AUS 57	5:01.3		m(1)		Adelaide	22 Dec 79
Steve	Prefontaine	USA 51	5:01.4		m(1)		Coos Bay	9 May 75
Rodney	Dixon	NZL 50	5:01.67		(2)		London	4 Jul 75
Sydney	Maree	USA 56	5:01.69		(2)		Stuttgart	29 Aug 82
Laszlo	Kispal	HUN 53	5:01.9		m(1)		Budapest	17 May 78
Jack	Buckner	UK 61	5:01.90		(4)		London	29 Aug 83
Uwe	Becker	FRG 55	5:02.00		(1)		Munchen	20 Jul 84
Anders	Garderud	SWE 46	5:02.09		(3)		London	4 Jul 75
Boguslaw	Maminski	POL 55	5:02.12		(3)		Stuttgart	29 Aug 82
(50)								

3000 METRES

Henry	Rono	KEN 52	7:32.1	m	(1)	BISL	Oslo	27 Jun 78
David	Moorcroft	UK 53	7:32.79		(1)		London	17 Jul 82
Said	Aouita	MOR 60	7:33.3	m	(1)	VD	Bruxelles	24 Aug 84
Sydney	Maree	USA 56	7:33.37		(2)		London	17 Jul 82
Brendan	Foster	UK 48	7:35.2		m(1)		Gateshead	3 Aug 74
Doug	Padilla	USA 56	7:35.84		(1)		Oslo	9 Jul 83
Steve	Scott	USA 56	7:36.69		(1)		Ingelheim	1 Sep 81
Thomas	Wessinghage	FRG 52	7:36.75		(2)		Ingelheim	1 Sep 81
John	Walker	NZL 52	7:37.49		(3)		London	17 Jul 82
Emiel	Puttemans	BEL 47	7:37.6	m	(1)		Arhus	14 Sep 72
Eamonn	Coghlan	IRL 52	7:37.60		(1)	BISL	Oslo	1 Jul 80
Rudy	Chapa	USA 57	7:37.70		(1)		Eugene	10 May 79
	Coghlan		7:38.39		(1)	VD	Bruxelles	26 Aug 83
	Wessinghage		7:38.89		(2)	BISL	Oslo	1 Jul 80
	Coghlan		7:39.08		(1)	BISL	Oslo	5 Jul 79
Peter	Koech	KEN 58	7:39.09		(4)		London	17 Jul 82
Filbert	Bayi	TAN 53	7:39.27		(3)	BISL	Oslo	1 Jul 80
	Wessinghage		7:39.34		(1)		Koln	22 Aug 82
Kipchoge	Keino	KEN 40	7:39.5		m(1)		Hasingborg	27 Aug 65
(20/16)								

193

All-time Lists – Men

Antonio	Leitao	POR 60	7:39.69		(2)	VD	Bruxelles	26 Aug 83
Bill	McChesney	USA 59	7:40.19		(2)		Koln	22 Aug 82
Suleiman	Nyambui	TAN 53	7:40.3	m	(2)	BISL	Oslo	27 Jun 78
Nick	Rose	UK 51	7:40.4	m	(3)	BISL	Oslo	27 Jun 78
Dragan	Zdravkovic	YUG 59	7:40.49		(2)		Oslo	9 Jul 83
(20)								
Wilson	Waigwa	KEN 49	7:40.52		(4)	VD	Bruxelles	26 Aug 83
Wodajo	Bulti	ETH 57	7:40.64		(5)	VD	Bruxelles	26 Aug 83
Eamonn	Martin	UK 58	7:40.94		(3)		Oslo	9 Jul 83
Rodney	Dixon	NZL 50	7:41.0	m	(1)		Milano	2 Jul 74
Francis	Gonzalez	FRA 52	7:41.00		(2)		Lausanne	18 Jul 79
Markus	Ryffel	SWZ 55	7:41.00		(3)		Lausanne	18 Jul 79
Karl	Fleschen	FRG 55	7:41.22		(1)		Koln	22 Jul 77
Steve	Ovett	UK 55	7:41.3		(1)		Wattenscheid	23 Sep 77
Ray	Flynn	IRL 57	7:41.60		(1)		London	13 Jul 84
Dmitriy	Dmitriyev	SU 56	7:42.05		(2)		London	13 Jul 84
(30)								
Boris	Kuznetsov	SU 48	7:42.1	m	(1)		Podolsk	20 Aug 78
Ralph	King	USA 56	7:42.11		(4)		Lausanne	18 Jul 79
Dan	Glans	SWE 47	7:42.24		(4)	BISL	Oslo	5 Jul 79
Graeme	Fell	UK 59	7:42.26		(4)		Oslo	9 Jul 83
Peter	Weigt	FRG 48	7:42.38		(2)		Koln	22 Jun 77
Bronislaw	Malinowski	POL 51	7:42.4	m	(3)	BISL	Oslo	4 Jul 74
Knut	Kvalheim	NOR 50	7:42.4	m	(4)	BISL	Oslo	4 Jul 74
Dave	Lewis	UK 61	7:42.47		(5)		Oslo	9 Jul 83
Steve	Prefontaine	USA 51	7:42.6	m	(2)		Milano	2 Jul 74
Steve	Cram	UK 60	7:43.1 +		(1)		London	29 Aug 83
(40)								
Eshetu	Tura	ETH 50	7:43.18		(1)		Viareggio	3 Aug 77
Ari	Paunonen	FIN 58	7:43.20		(3)		Koln	22 Jun 77
Lasse	Viren	FIN 49	7:43.2	m	(1)		Oulu	27 Jul 72
Marty	Liquori	USA 49	7:43.23		(2)	COKE	London	9 Sep 77
Dietmar	Millonig	AUT 55	7:43.66		(2)		Lausanne	15 Aug 80
Jacques	Boxberger	FRA 49	7:43.76		(2)		Koln	15 Sep 76
Alberto	Salazar	USA 58	7:43.79		(2)		Eugene	10 May 79
Ian	Stewart II	UK 60	7:43.90		(3)	BISL	Oslo	26 Jun 82
Fernando	Mamede	POR 51	7:43.94		(6)	VD	Bruxelles	26 Aug 83
Hansjorg	Kunze	GDR 59	7:44.05		(1)		Berlin	31 Jul 83
(50)								

5000 METRES

David	Moorcroft	UK 53	13:00.41		(1)		Oslo	7 Jul 82
Said	Aouita	MOR 60	13:04.78		(1)		Firenze	13 Jun 84
Henry	Rono	KEN 52	13:06.20		(1)		Knarvik	13 Sep 81
Wodajo	Bulti	ETH 57	13:07.29		(1)		Rieti	16 Sep 82
Markus	Ryffel	SWZ 55	13:07.54		(2)	OG	Los Angeles	11 Aug 84
Antonio	Leitao	POR 60	13:07.70		(2)		Rieti	16 Sep 82
H	Rono		13:08.4	m	(1)		Berkeley	8 Apr 78
Fernando	Mamede	POR 51	13:08.54		(1)		Tokyo	17 Sep 83
H	Rono		13:08.97		(1)	DNG	Stockholm	6 Jul 82
	Leitao		13:09.20		(3)	OG	Los Angeles	11 Aug 84
Peter	Koech	KEN 58	13:09.50		(2)	DNG	Stockholm	6 Jul 82
	Mamede		13:09.92		(1)		Rieti	4 Sep 83
	Bulti		13:10.08		(2)		Firenze	13 Jun 84
Hansjorg	Kunze	GDR 59	13:10.40		(1)		Rieti	9 Sep 81
Tim	Hutchings	UK 58	13:11.50		(4)	OG	Los Angeles	11 Aug 84
Alberto	Salazar	USA 58	13:11.93		(3)	DNG	Stockholm	6 Jul 82
Valeriy	Abramov	SU 56	13:11.99		(2)		Rieti	9 Sep 81
H	Rono		13:12.15		(1)		Koblenz	26 Aug 81
Suleiman	Nyambui	TAN 53	13:12.29		(1)		Stockholm	18 Jun 79
H	Rono		13:12.34		(1)	COKE	London	11 Sep 81
(20/13)								

All-time Lists – Men

Werner	Schildhauer	GDR 59	13:12.54		(2)	WK	Zurich	18 Aug 82
Thomas	Wessinghage	FRG 52	13:12.78		(3)	WK	Zurich	18 Aug 82
Dick	Quax	NZL 48	13:12.86		(1)	DNG	Stockholm	5 Jul 77
Matt	Centrowitz	USA 55	13:12.91		(1)	PRE	Eugene	5 Jun 82
Emiel	Puttemans	BEL 47	13:13.0	m	(1)		Bruxelles	20 Sep 72
Klaus-Peter	Hildenbrand	FRG 52	13:13.69		(2)		Stockholm	5 Jul 76
Alberto	Cova	ITA 58	13:13.71		(3)		Rieti	16 Sep 82
(20)								
Miruts	Yifter	ETH 44	13:13.82		(1)	WP	Dusseldorf	4 Sep 77
Karl	Fleschen	FRG 55	13:13.88		(2)	DNG	Stockholm	5 Jul 77
Ben	Jipcho	KEN 43	13:14.4		(1)	BCG	Christchurch	29 Jan 74
Paul	Kipkoech	KEN 62	13:14.40		(5)	OG	Los Angeles	11 Aug 84
Peter	Weigt	FRG 48	13:14:54		(3)	DNG	Stockholm	5 Jul 77
Brendan	Foster	UK 48	13:14.6		(2)	BCG	Christchurch	29 Jan 74
Bill	McChesney	USA 59	13:14.80		(5)	WK	Zurich	18 Aug 82
Ilie	Floroiu	RUM 52	13:15.0		(1)	NC	Bucuresti	23 Jul 78
Marty	Liquori	USA 49	13:15.06		(2)	WP	Dusseldorf	4 Sep 77
Dietmar	Millonig	AUT 55	13:15.31		(6)	WK	Zurich	18 Aug 82
(30)								
Julian	Goater	UK 53	13:15.59		(2)	COKE	London	11 Sep 81
Martti	Vainio	FIN 50	13:16.02		(2)	BISL	Oslo	28 Jun 84
Carlos	Lopes	POR 47	13:16.38		(3)	BISL	Oslo	28 Jun 84
Lasse	Viren	FIN 49	13:16.4	m	(1)		Helsinki	14 Sep 72
Ron	Clarke	AUS 37	13:16.6	m	(1)	DNG	Stockholm	5 Jul 66
John	Treacy	IRL 57	13:16.81		(4)	BISL	Oslo	28 Jun 84
Enn	Sellik	SU 54	13:17.2	m	(1)		Podolsk	28 Jun 76
David	Bedford	UK 49	13:17.21		(1)	AAA	London	14 Jul 72
Rod	Dixon	NZL 50	13:17.27		(3)		Stockholm	5 Jul 76
Dmitriy	Dmitriyev	SU 56	13:17.37		(1)	IZV	Kiev	23 Jun 84
(40)								
David	Fitzsimons	AUS 50	13:17.42		(3)	WP	Dusseldorf	4 Sep 77
Mohamed	Kedir	ETH 53	13:17.5		(2)	PTS	Bratislava	7 Jun 80
Anders	Garderud	SWE 46	13:17.59		(4)		Stockholm	5 Jul 76
Aleksandr	Fedotkin	SU 55	13:17.66		(1)	BGP	Budapest	10 Jul 79
Bronislaw	Malinowski	POL 51	13:17.69		(5)		Stockholm	5 Jul 76
Doug	Padilla	USA 56	13:17.69		(1)		Oslo	28 Jun 83
Aleksandr	Antipov	SU 55	13:17.9		(2)	PRAV	Sochi	8 Jun 79
Nat	Muir	UK 58	13:17.9	m	(1)		Oslo	15 Jul 80
Boris	Kuznyetsov	SU 48	13:18.0	m	(2)		Podolsk	28 Jun 76
Lasse	Orimus	FIN 50	13:18.19		(6)		Stockholm	5 Jul 76
(50)								
Ralph	King	USA 56	13:18.19		(3)	PRE	Eugene	5 Jun 82

10000 METRES

Fernando	Mamede	POR 51	27:13.81		(1)	DNG	Stockholm	2 Jul 84
Carlos	Lopes	POR 47	27:17.48		(2)	DNG	Stockholm	2 Jul 84
Henry	Rono	KEN 52	27:22.478		(1)		Wien	11 Jun 78
	Mamede		27:22.95		(1)	JB	Paris	9 Jul 82
	Lopes		27:33.44		(1)		Oslo	9 Jul 83
	Lopes		27:24.39		(1)	BISL	Oslo	26 Jun 82
Werner	Schildhauer	GDR 59	27:24.95		(1)	NC	Jena	28 May 83
	Mamede		27:25.13				Oslo	9 Jul 83
Alberto	Salazar	USA 58	27:25.61		(2)	BISL	Oslo	26 Jun 82
Alex	Hagelsteens	BEL 56	27:26.95		(3)	BISL	Oslo	26 Jun 82
	Mamede		27:27.7	m	(1)		Lisboa	30 May 81
	Rono		27:28.67*		(4)	BISL	Oslo	26 Jun 82
	Salazar		27:29.06		(2)	JB	Paris	9 Jul 82
Craig	Virgin	USA 55	27:29.16		(1)		Paris	17 Jul 80
	Rono		27:29.90		(1)		Eugene	10 Apr 82
	Salazar		27:30.00		(2)		Eugene	10 Apr 82
Brendan	Foster	UK 48	27:30.3	m	(1)	AAA	London	23 Jun 78

All-time Lists – Men

Samson	Kimobwa	KEN 55	27:30.47		(1)	WG	Helsinki	30 Jun 77
Hansjorg	Kunze	GDR 59	27:30.69		(2)	NC	Jena	28 May 83
David	Bedford	UK 49	27:30.80		(1)	AAA	London	13 Jul 73
(20/11)								
Martti	Vainio	FIN 50	27:30.99		(1)	EC	Praha	29 Aug 78
Nick	Rose	UK 51	27:31.19		(3)		Oslo	9 Jul 83
Venanzio	Ortis	ITA 55	27:31.48		(2)	EC	Praha	29 Aug 78
Aleksandr	Antipov	SU 55	27:31.50		(3)	EC	Praha	29 Aug 78
Julian	Goater	UK 53	27:34.58		(5)	BISL	Oslo	26 Jun 82
Gabriel	Kamau	KEN 58	27:36.2	m	(1)	MSR	Walnut	24 Apr 82
David	Black	UK 52	27:36.27		(5)	EC	Praha	29 Aug 78
Gerard	Tebroke	HOL 49	27:36.64		(6)	EC	Praha	29 Aug 78
Mark	Nenow	USA 57	27:36.7	m	(2)	MSR	Walnut	24 Apr 82
(20)								
Karl	Fleschen	FRG 55	27:36.8	m	(1)		Troisdorf	28 Apr 79
Alberto	Cova	ITA 58	27:37.59		(2)		Lausanne	30 Jun 83
Gidamis	Shahanga	TAN 57	27:38.1	m	(3)	MSR	Walnut	24 Apr 82
Lasse	Viren	FIN 49	27:38.35		(1)	OG	Munchen	3 Sep 72
Zakariah	Barie	TAN 53	27:38.6	m	(4)	MSR	Walnut	24 Apr 82
Steve	Jones	UK 55	27:39.14		(4)		Oslo	9 Jul 83
Ron	Clarke	AUS 37	27:39.4	m	(1)		Oslo	14 Jul 65
Mohamed	Kedir	ETH 53	27:39.44		(2)	WP	Roma	4 Sep 81
Emiel	Puttemans	BEL 47	27:39:58		(2)	OG	Munchen	3 Sep 72
Mike	McLeod	UK 52	27:39.76		(1)	VD	Bruxelles	4 Sep 79
(30)								
Ilie	Floroiu	RUM 52	27:40.06		(7)	EC	Praha	29 Aug 78
Enn	Sellik	SU 54	27:40.61		(8)	EC	Praha	29 Aug 78
Miruts	Yifter	ETH 44	27:40.96		(3)	OG	Munchen	3 Sep 72
Jos	Hermens	HOL 50	27:41.25		(2)	DNG	Stockholm	4 Jul 77
Knut	Kvalheim	NOR 50	27:41.26		(9)	EC	Praha	29 Aug 78
Leon	Schots	BEL 52	27:41.34		(3)	VD	Bruxelles	4 Sep 79
Aleksandr	Fedotkin	SU 55	27:41.89		(4)	VD	Bruxelles	4 Sep 79
Mike	Musyoki	KEN 56	27:41.92		(2)	WG	Helsinki	30 Jun 77
Dick	Quax	NZL 48	27:41.95		(4)	COKE	London	9 Sep 77
Detlef	Uhlemann	FRG 49	27:42.09		(3)	DNG	Stockholm	4 Jul 77
(40)								
Franco	Fava	ITA 52	27:42.65		(3)	WG	Helsinki	30 Jun 77
Frank	Zimmermann	FRG 53	27:42.8	m	(2)		Troisdorf	28 Apr 79
Dietmar	Millonig	AUT 55	27:42.98		(6)	BISL	Oslo	26 Jun 82
Ian	Stewart	UK 49	27:43.03		(6)	COKE	London	9 Sep 77
Toshihiko	Seko	JAP 56	27:43.44		(1)	DNG	Stockholm	7 Jul 80
Tony	Simmons	UK 48	27:43.59		(4)	WG	Helsinki	30 Jun 77
Steve	Prefontaine	USA 51	27:43.6	m	(1)		Eugene	27 Apr 74
Antonio	Prieto	SPA 58	27:43.66		(3)		Lausanne	30 Jun 83
Paul	Cummings	USA 53	27:43.7	m	(1)	MSR	Walnut	28 Apr 84
Bernie	Ford	UK 52	27:43.74		(7)	COKE	London	9 Sep 77
(50)								

3000 METRES STEEPLECHASE

Henry	Rono	KEN 52	8:05.4	m	(1)		Seattle	13 May 78
Joseph	Mahmoud	FRA 55	8:07.62		(1)	VD	Bruxelles	24 Aug 84
Anders	Garderud	SWE 46	8:08.02		(1)	OG	Montreal	28 Jul 76
Bronislaw	Malinowski	POL 51	8:09.11		(2)	OG	Montreal	28 Jul 76
Boguslaw	Maminski	POL 55	8:09.18		(2)	VD	Bruxelles	24 Aug 84
	Garderud		8:09.70		(1)	DNG	Stockholm	1 Jul 75
	Malinowski		8:09.70		(1)	OG	Moskva	31 Jul 80
Frank	Baumgartl	GDR 55	8:10.36		(3)	OG	Montreal	28 Jul 76
	Garderud		8:10.4	m	(1)	V GDR NOR	Oslo	25 Jun 75
	Malinowski		8:11.63		(1)	ISTAF	Berlin	18 Aug 78

196

All-time Lists – Men

	Mahmoud		8:11.64		(1)		Koblenz	29 Aug 84
Julius	Korir	KEN 60	8:11.80		(1)	OG	Los Angeles	10 Aug 84
George Kip	Rono	KEN 58	8:12.0		(1)	G. GALA	Roma	5 Aug 80
	Malinowski		8:12.23		(1)	DNG	Stockholm	10 Aug 76
Henry	Marsh	USA 54	8:12.37		(1)	ISTAF	Berlin	17 Aug 83
H	Rono		8:12.39		(1)	NCAA	Eugene	3 Jun 78
Filbert	Bayi	TAN 53	8:12.48		(2)	OG	Moskva	31 Jul 80
Mariano	Scartezzini	ITA 54	8:12.5		(2)	G. GALA	Roma	5 Aug 80
Tapio	Kantanen	FIN 49	8:12.60		(4)	OG	Montreal	28 Jul 76
	Malinowski		8:12.62		(2)	DNG	Stockholm	1 Jul 75
	Maminski		8:12.62		(2)	ISTAF	Berlin	17 Aug 83
(21/12)								
Brian	Diemer	USA 61	8:13:16		(2)		Koblenz	29 Aug 84
Eshetu	Tura	ETH 50	8:13.57		(3)	OG	Moskva	31 Jul 80
Colin	Reitz	UK 60	8:13.78		(2)		Oslo	21 Jul 84
Ben	Jipcho	KEN 43	8:13.91		(1)	WG	Helsinki	27 Jun 73
Michael	Karst	FRG 52	8:14.05		(1)	DNG	Stockholm	5 Jul 77
Peter	Renner	NZ 59	8:14.05		(3)		Koblenz	29 Aug 84
Patriz	Ilg	FRG 57	8:15.06		(1)	WORLD C.	Helsinki	12 Aug 83
Graeme	Fell	UK 59	8:15.16		(3)	ISTAF	Berlin	17 Aug 83
(20)								
Krzysztof	Wesolowski	POL 56	8:15.28		(3)		Oslo	21 Jul 84
Dan	Glans	SWE 47	8:15.32		(3)	DNG	Stockholm	10 Aug 76
Domingo	Ramon	SPA 58	8:15.74		(4)	OG	Moskva	31 Jul 80
Gheorghe	Cefan	RUM 47	8:16.10		(2)		Stockholm	8 Jun 76
Juan	Torres	SPA 57	8:16.25		(4)		Koblenz	29 Aug 84
Francisco	Sanchez	SPA 58	8:16.59		(4)	ISTAF	Berlin	17 Aug 83
Wolfgang	Konrad	AUT 58	8:17.22		(2)	ISTAF	Berlin	20 Aug 82
Julius	Kariuki	KEN 61	8:17.47		(7)	OG	Los Angeles	10 Aug 84
Gabor	Marko	HUN 60	8:17.97		(1)	OD	Potsdam	21 Jul 84
Richard	Tuwei	KEN 54	8:18.22		(1)	FBK	Hengelo	12 Jul 83
(30)								
Ismo	Toukonen	FIN 54	8:18.29		(3)	EC	Praha	3 Sep 78
John	Gregorek	USA 60	8:18.45		(3)	FOT	Los Angeles	23 Jun 84
Giuseppe	Gerbi	ITA 55	8:18.47		(6)	OG	Moskva	31 Jul 80
Amos	Korir	KEN 56	8:18.57		(1)	PRE	Eugene	6 Jun 81
Fethi	Baccouche	TUN 60	8:18.70		(6)S2	OG	Los Angeles	8 Aug 84
William	Van Dijck	BEL 61	8:18.75		(5)		Koblenz	29 Aug 84
Franco	Fava	ITA 52	8:18.85		(4)	EC	Roma	7 Sep 74
Dennis	Coates	UK 53	8:18.95		(1)H2	OG	Montreal	25 Jul 76
Greg	Duhaime	CAN 53	8:19.05		(2)		Koblenz	25 Aug 82
Farley	Gerber	USA 60	8:19.27		(1)	NCAA	Eugene	1 Jun 84
(40)								
Doug	Brown	USA 52	8:19.29		(2)	ISTAF	Berlin	18 Aug 78
Roger	Hackney	UK 57	8:19.38		(5)	WORLD C.	Helsinki	12 Aug 83
Tommy	Ekblom	FIN 59	8:19.40		(1)	WG	Helsinki	6 Jul 83
Gerd	Frahmcke	FRG 50	8:19.44		(5)		Stockholm	8 Jun 76
Masanari	Shintaku	JAP 57	8:19.52		(2)	DNG	Stockholm	8 Jul 80
Yohannes	Mohamed	ETH 48	8:19.57		(2)	PO	Montreal	26 Jul 75
Rainer	Schwarz	FRG 59	8:19.64		(3)		Munchen	26 Jul 83
Anatoliy	Dimov	SU 56	8:19.75		(8)	OG	Moskva	31 Jul 80
Jurgen	Straub	GDR 53	8:19.8	m	(3)	V SWE NOR	Oslo	25 Jun 75
Boulam	Rahoui	ALG 48	8:20.2		(1)	MED G	Al Jazair	26 Aug 75
(50)								

MARATHON

Steve	Jones	UK 55	2:08:05		(1)		Chicago	21 Oct 84
Alberto	Salazar	USA 58	2:08:13	*	(1)		New York	25 Oct 81
Robert	De Castella	AUS 57	2:08:18		(1)		Fukuoka	6 Dec 81
Derek	Clayton	AUS 42	2:08:34		(1)		Antwerpen	30 May 69
	De Castella		2:08:37		(1)		Rotterdam	9 Apr 83

All-time Lists – Men

Toshihiko	Seko	JAP 56	2:08:38		(1)		Tokyo	13 Feb 83
Carlos	Lopes	POR 47	2:08:39		(2)		Rotterdam	9 Apr 83
	Salazar		2:08:51		(1)		Boston	19 Apr 82
	Seko		2:08:52		(1)		Fukuoka	4 Dec 83
Dick	Beardsley	USA 56	2:08:53		(2)		Boston	19 Apr 82
Takeshi	Soh	JAP 53	2:08:55		(2)		Tokyo	13 Feb 83
Juma	Ikangaa	TAN 57	2:08:55		(2)		Fukuoka	4 Dec 83
Rod	Dixon	NZL 50	2:08:59		(1)		New York	23 Oct 83
Gerard	Nijboer	HOL 55	2:09:01		(1)		Amsterdam	26 Apr 80
Greg	Meyer	USA 55	2:09:01		(1)		Boston	19 Apr 83
Shigeru	Soh	JAP 53	2:09:06		(1)		Beppu	5 Feb 78
	Lopes		2:09:06		(2)		Chicago	21 Oct 84
Geoff	Smith	UK 53	2:09:08		(2)		New York	23 Oct 83
	De Castella		2:09:09		(3)		Chicago	21 Oct 84
(19/14)								
Ian	Thompson	UK 49	2:09:12		(1)	BCG	Christchurch	31 Jan 74
Rodolfo	Gomez	MEX 50	2:09:12		(3)		Tokyo	13 Feb 83
Jorg	Peter	GDR 55	2:09:14		(1)		Berlin–Grunau	21 Jul 84
Hugh	Jones	UK 55	2:09:24		(1)		London	9 May 82
Bill	Rodgers	USA 47	2:09:27		(1)		Boston	16 Apr 79
Ron	Hill	UK 38	2:09:28		(1)	BCG	Edinburgh	23 Jul 70
(20)								
John	Graham	UK 56	2:09:28		(1)		Rotterdam	23 May 81
Michael	Heilmann	GDR 61	2:09:30		(2)		Berlin–Grunau	21 Jul 84
Ron	Tabb	USA 54	2:09:32		(2)		Boston	19 Apr 83
Kumitsu	Itoh	JAP 55	2:09:35		(6)		Fukuoka	4 Dec 83
Ernest	Seleke	RSA 59	2:09:41		(1)		Port Elizabeth	31 Mar 84
Mike	Gratton	UK 54	2:09:43		(1)		London	18 Apr 83
Joseph	Nzau	KEN 50	2:09:45		(1)		Chicago	16 Oct 83
Waldemar	Cierpinski	GDR 50	2:09:55		(1)	OG	Montreal	31 Jul 76
John	Treacy	IRL 57	2:09:56		(2)	OG	Los Angeles	12 Aug 84
Armand	Parmentier	BEL 54	2:09:57		(4)		Rotterdam	9 Apr 83
(30)								
Charles	Spedding	UK 52	2:09:57		(1)		London	13 May 84
Benji	Durden	USA 51	2:09:58		(3)		Boston	19 Apr 83
Marc	Smet	BEL 51	2:10:00		(1)	NC	Berchem	14 Sep 79
Tekeyuki	Nakayama	JAP 60	2:10:00		(1)		Fukuoka	2 Dec 84
Kebede	Balcha	ETH 51	2:10:03		(1)		Montreal	25 Sep 83
Gabriel	Kamau	KEN 58	2:10:05		(4)		Chicago	21 Oct 84
Ed	Mendoza	USA 52	2:10:07		(4)		Boston	19 Apr 83
Jerome	Drayton	CAN 45	2:10:09		(1)		Fukuoka	7 Dec 75
Garry	Henry	AUS 55	2:10:09		(4)		Fukuoka	7 Dec 80
Gerry	Helme	UK 57	2:10:12		(2)		London	18 Apr 83
(40)								
Jeff	Wells	USA 54	2:10:15		(2)		Boston	17 Apr 78
Paul	Ballinger	NZL 53	2:10:15		(1)		Fukuoka	5 Dec 82
Simeon	Kigen	KEN 61	2:10:18		(1)		San Francisco	19 Aug 84
Tony	Sandoval	USA 54	2:10:19		(1)	FOT	Niagara Falls	24 May 80
Gidamis	Shahanga	TAN 57	2:10:19		(1)		Los Angeles	19 Feb 84
David	Chettle	AUS 51	2:10:20		(1)		Fukuoka	7 Dec 75
Garry	Bjorklund	USA 51	2:10:20		(1)		Duluth	21 Jun 80
Craig	Virgin	USA 55	2:10:26		(2)		Boston	20 Apr 81
Kirk	Pfeffer	USA 56	2:10:29		(7)		Fukuoka	7 Dec 80
Martin	Pitayo	MEX 60	2:10:29		(6)		Chicago	21 Oct 84
(50)								

* 1981 New York course recently found to be short

110 METRES HURDLES

Renaldo	Nehemiah	USA 59	12.93	−0.2	(1)	WK	Zurich	19 Aug 81
	Nehemiah		13.00	0.9	(1)	PEPSI	Westwood	6 May 79
Greg	Foster	USA 58	13.03	−0.2	(2)	WK	Zurich	19 Aug 81

All-time Lists – Men

	Nehemiah		13.04	0.0	(1)		Koblenz	26 Aug 81
	Nehemiah		13.07	−0.1	(1)		Koln	23 Aug 81
	Nehemiah		13.07	0.3	(1)	VD	Bruxelles	28 Aug 81
G	Foster		13.10	0.8	(1)	PEPSI	Westwood	10 May 81
G	Foster		13.11	−0.4	(1)	PEPSI	Westwood	15 May 83
G	Foster		13.15	−0.8	(1)	TAC	Indianapolis	18 Jun 83
G	Foster		13.15	−1.1	(1)	WK	Zurich	22 Aug 84
	Nehemiah		13.16	1.7			San Jose	14 Apr 79
G	Foster		13.16	−0.1	(1)	ISTAF	Berlin	17 Aug 84
Roger	Kingdom	USA 62	13.16	−1.1	(2)	WK	Zurich	22 Aug 84
	Nehemiah		13.17	0.8	(1)	AAA	London	8 Aug 81
Sam	Turner	USA 57	13.17	−0.4	(2)	PEPSI	Westwood	15 May 83
	Kingdom		13.17	−0.1	(2)	ISTAF	Berlin	17 Aug 84
G	Foster		13.18	2.0	(1)	CAL R.	Modesto	16 May 81
	Nehemiah		13.19	1.5	(1)	AAU	Walnut	16 Jun 79
G	Foster		13.19	0.5	(1)H1	FOT	Los Angeles	18 Jun 84
	Kingdom		13.19	0.6	(1)	NIK	Nice	20 Aug 84
(20/4)								
Alejandro	Casanas	CUB 54	13.21	0.6	(1)	WUG	Sofia	21 Aug 77
Tonie	Campbell	USA 60	13.23	1.1	(2)	PEPSI	Westwood	13 May 84
Rod	Milburn	USA 50	13.24	0.3	(1)	OG	Munchen	7 Sep 72
Willie	Gault	USA 60	13.26	1.6	(1)	USOC SF	Indianapolis	25 Jul 82
Mark	McKoy	CAN 61	13.27	1.5	(1)R2		Walnut	25 Jul 84
Guy	Drut	FRA 50	13.28	1.1	(1)		Saint Etienne	29 Jun 75
(10)								
Willie	Davenport	USA 43	A 13.33	0.0	(1)	OG	Mexico, D.F.	17 Oct 68
Dedy	Cooper	USA 56	13.34	1.8	(2)	LITE	Houston	3 May 80
Arto	Bryggare	FIN 58	13.35	2.0	(1)H1	OG	Los Angeles	5 Aug 84
Thomas	Munkelt	GDR 52	13.37	2.0	(1)	EP	Helsinki	14 Aug 77
Ervin	Hall	USA 47	A 13.38	1.8	(1)S1	OG	Mexico, D.F.	17 Oct 68
Jerry	Wilson	USA 50	13.38	1.6	(1)	AAU	Eugene	20 Jun 75
Larry	Cowling	USA 60	13.39	1.9	(1)	V GDR	Karl-Marx-Stadt	10 Jul 82
Charles	Foster	USA 53	13.41	0.0	(4)	OG	Montreal	28 Jul 76
Cletus	Clark	USA 62	13.41	−0.7	(2)	MSR	Walnut	29 Apr 84
Tom	Hill	USA 49	13.42*	0.0	(1)	AAU	Bakersfield	26 Jun 70
(20)								
Earl	McCullouch	USA 46	13.43	1.8	(1)	PAT	Minneapolis	16 Jul 67
Marcus	Walker	USA 49	13.43*	0.0	(2)	AAU	Bakersfield	26 Jun 70
Mark	Holtom	UK 58	13.43	1.9	(2)	CG	Brisbane	4 Oct 82
Stephane	Caristan	FRA 64	13.43	1.4	(1)		San Diego	30 Jul 84
Aleksandr	Puchkov	SU 57	13.44	0.9	(3)	OG	Moskva	27 Jul 80
Leon	Coleman	USA 44	13.45*	0.7	(1)=	AAU	Miami	28 Jun 69
Kerry	Bethel	USA 57	A 13.45	1.6	(1)	USOC SF	Colorado Springs	30 Jul 78
Henry	Andrade	USA 62	13.45	1.8	(3)S2	FOT	Los Angeles	19 Jun 84
Georgy	Bakos	HUN 60	13.45	1.4	(2)	8 NAT	Tokyo	14 Sep 84
Eddy	Ottoz	ITA 44	A 13.46	0.0	(3)	OG	Mexico, D.F.	17 Oct 68
(30)								
James	Owens	USA 55	13.46	1.8	(3)	NCAA	Eugene	2 Jun 78
Milan	Stewart	USA 60	13.46	1.7	(3)	MSR	Walnut	25 Apr 82
Andrey	Prokofyev	SU 59	13.46	−0.9	(2)	EC	Athinai	11 Sep 82
Plamen	Krastev	BUL 58	13.46	−0.3	(1)	V HUN GRE FRG	Athinai	10 Jul 84
Frank	Siebeck	GDR 49	13.47	1.8	(1)	DNG	Stockholm	1 Jul 75
Viktor	Myasnikov	SU 48	13.47	1.8	(2)	V USA	Berkeley	Jul 78
Holger	Pohland	GDR 63	13.47	1.9	(2)	V USA	Karl-Marx-Stadt	10 Jul 82
John	Johnston	USA 60	13.47	1.6	(1)H4	NCAA	Eugene	31 May 84
Garnett	Edwards	USA 56	13.48	1.7	(2)S1	NCAA	Champaign	1 Jun 79
John	Timpson	USA 62	13.48	1.8	(1)		Baton Rouge	21 Apr 84
(40)								
Andreas	Oschkenat	GDR 62	13.50	0.9	(2)	NC	Karl-Marx-Stadt	16 Jun 83
Javier	Moracho	SPA 57	13.52	0.0	(4)		Koblenz	26 Aug 81
Richmond	Flowers	USA 47	A 13.53*	−0.2	(2)	NCAA	Provo	16 Jun 67

199

All-time Lists – Men

Jan	Pusty	POL 52	13.53	0.6	(2)	WUG	Sofia	21 Aug 77	
Dan	Lavitt	USA 58	13.53	0.9	(1)		Waco	18 Apr 80	
James	Quinn	USA 63	13.53	0.4	(1)		Athens, GA.	5 May 84	
Yuriy	Chervanyev	SU 58	13.54	−0.3	(1)H1	PRAV	Moskva	11 Jun 80	
Karl Werner	Donges	FRG 58	13.54	0.8	(1)	8 NAT	Tokyo	24 Sep 82	
Nikolay	Shilev	BUL 63	13.54	1.2	(1)		Sofia	6 May 84	
Ricky	Stubbs	USA 51	13.55*	0.0	(2)S2	NCAA	Baton Rouge	8 Jun 73	
(50)									
Larry	Shipp	USA 54	13.55*	0.9	(1)S1	TEX R.	Austin	4 Apr 75	
Miroslaw	Wodzynski	POL 51	13.55		(1)		Warszawa	29 May 75	
Vyacheslav	Kulebyakin	SU 50	13.55	0.6	(3)	WUG	Sofia	21 Aug 77	
Julius	Ivan	CS 54	13.55	0.0	(1)	NC	Ostrava	30 Aug 81	
James	McCraney	USA 55	13.55	1.3	(1)		Walnut	3 Jun 84	
(55)									

Marks made with assisting wind

Renaldo	Nehemiah	USA 59	12.91	3.5	(1)	NCAA	Champaign	1 Jun 79	
	Nehemiah		13.00	3.5	(1)	USOC SF	Syracuse	26 Jul 81	
Roger	Kingdom	USA 62	13.00	2.7	(1)		Sacramento	21 Jul 84	
Mark	McKoy	CAN 61	13.16	2.7	(2)		Sacramento	21 Jul 84	
	Nehemiah		13.18	2.1	(1)	ISTAF	Berlin	21 Aug 81	
(5/3)									
Henry	Andrade	USA 62	13.28	2.7	(3)		Sacramento	21 Jul 84	
Ricky	Stubbs	USA 51	13.36*	3.5	(1)	TEX R	Austin	13 Apr 74	
Charles	Foster	USA 53	13.38*	2.3	(1)	NCAA	Austin	7 Jun 74	
Albert	Lane	USA 62	13.38	3.4	(1)H3	NCAA	Eugene	31 May 84	
Colin	Williams	USA	13.39		(1)		Dallas	1 Apr 78	
Cletus	Clark	USA 62	13.39	3.3	(1)		Edinburgh	17 Jul 84	
Efrem	Gipson	USA 49	13.41*	3.5	(2)	TEX R	Austin	13 Apr 74	
(10)									
James	McCraney	USA 55	13.43	3.2	(4)		Modesto	12 May 84	
Milan	Stewart	USA 60	13.44	4.5	(1)	CAL R	Modesto	15 May 82	
Jack	Pierce	USA 62	13.44	2.4	(1)H3	WUG	Edmonton	10 Jul 83	
Rodney	Wilson	USA 61	13.46	2.3	(1)		Houston	28 May 83	
Larry	Shipp	USA 54	13.48*	2.3	(2)	NCAA	Austin	7 Jun 74	
Orlando	McDaniel	USA 60	13.53	3.0	(1)H1	NCAA	Austin	6 Jun 80	
Julius	Ivan	CS 54	13.54	4.3	(1)	EP/REP	Athinai	2 Aug 81	
Malcom	Dixon	USA 59	13.54	2.3	(2)		Houston	28 May 83	
Romuald	Giegel	POL 57	13.54	4.0	(1)	KUSOC	Lublin	17 Jun 83	
Dan	Oliver	USA 57	13.55	3.5	(2)	NCAA	Champaign	1 Jun 79	
(20)									
Carlos	Sala	SPA 60	13.55	5.2	(2)	MED G	Dar-el-Beida	16 Sep 83	
(21)									

400 METRES HURDLES

Edwin	Moses	USA 55	47.02		(1)		Koblenz	31 Aug 83	
	Moses		47.13		(1)		Milano	3 Jul 80	
	Moses		47.14		(1)		Lausanne	14 Jul 81	
	Moses		47.17		(1)	ISTAF	Berlin	8 Aug 80	
	Moses		47.27		(1)	ISTAF	Berlin	21 Aug 81	
	Moses		47.32		(1)		Koblenz	29 Aug 84	
	Moses		47.37		(1)	WP	Roma	4 Sep 81	
	Moses		47.37		(1)	WK	Zurich	24 Aug 83	
	Moses		47.43		(1)		Koln	28 Aug 83	
	Moses		47.45		(1)	AAU	Westwood	11 Jun 77	
Harald	Schmid	FRG 57	47.48		(1)	EC	Athinai	8 Sep 82	
	Moses		47.50		(1)	WORLD C.	Helsinki	9 Aug 83	
	Moses		47.53		(1)	WP	Montreal	24 Aug 79	
	Moses		47.58		(1)	WP	Dusseldorf	2 Sep 77	
	Moses		47.58		(1)S1	FOT	Los Angeles	17 Jun 84	

All-time Lists – Men

	Moses		47.59	(1)	TAC	Sacramento	21 Jun 81
	Moses		47.63	(1)	OG	Montreal	25 Jul 76
	Moses		47.64	(1)	WK	Zurich	19 Aug 81
	Moses		47.67	(1)		Oslo	17 Jul 79
	Moses		47.69	(1)	LITE	Durham	19 May 79
	Schmid		47.69	(1)		Lausanne	10 Jul 84
(21/2)							
Andre	Phillips	USA 59	47.48	(2)		Koln	28 Aug 83
John	Akii-Bua	UGA 49	47.82	(1)	OG	Munchen	2 Sep 72
Danny	Harris	USA 65	48.02	(2)S1	FOT	Los Angeles	17 Jun 84
David	Patrick	USA 60	48.05	(2)	WK	Zurich	24 Aug 83
David	Hemery	UK 44	A 48.12	(1)	OG	Mexico D.F.	15 Oct 68
Tony	Rambo	USA 60	48.16	(3)S1	FOT	Los Angeles	17 Jun 84
Tranel	Hawkins	USA 62	48.28	(3)	FOT	Los Angeles	18 Jun 84
Vasiliy	Arkhipyenko	SU 57	48.34	(2)	EP	Torino	4 Aug 79
(10)							
Quentin	Wheeler	USA 55	48.39	(2)	AAU	Walnut	17 Jun 79
David	Lee	USA 59	48.42	(4)	WK	Zurich	24 Aug 83
Harry	Schulting	HOL 56	A 48.44	(1)	WUG	Mexico, D.F.	12 Sep 79
Aleksandr	Vasilyev	SU 61	48.45	(1)	IZV	Kiev	22 Jun 84
Larry	Cowling	USA 60	A 48.46	(2)	NCAA	Provo	4 Jun 82
James	Walker	USA 57	48.48	(1)	SEC	Tuscaloosa	13 May 79
Uwe	Ackermann	GDR 60	48.50	(1)	V USA	Karl-Marx-Stadt	9 Jul 82
Ralph	Mann	USA 49	48.51	(2)	OG	Munchen	2 Sep 72
Jim	Bolding	USA 49	48.55	(1)		Paris	8 Jul 75
Tom	Andrews	USA 54	48.55	(1)	AAU	Westwood	12 Jun 76
(20)							
Volker	Beck	GDR 56	48.58	(3)	EP	Torino	4 Aug 79
Alan	Pascoe	UK 47	48.59	(1)	DNG	Stockholm	30 Jun 75
Aleksandr	Yatsevich	SU 56	48.60	(2)	EC	Athinai	8 Sep 82
Bart	Williams	USA 56	48.63	(2)		Lausanne	10 Jul 84
Jim	Seymour	USA 49	48.64	(4)	OG	Munchen	2 Sep 72
Mike	Shine	USA 53	48.69	(2)	OG	Montreal	25 Jul 76
Paul	Montgomery	USA 61	A 48.73	(3)	NCAA	Provo	4 Jun 82
Elhadj	Amadou Dia Ba	SEN 58	48.73	(1)	VD	Bruxelles	24 Aug 84
Vladimir	Budko	SU 65	48.74	(2)		Moskva	18 Aug 84
Aleksandr	Kharlov	SU 58	48.78	(1)	SPART	Moskva	20 Jun 83
(30)							
Sven	Nylander	SWE 62	48.88	(1)	NCAA	Houston	3 Jun 83
Geoff	Vanderstock	USA 46	A 48.94	(1)	FOT	Echo Summit	11 Sep 68
Jean-Claude	Nallet	FRA 47	48.94	(2)	EC	Roma	4 Sep 74
Nikolay	Vasilyev	SU 56	A 48.98	(1)S2	WUG	Mexico, D.F.	11 Sep 79
Toma	Tomov	BUL 58	48.99	(1)		Sofia	8 Aug 84
Wesley	Williams	USA 48	49.00	(5)	AAU	Westwood	12 Jun 76
James	King	USA 49	49.00	(2)		Bratislava	7 Sep 79
Gerhard	Hennige	FRG 40	A 49.02	(2)	OG	Mexico, D.F.	15 Oct 68
Yevgeniy	Gavrilyenko	SU 51	49.02	(1)	V FRG	Munchen	30 May 76
John	Sherwood	UK 45	A 49.03	(3)	OG	Mexico, D.F.	15 Oct 68
(40)							
Sam	Turner	USA 57	49.04	(3)		Lausanne	13 Jul 78
Jon	Thomas	USA 63	49.04	(2)	NCAA	Houston	3 Jun 83
Ron	Whitney	USA 42	A 49.06	(1)H3	OG	Mexico, D.F.	13 Oct 68
Hartmut	Weber	FRG 60	49.10	(1)		Dortmund	15 May 82
Bernie	Holloway	USA 61	A 49.10	(4)	NCAA	Provo	4 Jun 82
Rok	Kopitar	YUG 59	49.11	(1)		Maribor	3 Jun 80
Gary	Oakes	UK 58	49.11	(3)	OG	Moskva	26 Jul 80
Vyacheslav	Skomorokhov	SU 40	A 49.12	(5)	OG	Mexico, D.F.	15 Oct 68
Roberto	Frinolli	ITA 40	A 49.14	(1)S1	OG	Mexico, D.F.	14 Oct 68
Rainer	Schubert	FRG 41	A 49.15	(2)H3	OG	Mexico, D.F.	13 Oct 68
(50)							

All-time Lists – Men

Hand timing

Jim	Bolding	USA 49	48.1	1		Milano	2 Jul 74	48.55
Ralph	Mann	USA 49	48.4	1	FOT	Eugene	2 Jul 72	48.51
Aleksandr	Yatsevich	SU 56	48.5	1		Kiev	9 Aug 82	48.60
Jean-Claude	Nallet	FRA 47	48.6	1	vUSA	Colombes	8 Jul 70	48.94
Aleksandr	Cheshko	SU 58	48.7	1		Cherkassy	3 Sep 82	(49.65)
Wayne	Collett	USA 49	48.9*	2	NCAA	Des Moines	20 Jun 70	
Gerhardus	Potgieter	RSA 37	A49.0*	1	NC	Bloemfontein	16 Apr 60	(49.46)
William	Koskei	KEN 47	A49.0	1		Nairobi	27 May 72	(49.34)

HIGH JUMP

Zhu	Jianhua	CHN 63	2.39		(1)		Eberstadt	10 Jun 84
	Jianhua		2.38		(1)	NC	Shangai	22 Sep 83
	Jianhua		2.37		(1)		Beijing	11 Jun 83
Carlo	Thranhardt	FRG 57	2.37 i		(1)		Berlin	24 Feb 84
Valeriy	Sereda	SU 59	2.37		(1)		Rieti	2 Sep 84
	Thranhardt		2.37		(2)		Rieti	2 Sep 84
Gerd	Wessig	GDR 59	2.36		(1)	OG	Moskva	1 Aug 80
Igor	Paklin	SU 63	2.36 i		(1)	V ITA SPA	Milano	1 Feb 84
Sergey	Zasimovich	SU 62	2.36		(1)		Tashkent	5 May 84
	Thranhardt		2.36		(2)		Eberstadt	10 Jun 84
Dietmar	Mogenburg	FRG 61	2.36		(3)		Eberstadt	10 Jun 84
Vladimir	Yaschenko	SU 59	2.35 i		(1)	EC	Milano	12 Mar 78
Jacek	Wszola	POL 56	2.35		(1)		Eberstadt	25 May 80
	Mogenburg		2.35		(1)		Rehlingen	26 May 80
	Sereda		2.35		(1)	SPART	Moskva	19 Jun 83
	Jianhua		2.35		(1)		Guangzhou	5 Mar 84
	Mogenburg		2.35		(1)	OG	Los Angeles	11 Aug 84
	Jianhua		2.35		(1)		Shangai	22 Sep 84
(18/9)								
Paul	Frommeyer	FRG 57	2.34		(1)		Recke	17 Jun 83
Eddy	Annys	BEL 58	2.34		(1)	NC	Bruxelles	23 Jul 83
Sorin	Matei	RUM 63	2.34		(1)		Bucuresti	9 Jun 84
Dwight	Stones	USA 53	2.34		(1)	FOT	Los Angeles	24 Jun 84
Jeff	Woodard	USA 58	2.33 i		(1)	TAC	New York	27 Feb 81
Aleksey	Demyanyuk	SU 58	2.33		(1)	V USA	Leningrad	11 Jul 81
Patrik	Sjoberg	SWE 65	2.33		(1)		Oslo	9 Jul 83
Tyke	Peacock	USA 61	2.33		(1)	ISTAF	Berlin	17 Aug 83
Javier	Sotomayor	CUB 67	2.33		(1)	BARR	Habana	19 May 84
Aleksandr	Kotovich	SU 61	2.33		(1)	NAR	Sofia	20 May 84
Vladimir	Granyenkov	SU 59	2.33		(1)		Moskva	5 Aug 84
(20)								
Jim	Howard	USA 59	2.33		(1)		London	18 Aug 84
Franklin	Jacobs	USA 57	2.32 i		(1)		New York	27 Jan 78
Janusz	Trzepizur	POL 59	2.32 i		(2)	EC	Milano	6 Mar 82
Roland	Dalhauser	SWZ 58	2.32 i		(3)	EC	Milano	6 Mar 82
Gennadiy	Byelkov	SU 56	2.32		(1)		Tashkent	29 May 82
Milton	Ottey	CAN 59	2.32		(1)	NCAA	Provo	4 Jun 82
Del	Davis	USA 60	2.32		(2)	NCAA	Provo	4 Jun 82
J. Fransisco	Centelles	CUB 61	2.32		(1)	PTS	Bratislava	4 Jun 83
Gennadiy	Avdeyenko	SU 63	2.32		(1)	WORLD C.	Helsinki	13 Aug 83
Franck	Verzy	FRA 61	2.32		(1)	EP	London	20 Aug 83
(30)								
Rolf	Beilschmidt	GDR 53	2.31		(1)	EP	Helsinki	13 Aug 77
Greg	Joy	CAN 56	2.31 i		(1)		College Park	13 Jan 78
Jorg	Freimuth	GDR 61	2.31		(3)	OG	Moskva	1 Aug 80
Gerd	Nagel	FRG 57	2.31		(2)		Eberstadt	7 Jun 81
Milton	Goode	USA 60	2.31 i		(1)		New York	12 Feb 82
Stephen	Wray	BAH 62	2.31		(2)	CG	Brisbane	7 Oct 82
Jerome	Carter	USA 63	2.31 i		(1)		Fairfax	16 Jan 83
Constantin	Militaru	RUM 63	2.31 i		(1)		Sofia	11 Feb 84

All-time Lists – Men

Dennis	Lewis	USA 59	2.31 i		(1)	TAC	New York	24 Feb 84	
Doug	Nordquist	USA 58	2.31		(2)	FOT	Los Angeles	24 Jun 84	
(40)									
Dariusz	Zielke	POL 60	2.31		(1)		Warszawa	12 Aug 84	
Andreas	Sam	GDR 60	2.31		(1)		Praha	28 Aug 84	
Brent	Harken	USA 61	2.31		(2)	G. GALA	Roma	31 Aug 84	
Aleksandr	Grigoryev	SU 55	2.30		(1)		Riga	5 Jun 77	
Henry	Lauterbach	GDR 57	2.30		(1)		Potsdam	19 Aug 78	
Benn	Fields	USA 54	2.30		(1)		Valparaiso	1 Nov 78	
Andre	Schneider	FRG 58	2.30		(1)	ISTAF	Berlin	17 Aug 79	
Massimo	Di Giorgio	ITA 58	2.30		(1)		Udine	13 Jun 81	
Nick	Saunders	BER 63	2.30 i		(1)	IC4A	Princeton	6 Mar 83	
Ricky	Thompson	USA 59	2.30		(1)		Houston	28 May 83	
(50)									
James	Barrineau	USA 55	2.30		(2)	USOC SF	Colorado Springs	2 Jul 83	
Takao	Sakamoto	JAP 58	2.30		(1)		Tokyo	6 May 84	
Vadim	Oganyan	SU 63	2.30		(2)		Tashkent	13 May 84	
(53)									

POLE VAULT

Sergey	Bubka	SU 63	5.94		(1)	G. GALA	Roma	31 Aug 84	
Thierry	Vigneron	FRA 60	5.91		(2)	G. GALA	Roma	31 Aug 84	
	Bubka		5.90		(1)	TALBOT	London	13 Jun 84	
	Bubka		5.88		(1)		Saint Denis	2 Jun 84	
	Vigneron		5.85 i		(1)	EC	Goteborg	4 Mar 84	
	Bubka		5.85		(1)	PTS	Bratislava	26 May 84	
Konstantin	Volkov	SU 60	5.85		(1)	IZV	Kiev	22 Jun 84	
	Vigneron		5.83		(1)	G. GALA	Roma	1 Sep 83	
	Bubka		5.83 i		(1)		Inglewood	10 Feb 84	
Pierre	Quinon	FRA 62	5.82		(1)		Koln	28 Aug 83	
	Bubka		5.82 i		(1)	V ITA SPA	Milano	1 Feb 84	
Mike	Tully	USA 56	5.82		(1)	PRE	Eugene	21 Jul 84	
Aleksandr	Krupskiy	SU 60	5.82		(1)	BGP	Budapest	20 Aug 84	
Vladimir	Polyakov	SU 60	5.81		(1)	V GDR	Tbilisi	26 Jun 81	
	Bubka		5.81 i		(1)		Vilnius	15 Jan 84	
	Tully		5.81		(1)	FOT	Los Angeles	21 Jun 84	
	Vigneron		5.80		(1)	V UK SPA	Macon	20 Jun 81	
Billy	Olson	USA 58	5.80 i		(1)		Toronto	4 Feb 83	
	Quinon		5.80		(1)	NIK	Nice	18 Jul 83	
	Olson		5.80 i		(2)		Inglewood	10 Feb 84	
	Krupskiy		5.80		(1)	ZNAM	Sochi	9 Jun 84	
Earl	Bell	USA 55	5.80		(1)	TAC	San Jose	9 Jun 84	
	Quinon		5.80		(1)		Lausanne	10 Jul 84	
	Polyakov		5.80		(1)		Moskva	19 Jul 84	
	Volkov		5.80		(1)		Moskva	17 Aug 84	
	Bubka		5.80		(1)	NC	Donyetsk	8 Sep 84	
(26/9)									
Wladyslaw	Kozakiewicz	POL 53	5.78		(1)	OG	Moskva	30 Jul 80	
Philippe	Houvion	FRA 57	5.77		(1)		Paris	17 Jul 80	
Jeff	Buckingham	USA 60	5.76		(1)		Lawrence	16 Jul 83	
Dave	Volz	USA 62	5.75		(1)	NIK	Nice	14 Aug 82	
Jean Michel	Bellot	FRA 53	5.75		(1)		Colombes	25 Sep 82	
Brad	Pursley	USA 60	5.75		(1)		Abilene	29 Mar 83	
Pavel	Bogatyryov	SU 61	5.75		(2)	ZNAM	Sochi	9 Jun 84	
Aleksandr	Obizhayev	SU 59	5.74 i		(1)		Moskva	12 Feb 83	
Larry	Jessee	USA 52	5.73		(1)		Vanves	27 Apr 84	
Dan	Ripley	USA 53	5.72		(1)T	TAC	Knoxville	20 Jun 82	
Atanas	Tarev	BUL 58	5.72		(1)	NC	Sofia	2 Jun 84	
(20)									
Felix	Bohni	SWZ 58	5.71		(1)		Bern	11 Jun 83	

203

All-time Lists – Men

Aleksandr	Chernyayev	SU 60	5.71		(1)		Chernigov	2 Jul 83
Doug	Lytle	USA 62	5.71		(2)	FOT	Los Angeles	21 Jun 84
Serge	Ferreira	FRA 59	5.71		(1)		Creteil	23 Jun 84
Dave	Roberts	USA 51	5.70		(1)	FOT	Eugene	22 Jun 76
Sergey	Kulibaba	SU 59	5.70		(1)	V USA	Leningrad	10 Jul 81
Viktor	Spasov	SU 59	5.70 i		(1)	EC	Milano	7 Mar 82
Nikolay	Selivanov	SU 58	5.70		(1)		Moskva	16 Jun 83
Patrick	Abada	FRA 54	5.70		(1)	VD	Bruxelles	26 Aug 83
Tadeusz	Slusarski	POL 50	5.70		(2)	VD	Bruxelles	26 Aug 83
(30)								
Vasiliy	Bubka	SU 60	5.70 i		(1)		Moskva	1 Mar 84
Sergey	Smolyakov	SU 62	5.70		(3)		Moskva	19 Jul 84
Antti	Kalliomaki	FIN 47	5.66		(1)		Raahe	13 Jul 80
Jurgen	Winkler	FRG 59	5.66		(1)		Rhede	29 Jul 83
Joe	Dial	USA 62	5.66		(1)		Norman	27 Apr 84
Keith	Stock	UK 57	5.65		(1)	DNG	Stockholm	7 Jul 81
Gunther	Lohre	FRG 53	5.65		(1)	NC	Munchen	25 Jul 82
Ivo	Yanchev	BUL 60	5.65		(1)	V POL HUN	Sofia	23 Jul 83
Peter	Volmer	FRG 58	5.65 i		(1)		Nordlingen	23 Feb 84
Rodion	Gataullin	SU 65	5.65		(2)	NC	Donyestsk	8 Sep 84
(40)								
Bob	Seagren	USA 46	5.63		(1)	FOT	Eugene	2 Jul 72
Frantisek	Jansa	CSR 62	5.62		(1)		Praha	3 Sep 83
Steve	Smith	USA 51	5.61 i		(1)	ITA	New York	28 May 75
Vladimir	Trofimenko	SU 53	5.61		(1)	V GDR POL	Vilnius	24 Jun 78
Miro	Zalar	SWE 57	5.61		(2)	WK	Zurich	24 Aug 83
Dave	Kenworthy	USA 60	5.61		(4T)	FOT	Los Angeles	21 Jun 84
Yuriy	Prokhoryenko	SU 51	5.60		(1)		Leningrad	21 Jun 80
Tom	Hintnaus	USA 58	5.60		(1)	FOT	Eugene	27 Jun 80
Rauli	Pudas	FIN 54	5.60		(2)		Raahe	13 Jul 80
Mariusz	Klimczyk	POL 56	5.60		(3)	NIK	Nice	17 Aug 80
(50)								
Patrick	Desruellees	BEL 57	5.60 i		(4)	EC	Grenoble	22 Feb 81
Viktor	Sobolyev	SU 60	5.60		(1)		Donyetsk	30 Jul 81
Aleksandr	Parnov	SU 59	5.60		(2)	SPART	Moskva	22 Jun 83
Vladimir	Shulgin	SU 61	5.60		(3)	SPART	Moskva	22 Jun 83
Philippe	Collet	FRA 63	5.60		(1)		Pescara	11 Aug 83
Leonid	Ivanushkin	SU 61	5.60		(1)		Minsk	27 Aug 83
Greg	Woepse	USA 57	5.60		(1)		Long Beach	24 Mar 84
Steve	Stubblefield	USA 61	5.60		(1)	KANSAS R.	Lawrence	21 Apr 84
Anton	Paskalev	BUL 58	5.60		(3)	NC	Sofia	2 Jun 84
Marian	Kolasa	POL 59	5.60		(1)		Sopot	6 Jul 84
(60)								
Arkadiy	Shkvira	SU 60	5.60		(3T)	NC	Donyetsk	8 Sep 84
Nat	Durham	USA 54	5.60 i		(1)		Saskatoon	29 Dec 84
(62)								

LONG JUMP

Bob	Beamon	USA 46	A 8.90	2.0	(1)	OG	Mexico, D.F.	18 Oct 68
Carl	Lewis	USA 61	8.79	1.9	(1)	TAC	Indianapolis	19 Jun 83
	Lewis		8.79 i		(1)		New York	27 Jan 84
	Lewis		8.76	1.0	(1)	USOC SF	Indianapolis	24 Jul 82
	Lewis		8.71	−0.4	(1)	PEPSI	Westwood	13 May 84
	Lewis		8.71	0.1	(1)	FOT	Los Angeles	19 Jun 84
	Lewis		8.65	0.2	(1)	VD	Bruxelles	24 Aug 84
	Lewis		8.62	0.8	(1)	TAC	Sacramento	20 Jun 81
	Lewis		8.61	0.5	(1)	PEPSI	Westwood	16 May 82
Larry	Myricks	USA 56	8.59	1.3	(1)		Rhede	5 Sep 84
	Lewis		8.58	0.0	(1)	WK	Zurich	18 Aug 82
	Lewis		8.56 i		(1)		East Rutherford	16 Jan 82
	Myricks		8.56	0.5	(1)		Rhede	1 Sep 82

204

All-time Lists – Men

#	First	Last	Club/Nat	Mark	Wind	(n)	Meet	Venue	Date
		Lewis		8.56	1.0	(1)	PEPSI	Westwood	15 May 83
		Lewis		8.55 i		(1)	TAC	New York	26 Feb 82
		Lewis		8.55	1.2	(1)	WORLD C.	Helsinki	10 Aug 83
		Lewis		8.55 i		(1)		East Rutherford	11 Feb 84
		Lewis		8.55	−1.6	(1)	OG	Los Angeles	6 Aug 84
Lutz		Dombrowski	GDR 59	8.54	0.9	(1)	OG	Moskva	28 Jul 80
		Lewis		8.54 i		(1)		New York	28 Jan 83
(20/4)									
Nenad		Stekic	YUG 51	8.45	2.0	(1)	PO	Montreal	25 Jul 75
Jason		Grimes	USA 59	8.39	1.1	(2)	TAC	Indianapolis	19 Jun 83
Konstantin		Syemikin	SU 60	8.38	0.4	(1)		Moskva	17 Aug 84
Jaime		Jefferson	CUB 62	8.37	0.4	(2)		Moskva	17 Aug 84
Joao Carlos		De Oliveira	BRA 54	8.36	1.0	(1)		Rieti	21 Jul 79
Frank		Paschek	GDR 56	8.36	1.6	(1)	OD	Berlin	28 May 80
(10)									
Ralph		Boston	USA 39	8.35	0.0	(1)	CAL R.	Modesto	29 May 65
Igor		Ter-Ovanesyan	SU 38	A 8.35	0.0	(1)	PO	Mexico, D.F.	19 Oct 67
Josef		Schwarz	FRG 35	8.35	0.8	(1)	V USA	Stuttgart	15 Jul 70
Arnie		Robinson	USA 48	8.35	−0.6	(1)	OG	Montreal	29 Jul 76
Henry		Lauterbach	GDR 57	8.35	2.0	(1)		Erfurt	2 Aug 81
Randy		Williams	USA 53	8.34	0.0	(Q)	OG	Munchen	8 Sep 72
Sergey		Rodin	SU 63	8.33	1.0	(1)		Leningrad	27 Jul 83
Reggie		Kelly	USA 62	8.33 i		(1)		Jackson	3 Dec 83
Sergey		Layevskiy	SU 59	8.32	0.1	(1)	NC	Donyetsk	8 Sep 84
Atanas		Atanasov	BUL 56	8.31	0.7	(1)		Sofia	4 Jul 84
(20)									
Aleksandr		Beskrovniy	SU 60	8.28		(1)		Moskva	29 May 83
Mike		Conley	USA 62	8.28	0.5	(2)	NCAA	Houston	3 Jun 83
Vadim		Kobyalyanskiy	SU 61	8.28	0.1	(2)	NC	Donyetsk	8 Sep 84
Grzegorz		Cybulski	POL 51	8.27	0.5	(1)	KUSOC	Warszawa	20 Jun 75
Mike		Mcrae	USA 55	8.27	2.0	(1)	TAC	San Jose	9 Jun 84
Gary		Honey	AUS 59	8.27	1.2	(1)	BGP	Budapest	20 Aug 84
Laszlo		Szalma	HUN 57	8.27	−0.7	(2)		Koln	26 Aug 84
Charlton		Ehizuelen	NIG 53	8.26 i		(1)		Bloomington	7 Mar 75
Jacques		Rousseau	FRA 51	8.26	1.4	(-)	NC	Lille	26 Jun 76
Henry		Hines	USA 49	8.25 i		(1)	ITA	New York	6 Jun 73
(30)									
James		McAlister	USA 51	8.24	1.7	(1)		Westwood	5 May 73
Giovanni		Evangelisti	ITA 61	8.24	−0.7	(3)	OG	Los Angeles	6 Aug 84
Lynn		Davies	UK 42	8.23	2.0	(1)		Bern	30 Jun 68
James		Lofton	USA 56	8.23	2.0	(2)	AAU	Westwood	9 Jun 78
Antonio		Corgos	SPA 60	8.23	0.2	(1)	NC	Madrid	24 Aug 80
Yuriy		Samarin	SU 60	8.23	0.0	(3)	NC	Donyetsk	8 Sep 84
Preston		Carrington	USA 49	8.22	0.1	(Q)	OG	Munchen	8 Sep 72
Larry		Doubley	USA 58	8.22		(1)	NCAA	Champaign	3 Jun 77
Lamonte		King	USA 59	8.22		(1)		San Jose	12 May 79
David		Giralt	CUB 59	8.22	0.6	(3)	WP	Montreal	26 Aug 79
(40)									
Uwe		Lange	GDR 54	8.22	1.6	(1)		Dresden	19 May 84
Gyula		Paloczi	HUN 62	8.22	1.7	(1)	NC	Budapest	27 Jul 84
Yuriy		Kharitonov	SU 59	8.22		(1)		Gorkiy	11 Aug 84
Valdemar		Stepien	POL 46	8.21	1.9	(1)	V GDR SU	Chorzow	12 Jul 69
Aleksey		Pereverzyev	SU 49	8.21		(1)	V UK	Kiev	22 May 76
Winifred		Klepsch	FRG 56	8.21 i		(1)	NC	Sindelfingen	7 Feb 81
Vance		Johnson	USA 63	A 8.21	2.0	(1)	NCAA	Provo	4 Jun 82
Yusuf		Alli	NIG 60	8.21	1.5	(1)	WUG	Edmonton	7 Jul 83
James		Moore	USA 51	8.20	1.5	(2)	CAL R.	Modesto	25 May 74
Andrzej		Klimaszewski	POL 60	8.20	1.9	(1)		Sopot	5 Jul 80
(50)									
Viktor		Belskiy	SU 55	8.20	1.3	(1)	NC	Kiev	21 Aug 82
(51)									

All-time Lists – Men

Marks made with assisting wind

Carl	Lewis	USA 61	8.73	4.6	(Q)	TAC	Sacramento	19 Jun 81	
	Lewis		8.73	3.2	(Q)	TAC	Indianapolis	17 Jun 83	
Larry	Myricks	USA 56	A 8.64	3.1	(1)	USOC SF	Air F. Academy	2 Jul 83	
	Lewis		8.63	2.1	(1)	PEPSI	Westwood	10 May 81	
Jason	Grimes	USA 59	8.57	5.2	(1)	V FRG AFR	Durham	27 Jun 82	
	Lewis		8.56	8.9	(1)		Sacramento	21 Jul 84	
(6/3)									
Ralph	Boston	USA 39	8.49	2.6	(1)	FOT	Los Angeles	12 Sep 64	
Randy	Williams	USA 53	8.46	3.4	(1)		Eugene	18 May 73	
Shamil	Abbyasov	SU 57	8.41	4.3	(2)	V USA	Indianapolis	3 Jul 82	
Lutz	Dombrowski	GDR 59	8.41	2.9	(1)	EC	Athinai	9 Sep 82	
Henry	Hines	USA 49	8.40	4.3	(1)	CAL R.	Modesto	27 May 72	
Gary	Honey	AUS 59	8.39	6.2	(2)		Sacramento	21 Jul 84	
Mike	Conley	USA 62	8.38	2.6	(3)	TAC	Indianapolis	18 Jun 83	
(10)									
Arnie	Robinson	USA 48	8.37	3.5	(1)	FOT	Eugene	25 Jun 76	
Jacques	Rousseau	FRA 51	8.37	2.8	(1)	NC	Lille	25 Jun 76	
Sergey	Rodin	SU 63	8.37		(1)		Moskva	6 Jul 84	
Ralph	Spry	USA 60	8.36	5.2	(1)	NCAA	Houston	3 Jun 83	
Mike	McRae	USA 55	8.34		(1)		Modesto	12 May 84	
Phil	Shinnick	USA 43	8.33		(1)	CAL R.	Modesto	25 May 63	
Charlton	Ehizuelen	NIG 53	8.33	2.1	(1)	KANS R.	Lawrence	19 Apr 75	
Andrzej	Klimaszewski	POL 60	8.33	3.7	(1)	KUSOC	Warszwa	13 Jun 80	
David	Giralt	CUB 59	8.32	3.8	(1)	WPT	Quebec	11 Aug 79	
Carl	Williams	USA 57	8.26	4.0	(1)	NAIA	Abilene	19 May 78	
(20)									
Larry	Doubley	USA 58	8.26	3.4	(1)		Los Angeles	15 Mar 80	
Lamonte	King	USA 59	8.25		(1)		Tempe	26 May 79	
Gordon	Laine	USA 58	8.24		(2)		Knoxville	19 May 84	
Norman	Tate	USA 42	A 8.23		(1)		El Paso	22 May 71	
Darrell	Horn	USA 39	8.22	5.9	(2)	SFOT	New York	3 Jul 64	
Jerry	Proctor	USA 49	8.22	3.0	(1)	NCAA	Knoxville	20 Jun 82	
Jacques	Pani	FRA 46	8.22	3.0	(1)		Colombes	5 Jul 69	
Liu	Yuhuang	CHN 59	8.22		(1)	NC	Beijing	21 Sep 81	
Danny	Seay	USA 53	8.21		(2)	CAL R.	Modesto	24 May 75	
Josh	Owusu	GHA 48	A 8.20		(2)		El Paso	22 May 71	
(30)									
Valeriy	Podluzhniy	SU 52	8.20	3.6	(1)	EP	Edinburgh	8 Sep 73	
Rolf	Bernhard	SWZ 49	8.20	2.2	(1)		Zofingen	30 May 77	
(32)									

Marks made with unknown irregularity

Yuriy	Samarin	SU 60	8.28		(1)		Kharkov	8 Jul 84	

TRIPLE JUMP

Joao Carlos	De Oliveira	BRA 54	A 17.89	0.0	(1)	PAG	Mexico, D.F.	15 Oct 75	
Keith	Connor	UK 57	A 17.57	−0.1	(1)	NCAA	Provo	5 Jun 82	
Willie	Banks	USA 56	17.56	0.8	(1)	TAC	Sacramento	21 Jun 81	
	Banks		17.55	−0.5	(1)	DNG	Stockholm	8 Jul 81	
Vasiliy	Grishchenkov	SU 58	17.55	0.3	(1)	SPART	Moskva	19 Jun 83	
Aleksandr	Beskrovniy	SU 60	17.53	1.0	(2)	SPART	Moskva	19 Jun 83	
Olyeg	Protsenko	SU 63	17.52	−0.6	(1)	IZV	Kiev	21 Jun 84	
Aleksandr	Yakovlyev	SU 57	17.50	2.0	(1)	ZNAM	Sochi	10 Jun 84	
Mike	Conley	USA 62	17.50	−0.5	(1)	FOT	Los Angeles	17 Jun 84	
Gennadiy	Valyukyevich	SU 58	17.47	−0.5	(1)		Moskva	19 Jul 84	
Ken	Lorraway	AUS 56	17.46	1.7	(1)		London	7 Aug 82	
	Valyukyevich		17.46		(1)		Moskva	7 Jul 84	

All-time Lists – Men

	Protsenko		17.46	0.5	(1)	DRZ	Moskva	18 Aug 84
	Yakovlyev		17.45	1.0	(1)		Sochi	20 May 84
Lazaro	Betancourt	CUB 63	17.45	0.1	(1)		Koln	26 Aug 84
Viktor	Sanyeyev	SU 45	17.44		(1)		Sukhumi	17 Oct 72
	De Oliveira		17.44		(1)	PTS	Bratislava	10 Jun 78
	Valyukyevich		17.42	2.0	(1)	NC	Kiev	22 Aug 82
Zdzislaw	Hoffmann	POL 59	17.42	0.6	(1)	WORLD C.	Helsinki	8 Aug 83
Khristo	Markov	BUL 65	17.42	1.3	(1)	NAR	Sofia	19 May 84
(20/14)								
Pedro	Perez Duenas	CUB 52	A 17.40	0.4	(1)	PAG	Cali	5 Aug 71
Vyacheslav	Bordukov	SU 59	17.37	0.7	(2)	NAR	Sofia	19 May 84
Jaak	Uudmae	SU 54	17.35	−0.3	(1)	OG	Moskva	25 Jul 80
Zhenxian	Zou	CHN 55	17.34	0.3	(2)	WP	Roma	5 Sep 81
Jan	Cado	CS 63	17.34	0.1	(1)	PTS	Bratislava	26 May 84
Peter	Bouschen	FRG 60	17.33	0.8	(1)	NC	Bremen	25 Jun 83
(20)								
Grigoriy	Yemets	SU 57	17.33 i		(1)	EC	Grenoble	3 Mar 84
Jorg	Drehmel	GDR 45	17.31	1.5	(2)	OG	Munchen	4 Sep 72
Shamil	Abbyasov	SU 57	17.30 i		(1)	EC	Grenoble	21 Feb 81
Nelson	Prudencio	BRA 44	A 17.27	2.0	(2)	OG	Mexico, D.F.	17 Oct 68
Bedros	Bedrosian	RUM 58	17.27	1.2	(1)		Bucuresti	9 Jun 84
Ajayi	Agbebaku	NIG 55	17.26	1.5	(1)	WUG	Edmonton	8 Jul 83
James	Butts	USA 50	17.24	0.8	(1)	WG	Helsinki	29 Jun 78
Nikolay	Musiyenko	SU 59	17.24	1.2	(1)		Sochi	27 May 84
Jaroslav	Priscak	CS 56	17.23		(1)		Praha	13 May 84
Giuseppe	Gentile	ITA 43	A 17.22	0.0	(3)	OG	Mexico, D.F.	17 Oct 68
(30)								
Vasiliy	Isayev	SU 59	17.22	1.9	(4)	ZNAM	Sochi	10 Jun 84
Aleksandr	Pokusayev	SU 60	17.21	1.6	(1)		Krasnodar	26 May 83
Vlastimil	Marinec	CS 57	17.21	0.9	(1)	PTS	Bratislava	4 Jun 83
Mikhail	Bariban	SU 49	17.20	0.1	(1)	WUG	Moskva	19 Aug 73
Tommy	Haynes	USA 52	A 17.20	0.0	(2)	PAG	Mexico, D.F.	15 Oct 75
Bela	Bakosi	HUN 57	17.20	1.8	(1)	V CSR	Budaspest	21 Aug 82
Vladimir	Brigadniy	SU 55	17.20		(1)		Ashkhabad	2 May 83
Ron	Livers	USA 55	17.19	1.0	(1)	V SU	Sochi	1 Jul 77
Paul	Jordan	USA 56	17.19	−0.3	(Q)	FOT	Los Angeles	16 Jun 84
Al	Joyner	USA 60	17.19	−0.8	(2)	FOT	Los Angeles	17 Jun 84
(40)								
Joseph	Taiwo	NIG 59	17.19		(1)	AFR CH	Rabat	13 Jul 84
Vladimir	Chernikov	SU 59	17.19	0.1	(3)	NC	Donyetsk	9 Sep 84
Robert	Cannon	USA 58	17.18	0.7	(1)	USOC SF	Indianapolis	25 Jul 82
Mike	Marlow	USA 56	17.17	0.8	(2)	TAC	Sacramento	21 Jun 81
Maris	Bruziks	SU 62	17.15		(1)		Riga	17 Jun 84
Carol	Corbu	RUM 46	17.12		(1)	V ITA GDR NOR	Torino	13 Jun 71
Volker	Mai	GDR 66	17.12	1.2	(2)	OD	Potsdam	21 Jul 84
Aleksey	Roganin	SU 59	17.10		(1)		Sochi	22 May 82
Nate	Cooper	USA 57	17.10		(1)	NCAA	Champaign	2 Jun 79
Viktor	Gerasimenya	SU 60	17.10		(1)		Riga	7 Jul 84
(50)								

Marks made with assisting wind

Keith	Connor	UK 57	17.81	4.6	(1)	CG	Brisbane	9 Oct 82
Ron	Livers	USA 55	17.56	3.7	(1)	AAU	Walnut	17 Jun 79
Zdislaw	Hoffmann	POL 59	17.55	3.6	(1)	KUSOC	Warszawa	9 Jun 84
Ken	Lorraway	AUS 56	17.54	3.2	(2)	CG	Brisbane	9 Oct 82
Lazaro	Betancourt	CUB 63	17.50	3.0	(1)	BARR	Habana	22 May 83
	Connor		17.48		(1)	JENNER	San Jose	28 May 83
Willie	Banks	USA 56	17.43	3.5	(2)	AAU	Walnut	17 Jun 79
	Yakovlyev		17.41	2.4	(2)		Moskva	18 Aug 84
(8/7)								
Milan	Tiff	USA 49	17.38	4.2	(1)	AAU	Westwood	11 Jun 77
Anatoliy	Piskulin	SU 52	17.30	3.2	(1)	WUG	Sofia	22 Aug 77
(10)								

207

All-time Lists – Men

James	Butts	USA 50	17.29	2.9	(1)	FOT	Eugene	26 Jun 76	
Bela	Bakosi	HUN 57	17.29	3.4	(1)		Hiroshima	6 May 82	
Al	Joyner	USA 60	17.26	2.1	(1)	OG	Los Angeles	4 Aug 84	
Henry	Ellard	USA 61	17.23	2.5	(1)		Fresno	1 May 82	
Ray	Kimble	USA 53	17.21	2.2	(1)		Berkeley	12 Jun 83	
David	McFadgen	USA 60	A 17.21	3.6	(1)	USOC SF	Air F. Academy	3 Jul 83	
Mike	Marlow	USA 58	17.20	2.2	(1)		Auckland	25 Jan 81	
Ian	Campbell	AUS 57	17.19	4.7	(2)		Perth	13 Jan 80	
Charles	Simpkins	USA 63	17.18	2.6	(3)	NCAA	Eugene	2 Jun 84	
Art	Walker	USA 41	A 17.12	2.5	(4)	OG	Mexico, D.F.	17 Oct 68	
(20)									
John	Craft	USA 47	17.12	2.4	(1)	FOT	Eugene	1 Jul 72	
Phil	May	AUS 45	17.10	3.0	(1)		Perth	9 Jan 71	
(22)									

Unknown irregularity

Aleksey	Roganin	SU 59	17.11		(1)		Kharkov	7 Jul 84

SHOT PUTT

Brian	Oldfield	USA 45	22.86		(1)	ITA	El Paso	10 May 75
	Oldfield		22.45		(1)	ITA	El Paso	22 May 76
	Oldfield		22.28		(1)	ITA	Edinburgh	18 Jun 75
Udo	Beyer	GDR 55	22.22		(1)	V USA	Los Angeles	25 Jun 83
	Oldfield		22.19		(1)	JENNER	San Jose	26 May 84
	Beyer		22.15		(1)		Goteborg	6 Jul 78
	Oldfield		22.11 i		(1)	ITA	Daly City	4 Apr 75
	Beyer		22.04		(1)		Rehlingen	11 Jun 84
George	Woods	USA 43	22.02 i		(1)		Inglewood	8 Feb 74
	Oldfield		22.02		(1)	CAL R.	Modesto	16 May 81
Dave	Laut	USA 56	22.02		(1)		Koblenz	25 Aug 82
Aleksandr	Baryshnikov	SU 48	22.00		(1)	V FRA	Colombes	10 Jul 76
	Beyer		22.00		(1)		Dresden	26 Jul 84
	Beyer		21.98		(1)	OT	Erfurt	18 May 80
	Beyer		21.98		(1)		Split	30 Apr 84
	Beyer		21.94		(1)	V USA	Karl-Marx-Stadt	9 Jul 82
	Laut		21.94		(1)	JENNER	San Jose	28 May 83
John	Brenner	USA 61	21.92		(1)	NCAA	Eugene	2 Jun 84
	Beyer		21.89		(1)	NC	Leipzig	30 Jun 78
(20/7)								
Terry	Albritton	USA 55	21.85		(1)		Honolulu	21 Feb 76
Al	Feuerbach	USA 48	21.82		(1)		San Jose	5 May 73
(10)								
Randy	Matson	USA 45	21.78		(1)		College Station	22 Apr 67
Mike	Carter	USA 60	21.76		(2)	NCAA	Eugene	2 Jun 84
Ulf	Timmermann	GDR 62	21.75		(1)	OD	Potsdam	21 Jul 84
Remigius	Machura	CSR 60	21.74		(1)	ROS	Praha	16 Aug 82
Janis	Bojars	SU 56	21.74		(1)		Riga	14 Jul 84
August	Wolf	USA 61	21.73		(1)		Leverkusen	12 Apr 84
Reijo	Stahlberg	FIN 52	21.69		(1)	WCR	Fresno	5 May 79
Geoff	Capes	UK 49	21.68		(1)	V HOL HUN WAL	Cwmbran	18 May 80
Edward	Sarul	POL 58	21.68		(1)		Sopot	31 Jul 83
Hartmut	Briesenick	GDR 49	21.67		(1)		Potsdam	1 Sep 73
Sergey	Kasnauskas	SU 61	21.64		(1)	DRZ	Moskva	17 Aug 84
Sergey	Smirnov	SU 60	21.63		(1)		Leningrad	18 Jun 84
(20)								
Kevin	Akins	USA 60	21.61		(1)		Modesto	14 May 83
Sergey	Gavrushin	SU 60	21.60		(1)		Moskva	19 Aug 84
Vladimir	Kiselyov	SU 57	21.58		(3)	DRZ	Moskva	17 Aug 84
Yevgeniy	Mironov	SU 49	21.53		(1)	NC	Kiev	24 Jun 76

All-time Lists – Men

Ralf	Reichenbach	FRG 50	21.51	(1)	ISTAF	Berlin	8 Aug 80
Alessandro	Andrei	ITA 59	21.50	(1)	NC	Roma	11 Jul 84
Mike	Lehmann	USA 60	21.43	(2)	JENNER	San Jose	28 May 83
Fred	Debernardi	USA 49	21.42 i	(1)	ITA	Portland	20 Apr 74
(30)							
Ron	Semkiw	USA 54	21.35	(1)		Mesa, Az.	5 Mar 74
Hans	Hoglund	SWE 52	21.33	(1)	NCAA	Provo	6 Jun 75
Heinz-Joachim	Rothenburg	GDR 44	21.32	(1)		Potsdam	3 Jun 72
Hans-Peter	Gies	GDR 47	21.31	(2)		Potsdam	25 Aug 72
Hans-Jurgen	Jacobi	GDR 50	21.25	(2)	NC	Cottbus	16 Jul 80
Greg	Tafralis	USA 58	21.25	(5)	JENNER	San Jose	26 May 84
Josef	Kubes	CSR 57	21.20	(2)	NC	Praha	24 Jul 83
Wladyslaw	Komar	POL 40	21.19	(1)		Warszawa	17 Aug 74
(40)							
Vladimir	Milic	YUG 55	21.19	(1)		Beograd	18 Aug 82
Zlatko	Saracevic	YUG 56	21.11	(1)		Zagreb	16 Jun 84
Pete	Shmock	USA 50	21.10	(1)	PRE	Eugene	5 Jun 76
Hreinn	Halldorsson	ICE 49	21.09	(1)	DNG	Stockholm	4 Jul 77
Sergey	Donskikh	SU 56	21.09	(1)		Leningrad	13 Aug 84
Colin	Anderson	USA 51	21.08	(2)	TAC	Walnut	15 Jun 80
Dean	Crouser	USA 60	21.07	(2)	TAC	Knoxville	19 Jun 82
Mac	Wilkins	USA 50	21.06 i	(1)	AAU	New York	25 Feb 77
Jaroslav	Brabec	CSR 49	21.04	(1)		Banska Bystrica	1 Sep 73
Peter	Block	GDR 55	21.04	(1)		Halle	16 May 82
Helmut	Krieger	POL 58	21.03	(5)	DRZ	Moskva	17 Aug 84
Sergey	Solomko	SU 58	21.02	(1)		Kiev	10 Aug 84
Neal	Steinhauer	USA 44	21.01	(1)		Sacramento	25 Mar 67
Nikolay	Borodkin	SU 55	21.00	(3)	ZNAM	Sochi	10 Jun 84
(50)							

Light implement

Sergey	Kasnauskas	sU 61	22.09	(1)		Minsk	23 Aug 84

DISCUS

Ben	Pluckneft	USA 54	72.34*	(1)	DNG	Stockholm	7 Jul 81
Yuriy	Dumchev	SU 58	71.86	(1)		Moskva	29 May 83
	Pluckneft		71.32	(1)	PRE	Eugene	4 Jun 83
John	Powell	USA 47	71.26	(1)	TAC	San Jose	9 Jun 84
Ricky	Bruch	SWE 46	71.26	(1)		Malmo	16 Nov 84
	Pluckneft		71.20*	(1)	CAL R.	Modesto	16 May 81
Art	Burns	USA 54	71.18	(1)		San Jose	19 Jul 83
Wolfgang	Schmidt	GDR 54	71.16	(1)		Berlin	9 Aug 79
	Pluckneft		71.14	(1)		Berkeley	12 Jun 83
Luis Mariano	Delis	CUB 57	71.06	(1)	BARR	Habana	21 May 83
	Bruch		71.00	(1)		Malmo	14 Oct 84
Mac	Wilkins	USA 50	70.98	(1)	WG	Helsinki	9 Jul 80
	Burns		70.98	(1)	PRE	Eugene	21 Jul 84
	Wilkins		70.86	(1)		San Jose	1 May 76
	Pluckneft		70.82	(1)		Salinas	1 Jun 83
Imrich	Bugar	CSR 55	70.72	(1)	V HUN AUT	Schwechat	18 Jun 83
	Wilkins		70.66	(1)	AAU	Walnut	16 Jun 79
	Delis		70.58	(1)		Salinas	19 May 82
	Wilkins		70.48	(1)		San Jose	29 Apr 78
	Wilkins		70.48	(1)	PRE	REugene	31 May 78
	Bruch		70.48	(1)		Malmo	12 Sep 84
(21/9)							
Jay	Silvester	USA 37	70.38	(1)		Lancaster	16 May 71
Juan	Martinez	CUB 58	70.00	(2)	BARR	Habana	21 May 83
Gejza	Valent	CSR 53	69.70	(2)		Nitra	26 Aug 84

All-time Lists – Men

Knut	Hjeltnes	NOR 51	69.50	(1)	CAL R.	Modesto	12 May 79
Al	Oerter	USA 36	69.46	(1)	TFA	Wichita	31 May 80
Georgiy	Kolnootchenko	SU 59	69.44	(1)	V USA	Indianapolis	3 Jul 82
Art	Swarts	USA 45	69.40	(1)		Scotch Plains	8 Dec 79
Ken	Stadel	USA 52	69.26	(2)	AAU	Walnut	16 Jun 79
Jurgen	Schult	GDR 60	68.82	(1)		Berlin	15 Jul 84
Dmitriy	Kovtsun	SU 55	68.64	(1)		Riga	6 Jul 84
Igor	Duginyets	SU 56	68.52	(1)	NC	Kiev	21 Aug 82
(20)							
Armin	Lemme	GDR 55	68.50	(1)	V USA	Karl-Marx-Stadt	10 Jul 82
John	Van Reenen	RSA 47	68.48	(1)E2		Stellenbosch	14 Mar 75
Markku	Tuokko	FIN 51	68.12	(1)	WCR	Fresno	5 May 79
Iosif	Nagy	RUM 46	68.12	(2)		Zaragoza	22 May 83
Hein-Direck	Neu	FRG 44	68.08	(1)		Bremerhaven	27 May 77
Svein Inge	Valvik	NOR 56	68.00	(1)		Juarez	31 May 82
Velko	Velev	BUL 48	67.82	(1)		Riga	13 Aug 78
Vitaliy	Pishchalnikov	SU 58	67.76	(1)		Stavropol	9 May 84
Wolfgang	Warnemunde	GDR 53	67.56	(1)		Rostock	2 Jun 80
Siegfried	Pachale	GDR 49	67.54	(1)		Karl-Marx-Stadt	29 May 76
(30)							
Hilmar	Hossfeld	GDR 54	67.54	(2)	OT	Jena	17 May 80
Werner	Hartmann	FRG 59	67.54	(1)		Georgsheil	29 Apr 82
Rolf	Danneberg	FRG 53	67.40	(1)		Stade	5 May 84
Tim	Vollmer	USA 46	67.38	(2)		Lancaster	16 May 71
Ferenc	Tegla	HUN 47	67.38	(1)		Szentes	12 Oct 77
Rob	Gray	CAN 56	67.32	(1)		Etobicoke	30 Apr 84
Ludvik	Danek	CSR 37	67.18	(1)		Praha	10 Jul 74
Borislav	Tashev	BUL 56	67.14	(1)		Pleven	31 Jul 82
Igor	Avrunin	SU 57	67.14	(1)		Smolininkay	9 May 84
Alwin	Wagner	FRG 50	67.10	(1)		Felsberg	7 Sep 82
(40)							
Marco	Bucci	ITA 60	66.96	(2)		Formia	30 Jun 84
Geza	Fejer	HUN 45	66.92	(1)	V RUM	Budapest	3 Jul 71
Romas	Ubartas	SU 60	66.92	(1)	V ITA POL HUN	Torino	2 Jun 84
Norbert	Thiede	GDR 49	66.90	(1)		Rostock	25 Apr 76
Marco	Martino	ITA 60	66.90	(3)		Formia	30 Jun 84
Pentti	Kahma	FIN 43	66.82	(1)	CAL R.	Modesto	24 May 75
Brad	Cooper	BAH 57	66.72	(2)	CAC CH	Habana	8 Aug 82
Vladimir	Zinchenko	SU 59	66.70	(1)		Alushta	27 Apr 83
Viktor	Rashchupkin	SU 50	66.64	(1)	OG	Moskva	28 Jul 80
Sergey	Lukashok	SU 58	66.64	(1)		Odessa	10 Sep 83
(50)							
Stefan	Fernholm	SWE 59	67.00	(1)		Provo	16 May 84

HAMMER THROW

Yuriy	Syedikh	SU 55	86.34	(1)		Cork	3 Jul 84
	Syedikh		85.60	(1)	TALBOT	London	13 Jul 84
	Syedikh		85.60	(1)	DRZ	Moskva	17 Aug 84
Sergey	Litvinov	SU 58	85.20	(2)		Cork	3 Jul 84
	Syedikh		85.02	(1)	BGP	Budapest	20 Aug 84
	Syedikh		84.60	(1)	8 NAT	Tokyo	14 Sep 84
Juri	Tamm	SU 57	84.40	(1)		Banska Bystrica	9 Sep 84
	Litvinov		84.14	(1)	SPART	Moskva	21 Jun 83
	Litvinov		83.98	(1)		Moskva	4 Jun 82
	Syedikh		83.90	(1)	G. GALA	Roma	31 Aug 84
	Litvinov		83.58			Moskva	8 Jul 84
Igor	Nikulin	SU 60	83.54	(1)	PEC	Athinai	2 Sep 82
	Tammq		83.32	(2)	BGP	Budapest	20 Aug 84
	Litvinov		83.10	(1)		Khania	22 May 83
	Nikulin		82.92	(1)		Leningrad	3 Jun 83

All-time Lists – Men

	Name	Surname	Country	Mark		Extra	Location	City	Date
		Litvinov		82.68		(1) W	ORLD C.	Helsinki	9 Aug 83
		Syedikh		82.60		(1)	IZV	Kiev	21 Jun 84
		Litvinov		82.60		(2)	IZV	Kiev	21 Jun 84
		Nikulin		82.56		(2)	DRZ	Moskva	17 Aug 84
		Nikulin		82.20		(1)	ZNAM	Moskva	11 Jun 83
(20/4)									
Juha	Tiainen	FIN 55	81.52		(1)		Tampere	11 Jun 84
Yuriy	Tarasyuk	SU 57	81.44		(1)		Minsk	10 Aug 84
Igor	Grigorash	SU 59	81.20		(1)		Kiev	23 Aug 84
Karl-Hans	Riehm	FRG 51	80.80		(1)		Rhede	30 Jul 80
Viktor	Litvinyenko	SU 57	80.68		(2)		Kiev	23 Aug 84
Emanuil	Dyulgerov	BUL 55	80.64		(1)		Sofia	25 Aug 84
(10)									
Klaus	Ploghaus	FRG 56	80.56		(1)		Obersuhl	27 Jun 81
Detlef	Gerstenberg	GDR 57	80.50		(1)		Berlin	15 Jul 84
Boris	Zaichuk	SU 47	80.48		(2)		Sochi	24 May 80
Grigoriy	Shevtsov	SU 58	80.24		(1)		Volgograd	9 May 83
Gunther	Rodehau	GDR 59	80.20		(1)		Celje	5 May 84
Zdzislaw	Kwasny	POL 60	80.18		(2)	EP	London	21 Aug 83
Anatoliy	Chyuzhas	SU 56	80.16		(2)		Klaipeda	27 May 84
Igor	Astapkovich	SU 63	79.98		(1)		Vitebsk	15 Jul 84
Roland	Steuk	GDR 59	79.90		(1)		Sofia	16 Jun 84
Anatoliy	Yefimov	SU 56	79.56		(1)		Adler	24 Apr 83
(20)									
Mariusz	Tomaszewski	POL 56	79.46		(1)		Zabrze	1 Jul 84
Ralf	Haber	GDR 62	79.38		(3)		Berlin	15 Jul 84
Matthias	Moder	GDR 63	79.38		(4)		Berlin	15 Jul 84
Walter	Schmidt	FRG 48	79.30		(1)		Frankfurt/M.	14 Aug 75
Manfred	Huning	FRG 53	79.16		(1)		Dortmund	22 Aug 79
Jozsef	Vida	HUN 63	79.06		(1)		Szombathely	28 Aug 84
Frantisek	Vrbka	CSR 58	78.84		(1)		Praha	2 Jun 84
Imre	Szitas	HUN 61	78.84		(1)		Miskolc	26 Aug 84
Harri	Huhtala	FIN 52	78.74		(2)	NURMI	Turku	26 Jun 84
Aleksey	Spiridonov	SU 51	78.62		(1)	V UK	Kiev	22 May 76
(30)									
Sergey	Dvoretskiy	SU 57	78.62		(1)		Gorkiy	12 Aug 84
Henryk	Krolak	POL 60	78.60		(1)		Warszawa	9 Jun 84
Aleksandr	Kozlov	SU 52	78.58		(5)		Sochi	24 May 80
Aleksandr	Bunyeyev	SU 50	78.56		(1)		Togliatti	28 Aug 82
Aleksey	Malyukov	SU 50	78.52		(6)		Sochi	24 May 80
Viktor	Bobryshev	SU 57	78.28		(1)		Leningrad	19 Aug 83
Benjaminas	Viluckis	SU 61	78.20		(3)		Klaipeda	27 May 84
Giampaolo	Urlando	ITA 45	78.16		(1)		Walnut	25 Jul 84
Christoph	Sahner	FRG 63	78.04		(Q)	NC	Dusseldorf	23 Jun 84
Sergey	Dorozhon	SU 64	78.00		(1)		Moskva	7 Aug 83
(40)									
Orlando	Bianchini	ITA 55	77.94		(1)		Milano	27 Jun 84
Pavel	Ryepin	SU 54	77.84		(1)		Leningrad	30 Aug 81
Yuriy	Kashchenko	SU 59	77.80		(2)		Dnyepropetrovsk	25 Sep 83
Dzhumber	Pkhakadze	SU 51	77.64		(1)		Tbilisi	26 May 75
Vladimir	Lyesovoy	SU 47	77.60		(1)		Alma-Ata	27 Jun 77
Valentin	Dmitrenko	SU 51	77.58		(1)		Stuttgart	26 Aug 75
Yuriy	Pastukhov	SU 61	77.56		(7)		Leselidze	21 May 83
Martin	Girvan	UK 60	77.54		(1)		Wolverhampton	12 May 84
Anatoliy	Bondarchuk	SU 40	77.42		(2)	NC	Kiev	24 Jun 76
Sergey	Abramov	SU 59	77.40		(3)		Tula	7 Aug 82
(50)									

211

All-time Lists – Men

JAVELIN

Uwe	Hohn	GDR 62	104.80		(1)	OD	Berlin	20 Jul 84
Tom	Petranoff	USA 58	99.72		(1)	PEPSI	Westwood	15 May 83
	Hohn		99.52		(1)		Potsdam	25 May 84
	Hohn		97.12		(1)		Berlin	15 Jul 84
Ferenc	Paragi	HUN 53	96.72		(1)		Tata	23 Apr 80
Detlef	Michel	GDR 55	96.72		(1)	OD	Berlin	8 Jun 83
	Paragi		96.20		(1)	V ENG WAL HOL	Cwmbran	18 May 80
	Michel		96.08		(1)	PTS	Bratislava	4 Jun 83
Bob	Roggy	USA 56	95.80		(1)		Stuttgart	29 Aug 82
	Michel		95.66		(1)		Berlin	31 Jul 83
	Petranoff		94.88		(1)	NURMI	Turku	28 Jul 83
	Hohn		94.82		(1)		Jena	13 May 84
	Petranoff		94.62		(1)	V GDR	Los Angeles	25 Jun 83
Miklos	Nemeth	HUN 46	94.58		(1)	OG	Montreal	26 Jul 76
	Michel		94.52		(1)		Berlin	9 May 82
	Roggy		94.46		(1)	FIN CH	Kuovola	15 Aug 82
	Hohn		94.44		(1)	DRZ	Moskva	17 Aug 84
	Michel		94.26		(1)		Berlin	26 May 82
Michael	Wessing	FRG 52	94.22		(1)		Oslo	3 Aug 78
Heino	Puuste	SU 55	94.20		(1)	V UK	Birmingham	5 Jun 83
(10/8)								
Klaus	Wolfermann	FRG 46	94.08		(1)		Leverkusen	5 May 73
Hannu	Siitonen	FIN 49	93.90		(1)		Helsinki	6 Jun 73
(10)								
Pentti	Sinersaari	FIN 56	93.84		(1)		Auckland	27 Jan 79
Janis	Lusis	SU 39	93.80		(1)	DNG	Stockholm	6 Jul 72
Seppo	Hovinen	FIN 51	93.54		(1)	WG	Helsinki	23 Jun 76
Duncan	Atwood	USA 55	93.44		(1)	FOT	Los Angeles	18 Jun 84
Raimo	Manninen	FIN 55	93.42		(1)		Pihtipudas	1 Jul 84
Antero	Puranen	FIN 52	92.74		(1)		Saarijarvi	24 Jun 79
Helmut	Schreiber	FRG 55	92.72		(1)		Ulm	27 Jul 79
Jorma	Kinnunen	FIN 41	92.70		(1)		Tampere	18 Jun 69
Pauli	Nevala	FIN 40	92.64		(1)	V SWE	Helsinki	6 Sep 70
Einar	Vilhjalmsson	ICE 60	92.42		(1)	TEX R./U.D.	Austin	6 Apr 84
(20)								
Arto	Harkonen	FIN 59	92.40		(2)		Pihtipudas	1 Jul 84
Dainis	Kula	SU 59	92.06		(1)		Moskva	21 Jun 80
Terje	Pedersen	NOR 43	91.72		(1)	V CSR	Oslo	2 Sep 64
Mark	Murro	USA 49	91.44		(1)		Tempe	27 Mar 70
Klaus	Tafelmeier	FRG 58	91.44		(1)		Kevelaer	23 May 83
Koos	Van Der Merwe	RSA 56	91.24		(1)		Middelburg	5 Feb 83
Wolfgang	Hanisch	GDR 51	91.14		(1)	WG	Helsinki	28 Jun 78
Kent	Eldebrink	SWE 55	91.14		(1)	V FIN	Stockholm	4 Sep 83
Zdenek	Adamec	CSR 56	91.12		(1)		Lille	27 Sep 84
Esa	Utriainen	FIN 53	90.94		(1)	NC	Helsinki	13 Aug 79
(30)								
Viktor	Yevsyukov	SU 56	90.94		(1)		Moskva	6 Aug 84
Cary	Feldmann	USA 50	90.92		(1)		Bakersfield	19 May 73
Jorma	Jaakola	FIN 50	90.86		(1)		Kaarlela	8 Aug 76
Piotr	Bielzkyk	POL 52	90.78		(1)	KUSOC	Bydgoszcz	22 Jun 76
Manfred	Stolle	GDR 37	90.68		(1)	NC	Erfurt	4 Jul 70
Rod	Ewaliko	USA 54	90.66		(1)		Goleta	25 Feb 84
Mike	O'Rourke	NZL 55	90.58		(1)		Auckland	22 Jan 83
Mike	Barnett	USA 61	90.34		(1)	MSR	Walnut	24 Apr 83
Per Erling	Olsen	NOR 58	90.30		(2)	BISL	Oslo	28 Jun 83
Jorma	Markus	FIN 52	90.18		(1)		Tyrnava	6 Jun 82
(40)								
Gerlad	Weiss	GDR 60	90.06		(1)		Sofia	17 Jun 84
Leif	Lundmark	SWE 53	89.92		(1)		Karlskrona	20 Jun 79
Nikolay	Grebnyev	SU 48	89.82		(1)	V FRG	Dortmund	1 Jul 78
Aleksandr	Makarov	SU 51	89.64		(2)	OG	Moskva	27 Jul 80

All-time Lists – Men

Karl	Heller	GDR 53	89.56		(1)		OT		Karl-Marx-Stadt	25 May 80
Janis	Zirnis	SU 47	89.48		(1)				Ventspils	27 Sep 81
Detlef	Fuhrmann	GDR 53	89.46		(2)		OT		Potsdam	31 May 80
Aimo	Aho	FIN 51	89.42		(1)				Reisjarvi	21 May 77
Janis	Donins	SU 46	89.32*		(1)		V USA		Berkeley	3 Jul 71
Brian	Crouser	USA 62	89.20		(1)				Eugene	13 Jul 84

(50)
* = actually measured in odd centimetres

DECATHLON

8798e	1)	Jurgen	Hingsen	FRG 58	Manheim		9 Jun 84
10.70w 7.76 16.42 2.07 48.05 14.07 49.36 4.90 59.86 4.19.75
8797e	1)	Daley	Thompson	UK 58	Los Angeles	OG	9 Aug 84
10.44 8.01 15.72 2.03 46.97 14.34 46.56 5.00 65.24 4.35.00
8779e	1)		Hingsen		Bernhausen		5 Jun 83
10.92 7.74 15.94 2.15 47.89 14.10 46.80 4.70 67.26 4.19.74
8743e	1)		Thompson		Athinai	EC	8 Sep 82
10.51 7.80 15.44 2.03 47.11 14.39 45.48 5.00 63.56 4.23.71
8723e	1)		Hingsen		Ulm		15 Aug 82
10.74w 7.85 16.00 2.15 47.65 14.64 44.92 4.60 63.10 4.15.13
8718e	2)	Siegfried	Wentz	FRG 60	Bernhausen		5 Jun 83
10.89 7.49 15.35 2.09 47.38 14.00 46.90 4.80 70.68 4.24.90
8704e	1)		Thompson		Gotzis		23 May 82
10.50w 7.95 15.31 2.08 46.86 14.31 44.34 4.90 60.52 4.30.55
87004e	1)	Uwe	Freimuth	GDR 61	Potsdam	OD	21 Jul 84
11.07 7.79 16.30 2.03 48.43 14.66 46.58 5.15 72.42 4.25.19
8673e	2)		Hingsen		Los Angeles	OG	9 Aug 84
10.91 7.80 15.87 2.12 47.69 14.29 50.80 4.50 60.44 4.22.60
8666e	1)		Thompson		Helsinki	WC	13 Aug 83
10.60 7.88 15.35 2.03 48.12 14.37 44.46 5.10 65.24 4.29.72
8652e	1)	Grigoriy	Degtyarev	SU 58	Kiev	NC	22 Jun 84
10.87 7.42 16.03 2.10 49.75 14.53 51.20 4.90 67.08 4.23.09
8649e	1)	Guido	Kratschmer	FRG 53	Bernhausen		14 Jun 80
10.58 7.80 15.47 2.00 48.04 13.92 45.52 4.60 66.50 4.24.15
8643e	1)	Aleksandr	Apaychev	SU 61	Neubrandenburg	V GDR	2 Jun 84
10.96 7.57 16.00 1.97 48.72 13.93 48.00 4.90 72.24 4.26.51
8622e	1)		Thompson		Gotzis		18 May 80
10.55 7.72 14.46 2.11 48.04 14.37 42.98 4.90 65.38 4.25.49
8618e	1)	Bruce	Jenner	USA 49	Montreal	OG	30 Jul 76
10.94 7.22 15.35 2.03 47.51 14.84 50.04 4.80 68.52 4.12.61
8579e	1)		Degtyaryev		Gotzis		20 May 84
11.05 7.73 15.83 2.08 49.76 14.45 49.90 4.90 60.70 4.20.49
8560e	1)		Apaychev		Kiev		6 May 84
10.97 7.61 15.91 1.95 48.40 14.11 45.07 4.80 68.88 4.18.78
8553e	2)		Freimuth		Neubrandenburg	V SU	2 Jun 84
11.10 7.79 16.42 1.94 48.93 14.54 51.54 4.90 66.32 4.27.95
8542e	1)		Freimuth		Potsdam		6 May 84
11.06 7.69 16.06 1.97 48.78 14.75 47.54 4.80 73.02 4.24.46
8535e	2)	Torsten	Voss	GDR 63	Potsdam		6 May 84
10.56 7.73 14.56 2.09 47.50 14.84 42.60 5.00 59.92 4.25.68

(20/9)

8530e	2)	Igor	Sobolevskiy	SU 62	Kiev	NC	22 Jun 84
10.64 7.71 15.93 2.01 48.24 14.82 50.54 4.40 67.40 4.32.84
8512e	3)	Yuriy	Kutsenko	SU 52	Kiev		22 Jun 84
11.07 7.54 15.11 2.13 49.07 14.94 50.38 4.60 61.70 4.12.68
8480e	1)	Siegfried	Stark	GDR 55	Halle		4 May 80
11.10w 7.64 15.81 2.03 49.53 14.86w 47.20 5.00 68.70 4.27.70
8476e	2)	Aleksandr	Nevskiy	SU 58	Gotzis		20 May 84
10.97 7.24 15.04 2.08 48.44 14.67 46.06 4.70 69.56 4.19.62
8458e	1)	Konstantin	Achapkin	SU 56	Moskva		2 Aug 82
11.10 7.72 15.25 2.02 49.14 14.38 45.68 4.90 62.42 4.19.30

213

All-time Lists – Men

8454e	1)	Nikolay	Avilov	SU 48	Munchen	OG	8 Sep 72
	11.00 7.68 14.36 2.12 48.45 14.31 46.98 4.55 61.66 4.22.82						
8390e	1)	Fred	Dixon	USA 49	Bloomington	V SU	14 Aug 77
	10.85 7.44 15.20 2.04 48.54 14.94 47.14 4.60 67.88 4.30.21						
8376e	4)	Sergey	Zhelanov	SU 57	Kiev	NC	22 Jun 84
	11.04 7.50 14.31 2.13 48.94 14.40 43.44 5.00 65.90 4.37.24						
8369e	4)	Andreas	Rizzi	GFR 59	Bernhausen		5 Jun 83
	10.52 7.73 14.78 2.00 46.82 14.91 43.62 4.70 50.92 4.21.04						
8340e	1)	Aleksandr	Grebenyuk	SU 51	Praha	EC	31 Aug 78
	11.02 6.94 15.93 2.01 48.88 14.43 48.42 4.50 67.74 4.24.4						
8337e	1)	Stefan	Niklaus	SWZ 58	Lausanne	NC	3 Jul 83
	20.82 7.32 15.44 2.01 47.47 14.79 48.68 4.40 67.84 4.41.29						
(20)							
8337e	5)	Viktor	Gruzenkin	SU 51	Kiev		22 Jun 84
	10.92 7.67 15.98 2.07 50.06 14.65 46.70 4.60 65.74 4.43.00						
8311e	1)	Rainer	Pottel	GDR 53	Birmingham		30 Jun 81
	11.06 7.68 14.38 2.01 48.35 14.57 39.52 4.80 67.46 4.22.67						
8306e	2)	Valeriy	Kachanov	SU 54	Moskva		21 Jun 80
	11.08 7.54 14.53 2.08 48.70 14.61 46.10 4.50 58.10 4.17.4						
8302e	4)	Jens	Schulze	FRG 56	Mannheim		9 Jun 84
	10.56w 7.33 15.00 2.01 48.58 14.44w 45.32 4.60 53.70 4.22.95						
8294e	1)	Aleksandr	Shablenko	SU 57	Potsdam		1 Jun 80
	10.95 7.25 15.23 2.03 48.85 14.25 47.14 5.00 50.64 4.25.9						
8279e	1)	Tito	Steiner	ARG 52	Baton Rouge		3 Jun 81
	11.19w 7.37 15.20 2.09 49.85 14.97 45.20 4.70 70.28 4.31.98						
8274e	1)	Bobby	Coffman	USA 51	Quebec City		12 Aug 79
	10.71 7.37 15.92 1.90 48.85 13.91 49.52 4.50 56.36 4.36.5						
8274e	1)	Steffen	Grummt	GDR 59	Halle		20 Jun 82
	10.99w 7.26 16.32 1.91 49.16 14.38w 48.76 4.40 63.56 4.24.68						
8266e	5)	William	Motti	FRA 64	Los Angeles	OG	9 Aug 84
	11.28 7.45 14.42 2.06 48.13 14.71 50.92 4.50 63.76 4.35.15						
8265e	2)	Jorg–Peter	Schaperkotter	GDR 58	Neubrandenburg.	NC	22 May 83
	10.93 7.62 15.46 2.03 47.74 14.58 49.72 4.40 47.62 4.25.73						
(30)							
8250e	1)	Mark	Anderson	USA 58	Walnut	MSR	22 Apr 83
	11.11 7.03 14.86 2.10 49.21 15.77 42.50 4.70 76.42 4.21.75						
8243e	1)	Dave	Steen	CAN 59	Los Angeles		24 May 84
	11.10 7.39 12.92 2.05 47.96 15.09 42.88 5.00 62.84 4.17.83						
8233e	7)	Pavel	Tarnavetskiy	SU 61	Kiev	NC	22 Jun 84
	11.03 7.19 15.12 1.95 48.49 14.60 48.18 4.70 56.96 4.20.19						
8229e	1)	Georg	Werthner	AUT 56	Schielleiten		8 Aug 82
	11.12 7.13 14.84 2.07 49.68 14.89 40.46 4.70 68.86 4.15.89						
8227e	1)	Rob	Muzzio	USA 64	Eugene	NCAA	29 May 84
	10.90 7.02 16.67 2.00 49.64 14.65 50.80 4.60 57.84 4.36.35						
8222e	1)	Dariusz	Ludwig	POL 55	Bruxelles		12 Jul 81
	10.92 7.64 15.06 2.07 50.11 15.11 46.76 4.50 58.88 4.26.90						
8220e	1)	Atanas	Andonov	BUL 55	Sofia		2 Aug 81
	11.02 7.18 15.94 2.05 49.54 14.60 48.88 4.50 55.12 4.25.75						
8218e	4)	Raimo	Pihl	SWE 49	Montreal	OG	30 Jul 76
	10.93 6.99 15.55 2.00 47.97 15.81 44.30 4.40 77.34 4.28.76						
8212e	4)	Hans–Ulrich	Riecke	GDR 63	Potsdam	OD	21 Jul 84
	10.66 7.63 14.45 1.97 48.46 15.02 44.62 4.60 57.44 4.27.41						
8210e	7)	Sergey	Pugach	SU 59	Moskva	SPART	19 Jun 83
	11.28 7.51 14.57 2.00 48.31 14.82 42.44 4.90 56.42 4.14.49						
(40)							
8207e	1)	Ryszard	Skowronek	POL 49	Roma	EC	7 Sep 74
	10.97 7.49 13.10 1.95 47.91 14.79 43.26 5.10 64.14 4.30.9						
8207e	1)	Andreas	Rizzi	FRG 59	Lage		9 Aug 81
	10.79 7.59 14.63 1.97 46.79 15.34 43.62 4.60 51.84 4.18.07						
8201e	2)	Sergey	Popov	SU 57	Kiev		6 May 84
	11.50 7.27 14.64 2.01 50.30 15.12 49.60 4.80 66.78 4.19.0						
8198e	1)	Josef	Zeilbauer	AUT 52	Mexico, D.F.	WUG	11 Sep 79
	10.99 7.39 16.12 2.09 49.52 14.31 43.28 4.60 62.24 4.51.2						
8196e	1)	Joachim	Kirst	GDR 47	Helsinki	EC	12 Aug 71
	11.02 7.68 16.59 2.13 49.0 16.12 47.21 4.20 65.51 4.44.7						

All-time Lists – Men

8187e	1)	Herbert	Peter	FRG 57	Baton Rouge			28 Jun 82
	11.19 6.90 13.04 2.10 48.83 14.80 44.04 4.60 64.36 4.15.49							
8181e	1)	Bill	Toomey	USA 39	Mexico, D.F.	OG		19 Oct 68
	10.41 7.87 13.75 1.95 45.68 14.95 43.68 4.20 62.80 4.57.18							
8171e	2)	Mark	Anderson	USA 58	Baton Rouge			3 Jun 81
	10.67 7.03 14.19 2.04 48.02 16.34 43.32 4.30 75.92 4.23.42							
8161e	1)	Thierry	Dubois	FRA 56	Gotzis			27 May 79
	10.86 7.17 14.91 2.08 48.66 14.56 44.40 4.70 60.70 4.48.3							
8159e	2)	Lee	Palles	USA 56	Eugene			22 Jun 80
	10.87 7.10 14.63 2.13 48.34 14.96 44.12 4.15 62.34 4.26.06							

(50)
w = wind assistance exceeding +4.0 m/s

Decathlon – scores made with manual timing
Best auto scores are shown in parenthesis

8524	1)		Jenner		Eugene	V SU P	10 Aug 75	(8617)
	10.7 7.17 15.25 2.01 48.7 14.6 50.00 4.70 65.52 4.16.6							
8478	1)	Aleksandr	Grebenyuk	SU 51	Riga		3 Jul 77	(8340)
	10.7 7.12 15.50 2.02 48.8 14.3 45.52 4.70 71.52 4.27.3							
8417	1)	William	Toomey	USA 39	Los Angeles		11 Dec 69	(8181)
	10.3 7.76 14.38 1.93 47.1 14.3 46.49 4.27 65.74 4.39.4							
8319	1)	Kurt	Bendlin	FRG 43	Heidelberg		14 May 67	
	10.6 7.55 14.50 1.84 47.9 14.8 46.31 4.10 74.85 4.19.4							
8310	2)	Josef	Zeilbauer	AUT 52	Gotzis		16 May 76	(8198)
	10.9 7.21 14.68 2.10 49.4 14.2 44.62 4.70 64.04 4.32.6							
8310	1)	Mikhail	Romanyuk	SU 62	Kiev		10 Aug 84	
	10.8 7.29 14.24 1.80 48.0 14.3 46.53 4.80 63.50 4.12.8							
8308	1)	Igor	Kolovanov	SU 58	Kiev		12 May 83	(8018)
	10.9 7.53 14.48 2.07 49.9 14.4 44.24 4.80 61.70 4.28.3							
8300	1)	Nikolay	Parakhovskiy	SU 57	Minsk		30 Jun 83	
	10.5 7.30 15.87 1.94 48.7 15.4 48.68 4.50 65.76 4.34.4							
8279	1)	Joachim	Kirst	GDR 47	Schielleiten		1 Jun 69	(8196)
	10.7 7.72 17.40 2.11 49.5 15.5 47.01 4.30 63.03 4.55.4							
8258	1)	Sergey	Pugach	SU 59	Chelyabinsk		4 Sep 82	(8210)
	10.7 7.36 14.51 1.98 48.1 13.9 39.40 5.00 55.82 4.30.6							
8249	2)	Leonid	Litvinenko	SU 49	Kiev		11 Jun 76	(8122)
	10.9 7.08 14.12 1.85 48.6 14.3 49.62 4.50 64.90 4.13.3							
8237	1)	Boris	Ivanov	SU 47	Nalcik		31 May 71	
	10.6 7.34 15.02 2.01 50.2 14.1 43.62 4.30 75.30 4.50.0							
8230	1)	Russ	Hodge	USA 39	Los Angeles		24 Jul 66	
	10.5 7.51 17.25 1.85 48.9 15.2 50.44 4.10 64.49 4.40.4							
8229	1)	Yves	Le Roy	FRA 51	Colombes		29 Sep 74	
	10.8 7.44w 14.59 1.96 48.4 14.7 46.50 4.70 64.66 4.41.9							
8221	1)	Valter	Kulvet	SU 54	Viimsi		23 Aug 81	
	10.7 7.26 13.86 2.09 48.5 14.8 47.92 4.50 60.34 4.37.8							
8206	1)	Aleksandr	Areshin	SU 61	Tashkent		25 May 83	
	10.7 7.17 14.00 2.06 47.7 14.2 42.64 4.50 59.66 4.34.8							
8188	1)	Lennart	Hedmark	SWE 44	Stockholm		17 Jun 73	
	10.8 7.16 15.43 1.90 49.4 14.4 49.08 4.30 78.68 4.54.6							
8157	1)	Aleksandr	Pismennyj	SU 58	Charnkov		15 Aug 81	
	10.7 7.03 14.82 1.94 49.3 14.8 49.76 4.60 56.66 4.25.9							
8155	1)	Phil	Mulkey	USA 33	Memphis		17 Jun 61	
	10.7 7.34 15.32 1.99 51.0 14.6 47.03 4.39 67.45 4.43.8							

(18)

All-time Lists – Men
4 x 100 METRES RELAY

USA	37.83	(1)	OG	Los Angeles	10 Aug 84	
(Graddy, Brown, C. Smith, Lewis)						
USA	37.86	(1)	WORLD C	Helsinki	10 Aug 83	
(King, Gault, C. Smith, Lewis)						
USA	38.03	(1)	WP	Dusseldorf	3 Sep 77	
(Collins, Riddick, Wiley, S. Williams)						
USA	38.13	(1)	WK	Zurich	18 Aug 82	
(Lattany, Floyd, C. Smith, Lewis)						
USA	38.19	(1)	OG	Mexico, D.F.	20 Oct 68	
(Greene, Pender, R.R. Smith, Hines)						
USA	38.19	(1)	OG	Munchen	10 Sep 72	
(Black, R. Taylor, Tinker, Hart)						
USA	38.22	(1)	V GDR	Karl–Marx–Stadt	9 Jul 82	
(Wright, Miller, Cook, C. Smith)						
USA	38.24	(1)	ISTAF	Berlin	20 Aug 82	
(Lattany, Floyd, C. Smith, Lewis)						
SU	38.26	(1)	OG	Moskva	1 Aug 80	
(Muravyev, Sidorov, Aksinin, Prokofyev)						
USOC SOUTH(USA)	38.27	(1)	USOC SF	Indianapolis	24 Jul 82	
(Miller, Lewis, C. Smith, Floyd)						
(10)						
GDR	38.29	(2)	V USA	Karl–Marx–Stadt	9 Jul 82	
(Schroder, Kubeck, Prenzler, Emmelmann)						
USOC SOUTH(USA)	38.30	(1)	USOC SF	Colorado Springs	30 Jul 79	
(Roberson, Glance, Collins, Lattany)						
GDR	38.30	(1)	OD	Berlin	8 Jun 83	
(Schroder, Bringmann, Prenzler, Emmelmann)						
USA	38.31	(1)	PAG	Mexico, D.F.	20 Oct 75	
(Edwards, L. Brown, Merrick, Collins)						
SU	38.32	(1)	DRZ	Moskva	17 Aug 84	
(Yevgenyev, Sokolov, Muravyev, Sidorov)						
USA	38.33	(1)	OG	Montreal	31 Jul 76	
(Glance, J. Jones, Hampton, Riddick)						
POL	38.33	(2)	OG	Moskva	1 Aug 80	
(Zwolinski, Licznerski, Dunecki, Woronin)						
ITA	38.37	(2)	WORLD C.	Helsinki	10 Aug 83	
(Tilli, Simionato, Pavoni, Mennea)						
JAM	38.39	(2)S1	OG	Mexico, D.F.	19 Oct 68	
(Stewart, Fray, Forbes, Miller)						
CUB	38.39	(2)	OG	Mexico, D.F.	20 Oct 68	
(Ramirez, Morales, Montes, Figuerola)						
(20)						
SU	38.41	(3)	WORLD C.	Helsinki	10 Aug 83	
(Prokofyev, Sidorov, Muravyev, Bryzgin)						
FRA	38.42	(3)	OG	Mexico, D.F.	20 Oct 68	
(Fenouil, Delecour, Piquemal, Bambuck)						
ITA	38.42	(1)	WUG	Mexico, D.F.	13 Sep 79	
(Lazzer, Caravani, Grazioli, Mennea)						
SU	38.42	(1)	NAR	Sofia	19 May 84	
(Yevgenyev, Aa. Fyodorov, Muravyev, Sokolov)						
CAN	38.43	(1)		Colorado Springs	19 Jul 82	
(Johnson, Sharpe, D. Williams, S. Hinds)						
USA	38.44	(1)S1	OG	Los Angeles	11 Aug 84	
(Graddy, Brown, C. Smith, Lewis)						
SU	38.45	(1)	OD	Berlin	20 Jul 84	
(Yevgenyev, Sokolov, Muravyev, Sidorov)						
JAM	38.46	(4)	OG	Mexico, D.F.	20 Oct 68	
(Stewart, Fray, Forbes, Miller)						
CUB	38.46	(2)	PAG	Mexico, D.F.	20 Oct 75	
(Ramirez, Casanas, Montes, Triana Matamoros)						
GDR	38.46	(2)	OD	Berlin	20 Jul 84	
(Hubler, Schroeder, Prenzler, Emmelmann)						

All-time Lists – Men

4 x 400 METRES RELAY

USA	2:56.16	(1)	OG	Mexico, D.F.	20 Oct 68
(Matthews, Freeman, James, Evans)					
USA	2:57.91	(1)	OG	Los Angeles	11 Aug 84
(Nix, Armstead, Babers, McKay)					
USA	2:58.65	(1)	OG	Montreal	31 Jul 76
(Frazier, B. Brown, Newhouse, Parks)					
USA	2:59.12	(1)	WP	Roma	6 Sep 81
(McCoy, Wiley, W. Smith, Darden)					
UK	2:59.13	(2)	OG	Los Angeles	11 Aug 84
(Akabusi, Cook, T. Bennett, Brown)					
NIG	2:59.32	(3)	OG	Los Angeles	11 Aug 84
(Uti, Ugbisie, Peters, Egbunike)					
USA	2:59.52	(1)H1	OG	Montreal	30 Jul 76
(Frazier, B. Brown, Newhouse, Parks)					
USA	2:59.6	(1)		Los Angeles	24 Jul 66
(Frey, Evans, T. Smith, Lewis)					
AUS	2:59.64	(2)	OG	Mexico, D.F.	20 Oct 68
(Frayne, Clark, Minihan, Mitchell)					
(10)					
KEN	2:59.83	(1)	OG	Munchen	10 Sep 72
(Asati, Nyamau, Ouko, Sang)					
USOC SOUTH(USA)	2:59.91	(1)	USOC SF	Air F. Academy	3 Jul 83
(L. Brown, Brooks, Rolle, McCoy)					
GDR	3:00.7	(1)		Erfurt	3 Jun 84
(Lieske, Schersing, Carlowitz, Schonlebe)					
SU	3:00.16	(1)	DRZ	Moskva	18 Aug 84
(Lovachev, Lomtyev, Kurochkin, Markin)					
USOC NORTH(USA)	3:00.18	(2)	USOC SF	Air F. Academy	3 Jul 83
(Wiley, S. Davis, Bradley, Babers)					
USA	3:00.19	(1)S1	OG	Los Angeles	10 Aug 84
(Nix, McCoy, W. Smith, McKay)					
GDR	3:00.27	(1)		Dresden	27 Jul 84
(Niestadt, Schersing, Carlowitz, Schonlebe)					
UK	3:00.46	(2)	OG	Munchen	10 Sep 72
(Reynolds, Pascoe, Hemery, Jenkins)					
USA	3:00.47	(1)	PAG	Caracas	28 Aug 83
(Babers, Bradley, Rolle, Carey)					
GDR	3:00.47	(2)	DRZ	Moskva	18 Aug 84
(Niestadt, Schersing, Schonlebe, Carlowitz)					
(20)					
FRG	3:00.50	(1)	EC	Athinai	11 Sep 82
(Skamrahl, Schmid, Giessing, Weber)					
FRG	3:00.57	(3)	OG	Mexico, D.F.	20 Oct 68
(H. Muller, Kinder, Hennige, Jellinghaus)					
POL	3:00.58	(4)	OG	Mexico, D.F.	20 Oct 68
(Gredzinski, Balachowski, Werner, Badenski)					
USA	3:00.63	(1)	PAG	Cali	5 Aug 71
(Alexander, Newhouse, T. Turner, J. Smith)					
FRA	3:00.65	(3)	OG	Munchen	10 Sep 72
(Bertould, Velasquez, Kerbiriou, Carette)					
UK	2:56.10	(1)	OG	Mexico, D.F.	20 Oct 68
(Jenkins, Cook, T. Bennett, P. Brown)					
USOC SOUTH(USA)	3:00.69	(1)	USOC SF	Indianapolis	25 Jul 82
(Taylor, Ketchum, Vaughns, McCoy)					
USA	3:00.7	(1)		Munchen	23 Aug 72
(Matthews, Collett, J. Smith, Evans)					
USA	3:00.70	(1)	WP	Montreal	26 Aug 79
(Frazier, Green, W. Smith, Darden)					
USA	3:00.71	(1)H1	OG	Mexico, D.F.	19 Oct 68
(Matthews, Freeman, James, Evans)					
(30)					

All-time Lists – Men

20,000 METRES WALK (ROAD)

Jozef	Pribilinec	CS 60	1:19:30	(1)	LT	Bergen	24 Sep 83
Domingo	Colin	Mex 52	1:19:35	(1)		Cherkassy	27 Apr 80
Ernesto	Canto	Mex 59	1:19:41	(2)	LT	Bergen	24 Sep 83
Anatoliy	Solomin	SU 52	1:19:43	(3)	LT	Bergen	24 Sep 83
	Pribilinec		1:19:49	(1)		Barcelona	17 Apr 83
Yevgeniy	Yevsyukov	SU 54	1:19:53	(2)		Cherkassy	27 Apr 80
Ronald	Weigel	GDR 58	1:19:56	(1)		Berlin	27 Jul 84
Jose	Marin	Spa 50	1:20:00	(2)		Barcelona	17 Apr 83
	Canto		1:20:02	(3)		Cherkassy	27 Apr 80
Maurizio	Damilano	Ita 57	1:20:09	(1)		Piacenza	13 May 84
	Damilano		1:20:10	(4)	LT	Bergen	24 Sep 83
Alessandro	Pezzatini	Ita 57	1:20:18	(2)		Piacenza	13 May 84
David	Smith	Aus 55	1:20:23	(1)		Melbourne	17 Dec 83
	Yevsyukov		1:20:30	(5)	LT	Bergen	24 Sep 83
	Solomin		1:20:35	(4)		Cherkassy	27 Apr 80
Ralf	Kowalsky	GDR 62	1:20:35	(1)	OD	Berlin	20 Jul 84
Marcelino	Colin	Mex 61	1:20:40	(6)	LT	Bergen	24 Sep 83
	Smith		1:20:40	(1)		Sdr. Omme	21 Apr 84
	Canto		1:20:49	(1)	WCh	Helsinki	7 Aug 83
Nikolay	Polozov	SU 51	1:20:50	(5)		Cherkassy	27 Apr 80
	Smith		1:20:52	(1)		Pentage	21 Aug 83
Aivars	Rumbenieks	SU 51	1:20:53	(6)		Cherkassy	27 Apr 80
	Weigel		1:20:54	(1)	IPM	Kobenhavn	12 May 84
	Pribilinec		1:20:59	(2)	WCh	Helsinki	7 Aug 83
Daniel	Bautista	Mex 52	1:21:00	(1)		Xalapa	30 Mar 80
Reima	Salonen	Fin 55	1:21:01	(1)		Raisio	9 Sep 79
	Bautista		1:21:04	(1)		Vretstorp	9 Jun 79
	Yevsyukov		1:21:08	(3)	WCh	Helsinki	7 Aug 83
Carlo	Mattioli	Ita 54	1:21:11	(7)	LT	Bergen	24 Sep 83
Andrey	Perlov	SU 61	1:21:16	(7)		Cherkassy	27 Apr 80
	Smith		1:21:17	(2)	IPM	Kobenhavn	12 May 84
Nikolay	Matveyev	SU 55	1:21:18	(1)		Ruse	17 Apr 83
Felix	Gomez	Mex 55	1:21:19	(2)		Vretstorp	9 Jun 79
	Weigel		1:21:20	(2)		Ruse	17 Apr 83
Aleksandr	Potashov	SU 62	1:21:21	(8)		Cherkassy	27 Apr 80
	Marin		1:21:21	(4)	WCh	Helsinki	7 Aug 83
Anatoliy	Gorshkov	SU 52	1:21:26	(8)	LT	Bergen	24 Sep 83
Hartwig	Gauder	GDR 54	1:21:33	(1)		Berlin	29 May 83
Willi	Sawall	Aus 41	1:21:36	(1)		Melbourne	4 Jul 82
Gerard	Lelievre	Fra 49	1:21:37	(5)	WCh	Helsinki	7 Aug 83
Pavol	Blazek	CS 58	1:21:37	(9)	LT	Bergen	24 Sep 83
Bo	Gustafsson	Swe 54	1:21:38	(1)		Kobenhavn	16 Jul 83
	Gauder		1:21:39	(3)		Vretstorp	9 Jun 79
	Smith		1:21:39	(1)		Melbourne	17 May 81
Maris	Petersons	SU 48	1:21:40	(9)		Cherkassy	27 Apr 80
	Kowalsky		1:21:40	(1)		Jena	7 Aug 81
Mykola	Vynnychenko	SU 58	1:21:41	(2)		Xalapa	30 Mar 80
	Kowalsky		1:21:43	(3)	IPM	Kobenhavn	12 May 84
Ivan	Sankovskiy	SU 58	1:21:43	(1)		Moskva	13 May 84
Aleksandr	Pankov	SU 52	1:21:44	(10)		Cherkassy	27 Apr 80

(50/31)

Michael	Boenke	GDR 57	1:21:45	(2)		Berlin	29 May 83
Uwe	Dunkel	GDR 60	1:21:48	(3)		Berlin	29 May 83
Sergiy	Protsyshyn	SU 59	1:21:57	(1)	Drzh	Moskva	17 Aug 84
Lyubomir	Ivanov	Bul 60	1:22:03	(2)	OD	Berlin	20 Jul 84
Guillaume	Leblanc	Can 62	1:22:04	(8)	WCh	Helsinki	7 Aug 83
Yevgeniy	Saykin	SU 57	1:22:05	(11)		Cherkassy	27 Apr 80
Aleksandr	Starchenko	SU 50	1:22:08	(1)		Chelyabinsk	7 Oct 79

218

All-time Lists – Men

Roland	Wieser	GDR 56	1:22:12	(2)		Naumburg	1 May 81
Gennadiy	Mironov	SU 54	1:22:16	(13)		Cherkassy	27 Apr 80
Vladimir	Gerus	SU 49	1:22:16	(14)		Cherkassy	27 Apr 80
Werner	Heyer	GDR 56	1:22:17	(2)		Karl-Marx-Stadt	17 Jun 83
Vadim	Tsvetkov	SU 46	1:22:19	(1)		Klaipeda	13 May 79
Valdas	Kazlauskas	SU 58	1:22:19	(3)		Cherkassy	27 Apr 80
Karl-Heinz	Stadtmuller	GDR 53	1:22:25	(1)		Eisenhutenstadt	31 May 80
Angel	Flores	Mex 55	1:22:28	(3)		Xalapa	30 Mar 80
Martin	Bermudez	Mex 58	1:22:30	(1)		Zaragosa	11 Oct 81
Yevgeniy	Misyulya	SU 64	1:22:31	(1)		Cheboksary	13 May 84
Aleksandr	Boryashinov	SU 63	1:22:31	(2)		Cheboksary	13 May 84
Aleksandr	Novoselov	SU 57	1:22:36	(1)		Tula	18 Aug 82

Not included (doubtful distance): Eschborn (29 Sep 79); Ruse (13 Apr 80); Yesentuki (5 Apr 81)

50,000 METRES WALK (ROAD)

Ronald	Weigel	GDR 58	3:38:31	(1)	OD	Berlin	20 Jul 84
Jose	Marin	Spa 50	3:40:46	(1)	NCh	Valencia	13 Mar 83
Raul	Gonzalez	Mex 52	3:41:20	(1)	PP	Podebrady	11 Jun 78
Hartwig	Gauder	GDR 54	3:41:24	(2)	OD	Berlin	20 Jul 84
	Weigel		3:41:31	(1)		Naumburg	1 May 83
Andrey	Perlov	SU 61	3:43:06	(1)	Drzh	Moskva	17 Aug 84
	Weigel		3:43:08	(1)	WCh	Helsinki	12 Aug 83
	Gauder		3:43:23	(2)		Naumburg	1 May 83
	Weigel		3:43:25	(1)		Naumburg	1 May 84
Dietmar	Meisch	GDR 59	3:43:33	(3)	OD	Berlin	20 Jul 84
	Marin		3:43:35	(1)	NCh	Barcelona	9 Mar 80
Martin	Bermudez	Mex 58	3:43:36	(1)	LT	Eschborn	30 Sep 79
Enrique	Vera-Ybanez	Mex 54	3:43:59	(2)	LT	Eschborn	30 Sep 79
	Weigel		3:44:20	(1)		Naumburg	1 May 82
Jorge	Llopart	Spa 52	3:44:33	(1)		Reus	26 Aug 79
	Gonzalez		3:45:18	(1)	MRWW	Mixhuca	23 Mar 80
	Gonzalez		3:45:23	(1)	MRWW	Mixhuca	18 Apr 82
	Gonzalez		3:45:37	(1)	LT	Bergen	25 Sep 83
	Gauder		3:45:37	(2)		Naumburg	1 May 84
	Perlov		3:45:49	(1)		Sochi	17 Apr 83
Viktor	Dorovskikh	SU 50	3:45:51	(3)	LT	Eschborn	30 Sep 79
Uwe	Dunkel	GDR 60	3:45:51	(1)	NCh	Berlin	18 Jul 81
	Gonzalez		3:45:52	(1)	MRWW	Mixhuca	23 Apr 78
Pavol	Szikora	CS 52	3:45:53	(2)	Drzh	Moskva	17 Aug 84
	Llopart		3:45:55	(2)	NCh	Barcelona	9 Mar 80
	Dunkel		3:45:56	(1)		Naumburg	1 May 81
	Meisch		3:46:12	(3)		Naumburg	1 May 83
	Dorovskikh		3:46:25	(1)	SpOT	Moskva	27 Jul 79
Willi	Sawall	Aus 41	3:46:34	(1)		Adelaide	6 Apr 80
Valeriy	Suntsov	SU 55	3:46:34	(1)		Cherkassy	25 Sep 83
	Gonzalez		3:46:36	(4)	LT	Eschborn	30 Sep 79
	Gonzalez		3:46:41	(3)		Naumburg	1 May 84
	Marin		3:46:42	(2)	WCh	Helsinki	12 Aug 83
	Dorovskikh		3:46:54	(1)	NCh	Moskva	3 Jul 82
Vyacheslav	Fursov	SU 54	3:46:55	(5)	LT	Eschborn	30 Sep 79
Vladimir	Rezayev	SU 50	3:46:57	(2)	SpOT	Moskva	27 Jul 79
	Gauder		3:46:57	(2)	NCh	Berlin	18 Jul 81
	Suntsov		3:46:58	(2)	NCh	Moskva	3 Jul 82
Pyotr	Gaus	SU 52	3:47:13	(3)	NCh	Moskva	3 Jul 82
	Gonzalez		3:47:16	(1)	MJI	Quebec	20 Jun 81
Sergey	Yung	SU 55	3:47:16	(4)	NCh	Moskva	3 Jul 82
Domingo	Colin	Mex 52	3:47:18	(1)		Valencia	20 May 79
	Perlov		3:47:20	(1)	Znam	Sochi	10 Jun 84

219

Aleksandr	Starchenko	SU 51	3:47:25	(2)		Sochi	17 Apr 83
	Gonzalez		3:47:26	(1)	OG	Los Angeles	11 Aug 84
	Meisch		3:47:38	(1)		Lille	31 May 80
	Suntsov		3:47:44	(2)	Znam	Sochi	10 Jun 84
Marcel	Jobin	Can 42	3:47:48	(2)	MJI	Quebec	20 Jun 81
	Llopart		3:47:48	(2)	NCh	Valencia	13 Mar 83
	Fursov		3:47:56	(3)	SpOT	Moskva	27 Jul 79

(50/21)

Viktor	Shchernov	SU 52	3:47:59	(1)		Cherkassy	8 Oct 82
Petro	Melnyk	SU 51	3:48:19	(4)	SpOT	Moskva	27 Jul 79
Reima	Salonen	Fin 55	3:48:36	(1)	UCp	Zhytomyr	30 Sep 84
Valeriy	Yarets	SU 56	3:48:50	(2)	UCp	Zhytomyr	30 Sep 84
Felix	Gomez	Mex 55	3:49:06	(2)	MRWW	Mixhuca	18 Apr 82
Vladimir	Nefyodov	SU 55	3:49:08	(1)		Kiyev	29 Aug 83
Mykola	Udovenko	SU 56	3:49:25	(3)	MRWW	Mixhuca	18 Apr 82
Venyamin	Nikolayev	SU 58	3:49:38	(3)	Znam	Sochi	10 Jun 84
Ivan	Tikhonov	SU 50	3:49:52	(3)		Sochi	17 Apr 83
Viktor	Grodovchuk	SU 52	3:49:58	(5)	NCh	Moskva	3 Jul 82
Artur	Shumak	SU 63	3:49:58	(4)	UCp	Zhytomyr	30 Sep 84
Nikolay	Frolov	SU 56	3:50:00	(4)		Sochi	17 Apr 83
Yevgeniy	Ivchenko	SU 38	3:50:24	(5)	SpOT	Moskva	27 Jul 79
Paolo	Grecucci	Ita 51	3:50:51	(9)	LT	Eschborn	30 Sep 79
Vladimir	Dushko	SU 56	3:50:51	(5)	Znam	Sochi	10 Jun 84
Vadim	Tsvetkov	SU 46	3:50:59	(7)	NCh	Moskva	3 Jul 82
Ernesto	Canto	Mex 59	3:51:10	(1)	PP	Podebrady	12 Jun 82
Sandro	Bellucci	Ita 55	3:51:20	(11)	LT	Eschborn	30 Sep 79
Horst	Matern	GDR 54	3:51:27	(2)		Naumburg	1 May 81
Anatoliy	Ovchinnikov	SU 57	3:51:28	(8)	NCh	Moskva	3 Jul 82
Francois	Lapointe	Can 61	3:51:38	(1)	NCh	Montreal	24 Oct 82
Boris	Yakovlev	SU 45	3:51:43	(9)	NCh	Moskva	3 Jul 82
Oleg	Andreyev	SU 56	3:51:44	(6)	Znam	Sochi	10 Jun 84
Bo	Gustafsson	Swe 54	3:51:49	(1)	NCh	Goteborg	24 Apr 83
Sergiy	Tsymbalyuk	SU 58	3:51:54	(10)	NCh	Moskva	3 Jul 82
Otto	Barch	SU 43	3:52:05	(7)	SpOT	Moskva	27 Jul 79
Matthias	Kroel	GDR 50	3:52:10	(12)	LT	Eschborn	30 Sep 79
Domingo	Carpentieri	Ita 46	3:52:10	(14)	LT	Eschborn	30 Sep 79
Pedro	Aroche	Mex 46	3:52:31	(2)	MRWW	Mixhuca	1 Apr 79

Not included (doubtful distance): Moskva, 23 May 80

1984 WORLD LISTS

100 METRES

Mel	Lattany	USA 59	9.96	0.1	1r1		Athens,Ga	5 May
Carl	Lewis	USA 61	9.99	1.3	1r1		Houston	6 May
	Lewis		9.99	0.2	1	OG	Los Angeles	4 Aug
	Lewis		9.99	0.9	1	WK	Zürich	22 Aug
Marian	Woronin	POL 56	10.00	2.0	1	Kuso	Warszawa	9 Jun
	Lewis		10.04	0.8	1q5	OG	Los Angeles	3 Aug
	Lewis		10.05	1.1	1	BGP	Budapest	20 Aug
	Lewis		10.06	0.0	1	MSR	Walnut	29 Apr
	Lewis		10.06	−2.2	1	FOT	Los Angeles	17 Jun
Sam	Graddy	USA 64	10.09	1.4	1h2		Baton Rouge	12 May
Harvey	Glance	USA 57	10.09	0.9	2	WK	Zürich	22 Aug
	Glance		10.11	−0.5	1q3	FOT	Los Angeles	16 Jun
Calvin	Smith	USA 61	10.11	0.0	1r5		Walnut	25 Jul
Ron	Brown	USA 61	10.12	0.0	2	MSR	Walnut	29 Apr
Ben	Johnson	CAN 61	10.12	0.9	3	WK	Zürich	22 Aug
	Smith		10.13	0.9	4	WK	Zürich	22 Aug
	Lewis		10.13	0.2	1	8−N	Tokyo	14 Sep
Osvaldo	Lara	CUB 55	10.14	1.1	1r1		Fürth	9 Jun
Leandro	Penalver	CUB 61	10.14	1.1	2r1797,	Fürth	9 Jun	
	Lewis		10.14	−0.5	1q2	FOT	Los Angeles	16 Jun
	Lewis		10.14	−1.5	1s2	OG	Los Angeles	4 Aug
	Glance		10.14	1.4	1h2	WK	Zürich	22 Aug
Innocent	Egbunike	NIG 61	10.15		1		Charleston	25 May
	Woronin		10.15	0.3	1	vITA,SU,HUN	Torino	2 Jun
	Lewis		10.15	−2.1	1s2	FOT	Los Angeles	17 Jun
	Graddy		10.15	0.1	1q2	OG	Los Angeles	3 Aug
	Lara		10.16	1.6	1		Madrid	21 Jun
Stefano	Tilli	ITA 62	10.16	1.7	1h1	WK	Zürich	22 Aug
	Johnson		10.16	1.8	1h4	WK	Zürich	22 Aug
Kirk	Baptiste	USA 62	10.16	0.9	1	GGala	Roma	31 Aug

(30 Marks by 13 Athletes)

Emmit	King	USA 59	10.18	0.6	1		Fort de France	28 Apr
Viktor	Bryzgin	SU 62	10.18	0.1	1r1		Sochi	19 May
Allan	Wells	UK 52	10.18	2.0	1		Edinburgh	17 Jul
Attila	Kovacs	HUN 60	10.18	−0.4	2	DRZ	Moskva	17 Aug
Frank	Emmelmann	GDR 61	10.19	1.3	1r1		Erfurt	12 May
Ray	Stewart	JAM 65	10.19		1h		Port of Spain	19 May
Christian	Haas	FRG 58	10.20	1.1	3r1		Fürth	9 Jun
Norman	Edwards	JAM 62	10.21	−0.1	1r2		Athens,Ga	24 Mar
Aleksandr	Yevgenyev	SU 61	10.22	0.0	1s1	Izv	Kiev	21 Jun
Elliston	Stinson	USA 62	10.23	1.8	1	TexR	Austin	7 Apr
Mark	McNeil	USA 61	10.23	1.3	2r1		Houston	6 May
Vladimir	Muravyev	SU 59	10.23	0.0	1r1		Sochi	26 May
Albert	Robinson	USA 64	10.24	−0.5	2q3	FOT	Los Angeles	16 Jun
Michael	Franks	USA 63	10.25	1.5	1		Carbondale	31 Mar
Nikolay	Yushmanov	SU 61	10.25	0.1	2r1		Sochi	19 May
Hasely	Crawford	TRI 50	10.25		3		Port of Spain	19 May
Thomas	Jefferson	USA 62	10.25	1.9	1		Kent,Ohio	19 May
Ronald	Desruelles	BEL 55	10.25	0.4	1		Hechtel	20 May
Andres	Simon	CUB 61	10.25	1.6	2		Madrid	21 Jun
Ernest	Obeng UK/	GHA 56	10.25	1.8	3h4	WK	Zürich	22 Aug
Paul	Narracott	AUS 59	10.26	0.8	1		Melbourne	6 Mar
Darwin	Cook	USA 62	10.26	1.5	1		Los Angeles(Ww)	5 May
Mikhail	Zalutskiy	SU 57	10.26	0.1	3r1		Sochi	19 May
Jere	Wheeler	USA 64	10.26	−0.5	3q3	FOT	Los Angeles	16 Jun
Leszek	Dunecki	POL 56	10.26	1.4	1	NC	Lublin	22 Jun
Henry	Thomas	USA 67	10.27	0.2	1		Norwalk	19 May
Thomas	Schroder	GDR 62	10.27	0.2	1	NC	Erfurt	1 Jun

221

1984 Lists – Men

Desai	Williams	CAN 59	10.27	0.8	2q5	OG	Los Angeles	3 Aug
Mike	McFarlane	UK 60	10.27	0.2	5	OG	Los Angeles	4 Aug
Ken	Robinson	USA 63	10.28	1.7	1		Austin	24 Mar
Mike	Morris	USA 63	10.28	1.2	1		University Pk	11 May
Silvio	Leonard	CUB 55	10.28	1.1	4r1		Fürth	9 Jun
Pietro	Mennea	ITA 52	10.28	0.3	1		Ostia	22 Sep
Frank	Moller	GDR 60	10.29		3		Split	30 Apr
Sam	Palmer	USA 63	10.29	0.1	2r1		Athens,Ga	5 May
Ainsley	Armstrong	TRI 52	10.29		4		Port of Spain	19 May
Lee	Gordon	USA 63	10.29	1.5	2	NCAA	Eugene	2 Jun
James	Sanford	USA 57	10.29	1.1	1r1		Walnut	3 Jun
Bruno	Marie-Rose	FRA 65	10.29	2.0	1s1	NC (a)	Villeneuve D'A.	30 Jun
Arkadiusz	Janiak	POL 63	10.29	−0.4	4	DRZ	Moskva	17 Aug
Howard	Henley	USA 61	10.30	1.0	1		Las Vegas	3 Mar
Neal	Jessie	USA 64	10.30	0.1	3r1		Athens,Ga	5 May
Greg	Foster	USA 58	10.30	1.5	2		Los Angeles(Ww)	5 May
Chidi	Imo	NIG 65	10.30	0.4	1		Lincoln	12 May
George	Nicholas	USA 63	10.30	1.4	1h3		Columbus	19 May
Stanley	Blalock	USA 64	10.30	−0.5	4q3	FOT	Los Angeles	16 Jun
Luis	Morales USA	/PR 64	10.30	−0.5	5q3	FOT	Los Angeles	16 Jun
Rod	Richardson	USA 62	10.30	−0.5	6q3	FOT	Los Angeles	16 Jun
Aleksandr	Afteni	SU 58	10.30	0.4	2		Moskva	19 Jul
Bobby	Bankston	USA	10.31	1.0	1		San Angelo	18 May
Alvin	McNair	USA 62	10.31	1.2	2		Indianapolis	5 May
Marty	Krulee	USA 56	10.31	1.9	1		Ylivieska	1 Jul
Roy	Martin	USA 66	10.32		1		Dallas	19 Apr
Boris	Nikulin	SU 60	10.32	0.1	4r1		Sochi	19 May
Nikolay	Sidorov	SU 56	10.32	0.1	2	Izv	Kiev	21 Jun
Donovan	Reid	UK 63	10.32	0.7	3s1	OG	Los Angeles	4 Aug
Valentin	Atanasov	BUL 61	10.32	0.4	1		Sofia	25 Aug
Mario	Johnson	USA 61	10.33	1.9	1		Natchitoches	2 Mar
J.-Jacques	Boussemart	FRA 63	10.33	0.6	3		Les Abymes	28 Apr
Lester	Washington	USA 55	10.33		1		Champaign	4 May
Greg	Walker	USA 63	10.33	1.3	3r1		Houston	6 May
Lester	Benjamin	ANT 63	10.33	1.4	2h2		Baton Rouge	12 May
Dannie	Carter	USA 60	10.33	0.4	2		Lincoln	12 May
Walter	Monroe	USA 62	10.33	−1.0	2r1		Tuscaloosa	19 May
Richard	Luxenburger	FRG 58	10.33	1.1	5r1		Fürth	9 Jun
Tony	Sharpe	CAN 61	10.33	0.1	2q2	OG	Los Angeles	3 Aug
Gus	Young	JAM 61	10.34	1.8	1		Chapel Hill	21 Apr
Larnell	Thomas	USA 64	10.34		2		Pasadena,Tex	27 Apr
Dwayne	Evans	USA 58	10.34	0.9	1		Tucson	5 May
Hiroki	Fuwa	JAP 66	10.34	0.0	1		Tokyo	6 May
Donald	Bly	USA 62	10.34	0.4	3		Lincoln	12 May
Terry	Scott	USA 64	10.34	−1.8	1		Knoxville	25 May
Steve	Williams	USA 53	10.34	−0.5	5q2	FOT	Los Angeles	16 Jun
Mikhail	Uryadnikov	SU 59	10.34	1.1	2q2	Izv	Kiev	20 Jun
Mladen	Nikolic	YUG 59	10.34	0.7	1	Balk	Athinai	7 Sep
	Purnomo	INA 61	10.34		1		Taipei	8 Sep
Aleksandr	Semyonov	SU 62	10.34	2.0	1		Baku	14 Sep
Kipper	Bell	USA	10.35	1.7	1r2	MSR	Walnut	28 Apr
Steve	Bridges	USA 60	10.35	0.1	5r1		Athens,Ga	5 May
Antoine	Richard	FRA 60	10.35	1.9	2h6	OG	Los Angeles	3 Aug
František	Ptáčnik	CS 62	10.35	−0.4	7	DRZ	Moskva	17 Aug
Daley	Thompson	UK 57	10.36	0.1	1		Pomona	24 Mar
Colin	Bradford	JAM 55	10.36	0.0	1r2	MSR	Walnut	29 Apr
Doug	Harris	USA 62	10.36	0.6	1		West Point	6 May
John	Gilchrest	USA	10.36		1		Piscataway	12 May
Werner	Bastians	FRG 57	10.36	1.1	7r1		Fürth	9 Jun
Mikhail	Kulikov	SU 61	10.36	0.1	1		Kiev	3 Jul
Greg	Meghoo	JAM 65	10.36	1.1	1r2		Walnut	25 Jul
Antonio	Ullo	ITA 63	10.36	1.9	3h6	OG	Los Angeles	3 Aug
Charles	Seck	SEN 65	10.36	1.7	3		Riccione	26 Aug

1984 Lists – Men

Kenneth	Sutton	USA 62	10.37	7 Apr	1.8
Bernie	Jackson	USA 61	10.37	7 Apr	0.1
Ken	Zachery	USA 63	10.37	28 Apr	−0.1
Igor	Groshev	SU 64	10.37	19 May	0.1
John	Williams	USA	10.37	26 May	0.4
Paulo	Correia	BRA 60	10.37	16 Jun	0.2
Andrey	Shlyapnikov	SU 59	10.37	21 Jun	1.1
Darryl	Clack	USA 63	10.38	14 Apr	
Joe	DeLoach	USA 67	10.38	27 Apr	
Lamar	Smith	USA 64	10.38	12 May	1.3
Aleksandr	Shumilov	SU 61	10.38	19 May	−0.5
Byron	Harris	USA 61	10.38	19 May	
Bogomil	Karadimov	BUL 57	10.38	2 Jun	0.5
Marc	Gasparoni	FRA 59	10.38	6 Jun	1.6
Lincoln	Asquith	UK 64	10.38	2 Sep	−0.3
Verril	Young	USA 60	10.39	17 Mar	0.6
Andre	Freeman	USA	10.39	24 Mar	
Reggie	Bright	USA 65	10.39	30 Mar	
Peter	Ngobeni	RSA 62	A10.39	21 Apr	
Jerry	Lacy	USA 62	10.39	27 Apr	1.7
Vance	Johnson	USA 63	10.39	28 Apr	1.7
Ray	Brown	USA	10.39	29 Apr	0.4
Frank	Hollender	GDR 59	10.39	5 May	0.4
Kelly	Johnson	USA 62	10.39	12 May	0.4
Henry	Williams	USA	10.39	19 May	1.8
Krzysztof	Zwolinski	POL 59	10.39	25 Jul	
Steve	Riddick	USA 51	10.40	28 Apr	0.5
Hermann	Lomba	FRA 60	10.40	28 Apr	0.6
Troy	Amboree	USA 62	10.40	28 Apr	1.6
Rod	Barksdale	USA 62	10.40	5 May	0.9
Daron	Council	USA 64	10.40	12 May	1.4
Clark	Waddell	USA 65	10.40	18 May	1.0
Konstantin	Osadchenko	SU 58	10.40	19 May	0.1
Fred	Johnson	USA 62	10.40	26 May	0.7
Don	Quarrie	JAM 51	10.40	25 Jul	0.0
Elliot	Bunney	UK 66	10.40	11 Aug	1.4
Donnie	Young	USA 62	10.41	7 Apr	
Bruce	Davis	USA 63	10.41	28 Apr	−0.2
William	Snoddy	USA 57	10.41	28 Apr	1.7
Guido	Lieske	GDR 64	10.41	5 May	
John	Mair	JAM	10.41	5 May	1.4
Byron	Stroud	USA	10.41	18 May	1.0
Robert	Hackett	USA 64	10.41	19 May	1.4
Elliot	Quow	USA 62	10.41	25 May	1.8
Vadim	Davydov	SU 62	10.41	20 Jun	0.2
Endre	Havas	HUN 66	10.41	4 Aug	
Greg	Colin	RSA 58	A10.41	14 Nov	0.4
Curtis	Hardy	USA	10.42	24 Mar	−0.1
Kenny	Shannon	USA 62	10.42	15 May	1.9
Sergey	Poduzdov	SU 66	10.42	26 May	
Ikpoto	Eseme	NIG 57	10.42	11 Jun	0.4
José	Arques	SPA 60	10.42	21 Jun	1.6
Ralf	Lübke	FRG 65	10.42	22 Jun	−1.0
František	Břečka	CS 58	10.42	21 Jul	0.3
Mike	Dexter	USA 64	10.43	3 Mar	1.0
Sterling	Hinds	CAN 61	10.43	14 Apr	1.4
Chris	Brathwaite	TRI 48	10.43	28 Apr	1.7
Al	Miller	USA 63	10.43	29 Apr	0.0
Steve	Morgan	JAM	10.43	5 May	0.6
Emerson	Williams	USA 65	10.43	5 May	0.1

Tomás	González	CUB 59	10.43	11 May	
Carl	Dale	USA 64	10.43	18 May	1.0
Viktor	Fyodorov	SU 55	10.43	19 May	0.1
Yoshihiro	Shimizu	JAP 59	10.43	2 Jun	0.0
Hideki	Arikawa	JAP 60	10.43	2 Jun	0.0
Zhang	Chen	CHN 65	10.43	6 Jun	
Arnaldo	de Oliveira	BRA 64	10.43	6 Jun	0.5
Jens	Hübler	GDR 61	10.43	9 Jun	1.9
Detlef	Kübeck	GDR 57	10.43	16 Jun	0.5
James	Butler	USA 60	10.43	16 Jun	−0.1
Fabian	Whymns	BAH 61	10.43	1 Jul	1.9
Brady	Crain	USA 56	10.43	8 Jul	0.6
Peter	Klein	FRG 59	10.43	20 Jul	0.7
István	Tatár	HUN 58	10.43	26 Jul	−0.7
Steffen	Bringmann	GDR 64	10.43	17 Aug	0.3
Bo	Jackson	USA	10.44	17 Mar	1.1
Ollie	Anderson	USA 63	10.44	24 Mar	−0.1
Byron	Howell	USA 62	10.44	14 Apr	1.4
Steven	Hall	USA 63	10.44	7 Apr	1.8
Vince	Scott	USA	10.44	10 Apr	
Lucius	Miller	USA 63	10.44	5 May	0.9
Nikolay	Markov	BUL 60	10.44	6 May	1.4
Mike	McRae	USA 55	10.44	12 May	0.2
Marek	Hulbój	POL 63	10.44	9 Jun	2.0
Piotr	Waszek	POL 60	10.44	9 Jun	2.0
Andrius	Kornikas	SU 64	10.44	3 Jul	0.1
Kimmo	Saaristo	FIN 62	10.44	6 Jul	1.8
Stanley	Davis	USA	A10.44	13 Jul	
Jürgen	Evers	FRG 65	10.44	20 Jul	0.8
Linford	Christie	UK 60	10.44	18 Aug	−0.3

Doubtful Timing

Leone	Ricciardi	ITA	10.41	4 Jul

Unconfirmed Marks

Dudley	Parker	BAH 62	10.40	16 Jun
Audrick	Lightbourne	BAH 60	10.37	16 Jun
Neville	Hodge	UVI 56	10.41	3 Mar
Charles	Mbazira	UGA 58	10.41	28 Apr
Florencio	Aguilar	PAN 59	10.44	8 Jul

Auto-times during 200m race

Don	Quarrie	JAM 51	10.31	6 Aug
Leroy	Reid	JAM 63	10.35	6 Aug
Elliot	Quow	USA 62	10.39	21 Jun
Larry	Myricks	USA 56	10.39	21 Jun

(a) Marie–Rose also 10.29   1.5   1   NC   Villeneuve d'Ascq 30 Jun

1984 Lists – Men

100 METRES

Wind-Assisted Marks

Calvin	Smith	USA 61	9.94	4.6	1		Sacramento	21 Jul
	Smith		9.99	4.1	1		Knoxville	14 Apr
	Lewis		10.00	2.1	1		San Jose	26 May
	Lattany		10.01	4.0	1r1	CalR	Modesto	12 May
Ben	Johnson	CAN 61	10.01	5.5	1	NC/OT	Winnipeg	30 Jun
Ron	Brown	USA 61	10.05	4.0	2r1	CalR	Modesto	12 May
	Smith		10.05	4.0	1h1	TAC	San Jose	7 Jun
Harvey	Glance	USA 57	10.07	4.1	2		Knoxville	14 Apr
	Brown		10.07	2.1	2		San Jose	26 May
	Smith		10.08	4.0	3r1	CalR	Modesto	12 May
Sam	Graddy	USA 64	10.08	2.4			Knoxville	19 May
Mike	McFarlane	UK 60	10.08	>4.5	1	NC	Cwmbran	27 May
Tony	Sharpe	CAN 61	10.09	5.5	2	NC/OT	Winnipeg	30 Jun
	Lattany		10.11	3.0	1r2	FlaR	Gainesville	31 Mar
	Johnson		A10.11	2.2	1r1		Provo	19 May
Innocent	Egbunike	NIG 61	10.12	3.4			Pomona	31 Mar
Carl	Carter	USA 64	10.12	6.5	1h3		Arlington	5 May
Luke	Watson	UK 57	10.12	>4.5	2	NC	Cwmbran	27 May
	Lattany		10.12	5.1	1s2	TAC	San Jose	7 Jun
	Brown		10.13	3.6	1	Pepsi	Los Angeles(Ww)	13 May
Kirk	Baptiste	USA 63	10.13	4.6	2		Sacramento	21 Jul
Roy	Martin	USA 66	10.14	4.0	1	TexR	Austin	6 Apr
	Smith		10.14&	2.8	1s1	TAC	San Jose	7 Jun
	Graddy		10.14	2.8	2s1	TAC	San Jose	7 Jun

(24/14)

Greg	Sholars	USA 66	10.16	4.0	1		Austin 12 May	
Dwayne	Evans	USA 58	10.16	4.0	4r1	CalR	Modesto	12 May
Bruce	Davis	USA 63	10.16	3.5	1		Austin	12 May
Claude	Magee	USA 62	10.16	2.4	2		Knoxville	19 May
Elliston	Stinson	USA 62	10.16	3.2	1h3	NCAA	Eugene	31 May
Donovan	Reid	UK 63	10.17	>4.5	3	NC	Cwmbran	27 May
Jere	Wheeler	USA 64	10.17	4.0	2h1	TAC	San Jose	7 Jun
Thomas	Jefferson	USA 62	10.17	5.1	2s2	TAC	San Jose	7 Jun
Emmit	King	USA 59	10.17	4.6	3		Sacramento	21 Jul
Darwin	Cook	USA 62	10.19	3.6	1		San Jose	21 Apr
Desai	Williams	CAN 59	10.19	5.5	3	NC/OT	Winnipeg	30 Jun
Kenneth	Sutton	USA 62	10.20	6.1	1		San Angelo	22 Mar
Mike	Morris	USA 63	10.20	4.1	4		Knoxville	14 Apr
Lee	Gordon	USA 63	10.21	5.2	1		Boise	14 Apr
Jerry	Lacy	USA 62	10.22	5.3	1h5		Arlington	5 May
James	Sanford	USA 57	10.22	3.6	2	Pepsi	Los Angeles(Ww)	13 May
Albert	Robinson	USA 64	10.23	4.1	5		Knoxville	14 Apr
Stanley	Blalock	USA 64	10.24	3.5	2r2	FlaR	Gainesville	31 Mar
Bobby	Bankston	USA	10.24	2.6	1h2		San Angelo	17 May
Fred	Johnson	USA 62	10.24	4.0	2h2	NCAA	Eugene	31 May
Lester	Washington	USA 55	10.24	4.6	1h4	NCAA	Eugene	31 May
Ken	Robinson	USA 63	10.24	5.1	3s2	TAC	San Jose	7 Jun
Arkadiusz	Janiak	POL 63	10.24	3.2	1		Bydgoszcz	25 Aug
Chidi	Imo	NIG 65	10.25	2.2	2r2	TexR	Austin	7 Apr
Wallace	Spearmon	USA 62	10.25	3.5	4		Austin	12 May
Roscoe	Tatum	USA 66	10.26	4.0	3	TexR	Austin	6 Apr
Greg	Moore	USA 59	10.26	2.3	1r3	MSR	Walnut	28 Apr
Steve	Williams	USA 53	10.26	3.1	1r2	CalR	Modesto	12 May
Larnell	Thomas	USA 64	10.26	2.5	1h3		San Angelo	17 May
Jason	Leach	USA 66	10.26	4.5	1		Sacramento	9 Jun

224

1984 Lists – Men

First	Last	Nat/Yr	Time	w	r	Meet	Place	Date
Dave	Smith	JAM	10.27	4.4	1		Bozeman	19 May
Mark	Witherspoon	USA 63	10.27		1		Arlington	5 May
Verril	Young	USA 60	10.27	3.1	2r2	CalR	Modesto	12 May
Johnny	Thomas	USA 63	10.28	6.5	2h3		Arlington	5 May
Daley	Thompson	UK 57	10.28	4.0	6r1	CalR	Modesto	12 May
Kaoru	Matsubara	JAP 60	10.28	4.6	1	NC	Tokyo	21 Oct
Elliot	Bunney	UK 66	10.29	>4.5	4	NC	Cwmbran	27 May
Marty	Krulee	SU 56	10.29	3.4	2h3	TAC	San Jose	7 Jun
Keith	Stubblefield	USA 65	10.29	4.5	2		Sacramento	9 Jun
Delroy	Poyser	JAM 62	10.30	6.5	3h3		Arlington	5 May
LaNoris	Marshall	USA 60	10.30	3.1	4r2	CalR	Modesto	12 May
Elliot	Quow	USA 62	10.30	2.4	3		Knoxville	19 May
Steffen	Bringmann	GDR 64	10.30	3.2	1		Dresden	26 Jul
Cameron	Sharp	UK 58	10.30	2.4	2h3	WK	Zurich	22 Aug
Mario	Johnson	USA 61	10.31	4.0	1h1	TexR	Austin	6 Apr
Don	Quarrie	JAM 51	10.31	3.1	5r2	CalR	Modesto	12 May
Terry	Scott	USA 64	10.31	2.4	4		Knoxville	19 May
Linford	Christie	UK 60	10.31	3.4	2s1	NC	Cwmbran	27 May
Max	Moriniere	FRA 64	10.32		1		Fort-de-France	21 Mar
Darrell	Austin	USA 63	10.32		1r2		Houston	6 May
Kelly	Reed	USA 65	10.32	2.6	2h2		San Angelo	17 May
Czeslaw	Prądzyński	POL 62	10.32	4.8	1h2		Sopot	29 Jul
Steven	Hall	USA 63	10.33	3.5	5		Austin	12 May
Tomas	Gonzales	CUB 59	10.33	3.2	1h4	Barr	Habana	19 May
Mike	Sanford	USA 60	10.33	3.0	1r2		Walnut	3 Jun
Mladen	Nikolic	YUG 59	10.33	3.5	3		Woluwe	1 Jul
Albert	Lawrence	JAM 61	10.34		1		Kingsville	28 Apr
Joe	DeLoach	USA 67	10.34		1		Pasadena	5 May
Desmond	Ross	USA 61	10.34	7.2	2h1		Arlington	5 May
Mike	McRae	USA 55	10.34	3.1	6r2	CalR	Modesto	12 May
Rolf	Kistner	FRG 62	10.34	2.7	1r2		Fürth	9 Jun
Andrew	Mowatt	CAN 64	10.34	5.1	1		North York	10 Jun
Ken	Zachery	USA 63	10.35	2.8	1h2		Arlington	5 May
Keith	McCoy	USA	10.35				Norwalk	12 May
Marc	Gasparoni	FRA 59	10.35	2.4	1s2	NC	Villeneuve D'A.	30 Jun
Frank	Hollender	GDR 59	10.35	3.2	3		Dresden	26 Jul
Darrell	Wyatt	USA	10.36		14 Apr			
Gerald	White	USA 63	10.36	2.3	28 Apr			
Victor	Scott	USA 62	10.36	4.1	5 May			
Byron	Stroud	USA	10.36	2.6	17 May			
Carl	Dale	USA 64	10.36	2.2	18 May			
Philip	Attipoe	GHA 62	10.36	4.4	19 May			
Peter	v.d.Heyden	HOL 62	10.36	3.2	9 Jun			
Anthony	Small	CAN 62	10.36	5.1	10 Jun			
Archie	Williams	USA	10.37	6.1	23 Mar			
Christian	Zirkelbach	FRG 61	10.37	2.7	9 Jun			
Wilfred	Shepherd	USA	10.38		14 Apr			
Mike	Hill	USA	10.38	6.5	5 May			
Clark	Waddell	USA 65	10.38	2.6	18 May			
Endre	Havas	HUN 66	10.38	2.8	7 Jul			
Hideyuki	Arikawa	JAP 60	10.38	4.6	21 Oct			
Gerrard	Keating	AUS 62	10.39	2.4	3 Mar			
Bo	Jackson	USA	10.39	3.5	31 Mar			
Frank	Booker	USA	10.39		14 Apr			
Leonard	Harrison	USA 63	10.39		5 May			
Mike	Conley	USA 62	10.39	2.4	19 May			
Satoshi	Yonai	JAP 64	10.39		20 May			
Trevor	McKenzie	UK 66	10.39	3.2	21 Jul			
Jörg	Treffer	GDR 65	10.39	4.6	26 Jul			
Olaf	Prenzler	GDR 58	10.39	3.2	26 Jul			
Hirofumi	Miyazaki	JAP 59	10.39	21 Oct	4.6			
James	Barham	USA	10.40	14 Apr	3.2			
Jouko	Lehtinen	FIN 58	10.40	31 Mar	3.4			
Erskine	Evans	USA 63	10.40	14 Apr	4.1			
Al	Miller	USA 63	10.40	12 May	4.0			
Ralf	Lübke	FRG 65	10.40	2 Jun	2.6			
Anthony	Small	CAN 64	10.40	30 Jun	5.5			
Rene	Mangold	SWZ 63	10.40	20 Jul	5.4			
Lucius	Miller	USA 63	10.41	28 Apr	2.3			
Mike	Lawson	USA 58	10.41	19 May	2.4			
Atlee	Mahorn	CAN 65	10.41	26 May	5.9			
Vincent	Jones	UK 65	10.41	27 May	>4.5			
Clayton	Kearney	AUS 64	10.41	15 Dec	3.0			
Mike	Ransby	USA	10.42	31 Mar	2.9			
Brady	Crain	USA 56	10.42	21 Apr	3.6			
James	Washington	USA 60	10.42	6 May				
Clancy	Edwards	USA 55	10.42	12 May				
Johnny	Holloway	USA	10.42	17 May	2.5			
Stephen	Graham	UK 65	10.43	21 Apr				
LaMonte	King	USA 59	10.43	21 May	3.6			
Art	Williams	USA 63	10.43	28 Apr				
Kerwin	Johnson	USA	10.43	5 May	4.1			
Bobby	Ellis	USA	10.43	Jul				

& – Smith's time was actually 9.9 hand timed; his slowest possible time is therefore 10.14, the time of the 2nd placed man.

225

1984 Lists – Men

Short course (98.5 Metres) – Wind Assisted

Verril	Young	USA 60	9.84	2.2	1r2	Baton Rouge		21 Apr
Reggie	Bright	USA 65	10.10		1r1	Baton Rouge		21 Apr
Bill	Collins	USA 50	10.11	2.2	2r2	Baton Rouge		21 Apr
Moses	Ugbisie	NIG 64	10.13	2.2	3r2	Baton Rouge		21 Apr
Travis	Johnson	USA	10.14	2.2	4r2	Baton Rouge		21 Apr
Frank	Booker	USA	10.23		2r1	Baton Rouge		21 Apr

Manual Timing

Auto Best

Paul	Narracott	AUS 59	9.9	1.2	1	Brisbane	4 Jan		10.26
Osvaldo	Lara	CUB 55	10.0		1	Habana	27 Jan		10.14
Peter	Ngobeni	RSA 62	A10.0		1	Libanon	18 Mar		10.39
Harvey	Glance	USA 57	10.0	1.7	1	Tallahassee	26 May		10.09
Sergey	Polevoy	SU 57	10.0		1	Leningrad	4 Aug		
Boris	Nikulin	SU 60	10.0	0.2	1	Gorkiy	11 Aug		10.32
Ronald	Desruelles	BEL 55	10.0		D	Luik	22 Sep		10.25
Silvio	Leonard	CUB 55	10.1		2	Habana	27 Jan		10.28
Oumar	Fye	GAM 60	10.1		1	Banjul	4 Mar		
Jerry	Lacy	USA 62	10.1	−0.2	1h2	Baton Rouge	23 Mar		10.39
Frank	Emmelmann	GDR 61	10.1		1 (&)	Split	30 Apr		10.19
Nat	Johnson	USA 63	10.1	1.5	1	Baton Rouge	5 May		(10.46)
Frank	Booker	USA	10.1	1.5	2	Baton Rouge	5 May		
Moses	Adebanji	NIG 56	10.1		1	Ames	5 May		
Mikhail	Kulikov	SU 61	10.1		1	Leningrad	9 Jun		10.36
Aleksey	Zasypkin	SU 59	10.1		2	Leningrad	9 Jun		(10.57)
Viktor	Bryzgin	SU 62	10.1	−0.1	1h2 (a)	Kiev	20 Jun		10.18
Mikhail	Zalutskiy	SU 57	10.1	1.6	1h5 (a)	Kiev	20 Jun		10.26
Aleksandr	Naduda	SU 61	10.1	−0.1	2h2 (a)	Kiev	20 Jun		(10.45)
Aleksandr	Ryzhkov	SU 56	10.1		1h	Komsomolsk	14 Jul		
Antonio	Ullo	ITA 63	10.1		1 (b)	Alexandria	14 Oct		10.36
Faraj	Marzouk	QAT	10.1		2 (b)	Alexandria	14 Oct		
Jamal	Suliman	QAT	10.1		3 (b)	Alexandria	14 Oct		
Marty	Krulee	USA 56	10.2	11 Feb		Ed	Cutting	UK 59	10.2 20 May
Hermann	Bohmer	RSA 59	A10.2	25 Feb		Vladimir	Kravtsov	SU 56	10.2 2 Jun
Keith	Stubblefield	USA 65	10.2	Mar		Yuriy	Kravets	SU 65	10.2 2 Jun
John	Simpson	USA	10.2	17 Mar		Aleksey	Golovin	SU 61	10.2 20 Jun
Kipper	Bell	USA	10.2	17 Mar		Viktor	Panov	SU 60	10.2 20 Jun
Desmond	Ross	USA 61	10.2	24 Mar		Aleksandr	Afteni	SU 58	10.2 20 Jun
Wessel	Oosthuizen	RSA 61	A10.2	31 Mar		Igor	Ivanneyev	SU 58	10.2 6 Jul
Kenny	Shannon	USA 62	10.2	6 Apr		Yevgeniy	Fedotov	SU 65	10.2 12 Jul
Dmitriy	Petrov	SU 58	10.2	7 Apr		Peter	v.Miltenberg	AUS 57	10.2 13 Jul
Andrey	Murinovich	SU 59	10.2	7 Apr		Sergey	Konstantinov	SU 60	10.2 14 Jul
Tim	Worley	USA 66	10.2	12 Apr		Aleksandr	Osipov	SU 63	10.2 14 Jul
Emerson	Williams	USA 65	10.2	14 Apr		Viktor	Khrishchuk	SU 58	10.2 24 Jul
Darren	Holmes	USA	10.2	Apr		Oleg	Mamayev	SU 58	10.2 4 Aug
Curtis	Hardy	USA	10.2	14 Apr		Josef	Lomicky	CS 58	10.2 8 Aug
Olaf	Prenzler	GDR 58	10.2	30 Apr		Yuriy	Yordanov	SU 58	10.2 10 Aug
Gabriel	Okon	NIG	10.2	5 May		Aleksandr	Zolotaryev	SU 57	10.2 11 Aug
Keith	Stanton	USA	10.2	5 May		Sergey	Pakhar	SU 62	10.2 28 Aug
Vitaliy	Boiko	SU 58	10.2	12 May		Andrey	Razin	SU 62	10.2 22 Sep
Eliot	Tabron	USA 60	10.2	12 May					
Donnie	Young	USA 62	10.2	19 May					

(a) – Izvestia meeting. (b) – CISM championship.
(&) – Timed by hand (3 at 10.1), photo-cell (10.28) and semi-automatic timing (10.11).

Manual Timing – Wind Assisted

Thomas	Jefferson	USA 62	9.9		1		Muncie	28 Apr
Jerry	Lacy	USA 62	10.0	4.0	1h2	TexR	Austin	6 Apr
Steve	Bridges	USA 60	10.0		2		Muncie	28 Apr
Joe	DeLoach	USA 67	10.0		1		Austin	11 May
Roy	Martin	USA 66	10.1		1		Dallas	3 Mar
Peter	V.Miltenberg	AUS 57	10.1		1h1		Melbourne	10 Mar

1984 Lists – Men

Vince	Scott	USA 62	10.1		1		Richmond,Ky.	31 Mar
Bruce	Davis	USA 63	10.1		1		Arlington	31 Mar
Tony	Allen	USA 67	10.1		1		Bridge City	12 Apr
Jason	Leach	USA 66	10.1		1		Odessa	13 Apr
Donnie	Young	USA 62	10.1		1		Jackson	14 Apr
Steve	Williams	USA 53	10.1	2.1	1h2	CalR	Modesto	12 May
Floyd	Heard	USA 66	10.1		1		Brookfield	24 May
David	Cassuto	USA 66	10.1		1		New York	4 Jun

Rolling Start
| Peter | Ngobeni | RSA 62 | 9.9 | 1 | Welkom | 24 Nov |

Doubtful Timing
| Alfonso | Pitters | PAN 63 | 10.1 | 1 | Panama City | 14 Mar |

Unknown Irregularity
| Vadim | Davydov | SU 60 | 10.1 | 1 | Kharkov | 7 Jul |

Unconfirmed Marks
Barnabe	Messomo	CAM 56	10.2	29 Jan
Emmanuel	Bitanga	CAM 53	10.2	5 Feb
Yu	Zhanghui	TAI 62	10.2	21 Apr
Philip	Attipoe	GHA 63	10.2	14 May
Collins	Mensah	GHA 61	10.2	22 May

	1	10	20	30	50	100	Under 10.30	Under 10.40
1980	10.02	10.18	10.21	10.29	10.33	10.44	32	71
1981	10.00	10.18	10.23	10.28	10.35	10.43	33	77
1982	10.00	10.15	10.20	10.26	10.32	10.40	41	91
1983	9.93	10.15	10.19	10.22	10.30	10.37	48	111
1984	9.96	10.14	10.20	10.25	10.29	10.36	53	129

200 METRES

(* = 220 yards time less 0.11 sec)

Carl	Lewis	USA 61	19.80	−0.9	1	OG	Los Angeles	8 Aug
	Lewis		19.84	0.2	1q3	FOT	Los Angeles	19 Jun
	Lewis		19.86	−0.2	1	FOT	Los Angeles	21 Jun
Kirk	Baptiste	USA 63	19.96	−0.9	2	OG	Los Angeles	8 Aug
	Baptiste		20.05	−0.2	2	FOT	Los Angeles	21 Jun
Albert	Robinson	USA 64	20.07	0.3	1		Indianapolis	5 May
Pietro	Mennea	ITA 52	20.07	1.2	1		Brindisi	3 Oct
	Lewis		20.09	−1.3	1s1	FOT	Los Angeles	21 Jun
	Mennea		20.09	0.8	1		Brindisi	14 Oct
	Baptiste		20.16	1.9	1		Austin	12 May
	Baptiste		20.16	0.0	1	WK	Zürich	22 Aug
	Lewis		20.21	−0.3	1		Köln	26 Aug
	Mennea		20.21	−0.8	1		Brindisi	13 Oct
	Mennea		20.25	0.5	1	vCS	Cagliari	9 Sep
Thomas	Jefferson	USA 62	20.26	−0.9	3	OG	Los Angeles	8 Aug
	Lewis		20.27	0.7	1s2	OG	Los Angeles	8 Aug
	Baptiste		20.28	1.4	1h1		Austin	11 May
Roy	Martin	USA 66	20.28	1.0	1q2	FOT	Los Angeles	19 Jun
	Baptiste		20.29	−2.2	1s1	OG	Los Angeles	8 Aug
	Baptiste		20.29	0.9	1	BGP	Budapest	20 Aug
João B.	da Silva	BRA 63	20.30	−0.9	4	OG	Los Angeles	8 Aug
James	Butler	USA 60	20.31	0.9	1	GGala	Roma	31 Aug
	Baptiste		20.33	−0.7	1q1	FOT	Los Angeles	19 Jun
Calvin	Smith	USA 61	20.33	0.5	1q4	FOT	Los Angeles	19 Jun
Vladimir	Muravyev	SU 59	20.34	−1.2	1	DRZ	Moskva	18 Aug
Rod	Barksdale	USA 62	20.35		1		Tempe	21 Apr

227

1984 Lists – Men

	Mennea		20.35	0.4	1	NC	Roma	11 Jul
	Baptiste		20.35	0.9	1		Rieti	2 Sep
Dwight	Williams	USA 60	20.36	0.3	2		Indianapolis	5 May
Wallace	Spearmon	USA 62	20.36	1.9	2		Austin	12 May
Todd	Bennett	UK 62	20.36	1.8	1	NC	Cwmbran	28 May
	Mennea		20.36	0.9	2	GGala	Roma	31 Aug
(32/14)								
Donald	Bly	USA 62	20.37	1.6	1		Norman	14 Apr
Mike	Conley	USA 62	20.37	1.9	3		Austin	12 May
Dwayne	Evans	USA 58	20.38	-0.2	1		Lausanne	10 Jul
Stefano	Tilli	ITA 62	20.40	0.5	2	vCS	Cagliari	9 Sep
J.–Jacques	Boussemart	FRA 63	20.41	1.6	1s1	NC	Villeneuve D'A.	1 Jul
Aleksandr	Yevgenyev	SU 61	20.41	-1.2	2	DRZ	Moskva	18 Aug
Harvey	Glance	USA 57	20.42	0.8	2	VD	Bruxelles	24 Aug
Desai	Williams	CAN 59	20.45	0.0	2	WK	Zürich	22 Aug
Frank	Emmelmann	GDR 61	20.46	0.6	1r1	OD	Potsdam	21 Jul
Gus	Young	JAM 61	20.47	0.0	1	NC	Kingston	16 Jun
Elliot	Quow	USA 62	20.47	-0.2	5	FOT	Los Angeles	21 Jun
Don	Quarrie	JAM 51	20.48	0.0	2	NC	Kingston	16 Jun
Aubrey	Jones	USA 63	20.50	1.6	2		Norman	14 Apr
Larry	Myricks	USA 56	20.50	-0.2	6	FOT	Los Angeles	21 Jun
Ralf	Lübke	FRG 65	20.51	-0.9	5	OG	Los Angeles	8 Aug
Sam	Turner	USA 57	20.52	-0.2	1		San Jose	21 Apr
Gary	Roberson	USA 61	20.52	1.9	4		Austin	12 May
Sergey	Sokolov	SU 61	20.52	-0.1	1	Izv	Kiev	23 Jun
Dannie	Carter	USA 60	20.53	1.6	3		Norman	14 Apr
Tony	Dees	USA 63	20.54	1.9	1		Baton Rouge	13 May
Stanley	Blalock	USA 64	20.54	0.2	3q3	FOT	Los Angeles	19 Jun
Johnny	Thomas	USA 63	20.56	1.9	5		Austin	12 May
Thomas	Schröder	GDR 62	20.56	0.1	2	NC	Erfurt	3 Jun
Olaf	Prenzler	GDR 58	20.57	1.0	1		Karl Marx St.	20 May
Greg	Moore	USA 59	20.57	0.1	2h2	TAC	San Jose	7 Jun
Brady	Crain	USA 56	20.57	-0.7	3q1	FOT	Los Angeles	19 Jun
Ade	Mafe	UK 66	20.57	1.5	2	8–N	Tokyo	14 Sep
Innocent	Egbunike	NIG 61	20.59	0.6	2	FBK	Hengelo	6 Jul
Attila	Kovács	HUN 60	20.60	0.9	2	BGP	Budapest	20 Aug
Christian	Haas	FRG 58	20.61	-0.7	1		Schweinfurt	3 Jun
František	Břečka	CS 58	20.61	0.5	3 v	ITA	Cagliari	9 Sep
Wessel	Oosthuizen	RSA 61	A20.62				Sasolburg	21 Jan
Allan	Wells	UK 52	20.62	0.5	1		Auckland	28 Jan
Michael	Franks	USA 63	20.62	0.4	1		Carbondale	31 Mar
Robert	Hackett	USA 64	20.62	0.3	3		Indianapolis	5 May
Sam	Graddy	USA 64	20.62	1.9	2		Baton Rouge	13 May
Donovan	Reid	UK 63	20.62	1.8	2	NC	Cwmbran	28 May
Arnaldo S.	de Oliveira	BRA 64	20.62	0.0	1		São Paulo	17 Jun
Leszek	Dunecki	POL 56	20.62	1.7	1	NC	Lublin	23 Jun
Leroy	Reid	JAM 63	20.62	0.6	1h2	OG	Los Angeles	6 Aug
Mark	Witherspoon	USA 63	20.63	0.3	1		Arlington	5 May
Jens	Hubler	GDR 63	20.63	0.1	3	NC	Erfurt	3 Jun
Guido	Lieske	GDR 64	20.63	0.5	1r2	OD	Potsdam	21 Jul
Donnie	Young	USA 62	20.64	1.0	1		Tuscaloosa	19 May
Tony	Sharpe	CAN 61	A20.64	1.4	1		Provo	26 May
William	Snoddy	USA 57	A20.64		1		Colorado Spr.	5 Jun
Curtis	Thomas	USA 62	20.65	0.3	2		Arlington	5 May
Leandro	Peñalver	CUB 61	20.65	0.5	4	DRZ	Moskva	18 Aug
Nat	Johnson	USA 63	20.66	-0.7	1		Baton Rouge	4 May
Steven	Hall	USA 63	20.66	1.9	6		Austin	12 May
Colin	Bradford	JAM 55	20.66	0.0	3	NC	Kingston	16 Jun
Ronald	Desruelles	BEL 55	20.66				Grosseto	18 Jul
Alvin	McNair	USA 62	20.67	-0.4	2	DrakeR	Des Moines	28 Apr
Luis	Morales USA	/PR 64	20.67	1.0	1h1		Pullman	18 May
Antonio	Sanchez	SPA 63	20.67	1.7	1		Madrid	21 Jun

1984 Lists – Men

Marc	Gasparoni	FRA 59	20.67	0.3	1s2	NC	Villeneuve D'A.	1 Jul	
Deon	Hogan	USA 60	20.68	1.6	4		Norman	14 Apr	
Elliston	Stinson	USA 62	20.68	1.4	2h1		Austin	11 May	
Daron	Council	USA 64	20.68	1.9	4		Baton Rouge	13 May	
Claude	Magee	USA 62	20.68	1.4	2		Knoxville	19 May	
Tomás	Gonzalez	CUB 59	20.68	1.7	2		Madrid	21 Jun	
Peter	V.Miltenberg	AUS 57	20.69	2.0	1		Melbourne	6 Mar	
Bill	Collins	USA 50	20.69	0.5	1h1		Houston	26 May	
Aldo	Canti	FRA 61	20.69	0.3	2s2	NC	Villeneuve D'A.	1 Jul	
Atlee	Mahorn	CAN 65	20.69	−0.5	3q1	OG	Los Angeles	6 Aug	
Czeslaw	Prądzyński	POL 60	20.70	1.7	2	NC	Lublin	23 Jun	
Fred	Martin	AUS 66	20.71	2.0	1		Brisbane	4 Mar	
Gabriel	Tiacoh	IVC 63	20.71	1.2	1h2		Pullman	18 May	
Robson C.	da Silva	BRA 64	20.71	0.0	2		São Paulo	17 Jun	
Mel	Lattany	USA 59	20.73		1		Dallas	14 Apr	
Carlton	Young	USA 61	20.73		1r1		Piscataway	12 May	
Darwin	Cook	USA 62	20.73	1.2	2h2		Pullman	18 May	
Henry	Thomas	USA 67	20.73	0.9	1		Norwalk	19 May	
Fabian	Cooper	USA 64	20.73	1.0	1		Bakersfield	26 May	
Frank	Möller	GDR 60	20.73	0.1	4	NC	Erfurt	3 Jun	
John	Gilchrest	USA	20.74		1r2		Piscataway	12 May	
George	Crunkleton	USA 56	A20.74	0.7	1		Provo	19 May	
Patrick	Barré	FRA 59	20.74	1.7	1		Colombes	10 Jul	
Mladen	Nikolić	YUG 59	20.74	1.2	1	Balk	Athinai	9 Jul	
Lester	Washington	USA 55	20.75	1.9	1		Stuttgart	21 Jul	
Arkadiusz	Janiak	POL 63	20.75	1.9	2		Sopot	5 Aug	
Darren	Clark	AUS 65	20.76	1.5	1		Sydney	7 Jan	
Carlo	Simionato	ITA 61	20.76	1.9	1		Milano	10 Jun	
Mark	McNeil	USA 61	20.77	1.3	1		Houston	6 May	
James	Maness	USA 63	20.77	1.4	3h1		Austin	11 May	
Marian	Woronin	POL 56	20.78	0.0	4	vITA,SU,HUN	Torino	3 Jun	
Marty	Krulee	USA 56	20.78	1.9	2		Stuttgart	21 Jul	
Dave	Smith	JAM	20.79	0.0	1h2		Bozeman	18 May	
Clark	Waddell	USA 65	20.79	0.1	1		San Angelo	19 May	
Mike	Ransby	USA	20.79		1h4		Cape Girardeau	23 May	
James	Sanford	USA 57	20.79	1.7	1r2		Walnut	3 Jun	
Art	Williams	USA 63	20.80	0.3	3		Arlington	5 May	
Carl	Carter	USA 64	20.80	0.4	3h4		Austin	11 May	
Walter	Monroe	USA 62	20.80	1.9	5		Baton Rouge	13 May	
Luke	Watson	UK 57	20.80	1.0	2	OT	Gateshead	10 Jun	
Fred	Johnson	USA 62	20.81		2h4		Cape Girardeau	23 May	
Jere	Wheeler	USA 64	20.81		2		Bakersfield	26 May	
Courtney	Brown	CAN 65	20.81	1.3	1s1	NC/OT	Winnipeg	1 Jul	
Frank	Hollender	GDR 59	20.81	0.5	3r2	OD	Potsdam	21 Jul	
Steve	Williams	USA 53	20.82	21 Apr	−0.2				
Erwin	Skamrahl	FRG 58	20.82	31 May	0.5	Ed	Frazier	USA 64	20.86	26 May
Silvio	Leonard	CUB 55	20.82	18 Aug	−1.2	Angus	McCuaig	UK 58	20.86	28 May	1.8
Alonzo	Babers	USA 61	20.82	19 Aug		Torsten	Strassburger	GDR 62	20.87	20 May	0.6
Kimmo	Saaristo	FIN 62	20.83	7 Jul	0.3	Boris	Nikulin	SU 60	20.87	23 Jun	−0.1
Peter	Ngobeni	RSA 62	A20.84	21 Apr		Troy	Amboree	USA 62	20.88	26 May	
Mathias	Schersing	GDR 64	20.84	30 Apr		Phil	Brown	UK 62	20.88	28 May	1.8
Andrey	Fyodorov	SU 63	20.84	20 May	0.7	Mikhail	Kulikov	SU 61	20.88	4 Jul	0.4
Gerald	White	USA 63	20.85	28 Apr	1.6	Mike	McFarlane	UK 60	20.88	13 Jul	−1.2
Andre	Freeman	USA	20.85	12 May		Ansell	Cole	USA 62	20.89	11 May	1.4
						Elvis	Forde	BAR 59	20.89	12 May	
Ronnie	Dennis	USA 65	20.85	13 May		Detlef	Kübeck	GDR 57	20.89	3 Jun	0.1
Bernie	Jackson	USA 61	20.85	19 Jun	0.2	Aleksandr	Knysh	SU 64	20.89	23 Jun	−0.1
Boguslaw	Szpiech	POL 63	20.85	23 Jun	1.7	Dennis	Wallace	JAM 62	20.90	11 May	1.4
Walter	McCoy	USA 58	20.86	6 Mar	2.0	James	Washington	USA 60	20.90	11 May	1.4
Ken	Robinson	USA 63	20.86	14 Apr		John	Williams	USA	20.90	12 May	
LaMonte	King	USA 59	20.86	21 Apr	−0.2	Dwight	Johnson	USA 64	20.90	15 May	2.0
Roger	Hunter	UK 65	20.86	5 May	0.3	Kevin	Wilson	USA 57	20.90	20 May	
Charles	Ricks	USA 63	20.86	11 May	1.9	Jack	Pierce	USA 62	20.90	23 May	
Cyprean	Enweani	CAN 64	A20.86	26 May	1.4						

229

1984 Lists – Men

LaNoris	Marshall	USA 60	20.90	7 Jun	0.1	Vesiki	Gotsiridze	SU 61	20.94	20 Jul	−0.7
Viktor	Khrishchuk	SU 58	20.90	23 Jun	−2.1	Sunday	Uti	NIG 62	20.94	25 Jul	0.0
Gusztav	Menczer	HUN 59	20.90	24 Jun	−0.4	Philip	Attipoe	GHA 62	20.95	7 Apr	
Ikpoto	Eseme	NIG 57	20.90	6 Jul	0.6	Merritt	Robinson	USA	20.95	Apr	
Giovanni	Bongiorni	ITA 56	20.90	11 Jul	0.4	Darrell	Austin	USA 63	20.95	11 May	1.9
Joe	DeLoach	USA 67	20.91	27 Apr		René	Gloor	SWZ 56	20.95	26 May	0.3
Danny	Harris	USA 65	20.91	26 May		Jeff	Thorbs	USA 65	20.95	26 May	
Mike	Dexter	USA 64	20.92	7 Apr		Luís	Barroso	POR 66	20.95	8 Jul	2.0
Byron	Howell	USA 62	20.92	28 Apr		Torsten	Heimrath	GDR 63	20.95	21 Jul	1.6
Calvin	Brooks	USA 63	20.92	19 May	1.4	Herman	Venske	RSA 60	A20.96	21 Mar	
Greg	Walker	USA 63	20.92	26 May	1.7	Daron	Early	USA	20.96	21 Apr	
Steve	Riddick	USA 51	20.92	3 Jun		Vladimir	Prosin	SU 59	20.96	10 Jun	−1.0
Aleksandr	Zolotaryov	SU 57	20.92	23 Jun	0.4	Krzysztof	Zwoliński	POL 59	20.96	5 Aug	1.9
Howard	Henley	USA 61	20.93	28 Jan	0.5	Pascal	Barré	FRA 59	20.96	30 Sep	0.0
Clancy	Edwards	USA 55	20.93	14 Apr	0.3	Len	Russell	USA	20.97	21 Apr	
Steve	Morgan	JAM	20.93	6 May	0.7	Nat	Page	USA 57	20.97	3 Jun	1.5
Achim	Piasetzki	FRG 61	20.93	31 May	0.5	Mike	Ricks	USA 59	A20.97	5 Jun	
George	McCallum	UK 63	20.93	30 Jun		Lucius	Miller	USA 63	20.98	24 Mar	
	Purnomo	INA 61	20.93	6 Aug	−0.5	Doug	Hinds	CAN 58	20.98	6 May	1.3
Richard	Wilson	JAM 59	20.93	11 May	1.9	Theodis	Windham	USA 61	A20.98	May	
Lee	Gordon	USA 63	20.94	18 May	1.0	Miroslav	Púchovský	CS 62	20.98	22 Jul	0.8
Rolf	Kistner	FRG 62	20.94	19 May							
John	Bodine	USA 63	20.94	23 May							

Unconfirmed Mark
Dudley   Parker   BAH 62   20.88   15 Jun

Indoor Mark
Roland   Jokl   AUT 62   20.98   2 Feb

Disqualified (Lane Infraction)
Harold   Todd   USA 64   20.89   12 May

Low Altitude Mark
(20.64)   Snoddy   20.77   0.5   3q4   FOT   Los Angeles   19 Jun

Wind Assisted Marks

	Lewis		20.01	2.1	1		San Jose	26 May	
Brady	Crain	USA 56	20.09	3.7	1	TAC	San Jose	9 Jun	
	Baptiste		20.16	3.9	1	NCAA	Eugene	1 Jun	
Dwayne	Evans	USA 58	20.21		1r1	MSR	Walnut	29 Apr	
Thomas	Jefferson	USA 62	20.21	3.8	1s2	TAC	San Jose	9 Jun	
Dave	Smith	JAM	20.22	5.9	1		Bozeman	19 May	
Innocent	Egbunike	NIG 61	20.23	4.5	1		Pomona	31 Mar	
Roy	Martin	USA 66	20.25*				Mesquite	5 May	
	Jefferson		20.26	3.7	2	TAC	San Jose	9 Jun	
	Evans		20.29	2.1	2		San Jose	26 May	
	Evans		20.32	4.9	1	CalR	Modesto	12 May	
Larry	Myricks	USA 56	20.34	3.7	3	TAC	San Jose	9 Jun	
	Mennea		20.34	2.1	1		Riccione	26 Aug	
	Crain		20.35	3.5	1h3	TAC	San Jose	7 Jun	

(14/10)

Elliot	Quow	USA 62	20.40	3.7	4	TAC	San Jose	9 Jun	
Desai	Williams	CAN 59	20.40	2.2	1q2	OG	Los Angeles	6 Aug	
Mel	Lattany	USA 59	20.41	4.9	4	CalR	Modesto	12 May	
Don	Quarrie	JAM 51	20.41	4.9	5	CalR	Modesto	12 May	
Luis	Morales	USA/PR 64	20.42	3.7	5	TAC	San Jose	9 Jun	
Kenneth	Sutton	USA 62	20.44		1h1		Arlington	5 May	

230

1984 Lists – Men

Dannie	Carter	USA 60	20.45	3.9	3	NCAA	Eugene	2 Jun	
Greg	Foster	USA 58	20.47		3r2	MSR	Walnut	29 Apr	
Brad	McDonald	USA 58	20.47	3.7	6	TAC	San Jose	9 Jun	
Mark	Monoco	USA	20.49	5.9	2		Bozeman	19 May	
Attila	Kovács	HUN 60	20.51	4.2	1	NC	Budapest	27 Jul	
Curtis	Thomas	USA 62	20.53		2h1		Arlington	5 May	
Leroy	Reid	JAM 63	20.53	3.9	4	NCAA	Eugene	1 Jun	
Art	Williams	USA 63	20.54	3.7	7	TAC	San Jose	9 Jun	
Ferenc	Kiss	HUN 55	20.54	4.2	2	NC	Budapest	27 Jul	
Allan	Wells	UK 52	20.55	2.1	1		Hamilton	26 Jan	
Charles	Ricks	USA 63	20.55		1h2		Arlington	5 May	
Mark	Witherspoon	USA 63	20.55	2.8	1	Pepsi	Los Angeles(Ww)	13 May	
Tomás	González	CUB 59	20.55	2.7	1		Brest	6 Jun	
Ade	Mafe	UK 66	20.55	2.2	3q2	OG	Los Angeles	6 Aug	
Tony	Sharpe	CAN 61	20.56	3.6	1	NC/OT	Winnipeg	1 Jul	
Michael	Franks	USA 63	20.58	2.8	2h4	NCAA	Eugene	30 May	
Clancy	Edwards	USA 55	20.61		2r1	MSR	Walnut	29 Apr	
Bernie	Jackson	USA 61	20.63	3.5	3h3	TAC	San Jose	7 Jun	
Lester	Washington	USA 55	20.65	2.6	2		Columbus	20 May	
Gusztav	Menczer	HUN 59	20.65	4.2	3	NC	Budapest	27 Jul	
Nikolay	Sidorov	SU 56	20.65	3.9	1		Moskva	5 Aug	
Alvin	McNair	USA 62	20.66	3.5	4h3	TAC	San Jose	7 Jun	
Patrick	Barre	FRA 59	20.67	2.7	2		Brest	6 Jun	
Willie	Hudson	USA 61	20.69		1		Starkville	31 Mar	
Carl	Carter	USA 64	20.69		1h3		Arlington	5 May	
Steve	Morgan	JAM	20.71	4.9	2		College Park	26 May	
Desmond	Ross	USA 61	20.77		1h1		Norman	14 Apr	
Victor	Greer	USA 62	20.77	2.6	2		Columbus	20 May	
Joe	DeLoach	USA 67	20.79		1		Pasadena	5 May	
Ronnie	Dennis	USA 65	20.80		2		Starkville	31 Mar	
Howard	Henley	USA 61	20.80		3r1	MSR	Walnut	29 Apr	
Erwin	Skamrahl	FRG 58	20.80	3.9	1		Wilhelmshaven	1 May	
Henry	Williams	USA	20.82	13 May		Edgar	Washington	USA 62	20.89	27 Apr	
Laron	Brown	USA 63	20.82	25 May	2.2	Mike	Adams	USA	20.89*	5 May	
Laszlo	Babaly	HUN 57	20.82	27 Jul	4.2	Greg	Walker	USA 63	20.89	6 May	
Doug	Hinds	CAN 58	20.83	1 Jul	3.6	Ron	Brown	USA 61	20.89	20 May	2.2
Stanislav	Sajdok	CS 57	20.84	19 May	2.7	Greg	Sholars	USA 66	20.90	9 Jun	3.3
Yura	Bryant	USA 64	20.85	31 Mar		Roscoe	Tatum	USA 66	20.93	5 May	
Eliot	Tabron	USA 60	20.85	12 May		Jason	Leach	USA 66	20.93	9 Jun	3.3
Phil	Brown	UK 62	20.85	28 May	2.6	Jouko	Lehtinen	FIN 58	20.94	31 Mar	4.5
Sam	Koduah	GHA	20.86	19 May	5.9	Jurgen	Evers	FRG 65	20.95	6 Aug	2.2
Terrence	Duckett	USA 62	20.87	19 May	2.9	Mark	McKoy	CAN 61	20.96	1 Jul	3.6
Keith	Stubblefield	USA 65	20.87	9 Jun	3.3	Darren	Holmes	USA	20.97	14 Apr	2.1
Clayton	Kearney	AUS 64	20.87	10 Nov	2.9	Javarro	Sims	USA 60	20.99	17 Mar	2.3
David	Cassuto	USA 66	20.88	9 Jun	3.3						

Disqualified (Lane infraction)

Greg	Moore	USA 59	20.41	4.3	1s2	TAC	San Jose	9 Jun

	1	10	20	30	50	100	Under 20.70	Under 20.90
1980	19.96	20.36	20.55	20.61	20.76	20.94	43	82
1981	20.20	20.46	20.60	20.67	20.79	20.96	35	78
1982	20.15	20.39	20.47	20.58	20.74	20.88	43	108
1983	19.75	20.32	20.46	20.52	20.65	20.85	53	117
1984	19.80	20.34	20.41	20.52	20.62	20.78	79	143

Manual Timing

Mike	Conley	USA 62	20.0		–0.8	1h3		Austin	11 May	20.37
	Robinson		20.1			1		Bloomington	12 May	
Brad	McDonald	USA 58	20.2		1.8	1h1(a)		San Jose	7 Jun	
Harvey	Glance	USA 57	20.3			1		Tallahassee	26 May	20.42

1984 Lists – Men

Name	Surname	Nat/YOB	Mark	Wind	Pos	Venue	Date	Add'l
Alvin	McNair	USA 62	20.4		2	Bloomington	12 May	20.67
Nikolay	Sidorov	SU 56	20.4		1	Moskva	7 Jul	(21.35)
Elliot	Quow	USA 62	20.4	-2.4	1	Atlanta	8 Jul	20.47
Stanley	Blalock	USA 64	20.4	-2.4	2	Atlanta	8 Jul	20.54
Peter	Ngobeni	RSA 62	A20.5		1	Libanon	18 Mar	20.84
Wessel	Oosthuizen	RSA 61	A20.5		1	Pretoria	19 Mar	20.62
Mike	Dexter	USA 64	20.5	2.0	1	Pomona	24 Mar	20.92
Terrence	Duckett	USA 62	20.5		3	Bloomington	12 May	
Dave	Smith	JAM	20.5		1	Pullman	12 May	20.79
Mladen	Nikolic	YUG 59	20.5		1h	Beograd	3 Jun	20.74
Peter	V.Miltenberg	AUS 57	20.6		1	Melbourne	26 Jan	20.69
Fred	Martin	AUS 66	20.6	2.0	1	Sydney	29 Jan	20.71
Claude	Magee	USA 62	20.6		1	Starkville	24 Mar	20.68
Larnell	Thomas	USA 64	20.6		1	Kingsville	31 Mar	
Sunday	Uti	NIG 62	20.6		1	Ames	5 May	20.94
Dudley	Parker	BAH 62	20.6		1	Raleigh	9 May	
Alfred	Nyambane	KEN 56	A20.6		1	Kisumu	19 May	
Simon	Kipkemboi	KEN 61	A20.6		1	Thika	9 Jun	
Sergey	Strebkov	SU 55	20.6	-0.1	1	Omsk	17 Jun	
Donovan	Reid	UK 63	20.6	0.2	1	Woluwe	1 Jul	20.62
Ali	Bakhta	ALG 61	20.6		1	Algiers	5 Jul	(21.14)
Viktor	Khrishchuk	SU 58	20.6		1	Alma Ata	29 Jul	20.90
Jamal	Suliman	QAT	20.6		1 (b)	Alexandria	16 Oct	(21.10)
Ludwig	Myburgh	RSA 62	A20.6		1	Welkom	24 Nov	
Marty	Krulee	USA 56	20.7	11 Feb	Andrey	Dokanyev	SU 64	20.7	7 Jul
Paul	Narracott	AUS 59	20.7	11 Feb	Mikhail	Uryadnikov	SU 59	20.7	7 Jul
Jere	Wheeler	USA 64	20.7	23 Mar	Aleksey	Golovin	SU 61	20.7	15 Jul
Desmond	Ross	USA 61	20.7	24 Mar	Ilya	Ivanov	SU 65	20.7	26 Aug
Hermann	Lomba	FRA 60	20.7	24 Mar	John	Anzrah	KEN 54	A20.7	26 Aug
Neal	Jessie	USA 64	20.7	5 May					
Edgar	Washington	USA 62	20.7	5 May					
Aleksandr	Kazmerchuk	SU 62	20.7	16 Jun					

(a) = TAC. (b) = CISM.

Wind Assisted Marks

Name	Surname	Nat/YOB	Mark	Wind	Pos	Venue	Date
Paul	Narracott	AUS 59	20.3	4.0	1	Brisbane	7 Jan
James	Butler	USA 60	20.3	2.1	1	Knoxville	14 Apr
Stanley	Blalock	USA 64	20.3	2.1	2	Knoxville	14 Apr
Ronnie	Dennis	USA 65	20.3	2.4	1	Starkville	21 Apr
Kenneth	Sutton	USA 62	20.4		1	San Angelo	22 Mar
Johnny	Thomas	USA 63	20.4		1	Arlington	31 Mar
Peter	V.Miltenberg	AUS 57	20.5	2.1	1	Melbourne	22 Mar
Luke	Watson	UK 57	20.5	3.9	1	Wolverhampton	12 May
Brett	Leavy	AUS 65	20.6	4.0	2	Brisbane	7 Jan
Jouko	Lehtinen	FIN 58	20.6		1	Goleta	5 May
Byron	Stroud	USA	20.6		1	Abilene	10 May

400 METRES

Name	Surname	Nat/YOB	Mark	Pos	Meet	Venue	Date
Alonzo	Babers	USA 61	44.27	1	OG	Los Angeles	8 Aug
Gabriel	Tiacoh	IVC 63	44.54	2	OG	Los Angeles	8 Aug
	Tiacoh		44.64	1s2	OG	Los Angeles	6 Aug
Antonio	McKay	USA 64	44.71	1	FOT	Los Angeles	21 Jun
	McKay		44.71	3	OG	Los Angeles	8 Aug
	McKay		44.72	1q1	OG	Los Angeles	5 Aug
	Babers		44.74	1	WK	Zurich	22 Aug
	Babers		44.75	1q3	OG	Los Angeles	5 Aug
Darren	Clark	AUS 65	44.75	4	OG	Los Angeles	8 Aug
Sunder	Nix	USA 61	44.75	5	OG	Los Angeles	8 Aug

1984 Lists – Men

Walter	McCoy	USA 58	44.76	2	WK	Zurich	22 Aug
	Clark		44.77	2q1	OG	Los Angeles	5 Aug
Viktor	Markin	SU 57	44.78	1	DRZ	Moskva	17 Aug
Innocent	Egbunike	NIG 61	44.81	1	Pepsi	Los Angeles (Ww)	13 May
	McKay		44.83	1	NCAA	Eugene	2 Jun
Sunday	Uti	NIG 62	44.83	2s2	OG	Los Angeles	6 Aug
Ray	Armstead	USA 60	44.83	3	WK	Zurich	22 Aug
	Babers		44.86	2	FOT	Los Angeles	21 Jun
Mathias	Schersing	GDR 64	44.86	1	OD	Potsdam	21 Jul
	Uti		44.90	1		Knoxville	19 May
	Markin		44.92	1	Izv	Kiev	22 Jun
	McKay		44.92	3s2	OG	Los Angeles	6 Aug
	Nix		44.93	1s2	FOT	Los Angeles	19 Jun
	Uti		44.93	6	OG	Los Angeles	8 Aug
Rod	Jones	USA 64	44.94	1		Austin	12 May
	McKay		44.95	1q2	FOT	Los Angeles	18 Jun
	Babers		44.95	1s1	FOT	Los Angeles	19 Jun
Jens	Carlowitz	GDR 64	44.95	2	OD	Potsdam	21 Jul
Thomas	Schonlebe	GDR 65	45.01	1		Berlin	15 Jul
	Uti		45.01	2q3	OG	Los Angeles	5 Aug
(30/14)							
Yevgeniy	Lomtyev	SU 61	45.05	2	Izv	Kiev	22 Jun
Bert	Cameron	JAM 59	45.07	1	NC	Kingston	16 Jun
Willie	Smith	USA 56	45.07	1		Koln	26 Aug
Aldo	Canti	FRA 61	45.09	4	WK	Zurich	22 Aug
El Kashief	Hassan	SUD 56	45.19	1		Furth	9 Jun
Chris	Whitlock	USA 59	45.19	3q2	FOT	Los Angeles	18 Jun
Michael	Franks	USA 63	45.20	2	NCAA	Eugene	2 Jun
Bruce	Frayne	AUS 58	45.21	5s2	OG	Los Angeles	6 Aug
Allen	Ingraham	BAH 62	45.26	2		Austin	12 May
Mark	Rowe	USA 60	45.30	4s2	FOT	Los Angeles	19 Jun
Elvis	Forde	BAR 59	45.32	6s2	OG	Los Angeles	6 Aug
James	Rolle	USA 64	45.34	1		Tallahassee	26 May
Oddur	Sigurdsson	ICE 59	45.36	=3		Austin	12 May
Willie	Caldwell	USA 63	45.36	=3		Austin	12 May
Harald	Schmid	FRG 57	45.36	1		Luxemburg	8 Jul
Mark	Witherspoon	USA 63	45.37	5s1	FOT	Los Angeles	19 Jun
Sergey	Lovachev	SU 59	45.37	3	Izv	Kiev	22 Jun
Marcel	Arnold	SWZ 62	45.37	1	NC	Zofingen	22 Jul
Brad	McDonald	USA 58	45.38	1q3	FOT	Los Angeles	18 Jun
Clarence	Daniel	USA 61	45.39	1		Baton Rouge	13 May
Darrell	Robinson	USA 63	45.40	1h6	FOT	Los Angeles	17 Jun
Mike	Paul	TRI 57	45.42	1		Port of Spain	20 May
Kriss	Akabusi	UK 58	45.43	3q1	OG	Los Angeles	5 Aug
Gerson	A.Souza	BRA 59	45.44	2	Pepsi	Los Angeles (Ww)	13 May
Oliver	Bridges	USA 62	45.45	2q1	FOT	Los Angeles	18 Jun
Todd	Bennett	UK 62	45.45	5		Koblenz	29 Aug
Harry	Reynolds	USA 64	45.47	1s1		San Angelo	18 May
Vladimir	Prosin	SU 59	45.47	4	Izv	Kiev	22 Jun
Edwin	Modibede	RSA 61	A45.51	1		Potchefstroom	2 Mar
Aleksandr	Troshchilo	SU 60	45.51	2	DRZ	Moskva	17 Aug
Aleksandr	Kurochkin	SU 61	45.52	3	DRZ	Moskva	17 Aug
Jeff	Gross	USA 63	45.54	3		Cape Girardeau	26 May
Angel	Heras	SPA 58	45.54	1		Milano	9 Jun
Davison	Lishebo	ZAM 55	45.57	4q1	OG	Los Angeles	5 Aug
Isidro	del Prado	PHI 59	45.57	1		Manila	1 Dec
David	Kitur	KEN 62	45.62	7s2	OG	Los Angeles	6 Aug
Carlos	Reyte	CUB 56	45.63	1h	Barr	Habana	19 May
Bill	Green	USA 61	45.65	2s1	TAC	San Jose	8 Jun
Roddie	Haley	USA 64	45.66	1		Austin	12 May
Ed	Yearwood	USA 59	45.66	1		Charlottesville	13 May
Ludwig	Myburgh	RSA 62	A45.66	1		Bloemfontein	7 Nov

1984 Lists – Men

John	Anzrah	KEN 54	45.67	5q1	OG	Los Angeles	5 Aug
Calvin	Brooks	USA 63	45.69	2		Baton Rouge	13 May
Alberto	Juantorena	CUB 50	45.69	2		Rieti	2 Sep
Susumu	Takano	JAP 61	45.69	1	8-N	Tokyo	14 Sep
Willie	McLaughlin	USA 63	45.70	1		Villanova	20 May
Donato	Sabia	ITA 63	45.73	2		Milano	9 Jun
Jackie	Harris	USA 61	45.74	1		Ruston	28 Apr
Eddie	Carey	USA 60	45.74	5q1	FOT	Los Angeles	18 Jun
Erwin	Skamrahl	FRG 58	45.74	3		Munchen	20 Jul
Mark	Senior	JAM 63	45.75	1		Tucson	5 May
Jeff	White	USA 61	45.75	2		Charlottesville	13 May
Antonio	Sanchez	SPA 63	45.76	1		Madrid	29 May
Phil	Brown	UK 62	45.76	2		London	6 Jun
Jan	Tomko	CS 62	45.76	1h3	NC	Praha	21 Jul
Ed	Frazier	USA 64	45.77	1		Bakersfield	26 May
Cedric	Vaughans	USA 61	45.78	4h1	FOT	Los Angeles	17 Jun
Danny	Harris	USA 65	45.79	1h1		Lincoln	11 May
Reggie	Henderson	USA 60	45.80	3		Charlottesville	13 May
Devon	Morris	JAM 61	45.80	4h10	OG	Los Angeles	4 Aug
Henry	Thomas	USA 67	45.82	4	Pepsi	Los Angeles (Ww)	13 May
Eugene	McDaniel	USA 63	45.82	4		Cape Girardeau	26 May
Jeff	Jackson	USA 63	45.84	1		West Lafayette	24 Mar
Kris	Durr	USA 64	45.84	2		Pullman	19 May
Mike	Cannon	USA 64	45.85	5		Austin	12 May
Perry	Cartlidge	USA 63	45.86	4		Baton Rouge	13 May
Cliff	Wiley	USA 55	45.86	4h5	FOT	Los Angeles	17 Jun
Toma	Tomov	BUL 58	45.86	1		Sofia	8 Aug
Gary	Minihan	AUS 62	45.87	1		Adelaide	14 Mar
Donald	Bly	USA 62	45.87	1r2		Austin	20 May
Lamar	Smith	USA 64	45.90	3s1	TAC	San Jose	8 Jun
Athanassios	Kalogiannis	GRE 65	45.90	1	Balk	Athinai	8 Sep
Guido	Lieske	GDR 64	45.91	4	NC	Erfurt	2 Jun
Desai	Williams	CAN 59	A45.92	1		Provo	22 May
Andrew	Valmon	USA 65	45.92	1s2	TAC-jr	Los Angeles	23 Jun
David	Peltier	BAR 63	45.94	2		Ruston	28 Apr
Andre	Phillips	USA 59	45.94	1		Los Angeles(Ww)	5 May
Laron	Brown	USA 63	45.94	5		Baton Rouge	13 May
Robin	Thomas	USA 62	45.95	5		Cape Girardeau	26 May
John	Patterson	USA 65	45.96	6		Austin	12 May
Lazaro	Martinez	CUB 62	45.97	1		Sofia	16 Jun
Aubrey	Jones	USA 63	45.99	2r2		Austin	20 May
Hartmut	Weber	FRG 60	45.99	1		Lage	31 May
Mike	Okot	UGA 58	45.99	1		Boras	19 Jun
Dennis	Mitchell	USA 66	46.02	1		Elmshurst	16 Jun
Billy	Mullins	USA 58	46.03	1		San Diego	25 May
Aivar	Ojastu	SU 61	46.03	6	Izv	Kiev	22 Jun
Roberto	Tozzi	ITA 58	46.03	3		Rieti	2 Sep
Kevin	Robinzine	USA 66	46.04	1s1	TAC-jr	Los Angeles	23 Jun
Amadou	Dia Ba	SEN 58	46.04	2	NC-FRA	Villeneuve D'Ascq	1 Jul
Vladimir	Krylov	SU 64	46.05	2	NC	Donyetsk	7 Sep
Johan	Oosthuizen	RSA 61	46.06	3	NC	Durban	13 Apr
Sammy	Epps	USA 62	46.06	4h1		Knoxville	18 May
Frank	Schaffer	GDR 58	46.07	5		Potsdam	25 May
Carlo	Niestedt	GDR 63	46.07	5	NC	Erfurt	2 Jun
Boubacar	Diallo	SEN 60	46.07	3	WG	Helsinki	4 Jul
Gusztav	Menczer	HUN 59	46.07	3	BGP	Budapest	20 Aug
Dimitar	Rangelov	BUL 63	46.08	1		Sofia	12 May
Steve	Griffiths	JAM 64	46.08	6		Baton Rouge	13 May
Martin	Weppler	FRG 58	46.08	1		Waiblingen	3 Jun
Rick	Mitchell	AUS 55	46.09	2h2	NC	Melbourne	30 Mar
Daniel	Shannon	USA 63	46.09	3		Villanova	20 May
Moses	Ugbisie	NIG 64	46.09	1r2		Walnut	25 Jul

1984 Lists – Men

Eliot	Tabron	USA 60	46.10	6 May	Victor	Lacey	USA	46.28	12 May
Klaus	Just	FRG 64	46.10	18 Aug	Peter	Howard	USA 63	46.28	19 May
Fonnie	Kemp	USA	46.12	12 May	Alan	Slack	UK 60	46.28	6 Jun
Arkadiy	Kornilov	SU 63	46.12	7 Sep	Vasiliy	Polikashin	SU 58	46.29	9 Jun
Kenneth	Lowery	USA 61	46.13	6 May	Henry	Amike	NIG 61	46.29	11 Jun
Hector	Daley	PAN 61	46.13	19 May	Robert	Kseniak	POL 60	46.29	5 Aug
Terry	Ivey	USA 64	46.14	5 May	Anton	Skerritt	TRI 64	46.30	4 Aug
Nate	Williams	USA 61	46.15	18 May	Uwe	Schmitt	FRG 61	46.31	20 Jul
Tim	Bethune	CAN 62	A46.15	1 Jun	David	McKinzie	USA 63	46.32	20 May
Kevin	Hawkins	USA 65	46.16	5 Jun	Derek	Redmond	UK 65	46.32	9 Sep
David	Johnston	AUS 61	46.17	11 Feb	Earl	Jones	USA 64	46.33	25 Jul
Alan	Ellsworth	HOL 64	46.17	4 Jul	Wally	Bumpas	USA 62	46.34	13 May
Rod	Barksdale	USA 62	46.18	21 Apr	Harold	Spells	USA 65	46.34	19 May
Roy	Dickens	UK 61	46.19	28 May	Sylvester	Davis	USA 62	46.36	18 May
Tony	Darden	USA 57	46.19	8 Jun	Mike	Spangler	USA 66	46.36	26 May
Doug	Hinds	CAN 58	46.19	5 Aug	Fabian	Cooper	USA 64	46.36	26 May
Tommy	Johansson	SWE 61	46.19	25 Aug	Chip	Rish	USA 67	46.37	26 May
Vince	Bostic	USA 64	46.20	20 Apr	Kirk	Baptiste	USA 63	46.38	17 Mar
Aaron	Philips	VEN 65	46.20	17 Jun	Greg	Moore	USA 59	46.39	31 May
Dusan	Malovec	CS 57	46.21	19 May	Bill	Hartson	USA 61	46.39	Apr
Reggie	Ross	USA 62	46.21	7 Jun	Curtis	Thomas	USA 62	46.39	5 May
Nikolay	Chernyetskiy	SU 59	46.21	20 Jul	James	King	USA 49	46.39	25 May
Thomas	Giessing	FRG 61	46.21	20 Jul	Willie	Atterberry	USA 63	46.39	25 May
Andrzej	Stepien	POL 53	46.22	22 Jul	Sergey	Kutsebo	SU 61	46.40	5 Jul
Pavel	Roshchin	SU 56	46.22	7 Sep	Olurotimi	Peters	NIG 55	46.42	6 Jul
Zeljko	Knapic	YUG 57	46.22	8 Sep	Terrence	Duckett	USA 62	46.43	19 May
Stanley	Blalock	USA 64	46.24	21 Apr	Willie	Jones	USA 60	46.43	3 Jun
Earl	Bates	USA	46.25	28 Apr	Elijah	Sogomo	KEN 54	46.43	25 Jul
Yann	Quentrec	FRA 62	46.25	1 Jul	Roberto	Hernandez	CUB 67	A46.44	16 Jun
Alfonzo	Henson	USA	46.26	19 May	Nafi	Mersal	EGY 60	46.46	4 Aug
Jörg	Vaihinger	FRG 62	46.26	10 Jul	Roberto	Ramos	CUB 65	46.47	19 May
Dwight	Williams	USA 60	46.27	12 May	Roger	Hunter	UK 65	46.48	20 May
Vladimir	Dyomin	SU 59	46.27	22 Jun	Ali	St Louis	TRI 59	46.48	14 Jul
Bozidar	Konstantinov	BUL 63	46.27	8 Sep					

Best low altitude marks for athletes with seasonal bests at altitude

| Myburgh | 45.78 | 2 | NC | Durban | 13 Apr | (45.66A) |

	1	10	20	30	50	100	Under 46.00	Under 46.30
1980	44.60	45.33	45.57	45.80	46.03	46.35	45	86
1981	44.58	45.18	45.54	45.79	46.02	46.31	46	96
1982	44.68	45.09	45.46	45.65	45.89	46.23	65	106
1983	44.50	44.98	45.29	45.48	45.74	46.16	80	117
1984	44.27	44.83	45.19	45.37	45.62	46.03	98	157

Indoor Marks

Hartmut	Weber	FRG 60	45.97	1	NC	Stuttgart	11 Feb
Willie	Hudson	USA 61	46.08	1		Murfreesboro	13 Mar
Dave	Smith	JAM	46.40	25 Feb			

Manual Timing

	Babers		A44.8	1		Colorado Springs	4 Jun
David	Kitur	KEN 62	A45.1	1	NC	Nairobi	16 Jun
Danny	Harris	USA 65	45.3	1		Lincoln	12 May
John	Anzrah	KEN 54	A45.3	2	NC	Nairobi	16 Jun
Aleksandr	Kurochkin	SU 61	45.3	1		Moskva	8 Jul
Willie	McLaughlin	USA 63	45.4	1	King	Atlanta	22 Apr
Gerson	A.Souza	BRA 59	45.4	1		Sao Paulo	28 Apr
Herman	Vaughans	USA 61	45.6	3		Athens	5 May

1984 Lists – Men

Kevin	Robinzine	USA 66	45.8	1		Austin	11 May
Elijah	Sogomo	KEN 54	A45.8	1h	NC	Nairobi	15 Jun
Sam	Koduah	GHA	45.9	1		Bozeman	19 May
Uwe	Schmitt	FRG 61	45.9	1		Wetzlar	3 Jun
Mike	Ricks	USA 59	A45.9	2		Colorado Springs	4 Jun
James	Atuti	KEN 54	A45.9	3	NC	Nairobi	16 Jun
Nikolay	Chernyetskiy	SU 59	45.9	2		Moskva	8 Jul
Boris	Makhotkin	SU 60	45.9	1		Tula	24 Jul
Carter	Williams	USA	46.0	1		Miami	18 Feb
Nafi	Mersal	EGY 60	46.0	1		Cairo	5 Apr
Sylvester	Davis	USA 62	46.0	3	King	Atlanta	22 Apr
William	White	USA	A46.0	3		Colorado Springs	4 Jun
Reuben	Amimo	KEN 63	A46.0	2		Nairobi	26 Aug
Marcus	Sanders	USA 63	46.1	22 Apr	Javarro	Sims	USA 60	46.3	14 Apr
Alfred	Nyambane	KEN 56	A46.1	12 May	Lorenzo	Brown	USA	A46.3	4 Jun
Jason	Opicho	KEN 60	A46.1	16 Jun	Elkana	Nyangau	KEN 64	46.3	30 Jun
Anatoliy	Melnikov	SU 60	46.2	8 Jul	Valeriy	Boychuk	SU 56	46.3	11 Aug

800 METRES

Joaquim C.	Cruz	BRA 63	1:41.77	1		Koln	26 Aug
Sam	Koskei	KEN 61	1:42.28	2		Koln	26 Aug
	Cruz		1:42.34	1r1	WK	Zurich	22 Aug
	Cruz		1:42.41	1	VD	Bruxelles	24 Aug
Johnny	Gray	USA 60	1:42.96	1		Koblenz	29 Aug
	Cruz		1:43.00	1	OG	Los Angeles	6 Aug
	Gray		1:43.28	2	VD	Bruxelles	24 Aug
	Gray		1:43.28	3		Koln	26 Aug
	Koskei		1:43.28	2		Koblenz	29 Aug
	Koskei		1:43.51	2r1	WK	Zurich	22 Aug
	Gray		1:43.59	1		Rieti	2 Sep
Agberto	Guimaraes	BRA 57	1:43.63	3		Koblenz	29 Aug
Sebastian	Coe	UK 56	1:43.64	2	OG	Los Angeles	6 Aug
Earl	Jones	USA 64	1:43.74	1	FOT	Los Angeles	19 Jun
	Gray		1:43.74	2	FOT	Los Angeles	19 Jun
	Cruz		1:43.82	1s1	OG	Los Angeles	5 Aug
	Jones		1:43.83	3	OG	Los Angeles	6 Aug
	Coe		1:43.84	1	Bisl	Oslo	28 Jun
Donato	Sabia	ITA 63	1:43.88	1		Firenze	13 Jun
	Guimaraes		1:43.91	4		Koln	26 Aug
John	Marshall	USA 63	1:43.92	3	FOT	Los Angeles	19 Jun
James	Robinson	USA 54	1:43.92	4	FOT	Los Angeles	19 Jun
William	Wuycke	VEN 58	1:43.93	2		Rieti	2 Sep
Billy	Konchellah	KEN 61	1:44.03	4	OG	Los Angeles	6 Aug
Edwin	Koech	KEN 61	1:44.12	2s1	OG	Los Angeles	5 Aug
	Robinson		1:44.24	3	VD	Bruxelles	24 Aug
Vasiliy	Matveyev	SU 62	1:44.25	1	Izv	Kiev	22 Jun
	Jones		1:44.51	3s1	OG	Los Angeles	5 Aug
	Sabia		1:44.53	5	OG	Los Angeles	6 Aug
Garry	Cook	UK 58	1:44.55	4		Koblenz	29 Aug
	Guimaraes		1:44.58	3r1	WK	Zurich	22 Aug
(31/14)							
Rob	Druppers	HOL 62	1:44.60	2		Firenze	13 Jun
James	Mays	USA 59	1:44.62	1	DNG	Stockholm	2 Jul
Ikem	Billy	UK 64	1:44.65	1		Oslo	21 Jul
Viktor	Kalinkin	SU 60	1:44.73	2	Izv	Kiev	22 Jun
Steve	Ovett	UK 55	1:44.81	4s1	OG	Los Angeles	5 Aug
Stanley	Redwine	USA 61	1:44.87	2		Oslo	21 Jul

1984 Lists – Men

Omer	Khalifa	SUD 56	1:44.87	5s1	OG	Los Angeles	5 Aug
Alberto	Juantorena	CUB 50	1:44.88	3*		Firenze	13 Jun
Matthias	Assmann	FRG 57	1:44.93	6		Koblenz	29 Aug
Jose-Luis	Barbosa	BRA 61	1:44.98	1		London	18 Aug
Moussa	Fall	SEN 63	1:45.03	6s1	OG	Los Angeles	5 Aug
Leonid	Masunov	SU 62	1:45.08	3	Izv	Kiev	22 Jun
Hans-Peter	Ferner	FRG 56	1:45.11	7		Koblenz	29 Aug
Coloman	Trabado	SPA 58	1:45.15	3		Oslo	21 Jul
Don	Paige	USA 56	1:45.17	5	FOT	Los Angeles	19 Jun
Aleksandr	Kostetskiy	SU 60	1:45.17	4	Izv	Kiev	22 Jun
Rob	Harrison	UK 59	1:45.31	4		Oslo	21 Jul
Detlef	Wagenknecht	GDR 59	1:45.44	1h2	NC	Erfurt	1 Jun
Peter	Elliott	UK 62	1:45.49	4q1	OG	Los Angeles	4 Aug
Juma	N'diwa	KEN 60	1:45.59	3q4	OG	Los Angeles	4 Aug
Paul	Gilbert	AUS 60	1:45.6m	1		Melbourne	22 Mar
Peter	Braun	FRG 62	1:45.62	5		Lausanne	10 Jul
Faouzi	Lahbi	MOR 60	1:45.67	5q1	OG	Los Angeles	4 Aug
Ryszard	Ostrowski	POL 61	1:45.68	=1	DRZ	Moskva	18 Aug
Babacar	Niang	SEN 58	1:45.71	6q1	OG	Los Angeles	4 Aug
Pat	Scammell	AUS 61	1:45.74	2	Jerome	Burnaby	16 Jul
Marco	Mayr	SWZ 60	1:45.75	6		Lausanne	10 Jul
Andreas	Hauck	GDR 61	1:45.78	2		Dresden	19 May
Mohamed	Alouini	TUN 57	1:45.78	5q4	OG	Los Angeles	4 Aug
Steve	Crabb	UK 63	1:45.80	5		London	18 Aug
Chris	McGeorge	UK 62	1:45.85	5		Oslo	21 Jul
Peter	Pearless	NZ 57	1:45.9m	3		Melbourne	22 Mar
Steve	Cram	UK 60	1:46.0m	1	(a)	Coventry	2 Sep
Owen	Hamilton	JAM 59	1:46.02	2		Hannover	19 Aug
Riccardo	Materazzi	ITA 63	1:46.03	4h2	OG	Los Angeles	3 Aug
Axel	Harries	FRG 64	1:46.04	2		Munchen	20 Jul
Mike	Hillardt	AUS 61	1:46.06	1r2		Walnut	25 Jul
Abdi	Bile	SOM 63	1:46.1m	1		Charlottesville	13 May
Yakov	Shenkerman	SU 60	1:46.16	5	Izv	Kiev	22 Jun
Gareth	Brown	UK 61	1:46.16	6	DNG	Stockholm	2 Jul
Jack	McIntosh	USA 59	1:46.16	2r2	WK	Zurich	22 Aug
Jose	Marajo	FRA 54	1:46.18	7		Oslo	21 Jul
Marcus	O'Sullivan	IRL 61	1:46.21	6q4	OG	Los Angeles	4 Aug
Valeriy	Starodubtsev	SU 62	1:46.24	3		Sochi	27 May
Ronny	Olsson	SWE 61	1:46.28	6	BisI	Oslo	28 Jun
Igor	Lotarev	SU 64	1:46.34	4	vITA,POL,HUN	Torino	2 Jun
Chuck	Aragon	USA 59	1:46.34	2		Eugene	4 Jun
Sotirios	Moutsanas	GRE 58	1:46.34	7q1	OG	Los Angeles	4 Aug
Rob	Webster	USA 60	1:46.35	1		San Diego	25 May
James	Maina Boi	KEN 54	1:46.39	2r2		Walnut	25 Jul
Oslen	Barr	GUY 61	1:46.42	1	King	Atlanta	22 Apr
Didier	Marquant	FRA 58	1:46.46	7		Lausanne	10 Jul
John	Gladwin	UK 63	1:46.48	7		London	18 Aug
Anatoliy	Millin	SU 59	1:46.50	4		Sochi	27 May
Brian	Theriot	USA 57	1:46.50	7		Luxemburg	8 Jul
Philippe	Dupont	FRA 58	1:46.51	1		St Maur	6 Jun
Mark	Handelsman	ISR 61	1:46.53	3	Pepsi	Los Angeles (Ww)	13 May
Bruce	Roberts	CAN 57	1:46.53	1		Burnaby	26 May
Istvan	Szalai	HUN 62	1:46.54	1		Budapest	11 Jul
Jeff	West	USA 61	1:46.57	2		San Jose	26 May
Benjamin	Gonzalez	SPA 58	1:46.58	5		Gateshead	6 Jul
Stefano	Cecchini	ITA 61	1:46.60	1		Caravaggio	27 May
Olaf	Beyer	GDR 57	1:46.60	3	NC	Erfurt	2 Jun
Pete	Richardson	USA 63	1:46.62	7	FOT	Los Angeles	19 Jun
Vladimir	Samoylenko	SU 61	1:46.7m	1		Kiev	12 Aug
Ferenc	Reichnach	HUN 64	1:46.72	5	BGP	Budapest	20 Aug
Simon	Hoogewerf	CAN 63	1:46.73	4	Jerome	Burnaby	16 Jul
Steve	Scott	USA 56	1:46.73	3r2		Walnut	25 Jul

1984 Lists – Men

James	Garrett	USA 64	1:46.77	2		San Diego	25 May
Eugene	Sanders	USA 60	1:46.77	5q1	FOT	Los Angeles	17 Jun
Peter	Bourke	AUS 58	1:46.8m	4		Melbourne	22 Mar
Said	Aouita	MOR 60	1:46.81	1r2		Torino	2 Jun
Petru	Dragoescu	RUM 62	1:46.81	4		Firenze	13 Jun
Christoph	Ulmer	SWZ 61	1:46.82	8		Lausanne	10 Jul
John	Walker	NZ 52	1:46.83	3		Hamilton	26 Jan
Fred	Williams	RSA 62	1:46.85	1		Arlington	5 May
Andres	Vera	SPA 60	1:46.85	2		Madrid	21 Jun
Eckardt	Ruter	FRG 63	1:46.85	1		Monchen Gladba.	19 Aug
Johnny	Walker	USA 63	1:46.86	2		Arlington	5 May
Doug	Wournell	CAN 61	1:46.87	2		Burnaby	26 May
Mike	Solomon	TRI 54	1:46.88	9		London	18 Aug
Oki	Clark	USA 60	1:46.90	1		San Angelo	19 May
Neil	Moore	USA 57	1:46.9m	4		Burnaby	26 May
Andre	Lavie	FRA 59	1:46.92	2		St Maur	6 Jun
Holger	Bottcher	FRG 63	1:46.94	3		Athinai	10 Jul
Mario	Monien	GDR 61	1:46.97	4	NC	Erfurt	2 Jun
Ken	Wynn	USA 61	1:46.97	2s1	TAC	San Jose	8 Jun

Mohamed	Zahafi	MOR 59	1:47.00	13 Jul	Wieslaw	Wojciechowski	POL 60	1:47.44	24 Jun
Melvin	Beckman	RSA 61	1:47.0m	21 Mar	Costel	Ene	RUM 62	1:47.44	12 Jul
Stan	Whitaker	USA 57	1:47.02	18 Jul	Tony	Davis	USA 63	1:47.49	13 May
Ray	Brown	USA 61	1:47.05	17 Jun	Ian	Lewis	RSA 62	1:47.5m	21 Mar
Anatoliy	Ivanov	SU 62	1:47.06	27 May	Aleksey	Litvinov	SU 59	1:47.5m	16 Jun
Larry	Mangan	USA 59	1:47.07	4 Jun	Dub	Myers	USA 64	1:47.51	19 May
Roger	Moore	USA 60	1:47.08	8 Jun	Johan	Fourie	RSA 59	1:47.56	14 Apr
Zsolt	Szabo	HUN 61	1:47.09	17 Jun	Morten	Jurs	NOR 60	1:47.56	21 Jul
Krzysztof	Pradzynski	POL 58	1:47.09	24 Jun	Andreas	Busse	GDR 59	1:47.58	9 Jun
Thierry	Tonnellier	FRA 59	1:47.10	6 Jun	Batuimalu	Rajakumar	MAL 64	1:47.59	8 Jul
Charles	Onsare	KEN 58	A1:47.1m	16 Jun	Ralph	Schumann	GDR 66	1:47.59	5 Aug
Joseph	Chesire	KEN 57	A1:47.1m	16 Jun	Vadim	Laushkin	SU 65	1:47.6m	7 Jul
Pascal	Thiebaut	FRA 59	1:47.1m	25 Jul	Deon	Brummer	RSA	A1:47.6m	7 Nov
Paul	Larkins	UK 63	1:47.13	20 May	Scott	Rider	USA 59	1:47.62	16 Jul
Randy	Wilson	USA 55	1:47.14	26 May	Darrell	Sargent	USA 59	1:47.65	25 May
Jose Luis	Gonzalez	SPA 57	1:47.14	29 May	Tonino	Viali	ITA 60	1:47.65	20 Jun
Alberto	Barsotti	ITA 64	1:47.14	13 Jun	Dan	Futrell	USA 56	1:47.66	18 May
Luis	Migueles	ARG 65	1:47.14	28 Oct	Darryl	Taylor	UK 65	1:47.70	13 Jul
Jozsef	Bereczki	HUN 62	1:47.19	10 Jul	Rodney	Lessing (b)	RSA	1:47.7m	25 Feb
Vladimir	Skutov	SU 59	1:47.2m	15 Jul	Garland	Brown	USA 62	1:47.7m	13 May
Aleksandr	Toyshev	SU 59	1:47.2m	23 Sep	Viktor	Minyenko	SU 60	1:47.7m	16 Jun
Bernd	Wulf	GDR 59	1:47.21	2 Jun	Sergey	Artyemenko	SU 61	1:47.7m	12 Aug
Mike	Shea	USA 60	1:47.24	17 Jun	John	Blackledge	UK 61	1:47.71	23 Jun
Hans-Joach.	Mogalle	GDR 59	1:47.25	19 May	Kim	Bok-Joo	TAI 60	1:47.72	29 Apr
Rob	McVicar	AUS 60	1:47.26	22 Jan	Pavel	Troshchilo	SU 60	1:47.72	19 Jul
Ahmed	Belkessam	ALG 62	1:47.28	13 Jul	Ian	Marron	IRL 63	1:47.74	24 Jun
Bill	Martin	USA 57	1:47.3m	26 May	Frank	O'Mara	IRL 60	1:47.75	18 May
Brett	Crew	AUS 62	1:47.31	6 Mar	Sandy	Chapman	USA 61	1:47.75	19 May
Scott	Davis	USA 61	1:47.31	17 Jun	Jurgen	Grothe	FRG 60	1:47.75	4 Sep
John	Hinton	USA 62	1:47.33	18 May	Gerald	Masterson	USA 54	1:47.78	22 Apr
Raivo	Magi	SU 60	1:47.33	27 May	Rudi	De Wijngaert	BEL 59	1:47.78	14 Aug
Eero	Kytola	FIN 62	1:47.33	28 Jun	Henning	Gericke	RSA 60	1:47.8m	21 Mar
Mike	Armour	USA 62	1:47.34	18 May	Kipkoech	Cheruiyot	KEN 64	1:47.8m	12 May
Slobodan	Popovic	YUG 62	1:47.35	21 Jun	Sergey	Lapetin	SU 60	1:47.8m	6 Jul
Binko	Kolev	BUL 58	1:47.40	10 Jul	Brian	Thompson	CAN 63	1:47.8m	16 Jul
Willie	Singleton	USA 63	1:47.4m	21 Apr	Johnny	Kroon	SWE 60	1:47.85	25 Aug
Pyotr	Pilipchuk	SU 58	1:47.4m	6 Jul	Werner	Busshof	FRG 65	1:47.9m	30 May
Espen	Borge	NOR 61	1:47.41	18 Jul	Dominique	Bouchard	FRA 63	1:47.9m	25 Jul
Herbert	Wursthorn	FRG 57	1:47.41	29 Aug	Andreas	Kaliebe	GDR 62	1:47.91	2 Jun
Mel	Trahan	USA 61	1:47.42	4 May	Said	Oukali	ALG 57	1:47.93	20 Jun
Pascal	Thomas	FRA 56	1:47.42	6 Jun	Hans	Kulker	HOL 59	1:47.94	6 Jul
Nikolay	Kirov	SU 57	1:47.43	9 Jun	Milovan	Savic	YUG 53	1:47.95	5 May

238

1984 Lists – Men

Uwe	Bergmann	GDR 61	1:47.95	6 May
Joe	Kapheim	USA 62	1:47.96	5 May
Marian	Rados	RUM 62	1:47.96	12 Jul
Gert	Kilbert	SWZ 65	1:47.97	31 May
Peter	Wirz	SWZ 60	1:47.98	26 May
Tony	Gamble	USA 64	1:47.99	12 May

Indoor Marks

| Andreas | Kaliebe | GDR 62 | 1:47.55 | 15 Jan |
| Torsten | Lenhardt | GDR 63 | 1:47.92 | 15 Jan |

(a) Cram also 1:46.05 6 London 18 Aug
(b) Lessing also A1:47.74 21 Apr

	1	10	20	30	50	100	Under 1:47.0	Under 1:47.5
1980	1:44.53	1:45.6	1:46.11	1:46.6	1:46.9	1:47.85	52	80
1981	1:41.8	1:45.30	1:46.0	1:46.29	1:46.89	1:47.66	55	90
1982	1:44.45	1:45.05	1:45.44	1:45.90	1:46.5	1:47.33	76	111
1983	1:43.61	1:44.32	1:45.13	1:45.58	1:46.29	1:47.14	89	126
1984	1:41.77	1:43.93	1:44.87	1:45.17	1:46.04	1:46.97	101	146

1000 METRES

Joaquim C.	Cruz	BRA 63	2:14.09	1	Nik	Nice	20 Aug
	Cruz		2:14.54	1	Pre	Eugene	21 Jul
Steve	Cram	UK 60	2:15.98	1		Loughborough	17 Jun
Andreas	Hauck	GDR 60	2:16.3m	1		Potsdam	12 Jul
Andreas	Busse	GDR 59	2:16.3m	2		Potsdam	12 Jul
Jim	Spivey	USA 60	2:16.54	2	Pre	Eugene	21 Jul
Graham	Williamson	UK 60	2:16.82	1		Edinburgh	17 Jul
	Williamson		2:16.86	2	Nik	Nice	20 Aug
Rob	Druppers	HOL 62	2:17.07	3	Pre	Eugene	21 Jul
Riccardo	Materazzi	ITA 63	2:17.14	1		Pisa	20 Jun
Rob	Harrison	UK 59	2:17.20	1		London	18 Aug
Johnny	Gray	USA 60	2:17.27	2		London	18 Aug
Johan	Fourie	RSA 59	A2:17.34	1		Pretoria	14 Mar
Gareth	Brown	UK 61	2:17.43	3		London	18 Aug
Chris	McGeorge	UK 62	2:17.45	3	Nik	Nice	20 Aug
Mike	Hillardt	AUS 61	2:17.49	4		London	18 Aug
Agberto	Guimäraes	BRA 57	2:17.52	4	Pre	Eugene	21 Jul
	Cram		2:17.58	2		Edinburgh	17 Jul
James	Mays	USA 59	2:17.67	3		Edinburgh	17 Jul
Hans-Peter	Ferner	FRG 56	2:17.83	1		München	20 Jul
Mark	Scruton	UK 58	2:17.95	4		Edinburgh	17 Jul

(21/18)

Steve	Crabb	UK 63	2:18.13	1		London	13 Jul
Don	Paige	USA 56	2:18.18	4	Nik	Nice	20 Aug
Wolfgang	Frombold	FRG 59	2:18.22	2		München	20 Jul
Abdi	Bile	SOM 63	2:18.32	6		London	18 Aug
Henning	Gericke	RSA 60	A2:18.38	2		Pretoria	14 Mar
Matthias	Assmann	FRG 57	2:18.61	2		Köln	26 Aug
Pascal	Thiébaut	FRA 59	2:18.7m	1		Metz	21 Jun
Detlef	Wallow	FRG 63	2:18.86	3		München	20 Jul
Brian	Theriot	USA 57	2:18.91	3		London	13 Jul
Kevin	Johnson	USA 60	2:18.93	3		Köln	26 Aug
Deon	Brummer	RSA	A2:19.00	3		Pretoria	14 Mar
Simon	Hoogewerf	CAN 63	2:19.05	5	Nik	Nice	20 Aug
John	Gladwin	UK 63	2:19.14	4		London	13 Jul
Said	Aouita	MOR 60	2:19.17	1		Viareggio	15 Aug
Richard	Block	USA 60	2:19.23	4		München	20 Jul
Stuart	Paton	UK 63	2:19.36	7		London	18 Aug
John	Walker	NZ 52	2:19.37	1		San Diego	30 Jul
Jeff	West	USA 61	2:19.49	5	•	Edinburgh	17 Jul
Jack	McIntosh	USA 59	2:19.57	6		Köln	26 Aug

1984 Lists – Men

John	Blackledge	UK 61	2:19.65	5		Edinburgh	17 Jul
Jürgen	Grothe	FRG 59	2:19.69	7		Köln	26 Aug
Andres	Vera	SPA 60	2:19.83	1		Zaragoza	3 Jun

No Curb to track
| Ryszard | Ostrowski | POL 61 | | 2:18.0m | 1 | | Poznan | 12 May |

Indoor Marks
| Sam | Koskei | KEN 61 | | 2:19.26 | 2 | | East Rutherford | 11 Feb |
| Viktor | Kalinkin | SU 60 | | 2:19.89 | 1 | | Moskva | 11 Feb |

1500 METRES

(# = During Mile race)

Said	Aouita	MOR 60	3:31.54	1	FBK	Hengelo	6 Jul
Sebastian	Coe	UK 56	3:32.39	1	WK	Zürich	22 Aug
	Coe		3:32.53	1	OG	Los Angeles	11 Aug
Steve	Cram	UK 60	3:33.13	1	BGP	Budapest	20 Aug
	Cram		3:33.40	2	OG	Los Angeles	11 Aug
Steve	Scott	USA 56	3:33.46	2	WK	Zürich	22 Aug
Pierre	Délèze	SWZ 58	3:33.64	3	WK	Zürich	22 Aug
José Manuel	Abascal	SPA 58	3:33.69	4	WK	Zürich	22 Aug
	Cram		3:34.08	1	VD	Bruxelles	24 Aug
Andreas	Busse	GDR 59	3:34.10	1	OD	Potsdam	21 Jul
	Aouita		3:34.10	1		Koblenz	29 Aug
Graham	Williamson	UK 60	3:34.13#	1		Oslo	21 Jul
	Aouita		3:34.13	1		Paris	4 Sep
Jim	Spivey	USA 60	3:34.19	5	WK	Zürich	22 Aug
Mike	Hillardt	AUS 61	3:34.20	1		Sydney	11 Mar
David	Moorcroft	UK 53	3:34.2 #	2		Oslo	21 Jul
	Abascal		3:34.30	3	OG	Los Angeles	11 Aug
Johan	Fourie	RSA 59	3:34.3m	1		Port Elizabeth	21 Mar
Steve	Ovett	UK 55	3:34.50	1	Bisl	Oslo	28 Jun
	Fourie		3:34.5m	1		Stellenbosch	22 Feb
Joséph	Chesire	KEN 57	3:34.52	4	OG	Los Angeles	11 Aug
Omer	Khalifa	SUD 56	3:34.59	2		Koblenz	29 Aug
José Luis	Gonzalez	SPA 57	3:34.61	2	Bisl	Oslo	28 Jun
	Abascal		3:34.66	3		Koblenz	29 Aug
Chuck	Aragon	USA 59	3:34.7 #	3		Oslo	21 Jul
	Abascal		3:34.74	2		Paris	4 Sep
	Aouita		3:34.82	1		Grosseto	18 Jul
Igor	Lotarev	SU 64	3:34.88	2	OD	Potsdam	21 Jul
	Fourie		3:34.9m#	1		Port Elizabeth	7 Mar
	Fourie		3:34.9m#	1		Port Elizabeth	10 Dec

(30/18)

Ray	Flynn	IRL 57	3:35.06	3	Bisl	Oslo	28 Jun
Steve	Crabb	UK 63	3:35.16	4	Bisl	Oslo	28 Jun
Uwe	Becker	FRG 55	3:35.51	5		Koblenz	29 Aug
Riccardo	Materazzi	ITA 63	3:35.79	6	WK	Zürich	22 Aug
Robert	Nemeth	AUT 58	3:35.80	6		Koblenz	29 Aug
Pascal	Thiébaut	FRA 59	3:35.8 #	4		Oslo	21 Jul
Peter	Wirz	SWZ 60	3:35.83=	4s1	OG	Los Angeles	10 Aug
John	Walker	NZ 52	3:35.93	2		Sydney	22 Jan
Kevin	Johnson	USA 60	3:36.04	8	WK	Zürich	22 Aug
Rich	Harris	USA 59	3:36.05	2	BGP	Budapest	20 Aug
José	Marajo	FRA 54	3:36.23	3		Paris	4 Sep
Anatoliy	Kalutskiy	SU 60	3:36.36	1	Izv	Kiev	24 Jun
Joaquim C.	Cruz	BRA 63	3:36.48	1	NCAA	Eugene	2 Jun
Tony	Rogers	NZ 57	3:36.48	6s1	OG	Los Angeles	10 Aug

240

1984 Lists – Men

Dmitriy	Dmitriyev	SU 63	3:36.50	1r1	ZN	Sochi	10 Jun
Andres	Vera	SPA 60	3:36.55	3s2	OG	Los Angeles	10 Aug
Ste´´no	Mei	ITA 63	3:36.62	4		Paris	4 Sep
Claudio	Patrignani	ITA 59	3:36.68	3	VD	Bruxelles	24 Aug
Adam	Dixon	USA 60	3:36.71	1	PennR	Philadelphia	28 Apr
István	Knipl	HUN 61	3:36.74	3	BGP	Budapest	20 Aug
Vitaliy	Tishchenko	SU 57	3:36.91	2r1		Sochi	26 May
Ross	Donoghue	USA 59	3:36.95	3	PennR	Philadelphia	28 Apr
Uwe	Monkemeyer	FRG 59	3:36.95	2		St Maur	6 Jun
Bob	Verbeeck	BEL 60	3:36.96	1		Woluwe	1 Jul
Peter	Elliott	UK 62	3:36.97	2		Woluwe	1 Jul
Pavel	Yakovlev	SU 58	3:36.99	2	Izv	Kiev	24 Jun
Kipkoech	Cheruiyot	KEN 64	3:37.0m	1	OT	Kisumu	30 Jun
Brian	Theriot	USA 57	3:37.0 #	6		Oslo	21 Jul
Sydney	Maree	USA 56	3:37.02	3	FOT	Los Angeles	24 Jun
Abderrahmane	Morceli	ALG 57	3:37.03	3		St Maur	6 Jun
Peter	O'Donoghue	NZ 61	3:37.08	1		Melbourne	6 Mar
Viktor	Kalinkin	SU 60	3:37.1m	1r2		Moskva	7 Jul
Anatoliy	Legeda	SU 62	3:37.17	3	Izv	Kiev	24 Jun
Mike	Boit	KEN 49	3:37.29	9		Koblenz	29 Aug
Jack	Buckn	UK 61	3:37.32	6		Rieti	2 Sep
Marcus	O'Sullivan	IRL 61	3:37.40	2	NCAA	Eugene	2 Jun
Vladimir	Kalsin	SU 58	3:37.54	4	Izv	Kiev	24 Jun
Alex	Gonzalez	FRA 51	3:37.58	4		St Maur	6 Jun
Antti	Loikkanen	FIN 55	3:37.63	2	WG	Helsinki	4 Jul
Jaime	Lopez Egea	SPA 55	3:37.64	1		Grosseto	18 Jul
Deon	Brummer	RSA	3:37.7m#	2		Port Elizabeth	10 Dec
Tim	Hacker	USA 62	3:37.78	5	FOT	Los Angeles	24 Jun
Pat	Scammell	AUS 61	3:37.86	3		Melbourne	6 Mar
Dub	Myers	USA 64	3:37.89	6	FOT	Los Angeles	24 Jun
Frank	O'Mara	IRL 60	3:37.91	5	PennR	Philadelphia	28 Apr
Rudi	De Wijngaert	BEL 59	3:37.94	4		Woluwe	1 Jul
Tom	Byers	USA 55	3:37.95	6	PennR	Philadelphia	28 Apr
Mirosaw	Zerkowski	POL 56	3:38.00	1		Sopot	5 Aug
Henning	Gericke	RSA 60	3:38.0m#	2		Port Elizabeth	7 Mar
Terry	Brahm	USA 62	3:38.0m#		Jerome	Burnaby	16 Jul
Didier	Begouin	FRA 56	3:38.06	5		St Maur	6 Jun
Tim	Hutchings	UK 58	3:38.06	4	GGala	Roma	31 Aug
Vasiliy	Matveyev	SU 62	3:38.1m	3r1		Moskva	7 Jul
Leonid	Masunov	SU 62	3:38.11	5r1		Sochi	26 May
Valeriy	Abramov	SU 56	3:38.2m	4r1		Moskva	7 Jul
Todd	Harbour	USA 59	3:38.22	4	BGP	Budapest	20 Aug
Marek	Adamski	POL 61	3:38.28	2		Sopot	5 Aug
Matthew	Temane	RSA 60	3:38.3m	2		Stellenbosch	22 Feb
Paul	Donovan	IRL 63	3:38.31	4	NCAA	Eugene	2 Jun
Yevgeniy	Nechayev	SU 59	3:38.32	5	Izv	Kiev	24 Jun
Doug	Padilla	USA 56	3:38.39	1	CalR	Modesto	12 May
Joseph	Mahmoud	FRA 55	3:38.39	6		St Maur	6 Jun
Mike	Gilchrist	NZ 60	3:38.42	1		Christchurch	24 Mar
Klaus-Peter	Nabein	FRG 60	3:38.42	5		Firenze	13 Jun
Paul	Larkins	UK 63	3:38.44	5	NCAA	Eugene	2 Jun
Larry	Mangan	USA 59	3:38.44	5	WG	Helsinki	4 Jul
Aleksandr	Lysenko	SU 55	3:38.55	1r2		Sochi	26 May
Don	Volkey	USA 62	3:38.59	6	NCAA	Eugene	2 Jun
Aleksandr	Kostetskiy	SU 60	3:38.59	6	Znam	Sochi	10 Jun
József	Bereczki	HUN 62	3:38.6m	1		Debrecen	4 Aug
Thomas	Wessinghage	FRG 52	3:38.61	3		Madrid	29 May
Uwe	Bergmann	GDR 61	3:38.65	6	BGP	Budapest	20 Aug
Ashley	Johnson	RSA 61	3:38.66	7	NCAA	Eugene	2 Jun
Stefano	Cecchini	ITA 61	3:38.67	7		Firenze	13 Jun
Mark	Scruton	UK 58	3:38.78	1		Loughborough	17 Jun
José Luis	Carreira	SPA 62	3:38.79	1		Madrid	14 Jul
Tom	Smith	USA 57	3:38.8m#	4	Pepsi	Los Angeles(Ww)	13 May

241

1984 Lists – Men

László	Tóth	HUN 55	3:38.8m	2		Debrecen	4 Aug
Cyrille	Laventure	FRA 64	3:38.82	7		St Maur	6 Jun
Krzysztof	Prądzynski	POL 58	3:38.85	3		Sopot	5 Aug
Colin	Reitz	UK 60	3:38.86	2		Edinburgh	17 Jul
John	Robson	UK 57	3:38.89	3		London	18 Aug
Timo	Lehto	FIN 56	3:38.92	4	DNG	Stockholm	2 Jul
Raf	Wijns	BEL 64	3:38.96	5		Woluwe	1 Jul
Aleksey	Litvinov	SU 59	3:39.14	7	Izv	Kiev	24 Jun
Iosif	Leonard	SU 60	3:39.15	8	Izv	Kiev	24 Jun
Kevin	King	USA 63	3:39.19	8	NCAA	Eugene	2 Jun

Mike	Wyatt	USA 56	3:39.2m	28 Apr	Espen	Borge	NOR 61	3:40.46	2 Jun
Olaf	Beyer	GDR 57	3:39.28	5 May	Bruno	Levant	FRA 60	3:40.47	6 Jun
Rob	Druppers	HOL 62	3:39.3m	30 May	Feófilio	Benito	SPA 66	3:40.48	30 Jun
Kelly	Britz	CAN 58	3:39.3m#	16 Jul	Jon	Richards	UK 64	3:40.50	17 Jun
László	Zöld	HUN 56	3:39.3m	4 Aug	Ron	Roberts	USA 61	3:40.5m	25 May
Dominique	Bouchard	FRA 63	3:39.32	4 Sep	Hans	Allmandinger	FRG 58	3:40.5m	30 May
Mark	Fricker	USA 59	3:39.33	22 Jun	Marc	Mohr	FRG 62	3:40.53	6 Jun
Josephat	Muraya	KEN 57	3:39.4m	30 Jun	Vince	Draddy	USA 61	3:40.58	6 Jul
Steve	Foley	AUS 57	3:39.41	11 Mar	Jurgen	Grothe	FRG 60	3:40.6m	30 May
Mike	Chorlton	UK 63	3:39.43	17 Jun	Vinko	Pokrajčić	YUG 53	3:40.62	8 Sep
John	Gladwin	UK 63	3:39.47	17 Jul	Hagen	Melzer	GDR 59	3:40.68	15 Jul
Grzegorz	Basiak	POL 62	3:39.59	5 Aug	Ari	Paunonen	FIN 58	3:40.68	8 Sep
Dave	Campbell	CAN 60	3:39.6m#	16 Jul	Mehdi	Aidet	ALG 53	3:40.71	26 Jun
Ken	Lucks	CAN 62	3:39.6m#	16 Jul	István	Szalai	HUN 62	3:40.72	10 Jul
Attila	Sulyok	HUN 59	3:39.6m	4 Aug	Krzysztof	Wesolowski	POL 56	3:40.74	5 Aug
James	Igohe	TAN 62	3:39.62	9 Aug	Tom	Moloney	IRL 60	3:40.77	18 Aug
Steve	Martin	UK 59	3:39.62	18 Aug	Ivan	Konovalov	SU 61	3:40.80	19 May
Doug	Peterson	USA 58	3:39.7m	28 Apr	Omar	Ortega	ARG 60	3:40.8m	7 Apr
Samson	Obwocha	KEN 54	3:39.7m	30 Jun	Andreas	Baranski	FRG 60	3:40.8m	30 May
Abderrazak	Bounour	ALG 57	3:39.75	26 Jun	Sisa	Kirati	KEN 57	3:40.8m	30 Jun
Craig	Masback	USA 55	3:39.79	22 Jun	Sam	Koskei	KEN 61	3:40.83	14 Apr
Geoff	Turnbull	UK 61	3:39.84	17 Jun	Torstein	Brox	NOR 59	3:40.84	29 Apr
Andy	Clifford	USA 56	3:39.85	22 Jun	Paul	Rugut	KEN 62	3:40.87	5 May
Abdi	Bile	SOM 63	3:39.86	20 Aug	Kevin	Ryan	USA 57	3:40.87	7 Jun
David	Forbes	AUS 60	3:39.89	11 Mar	Leszek	Witkowski	POL 58	3:40.90	5 Aug
Benjamin	Fernandez	SPA 55	3:39.89	30 Jun	Rob	Lonergan	CAN 59	3:40.9m	11 Jul
Agberto	Guimaraes	BRA 57	3:39.9m	17 Jun	Petr	Klimeš	CS 58	3:40.9m	30 Aug
Mohamed	Zahafi	MOR 59	3:39.92	13 Jun	Zsolt	Mallár	HUN 62	3:40.92	10 Jul
João	Campos	POR 58	3:39.94	29 May	John	Hinton	USA 62	3:40.93	13 May
Mohamed	Henchiri	TUN 57	3:39.96	4 Jul	Tomasz	Kozlowski	POL 60	3:40.96	5 Aug
Valeriy	Gogolev	SU 63	3:39.97	24 Jun	Stijn	Jaspers	HOL 61	3:40.99	10 Sep
Sergey	Lapetin	SU 60	3:40.0m	7 Jul	Roosevelt	Jackson	USA 62	3:41.00	22 Jun
Ivan	Buriy	SU 58	3:40.0m	7 Jul	Eamonn	Martin	UK 58	3:41.00	24 Jun
Stuart	Paton	UK 63	3:40.04	17 Jul	Nikolaos	Tsiakoulas	GRE 59	3:41.00	8 Sep
Johnny	Kroon	SWE 60	3:40.10	2 Jul	John	Gregorek	USA 60	3:41.01	13 May
Vladimir	Samoylenko	SU 61	3:40.1m	10 Aug	P.-Erling	Kristoffersen	NOR 59	3:41.02	28 Jun
Wayne	Dyer	AUS 58	3:40.13	6 Mar	Mike	Parkinson	USA 62	3:41.04	2 Jun
Amar	Brahmia	ALG 54	3:40.17	6 Jun	Tim	Redman	UK 60	3:41.05	17 Jun
Farley	Gerber	USA 60	3:40.2m	12 May	Alberto	Corvo	ITA 63	3:41.12	18 Jul
Richard	Callan	UK 55	3:40.21	17 Jun	Francisco	Pascual	SPA 61	3:41.17	30 Jun
Emmanuel	Goulin	FRA 62	3:40.27	1 Jul	Csaba	Szatzker	HUN 63	3:41.17	10 Jul
Boguslaw	Psujek	POL 56	3:40.37	2 Sep	Raymond	van Paemel	BEL 56	3:41.20	17 May
Petru	Dragoescu	RUM 62	3:40.38	8 Sep	Béla	Énekes	HUN 63	3:41.20	20 Aug
Dietmar	Millonig	AUT 55	3:40.4m	12 Aug	Evgeni	Ignatov	BUL 57	3:41.25	5 Aug
Tapfumaneyi	Jonga	ZIM 59	3:40.42	9 Aug					

Irregular conditions
Dragan   Zdravkovic   YUG 59   3:40.3m   24 Jun

Disqualified
Abdi   Bile   SOM 63   3:36.0   6s1   OG   Los Angeles   10 Aug

1984 Lists – Men

	1	10	20	30	50	100	Under 3:38.0	Under 3:40.0
1980	3:31.36	3:34.11	3:36.3	3:37.33	3:38.64	3:40.41	35	83
1981	3:31.57	3:34.96	3:36.6	3:37.72	3:38.87	3:40.86	33	82
1982	3:32.12	3:34.40	3:37.02	3:37.96	3:38.88	3:40.3	30	86
1983	3:30.77	3:34.01	3:35.2	3:36.77	3:38.18	3:39.86	48	100
1984	3:31.54	3:34.20	3:35.16	3:36.36	3:37.1	3:38.89	65	136

MILE

Said	Aouita	MOR 60	3:49.54	1	WK	Zurich	22 Aug
Steve	Cram	UK 60	3:49.65	1		Koblenz	29 Aug
John	Walker	NZ 52	3:49.73	2		Koblenz	29 Aug
	Walker		3:50.27	2	WK	Zurich	22 Aug
David	Moorcroft	UK 53	3:50.95	1		Oslo	21 Jul
Johan	Fourie	RSA 59	3:51.23	1		Port Elizabeth	7 Mar
Rich	Harris	USA 59	3:51.39	3		Koblenz	29 Aug
Jack	Buckner	UK 61	3:51.57	4		Koblenz	29 Aug
Graham	Williamson	UK 60	3:51.60	2		Oslo	21 Jul
Chuck	Aragon	USA 59	3:51.62	3		Oslo	21 Jul
	Fourie		3:51.99	1		Port Elizabeth	10 Dec
Pascal	Thiebaut	FRA 59	3:52.02	4		Oslo	21 Jul
Mike	Hillardt	AUS 61	3:52.34	1	Jerome	Burnaby	16 Jul
	Walker		3:52.37	2	Jerome	Burnaby	16 Jul
	Aragon		3:52.66	3	WK	Zurich	22 Aug
Ray	Flynn	IRL 57	3:52.79	4	WK	Zurich	22 Aug
	Walker		3:52.82	1		Auckland	28 Jan
Steve	Scott	USA 56	3:52.99	1	Pepsi	Los Angeles(Ww)	13 May
Joaquim C.	Cruz	BRA 63	3:53.00	2	Pepsi	Los Angeles(Ww)	13 May
	Fourie I.		3:53.45	1		Durban	15 Dec
	Scott		3:53.66	1	ISTAF	Berlin	17 Aug
Omer	Khalifa	SUD 56	3:53.74	2	ISTAF	Berlin	17 Aug
	Aragon		3:53.79	3	ISTAF	Berlin	17 Aug
Jim	Spivey	USA 60	3:53.88	3	Pepsi	Los Angeles(Ww)	13 May
(24/16)							
Kevin	Johnson	USA 60	3:54.06	4	ISTAF	Berlin	17 Aug
Steve	Crabb	UK 63	3:54.36	5		Oslo	21 Jul
Terry	Brahm	USA 62	3:54.56	3	Jerome	Burnaby	16 Jul
Sebastian	Coe	UK 56	3:54.6m	1		London	4 Jul
Tom	Smith	USA 57	3:54.65	4	Pepsi	Los Angeles(Ww)	13 May
Uwe	Becker	FRG 55	3:54.95	6	ISTAF	Berlin	17 Aug
Istvan	Knipl	HUN 61	3:55.13	5		Koblenz	29 Aug
Tony	Rogers	NZ 57	3:55.18	4	Jerome	Burnaby	16 Jul
Ross	Donoghue	USA 59	3:55.26	5	Pepsi	Los Angeles(Ww)	13 May
Todd	Harbour	USA 59	3:55.29	5	WK	Zurich	22 Aug
Andres	Vera	SPA 60	3:55.33	6		Oslo	21 Jul
Deon	Brummer	RSA	3:55.62	3		Durban	15 Dec
Peter	Elliott	UK 62	3:55.71	1		Gateshead	10 Jun
Paul	Donovan	IRL 63	3:55.82	3		Cork	3 Jul
Marcus	O'Sullivan	IRL 61	3:55.82	7		Oslo	21 Jul
Brian	Theriot	USA 57	3:56.10	8		Oslo	21 Jul
Henning	Gericke	RSA 60	3:56.17	2		Port Elizabeth	7 Mar
Jose Luis	Gonzalez	SPA 57	3:56.41	7	ISTAF	Berlin	17 Aug
Matthew	Temane	RSA 60	3:56.58	2		Port Elizabeth	10 Dec
Steve	Martin	UK 59	3:56.71	2		Gateshead	10 Jun
Rob	Harrison	UK 59	3:56.76	3		Gateshead	10 Jun
Pierre	Deleze	SWZ 58	3:56.81	4	Coke	London	7 Sep
Uwe	Monkemeyer	FRG 59	3:56.84	8	ISTAF	Berlin	17 Aug
Tim	Hutchings	UK 58	3:56.88	6		Cork	3 Jul

243

1984 Lists – Men

Abdi	Bile	SOM 63	3:57.43	1		Atlanta	20 Jul	
Mike	Boit	KEN 49	3:57.44	9	ISTAF	Berlin	17 Aug	
Peter	O'Donoghue	NZ 61	3:57.69	5	Jerome	Burnaby	16 Jul	
Markus	Ryffel	SWZ 55	3:58.05	6		Koblenz	29 Aug	
Dub	Myers	USA 64	3:58.24	1		Eugene	12 May	
Bob	Verbeeck	BEL 60	3:58.34	6	Coke	London	7 Sep	
Jose	Marajo	FRA 54	3:58.35	7	Coke	London	7 Sep	
Larry	Mangan	USA 59	3:58.36	2		Eugene	12 May	
John	Robson	UK 57	3:58.38	8	Coke	London	7 Sep	
Kevin	Ryan	USA 57	3:58.4m	3		Scarborough	10 Jul	
Craig	Lambert	RSA 57	3:58.41	3		Durban	15 Dec	
Kelly	Britz	CAN 58	3:58.46	6	Jerome	Burnaby	16 Jul	
Randy	Wilson	USA 55	3:58.74	3		Eugene	12 May	
Jose Manuel	Abascal	SPA 58	3:58.82	9 Jul	Wilson	Waigwa	KEN 49	3:59.15	10 Jun
Colin	Reitz	UK 60	3:58.92	10 Jun	Mark	Fricker	USA 59	3:59.25	14 Jul
Mark	Scruton	UK 58	3:58.95	10 Jun	Aleksandr	Kostetskiy	SU 60	3:59.32	3 Jul
Ken	Lucks	CAN 62	3:58.96	16 Jul	Jose Luis	Carreira	SPA 62	3:59.32	8 Jul
James	Igohe	TAN 62	3:59.06	21 Jul					

Indoor Marks

Jose Manuel	Abascal	SPA 58	3:55.69	1	E. Rutherford	11 Feb	
Tom	Byers	USA 55	3:55.7m	1	San Diego	17 Feb	
Adam	Dixon	USA 60	3:57.2m	1	Boston	22 Jan	
Jay	Woods (a)	USA 57	3:58.3m	3	Daly City	2 Mar	
Thomas	Wessinghage	FRG 52	3:58.86	1	Los Angeles	20 Jan	

(a) Woods also 3:58.36i 4 Feb

2000 METRES

(* = During 3000 metres race)

Johan	Fourie	RSA 59	4:56.5m	1		Stellenbosch	23 Apr
Pierre	Délèze	SWZ 58	4:57.27	1		Langenthal	27 Jul
Peter	Wirz	SWZ 60	4:58.29	2		Langenthal	27 Jul
Stefano	Mei	ITA 63	4:58.65	1		Viareggio	15 Aug
Rich	Harris	USA 59	4:59.04	2		Viareggio	15 Aug
Markus	Ryffel	SWZ 55	4:59.54	3		Langenthal	27 Jul
Robert	Nemeth	AUT 58	4:59.56	1		Klagenfurt	6 Aug
	Fourie		5:00.76			Stellenbosch	5 Jan
Fernando	Mamede	POR 51	5:00.8m	1		Lisboa	10 Jun
João	Campos	POR 58	5:00.8m	2		Lisboa	10 Jun

(10/9)

Eamonn	Martin	UK 58	5:01.09	1		Belfast	19 Jun
Jose Manuel	Abascal	SPA 58	5:01.1m	1		Santander	27 Jul
Uwe	Becker	FRG 55	5:02.00	1		München	20 Jul
Uwe	Mönkemeyer	FRG 59	5:02.37	2		München	20 Jul
Olaf	Beyer	GDR 57	5:02.6m	1		Potsdam	12 Jul
Jack	Buckner	UK 61	5:02.6m*	1	VD	Bruxelles	24 Aug
Steve	Martin	UK 59	5:02.61	2		Belfast	19 Jun
Said	Aouita	MOR 60	5:03.0m*	3	VD	Bruxelles	24 Aug
Evgeni	Ignatov	BUL 59	5:04.2m	1		Sofia	16 Jul
Dragan	Adravkovic	YUG 59	5:04.61	3		München	20 Jul
Chris	Fox	USA 58	5:04.68	1		Eugene	4 Jun
Petr	Klimeš	CS 58	5:04.8m	1		Ostrava	9 Aug
Christoph	Herle	FRG 55	5:05.14	4		München	20 Jul
Herbert	Stephan	FRG 59	5:05.23	5		München	20 Jul
Pavel	Klimeš	CS 58	5:05.3m	2		Ostrava	9 Aug
Omer	Khalifa	SUD 56	5:05.78	3		Viareggio	15 Aug
Dragan	Sekulić	YUG 57	5:05.91	6		München	20 Jul

1984 Lists – Men

Béla	Énekes	HUN 63	5:06.05	7		München	20 Jul
Dan	Aldridge	USA 56	5:06.15	3		Eugene	4 Jun
Deon	Brummer	RSA	5:06.3m	2		Stellenbosch	23 Apr
Henning	Gericke	RSA 60	5:06.3m	3		Stellenbosch	23 Apr
Carlos	Cabral	POR 52	5:06.4m	3		Lisboa	10 Jun
Franco	Boffi	ITA 58	5:06.65	4		Viareggio	15 Aug
Antonio	Selvaggio	ITA 58	5:06.80	5		Viareggio	15 Aug
Josef	Vedra	CS 56	5:07.83	1		Praha	10 Aug
Thomas	Wessinghage	FRG 52	5:08.34	8		München	20 Jul
Lubomír	Tesáček	CS 57	5:08.46	2		Praha	10 Aug
Attila	Sulyok	HUN 59	5:08.98	9		München	20 Jul
Herb	Lindsay	USA 54	5:09.12	4		Eugene	4 Jun
Robbie	Perkins	USA 55	5:09.71	5		Eugene	4 Jun
Enda	Fitzpatrick	IRL 65	5:09.73	3		Belfast	19 Jun

Indoor Marks

Patriz	Ilg	FRG 57	5:05.84	1		Sindelfingen	1 Feb

3000 METRES

Said	Aouita	MOR 60	7:33.3m	1	VD	Bruxelles	24 Aug
Ray	Flynn	IRL 57	7:41.60	1		London	13 Jul
Dmitriy	Dmitriyev	SU 55	7:42.05	2		London	13 Jul
Robert	Nemeth	AUT 58	7:44.08	1	ISTAF	Berlin	17 Aug
Dietmar	Millonig	AUT 55	7:44.10	2	ISTAF	Berlin	17 Aug
Martti	Vainio	FIN 50	7:44.42	1		Varkaus	12 Jul
Tim	Hutchings	UK 58	7:44.55	3		London	13 Jul
Jack	Buckner	UK 61	7:45.19	1		Loughborough	17 Jun
Jose Luis	Gonzalez	SPA 57	7:45.44	1		Zaragoza	3 Jun
Paul	Davies–Hale	UK 62	7:45.45	4		London	13 Jul
John	Robson	UK 57	7:45.81	5		London	13 Jul
Frank	O'Mara	IRL 60	7:46.54	1		Oslo	21 Jul
Pascal	Thiebaut	FRA 59	7:46.89	1		St.Maur	23 May
Doug	Padilla	USA 56	7:47.09	2	GGala	Roma	31 Aug
Bob	Verbeeck	BEL 60	7:47.22	3	GGala	Roma	31 Aug
Stijn	Jaspers	HOL 61	7:47.4m	2	VD	Bruxelles	24 Aug
Chris	Fox	USA 58	7:47.18	6		London	13 Jul
Joseph	Mahmoud	FRA 55	7:47.58	3		Oslo	21 Jul
Evgeni	Ignatov	BUL 59	7:47.74	5	GGala	Roma	31 Aug
Eamonn	Martin	UK 58	7:47.8m	1		Walnut	25 Jul
Rich	Harris	USA 59	7:47.87	6	GGala	Roma	31 Aug
Geoff	Turnbull	UK 61	7:47.88	7		London	13 Jul
Antonio	Selvaggio	ITA 58	7:48.14	1	4–N (a)	Torino	2 Jun
Nick	Rose	UK 51	7:48.39	8		London	13 Jul
Tim	Redman	UK 60	7:48.81	3		London	18 Aug
Jim	Hill	USA 61	7:48.82	1		Eugene	12 May
David	Moorcroft	UK 53	7:48.88	1		Gateshead	6 Jul
Joseph	Chesire	KEN 57	7:49.4m	2		Walnut	25 Jul
Viktor	Chumakov	SU 57	7:49.47	2	4–N (a)	Torino	2 Jun
Roger	Hackney	UK 57	7:49.47	9		London	13 Jul
Thomas	Wessinghage	FRG 52	7:49.49	1	4–N (b)	Hannover	16 Jun
Vince	Draddy	USA 61	7:49.55	5		Oslo	21 Jul
Thierry	Watrice	FRA 57	7:49.56	3		St.Maur	23 May
J.–Louis	Prianon	FRA 60	7:49.58	4		St.Maur	23 May
Mike	McLeod	UK 52	7:49.59	4		London	18 Aug
William	Van Dijck	BEL 61	7:49.7m	1		Bruxelles	24 Jul
Dave	Lewis	UK 61	7:49.77	6		Oslo	21 Jul
Steve	Jones	UK 55	7:49.80	10		London	13 Jul
Ezequiel	Canario	POR 60	7:49.8m	3	VD	Bruxelles	24 Aug
Dragan	Sekulic	YUG 57	7:49.85	11		London	13 Jul

245

1984 Lists – Men

Uwe	Monkemeyer	FRG 59	7:49.86	2	4–N (b)	Hannover	16 Jun
Vincent	Rousseau	BEL 62	7:50.3m	2		Bruxelles	24 Jul
Pavel	Klimes	CS 58	7:50.37	3	4–N (b)	Hannover	16 Jun
Rob	Lonergan	CAN 59	7:50.44	5		London	18 Aug
Markus	Ryffel	SWZ 55	7:50.59	1		Koln	26 Aug
Czeslaw	Mojzysz	POL 58	7:50.67	3	4–N (a)	Torino	2 Jun
Antti	Loikkanen	FIN 55	7:50.77	1		Tampere	11 Jun
Alberto	Cova	ITA 58	7:51.18	1		Busto Arsizio	26 May
Ibrahim	Hussein	KEN 59	7:51.19	2		Tampere	11 Jun
Bruce	Bickford	USA 57	7:51.34	7	GGala	Roma	31 Aug
Hannu	Okkola	FIN 54	7:51.82	2		Varkaus	12 Jul
Kevin	Jacques	UK 58	7:51.88	7		London	18 Aug
Antonio	Leitao	POR 60	7:51.94	1		Madrid	21 Jun
Gabor K.	Szabo	HUN 62	7:52.0m	17 Jun	Boguslaw	Maminski	POL 55	7:53.64	18 Jul
Petr	Klimes	CS 58	7:52.02	16 Jun	Jon	Richards	UK 64	7:53.65	15 Jul
Igor	Lotarev	SU 64	7:52.15	20 May	Fethi	Baccouche	TUN 60	7:53.86	9 Jun
Mike	Hillardt	AUS 61	7:52.17	20 Aug	Niels Kim	Hjort	DEN 59	7:53.86	9 Jun
Gennadiy	Fishman	SU 59	7:52.39	10 Jun	Raf	Wijns	BEL 64	7:54.04	26 Aug
Vitaliy	Tishchenko	SU 57	7:52.45	10 Jun	Salvatore	Antibo	ITA 62	7:54.04	31 Aug
Jim	Cooper	USA 59	7:52.50	13 Jul	Gennadiy	Temnikov	SU 61	7:54.06	10 Jun
Adrian	Royle	UK 59	7:52.57	18 Aug	Alfons	Schellens	BEL 56	7:54.1m	24 Jul
Stig Roar	Husby	NOR 54	7:52.60	22 May	Kipsubai	Koskei	KEN 51	7:54.1m	25 Jul
Piero	Selvaggio	ITA 58	7:52.61	2 Jun	Dave	Clarke	UK 58	7:54.13	18 Aug
John	Doherty	UK 61	7:52.61	13 Jul	Christoph	Herle	FRG 55	7:54.22	9 Jun
A	Verin	SU	7:52.65	10 Jun	Hansjörg	Kunze	GDR 59	7:54.27	9 Jun
Peter	Daenens	BEL 60	7:52.7m	24 Jul	Stephen	James	UK 62	7:54.30	18 Aug
Spiridon	Andriopoulos	GRE 62	7:52.72	20 Aug	Benjamin	Fernandez	SPA 55	7:54.31	21 Jun
Franco	Boffi	ITA 58	7:52.78	31 Aug	Abderrazak	Bounour	ALG 57	7:54.34	9 Jun
Julius	Kariuki	KEN 61	7:52.87	9 Jun	Dmitriy	Korneyev	SU 56	7:54.39	10 Jun
Didier	Begouin	FRA 56	7:52.96	16 Jun	Mark	Nenow	USA 57	7:54.39	8 Jul
Pascal	Debacker	FRA 60	7:52.96	21 Jul	Valeriy	Abramov	SU 56	7:54.44	20 May
Viktor	Dolgopolov	SU 60	7:52.97	10 Jun	Paul	McCloy	CAN 63	7:54.46	18 Aug
Stanislav	Rozman	YUG 60	7:53.00	1 Jul	Paul	Rugut	KEN 62	7:54.50	13 Jul
Dan	Aldridge	USA 56	7:53.10	12 May	José Manuel	Abascal	SPA 58	7:54.56	19 May
Ranieri	Carenza	ITA 63	7:53.12	31 Aug	Jerzy	Kowol	POL 51	7:54.72	26 Aug
Krzysztof	Wesolowski	POL 56	7:53.16	20 May	Aleksandr	Khudyakov	SU 60	7:54.75	26 May
Jef	Gees	BEL 56	7:53.20	18 Aug	Steve	Lacy	USA 56	7:54.89	21 Jul
Dragan	Zdravkovic	YUG 59	7:53.29	9 Jun	Jon	Solly	UK 63	7:54.97	18 Aug
Paul	Williams	CAN 56	7:53.3m	20 Jun					
Ivan	Konovalov	SU 59	7:53.36	20 May	4–N (a) ITA v SU v POL v HUN				
Lubomir	Tesacek	CS 57	7:53.38	26 Aug	4–N (b) FRG v CS v POL v FRA				

Indoor Marks

Doug	Padilla	USA 56	7:46.87	1		E.Rutherford	11 Feb
Hansjörg	Kunze	GDR 59	7:47.5m	1	NC	Senftenberg	21 Jan
Axel	Krippschock	GDR 62	7:48.38	1		Budapest	4 Feb
Gabor K.	Szabo	HUN 62	7:48.93	3		Budapest	4 Feb
John	Gregorek	USA 60	7:49.12	2		E.Rutherford	11 Feb
Thomas	Wessinghage	FRG 52	7:49.13	3		E.Rutherford	11 Feb
Lubomir	Tesacek	CS 57	7:49.20	4		Budapest	4 Feb
Markus	Ryffel	SWZ 55	7:49.27	4		E.Rutherford	11 Feb
Wolfgang	Konrad	AUT 58	7:50.07	5		Budapest	4 Feb
Zakariah	Barie	TAN 53	7:51.46	5		E.Rutherford	11 Feb

Bill	Krohn	USA 58	7:52.17	11 Feb
Francis	Gonzalez	FRA 52	7:52.5m	4 Feb
Karl	Fleschen	FRG 55	7:54.45	4 Mar
Todd	Harbour	USA 59	7:54.86	11 Feb
Patriz	Ilg	FRG 57	7:54.88	11 Feb

1984 Lists – Men

5000 METRES

Name	Surname	Nat/Yr	Time	Pos	Meet	Venue	Date
Said	Aouita	MOR 60	13:04.78	1		Firenze	13 Jun
	Aouita		13:05.59	1	OG	Los Angeles	11 Aug
Markus	Ryffel	SWZ 55	13:07.54	2	OG	Los Angeles	11 Aug
Antonio	Leitao	POR 60	13:09.20	3	OG	Los Angeles	11 Aug
Wodago	Bulti	ETH 57	13:10.08	2		Firenze	13 Jun
Tim	Hutchings	UK 58	13:11.50	4	OG	Los Angeles	11 Aug
	Aouita		13:12.51	1		Lausanne	10 Jul
Fernando	Mamede	POR 51	13:12.83	1	Bisl	Oslo	28 Jun
	Leitao		13:13.17	1		Barcelona	8 Jul
Paul	Kipkoech	KEN 62	13:14.40	5	OG	Los Angeles	11 Aug
Martti	Vainio	FIN 50	13:16.02	2	Bisl	Oslo	28 Jun
	Ryffel		13:16.20	2		Lausanne	10 Jul
Carlos	Lopes	POR 47	13:16.38	3	Bisl	Oslo	28 Jun
	Hutchings		13:16.57	1		Koblenz	29 Aug
John	Treacy	IRL 57	13:16.81	4	Bisl	Oslo	28 Jun
Dmitriy	Dmitriyev	SU 56	13:17.37	1	Izv	Kiev	23 Jun
	Mamede		13:18.18	1		Rieti	2 Sep
Alberto	Cova	ITA 58	13:18.24	1		Oslo	21 Jul
Charles	Cheruiyot	KEN 64	13:18.41	6	OG	Los Angeles	11 Aug
Gennadiy	Fishman	SU 59	13:18.46	2	Izv	Kiev	23 Jun
Mark	Nenow	USA 57	13:18.54	5	Bisl	Oslo	28 Jun
Nick	Rose	UK 51	13:18.91	6	Bisl	Oslo	28 Jun
Joao	Campos	POR 58	13:19.10	7	Bisl	Oslo	28 Jun
Ray	Flynn	IRL 57	13:19.52	1	AAA	London	24 Jun
	Hutchings		13:20.24	2		Oslo	21 Jul
	Mamede		13:20.61	1	WK	Zurich	22 Aug
	Leitao		13:21.51	2	WK	Zurich	22 Aug
	Rose		13:22.00	2	AAA	London	24 Jun
Eamonn	Martin	UK 58	13:23.33	1	OT	Gateshead	10 Jun
Doug	Padilla	USA 56	13:23.56	7	OG	Los Angeles	11 Aug

(30/20)

Name	Surname	Nat/Yr	Time	Pos	Meet	Venue	Date
Zephaniah	Ncube	ZIM 57	13:24.07	1	Jerome	Burnaby	16 Jul
Stijn	Jaspers	HOL 61	13:24.46	1		Kessel-Lo	1 Jun
John	Walker	NZ 52	13:24.46	8	OG	Los Angeles	11 Aug
Paul	Davies-Hale	UK 62	13:24.59	2		Kessel-Lo	1 Jun
Bob	Verbeeck	BEL 60	13:24.73	3		Kessel-Lo	1 Jun
Dan	Henderson	USA 58	13:24.75	2	Jerome	Burnaby	16 Jul
Vincent	Rousseau	BEL 62	13:24.81	3		Firenze	13 Jun
Abderrazak	Bounour	ALG 57	13:25.26	4		Firenze	13 Jun
Antonio	Selvaggio	ITA 58	13:25.63	1		Pisa	20 Jun
Chris	Fox	USA 58	13:25.78	3		Oslo	21 Jul
Jef	Gees	BEL 56	13:26.13	4		Kessel-Lo	1 Jun
Mike	McLeod	UK 58	13:26.14	2	OT	Gateshead	10 Jun
Francis	Gonzalez	FRA 52	13:26.22	5		Firenze	13 Jun
John	Doherty	UK 61	13:26.23	3	OT	Gateshead	10 Jun
Werner	Schildhauer	GDR 59	13:26.23	1		Dresden	26 Jul
Evgeni	Ignatov	BUL 59	13:26.35	1	DRZ	Moskva	18 Aug
Ezequiel	Canario	POR 60	13:26.50	9	OG	Los Angeles	11 Aug
Mats	Erixon	SWE 58	13:26.96	9	Bisl	Oslo	28 Jun
Dave	Lewis	UK 61	13:27.03	4	AAA	London	24 Jun
Uwe	Monkemeyer	FRG 59	13:27.05	1		Koblenz	16 May
Piero	Selvaggio	ITA 58	13:27.08	6		Firenze	13 Jun
Fethi	Baccouche	TUN 60	13:27.1m	1		St.Maur	6 Jun
Dietmar	Millonig	AUT 55	13:27.13	5	WK	Zurich	22 Aug
Wilson	Waigwa	KEN 49	13:27.34	10	OG	Los Angeles	11 Aug
Stig Roar	Husby	NOR 54	13:27.53	5		Oslo	21 Jul
Richard	Callan	UK 55	13:27.67	4	OT	Gateshead	10 Jun
Steve	Lacy	USA 56	13:27.72	2	FOT	Los Angeles	24 Jun

247

1984 Lists – Men

Antti	Loikkanen	FIN 55	13:27.76	10	Bisl	Oslo	28 Jun
Steve	Jones	UK 55	13:27.84	5	OT	Gateshead	10 Jun
Abel	Anton	SPA 62	13:27.95	6		Oslo	21 Jul
David	Moorcroft	UK 53	13:28.44	2s2	OG	Los Angeles	9 Aug
Don	Clary	USA 57	13:28.62	3	FOT	Los Angeles	24 Jun
Christoph	Herle	FRG 55	13:28.73	2		Koblenz	16 May
Paul	Williams	CAN 56	13:29.18	4	Jerome	Burnaby	16 Jul
Stefano	Mei	ITA 63	13:29.61	3		Pisa	20 Jun
Viktor	Chumakov	SU 57	13:29.68	3	Izv	Kiev	23 Jun
Mark	Roberts	UK 59	13:29.93	6	OT	Gateshead	10 Jun
Karl	Fleschen	FRG 55	13:30.08	3		Koblenz	16 May
Julian	Goater	UK 53	13:30.13	7	OT	Gateshead	10 Jun
Todd	Harbour	USA 59	13:30.57	1	MSR	Walnut	28 Apr
Peter	Koech	KEN 58	13:30.59	2	MSR	Walnut	28 Apr
Eduardo	Castro	MEX 54	13:30.59	2	PTS	Bratislava	25 May
Lubomir	Tesacek	CS 57	13:30.88	3	PTS	Bratislava	25 May
Tony	Milovsorov	UK 58	13:30.88	8	OT	Gateshead	10 Jun
Oleg	Strizhakov	SU 63	13:30.88	4	Izv	Kiev	23 Jun
Jon	Solly	UK 63	13:30.91	9	OT	Gateshead	10 Jun
Tom	Smith	USA 57	13:30.93	3	MSR	Walnut	28 Apr
Anatoliy	Krakhmalyuk	SU 60	13:30.95	5	Izv	Kiev	23 Jun
Aleksandr	Fedotkin	SU 55	13:31.08	6	Izv	Kiev	23 Jun
Franco	Boffi	ITA 58	13:31.27	7		Oslo	21 Jul
Steve	Plasencia	USA 56	13:31.28	8		Oslo	21 Jul
Steve	Harris	UK 61	13:31.45	10	OT	Gateshead	10 Jun
Raymond	Van Paemel	BEL 56	13:31.93	6		Kessel-Lo	1 Jun
Kassa	Balcha	ETH 55	13:32.01	5	DRZ	Moskva	18 Aug
Nat	Muir	UK 58	13:32.06	11	OT	Gateshead	10 Jun
Filbert	Bayi	TAN 53	13:32.11	5	MSR	Walnut	28 Apr
Jorge	Garcia	SPA 61	13:32.17	2		Barcelona	8 Jul
Boguslaw	Maminski	POL 55	13:32.26	6		Lausanne	10 Jul
Kelly	Jensen	USA 54	13:32.47	6	MSR	Walnut	28 Apr
Kevin	Ryan	USA 57	13:32.50	7	MSR	Walnut	28 Apr
Jerald	Jones	USA 53	13:32.5m	8	MSR	Walnut	28 Apr
Ed	Eyestone	USA 61	13:32.52	4	WG	Helsinki	4 Jul
Vince	Draddy	USA 61	13:32.6m	2		Burnaby	26 May
Mike	Chorlton	UK 63	13:32.71	12	OT	Gateshead	10 Jun
William	Van Dijck	BEL 61	13:32.77	7		Kessel-Lo	1 Jun
Ross	Donoghue	USA 59	13:33.37	2		Knoxville	18 May
Gerardo	Alcala	MEX 61	13:33.4m	10	MSR	Walnut	28 Apr
Salvatore	Antibo	ITA 62	13:33.65	3		Firenze	7 Jun
Bekele	Debele	ETH 63	13:33.74	6	DRZ	Moskva	18 Aug
Bruce	Bickford	USA 57	13:33.78	4	FOT	Los Angeles	24 Jun
Geoff	Turnbull	UK 61	13:33.86	2	NC	Cwmbran	28 May
Jose	Gomez	MEX 56	13:34.1m	11	MSR	Walnut	28 Apr
Aleksandr	Khudyakov	SU 60	13:34.19	8	Izv	Kiev	23 Jun
Valeriy	Abramov	SU 56	13:34.24	1		Cork	3 Jul
Jim	Hill	USA 61	13:34.5m	1		Berkeley	21 Apr
Thierry	Watrice	FRA 57	13:34.62	1		St Maur	6 Jun
Niels Kim	Hjort	DEN 59	13:34.63	4		Koblenz	16 May
Greg	Duhaime	CAN 53	13:34.7m	3		Burnaby	26 May
Ivan	Huff	USA 59	13:34.8m	12	MSR	Walnut	28 Apr
Alex	Hagelsteens	BEL 56	13:35.1m	1		Louvain	22 Jun
Robert	Schneider	FRG 60	13:35.15	5		Koblenz	29 Aug
Jon	Sinclair	USA 57	13:35.3m	4		Burnaby	26 May
Francesco	Panetta	ITA 63	13:35.32	4		Pisa	20 Jun
Peter	Daenens	BEL 60	13:35.4m	1		Louvain	6 May
Jon	Richards	UK 64	13:35.50	13	OT	Gateshead	10 Jun
Rob	Lonergan	CAN 59	13:35.76	5		Eugene	4 Jun
Robert	Nemeth	AUT 58	13:35.90	5		Koblenz	16 May
J-Louis	Prianon	FRA 60	13:35.95	2		St Maur	6 Jun

1984 Lists – Men

Gerard	Donakowski	USA 60	13:36.0m	28 Apr
Sergey	Navolokin	SU 59	13:36.10	20 Jul
Hansjorg	Kunze	GDR 59	13:36.22	26 Jul
Ahmed Musa	Juda	SUD 57	13:36.34	4 Jul
Karl	Harrison	UK 56	13:36.48	13 Jul
Steve	Anders	UK 59	13:36.55	10 Jun
Antonio	Prieto	SPA 58	13:36.71	18 Jul
Ivan	Konovalov	SU 59	13:36.72	27 May
Ray	Wicksell	USA 56	13:36.8m	28 Apr
Herb	Lindsay	USA 54	13:36.9m	28 Apr
Erin	Rankin	USA 58	13:37.20	4 Jun
Paul	McCloy	CAN 63	13:37.27	4 Jun
Jim	Spivey	USA 60	13:37.51	18 May
Ralf	Salzmann	FRG 55	13:37.74	16 May
Sergio	Pesavento	ITA 58	13:37.75	20 Jun
Raf	Wijns	BEL 64	13:37.79	1 Jun
Matthews	Temane	RSA 60	13:38.27	7 Mar
Mauricio	Gonzalez	MEX 60	13:38.28	25 May
Steve	Ortiz	USA 59	13:38.28	22 Jun
Fernando	Couto	POR 59	13:38.3m	3 Jun
Eamonn	Coghlan	IRL 52	13:38.35	3 Jul
Algis	Dabulskis	SU 61	13:38.65	23 Jun
Theo	V.den Abeele	BEL 60	13:38.72	14 Aug
Vladimir	Shesterov	SU 54	13:39.22	23 Jun
Jose Manuel	Abascal	SPA 58	13:39.27	23 May
Nikolay	Chameyev	SU 62	13:39.27	27 May
Seppo	Liuttu	FIN 56	13:39.31	17 Jul
Peter	Butler	CAN 58	13:39.4m	18 Jun
Sergey	Litvinov	SU 61	13:39.50	3 Aug
Ibrahim	Kivina	TAN 58	13:39.5m	28 Apr
Alan	Guilder	UK 61	13:39.52	13 Jul
Giuseppe	Pambianchi	ITA 57	13:39.62	20 Jun
Rafael	Marques	POR 57	13:39.7m	12 May
Lars	Ericsson	SWE 57	13:39.76	17 Jul
Gianni	De Madonna	ITA 54	13:39.94	21 Jul
Robbie	Perkins	USA 55	13:39.97	18 May
Sergey	Sedov	SU 58	13:40.12	27 May
Giovanni	D'Aleo	ITA 59	13:40.22	20 Jun
Craig	Virgin	USA 55	13:40.26	18 May
Berhanu	Girma	ETH 60	13:40.41	25 May
Mark	Curp	USA 59	13:40.65	18 May
Jed	Hopfsenberger	USA 57	13:40.74	18 May
Kurt	Stenzel	FRG 62	13:40.96	29 Aug
Boguslaw	Psujek	POL 56	13:41.14	23 May
Antoni	Niemczak	POL 55	13:41.16	24 Jun
Walter	Merlo	ITA 65	13:41.17	7 Jun
Rodolfo	Gomez	MEX 50	13:41.2m	28 Apr
Brad	Erickstad	USA 59	13:41.28	24 Jun
Klaas	Lok	HOL 55	13:41.33	6 Jul
Chris	Buckley	UK 61	13:41.34	13 Jul
Charlie	Bevier	USA 59	13:41.37	10 Jul
David	Barney	USA 60	13:41.6m	28 Apr

Gabor K.	Szabo	HUN 62	13:41.66	25 May
Masami	Ohtsuka	JAP 60	13:41.7m	22 Apr
Barry	Smith	UK 53	13:41.7m	16 May
Jorg	Peter	GDR 55	13:41.81	13 May
Art	Boileau	CAN 57	13:41.9m	28 Apr
Joseph	Kipsang	KEN 62	13:41.9m	18 May
Samson	Obwocha	KEN 54	13:41.98	14 Jul
Kipsubai	Koskei	KEN 51	13:42.05	15 Jul
Roy	Kissin	USA 57	13:42.2m	26 May
Pavel	Klimes	CS 58	13:42.26	23 May
Jackson	Ruto	KEN 59	13:42.3m	16 Jun
Toomas	Turb	SU 57	13:42.42	27 May
Troy	Billings	USA 60	13:42.5m	28 Apr
Frank	Heine	GDR 63	13:42.53	21 Jul
Gennadiy	Temmnikov	SU 61	13:42.70	27 May
Wieslaw	Ziembicki	POL 60	13:42.78	24 Jun
Martin	ten Kate	HOL 58	13:42.90	6 Jul
Arye	Gamliel	ISR 57	13:43.04	12 Aug
Marc	Ruell	BEL 58	13:43.1m	22 Jun
Gyorgy	Marko	RUM 60	13:43.11	25 May
Alain	Bordeleau	CAN 56	13:43.17	16 Jul
John	Idstrom	USA 59	13:43.32	4 Jun
Ed	Spinney	USA 53	13:43.4m	26 May
Zakariah	Barie	TAN 53	13:43.49	9 Aug
Tom	Downs	USA 61	13:43.5m	21 Apr
Mark	Scrutton	UK 60	13:43.51	13 Apr
John	Bowden	NZ 55	13:43.57	26 Jan
Pat	Vaughn	USA 59	13:43.6m	18 May
Ranieri	Carenza	ITA 63	13:43.61	7 Jun
Miroslaw	Dzienisik	POL 58	13:43.67	24 Jun
Petr	Klimes	CS 58	13:43.81	23 May
Hans-Jurgen	Orthmann	FRG 54	13:43.86	29 Aug
Ken	Martin	USA 58	13:43.94	22 Jul
Dirk	Sander	FRG 56	13:43.97	6 Jul
Robert	de Castella	AUS 57	13:44.00	21 Jul
Jose Manuel	Albentosa	SPA 64	13:44.1m	16 Jun
Shozo	Shimojuu	JAP 57	13:44.1m	22 Apr
Ashley	Johnson	RSA 61	13:44.15	13 Apr
Paul	Rugut	KEN 62	13:44.17	4 Jul
Dan	Dillon	USA 57	13:44.21	4 Jun
Patrick	Aris	BEL 56	13:44.21	6 Jul
Lars-Erik	Nilsson	SWE 61	13:44.43	6 Jul
Gennadiy	Temnikov	URS 61	13:44.44	23 Jun
Kenji	Ide	JAP 59	13:44.5m	22 Apr
Greg	Lautenslager	USA 57	13:44.6m	26 May
Ibrahim	Hussein	KEN 59	13:44.65	18 Jun
Bogumil	Kus	POL 57	13:44.69	23 May
Ivan	Uvizl	CS 58	13:44.69	23 May
Vladimir	Mayfat	SU 63	13:44.72	23 Jun
Alfons	Schellens	BEL 56	13:44.90	14 Aug
Hannu	Okkola	FIN 54	13:44.94	17 Jul

Indoor Marks

Hansjorg	Kunze	GDR 59	13:33.90	2	New York	27 Jan
Sosthenes	Bitok	KEN 57	13:34.06	3	New York	27 Jan

Gidamis	Shahanga	TAN 57	13:38.62	27 Jan
Graeme	Fell	UK 59	13:40.25	27 Jan
Geoff	Smith	UK 53	13:41.66	27 Jan
Greg	Meyer	USA 55	13:43.5m	22 Jan

1984 Lists – Men

	1	10	20	30	50	100	Under 13:30	Under 13:40
1980	13:16.34	13:19.8	13:22.1	13:24.1	13:29.47	13:40.1	51	97
1981	13:06.20	13:19.74	13:23.79	13:26.41	13:31.52	13:38.4	45	110
1982	13:00.41	13:12.91	13:19.62	13:26.8	13:30.88	13:39.74	41	103
1983	13:08.54	13:20.94	13:22.67	13:26.61	13:31.43	13:38.8	39	109
1984	13:04.78	13:16.81	13:23.56	13:25.78	13:27.95	13:35.1	57	144

10000 METRES

Fernando	Mamede	POR 51	27:13.81	1	DNG	Stockholm	2 Jul
Carlos	Lopes	POR 47	27:17.48	2	DNG	Stockholm	2 Jul
Hansjorg	Kunze	GDR 59	27:33.10	1	NC	Potsdam	5 May
Mark	Nenow	USA 57	27:40.56	3	DNG	Stockholm	2 Jul
Martti	Vainio *	FIN 50	27:41.75	1		Firenze	13 Jun
Paul	Cummings	USA 53	27:43.7m	1	MSR	Walnut	28 Apr
Alberto	Salazar	USA 58	27:45.5m	2	MSR	Walnut	28 Apr
Mike	Musyoki	KEN 56	27:46.0m	3	MSR	Walnut	28 Apr
Garry	Bjorklund	USA 51	27:46.9m	4	MSR	Walnut	28 Apr
Tony	Sandoval	USA 54	27:47.0m	5	MSR	Walnut	28 Apr
	Mamede		27:47.19	1		Paris	4 Sep
Alberto	Cova	ITA 58	27:47.54	1	OG	Los Angeles	6 Aug
Bruce	Bickford	USA 57	27:47.91	1	VD	Bruxelles	24 Aug
Salvatore	Antibo	ITA 62	27:48.02	2		Firenze	13 Jun
Pat	Porter	USA 59	27:49.5m	6	MSR	Walnut	28 Apr
Sosthenes	Bitok	KEN 57	27:50.0m	1r1	PennR	Philadelphia	26 Apr
	Vainio		27:51.10*	2	OG	Los Angeles	6 Aug
	Bickford		27:51.6m	2r1	PennR	Philadelphia	26 Apr
Valeriy	Abramov	SU 56	27:55.17	1	DRZ	Moskva	17 Aug
Paul	Williams	CAN 56	27:55.92	1		Eugene	7 Apr
Ed	Eyestone	USA 61	27:56.06	2		Eugene	7 Apr
	Salazar		27:56.47	3		Eugene	7 Apr
Mohamed	Kedir	ETH 54	27:57.09	1	PTS	Bratislava	26 May
	Cova		27:57.38	2	VD	Bruxelles	24 Aug
	Nenow		27:57.49	1	Pre	Eugene	21 Jul
Simeon	Kigen	KEN 61	27:57.68	2	Pre	Eugene	21 Jul
Berhanu	Girma	ETH 60	27:57.89	2	PTS	Bratislava	26 May
Wodajo	Bulti	ETH 57	27:58.24	3	PTS	Bratislava	26 May
	Salazar		27:58.25	3	Pre	Eugene	21 Jul
Steve	Jones	UK 55	27:58.64	3	VD	Bruxelles	24 Aug
	Bulti		27:58.97	2	DRZ	Moskva	17 Aug

(31/23)

Masanari	Shintaku	JAP 57	27:59.79	1	NC	Tokyo	21 Oct
Nick	Rose	UK 51	28:00.70	1	NC	Cwmbran	27 May
Mark	Curp	USA 59	28:01.02	4		Eugene	7 Apr
John	Treacy	IRL 57	28:01.3m	3r1	PennR	Philadelphia	26 Apr
Craig	Virgin	USA 55	28:02.27	2	FOT	Los Angeles	19 Jun
Dan	Henderson	USA 58	28:02.41	4	Pre	Eugene	21 Jul
Bekele	Debele	ETH 63	28:03.06	3	DRZ	Moskva	17 Aug
Zakariah	Barie	TAN 53	28:03.17	5	Pre	Eugene	21 Jul
Gidamis	Shahanga	TAN 57	28:03.24	3		Firenze	13 Jun
Gerard	Donakowski	USA 60	28:03.92	5		Eugene	7 Apr
Francesco	Panetta	ITA 63	28:03.99	4		Firenze	13 Jun
Gianni	De Madonna	ITA 54	28:04.60	4	DNG	Stockholm	2 Jul
Thierry	Watrice	FRA 57	28:04.61	5		Firenze	13 Jun
Christoph	Herle	FRG 55	28:05.0m	1		Aachen	30 May
Herb	Lindsay	USA 54	28:05.07	6		Eugene	7 Apr
Salvatore	Nicosia	ITA 63	28:05.35	5	DNG	Stockholm	2 Jul

1984 Lists – Men

Paul	Kipkoech	KEN 62	28:05.4m	2		Aachen	30 May
Ibrahim	Kivina	TAN 58	28:06.00	2	NCAA	Eugene	1 Jun
Mike	McLeod	UK 52	28:06.22	3	OG	Los Angeles	6 Aug
Joseph	Kiptum	KEN 56	28:06.5m	3		Aachen	30 May
Seppo	Liuttu	FIN 56	28:06.58	6	DNG	Stockholm	2 Jul
Joseph	Nzau	KEN 50	28:06.63	2	TexR	Austin	5 Apr
Don	Clary	USA 57	28:07.01	7		Eugene	7 Apr
Mohamed Ali	Chouri	TUN 62	28:07.24	7	DNG	Stockholm	2 Jul
Aleksandr	Khudyakov	SU 60	28:07.30	4	DRZ	Moskva	17 Aug
Mats	Erixon	SWE 58	28:07.49	9	DNG	Stockholm	2 Jul
Pierre	Levisse	FRA 52	28:08.11	10	DNG	Stockholm	2 Jul
Alain	Bordeleau	CAN 56	28:08.87	6	Pre	Eugene	21 Jul
Yutaka	Kanai	JAP 59	28:09.04	2	NC	Tokyo	21 Oct
Werner	Schildhauer	GDR 59	28:09.05	2	NC	Potsdam	5 May
Lars-Erik	Nilsson	SWE 61	28:09.22	11	DNG	Stockholm	2 Jul
Cor	Lambregts	HOL 58	28:09.5m	4		Aachen	30 May
Jose Joao	da Silva	BRA 54	28:09.59	6		Firenze	13 Jun
Martin	Pitayo	MEX 60	28:11.4m	7	MSR	Walnut	28 Apr
Kipsubai	Koskei	KEN 51	28:11.7m	1	AfrC	Rabat	12 Jul
Paul	McCloy	CAN 63	28:11.72	1		Eugene	4 May
Sergio	Pesavento	ITA 58	28:11.99	7		Firenze	13 Jun
Julian	Goater	UK 53	28:13.02	3	NC	Cwmbran	27 May
Giovanni	D'Aleo	ITA 59	28:14.62	8		Firenze	13 Jun
Tom	Ansberry	USA 63	28:14.8m	8	MSR	Walnut	28 Apr
Geoff	Smith	UK 53	28:14.87	4	NC	Cwmbran	27 May
Ralf	Salzmann	FRG 55	28:15.3m	5		Aachen	30 May
Joseph	Kipsang	KEN 62	28:15.35	3	NCAA	Eugene	1 Jun
Alex	Hagelsteens	BEL 56	28:17.00	4	VD	Bruxelles	24 Aug
Ahmed	Saleh	DJI 56	28:17.4m	2	AfrC	Rabat	12 Jul
Jose	Sena	POR 55	28:17.83	12	DNG	Stockholm	2 Jul
Jorg	Peter	GDR 55	28:17.95	3	NC	Potsdam	5 May
Luis	Horta	POR 58	28:18.13	13	DNG	Stockholm	2 Jul
Andrew	Lloyd	AUS 59	28:18.6m	1	NC (a)	Melbourne	13 Dec
Theo	V.den Abeele	BEL 60	28:18.65	5	VD	Bruxelles	24 Aug
Thom	Hunt	USA 58	28:18.8m	9	MSR	Walnut	28 Apr
Pat	Petersen	USA 59	28:19.3m	4r1	PennR	Philadelphia	26 Apr
Roy	Kissin	USA 57	28:19.5m	10	MSR	Walnut	28 Apr
Martin	Vrabel	CS 55	28:19.66	5	DRZ	Moskva	17 Aug
Bill	Donakowski	USA 56	28:20.1m	11	MSR	Walnut	28 Apr
Ahmed Musa	Juda	SUD 57	28:20.26	8h3	OG	Los Angeles	3 Aug
Toomas	Turb	SU 57	28:20.35	1	Znam	Sochi	9 Jun
Robbie	Perkins	USA 55	28:20.4m	9		Eugene	7 Apr
Pat	Vaughn	USA 59	28:21.7m	10		Eugene	7 Apr
Jari	Hemmila	FIN 59	28:21.74	14	DNG	Stockholm	2 Jul
Francisco	Pacheco	MEX 61	28:21.8m	12	MSR	Walnut	28 Apr
Jef	Gees	BEL 56	28:22.13	15	DNG	Stockholm	2 Jul
Antoni	Niemczak	POL 55	28:22.24	2	Znam	Sochi	9 Jun
Garry	Henry	AUS 55	28:22.5m	2	NC (a)	Melbourne	13 Dec
Pavel	Klimes	CS 58	28:23.16	4	PTS	Bratislava	26 May
Juma	Ikangaa	TAN 57	28:23.29	2		Tokyo	6 May
Oleg	Strizhakov	SU 63	28:23.80	3	Znam	Sochi	9 Jun
algis	Dabulskis	SU 61	28:24.13	4	Znam	sochi	9 Jun
Robert	Hodge	USA 55	28:24.6m	5r1	PennR	Philadelphia	26 Apr
Evgeni	Ignatov	BUL 59	28:24.73	5	Znam	Sochi	9 Jun
Mark	Scrutton	UK 60	28:25.6m	1	FlaR	Gainesville	30 Mar
John	Moreno	USA 55	28:25.6m	13 MSR	Walnut	28 Apr	
Francis	Gonzalez	FRA 52	28:26.04	2	Paris	4 Sep	
Rex	Wilson	NZ	28:26.1m	3	Aus Ch	Melbourne	13 Dec
Vladimir	Shesterov	SU 54	28:26.31	6	Znam	Sochi	9 Jun
Gary	Tuttle	USA 47	28:26.4m	14	MSR	Walnut	28 Apr
Bogumil	Kus	POL 57	28:26.92	7	Znam	Sochi	9 Jun
Carmelo	Rios	PR 59	28:27.1m	15	MSR	Walnut	28 Apr
Kirk	Pfeffer	USA 56	28:27.8m	16	MSR	Walnut	28 Apr

1984 Lists – Men

Miroslaw	Dzienisik	POL 58	28:28.03	1		Sopot	29 Jul
Raf	Wijns	BEL 64	28:28.1m	1		Kessel-Lo	15 Jun
Jose	Gomez	MEX 56	28:28.50	6h1	OG	Los Angeles	3 Aug
Zephaniah	Ncube	ZIM 57	28:28.53	2h2	OG	Los Angeles	3 Aug
Dan	Aldridge	USA 56	28:28.7m	11		Eugene	7 Apr
Peter	Butler	CAN 58	28:28.7m	17	MSR	Walnut	28 Apr
Omar	Aguilar	CHL 59	28:29.06	7h1	OG	Los Angeles	3 Aug
John	Easker	USA 63	28:29.2m	1r2	PennR	Philadelphia	26 Apr
Vesa	Kahkola	FIN 59	28:29.54	1		Lahti	21 Aug
Art	Boileau	CAN 57	28:29.91	1		Eugene	17 Mar

Name		Nat/Yr	Time	Date
Charlie	Bevier	USA 59	28:30.4m	26 Apr
Esa	Liedes	FIN 50	28:30.53	21 Aug
Viktor	Chumakov	SU 57	28:30.56	19 Jul
Dean	Matthews	USA 55	28:30.6m	7 Apr
Karl	Harrison	UK 56	28:30.75	23 Jun
John	Idstrom	USA 59	28:30.9m	28 Apr
Adugna	Lema	ETH 63	28:31.34	26 May
Vladimir	Mayfat	SU 63	28:31.51	9 Jun
Wieslaw	Perszke	POL 60	28:31.88	29 Jul
Greg	Lautenslager	USA 57	28:32.04	17 Mar
Orlando	Pizzolato	ITA 58	28:32.2m	30 May
Ezequiel	Canario	POR 60	28:32.37	4 Sep
Spiridon	Andriopoulos	GRE 62	28:32.46	26 May
Toshihiko	Seko	JAP 56	28:32.49	21 Oct
Kazuyoshi	Kudoh	JAP 61	28:32.5m	13 May
Richard	O'Flynn	IRL	28:32.6m	26 Apr
Jerszy	Skarzynski	POL 56	28:33.26	29 Jul
Tony	Milovsorov	UK 58	28:33.29	27 May
Kunimitsu	Itoh	JAP 55	28:33.33	30 Apr
Greg	Fredericks	USA 50	28:33.6m	26 Apr
Dan	Schlesinger	USA 55	28:33.7m	28 Apr
Tadeusz	Lawicki	POL 56	28:33.83	29 Jul
Masami	Ohtsuka	JAP 60	28:34.37	30 Apr
Tom	Wysocki	USA 56	28:34.39	17 Mar
Tetsuo	Urakawa	JAP	28:34.49	30 Apr
Savas	Koubouras	GRE 60	28:34.50	26 May
Tom	Raunig	USA 59	28:34.6m	28 Apr
Petr	Klimes	CS 58	28:34.69	26 May
Steve	Ortiz	USA 59	28:34.69	16 Jun
Charles	Cheruiyot	KEN 64	28:34.74	6 May
Jackson	Ruto	KEN 59	28:35.0m	15 Jun
Steve	McCormack	USA 60	28:35.1m	28 Apr
Sergey	Sedov	SU 58	28:36.28	9 Jun
Dan	Dillon	USA 57	28:36.7m	28 Apr
John	Woods	IRL 55	28:37.55	17 Jun
Axel	Krippschock	GDR 62	28:37.67	5 May
Jozef	Ziubrak	POL 51	28:38.16	29 Jul
Steve	Anders	UK 59	28:38.20	27 May
Tommy	Ekblom	FIN 59	28:38.46	24 May
Carlos	Retiz	MEX 61	28:38.5m	28 Apr
Anatoliy	Krakhmalyuk	SU 60	28:38.78	7 Sep
Gennadiy	Fishman	SU 59	28:38.80	7 Sep
Allister	Hutton	UK 54	28:38.82	27 May
Giuseppe	Pambianchi	ITA 57	28:38.9m	30 May
Derrick	May	RSA 55	28:39.1m	28 Apr
Dan	Grimes	USA 59	28:39.38	17 Mar
Walter	Merlo	ITA 65	28:39.4m	13 Oct
Giuseppe	Gerbi	ITA 55	28:39.5m	13 Oct
Ilie	Floroiu	RUM 52	28:39.56	7 Sep

Peter	Koech	KEN 58	28:39.65	1 Jun
Keith	Brantly	USA 62	28:39.82	1 Jun
Ghislain	Fourrier	BEL 54	28:40.1m	15 Jun
Jed	Hopfsenberger	USA 57	28:40.5m	13 Apr
Marc	Ruell	BEL 60	28:40.59	24 Aug
Gheorge	Motorca	RUM 55	28:40.82	7 Sep
Steve	Austin	AUS 51	28:41.04	30 Mar
Jeff	Drenth	USA 61	28:41.11	13 Apr
Agapius	Masong	TAN 60	28:41.55	13 Jun
Gyorgy	Marko	RUM 60	28:41.67	9 Jun
Mike	Buhmann	USA 57	28:42.05	16 Jun
Jon	Sinclair	USA 57	28:42.54	8 Jun
Dean	Kimball	USA 58	28:42.6m	26 Apr
Antti	Loikkanen	FIN 55	28:42.77	24 May
Steve	Morake	RSA 54	28:42.79	13 Apr
Christian	Geffray	FRA 54	28:42.92	4 Sep
Ron	Tabb	USA 54	28:43.11	4 May
Mark	Conover	USA 60	28:43.45	4 May
John	Flora	USA 56	28:43.9m	26 Apr
Kurt	Hurst	SWZ 51	28:44.04	4 Sep
Nikolay	Nikolayenko	SU 54	28:44.12	7 Sep
Olof	Salmi	FIN 52	28:44.37	21 Aug
Graham	Payne	UK 57	28:44.4m	27 May
Jean-Pierre	Paumen	BEL 56	28:44.69	24 Aug
Silvio	Salazar	COL 58	28:44.89	27 Oct
Vladimir	Anisimov	SU 56	28:45.0m	11 Aug
Ivan	Huff	USA 59	28:45.1m	7 Apr
John	Andrews	AUS 58	28:45.18	6 Mar
Karl	Fleschen	FRG 55	28:45.4m	30 May
Chris	Hamilton	USA 63	28:45.56	17 Mar
Gennadiy	Temnikov	SU 61	28:45.6m	11 Aug
Frank	Heine	GDR 63	28:45.68	5 May
Mark	Stickley	USA 62	28:45.97	8 Jun
Philippe	Legrand	FRA 58	28:45.98	29 Jun
Antonio	Prieto	SPA 58	28:46.0m	21 Apr
Don	Janicki	USA 60	28:46.2m	28 Apr
Vladimir	Solovyev	SU 59	28:46.2m	11 Aug
Leonid	Tikhonov	SU 56	28:46.4m	11 Aug
Peter	Ffitch	USA	28:46.6m	4 May
Douglas	Wakiihura	KEN 62	28:46.82	11 Mar
Renat	Altynguzhin	SU 56	28:46.92	19 Jul
Stanislav	Tabor	CS 56	28:47.04	26 May
Yasuhiro	Sakaguchi	JAP	28:47.09	11 Mar
Takao	Nakamura	JAP 58	28:47.10	30 May
Dirk	Sander	FRG 56	28:47.3m	30 May
Mehmet	Yurdadon	TUR 54	28:47.6m	30 May

*= Disqualified for drug abuse.
(a) = Australian Championship 1985.

1984 Lists – Men

	1	10	20	30	50	100	Under 28:00	Under 28:30
1980	27:29.16	27:46.71	27:55.41	28:04.0	28:16.12	28:36.6	22	84
1981	27:27.7	27:47.54	28:00.58	28:09.9	28:26.31	28:41.8	19	59
1982	27:22.95	27:38.1	28:01.00	28:09.7	28:17.71	28:35.01	19	87
1983	27:23.44	27:46.93	27:59.14	28:06.7	28:19.97	28:38.40	22	69
1984	27:13.81	27:47.0	27:57.68	28:03.06	28:08.11	28:26.92	24	112

3000 METRES STEEPLECHASE

Joseph	Mahmoud	FRA 55	8:07.62	1	VD	Bruxelles	24 Aug
Boguslaw	Maminski	POL 55	8:09.18	2	VD	Bruxelles	24 Aug
	Mahmoud		8:11.64	1		Koblenz	29 Aug
Julius	Korir	KEN 60	8:11.80	1	OG	Los Angeles	10 Aug
Brian	Diemer	USA 61	8:13.16	2		Koblenz	29 Aug
	Mahmoud		8:13.31	2	OG	Los Angeles	10 Aug
	Maminski		8:13.43	1		Oslo	21 Jul
Colin	Reitz	UK 60	8:13.78	2		Oslo	21 Jul
Peter	Renner	NZ 59	8:14.05	3		Koblenz	29 Aug
	Diemer		8:14.06	3	OG	Los Angeles	10 Aug
Henry	Marsh	USA 54	8:14.25	4	OG	Los Angeles	10 Aug
Krzysztof	Wesolowski	POL 56	8:15.28	3		Oslo	21 Jul
	Reitz		8:15.48	5	OG	Los Angeles	10 Aug
	Maminski		8:15.68	1	FBK	Hengelo	6 Jul
	Marsh		8:15.91	1	FOT	Los Angeles	23 Jun
Juan	Torres	SPA 57	8:16.25	4		Koblenz	29 Aug
	Mahmoud		8:16.33	1		Hannover	16 Jun
	Maminski		8:16.46	1		Koln	26 Aug
	Mahmoud		8:16.68	1		Paris	4 Sep
	Wesolowski		8:16.83	2		Hannover	16 Jun
	Diemer		8:17.00	2	FOT	Los Angeles	23 Jun
Domingo	Ramon	SPA 58	8:17.27	6	OG	Los Angeles	10 Aug
	Korir		8:17.40	1s2	OG	Los Angeles	8 Aug
Julius	Kariuki	KEN 61	8:17.47	7	OG	Los Angeles	10 Aug
	Mahmoud		8:17.60	1		Beaupreau	31 May
Graeme	Fell	UK 59	8:17.71	3	VD	Bruxelles	24 Aug
	Diemer		8:17.77	4	VD	Bruxelles	24 Aug
Gabor	Marko	HUN 60	8:17.97	1	OD	Potsdam	21 Jul
	Renner		8:18.12	2s2	OG	Los Angeles	8 Aug
	Diemer		8:18.36	3s2	OG	Los Angeles	8 Aug

(30/13)

John	Gregorek	USA 60	8:18.45	3	FOT	Los Angeles	23 Jun
Fethi	Baccouche	TUN 60	8:18.70	6s2	OG	Los Angeles	8 Aug
William	van Dijck	BEL 61	8:18.75	5		Koblenz	29 Aug
Farley	Gerber	USA 60	8:19.27	1	NCAA	Eugene	1 Jun
Roger	Hackney	UK 57	8:20.16	1	OT	Gateshead	10 Jun
Pascal	Debacker	FRA 60	8:20.34	2s1	OG	Los Angeles	8 Aug
Ken	Martin	USA 58	8:20.40	6	VD	Bruxelles	24 Aug
Tommy	Ekblom	FIN 59	8:20.54	3s1	OG	Los Angeles	8 Aug
Peter	Daenens	BEL 60	8:20.7m	2		Louvain	22 Jun
Paul	Davies–Hale	UK 62	8:20.83	2	OT	Gateshead	10 Jun
Hagen	Melzer	GDR 59	8:21.32	2	OD	Potsdam	21 Jul
Andrey	Popelyayev	SU 63	8:21.75	1		Moskva	19 Jul
Patrick	Sang	KEN	8:22.45	2		Stockholm	17 Jul
Ivan	Huff	USA 59	8:22.80	5	FOT	Los Angeles	23 Jun
Hans	Koeleman	HOL 57	8:23.73	2		Lausanne	10 Jul
Dave	Daniels	USA 58	8:24.77	6	FOT	Los Angeles	23 Jun

253

1984 Lists – Men

Kelly	Jensen	USA 54	8:25.13	4s1	FOT	Los Angeles	21 Jun
Tom	Stevens	USA 61	8:25.21	7	FOT	Los Angeles	23 Jun
Bret	Hyde	USA 59	8:25.39	6s1	FOT	Los Angeles	21 Jun
Jeff	Hess	USA 60	8:25.48	7s1	FOT	Los Angeles	21 Jun
Ivan	Konovalov	SU 59	8:25.81	3	vITA,POL,FRG	Torino	3 Jun
Ricky	Pittman	USA 61	8:26.03	8s1	FOT	Los Angeles	21 Jun
Antonio	Leitao	POR 60	8:26.19	3	WA	Lisboa	17 Jun
Greg	Duhaime	CAN 53	8:26.32	9s1	OG	Los Angeles	8 Aug
Valeriy	Gryaznov	SU 61	8:26.43	3		Moskva	19 Jul
Vasile	Bichea	RUM 50	8:26.56	1		Bucuresti	10 Jun
Francesco	Panetta	ITA 63	8:26.90	4	vSU,POL,FRG	Torino	3 Jun
Sergey	Yepishin	SU 58	8:26.92	2	Znam	Sochi	10 Jun
Eddie	Wedderburn	UK 60	8:27.17	3		Gateshead	6 Jul
Liam	O'Brien	IRL 54	8:27.24	4	AAA	London	24 Jun
Lars	Sorensen	FIN 59	8:27.27	5		Stockholm	17 Jul
Czeslaw	Mojzysz	POL 58	8:27.58	4	vFRG,CS,FRA	Hannover	16 Jun
Franco	Boffi	ITA 58	8:27.66	6	WG	Helsinki	4 Jul
Joshua	Kipkemboi	KEN 59	8:27.88	1	AfrC	Rabat	13 Jul
Panayot	Kashanov	BUL 57	8:28.02	3	OD	Potsdam	21 Jul
Jan	Hagelbrand	SWE 54	8:28.28	6		Stockholm	17 Jul
Torsten	Tiller	FRG 62	8:28.95	5	vPOL,CS,FRA	Hannover	16 Jun
Emilio	Ulloa	CHL 54	8:28.99	8s2	OG	Los Angeles	8 Aug
Peter	Koech	KEN 58	8:29.09	2		Eugene	4 May
George Kip	Rono	KEN 58	A8:29.4m	1	NC	Nairobi	16 Jun
Frank	Ruhkieck	GDR 61	8:29.93	2		Potsdam	6 May
Randy	Jackson	USA 58	8:29.95	1		Knoxville	19 May
Filippos	Filippou	CYP 56	8:30.09	7h3	OG	Los Angeles	6 Aug
Jim	Cooper	USA 59	8:30.10	4		Eugene	4 Jun
Phil	Laheurte	CAN 57	8:30.39	3	Jerome	Burnaby	16 Jul
Bruce	Bickford	USA 57	8:30.43	1	King	Atlanta	22 Apr
Wieslaw	Ziembicki	POL 60	8:30.50	1		Lublin	8 Jun
Wilson	Musonik	KEN 56	A8:30.5m	3	NC	Nairobi	16 Jun
Aleksandr	Vitshel	SU 58	8:30.76	3	Izv	Kiev	24 Jun
Filbert	Bayi	TAN 53	8:30.97	1		Sollentuna	12 Jun
Mike	Vanatta	USA 61	8:31.14	6		Eugene	4 Jun
Rainer	Schwarz	FRG 59	8:31.8m	1		Koblenz	25 Jul
Carmelo	Rios	PR 59	8:31.88	6h2	OG	Los Angeles	6 Aug
Karl-Heinz	Seck	FRG 54	8:32.06	6		Hannover	16 Jun
Boris	Pruss	SU 58	8:32.07	4	Izv	Kiev	24 Jun
Eshetu	Tura	ETH 50	8:32.08	3	PTS	Bratislava	26 May
Guilherme	Alves	POR 61	8:32.21	11	WG	Helsinki	4 Jul
Jorge	Bello	SPA 63	8:32.35	4		Barcelona	8 Jul
Augustin	Barbu	RUM 63	8:32.83	2	NC	Bucuresti	10 Jul
Aleksandr	Zagoruyko	SU 55	8:32.94	3	NC	Donyetsk	8 Sep
Mikhail	Romanov	SU 59	8:32.94	4	NC	Donyetsk	8 Sep
Matt	McGuirk	USA 64	8:33.03	5	NCAA	Eugene	1 Jun
Vaclav	Patek	CS 59	8:33.11	4	DRZ	Moskva	17 Aug
Harrison	Koroso	KEN 56	8:33.29	1		Tucson	5 May
Kregg	Einspahr	USA 60	8:33.46	4		Eugene	4 May
Gyula	Balogh	HUN 61	8:33.7m	1		Miskolc	17 Jun
Romeo	Zivko	YUG 62	8:34.01	2		Bruxelles	1 Jul
Norbert	Brotzmann	GDR 61	8:34.02	3		Potsdam	6 May
David	Barney	USA 60	8:34.12	1	TexR	Austin	7 Apr
Richard	Garcia	USA 61	8:34.13	3h1	FOT	Los Angeles	19 Jun
Mati	Uusmaa	SU 59	8:34.20	5	Znam	Sochi	10 Jun
Vyacheslav	Groshev	SU 58	8:34.2m	1		Sochi	27 May
Igor	Pavlov	SU 60	8:34.2m	1		Ryazan	11 Aug
Roland	Hertner	SWZ 57	8:34.25	8		Koblenz	29 Aug
Nollie	Meintjies	RSA 57	8:34.3m	1		Stellenbosch	23 Apr
Raymond	Pannier	FRA 61	8:34.47	3	NC	Villeneuve D'As.	1 Jul
Gary	Zeuner	AUS 53	8:34.52	1	NC	Melbourne	31 Mar
Joe	Hartnett	IRL 56	8:34.52	2	NC	Dublin	8 Jul
Roger	Gjovaag	NOR 56	8:34.70	12	WG	Helsinki	4 Jul
Ken	Baker	UK 63	8:34.83	3		Bruxelles	1 Jul

1984 Lists – Men

Harold	Kuphaldt	USA 64	8:34.86	6	NCAA	Eugene	1 Jun
Bela	Vago	HUN 63	8:34.90	2	NC	Budapest	26 Jul
Vern	Iwancin	CAN 60	8:34.9m	1		Burnaby	18 Jun
Boris	Petunin	SU 58	8:34.9m	2		Ryazan	11 Aug
Wayne	Dyer	AUS 58	8:35.02	3	NC	Melbourne	31 Mar
Marek	Stepnicki	POL 55	8:35.18	2		Lublin	8 Jun
Jorge	Castello	SPA 60	8:35.35	2	NC	Barcelona	1 Jul
Ibrahim	Hussein	KEN 59	8:35.4m	2r1	MSR	Walnut	28 Apr
Yehuda	Zadok	ISR 58	8:35.41	3	PNG	Turku	26 Jun
Bob	Ingram	USA 62	8:35.43	7	NCAA	Eugene	1 Jun
Sam	Ngatia	KEN 57	8:35.47	8	NCAA	Eugene	1 Jun
Steve	James	USA 60	8:35.5m	5		Seattle	21 Apr
Yuriy	Konovalov	SU 57	8:35.6m	3		Ryazan	11 Aug
Aleksandr	Mavrin	SU 58	8:35.62	6		Moskva	19 Jul
Guillermo	Serrano	MEX 60	8:35.64	2	GS	Ostrava	23 May
Alain	Boucher	CAN 63	8:36.0m	29 Jun	Slawomir	Gorny	POL 64	8:38.86	29 Jul
Lars	Abrahmsen	SWE 57	8:36.09	26 Jun	David	Frank	USA 61	8:38.89	24 May
Kari	Hanninen	FIN 62	8:36.11	7 Jul	Brendan	Hewitt	AUS 64	8:38.9m	8 Feb
Ahcene	Babaci	ALG 57	8:36.30	13 Jul	Atila	Barus	CS 60	8:38.99	21 Jul
Joseph	Chelelgo	KEN 61	8:36.50	20 May	Dave	Dobler	USA 62	8:39.04	24 Mar
Sandor	Paczuk	HUN 58	8:36.5m	2 Sep	Andreas	Pichler	FRG 59	8:39.05	29 Aug
Miroslaw	Zerkowski	POL 56	8:36.68	16 Sep	Anatoliy	Dimov	SU 56	8:39.26	4 Aug
Henryk	Jankowski	POL 61	8:36.76	22 Jun	Viktor	Yaroshenko	SU 58	8:39.30	10 Jun
Stanislav	Stit	CS 58	8:36.77	21 Jul	Csaba	Szucs	HUN 65	8:39.37	26 Jul
Valeriy	Vandyak	SU 62	8:36.8m	27 May	Terry	Drake	USA 57	8:39.4m	21 Apr
Sergey	Bagdasaryan	SU 61	8:36.8m	8 Jul	Jos	Maes	BEL 61	8:39.4m	22 Jun
Jozsef	Orosz	HUN 57	8:36.9m	2 Sep	Vladimir	Sharmanov	SU 60	8:39.46	19 Jul
Piotr	Zgarda	POL 56	8:36.96	22 Jun	Rainer	Wachenbrunner	GDR 62	8:39.47	1 Jun
Kirill	Laktionov	SU 60	8:37.0m	27 May	Frank	Fischer	GDR 63	8:39.47	1 Jun
Richard	Tuwei	KEN 54	8:37.2m	21 Apr	Vitautas	Jezerskis	SU 61	8:39.5m	30 Sep
Ron	Addison	USA 54	8:37.21	4 Jun	Ismo	Toukonen	FIN 54	8:39.59	14 Jun
Algis	Stancius	SU 58	8:37.37	8 Sep	Ivan	Danu	SU 61	8:39.59	1 Jun
Milan	Behun	CS 58	8:37.47	21 Jul	Ahmed	Homada	MOR 58	8:39.66	13 Jul
Don	Clary	USA 57	8:37.56	17 Mar	Kieran	Stack	IRL 63	8:39.80	31 Mar
Vladimir	Shtyrts	SU 62	8:37.6m	11 Aug	Janos	Papp	HUN 59	8:39.8m	27 Sep
Manuel	Salvador	SPA 59	8:37.68	1 Jul	Karl	Van Calcar	USA 65	8:39.81	30 May
Aleksandr	Boloto	SU 56	8:37.74	19 Jul	Bill	McCullough	USA 53	8:39.84	12 May
Sam	Sitonik	KEN 55	8:37.83	20 May	Gheorge	Neamtu	RUM 57	8:39.89	10 Jul
Jan	Karol	POL 59	8:37.85	8 Aug	Peter	Larkins	AUS 54	8:39.94	31 Mar
Cory	Randall	USA 63	8:37.94	19 Jun	Bruno	Le Stum	FRA 59	8:39.95	6 Jun
Istvan	Szenegeto	HUN 56	8:38.20	26 Jul	Vasiliy	Andronakiy	SU 62	8:40.0m	27 May
Arrie	Van Heerden	RSA 59	8:38.20	7 Dec	Martin	Fiz	SPA 63	8:40.01	1 Jul
Rex	Hohnholt	USA 58	8:38.2m	21 Apr	Artur	Koleczek	POL 63	8:40.35	8 Jun
Habib	Cherif	ALG 62	8:38.26	13 Jul	Vinko	Pokrajcic	YUG 53	8:40.35	16 Sep
Gary	Gregory	USA 60	8:38.27	16 Jul	Patriz	Ilg	FRG 57	8:40.53	23 Jun
Pete	Warner	USA 62	8:38.42	17 Mar	Tony	Blackwell	UK 58	8:40.58	28 May
Christian	Schieber	FRG 59	8:38.53	29 Aug	Marcel	Martinas	RUM 64	8:40.60	1 May
Laszlo	Szasz	HUN 61	8:38.6m	13 Sep	Wolfgang	Konrad	AUT 58	8:40.64	17 Jun
Danie	Prinsloo	RSA	8:38.64	7 Dec					
Jozsef	Szeleczky	HUN 57	8:38.7m	27 Sep	Pavlov (8:34.2m) also 8:34.25	4	Moskva	19 Jul
Maks	Skubic	YUG 57	8:38.73	17 Jun					

Short Course (2985m)

| Greg | Duhaime | CAN 53 | 8:24.9 | 1 | Burnaby | 9 Jun | (8:26.32) |

	1	10	20	30	50	100	Under 8:30	Under 8:35
1980	8:09.70	8:18.78	8:22.81	8:25.89	8:29.1	8:36.3	55	87
1981	8:13.2	8:21.93	8:25.79	8:28.93	8:30.7	8:37.1	45	75
1982	8:16.17	8:21.15	8:23.94	8:27.36	8:31.0	8:35.7	42	94
1983	8:12.37	8:19.38	8:21.72	8:25.05	8:28.77	8:36.09	60	94
1984	8:07.62	8:17.27	8:20.40	8:25.13	8:28.95	8:35.35	55	97

1984 Lists – Men

110 METRES HURDLES

Greg	Foster	USA 58	13.15	−1.1	1r1	WK	Zurich	22 Aug
	Foster		13.16	−0.1	1	ISTAF	Berlin	17 Aug
Roger	Kingdom	USA 62	13.16	−1.1	2	WK	Zurich	22 Aug
	Kingdom		13.17	−0.1	2	ISTAF	Berlin	17 Aug
	Foster		13.19	0.5	1h1	FOT	Los Angeles	18 Jun
	Kingdom		13.19	0.6	1	Nik	Nice	20 Aug
	Kingdom		13.20	−0.4	1	OG	Los Angeles	6 Aug
	Foster		13.21	1.1	1	Pepsi	Los Angeles(Ww)	13 May
	Foster		13.21	−1.1	1	FOT	Los Angeles	19 Jun
	Foster		13.22	−2.7	1s1	FOT	Los Angeles	19 Jun
Tonie	Campbell	USA 60	13.23	1.1	2	Pepsi	Los Angeles(Ww)	13 May
	Foster		13.23	−0.4	2	OG	Los Angeles	6 Aug
	Kingdom		13.23	−0.6	1		Koln	26 Aug
	Foster		13.24	1.7	1h4	OG	Los Angeles	5 Aug
	Kingdom		13.24	0.7	1s1	OG	Los Angeles	6 Aug
	Foster		13.24	−1.1	1s2	FOT	Los Angeles	6 Aug
	Campbell		13.26	−0.6	1	TAC	San Jose	8 Jun
Mark	McKoy	CAN 61	13.27	1.5	1		Walnut	25 Jul
	Foster		13.29	0.4	1q1	FOT	Los Angeles	18 Jun
	Campbell		13.29	−0.6	2		Koln	26 Aug
	Campbell		13.29	0.7	1	GGala	Roma	31 Aug
	Campbell		13.29	−1.0	1		Seoul	29 Sep
	Campbell		13.30	0.6	1s1	TAC	San Jose	7 Jun
	McKoy		13.30	−1.1	2s2	OG	Los Angeles	6 Aug
	Campbell		13.30	1.4	1	8-N	Tokyo	14 Sep
	Campbell		13.31	1.8	1s2	FOT	Los Angeles	19 Jun
	Kingdom		13.32	−1.5	1		Villanova	14 Jul
	Campbell		13.33	1.1	1h2	FOT	Los Angeles	18 Jun
	Campbell		13.34	−1.1	2	FOT	Los Angeles	19 Jun
	Campbell		13.34	0.6	2	Nik	Nice	20 Aug

(30/4)

Arto	Bryggare	FIN 58	13.35	2.0	1h1	OG	Los Angeles	5 Aug
Cletus	Clark	USA 62	13.41	−0.7	2r1	MSR	Walnut	29 Apr
Larry	Cowling	USA 60	13.43	0.6	2s1	TAC	San Jose	7 Jun
Stephane	Caristan	FRA 64	13.43	1.4	1		San Diego	30 Jul
Henry	Andrade	USA 62	13.45	1.8	3s2	FOT	Los Angeles	19 Jun
Gyorgy	Bakos	HUN 60	13.45	1.4	2	8-N	Tokyo	14 Sep
Plamen	Krastev	BUL 58	13.46	−0.3	1	4-N(a)	Athinai	10 Jul
John	Johnson	USA 60	13.47	1.6	1h4	NCAA	Eugene	31 May
John	Timpson	USA 62	13.48	1.8	1r1		Baton Rouge	21 Apr
Milan	Stewart	USA 60	13.48	0.7	4		Koblenz	29 Aug
Sam	Turner	USA 57	13.49	−0.7	3r1	MSR	Walnut	29 Apr
Thomas	Munkelt	GDR 52	13.51	0.9	1	NC	Erfurt	1 Jun
James	Quinn	USA 63	13.53	0.4	1		Athens	5 May
Alejandro	Casanas	CUB 54	13.53	1.9	1	Barr	Habana	19 May
Nikolay	Shilev	BUL 63	13.54	1.2	1		Sofia	5 May
James	McCraney	USA 55	13.55	1.3	1		Walnut	3 Jun
Carlos	Sala	SPA 60	13.56	0.7	5	GGala	Roma	31 Aug
Andrey	Prokofyev	SU 59	13.57	−2.0	1	Izv	Kiev	21 Jun
Javier	Moracho	SPA 57	13.57	0.6	1	NC	Barcelona	30 Jun
Vyacheslav	Ustinov	SU 57	13.57	−0.6	2	DRZ	Moskva	18 Aug
Igor	Kazanov	SU 63	13.59	−0.3	1	NC	Donyetsk	9 Sep
Jack	Pierce	USA 62	13.60	0.6	1	PennR	Philadelphia	28 Apr
Al	Lane	USA 62	13.60	0.6	2	PennR	Philadelphia	28 Apr
Stefan	Baker	USA 61	13.63	0.1	2		Houston	6 May
Jacek	Rutkowski	POL 59	13.64	−0.8	1h2		Zabrze	20 May
Wayne	Roby	USA 62	13.64	1.8	7s2	FOT	Los Angeles	19 Jun
Kerry	Bethel	USA 57	13.65	0.2	2		Charlottesville	13 May
Tony	Dees	USA 63	13.65	1.3	1		Baton Rouge	13 May

1984 Lists – Men

Sansiski	Daniels	USA 63	13.66	1.4	1		Ruston	28 Apr
Rod	Wilson	USA 61	13.66	0.4	3q1	FOT	Los Angeles	18 Jun
Venzislav	Radev	BUL 61	13.66	1.9	2		Barcelona	8 Jul
Charles	James	USA 64	13.67	1.6	4h4	NCAA	Eugene	31 May
Steve	Kerho	USA 64	13.68	1.7	1	MSR	Walnut	28 Apr
Eugene	Miller	USA 59	13.68	0.4	2		Athens	5 May
Andreas	Schlisske	GDR 57	13.68		2		Sofia	16 Jun
Keith	Talley	USA 64	13.69	2.0	1s1		San Angelo	18 May
Romuald	Giegiel	POL 57	13.69	-1.5	1	NC	Lublin	24 Jun
Rod	Woodson	USA 65	13.71		2r1		Tallahassee	17 Mar
Nat	Page	USA 57	13.71		3r2	MSR	Walnut	29 Apr
Daniele	Fontecchio	ITA 60	13.71		1		Molfetta	1 Jul
Don	Wright	AUS 59	13.72	0.5	1		Sydney	11 Feb
Anatoliy	Titov	SU 56	13.72	-2.0	1		Kiev	5 Jul
Jeff	Glass	CAN 62	A13.73	1.6	1		Provo	19 May
Holger	Pohland	GDR 63	13.73	-0.4	5	OD	Berlin	20 Jul
Eugene	Norman	USA 61	13.74	0.3	4		Columbus	6 May
Sergey	Usov	SU 63	13.74	-0.8	2		Moskva	4 Aug
Dennis	Brantley	USA 61	13.75	1.8	2r1		Baton Rouge	21 Apr
Boris	Pendergrass	USA 63	13.75	1.7	1h2		Villanova	20 May
Kenny	Link	USA 61	13.76	0.6	3		Baton Rouge	24 Mar
Barry	McClain	USA 62	13.77	-2.2	1		Athens	24 Mar
Thomas	Nnakwe	NIG 58	13.78	-2.2	2		Athens	24 Mar
Nigel	Walker	UK 63	13.78	-0.8	1	AAA	London	24 Jun
Jiri	Hudec	CS 64	13.78	-1.1	4h1	DRZ	Moskva	18 Aug
Jean-Marc	Muster	SWZ 61	13.78	1.0	1		Chaux-de-Fonds	18 Aug
Rod	Milburn	USA 50	13.79	1.0	3		Houston	26 May
Robert	Thomas	USA 60	13.80	1.8	1r2		Baton Rouge	21 Apr
Albert	Jones	USA 62	13.80	1.1	5	NCAA	Eugene	2 Jun
John	Lenstrohm	USA 61	13.80	1.3	2h3	TAC	San Jose	7 Jun
Thomas	Wilcher	USA 64	13.80	1.1	3h2	FOT	Los Angeles	18 Jun
Leander	McKenzie	USA 63	13.81		2h2		Tallahassee	16 Mar
Lamar	Hurd	USA 64	13.81	1.8	1		Eugene	28 Apr
Martin	Booker	USA 63	13.81		1		Philadelphia	11 May
David	Ashford	USA 64	13.82	2.0	2s1		San Angelo	18 May
Mark	Holtom	UK 58	13.82	-1.5	4		London	13 Jul
Janis	Saulite	SU 58	13.82	-0.3	3	NC	Donyetsk	9 Sep
Ricky	Alexander	USA 60	13.83	1.8	2r2		Baton Rouge	21 Apr
Craig	White	USA 64	13.83	-0.9	3h1	PennR	Philaelphia	27 Apr
Ed	Ross	USA 61	13.83	1.8	6h4	FOT	Los Angeles	18 Jun
Alex	Washington	USA 62	13.83	0.5	3q2	FOT	Los Angeles	18 Jun
Roberto	Schneider	SWZ 58	13.83	2.0	1h		Chaux-de-Fonds	27 Jun
Al	Joyner	USA 60	13.83	0.7	8	GGala	Roma	31 Aug
Jerome	Wilson	USA 62	13.84	1.3	2		Baton Rouge	13 May
Arthur	Blake	USA 66	13.84	-0.4	1s2	TAC-jr	Los Angeles	22 Jun
Gianni	Tozzi	ITA 62	13.84	-0.5	2r2		Rieti	2 Sep
Elliott	White	USA 63	13.85	0.0	1		Fresno	12 May
Jonas	Jakstis	SU 59	13.85	0.0	1		Tallinn	28 Jun
Franck	Chevallier	FRA 64	13.85	1.0	1s2	NC	Villeneuve D'A.	30 Jun
Wojciech	Zawila	POL 61	13.86	-1.5	3	NC	Lublin	24 Jun
Wilbert	Greaves	UK 56	13.86	-1.1	5s2	OG	Los Angeles	6 Aug
William	Cooper	USA 62	13.87	1.0	2	FlaR	Gainesville	31 Mar
Igor	Perevedentsev	SU 64	13.87	0.2	2h1		Sochi	19 May
Pavel	Voronkov	SU 58	13.87		h		Sochi	19 May
Jurgen	Schoch	FRG 62	13.87	1.8	1		Stuttgart	21 Jul
Petar	Vukicevic	YUG 56	13.87	1.3	2	Balk	Athinai	9 Sep
Mike	Roberson	USA 56	13.88		4		Tallahassee	17 Mar
Vitaliy	Sklyarov	SU 60	13.88	0.6	2h3	Izv	Kiev	20 Jun
Vladimir	Zayka	SU 57	13.88	-0.7	4		Moskva	19 Jul
Frank	Williamson	USA 62	13.89	0.0	2		Fresno	12 May
Barry	Word	USA 64	13.89	0.2	5		Charlottesville	13 May
Andreas	Oschkenat	GDR 62	13.89	1.2	1h		Potsdam	25 May

257

1984 Lists – Men

Malcolm	Dixon	USA 59	13.89	0.6	5s1	TAC	San Jose	7 Jun	
Jeff	Powell	USA 63	13.90		2h3	PennR	Philadelphia	27 Apr	
Charles	Foster	USA 53	13.90	1.6	1		Raleigh	23 May	
Bela	Bodo	HUN 59	13.90	1.8	2		Tampere	14 Jun	
Victor	Moore	USA 64	13.91		2		Fayetteville	21 Apr	
Reyna	Thompson	USA 63	13.91	1.3	4h1	NCAA	Eugene	31 May	
Nikolay	Kulyasha	SU 59	13.91	-2.0	2		Kiev	5 Jul	
Krzysztof	Platek	POL 62	13.91	1.9	1h1		Sopot	29 Jul	
Wu	ChingChin	TAI 58	13.91	1.7	3h4	OG	Los Angeles	5 Aug	
Reggie	Towns	USA 61	13.92	0.5	5h1	FOT	Los Angeles	18 Jun	
Jonathon	Ridgeon	UK 66	13.92	1.0	1		Birmingham	12 Aug	
Angelo	Booker	USA 59	13.93		4r2	MSR	Walnut	29 Apr	
Aleksandr	Markin	SU 62	13.93	0.0	4		Sochi	26 May	
Aleksandr	Apaychev	SU 61	13.93		D v	GDR	Neubrandenburg	3 Jun	
Viktor	Batrachenko	SU 63	13.93	0.9	4s2	Izv	Kiev	21 Jun	
Jan	Tesitel	CS 58	13.93	0.4	2	NC	Praha	22 Jul	
Allen	Cooper	USA 61	13.94	21 Apr	1.8	Ion	Oltean	RUM 58	14.05	11 Jul	-0.9
Fred	Cleary	USA 62	13.94	21 Apr		Modesto	Castillo	DOM 61	14.05	5 Aug	1.7
Albert	Toon	USA 63	13.94	12 May	1.8	Anton	Isayev	SU 62	14.06	9 Jun	-1.4
Frank	Rossland	GDR 60	13.94	24 May	1.0	Yuriy	Myshkin	SU 63	14.06	9 Sep	0.3
Ales	Hoffer	CS 62	13.94	2 Jun	0.4	Geoff	Caldarone	USA	14.07	13 May	
Istvan	Simon-Balla	HUN 58	13.94	10 Jul	-0.3	Clifton	Franklin	USA 65	14.07	13 May	1.3
Vladimir	Shishkin	SU 64	13.94	9 Sep	-0.3	Jurgen	Hingsen	FRG 58	14.07	8 Jun	0.2
Len	Robinson	USA 62	13.95	31 Mar	1.5	Igor	Podmaryov	SU 61	14.07	5 Jul	-2.0
Tadeusz	Zakoscielny	POL 58	13.95	6 May	0.1	Jeff	Nichols	USA	14.08	6 May	
Yu	Zhicheng	CHN 63	13.95	10 Jun		Forika	McDougall	USA 62	14.08	13 May	1.3
Georgiy	Shabanov	SU 60	13.95	19 Jul	-0.9	Miguel	Williams	USA 60	14.08	7 Jun	1.3
Guido	Kratschmer	FRG 53	13.95	21 Jul	1.8	Carlos	Lloveras	SPA 61	14.08	24 Jun	1.1
Colin	Jackson	UK 67	13.95	12 Aug	1.0	Michele	Ventura	ITA 61	14.08	10 Jul	0.6
Greg	Smith	USA 60	13.96	31 Mar	1.9	Mike	Wilson	AUS 60	14.09	6 Mar	0.0
Gus	Young	JAM 61	13.96	21 Apr	1.8	Steve	Martin	USA	14.09	21 Apr	
Ray	Hollier	USA 61	13.96	21 Apr	1.8	Stephan	Fletcher	USA 64	14.09	12 May	0.3
Kenny	Nesbitt	USA 62	13.97	17 Mar	1.9	Derrick	Gentry	USA 62	14.09	20 May	1.7
Joe	Pugh	USA 63	13.97	14 Apr		Daryl	Hill	USA	14.09	26 May	0.4
Fred	Smith	USA	13.97	14 Apr	0.6	Georg	Prast	ITA 59	14.09	27 May	
Julius	Ivan	CS 54	13.97	13 May		Siegfried	Wentz	FRG 60	14.09	9 Jun	0.2
Peter	Scholz	FRG 59	13.97	23 Jun	-0.7	Torsten	Voss	GDR 63	14.09	16 Sep	
Aleksandr	Kuznetsov	SU 57	13.97	19 Jul	0.2	Luigi	Bertocchi	ITA 65	14.09	29 Sep	0.5
Dedy	Cooper	USA 56	13.98	7 Apr	1.8	Wessel	Bosman	RSA 58	A14.10	3 Apr	
Mark	Boyd	USA 65	13.98	5 May	0.0	Ricky	Davenport	USA 56	14.10	21 Apr	1.8
Micah	Williams	USA	13.99	28 Apr	1.7	Kevin	McKinley	USA 64	14.10	25 May	
Angel	Bueno	CUB 63	13.99	19 May	1.9	Franciszek	Jozwicki	POL 60	14.10	2 Jun	0.8
Robert	Ekpete	NOR 63	13.99	16 Jun	1.6	Herbert	Kreiner	AUT 55	14.10	10 Jun	0.5
Aivars	Ikaunieks	SU 59	13.99	9 Sep	0.3	Hannu	Parssinen	FIN 60	14.10	24 Jun	0.8
Eric	Reid	USA 65	14.01	13 May	1.3	Jim	Scanella	USA 61	14.11	24 Mar	0.0
Darryl	Shepherd	USA	14.01	31 May	1.3	Jurie	v.der Walt	RSA 60	A14.11	21 Apr	
Gennadiy	Chugunov	SU 63	14.01	9 Sep	0.3	Sergey	Strelchenko	SU 61	14.11	28 Apr	
Lorenzo	Zackery	USA 60	A14.02	14 Apr		Doug	Rosado	PR 63	14.11	28 Apr	
Wellington	Araujo	BRA 60	14.02	9 Jun	1.1	Hugh	Teape	UK 63	14.11	1 Jul	2.0
Mikael	Ylostalo	FIN 63	14.02	8 Jul	0.3	Georgios	Tsiandas	GRE 63	14.11	9 Sep	1.3
Arne	Rincklebe	GDR 62	14.02	27 Jul	2.0	Damon	Polk	USA	14.12	14 Apr	
Jiri	Cerovsky	CS 55	14.02	1 Aug		Owen	Herrera	USA 64	14.12	26 May	1.0
Philippe	Hatil	FRA 58	14.02	12 Aug	1.7	Philippe	Aubert	FRA 57	14.12	30 Jun	1.9
Arend	de Waal	RSA 60	A14.03	24 Mar		Ralph	Schroeder	RSA	A14.12	14 Nov	
Claudell	Anderson	USA 63	14.04	14 Apr		Craig	Easley	USA	14.13	5 May	1.2
Eric	Spence	CAN 61	A14.04	19 May	1.6	Doug	Jones	USA 64	14.14	19 May	2.0
Reggie	Davis	USA	14.05	17 Mar	1.9	Pedro	Chiamulera	BRA 64	14.14	17 Jun	0.0
Barry	Malloyd	USA 64	14.05	28 Apr	1.4	Li	Jieqiang	CHN 59	14.14	25 Jul	1.5
Terron	Wright	USA 58	14.05	29 Apr							
Ronnie	McCoy	USA 63	14.05	31 May	1.3						

(a) 4-N = BUL v HUN v FRG v GRE.

1984 Lists – Men

Low Altitude Marks

| Glass | 13.79 | 1.5 | 5 | Walnut | 25 Jul | Altitude Best 13.73 |

Wind Assisted Marks

Roger	Kingdom	USA 62	13.00	2.7	1			Sacramento	21 Jul
Mark	McKoy	CAN 61	13.16	2.7	2			Sacramento	21 Jul
	Campbell		13.23	2.2	1			Knoxville	19 May
	Kingdom		13.23	2.8	1			San Jose	26 May
	Campbell		13.25	2.8	2			San Jose	26 May
Henry	Andrade	USA 62	13.28	2.7	3			Sacramento	21 Jul
	Campbell		13.30	3.2	1r1		CalR	Modesto	12 May
	McKoy		13.31	2.2	2			Knoxville	19 May
Sam	Turner	USA 57	13.38	2.2	1			San Jose	21 Apr
Al	Lane	USA 62	13.38	3.4	1h3		NCAA	Eugene	31 May
Cletus	Clark	USA 62	13.39	3.3	1			Edinburgh	17 Jul
Alejandro	Casanas	CUB 54	13.40	2.6	1			Brest	6 Jun
James	McCraney	USA 55	13.43	3.2	4r1		CalR	Modesto	12 May
Keith	Talley	USA 64	13.50	2.8	1			San Angelo	18 May
Stefan	Baker	USA 61	13.57	2.6	2			Austin	12 May
Jacek	Rutkowski	POL 60	13.59	4.7	1		Kuso	Warszawa	9 Jun
Albert	Jones	USA 62	13.60	3.4	2h3		NCAA	Eugene	31 May
Mark	Holtom	UK 58	13.60	3.3	3			Edinburgh	17 Jul
Eugene	Norman	USA 61	13.62	4.1	1			Knoxville	14 Apr
Reyna	Thompson	USA 63	13.64	6.9	1h1			Arlington	5 May
Romuald	Giegiel	POL 57	13.64	3.4	1			Warszawa	2 Jun
Alex	Washington	USA 62	13.64	2.6	2h5		FOT	Los Angeles	18 Jun
Sansiski	Daniels	USA 63	13.65	4.6	1			Arlington	14 Apr
Bela	Bodo	HUN 58	13.69	2.8	1			Budapest	24 Jun
Wojciech	Zawila	POL 61	13.70	4.7	3		Kuso	Warszawa	9 Jun
Kenny	Link	USA 61	13.71	4.6	2			Arlington	14 Apr
David	Ashford	USA 64	13.72	2.8	2			San Angelo	18 May
Damon	Polk	USA	13.72	2.8	3			San Angelo	18 May
Joe	Pugh	USA 63	13.79	2.8	4			San Angelo	18 May
Reggie	Towns	USA 61	13.80	2.2	5			Knoxville	19 May
Miguel	Williams	USA 60	13.81	7.1	1s1			Knoxville	14 Apr
Mike	Benjamin	USA 61	13.81	5.6	2s2			Knoxville	14 Apr
Ed	Ross	USA 61	13.82	2.8	1			Baton Rouge	14 Apr
Elliott	White	USA 63	13.82	2.5	4h2		NCAA	Eugene	31 May
Wilbert	Greaves	UK 56	13.82	4.4	5			Birmingham	15 Jul
Krzysztof	Platek	POL 62	13.83	4.7	5		Kuso	Warszawa	9 Jun
Ronnie	McCoy	USA 63	13.84	4.1	1h2			Columbus	19 May
Jurgen	Hingsen	FRG 58	13.84	2.4	1			Ludenscheid	26 May
Franck	Chevallier	FRA 64	13.84	2.2	2		NC	Villeneuve D'A.	30 Jun
Dedy	Cooper	USA 56	13.85	2.2	5			San Jose	21 Apr
Jeff	Nichols	USA	13.86	7.1	2s1			Knoxville	14 Apr
Chappelle	Henderson	USA 61	13.86	4.6	4			Arlington	14 Apr
Malcolm	Dixon	USA 59	13.86	2.7	5			Sacramento	21 Jul
Barry	Word	USA 64	13.88	2.2	7			Knoxville	19 May
Angel	Bueno	CUB 63	13.89	5.0	1h		Barr	Habana	19 May
Michel	Brodeur	CAN 62	13.89	3.0	1			Montreal	14 Jul
Albert	Toon	USA 63	13.90		3h2			Columbus	19 May
Craig	Moody	USA 62	13.91	4.6	5			Arlington	14 Apr
Frank	Rossland	GDR 60	13.92	4.7	6		Kuso	Warszawa	9 Jun
Li	Jieqiang	CHN 59	13.92		2			Eugene	21 Jul

Derrick	Stinson	USA 64	13.93	14 Apr	5.6	Ron	Kennedy	USA 57	13.96	7 Jun	4.4
Andrew	Parker	USA	13.93	18 May	2.8	Hugh	Teape	UK 63	13.98	27 May	2.7
Robert	Ekpete	NOR 63	13.93	1 Jun	2.9	Jake	Jacoby	USA 61	13.99	14 Apr	3.1
Philippe	Hatil	FRA 58	13.93	30 Jun	2.7	Greg	Culp	USA 60	13.99	28 Apr	
Greg	Smith	USA 60	13.94	26 May	4.3	Jesse	Rider	USA 65	13.99	18 May	2.7
Reggie	Davis	USA	13.95	14 Apr	4.1						

259

1984 Lists – Men

John	Long	USA 52	14.00	14 Apr	5.6	Reijo	Byman	FIN 55	14.05	8 Jul	3.0
Kazuhiko	Mizuno	JAP 61	14.01	29 Apr	3.8	Anton	Isayev	SU 62	14.05	15 Sep	2.3
Philippe	Aubert	FRA 57	14.01	30 Jun	2.2	Albert	Kelly	USA	14.06	19 May	3.4
Stephan	Fletcher	USA 64	14.02	14 Apr	2.8	Lajos	Vaszil	HUN 58	14.07	24 Jun	2.8
Owen	Herrera	USA 64	14.02	12 May		King	Simmons	USA 63	14.11	20 Apr	
John	Bell	USA 62	14.03	14 Apr		Terry	Brooks	USA	14.13	28 Apr	
Yuriy	Myshkin	SU 63	14.03	15 Sep	2.3	Matt	Morris	USA	14.13	18 May	2.8
Craig	Easley	USA	14.04	5 May	3.5						
Wolfgang	Muders	FRG 57	14.05	2 Jun	2.7						

Unclear Photo

	Kingdom		13.25		0.6	1r2	Tillsonburg		7 Jul
	McKoy		13.31		0.6	2r2	Tillsonburg		7 Jul
Michel	Brodeur	CAN	14.08						7 Jul

Manual Timing

Roger	Kingdom	USA 62	13.1	-0.9	1r1	Tillsonburg	7 Jul	13.16	
Tonie	Campbell	USA 60	13.1	1.8	1	Berkeley	14 Jul	13.23	
Milan	Stewart	USA 60	13.4	1.8	2	Berkeley	14 Jul	13.48	
James	McCraney	USA 55	13.4	1.8	3	Berkeley	14 Jul	13.55	
Janis	Saulite	SU 58	13.4		1=(a)	Riga	10 Aug	13.82	
Aivars	Ikaunieks	SU 59	13.4		1=(a)	Riga	10 Aug	13.99	
Anton	Isayev	SU 62	13.4		1	Leningrad	12 Aug	14.06	
Plamen	Krastev	BUL 58	13.4	0.2	1	Sofia	25 Aug	13.46	
Aleksandr	Kuznetsov	SU 57	13.5		1	Leningrad	15 Jun	13.97	
Al	Lane	USA 62	13.5	-0.9	2r1	Tillsonburg	7 Jul	13.60	
Vitaliy	Sklyarov	SU 60	13.5		1	Leningrad	12 Aug	13.88	
Venzislav	Radev	BUL 61	13.5	0.2	2	Sofia	25 Aug	13.66	
Anatoliy	Titov	SU 56	13.6i		1	Moskva	3 Feb	13.72	
Sergey	Strelchenko	SU 61	13.6i		1	Donyetsk	4 Mar	14.11	
Sansiski	Daniels	USA 63	13.6	0.8	2	Austin	20 May	13.82	
Al	Joyner	USA 60	13.6	1.8	4	Berkeley	14 Jul	13.83	
Yuriy	Nedosekov	SU 58	13.6		1	Vitebsk	16 Jul	(14.22)	
Petar	Vukicevic	YUG 56	13.6	0.2	1	Sarajevo	21 Jul	13.87	
Ales	Hoffer	CS 62	13.6		1	Praha	8 Aug	13.94	
Jiri	Hudec	CS 64	13.6		2	Praha	8 Aug	13.78	
Ainars	Loris	SU 61	13.6		3	Riga	10 Aug	(14.27)	
Vladimir	Zayka	SU 57	13.6	2.0	1	Kiev	10 Aug	13.88	
Sergey	Krasovskiy	SU 63	13.6	2.0	2	Kiev	10 Aug	(14.17)	
Igor	Perevedentsev	SU 64	13.6		1	Gorkiy	12 Aug	13.87	
Luigi	Bertocchi	ITA 65	13.6		1 (b)	Alexandria	16 Oct	14.09	
Don	Wright	USA 59	13.7	2.0	1	Canberra	4 Jan	13.72	
David	Ashford	USA 64	13.7		1	Walnut	7 Jan	13.82	
Angelo	Booker	USA 59	13.7		1	Los Angeles	21 Jan	13.94	
Fred	Smith	USA	13.7		1	Bakersfield	11 Feb	13.98	
Kobus	Schoeman	RSA 65	A13.7		1	Johannesburg	25 Feb		
Yuriy	Myshkin	SU 63	13.7i		2	Moskva	3 Mar	14.06	
Oleg	Degtyar	SU 64	13.7		1	Chernovtsy	16 Jun		
Jonas	Jakstis	SU 59	13.7		1	Riga	6 Jul	13.85	
Georgiy	Shabanov	SU 60	13.7		3	Moskva	6 Jul	13.95	
Igor	Podmaryov	SU 61	13.7		3	Leningrad	6 Jul	14.07	
Sergey	Usov	SU 64	13.7		2	Moskva	8 Jul	13.74	
Nikolay	Kulyasha	SU 59	13.7		2	Dnepropetrovsk	Gaug	13.91	
Aleksandr	Kuzmenko	SU 55	13.7	2.0	3	Kiev	10 Aug	(14.32)	
Viktor	Batrachenko	SU 63	13.7					13.93	
Jurie	v. der Walt	RSA 60	A13.8	18 Feb	Zoven	Danilyants	SU 62	13.8	15 Jun
Arend	de Waal	RSA 63	A13.8	25 Feb	Sergey	Ryzhkov	SU 56	13.8	13 Jul
Martin	Booker	USA 63	13.8	7 Apr	Sergey	Novikov	SU 63	13.8	4 Aug
Vladimir	Shishkin	SU 64	13.8	23 Apr	Sergey	Tesunov	SU 59	13.8	10 Aug
Giovanni	Tozzi	ITA 62	13.8	19 May	Aleksandr	Polyantsev	SU 60	13.8	10 Aug

1984 Lists – Men

Best Outdoor Mark

| Strelchenko | 13.6 | 1 | Shakty | 14 Jul | (13.6i) |
| Myshkin | 13.8 | | | 15 Jul | |

(a) = Latvian SSR Championships   (b) = CISM championships.

World list 110 metres hurdles: **Wind Assisted Marks**

David	Ashford	USA 64	13.5		1		Tucson	18 Feb
Darryl	Shepherd	USA	13.5		1		Pittsburgh	12 May
John	Lenstrohm	USA 61	13.6	2.9	1r2	CalR	Modesto	12 May
Nat	Page	USA 57	13.6	2.9	2r2	CalR	Modesto	12 May
Yuriy	Myshkin	SU 63	13.6	2.2	2		Chelyabinsk	29 Jul
Leander	McKenzie	USA 63	13.7	3.4	1h5	TexR	Austin	6 Apr
Victor	Moore	USA 64	13.7		2		Wichita	14 Apr
Craig	Easley	USA	13.7		2		Pittsburgh	12 May
Sergey	Ryzhkov	SU 56	13.7	2.2	3		Chelyabinsk	29 Jul

	1	10	20	30	50	100	Under 13.80	Under 14.00
1980	13.21	13.53	13.68	13.79	13.90	14.07	31	77
1981	12.93	13.59	13.70	13.75	13.87	14.04	39	83
1982	13.22	13.46	13.65	13.72	13.82	14.02	45	94
1983	13.11	13.50	13.60	13.68	13.79	13.96	50	106
1984	13.15	13.45	13.55	13.64	13.74	13.91	59	138

400 METRES HURDLES

Edwin	Moses	USA 55	47.32	1		Koblenz	29 Aug
	Moses		47.58	1s1	FOT	Los Angeles	17 Jun
Harald	Schmid	FRG 57	47.69	1		Lausanne	10 Jul
	Moses		47.75	1	OG	Los Angeles	5 Aug
	Moses		47.76	1	FOT	Los Angeles	18 Jun
	Moses		47.95	1		Koln	26 Aug
	Moses		48.01	1	GGala	Roma	31 Aug
Danny	Harris	USA 65	48.02	2s1	FOT	Los Angeles	17 Jun
	Schmid		48.04	2		Koblenz	29 Aug
	Harris		48.11	2	FOT	Los Angeles	18 Jun
	Harris		48.13	2	OG	Los Angeles	5 Aug
Tony	Rambo	USA 60	48.16	3s1	FOT	Los Angeles	17 Jun
	Schmid		48.19	3	OG	Los Angeles	5 Aug
	Moses		48.25	1s1	TAC	San Jose	8 Jun
	Schmid		48.26	1	Nik	Nice	20 Aug
Tranel	Hawkins	USA 62	48.28	3	FOT	Los Angeles	18 Jun
Andre	Phillips	USA 59	48.42	1r1	WK	Zurich	22 Aug
Aleksandr	Vasilyev	SU 61	48.45	1	Izv	Kiev	22 Jun
	Hawkins		48.48	2r1	WK	Zurich	22 Aug
	Moses		48.49	1	ISTAF	Berlin	17 Aug
	Moses		48.51	1s1	OG	Los Angeles	4 Aug
	Hawkins		48.52	1s2	FOT	Los Angeles	17 Jun
	Phillips		48.61	2		Koln	26 Aug
	Phillips		48.62	4	FOT	Los Angeles	18 Jun
Bart	Williams	USA 56	48.63	2		Lausanne	10 Jul
	Vasilyev		48.63	1	DRZ	Moskva	18 Aug
	Schmid		48.66	2	GGala	Roma	31 Aug
	Phillips		48.73	1		San Jose	26 May
Amadou	Dia Ba	SEN 58	48.73	1	VD	Bruxelles	24 Aug
Vladimir	Budko	SU 65	48.74	2	DRZ	Moskva	18 Aug

261

1984 Lists – Men

(30/10)

David	Patrick	USA 60	48.80	4s1	FOT	Los Angeles	17 Jun
Vasiliy	Arkhipenko	SU 57	48.81	1		Sochi	27 May
Sven	Nylander	SWE 62	48.97	4	OG	Los Angeles	5 Aug
Toma	Tomov	BUL 58	48.99	1		Sofia	8 Aug
Aleksandr	Kharlov	SU 58	49.15	1		Moskva	20 Jul
Ray	Smith	USA 57	49.18	2h1	FOT	Los Angeles	16 Jun
David	Lee	USA 59	49.29	1		Athens	24 Mar
Henry	Amike	NIG 61	49.33	2		Lincoln	12 May
James	Walker	USA 57	49.40	5s	FOT	Los Angeles	17 Jun
Valeriy	Vikhrov	SU 61	49.40	2	Izv	Kiev	22 Jun
Franz	Meier	SWZ 56	49.42	5r1	WK	Zurich	22 Aug
Sergey	Melnikov	SU 60	49.45	3	Izv	Kiev	22 Jun
Belfrab	Clark	USA 65	49.45	1	TAC-jr	Los Angeles	24 Jun
Peter	Scholz	FRG 59	49.45	1		Stuttgart	21 Jul
Volker	Beck	GDR 56	49.46	1		Potsdam	25 May
Uwe	Schmitt	FRG 61	49.48	3r2	WK	Zurich	22 Aug
Leander	McKenzie	USA 63	49.51	6s1	FOT	Los Angeles	17 Jun
Karl	Smith	JAM 59	49.58	5s2	OG	Los Angeles	4 Aug
Julio	Prado	CUB 60	49.61	3		Rieti	2 Sep
Hannes	Pienaar	RSA 60	A49.63	1		Sasolburg	21 Apr
Jon	Thomas	USA 63	49.63	1	Jerome	Burnaby	16 Jul
Rik	Tommelein	BEL 62	49.64	1		Louvain	22 Jun
Michel	Zimmerman	BEL 60	49.64	1	NC	Bruxelles	8 Jul
Antonio E.	Diaz Ferreira	BRA 60	49.65	1		Sao Paulo	17 Jun
Hennie	Kotze	RSA 60	A49.66	1		Germiston	8 Mar
Greg	Rolle	BAH 59	49.66	1	TexR	Austin	6 Apr
Tony	Valentine	USA 64	49.66	3h1	FOT	Los Angeles	16 Jun
Simon	Kitur	KEN 59	49.70	2h4	OG	Los Angeles	3 Aug
James	King	USA 49	49.72	4	Pepsi	Los Angeles (Ww)	13 May
Ryoichi	Yoshida	JAP 65	49.75	1	NC	Tokyo	20 Oct
Bernie	Holloway	USA 61	49.78	3	MSR	Walnut	29 Apr
Nikolay	Chernyetskiy	SU 59	49.78	3		Sochi	20 May
Manfred	Konow	GDR 58	49.78	1	NC	Erfurt	2 Jun
Ryszard	Szparak	POL 51	49.81	1	NC	Lublin	23 Jun
Len	Robinson	USA 62	49.83	1		Los Angeles (Ww)	31 Mar
Martin	Briggs	UK 64	49.86	1	OT	London	6 Jun
Ed	Brown	USA 61	49.89	7s1	FOT	Los Angeles	17 Jun
Ken	Gray	JAM 60	49.91	2		London	18 Aug
Chappelle	Henderson	USA 61	49.92	1		Austin	12 May
Thomas	Futterknecht	AUT 62	49.92	6r1	WK	Zurich	22 Aug
Kevin	Henderson	USA 65	49.94	2	TAC-jr	Los Angeles	24 Jun
Jose	Alonso	SPA 57	49.94	4	Nik	Nice	20 Aug
Lloyd	Guss	CAN 59	50.01	2	Jerome	Burnaby	16 Jul
Patrick	Mann	USA 66	50.02	3	TAC-jr	Los Angeles	24 Jun
Horia	Toboc	RUM 55	50.02	1	NC	Bucuresti	12 Jul
Bozhidar	Konstantinov	BUL 63	50.03	2	Balk	Athinai	8 Sep
Kobus	Burger	RSA 62	50.04	1		Port Elizabeth	8 Dec
Tagir	Zemskov	SU 62	50.05	2	NC	Donyetsk	8 Sep
Jozsef	Szalai	HUN 61	50.05	2	8-N	Tokyo	14 Sep
Ed	Cooper	USA 63	50.09	1		Tucson	17 Mar
Jim	Scanella	USA 61	50.09	1		Berkeley	21 Apr
Terry	Menefee	USA 62	50.10	1		Baton Rouge	13 May
Reggie	Davis	USA	50.10	1		Tallahassee	26 May
Forika	McDougald	USA 62	50.11	2		Baton Rouge	13 May
Gerard	Brunel	FRA 57	50.11	1	NC	Villeneuve D'Ascq	1 Jul
Markus	Konig	FRG 62	50.11	1		Saarbrucken	15 Jul
Sven	Mikisch	FRG 65	50.11	1		Monchen Gladbach	19 Aug
Shigenobu	Ohmori	JAP 60	50.12	1		Tokyo	2 Jun
Andri	Hargrove	USA 58	50.12	4s2	TAC	San Jose	8 Jun
Vladimir	Titov	SU 59	50.12	h		Moskva	19 Jul
Don	Ward	USA 62	50.19	2		Berkeley	21 Apr

262

1984 Lists – Men

Takashi	Nagao	JAP 57	50.21	2		Tokyo	6 May
Athanassios	Kalogiannis	GRE 65	50.22	1		Athinai	4 Jul
Sylvester	Davis	USA 62	50.23	2r2		Knoxville	14 Apr
Istvan	Takacs	HUN 59	50.23	2		Munchen	20 Jul
Martin	Gillingham	UK 63	50.24	1	AAA	London	24 Jun
Gary	Oakes	UK 58	50.24	3		London	18 Aug
Matthias	Kaulin	FRG 63	50.24	2		Monchen Gladbach	19 Aug
Wendell	Angel	USA 52	50.25	1r2	CalR	Modesto	12 May
Sergey	Kutsebo	SU 61	50.25	1		Kiev	4 Jul
Harry	Schulting	HOL 56	50.26	3	FBK	Hengelo	6 Jul
Istvan	Simon-Balla	HUN 58	50.26	2		Riccione	26 Aug
R.Meledje	Djedjemel	IVC 58	50.27	3h3	OG	Los Angeles	3 Aug
Georgios	Vamvakas	GRE 60	50.30	2		Athinai	4 Jul
Franck	Jonot	FRA 61	50.31	1h1	NC	Villeneuve D'Ascq	29 Jun
Floyd	Johnson	USA 59	50.32	4		Tallahassee	17 Mar
Pierre	Leveille	CAN 62	A50.32	1		Provo	23 May
Fred	Cleary	USA 62	50.34	1		Fayetville	21 Apr
Yuriy	Chashchin	SU 63	50.34	6	Izv	Kiev	22 Jun
Phil	Beattie	UK 63	50.43	2	OT	London	6 Jun
Peter	Rwamuhanda	UGA 53	50.46	1		Atlanta	14 Jul
Walter	Morrison	USA 59	50.47	2		Austin	12 May
Thomas	Nyberg	SWE 62	50.47	5h1	OG	Los Angeles	3 Aug
Ryszard	Stoch	POL 62	50.50	1		Zabrze	20 May
Krasimir	Demirev	BUL 62	50.51	2		Schwechat	30 May
Giorgio	Rucli	ITA 63	50.51	3		Grosseto	14 Jul
Garry	Brown	AUS 54	50.52	1		Sydney	11 Mar
Craig	Moody	USA 62	50.52	4	TexR	Austin	6 Apr
Martin	Booker	USA 63	50.52	2		Philadelphia	12 May
Daniel	Hejret	CS 62	50.52	1		Praha	28 Aug
Arend	de Waal	RSA 63	A50.53	2		Pretoria	18 Feb
Jorg	Steinbrecher	GDR 63	50.53	3		Potsdam	25 May
Thomas	Burkle	FRG 58	50.53	2		Saarbrucken	15 Jul
Stefan	Schnabel	FRG 63	50.56	3		Saarbrucken	15 Jul
Nick	Ross	USA 60	50.58	1		Ruston	28 Apr
Daniel	Ogidi	NIG 63	50.58	1h2		Knoxville	18 May
Piotr	Karczmarek	POL 57	50.58	2	NC	Lublin	23 Jun

Rob	Cassleman	USA 52	50.60	4 May
Rimantas	Jurjevicius	SU 64	50.61	19 Jul
Ahmed	Hamada	BHN 61	50.62	3 Aug
Hawie	Engels	RSA 62	50.62	8 Dec
Parry	Duncan	USA 61	50.65	12 May
Oswaldo	Zea	VEN 63	50.65	18 May
Nathaniel	Hale	USA 61	50.65	26 May
Stanislav	Navesnak	CS 65	50.65	22 Jul
Arthur	Blake	USA 66	50.66	9 Jun
Julius	Mercer	USA 60	50.68	6 Apr
Walter	Murray	USA 62	50.68	8 Jun
Fujihide	Nakajyo	JAP 63	50.69	6 May
Ian	Newhouse	CAN 56	A50.69	16 Jun
Thomas	Wild	SWZ 57	50.69	22 Jul
Steve	Sole	UK 59	50.70	24 Jun
Eric	Riley	USA 62	50.71	11 May
John	Lenstrohm	USA 61	50.71	16 Jun
Sam	Nwosu	NIG 61	50.72	12 May
Patrick	Cheruiyot	KEN 64	50.72	26 May
Jaco	Pienaar	RSA 58	A50.73	5 Mar
Aleksandr	Cheshko	SU 58	50.73	26 May
Garrett	Shumway	USA 60	50.76	27 May
Pablo	Squella	CHL 63	50.76	25 Jul
Petter	Hesselberg	NOR 59	50.76	28 Jun
Ahmed	Ghanem	EGY 59	50.77	13 Jul

Victor	Gomez	CUB 64	50.78	20 May
Dmitriy	Matsulevich	SU 62	50.79	5 Aug
Rudik	Matevosyan	SU 62	50.79	5 Aug
Rob	Archer	USA 62	50.80	13 May
Rok	Kopitar	YUG 59	50.80	17 Jun
Mike	Whittingham	UK 54	50.80	24 Jun
Dale	Laverty	USA 65	50.82	24 Jun
Lorenzo	Zackery	USA 60	50.83	4 May
Charlie	Ca	USA 64	50.83	26 May
James	Ferreira	USA 65	50.84	26 May
Mark	Whitby	UK 64	50.84	6 Jun
Don	Burrell	USA 62	50.85	26 May
Joe	Pugh	USA 63	50.87	5 May
Sergey	Sedov	SU 60	50.88	20 May
Roger	Coleman	USA 61	50.90	6 Apr
H.-Jurgen	Ende	GDR 62	50.90	6 May
Bernard	Williams	USA 65	50.90	12 May
Paul	Atherton	UK 57	50.91	6 Jun
Dimitar	Ivanov	BUL 60	50.93	17 Jun
Carlos	Leal	MEX 59	A50.93	24 Jun
Carsten	Fischer	FRG 62	50.93	15 Jul
Nate	Grier	USA 61	50.94	20 Apr
Frank	Montie	CUB 59	50.96	12 Jun
Kenny	Nesbitt	USA 62	50.97	18 May
Yakov	Merchuk	SU 59	50.97	26 May

263

1984 Lists – Men

John	Graham	CAN 65	A50.98	23 May	Mike	Kinney	USA 61	51.09	4 May
Luca	Cosi	ITA 63	50.98	26 May	Payton	Hines	USA	51.09	13 May
Anthony	Bell	USA 65	50.99	28 Apr	Jerome	Wilson	USA 62	51.10	13 May
Charles	DeRouselles	USA	50.99	26 May	Jesus	Arino	SPA 63	51.10	30 Jun
Wang	Guihua	CHN 61	50.99	6 Sep	Ken	Gordon	AUS 62	51.11	3 Mar
Dale	Horrobin	AUS 60	51.00	31 Mar	Rolf	Dresen	FRG 57	51.11	9 Jun
Randy	Cox	USA	51.00	11 May	Stefano	Bizzaglia	ITA 60	51.11	1 Jul
Nikolay	Ilchenko	SU 63	51.00	19 May	Vladimir	Musil	CS 59	51.11	22 Jul
Duane	Bright	USA	51.00	26 May	Sansiski	Daniels	USA 63	51.12	27 Apr
Sergey	Lukyanov	SU 61	51.03	4 Jul	Lajos	Csapo	HUN 62	51.12	17 Jun
Mark	Campbell	USA 63	51.04	21 Apr	Thierry	Fromont	FRA 59	51.12	1 Jul
Frank	Williamson	USA 62	51.04	12 May	Charles	Moss	USA 63	51.15	11 May
Steve	Patterson	USA 63	51.05	14 Apr	Michael	Chukes	USA 61	51.16	12 May
Martin	Burkle	FRG 57	51.05	20 May	Vladislav	Pecen	CS 60	51.16	22 Jul
Jan	Wiberg	SWE 61	51.06	26 Aug	Christer	Gullstrand	SWE 59	51.16	2 Sep
Max	Robertson	UK 63	51.08	1 Jul					

Low altitude mark for athlete with seasonal best at high altitude

| Kotze | 50.02 | 2 | NC | Durban | 13 Apr | (49.66A) | |

Manual Timing

Tagir	Zemskov	SU 62	49.7	1		Moskva		5 Aug
Ed	Cooper	USA 63	49.8	1		San Diego		25 May
John	Lenstrohm	USA 61	49.9	2		San Diego		25 May
Meshak	Munyoro	KEN 58	A49.9	1	NC	Nairobi		16 Jun
Jaco	Pienaar	RSA 58	A50.0	2		Johannesburg		15 Feb
Kobus	Burger	RSA 62	50.0	1		Stellenbosch		23 Apr
Vladimir	Titov	SU 59	50.0	1		Leningrad		18 Jun
Sergey	Dedukhov	SU 63	50.1	2		Kiev		12 Aug
Rimantas	Jurjevicius	SU 64	50.1	1		Gorkiy		12 Aug
Arend	de Waal	RSA 63	A50.2	3		Johannesburg		15 Feb
R.Meledje	Djedjemel	IVC 58	50.2	1	CISM	Alexandria		15 Oct
Garry	Brown	AUS 54	50.4	1		Canberra		19 Feb
Hawie	Engels	RSA 62	A50.4	1		Germiston		14 Nov
Yakov	Merchuk	SU 63	50.5	3 Jun	Max	Robertson	UK 63	50.7	19 Aug
Izel	Jenkins	USA 64	50.6	16 May	Thomas	Giessing	FRG 61	50.8	30 May
Shem	Ochako	KEN 63	A50.6	16 Jun	Frank	Anderson	USA	50.9	16 May
Anatoliy	Gladkovskiy	SU 59	50.7	5 Aug	Doug	Lalicker	USA 60	50.9	25 May
Sergey	Sedov	SU 61	50.7	12 Aug					

Best Low Altitude Mark

| H.Pienaar | 50.1 | 1 | Stellenbosch | 29 Feb | (A49.63) | |

	1	10	20	30	50	100	Under 50.00	Under 51.00
1980	47.13	49.24	49.69	50.00	50.25	50.99	28	100
1981	47.14	49.33	49.72	50.11	50.41	50.94	23	109
1982	47.48	48.90	49.64	49.88	50.19	50.89	34	111
1983	47.02	49.03	49.35	49.59	50.02	50.72	48	137
1984	47.32	48.74	49.40	49.63	49.92	50.52	52	162

HIGH JUMP

Zhu	Jianhua	CHN 63	2.39	1		Eberstadt	10 Jun
Carlo	Thranhardt	FRG 57	2.37i	1		Berlin	24 Feb
Valeriy	Sereda	SU 59	2.37	1		Rieti	2 Sep

1984 Lists – Men

Igor	Thranhardt Paklin	SU 63	2.37 2.36i	2 1	vITA,SPA	Rieti Milano	2 Sep 1 Feb
Sergey	Zasimovich	SU 62	2.36	1		Tashkent	5 May
	Thranhardt		2.36	2		Eberstadt	10 Jun
Dietmar	Mogenburg	FRG 61	2.36	3		Eberstadt	10 Jun
	Zhu		2.35	1		Guangzhou	5 Mar
	Mogenburg		2.35	1	OG	Los Angeles	11 Aug
	Zhu		2.35	1		Shanghai	22 Sep
Sorin	Matei	RUM 63	2.34	1		Bucuresti	9 Jun
	Sereda		2.34	1	Izv	Kiev	24 Jun
Dwight	Stones	USA 53	2.34	1	FOT	Los Angeles	24 Jun
	Mogenburg		2.34	1		Rhede	5 Sep
	Mogenburg		2.33i	1	EC	Goteborg	3 Mar
	Zasimovich		2.33	1		Tashkent	13 May
Javier	Sotomayor	CUB 67	2.33	1	Barr	Habana	19 May
Aleksandr	Kotovich	SU 61	2.33	1	Nar	Sofia	20 May
Patrik	Sjoberg	SWE 65	2.33	4		Eberstadt	10 Jun
	Zhu		2.33	1		Walnut	25 Jul
	Stones		2.33	1		Pasadena	2 Aug
Vladimir	Granyenkov	SU 59	2.33	1		Moskva	5 Aug
Aleksey	Demyanyuk	SU 58	2.33	2		Moskva	5 Aug
	Sjoberg		2.33	2	OG	Los Angeles	11 Aug
Jim	Howard	USA 59	2.33	1		London	18 Aug
	Kotovich		2.32i	1		Minsk	15 Jan
	Matei		2.32i	1		Bucuresti	19 Feb
	Mogenburg		2.32i	2		Berlin	24 Feb
	Zasimovich		2.32	1		Sochi	20 May
	Howard		2.32	1	TAC	San Jose	9 Jun
	Demyanyuk		2.32	1	Znam	Sochi	10 Jun
Eddy	Annys	BEL 58	2.32	1		Woluwe	1 Jul
	Stones		2.32	1	WK	Zurich	22 Aug

(34/15)

Cotantin	Militaru	RUM 63	2.31i	1		Sofia	11 Feb
Dennis	Lewis	USA 59	2.31i	1	TAC	New York	24 Feb
Doug	Nordquist	USA 58	2.31	2	FOT	Los Angeles	24 Jun
Gennadiy	Avdeyenko	SU 63	2.31	1		Moskva	19 Jul
Dariusz	Zielke	POL 60	2.31	1		Warszawa	12 Aug
Jacek	Wszola	POL 56	2.31	2	VD	Bruxelles	24 Aug
Andreas	Sam	GDR 60	2.31	1		Praha	28 Aug
Brent	Harken	USA 61	2.31	2	GGala	Roma	31 Aug
Roland	Dalhauser	SWZ 58	2.30i	1	NC	Magglingen	19 Feb
Takao	Sakamoto	JAP 58	2.30	1		Tokyo	6 May
Vadim	Oganyan	SU 63	2.30	2		Tashkent	13 May
Gerd	Nagel	FRG 57	2.30	5		Eberstadt	10 Jun
J.Francisco	Centelles	CUB 61	2.30	1	AAA	London	24 Jun
Jerome	Carter	USA 63	2.30	1		Oslo	21 Jul
Gerd	Wessig	GDR 59	2.30	1		Nanjing	17 Sep
Del	Davis	USA 60	2.29	1		Los Angeles (Ww)	20 May
Milton	Ottey	CAN 59	2.29	6	OG	Los Angeles	11 Aug
Liu	Yunpeng	CHN 62	2.29	7	OG	Los Angeles	11 Aug
Jake	Jacoby	USA 61	2.285	1		Los Angeles	24 Mar
Gennadiy	Belkov	SU 56	2.28i	2		Vilnius	15 Jan
Oleg	Palashevskiy	SU 62	2.28i	2		Moskva	11 Feb
Sasa	Apostolovski	YUG 63	2.28i	1		Ljubljana	18 Feb
Alain	Metellus	CAN 65	2.28i	1	NC	Toronto	26 Feb
John	Atkinson	AUS 63	2.28	1	NC	Melbourne	31 Mar
Thomas	Eriksson	SWE 63	2.28	1		Ruston	27 Apr
Jorge	Alfaro	CUB 62	2.28	2		Habana	11 May
Tyke	Peacock	USA 61	2.28	1		San Jose	26 May
Anatoliy	Korobenko	SU 57	2.28	3	Znam	Sochi	10 Jun
Milton	Goode	USA 60	2.28	3	FOT	Los Angeles	24 Jun
Leo	Williams	USA 60	2.28	4	FOT	Los Angeles	24 Jun

1984 Lists – Men

Joe	Radan	USA 57	2.28	5	FOT	Los Angeles	24 Jun
Erkki	Niemi	FIN 62	2.28	1	NC	Kajaani	7 Jul
Viktor	Malchugin	SU 62	2.28	3		Moskva	19 Jul
Nick	Saunders	BER 63	2.28	7	VD	Bruxelles	24 Aug
Bill	Jasinski	USA 64	2.27i	1		Fayetteville	28 Jan
Josef	Hrabal	CS 58	2.27i	1		Budapest	8 Feb
Krzysztof	Krawczyk	POL 62	2.27i	2		Praha	21 Feb
Dothel	Edwards	USA 66	2.27	1e2		Athens	24 Mar
James	Lott	USA 65	2.27	1		Baton Rouge	14 Apr
Brian	Tietjens	USA 62	2.27	1		Ames	5 May
Matthias	Grebenstein	GDR 64	2.27	1		Potsdam	25 May
John	Morris	USA 64	2.27	3	TAC	San Jose	9 Jun
Cai	Shu	CHN 62	2.27	7		Eberstadt	10 Jun
Novica	Canovic	YUG 61	2.27	1	vGRE	Zagreb	21 Jun
Lee	Balkin	USA 61	2.27	3		Pasadena	2 Aug
Sergey	Ilnitskiy	SU 62	2.26i	1		Kharkov	18 Feb
Igor	Samylov	SU 62	2.26i	1		Klaipeda	28 Jan
Yuriy	Sergiyenko	SU 65	2.26i	2		Kiev	3 Feb
Tom	McCants	USA 62	2.26i	1		Gainesville	11 Feb
Jim	Pringle	USA 58	2.26i	2		Gainesville	11 Feb
Dariusz	Biczysko	POL 62	2.26	1		Zielona Gora	20 May
Marc	Borra	BEL 57	2.26	1		Bruxelles	12 Jun
Mikko	Levola	FIN 59	2.26	1		Salo	17 Jun
Oleg	Azizmuradov	SU 62	2.26	4	Izv	Kiev	24 Jun
Franck	Verzy	FRA 61	2.26	1	NC	Villeneuve D'Ascq	30 Jun
Hrvoje	Fizuleto	YUG 63	2.26	2		Woluwe	1 Jul
Istvan	Gibicsar	HUN 57	2.26	1		Debrecen	4 Jul
Geoff	Parsons	UK 64	2.26	2		London	13 Jul
Greg	Gonsalves	USA 63	2.26i	1		New Haven	8 Dec
Joe	Patrone	USA 62	2.26i	1		Princeton	16 Dec
Andrey	Morozov	SU 60	2.25i	2		Leningrad	8 Jan
Yuriy	Gotovskiy	SU 61	2.25i	5		Leningrad	22 Jan
Gianni	Davito	ITA 57	2.25i	1		Genova	25 Jan
Scott	Budnik	USA 62	2.25i	2e2		Dallas	4 Feb
Franklin	Jacobs	USA 57	2.25i	1		E.Rutherford	11 Feb
Dave	Puvogel	USA 62	2.25i	1		Colorado Springs	25 Feb
Takashi	Katamine	JAP 58	2.25	1		Shizuoka	22 Apr
Ben	Lucero	USA 62	2.25	2		Ames	5 May
Marshall	Broadway	USA 62	2.25	2		Houston	6 May
Rick	Noji	USA 67	2.25	1		Seattle	12 May
Mel	Baker	USA 60	2.25	1		Scottsdale	26 May
Anthony	Caire	USA 63	2.25	1		Compton	28 May
Rick	Watkins	USA 60	2.25	1		Abilene	2 Jun
Andre	Schneider-Laub	FRG 58	2.25	1		Dortmund	3 Jun
Paolo	Borghi	ITA 61	2.25	1		Piacenza	16 Jun
Brad	Speer	USA 65	2.25	1		Chicago	16 Jun
James	Barrineau	USA 55	2.25	Q	FOT	Los Angeles	23 Jun
Bob	Hopson	USA 61	2.25	Q	FOT	Los Angeles	23 Jun
Yuriy	Shevchenko	SU 60	2.25	4		Moskva	19 Jul
Sergey	Malchenko	SU 63	2.25	5		Moskva	19 Jul
Eugen	Popescu	RUM 62	2.25	1		Saloniki	12 Sep
Paul	Frommeyer	FRG 57	2.24i	3		Simmerath	13 Jan
Paul	Piwinski	USA 61	2.24i	2		Johnson City	21 Jan
Mike	Pascuzzo	USA 61	2.24i	1		Allston	29 Jan
James	Cunningham	USA 62	2.24i	1		Cheney	11 Feb
Chuck	Perry	USA 62	2.24i	2		Ft.Worth	17 Feb
Edwin	Ludick	RSA 64	2.24	1		Pretoria	18 Feb
Ron	Jones	USA 62	2.24i	1		Bloomington	18 Feb
Vladimir	Tsyplyakov	SU 56	2.24i	3		Moskva	2 Mar
Miroslaw	Wlodarczyk	POL 59	2.24i	5=	EC	Goteborg	3 Mar
Dale	Davis	USA 60	2.24	2		Tallahassee	17 Mar
Charles	Willbanks	USA 63	2.24	1		Athens	24 Mar

266

1984 Lists – Men

James	Frazier	USA 59	2.24	1		Tempe	7 Apr
Yevgeniy	Nikitin	SU 58	2.24	1		Yevpatoria	14 Apr
Darren	Burton	USA 63	2.24	2		Baton Rouge	14 Apr
Brian	Whitehead	USA 62	2.24	1		Knoxville	14 Apr
Jens-Uwe	Austel	GDR 61	2.24	2		Karl-Marx-Stadt	20 May
Jim	Moran	USA 62	2.24	1		Cape Girardeau	25 May
Aldis	Vanags	SU 60	2.24	1		Tartu	27 May
Kenny	Smith	USA 62	2.24	5=	NCAA	Eugene	1 Jun
Dimitrios	Kattis	GRE 56	2.24	1		Nicosia	15 Sep
Kalev	Martsepp	SU 59	2.24	1		Tbilisi	28 Sep

Vyacheslav	Prosvirin	SU 56	2.23i	21 Jan	Krzysztof	Przybyla	POL 62	2.22	8 Sep
Valeriy	Glinchak	SU 62	2.23i	3 Feb	Maurice	Crumby	USA 65	2.21	7 Jan
Evgeni	Peev	BUL 65	2.23i	18 Feb	Mike	Ripberger	USA 61	2.21i	14 Jan
Georgi	Gadzhev	BUL 60	2.23i	18 Feb	Mikhail	Latishev	SU 62	22 Jan
Atsushi	Inaoka	JAP 62	2.23	6 May	Michal	Pogany	CS 61	2.21i	28 Jan
Jindrich	Vondra	CS 57	2.23	14 Jun	Bruce	Beckel	USA	2.21i	28 Jan
Oleg	Dzuzhov	SU 62	2.23	24 Jun	Pyotr	Kostrykin	SU 63	2.21i	29 Jan
Phil	McDonnell	UK 62	2.23	29 Jul	Guy	Moreau	BEL 54	2.21i	29 Jan
Vladimir	Sokolov	SU 63	2.23	12 Aug	Panagiotis	Panagos	GRE 58	2.21i	11 Feb
Bernhard	Bensch	FRG 64	2.23	1 Sep	Heinrich	Rix	RSA 63	2.21	18 Feb
Karoly	Raus	HUN 63	2.22i	3 Feb	Christo	Vrey	RSA 61	2.21	18 Feb
Sergey	Zhelanov	SU 57	2.22i	11 Feb	Dominique	Hernandez	FRA 60	2.21i	19 Feb
Jeff	Loescher	USA 63	2.22i	3 Mar	Rudolf	Povarnitsin	SU 62	2.21	2 Mar
Steven	Wray	BAH 62	2.22	24 Mar	Mikhail	Barnikov	SU 60	2.21i	2 Mar
Mark	Reed	USA 65	2.22	7 Apr	Vadim	Novikov	SU 62	2.21i	3 Mar
Ethan	Glass	USA 62	2.22	7 Apr	Gennadiy	Savchenko	SU 59	2.21i	9 Mar
Ron	Kamaka	USA 63	2.22	7 Apr	Gary	Duncan	USA 61	2.21	24 Mar
Hitoshi	Masuda	JAP 61	2.22	29 Apr	Carsten	Siebert	GDR 62	2.21	19 May
Vic	Smalls	USA 64	2.22	5 May	Roman	Wozny	POL 59	2.21	20 May
Marcello	Croci	ITA 65	2.22	6 May	Uwe	Rudiger	GDR 61	2.21	21 May
Roland	Mitchell	USA 64	2.22	12 May	Jorg	Freimuth	GDR 61	2.21	25 May
Rickie	Thompson	USA 59	2.22	12 May	Des	Morris	JAM 61	2.21	16 May
Peter	Blank	FRG 62	2.22	20 May	Sergey	Zaytsev	SU 65	2.21	27 May
Mike	Winsor	USA 56	2.22	20 May	Maris	Reinsons	SU 64	2.21	3 Jun
Ernie	Patterson	USA 61	2.22	25 May	Stevan	Filipovic	YUG 59	2.21	3 Jun
Gyula	Nemeth	HUN 59	2.22	3 Jun	Pavel	Filipov	SU 64	2.21	24 Jun
Mark	Naylor	UK 57	2.22	6 Jun	Michail	Minoudis	GRE 60	2.21	10 Jul
Jouko	Kilpi	FIN 61	2.22	23 Jun	Grigoriy	Chomiy	SU 59	2.21	14 Jul
Seppo	Haavisto	FIN 60	2.22	7 Jul	Gian Piero	Palomba	ITA 63	2.21	22 Jul
Panagiotis	Kontaxakis	GRE 64	2.22	23 Aug	Klaus	Trapka	FRG 61	2.21	22 Aug
Roland	Egger	SWZ 60	2.22	25 Aug	Bengt-Goran	Ernstrom	SWE 63	2.21	25 Aug
Karel	Svestka	CS 63	2.22	28 Aug	Gennadiy	Golubyev	SU 60	2.21	27 Aug
Karol	Getek	POL 62	2.22	6 Sep	Tarmo	Valgepea	SU 57	2.21	27 Aug

Best outdoor marks for athletes with indoor seasonal bests

Dalhauser	2.30	2		Lausanne	10 Jul	(2.30i)
Paklin	2.30	3		Moskva	5 Aug	(2.36i)
Lewis	2.28	2		Walnut	25 Jul	(2.31i)
Jasinski	2.26	1		Austin	12 May	(2.27i)
Militaru	2.26	1	Balk	Athinai	9 Sep	(2.31i)
Metellus	2.25	1		Provo	19 May	(2.28i)
Ilnitskiy	2.25	1		Simperapol	15 Jul	(2.26i)
Hrabal	2.25	4=	PTS	Bratislava	26 May	(2.27i)
Piwinski	2.24	1		Tallahassee	17 Mar	(2.24i)
Wlodarczyk	2.24	2		Zabrze	20 May	(2.24i)
Belkov	2.24	5=		Riga	3 Jun	(2.28i)
Frommeyer	2.24	10=		Eberstadt	10 Jun	(2.24i)
Sergiyenko	2.24	1	NC–j	Riga	14 Jul	(2.26i)
Palashevskiy	2.24	3	NC	Donyetsk	9 Sep	(2.28i)
Apostolovski	2.24	1		Ravenna	23 Sep	(2.28i)

1984 Lists – Men

Borghi	2.23	19 May	(2.23i)	Morozov	2.21	2 Jun	(2.25i)
Patrone	2.23	20 May	(2.26i)	Moreau	2.21	2 Jun	(2.25i)
Davito	2.23	26 May	(2.25i)	Krawczyk	2.21	23 Jun	(2.27i)
Gotovskiy	2.23	9 Jul	(2.25i)	McCants	2.21	23 Jun	(2.26i)
Puvogel	2.22	7 Apr	(2.25i)	Ilnitskiy	2.21	29 Jul	(2.25i)
Gadzhev	2.22	19 May	(2.23i)	Kostrykin	2.21	29 Jul	(2.21i)
Cunningham	2.21	31 May	(2.24i)				

Extra Trial

Zhu	2.33	1		Pre	Eugene	21 Jul
Dalhauser	2.30	–			Boswil	30 Jun

Ancillary jumps over 2.32

Zhu	2.36	10 Jun		Paklin	2.33	1 Feb
Thranhardt	2.34i	24 Feb		Zhu	2.33	10 Jun
Sereda	2.34	2 Sep		Mogenburg	2.33	11 Aug

	1	10	20	30	50	100	Over 2.26	Over 2.22
1980	2.36	2.29	2.27	2.25	2.24	2.20	28	66
1981	2.33	2.30	2.27	2.26	2.24	2.21	32	88
1982	2.34	2.31	2.28	2.27	2.25	2.22	44	104
1983	2.38	2.32	2.30	2.285	2.27	2.24	68	134
1984	2.39	2.33	2.31	2.30	2.27	2.24	75	151

POLE VAULT

Sergey	Bubka	SU 63	5.94	1	GGala	Roma	31 Aug
Thierry	Vigneron	FRA 60	5.91	2	GGala	Roma	31 Aug
	Bubka		5.90	1		London	13 Jul
	Bubka		5.88	1		St.Denis	2 Jun
	Vigneron		5.85i	1	EC	Goteborg	4 Mar
	Bubka		5.85	1	PTS	Bratislava	26 May
Konstantin	Volkov	SU 60	5.85	1	Izv	Kiev	22 Jun
	Bubka		5.83i	1		Inglewood	10 Feb
	Bubka		5.82i	1	vITA,SPA	Milano	1 Feb
Mike	Tully	USA 56	5.82	1	Pre	Eugene	21 Jul
Aleksandr	Krupskiy	SU 60	5.82	1	BGP	Budapest	20 Aug
	Bubka		5.81i	1		Vilnius	15 Jan
	Tully		5.81	1	FOT	Los Angeles	21 Jun
Billy	Olson	USA 58	5.80i	2		Inglewood	10 Feb
	Krupskiy		5.80	1	Znam	Sochi	9 Jun
Earl	Bell	USA 55	5.80	1	TAC	San Jose	9 Jun
Pierre	Quinon	FRA 62	5.80	1		Lausanne	10 Jul
Vladimir	Polyakov		5.80	1		Moskva	19 Jul
	Volkov		5.80	1	DRZ	Moskva	17 Aug
	Bubka		5.80	1	NC	Donyetsk	8 Sep
	Tully		5.77	1		Los Angeles (Ww)	20 May
	Quinon		5.75i	2	EC	Goteborg	4 Mar
	Polyakov		5.75	1		Moskva	11 May
Pavel	Bogatyryov	SU 61	5.75	2	Znam	Sochi	9 Jun
	Volkov		5.75	3	Znam	Sochi	9 Jun
Wladyslaw	Kozakiewicz	POL 53	5.75	1		Edinburgh	17 Jul
	Vigneron		5.75	1		Sacramento	21 Jul
	Quinon		5.75	1	OG	Los Angeles	8 Aug

1984 Lists – Men

Larry	Vigneron Jessee	USA 52	5.75 5.73	1 1	VD	Bruxelles Vanves	24 Aug 27 Apr
	Vigneron		5.73i	1	vUK	Vittel	4 Feb

(31/12)

Atanas	Tarev	BUL 58	5.72	1	NC	Sofia	2 Jun
Doug	Lytle	USA 62	5.71	2	FOT	Los Angeles	21 Jun
Serge	Ferreira	FRA 59	5.71	1		Creteil	23 Jun
Vasiliy	Bubka	SU 60	5.70i	1		Moskva	1 Mar
Aleksandr	Obizhayev	SU 59	5.70	1		Riga	3 Jun
Aleksandr	Chernyayev	SU 60	5.70	1		Moskva	7 Jul
Sergey	Smolyakov	SU 62	5.70	3		Moskva	19 Jul
Joe	Dial	USA 62	5.66	1		Norman	27 Apr
Jeff	Buckingham	USA 60	5.65i	1		Johnson City	21 Jan
Peter	Volmer	FRG 58	5.65i	1		Nordlingen	26 Feb
Brad	Pursley	USA 60	5.65	3	Pre	Eugene	21 Jul
Ivo	Yanchev	BUL 60	5.65	1		Rovereto	29 Aug
Rodion	Gataullin	SU 65	5.65	2	NC	Donyetsk	8 Sep
Dave	Kenworthy	USA 60	5.61	4=	FOT	Los Angeles	21 Jun
Nikolay	Selivanov	SU 58	5.60i	3		Leningrad	22 Jan
Dan	Ripley	USA 53	5.60i	4		New York	27 Jan
Philippe	Houvion	FRA 57	5.60i	2	vUK	Vittel	4 Feb
Felix	Bohni	SWZ 58	5.60i	5		Inglewood	10 Feb
Aleksandr	Parnov	SU 59	5.60i	1		Donyetsk	4 Mar
Greg	Woepse	USA 57	5.60	1		Long Beach	4 Mar
Steve	Stubblefield	USA 61	5.60i	1	KansR	Lawrence	21 Apr
Viktor	Spasov	SU 59	5.60	1		Kiev	3 May
Anton	Paskalev	BUL 58	5.60	3	NC	Sofia	2 Jun
Vladimir	Shulgin	SU 61	5.60	4	Znam	Sochi	9 Jun
Marian	Kolasa	POL 59	5.60	1		Sopot	6 Jul
Kasimir	Zalar	SWE 57	5.60	1		Gateshead	6 Jul
Philippe	Collet	FRA 63	5.60	1	NC–j	Fontainebleau	15 Jul
Arkadiy	Shkvira	SU 60	5.60	3=	NC	Donyetsk	8 Sep
Nat	Durham	USA 54	5.60i	1		Saskatoon	29 Dec
Tom	Hintnaus	BRA 58	5.56	1		Redondo Beach	15 Jun
Gunther	Lohre	FRG 53	5.55i	1=		Sindelfingen	1 Feb
Leonid	Ivanushkin	SU 61	5.55i	6	NC	Moskva	19 Feb
Tadeusz	Slusarski	POL 50	5.55i	1	NC	Zabrze	19 Feb
Gerhard	Schmidt	FRG 61	5.55i	2		Nordlingen	26 Feb
David	Hodge	USA 62	5.55	1		Austin	12 May
Andreas	Kramss	GDR 62	5.55	1		Dresden	19 May
Frantisek	Jansa	CS 62	5.55	1	PTS	Bratislava	25 May
Alberto	Ruiz	SPA 61	5.55	1	NC	Barcelona	30 Jun
Zdzislaw	Panasiuk	POL 58	5.55	1		Warszawa	25 Jul
Dale	Jenkins	USA 63	5.54	1		Cape Girardeau	26 May
Patrick	Abada	FRA 54	5.53i	3		Albuquerque	3 Feb
Gennadiy	Sukharev	SU 65	5.53i	2	NC–j	Leningrad	12 Feb
Tomomi	Takahashi	JAP 56	5.53	1		Tokyo	6 May
Grey	Rappe	USA 59	5.51i	1		Baton Rouge	4 Feb
Paul	Babits	USA 59	5.51	1		Chicago	3 Jun
Kimmo	Kuusela	FIN 62	5.51	1		Tuusula	26 Aug
Dominique	Heber-Suffrin	FRA 55	5.50i	2		Paris	15 Jan
Mariusz	Klimczyk	POL 56	5.50i	1	vITA	Torino	11 Feb
Philippe	Sivillon	FRA 58	5.50i	7	NC	Paris	18 Feb
Mikhail	Voronin	SU 60	5.50i	10	NC	Moskva	19 Feb
Bob	Phillips	USA 59	5.50i	3		Cleveland	19 Feb
Tim	Bright	USA 60	5.50i	4		Cleveland	19 Feb
Serge	Leveur	FRA 57	5.50i	1		Paris	25 Feb
Patrick	Desruelles	BEL 57	5.50i	1=		Cosford	7 Mar
Dave	Volz	USA 62	5.50	1		Knoxville	14 Apr
David	Swezey	USA 59	5.50	2		Norman	27 Apr
Alain	Donias	FRA 60	5.50	1		Fontenay	13 May

269

1984 Lists – Men

Jerry	Mulligan	USA 58	5.50	4			Los Angeles (Ww)	20 May
Stanimir	Penchev	BUL 59	5.50	4	NC		Sofia	2 Jun
Kory	Tarpenning	USA 62	5.50	2	NCAA		Eugene	2 Jun
Asko	Peltoniemi	FIN 63	5.50	1			Valkeakoski	5 Jun
Yevgeniy	Laptyev	SU 62	5.50	1			Yaroslavl	15 Jun
Mark	Strawderman	USA 60	5.50	3			Redondo Beach	15 Jun
Ferenc	Salbert	HUN 60	5.50	1			Zagreb	20 Jun
Kimmo	Pallonen	FIN 59	5.50	1			Saarijarvi	24 Jun
Timo	Kuusisto	FIN 59	5.50	1			Ylivieska	1 Jul
Veijo	Vannesluoma	FIN 58	5.50	2	WG		Helsinki	4 Jul
Ryszard	Kolasa	POL 64	5.50	2			Sopot	6 Jul
Alfonso	Cano	SPA 60	5.50	2			Gateshead	6 Jul
Mauro	Barella	ITA 56	5.50	1	NC		Roma	11 Jul
Viktor	Sobolev	SU 60	5.50	1			Gorkiy	11 Aug
Aleksandr	Arendar	SU 58	5.50	1			Kiev	Aug
John	Sayre	USA 61	5.49i	1			W.Lafayette	14 Jan
Todd	Cooper	USA 63	5.49	1			Brownwood	4 Aug
Yang	Weimin	CHN 58	5.46i	1			Beijing	25 Feb
Ji	Zebiao	CHN 64	5.46	1			Guangzhou	11 Apr
Ross	McAlexander	USA 60	5.45	2			Los Gatos	5 May
Grigoriy	Yegorov	SU 67	5.45	1			Simferopol	26 May
Hermann	Fehringer	AUT 62	5.45	1			Amstetten	21 Jun
Ilkka	Pekkala	FIN 55	5.45	2	NC		Kajaani	8 Jul
Jurgen	Winkler	FRG 59	5.43i	3			Zweibrucken	15 Feb
Eric	Forney	USA 62	5.43	2			Abilene	24 Mar
Chuck	Suey	USA 60	5.42	1			Pomona	19 May
Arto	Peltoniemi	FIN 66	5.42	1			Raahe	8 Aug
Keith	Stock	UK 57	5.42i	1			Cosford	8 Dec
Glen	Loontjer	USA 61	5.41i	2	KansR		Lawrence	21 Apr
Steve	Thaxton	USA 64	5.41	1			Abilene	10 May
Randy	Hall	USA 59	5.41	1			Dallas	22 May
Bubba	Kavanaugh	USA 60	5.41	2			San Jose	26 May
Doug	Fraley	USA 65	5.41	1			Fresno	13 Jul
Brian	Hooper	UK 53	5.41	1	vYUG		Karlovac	16 Sep
Igor	Nazarov	SU 62	5.40i	1			Leningrad	14 Jan
Vasiliy	Trofimenko	SU 62	5.40i				Klaipeda	28 Jan
Aleksey	Surguchev	SU 58	5.40i	2			Chelyabinsk	4 Feb
Andrey	Pogoreliy	SU 59	5.40i	3			Chelyabinsk	4 Feb
Zbigniew	Radzikowski	POL 60	5.40i	4	NC		Zabrze	19 Feb
Greg	Duplantis	USA 62	5.40	4	TexR		Austin	7 Apr
Baker	Vinci	USA 62	5.40	1			Baton Rouge	13 May
Olaf	Kasten	GDR 62	5.40	2			Dresden	19 May
Anthony	Curran	USA 59	5.40	6			Los Angeles (Ww)	20 May
Laszlo	Fulop	FRA/HUN 58	5.40	2			Fontainebleau	23 May
Ed	Lipscomb	USA 51	5.40	1			Corvallis	24 May
Valeriy	Rybin	SU 54	5.40	1			Leningrad	2 Jun
Mark	Klee	USA 62	5.40	5	NCAA		Eugene	2 Jun
Gary	Hunter	USA 56	5.40	2			Chicago	3 Jun
Valentin	Videv	BUL 63	5.40	3			Sofia	16 Jun
Jeff	Gutteridge	UK 56	5.40	1	AAA		London	24 Jun
Gerald	Heinrich	FRG 56	5.40	3			Bern	28 Jun
Detlef	de Raad	FRG 60	5.40	4			Bern	28 Jun
Reijo	Siitonen	FIN 61	5.40	3			Ylivieska	1 Jul
Daniel	Aebischer	SWZ 57	5.40	7			Lausanne	10 Jul
Antti	Kalliomaki	FIN 47	5.40	1			Varkaus	12 Jul
Valeriy	Ishutin	SU 65	5.40	1			Riga	13 Jul
Valeriy	Osipenko	SU 57	5.40	2			Leningrad	14 Jul
Viktor	Komarov	SU 66	5.40	1			Kharkov	21 Jul
Oleg	Isakin	SU 60	5.40	1			Kislovodsk	21 Sep
Liang	Xuereng	CHN 65	5.40	1			Shanghai	8 Oct

1984 Lists – Men

Valeriy	Bukreyev	SU 64	5.39	23 Jun
Doug	Wicks	USA	5.36	12 May
Dave	Sanderson	USA 57	5.35	27 Jul
Jim	Metzger	USA 62	5.34	27 Apr
Bobby	Williams	USA 61	5.33	22 Mar
Sergey	Belyayev	SU 62	5.32i	14 Jan
Sigurdur	Sigurdsson	ICE 57	5.31	31 May
Chris	Leeuwenburgh	HOL 62	5.31	2 Sep
Detlef	Pilz	GDR 62	5.30i	11 Jan
Rumen	Stoyanov	BUL 59	5.30i	29 Jan
Viktor	Drechsel	ITA 60	5.30i	1 Feb
Boleslav	Patera	CS 63	5.30i	4 Feb
Aleksandr	Grigoryev	SU 64	5.30i	5 Feb
Erno	Mako	HUN 55	5.30i	8 Feb
Aleksandr	Isachenko	SU 65	5.30i	12 Feb
Bernhard	Zintl	FRG 65	5.30i	26 Feb
Steve	Tully	USA 60	5.30	31 Mar
Aleksandr	Dolgov	SU 58	5.30	27 Apr
Aleksandr	Morozov	SU 63	5.30	27 Apr
Thibaut	Cattiau	FRA 57	5.30	29 Apr
Scott	Davis	USA 61	5.30	24 May
Sergey	Ponomarenko	SU 63	5.30	3 Jun
Chen	Guoming	CHN 59	5.30	9 Jun
Yevgeniy	Bondarenko	SU 66	5.30	9 Jun
Zdenek	Lubensky	CS 62	5.30	9 Jun
Corrado	Alagona	ITA 60	5.30	13 Jun
Manfred	Reichert	FRG 63	5.30	16 Jun
Oleg	Kritaryov	SU 64	5.30	30 Jun
Gilles	LeBris	FRA 60	5.30	5 Jul
Marco	Andreini	ITA 61	5.30	11 Jul
Gianni	Stecchi	ITA 58	5.30	11 Jul
Alain	Auclair	FRA 62	5.30	14 Jul
Dmitriy	Shmarlin	SU 64	5.30	22 Jul
Sergey	Korablyev	SU 61	5.30	28 Jul
Kjell	Isaksson	SWE 48	5.30	3 Aug
Helmar	Schmidt	FRG 63	5.30	18 Aug
Miroslaw	Chmara	POL 64	5.30	25 Aug
Viktor	Loshchev	SU 65	5.30	8 Sep
Viktor	Ryzhenkov	SU 66	5.30	19 Sep
Igor	Trandenkov	SU 66	5.30	19 Sep
Scott	Shaffer	USA 64	5.28i	28 Feb
Jay	Novacek	USA 63	5.28i	3 Mar
Ralph	Preimann	USA 58	5.28	17 Mar
John	Fewell	USA 62	5.28	7 Apr
Greg	Stull	USA 62	5.28	7 Apr
Jim	Johnston	USA 62	5.28	28 Apr
Bill	Butler	USA	5.26i	12 Feb
Edgardo	Rivero	PR 53	5.25	28 Jun
Dietmar	Wesp	FRG 65	5.25	8 Jul
Jari	Holttinen	FIN 65	5.25	14 Jul

Best outdoor marks for athletes with seasonal bests indoors

Bohni (a)	5.60	1	CalR	Modesto	12 May	(5.60i)
Parnov	5.60	1		Tashkent	13 May	(5.60i)
Ripley	5.60	2		Los Angeles(Ww)	20 May	(5.60i)
Durham	5.55	1		Eugene	6 Jul	(5.60i)
Olson	5.54	1		Austin	20 May	(5.80i)
Lohre	5.53	1		Lubeck	13 Jul	(5.55i)
Schmidt	5.52	1		Recklinghausen	11 Jun	(5.55i)
Abada	5.50	1=		Colombes	24 Apr	(5.53i)
Leveur	5.50	1		Querqueville	29 Apr	(5.50i)
Voronin	5.50	1		Volgograd	13 May	(5.50i)
Volmer	5.50	1		Ludenscheid	26 May	(5.65i)
Slusarski	5.50	3	NC	Lublin	24 Jun	(5.55i)
V.Bubka	5.50	4		Moskva	7 Jul	(5.70i)
Selivanov	5.50	5		Moskva	7 Jul	(5.60i)
Stubblefield	5.50	4=	Pre	Eugene	21 Jul	(5.60i)
Sivillon	5.50	5		Walnut	25 Jul	(5.50i)
Buckingham	5.42	4=		Berkeley	14 Jul	(5.65i)
Rappe	5.41	2	Drake	Des Moines	28 Apr	(5.51i)
Loontjer	5.40	2		Baton Rouge	14 Apr	(5.41i)
Surguchev	5.40	1		Sochi	27 Apr	(5.40i)
Heber-Suffrin	5.40	4		Querqueville	29 Apr	(5.50i)
Pogoreliy	5.40	3		Sochi	19 May	(5.40i)
Houvion	5.40	7		Creteil	23 Jun	(5.60i)
Trofimenko	5.40	8		Moskva	7 Jul	(5.40i)
Stock	5.40	4		Edinburgh	17 Jul	(5.42i)
Winkler	5.40	3		Munchen	20 Jul	(5.43i)
Bright	5.40	D	OG	Los Angeles	9 Aug	(5.50i)
Klimczyk	5.40	1		Zabrze	13 Sep	(5.50i)
Desruelles	5.35	16 Jun	(5.50i)				
Stoyanov	5.30	12 May	(5.30i)				
Radzikowski	5.30	29 May	(5.40i)				
Drechsel	5.30	10 Jun	(5.30i)				
Nazarov	5.30	7 Jul	(5.40i)				
Weimin	5.30	6 Aug	(5.46i)				
Isachenko	5.30	8 Aug	(5.30i)				
Sukharev	5.30	8 Sep	(5.53i)				

(a) Bohni 5.60 18'4 1/2" at Modesto, 5.60 18'4 3/4 (1) San Jose 26 May

1984 Lists – Men

Exhibition

Ivo	Vigneron Yanchev	BUL 60	5.75 5.70	1 2=	Bologna Bologna	6 Sep 6 Sep	

Ancillary marks at 5.72 or better

Bubka	5.84	31 Aug	Bubka	5.80	2 Jun
Vigneron	5.84	31 Aug	Bubka	5.75i	10 Feb
Vigneron	5.80i	4 Mar	Bubka	5.75	26 May

	1	10	20	30	50	100	Over 5.50	Over 5.40
1980	5.78	5.65	5.57	5.50	5.41	5.28	39	66
1981	5.81	5.65	5.55	5.50	5.48	5.30	49	73
1982	5.75	5.70	5.60	5.55	5.51	5.33	63	85
1983	5.83	5.71	5.65	5.60	5.50	5.36	65	97
1984	5.94	5.75	5.66	5.60	5.55	5.41	84	129

LONG JUMP

Carl	Lewis	USA 61	8.79i		1		New York	27 Jan
	Lewis		8.71	−0.4	1	Pepsi	Los Angeles (Ww)	13 May
	Lewis		8.71	0.1	1	FOT	Los Angeles	19 Jun
	Lewis		8.65	0.2	1	VD	Bruxelles	24 Aug
Larry	Myricks	USA 56	8.59	1.3	1		Rhede	5 Sep
	Lewis		8.55i		1		East Rutherford	11 Feb
	Lewis		8.54	−1.6	1	OG	Los Angeles	6 Aug
	Lewis		8.50i		1	TAC	New York	24 Feb
Lutz	Dombrowski	GDR 59	8.50	2.0	1		Dresden	27 Jul
	Myricks		8.48	0.1	1		Koln	26 Aug
	Myricks		8.45	0.2	2	Pepsi	Los Angeles (Ww)	13 May
	Myricks		8.45	−0.3	2	VD	Bruxelles	24 Aug
	Myricks		8.44i		2	TAC	New York	24 Feb
	Myricks		8.42	0.0	1	WK	Zurich	22 Aug
	Myricks		8.42	0.2	1		Koblenz	29 Aug
	Lewis		8.39	1.3	Q	FOT	Los Angeles	18 Jun
	Myricks		8.38i		2		New York	27 Jan
Konstantin	Semykin	SU 60	8.38	0.4	1	DRZ	Moskva	17 Aug
Jaime	Jefferson	CUB 62	8.37	0.4	2	DRZ	Moskva	17 Aug
	Dombrowski		8.36	0.2	1		Berlin	20 Jul
	Myricks		8.32		−	MSR	Walnut	29 Apr
Jason	Grimes	USA 59	8.32		2	CalR	Modesto	12 May
	Myricks		8.32	0.2	1	ISTAF	Berlin	17 Aug
Sergey	Layevskiy	SU 59	8.32	0.1	1	NC	Donyetsk	8 Sep
Atanas	Atanasov	BUL 56	8.31	0.7	1		Sofia	4 Jul
	Myricks		8.31		1		Rieti	2 Sep
	Jefferson		8.29	0.0	2	WK	Zurich	22 Aug
	Dombrowski		8.28	1.6	1	NC	Erfurt	3 Jun
	Semykin		8.28		2		Moskva	6 Jul
	Myricks		8.28		1		Hannover	19 Aug
Vadim	Kobylyanskiy	SU 61	8.28	0.1	2	NC	Donyetsk	8 Sep

(31/9)

Mike	McRae	USA 55	8.27	2.0	1	TAC	San Jose	9 Jun
Gary	Honey	AUS 59	8.27	1.2	1	BGP	Budapest	20 Aug
Laszlo	Szalma	HUN 57	8.27	−0.7	2		Koln	26 Aug
Giovanni	Evangelisti	ITA 61	8.24	−0.7	3	OG	Los Angeles	6 Aug
Yuriy	Samarin	SU 60	8.23	0.0	3	NC	Donyetsk	8 Sep
Mike	Conley	USA 62	8.22	0.7	1		Austin	11 May

1984 Lists – Men

Name	Surname	Nat/Yr	Mark	Wind	Pos	Meet	Venue	Date
Uwe	Lange	GDR 54	8.22	1.6	1		Dresden	19 May
Gyula	Paloczi	HUN 62	8.22	1.7	1	NC	Budapest	27 Jul
Yuriy	Kharitonov	SU 59	8.22		1		Gorkiy	11 Aug
Ralph	Spry	USA 60	8.16		1		Riccione	26 Aug
Ken	Frazier	USA 63	8.14		1		Tempe	21 Apr
Ubaldo	Duany	CUB 60	8.14	1.5	2		Furth	9 Jun
Vance	Johnson	USA 63	8.13	0.2	3	Pepsi	Los Angeles (Ww)	13 May
Andre	Reichelt	GDR 62	8.13	2.0	2		Dresden	27 Jul
Robert	Emmiyan	SU 65	8.13	1.1	1		Baku	14 Sep
Viktor	Belskiy	SU 55	8.12		1		Riga	6 Jul
Frank-Peter	Kulske	GDR 60	8.10i		1		Berlin	25 Jan
Aleksandr	Yakovlev	SU 57	8.10i		1		Kiev	4 Feb
Nenad	Stekic	YUG 51	8.10		1	vGRE	Zagreb	20 Jun
Oganes	Stepanyan	SU 56	8.10	1.6	3	Izv	Kiev	24 Jun
Jan	Leitner	CS 53	8.10	1.6	2	vITA	Cagliari	8 Sep
Mathias	Koch	GDR 62	8.09i		2		Berlin	25 Jan
Jan	Cado	CS 63	8.09		1		Barcelona	8 Jul
Moses	Kiyai	KEN 60	8.08		1		Lincoln	11 May
Keith	Taylor	USA 56	8.08		1		Walnut	3 Jun
Oleg	Mamayev	SU 58	8.08		1		Leningrad	15 Jul
Ivan	Tuparov	BUL 59	8.07	0.8	1	NC	Sofia	3 Jun
Oleg	Semiraz	SU 61	8.07	0.0	5	NC	Donyetsk	8 Sep
Wlodzimierz	Wlodarczyk	POL 57	8.06	1.8	1	Malin	Grudziadz	29 May
Ron	Beer	GDR 65	8.06	0.2	3		Berlin	9 Jun
Charles	Smith	USA 66	8.06		1		Las Vegas	9 Jun
Andrey	Balashov	SU 62	8.06		2		Riga	6 Jul
Stanislaw	Jaskulka	POL 58	8.06	1.9	1		Sopot	29 Jul
Rene	Gloor	SWZ 56	8.06	0.3	4		Rieti	2 Sep
Uwe	Vogel	GDR 58	8.05	1.1	2		Dresden	19 May
Vladimir	Tsepelyov	SU 56	8.05	1.9	3	Znam	Sochi	10 Jun
Troy	Amboree	USA 62	8.04		1		Lake Charles	31 Mar
Antonio	Corgos	SPA 60	8.02i		2	vSU,ITA	Milano	1 Feb
Lester	Benjamin	ANT 63	8.02		1		Baton Rouge	12 May
George	Gaffney	USA 60	8.02		1		Fresno	12 May
Vesco	Bradley	USA 53	8.02		–	CalR	Modesto	12 May
Junichi	Usui	JAP 57	8.02	1.8	Q	OG	Los Angeles	5 Aug
Torsten	Voss	GDR 63	8.02		D	DRZ	Moskva	17 Aug
Zdenek	Hanacek	CS 62	8.02	−0.9	1		Praha	28 Aug
John	Parker	USA 64	8.01i		1		Princeton	3 Mar
Joachim	Busse	FRG 54	8.01	1.4	3		Furth	9 Jun
Daley	Thompson	UK 58	8.01	0.4	D	OG	Los Angeles	8 Aug
Francois	Fouche	RSA 63 A	8.00		1		Pretoria	14 Mar
Winfried	Klepsch	FRG 56	8.00	1.3	3		Stuttgart	17 Jun
Yuriy	Morkovkin	SU 57	7.99i		2	NC	Moskva	19 Feb
Jurgen	Worner	FRG 59	7.99	1.7	1		Stuttgart	21 Jul
Grigoriy	Petrosyan	SU 58	7.99	0.0	2		Dnepropetrovsk	5 Aug
Liu	Yuhuang	CHN 59	7.99	0.6	5	OG	Los Angeles	6 Aug
Pang	Yan	CHN 63	7.99	0.0	1		Nanjing	18 Sep
James	Washington	USA 62	7.98		2		Austin	11 May
Mike	Powell	USA 63	7.98	−1.0	6	FOT	Los Angeles	19 Jun
Igor	Sobolevskiy	SU 62	7.98		D	DRZ	Moskva	17 Aug
Ed	Tave	USA 63	7.97		2		Los Angeles	31 Mar
Brian	Cooper	USA 65	7.97		1		Houston	6 May
Norbert	Brige	FRA 64	7.97	2.0	1		Creteil	23 Jun
Joey	Wells	BAH 65	7.97	−0.8	6	OG	Los Angeles	6 Aug
Aleksandr	Katkov	SU 59	7.97	−0.3	Q	NC	Donyetsk	7 Sep
Stephen	Walsh	NZ 60	7.96		1		Hamilton	21 Jan
Reggie	Kelly	USA 62	7.95i		2		Rosemont	29 Jan
Elton	Slater	USA 64	7.95		2		Houston	6 May
Keith	Talley	USA 64	7.95	1.5	–		San Angelo	18 May
Khristo	Markov	BUL 65	7.95	0.3	2		Sofia	3 Jun
Randy	Williams	USA 53 A	7.95		1		Colorado Springs	4 Jun

273

1984 Lists – Men

Yordan	Yanev	BUL 54	7.95		1		Pleven	8 Jul
Yuriy	Churilin	SU 59	7.94i		1		Moskva	5 Feb
Ronald	Desruelles	BEL 55	7.94		1		Louvain	15 May
Joe	Richardson	USA 66	7.94		1		Sacramento	9 Jun
Vladimir	Potapenko	SU 61	7.94		3 (a)		Moskva	6 Jul
Marco	Piochi	ITA 57	7.93i		3	vSU,SPA	Milano	1 Feb
Lyndon	Sands	BAH 64	7.93		3		Houston	6 May
Anatoliy	Kim	SU 58	7.93		3		Riga	6 Jul
Yussuf	Alli	NIG 60	7.93	0.6	1	FBK	Hengelo	6 Jul
Nick	Rahal	USA 63	7.92		2		Baton Rouge	12 May
Bernd	Bieber	FRG 59	7.92		1		Monchengladbach	19 May
Malcolm	Grimes	USA 57 A	7.92		2		Colorado Springs	4 Jun
Johnny	Cleveland	USA 66	7.92		2		Sacramento	9 Jun
Markus	Kessler	FRG 62	7.92	1.9	6		Stuttgart	17 Jun
Vladimir	Puzyrev	SU 62	7.91i		1		Gomel	26 Feb
Danny	Little	USA 60	7.91		1		University Park	26 May
Maris	Bruzikis	SU 62	7.91	0.1	8	NC	Donyetsk	7 Sep
Ron	Waynes	USA 60	7.90i		1		Champaign	11 Feb
Leotha	Stanley	USA 56	7.90		3	FlaR	Gainesville	31 Mar
Mike	Davis	USA 64	7.90		3		Austin	11 May
Kerry	Zimmerman	USA 59	7.90		1		Bloomington	12 May
Jarmo	Karna	FIN 58	7.90	0.6	–		Heinola	3 Jun
Sergey	Rodin	SU 63	7.90	1.8	5	Znam	Sochi	10 Jun
Paul	Emordi	NIG 65	7.90		1	AfrC	Rabat	15 Jul
Derek	Harper	USA 61	7.89i		1		Ann Arbor	2 Mar
Stan	Holmes	USA 57	7.89		2		Tallahassee	17 Mar
Torsten	Kottke	GDR 65	7.88i		3		Berlin	25 Jan
Tim	Leach	USA 64	7.88		1		Pembroke	13 Apr
Russell	Mitchell	USA 60	7.88	1.6	8	TAC	San Jose	9 Jun
Gordon	Laine	USA 58	7.88	–0.6	Q	FOT	Los Angeles	18 Jun
Sergey	Kirilov	SU 62	7.88		2		Leningrad	15 Jul
Igor	Aleksandrov	SU 57	7.88	0.3	1		Dnepropetrovsk	28 Jul
Warren	Wilhoite	USA 61	A7.87i	11 Feb
Deon	Mayfield	USA 62	7.87	21 Apr
Dannie	Jackson	USA 58	7.87	1 Jun
Laurentiu	Budur	RUM 63	7.87	11 Jul
Marco	Delonge	GDR 66	7.87	14 Aug
Wang	Shijie	CHN 63	7.87	22 Sep
Verril	Young	USA 60	7.86	31 Mar
Valeriy	Bakunin	SU 62	7.86	28 Apr
Adolf	Ronge	AUT 57	7.86	20 May
Vasile	Dima	RUM 58	7.86	11 Jul
Kim	Yongil	SKO 62	7.86	5 Aug
Jurgen	Hingsen	FRG 58	7.85	19 May
Grzegorz	Cybulski	POL 51	7.85	14 Jun
Yevgeniy	Shtyflyuk	SU 58	7.85	6 Jul
Zsolt	Szabo	HUN 64	7.85	4 Aug
Volker	Mai	GDR 66	7.85	29 Aug
Greg	Johnson	USA 62	7.84	12 May
Emiel	Mellaard	HOL 66	7.84	23 Jun
Igor	Kharitonov	SU 62	7.83i	19 Feb
Roman	Zrun	CS 60	7.83	5 May
Kerry	Harrison	USA 65	7.83	11 May
Thomas	Selmon	USA 62	7.83	30 May
Uwe	Palm	FRG 63	7.83	9 Jun
Kevin	Wilson	USA 57	7.83	9 Jun
Gheorge	Cojocaru	RUM 60	7.83	10 Jun
Vladimir	Amidzhinov	BUL 63	7.83	14 Jun
Mario	Lega	ITA 57	7.83	4 Jul
Artem	Tsygankov	SU 64	7.82i	8 Jan
Sergey	Lapko	SU 60	7.82i	28 Jan
John	King	UK 63	7.82	19 May
Frank	Wodars	GDR 61	7.82	3 Jun
Richard	Rock	CAN 57	7.82	30 Jun
Joshua	Kio	NIG 57	7.82	15 Jul
Arvidas	Sabonis	SU 54	7.81i	19 Feb
Philippe	Deroche	FRA 54	7.81i	19 Feb
Yevgeniy	Anikin	SU 58	7.81	21 May
Janusz	Banas	POL 54	7.81	29 May
Noboyuki	Itoh	JAP 64	7.81	2 Jun
Aleksandr	Nevskiy	SU 58	7.81	21 Jun
Pentti	Raitanen	FIN 56	7.81	7 Jul
Sergey	Zaozerskiy	SU 63	7.81	7 Sep
Serge	Helan	FRA 64	7.81	12 Sep
Ivan	Malko	SU 57	7.80i	4 Mar
Earl	Bridges	USA 62	7.80	12 May
Yuriy	Slonov	SU 60	7.80	21 May
Chen	Zunrong	CHN 62	7.80	25 May
Ling	Rongliang	CHN 63	7.80	10 Jun
Juris	Tone	SU 61	7.80	6 Jul
Stephane	Caristan	FRA 64	7.79i	29 Jan
Kristjan	Hardarsson	ICE 63	7.79	3 Mar
Gilbert	Smith	USA 60	7.79	6 May
Vakhtang	Minashvili	SU 65	7.79	5 Jul
Ivan	Mafienya	SU 57	7.79	6 Jul
Jorg	Freimuth	GDR 61	7.79	20 Jul
Frank	Nowak	GDR 56	7.79	27 Jul

274

1984 Lists – Men

Name	Surname	Nat	Mark	Date
Laszlo	Szenczi	HUN 59	7.79	27 Jul
Sergey	Sorokin	SU 63	7.79	11 Aug
Vladimir	Sidorov	SU 58	7.79	12 Aug
H-Ulrich	Riecke	GDR 63	7.79	16 Sep
Charles	Powell	USA 64	7.78	11 May
Atanas	Chochev	BUL 57	7.78	20 May
Aleksandr	Areshin	SU 61	7.78	2 Jun
Denis	Pinabel	FRA 58	7.78	3 Jun
Claude	Moriniere	FRA 60	7.78	1 Jul
Valeriy	Bereglazov	SU 58	7.77i	4 Feb
Rob	Boulware	USA 64	7.77	19 May
Bill	Rea	AUT 52	A7.77	24 Mar
Ken	Smith	USA 63	7.77	12 May
Albert	Peacock	USA	7.77	19 May
Frank	Liek	GDR 65	7.77	3 Jun
Vadim	Pugachev	SU 63	7.77	15 Jul
Anton	Zhivitskiy	SU 67	7.77	
Radoslav	Olzetenov	BUL 65	7.77	10 Sep
Aleksandr	Aushev	SU 60	7.76i	Feb

Name	Surname	Nat	Mark	Date
Skeeter	Jackson	USA 61	7.76i	19 Feb
Vince	Bean	USA	7.76i	2 Mar
Kayode	Elegbede	NIG 55	7.76	14 Mar
Nat	Peterkin	USA 65	7.76	17 Apr
Von	Sheppard	USA 65	7.76	12 May
Anthony	Bailous	USA 65	7.76	18 May
Wang	Wenhao	CHN 60	7.76	5 Jul
Vladimir	Sokolov	SU 65	7.76	14 Jul
Wolfgang	Bohringer	FRG 63	7.76	14 Jul
Oleg	Oleshko	SU 60	7.76	14 Jul
Willie	Prinsloo	RSA 55	7.75	14 Apr
Cilliers	Botha	RSA 63	A7.75	21 Apr
Trevor	Hoyte	UK 57	7.75	6 May
Sergey	Podgayniy	SU 63	7.75	3 Jun
Emil	Mikhailov	BUL 64	7.75	3 Jun
Alberto	Solanas	SPA 55	7.75	3 Jun
Igor	Prikhodko	SU 65	7.75	10 Jun
Vache	Movsepyan	SU 58	7.75	7 Sep
Oleg	Koptelov	SU 63	7.75	30 Sep

Best low altitude mark

Fouche	7.90	15 Dec	(8.00A)
R.Williams	7.83	18 Jun	(7.95A)

Best outdoor marks for athletes with indoor seasonal bests

Koch	8.08	0.3	2			Berlin	9 Jun	(8.09i)
Corgos	8.02	1.5	Q	OG		Los Angeles	5 Aug	(8.02i)
Churilin	7.92		6			Moskva	6 Jul	(7.94i)
Kottke	7.88	0.4	4	NC		Erfurt	3 Jun	(7.88i)

Wilhoite	7.85	5 May	(7.87i)	Deroche	7.79	16 Jun	(7.81i)
Puzyrev	7.85	10 Jun	(7.91i)	I.Kharitonov	7.78	19 Apr	(7.83i)
Yakovlev	7.84	19 May	(8.10i)	Malko	7.77	26 May	(7.80i)
Waynes	7.83	18 Jun	(7.90i)	Aushev	7.75	10 Jun	(7.76i)
Piochi	7.82	2 Jun	(7.93i)				
Tsygankov	7.82	6 Aug	(7.82i)	(a) Potapenko also 7.94 −0.1 Q NC Donyetsk 7 Sep			

Wind assisted marks

	Lewis		8.56	8.9	1		Sacramento	21 Jul
Jason	Grimes	USA 59	8.40		1		Knoxville	19 May
Gary	Honey	AUS 59	8.39	6.2	2		Sacramento	21 Jul
Sergey	Rodin	SU 63	8.37		1		Moskva	6 Jul
	Myricks		8.36	3.0	1	MSR	Walnut	29 Apr
Mike	McRae	USA 55	8.34		1	CalR	Modesto	12 May
	Lewis		8.30	2.2	Q	OG	Los Angeles	5 Aug
Gordon	Laine	USA 58	8.24		2		Knoxville	19 May
Mike	Conley	USA 62	8.23	5.2	1	NCAA	Eugene	1 Jun
Vance	Johnson	USA 63	8.18	3.2	2	NCAA	Eugene	1 Jun
Wlodzimierz	Wlodarczyk	POL 57	8.18	3.7	1		Birmingham	15 Jul
Thomas	Selmon	USA 62	8.17		1		San Angelo	14 Apr
Mike	Powell	USA 63	8.14	2.4	2	TAC	San Jose	9 Jun
Mike	Davis	USA 64	8.11	6.4	3	NCAA	Eugene	1 Jun
Rene	Gloor	SWZ 56	8.11	2.8	1	NC	Zofingen	21 Jul
Vladimir	Sidorov	SU 58	8.11		1		Poltava	30 Sep

1984 Lists – Men

Stephen	Walsh	NZ 60	8.10		1		Auckland	28 Jan
Oleg	Semiraz	SU 61	8.10		2		Poltava	30 Sep
Kim	Yongil	KOR 62	8.09		1		Eugene	21 Jul
Vesco	Bradley	USA 53	8.08		3	CalR	Modesto	12 May
Ed	Tave	USA 63	8.07		1		Los Angeles	17 Mar
Vernon	George	USA 64	8.07		1		Abilene	10 May
Tim	Leach	USA 64	8.06		1		Cape Girardeau	25 May
Junichi	Usui	JAP 57	8.03	3.2	1		Shizuoka	22 Apr
Jarmo	Karna	FIN 58	8.02	3.9	1		Heinola	3 Jun
Kevin	Wilson	USA 57	8.00		3	MSR	Walnut	29 Apr
Keith	Talley	USA 64	7.97	2.3	1		San Angelo	18 May
Nick	Rahal	USA 63	7.96	3.1	4	TAC	San Jose	9 Jun
Marco	Delonge	GDR 66	7.96	3.5	1	NC–y	Magdeburg	21 Jul
Kerry	Therwanger	USA	7.95		2		San Angelo	14 Apr
Henry	Lauterbach	GDR 57	7.95	2.3	1		Erfurt	12 May
Bernd	Bieber	FRG 59	7.94	2.8	5		Furth	9 Jun
Zsolt	Szabo	HUN 64	7.93	3.0	1		Budapest	10 Jul
Craig	Stewart	USA	7.92		3		Walnut	3 Jun
Alberto	Solanas	SPA 55	7.92	2.2	1	vFIN,POR	Santiago	9 Sep
Leotha	Stanley	USA 56	7.91	2.4	6	TAC	San Jose	9 Jun
Mario	Lega	ITA 57	7.89	2.3	3	vCS	Cagliari	8 Sep

Greg	Johnson	USA 62	7.88	27 Apr
Dimitrios	Araouzos	CYP 61	7.86	14 Apr
Derrick	Brown	UK 63	7.85	17 Jun
Denis	Pinabel	FRA 58	7.84	29 Apr
Gilbert	Smith	USA 60	7.84	6 May
Janusz	Banas	POL 54	7.84	29 May
Evangelos	Tsoulias	GRE 59	7.84	21 Sep
Bernd	Rebischke	FRG 55	7.82	20 May
Philippe	Deroche	FRA 54	7.82	26 May

Thomas	Eriksson	SWE 63	7.81	27 Apr
Emmanouil	Filandarakis	GRE 64	7.81	3 Jun
Delroy	Poyser	JAM 62	7.80	20 Apr
Gennadiy	Danilov	SU 61	7.80	6 Aug
Bjorn	Johansson	SWE 63	7.79	2 Jun
Erik	Thomas	USA 64	7.78	26 Apr
Michael	Harris	USA	7.78	12 May
Robert	Szeli	CS 65	7.78	16 Jun

Wind Assisted and Unknown Irregularity
| Yuriy | Samarin | SU 60 | 8.28 | 1 | Kharkov | 8 Jul |

Ancillary marks
Lewis	8.59	0.3	24 Aug	Myricks	8.42		26 Aug
Lewis	8.50i		11 Feb	Myricks	8.40		26 Aug
Lewis	8.49	0.4	24 Aug	Lewis	8.39		13 May
Dombrowski	8.48	1.8	27 Jul	Lewis	8.35i		11 Feb
Lewis	8.46i		24 Feb	Myricks	8.34	0.0	22 Aug
Myricks	8.45		5 Sep	Myricks	8.34		5 Sep
Lewis	8.44i		11 Feb	Myricks	8.34		5 Sep
Lewis	8.44	0.7	24 Aug	Myricks	8.32		5 Sep
Myricks	8.44	0.3	24 Aug	Myricks	8.31i		27 Jan
Myricks	8.43	−0.4	24 Aug	Lewis	8.30i		27 Jan
Dombrowski	8.42	1.8	27 Jul	Myricks	8.30		29 Aug

Ancillary Marks – Wind assisted
| Myricks | 8.33 | 12 May |

1984 Lists – Men

	1	10	20	30	50	100	Over 8.00	Over 7.80
1980	8.54	8.13	8.09	8.03	7.91	7.78	36	91
1981	8.62	8.12	8.08	8.00	7.91	7.77	30	82
1982	8.76	8.19	8.12	8.07	7.95	7.85	41	124
1983	8.79	8.19	8.10	8.06	7.99	7.86	47	135
1984	8.79	8.27	8.14	8.10	8.02	7.90	58	157

TRIPLE JUMP

Oleg	Protsenko	SU 63	17.52	−0.6	1	Izv	Kiev	21 Jun
Aleksandr	Yakovlev	SU 57	17.50	2.0	1	Znam	Sochi	10 Jun
Mike	Conley	USA 62	17.50	−0.5	1	FOT	Los Angeles	17 Jun
Gennadiy	Valyukevich	SU 58	17.47	−0.5	1		Moskva	19 Jul
	Valyukevich		17.46		1		Moskva	7 Jul
	Protsenko		17.46	0.5	1	DRZ	Moskva	18 Aug
	Yakovlev		17.45	1.0	1		Sochi	20 May
Lazaro	Betancourt	CUB 63	17.45	0.1	1		Koln	26 Aug
	Conley		17.44	1.3	1	ISTAF	Berlin	17 Aug
	Betancourt		17.43	2.0	1	Barr	Habana	19 May
Khristo	Markov	BUL 65	17.42	1.3	1	Nar	Sofia	19 May
Willie	Banks	USA 56	17.39	−0.6	1		Koblenz	29 Aug
	Betancourt		17.39	0.0	1		Paris	4 Sep
	Valyukevich		17.38	0.1	1	NC	Donyetsk	9 Sep
Vyacheslav	Bordukov	SU 59	17.37	0.7	2	Nar	Sofia	19 May
	Betancourt		17.37	1.8	1		Stuttgart	17 Jun
	Betancourt		17.37	0.5	1	BGP	Budapest	20 Aug
	Conley		17.36	1.3	1	NCAA	Eugene	2 Jun
	Conley		17.36	0.8	Q	OG	Los Angeles	3 Aug
Jan	Cado	CS 63	17.34	0.1	1	PTS	Bratislava	26 May
Zdzislaw	Hoffmann	POL 59	17.34	−0.8	1		St.Denis	2 Jun
	Betancourt		17.34	1.7	2	Znam	Sochi	10 Jun
Grigoriy	Yemets	SU 57	17.33i		1	EC	Goteborg	3 Mar
	Valyukevich		17.32	0.4	3	Znam	Sochi	10 Jun
	Yakovlev		17.32	0.1	2	Izv	Kiev	21 Jun
	Yemets		17.30	0.2	2	NC	Donyetsk	9 Sep
	Betancourt		17.29	0.1	2	PTS	Bratislava	26 May
	Markov		17.29	−0.9	3	DRZ	Moskva	18 Aug
	Banks		17.29	0.1	1	Coke	London	7 Sep
	Banks		17.28	0.7	2	BGP	Budapest	20 Aug

(30/11)

Bedros	Bedrosian	RUM 58	17.27	1.2	1		Bucuresti	9 Jun
Nikolay	Musiyenko	SU 59	17.24	1.2	1		Sochi	27 May
Jaroslav	Priscak	CS 56	17.23		1		Praha	13 May
Vasiliy	Isayev	SU 59	17.22	1.9	4	Znam	Sochi	10 Jun
Peter	Bouschen	FRG 60	17.20	1.1	2		London	13 Jul
Paul	Jordan	USA 56	17.19	−0.3	Q	FOT	Los Angeles	16 Jun
Al	Joyner	USA 60	17.19	−0.8	2	FOT	Los Angeles	17 Jun
Joseph	Taiwo	NIG 59	17.19		1	AfrC	Rabat	13 Jul
Vladimir	Chernikov	SU 59	17.19	0.1	3	NC	Donyetsk	9 Sep
Vlastimil	Marinec	CS 57	17.16i		2	EC	Goteborg	3 Mar
Bela	Bakosi	HUN 57	17.15i		3	EC	Goteborg	3 Mar
Maris	Bruziks	SU 62	17.15		1		Riga	17 Jun
Volker	Mai	GDR 66	17.12	1.2	2	OD	Potsdam	21 Jul
Viktor	Gerasimenya	SU 60	17.10		1		Riga	5 Jul
Vladimir	Plekhanov	SU 58	17.09i		1	NC	Moskva	18 Feb
Stoitsa	Iliev	BUL 60	17.09	−0.3	2	NC	Sofia	2 Jun
Robert	Cannon	USA 58	17.04	0.4	1		Munchen	20 Jul

277

1984 Lists – Men

Name	Surname	Nat/Age	Mark	Wind	Pos	Meet	Venue	Date
Sergey	Belevskiy	SU 59	17.03		4		Moskva	7 Jul
Sergey	Tkachev	SU 58	17.02		1		Bryansk	1 Jul
Eric	McCalla	UK 60	17.01	2.0	Q	OG	Los Angeles	3 Aug
Dario	Badinelli	ITA 60	17.00	1.7	1	vCS	Cagliari	9 Sep
Ray	Kimble	USA 53	16.99	-0.9	4	FOT	Los Angeles	17 Jun
Ajayi	Agbebaku	NIG 55	16.96		2	AfrC	Rabat	13 Jul
Mahmed	Akhundov	SU 64	16.96	1.8	1		Chelyabinsk	29 Jul
Aleksandr	Lisichonok	SU 58	16.95		6	Znam	Sochi	10 Jun
Lazaro	Balcindes	CUB 63	16.93	1.8	2		Stuttgart	17 Jun
Aleksandr	Beskrovniy	SU 60	16.92		1		Moskva	11 May
Jorge	Reyna	CUB 63	16.87	1.0	3		Stuttgart	17 Jun
Keith	Connor	UK 57	16.87	0.4	3	OG	Los Angeles	4 Aug
Sergey	Tarasov	SU 62	16.85		1		Omsk	16 Jun
Francisco	A. Santos	BRA 60	16.83	0.1	4	PTS	Bratislava	26 May
Zou	Zhenxian	CHN 55	16.83	-1.0	4	OG	Los Angeles	4 Aug
Ken	Lorraway	AUS 56	16.81i		2		Osaka	16 Jan
Ralf	Jaros	FRG 65	16.81	-0.1	1	NC	Dusseldorf	23 Jun
Aston	Moore	UK 56	16.80	2.0	1	NC	Cwmbran	28 May
Aleksandr	Orlov	SU 58	16.80		1		Kiev	10 Aug
John	Herbert	UK 62	16.79i		1	vUSA	Cosford	10 Mar
Dimitrios	Mihas	GRE 58	16.79		1		Patra	1 Jul
Paul	Emordi	NIG 65	16.78		1		Baton Rouge	5 May
Charles	Simpkins	USA 63	16.76	-1.6	5	FOT	Los Angeles	17 Jun
Abcelvio	Rodrigues	BRA 57	16.76		1		Rio de Janeiro	5 Jul
Sergey	Usov	SU 61	16.76		1		Alma Ata	29 Jul
Vladimir	Bereglazov	SU 59	16.75i		3		Moskva	10 Feb
Mihai	Ene	RUM 60	16.73		2		Bucuresti	9 Jun
Yevgeniy	Anikin	SU 58	16.73		1		Kazan	14 Jul
Jorg	Elbe	GDR 64	16.72	0.7	2	NC	Erfurt	1 Jun
Yasushi	Ueta	JAP 55	16.71	1.7	1		Tokyo	6 May
Sergey	Abramov	SU 58	16.71	0.1	5	NC	Donyetsk	9 Sep
Greg	Caldwell	USA 57	16.70	1.9	6	FOT	Los Angeles	17 Jun
Vasiliy	Grishchenkov	SU 59	16.69	-0.2	8	Izv	Kiev	21 Jun
Vladimir	Inozemtsev	SU 64	16.68	-1.3	Q	Izv	Kiev	20 Jun
Axel	Gross	GDR 60	16.68	1.0	1		Neubrandenburg	4 Jul
Mamadou	Diallo	SEN 54	16.68		3	AfrC	Rabat	13 Jul
Ken	Hays	USA 56	16.67		3	MSR	Walnut	29 Apr
Ravil	Bakirov	SU 58	16.67		1		Omsk	16 Jun
Shamil	Abbyasov	SU 57	16.66i		1		Vilnius	15 Jan
Serge	Helan	FRA 64	16.66	0.4	2		St.Denis	2 Jun
Viktor	Panych	SU 60	16.66		1		Poltava	29 Sep
Dirk	Gamlin	GDR 63	16.64i		1		Senftenberg	7 Jan
Juan A.	Gonzalez	SPA 60	16.64	2.0	1		Salamanca	15 Sep
Bodo	Behmer	GDR 61	16.60	1.7	3	NC	Erfurt	1 Jun
Vasile	Dima	RUM 58	16.60		1		Bucuresti	19 Aug
Doug	Garner	USA 54	16.59		1		Tucson	5 May
Mihai	Bran	RUM 62	16.59		2	NC	Bucuresti	11 Jul
Boris	Khokhlov	SU 58	16.59		1		Alma Ata	29 Jul
Byron	Criddle	USA 62	16.58		2		Houston	6 May
David	McFadgen	USA 60	16.58		1		University Pk	26 May
Rayfield	Dupree	USA 53	16.58		1		Compton	28 May
Mike	Marlow	USA 57	16.58	-0.4	- T	AC	San Jose	9 Jun
Vladimir	Zubrilin	SU 63	16.58		2		Kazan	14 Jul
Waldemar	Golanko	POL 61	16.57		1		Bydgoszcz	18 Aug
Joshua	Kio	KEN 57	16.56		1		Houston	26 May
Tibor	Kiss	HUN 55	16.56	-0.9	2		Athinai	10 Jul
Igor	Lapshin	SU 63	16.56		1		Minsk	9 Aug
Georgi	Pomashki	BUL 60	16.55i		1		Budapest	4 Feb
Dmitriy	Litvinenko	SU 63	16.55i		1		Moskva	3 Mar
Aleksandr	Vanichkin	SU 55	16.55i		1		Rostov	9 Mar
Mikhail	Bezruchko	SU 62	16.55	0.2	8	NC	Donyetsk	9 Sep
David	Siler	USA 61	16.53		4		Knoxville	18 May
Kerry	Harrison	USA 65	16.50		1		Lincoln	12 May

1984 Lists – Men

Alain	Rene-Corail	FRA 62	16.49		1		Les Abymes	21 Mar
Michael	Makin	UK 62	16.47	0.4	1		Bruxelles	1 Jul
Igor	Chekmaryov	SU 58	16.46i		2		Moskva	3 Feb
Francis	DoDoo	GHA 60	16.45i		Q	NCAA	Syracuse	9 Mar
Leonid	Levchenko	SU 58	16.45					
Jose	Salazar	VEN 57		16.43i	1		Albuquerque	4 Feb
Thomas	Eriksson	SWE 63	16.43	−1.9	1		Ruston	28 Apr
Andrey	Kayumov	SU 64	16.43	.	3		Omsk	16 Jun
Delroy	Poyser	JAM 62	16.42i		Q	NCAA	Syracuse	9 Mar
Vyacheslav	Sladinov	SU 59	16.42		1		Leningrad	15 Jun
Cary	Tyler	USA 59	16.42	−1.1	Q	FOT	Los Angeles	16 Jun
Jerzy	Kaduskiewicz	POL 52	16.42	2.0	2	NC	Lublin	23 Jun
Aleksandr	Grushnik	SU 59	16.42		1		Minsk	4 Jul
Harri	Pesonen	FIN 62	16.42	1.0	1	vSWE	Helsinki	2 Sep
Vasil	Asadov	SU 65	16.42	0.1	Q	NC	Donyetsk	8 Sep
Aleksey	Shcherbakov	SU 65	16.41				2 Jun	
Stanislav	Timofeyev	SU 56	16.40i				5 Feb	
Pierre	Camara	FRA 65	16.40				13 May	
Aleksandr	Kovalenko	SU 63	16.40				4 Jul	
Roberto	Mazzucato	ITA 54	16.40				16 Sep	
Steve	Hanna	BAH 58	16.39				28 Apr	
Ivo	Bilik	CS 62	16.38i				28 Jan	
Kalman	Sari	HUN 60	16.38				13 Sep	
Greg	Neal	USA 63	16.37i				20 Jan	
Deon	Mayfield	USA 62	16.37				21 Apr	
Frank	Rutherford	BAH	16.37				26 May	
Arne	Holm	SWE 61	16.37				26 Aug	
Dwayne	Rudd	USA 61	A16.36				28 Jan	
Jacek	Pastusinski	POL 64	16.36				29 May	
Nikolay	Prokhorov	SU 64	16.36				19 Jul	
Sergey	Frolenkov	SU 62	16.35i				14 Jan	
Al	Toon	USA 63	16.35i				25 Feb	
Ken	Frazier	USA 63	16.35				14 Apr	
Didier	Falise	BEL 61	16.35				1 Jul	
Haralambos	Giannoulis	GRE 63	16.34				29 Aug	
Tian	Hungxian	CHN 61	16.33				14 Mar	
Stanislav	Zubar	SU 64	16.33				10 Aug	
Markku	Rokala	FIN 60	16.32i				19 Feb	
Joe	Richardson	USA 66	16.32				9 Jun	
Damir	Tashpulatov	SU 64	16.32				5 Jul	
Stanislaw	Oporski	USA 59	16.31				18 May	
Gennadiy	Kakhno	SU 64	16.31				9 Aug	
Viktor	Lysikov	SU 55	16.30				16 Jun	
Claes	Rahm	SWE 64	16.30				9 Jul	
Barbaro	Torres	CUB 63	16.30				10 Jul	
Igor	Andrievskiy	SU 59	16.29i				7 Jan	
Gintautas	Zizis	SU 60	16.29				20 May	
Francisco	Olivarez	MEX 62 A	16.29				28 May	
Ed	Williams	USA	16.28				26 May	
Byron	Gray	USA 59	16.28				3 Jun	
Fred	Brooks	USA 56 A	16.28				4 Jun	
George	Wright	CAN 63	16.28				14 Jul	
Ivan	Slanar	CS 61	16.28				1 Sep	
Ed	Roskiewicz	USA 60	16.27				26 May	
Sergey	Taratukhin	SU 59	16.26i				25 Feb	
Masao	Ikegami	JAP 57	16.26				2 Jun	
Milan	Korinek	CS 60	16.26				21 Jul	
Gerald	McNair	USA	16.25				19 May	
Jimmy	Washington	USA 52	16.25				26 May	
Assatur	Aroyan	SU 59	16.24i				25 Feb	
Norbert	Elliott	BAH 62	16.24				7 Apr	
Sanya	Owolabi	USA 60	16.24				26 May	
Esa	Viitasalo	FIN 60	16.24				2 Sep	
Atanas	Chochev	BUL 57	16.23i				2 Feb	
Brad	Johnson	BAH 62	16.23				5 May	
Michael	Patton	USA 66	16.23				16 Jun	
Peter	Beames	AUS 63	16.22				11 Feb	
Sergey	Omelchenko	SU 59	16.21				10 Aug	
Jorge	Vila	SPA 55	16.20				29 Jun	
Igor	Kolomagin	SU 60	16.20				14 Jul	
Vladimir	Chernota	SU 61	16.20				10 Aug	
Patrice	Louis Marie	FRA 63	16.19				13 May	
Tanner	Cronic	USA 62	16.19				26 May	
Alain	Wanlin	BEL 64	16.19				17 Jun	
Earl	Bridges	USA 62	16.18				18 May	
Keith	Gilreath	USA 59	16.18				26 May	
Aleksandr	Gassanov	SU 63	16.18				1 Jun	
Alfred	Stummer	AUT 62	16.18				14 Oct	
Henri	Dorina	FRA 58	16.17i				18 Feb	
Cameron	Gary	USA 60	16.17				3 Mar	
Leon	Hutchins	USA 58	16.17				17 Mar	
Ken	Williams	USA 64	16.16				14 Apr	
Ronald	Stein	GDR 63	16.16				19 May	
Janos	Hegedis	YUG 55	16.16				10 Jun	
Mai	Guoqiang	CHN 62	16.16				6 Sep	

Best Outdoor Marks

Marinec	17.06	1.5	5		DRZ	Moskva	18 Aug	(17.16i)
Bakosi	16.85	0.9	4		4–N	Stuttgart	17 Jun	(17.15i)
Herbert	16.77	1.0	1			Loughborough	17 Jun	(16.79i)
Bereglazov	16.69	0.0	4			Sochi	20 May	(16.75i)
Lorraway	16.59	1.6	–			Melbourne	1 Apr	(16.81i)
Pomashki	16.54	0.4	3			Athinai	10 Jul	(16.55i)
Abbyasov	16.53		Q			Sochi	19 May	(16.66i)
Chekmaryov	16.44		4			Moskva	10 May	(16.46i)
Gamlin	16.42	0.5	3			Neubrandenburg	4 Jul	(16.64i)

1984 Lists – Men

Gamlin	16.32	19 May	(16.64i)	Bilik	16.27	9 Sep	(16.38i)
Zubrilin	16.30	20 May	(16.47i)	Salazar	16.26	26 May	(16.43i)
Litvinenko	16.29	27 May	(16.55i)	Plekhanov	16.16	27 May	(17.09i)
Rokala	16.28	8 Jul	(16.32i)				

Unknown Irregularity

Aleksey	Roganin	SU 59	17.11	1	Kharkov	7 Jul
Aleksandr	Lisichonok	SU 58	17.05	2	Kharkov	7 Jul
Vyacheslav	Sladinov	SU 59	16.48	3	Kharkov	7 Jul
Aleksandr	Shumilin	SU 53	16.43	4	Kharkov	7 Jul

Marks made with assisting wind

Zdzislaw	Hoffmann	POL 59	17.55	3.6	1	Kuso	Warszawa	9 Jun
	Yakovlev		17.41	2.4	2	DRZ	Moskva	18 Aug
	Hoffmann		17.28	2.8	1		Sevilla	19 May
	Hoffmann		17.28	3.6	1	NC	Lublin	23 Jun
Al	Joyner	USA 60	17.26	2.1	1	OG	Los Angeles	4 Aug
Charles	Simpkins	USA 63	17.18	2.6	3	NCAA	Eugene	2 Jun
Byron	Criddle	USA 62	17.08		1		Houston	14 Apr
Ken	Lorraway	AUS 56	17.07	4.0	1		Canberra	19 Feb
Dwayne	Rudd	USA 61	16.68	3.7	Q	NCAA	Eugene	31 May
Vasil	Asadov	SU 65	16.68		1	NC-Y	Simferopol	26 May
John	Tillman	USA 65	16.61	1.9*	1	PAG–j	Nassau	23 Aug
Waldemar	Golanko	POL 61	16.60	4.0	2	Kuso	Warszawa	9 Jun
Mike	Marlow	USA 57	16.60	4.2	3	TAC	San Jose	9 Jun
Esa	Viitasalo	FIN 60	16.53	4.4	1	NC	Kajaani	8 Jul
Alain	Rene-Corail	FRA 62	16.52	3.1	1	NC	Villeneuve D'.	30 Jun
Thomas	Eriksson	SWE 63	16.51	2.4	1		Vaxjo	26 Aug
Norifumi	Yamashita	JAP 62	16.50	1.7*	1		Tokyo	20 May
Hassan	Badra	EGY 59	16.48	2.2	Q	OG	Los Angeles	3 Aug
Masao	Ikegami	JAP 57	16.46	3.4	3		Hiroshima	29 Apr
Ryszard	Juszczak	POL 58	16.43	3.0	1		Grudziadz	29 May
Harri	Pesonen	FIN 62	16.43		1	vPOR,SPA	Santiago de C.	8 Sep

*Note – move Tillman and Yamashita to main section

Arne	Holm	SWE 61	16.39	2 Sep	Morgan	Tharpe	USA 62	16.24	5 May
Ken	Williams	USA 64	16.37	31 Mar	Jorge	Vila	SPA 55	16.22	8 Jul
Byron	Gray	USA 59	16.37	3 Jun	Masami	Nakanishi	JAP 58	16.21	6 May
Claes	Rahm	SWE 64	16.36	26 Aug	Shawn	Akridge	USA 64	16.20	13 Apr
Alton	Henry	USA 63	16.35	12 May	Vladimir	Khlebnikov	SU 62	16.20	5 Jul
Markku	Rokala	FIN 60	16.34	10 Jun	Vernon	Samuels	UK 64	16.19	6 May
Tetsushi	Kanamaru	JAP 60	16.31	29 Apr	Jean-Louis	Tahon	FRA 59	16.19	12 May
Dorant	Bartlett	BAH	16.31	24 May	Paolo	Challancin	ITA 63	16.19	22 Jul
Eddie	Loyd	USA 58	16.31	9 Jun					

Ancillary jumps

Yakovlev	17.43	20 May	Conley	17.32	−0.6	17 Jun
Valyukevich	17.42	7 Jul	Conley	17.31	−0.6	17 Jun
Valyukevich	17.39	19 Jul	Valyukevich	17.28		9 Sep
Yakovlev	17.36	10 Jun				

Ancillary jumps – wind assisted

Conley	17.34	2.3	2 Jun

1984 Lists – Men

	1	10	20	30	50	100	Over 17.00	Over 16.50
1980	17.35	17.03	16.81	16.71	16.51	16.22	11	51
1981	17.56	17.13	16.97	16.76	16.59	16.30	18	68
1982	17.57	17.16	17.02	16.91	16.69	16.38	24	74
1983	17.55	17.27	17.12	17.05	16.74	16.42	33	87
1984	17.52	17.34	17.19	17.02	16.78	16.42	32	91

SHOT PUT

Brian	Oldfield	USA 45	22.19	1		San Jose	26 May
Udo	Beyer	GDR 55	22.04	1		Rehlingen	11 Jun
	Beyer		22.00	1		Dresden	27 Jul
	Beyer		21.98	1		Split	30 Apr
John	Brenner	USA 61	21.92	1	NCAA	Eugene	2 Jun
Mike	Carter	USA 60	21.76	2	NCAA	Eugene	2 Jun
Ulf	Timmermann	GDR 62	21.75	1	OD	Potsdam	21 Jul
Janis	Bojars	SU 56	21.74	1		Riga	14 Jul
Augie	Wolf	USA 61	21.73	1		Leverkusen	12 Apr
	Brenner		21.72	1		Los Angeles (Ww)	5 May
	Beyer		21.72	1	NC	Erfurt	1 Jun
	Beyer		21.71	2	OD	Potsdam	21 Jul
	Bojars		21.67	1		Sochi	26 May
	Beyer		21.66	1		Celje	5 May
Dave	Laut	USA 56	21.64	1		Eugene	4 Jun
Sergey	Kasnauskas	SU 61	21.64	1	DRZ	Moskva	17 Aug
Sergey	Smirnov	SU 60	21.63	1		Leningrad	18 Jun
	Laut		21.60	Q	TAC	San Jose	7 Jun
	Beyer		21.60	1		Berlin	15 Jul
	Beyer		21.60	2	DRZ	Moskva	17 Aug
Sergey	Gavryushin	SU 59	21.60	1		Moskva	19 Aug
	Brenner		21.59	2		San Jose	26 May
	Laut		21.58	3		San Jose	26 May
	Laut		21.58	1		Berkeley	14 Jul
Vladimir	Kiselyov	SU 57	21.58	3	DRZ	Moskva	17 Aug
	Bojars		21.57	1		Sochi	19 May
	Timmermann		21.56	1		Dresden	19 May
	Beyer		21.54	1		Erfurt	12 May
	Oldfield		21.53	1	MSR	Walnut	29 Apr
	Timmermann		21.52	1		Split	30 Apr
	Wolf		21.52	1		Stuttgart	21 Jul
Remigius	Machura	CS 60	21.52	1	WK	Zurich	22 Aug

(32/13)

Alessandro	Andrei	ITA 59	21.50	1	NC	Roma	11 Jul
Aleksandr	Baryshnikov	SU 48	21.35	1	Znam	Sochi	10 Jun
Mike	Lehmann	USA 60	21.27	1		Knoxville	19 May
Greg	Tafralis	USA 58	21.25	5		San Jose	26 May
Zlatan	Saracevic	YUG 56	21.11*	1		Zagreb	16 Jun
Sergey	Donskikh	SU 56	21.09	1		Leningrad	13 Aug
Helmut	Krieger	POL 58	21.03	5	DRZ	Moskva	17 Aug
Sergey	Solomko	SU 58	21.02	1		Kiev	10 Aug
Nikolay	Borodkin	SU 55	21.00	3	Znam	Sochi	10 Jun
Mikhail	Kostin	SU 59	20.96	1		Tula	24 Jul
Mike	Smith	USA 58	20.90	4	CalR	Modesto	12 May
Edward	Sarul	POL 58	20.89	1		Seville	19 May
Janusz	Gassowski	POL 58	20.85	2		Seville	19 May
Werner	Gunthor	SWZ 61	20.80	1	WA	Lisboa	16 Jun

1984 Lists – Men

Algis	Pusinaitis	SU 57	20.71	4		Sochi	19 May
Kevin	Akins	USA 60	20.70i	2	TAC	Princeton	24 Feb
Vladimir	Milic	YUG 55	20.66	1		Beograd	2 Jun
Josef	Kubes	CS 57	20.64	1	PTS	Bratislava	26 May
Soren	Tallhem	SWE 64	20.60i	1		Colorado Springs	24 Feb
Marco	Montelatici	ITA 53	20.59	2		Milano	27 Jun
Brian	Muir	USA 60	20.58	1		Los Angeles (Ww)	18 Mar
Erik	de Bruin	HOL 63	20.58i	1		Dortmund	9 Dec
Tony	Harlin	USA 59	20.57	2		Piscataway	21 Apr
Dimitrios	Koutsoukis	GRE 62	20.51	1		Palo Alto	7 Apr
Igor	Avrunin	SU 57	20.50	2		Riga	2 Jun
Rob	Suelflohn	USA 59	20.46	1		Los Gatos	5 May
Viktor	Sosnin	SU 54	20.44	1		Sochi	27 Apr
Yevgeniy	Mironov	SU 49	20.43	7	Znam	Sochi	10 Jun
Torsten	Pelzer	GDR 63	20.39	1		Potsdam	5 May
Mikhail	Domorosov	SU 55	20.38	3		Riga	2 Jun
Peter	Block	GDR 55	20.38	1		Sofia	17 Jun
Yngve	Wahlander	SWE 58	20.35	1		Vasteras	20 May
Zane	Hubbard	USA 58	20.30	7	TAC	San Jose	8 Jun
Georgi	Todorov	BUL 60	20.30	2		Sofia	17 Jun
Jovan	Lazarevic	YUG 52	20.29i*	2	vITA,POL	Torino	11 Feb
Igor	Palchikov	SU 61	20.25	1		Stavropol	19 Apr
Aleksandr	Boreyko	SU 56	20.23	2		Tallinn	28 Jun
Gary	Williky	USA 59	20.22	2		Eugene	4 Jun
Nikolay	Gemizhev	BUL 56	20.20	1	NC	Sofia	3 Jun
Matthias	Schmidt	GDR 56	20.19i	3		Jablonec	28 Jan
Aulis	Akonniemi	FIN 58	20.18	3		Hameenkyro	1 Jul
Ivan	Ivancic	YUG 37	20.17*	1		Hainfeld	11 Jun
Donatas	Stukonis	SU 57	20.14	6	NC	Donyetsk	8 Sep
Aleksandr	Stepankov	SU 58	20.11	2		Sochi	1 Apr
Ian	Pyka	USA 56	20.11	8	TAC	San Jose	8 Jun
Kelly	Brooks	USA 58	20.09	1	TexR	Austin	7 Apr
Vladimir	Kisheyev	SU 58	20.07	4		Moskva	5 Aug
Viktor	Stepanskiy	SU 59	20.05	2		Kiev	10 Aug
Sergey	Belkov	SU 61	20.03	2		Stavropol	19 Apr
Jozef	Lacika	CS 61	20.02	1		Praha	2 Jun
Colin	Anderson	USA 51	20.01	8		San Jose	26 May
Hank	Kraychir	USA 60	20.00	1		Compton	28 May
Udo	Gelhausen	FRG 56	20.00	1		Bonn	3 Jun
Jim	Doehring	USA 62	19.97	3		Salinas	23 May
Vyacheslav	Yemelyanov	SU 58	19.94	3		Sochi	1 Apr
Gert	Weil	CHL 60	19.94	Q	OG	Los Angeles	10 Aug
Scott	Lofquist	USA 60	19.92	1	KansR	Lawrence	21 Apr
Bob	Otrando	USA 56	19.91	1		Taunton,Mass.	6 May
Knut	Hjeltnes	NOR 51	19.91	1	vSWE,GRE	Malmo	17 Jun
Detlef	Last	GDR 60	19.90i	4		Jablonec	28 Jan
Laszlo	Szabo	HUN 55	19.87	1		Budapest	19 May
Milton	Williams	USA 56	19.86	1		Monroe	31 Mar
Erwin	Weitzl	AUT 60	19.86	1	NC	Vienna	22 Jul
John	Dupuis	USA 54	19.85	1		Fitchburg	28 May
Marty	Kobza	USA 62	19.84	5		Knoxville	19 May
Oskar	Jakobsson	ICE 55	19.80	1		Austin	20 May
Vladislav	Koncicky	CS 58	19.79	5	PTS	Bratislava	26 May
Nikolay	Valakhanovich	SU 57	19.77	1		Minsk	17 Jun
Art	McDermott	USA 61	19.76i	1		Boston	10 Feb
Bishop	Dolegiewicz	CAN 53	19.74	3		Eugene	4 Jun
Karsten	Stolz	FRG 64	19.73	1	NC	Dusseldorf	24 Jun
Jesse	Stuart	USA 51	19.71	1		Houston	6 May
Kari	Toyryla	FIN 56	19.70	1		Lahti	19 May
Karel	Sula	CS 59	19.69i	3	NC	Jablonec	18 Feb
Ventsislav	Khristov	BUL 62	19.68	1		Sofia	28 Jul
Fernando	Baroni	ITA 57	19.67	1		Roma	12 May

1984 Lists – Men

Vladimir	Yaryshkin	SU 63	19.67	2		Moskva	19 Aug
Yuriy	Kuyumdzhan	SU 61	19.65i	2		Moskva	4 Feb
Zsigmond	Ladanyi	HUN 61	19.60	1		Szeged	29 Sep
Valeriy	Voykin	SU 45	19.59	1		Kharkov	7 Jul
Ron	Backes	USA	19.58	4	NCAA	Eugene	2 Jun
Mike	Weeks	USA 54	19.57	2		Salinas	21 Apr
Edmund	Wenta	POL 53	19.57	1		Sopot	22 Jul
Ahmed Kamel	Chatta	EGY 61	19.56	1		Cairo	25 Feb
Trent	Eddings	USA	19.53	1		Davis	14 Apr
Mike	Buncic	USA 62	19.50i	2		Columbus	18 Feb
Joe	Zelezniak	USA 51	19.48	1		Williamsburg	7 Apr

Stefan	Fernholm	SWE 59	19.47	20 Jun	Janne	Ronkainen	FIN 63	19.06	18 Jun
Jari	Kuoppa	FIN 60	19.47	10 Jul	Igor	Medkov	SU 60	19.06	14 Jul
Vladimir	Zinchenko	SU 59	19.47	29 Sep	Sergey	Babanin	SU 59	19.05	28 Jul
Aleksandr	Zaytsev	SU 57	19.46i	29 Jan	Aivars	Plugis	SU 63	19.05	8 Aug
Holger	Grell	GDR 60	19.45i	7 Jan	Valeriy	Zotin	SU 60	19.04	15 Jul
Aleksandr	Burin	SU 60	19.45	15 Jul	Luis M.	Delis	CUB 57	19.04	29 Aug
Brian	Faul	USA 60	19.44	19 May	Brian	Donohue	USA 62	19.01	19 May
Matt	Catalano	CAN 58	19.44	15 Jun	Pyotr	Frizen	SU 51	19.01	22 Sep
Sergey	Kozhukhov	SU 54	19.42	1 Jul	John	Frazier	USA 63	19.00	28 Apr
Mohamed	Achouche	EGY 55	19.41	11 May	Albert	Czyz	POL 57	19.00	30 Sep
Joe	Maciejczyk	USA 58	19.40i	27 Jan	Cameron	Baxter	USA 62	18.96	7 Apr
Arnold	Campbell	USA 66	19.40	16 May	Sergey	Korobeynikov	SU 56	18.95	27 Apr
Nikolay	Khristov	BUL 52	19.40	3 Jun	Enn	Rohula	SU 53	18.94	26 May
Anatoliy	Samolyuk	SU 58	19.40	10 Aug	Luciano	Zerbini	ITA 60	18.93	20 Jun
Andreas	Horn	GDR 62	19.39	13 Jul	Vladimir	Kiselyov-2	SU 57	18.92	5 Aug
Viktor	Lazarev	SU 54	19.37	1 Apr	Aleksandr	Valov	SU 63	18.92	5 Aug
Ron	Semkiw	USA 54	19.34	7 Apr	Mieczyslaw	Kropelnicki	POL 51	18.90	20 May
Paul	Ruiz	CUB 62	19.30	20 Jun	Mario	Hoyer	GDR 65	18.88i	12 Feb
Bernd	Kneissler	FRG 62	19.30	25 Jul	Luby	Chambul	CAN 58	18.88	15 Jun
Mikhail	Gusev	SU 57	19.28	7 Jul	Trond	Ulleberg	NOR 62	18.88	16 May
Clint	Johnson	USA 61	19.26i	21 Jan	Nikolay	Matveyev	SU 62	18.87	8 Apr
Aulis	Toivonen	FIN 56	19.26	30 Jun	Thomas	Kleeberg	GDR 63	18.87	15 Jul
Luigi	De Santis	ITA 57	19.24i	22 Jan	Wolfgang	Warnemunde	GDR 53	18.85	18 Jul
Lennart	Flyman	SWE 56	19.21	22 Mar	Vladimir	Yeliseyev	SU 53	18.84	7 Jul
Anders	Jonsson	SWE 60	19.20	23 Jun	Flip	Jones	USA	18.83	31 Mar
Claus-Dieter	Fohrenbach	FRG 55	19.19	9 Jun	Al	Feuerbach	USA 48	18.83	19 May
Maris	Petrashko	SU 61	19.17	8 Sep	Yaroslav	Malinin	SU 61	18.83	25 Aug
Jeff	Lehmann	USA 62	19.16	28 Apr	Werner	Hartmann	FRG 59	18.80i	3 Feb
John	Smith	USA 61	19.14i	4 Feb	Aleksandr	Gluberman	SU 59	18.80	5 Aug
Sergey	Belkin	SU 62	19.14	2 May	Mikhail	Kulesh	SU 64	18.80	29 Sep
Viktor	Beliy	SU 64	19.14	7 Jul	Steve	Cate	USA 63	18.76	20 Apr
Mike	Spiritoso	CAN 63	19.12	15 Jun	Mike	Winch	UK 48	18.75	6 Jun
Tom	Newberry	USA 62	19.08	2 Jun	Mikhail	Petrov	SU 65	18.75	14 Jul
Gennadiy	Vasyuk	SU 61	19.08	10 Aug	Aleksey	Gerenko	SU 62	18.75	Jul
Sorin	Tirichita	RUM 60	19.07	9 Jun					

* = Athlete subsequently suspended for failing doping test.

Best outdoor marks for athletes with seasonal bests indoors

Tallhem	20.26	1		Provo	19 May	(20.60i)
de Bruin	20.20	1	FBK	Hengelo	6 Jul	(20.58i)
Akins	20.13	4		Knoxville	19 May	(20.70i)
Schmidt	19.82	2		Rijeka	2 May	(20.19i)
McDermott	19.68	1		Villanova	19 May	(19.76i)
Kuyumzdhan	19.49	1		Moskva	2 May	(19.65i)

283

1984 Lists – Men

Maciejczyk	19.38	7 Apr	(19.40i)	Smith	18.98	13 Mar	(19.14i)
Sula	19.42	28 May	(19.69i)	Grell	18.91	5 May	(19.45i)
Buncic	19.12	12 May	(19.50i)	Hartmann	18.77	2 Jun	(18.80i)
Last	19.04	1 Jun	(19.90i)	Zaytsev	18.77	16 Jun	(19.46i)
Johnson	19.02	21 Apr	(19.26i)				

Light Implement

Sergey	Kasnauskas	SU 61	22.09	1	Minsk	23 Aug

Ancillary Marks

Beyer	21.98	30 Apr	Beyer	21.62	5 May
Beyer	21.83	26 Jul	Laut	21.61	4 Jun
Beyer	21.81	26 Jul	Bojars	21.61	14 Jul
Beyer	21.78	30 Apr	Beyer	21.59	1 Jun
Bojars	21.65	14 Jul	Bojars	21.57	14 Jul
Timmermann	21.64	21 Jul	Beyer	21.56	5 May

Light Implement – Ancillary marks

Kasnauskas	22.02	23 Aug
Kasnauskas	21.98	23 Aug
Kasnauskas	21.69	23 Aug
Kasnauskas	21.56	23 Aug

	1	10	20	30	50	100	Over 20.00	Over 19.00
1980	21.98	21.10	20.67	20.48	19.90	19.15	43	116
1981	22.02	20.60	20.33	20.08	19.88	19.06	38	107
1982	22.02	21.04	20.62	20.32	19.98	19.22	47	113
1983	22.22	21.20	20.81	20.64	20.13	19.37	64	150
1984	22.19	21.63	21.03	20.66	20.23	19.48	66	145

DISCUS

John	Powell	USA 47	71.26	1	TAC	San Jose	9 Jun
Ricky	Bruch	SWE 46	71.26	1		Malmo	15 Nov
	Bruch		71.00	1		Malmo	14 Oct
Art	Burns	USA 54	70.98	1	Pre	Eugene	21 Jul
	Bruch		70.48	1		Malmo	12 Sep
Mac	Wilkins	USA 50	70.44	2	TAC	San Jose	9 Jun
Imrich	Bugar	CS 55	70.26	1	vITA	Cagliari	8 Sep
	Bugar		70.24	1		Nitra	26 Aug
	Bugar		69.94	1	VD	Bruxelles	24 Aug
	Bugar		69.88	1		Praha	8 Aug
	Bruch		69.86	1		Ystad	27 Oct
Luis M.	Delis	CUB 57	69.74	1	Barr	Habana	19 May
Gejza	Valent	CS 53	69.70	2		Nitra	26 Aug
	Bruch		69.68	1		Ystad	21 Oct
	Bugar		69.60	1		Znojmo	15 Sep
	Wilkins		69.42	2	Pre	Eugene	21 Jul
	Bruch		69.38	1		Malmo	7 Oct
	Valent		69.36	1		Zaragoza	3 Jun
	Bugar		69.26	1		Los Angeles (Ww)	5 May
	Wilkins		69.20	1		San Jose	26 May

1984 Lists – Men

	Bugar		69.18	1	OD	Potsdam	21 Jul
	Bruch		69.10	1		Malmo	12 Jul
	Delis		69.02	1		Sofia	16 Jun
	Burns		68.96	1		Berkeley	14 Jul
	Bruch		68.86	1		Malmo	18 Oct
Jurgen	Schult	GDR 60	68.82	1		Berlin	15 Jul
	Burns		68.68	1		Salinas	23 May
Dmitriy	Kovtsun	SU 55	68.64	1		Riga	6 Jul
	Delis		68.60	1	BGP	Budapest	20 Aug
	Bugar		68.50	1		Formia	30 Jun

(30/9)

Vitaliy	Pischalnikov	SU 58	67.76	1		Stavropol	9 May
Yuriy	Dumchev	SU 58	67.42	1		Sochi	20 May
Rolf	Danneberg	FRG 53	67.40	1		Stade	5 May
Rob	Gray	CAN 56	67.32	1		Etibicoke	30 Apr
Juan	Martinez	CUB 58	67.32	2	GGala	Roma	31 Aug
Wolfgang	Warnemunde	GDR 53	67.30	1		Rostock	11 Jul
Knut	Hjeltnes	NOR 51	67.30	1	vSWZ,HOL	Romedal	8 Sep
Igor	Avrunin	SU 57	67.14	1		Smolininkay	9 May
Marco	Bucci	ITA 60	66.96	2		Formia	30 Jun
Romas	Ubartas	SU 60	66.92	1	vITA,POL,HUN	Torino	2 Jun
Marco	Martino	ITA 60	66.90	3		Formia	30 Jun

Ion	Zamfirache	RUM 53	66.84	1		Bucuresti	5 Aug
Alwin	Wagner	FRG 50	66.58	1		Hainsfeld	11 Jun
Igor	Duginyets	SU 56	66.56	1		Chernovtsy	4 Sep
Georgiy	Kolnootchenko	SU 59	66.52	4	GGala	Roma	31 Aug
Stefan	Fernholm	SWE 59	66.30	1		Gateshead	6 Jul
Gennadiy	Samarin	SU 55	66.16	1		Chelyabinsk	28 Jul
Vladimir	Zinchenko	SU 59	66.16	1		Yalta	29 Sep
Georgi	Taushanski	BUL 57	65.78	2		Sofia	16 Jun
Armin	Lemme	GDR 55	65.76	2		Berlin	15 Jul
Velko	Velev	BUL 48	65.70	1		Sofia	28 Jul

Mitch	Crouser	USA 57	65.62	1		Eugene	27 Jul
Werner	Hartmann	FRG 59	65.60	2	vFIN	Aachen	30 May
Hilmar	Hossfeld	GDR 54	65.32	3	OD	Potsdam	21 Jul
Marcus	Gordien	USA 55	65.28	1		Santa Barbara	14 Mar
Iosif	Nagy	RUM 46	65.20	1		Tirgu Mures	17 Jun
Alois	Hannecker	FRG 61	64.82	1		Altotting	5 May
Mike	Buncic	USA 62	64.74	1	MSR	Walnut	28 Apr
Art	Swarts	USA 45	64.66	4		San Jose	26 May
Richard	Slaney	UK 56	64.66	1		Eugene	6 Jul
Kamen	Dimitrov	BUL 62	64.56	1		Pleven	8 Jul

Vitaliy	Sokolov	SU 55	64.40	1		Vitebsk	16 Jul
Aleksandr	Nazhimov	SU 52	64.16	2		Adler	26 Feb
Jim	McGoldrick	USA 53	64.14	4	TAC	San Jose	9 Jun
Brad	Cooper	BAH 57	64.08	5		San Jose	26 May
Art	McDermott	USA 61	64.04	6		San Jose	26 May
Ole	Haugom	NOR 57	64.02	1		El Paso	23 Jun
Luciano	Zerbini	ITA 60	64.00	1		Verona	30 May
Al	Oerter	USA 36	63.92	Q	TAC	San Jose	8 Jun
Svein Inge	Valvik	NOR 56	63.82	1		Lund	22 May
Erik	de Bruin	HOL 63	63.66	1		Vught	13 May

Ari	Huumonen	FIN 56	63.66	1		Ylivieska	1 Jul
Paul	Bender	USA 61	63.64	1		Walnut	3 Jun
Judd	Binley	USA 55	63.62	2		Walnut	3 Jun
Vesteinn	Hafsteinsson	ICE 60	63.60	1		Tuscaloosa	25 Mar
Stanislaw	Grabowski	POL 55	63.50	1		Brzeszce	18 Sep
John	Brenner	USA 61	63.44	1	NCAA	Eugene	1 Jun
Mohamed	Naguib	EGY 53	63.30	1		Cairo	6 Jul
Velislav	Prokhaska	BUL 53	63.28	2		Sofia	4 Jul
Andrey	Osipov	SU 58	63.24	2		Chelyabinsk	28 Jul
Alfonz	Saskoi	HUN 58	63.24	1		Szeged	8 Oct

285

1984 Lists – Men

Raul	Calderon	CUB 62	63.18	2		Habana	10 Jul
Greg	McSeveney	USA 59	63.16	4	CalR	Modesto	12 May
Ben	Plucknett	USA 54	63.16	Q	FOT	Los Angeles	21 Jun
Viktor	Rashchupkin	SU 50	63.14	3	Izv	Kiev	22 Jun
Paul	Bishop	USA 57	62.86	7	TAC	San Jose	9 Jun
Stanislaw	Wolodko	POL 50	62.82	1		Warszawa	23 Sep
Pat	McCulla	USA 58	62.74	1		Houston	31 May
Viktor	Sinitsyn	SU 59	62.64	1		Krasnodar	30 Jan
Robert	Weir	UK 61	62.50	1	AAA	London	23 Jun
Juhani	Tuomola	FIN 42	62.48	2		Ylivieska	1 Jul
Ference	Tegla	HUN 47	62.44	1		Debrecen	5 Aug
Lutz	Friedrich	GDR 61	62.40	5	NC	Erfurt	2 Jun
Csaba	Hollo	HUN 58	62.40	1		Papa	6 Oct
Ferenc	Szegletes	HUN 48	62.26	2		Papa	6 Oct
Lajos	Gyori	HUN 56	62.24	1		Miskolc	22 Sep
Randy	Heisler	USA 61	62.22	6	NCAA	Eugene	1 Jun
Konstantinos	Georgakopoulos	GRE 63	62.14	1		Athinai	28 Apr
Izak	Kotze	RSA 56	62.12	1		Stellenbosch	27 Mar
Aleksandr	Parakhnenko	SU 61	62.10				
Josef	Kubes	CS 57	62.00	* 1		Praha	13 May
Christian	Okoye	NIG 61	61.92	1		Goleta	5 May
Kostrzewski	Daniel	POL 54	61.92	1		Slupsk	19 Sep
Kyle	Jenner	USA 59	61.90	1		Champaign	4 May
Paul	Mardle	UK 62	61.86	1		Birmingham	13 Jun
Vladimir	Turanok	SU 57	61.86	7	NC	Donyetsk	8 Sep
Jonas	Siaudinis	SU 58	61.80	2		Klaipeda	18 Aug
Lance	Deal	USA 61	61.62	8	NCAA	Eugene	1 Jun
Bernd	Kneissler	FRG 62	61.62	3		Rehlingen	11 Jun
Jim	Reardon	USA 47	61.60	1		Columbus	27 May
Scott	Lofquist	USA 60	61.44	Q	TAC	San Jose	8 Jun
Vladimir	Milic	YUG 55	61.44	1		Zagreb	17 Jun
Boris	Priymak	SU 57	61.42	1		Poltava	30 Sep
Anatoliy	Lang	SU 55	61.32	3		Sochi	31 Mar
Czeslaw	Lis	POL 56	61.32	1		Sopot	22 Jul
Paul	Nandapi	AUS 61	61.28	1		Melbourne	10 Nov
Jay	Kovar	USA 60	61.26	3	MSR	Walnut	28 Apr
Nikolay	Vostrikov	SU 60	61.24	1		Voroshilovgrad	2 Aug
Mieczyslaw	Szpak	POl 61	61.10	1		Slupsk	15 Sep
Eligiusz	Pukownik	POL 62	61.04	2		Zabrze	14 Sep
Aleksandr	Andrianov	SU 58	60.96	1		Leningrad	2 Aug
Angelos	Nikolaidis	GRE 56	60.84	1		Saloniki	9 Jun
Georg	Frank	AUT 51	60.78	1		Klagenfurt	22 May
Dmitriy	Gerson	SU 60	60.74	1		Rovno	6 May
Wulf	Brunner	FRG 62	60.72	1		Bad Kreuznach	7 Apr
Oskar	Jakobsson	ICE 55	60.68	4		Walnut	15 Jul
Li	Weinan	CHN 57	60.64	1		Beijing	21 Apr
Sergey	Andryushchenko	SU 60	60.62	1		Odessa	8 Jun
Oystein	Bjorbaek	NOR 53	60.54	1		Bodo	7 Jun
Nikolay	Zelenov	SU 60	60.54	2		Leningrad	2 Aug
Janusz	Sargalski	POL 58	60.54	3		Slupsk	19 Sep
Goran	Berqvist	SWE 60	60.52	1		Boise	21 Apr
Hank	Kraychir	USA 60	60.52	9	NCAA	Eugene	1 Jun

Risto	Myyra	FIN 42	60.36	18 Jun	Goran	Svensson	SWE 59	60.12	26 Aug
Vaclavas	Kidikas	SU 61	60.28	18 Aug	Sergey	Ivanov	SU 59	60.10	31 Mar
Andreas	Becker	GDR 62	60.26	4 Jul	Scott	Erikson	USA	60.10	19 May
Tadeusz	Majewski	POL 54	60.22	2 Jun	Geza	Fejer	HUN 45	60.08	27 Jul
Albert	Reinaste	SU 59	60.22	6 Jul	Jacek	Strychalski	POL 62	60.08	1 Sep
Sandor	Katona	HUN/FRA 53	60.22	9 Sep	Jozsef	Ficsor	HUN 65	60.06	12 Jun
Marek	Polewany	POL 61	60.18	10 Jun	Roger	Axelsson	SW‹E 57	60.06	4 Jul
Sergey	Seryogin	SU 59	60.14	11 Feb					

1984 Lists – Men

Kalev	Kulv	SU 53	60.06	15 Aug	David	Kielty	USA	58.80	19 May
Konstantinos	Spanidis	GRE 59	60.00	2 Jun	Rick	Meyer	USA 61	58.78	31 May
Augie	Wolf	USA 61	59.98	11 Sep	Yuriy	Kuyumdzhan	SU 61	58.78	7 Jul
Jean-Marc	David	FRA 57	59.94	27 May	David	Simmons	USA 62	58.76	7 Nov
Dietmar	Krause	GDR 63	59.92	11 Jul	Yevgeniy	Burin	SU 64	58.74	28 Jul
Marty	Davenport	USA 63	59.84	11 May	Frederic	Selle	FRA 57	58.68	3 Jun
Borislav	Tashev	BUL 56	59.76	5 May	Aleksandr	Gluberman	SU 59	58.66	21 Jul
Bodo	Ferl	GDR 63	59.70	24 May	Ferenc	Csiszar	HUN 55	58.66	27 Jul
Lars	Sundin	SWE 61	59.70	30 May	Nikolay	Vikhor	SU 54	58.64	2 May
Rene Jean	Coquin	FRA 56	59.68	28 Apr	Sergey	Kokoryev	SU 60	58.64	29 Jul
Nonah	Hadnot	USA 61	59.62	30 May	Tim	Scott	USA 58	58.62	31 May
Andrey	Kuzyanin	SU 60	59.48	14 Sep	Frantisek	Krejci	CS 56	58.58	6 May
Vasiliy	Zamfirov	SU 62	59.48	22 Sep	Andrzej	Maliszewski	POL 57	58.54	18 Sep
Sergey	Grishkin	SU 62	59.42	28 Jul	Uldis	Mejers	SU 63	58.50	22 Aug
Nikolay	Gemizhev	BUL 56	59.40	5 May	Aleksandr	Kuklin	SU 58	58.48	31 Mar
Jack	Harkness	CAN 59	59.40	29 Jun	Markus	Begerow	FRG 58	58.40	2 Sep
Remigius	Machura	CS 60	59.36	13 May	JR	Hanley	USA 59	58.30	10 May
Zeljko	Tarabaric	YUG 55	59.36	26 Aug	Yuriy	Kharchenko	SU 58	58.30	14 Jul
Urmas	Rakhnel	SU 59	59.30	5 Sep	Sergey	Poryadkin	SU 63	58.30	21 Jul
Todd	Kaufman	USA 61	59.28	4 Mar	Per	Ortmann	SWE 55	58.30	4 Sep
Aleksandr	Klimenko	SU 55	59.28	6 Jul	Edward	Rikert	POL 61	58.28	2 Jun
Jurgen	Riese	FRG 62	59.24	7 Apr	Eggert	Bogarsson	ICE 60	58.28	
Gary	Williky	USA 59	59.24	20 May	Laszlo	Nemeth	HUN 60	58.24	13 Aug
John	Garvey	USA	59.20	31 Mar	Dirk	Wippermann	FRG 46	58.22	24 Mar
Steve	Davis	USA 60	59.16	12 May	Aleksandr	Grechko	SU 62	58.20	6 May
Valeriy	Khaustov	SU 61	59.10	Jul	Mikhail	Vdovin	SU 59	58.10	6 May
Vladislav	Popov	SU 62	59.08	15 Jul	Peter	Gordon	UK 51	58.10	27 May
Mike	Carter	USA 60	59.02	11 May	Igor	Latukhov	SU 59	58.08	6 Jul
Sergey	Gorislavtsev	SU 62	59.02	6 Jul	Aleksandr	Selenyev	SU 64	58.04	18 Jun
Borys	Chambul	CAN 53	58.92	12 May	Klaus	Thormann	GDR 60	58.02	15 Jul
Chris	Waltman	USA 61	58.88	12 May	Valeriy	Ushakov	SU 58	58.02	28 Jul
Rob	James	USA 61	58.82	21 Apr	Ron	Schmidt	USA	58.00	21 Apr
Brian	Muir	USA 60	58.80	18 Mar					
Brad	Boland	USA	58.80	24 Mar					

Exhibition

Stefan	Fernholm	SWE 59	67.00	–	Provo	16 May	(66.30)

Sloping ground

Jack	Harkness	CAN 58	61.58	2	North York	10 Jun
Ray	Lazdins	CAN 64	61.02	1	North York	16 Sep

Ancillary marks

Bruch	70.18	14 Oct	Wilkins	68.74	9 Jun
Powell	69.84	9 Jun	Bruch	68.74	12 Sep
Bruch	69.82	14 Oct	Bruch	68.64	14 Oct
Bruch	69.78	27 Oct	Bruch	68.60	7 Oct
Bruch	69.68	14 Oct	Wilkins	68.56	21 Jul
Delis	69.54	19 May	Bruch	68.54	18 Oct
Bruch	68.92	12 Jul			

	1	10	20	30	50	100	Over 62.00	Over 62.00
1980	70.98	67.68	66.34	65.28	62.86	60.32	70	108
1981	72.34	67.26	65.62	64.10	62.00	60.02	51	104
1982	70.58	68.20	66.36	64.62	62.92	60.26	62	104
1983	71.86	68.12	66.24	64.56	62.98	60.48	73	119
1984	71.26	67.76	66.90	65.70	63.66	60.96	80	128

HAMMER THROW

1984 Lists – Men

Yuriy	Sedykh	SU 55	86.34	1		Cork	3 Jul
	Sedykh		85.60	1		London	13 Jul
	Sedykh		85.60	1	DRZ	Moskva	17 Aug
Sergey	Litvinov	SU 58	85.20	2		Cork	3 Jul
	Sedykh		85.02	1	BGP	Budapest	20 Aug
	Sedykh		84.60	1		Tokyo	14 Sep
Juri	Tamm	SU 57	84.40	1		Banska Bystrica	9 Sep
	Sedykh		83.90	1	GGala	Roma	31 Aug
	Litvinov		83.58	1		Moskva	8 Jul
	Tamm		83.32	2	BGP	Budapest	20 Aug
	Sedykh		82.60	1	Izv	Kiev	21 Jun
	Litvinov		82.60	2	Izv	Kiev	21 Jun
Igor	Nikulin	SU 60	82.56	2	DRZ	Moskva	17 Aug
	Nikulin		82.18	3	Izv	Kiev	21 Jun
	Tamm		82.02	1	OD	Berlin	20 Jul
	Tamm		81.56	2		Moskva	8 Jul
	Sedykh		81.52	1	4–N	Torino	2 Jun
Juha	Tiainen	FIN 55	81.52	1		Tampere	11 Jun
Yuriy	Tarasyuk	SU 57	81.44	1		Minsk	10 Aug
	Tiainen		81.36	1		Joutseno	26 May
	Sedykh		81.34	1	Znam	Adler	10 Jun
	Litvinov		81.30	3	DRZ	Moskva	17 Aug
	Nikulin		81.20	3	BGP	Budapest	20 Aug
Igor	Grigorash	SU 59	81.20	1		Kiev	23 Aug
	Nikulin		81.16	1		Leningrad	May
	Tarasyuk		81.14	1		Klaipeda	27 May
	Tiainen		81.12	1		Lappeenranta	28 Jun
	Tamm		81.06	1		Rovno	5 May
	Tiainen		80.88	1	PNG	Turku	26 Jun
	Nikulin		80.84	1	WG	Helsinki	4 Jul

(30/7)

Viktor	Litvinenko	SU 57	80.68	2		Kiev	23 Aug
Emanuil	Dyulgherov	BUL 55	80.64	1		Sofia	25 Aug
Detlef	Gerstenberg	GDR 57	80.50	1		Berlin	15 Jul
Gunther	Rodehau	GDR 59	80.20	1		Celje	5 May
Anatoliy	Chyuzhas	SU 56	80.16	2		Klaipeda	27 May
Igor	Astapkovich	SU 63	79.98	1		Vitebsk	16 Jul
Roland	Steuk	GDR 59	79.90	1		Sofia	16 Jun
Mariusz	Tomaszewski	POL 56	79.46	1		Zabrze	1 Jul
Karl-Hans	Riehm	FRG 51	79.44	1		Augsburg	5 May
Ralf	Haber	GDR 62	79.38	3		Berlin	15 Jul
Matthias	Moder	GDR 63	79.38	4		Berlin	15 Jul
Klaus	Ploghaus	FRG 56	79.36	2		Augsburg	5 May
Jozsef	Vida	HUN 63	79.06	1		Szombathely	28 Aug
Anatoliy	Yefimov	SU 56	78.86	1		Leningrad	15 Jul
Frantisek	Vrbka	CS 58	78.84	1		Praha-Juliska	2 Jun
Imre	Szitas	HUN 61	78.84	1		Miskolc-Diosgyor	26 Aug
Harri	Huhtala	FIN 52	78.74	2	PNG	Turku	26 Jun
Sergey	Dvoretskiy	SU 57	78.62	1		Gorkiy	12 Aug
Henryk	Krolak	POL 60	78.60	1	Kuso	Warszawa	9 Jun
Benjaminas	Viluckis	SU 61	78.20	3		Klaipeda	27 May
Giampaolo	Urlando	ITA 45	78.16	1		Walnut	25 Jul
Christoph	Sahner	FRG 63	78.04	Q	NC	Dusseldorf	23 Jun
Orlando	Bianchini	ITA 55	77.94	1		Milano	27 Jun
Martin	Girvan	UK 60	77.54	1		Wolverhampton	12 May
Vyacheslav	Korovin	SU 62	77.32	2		Adler	27 Apr
Aleksandr	Puchkov	SU 60	77.28	5		Moskva	8 Jul
Matt	Mileham	UK 56	77.02	1		Fresno	11 May

1984 Lists – Men

Nikolay	Pichugin	SU 59	77.00	1		Irpinsk	12 May
Ireneusz	Golda	POL 55	77.00	4	Kuso	Warszawa	9 Jun
Sergey	Vashchenko	SU 58	76.96	1		Leningrad	13 Aug
Vladimir	Nagurniy	SU 58	76.94	1		Molodechno	19 May
Vladimir	Gudilin	SU 52	76.94	1		Poltava	30 Sep
Leszek	Woderski	POL 58	76.88	1		Bydgoszcz	18 Aug
Vasiliy	Sidorenko	SU 61	76.80	1		Volgograd	15 May
Tibor	Tanczi	HUN 58	76.80	2	NC	Budapest	25 Jul
Pavel	Dmitriyev	SU 57	76.66	1		Alma Ata	19 May
Jorg	Schaefer	FRG 59	76.58	1		Palo Alto	23 Apr
Sergey	Dorozhon	SU 64	76.54	1		Dnepropetrovsk	7 Aug
Bill	Green	USA 60	76.52	1		Walnut	15 Jul
Ivan	Tanev	BUL 57	76.50	1		Sofia	4 Jul
Walter	Ciofani	FRA 62	76.38	1		Colombes	6 May
Mikhail	Lavrenyev	SU 64	76.36	1		Leningrad	25 Aug
Declan	Hegarty	IRL 60	76.34	3		Walnut	15 Jul
Igor	Shchegolev	SU 60	76.18	5	NC	Donyetsk	8 Sep
Johann	Lindner	AUT 56	76.12	1		Hainsfeld	11 Jun
Valeriy	Reshetnikov	SU 59	76.10	2		Dnepropetrovsk	5 Aug
Shigenobu	Murofushi	JAP 45	75.94	4		Walnut	15 Jul
Peter	Farmer	USA 52	75.88	1		Lillestrom	5 Jul
Eckbert	Brauer	GDR 59	75.86	1		Berlin	16 May
Aleksandr	Seleznyev	SU 64	75.80	1		Bryansk	2 Jul
Lucio	Serrani	ITA 61	75.76	3	4–N	Torino	2 Jun
Igor	Kuprishenkov	SU 59	75.68	4		Poltava	30 Sep
Ari	Taavitsainen	FIN 58	75.62	1		Oslo	21 Jun
Viktor	Bobryshev	SU 57	75.48	2		Leningrad	25 Aug
Oleg	Dyatlov	SU 49	75.46	6		Adler	26 Feb
Ivan	Petkov	BUL 60	75.38	3		Sofia	25 Aug
Gian Maria	Zichichi	ITA 64	75.02	1		Palermo	8 Sep
Dave	McKenzie	USA 49	74.98	1	Pre	Eugene	21 Jul
Igor	Kucherenko	SU 60	74.94	2		Krasnodar	23 Sep
Sergey	Ishchenko	SU 54	74.88	1		Alushta	4 Apr
Sergey	Ivanov	SU 62	74.86	6		Adler	27 Apr
Vitaliy	Bychkov	SU 60	74.68	4		Kharkov	12 Aug
Vladimir	Dubinin	SU 63	74.64	2		Leningrad	7 Jul
Kjell	Bystedt	SWE 60	74.62	le2		Palo Alto	7 Apr
Dave	Smith	UK 62	74.62	4		Birmingham	15 Jul
Sandor	Fuzesi	HUN 59	74.62	1		Budapest	4 Aug
Jud	Logan	USA 59	74.56	1		Columbus	6 May
Ed	Burke	USA 40	74.34	2		Stanford	28 Apr
Maco	Gerloff	GDR 64	74.26	1		Potsdam	3 May
Igor	Lebedyev	SU 55	74.26	1		Moskva	20 Aug
Sergey	Koptilov	SU 60	74.06	2		Leningrad	3 Jun
Tore	Johnsen	NOR 61	73.86	1		Lillestrom	14 Jul
Marc	Odenthal	FRG 63	73.80	1		Leverkusen	19 May
Aleksey	Tsvetikov	SU 62	73.78	1		Cherepovets	20 May
Zdzislaw	Kwasny	POL 60	73.76	4	NC	Lublin	24 Jun
John	McArdle	USA 57	73.70	5		Walnut	15 Jul
Robert	Weir	UK 61	73.70	1		San Diego	30 Jul
Valentin	Chaliy	SU 58	73.70	Q		Donyetsk	7 Sep
Aleksandr	Kozlov	SU 52	73.66	7		Adler	27 Apr
Tibor	Gecsek	HUN 64	73.66	4	NC	Budapest	25 Jul
Vladimir	Styopochkin	SU 64	73.64	2		Irpinsk	12 May
Hannu	Polvi	FIN 48	73.64	3		Ylivieska	1 Jul
Ajet	Toska	ALB 61	73.62	1		Tirana	9 Aug
Sergey	Pyshkin	SU 55	73.38	2		Odessa	14 Apr
Fyodor	Makovskiy	SU 65	73.34	2		Volgograd	15 May
Lutz	Schafer	GDR 61	73.34	4		Berlin	16 May
Albert	Sinka	HUN 62	73.30	1		Budapest	12 Feb
Vidmantas	Sevinskas	SU 60	73.30	1		Klaipeda	19 Aug
Zdenek	Bednar	CS 57	73.10	2	GS	Ostrava	23 May

289

1984 Lists – Men

Burkhard	Sommerfeld	GDR 62	73.10	6	NC	Erfurt	3 Jun
Vladimir	Kuprovskiy	SU 57	73.08	3		Irpinsk	12 May
Plamen	Minev	BUL 65	73.08	2		Sofia	4 Jul
Giuliano	Zanello	ITA 63	73.06	3		Forli	19 May
Aleksandr	Silanchenko	SU 57	73.06	2		Moskva	15 Jul
Valentin	Doshev	BUL 63	73.02	4	Nar	Sofia	19 May
Tudor	Stan	RUM 53	73.02	1	NC	Bucuresti	11 Jul

Waclaw	Filek	POL 59	72.92	1 Sep	Georg	Markaryan	SU 62	71.48	2 Jun
Yevgeniy	Gribov	SU 62	72.86	12 Aug	Raul	Jimeno	SPA 59	71.42	1 Jul
Gennadiy	Vovk	SU 62	72.82	10 Aug	Srecko	Stiglic	YUG 43	71.36	21 Jun
Vladimir	Mishin	SU 62	72.80	31 Jan	Sergey	Botov	SU 61	71.34	27 Apr
Kleanthis	Ierissiotis	GRE 53	72.80*	20 Jun	Aleksandr	Fedorenko	SU 62	71.32	15 Jun
Vladimir	Glubokov	SU 64	72.80	22 Sep	Sergey	Alay	SU 65	71.26	14 Jul
Nicolae	Bindar	RUM 56	76.68	10 May	Karoly	Povaszon	HUN 60	71.16	20 May
Romeo	Budai	ITA 58	72.68	19 May	Ioannis	Maggos	GRE 61	71.16	22 Sep
Paul	Dickenson	UK 49	72.62	5 May	Tsvetan	Stoyanov	BUL 62	71.14	7 Jul
Jukka	Olkkonen	FIN 58	72.58	1 Jul	Jouni	Olkkonen	FIN 57	71.08	1 Jul
Oleg	Talanov	SU 57	72.56	2 Jun	Vyacheslav	Kuznyetsov	SU 59	71.00	7 Apr
Albert	Mehes	RUM 60	72.52	30 May	Hakim	Toumi	ALG 61	70.86	5 Jul
Andrey	Makarov	SU 62	72.42	20 May	Thomas	Grogorick	GDR 62	70.72	29 Apr
Donatas	Plunge	SU 60	72.34	4 Aug	Rainer	Schons	FRG 62	70.70	8 Sep
Aleksandr	Gurmazhenko	SU 57	72.20	10 May	Norbert	Radefeld	FRG 62	70.52	21 Jul
Yuriy	Pastukhov	SU 61	72.08	4 Jul	Chris	Black	UK 50	70.50	20 Jun
Jens	Geisensetter	GDR 64	72.06	17 May	Klaus	Streckenbach	GDR 60	70.50	12 Apr
Conor	McCullough	IRL 61	72.06	11 Jul	Valentin	Kirov	BUL 66	70.46	3 Aug
Aleksandr	Sinitsyn	SU 56	72.04	27 Jan	Gabor	Tamas	HUN 51	70.46	11 Aug
Kalman	Zeitler	HUN 50	71.88	25 Jul	Roman	Bychkin	SU 60	70.42	28 Jul
Vadim	Poklonov	SU 63	71.86	5 Aug	Gennadiy	Shalupenko	SU 58	70.30	15 Jun
Sandor	Voros	HUN 54	71.84	25 Jul	Philippe	Suriray	FRA 56	70.24	10 Jul
Michael	Beierl	AUT 63	71.80	10 Jun	Radomil	Skoumal	CS 55	70.18	2 Jun
Aleksandr	Zinchenko	SU 57	71.80	16 Jun	Al	Schoterman	USA 50	70.14*	6 May
Vasiliy	Vesselov	SU 61	71.72	5 Aug	Wolfgang	Heinrich	FRG 59	70.08	19 Sep
Nikolay	Lyssenko	SU 66	71.62	25 Aug	Mikko	Valimaki	FIN 61	70.02	4 May
Leszek	Kowalski	POL 61	71.58	24 Jun	Ken	Flax	USA 63	70.02	4 May
Andrey	Abduvaliyev	SU 66	71.54	8 Sep	Jari	Matinolli	FIN 65	70.02	9 Sep
Yuriy	Esayan	SU 56	71.50	11 Feb					
Aleksey	Afanasyev	SU 66	71.50	8 Sep					

* = Athlete subsequently disqualified for failing doping test.

Extra Trial
Mariusz   Tomaszewski   POL 56   81.04   –   Zabrze   1 Jul

Ancillary Marks

Sedykh	86.00	3 Jul	Sedykh	83.06	20 Aug
Sedykh	85.52	13 Jul	Sedykh	82.96	13 Jul
Sedykh	85.20	3 Jul	Sedykh	82.96	20 Aug
Sedykh	85.04	13 Jul	Litvinov	82.94	9 Jul
Litvinov	84.84	3 Jul	Sedykh	82.52	21 Jun
Sedykh	84.84	17 Aug	Litvinov	82.42	21 Jun
Sedykh	84.58	14 Sep	Litvinov	81.94	21 Jun
Sedykh	84.48	14 Sep	Litvinov	81.84	21 Jun
Sedykh	84.44	17 Aug	Tamm	81.84	20 Aug
Sedykh	84.18	3 Jul	Sedykh	81.82	21 Jun
Sedykh	83.90	31 Aug	Sedykh	81.80	21 Jun
Sedykh	83.88	17 Aug	Tamm	81.78	20 Jul
Sedykh	83.86	20 Aug	Sedykh	81.72	14 Sep
Sedykh	83.84	31 Aug	Sedykh	81.70	21 Jun
Litvinov	83.74	3 Jul	Tamm	81.70	20 Jul
Sedykh	83.52	20 Aug	Sedykh	81.66	21 Jun

1984 Lists – Men

Sedykh	83.50	31 Aug	Tamm	81.62	20 Jul
Sedykh	83.44	31 Aug	Litvinov	81.38	9 Jul
Litvinov	83.38	9 Jul	Tamm	81.28	20 Aug
Sedykh	83.38	17 Aug	Tamm	81.26	20 Jul
Litvinov	83.34	9 Jul	Nikulin	81.20	20 Aug
Sedykh	83.30	3 Jul	Nikulin	81.14	20 Aug
Sedykh	83.20	31 Aug	Tamm	81.02	20 Aug
Sedykh	83.10	17 Aug			

	1	10	20	30	50		100 75.00	Over 72.00
1980	81.80	77.96	76.02	75.08	73.08	69.98	23	56
1981	80.56	76.84	75.90	74.50	72.32	69.88	31	63
1982	83.98	77.92	76.60	75.90	74.56	71.62	43	94
1983	84.14	80.00	77.98	77.30	75.30	72.40	55	109
1984	86.34	80.50	79.06	77.94	76.34	73.06	64	122

JAVELIN THROW

Uwe	Hohn	GDR 62	104.80	1	OD	Berlin	20 Jul
	Hohn		99.52	1		Potsdam	25 May
	Hohn		97.12	1		Berlin	15 Jul
	Hohn		94.82	1		Jena	13 May
	Hohn		94.44	1	DRZ	Moskva	17 Aug
	Hohn		93.80	1	NC	Erfurt	2 Jun
Detlef	Michel	GDR 55	93.68	2	NC	Erfurt	2 Jun
Duncan	Atwood	USA 55	93.44	1	FOT	Los Angeles	18 Jun
Raimo	Manninen	FIN 55	93.42	1e1		Pihtipudas	1 Jul
	Hohn		93.16	1	BGP	Budapest	20 Aug
	Hohn		92.76	1	8-N	Tokyo	14 Sep
	Michel		92.48	2	OD	Berlin	20 Jul
Einar	Vilhjalmsson	ICE 60	92.42	1	TexR	Austin	6 Apr
Arto	Harkonen	FIN 59	92.40	2e1		Pihtipudas	1 Jul
Heino	Puuste	SU 55	91.86	1		Oulu	16 Jun
	Michel		91.80	1		Split	30 Apr
	Michel		91.38	2	BGP	Budapest	20 Aug
	Hohn		91.24	1		Dresden	26 Jul
Zdenek	Adamec	CS 56	91.12	1		Lille	27 Sep
	Michel		91.04	1		Rijeka	2 May
Klaus	Tafelmeier	FRG 58	91.04	1		Seoul	29 Sep
Viktor	Yevsyukov	SU 56	90.94	1		Moskva	6 Aug
Bob	Roggy	USA 56	90.80	3	BGP	Budapest	20 Aug
	Michel		90.78	2		Dresden	26 Jul
Rod	Ewaliko	USA 54	90.66	1		Goleta	25 Feb
	Yevsyukov		90.50	1	NC	Donyetsk	9 Sep
	Roggy		90.28	1	ISTAF	Berlin	17 Aug
	Manninen		90.26	1		Aanekoski	14 May
	Tafelmeier		90.10	1	NC	Dusseldorf	24 Jun
	Tafelmeier		90.10	1	WG	Helsinki	4 Jul

(30/12)

Gerald	Weiss	GDR 60	90.06	1		Sofia	17 Jun
Tom	Petranoff	USA 58	89.50	1	Pepsi	Los Angeles (Ww)	13 May
Brian	Crouser	USA 62	89.20	1		Eugene	13 Jul
Dainis	Kula	SU 59	88.80	1		Adler	25 Feb
Reidar	Lorentzen	NOR 56	88.46	1		Larvik	18 Jul
Roald	Bradstock	UK 62	88.26	1		Arlington	5 May
Stanislaw	Gorak	POL 59	88.10	1		Praha	28 Aug

1984 Lists – Men

Zakayo	Malekwa	TAN 51	87.68	1		Plainview,Tex	20 Apr	
Joachim	Lange	GDR 60	87.42	2		Rijeka	2 May	
Tapio	Korjus	FIN 61	87.24	1		Mantta	29 Jul	
Yuriy	Smirnov	SU 61	87.10	2	NC	Donyetsk	9 Sep	
Kenth	Eldebrink	SWE 55	87.08	1		Vasteras	26 Jun	
Jorma	Markus	FIN 52	86.90	1		Karjaa	3 Jun	
Laslo	Babits	CAN 58	86.90	2		Koln	26 Aug	
Ramon	Gonzalez	CUB 65	86.82	1		Habana	27 Jan	
Tero	Saviniemi	FIN 63	86.78	1	NC	Kajaani	8 Jul	
Ray	Hansen	USA 61	86.26	1		Norman	27 Apr	
Matti	Kiilunen	FIN 62	86.20	1		Ahtari	17 Jun	
Sergey	Gavras	SU 57	86.18	2		Sochi	20 May	
Peter	Yates	UK 57	85.92	1		Wolverhampton	12 May	
Zbigniew	Bednarski	POL 60	85.88	1		Poznan	5 May	
Nicu	Roata	RUM 61	85.86	1		Bucuresti	2 Jun	
David	Ottley	UK 55	85.86	1	OT	Gateshead	10 Jun	
Kari	Ihalainen	FIN 54	85.84	2		Aanekoski	30 Sep	
Wolfram	Gambke	FRG 59	85.80	1	vCS,POL,FRA	Hannover	15 Jun	
Vladislav	Korolyov	SU 60	85.80	3	NC	Donyetsk	9 Sep	
Agostino	Ghesini	ITA 58	85.68	1		Caorle	15 Jul	
Masami	Yoshida	JAP 58	85.52	1	NC	Tokyo	20 Oct	
Vladimir	Furdylo	SU 58	85.42	1		Ventspils	30 Sep	
Stanislaw	Witek	POL 60	85.10	1		Bialogard	22 Sep	
Jean-Paul	Lakafia	FRA 61	85.08	1	NC	Villeneuve D'Ascq	1 Jul	
Steve	Pearson	UK 59	84.96	1		Hong Kong	27 Oct	
Janis	Zirnis	SU 47	84.84	1		Klaipeda	26 May	
Matti	Korte	FIN 56	84.80	1		Lieto	10 Jun	
Kauko	Koivuniemi	FIN 59	84.78	1		Kauhajoki	20 Jun	
Per Erling	Olsen	NOR 58	84.76	1	NC	Ovre Ardal	24 Aug	
Yuriy	Novikov	SU 58	84.72	1		Sochi	28 Apr	
Reinaldo	Patterson	CUB 56	84.64	1		Habana	9 Jul	
Dumitru	Negoita	RUM 60	84.58	2	Malin	Grudziadz	29 May	
Curt	Ransford	USA 57	84.40	1	TAC	San Jose	9 Jun	
Zhao	Ming	CHN 63	84.38	2		Hong Kong	27 Oct	
Tamas	Bolgar	HUN 55	84.32	1		Szeged	29 Sep	
Thomas	Paetow	GDR 63	84.00	2		Sofia	17 Jun	
Steve	Roller	USA 54	83.94	1		Fresno	7 Apr	
Jyrki	Blom	FIN 62	83.94	2		Lahti	21 Aug	
Martin	Alvarez	CUB 60	83.80	3		Habana	9 Feb	
Leif	Lundmark	SWE 53	83.76	1		Ostersund	11 Jul	
Sead	Krdzalic	YUG 60	83.70	1	vGRE	Zagreb	20 Jun	
Hannu	Holopainen	FIN 58	83.66	1		Juuka	10 Jun	
Narve	Hoff	NOR 57	83.64	1		Liabygda	25 Sep	
Andras	Temesi	HUN 50	83.62	5	BGP	Budapest	20 Aug	
Antonios	Papadimitriou	GRE 65	83.56	2	vSWE,NOR	Malmo	17 Jun	
Charlus-Mi.	Bertimon	FRA 57	83.50	1		Nicosia	15 Sep	
Chris	de Beer	RSA 61	83.44	1		Port Elizabeth	10 Dec	
Aimo	Aho	FIN 51	83.38	3		Valkeakoski	5 Jun	
Mike	Barnett	USA 61	83.34	3	DNG	Stockholm	2 Jul	
Marek	Kaleta	SU 61	83.30	1		Kiev	4 Jul	
Mike	Mahovlich	CAN 60	83.22	2		Seattle	24 Mar	
Tom	Jadwin	USA 58	83.20	1		Sacramento	21 Jul	
John	Stapylton-Smith	NZ 61	83.10	1		Christchurch	15 Dec	
Viktor	Bochin	SU 60	83.08	4		Moskva	20 Jul	
Urpo	Pollari	FIN 53	82.82	1		Alavus	3 Jun	
Sigurdur	Einarsson	ICE 62	82.76	1		Tallahasee	17 Mar	
Kazuhiro	Mizoguchi	JAP 61	82.74	1		Walnut	25 Jul	
Mark	Anderson	USA 58	82.68	1		Los Angeles (Ww)	15 Apr	
Thomas	Schaffner	GDR 63	82.68	3		Jena	13 May	
Seppo	Raty	FIN 62	82.60	1		Joensuu	12 Jul	
Perry	Puccetti	USA 61	82.52	1		Colorado Springs	5 Jun	
Werner	Kalb	FRG 60	82.50	3		Munster	20 May	

1984 Lists – Men

First	Last	Nation/Club	Mark			City	Date
Paul	Kulak	USA 59	82.48	1		Northridge	12 Feb
Juan	de la Garza	MEX 61	82.44	1		Mexico City	30 Jun
Raicho	Dimitrov	BUL 55	82.42	1		Sofia	6 May
Dag	Wennlund	SWE 63	82.34	2		Vasteras	26 Jun
Burkhardt	Looks	GDR 58	82.26	4		Celje	5 May
Herman	Potgieter	RSA 53	82.22	1		Potchefstroom	8 Feb
Olavi	Kohlemainen	SWE 57	82.20	1		Stockholm	26 May
Bernard	Werner	POL 51	82.20	1		Slupsk	26 Aug
Aleksey	Gritskevich	SU 62	82.18	3		Adler	25 Feb
Vladimir	Pinchuk	SU 54	82.16	1		Vitebsk	16 Jul
Jan-Olov	Johansson	SWE 62	82.10	2		Seattle	21 Apr
Jorgen	Jelstrom	DEN 63	82.04	1		Lyngby	22 Jul
Steve	Kreider	USA 58	82.02	3	MSR	Walnut	29 Apr
Peter	Blank	FRG 62	81.98	6	vFIN	Aachen	30 May
Yuriy	Zhirov	SU 60	81.94	2		Gorkiy	12 Aug
Vasiliy	Yershov	SU 49	81.86	4		Sochi	20 May
Jorg	Murawa	GDR 64	81.84	4	OD	Berlin	20 Jul
Andris	Keiss	SU 58	81.74	1		Valmiera	28 Jul
Helmut	Schreiber	FRG 55	81.52	1		Waiblingen	2 Jun
Uwe	Trinks	GDR 62	81.44	4		Potsdam	25 May
Vladimir	Gavrilyuk	SU 60	81.42	1		Kiev	23 Aug
Vladimir	Shopin	SU 63	81.40	2		Gorkiy	12 Aug
Bob	Rockett	USA 64	81.38	2		Seattle	3 Mar
Jason	Bender	USA 60	81.38	6	FOT	Los Angeles	18 Jun
Antero	Toivonen	FIN 48	81.38	1		Lahti	30 Jun
Ivan	Gromov	SU 56	81.36			Krasnodar	30 Jan
Olavi	Malts	SU 59	81.36	1		Tartu	1 Aug
Peter	Borglund	SWE 64	81.34	2		Baton Rouge	13 Apr
Aleksandr	Zaytsev	SU 57	81.30	4		Adler	25 Feb
Mickey	Cutler	USA 59	81.20	4	TAC	San Jose	9 Jun
Miroslaw	Szybowski	POL 60	81.18	1		Sopot	29 Jul
Nikolay	Kalitukha	SU 58	80.96				25 Feb
Michal	Waclawik	POL 54	80.76				29 May
Juha	Hentunen	FIN 60	80.68				1 Jul
Pubu	Ciren	CHN 56	80.66				6 Jun
John	Amabile	USA 62	80.64				3 Mar
Vladimir	Konovalov	SU 55	80.56				14 Jul
Emil	Tsvetanov	BUL 63	80.54				20 May
Mikko	Hannula	FIN 63	80.50				8 Jul
Josef	Schaffarzik	FRG 55	80.44				1 Sep
Vladimir	Polishko	SU 59	80.40				25 Feb
Stasis	Toleikis	SU 58	80.38				6 Jul
Jan	Kolar	CS 57	80.34				2 Jun
Marcus	Humphries	UK 61	80.34				16 Sep
Ivan	Angelov	BUL 59	80.32				10 Jul
Jan	Zelezny	CS 66	80.32				8 Sep
Jiri	Cettl	SWZ 58	80.26				8 Jul
Stanislaw	Zabinski	POL 54	80.24				28 Aug
Matti	Napari	FIN 58	80.10				22 Aug
Bengt	Gustafsson	SWE 50	80.08				31 May
Masaji	Okada	JAP 61	80.08				2 Jun
Nikolay	Kosyanok	SU 58	80.04				14 Jun
Andrey	Chizov	SU 64	80.02				14 Jul
Arto	Manninen	FIN 62	80.00				7 Jul
Jukka	Miettinen	FIN 54	79.96				8 Jul
Jouni	Seppala	FIN 61	79.94				14 Jun
Jukka	Kunnas	FIN 63	79.86				26 Jul
Shawn	Denton	USA 63	79.82				21 Apr
Vladimir	Tretyakov	SU 62	79.74				12 Aug
Dariusz	Adamus	POL 57	79.72				20 May
Dave	Stephens	USA	79.70				26 May
Oleg	Pakhol	SU 64	79.64				25 Feb
Yuriy	Subbotin	SU 56	79.64				12 Aug
Sergey	Glebov	SU 64	79.64				29 Sep
Seppo	Valla	FIN 57	79.60				15 Sep
Marcis	Strobinders	SU 66	79.60				30 Sep
Vladimir	Grinchenko	SU 65	79.52				12 May
Konstantin	Azhemshev	SU 64	79.52				23 Jun
Simon	Osborne	UK 55	79.36				2 Jun
Vladimir	Ivanov	SU	79.36				9 Jun
Thomas	Lindell	SWE 57	79.34				14 Aug
Kari	Uitto	FIN 61	79.32				26 May
John	Ward	USA 61	79.30				20 May
Bobby	George	USA 61	79.28				18 May
Peter	Schreiber	FRG 64	79.26				7 Oct
Tudorel	Pirvu	RUM 55	79.24				9 Sep
Paul	Dubyoski	USA 56	79.16				13 May
Jari	Montonen	FIN 65	79.16				12 Aug
Istvan	Csider	HUN 64	79.14				25 Jul
Barry	Darling	CAN 58	79.04				22 Aug
Czeslaw	Uhl	POL 58	79.00				2 Sep
Gary	England	USA 54	78.90				16 May
Alfred	Grossenbacher	SWZ 59	78.90				8 Sep
Soren	Tallhem	SWE 64	78.86				7 Apr
Aleksey	Titov	SU 61	78.82				29 Sep
Oytsein	Slettevold	NOR 62	78.76				24 Aug
Milan	Sobotka	CS 61	78.74				22 Jul
Chuck	Greene	USA	78.68				12 May

1984 Lists – Men

Pentti	Sinersaari	FIN 56	78.68	1 Jul	Andrey	Maznichenko	SU 66	78.38		
Ole Jorgen	Simonsen	NOR 63	78.68	21 Sep	Gerald	Lyons	USA 60	78.34	21 Apr	
Octavian	Sandru	RUM 56	78.64	16 Jun	Yuriy	Kopylov	SU 56	78.34	12 Aug	
Nikolay	Gervasov	SU 64	78.64	12 Aug	Jim	Connolly	USA 63	78.28	2 Jun	
Ji	Zhangzheng	CHN 63	78.60	30 Mar	Oleg	Litvinov	SU 65	78.26	1 Jun	
Paul	de Roo	BEL 59	78.60	27 May	Fabiano	Fakataulavelua	FRA 62	78.26	1 Jul	
Mahour	Bacha	ALG 61	78.60	4 Jul	Thierry	Prevel	FRA 61	78.24	13 May	
Ilpo	Poutiainen	FIN 64	78.58	22 Jul	Rob	Curtis	USA 62	78.24	13 May	
Dan	Barton	USA 60	78.52	12 May	Dave	Dixon	AUS 65	78.22	14 Mar	
Arto	Helminen	FIN 59	78.50	14 May	Ken	Asakura	JAP 61	78.22	16 Oct	
Igor	Avdeyev	SU 63	78.48	22 May	Jeff	Field	USA 62	78.20	13 May	
Toralf	Herbst	GDR 63	78.46	30 May	Lutz	Obelgonner	FRG 63	78.10	3 Jun	
German	Gulbit	SU 55	78.44	6 Aug	Bobby	Lohse	SWE 58	78.00	9 Jun	

Ancillary Marks at 90.10 or better

Hohn	96.96	15 Jul	Hohn	92.12	2 Jun
Hohn	93.48	13 May	Michel	91.84	2 Jun
Hohn	93.22	17 Aug	Hohn	91.42	17 Aug
Hohn	93.14	25 May	Michel	90.70	20 Jul
Michel	93.68	2 Jun	Hohn	90.56	2 Jun
Michel	92.20	20 Jul	Tafelmeier	90.10	29 Sep

	1	10	20	30	50	100	Over 85.00	Over 80.00
1980	96.72	89.46	87.90	85.80	84.32	80.68	41	107
1981	92.48	89.48	88.02	86.56	83.66	80.24	39	107
1982	95.80	88.40	86.78	85.82	84.00	80.48	41	108
1983	99.72	90.58	87.80	86.16	84.56	81.14	42	125
1984	104.80	90.94	87.68	86.20	84.60	81.52	42	135

DECATHLON

w = Wind aided, between 2 and 4 metres per second.
# = Wind aided, in excess of 4 metres per second
* = Automatic timing in 100m and 400m

Date shown is second day of performance
(1985 Tables Scores in parentheses)

8798 (8832) Jurgen Hingsen FRG 58 1 Mannheim 9 Jun
(10.70w 7.76 16.42 2.07 48.05 14.07 49.36 4.90 59.86 4:19.75)
8798 (8847) Daley Thompson UK 58 1 OG Los Angeles 9 Aug
(10.44 8.01 15.72 2.03 46.97 14.34 46.56 5.00 65.24 4:35.00)
8704 (8792) Uwe Freimuth GDR 61 1 OD Potsdam 21 Jul
(11.06 7.79 16.30 2.03 48.43 14.66 46.58 5.15 72.42 4:25.19)
8673 (8695) Hingsen 2 OG Los Angeles 9 Aug
(10.91 7.80 15.87 2.12 47.69 14.29 50.82 4.50 60.44 4:22.60)
8652 (8698) Grigoriy Degtyaryev SU 58 1 NC Kiev 22 Jun
(10.87 7.42 16.03 2.10 49.75 14.53 51.20 4.90 67.08 4:23.09)
8642 (8709) Aleksandr Apaychev SU 61 1. vGDR Neubranden. 3 Jun
(10.96 7.57 16.00 1.97 48.72 13.93 48.00 4.90 72.24 4:26.51)
8579 (8617) Degtyaryev 1 Gotzis 20 May
(11.05 7.73 16.14 2.08 49.76 14.45 49.40 4.90 60.70 4:20.49)
8560 (8592) Apaychev 1 Kiev 6 May
(10.97 7.61 15.91 1.95 48.40 14.11 45.08 4.80 68.88 4:18.70)
8553 (8616) Freimuth 2 vSU Neubranden. 3 Jun
(11.10 7.79 16.42 1.94 48.93 14.54w 51.54 4.90 66.32 4:27.95)

294

1984 Lists – Men

Score	(prev)	Name	Event	Pos	Club	City	Date
8542	(8597)	Freimuth		1		Potsdam	6 May
(11.06 7.69w 16.06 1.97 48.78 14.75 47.54 4.80 73.02 4:24.46)
8535	(8543)	Torsten Voss	GDR 63	2		Potsdam	6 May
(10.56 7.73 14.56 2.09 47.50 14.84 42.60 5.00 59.92 4:25.68)
8530	(8547)	Igor Sobolevskiy	SU 62	2	NC	Kiev	22 Jun
(10.64 7.71 15.93 2.01 48.24 14.82 50.54 4.40 67.40 4:32.84)
8523	(8572)	Degtyaryev		1	DRZ	Moskva	18 Aug
(10.99 7.58 15.54 2.09 50.29 14.60 49.20 5.10 63.20 4:27.14)
8512	(8519)	Yuriy Kutsenko	SU 52	3	NC	Kiev	22 Jun
(11.07 7.54 15.11 2.13 49.07 14.94 50.38 4.60 61.70 4:12.68)
8505	(8513)	Voss		3	vSU	Neubranden.	3 Jun
(10.62 7.70 15.10 2.09 48.24 14.50w 44.74 4.80 61.42 4:33.79)
8482	(8497)	Siegfried Wentz	FRG 60	2		Mannheim	9 Jun
(10.85w 7.26 14.96 1.98 47.59 14.09 43.94 4.80 69.58 4:23.84)
8476	(8491)	Aleksandr Nevskiy	SU 58	2		Gotzis	20 May
(10.97 7.24 15.04 2.08 48.44 14.67 46.06 4.70 69.56 4:19.62)
8450	(8482)	Voss		2	DRZ	Moskva	18 Aug
(10.59 8.02 15.39 2.06 48.06 14.44 42.34 5.10 58.22 4:52.96)
8444	(8437)	Voss		2	OD	Potsdam	21 Jul
(10.54 7.74 15.19 2.06 47.86 14.32 42.58 4.80 57.04 4:35.84)
8433	(8456)	Sobolevskiy		3	DRZ	Moskva	18 Aug
(10.67 7.98 16.07 2.00 48.34 15.08 46.46 4.70 64.86 4:45.58)
8428	(8435)	Voss		1		Talence	16 Sep
(10.57 7.78 15.30 2.07 48.58 14.09 43.32 4.90 56.72 4:44.92)
8420	(8429)	Guido Kratschmer	FRG 53	3		Mannheim	9 Jun
(10.63w 7.15 16.67 1.98 49.07 14.15 46.48 4.80 67.52 4:45.75)
8412	(8416)	Wentz		3	OG	Los Angeles	9 Aug
(10.99 7.11 15.87 2.09 47.78 14.35 46.60 4.50 67.68 4:33.96)
8401	(8408)	Wentz		3		Gotzis	20 May
(10.99 7.45 14.78 2.08 47.68 14.16 43.76 4.50 66.50 4:28.71)
8376	(8417)	Sergey Zhelanov	SU 57	4	NC	Kiev	22 Jun
(11.04 7.50 14.31 2.13 48.94 14.40 43.44 5.00 65.90 4:37.24)
8356	(8375)	Nevskiy		4	DRZ	Moskva	18 Aug
(11.01 7.46 15.57 2.03 50.06 14.90 46.98 4.70 68.32 4:25.98)
8337	(8356)	Viktor Gruzenkin	SU 51	5	NC	Kiev	22 Jun
(10.92 7.67 15.98 2.07 50.06 14.65 46.70 4.60 65.74 4:43.00)
8327	(8363)	Konstantin Akhapkin	SU 56	4	vGDR	Neubranden.	3 Jun
(11.18 7.66 15.84 1.91 50.37 14.48 50.22 5.00 60.60 4:27.70)
8326	(8357)	Kratschmer		4	OG	Los Angeles	9 Aug
(10.80 7.40 15.93 1.94 49.25 14.66 47.28 4.90 69.40 4:47.99)
8302	(8255)	Jens Schulze	FRG 56	4		Mannheim	9 Jun
(10.56w 7.33 15.00 2.01 48.58 14.44w 45.32 4.60 53.70 4:22.95)
(30/15)
8266	(8278)	William Motti	FRA 64	5	OG	Los Angeles	9 Aug
(11.28 7.45 14.42 2.06 48.13 14.71 50.92 4.50 63.76 4:35.15)
8242	(8248)	Dave Steen	CAN 1			Los Angeles	24 May
(11.10 7.39 12.92 2.05 47.96 15.09 42.88 5.00 62.84 4:17.83)
8233	(8207)	Pavel Tarnavetskiy	SU 61	7	NC	Kiev	22 Jun
(11.03 7.19 15.12 1.95 48.49 14.60 48.18 4.70 56.96 4:20.19)
8227	(8205)	Rob Muzzio	USA 64	1	NCAA	Eugene	29 May
(10.90 7.02w 16.67 2.00 49.64 14.65 50.80 4.60 57.84 4:36.35)
8212	(8181)	Hans-Ullrich Riecke	GDR 63	4	OD	Potsdam	21 Jul
(10.66 7.63 14.45 1.97 48.46 15.02 44.62 4.60 57.44 4:27.41)
8201	(8217)	Sergey Popov	SU 57	2		Kiev	6 May
(11.50 7.27 14.64 2.01 50.30 15.12 49.60 4.80 66.78 4:19.0)
8186	(8172)	Steffen Grummt	GDR 59	6	vSU	Neubranden.	3 Jun
(11.18 7.34 16.81 1.91 49.46 14.37w 46.50 4.40 62.20 4:27.04)
8132	(8176)	Sven Reintak	SU 63	1		Tartu	3 Jun
(11.39 7.23 13.18 2.05 50.90 14.54 45.26 5.10 67.90 4:28.71)
8132	(8097)	Trond Skramstad	NOR 60	1		Emmitsburg	11 Jun
(10.94 7.33 14.62 2.00 49.22 14.52 41.12 4.50 61.08 4:21.51)
8130	(8115)	John Crist	USA 64	6	OG	Los Angeles	9 Aug
(11.33 6.98w 14.05 2.06 48.45 15.01 46.18 4.80 61.88 4:23.78)
8121	(8107)	Vadim Podmaryov	SU 58	4		Gotzis	20 May
(11.14 7.66 15.11 2.11 50.23 14.87 47.38 4.40 56.06 4:36.14)

1984 Lists – Men

8098	(8106)	Tim	Bright	USA 60	2	FOT	Los Angeles	22 Jun
(11.00 6.81 13.59 2.06 48.93 14.21 43.50 5.30 56.06 4:39.69)								
8091	(8054)	Jim	Wooding	USA 54	7	OG	Los Angeles	9 Aug
(11.04 7.01 13.90 1.97 47.62 14.57 47.38 4.60 57.20 4:28.31)								
8075	(8069)	Yevgeniy	Ovsyannikov	SU 63	9		Neubranden.	3 Jun
(11.23 7.43 14.39 2.06 50.03 15.05 46.34 4.90 56.16 4:33.82)								
8067*	(8004)	Fred	Dixon	USA 49	1	MSR	Walnut	27 Apr
(10.88 7.27 14.52 1.95 48.43 14.8 45.48 4.70 57.26 4:37.8)								
8065	(8064)	Igor	Kolovanov	SU 58	8	NC	Kiev	22 Jun
(11.14 7.47 14.30 2.01 50.68 14.49 47.90 4.80 57.40 4:40.75)								
8061	(8083)	Georg	Werthner	AUT 56	1	NC	Innsbruck	8 Jul
(11.16 7.04 14.03 1.99 48.91 14.99 37.54 4.80 75.48 4:28.07)								
8053	(8020)	Hans-Joachim	Haberle	FRG 59	6		Gotzis	20 May
(11.05 7.24w 14.34 1.90 47.86 15.25 43.10 4.30 67.14 4:18.22)								
8053	(8036)	Christian	Plaziat	GDR 65	5	OD	Potsdam	21 Jul
(11.54 7.18 14.26 2.16 49.23 15.06 44.74 4.20 65.98 4:24.11)								
8051	(8018)	Janusz	Lesniewicz	POL 55	1		Zabrze	14 Sep
(11.09 7.12 13.52 2.10 48.36 15.01 44.22 4.60 58.24 4:29.31)								
8045	(7972)	Ulf	Behrendt	GDR 62	4		Potsdam	6 May
(10.92 7.05w 15.88 1.97 47.55 15.36 44.54 4.20 56.98 4:23.61)								
8042	(8000)	Fritz	Mehl	FRG 55	7		Gotzis	20 May
(11.21 7.33w 14.67 1.96 48.38 14.90 43.82 4.10 63.02 4:16.81)								
8036	(8015)	Stephan	Niklaus	SWZ 58	8		Gotzis	20 May
(10.96 7.13 15.00 2.02 49.00 15.17 46.58 4.20 69.94 4:46.89)								
8018	(7998)	Orville	Peterson	USA 61	1		Raleigh	2 Jun
(10.96 7.31 13.55 2.02 49.89 14.52 44.64 4.40 64.70 4:38.5)								
8017	(7987)	Wojciech	Podsiadlo	POL 58	1	NC	Lublin	23 Jun
(11.28 7.09w 14.65 2.10 50.41 14.70 45.06 4.50 58.96 4:28.17)								
8017	(7974)	Viktor	Gartung	SU 60	1		Kiev	5 Jul
(10.75 7.40 14.82 1.99 48.93 15.66 40.94 4.60 61.70 4:36.85)								
8009	(7958)	Herbert	Peter	FRG 57	5		Mannheim	9 Jun
(11.22w 6.88 13.23 1.95 48.61 15.15w 42.72 4.50 65.28 4:05.50)								
7995	(7987)	Mike	Ramos	USA 62	4	FOT	Los Angeles	22 Jun
(11.08 7.02 13.98 2.09 50.89 15.01 45.70 4.70 66.52 4:44.21)								
7979	(7961)	Marek	Kubiszewski	POL 55	1		Sopot	15 Jul
(11.16 6.76 15.62 2.01 49.78 14.59 46.32 4.30 69.20 4:46.49)								
7978	(7997)	Viktor	Vashchenko	SU 58	11		Kiev	22 Jun
(11.29 7.17 15.25 1.85 51.25 15.36 50.34 4.40 74.76 4:31.36)								
7975	(7922)	Brad	McStravick	UK 56	1	NC	Cwmbran	28 May
(10.63w 7.05# 13.53 1.87 49.64 14.62w 44.80 4.40 61.52 4:24.35)								
7960	(7948)	Mike	Gonzales	USA 64	5	FOT	Los Angeles	22 Jun
(11.43 7.07 13.76 2.09 50.92 14.67 47.06 4.30 66.12 4:29.83)								
7949	(7941)	Mikhail	Romanyuk	SU 62	12	NC	Kiev	22 Jun
(11.34 7.05 14.44 1.85 49.98 14.58 44.06 4.90 62.00 4:23.08)								
7947	(7932)	Vladimir	Shmakov	SU 58	13	NC	Kiev	22 Jun
(11.16 7.27 13.98 2.07 51.40 14.96 48.78 4.90 53.94 4:43.69)								
7945	(7910)	Aleksandr	Areshin	SU 61	11	vGDR	Neubranden.	3 Jun
(10.95 7.78 14.00 1.94 48.93 14.42 41.04 4.20 55.78 4:31.36)								
7943	(7946)	Nikolay	Poptsov	SU 57	14	NC	Kiev	22 Jun
(11.39 7.07 15.54 2.07 51.72 14.76 45.10 5.00 60.66 4:52.16)								
7924	(7855)	Michele	Rufenacht	SWZ 59	10	OG	Los Angeles	9 Aug
(10.72 6.96 13.86 2.00 48.63 14.57 45.30 4.30 55.10 4:39.47)								
7922	(7899)	Michael	Neugebauer	FRG 62	3		Talence	16 Sep
(11.24 7.40 12.78 2.10 49.31 14.15 42.84 4.20 60.00 4:37.46)								
7918	(7869)	Valeriy	Kachanov	SU 54	2		Baku	15 Sep
(11.34w 7.19 14.72 2.06 49.58 15.20w 46.16 4.40 55.44 4:30.26)								
7891	(7884)	Lane	Maestretti	USA 59	1		S.Barbara	15 Apr
(11.41 7.01 13.70 1.97 51.43 15.55 48.20 5.10 60.22 4:27.4)								
7891	(7891)	John	Sayre	USA 61	2	NCAA	Eugene	29 May
(11.12 7.00w 13.25 2.00 49.88 14.90w 43.32 5.10 62.38 4:48.25)								
7884	(7831)	Colin	Boreham	UK 54	2	NC	Cwmbran	28 May
(11.24w 7.17# 13.99 2.02 50.28 14.59w 44.92 4.20 56.98 4:23.80)								
7881	(7852)	Andrzej	Wyzykowski	POL 60	3		Zabrze	14 Sep
(11.06 6.71 14.11 1.98 49.25 14.75 48.04 4.40 66.86 4:52.00)								

1984 Lists – Men

7877	(7842)	Conny	Silfver	SWE 57	1	TexR	Austin	5 Apr
(11.24 6.89 15.83 1.91 50.70 15.07 48.94 4.55 59.60 4:36.41)								
7864	(7827)	Patrick	Vetterli	SWZ 61	2	NC	Winterthur	23 Jun
(11.19w 7.09w 14.57 2.04 49.52 15.21 47.70 4.30 62.96 4:52.77)								
7855	(7824)	Adam	Baginski	POL 59	8		Mannheim	9 Jun
(11.30 7.02 13.65 2.01 49.83 14.98 46.56 4.80 55.40 4:36.83)								
7845	(7852)	Aleksey	Lyakh	SU 62	15	NC	Kiev	22 Jun
(11.43 7.06 14.73 1.95 50.34 15.03 41.60 5.10 64.68 4:47.24)								
7844	(7827)	Igor	Maryin	SU 65	1		Frunze	9 Sep
(11.30 7.25 13.55 2.04 50.65 15.21 43.70 4.70 62.92 4:42.05)								
7840	(7769)	Andrey	Fomochkin	SU 63	2		Kiev	5 Jul
(10.66 7.25 12.52 1.99 48.12 15.05 42.58 4.30 54.64 4:36.52)								
7837	(7812)	Greg	Culp	USA 60	2		C.Girardeau	22 May
(11.07 7.04 13.59 2.03 51.10 14.31 39.50 4.90 57.14 4:39.92)								
	(7776)	Holger	Schmidt	FRG 57	9		Gotzis	20 May
(10.98 7.25 15.03 1.99 49.99 14.83 46.42 4.20 59.46 4:58.77)								
7829	(7790)	Tsetsko	Mitrakyev	BUL 56	1	NC	Sofia	16 Jun
(11.34 7.03 14.28 2.03 50.39 14.78 43.44 4.70 55.98 4:36.56)								
7829	(7790)	Patrick	Gellens	FRA 59	1	vUK,BEL	Dombasle	19 Aug
(10.96 7.15 13.05 2.07 48.71 15.53 39.24 4.90 52.84 4:35.40)								
7823	(7802)	Atanas	Andonov	BUL 55	2	NC	Sofia	16 Jun
(11.47 6.85 16.08 2.06 52.64 14.93 48.36 4.60 63.26 4:56.09)								
7788	(7730)	Ion	Buliga	RUM 63	1	NC	Bucuresti	12 Jul
(11.30 6.77 13.47 2.14 49.19 15.56 43.08 4.40 57.68 4:29.30)								
7785	(7718)	Mike	Brown	USA 57	2		S.Barbara	15 Apr
(10.93 7.10 13.80 2.09 49.39 14.89 40.40 4.40 51.10 4:39.1)								
7783	(7769)	Siegfried	Stark	GDR 55	5		Potsdam	6 May
(11.57 6.90 14.69 1.91 49.48 15.43 48.22 5.00 59.56 4:47.20)								
7781	(7716)	Ivan	Babiy	SU 63	4		Kiev	6 May
(11.01 7.07 13.05 2.01 48.74 14.50 37.80 4.60 46.08 4:18.86)								
7777	(7717)	Shannon	Sullivan	USA 59	1		Tucson	12 Mar
(11.05 6.77w 15.22 1.95 49.51 15.30 43.42 4.70 55.32 4:41.02)								
7768	(7728)	Tom	Harris	USA 57	6	FOT	Los Angeles	22 Jun
(11.32 7.19 12.86 2.00 49.18 14.87 40.74 4.10 63.68 4:24.66)								
7767	(7745)	Steve	Erickson	USA 61	7	FOT	Los Angeles	22 Jun
(11.54 6.76 13.79 1.97 50.14 15.24 44.84 4.60 67.18 4:33.13)								
7763	(7708)	Fidelis	Obikwu	UK 60	3	NC	Cwmbran	28 May
(11.40w 6.95w 14.42 2.02 50.54 15.99w 42.10 4.60 61.12 4:24.65)								
7762	(7738)	Jay	Novacek	USA 62	4	NCAA	Eugene	29 May
(11.21 6.72w 14.88 1.88 51.06 15.07w 45.58 5.00 59.72 4:42.00)								
7760	(7718)	Ilyas	Abdulin	SU 58	3		Baku	15 Sep
(11.30 6.71 14.30 2.00 50.11 15.66w 43.58 4.40 67.42 4:32.89)								
7751	(7704)	Frederic	Sacco	FRA 61	1	NC	Lons-le-Sau.	24 Jun
(11.29 7.27 15.28 1.92 50.29 15.40 42.08 4.30 62.68 4:36.78)								
7746	(7710)	Jim	Connolly	USA 63	8	FOT	Los Angeles	22 Jun
(11.15 6.81 15.08 2.00 49.07 15.38 34.68 4.50 67.04 4:37.98)								
7721	(7651)	Lee	Palles	GRE/USA 56	9	FOT	Los Angeles	22 Jun
(11.18 6.98 14.42 2.03 51.13 14.96 47.54 4.30 49.54 4:34.38)								
7718	(7691)	Gary	Gefre	USA 57	2		Tucson	12 Mar
(11.14 6.87w 15.12 1.85 49.79 15.46 48.58 3.80 72.10 4:41.96)								
7718	(7607)	Eugene	Gilkes	UK 62	4	NC	Cwmbran	28 May
(10.64w 6.58w 13.81 1.84 47.80 15.39w 43.28 4.10 52.38 4:14.71)								
7717	(7684)	Jean-Bernard	Royer	FRA 62	2	vUK,BEL	Dombasle	19 Aug
(11.07 7.02 12.68 2.04 49.19 14.82 43.00 4.60 62.88 5:08.34)								
7715	(7655)	Ivan	Sidorov	SU 62	6		Kiev	6 May
(11.37 7.31 14.20 1.98 49.41 15.25 43.76 4.40 50.84 4:32.90)								
7709	(7630)	Staffan	Blomstrand	SWE 60	1		Tallahassee	28 Apr
(10.93 6.59 14.21 1.90 48.30 16.49 48.42 4.16 64.34 4:36.2)								
7708	(7630)	Rolf	Muller	FRG 61	9		Mannheim	Jun
(10.76w 7.03 13.31 1.95 49.68 14.81 40.82 4.50 49.18 4:32.05)								
7708	(7658)	Jens	Petersson	GDR 64	6	OD	Potsdam	21 Jul
(11.13 7.63 14.27 1.97 48.98 14.92 40.24 4.30 53.48 4:52.15)								
7701	(7665)	Wes	Herbst	USA 56	3		Tucson	12 Mar
(11.38 7.02 15.94 1.95 53.52 15.71 49.58 4.40 64.46 4:46.72)								
7701	(7645)	Wolfgang	Muders	FRG 57	9		Talence	16 Sep
(11.28 6.80 14.83 1.98 50.68 14.43 43.62 4.60 53.20 4:45.29)								

297

1984 Lists – Men

7694	(7667)	Alain	Blondel	FRA 62	16 Sep
7692	(7643)	Peter	Hadfield	AUS 55	15 Apr
7691	(7676)	Gary	Kinder	USA 62	2 Mar
7691	(7666)	Krzysztof	Krakowiak	POL 61	14 Sep
7690	(7617)	Vladimir	Zavyalov	SU 58	22 Jun
7687	(7658)	Karl–Heinz	Fichtner	FRG 62	29 Jul
7684	(7605)	Robert	Baker	USA 55	5 Apr
7672	(7586)	Piet	v.Vaerenberghe	BEL 56	19 Aug
7670	(7641)	Dave	Johnson	USA 63	22 Jun
7670	(7609)	Jon	Hallingstad	USA 58	28 Apr
7670	(7628)	Sergey	Makarov	SU 58	15 Sep
7663	(7599)	Scott	Daniels	USA 60	22 Jun
7662		Jeff	Montpas	USA 58	24 May
7662	(7662)	Weng	Kangqiang	CHN 59	9 Aug
7660	(7645)	Marty	Neibauer	USA 61	3 Jun
7660	(7581)	Martin	Machura	CS 58	10 Jun
7659	(7611)	Jozsef	Hoffer	HUN 56	8 Jul
7658	(7644)	Guu	Jinshoei	TAI 60	9 Aug
7657	(7609)	Trond	Knaplund	NOR 60	29 May
7655	(7603)	Leszek	Smajdor	POL 58	23 Jun
7653	(7599)	Keith	Robinson	USA 64	29 Mar
7652	(7589)	Armin	Sporri	SWZ 55	23 Jun
7652	(7623)	Janusz	Szczerkowski	POL 54	14 Sep
7642	(7563)	Frank	Harrison	USA 59	13 May
7636	(7550)	Grant	Niederhaus	USA 54	22 Jun
7634	(7565)	Willy	Pirtle	USA 60	2 Jun
7634	(7567)	Harri	Sundell	FIN 53	9 Sep
7631	(7581)	Pete	Mansur	USA 62	12 May
7628	(7570)	Tom	Leutz	USA 63	22 May
7623		Doug	Loisel	USA 62	25 May
7615	(7577)	Steve	Jacobs	USA 56	22 Jun
7613	(7543)	Gary	Armstrong	USA 60	18 May
7609	(7570)	Beat	Gahwiler	SWZ 65	23 Jun
7606		Roland	Marloye	BEL 62	3 Jun
7596	(7551)	Andrzej	Langowski	POL 59	15 Jul
7593		Xi	Xiashun	CHN 59	6 Sep
7587	(7512)	Enno	Tjepkema	HOL 65	10 Jun
7571	(7526)	Sergey	Potapov	SU 62	22 Jun
7566	(7491)	J.Francois	Raffali	FRA 57	29 Apr
7561	(7509)	Tonu	Kaukis	SU 56	9 Sep
7558	(7496)	Kalev	Oja	SU 59	3 Jun
7557	(7472)	John	Hunt	NZ 63	25 Nov
7556	(7485)	Rob	Town	CAN 58	10 Jun
7556	(7462)	Jurdanas	Radzius	SU 61	3 Jun
7554	(7496)	Mikael	Olander	SWE 63	9 Sep
7553	(7505)	Douglas	Fernandez	VEN 59	9 Aug
7550	(7478)	Didier	Claverie	FRA 59	19 Aug
7538	(7475)	Milan	Popadich	CAN 59	1 Jul
7533	(7462)	Gary	Bastien	USA 59	28 Apr
7525	(7477)	Stan	Vegar	USA 55	22 Jun
7521	(7439)	Kevan	Lobb	UK 60	19 Aug
7517	(7467)	Roman	Hraban	CS 62	16 Sep

Manually timed scores

8310 (8212) *Mikhail Romanyuk SU 62 1 Kiev 11 Aug
(10.8 7.29 14.24 1.80 48.0 14.3 46.52 4.80 63.50 4:12.8)

8273 (8175) *Pavel Tarnavetskiy SU 61 1 Moskva 7 Jul
(11.0 7.30 14.70 2.05 48.8 14.6 46.28 4.80 59.54 4:28.6)

8092 (7989) "Peter Hadfield AUS 55 1 Adelaide 8 Apr
(10.7 7.44w 13.66 1.85 48.8 14.6 44.84 4.81 61.50 4:35.4)

298

1984 Lists – Men

8061	(7919)	Vladimir	Novikov	SU 60	2		Moskva	7 Jul
(10.5 7.39 12.55 1.90 47.2 15.1 38.30 4.50 61.76 4:16.8)								
8054	(7930)	Vladimir	Kuchmenko	SU 58	1		Alma-Ata	29 Jul
(10.8 7.25 14.00 2.06 49.1 15.1 42.56 4.80 56.70 4:36.2)								
8045	(7918)	Galvidas	Skalidas	SU 60	1		Vilnius	5 Aug
(10.9 7.39 16.28 1.90 50.1 15.6 47.80 4.30 61.70 4:28.5)								
8043	(7933)	"Dave	Johnson	USA 63	1		Pomona	27 Apr
(10.9 6.77 13.34 2.04 48.5 14.3 43.56 4.30 69.68 4:35.6)								
8021	(7862)	"Grant	Niederhaus	USA 54	1		Bakersfield	13 Apr
(10.7 6.88 13.23 1.98 47.4 14.2 41.18 4.50 55.32 4:26.1)								
8018	(7885)	*Brad	McStravick	UK 56	1		Birmingham	6 May
(10.8 6.64 13.91 1.96 48.3 14.9 45.78 4.70 60.56 4:30.0)								
8001	(7849)	Nikolay	Parakhovskiy	SU 57	2		Minsk	9 Jun
(10.4 7.20 16.10 1.88 50.3 15.6 47.44 4.20 63.90 4:43.2)								
7958	(7862)	*Vladimir	Shmakov	SU 58	1		Tula	26 Aug
(11.0 7.30 13.33 2.04 51.6 14.5 46.76 5.10 51.90 4:42.5)								
7954	(7804)	"Jurdanas	Radzius	SU 61	2		Vilnius	3 Jun
(11.0 6.97 13.92 2.02 50.2 15.2 45.72 4.60 54.00 4:17.6)								
7946	(7849)	Yuriy	Karpov	SU 57	2		Tula	26 Aug
(11.0 7.44 14.31 2.10 51.0 14.8 41.20 4.20 70.00 4:49.9)								
7937	(7844)	Dannie	Jackson	USA 58	1		Tempe	2 Jun
(10.9 7.87 14.28 1.98 49.3 14.3 44.74 4.10 53.54 4:47.8)								
7930#	(7723)	*Eugene	Gilkes	UK 62	1	vNOR	Oslo	8 Jul
(10.2w 6.84w 14.41 1.87 47.3 15.0 41.30 4.30 50.64 4:26.1)								
7930	(7776)	Vladimir	Romanov	SU 61	2		Kiev	11 Aug
(11.1 7.10 15.00 2.01 49.0 15.9 47.44 4.00 60.30 4:21.5)								
7927	(7859)	Tim	Taft	USA 58	1		Lawrence	3 Jun
(11.0 7.01 13.57 2.02 52.1 15.2 41.68 5.06 71.66 4:43.8)								
7922	(7733)	"Scott	Daniels	USA 60	1		Los Angeles	18 Mar
(11.2 7.16 13.90 2.00 49.2 14.8 45.46 4.10 57.04 4:17.8)								
7918	(7783)	Nikolay	Kulinkovich	SU 60	1		Riga	6 Jul
(10.7 7.26 13.94 2.15 50.6 14.8 46.32 4.50 54.70 5:05.8)								
7912	(7750)	Andrey	Fomochkin	SU 63	1		Minsk	11 Aug
(10.6 7.49 13.76 1.99 49.0 14.9 43.70 4.20 52.32 4:38.3)								
7907	(7721)	Viktor	Kulesh	SU 60	3		Minsk	9 Jun
(10.4 6.92 14.92 1.97 50.5 14.0 42.92 4.20 52.44 4:41.3)								
7881	(7745)	Mikhail	Medved	SU 64	3		Moskva	7 Jul
(11.0 7.12 14.62 2.05 51.2 14.7 43.96 4.50 56.68 4:40.9)								
7880	(7732)	Nikolay	Tokarev	SU 60	3		Alma-Ata	29 Jul
(10.7 7.14 15.62 1.95 50.8 14.7 48.04 4.20 58.52 4:57.0)								
7867	(7717)	Jim	Schnur	USA 54	1		Emmitsburg	13 May
(10.6 7.16 14.16 1.91 49.2 15.6 41.68 4.60 60.38 4:40.4)								
7858	(7740)	Vasiliy	Potapenko	SU 64	1		Angarsk	17 Jun
(11.0 7.19 13.68 2.02 52.0 14.5 45.14 4.70 58.72 4:47.4)								
7852	(7716)	*Ilyas	Abdulin	SU 58	3		Tula	26 Aug
(10.9 6.92 14.70 1.95 50.3 15.6 44.36 4.60 63.20 4:38.9)								
7842	(7717)	Aleksandr	Stavro	SU 63	1		Riga	10 Aug
(11.2 6.91 13.17 2.00 49.8 15.0 42.02 4.65 61.94 4:27.0)								
7837	(7694)	Owen	Buckley	USA 59	2		Lawrence	3 Jun
(10.4 7.11 12.73 1.93 49.0 15.8 44.28 5.06 54.80 4:53.6)								
7821	(7671)	Yuriy	Pavlyuk	SU 60	4		Tula	26 Aug
(10.8 7.12 14.50 1.95 50.4 15.1 45.06 4. 52.88 4:41.3)								
7821	(7699)	Sergey	Chuntonov	SU 59	5		Tula	26 Aug
(10.8 7.14 14.27 1.85 49.7 14.5 48.46 3.80 66.16 4:44.7)								
7819	(7689)	*Gary	Gefre	USA 57	1		Lawrence	19 Apr
(10.9 6.87 15.49 1.88 50.0 15.5 50.74 4.14 65.08 4:47.6)								
7813	(7701)	"Sergey	Potapov	SU 62	1		Leningrad	13 Aug
(11.1 7.01 14.98 1.95 50.8 14.9 47.38 4.60 57.06 4:48.1)								
7806	(7685)	Joe	Schneider	USA 57	2		Los Angeles	18 Mar
(11.2 7.02 14.15 1.90 51.9 15.2 42.08 4.70 64.46 4:21.8)								
7804	(7686)	"Sergey	Makarov	SU 58	1		Chelyabinsk	29 Jul
(11.3 6.98 14.25 1.90 50.7 15.3 44.80 4.80 60.60 4:28.4)								
7803	(7646)	David	Saye	USA 59	1		Houston	31 May
(10.6 7.10 12.92 2.03 50.0 14.4 40.58 4.30 56.90 4:45.4)								

299

1984 Lists – Men

7781	(7634)	"Harri	Sundell	FIN 53	1 Jul
7776	(7623)	Aleksandr	Nevadovskiy	SU 61	20 May
7763	(7667)	"Stan	Vegar	USA 55	18 Mar
7756	(7621)	Ken	Terry	USA 59	30 Jan
7756	(7592)	Paulo	Lima	BRA 58	1 Apr
7753	(7584)	Aleksandr	Tsyoma	SU 61	27 May
7743	(7598)	Mike	Moore	USA 55	12 May
7741	(7609)	"Gary	Armstrong	USA 60	2 Jun
7739	(7599)	Sergey	Pogrebnyuk	SU 61	7 Jul
7738	(7584)	Konstantin	Shultyatinov	SU 60	21 Jun
7737	(7595)	"Pete	Mansur	USA 62	18 Apr
7736	(7594)	Bob	Stebbins	USA 60	21 Apr
7735	(7567)	Ivan	Khorin	SU 62	27 May
7733		Lee	Foo-yen	TAI 64	20 May
7731	(7576)	Eric	Lammi	USA 56	12 May
7728	(7566)	Sergey	Gavrikov	SU 59	26 Aug
7726	(7535)	Heinz	Heinrichs	USA 61	12 May
7726	(7570)	Keith	Stewart	USA 61	3 Jun
7724	(7568)	Vladislav	Pastukhov	SU 62	15 Jul
7717	(7560)	Paul	Mainz	FRG 61	12 Aug
7705		Vladimir	Zavyalor	SU 55	17 Jul
7702		"Roland	Marloye	BEL 62	23 Sep
7693	(7523)	Knut Harald	Gunderson	NOR 64	23 Sep
7692	(7551)	Aleksey	Urdayev	SU 60	8 Jul
7684	(7532)	Heimar	Lipp	SU 63	6 Jul
7683	(7534)	Sergey	Strinkevich	SU 61	17 Jun
7654	(7501)	Igor	Paptchonok	SU 61	29 Jul
7650	(7511)	Sergey	Zaretskiy	SU 60	27 May
7646	(7527)	Nikolay	Lesnoy	SU 62	26 Aug
7645	(7494)	Sergey	Koshar	SU 61	11 Aug
7632	(7486)	Ed	Brown	USA 58	2 Jun
7628	(7491)	Petri	Keskitalo	FIN 67	1 Jul
7628	(7446)	Vladimir	Pastukhov	SU 64	6 Jul
7623	(7451)	Martin	Szafranski	FRG 58	29 Jul
7622	(7488)	Andrey	Ivanov	SU 62	
7621	(7469)	Antonio	Iacocca	ITA 61	29 Jul
7611	(7467)	Steve	Odgers	USA 62	18 Mar

* = Athlete also appears in auto-timed list.
" = Athlete also appears in supplementary auto-timed list.

Unknown Irregularity

| 7687 | (7532) | Vasiliy | Losyev | SU 62 | 8 Jul |

400 METRES RELAY

37.83	USA	1	OG	Los Angeles	11 Aug
(Graddy,Brown,C.Smith,Lewis)					
38.32	Soviet Union	1	DRZ	Moskva	17 Aug
(Yevgenyev,Sokolov,Muravyev,Sidorov)					
38.42	Soviet Union	1	Nar	Sofia	19 May
(Yevgenyev,A.Fyodorov,Muravyev,Sokolov)					
38.44	USA	1s1	OG	Los Angeles	11 Aug
(Graddy,Brown,C.Smith,Lewis)					
38.45	Soviet Union	1	OD	Berlin	20 Jul
(Yevgenyev,Sokolov,Muravyev,Sidorov)					

1984 Lists – Men

38.46	GDR	2	OD	Berlin	20 Jul
(Hubler,Schroder,Prenzler,Emmelmann)						
38.48	Bud Lite TC (USA)	1		Tempe	7 Apr
(Butler,Myricks,C.Smith,Lattany)						
38.54	GDR "A"	1		Karl Marx St.	20 May
(Hubler,Schroder,Prenzler,Hollender)						
38.58	USA	1		Koln	26 Aug
(Glance,McNeil,Baptiste,Lewis)						
38.62	Jamaica	2	OG	Los Angeles	11 Aug
(A.Lawrence,Meghoo,Quarrie,Stewart)						
38.62	Canada	2		Koln	26 Aug
(B.Johnson,Sharpe,D.Williams,Mahorn)						
38.67	Jamaica	1s2	OG	Los Angeles	11 Aug
(A.Lawrence,Meghoo,Quarrie,Stewart)						
38.68	United Kingdom	2s2	OG	Los Angeles	11 Aug
(Thompson,Reid,McFarlane,Wells)						
38.70	FRG	3s2	OG	Los Angeles	11 Aug
(Koffler,Klein,Evers,Lubke)						
38.70	Canada	3	OG	Los Angeles	11 Aug
(B.Johnson,Sharpe,D.Williams,S.Hinds)						
38.70	Soviet Union	1	8–N	Tokyo	14 Sep
(Yevgenyev,Sokolov,Muravyev,Sidorov)						
38.75	GDR	1		Celje	5 Aug
(Hubler,Moller,Prenzler,Emmelmann)						
38.78	GDR	1		Berlin	15 Jul
(Hubler,Schroder,Prenzler,Hollender)						
38.79	Cuba	2	DRZ	Moskva	17 Aug
(Gonzalez,Penalver,Leonard,Lara)						
38.81	Poland	3	DRZ	Moskva	17 Aug
(Zwolinski,Woronin,Pradzynski,Janiak)						
38.82	GDR "B"	2		Karl Marx St.	20 May
(Schulz,Moller,Kubeck,Strassburger)						
38.87	Italy	4	OG	Los Angeles	11 Aug
(Ullo,Bongiorni,Tilli,Mennea)						
38.89	USA	1h1	OG	Los Angeles	10 Aug
(Graddy,Brown,C.Smith,Lewis)						
38.90	GDR	1		Dresden	27 Jul
(Bringmann,Schroder,Prenzler,Emmelmann)						
38.91	USA	1		Berkeley	14 Jul
(Graddy,Brown,C.Smith,Glance)						
38.91	France	4s2	OG	Los Angeles	11 Aug
(Richard,Boussemart,Gasparoni,Marie-Rose)						
38.93	Jamaica	1h3	OG	Los Angeles	10 Aug
(Edwards,Meghoo,Quarrie,A.Lawrence)						
38.95	Canada	1		Walnut	25 Jul
(Johnson,Sharpe,D.Williams,S.Hinds)						
38.97	USA	2		Walnut	25 Jul
(W.Smith,Jefferson,C.Smith,Glance)						
38.98	Santa Monica TC (USA)	2		Tempe	7 Apr
(Reed,McNeil,Ketchum,Lewis)						
38.98	Nigeria	5s2	OG	Los Angeles	11 Aug
(Adeyanju,Ikpoto,Oyeledun,Imo)						

(31 Performances/10 Countries)

39.14	Czechoslovakia	4	DRZ	Moskva	17 Aug
(Lomicky,Ptacnik,Puchovsky,F.Brecka)						
39.21	Hungary	5	DRZ	Moskva	17 Aug
(Kiss,Havas,Tatar,Kovacs)						
39.27	Brasil	2h2	OG	Los Angeles	10 Aug
(A.Oliveira,R. Caetano da Silva,Correia,Nakaya)						
39.34	Bulgaria	1		Sofia	8 Aug
(Sarbakov,A.Atanasov,Karadimov,N.Markov)						
39.93	Belgium	1	WA	Lisboa	16 Jun
(Cincinatis,Borlee,Desruelles,Van Hamme)						

1984 Lists – Men

39.94	Ivory Coast	2	AfrC	Rabat	15 Jul
(Otokpa,Koffi,Kablan,Tiacho)						
39.95	Yugoslavia	2	Balk	Athinai	8 Sep
(Jovanovic,Nikolic,Popovic,Stanicic)						
40.01	Greece	3		Athinai	10 Jul
(Stratos,Gatzios,Stratopoulos,Vamvakas)						
40.05	Finland	1	WG	Helsinki	4 Jul
(Pyy, Hassi,Anias,Saaristo)						
40.12	China	1		Nanjing	17 Sep
40.14	Antigua	6s2	OG	Los Angeles	10 Aug
(Henry,Benjamin,Browne,Miller)						
40.15	Senegal	4h1	OG	Los Angeles	10 Aug
(Sene,Diawara,S.Seck,C.Seck)						
40.18	Barbados	7s2	OG	Los Angeles	11 Aug
(Mayers,H.Grimes,C.Edwards,A.Jones)						
40.18	Japan	6	8–N	Tokyo	14 Sep
(Matsubara,Shimizu,Arikawa,Fuwa)						

(24 Countries)

Manual Timing

38.5	USA	1		Sacramento	21 Jul
(Graddy,Brown,C.Smith,Glance)					
38.8	Brasil	1		Sao Paulo	1 May
(A.Oliveira,R.Caetano da Silva,Nakaya,Correia)					

1600 METRES RELAY

(* = Mile relay less 1.05 seconds)

2:57.91	USA	1	OG	Los Angeles	11 Aug
(Nix 45.59,Armstead 43.97,Babers 43.75,McKay 44.60)					
2:59.13	United Kingdom	2	OG	Los Angeles	11 Aug
(Akabusi 45.87,Cook 44.74,T.Bennett 44.17,Brown 44.35)					
2:59.32	Nigeria	3	OG	Los Angeles	11 Aug
(Uti 45.34,Ugbisie 44.48,Peters 44.94,Egbunike 44.56)					
2:59.70	Australia	4	OG	Los Angeles	11 Aug
(Frayne 45.38,Clark 43.86,Minihan 45.07,Mitchell 45.39)					
3:00.07	GDR	1		Erfurt	3 Jun
(Lieske,Schersing,Carlowitz,Schonlebe)					
3:00.11	USA	1		Berkeley	14 Jul
(W.Smith 45.4, Armstead 45.0, Babers 45.0, McCoy 44.8)					
3:00.16	Soviet Union	1	DRZ	Moskva	18 Aug
(Lovachov ,Lomtyev ,Kurochkin ,Markin 43.9)					
3:00.19	USA	1s1	OG	Los Angeles	10 Aug
(Nix 45.93,McCoy 44.65,W.Smith 44.81,Mckay 44.80)					
3:00.27	GDR	1		Dresden	27 Jul
(Niestadt,Schersing,Carlowitz,Schonlebe)					
3:00.47	GDR	2		Moskva	18 Aug
(Niestadt,Schersing,Schonlebe,Carlowitz)					
3:00.78	Southern Illinois (USA/BAR)	1	DrakeR	Des Moines	28 Apr
(Duncan 45.6,Adams 45.6,Forde 45.1,Franks 44.5)					
3:01.44	USA	1h4	OG	Los Angeles	10 Aug
(W.Smith 45.2,Armstead 44.7,Babers 46.5,McCoy 45.1)					
3:01.44	Italy	5	OG	Los Angeles	11 Aug
(Tozzi 45.69,Nocco 45.07,Ribaud 45.73,Mennea 44.95)					
3:01.46	Oklahoma Un. (USA)	2	DrakeR	Des Moines	28 Apr
(A.Jones 45.7,Kemp 44.9,Carter 45.8,Bly 45.1)					
3:01.60	Barbados	6	OG	Los Angeles	11 Aug
(Louis 46.67,Peltier 44.97,Edwards 45.04,Forde 44.92)					

1984 Lists – Men

3:01.95	GDR	1	8–N	Tokyo	14 Sep
(Niestadt,Carlowitz,Schersing,Schonlebe)						
3:02.01*	Oklahoma Un.(USA)	1	NCAA	Eugene	2 Jun
(A.Jones 46.7,Kemp 45.5,Carter 44.8,Bly 45.1)						
3:02.09	Uganda	7	OG	Los Angeles	11 Aug
(Govile 46.72,Kyeswa 44.60,Rwamu 46.40,Okot 44.37)						
3:02.1m	Australia	1		Melbourne	26 Feb
(Van Miltenberg 46.3,Minihan 45.1,Frayne 45.3,Mitchell 45.4)						
3:02.20	Bud Lite TC (USA)	1		Tempe	7 Apr
(McCoy 45.9,C.Smith 45.1,Rolle 45.9,Babers 45.3)						
3:02.20	Accusplit Sp.Club (USA/Sudan)	2		Tempe	7 Apr
(Wiley 45.6,Henley 45.6,Whitlock 46.3,Hassan 44.7)						
3:02.20	United Kingdom	2	8–N	Tokyo	14 Sep
(R.Dickens,Akabusi,T.Bennett,Brown)						
3:02.22	Nigeria	1s2	OG	Los Angeles	11 Aug
(Uti 45.63,Ugbisie 45.62,Peters 45.75,Egbunike 45.22)						
3:02.63	Tiger Int. (USA/Trinidad)	3		Tempe	7 Apr
(Moore 46.3,Paul 45.0,Bradley 46.5,Rowe 44.9)						
3:02.67*	Lamar Un. (USA)	2	NCAA	Eugene	2 Jun
(Nichols 47.2,Amboree 45.6,Guiton 45.0,J.Harris 45.0)						
3:02.69*	Baylor Un. (USA)	1		Waco	20 Apr
(Graham,Thomas,Jefferson,Caldwell)						
3:02.71	Southern Illinois (USA/BAR)	1		Baton Rouge	24 Mar
(Duncan 46.8,Adams 46.4,Forde 44.8,Franks 44.8)						
3:02.82	Canada	8	OG	Los Angeles	11 Aug
(Sokolowski 46.09,D.Hinds 45.04,Saunders 45.43,Bethune 46.26)						
3:02.83	Oklahoma Un. (USA)	1		Lincoln	12 May
(Jones, Kemp, Carter, Bly)						
3:02.85*	Alabama Un. (USA/VEN)	3	NCAA	Eugene	2 Jun
(Menefee 46.5,Wuycke 45.9,Vaughans 45.1,L.Smith 45.4)						

(30 Performances by 10 Countries)

3:03.33	FRG	2h3	OG	Los Angeles	10 Aug
(Weppler 46.7,Schmitt 45.7,Giessing 45.5,Skamrahl 45.5)					
3:03.50	Ivory Coast	3h3	OG	Los Angeles	10 Aug
(Kablan 46.5,Nogboum 46.3,Djedjemel 46.3,Tiacoh 44.4)					
3:03.85	Jamaica	4h3	OG	Los Angeles	10 Aug
(Griffiths 46.8,Senior 45.6,Wallace 45.5,Morris 46.0)					
3:03.99	Brasil	5s2	OG	Los Angeles	10 Aug
(J.B.da Silva 46.12,A.Ferreira 46.35,Barbosa 46.35,Souza 45.17)					
3:04.32	Switzerland	1		Lausanne	10 Jul
(R.Gisler,Baumeler,Arnold,Fahndrich)					
3:04.44	Cuba	1		Sofia	17 Jun
(Juantorena,Martinez,Alfonso,Ramos)					
3:04.74	Kenya	7s2	OG	Los Angeles	10 Aug
(Anzrah 45.69,Sogomo 46.62,Opicho 46.93,D.Kitur 45.50)					
3:04.76	Senegal	1	AfrC	Rabat	15 Jul
(Diallo,Niang,Fall,Dia Ba 44.8)					
3:05.48	Bulgaria	1		Athinai	11 Jul
(Demirev,Penev,Tomov,Rangelov)					
3:05.51	Spain	1	WA	Lisboa	17 Jun
(Prado,Sanchez,Gonzalez,Heras)					
3:05.51	Hungary	2		Athinai	11 Jul
(Menczer,Banko,Nagy,Takacs)					
3:05.53	Holland	2		Lausanne	10 Jul
(Schulting,Cools,Brouwer,Ellsworth)					
3:05.69	Czechoslovakia	4	DRZ	Moskva	18 Aug
(Puchovsky,F.Brecka,Malovec,Tomko)					

(23 Countries)

Manual Timing
A3:04.0   Kenya

1984 Lists – Men

20,000 METRES WALK (TRACK)

Ernesto	Canto	Mex 59	1:18:40.0	(1)	SGP	Fana	5 May
Erling	Andersen	Nor 60	1:20:36.7	(2)	SGP	Fana	5 May
Ronald	Weigel	GDR 58	1:21:13.2	(1)		Potsdam	24 Mar
Pavol	Blazek	CS 58	1:21:23.5	(3)	SGP	Fana	5 May
Raul	Gonzalez	Mex 52	1:21:48.8	(4)	SGP	Fana	5 May
Gerard	Lelievre	Fra 49	1:22:14.0	(1)		Epinay-sur-Seine	15 Apr
Alessandro	Pezzatini	Ita 57	1:24:02.0	(1)		Bov.Masciago	14 Apr
Phil	Vesty	UK 63	1:24:07.6	(1)		Leicester	1 Dec
Martial	Fesselier	Fra 61	1:24:35.6	(1)	SGP	Fana	5 May
Maurizio	Damilano	Ita 57	1:24:50.0	(1)		Torino	15 Apr
Marcel	Jobin	Can 42	1:24:58.8	(1)	IM	Quebec	12 May
Andrey	Ivanov	SU 57	1:25:07.8	(1)		Klaipeda	19 Aug
Alfons	Schwarz	FRG 54	1:25:13.6	(1)	IM	Ahlen	22 Sep
Marcelino	Colin	Mex 61	1:25:39.3	(6)	SGP	Fana	5 May
Walter	Arena	Ita 64	1:25:50.4	(1)		Roma	14 Apr
Martin	Bermudez	Mex 58	1:25:56.4	(7)	SGP	Fana	5 May
Enrique	Vera-Ybanez	Mex 54	1:25:56.5	(8)	SGP	Fana	5 May
Sandro	Bellucci	Ita 55	1:25:56.7	(2)		Roma	14 Apr
Carlo	Mattioli	Ita 54	1:25:57.7	(1)		Bologna	14 Apr
Zhaudat	Aydarov	SU 56	1:25:59.0	(1)		Kiyev	4 Jul
Jim	Heiring	USA 55	1:26:15.2	(2)	IM	Quebec	12 May
Arturo	Bravo	Mex 58	1:26:15.9	(9)	SGP	Fana	5 May
Jorge	Llopart	Spa 52	1:26:22.9	(10)	SGP	Fana	5 May
	Fesselier		1:26:25.3	(2)		Epinay-sur-Seine	15 Apr
Kastitis	Stasiunas	SU 62	1:26:31.4	(2)		Klaipeda	19 Aug
Simon	Baker	Aus 58	1:26:31.5	(1)		Winnipeg	30 Jun
Benamar	Kachkouche	Alg 51	1:26:39.93	(1)		Thonon-les-Bains	20 Jun
Abdelwahab	Ferguene	Alg 58	1:26:39.95	(2)		Thonon-les-Bains	20 Jun
Guillaume	Leblanc	Can 62	1:26:41.7	(3)	IM	Quebec	12 May
Marco	Evoniuk	USA 57	1:26:42.9	(11)	SGP	Fana	5 May
Joes	Martens	Bel 64	1:26:45.0	(12)	SGP	Fana	5 May
Bo	Gustafsson	Swe 54	1:26:49.3	(1)	NCh	Solleftea	19 Aug
Steve	Pecinkovsky	USA 54	1:27:09.0	(1)		Dearborn	14 Apr
Vyacheslav	Popovich	SU 62	1:27:09.2	(2)		Kiyev	4 Jul
Dominique	Guebey	Fra 52	1:27:12.1	(3)		Epinay-sur-Seine	15 Apr
Shoahong	Jiang	Chn 60	1:27:14.0	(13)	SGP	Fana	5 May
Aivars	Rumbenieks	SU 51	1:27:15.9	(1)		Tartu	27 Aug
Antanas	Grigaliunas	SU 61	1:27:22.4	(3)		Klaipeda	19 Aug
Dietmar	Meisch	GDR 59	1:27:24.6	(2)		Potsdam	24 Mar
Raffaello	Ducceschi	Ita 62	1:27:28.0	(1)		Mestre	14 Apr
Sergio	Spagnulo	Ita 62	1:27:38.8	(2)		Bov.Masciago	14 Apr
Francois	Lapointe	Can 61	1:27:47.0	(3)		Winnipeg	30 Jun
Philippe	Lafleur	Fra 60	1:27:59.3	(14)	SGP	Fana	5 May
Miguel Angel	Prieto	Spa 64	1:28:13.0	(15)	SGP	Fana	5 May
Jan	Staaf	Swe 62	1:28:55.1	(2)	NCh	Solleftea	19 Aug
Miroslav	Svoboda	CS 61	1:28:59.8	(1)		Bratislava	7 Jul
Roberto	Giamogante	Ita 63	1:28:59.9	(3)		Roma	14 Apr
Manuel	Alcalde	Spa 56	1:29:05.0	(1)	NCh	Serrahima	30 Jun
Jose	Pinto	Por 56	1:29:08.0	(1)		Beja	9 Jun
Tor Ivar	Guttulsrod	Nor 63	1:29:15.0	(2)	NCh	Kyrksaterrora	Aug
Christos	Karayorgos	Gre 53	1:29:16.0	(1)		Salonika	2 Jun

304

1984 Lists – Men

20,000 METRES WALK (ROAD)

Ronald	Weigel	GDR 58	1:19:56	(1)		Berlin	27 Jul
Maurizio	Damilano	Ita 57	1:20:09	(1)		Piacenza	13 May
Alessandro	Pezzetini	Ita 57	1:20:18	(2)		Piacenza	13 May
Ralf	Kowalsky	GDR 62	1:20:35	(1)	IM	Berlin	20 Jul
David	Smith	Aus 55	1:20:40	(1)	IM	Sdr.Omme	21 Apr
	Weigel		1:20:54	(1)	IPM	Kobenhavn	12 May
	Smith		1:21:17	(2)	IPM	Kobenhavn	12 May
	Kowalsky		1:21:43	(3)	IPM	Kobenhavn	12 May
Ivan	Sankovskiy	SU 58	1:21:43	(1)		Moskva	13 May
Sergiy	Protsyshyn	SU 59	1:21:57	(1)	Drzh	Moskva	17 Aug
Lyubomir	Ivanov	Bul 60	1:22:03	(2)	IM	Berlin	20 Jul
Carlo	Mattioli	Ita 54	1:22:07	(3)		Piacenza	13 May
	Weigel		1:22:16	(1)	NCh	Erfurt	2 Jun
	Ivanov		1:22:19	(1)	NCh	Sofiya	16 Jun
Anatoliy	Solomin	SU 52	1:22:21	(2)	Drzh	Moskva	17 Aug
Yevgeniy	Misyulya	SU 64	1:22:31	(1)		Cheboksary	13 May
Aleksandr	Boryashinov	SU 63	1:22:31	(2)		Cheboksary	13 May
Mykola	Vynnychenko	SU 58	1:22:34	(2)		Moskva	13 May
	Kowalsky		1:22:36	(1)	IM	Naumburg	1 May
Nikolay	Polozov	SU 51	1:22:40	(3)	Drzh	Moskva	17 Aug
Aivars	Rumbenieks	SU 51	1:22:43	(3)		Moskva	13 May
Roland	Wieser	GDR 56	1:22:43	(2)	NCh	Erfurt	2 Jun
	Vynnychenko		1:22:50	(4)	Drzh	Moskva	17 Aug
Hartwig	Gauder	GDR 54	1:22:53	(3)	NCh	Erfurt	2 Jun
Viktor	Mostovik	SU 63	1:22:57	(3)		Cheboksary	13 May
	Boryashinov		1:22:57	(1)	RC	Moskva	7 Jul
Pyotr	Kakhnovich	SU 61	1:22:57	(1)		Leningrad	10 Aug
	Smith		1:22:58	(1)	IM	Eshborn	3 Jun
	Smith		1:23:00	(1)		Sydney	4 Mar
Reima	Salonen	Fin 55	1:23:04	(1)	GP	Ruse	15 Apr
Stanislav	Vezhel	SU 58	1:23:05	(4)		Cheboksary	13 May
	Rumbenieks		1:23:05	(5)		Cheboksary	13 May
Volodymyr	Stykulin	SU 58	1:23:06	(6)		Cheboksary	13 May
Sergey	Abiralo	SU 61	1:23:07	(7)		Cheboksary	13 May
	Mostovik		1:23:07	(2)	RC	Moskva	7 Jul
Artur	Shumak	SU 63	1:23:08	(8)		Cheboksary	13 May
Vitaliy	Popovych	SU 62	1:23:08	(3)	RC	Moskva	7 Jul
	Sankovskiy		1:23:11	(4)	RC	Moskva	7 Jul
Andrey	Perlov	SU 61	1:23:12	(2)	IM	Naumburg	1 May
Nikolay	Matveyev	SU 55	1:23:13	(5)	RC	Moskva	7 Jul
Frants	Kostyukevich	SU 63	1:23:13	(6)	RC	Moskva	7 Jul
Ernesto	Canto	Mex 59	1:23:13	(1)	OG	Los Angeles	3 Aug
Andrey	Evel	SU 59	1:23:16	(9)		Cheboksary	13 May
Vladimir	Obukhov	SU 58	1:23:19	(10)		Cheboksary	13 May
Raul	Gonzalez	Mex 52	1:23:20	(2)	OG	Los Angeles	3 Aug
Pyotr	Pochenchuk	SU 54	1:23:21	(7)	RC	Moskva	7 Jul
	Polozov		1:23:22	(1)		Armavir	22 Apr
Antanas	Grigaliunas	SU 61	1:23:22	(3)	IM	Naumburg	1 May
Nikolay	Baskirtsev	SU 53	1:23:22	(11)		Cheboksary	13 May
Aleksandr	Starchenko	SU 51	1:23:26	(2)		Armavir	22 Apr
	Damilano		1:23:26	(3)	OG	Los Angeles	3 Aug

(51/35)

Willi	Sawall	Aus 41	1:23:27	(1)		Melbourne	8 Apr
Marat	Akopyan	SU 54	1:23:29	(3)		Armavir	22 Apr
Oleg	Andreyev	SU 56	1:23:29	(12)		Cheboksary	13 May
Aleksandr	Khmelnitskiy	SU 64	1:23:30	(13)		Cheboksary	13 May
Yevgeniy	Zaykin	SU 57	1:23:30	(14)		Cheboksary	13 May
Vyacheslav	Fursov	SU 54	1:23:40	(3)		Sochi	9 Jun

1984 Lists – Men

Sergio	Spagnulo	Ita 62	1:23:41	(4)		Piacenza	13 May
Gerard	Lelievre	Fra 49	1:23:41	(1)		Laval	7 Oct
Alfons	Schwarz	Fra 54	1:23:44	(1)		Lippstadt	18 Mar
Sergey	Bantikov	SU 57	1:23:48	(8)		Moskva	7 Jul
Anatoliy	Gorshkov	SU 52	1:23:50	(1)		Zhytomyr	30 Sep
Giorgio	Damilano	Ita 57	1:23:54	(5)		Piacenza	13 May
Aleksandr	Udalov	SU 53	1:23:59	(4)		Moskva	13 May
Aleksey	Pershin	SU 62	1:24:04	(16)		Cheboksary	13 May
Volodymyr	Pyshko	SU 62	1:24:05	(17)		Cheboksary	13 May
Yevgeniy	Rengold	SU 62	1:24:13	(18)		Cheboksary	13 May
Ian	McCombie	UK 61	1:24:14	(1)		Dartford	25 Feb
Vladimir	Myakotnykh	SU 52	1:24:15	(19)		Cheboksary	13 May
Jan	Klos	Pol 60	1:24:17	(1)	NCh	Lublin	23 Jun
Roman	Mrazek	CS 62	1:24:19	(5)	IM	Naumburg	1 May
Ladislaw	Szlapkin	Pol 61	1:24:23	(2)	GP	Ruse	15 Apr
Sergey	Kostyukevich	SU 64	1:24:23	(20)		Cheboksary	13 May
Vyacheslav	Smirnov	SU 57	1:24:26	(4)		Armavir	22 Apr
Simon	Baker	Aus 58	1:24:29	(1)		Melbourne	21 Jan
Guillaume	Leblanc	Can 62	1:24:29	(4)	OG	Los Angeles	3 Aug
Walter	Arena	Ita 64	1:24:36	(6)		Piacenza	13 May
Steve	Barry	UK 50	1:24:37	(1)		London	7 Apr
Andrew	Jackno	Aus 62	1:24:40	(2)		Melbourne	21 Jan
Igor	Malukha	SU 58	1:24:41	(6)		Zhytomyr	30 Sep
Yevgeniy	Yevsyukov	SU 50	1:24:43	(5)		Armavir	22 Apr
Laszlo	Sator	Hun 53	1:24:46	(1)	IM	Schutterwald	6 Oct
Alik	Ibryamov	Bul 59	1:24:54	(3)	GP	Ruse	15 Apr
Raffaello	Ducceschi	Ita 62	1:24:55	(7)		Piacenza	13 May
Alessandro	Bellucci	Ita 55	1:24:55	(8)		Piacenza	13 May
Phil	Vesty	UK 63	1:24:58	(1)		Douglas	25 Feb
Dominique	Guebey	Fra 52	1:25:02	(2)	NCh	Villeneuve d'Asq	30 Jun
Josef	Pribilinec	CS 60	1:25:07	(1)	NCh	Praha	21 Jul
Pavol	Blazek	CS 58	1:25:12	(2)	NCh	Praha	21 Jul
Pyotr	Kakhmovich	SU ..	1:25:15	( )		Grodno	18 Apr
Werner	Heyer	GDR 56	1:25:16	(7)	IM	Naumburg	1 May
Jose	Marin	Spa 50	1:25:17	(1)	IM	L'Hospitalet	8 Apr
Giacomo	Poggi	Ita 60	1:25:19	(9)		Piacenza	13 May
Querubin	Moreno	Col 59	1:25:19	(1)	PAC	Bucaramanga	4 Nov
Marco	Evoniuk	USA 54	1:25:23	(5)	IPM	Kobenhavn	12 May
Vasiliy	Matveyev	SU 57	1:25:26	(9)		Moskva	7 Jul
Ravil	Ibryamov	Bul 61	1:25:34	(2)	NCh	Sofiya	16 Jun
Igor	Lyubomirov	SU 61	1:25:35	(10)		Zhytomyr	30 Sep
Zhaudat	Aydarov	SU 56	1:25:40	(11)		Zhytomyr	30 Sep
Erling	Andersen	Nor 60	1:25:42	(1)		Valer	15 Sep
Viktor	Semyonov	SU 49	1:25:43	(7)		Armavir	22 Apr
Valdas	Kazlauskas	SU 58	1:25:46	(4)	GP	Ruse	15 Apr
Vyacheslav	Frantsuzov	SU 56	1:25:46	(1)		Gagarin	22 Apr
Martin	Toporek	Aut 61	1:25:46	(1)	IM	Fredrikstad	9 Jun
Lars Ove	Moen	Nor 59	1:25:46	(2)		Valer	15 Sep
Vitaliy	Bazheno	SU 59	1:25:49	(2)		Gagarin	22 Apr
Valeriy	Medved	SU 64	1:25:50	(5)		Moskva	13 May
Ivan	Tikhonov	SU 50	1:25:52	(8)		Armavir	22 Apr
Imre	Stankovics	Hun 50	1:25:53	(6)	GP	Ruse	15 Apr
Dan	O'Connor	USA 52	1:25:56	(1)		Long Beach	10 Mar
Karl	Degener	FRG 43	1:25:57	(1)		Wolfsburg	17 Mar
Janos	Szalas	Hun 60	1:26:00	(1)	NCh	Ozd	26 May
Giuseppe	Sciute	Ita 65	1:26:00	(1)		S.Agata M.	23 Sep
Vladimir	Tarasov	SU ..	1:26:09	(6)		Moskva	13 May
Tim	Berrett	UK 65	1:26:13	(2)		Dartford	25 Feb

1984 Lists – Men

50,000 METRES WALK (ROAD)

Ronald	Weigel	GDR 58	3:38:31	(1)	OD	Berlin	20 Jul
Hartwig	Gauder	GDR 54	3:41:24	(2)	OD	Berlin	20 Jul
Andrey	Perlov	SU 61	3:43:06	(1)	Drzh	Moskva	17 Aug
	Weigel		3:43:25	(1)	IM	Naumburg	1 May
Dietmar	Meisch	GDR 59	3:43:33	(3)	OD	Berlin	20 Jul
	Gauder		3:45:37	(2)	IM	Naumburg	1 May
Pavol	Szikora	CS 52	3:45:53	(2)	Drzh	Moskva	17 Aug
Raul	Gonzalez	Mex 52	3:46:41	(3)	IM	Naumburg	1 May
	Perlov		3:47:20	(1)	Znam	Sochi	10 Jun
	Gonzalez		3:47:26	(1)	OG	Los Angeles	11 Aug
Valeriy	Suntsov	SU 55	3:47:44	(2)	Znam	Sochi	10 Jun
Martin	Bermudez	Mex 58	3:48:03	(4)	IM	Naumburg	1 May
	Suntsov		3:48:18	(5)	IM	Naumburg	1 May
Reima	Salonen	Fin 55	3:48:36	(1)	UCp	Zhytomyr	30 Sep
Valeriy	Yarets	SU 56	3:48:50	(2)	UCp	Zhytomyr	30 Sep
	Suntsov		3:49:13	(3)	UCp	Zhytomyr	30 Sep
	Szikora		3:49:38	(6)	IM	Naumburg	1 May
Venyamin	Nikolayev	SU 58	3:49:38	(3)	Znam	Sochi	10 Jun
Artur	Shumak	SU 63	3:49:58	(4)	UCp	Zhytomyr	30 Sep
	Yarets		3:49:59	(4)	Znam	Sochi	10 Jun
Jose	Marin	Spa 60	3:50:12	(1)	IM	Vilanova	18 Mar
Vladimir	Dushko	SU 56	3:50:51	(5)	Znam	Sochi	10 Jun
	Gonzalez		3:50:54	(1)	MRWW	Chapultepec	8 Apr
Oleg	Andreyev	SU 56	3:51:44	(6)	Znam	Sochi	10 Jun
Francois	Lapointe	Can 61	3:52:16	(1)		Hull	20 Oct
	Salonen		3:52:18	(7)	IM	Naumburg	1 May
	Andreyev		3:52:59	(3)	Drzh	Moskva	17 Aug
Erling	Andersen	Nor 60	3:53:16	(1)	NCh	Norrkoping	28 Apr
Bo	Gustafsson	Swe 54	3:53:19	(2)	OG	Los Angeles	11 Aug
Alessandro	Bellucci	Ita 55	3:53:45	(3)	OG	Los Angeles	11 Aug
Viktor	Dorovskikh	SU 50	3:53:53	(7)	Znam	Sochi	10 Jun
	Nikolayev		3:54:10	(4)	Drzh	Moskva	17 Aug
	Gauder		3:54:24	(1)	IM	Stockholm	26 May
Leonid	Sivakov	SU 56	3:54:25	(8)	Znam	Sochi	10 Jun
Ernesto	Canto	Mex 59	3:54:31	(2)	MRWW	Chapultepec	8 Apr
Vladimir	Nefyodov	SU 55	3:54:35	(5)	UCp	Zhytomyr	30 Sep
Lars Ove	Moen	Nor 59	3:54:53	(2)	IM	Vilanova	18 Mar
Viktor	Horodovchuk	SU 53	3:55:13	(9)	Znam	Sochi	10 Jun
Marcel	Jobin	Can 42	3:55:16	(1)	NCh	Ontario	15 Apr
Pavel	Karkhardin	SU 51	3:55:41	(10)	Znam	Sochi	10 Jun
	Meisch		3:55:44	(2)	IM	Stockholm	26 May
Bernd	Gummelt	GDR 63	3:55:44	(4)	OD	Berlin	20 Jul
Laszlo	Sator	Hun 53	3:56:16	(1)	IM	Bekescsaba	8 Apr
Bengt	Simonsen	Swe 58	3:56:32	(3)	IM	Stockholm	26 May
Vyacheslav	Fursov	SU 54	3:56:48	(11)	Znam	Sochi	10 Jun
Petro	Palagitskiy	SU 62	3:57:06	(6)	UCp	Zhytomyr	30 Sep
Paolo	Grecucci	Ita 51	3:57:18	(4)	IM	Stockholm	26 May
Walter	Schwoche	FRG 53	3:57:26	(1)	NCh	Bad Krozingen	15 Apr
	Salonen		3:57:42	(1)	NCh	Konnevesi	2 Jun
Arturo	Bravo	Mex 58	3:57:55	(1)	IM	Asch/Alz.	20 May

(50/35)

Manuel	Alcalde	Spa 56	3:58:03	(3)	IM	Vilanova	18 Mar
Ivan	Sakovits	SU 53	3:58:16	(1)		Grodno	19 Apr
Sergey	Soroka	SU 60	3:58:35	(13)	Znam	Sochi	10 Jun
Ivo	Pitak	CS 58	3:58:48	(2)	IM	Bekescsaba	8 Apr
Josef	Hudak	CS 62	3:59:16	(7)	Drzh	Moskva	17 Aug
Ignat	Olikh	SU 58	3:59:16	(7)	UCp	Zhytomyr	30 Sep
Roland	Nilsson	Swe 48	3:59:24	(4)	IM	Vilanova	18 Mar

1984 Lists – Men

Raffaello	Ducceschi	Ita 62	3:59:26	(5)	OG	Los Angeles	11 Aug
Carl	Schueler	USA 56	3:59:46	(6)	OG	Los Angeles	11 Aug
Heinrich	Schubert	FRG 51	3:59:47	(2)	NCh	Bad Krozingen	15 Apr
Aleksandr	Kitanov	SU 57	3:59:50	(15)	Znam	Sochi	10 Jun
Aleksandr	Udalov	SU 53	3:59:56	(16)	Znam	Sochi	10 Jun
Pyotr	Gaus	SU 52	4:00:17	(1)	RC	Penza	4 Aug
Jan	Klos	Pol 60	4:00:19	(1)	NCh	Szczecin	15 Apr
Jaroslav	Makovec	CS 60	4:00:24	(9)		Naumburg	1 May
Sergiy	Tsymbalyuk	SU 58	4:00:31	(8)	UCp	Zhytomyr	30 Sep
Mykola	Udovenko	SU 56	4:00:32	(9)	UCp	Zhytomyr	30 Sep
Axel	Noack	GDR 61	4:00:41	(1)	NCh	Magdeburg	14 Oct
Aleksandr	Potashov	SU 61	4:00:46	(2)		Grodno	19 Apr
Andrew	Jackno	Aus 62	4:01:02	(1)		Adelaide	18 Mar
Valeriy	Solovyov	SU 60	4:01:03	(19)	UCp	Zhytomyr	30 Sep
Jose	Pinto	Por 56	4:01:27	(5)	IM	Vilanova	18 Mar
Grzegorz	Ledzion	Pol 57	4:01:33	(2)	NCh	Szczecin	15 Apr
Nikolay	Pokatov	SU 56	4:01:53	(11)	UCp	Zhytomyr	30 Sep
Chris	Maddocks	UK 57	4:02:00	(6)	IM	Vilanova	18 Mar
Marco	Evoniuk	USA 57	4:02:25	(1)	FOT	Los Angeles	23 Jun
Ivan	Volgin	SU 62	4:02:53	(18)	Znam	Sochi	10 Jun
Jorge	Llopart	Spa 52	4:03:09	(7)	OG	Los Angeles	11 Aug
Grygoriy	Krasovsky	SU 59	4:03:23	(12)	UCp	Zhytomyr	30 Sep
Aleksandr	Kormilitsyn	SU 59	4:03:27	(19)	Znam	Sochi	10 Jun
Horst	Matern	FRG 51	4:03:45	(3)	NCh	Bad Krozingen	15 Apr
Oleksandr	Baranov	SU 61	4:03:59	(13)	UCp	Zhytomyr	30 Sep
Valdas	Marciauskas	SU 63	4:04:10	(1)		Vilnius	1 Jul
Fuxin	Zhang	Chn 61	4:04:16	(1)	NCh	Jiading	12 Mar
Ivan	Greben	SU 60	4:04:18	(14)	UCp	Zhytomyr	30 Sep
Qian	Ku	Chn 62	4:04:22	(2)	NCh	Jiading	12 Mar
Viktor	Balandin	SU 51	4:04:29	(20)	Znam	Sochi	10 Jun
Dominique	Guebey	Fra 52	4:04:45	(1)	NCh	Aye	6 May
Vladimir	Vasilenko	SU 62	4:04:46	(15)	UCp	Zhytomyr	30 Sep
Robert	Mildenberger	FRG 50	4:05:17	(4)	NCh	Bad Krozingen	15 Apr
Oleg	Kharitonov	SU 58	4:05:25	(16)	UCp	Zhytomyr	30 Sep
Michael	Harvey	Aus 62	4:05:41	(2)		Adelaide	18 Mar
Stanislav	Bakhanovich	SU 62	4:05:50	(18)	UCp	Zhytomyr	30 Sep
Giorgio	Damilano	Ita 57	4:05:52	(6)	IM	Stockholm	26 May
Stanislav	Vezhel	SU 62	4:05:54	(21)	Znam	Sochi	10 Jun
Alfons	Schwarz	FRG 54	4:06:03	(5)	NCh	Bad Krozingen	15 Apr
Guillaume	Leblanc	Can 62	4:06:04	(2)		Hull	0 Oct
Massimo	Qiriconi	Ita 63	4:06:27	(7)	IM	Stockholm	26 May
Petro	Melnyk	SU 51	4:06:30	(22)	Znam	Sochi	10 Jun
Volodymyr	Khomenko	SU 52	4:06:37	(22)	UCp	Zhytomyr	30 Sep
Vasiliy	Galinskiy	SU 56	4:06:42	(23)	UCp	Zhytomyr	30 Sep
Mikhail	Semyaninov	SU 56	4:06:55	(24)	Znam	Sochi	10 Jun
Ovksentiy	Granat	SU 57	4:07:15	(24)	UCp	Zhytomyr	30 Sep
Karl	Degener	FRG 43	4:07:22	(1)		Seelze-Letter	7 Oct
Aivars	Rumbenieks	SU 51	4:07:32	(1)		Riga	8 Jul
Oleksandr	Shtefan	SU 64	4:07:50	(25)	Znam	Sochi	10 Jun
Andrey	Ivanov	SU 58	4:08:21	(1)		Grodno	19 Apr
Matti	Katila	Fin 45	4:08:29	(11)	IM	Naumburg	1 May
Aleksandr	Meshcheryakov	SU 57	4:08:47	(26)	Znam	Sochi	10 Jun
Zoltan	Czukor	Hun 62	4:08:58	(3)	IM	Bekescsaba	8 Apr
Pavol	Jati	CS 59	4:08:59	(3)	NCh	Podebrady	3 Jun
Mikhail	Shishkin	SU 63	4:09:07	(25)	UCp	Zhytomyr	30 Sep
Vitaliy	Popovich	SU 62	4:09:09	(1)		Kiyev	8 Sep
Roman	Mrazek	CS 62	4:09:34	(4)	NCh	Podebrady	3 Jun
Georgiy	Budkevich	SU 53	4:09:40	(26)	UCp	Zhytomyr	30 Sep

Track performances

Alfons	Schwarz	FRG 54	4:01:21.7	(1)	IM	Fontenay	25 Mar
Chris	Maddocks	UK 57	4:05:47.3	(1)		Birmingham	22 Sep

1984 Lists – Men

Dennis	Terraz	Fra 58	4:10:29.8	(2)	IM	Fontenay	25 Mar
Dominique	Guebey	Fra 52	4:10:57.0	(3)	IM	Fontenay	25 Mar
Jan	Pilcuk	Pol 53	4:14:07.9	(1)		Zabrze	13 Oct

The Mexican Raul Gonzales(l) and Martin Bermudez(r) in the Olympic 50km walk. Between them is Willi Sarwall (Australia).

309

JUNIOR ALL-TIME LISTS

100 METRES

Stanley	Floyd	USA 61	10.07	2.0	(1)		Austin	24 May 80
Mel	Lattany	USA 59	10.09	1.8	(2)	USOCF	Colorado Springs	30 Jul 78
	Floyd		10.10	1.1	(1)	NCAA	Austin	6 Jun 80
Harvey	Glance	USA 57	10.11	1.9	(1)	FOT	Eugene	20 Jun 76
	Glance		10.12	1.6	(1)S1	FOT	Eugene	20 Jun 76
	Floyd		10.12	1.2	(1)		Den Haag	4 Jul 80
Ronnie R.	Smith	USA 49	10.14	0.8	(2)S1	AAU	Sacramento	20 Jun 68
Eugen	Ray	GDR 57	10.16 i		(1)		Berlin	25 Jan 76
	Glance		10.16	0.3	(1)	NCAA	Philadelphia	4 Jun 76
Houston	McTear	USA 57	10.16	1.9	(2)	FOT	Eugene	20 Jun 76
Calvin	Smith	USA 61	10.17	2.0	(2)		Austin	24 May 80
Sam	Graddy	USA 64	10.18	2.0	(3)	PAG	Caracas	24 Aug 83
Ray	Stewart	JAM 65	10.19		( )H		Port of Spain	19 May 84
Eric	Brown	USA 60	10.20	0.2	(2)		Westwood	28 Apr 79
Carl	Lewis	USA 61	10.21	-0.4	(1)	TAC-J	Knoxville	16 Jun 80
Terry	Scott	USA 64	10.21	0.3	(1)R1	PENN R	Philadelphia	30 Apr 83
Luis	Morales	USA 64	10.21	1.6	(1)R2	SW	Modesto	14 May 83
Bruce	Davis	USA 63	10.22	0.6	(2)		College Station	25 Apr 81
Johnny	Jones	USA 58	10.23	1.9	(4)	FOT	Eugene	20 Jun 76
Chidi	Imo	NIG 65	10.23	0.5	(2)S2	WUG	Edmonton	6 Jul 83
Silvio	Leonard	CUB 55	10.24	0.6	(1)		Praha	4 Sep 73
Pier-Francesco	Pavoni	ITA 63	10.2	-0.9	(2)	EC	Athinai	7 Sep 82
Herschel	Walker	USA 62	10.26	1.9	(1)		Athens	4 Apr 81
Dwayne	Strozier	USA 57	10.27	-0.9	(1)H1		Tempe	8 May 76
Ken	Robinson	USA 63	10.27	0.0	(1)		Tempe	27 Mar 82
Steffen	Bringmann	GDR 64	10.27	1.0	(3)	OD	Berlin	8 Jun 83
Henry	Thomas	USA 67	10.27	1.0	(1)		Norwalk	19 May 84

Doubtful timing

Renaldo	Dawson	USA 63	10.14		(1)		Prairie View	7 May 82

Marks made with assisting wind

Johnny	Jones	USA 58	10.08	4.0	(1)		Austin	20 May 77
Stanley	Blalock	USA 64	10.09	4.1	(1)		Athens	19 Mar 83
Rod	Richardson	USA 62	10.11	4.0	(1)		Austin	22 May 81
Calvin	Smith	USA 61	10.12	3.7	(1)H5	NCAA	Austin	5 Jun 80
Jerome	Harrison	USA 62	A10.12		(1)		Colorado Springs	25 Jul 81
Thomas	Schroder	GDR 62	10.14	3.6	(1)	EC-J	Utrecht	20 Aug 81
Roy	Martin	USA 66	10.14	4.0	(1)		Austin	6 Apr 84
Carl	Lewis	USA 61	10.16	2.8	(2)	MSR	Walnut	19 Apr 80
Sam	Graddy	USA 64	10.16	3.1	(1)H3	NVAA	Houston	2 Jun 83
Greg	Sholars	USA 66	10.16	4.0	(1)		Austin	12 May 84
Renaldo	Nehemiah	USA 61	10.18	4.2	(1)	IC4A	Philadelphia	21 May 78
Luis	Morales	USA 64	10.18	4.2	(1)H1	SW	Modesto	14 May 83
Ron	Brown	USA 61	10.19	2.2	(1)	CALR	Modesto	17 May 80
Mark	McNeil	USA 61	10.21	2.8	(1)		Austin	8 May 80
Herschel	Walker	USA 62	10.22	2.9	(2)S2	NCAA	Baton Rouge	5 Jun 81
Lincoln	Asquith	UK 64	10.22	8.5	(5)		Edinburgh	26 Jun 83
Darren	Walker	USA 62	10.23	4.2	(4)	USOCF	Syracuse	25 Jul 81
Prince	Fields	USA 63	10.23		(1)		Killeen	17 Apr 82
Don	Quarrie	JAM 51	10.24	3.6	(1)	CG	Edinburgh	18 Jul 70
Greg	Moore	USA 59	10.24	4.5	(4)H6	NCAA	Eugene	1 Jun 78
Adrian	Jones	USA 61	10.24		(2)R2		Cerritos	17 May 80
Ken	Robinson	USA 63	10.24	3.1	(1)H2		Norwalk	5 Jun 81
Jimmy	Daniel	USA 64	10.24	4.1	(1)H2		San Angelo	19 May 83

Junior All-time Lists – Men

200 METRES

Dwayne	Evans	USA 58	20.22	1.7	(2)		OT	Eugene	22 Jun 76
Roy	Martin	USA 66	20.28	1.0	(1)Q2		OT	Los Angeles	19 Jun 84
Clinton	Davis	USA 65	20.29	1.5	(1)		TAC-J	University Park	26 Jun 83
Jurgen	Evers	FRG 65	20.37	1.0	(1)		EC-J	Schwechat	28 Aug 83
Marshall	Dill	USA 52	A20.39	1.0	(2)		PAG	Cali	3 Aug 71
	Davis		20.39	-1.5	(1)		PAC-J	Barquisimeto	1 Aug 82
Silvio	Leonard	CUB 55	20.42	1.8	(2)			Potsdam	13 Jun 74
Dwayne	Strozier	USA 57	20.43	0.9	(2)			Tucson	1 May 76
	Evans		20.43	0.7	(3)		OG	Montreal	26 Jul 76
	Martin		20.43	-0.6	(4)		OT	Los Angeles	20 Jun 84
Stanley	Floyd	USA 61	20.46		(1)H2			Auburn	17 May 80
Darren	Clark	AUS 65	20.49	0.0	(1)			Sydney	12 Nov 83
Stanley	Blalock	USA 64	20.50	0.9	(2)		DRAKE R	Des Moines	30 Apr 83
Ralf	Lubke	FRG 65	20.50	1.0	(2)		EC-J	Schwechat	28 Aug 83
Harvey	Glance	USA 57	20.53	0.0	(1)H5		NCAA	Philadelphia	3 Jun 76
Don	Quarrie	JAM 51	20.56	1.7	(1)		CG	Edinburgh	12 Jul 70
Ade	Mafe	UK 66	20.57	1.5	(2)		8-N	Tokyo	14 Sep 84
Bernard	Hoff	GDR 59	20.59	0.0	(1)		EC-J	Donyetsk	21 Aug 77
Adrian	Jones	USA 61	20.59	-0.1	(1)			San Jose	31 May 80
La Monte	King	USA 59	20.61		(1)			Fresno	13 May 78
Bruno	Cherrier	FRA 53	20.62	0.4	(3)Q4		OG	Munchen	3 Sep 72
Danie	Zaayman	RSA 60	A20.63		(1)			Pretoria	31 Mar 78
Lamar	Preyor	USA 57	20.64"		(1)			Tempe	24 Mar 76
Calvin	Smith	USA 61	20.64	0.9	(2)			Tuscaloosa	5 Apr 80
Marks made with assisting wind									
Derald	Harris	USA 58	20.01	2.5	(1)			San Jose	9 Apr 77
Roy	Martin	USA 66	20.25"		(1)			Mesquite	5 May 84
Stanley	Floyd	USA 61	20.39	3.3	(1)H4		NCAA	Austin	5 Jun 80
Don	Quarrie	JAM 51	20.48	4.9	(1)Q4		CG	Edinburgh ·	21 Jul 70
Lamar	Preyor	USA 57	20.50	2.1	(2)			Westwood	21 Mar 76
Ade	Mafe	UK 66	20.55	2.2	(3)Q2		OG	Los Angeles	5 Aug 84
Mike	Dexter	USA 64	20.56	2.4	(1)			Modesto	21 Mar 83
Howard	Henley	USA 61	20.63	3.4	(4)H3		NCAA	Austin	5 Jun 80
Elliott	Quow	USA 62	20.63	2.3	(1)S3		NCAA	Baton Rouge	6 Jun 81

(" = 200 yards less 0.11 seconds)

400 METRES

Darrell	Robinson	USA 63	44.69		(2)		USOCF	Indianapolis	24 Jul 82
James	Rolle	USA 64	A44.73		(1)		USOCF	Colorado Springs	2 Jul 83
Darren	Clark	AUS 65	44.75		(4)		OG	Los Angeles	8 Aug 84
	Clark		44.77		(2)Q1		OG	Los Angeles	5 Aug 84
Thomas	Schonlebe	GDR 65	45.01		(1)			Berlin	15 Jul 84
Wayne	Collett	USA 49	A45.04		(1)Q2		OT	Echo Summit	13 Sep 68
	Clark		45.05		(1)		AAA	London	24 Jul 83
	Schonlebe		45.05		(3)		OD	Potsdam	21 Jul 84
	Schonlebe		45.13		(1)		NC	Erfurt	2 Jun 84
	Schonlebe		45.13		(1)H			Berlin	20 Jul 84
Dele	Udo	NIG 57	45.37		(1)			Lincoln	15 May 76
Bill	Green	USA 61	45.37		(2)		NCAA	Austin	7 Jun 80
Billy	Konchellah	KEN 61	A45.38		(2)			Nairobi	20 Jun 79
David	Jenkins	UK 52	45.45		(1)		EC	Helsinki	13 Aug 71
Felix	Imadyi	NIG 58	45.46		(1)		WPT	Tunis	12 Aug 77
Michael	Cannon	USA 64	A45.48		(1)			Colorado Springs	18 Jul 83
Tim	Dale	USA 57	45.51		(1)		IC4A	Philadelphia	22 May 76
Sunder	Nix	USA 62	45.56		(1)			East Lansing	23 May 81
Ed	Daniels	USA 60	A45.68		(1)			Albuquerque	5 May 79

311

Junior All-time Lists – Men

Anthony	Ketchum	USA 62	45.69	(2)S2	TAC	Sacramento	20 Jun 81
Jens	Carlowitz	GDR 64	45.72	(2)	EC-J	Schwechat	27 Aug 83
Hartmut	Weber	FRG 60	45.77	(1)	EC-J	Bydgoszcz	18 Aug 79
Leroy	Dixson	USA 63	45.77	(2)		Minneapolis	23 May 82
Danny	Harris	USA 65	45.79	(1)H1		Lincoln	11 May 84
Clinton	Davis	USA 65	45.80	(1)H1	TAC-J	University Park	25 Jun 83

Hand timed

Steve	Williams	USA 53	A44.9"	(1)		El Paso	13 May 72
Lee	Evans	USA 47	45.2	(1)		Los Angeles	23 Jul 66
Dave	Morton	USA 49	45.2"	(1)		Fort Worth	4 May 68
Edesel	Garrison	USA 50	45.2"	(2)S2	AAU	Knoxville	20 Jun 69
Al	Coffee	USA 50	45.3"	(1)		Knoxville	17 May 69
Benny	Brown	USA 53	45.3	(3)	NCAA	Eugene	3 Jun 72
Danny	Harris	USA 65	45.3	(1)		Lincoln	12 May 84
Evis	Jennings	USA 55	45.4"	(1)		Baton Rouge	4 May 74
Clinton	Davis	USA 65	45.4	(1)S		Towson	17 Jul 82
Ronnie	Ray	USA 54	45.5"	(1)		Charlottesville	27 May 72
Karl	Farmer	USA 54	45.5"	(2)	AAU	Bakersfield	16 Jun 73
Anthony	Ketchum	USA 62	45.5	(1)		Austin	16 May 81

(" = 440 yards time less 0.3)

800 METRES

Jim	Ryun	USA 47	1:44.3"	(1)	USTFF	Terre Haute	10 Jun 66
Joaquim	Cruz	BRA 63	1:44.3	(1)		Rioe de Janiero	27 Jun 81
Andreas	Busse	GDR 59	1:45.45	(1)	GS	Ostrava	7 Jun 78
	Ryun		1:45.5	(1)		Los Angeles	14 Jul 66
Steve	Ovett	UK 55	1:45.77	(2)	EC	Roma	4 Sep 74
Detlef	Wagenknecht	GDR 59	1:45.84	(1)	NC	Leipzig	2 Jul 78
Jozef	Plachy	CS 49	A1:45.96	(3)S2	OG	Mexico, D.F.	14 Oct 68
	Plachy		A1:45.99	(5)	OG	Mexico, D.F.	15 Oct 68
Jozsef	Bereczki	HUN 62	1:46.17	(1)	EC-J	Utrecht	13 Aug 81
Josef	Schmid	FRG 53	1:46.3	(2)		Waiblingen	2 Aug 72
George	Ghipu	RUM 54	1:46.37	(3)	EP/SF	Nice	5 Aug 73
Igor	Lotarev	SU 64	1:46.37	(3)	SPART	Moskva	20 Jun 83
Tony	Tufariello	USA 59	1:46.42	(3)	NCAA	Eugene	3 Jul 78
John	Gladwin	UK 63	1:46.46	(6)		Oslo	7 Jul 82
Mark	Winzenreid	USA 49	1:46.5	(2)	AAU	Sacramento	21 Jun 68
Neville	Myton	JAM 46	1:46.6"	(3)		Kingston	15 Aug 64
David	Mack	USA 61	1:46.67	(6)	FOT	Eugene	23 Jun 80
John	Davies	UK 49	1:46.7	(1)		London	3 Jun 68
Billy	Konchellah	KEN 61	1:46.79	(2)	MSR	Walnut	19 Apr 80
Olaf	Beyer	GDR 57	1:46.8	(1)	NC	Karl-Marx-Stadt	6 Aug 76
Rob	Druppers	HOL 62	1:46.88	(1)		Hengelo	26 Sep 81
Sammy	Koskei	KEN 61	1:46.90	(1)		San Angelo	17 May 80

(" = 880 yards time less 0.6)

1500 METRES

Kipkoech	Cheruiyot	KEN 64	3:34.92	(1)		Munchen	26 Jul 83
Jim	Ryun	USA 47	3:36.1	(1)		Berkeley	17 Jul 66
Graham	Williamson	UK 60	3:36.6	(3)		Oslo	17 Jul 79
Tom	Byers	USA 55	3:37.5	(3)		Torino	24 Jul 74
	Williamson		3:37.7	(2)		Warszawa	13 Aug 78
	Byers		3:37.9	(2)	AAU	Westwood	22 Jun 74
Ari	Paunonen	FIN 58	3:38.07	(1)	NC	Tampere	31 Jul 77
	Cheruiyot		3:38.09	(1)R2	WK	Zurich	24 Aug 83

312

Junior All-time Lists – Men

Jose M.	Abascal	SPA 58	3:38.2	(1)		Barcelona	10 Sep 77
Igor	Lotarev	SU 64	3:38.3	(1)		Krasnodar	7 Aug 83
Filbert	Bayi	TAN 53	3:38.9	(1)		Dar-es-Salam	3 Dec 72
Stefano	Mei	ITA 63	3:39.00	(2)		Bologna	12 Sep 81
Gheorghe	Ghipu	RUM 54	3:39.0	(1)		Athinai	30 Jun 73
Maik	Dreissigacker	GDR 64	3:39.05	(3)	NC	Karl-Marx-Stadt	18 Jun 83
Frank	Forster	GDR 57	3:39.3	(3)		Karl-Marx-Stadt	29 May 76
Mike	Hillardt	AUS 61	3:39.67	(1)	NC	Sydney	23 Mar 80
Leonid	Bruk	SU 60	3:39.95	(2)	EC-J	Bydgoszcz	16 Aug 79
Steve	Cram	UK 60	3:40.09	(1)	vFRG-J	London	27 Aug 78
Harald	Hudak	FRG 57	3:40.3	(5)		Dusseldorf	8 Jun 76
Andreas	Busse	GDR 59	3:40.3	(3)		Erfurt	28 May 78
Hansjorg	Kunze	GDR 59	3:40.33	(9)	VD	Bruxelles	18 Aug 78
Teofilo	Benito	SPA 66	3:40.48	(5)	NC	Barcelona	30 Jun 84
Randall	Markey	AUS 55	3:40.6	(1)	NC	Melbourne	30 Mar 74

3000 METRES

Ari	Paunonen	FIN 58	7:43.20	(3)		Koln	22 Jun 77
Charles	Cheruiyot	KEN 64	7:47.47	(3)	ISTAF	W. Berlin	17 Aug 83
Jon	Richards	UK 64	7:48.28	(9)		Oslo	9 Jul 83
Steve	Binns	UK 60	7:51.84	(2)		Gateshead	8 Sep 79
Eddy	De Pauw	BEL 60	7:53.4	(2)		Bornem	3 Aug 79
	Binns		7:53.6	(7)	ROTW	London	31 Aug 79
Raf	Wijns	BEL 64	7:54.2	(4)		Bosvoorde	4 Aug 83
Jean-Pierre	N'Dayisenga	BEL 62	7:55.3	(1)		Louvain	12 Jul 81
John	Doherty	UK 61	7:56.28	(10)		London	13 Jul 80
Hansjorg	Kunze	GDR 59	7:56.4	(2)		Karl-Marx-Stadt	27 Jun 76
Stefano	Mei	ITA 63	7:56.87	(5)	vENG,ETH	Gateshead	7 Jun 81
Rainer	Wachenbrunner	GDR 62	7:57.18	(1)	EC-J	Utrecht	23 Aug 81
Walter	Merlo	ITA 65	7:57.38	(6)		Busto Arsizio	26 May 84
Maik	Dreissigacker	GDR 64	7:57.5	(2)		Berlin	17 Aug 83
Paul	Jaspers	HOL 65	7:57.62	( )		Hechtel	12 Aug 84
Gerry	Lindgren	USA 46	7:58.0	(2)		Karlsruhe	5 Jul 65
Werner	Schildhauer	GDR 59	7:58.0	(4)		Erfurt	28 May 78
Jose M.	Abascal	SPA 58	7:58.3	(1)	EC-J	Donyetsk	21 Aug 77
Cyrille	Laventure	FRA 64	7:58.4	(1)		St Maur	29 Jun 83
Grigoriy	Mishurny	SU 62	7:59.01	(2)	vGDR-J	Cottbus	25 Jun 81
Frank	Heine	GDR 63	7:59.05	(2)	EC-J	Utrecht	23 Aug 81

5000 METRES

Charles	Cheruiyot	KEN 64	13:25.33	(1)		Munchen	26 Jul 83
Steve	Binns	UK 60	13:27.04	(3)	COKE	London	14 Sep 79
Berhanu	Girma	ETH 60	13:33.6	(2)R1		Sochi	8 Jun 79
Richard	Juma/Kivina	TAN 58	13:35.06	(4)		Den Haag	25 Jun 77
Paul	Davies-Hale	UK 62	13:35.95	(6)	COKE	London	11 Sep 81
Roberto	Lopez	MEX 65	13:37.22	(14)	MSR	Walnut	28 Apr 84
Dave	Black	UK 52	13:37.4	(4)	COKE	London	10 Sep 71
Jean-Pierre	N'Dayisenga	BEL 62	13:38.74	(7)	VD	Bruxelles	28 Aug 81
Steve	Prefontaine	USA 51	13:39.6	(2)	vFRG	Stuttgart	16 Jul 70
Eddy	De Pauw	BEL 60	13:39.77	(7)	VD	Bruxelles	4 Sep 79
Ari	Paunonen	FIN 58	13:41.03	(4)		Helsinki	7 Jun 77
Walter	Merlo	ITA 65	13:41.17	(4)		Firenze	7 Jun 84
Hansjorg	Kunze	GDR 59	13:42.2	(1)		Erfurt	27 May 78
Gabor	Szabo	HUN 62	13:42.87	(3)	vCS	Praha	24 Jun 81
Bruce	Kidd	CAN 43	13:43.8	(1)		Compton	2 Jun 62
Frank	Heine	GDR 63	13:43.86	(7)	OD	Berlin	9 Jun 82
Gerry	Lindgren	USA 46	13:44.0	(4)		Compton	5 Jun 64
Julian	Goater	UK 53	13:44.53	(10)	AAA	London	14 Jul 72
Don	Clary	USA 57	13:45.2	(1)		Eugene	17 Apr 76
Raineri	Carenza	ITA 63	13:45.45	(6)		Goteburg	2 Aug 82

313

Junior All-time Lists – Men

| Leonid | Schomsky | SU 59 | 13:42.8 | | (1) | | Voroshilovgrad | 9 Mar 77 |

3 Miles

| Gerry | Lindgren | USA 46 | 13:04.0 | | (2) | AAA | London | 10 Jul 65 |

2000 METRES STEEPLECHASE

Arsenios	Tsiminos	GRE 61	5:25.1		(1)		Athinai	20 Oct 80
Gaetano	Erba	ITA 60	5:27.44		(1)	EC-J	Bydgoszcz	18 Aug 79
Frank	Baumgartl	GDR 55	5:28.14		(1)	EC-J	Duisburg	26 Aug 73
Nikolay	Matyushenko	SU 66	5:28.15		(1)		Debrecen	19 Aug 84
Vladimir	Kanev	BUL 54	5:28.36		(2)	EC-J	Duisburg	26 Aug 73
Colin	Reitz	UK 60	5:29.61		(2)	EC-J	Bydgoszcz	18 Aug 79
Gyula	Balogh	HUN 61	5:29.91		(1)	vPOL,RUM-J	Budapest	5 Sep 80
Domingo	Ramon	SPA 58	5:30.2		(1)	vFRA,UK-J	Dôle	7 Aug 77
Vesa	Laukkanen	FIN 58	5:30.2		(1)	EC-J	Donyetsk	21 Aug 77
	Matyushenko		5:30.91		(1)	DRUZHBA	Plovdiv	5 Aug 84
Hagen	Melzer	GDR 59	5:31.1		(1)	vSU-J	Halle	16 Aug 78
Paul	Davies–Hale	UK 62	5:31.12		(1)	EC-J	Utrecht	22 Aug 81
Francesco	Panetta	ITA 63	5:31.2		(1)		Saronno	22 May 82
Michael	Langler	FRG 60	5:32.48		(3)	EC-J	Bydgoszcz	18 Aug 79
Frank	Fischer	GDR 63	5:32.58		(1)	vSU-J	Leningrad	19 Jun 82
Magnus	Tellander	SWE 54	5:32.6		(1)		Malmo	12 Aug 73
Peter	Daenens	BEL 60	5:32.75		(4)	EC-J	Bydgoszcz	18 Aug 79
Christoph	Engel	FRG 50	5:32.8		(1)		Schwetzingen	31 Aug 69
Frank	Fillaut	FRA 58	5:33.0		(2)	vSPA,UK-J	Dôle	7 Aug 77
Frank	Ruhkieck	GDR 61	5:33.02		(5)	EC-J	Bydgoszcz	18 Aug 79
Grigoriy	Mishurny	SU 62	5:33.77		(1)	vGDR-J	Cottbus	24 Jun 81

3000 METRES STEEPLECHASE

Ralf	Ponitzsch	GDR 57	8:29.50		(4)	vPOL,SU	Warszawa	19 Aug 76
Paul	Davies–Hale	UK 62	8:29.85		(3)	vPOL,SWI	London	31 Aug 81
	Ponitzsch		8:31.2		(1)	NC	Karl-Marx-Stadt	6 Aug 76
Shigeyuki	Aikyo	JAP 64	8:31.27		(9)H1	WC	Helsinki	9 Aug 83
Arsenios	Tsiminos	GRE 61	8:31.85		(3)	vSPA,BEL-J	Barcelona	31 Aug 80
Francesco	Panetta	ITA 63	8:33.24		(2)		Firenze	25 May 82
	Aikyo		8:33.29		(11)S2	WC	Helsinki	10 Aug 83
	Aikyo		8:33.44		(3)	WUG	Edmonton	8 Jul 83
John	Gregorek	USA 60	8:33.8		(2)	IC4A	Philadelphia	20 May 79
	Aikyo		8:34.48		(2)	PO	Los Angeles	26 Jun 83
Anders	Carlsson	SWE 59	8:34.84		(2)	NC	Stockholm	5 Aug 78
Frank	Baumgartl	GDR 55	8:35.99		(4)	vFIN,SU	Helsinki	16 Sep 73
Gyula	Balogh	HUN 61	8:36.2		(1)	NC	Budapest	30 Aug 80
Valeriy	Gryaznov	SU 61	8:38.5		(9)	NC	Donyetsk	7 Sep 80
Hagen	Melzer	GDR 59	8:38.66		(2)	NC	Leipzig	30 Jun 78
Bruce	Bickford	USA 57	8:38.67		(7)	NCAA	Philadelphia	5 Jun 76
Csaba	Szucs	HUN 65	8:39.37		(5)	NC	Budapest	26 Jul 84
Tommy	Ekblom	FIN 59	8:39.8		(3)		Kokkola	5 Aug 78
Karl	Van Calcar	USA 65	8:39.81		(3)H2	NCAA	Eugene	30 May 84
Said	Aouita	MOR 60	8:40.2		(2)	vTUN	Tunis	17 Jul 79
Grigoriy	Mishurny	SU 62	8:40.21			ZNAM	Leningrad	26 Jul 81
Todd	Lathers	USA 52	8:40.4		(2)		Seattle	21 May 71
Gabor	Marko	HUN 60	8:40.96		(1)		Budapest	28 Jul 79
Filbert	Bayi	TAN 53	8:41.34		(9)H1	OG	Munchen	1 Sep 72

110 METRES HURDLES

Renaldo	Nehemiah	USA 59	13.23	0.0	(1)R2	WK	Zurich	16 Aug 78
	Nehemiah		13.25	−0.1	(1)		Warszawa	13 Aug 78
	Nehemiah		13.27	1.8	(2)	NCAA	Eugene	2 Jun 78
	Nehemiah		13.28	0.2	(1)	AAU	Westwood	9 Jun 78

314

Junior All-time Lists – Men

	Nehemiah		13.28	0.6	(1)	DNG	Stockholm	4 Jul 78
	Nehemiah		• 13.35	1.4	(1)S1	AAU	Westwood	8 Jul 78
	Nehemiah		13.36	0.4	(1)		Stuttgart	22 Aug 78
	Nehemiah		13.37	0.8	(2)	PEPSI	Westwood	7 May 78
	Nehemiah		13.40	0.2	(1)		Dusseldorf	6 Jul 78
	Nehemiah		13.42		(1)		Milano	1 Jul 78
Holger	Pohland	GDR 63	13.47	1.9	(2)	vUSA	Karl-Marx-Stadt	10 Jul 82
Robert	Gaines	USA 57	13.57	1.4	(2)S1	OT	Eugene	14 Jun 76
Greg	Foster	USA 58	13.57"	0.5	(1)	WCR	Fresno	7 May 77
Arto	Bryggare	FIN 58	13.66	2.0	(4)	EP	Helsinki	14 Aug 77
James	Walker	USA 57	13.67	1.7	(1)	vFRG-J	Ludenscheid	8 Jul 76
Rod	Wilson	USA 61	13.71	0.6	(1)	PAG-J	Sudbury	31 Aug 80
Jorg	Naumann	GDR 63	13.71	1.3	(1)		Potsdam	10 Jun 82
Rod	Woodson	USA 65	13.71		(2)		Tallahassee	17 Mar 84
Don	Wright	AUS 59	A13.76		(1)H		Pocatello	19 May 78
Andrey	Prokofyev	SU 59	13.77		(1)	NC	Tbilisi	16 Sep 78
Roberto	Schneider	SWZ 57	13.78	0.8	(1)	NC	Zofingen	22 Aug 76
Reyna	Thompson	USA 63	13.80	1.9	(1)		College Station	20 Mar 82
Cletus	Clark	USA 62	13.81	1.5	(2)		Dallas	16 May 81
Steve	Darcus	USA 57	13.83	1.7	(4)S2	AAU	Westwood	10 Jun 76
Andreas	Oschkenat	GDR 62	13.83	−0.7	(1)	NC-J	Halle	5 Jul 81
Arthur	Blake	USA 66	13.84	−0.4	(1)S2	NC-J	Los Angeles	22 Jun 84
Milan	Stewart	USA 60	13.85	0.7	(2)		Westwood	28 Apr 79
Jiri	Hudec	CS 64	13.85	−0.5	(1)	EC-J	Schwechat	26 Aug 83
Rod	Chesley	USA 58	13.86		(2)		Charlottesville	23 Apr 77
Stephane	Caristan	FRA 64	13.86	1.4	(1)	NC	Bordeaux	23 Jul 83

Marks made with assisting wind

Arto	Bryggare	FIN 58	13.55	3.1	(1)	vUK	Oulo	10 Jul 77
Milan	Stewart	USA 60	13.70	4.0	(3)H1	NCAA	Champaign	31 May 79
Orlando	McDaniel	USA 60	13.77	4.0	(5)H1	NCAA	Champaign	31 May 79
Jiri	Hudec	CS 64	13.78	2.2	(1)H1	EC-J	Schwechat	26 Aug 83
Cletus	Clark	USA 62	13.79	3.1	(5)	NCAA	Baton Rouge	5 Jun 81
Al	Joyner	USA 61	13.81	4.0	(4)	TFA	Wichita	31 May 80
Dwayne	Allen	USA	13.81		(1)		Jonesboro	11 Apr 81
Steve	Kerho	USA 64	13.83	2.4	(3)		Berkeley	2 Apr 83

(" = 120 yards time plus 0.03 secs)

400 METRES HURDLES

Danny	Harris	USA 65	48.02		(2)S1	OT	Los Angeles	17 Jun 84
	Harris		48.11		(2)	OT	Los Angeles	18 Jun 84
	Harris		48.13		(2)	OG	Los Angeles	5 Aug 84
Vladimir	Budko	SU 65	48.74		(2)	FRI	Moskva	18 Aug 84
	Harris		48.81		(1)	NCAA	Eugene	1 Jun 84
	Harris		48.92		(1)S2	OG	Los Angeles	4 Aug 84
	Harris		49.16		(1)		Lincoln	12 May 84
	Harris		49.20		(1)		Knoxville	18 May 84
	Budko		49.27		(2)		Moskva	20 Jul 84
	Harris		49.44		(1)	TEXR	Austin	6 Apr 84

Belfred	Clark	USA 65	49.45		(1)	NC-J	Los Angeles	23 Jun 84
Harald	Schmid	FRG 57	49.61		(1)	vUSA-J	Ludenscheid	7 Jul 76
Dennis	Otono	NIG 58	49.62		(2)	NCAA	Champaign	4 Jun 77
Joszef	Szalai	HUN 61	49.64		(3)	BGP	Budapest	11 Aug 80
Ruslan	Mischenko	SU 64	49.71		(1)	EC-J	Schwechat	28 Aug 83
Ryoichi	Yoshida	JAP 65	49.75		(1)	NC	Tokyo	20 Oct 84
Hartmut	Weber	FRG 60	49.94		(1)		Cassino	8 Sep 79
Kevin	Henderson	USA 65	49.94		(2)	NC-J	Los Angeles	23 Jun 84
Rok	Kopitar	YUG 59	50.01		(1)	vSWZ,FRG	Olten	9 Sep 78
Patrick	Mann	USA 66	50.02		(3)	NC-J	Los Angeles	23 Jun 84

Jerzy	Pietrzyk	POL 55	50.07		(1)	EC-J	Duisburg	26 Aug 73
Sven	Mikisch	FRG 65	50.11		(1)	NC-J	Munchengladbach	19 Aug 84

Junior All-time Lists – Men

Carl	Young	USA 62	50.13		(1)		San Angelo	23 May 81
Martin	Briggs	UK 64	50.22		(3)	EC-J	Schwechat	28 Aug 83
Eddie	Southern	USA 38	*50.26		(1)S1	OG	Melbourne	24 Nov 56
Dmitry	Stukalov	SU 51	50.30		(1)	EC-J	Paris	13 Sep 70
Pablo	Squella	CHI 63	50.31		(1)		Santiago-de Chile	21 Nov 82
Jean-Pierre	Perrot	FRA 52	50.45		(2)	EC-J	Paris	13 Sep 70
Krasimir	Demirev	SU 51	50.45		(1)	EC-J	Utrecht	23 Aug 81

Hand timed

Danny	Harris	USA 65	49.4		(1)	Drake R	Des Moines	27 Apr 84
Eddie	Southern	USA 38	49.7		(2)	FOT	Los Angeles	29 Jun 56
Bob	Bornkessel	USA 50	A49.8		(2)R2		Echo Summit	31 Aug 68
James	Walker	USA 57	50.1		(2)		Atlanta	22 May 76
Juan	Pineira	CUB 63	50.3		(2)		Habana	27 May 81
Alberto	Queralta	CUB 64	0 50.3		(3)		Habana	27 May 81

HIGH JUMP

Vladimir	Yashchenko	SU 59	2.35I		(1)		Milano	12 Mar 78
Dietmar	Mogenburg	FRG 61	2.35		(1)		Rehlingen	26 May 80
	Yashchenko		2.34		(1)	PRAV	Tibilisi	16 Jun 78
	Yashchenko		2.33		(1)	vUSA-J	Richmond	3 Jul 77
	Mogenburg		2.33		(1)	NC	Hannover	16 Aug 80
Jianhua	Zhu	CHN 63	2.33		(1)	AIS:G	New Delhi	1 Dec 82
Patrik	Sjoberg	SWE 65	2.33		(1)		Oslo	9 Jul 83
Javier	Sotomayor	CUB 67	2.33		(1)	BARR	Habana	19 May 84
	Sjoberg		2.33		(4)		Eberstadt	10 Jun 84
	Sjoberg		2.33		(2)	OG	Los Angeles	11 Aug 84
Jorg	Freimuth	GDR 61	2.31		(3)	OG	Moskva	1 Aug 80
Yuriy	Sergiyenko	SU 65	2.29		(1)		Tashkent	25 Sep 83
Dothel	Edwards	USA 66	2.285		(1)		Athens	9 Jul 83
Paulo	Borghi	ITA 61	2.28		(1)		S.Lucia di Plave	25 May 80
Sergey	Zasimovich	SU 62	2.28		(1)		Alma-Ata	30 Jul 81
Sorin	Matei	RUM 63	2.28		(1)		Pitesti	12 Jun 82
Alain	Metellus	CAN 65	2.28i		(1)		Toronto	26 Feb 84
Thomas	Eriksson	SWE 63	2.27		(1)		Taipei	18 Sep 82
Luca	Tosa	ITA 64	2.27		(2)	NC	Roma	19 Jul 83
James	Lott	USA 65	2.27		(1)		Baton Rouge	14 Apr 84
Gail	Olson	USA 60	2.26i		(1)		Sterling	11 Mar 78
Krzysztof	Krawczyk	POL 62	2.26		(1)	EC-J	Utrecht	21 Aug 81
Valeriy	Brumel	SU 42	2.25		(1)	WUG	Sofia	31 Aug 61
Uwe	Rudiger	GDR 61	2.25		(2)	OT	Erfurt	18 May 80
Vadim	Oganyan	SU 63	2.25i		(1)	vGDR-J	Zaporozhe	21 Feb 82
Maurice	Crumby	USA 65	2.25		(1)		Stanford	2 Apr 83
Geoff	Parsons	UK 64	2.25		(1)		Plymouth	9 Jul 83
Evgeniy	Peew	BUL 65	2.25		(1)	vHUN,RUM-J	Plovdiv	15 Aug 83
Rick	Noji	USA 67	2.25		(1)		Seattle	12 May 84
Brad	Speer	USA 65	2.25		(1)		Elmhurst	16 Jun 84

POLE VAULT

Radion	Gataullin	SU 65	5.65		(2)	NC	Donyetsk	8 Sep 84
Thierry	Vigneron	FRA 60	5.61		(1)		Longwy	30 Sep 79
Konstantin	Volkov	SU 60	5.60		(1)	EP	Torino	5 Aug 79
	Gataullin		5.60i		(1)		Leningrad	12 Feb 84
	Gataullin		5.60i		(3)		Moskva	19 Feb 84
	Vigneron		5.57I		(1)		Paris	30 Nov 79
Dave	Volz	USA 62	5.57		(1)		Bloomington	18 Apr 81
	Volkov		5.55		(1)	SPART	Moskva	27 Jul 79
	Volz		5.55		(1)		Newhouse	27 Jul 81
Sergey	Bubka	SU 63	5.55		(1)		Kharkov	4 Sep 82

316

Junior All-time Lists – Men

	Bubka		5.55		(2)	SUP-NC	Tashkent	17 Sep 82
	Gataullin		5.55		(1)	EC-J	Schwechat	28 Aug 83
Gennadiy	Sukharev	SU 65	5.53i		(2)		Leningrad	12 Feb 84
Joe	Dial	USA 62	5.52		(1)		Stillwater	25 Aug 81
Aleksandr	Krupskiy	SU 60	5.50		(1)		Irkutsk	6 Aug 79
Pierre	Quinon	FRA 62	5.50		(2)		Haguenau	27 Sep 81
Dale	Jenkins	USA 63	5.50		(2)		Abilene	12 Nov 81
Aleksandr	Grigoryev	SU 64	5.50		(1)		Chelyabinsk	4 Sep 82
Greg	Duplantis	USA 62	5.48		(1)		Colorado Springs	25 Jul 81
Ryszard	Kolasa	POL 64	5.45		(1)		Gdynia	13 Sep 83
Grigoriy	Yegorov	SU 67	5.45		(1)	NC-Y	Simferopol	26 May 84
Mike	Tully	USA 56	5.43		(1)		Westwood	3 May 75
Ivo	Yanchev	BUL 60	5.42		(1)	vFRA,,HUN.,GRE-J	Sofia	5 Aug 79
Arto	Peltoniemi	FIN 66	5.42		(1)		Raahe	8 Aug 84
Jeff	Buckingham	USA 60	5.41		(1)	AAU-J	Bloomington	23 Jun 79
Doug	Fraley	USA 65	5.41		(1)		Fresno	14 Jul 84
Francois	Tracanelli	FRA 51	5.40		(1)	NC	Paris	26 Jul 70
Viktor	Spasov	SU 59	5.40		(2)		Kharkov	9 May 78
Vladimir	Polyakov	SU 60	5.40		(1)	EC-J	Bydgoszcz	19 Aug 79
Valeriy	Tkachenko	SU 61	5.40		(1)	NC-J	Tbilisi	7 Feb 80
Sergey	Dzemizhev	SU 64	5.40		(2)		Donyetsk	8 Feb 83
Valeriy	Ishutin	SU 65	5.40		(1)	NC-J	Riga	13 Jul 84
Viktor	Komarov	SU 66	5.40		(1)		Kharkov	21 Jul 84
Liang	Xuereng	CHN 65	5.40		(1)		Shanghai	8 Oct 84

LONG JUMP

Randy	Williams	USA 53	8.34	0.0	(q)	OG	Munchen	8 Sep 72
	Williams		8.24	0.0	(1)	OG	Munchen	9 Sep 72
Larry	Doubley	USA 58	8.22		(1)	NCAA	Champaign	3 Jul 77
Vance	Johnson	USA 63	A8.21	2.0	(1)	NCAA	Provo	4 Jun 82
La Monte	King	USA 59	8.18		(2)	CAL R	Modesto	20 May 78
Carl	Lewis	USA 61	8.13		(3)	PAG	San Juan	7 Jul 79
Robert	Emmiyan	SU 65	8.13	1.1	(1)		Baku	14 Sep 84
David	Giralt	CUB 59	8.12	0.3	(1)	OD	Berlin	15 Jun 77
Jerry	Herndon	USA 55	8.11	1.3	(3)	CAL R	Modesto	23 May 74
	Lewis		8.11		(-)	NCAA	Austin	6 Jun 80
Antonio	Corgos	SPA 60	8.09	1.8	(1)	vFIN,BEL	Bruxelles	17 Jun 79
Ron	Beer	GDR 65	8.06	0.2	(3)		Berlin	9 Jun 84
Charles	Smith	USA 66	8.06		(1)		Las Vegas	9 Jun 84
Juan	Ortiz	CUB 64	8.04	1.5	(1)	CAC	Habana	23 Jul 83
Joey	Wells	BAH 65	8.04	1.7	(2)	CAC	Habana	23 Jul 83
Sergey	Rodin	SU 63	8.03	0.7	(4)	NC	Kiev	21 Aug 82
Jerry	Proctor	USA 49	8.02		(1)		Claremont	30 Mar 68
Marek	Chludzinski	POL 57	8.02	0.6	(2)	NC	Bydgoszcz	26 Jun 76
Frank	Wartenburg	GDR 55	8.01i		(1)		Berlin	23 Feb 74
Waldemar	Golanko	POL 61	8.01	1.2	(1)	vFRG-J	Bielfield	16 Jun 79
Kenneth	Duncan	USA 53	7.98	1.4	(1)		Sacramento	17 Jun 72
Leszek	Dunecki	POL 56	7.98		(1)	EC-J	Athinai	24 Aug 75
Yong	Kim	NKO 62	A7.98	0.0	(1)		Mexico, D.F.	12 Jun 81

Marks made with assisting wind

Carl	Lewis	USA 61	8.35	2.2	(1)	NCAA	Austin	6 Jun 80
	Williams	USA 53	8.34	5.5	(1)	vSU-J	Sacramento	28 Jul 72
Jerry	Proctor	USA 49	8.07	5.1	(1)		Sacramento	17 Jun 67
Eugene	McCain	USA 60	8.05		(q)	NCAA	Eugene	1 Jun 78

Junior All-time Lists – Men

TRIPLE JUMP

Christo	Markov	BUL 65	17.42	1.3	(1)	NAR	Sofia	19 May 84
Pedro	Perez	CUB 52	A17.40	0.4	(1)	PAG	Cali	5 Aug 71
	Markov		17.29	−0.9	(3)	FRI	Moskva	18 Aug 84
	Markov		17.19	1.4	(1)	NC	Sofia	2 Jun 84
Volker	Mai	GDR 66	17.12	1.2	(2)	OD	Potsdam	21 Jul 84
	Markov		17.10	0.7	(1)		Furth	9 Jun 84
	Markov		17.05i		(1)		Sofia	11 Feb 84
	Markov		17.03		(1)		Ruse	5 May 84
	Markov		17.03	0.3	(3)	OD	Potsdam	21 Jul 84
	Mai		17.02		(3)	8-N	Tokyo	14 Sep 84
Gustavo	Platt	CUB 54	17.00		(1)		Habana	5 May 75
Aleksandr	Beskrovny	SU 60	16.83	0.8	(q)	EC-J	Bydgoszcz	18 Aug 79
Greg	Neal	USA 63	A16.81	0.0	(3)	NCAA	Provo	5 Jun 82
Ralf	Jaros	FRG 65	16.81	−0.1	(1)	NC	Dusseldorf	23 Jun 84
Willie	Banks	USA 56	16.79		(1)		Westwood	3 May 75
Jorge	Reyna	CUB 63	16.78		(1)		Stuttgart	29 Aug 82
Paul	Emordi	NIG 65	16.78		(1)		Baton Rouge	5 May 84
Oleg	Protsenko	SU 63	16.68	0.1	(1)	DRZ	Debrecen	2 Aug 81
Lazaro	Betancourt	CUB 63	16.64	0.2	(2)	CAC	Habana	12 Aug 82
Li	Mengchun	CHN 62	16.63		(1)	CHN IC	Peking	23 Sep 81
Lutz	Dombrowski	GDR 59	16.61		(1)		Berlin	19 Feb 77
John	Tillman	USA 65	16.61		(1)	PAG-J	Nassau	25 Aug 84
Aleksandr	Yakovlev	SU 57	16.60		(1)		Zaporozhe	22 Aug 76
Gennadiy	Valukevich	SU 58	16.60		(1)	EC-J	Donyetsk	19 Aug 77
Sergey	Akhvlediani	SU 62	16.58	1.9	(−)	EC-J	Utrecht	23 Aug 81
David	Giralt	CUB 59	16.57		(1)	HANZ	Zagreb	4 Jun 78
Ken	Williams	USA 64	16.56	1.6	(1)	vCAN-J	Sherbrooke	27 Jul 83

Marks made with assisting wind

Sergey	Akhvlediani	SU 62	16.76	4.0	(1)	EC-J	Utrecht	23 Aug 81
Jan	Cado	CS 63	16.66	2.4	(1)	ROS	Praha	16 Aug 82
Claes	Rahm	SWE 64	16.59	2.1	(1)	NC	Orebro	24 Jul 83
Aleksandr	Leonov	SU 62	16.54	3.4	(2)	EC-J	Utrecht	23 Aug 81

SHOT PUT

Terry	Albritton	USA 55	21.05l		(1)		New York	22 Feb 74
Mike	Carter	USA 60	20.65		(1)	vSU-J	Boston	4 Jul 79
	Albritton		20.38		(2)	MSR	Walnut	27 Apr 74
	Carter		20.31		(1)		Bakersfield	29 Jun 79
	Carter		20.22		(1)		Abilene	5 May 79
Randy	Matson	USA 45	20.20		(2)	OG	Tokyo	17 Oct 64
Udo	Beyer	GDR 55	20.20		(2)	NC	Leipzig	6 Jul 74
	Beyer		20.16		(1)		Potsdam	20 Jun 73
	Beyer		20.14		(2)		Berlin	24 Aug 74
Karl	Salb	USA 49	19.99		(4)	OT	South Lake Tahoe	10 Sep 68
Andreas	Horn	GDR 62	19.74		(2)	vSU-J	Cottbus	24 Jun 81
Vladimir	Kiselyov	SU 57	19.71		(1)		Yalta	15 May 76
Ron	Semkiw	USA 54	19.68		(1)	vAFR	Dakar	4 Aug 73
Viktor	Beliy	SU 64	19.51		(6)		Leningrad	26 Jul 83
Arnold	Campbell	USA 66	19.40		(1)		Shreveport	16 May 84
Jim	Neidhart	USA 55	19.39		(3)	CAL R	Modesto	25 May 74
Dallas	Long	USA 40	19.38		(1)		Los Angeles	2 May 59
Oleg	Zolotukhin	SU 64	19.25		(1)		Kharkov	5 May 83
Jens	Schroter	GDR 64	19.24i		(1)		Senftenburg	13 Feb 83
Wolfgang	Schmidt	GDR 54	19.19		(1)		Leipzig	30 Jun 73
Carlos	Scott	USA 60	19.03		(4)		Austin	18 May 79
Ulf	Timmermann	GDR 62	19.00		(3)		Cottbus	30 May 81
Valcho	Stoev	BUL 52	18.96		(1)		Warszawa	18 Sep 71
Dietmar	Krumm	GDR 58	18.87		(1)	EC-J	Donyetsk	21 Aug 77
Klaus	Gormer	GDR 63	18.85		(1)	vSU-J	Leningrad	20 Jun 82

Junior All-time Lists – Men

DISCUS THROW

Werner	Hartmann	FRG 59	63.64	(1)	vFRA	Strasbourg	25 Jun 78
Kent	Gardenkrans	SWE 55	62.04	(2)		Helsingborg	11 Aug 74
	Gardenkrans		61.98	(3)	CAL R	Modeesto	25 May 74
Wolfgang	Schmidt	GDR 54	61.30	(4)	NC	Dresden	22 Jul 73
	Hartmann		61.30	(4)		Dortmund	30 Jun 78
	Gardenkrans		61.02	(3)		Eskilstuna	5 Aug 74
Vladimir	Zinchenko	SU 59	60.60	(1)		Yalta	28 Sep 77
	Hartmann		60.34	(3)		Frankfurt	1 May 78
Juan	Martinez	CUB 59	60.34	(3)		Habana	25 Jun 78
Jozsef	Ficsor	HUN 65	60.06	(1)		Budapest	13 Jun 84
Marco	Martino	ITA 60	59.28	(1)		Cassino	8 Sep 79
Konstantinos	Georgakopoulos	GRE 63	59.08	(4)	BALK	Bucuresti	15 Aug 82
Aleksandr	Grechko	SU 62	58.92	(1)		Dnepropetrovsk	17 Jul 79
Laszlo	Kerkes	HUN 64	58.82	(1)		Uzhgorod	9 Oct 83
Darrell	Elder	USA 56	58.72	(1)		Lincoln	5 Jul 75
Igor	Duginyets	SU 56	58.58	(1)		Sevastopol	1 Oct 75
Yuriy	Dumchev	SU 58	58.52	(1)	vUSA-J	Richmond	3 Jul 77
Boris	Karayev	SU 50	58.28	(2)		Sochi	26 Oct 69
Mikhail	Gusev	SU 57	58.22	(3)		Kiev	30 May 76
Marshall	Smith	USA 53	58.00	(1)		Los Angeles	20 Jul 72
Doc	Luckie	USA 59	57.98	(q)	NCAA	Eugene	2 Jun 78
Helmut	Klink	GDR 56	57.92	(1)		Kharkov	16 Jun 75
Thomas	Christel	GDR 62	57.90	(6)	NC	Jena	8 Aug 81
Alfons	Saskoi	HUN 58	57.88	(1)		Budapest	7 Aug 77
Erik	de Bruin	HOL 63	57.88	(1)	NC	Amsterdam	7 Aug 82

HAMMER THROW

Roland	Steuk	GDR 59	78.14	(1)	NC	Leipzig	30 Jun 78
Sergey	Dorozhon	SU 64	78.00	(1)		Moskva	7 Aug 83
	Steuk		77.82	(1)	OD	Berlin	15 Jun 78
	Steuk		77.70	(1)		Potsdam	24 Aug 78
	Steuk		77.48	(1)		Erfurt	27 May 78
	Steuk		77.24	(2)	EC	Praha	2 Sep 78
	Steuk		77.04	(1)	vSU	Vilnius	25 Jun 78
	Steuk		76.92	(1)		Halle	17 Aug 78
	Steuk		76.76	(1)		Potsdam	18 Aug 78
	Steuk		76.38	(2)		Halle	27 Aug 77
Sergey	Litvinov	SU 58	76.32	(1)		Simferopol	7 Aug 77
Christoph	Sahner	FRG 63	75.24	(1)	vPOL-J	Gottingen	26 Jun 82
Igor	Nikulin	SU 60	75.20	(2)		Leselidze	1 Jun 79
Matthias	Moder	GDR 63	74.78	(1)	NC-J	Cottbus	24 Jul 82
Aleksandr	Seleznev	SU 64	74.28	(1)		Adler	22 Apr 83
Marc	Odenthal	FRG 63	73.60	(2)	vPOL-J	Gottingen	26 Jun 82
Fyodor	Makovskiy	SU 65	73.34	(2)		Volgograd	15 May 84
Vladimir	Dubinin	SU 63	73.20	(2)		Kharkov	30 May 82
Plamen	Minev	BUL 65	73.08	(2)		Sofia	4 Jul 84
Marco	Gerloff	GDR 64	72.64	(1)		Potsdam	20 Jul 83
Detlef	Gerstenberg	GDR 57	71.74	(3)		Berlin	12 May 76
Jozsef	Vida	HUN 63	71.66	(2)		Szombathely	21 Jul 82
Nikolay	Lysenko	SU 66	71.62	(1)		Frunze	25 Aug 84
Andrey	Abduvaliev	SU 66	71.54	(1)		Frunze	8 Sep 84
Alexey	Afanasyev	SU 66	71.50	(2)		Frunze	8 Sep 84
Sergey	Ivanov	SU 62	71.28	( )		Kislovodsk	29 Aug 80
Sergey	Alay	SU 65	71.26	(1)	NC-J	Riga	14 Jul 84
Ralf	Haber	GDR 62	70.88	(1)	vSU-J	Cottbus	25 Jun 81

319

Junior All-time Lists – Men

JAVELIN THROW

Ramon	Gonzalez	CUB 65	87.90		(1)		Habana	21 May 83
Phil	Olsen	CAN 57	87.76		(q)	OG	Montreal	25 Jun 76
	Gonzalez		86.82		(1)		Habana	27 Jan 84
Uwe	Hohn	GDR 62	86.56		(1)	EC-J	Utrecht	23 Aug 81
	Gonzalez		86.50		(1)		Habana	9 Feb 84
	Gonzalez		86.10		(1)		Habana	1 Feb 84
Arto	Harkonen	FIN 59	85.70		(1)		Kuortane	24 Jun 78
	Harkonen		85.54		(3)		Pihtipudas	2 Jul 78
Tero	Saviniemi	FIN 63	85.14		(1)		Alaharma	5 Sep 82
Charles	Clover	UK 55	84.92		(1)	OG	Christchurch	2 Feb 74
Klaus	Tafelmeier	FRG 58	81.14		(1)	EC-J	Donyetsk	21 Aug 77
Jean-Paul	Lakafia	FRA 61	83.56		(1)		Auckland	13 Dec 80
Antonios	Papadimitriou	GRE 65	83.56		(2)		Malmo	17 Jun 84
Mark	Murro	USA 49	83.21		(1)		Garden City	18 May 68
Roald	Bradstock	UK 62	83.20		(1)		Enfield	16 Aug 81
Roman	Zwierzchowski	POL 58	82.56		(3)	EC-J	Donyetsk	21 Aug 77
Georghe	Megelea	RUM 54	82.26		(1)		Kiev	29 Sep 73
Peter	Borglund	SWE 64	82.26		(1)		Karlstad	12 Jun 83
Aleksandr	Osipov	SU 59	82.24		(1)		Baku	24 Sep 78
Emil	Tsvetanov	BUL 63	82.14		(1)		Sofia	7 Aug 82
Gerald	Weiss	GDR 60	82.02		(5)	NC	Karl-Marx-Stadt	11 Aug 79
Jorgen	Jelstrom	DEN 63	81.74		(1)	NC	Aarhus	15 Aug 82
Oleg	Chasovitin	SU 64	81.52		(1)		Dnepropetrovsk	5 Oct 82
Bob	Rockett	USA 64	81.36		(1)		Corvallis	30 Apr 83

DECATHLON

Torsten	Voss	GDR 63	8387	(1)	NC	Erfurt	7 Jul 82
10.76 7.66 14.41 2.09 48.37 14.37 41.76 4.80 62.90 4:34.04							
Daley	Thompson	UK 58	8124	(1)	EP/SF	Sittard	31 Jul 77
10.70 7.54 13.84 2.01 47.31 15.26 41.70 4.70 54.48 4:30.4							
Valter	Kulvet	SU 64	8060	(6)		Gotzis	23 May 82
11.28 6.97 13.56 2.11 49.06 14.99 49.88 4.60 60.24 4:33.01							
Christian	Schenk	GDR 65	8053	(5)	OD	Potsdam	21 Jul 84
11.54 7.18 14.26 2.16 49.23 15.06 44.74 4.20 65.98 4:24.11							
	Voss		8044	(8)	vSU	Kiev	28 Jun 81
11.21 7.18 14.16 2.11 48.96 14.76 39.54 4.60 55.40 4:17.00							
	Voss		7997	(4)	NC	Halle	24 May 81
10.94 7.26 13.06 2.00 48.78 14.56 38.46 4.80 59.08 4:26.79							
	Thompson		7921	(3)		Gotzis	22 May 77
10.71 7.72 13.38 2.00 48.25 15.24 37.28 4.20 55.78 4:23.8							
Mikhail	Romanyuk	SU 62	7918	(1)	EC-J	Utrecht	21 Aug 81
11.26 7.11 13.50 1.98 49.98 14.72 42.94 4.90 59.74 4:30.63							
	Kulvet		7915	(1)	EC-J	Schwechat	26 Aug 83
11.30 6.99 14.75 2.10 50.40 15.27 48.74 4.40 59.70 4:39.63							
	Voss		7912	(2)	EC-J	Utrecht	21 Aug 81
10.89 7.35 14.26 2.07 48.97 14.50 36.66 4.60 48.80 4:31.21							
Sepp	Zeilbauer	AUT 52	7842	(5)	EC	Helsinki	12 Aug 71
10.96 7.38 13.49 2.04 48.8 15.06 39.70 4.00 48.96 4:27.5							
Hans-Ulrich	Riecke	GDR 63	7825	(1)	NC-J	Erfurt	7 Jul 82
10.87 7.53 13.74 1.95 49.93 15.88 39.56 4.40 58.26 4:22.28							
Siegfried	Wentz	FRG 60	7818	(1)	EC-J	Bydgoszcz	17 Aug 79
11.29 7.15 14.75 2.01 49.95 15.08 42.74 4.00 64.52 4:30.6							
Uwe	Freimuth	GDR 61	7772	(1)	NC-J	Cottbus	18 Jul 80
11.42w 7.20 14.24 2.10 50.91 15.42 42.08 4.50 59.18 4:37.2							
William	Motti	FRA 64	7745	(1)	NC	Montargis	25 Jul 82
11.23 6.94 13.28 2.13 50.89 15.04 41.84 4.50 70.38 5:02.66							
Dietmar	Jentsch	GDR 60	7715	(2)	EC-J	Bydgoszcz	17 Aug 79
11.38 7.19 12.70 2.01 48.34 15.37 35.18 4.70 49.98 4:09.6							
Keith	Robinson	USA 64	7709	(4)	NCAA	Houston	31 May 83
11.12 6.74 12.48 2.00 48.65 15.04 44.22 4.30 54.40 4:24.38							

320

Junior All-time Lists – Men

Eckart Muller	FRG	56	7706	(1)	EC-J	Athinai	23 Aug 75
11.37 7.41 13.22 2.10 50.9 15.39 41.64 4.40 59.82 4:43.0							
Yevgeniy	Ovsyannikov	SU 63	7698	(17)	NC	Moskva	2 Aug 82
11.56 7.27 13.05 2.02 50.62 15.32 41.54 4.60 59.88 4:31.29							
Jorg-Peter	Schaperkotter	GDR 58	7697	(1)	NC-J	Erfurt	10 Jul 77
10.94 6.94 13.80 2.04 48.48 15.27 42.54 4.20 51.14 4:39.7							
Ion	Buliga	RUM 63	7667	(1)	NC	Bucuresti	18 Jul 82
11.34 7.07 13.71 2.11 50.17 15.99 44.04 3.80 66.02 4:35.66							
Nikolay	Afanasyev	SU 65	7663	(1)	DRZ	Leningrad	12 Aug 83
11.11 6.88 12.26 2.08 49.80 14.82 37.70 4.30 59.68 4:30.47							
Aleksandr	Blinayev	SU 51	7632	(1)	EC-J	Paris	11 Sep 70
11.3 7.19 14.40 1.95 51.5 15.9 46.42 4.10 57.96 4:28.2							
Beat	Gahwiler	SWI 65	7609	(1)		Winterthur	23 Jun 84
11.17 7.06 13.46 1.83 50.51 15.55 40.40 4.50 65.46 4:30.23							
Aleksey	Lyakh	SU 62	7593	(1)		Moskva	28 May 81
11.52 7.22 13.60 1.98 51.16 15.30 39.62 4.70 54.60 4:31.38							

Hand timing

Valter	Kulvet	SU 64	8221w	(1)		Viimsi	23 Aug 81
10.7w 7.26w 13.86 2.09 48.5 14.8 47.92 4.50 60.34 4:37.8							
Daley	Thompson	UK 58	8190	(1)	vSPA,ITA,DEN	Madrid	26 Jun 77
10.5 7.60 13.85 2.07 47.4 15.1 39.60 4.80 50.32 4:29.0							
	Kulvet		8043	(1)		Kaariku	26 Jun 81
11.1 7.36 14.12 2.05 48.6 15.2 45.86 4.40 61.82 4:36.5							
Holger	Schmidt	FRG 57	7785	(1)		Hannover	5 Sep 76
10.6 7.22 15.01 1.90 50.0 14.9 44.60 4.10 60.90 5:00.6							
Robert	De Wit	HOL 62	7722	(1)		Blankenbe	rge 4 Oct 81
11.0 6.60 12.44 1.98 49.2 14.6 40.54 4.20 59.40 4:18.5							
Serge	Morth	FRA 57	7687	(5)		Talence	5 Sep 76
10.6 7.10 14.05 2.01 50.9 15.0 43.54 4.40 54.98 5:06.9							
Craig	Brigham	USA 54	7673	(1)		Eugene	19 May 73
11.3 6.75 14.80 2.07 52.5 16.0 46.52 4.80 58.10 4:47.4							
Igor	Sobolevskiy	SU 62	7659	(1)		Frunze	12 Oct 80
10.7 7.18 14.10 2.00 51.8 15.4 41.62 4.10 64.40 4:55.3							
Sven	Reintak	SU 63	7656	(3)		Tallinn	29 Aug 82
11.0 7.21 12.28 2.00 53.2 14.8 37.70 5.00 60.32 4:41.3							
Roland	Marloye	BEL 62	7655	(1)	NC	Naimette	24 May 81
10.7 7.60 12.44 2.00 50.2 14.5 38.88 4.00 52.74 4:42.2							

1984 WORLD JUNIOR LISTS

100 METRES

Ray	Stewart	JAM 65	10.19		(1)H		Port of Spain	19 May
Henry	Thomas	USA 67	10.27	0.2	(1)		Norwalk	19 May
Bruno	Marie-Rose	FRA 65	10.29	2.0	(1)S1	NC	Villeneuve	30 Jun
Chidi	Imo	NIG 65	10.30	0.4	(1)		Lincoln	12 May
Roy	Martin	USA 66	10.32		(1)		Dallas	19 Apr
Hiroki	Fuwa	JAP 66	10.34	0.0	(1)		Tokyo	6 May
Gregory	Meghoo	JAM 65	10.36	1.1	(1)R2		Walnut	25 Jul
Charles	Seck	SEN 65	10.36	1.7	(3)		Riccione	26 Aug
Joe	DeLoach	USA 67	10.38		(1)		Pasadena	27 Apr
Reggie	Bright	USA 65	10.39		(1)H1		Prairie View	30 Mar
Ray	Brown	USA	10.39	0.6	(1)		Walnut	29 Apr
Clark	Waddell	USA 65	10.40	1.0	(2)		San Angelo	18 May
Elliot	Bunney	UK 66	10.40	1.4	(1)	NC-J	Birmingham	11 Aug
Endre	Havas	HUN 66	10.41		(1)	DRZ	Plovdiv	4 Aug
Sergey	Poduzhov	SU 66	10.42		(1)	NC-Y	Simferopol	26 May
Ralf	Lubke	FRG 65	10.42	-1.0	(1)	NC	Dusseldorf	22 Jun
Emerson	Williams	USA 65	10.43	0.1	(6)R1		Athens	5 May
Zheng	Chen	CHN 65	10.43		(1)		Nanjing	6 Jun
Stanley	Davis	USA	A10.44		(1)H1		Provo	13 Jul
Jurgen	Evers	FRG 65	10.44	0.8	(2)		Munchen	20 Jul
Jason	Leach	USA 66	10.44	0.9	(2)	PAG-J	Nassau	25 Aug

Marks made with assisting wind

Roy	Martin	USA 66	10.14	4.0	(1)		Austin	6 Apr
Greg	Sholars	USA 66	10.16	4.0	(1)		Austin	12 May
Chidi	Imo	NIG 65	10.25	2.2	(2)		Austin	7 Apr
Roscoe	Tatum	USA 66	10.26	4.0	(3)		Austin	6 Apr
Jason	Leach	USA 66	10.26	4.5	(1)	TAC-J	Sacramento	9 Jun
Elliot	Bunney	UK 66	10.29	4.5	(4)	NC	Cwmbran	27 May
Keith	Stubblefield	USA 65	10.29	4.5	(2)	TAC-J	Sacramento	9 Jun
Kelly	Reed	USA 65	10.32	2.6	(2)H2		San Angelo	17 May
Joe	DeLoach	USA 67	10.34		(1)		Pasadena	5 May
Darrell	Wyatt	USA	10.36		(1)		Killeen	14 Apr
Wilfred	Shepherd	USA	10.38		(2)		Killeen	14 Apr
Clark	Waddell	USA 65	10.38	2.6	(3)S2		San Angelo	18 May
Endre	Havas	HUN 66	10.38	2.8	(1)		Miskolc	7 Jul
Trevor	McKenzie	UK 66	10.39	3.2	(1)		Birmingham	21 Jul
Jorg	Treffer	GDR 65	10.39	4.6	(2)H1		Dresden	26 Jul
Ralf	Lubke	FRG 65	10.40	2.6	(1)		Dormagen	2 Jun
Vincent	Jones	UK 65	10.41	4.5	(5)	NC	Cwmbran	27 May
Steven	Graham	UK 65	10.42		(1)		Edinburgh	21 Apr
Bobby	Ellis	USA 66	10.43		(1)			Jul

Hand Timing

Yergeniy	Fedorov	SU 65	10.2		(1)		Grodno	10 Jul
Joe	DeLoach	USA 67	10.2		(1)		Miami	20 Aug

Marks made with assisting wind

Joe	DeLoach	USA 67	10.0		(1)		Austin	11 May
Roy	Martin	USA 66	10.1		(1)		Dallas	3 Mar
Tony	Allen	USA 67	10.1		(1)		Bridge City	12 Apr
Jason	Leach	USA 66	10.1		(1)		Odessa	13 Apr
Chidi	Imo	NIG 65	10.1		(1)		Wichita	14 Apr
Floyd	Heard	USA 66	10.1		(1)		Brookfield	24 May
David	Cassuto	USA 66	10.1		(1)		New York	4 Jun

Junior 1984 Lists – Men

200 METRES

Roy	Martin	USA 66	20.28	1.0	(1)Q2	OT	Los Angeles	19 Jun
Ralf	Lubke	FRG 65	20.51	−0.9	(5)	OG	Los Angeles	8 Aug
Ade	Mafe	UK 66	20.57	1.5	(2)	8-N	Tokyo	14 Sep
Atlee	Mahorn	CAN 65	20.69	−0.5	(3)Q1	OG	Los Angeles	6 Aug
Fred	Martin	AUS 66	20.71	2.0	(1)		Brisbane	4 Mar
Henry	Thomas	USA 67	20.73	0.9	(1)		Norwalk	19 May
Darren	Clark	AUS 65	20.76	1.5	(1)		Sydney	7 Jan
Clark	Waddell	USA 65	20.79	0.1	(1)		San Angelo	19 May
Courtney	Brown	CAN 65	20.81	1.3	(1)S1	NC	Winnipeg	1 Jul
Roger	Hunter	UK 65	20.86	0.3	(4)		Indianapolis	5 May
Joe	DeLoach	USA 67	20.91		(1)		Pasadena	27 Apr
Danny	Harris	USA 65	20.91		(1)		Evanston	26 May
Jeff	Thorbs	USA 65	20.95		(4)		Bakersfield	26 May
Luis	Barroso	POR 66	20.95	2.0	(1)	NC	Lisboa	8 Jul
Kevin	Young	USA 65	21.00				Norman	14 Apr
Floyd	Heard	USA 66	21.00		(1)		Monona Grove	12 May
Clinton	Davis	USA 65	21.00	1.5	(4)H3	OT	Los Angeles	19 Jun
James	Hilliard	USA 66	21.00					
Jurgen	Evers	FRG 65	21.02	1.7	(2)		Ludenscheid	26 May
Lubos	Balosak	CS 65	21.05	2.0	(2)		Praha	13 May

Marks made with assisting wind

Roy	Martin	USA 66	20.25+		(1)		Mesquite	5 May
Ade	Mafe	UK 66	20.55	2.2	(3)Q2	OG	Los Angeles	6 Aug
Joe	DeLoach	USA 67	20.79		(1)		Pasadena	5 May
Keith	Stubblefield	USA 65	20.87	3.3	(1)		Sacramento	9 Jun
Michael	Adams	USA	20.88+		(1)R2		Mesquite	5 May
David	Cassuto	USA 66	20.88	3.3	(2)		Sacramento	9 Jun
Greg	Sholars	USA 66	20.90	3.3	(3)		Sacramento	9 Jun
Roscoe	Tatum	USA 66	20.93		(2)		Pasadena	5 May
Jason	Leach	USA 66	20.93	3.3	(4)		Sacramento	9 Jun
Jurgen	Evers	FRG 65	20.95	2.2	(5)Q2	OG	Los Angeles	6 Aug
Mark	Edwards	USA	20.99		(3)		Mesquite	5 May
Vincent	Jones	UK 65	21.02	2.7	(1)		Birmingham	1 Jul

Hand timing

Fred	Martin	AUS 66	20.6	2.0	(1)		Sydney	29 Jan
Henry	Thomas	USA 67	20.7		(1)		Los Angeles	4 Feb
Ilya	Ivanov	SU 65	20.7		( )		Frunze	26 Aug
Jurgen	Evers	FRG 65	20.8		(1)		Ludwigsburg	28 Apr
Chidi	Imo	NIG 65	20.8		(3)		Ames	5 May

Marks made with assisting wind

Brett	Leavy	AUS 65	20.6	4.0	(2)		Brisbane	7 Jan
Jason	Leach	USA 66	20.7					Apr
Donovan	Pitts	USA	20.7		(2)		Dallas	24 Mar
Richard	Willard	USA	20.7		(1)		Levelland	28 Apr
Danny	Mullany	AUS 66	20.8	4.0	(4)		Brisbane	7 Jan

400 METRES

Darren	Clark	AUS 65	44.75		(4)	OG	Los Angeles	8 Aug
Thomas	Schonlebe	GDR 65	45.01		(1)		Berlin	15 Jul
Danny	Harris	USA 65	45.79		(1)H1		Lincoln	11 May
Henry	Thomas	USA 67	45.82		(4)		Los Angeles	13 May
Athanassios	Kaloyannis	GRE 65	45.90		(1)	BALK	Athinai	8 Sep
Andrew	Valmon	USA 65	45.92		(1)S2	TAC-J	Los Angeles	23 Jun

323

Junior 1984 Lists – Men

John	Patterson	USA 65	45.96		(6)		Austin	12 May
Dennis	Mitchell	USA 66	46.02		(1)		Elmhurst	16 Jun
Kevin	Robinzine	USA 66	46.04		(1)S1	TAC-J	Los Angeles	23 Jun
Kevin	Hawkins	USA 65	46.16		(1)		S. Monica	5 May
Aaron	Phillips	VEN 65	46.20		(1)		Caracas	17 Jun
Derek	Redmond	UK 65	46.32		(2)		Jarrow	9 Sep
Harold	Spells	USA 65	46.34		(2)		Dallas	19 May
James	Cooper	USA 65	46.36		(2)		Bakersfield	26 May
Mike	Spangler	USA 66	46.36		(1)		Shippenburg	26 May
Chip	Rish	USA 67	46.37		(1)		Norwalk	26 May
Roberto	Hernandez	CUB 67	A46.44		(2)		Mexico, D.F.	16 Jun
Roger	Hunter	UK 65	46.48		(3)		Columbus	20 May
Mark	Thomas	UK 65	46.53		(2)	vYUG	Karlovac	15 Sep
Miles	Murphy	AUS 67	46.76		(1)		Brisbane	9 Dec

Hand timing

Danny	Harris	USA 65	45.3		(1)		Lincoln	12 May
Kevin	Robinzine	USA 66	45.8		(1)		Austin	11 May
Joe	Baker	USA 65	46.5		(2)		Austin	11 May
Jurgen	Evers	FRG 65	46.5		(1)		Aalen	5 May
Miles	Murphy	AUS 67	46.5		(1)		Brisbane	1 Dec

800 METRES

Luis	Migueles	ARG 65	1:47.14		(1)		Santiago de Chile	28 Oct
Ralph	Schumann	GDR 66	1:47.59		(1)	DRZ	Plovdiv	5 Aug
Vadim	Lauskin	SU 65	1:47.6		(2)		Leningrad	7 Jul
Darryl	Taylor	UK 65	1:47.70		(7)	TALBOT	London	13 Jul
Werner	Busshof	FRG 65	1:47.9		(4)		Aachen	30 May
Gert	Kilbert	SWI 65	1:47.97		(2)		Kusnacht	31 May
Marc	Cortsjens	BEL 65	1:48.23		(5)	VD	Bruxelles	24 Aug
Nikolay	Gombone	RUM 65	1:48.25		(2)	DRZ	Plovdiv	5 Aug
Thomas	Lauterbach	GDR 66	1:48.40		(3)	DRZ	Plovdiv	5 Aug
Paul	Williams	UK 67	1:48.42		(2)		Copenhagen	22 Jul
Arjen	Visserman	HOL 65	1:48.43		(2)		Grosseto	18 Jul
Sergey	Kolesnicenko	SU 65	1:48.5				Leningrad	16 Jun
Joey	Bunch	USA 65	1:48.55		(1)	PAG-J	Nassau	23 Aug
Yves	Gardes	FRA 65	1:48.61		(3)		Paris	4 Sep
Yuriy	Bukin	SU 66	1:48.76		(4)	DRZ	Plovdiv	5 Aug
Barry	Acers	AUS 65	1:48.8		(2)		Perth	18 Mar
Matt	Favier	AUS 65	1:48.85		(5)		Melbourne	6 Mar
James	Kimmie	USA 65	1:48.96		(4)		Tallahassee	28 Apr
Vance	Watson	USA 65	1:49.06		(3)		Villanova	20 May
Carl	Mayhand	USA 65	1:49.06					

1500 METRES

Teofilo	Benito	SPA 66	3:40.48		(5)	NC	Barcelona	30 Jun
Hans	V.D. Veen	RSA 66	3:42.1		(4)		Stellenbosch	29 Feb
Mika	Maaskola	FIN 66	3:42.49		(2)	NC	Kajaani	8 Jul
Sandor	Serfoz	HUN 66	3:42.7		(1)		Miskolc	25 Aug
Alastair	Currie	UK 65	3:42.89		(9)		Edinburgh	17 Jul
Gyula	Sarkozi	HUN 66	3:42.9		(2)		Miskolc	1 Sep
Enda	Fitzpatrick	IRL 65	3:43.05		(11)	DNG	Stockholm	2 Jul
Marius	Hugo-Schlechter	RSA 65	3:43.28		(4)	NC	Durban	13 Apr
Marc	Cortsjens	BEL 65	3:43.5		(1)		Neerpelt	2 Aug
Karl	Blaha	AUT 65	3:43.67		(5)R2	BGP	Budapest	20 Aug

324

Junior 1984 Lists – Men

Walter	Merlo	ITA 65	3:43.8	(2)		Piacenza	29 May
Paul	Jaspers	HOL 65	3:43.8	(2)		Neerpelt	2 Aug
Peter K	Rono	KEN 65	3:43.86	(1)		Seoul	25 Aug
Klaus	Klein	FRG 65	3:44.14	(8)	NC	Dusseldorf	23 Jun
Hauke	Fuhlbrugge	GDR 66	3:44.44	(4)		Dresden	26 Jul
Neil	Horsfield	UK 66	3:44.49	(4)	vYUG	Karlovac	15 Sep
Darryl	Taylor	UK 65	3:44.6	(2)		Stretford	14 Apr
Oleg	Kolesnicenko	SU 65	3:44.83	(9)	NC	Donyetsk	7 Sep
Valentas	Patapas	SU 65	3:44.88	(10)	NC	Donyetsk	7 Sep
Thomas	Andersson	SWE 65	3:45.31	(3)		Stockholm	2 Jul

3000 METRES

Walter	Merlo	ITA 65	7:57.38	(6)		Busto Arsizio	26 May
Paul	Jaspers	HOL 65	7:57.62	( )		Hechtel	12 Aug
Antonio	Rapisarda	ITA 65	8:02.4	(1)		Catania	27 Sep
Marcel	Versteeg	HOL 65	8:04.9	(3)		Den-Haag	15 Jun
Vladimir	Klimenko	SU 65	8:05.37	( )	ZNAM	Sochi	10 Jun
Dieter	Baumann	FRG 65	8:05.96	(4)		Munchen	20 Jul
Mika	Maaskola	FIN 66	8:07.01	(2)		Elaintarha	24 May
Sven	Wille	GDR 65	8:08.1 I	(1)		Senftenburg	11 Feb
Carlos	Monteiro	POR 65	8:08.2	(3)		Lisboa	1 Jul
Tim	Pugh	AUS 65	8:08.2	(1)		Melbourne	13 Dec
Gary	Castellano	CAN 66	8:09.20l	(1)		Toronto	26 Feb
Burkhard	Dahm	FRG 65	8:10.88	(1)		Koblenz	29 Aug
Alastair	Currie	UK 65	8:10.9	(2)		Edinburgh	22 Aug
Colin	Dalton	AUS 66	8:11.0	(4)		Sydney	5 Dec
Karl	Blaha	AUT 65	8:11.5	( )		Mannheim	7 Aug
Klaus	Jutten	FRG 66	8:12.65	(4)		Koblenz	29 Aug
Neil	Horsfield	GB 65	8:12.7	(4)		Cwmbran	20 Jun
Pedro	Casacubierta	SPA 65	8:12.87	(9)		Zaragoza	3 Jun
Michael	Heist	FRG 65	8:13.07	(5)		Koblenz	29 Aug
Steven	Marshall	UK 65	8:13.12	(3)		Edinburgh	6 Jun

5000 METRES

Roberto	Lopez	MEX 65	13:37.22	(14)	MSR	Walnut	28 Apr
Walter	Merlo	ITA 65	13:41.17	(4)		Firenze	7 Jun
Carlos	Monteiro	POR 65	13:54.54	(7)		Vigo	18 Jul
Gary	Castellano	CAN 66	13:59.01	(4)		Scarborough	10 Jul
Paul	Taylor	UK 66	14:00.85	(3)	vYUG	Karlovac	15 Sep
Pedro	Cascacubierta	SPA 65	14:01.61	(5)	NC	Barcelona	1 Jul
Antonio	Rapisarda	ITA 65	14:02.29	(12)		Pisa	20 Jun
Andre	Wessel	GDR 65	14:07.59	(4)		Dresden	26 Jul
Yuriy	Fedorov	SU 65	14:08.0	( )		Ryazan	11 Aug
Peter	Wasonga	KEN	14:09.29	(1)		Seoul	26 Aug
Anthony	Smith	USA 65	14:11.16	(1)	TAC-J	Los Angeles	23 Jun
Stephen	Karatalia	USA 65	14:12.71	(2)	TAC-J	Los Angeles	23 Jun
Volodomyr	Klimenko	SU 65	14:12.96			Moskva	20 Jul
Sergey	Klimakov	SU 66	14:16.4	( )		Tallinn	26 Aug
Kidkembo	Kimeli	KEN	14:16.70	(2)		Seoul	26 Aug
Alejandro	Gomez	SPA 67	14:16.7	(2)		Lisboa	25 Aug
Antonio	Perez	SPA 66	14:17.02	(1)S2	NC	Barcelona	29 Jun
Aleksandr	Burcev	SU 65	14:18.53	(1)	NC-J	Riga	13 Jul
Steffen	Brand	FRG 65	14:19.17	(3)		Bielefeld	27 May
Richard	Carter	UK 65	14:19.4	(2)		Luton	18 Aug

Junior 1984 Lists – Men

2000 METRES STEEPLECHASE

Nikolay	Matuschenko	SU 66	5:28.15		(1)		Debrecen	18 Aug
Sandor	Serfozo	HUN 66	5:37.08		(2)		Debrecen	18 Aug
Alessandro	Lamruschini	ITA 65	5:37.37		(1)		Bologna	23 Jun
Burkhard	Dahm	FRG 65	5:38.40		(1)		Wattenscheid	15 Jun
Benito	Nogales	SPA 65	5:39.98		(1)	NC-J	San Sebastian	22 Jul
Robert	Banai	HUN 67	5:40.10		(2)	DRUZHBA	Plovdiv	4 Aug
John	Hartigan	UK 65	5:40.2		(2)		Wolverhampton	27 Jun
Oliver	Hamsch	GDR 67	5:40.21		(2)	DRUZHBA	Plovdiv	4 Aug
Rostislav	Sevcu	CS 65	5:40.67		(1)		Praha	28 Jul
Spencer	Newport	UK 66	5:42.7		(2)		Thurrock	14 Jul
Ion	Nicolae	RUM 65	5:43.76		(1)		Bucuresti	2 Sep
Stephen	Male	UK 65	5:43.88		(4)		Loughborough	17 Jun
Igor	Zimin	SU 66	5:44.2		(1)		Tashkent	18 Sep
Romo	Zamfir	RUM 66	5:44.26		(4)		Debrecen	18 Aug
Vladimir	Belovs	SU 66	5:44.71		(2)	NC-J	Riga	13 Jul
Patrik	Wallin	SWE 66	5:44.75		(1)		Sollentuna	17 Jun
Attila	Kazsimir	HUN 66	5:45.44		(9)		Debrecen	19 Aug
Sergio	Magonara	ITA 65	5:45.5		(1)		Brescia	25 Apr
Lorenzo	Hidalgo	SPA 65	5:45.58		(2)	NC-J	San Sebastian	22 Jul
Michael	Heist	FRG 65	5:45.92		(3)		Bochum	15 Jun

3000 METRES STEEPLECHASE

Csaba	Szucs	HUN 65	8:39.37	(5)	NC	Budapest	26 Jul
Karl Van	Calcar	USA 65	8:39.81	(3)H2	NCAA	Eugene	30 May
Rostislav	Sevcu	CS 65	8:47.36	(5)		Praha	21 Jul
Burkhard	Dahm	FRG 65	8:48.10	(1)		Ingelheim	4 Sep
Dan	Bell	CAN 65	8:49.10	(1)		Eugene	6 May
Nikolay	Matuschenko	SU 66	8:52.1				
Robert	Banai	HUN 67	8:52.8	(1)		Debrecen	15 Sep
Klaus	Heist	FRG 65	8:53.31	(2)		Lausanne	10 Jul
Benito	Nogales	SPA 65	8:54.41	(6)S2	NC	Barcelona	30 Jun
Juan R.	Conde	CUB 65	8:54.5	(1)		Habana	9 Jul
Gavin	Gaynor	USA 65	8:56.94	(2)	TAC-J	Los Angeles	24 Jun
Juan A.	Conde	CUB 65	8:57.3	(2)		Habana	9 Jul
Ola	Torstensson	SWE 65	8:57.42	(2)H	NC	Vaxjo	24 Aug
John	Hartigan	UK 65	9:01.36	(6)	vYUG	Karlovac	16 Sep
Juha	Kettinen	FIN 66	9:02.90	(1)		Tuusula	18 Jun
Andy	Martin	USA 66	9:03.79	(4)	TAC-J	Los Angeles	24 Jun
Bob	Rice	CAN 65	9:05.0	(8)	NC	Winnipeg	29 Jun
Uwe	Raasch	GDR 65	9:06.00	(5)		Dresden	27 Jul
Jarmo	Ihalainen	FIN 66	9:06.35	(2)		Tuusula	18 Jun

110 METRES HURDLES

Rod	Woodson	USA 65	13.71		(2)		Tallahassee	17 Mar
Arthur	Blake	USA 66	13.84	-0.4	(1)S2	TAC-J	Los Angeles	22 Jun
Jon	Ridgeon	UK 67	13.92	1.0	(1)	NJ	Birmingham	12 Aug
Colin	Jackson	UK 67	13.95	1.0	(2)	NJ	Birmingham	12 Aug
Mark	Boyd	USA 65	13.98	0.0	(1)		Tucson	5 May
Eric	Reid	USA 65	14.01	1.3	(4)		Baton Rouge	13 May
Clifton	Franklin	USA 65	14.07	1.3	(5)		Baton Rouge	13 May
Daryl	Hill	USA 65	14.09	0.4	(2)		Cape Girarardeau	26 May
Luigi	Bertocchi	ITA 65	14.09	0.5	(1)R1		Novara	29 Sep
Kevin	Reid	CAN 66	14.22	1.0	(1)		Edmonton	21 Jul
Aleksey	Salnikov	SU 66	14.23		(1)		Debrecen	18 Aug
Jim	Purvis	USA	14.23		(2)		Syracuse	Aug

Junior 1984 Lists – Men

Gunter	Hagenbusch	FRG 65	14.25	2.0	(2)		Saar	14 Jul
Jorg	Rolz	GDR 65	14.26	1.3	(4)H		Erfurt	12 May
Thomas	Friedrich	GDR 65	14.26	0.9	(6)	NC	Erfurt	1 Jun
Gela	Veshapidze	SU 66	14.26		(1)	DRUZHBA	Plovdiv	4 Aug
Paul	Brice	UK 65	14.30	1.9	(2)H3	NC	Cwmbran	27 May
Zoltan	Varga	HUN 65	14.30		(2)		Debrecen	18 Aug
Calvin	Holmes	USA 65	14.33	−0.4	(2)S2	TAC-J	Los Angeles	22 Jun
Stefan	Mattern	FRG 65	14.33	0.0	(1)		Bochum	15 Jun

Marks made with assisting wind

Jessie	Rider	USA 65	13.99	2.7	(3)S2		San Angelo	18 May
Olivier	Vallaeys	FRA 66	14.18	2.6	(1)	NC-J	Fontainbleau	15 Jul
Zoltan	Varga	HUN 65	14.21	2.8	(4)		Budapest	23 Jun
Paul	Brice	UK 65	14.27	2.7	(3)	NC	Cwmbran	27 May

Hand timing

Luigi	Bertocchi	ITA 65	13.6		(1)		Alexandria	16 Oct
Stefan	Schoemann	RSA 65	A13.7		(1)		Pretoria	25 Feb
Gela	Veshapidze	SU 66	13.9				Alma Ata	19 May
Igor	Chitryakov	SU 65	13.9				Alma Ata	20 May
Luigi	Bertocchi	ITA 65	13.9				Fontainbleau	23 May
Aleksey	Salnikov	SU 66	13.9	1.9	(4)		Gorkiy	12 Aug
Gennadiy	Daskevic	SU 66	14.0				Leningrad	1 Aug
Andrey	Lednikov	SU 65	14.0		(1)		Dnepropetrovsk	8 Aug
Valdis	Norinsch	SU 65	14.0				Riga	10 Aug
Oscar	Duran	CUB 65	14.1		(1)		Habana	9 Jul
Olivier	Vallaeys	FRA 66	14.1		(1)		Caen	16 May

Marks made with assisting wind

Olivier	Vallaeys	FRA 66	14.0		(1)		Alencon	23 Sep

400 METRES HURDLES

Danny	Harris	USA 65	48.02		(2)S1	OT	Eugene	17 Jun
Vladimir	Budko	SU 65	48.74		(2)	DRZ	Moskva	18 Aug
Belfred	Clark	USA 65	49.45		(1)	TAC-J	Los Angeles	23 Jun
Ryoichi	Yoshida	JAP 65	49.75		(1)	NC	Tokyo	20 Oct
Kevin	Henderson	USA 65	49.94		(2)	TAC-J	Los Angeles	23 Jun
Patrick	Mann	USA 66	50.02		(3)	TAC-J	Los Angeles	23 Jun
Sven	Mikisch	FRG 65	50.11		(1)	NC-J	Munchengladbach	19 Aug
Athanassios	Kaloyannis	GRE 65	50.22		(1)		Athinai	4 Jul
Stanislav	Navesnak	CS 65	50.65		(1)	NC	Praha	22 Jul
Arthur	Blake	USA 66	50.66		(2)		Sacramento	9 Jun
Patrick	Cheruiyot	KEN 65	50.72		(1)		Evanston	26 May
Dale	Laverty	USA 65	50.82		(4)	TAC-J	Los Angeles	23 Jun
James	Ferreira	USA 65	50.84		(1)		Bakersfield	26 May
Bernard	Williams	USA 65	50.90		(3)H1		Baton Rouge	12 May
John	Graham	CAN 65	A50.98		(2)		Provo	23 May
Anthony	Bell	USA 65	50.99		(2)		Ruston	28 Apr
Aleksey	Bologutin	SU 65	51.26		(8)		Moskva	20 Jul
Sergey	Dobrovolskiy	SU 66	51.26		(1)	DRUZHBA	Plovdiv	5 Aug
Jorg	Reichel	FRG 66	51.39		(1)		Fulda	21 Jul
Andrez	Nowak	POL 67	51.44		(2)	DRUZHBA	Plovdiv	5 Aug

HIGH JUMP

Javier	Sotomayor	CUB 67	2.33		(1)	BARR	Habana	19 May
Patrik	Sjoberg	SWE 65	2.33		(4)		Eberstadt	10 Jun

Junior 1984 Lists – Men

Alain	Metellus	CAN 65	2.28i		(1)		Toronto	26 Feb
			2.25		(1)		Provo	19 May
Dothel	Edwards	USA 66	2.27		(1)		Athens	24 Mar
James	Lott	USA 65	2.27		(1)		Baton Rouge	27 Apr
Yuriy	Sergiyenko	SU 65	2.26i		(2)		Kiev	3 Feb
			2.24		(1)	NJ	Riga	14 Jul
Rick	Noji	USA 67	2.25		(1)		Seattle	12 May
Brad	Speer	USA 65	2.25		(1)		Elmhurst	16 Jun
Evgeni	Peev	BUL 65	2.23i		(1)		Sofia	18 Feb
Mark	Reed	USA 65	2.22		(1)		Austin	7 Apr
Marcello	Croci	ITA 65	2.22		(1)		Sesto S. Giov	6 May
Maurice	Crumby	USA 65	2.21		(1)		Berkeley	7 Jan
Sergey	Zaytsev	SU 65	2.21		(1)		Simferopol	27 May
Uwe	Hyckel	GDR 65	2.20i		(1)		Arnstadt	7 Jan
Konstantin	Galkin	SU 65	2.20		(1)		Vilnius	3 Jul
Oleg	Urmakayev	SU 65	2.20		(4)	NJ	Riga	14 Jul
Byron	Morrison	UK 66	2.20		(1)		Thurrock	14 Jul
Georgi	Dakov	BUL 67	2.20		(1)	DRUZHBA	Plovdiv	5 Aug
Raymond	Conzemius	LUX 66	2.20		(1)		Liege	29 Sep
Lambertus	de Wilzem	RSA 66	2.20		(1)		Cradock	13 Oct

POLE VAULT

Radion	Gataullin	SU 65	5.65		(2)	NC	Donyetsk	8 Sep
Gennadiy	Sukharev	SU 65	5.53i		(2)		Leningrad	12 Feb
			5.30		(10)	NC	Donyetsk	8 Sep
Grigoriy	Yegorov	SU 67	5.45		(1)	NC-Y	Simferopol	26 May
Arto	Peltoniemi	FIN 66	5.42		(1)		Raahe	8 Aug
Doug	Fraley	USA 65	5.41		(1)		Fresno	14 Jul
Valeriy	Ishutin	SU 65	5.40		(1)	NC-J	Riga	13 Jul
Viktor	Komarov	SU 66	5.40		(1)		Kharkov	21 Jul
Liang	Xuerang	CHN 65	5.40		(1)		Shanghai	8 Oct
Aleksandr	Isachenko	SU 65	5.30i		(3)		Leningrad	12 Feb
			5.30		(2)		Alma Ata	8 Aug
Bernhard	Zintl	FRG 65	5.30i		(4)		Nordlingen	26 Feb
			5.25		(2)	NC-J	Munchengladbach	18 Aug
Yevgeniy	Bondarenko	SU 66	5.30		(1)		Moskva	9 Jun
Viktor	Loscev	SU 65	5.30		(1)		Frunze	8 Sep
Igor	Tradenkov	SU 66	5.30		(3)		Tashkent	19 Sep
Viktor	Ryzenkov	SU 66	5.30		(1)		Tashkent	19 Sep
Jari	Holttinen	FIN 65	5.25		(1)		Somero	14 Jul
Dinitaz	Waltchev	BUL 66	5.21		(1)	DRUZHBA	Plovdiv	4 Aug
Andrew	Ashurst	UK 65	5.21		(1)		Coventry	2 Sep
Roman	Trosin	SU 65	5.20i		(1)		Leningrad	12 Feb
			5.20		( )		Leningrad	2 Jun
Sergey	Gavrin	SU 65	5.20I		(1)		Leningrad	17 Mar
Shivko	Shetchev	BUL 66	5.20		(1)		Plovdiv	26 May
Aleksandr	Kaschev	SU 65	5.20		( )		Alma Ata	8 Aug

LONG JUMP

Robert	Emmiyan	SU 65	8.13	1.1	(1)		Baku	14 Sep
Ron	Beer	GDR 65	8.06	0.2	(3)		East Berlin	9 Jun
Charles	Smith	USA 66	8.06		(1)		Las Vegas	9 Jun
Brian	Cooper	USA 65	7.97		(1)		Houston	6 May
Joey	Wells	BAH 65	7.97	−0.8	(6)	OG	Los Angeles	6 Aug
Khristo	Markov	BUL 65	7.95	0.3	(2)		Sofia	3 Jun
Joe	Richardson	USA 65	7.94		(1)		Sacramento	9 Jun
Johnny	Cleveland	USA 66	7.92		(2)		Sacramento	9 Jun

Junior 1984 Lists – Men

Paul	Emordi	NIG 65	7.90		(1)	AFR	Rabat	14 Jul
Torsten	Kottke	GDR 65	7.88	0.8	(4)	NC	Erfurt	3 Jun
Marco	Delonge	GDR 66	7.87	−0.6	(1)		Praha	14 Aug
Volker	Mai	GDR 66	7.85		(1)		Salonika	29 Aug
Emil	Mellaard	HOL 66	7.84	1.5	(1)		Sittard	23 Jun
Kerry	Harrison	USA 65	7.83		(2)		Lincoln	11 May
Vahtang	Minasvili	SU 65	7.79	0.7	(2)		Kiev	5 Jul
Frank	Liek	GDR 65	7.77		(7)	NC	Erfurt	3 Jun
Radoslav	Obzetenov	BUL 65	7.77		(1)		Ruse	10 Sep
Anton	Zivickiy	SU 67	7.77i					
Vladimir	Sokolov	SU 65	7.76		(2)	NJ	Riga	14 Jul
Nathaniel	Peterkin	USA 65	7.76		(1)		Winston-Salem	17 Apr
Von	Sheppard	USA 65	7.76		(3)		Lincoln	11 May
Anthony	Bailous	USA 65	7.76		(2)		San Angelo	18 May

Marks made with assisting wind

Marco	Delonge	GDR 66	7.96	3.5	(1)	NC-Y	Magdeburg	22 Jul
Robert	Szeli	CS 65	7.78		(1)		Nitra	16 Jun

TRIPLE JUMP

Khristo	Markov	BUL 65	17.42	1.3	(1)	NAR	Sofia	19 May
Volker	Mai	GDR 66	17.12	1.2	(2)	OD	Potsdam	21 Jul
Ralf	Jaros	FRG 65	16.81	-0.1	(1)	NC	Dusseldorf	23 Jun
Paul	Emordi	NIG 65	16.78		(1)		Baton Rouge	5 May
John	Tillman	USA 65	16.61	1.9	(1)	PAG-J	Nassau	25 Aug
Kerry	Harrison	USA 65	16.50		(1)		Lincoln	12 May
Vasil	Asadov	SU 65	16.42	0.1	(4)Q	NC	Donyetsk	8 Sep
Aleksey	Shcherbakov	SU 65	16.41		(1)		Cheboksary	2 Jun
Pierre	Camara	FRA 65	16.40		(2)		Fontenay le Comte	13 May
Joe	Richardson	USA 66	16.32		(1)		Sacramento	9 Jun
Michael	Patton	USA 66	16.23		(1)		Chicago	16 Jun
Yuriy	Gorbacenko	SU 66	16.09		(1)		Tashkent	22 Sep
Maksim	Gerasimov	SU 66	16.06		(2)	NC-Y	Simferopol	26 May
Tord	Henriksson	SWE 65	16.06		(4)	NC	Vaxjo	26 Aug
Daniel	Ciobanu	RUM 65	16.05		(4)	NC	Bucuresti	11 Jul
Jose	Leitao	POR 65	16.04	1.6	(2)		S. de Compostela	8 Sep
Dajins	Bessinsch	SU 66	16.03		(3)	NC-Y	Simferopol	26 May
Ramon	Herrera	CUB 65	15.96		(-)	BARR	Habana	19 May
Juan	N. Pena	CUB 65	15.96		(21)	ZNAM	Sochi	9 Jun
Andrey	Pisarenko	SU 65	15.93		(4)	NC-Y	Simferopol	26 May
Oleg	Sokirkin	SU 66	15.93		( )		Chikent	26 Jul
Andreja	Marinkovic	YUG 65	15.90		(4)	vUK	Karlovac	16 Sep

Wind assisted

Vasil	Asadov	SU 65	16.68		(1)	NC-Y	Simferopol	26 May
Ramon	Herrera	CUB 65	16.01		(3)	BARR	Habana	19 May

SHOT PUTT

Arnold	Campbell	USA 66	19.40		(1)		Shreveport	16 May
Mario	Hoyer	GDR 65	18.88i		(1)	NC-J	Senftenburg	12 Feb
			18.18		(1)	NC-J	Potsdam	1 Jul
Mikhail	Petrov	SU 65	18.75		(1)	NC-J	Riga	15 Jul
Tariel	Bicadze	SU 65	18.48i		(1)		Leningrad	
			18.39		(1)		Riga	4 Jul
Aleksandr	Bagatsch	SU 66	18.44		(1)	vGDR-J	Tallinn	24 Jun
	Ahmad	IRQ	18.41		(1)		Seoul	26 Aug

Junior 1984 Lists – Men

Aldis	Cupkovas	SU 66	18.27I		(2)		Leningrad	25 Feb
Vadim	Mensorov	SU 65	18.06		(3)	vGDR-J	Tallinn	24 Jun
Sergey	Lisicka	SU 65	17.97		(3)	NC-Y	Simferopol	26 May
Lars Arvid	Nilsen	NOR 65	17.87		(1)		Grimstad	14 Jul
Billy	Cole	UK 65	17.78i		(2)		Cosford	10 Mar
			17.72		(2)		London	2 Jun
Alexander	Woll	GDR 65	17.54		(2)		Leipzig	7 Jun
Vitalius	Mitkus	SU 65	17.49		( )		Tallinn	1 Sep
Attila	Hlavaty	HUN 65	17.45		(3)		Debrecen	18 Aug
Oleg	Gricenko	SU 65	17.38		( )		Sevastopol	9 Apr
Chris	Ellis	UK 66	17.36i		(1)		Cosford	3 Dec
			16.89		(1)		Bristol	18 Aug
Kwang-Yong	Ahn	SKo	17.25		(2)		Seoul	26 Aug
Michael	Mertens	FRG 65	17.21		(1)		Giessen	10 Jun
Maik	Prollius	GDR 66	17.16		(1)		Miskolc	7 Jul
Miklos	Barcsai	HUN 65	17.17		(1)		Nyiregyhaza	12 Sep

DISCUS

Jozsef	Ficsore	HUN 65	60.06		(1)		Budapest	12 Jun
Kristos	Papadopoulos	GRE 65	58.48		(1)		Athinai	19 Jul
Gero	Lautsch	GDR 65	56.64		(1)		Halle	30 May
Pasi	Heikkila	FIN 65	56.34		(4)		Hyvinkaa	23 Aug
Attila	Horvath	HUN 67	56.26		(1)		Debrecen	19 Aug
Aleksandr	Kondratyuk	SU 66	56.08		(2)		Tallinn	15 Jun
Frantisek	Petrovic	CS 65	55.04		(2)		Nitra	16 Jun
Costel	Grasu	ROM 67	54.52		(2)		Debrecen	19 Aug
Tariel	Bicadze	SU 66	54.18		(2)	NC-J	Riga	15 Jul
Witold	Duda	POL 65	54.04		(1)	vFRG-J	Bochum	15 Jun
Jens	Biermann	GDR 65	53.50		(1)		Halle	19 May
Venzislav	Stoyanov	BUL 65	53.04		(3)	DRUZHBA	Plovdiv	5 Aug
Gobinder	Singh	IND	53.04		(1)		Seoul	25 Aug
Rudiger	Pudenz	GDR 66	52.76		(2)	vSU-J	Tallinn	24 Jun
Andrey	Popov	SU 65	52.62		(3)	NC-J	Riga	15 Jul
Vassily	Petrov	SU 66	52.62		( )		Voroshilograd	28 Jul
Peter	Rickert	GDR 65	52.50		(3)		Rostock	18 Jul
Maksim	Kozlov	SU 66	53.38		( )		Smolensk	27 Jun
Oleg	Marin	SU 65	52.70		( )		Moskva	4 Aug
Mikhail	Alyusev	SU 65	52.56		( )		Tashkent	24 May

HAMMER THROW

Fyodor	Makovskiy	SU 65	73.34		(2)		Volgograd	15 May
Plamen	Minev	BUL 65	73.08		(2)		Sofia	4 Jul
Nikolay	Lysenko	SU 66	71.62		(1)		Frunze	25 Aug
Andrey	Abduvaliyev	SU 66	71.54		(1)		Frunze	8 Sep
Alexey	Afanasyev	SU 65	71.50		(2)		Frunze	8 Sep
Sergey	Alay	SU 65	71.26		(1)	NC-J	Riga	14 Jul
Valentin	Kirov	BUL 66	70.46		(1)	DRUZHBA	Plovdiv	4 Aug
Jari	Martinolli	FIN 65	70.02		(1)		Tyrnava	9 Sep
Vladimir	Voropayev	SU 65	69.02		(1)		Riga	4 Jul
Boris	Kotelnikov	SU 65	68.48		( )		Smolensk	27 Jun
Gintautas	Misevicks	SU 67	67.72					21 Aug
Paul	Head	UK 65	67.48		(2)	vYUG	Karlovac	16 Sep
Oleg	Ivanov	SU 65	67.34		(1)		Irkutsk	15 Jun
Aleksandr	Dregol	SU 66	67.06		(2)	vGDR-J	Tallinn	24 Jun
Vincente	Sanchez	CUB 66	66.52		(4)	BARR	Habana	20 May
Balazs	Lezsak	HUN 66	66.46		(2)		Debrecen	15 Sep
Yuriy	Alatovskiy	SU 66	66.32		( )		Cernovcy	17 Jun
Jacek	Dreger	POL 65	65.88		(1)		Bydgoszcz	25 Aug
Yaroslav	Cmyr	SU 66	65.62		( )		Lvov	9 Jun
Eduard	Piskunov	SU 67	65.16		(2)	NC-Y	Simferopol	27 May

Junior 1984 Lists – Men

JAVELIN

Ramon	Gonzalez	CUB 65	82.82		(1)		Habana	27 Jan
Atonios	Papadimitriou	GRE 65	83.56		(2)		Malmo	17 Jun
Jan	Zelezny	CS 66	80.32		(1)		Praha	8 Sep
Marcis	Shtrobinders	SU 66	79.60		(1)		Ventspils	30 Sep
Volodmyr	Grischenko	SU 65	79.52		(1)		Jevpatoris	12 May
Jari	Montonen	FIN 65	79.16		(1)		Sollentuna	12 Aug
Andrej	Maznicenko	SU 66	78.38					
Oleg	Litvinov	SU 65	78.26		(1)		Kishinyev	1 Jun
David	Dixon	AUS 65	78.22		(1)		Adelaide	14 Mar
Jamie	Highland	AUS 65	76.70		(1)		Perth	10 Nov
Paul	Morgan	UK 65	76.28		(3)		Haringey	19 Aug
Ragnar	Danielsen	NOR 65	75.92		(1)		Sollentuna	12 Aug
Francois	Demontigny	FRA 65	75.28		(1)		Montargis	8 Sep
Yuriy	Ivakin	SU 66	75.08		( )		Stavropol	11 Aug
Renat	Machmutov	SU 65	74.80		( )		Stavropol	11 Aug
Jong-Sam	Park	SKo	74.76		(1)		Seoul	26 Aug
Robert	Amabile	USA 65	74.72		( )			
Gavin	Lovegrove	NZ 67	74.70		( )			15 Dec
Andreas	Lang	GDR 65	74.28		(1)		Leipzig	7 Jun
Kenneth	Pedersen	DEN 65	74.12		(1)		Verden	8 Sep
Yki	Laine	FIN 65	73.96		(1)		Heinola	26 May

DECATHLON

Christian	Schenk	GDR 65	8053	(5)			Potsdam	21 Jul
11.54 7.18 14.26 2.16 49.23/ 15.06 44.74 4.20 65.98 4:24.11								
Igor	Marin	SU 65	7844	(1)			Frunze	9 Sep
11.30 7.25 13.55 2.04 50.65/ 15. 43.70 4.70 62.92 4:42.05								
Beat	Gahwiler	SWI 65	7609	(1)			Winterthur	23 Jun
11.17 7.06 13.46 1.83 50.51/ 15.55 40.40 4.50 65.46 4:30.23								
Petri	Keskitalo	FIN 67	7628H	(2)	NC		Huittinen	1 Jul
10.8 7.30 12.59 2.01 48.9/ 14.8 36.18 4.60 55.84 5:03.1								
Enno	Tjepkema	HOL 65	7587	(1)			Ottawa	10 Jun
10.83w 13.39 1.95 7.02w 50.53/ 14.77 40.56 4.00 56.98 4:38.8								
Rene	Gunther	GDR 65	7508	(15)	NC		Neubrandenburg	3 Jun
11.76 6.88 13.80 1.94 52.65/ 15.22w 46.56 4.40 58.92 4:31.87								
Veroslav	Valenta	65	7477	(2)			Praha	10 Jun
11.44 6.91 14.45 1.90 50.72/ 15.11 42.80 4.40 47.84 4:30.28								
Nikolay	Afanasyev	SU 65	7465	(2)	vGDR-J		Tallinn	24 Jun
11.55 6.85 13.00 1.95 51.02/ 15.19 38.02 4.30 65.40 4:32.18								
Jurgen	Mandl	AUT 65	7452	(11)			Gotzis	20 May
11.19 7.10 13.60 1.99 50.57/ 14.57 35.98 4.20 53.50 4:46.6								
Thomas	Fahner	GDR 65	7408	(1)			Plovdiv	5 Aug
11.46 6.72 12.51 1.92 51.03/ 15.43 38.90 4.60 61.78 4:34.01								
Igor	Sivoyedov	SU 65	7474H	( )			Mogilov	17 Jul
11.6 6.82 13.57 1.98 53.1/ 14.9 47.22 4.20 38.42 4:39.0								
Stefan	Remke	GDR 65	7360	(2)	DRUZHBA		Plovdiv	5 Aug
11.43 6.80 11.90 1.92 49.72/ 15.20 38.94 4.60 49.82 4:27.95								
Jann	Trefny	SWI 66	7351	(2)			Winterthur	23 Jun
11.04•7.06 12.06 2.04 49.71/ 15.20 37.36 4.00 47.66 4:36.76								
Andre	Preysing	GDR 66	7317	(3)	DRUZHBA		Plovdiv	5 Aug
11.36 6.99 11.17 1.98 48.78/ 15.00 34.58 4.40 49.10 4:30.96								
Sasa	Karan	YUG 65	7313	(1)	BALK-J		Maribor	29 Jul
11.53 7.04 12.52 2.01 50.20/ 15.54 46.04 3.80 51.40 4:42.56								
Christian	Deick	FRG 65	7342H	(1)			Kreutzal	27 May
10.8 6.95 14.29 1.88 50.2/ 16.2 43.28 3.60 55.94 4:44.7								
Jens	Kaden	GDR 66	7239	(1)	NC-J		Potsdam	1 Jul
11.20 6.51 14.00 1.89 50.07/ 15.58 39.94 4.20 49.14 4:40.23								
Igor	Malachovskiy	SU 65	7451H				Kharkov	12 Aug
11.3 6.99 12.93 2.00 51.6/ 15.3 37.66 4.50 58.74 4:43.6								
Sergey	Usmanov	SU 65	7396H				Kharkov	12 Aug
11.2 7.24 12.72 2.05 50.7/ 15.4 39.22 4.20 46.96 4:40.8								
Sergey	Zenger	SU 65	7373H				Alma Ata	8 Aug
10.9 6.47 11.22 1.99 47.3/ 15.4 33.88 4.00 44.50 4:13.4								

331

Valerie Brisco-Hooks – triple gold medallist.

ALL-TIME WORLD LISTS

100 METRES

Evelyn	Ashford	USA 57	10.76	1.7	1	WK	Zurich	22 Aug 84
	Ashford		A10.79	0.6	1	NSF	AF Academy, CO	3 Jul 83
Marlies	Oelsner-GOHR	GDR 58	10.81	1.7	1	OD	Berlin	8 Jun 83
Marita	Koch	GDR 57	10.83	1.7	2	OD	Berlin	8 Jun 83
	Gohr		10.84	1.7	2	WK	Zurich	22 Aug 84
	Gohr		10.86	0.4	1		Potsdam	5 May 84
	Gohr		10.87	1.9	1		Dresden	26 Jul 84
	Oelsner		10.88	2.0	1	NC	Dresden	1 Jul 77
	Gohr		10.88	1.9	1	v USA	Karl-Marx-Stadt	9 Jul 82
	Gohr		10.89	0.7	1	NC	Erfurt	1 Jun 84
	Ashford		A10.90	0.6	1r1		Colorado Springs	22 Jul 81
	Gohr		10.90	1.1	1	NC	Karl-Marx-Stadt	16 Jun 83
	Gohr		10.91	1.0	1	NC	Dresden	1 Jul 82
	Gohr		10.91	0.6	1		Berlin	31 Jul 83
	Gohr		10.91	−0.5	1	OD	Berlin	20 Jul 84
	Ashford		10.92	1.3	1h2	ISTAF	W Berlin	17 Aug 84
	Gohr		10.93	2.0	1	OT	Dresden	24 May 80
	Ashford		10.93	0.1	1		Westwood	7 Aug 82
	Ashford		10.93	1.6	1	GGala	Roma	31 Aug 84
	Gohr		10.94	1.4	1		Dresden	12 Aug 78
Diane	Williams	USA 61	A10.94	0.6	2	NSF	AF Academy, CO	3 Jul 83
	Ashford (22/4)		10.94	−0.1	1	ISTAF	W Berlin	17 Aug 84
(22/4)								
Barbel	Eckert-WOCKEL	GDR 55	10.95	1.0	2	NC	Dresden	1 Jul 82
Florence	Griffith	USA 59	10.99	−0.1	2	ISTAF	W Berlin	17 Aug 84
Angella	Taylor	CAN 58	11.00	1.4	1	CG	Brisbane	4 Oct 82
Annegret	Irrgang-RICHTER	FRG 50	11.01	0.6	1s1	OG	Montreal	25 Jul 76
Merlene	Ottey-PAGE	JAM 60	11.01	0.0	1r2		Walnut, CA	25 Jul 84
Romy	Schneider-MULLER	GDR 58	11.02	2.0	3	OT	Dresden	24 May 80
Lyudmila	Kondratyeva-SEDYKH	SU 58	11.02	−0.2	2	DRZ	Praha	16 Aug 84
Monika	Meyer-HAMANN	GDR 54	11.03	2.0	2	NC	Dresden	1 Jul 77
Silke	Gladisch	GDR 64	11.03	1.7	3	OD	Berlin	8 Jun 83
Inge	Helten	FRG 50	11.04	0.6	1h1		Furth	13 Jun 76
Ingrid	Brestrich-AUERSWALD	GDR 57	11.04	1.7	4	WK	Zurich	22 Aug 84
Renate	Meissner-STECHER	GDR 50	11.07	−0.2	1	OG	Munchen	2 Sep 72
Anelia	Nuneva	BUL 62	11.07	1.7	4	OD	Berlin	8 Jun 83
Wyomia	TYUS-Simburg	USA 45	A11.08	1.2	1	OG	Mexico, D.F.	15 Oct 68
Brenda	Morehead	USA 57	11.08	2.0	1	FOT	Eugene	21 Jun 76
Alice	Brown	USA 60	11.08	1.3	1	PO	Los Angeles	25 Jun 83
(20)								
Valerie	Brisco-HOOKS	USA 60	11.08	0.9	1		Koblenz	29 Aug 84
Jarmila	Kratochvilova	CS 51	11.09	1.7	1	PTS	Bratislava	6 Jun 81
Nadezhda	Georgieva	BUL 61	11.09	1.7	1	NC	Sofia	4 Jun 83
Kathy	SMALLWOOD-Cook	UK 60	11.10	0.1	2	WP	Roma	5 Sep 81
Barbel	Lockhoff-SCHOLZEL	GDR 59	11.11	1.7	5	OD	Berlin	8 Jun 83
Jackie	Washington	USA 62	A11.11	0.6	3	NSF	AF Academy, CO	3 Jul 83
Barbara	FERRELL-Edmondson	USA 47	A11.12	0.6	1q1	OG	Mexico, D.F.	14 Oct 68
Irena	Kirszenstein-SZEWINSKA	POL 46	11.13	−1.2	1	EC	Roma	3 Sep 74
Chandra	Cheeseborough	USA 59	11.13	2.0	2	FOT	Eugene	21 Jun 76
Gesine	Walther	GDR 62	11.13	1.8	1h2		Cottbus	21 Aug 82
(30)								
Helina	Laihorinne-MARJAMAA	FIN 56	11.13	1.0	1		Lahti	19 Jul 83
Lilieth	Hodges	JAM 53	11.14	1.7	1th1	AAU	Westwood	8 Jun 78
Chantal	Rega	FRA 55	11.15	2.0	1	NC	Lille	26 Jun 76
Sofka	Kazandzheva-POPOVA	BUL 53	11.15	1.4	1	Balk	Sofia	13 Jun 80
Jeanette	Bolden	USA 60	11.15	1.5	1	Pepsi	Westwood	13 May 84

333

All-time Lists – Women

Andrea	LYNCH-Saunders	UK 52	11.16	0.4	1		London	11 Jun 75
Silvia	Chivas	CUB 54	11.16	1.2	1s1	WUG	Sofia	20 Aug 77
Linda	Haglund	SWE 56	11.16	1.0	4	OG	Moskva	26 Jul 80
Rose-Aimee	Bacoul	FRA 52	11.16	1.8	1s1	NC	Bordeaux	23 Jul 83
Tatyana	Alekseyeva	SU 63	11.16	0.0	1		Sochi	19 May 84
(40)								
Wendy	Vereen	USA 66	A11.17	0.6	4	NSF	AF Academy, CO	3 Jul 83
Angela	Bailey	CAN 62	11.17	-1.7	3	VD	Bruxelles	26 Aug 83
Christina	BREHMER-Lathan	GDR 58	11.18	0.6	1r2	v SU	Leipzig	23 Jun 79
Elzbieta	Tomczak	POL 61	11.18	1.7	1	NC	Lublin	22 Jun 84
Mona Lisa	Strandvall-PURSIAINEN	FIN 51	11.19	1.8	1	EP-sf	Warszawa	4 Aug 73
Martina	Blos	GDR 57	11.19	1.3	3	OT	Karl-Marx-Stadt	29 May 76
Raelene	Boyle	AUS 51	A11.20	1.2	4	OG	Mexico, D.F.	15 Oct 68
Sonia	Lannaman	UK 56	11.20	0.4	2q3	OG	Moskva	25 Jul 80
Heather	HUNTE-Oakes	UK 59	11.20	0.0	1	8N-2	Beijing	26 Sep 80
Lyudmila	STOROZHKOVA-Bartenyeva	SU 55	11.21	0.8	1	WUG	Sofia	20 Aug 77
Ires	Schmidt	GDR 60	11.21	1.5	2h3	OD	Berlin	8 Jun 83
(50)								

Marks made with assisting wind greater than 2 m/s:

	Ashford		10.78	3.1	1		Modesto, CA	12 May 84
Marlies	Oelsner-GOHR	GDR 58	10.79	3.3	1	NC	Cottbus	16 Jul 80
	Ashford		10.85	5.2	1		Norwalk, CA	14 Jun 81
	Ashford		10.85	2.4	1		Modesto, CA	14 May 83
	Ashford		10.88	3.0	1	MSR	Walnut, CA	29 Apr 84
Barbel	Eckert-WOCKEL	GDR 55	10.92	3.3	2	NC	Cottbus	16 Jul 80
	Wockel		10.92	4.3	1		Cottbus	21 Aug 82
Angella	Taylor	CAN 58	10.92	3.4	1s2	CG	Brisbane	4 Oct 82
Sonia	Lannaman	UK 56	10.93	3.8	1	EP-sf	Dublin	17 Jul 77
Ingrid	Brestrich-AUERSWALD	GDR 57	10.93	3.3	3	NC	Cottbus	16 Jul 80
(10/6)								
Brenda	Morehead	USA 57	10.96	2.9	1s2	AAU	Walnut, CA	16 Jun 79
Florence	Griffith	USA 59	10.96	2.9	1	WK	Zurich	24 Aug 83
Gesine	Walther	GDR 62	10.97	3.3	4	NC	Cottbus	16 Jul 80
Merlene	OTTEY-Page	JAM 60	10.97	4.4	1h2	AIAW	Austin	28 May 81
(10)								
Chandra	Cheeseborough	USA 59	10.99	2.4	2		Modesto, CA	14 May 83
Heather	HUNTE-Oakes	UK 59	11.01	4.0	1		London	21 May 80
Valerie	Brisco-HOOKS	USA 60	11.02	2.3	1		Walnut, CA	3 Jun 84
Silvia	Chivas	CUB 54	A11.05	2.2	1	WPT	Guadalajara	12 Aug 77
Linda	Haglund	SWE 56	11.06	2.8	1	ISTAF	W Berlin	21 Aug 81
Randy	Givens	USA 62	11.06	3.7	1	NCAA	Eugene	1 Jun 84
Alice	Brown	USA 60	11.07	2.2	1s1	TAC	San Jose	8 Jun 84
Kathy	Smallwood-COOK	UK 60	11.08	2.9	4	WK	Zurich	24 Aug 83
Olga	Nasonova-ANTONOVA	SU 60	11.09	2.7	1		Leningrad	26 Jul 83
Angela	Williams	TRI 65	11.09		1		Nashville	14 Apr 84
(20)								
Wanda	Fort	USA 63	11.09		2		Nashville	14 Apr 84
Jeanette	Bolden	USA 60	A11.12	3.1	2	NCAA	Provo	4 Jun 82
Benita	FITZGERALD-Brown	USA 61	A11.13	3.1	3	NCAA	Provo	4 Jun 82
Bev	Kinch	UK 64	11.13	2.2	1	WUG	Edmonton	6 Jul 83
Shirley	Thomas	UK 63	11.13	3.8	2	NC	Cwmbran	27 May 84
Esther	Hope	TRI 60	11.14		1		Houston	2 May 81
Brenda	Cliette	USA 63	11.14	3.7	2	NCAA	Eugene	1 Jun 84
Sheila	LaBome	USA	11.15		2		Houston	2 May 81
Jennifer	Inniss	GUY 59	11.17	2.4	3		Modesto, CA	14 May 83
Wilma	RUDOLPH-Ward(30)	USA	11.18	2.8	1	OG	Roma	2 Sep 60
(40)								
Jacqueline	PUSEY-Perry	JAM 59	11.18	5.2	3		Norwalk, CA	14 Jun 81
Wendy	Hoyte	UK 57	11.18	3.4	2s2	CG	Brisbane	4 Oct 82
Rufina	Ubah	NIG 59	11.18	3.4	3s2	CG	Brisbane	4 Oct 82
Beverley	GODDARD-Callender	UK 56	11.19	4.0	4		London	21 May 80

All-time Lists – Women

Lyudmila	Zharkova-MASLAKOVA	SU 52	11.20		1	v USA	College Park, MD	6 Aug 76
Angela	Thacker	USA 64	11.20		1	KansR	Lawrence	22 Apr 83
Michelle	Finn	USA 65	11.20	3.7	4	NCAA	Eugene	1 Jun 84
Michele (38)	Glover	USA 63	11.21	3.8	1	TexR	Austin	6 Apr 84

200 METRES

Marita	Koch	GDR 57	21.71	0.7	1	v Can	Karl-Marx-Stadt	10 Jun 79
	Koch		21.71	0.3	1	OD	Potsdam	21 Jul 84
Marlies	Oelsner-GOHR	GDR 58	21.74	0.4	1	NC	Erfurt	3 Jun 84
	Koch		21.76	0.3	1	NC	Dresden	3 Jul 82
Valerie	Brisco-HOOKS	USA 60	21.81	−0.1	1	OG	Los Angeles	9 Aug 84
	Koch		21.82	1.3	1	NC	Karl-Marx-Stadt	18 Jun 83
Evelyn	Ashford	USA 57	21.83	−0.2	1	WP	Montreal	24 Aug 79
	Ashford		21.84	−1.1	1	VD	Bruxelles	28 Aug 81
Barbel	Eckert-WOCKEL	GDR 55	21.85	0.3	2	OD	Potsdam	21 Jul 84
	Koch		21.87	0.0	1	WK	Zurich	22 Aug 84
	Ashford		21.88	0.9	1	TAC	Indianapolis	19 Jun 83
	Koch		A21.91	1.9	1	WUG	Mexico, D.F.	12 Sep 79
Jarmila	Kratochvilova	CS 51	21.97	1.9	1	PTS	Bratislava	6 Jun 81
Chandra	Cheeseborough	USA 59	21.99	0.9	2	TAC	Indianapolis	19 Jun 83
	Wockel		22.01	0.6	1	NC	Cottbus	18 Jul 80
	Koch		22.02	−1.4	1		Leipzig	3 Jun 79
	Koch		22.02	−0.2	2	WP	Montreal	24 Aug 79
	Koch		22.02	0.3	1		Berlin	31 Jul 83
	Wockel		22.03	1.5	1	OG	Moskva	30 Jul 80
	Wockel		22.04	0.9	1	EC	Athinai	9 Sep 82
Florence (21/8)	Griffith	USA 59	22.04	−0.1	2	OG	Los Angeles	9 Aug 84
Merlene	Ottey-PAGE	JAM 60	22.09	−0.1	3	OG	Los Angeles	9 Aug 84
Kathy (10)	Smallwood-COOK	UK 60	22.10	−0.1	4	OG	Los Angeles	9 Aug 84
Natalya	Bochina	SU 62	22.19	1.5	2	OG	Moskva	30 Jul 80
Grace	Jackson	JAM 61	22.20	−0.1	5	OG	Los Angeles	9 Aug 84
Irena	Kirszenstein-SZEWINSKA	POL 46	22.21	1.9	1		Potsdam	13 Jun 74
Gesine	Walther	GDR 62	22.24	0.3	2	NC	Dresden	3 Jul 82
Angella	Taylor	CAN 58	A22.25	0.8	1		Colorado Springs	20 Jul 82
Lyudmila	KONDRATYEVA-Sedykh	SU 58	22.31	0.1	1		Moskva	12 Jun 80
Randy	Givens	USA 62	22.31	0.9	4	TAC	Indianapolis	19 Jun 83
Denise	Robertson-BOYD	AUS 52	22.35	1.8	1	NC	Sydney	23 Mar 80
Sabine	Rieger	GDR 63	22.37	1.3	2	v SU	Cottbus	26 Jun 82
Renate (20)	Meissner-STECHER	GDR 50	22.38	1.6	1	NC	Dresden	21 Jul 73
Brenda	Morehead	USA 57	22.38	1.7	1		Nashville	12 Apr 80
Mona Lisa	Strandvall-PURSIAINEN	FIN 51	22.39	0.6	1	WUG	Moskva	20 Aug 73
Annegret	Irrgang-RICHTER	FRG 50	22.39	0.0	2	OG	Montreal	28 Jul 76
Alice	Brown	USA 60	22.41	0.9	5	TAC	Indianapolis	19 Jun 83
Nadezhda	Georgieva	BUL 61	22.42	1.2	1	NarMl	Sofia	22 May 83
Ewa	Kasprzyk	POL 57	22.42	1.4	1		Sopot	5 Aug 84
Raelene	Boyle	AUS 51	22.45	1.1	2	OG	Munchen	7 Sep 72
Romy	Schneider-MULLER	GDR 58	22.47	1.5	4	OG	Moskva	30 Jul 80
Tatana	Kocembova	CS 62	22.47	0.2	1		Barcelona	8 Jul 84
Kirsten (30)	SIEMON-Emmelmann	GDR 61	22.50	0.0	2	NC	Jena	9 Aug 81
Rose-Aimee	Bacoul	FRA 52	22.53	1.4	4s2	OG	Los Angeles	9 Aug 84
Sonia	Lannaman	UK 56	22.58	1.5	1		Cwmbran	18 May 80
Anelia	Nuneva	BUL 62	22.58	1.2	1	v Hun,Pol	Sofia	24 Jul 83
Ingrid	Brestrich-AUERSWALD	GDR 57	22.60	1.1	2	OT	Erfurt	18 May 80
Christina	BREHMER-Lathan	GDR 58	22.61	1.9	2		Halle	14 Jun 79
Cheng	Chi	TAI 44	22.62	0.8	1	HB	Munchen	12 Jul 70

All-time Lists – Women

Lyudmila	Zharkova-MASLAKOVA	SU 52	22.62		1	NC	Tbilisi	17 Sep 78
Marita	Payne	CAN 60	22.62	0.1	2	WUG	Edmonton	10 Jul 83
Maya	Azarashvili	SU 64	22.63	0.1	2		Kiev	23 Jun 84
Carla	Rietig-BODENDORF	GDR 53	22.64	0.0	4	OG	Montreal	28 Jul 76
(40)								
Angela	Bailey	CAN 62	A22.64	0.1	1		Colorado Springs	19 Jul 83
Barbel	LOCKHOFF-Scholzel	GDR 59	22.65	1.1	3	OT	Erfurt	18 May 80
Pam	Marshall	USA 60	22.67	0.6	3	TAC	San Jose	9 Jun 84
Inge	Helten	FRG 50	22.68	0.0	5	OG	Montreal	28 Jul 76
Svetlana	Zhizdrikova	SU 60	22.69	0.1	3		Kiev	23 Jun 84
Silke	Gladisch	GDR 64	22.70	0.0	2		Jena	13 May 84
Marina	Nikiforova-SIDOROVA	SU 50	22.72	0.6	2	WUG	Moskva	20 Aug 73
Beverley	GODDARD-Callender	UK 56	22.72	1.5	6	OG	Moskva	30 Jul 80
Chantal	Rega	FRA 55	22.72	0.8	3		Les Abymes	15 May 81
Heide-Elke	Gaugel	FRG 59	22.72	0.4	1		Munchen	20 Jul 84
(50)								
Marks made with assisting wind greater than 2 m/s:								
	Koch		21.85	2.6	1		Karl-Marx-Stadt	27 May 79
	Wockel (2/2)		21.85	2.6	1	v USA	Karl-Marx-Stadt	10 Jul 82
Angella	Taylor	CAN 58	A22.19	3.1	1		Colorado Springs	21 Jul 82
Michelle	Probert-SCUTT	UK 60	22.48	4.0	1	WA	Dublin	4 Jul 82
Pam	Marshall	USA 60	22.59	2.4	1s2	TAC	San Jose	9 Jun 84
Diane	Williams	USA 61	22.65	2.7	3	MSR	Walnut, CA	24 Apr 83
Beverley	Goddard-CALLENDER	UK 56	22.69	2.5	2	v FRG,Pol	London	24 Jun 81
Molly	Killingbeck	CAN 59	A22.69		1r1		Provo	21 May 83
Annelies	Hirsch-WALTER	GDR 59	22.71	4.5	2	v UK	Dresden	14 Jun 81
(9)								

400 METRES

Jarmila	Kratochvilova	CS 51	47.99		1	WC	Helsinki	10 Aug 83
Marita	Koch	GDR 57	48.16		1	EC	Athinai	8 Sep 82
	Koch		48.16		1	DRZ	Praha	16 Aug 84
	Koch		48.26		1		Dresden	27 Jul 84
	Kratochvilova		48.45		1	NC	Praha	23 Jul 83
Tatana	Kocembova	CS 62	48.59		2	WC	Helsinki	10 Aug 83
	Koch		48.60		1	EP	Torino	4 Aug 79
	Kratochvilova		48.61		1	WP	Roma	6 Sep 81
	Kocembova		48.73		2	DRZ	Praha	16 Aug 84
	Koch		48.77		1	v USA	Karl-Marx-Stadt	9 Jul 82
	Kratochvilova		48.82			Ros	Praha	23 Jun 83
Valerie	Brisco-HOOKS	USA 60	48.83		1	OG	Los Angeles	6 Aug 84
	Kratochvilova		48.85		2	EC	Athinai	8 Sep 82
	Kratochvilova		48.86		1	WK	Zurich	18 Aug 82
	Koch		48.86		1	NC	Erfurt	2 Jun 84
	Koch		48.87		1	VD	Bruxelles	27 Aug 82
	Koch		48.88		1	OG	Moskva	28 Jul 80
	Koch		48.89		1		Potsdam	29 Jul 79
	Koch		48.89		1		Berlin	15 Jul 84
	Koch		48.94			EC	Praha	31 Aug 78
	Koch		48.97		1	WP	Montreal	26 Aug 79
Olga	Vladykina	SU 63	48.98		1		Kiev	22 Jun 84
(22/5)								
Chandra	Cheeseborough	USA 59	49.05		2	OG	Los Angeles	6 Aug 84
Maria	Kulchunova-PINIGINA	SU 58	49.19		3	WC	Helsinki	10 Aug 83
Sabine	Busch	GDR 62	49.24		2	NC	Erfurt	2 Jun 84
Irena	Kirszenstein-SZEWINSKA	POL 46	49.28		1	OG	Montreal	29 Jul 76
Kathy	Smallwood-COOK	UK 60	49.42		3	OG	Los Angeles	6 Aug 84
(10)								
Barbel	Eckert-WOCKEL	GDR 55	49.56		1		Erfurt	30 May 82
Dagmar	RUBSAM-Neubauer	GDR 62	49.58		3	NC	Erfurt	2 Jun 84

All-time Lists – Women

Christina	Brehmer-LATHAN	GDR 58	49.66	3	OG	Moskva	28 Jul 80	
Gaby	Bussmann	FRG 59	49.75	4	WC	Helsinki	10 Aug 83	
Marita	Payne	CAN 60	49.91	4	OG	Los Angeles	6 Aug 84	
Gesine	Walther	GDR 62	50.03	2		Jena	13 May 84	
Irina	Bagryantsova-NAZAROVA	SU 57	50.07	4	OG	Moskva	28 Jul 80	
Riitta	Hagman-SALIN	FIN 50	50.14	1	EC	Roma	4 Sep 74	
Ellen	Stropahl-STREIDT	GDR 52	50.15	2		Berlin	10 Jul 76	
Nina	Zyuskova (20)	SU 52	50.17	5	OG	Moskva	28 Jul 80	
(20)								
Irina	Baskakova	SU 56	50.19	2	Spart	Moskva	21 Jun 83	
Lillie	Leatherwood	USA 64	50.19	3	FOT	Los Angeles	19 Jun 84	
Brigitte	ROHDE-Kohn	GDR 54	50.26	1r2	v Yug,UK	Split	1 May 76	
Lilia	Tuznikova-NOVOSELTSOVA	SU 62	50.28	2		Moskva	20 Jul 84	
Doris	Maletzki	GDR 52	50.34	4		Berlin	10 Jul 76	
Ute	Finger-THIMM	FRG 58	50.37	6	OG	Los Angeles	6 Aug 84	
Sherri	Howard	USA 62	50.40	4	FOT	Los Angeles	19 Jun 84	
Charmaine	Crooks	CAN 61	50.45	7	OG	Los Angeles	6 Aug 84	
Tatyana	Nasonova-GOYSHCHIK	SU 52	50.49	3	Spart	Moskva	24 Jul 79	
Pirjo	Wilmi-HAGGMAN	FIN 51	50.56	4	OG	Montreal	29 Jul 76	
(30)								
Aurelia	Penton	CUB 43	A50.56	1	CAG	Medellin	16 Jul 78	
Larisa	Krylova	SU 55	50.60	1		Kiev	14 Aug 82	
Rosalyn	Bryant	USA 56	50.62	1s2	OG	Montreal	28 Jul 76	
Karoline	Steringer-KAFER	AUT 54	50.62	1		Klagenfurt	18 Jun 77	
Kirsten	Siemon-EMMELMANN	GDR 61	50.62	3	BGP	Budapest	20 Aug 84	
Michelle	Probert-SCUTT	UK 60	50.63	1	NC	Cwmbran	31 May 82	
Marina	Ivanova	SU 62	50.63	4	Spart	Moskva	21 Jun 83	
Lyudmila	Belova	SU 58	50.63	3		Moskva	4 Aug 84	
Gabriele	KOTTE-Lowe	GDR 58	50.70	1t	NC	Karl-Marx-Stadt	12 Aug 79	
Joslyn	Hoyte-SMITH	UK 54	50.75	1	v Bel,GDR	London	18 Jun 82	
(40)								
Yelena	Didilenko-KORBAN	SU 61	50.77	1		Leningrad	27 Jul 83	
Gisela	Anton	GDR 54	50.78	1		Halle	27 Jul 76	
Olga	Syrovatskaya-MINEYEVA	SU 52	50.78	2		Moskva	12 Jun 80	
Rositsa	Stamenova	BUL 55	50.82	4h1	DRZ	Praha	16 Aug 84	
Denean	Howard	USA 64	50.87	1	TAC	Knoxville	20 Jun 82	
Ana	Quirot	CUB 63	50.87	5h1	DRZ	Praha	16 Aug 84	
Rita	Jahn-WILDEN	FRG 47	50.88	3	EC	Roma	4 Sep 74	
Sheila	Ingram	USA 57	50.90	3s1	OG	Montreal	28 Jul 76	
Nadezhda	Aldoshina-LYALINA	SU 56	50.91	1		Krasnodar	24 May 83	
Lyudmila	Zenina-CHERNOVA	SU 55	50.91	2		Krasnodar	24 May 83	
(50)								
Margit	Sinzel	GDR 58	50.92	5		Berlin	10 Jul 76	
Florence	Griffith	USA 59	50.94	1	NCAA	Houston	4 Jun 83	
Nadezhda	Mushta-OLIZARENKO	SU 53	50.96	1		Moskva	12 Jul 80	
Mimmie	Theron-SNYMAN	RSA 56	A50.97	1		Germiston	17 Mar 82	
Jelica	PAVLICIC-Stefancic	YUG 54	50.98	1	Balk	Sofia	3 Aug 74	
Marina	Nikiforova-SIDOROVA	SU 50	50.98	1	NC	Moskva	27 Jul 77	
Easter	Gabriel	USA 60	50.99	2	NCAA	Houston	4 Jun 83	
(57)								

800 METRES

Jarmila	Kratochvilova	CS 51	1:53.28	1		Munchen	26 Jul 83	
Nadezhda	Mushta-OLIZARENKO	SU 53	1:53.43	1	OG	Moskva	27 Jul 80	
	Kratochvilova		1:54.68	1	WC	Helsinki	9 Aug 83	
Olga	Syrovatskaya-MINEYEVA	SU 52	1:54.81	2	OG	Moskva	27 Jul 80	
	Olizarenko		1:54.85	1		Moskva	12 Jun 80	
Tatyana	Kazankina	SU 51	1:54.94	1	OG	Montreal	26 Jul 76	
	Kratochvilova		1:55.04	1		Oslo	23 Aug 83	
Doina	Besliu-MELINTE	RUM 56	1:55.05	1	NC	Bucuresti	1 Aug 82	
	Mineyeva		1:55.1	1	Znam	Moskva	6 Jul 80	
	Mineyeva		1:55.41	1	EC	Athinai	8 Sep 82	

337

All-time Lists – Women

Nikolina	Shtereva	BUL 55	1:55.42		2	OG	Montreal	26 Jul 76
Tatyana	Providokhina	SU 53	1:55.46		3	OG	Moskva	27 Jul 80
	Mineyeva		1:55.5 m		1	Kuts	Podolsk	21 Aug 82
Elfi	Rost-ZINN	GDR 53	1:55.60		3	OG	Montreal	26 Jul 76
Irina	Podyalovskaya	SU 59	1:55.69		1		Kiev	22 Jun 84
Anita	Barkusky-WEISS	GDR 55	1:55.74		4	OG	Montreal	26 Jul 76
	Providokhina		1:55.80		1	EC	Praha	31 Aug 78
	Mushta		1:55.82		2	EC	Praha	31 Aug 78
	Providokhina		1:55.9		2	Znam	Moskva	6 Jul 80
Lyudmila	Samanyuta-VESELKOVA	SU 50	1:55.96		2	EC	Athinai	8 Sep 82
Yekaterina	Poryvkina-PODKOPAYEVA	SU 52	1:55.96		1		Leningrad	27 Jul 83
(21/12)								
Valentina	Gerasimova	SU 48	1:56.0 m		1	NC	Kiev	12 Jun 76
Ravilya	Agletdinova	SU 60	1:56.1 m		2	Kuts	Podolsk	21 Aug 82
Lyubov	Gurina	SU 57	1:56.11		2	WC	Helsinki	9 Aug 83
Totka	Petrova	BUL 56	1:56.2		1		Paris	6 Jul 79
Tatyana	Mishkel	SU 52	1:56.2 m		3	Kuts	Podolsk	21 Aug 82
Martina	KAMPFERT-Steuk	GDR 59	1:56.21		4	OG	Moskva	27 Jul 80
Zamira	Akhtyamova-ZAITSEVA	SU 53	1:56.21		2		Leningrad	27 Jul 83
Svetlana	Moshchenok-STYRKINA	SU 49	1:56.44		5	OG	Montreal	26 Jul 76
(20)								
Zoya	Shcherbakova-RIGEL	SU 52	1:56.57		3	EC	Praha	31 Aug 78
Tamara	Kazachkova-SOROKINA	SU 50	1:56.6 m		5	Kuts	Podolsk	21 Aug 82
Fita	Rafira-LOVIN	RUM 51	1:56.67		2		Moskva	12 Jun 80
Lyudmila	Ashikhmina-BORISOVA	SU 59	1:56.78		3		Kiev	22 Jun 84
Nina	Ruchayeva	SU 56	1:56.84		2r1		Moskva	19 Jul 84
Olga	Dvirna	SU 53	1:56.9 m		6	Kuts	Podolsk	21 Aug 82
Jolanta	Januchta	POL 55	1:56.95		1	BGP	Budapest	11 Aug 80
Zuzana	Moravcikova	CS 56	1:56.96		1		Leipzig	27 Jul 83
Valentina	Parkhuta-ZHUKOVA	SU 59	1:56.97		5		Kiev	22 Jun 84
Olga	Vakhrusheva	SU 47	1:57.0		1		Moskva	12 Jun 80
(30)								
Ulrike	KLAPEZYNSKI-Bruns	GDR 53	1:57.06				Berlin	10 Jul 76
Galina	Zakharova	SU 56	1:57.08		1		Baku	16 Sep 84
Hildegard	ULLRICH-Korner	GDR 59	1:57.20		5	OG	Moskva	27 Jul 80
Svetla	Zlateva-KOLEVA	BUL 52	1:57.21		6	OG	Montreal	26 Jul 76
Margrit	Klinger	FRG 60	1:57.22		7	EC	Athinai	8 Sep 82
Elzbieta	Skowronska-KATOLIK	POL 49	1:57.26		2	BGP	Budapest	11 Aug 80
Milena	Matejkovicova	CS 61	1:57.28		2		Leipzig	27 Jul 83
Ileana	Gergely-SILAI	RUM 41	1:57.39		1	NC	Bucuresti	28 Aug 77
Nadezhda	Zvyagintseva	SU 61	1:57.47		6		Kiev	22 Jun 84
Tatyana	Pozdnyakova	SU 56	1:57.5 m		9	Kuts	Podolsk	21 Aug 82
(40)								
Antje	Schroder	GDR 63	1:57.57		3		Leipzig	27 Jul 83
Christiane	Stoll-WARTENBERG	GDR 56	1:57.6		1		Potsdam	29 Jul 79
Mary	DECKER-Slaney	USA 58	1:57.60		1		Gateshead	31 Jul 83
Gabriella	Dorio	ITA 57	1:57.66		1		Pisa	5 Jul 80
Maricica	Luca-PUICA	RUM 50	1:57.8		2		Bucuresti	17 Jun 79
Maria	Enkina	SU 51	1:57.8 m		1		Volgograd	25 Sep 81
Katrin	Wuhn	GDR 65	1:57.86		1	Skok	Celje	5 May 84
Madeline	Manning-JACKSON	USA 48	1:57.9		3	v SU	College Park	7 Aug 76
Yelena	Medvedyeva	SU 59	1:57.90		h	Znam	Sochi	9 Jun 84
Svetlana	Popova	SU 59	1:57.9 m		1		Leningrad	19 Jul 83
(50)								

1000 METRES

Tatyana	Providokhina	SU 53	2:30.6 m		1		Podolsk	20 Aug 78
Martina	KAMPFERT-Steuk	GDR 59	2:30.85		1		Berlin	9 Jul 80
Beate	Ludtke-LIEBICH	GDR 58	2:31.5		2		Berlin	9 Jul 80
Olga	Dvirna	SU 53	2:31.65		1		Athinai	1 Sep 82

338

All-time Lists – Women

Anita	Barkusky-WEISS	GDR 55	2:31.74	1		Potsdam	13 Jul 80
	Dvirna		2:31.8	1	Kuts	Podolsk	5 Aug 79
Ulrike	Klapezynski-BRUNS	GDR 53	2:31.95	1	ISTAF	W Berlin	18 Aug 78
Christiane	Stoll-WARTENBERG	GDR56	2:32.29	2		Potsdam	13 Jul 80
Raisa Tatarintsera	BELOUSOVA	SU 52	2:32.6	2	Kuts	Podolsk	5 Aug 79
Jolanta	Januchta	POL 55	2:32.70	1	WK	Zurich	19 Aug 81
(10/9)							
Tamara	Kazachkova-SOROKINA	SU 50	2:32.8 m	1		Podolsk	24 Jul 76
(10)							
Lyudmila	Kalnitskaya	SU 53	2:32.9 m	2		Podolsk	20 Aug 78
Totka	Petrova	BUL 56	2:33.0 m	1		Sofia	13 Aug 78
Gabriella	Dorio	ITA 57	2:33.2 m	1		Formia	28 Aug 82
Brigitte	Kraus	FRG 56	2:33.44	1	ISTAF	W Berlin	17 Aug 79
Svetlana	Ulmasova	SU 53	2:33.6	3	Kuts	Podolsk	5 Aug 79
Nikolina	Shtereva	BUL 55	2:33.8 m	1		Sofia	4 Jul 76
Valentina	Ilyinykh	SU 56	2:34.1	4	Kuts	Podolsk	5 Aug 79
Tatyana	Pozdnyakova	SU 56	2:34.13	2		Athinai	1 Sep 82
Christina	Neumann-LIEBETRAU	GDR 53	2:34.8 m	1		Dresden	7 Aug 77
Hildegard	ULLRICH-Korner	GDR 59	2:34.8 m	2		Potsdam	12 Jul 84
(20)							
Margrit	Klinger	FRG 60	2:34.94	1		Letter	8 Sep 83
Karin	Burneleit-KREBS	GDR 43	2:35.0 m	1		Potsdam	28 Aug 74
Rositsa	Pekhlivanova	BUL 55	2:35.2 m	2		Sofia	4 Jul 76
Irina	Nikitina	SU 61	2:35.4	5	Kuts	Podolsk	5 Aug 79
Katrin	Wuhn	GDR 65	2:35.4 m	3		Potsdam	12 Jul 84
Christina	Boxer	UK 57	2:35.62	1		London	30 Aug 82
Vesela	Tasheva-YATSINSKA	BUL 51	2:35.65	2		Sofia	14 Aug 82
Maricica	Luca-PUICA	RUM 50	2:35.7 m	1		Poiana Brasov	1 Jun 84
Gunhild	Hoffmeister	GDR 44	2:35.9 m	1		Potsdam	20 Aug 72
Anna	Bukis	POL 53	2:35.96	2	Coke	London	11 Sep 81

1500 METRES

Tatyana	Kazankina	SU 51	3:52.47	1	WK	Zurich	13 Aug 80
Olga	Dvirna	SU 53	3:54.23	1	NC	Kiev	27 Jul 82
	Kazankina		3:55.0	1	Znam	Moskva	6 Jul 80
	Kazankina		3:56.0	1		Podolsk	28 Jun 76
Zamira	Akhtyamova-ZAITSEVA	SU 53	3:56.14	2	NC	Kiev	27 Jul 82
Tatyana	Pozdnyakova	SU 56	3:56.50	3	NC	Kiev	27 Jul 82
	Kazankina		3:56.56	1	OG	Moskva	1 Aug 80
Nadezhda	Raldugina	SU 57	3:56.63	1	DRZ	Praha	18 Aug 84
Yekaterina	Poryvkina-PODKOPAYEVA	SU 52	3:56.65	1		Rieti	2 Sep 84
Lyubov	Ruchka-SMOLKA	SU 52	3:56.7	2	Znam	Moskva	6 Jul 80
Nadezhda	Mushta-OLIZARENKO	SU 53	3:56.8	3	Znam	Moskva	6 Jul 80
	Zaitseva		3:56.9	4	Znam	Moskva	6 Jul 80
Svetlana	Guskova	SU 59	3:57.05	4	NC	Kiev	27 Jul 82
Mary	DECKER-Slaney	USA 58	3:57.12	1	v Scan	Stockholm	26 Jul 83
Maricica	Luca-PUICA	RUM 50	3:57.22	1		Bucuresti	1 Jul 84
Totka	Petrova	BUL 54	3:57.4	1	Balk	Athinai	11 Aug 79
	Podkopayeva		3:57.4	5	Znam	Moskva	6 Jul 80
	Puica		3:57.48	1	NC	Bucuresti	31 Jul 82
	Pozdnyakova		3:57.70	2		Rieti	2 Sep 84
Christiane	Stoll-WARTENBERG	GDR 56	3:57.71	2	OG	Moskva	1 Aug 80
Galina	Zakharova	SU 56	3:57.72	1		Baku	14 Sep 84
	Dvirna		3:57.78	1	BGP	Budapest	29 Jul 81
	Dvirna		3:57.80	1	EC	Athinai	11 Sep 82
	Puica		3:57.82	1		Tirrenia	25 Aug 82

(24/14)

All-time Lists – Women

Doina	Besliu-MELINTE	RUM 56	3:58.1 m	1	RumIC	Bucuresti	9 Jun 84
Natalia	Andrei-MARASESCU-Betini	RUM 52	3:58.2	1	NC	Bucuresti	13 Jul 79
Tatyana	Providokhina	SU 53	3:58.37	1	Kuts	Podolsk	22 Aug 82
Ileana	Gergely-SILAI	RUM 41	3:58.5	2	NC	Bucuresti	13 Jul 79
Gabriella	Dorio	ITA 57	3:58.65	2		Tirrenia	25 Aug 82
Ravilya	Agletdinova	SU 60	3:58.70	2	DRZ	Praha	18 Aug 84
(20)							
Svetlana	Ulmasova	SU 53	3:58.76	2	Kuts	Podolsk	22 Aug 82
Tamara	Kazachkova-SOROKINA	SU 50	3:58.89	1	Znam	Leningrad	26 Jul 81
Giana	ROMANOVA-Chernova	SU 55	3:59.01	1	EC	Praha	3 Sep 78
Yelena	Chernyshova-SIPATOVA	SU 55	3:59.48	4	Kuts	Podolsk	22 Aug 82
Anna	Bukis	POL 53	3:59.67	3	BGP	Budapest	29 Jul 81
Raisa	KATYUKOVA-Smekhnova	SU 50	3:59.8 m	2		Podolsk	28 Jun 76
Angelika	Kuhse-ZAUBER	GDR 58	3:59.90	1	NC	Jena	9 Aug 81
Ulrike	KLAPEZYNSKI-Bruns	GDR 53	3:59.9 m	1		Potsdam	14 Jul 76
Beate	Ludtke-LIEBICH	GDR 58	3:59.9 m	1		Potsdam	5 Jul 80
Fita	Rafira-LOVIN	RUM 51	4:00.12	1	RumIC	Bucuresti	4 Jun 83
(30)							
Valentina	Ilyinykh	SU 56	4:00.18	4	EC	Praha	3 Sep 78
Irina	Nikitina	SU 61	4:00.18	5	Kuts	Podolsk	22 Aug 82
Ruth	Kleinsasser-Caldwell-Wysocki	USA 57	4:00.18	1	FOT	Los Angeles	24 Jun 84
Alla	Yushina	SU 58	4:00.26	3	Znam	Leningrad	26 Jul 81
Lyudmila	Shesterova	SU 56	4:00.3	7		Moskva	6 Jul 80
Lyudmila	Medvedyeva	SU 57	4:00.42	3		Baku	14 Sep 84
Svetlana	Popova	SU 59	4:00.53	6	NC	Kiev	27 Jul 82
Grete	Andersen-WAITZ	NOR 53	4:00.55	5	EC	Praha	3 Sep 78
Christina	Boxer	UK 57	4:00.57	1		Gateshead	6 Jul 84
Maria	Radu	RUM 59	4:00.62	2	RumIC	Bucuresti	4 Jun 83
(40)							
Natalya	Rodina-BOBOROVA	SU 59	4:00.62	2		Moskva	20 Jul 84
Natalya	Artemova	SU 63	4:00.68	3		Rieti	2 Sep 84
Galina	Kireyeva	SU 56	4:01.22	8	NC	Kiev	27 Jul 82
Lyudmila	Bragina	SU 43	4:01.38	1	OG	Munchen	9 Sep 72
Gunhild	Hoffmeister	GDR 44	4:01.4 m	2		Potsdam	14 Jul 76
Christine	Tranter-BENNING	UK 55	4:01.53	3	WK	Zurich	15 Aug 79
Brigitte	Kraus	FRG 56	4:01.54	1	v SU	Dortmund	1 Jul 78
Tamara	Koba	SU 57	4:01.66	5	Znam	Leningrad	26 Jul 81
Zola	Budd	RSA 66	4:01.81	1		Port Elizabeth	21 Mar 84
Lyubov	Kremleva	SU 61	4:02.04	6		Kiev	24 Jun 84
(50)							
Lyudmila	Kalnitskaya	SU 53	4:02.1	1	Kuts	Podolsk	13 Aug 78
(51)							

ONE MILE

Natalya	Artemova	SU 63	4:15.8 m	1		Leningrad	5 Aug 84
Maricica	Luca-PUICA	RUM 50	4:17.44	1		Rieti	16 Sep 82
Mary	DECKER-Slaney	USA 58	4:18.08	1		Paris	9 Jul 82
Lyudmila	Samanyuta-VESELKOVA	SU 50	4:20.89	1		Bologna	12 Sep 81
Fita	Rafira-LOVIN	RUM 51	4:21.40	2		Bologna	12 Sep 81
	Decker		4:21.46	1	Bisl	Oslo	26 Jun 82
Vesela	Tasheva-YATSINSKA	BUL 51	4:21.52	1	BGP	Budapest	30 Jun 82
	Decker		4:21.65	1		Westwood	15 May 83
	Decker		4:21.68	1		Auckland	26 Jan 80
Vanya	Stoyanova	BUL 58	4:21.78	2	BGP	Budapest	30 Jun 82
Ruth	Kleinsasser-Caldwell-WYSOCKI	USA 57	4:21.78	1	Coke	London	7 Sep 84
	Puica		4:21.82	1		Viareggio	5 Aug 81
Tamara	Kazachkova-SOROKINA	SU 50	4:21.89	3	BGP	Budapest	30 Jun 82
(13/9)							
Natalia	Andrei-MARASESCU-Betini	RUM 52	4:22.09	1		Auckland	27 Jan 79
(10)							

All-time Lists – Women

Zamira	Akhtyamova-ZAITSEVA	SU 53	4:22.5 m	1		Kiev	15 Jun 81
Christina	Boxer	UK 57	4:22.64	2	Coke	London	7 Sep 84
Gabriella	Dorio	ITA 57	4:23.29	1		Viareggio	14 Aug 80
Svetlana	Ulmasova	SU 53	4:23.8 m	2		Kiev	15 Jun 81
Christine	Tranter-BENNING	UK 55	4:24.57	3	Coke	London	7 Sep 84
Silvana	Cruciata	ITA 53	4:24.6 m	1	DNG	Stockholm	8 Jul 81
Brigitte	Kraus	FRG 56	4:25.93	2		Rieti	16 Sep 82
Grete	Andersen-WAITZ	NOR 53	4:26.90	1		Gateshead	9 Jul 78
Francie	Larrieu	USA 52	4:27.52	2		Philadelphia	30 Jun 79
Margherita	Gargano	ITA 52	4:27.52	3		Rieti	16 Sep 82
(20)							
Wendy	Smith-SLY	UK 59	4:28.07	1		London	18 Aug 84
Jan	Merrill	USA 56	4:28.23	3		Philadelphia	30 Jun 79
Sarina	Mostert-CRONJE	RSA 55	4:28.4 m	1		Stellenbosch	15 Nov 80
Suzanne	Morley	UK 57	4:29.15	2		London	18 Aug 84
Cindy	Bremser	USA 53	4:29.21	1	Pepsi	Westwood	16 May 82
Agnese	Possamai	ITA 53	4:29.23	4		Rieti	16 Sep 82
Paola	Pigni-CACCHI	ITA 45	4:29.5 m	1		Viareggio	8 Aug 73
Debbie	Scott	CAN 58	4:29.67	2	Bisl	Oslo	26 Jun 82
Brit	McRoberts	CAN 57	4:29.90	2	Pepsi	Westwood	15 May 83
(29)							

3000 METRES

Tatyana	Kazankina	SU 51	8:22.62	1		Leningrad	26 Aug 84
Svetlana	Ulmasova	SU 53	8:26.78	1	NC	Kiev	25 Jul 82
Lyudmila	Bragina	SU 43	8:27.12	1	v USA	College Park, MD	7 Aug 76
Svetlana	Guskova	SU 59	8:29.36	2	NC	Kiev	25 Jul 82
	Guskova		8:29.59	1		Moskva	6 Aug 84
Mary	DECKER-Slaney	USA 58	8:29.71	1		Oslo	7 Jul 82
	Ulmasova		8:30.28	1	EC	Athinai	9 Sep 8
Maricica	Luca-PUICA	RUM 50	8:31.67	1	Balk	Bucuresti	14 Aug 82
Grete	Andersen-WAITZ	NOR 53	8:31.75	1		Oslo	17 Jul 79
Tatyana	Pozdnyakova	SU 56	8:32.0 m	1		Ryazan	11 Aug 84
	Kazankina		8:32.08	1		Leningrad	27 Jul 83
	Waitz		8:32.1 m	1		Oslo	27 Jun 78
	Kazankina		8:33.01	1	DRZ	Praha	16 Aug 84
	Ulmasova		8:33.16	1	EC	Praha	29 Aug 78
	Puica		8:33.33	2	EC	Athinai	9 Sep 82
Galina	Zakharova	SU 56	8:33.40	3	NC	Kiev	25 Jul 82
Natalia	Andrei-MARASESCU-Betini	RUM 52	8:33.53	1	EC	Praha	29 Aug 78
Yelena	Chernyshova-SIPATOVA	SU 55	8:33.53	1		Moskva	12 Jul 80
	Puica		8:33.57	1	NC	Bucuresti	10 Jul 84
	Puica		8:33.78	1		London	7 Aug 82
(20/11)							
Tatyana	Mekhanoshina-SYCHOVA	SU 53	8:33.9	2		Moskva	12 Jul 80
Faina	KRASNOVA-Andreyeva	SU 57	8:34.0	3		Moskva	12 Jul 80
Alla	Yushina	SU 58	8:34.02	2		Leningrad	27 Jul 83
Brigitte	Kraus	FRG 56	8:35.11	2	WC	Helsinki	10 Aug 83
Alla	Teslenko-LIBUTINA	SU 53	8:35.74	6	NC	Kiev	25 Jul 82
Lyubov	Ruchka-SMOLKA	SU 52	8:36.0	4		Moskva	12 Jul 80
Olga	Krentser-BONDARENKO	SU 60	8:36.20	2	Znam	Sochi	9 Jun 84
Ulrike	Klapezynski-BRUNS	GDR 53	8:36.38	1	OD	Berlin	20 Jul 84
Olga	Dvirna	SU 53	8:36.40	1		Sochi	30 May 82
(20)							
Wendy	Smith-SLY	UK 59	8:37.06	5	WC	Helsinki	10 Aug 83
Zola	Budd	RSA 66	8:37.5 m	1		Stellenbosch	29 Feb 84
Agnese	Possamai	ITA 53	8:37.96	6	WC	Helsinki	10 Aug 83
Olga	Kuzyukova	SU 53	8:38.22	8		Leningrad	27 Jul 83
Cindy	Bremser	USA 53	8:38.60	2	WK	Zurich	22 Aug 84
Natalya	Artemova	SU 63	8:38.84	1		Kiev	20 Jun 84
Yelena	Zhupiyeva	SU 60	8:39.52	3		Kiev	20 Jun 84

341

All-time Lists – Women

Ingrid	Christensen-KRISTIANSEN	NOR 56	8:39.56	1		Oslo	21 Jul 84
Nina	Yapeyeva	SU 56	8:40.4	5		Moskva	12 Jul 80
Raisa	Sadreydinova	SU 52	8:41.05	9		Leningrad	27 Jul 83
(30)							
Zhanna	Tursunova	SU 57	8:41.07	6		Kiev	20 Jun 84
Joan	Hansen	USA 58	8:41.43	3	FOT	Los Angeles	23 Jun 84
Raisa	KATYUKOVA-Smekhnova	SU 50	8:41.77	2	v USA	College Park, MD	7 Aug 76
Giana	ROMANOVA-Chernova	SU 55	8:41.8	6		Moskva	12 Jul 80
Lynn	Kanuka-WILLIAMS	CAN 60	8:42.14	3	OG	Los Angeles	10 Aug 84
Loa	Olafsson	DEN 58	8:42.3 m	2		Oslo	27 Jun 78
Jan	Merrill	USA 56	8:42.6 m	3		Oslo	27 Jun 78
Irina	Bondarchuk	SU 52	8:42.84	3		Sochi	30 May 82
Birgit	Friedmann	FRG 60	8:43.65	5	EC	Athinai	9 Sep 82
Christine	Tranter-BENNING	UK 55	8:44.46	3	WK	Zurich	22 Aug 84
(40)							
Raisa	Belousova	SU 52	8:44.7	4	Znam	Kaunas	11 Aug 79
Cornelia	de Vos-BURKI	SWZ 53	8:45.20	5	OG	Los Angeles	10 Aug 84
Anne	Garrett-AUDAIN	NZ 55	8:45.53	1	CG	Brisbane	4 Oct 82
Valentina	Ilyinykh	SU 56	8:45.6	1	Kuts	Podolsk	12 Aug 78
Olga	Ilyina	SU 58	8:45.6	5	NC	Donetsk	6 Sep 80
Jane	Furniss	UK 60	8:45.69	7	WC	Helsinki	10 Aug 83
Irina	Nikitina	SU 61	8:45.70	1	Kuts	Podolsk	21 Aug 82
Lyubov	Konyukhova	SU 56	8:45.88	2		Moskva	19 Jul 84
Nina	Konyakhina	SU 54	8:46.2	6	NC	Donetsk	6 Sep 80
Margherita	Gargano	ITA 52	8:46.31	2	GGala	Roma	14 Sep 82
(50)							
Lidia	Lunegova	SU 57	8:46.32	6	Znam	Sochi	9 Jun 84
Aurora	Cunha	POR 59	8:46.37	4h1	OG	Los Angeles	8 Aug 84
(52)							

5000 METRES

Ingrid	Christensen-KRISTIANSEN	NOR 56	14:58.89	1	Bisl	Oslo	28 Jun 84
Zola	Budd	RSA 66	15:01.83	1		Stellenbosch	5 Jan 84
Mary	DECKER-Slaney	USA 58	15:08.26	1	Pre	Eugene	5 Jun 82
Grete	Andersen-WAITZ	NOR 53	15:08.80	1	Bisl	Oslo	26 Jun 82
Loa	Olafsson	DEN 58	15:08.8 m	1		Sollerod	30 May 78
Aurora	Cunha	POR 59	15:09.07	2	Bisl	Oslo	28 Jun 84
	Budd		15:09.86	1		Port Elizabeth	7 Mar 84
	Budd		15:10.65	1		Port Elizabeth	17 Oct 83
Irina	Bondarchuk	SU 52	15:12.62	1	Znam	Moskva	11 Jun 82
Anne	Garrett-AUDAIN	NZ 55	15:13.22	1		Auckland	17 Mar 82
(10/8)							
Paula	Yeoman-FUDGE	UK 52	15:14.51	1		Knarvik	13 Sep 81
Anna	Domoradskaya	SU 53	15:19.0 m	1		Kiev	30 Sep 83
(10)							
Charlotte	Bernhardt-TESKE	FRG 49	15:19.54	2	Bisl	Oslo	26 Jun 82
Margherita	Gargano	ITA 52	15:21.0	1		Partinico	22 Sep 82
Angela	Tooby	UK 60	15:22.50	3	Bisl	Oslo	28 Jun 84
Brenda	Webb	USA 54	15:22.76	1		Knoxville	13 Apr 84
Tatyana	Kazankina	SU 51	15:23.12	1		Paris	4 Sep 84
Yelena	Chernyshova-SIPATOVA	SU 55	15:24.6 m	1	Kuts	Podolsk	6 Sep 81
Yelena	Tsukhlo	SU 54	15:25.13	2	Znam	Moskva	11 Jun 82
Monica	Joyce	IRE 58	15:27.5 m	1		San Diego	20 May 83
Marie-Louise	Hamrin	SWE 57	15:27.96	4	Bisl	Oslo	28 Jun 84
PattiSue	Plumer	USA 62	15:29.0 m	1	PennR	Philadelphia	26 Apr 84
(20)							
Barbara	Moore	NZ 57	15:29.65	2		Auckland	17 Mar 82
Dorthe	Rasmussen	DEN 60	15:29.7 m	1		Vallensbaek	31 May 83
Cathie	Twomey	USA 56	15:30.50	5	Bisl	Oslo	28 Jun 84
Jan	Merrill	USA 56	15:30.6	1		Palo Alto	22 Mar 80

All-time Lists – Women

Rosa	Mota	POR 58	15:30.63	6	Bisl	Oslo	28 Jun 84
Betty	Springs	USA 61	15:33.43	1		Oslo	9 Jul 83
Maggie	Keyes	USA 58	15:33.50	3	Pre	Eugene	5 Jun 82
Kathy	Hayes	USA 62	15:33.51	1		Eugene	30 Apr 83
Zhanna	Tursunova	SU 57	15:34.45	3	Znam	Moskva	11 Jun 82
Ellen	Tittel-WESSINGHAGE	FRG 48	15:34.76	2		Oslo	11 Jul 81
(30)							
Eva	Ernstrom	SWE 61	15:34.77	3		Oslo	9 Jul 83
Jane	Furniss	UK 60	15:34.92	5	Bisl	Oslo	26 Jun 82
(32)							

10000 METRES

Olga	Krentser-Bondarenko	SU 60	31:13.78	1		Kiev	24 Jun 84
Galina	Zakharova	SU 56	31:15.00	2		Kiev	24 Jun 84
Raisa	Sadreydinova	SU 52	31:27.58	1	NC	Odessa	7 Sep 83
Lyudmila	Baranova	SU 50	31:35.01	1		Krasnodar	29 May 83
Mary	DECKER-Slaney	USA 58	31:35.3 m	1		Eugene	16 Jul 82
	Krentser		31:35.61	2		Krasnodar	29 May 83
	Krentser		31:38.64	2	NC	Odessa	7 Sep 83
Loa	Olafsson	DEN 58	31:45.4 m	1		København	6 Apr 78
Anna	Domoradskaya	SU 53	31:48.23	1	NC	Kiev	27 Jul 82
Tatyana	Pozdnyakova	SU 56	31:48.94	3	NC	Odessa	7 Sep 83
(10/8)							
Lyudmila	Matveyeva	SU 57	31:51.80	4	NC	Odessa	7 Sep 83
Aurora	Cunha	POR 59	31:52.85	1	IAAF	Knarvik	4 Sep 83
(10)							
Zhanna	Tursunova	SU 57	31:53.53	3		Kiev	24 Jun 84
Lyubov	Konyukhova	SU 56	31:56.01	4		Kiev	24 Jun 84
Raisa	Katyukova-Smekhnova	SU 50	31:59.70	6		Kiev	24 Jun 84
Charlotte	Bernhardt-TESKE	FRG 49	32:00.26	2	IAAF	Knarvik	4 Sep 83
Dorthe	Rasmussen	DEN 60	32:02.89	3	IAAF	Knarvik	4 Sep 83
Joan	Benoit	USA 57	32:07.41	1	FOT	Los Angeles	17 Jun 84
Yelena	Chernyshova-SIPATOVA	SU 55	32:17.19	1	NC	Moskva	19 Sep 81
Yelena	Tsukhlo	SU 54	32:20.40	2	NC	Moskva	19 Sep 81
Anne	Garrett-AUDAIN	NZ 55	32:21.47	1		Auckland	14 Feb 83
Kellie	Cathey	USA 61	32:22.5 m	1	MSR	Walnut, CA	25 Apr 82
(20)							
Nancy	Rooks	CAN 59	32:23.04	4	IAAF	Knarvik	4 Sep 83
Tuija	Toivonen	FIN 58	32:23.1 m	1		Vantaa	7 Sep 83
Regina	Joyce	IRE 57	32:35.7 m	1	MSR	Walnut, CA	28 Apr 84
Anna	Ojun	SU 55	32:36.00	3	NC	Moskva	19 Sep 81
Zoya	Ivanova	SU 52	32:36.96	5	NC	Kiev	27 Jul 82
Katie	Ishmael	USA 64	32:37.37	2	FOT	Los Angeles	17 Jun 84
Maria	Klyukina	SU 50	32:37.40	4	NC	Moskva	19 Sep 81
Natalya	Rodina-BOBOROVA	SU 59	32:38.43	5	NC	Moskva	19 Sep 81
Karolin	Szabo	HUN 61	32:38.5 m	1	NC	Budapest	24 May 84
Margarita	Zhupikova	SU 65	32:40.85	8		Kiev	24 Jun 84
(30)							

100 METRES HURDLES

Grazyna	Rabsztyn	POL 52	12.36	1.9	1	Kuso	Warszawa	13 Jun 80
Vera	Nikitina-KOMISOVA	SU 53	12.39	1.5	1	GGala	Roma	5 Aug 80
Bettine	Gartz-JAHN	GDR 58	12.42	1.8	1	OD	Berlin	8 Jun 83
Lucyna	Langer-KALEK	POL 56	12.43	-0.9	1		Hannover	19 Aug 84
	Langer		12.44	1.9	2	Kuso	Warszawa	13 Jun 80
Yordanka	Donkova	BUL 61	12.44	1.0	1		Sofia	7 Aug 82
	Kalek		12.45	1.5	1h1	EC	Athinai	8 Sep 82
	Kalek		12.45	0.4	1	EC	Athinai	9 Sep 82
	Rabsztyn		12.48	1.9	1		Furth	10 Jun 78
	Rabsztyn		12.48	1.2	1	Kuso	Warszawa	18 Jun 79

343

All-time Lists – Women

	Jahn		12.48	0.5	1		Berlin	31 Jul 83
	Langer		12.49	1.9	1h1	Kuso	Warszawa	13 Jun 80
Ginka	Zagorcheva	BUL 58	12.49	1.0	1	NC	Sofia	4 Jun 83
	Kalek		12.49	0.8	1	GGala	Roma	31 Aug 84
Vera	Yeremeyeva-Tinkova-AKIMOVA	SU 59	12.50	0.0	1		Sochi	19 May 84
	Donkova		12.50	0.7	1		Sofia	8 Aug 84
	Rabsztyn		12.51	1.1	1	ISTAF	W Berlin	17 Aug 79
	Langer		12.51	2.0	1		Warszawa	1 Jun 80
	Akimova		12.51	-0.5	1		Kiev	22 Jun 84
	Rabsztyn		12.52	-2.4	1	WK	Zurich	15 Aug 79
(20/7)								
Kerstin	Claus-KNABE	GDR 59	12.54	0.4	3	EC	Athinai	9 Sep 82
Sabine	Mobius-PAETZ	GDR 57	12.54	0.9	1		Berlin	15 Jul 84
Johanna	Schaller-KLIER	GDR 52	12.56	1.2	1r2		Cottbus	17 Jul 80
(10)								
Cornelia	Riefstahl-OSCHKENAT	GDR 61	12.57	0.5	2	OD	Berlin	20 Jul 84
Anneliese	Jahns-EHRHARDT	GDR 50	12.59	-0.6	1	OG	Munchen	8 Sep 72
Zofia	Filip-BIELCZYK	POL 58	12.63	1.8	1h1	Kuso	Warszawa	18 Jun 79
Danuta	Wolosz-PERKA	POL 56	A12.65	0.0	1h3	WUG	Mexico, D.F.	9 Sep 79
Nadezhda	Korshunova	SU 61	12.65	0.0	2		Sochi	19 May 84
Yelena	Biserova	SU 62	12.66	0.0	3		Sochi	19 May 84
Tatyana	Poluboyarova-ANISIMOVA	SU 49	12.67	0.6	2	EC	Praha	2 Sep 78
Gudrun	BEREND-Wakan	GDR 55	12.73	0.6	3	EC	Praha	2 Sep 78
Svetlana	Gusarova	SU 59	12.74	-0.5	3		Kiev	22 Jun 84
Nina	Morgulina-DERBINA	SU 56	12.76		1		Leningrad	22 Jun 80
(20)								
Xenia	Siska	HUN 57	12.76	1.7	3	BGP	Budapest	20 Aug 84
Stephanie	Hightower	USA 58	12.79	1.9	3	v GDR	Karl-Marx-Stadt	10 Jul 82
Gloria	Kovarik	GDR 64	12.79	0.9	4		Berlin	15 Jul 84
Natalya	LEBEDYEVA-Monastyrskaya	SU 49	12.80	0.0	3	OG	Montreal	29 Jul 76
Elzbieta	RABSZTYN-Schmid	POL 56	12.80	1.9	5	Kuso	Warszawa	13 Jun 80
Maria	Kemenchedzhi-MERCHUK	SU 59	12.81	1.0	3	v GDR	Cottbus	26 Jun 82
Natalya	Kokulenko-PETROVA	SU 57	12.83	1.5	2s2	WC	Helsinki	13 Aug 83
Valeria	BUFANU-Stefanescu	RUM 46	12.84	0.0	1s1	OG	Munchen	7 Sep 72
Irina	Bondaryova-LITOVCHENKO	SU 50	12.84	1.2	3s2	OG	Moskva	28 Jul 80
Benita	FITZGERALD-Brown	USA 61	12.84	1.1	1	NCAA	Houston	4 Jun 83
(30)								
Deby	Lansky-LAPLANTE	USA 53	12.86	1.5	1	AAU	Walnut, CA	16 Jun 79
Cornelia	Feuerbach	GDR 63	12.86	0.4	3r2		Leipzig	27 Jul 83
Lyubov	KONONOVA-Nikitenko	SU 48	12.87	0.0	3	WP	Dusseldorf	3 Sep 77
Shirley	Strong	UK 58	12.87	1.1	1	WK	Zurich	24 Aug 83
Annerose	Krumpholz-FIEDLER	GDR 51	12.89	0.2	2	EC	Roma	7 Sep 74
Candy	Young	USA 62	12.89	0.4	2	VD	Bruxelles	27 Aug 82
Karin	Richert-BALZER	GDR 38	12.90	-0.6	3	OG	Munchen	8 Sep 72
Laurence	Elloy-MACHABEY	FRA 59	12.90	2.0	1	NC	Colombes	8 Aug 82
Danuta	STRASZYNSKA-Kossek	POL 42	12.91	0.5	2s2	OG	Munchen	7 Sep 72
Teresa	Gierczak-NOWAK	POL 42	12.91	0.2	3	EC	Roma	7 Sep 74
(40)								
Bozena	NOWAKOWSKA-Swierczynska	POL 55	12.91	0.2	1	v CS,GDR-J	Zielona Gora	9 Aug 75
Mihaela	Stoica	RUM 58	12.92	1.6	3	NarMl	Sofia	21 May 83
Cheng	Chi	TAI 44	12.93		1	HB	Munchen	12 Jul 70
Pamela	Kilborn-RYAN	AUS 39	12.93	0.0	2h1	OG	Munchen	4 Sep 72
Esther	Shakhamurov-ROT	ISR 52	12.93	0.6	1	ISTAF	W Berlin	20 Aug 76
Natalya	Shubenkova	SU 57	12.93	1.0	H	NC	Kiev	20 Jun 84
Kim	Turner	USA 61	12.95	1.1	2	NCAA	Houston	4 Jun 83
Michele	Chardonnet	FRA 56	12.97	2.0	2		Colombes	8 Aug 82
Ulrike	Denk	FRG 64	12.98	1.3	2		Furth	9 Jun 84
Pam	Page	USA 58	13.00		1		Walnut, CA	30 May 83
(50)								

All-time Lists – Women

Marks made with assisting wind greater than 2 m/s:

Bettine	Gartz-JAHN	GDR 58	12.35	2.4	1	WC	Helsinki	13 Aug 83
	Rabsztyn		12.39	2.8	1	v FRG,Swz,UK	Bremen	24 Jun 79
Kerstin	Claus-KNABE	GDR 59	12.42	2.4	2	WC	Helsinki	13 Aug 83
	Rabsztyn		12.45	2.8	1h2	Kuso	Warszawa	13 Jun 80
Johanna	Schaller-KLIER	GDR 52	12.51	3.2	1	NC	Cottbus	17 Jul 80
Sabine	Mobius-PAETZ	GDR 57	12.51	3.6	1		Dresden	27 Jul 84
(6/5)								
Natalya	Kokulenko-PETROVA	SU 57	12.67	2.4	4	WC	Helsinki	13 Aug 83
Laurence	Elloy	FRA 59	12.72	2.9	1	NC	Lille	1 Jul 84
Shirley	Strong	UK 58	12.78	4.5	1	CG	Brisbane	8 Oct 82
Stephanie	Hightower	USA 58	12.78	4.6	1		Modesto, CA	12 May 84
Lyudmila	Oliyar	SU 58	12.89	2.5	1h		Leningrad	26 Jul 83
Lorna	Boothe	UK 54	12.90	4.5	2	CG	Brisbane	8 Oct 82
Michele	Chardonnet	FRA 56	12.91	2.9	2	NC	Lille	1 Jul 84
Yekaterina	Smirnova	SU 56	12.95		P	v Can,USA	Quebec City	11 Aug 79
Silvia	Kawel-KEMPIN	FRG 55	12.96	3.4	1	NC	Gelsenkirchen	19 Jul 81
Heike	Terpe	GDR 64	12.99	4.1	3h1		Dresden	27 Jul 84
(15)								

400 METRES HURDLES

Margarita	Ponomaryova	SU 63	53.58		1		Kiev	22 Jun 84
Marina	Makeyeva-STEPANOVA	SU 50	53.67		1	DRZ	Praha	17 Aug 84
Anna	Kastetskaya-AMBRAZIENE	SU 55	54.02		1	Znam	Moskva	11 Jun 83
Yekaterina	FESENKO-Grun	SU 58	54.14		1	WC	Helsinki	10 Aug 83
	Ambraziene		54.15		2	WC	Helsinki	10 Aug 83
Ellen	Neumann-FIEDLER	GDR 58	54.20		1	EP	London	20 Aug 83
Karin	Regel-ROSSLEY	GDR 57	54.28		1	OT	Jena	17 May 80
	Stepanova		54.34		2		Kiev	22 Jun 84
	Grun		54.34		1		Moskva	20 Jul 84
	Ponomaryova		54.36		1	OD	Potsdam	21 Jul 84
	Stepanova		54.40		2	OD	Potsdam	21 Jul 84
	Grun		54.42		2	DRZ	Praha	17 Aug 84
Tatyana	Zubova	SU 58	54.43		3		Kiev	22 Jun 84
	Fiedler		54.52		1	NC	Karl-Marx-Stadt	16 Jun 83
Barbel	Klepp-BROSCHAT	GDR 57	54.55		1	WC	Sittard	16 Aug 80
	Fesenko		54.55		2	Znam	Moskva	11 Jun 83
	Fiedler		54.55		3	WC	Helsinki	10 Aug 83
	Neumann		54.56		2	WC	Sittard	16 Aug 80
Yelena	Filipishina	SU 62	54.56		2		Moskva	20 Jul 84
Ann-Louise	Skoglund	SWE 62	54.57		1	EC	Athinai	10 Sep 82
(20/10)								
Nawal	El Moutawakil	MOR 62	54.61		1	OG	Los Angeles	8 Aug 84
Petra	Pfaff	GDR 60	54.64		4	WC	Helsinki	10 Aug 83
Birgit	Sonntag-UIBEL	GDR 61	54.68		1		Dresden	19 May 84
Petra	Krug	GDR 63	54.76		5	WC	Helsinki	10 Aug 83
Genowefa	Nowaczyk-BLASZAK	POL 57	54.78		1	DNG	Stockholm	2 Jul 84
Tatyana	Storozheva	SU 54	54.80		1		Moskva	12 Jun 80
Tatyana	Klimchuk-ZELENTSOVA	SU 48	54.89		1	EC	Praha	2 Sep 78
Chantal	Rega	FRA 55	54.93		3	EC	Athinai	10 Sep 82
Judi	Brown	USA 61	54.93		1	FOT	Los Angeles	21 Jun 84
Margarita	Navickaite	SU 61	55.02		6		Kiev	22 Jun 84
(20)								
Silvia	Hollmann	FRG 55	55.14		2	EC	Praha	2 Sep 78
Mary	Wagner	FRG 61	55.19		1		Furth	21 May 83
Leslie	Maxie	USA 67	55.20		2	TAC	San Jose	9 Jun 84
Cristina	Cojocaru	RUM 62	55.24		2s1	OG	Los Angeles	6 Aug 84
Angela	Wright-SCOTT	USA 61	55.33		2	FOT	Los Angeles	21 Jun 84
P.T.	Usha	IND 64	55.42		4	OG	Los Angeles	8 Aug 84
Krystyna	Hryniewicka-KACPERCZYK	POL 48	55.44		1	ISTAF	W Berlin	18 Aug 78

345

All-time Lists – Women

Brigitte	Rohde-KOHN	GDR 54	55.46	4	EC	Praha	2 Sep 78
Natalya	Tsiruk	SU 55	55.49	1	NC	Moskva	18 Sep 81
Charmaine	Mennigke-FICK	RSA 59	A55.49	1	NC	Bloemfontein	16 Apr 83
(30)							
Radostina	Dimitrova	BUL 66	55.53	3	OD	Potsdam	21 Jul 84
Sharieffa	Barksdale	USA 61	55.58	3	FOT	Los Angeles	21 Jun 84
Lori	McCauley	USA 61	55.60	4	FOT	Los Angeles	21 Jun 84
Anita	Barkusky-WEISS	GDR 55	55.63	6	EC	Praha	2 Sep 78
Marina	Kotenyova	SU 64	55.64	7		Kiev	22 Jun 84
Natalya	Baranova	SU 60	55.67	1h		Krasnodar	25 May 83
Nicoleta	Vornicu	RUM 64	55.67	2	NC	Bucuresti	12 Jul 84
Myrtle	Simpson	RSA 64	A55.74	2	NC	Bloemfontein	16 Apr 83
Yelena	Goncharova	SU 63	55.76	2	v Rum	Bucuresti	16 Sep 84
Tatyana	Vasilenko	SU 57	55.78	4	NC	Kiev	21 Aug 82
(40)							
Valentina	Grishkina	SU 56	55.79	5		Moskva	20 Jul 84
Ina	van Rensburg	RSA 56	A55.81	1		Germiston	30 Apr 82
Ingrida	Verbele-BARKANE	SU 48	55.84	2h1	Znam	Kaunas	11 Aug 79
Debbie	Flintoff	AUS 60	55.89	1	CG	Brisbane	7 Oct 82
Nadezhda	Asenova	BUL 62	55.94	1		Klagenfurt	14 Jul 82
Latanya	Sheffield	USA 63	56.02	1	Pepsi	Westwood	13 May 84
Inka	Franke	GDR 62	56.03	3	OD	Berlin	8 Jun 83
Sue	Morley	UK 60	56.04	7	WC	Helsinki	10 Aug 83
Sandra	Farmer	JAM 62	56.05	4s1	OG	Los Angeles	6 Aug 84
Christine	Howell-WARDEN	UK 50	56.06	1	WAAA	London	28 Jul 79
(50)							

HIGH JUMP

Lyudmila	Zhecheva-ANDONOVA	BUL 60	2.07	1	OD	Berlin	20 Jul 84
Tamara	Bykova	SU 58	2.05	1		Kiev	22 Jun 84
	Bykova		2.04	1		Pisa	25 Aug 83
	Bykova		2.03	i1	EC	Budapest	6 Mar 83
Ulrike	Meyfarth	FRG 56	2.03	1	EP	London	21 Aug 83
	Bykova		2.03	2	EP	London	21 Aug 83
	Bykova		2.03	1		Moskva	6 Aug 84
	Andonova		2.03	1		Rieti	2 Sep 84
	Meyfarth		2.02	1	EC	Athinai	8 Sep 82
	Meyfarth		2.02	1	OG	Los Angeles	10 Aug 84
	Andonova		2.02	1	GGala	Roma	31 Aug 84
Sara	Simeoni	ITA 53	2.01	1	v Pol	Brescia	4 Aug 78
	Simeoni		2.01	1	EC	Praha	31 Aug 78
	Bykova		2.01	1	WC	Helsinki	9 Aug 83
Louise	Ritter	USA 58	2.01	1	GGala	Roma	1 Sep 83
Rosemarie	Witschas-						
	ACKERMANN	GDR 52	2.00	1	ISTAF	W Berlin	26 Aug 77
Coleen	Rienstra-SOMMER	USA 60	2.00	i1		Ottawa	14 Feb 82
	Meyfarth		2.00	1	NC	Munchen	25 Jul 82
	Bykova		2.00	1	NarMl	Sofia	21 May 83
	Ritter		2.00	1	v GDR	Los Angeles	25 Jun 83

	Meyfarth		2.00	1	NC	Bremen	26 Jun 83
	Bykova		2.00	i1	TAC	New York	24 Feb 84
	Bykova		2.00	1	Znam	Sochi	10 Jun 84
	Andonova		2.00	1		Sofia	8 Aug 84
	Simeoni		2.00	2	OG	Los Angeles	10 Aug 84
Stefka	Kostadinova	BUL 65	2.00	1		Sofia	25 Aug 84
	Andonova		2.00	1		Rovereto	29 Aug 84
(27/8)							
Debbie	Brill	CAN 53	1.99	i1		Edmonton	23 Jan 82
Andrea	Reichstein-BIENIAS	GDR 59	1.99	i2	EC	Milano	7 Mar 82
(10)							

346

All-time Lists – Women

Katalin	Sterk	HUN 61	1.99		i3	EC	Milano	7 Mar 82
Kerstin	Dedner-BRANDT	GDR 61	1.99		3	EP	London	21 Aug 83
Silvia	Costa	CUB 64	1.99		1		Verona	1 Jun 84
Andrea	Matay	HUN 55	1.98		i1	NC	Budapest	17 Feb 79
Larisa	Kositsyna	SU 63	1.98		2	NarMl	Sofia	21 May 83
Valentina	Akhramenko-POLUYKO	SU 55	1.98		1		Leningrad	26 Jul 83
Lyudmila	Butuzova	SU 57	1.98		2	Znam	Sochi	10 Jun 84
Pam	Spencer	USA 57	1.97		1	VD	Bruxelles	28 Aug 81
Zhanna	Gimmelfarb-NEKRASOVA	SU 57i	1.97		1	SU P	Moskva	13 Feb 82
Jutta	Krautwurst-KIRST	GDR 54	1.97		1	v USA	Karl-Marx-Stadt	10 Jul 82
(20)								
Yelena	Goloborodko-POPKOVA	SU 55	1.97		2	NC	Kiev	21 Aug 82
Niculina	Vasile	RUM 58	1.97		1	v RSFSR	Bucuresti	15 May 83
Susanne	Helm	GDR 61	1.97		1	OD	Berlin	8 Jun 83
Olga	Juha	HUN 62	1.97		4	EP	London	21 Aug 83
Marina	Doronina	SU 61	1.97		i1		Vilnius	14 Jan 84
Danuta	Bulkowska	POL 59	1.97		2		Worrstadt	9 Jun 84
Olga	Belkova	SU 56	1.97		2		Kiev	22 Jun 84
Joni	Huntley	USA 56	1.97		3	OG	Los Angeles	10 Aug 84
Nina	Serbina	SU 52	1.96		1		Chernigov	3 Jun 80
Charmaine	Gale	RSA 64	1.96		1	NC-j	Bloemfontein	4 Apr 81
(30)								
Olga	Turchak	SU 67	1.96		1	NC	Donetsk	7 Sep 84
Brigitte	Holzapfel	FRG 58	1.95		1	NC	Koln	12 Aug 78
Kristine	Nitzsche	GDR 59	1.95		P	EP-sf	Schielleiten	14 Jul 79
Urszula	Kielan	POL 60	1.95		1		Grudziadz	28 May 80
Diana	ELLIOTT-Davies	UK 61	1.95		1	Bisl	Oslo	26 Jun 82
Maryse	Ewanje-Epee	FRA 64	1.95		3		Rieti	4 Sep 83
Larisa	Petrus	SU 63	1.95		3		Kiev	22 Jun 84
Jolanta	Komsa	POL 58	1.95		1		Zabrze	14 Sep 84
Yordanka	Blagoeva-DIMITROVA	BUL 47	1.94		1		Zagreb	24 Sep 72
Elzbieta	Trylinska-KRAWCZUK	POL 60	1.94		1		Madrid	17 May 80
(40)								
Louise	Miller	UK 60	1.94		2		Napoli	25 May 80
Gaby	MEIER-Lindenthal	SWZ 59	1.94		2		Stuttgart	29 Aug 82
Vanessa	Browne	AUS 63	1.94		1		Adelaide	26 Fe
Christine	van Vliensberghe SOETEWEY	– BEL 57	1.94		1		Bruxelles	12 Jul 83
Yelena	Topchina	SU 66	1.94		1	EC-j	Schwechat	28 Aug 83
Chris	Annison-STANTON	AUS 59	1.94		1		Adelaide	14 Mar 84
Albina	Kazakova	SU 62	1.94		2		Chelyabinsk	29 Jul 84
Ilona	Majdan-GUSENBAUER	AUT 47	1.93		1		Wien	7 Oct 72
Cornelia	Popescu-POPA	RUM 50	1.93		1		Athinai	30 Jun 76
Katrina	GIBBS-Morrow	AUS 59	1.93		1	BCG	Edmonton	11 Aug 78
(50)								
Marina	Sysoyeva	SU 59	1.93		1	Znam	Moskva	5 Jul 80
Hisayo	Fukumitsu	JAP 60	1.93		1	AsiC	Tokyo	7 Jun 81
Andrea	Breder	FRG 64	1.93		1	NC-j	Koblenz	30 Aug 81
Olga	Bondarenko	SU 51	1.93		1		Yalta	1 Oct 81
Dazhen	Zheng	CHN 59	1.93		1		Beijing	23 Apr 82
Emese	Bela	HUN 58	1.93		1		Debrecen	7 Aug 82
Nina	Baranova	SU 64	1.93		1		Togliatti	30 Aug 82
Svetlana	Nikolayeva	SU 59	1.93		i2	NC	Moskva	19 Feb 84
Galina	Brigadnaya	SU 58	1.93		i3	NC	Moskva	19 Feb 84
Susanne	Lorentzon	SWE 61	1.93		1	NC	Vaxjo	26 Aug 84
(60)								

LONG JUMP

Anisoara	CUSMIR-Stanciu	RUM 62	7.43	1.4	1	RumIC	Bucuresti	4 Jun 83
Heike	DAUTE-Drechsler	GDR 64	7.40	1.8	1		Dresden	26 Jul 84
	Daute		7.34	1.6	1		Dresden	19 May 84
	Daute		7.32	−0.2	1	OD	Berlin	20 Jul 84

347

All-time Lists – Women

	Daute		7.29	0.0	1		Jena	13 May 84
Galina	Chistyakova	SU 62	7.29	-0.5	1		Moskva	6 Aug 84
	Stanciu		7.27	1.0	1	v Bul,GDR	Sofia	17 Jun 84
	Cusmir		7.21	0.6	1	v RSFSR	Bucuresti	15 May 83
	Chistyakova		7.21	1.6	1		Moskva	14 Jul 84
Helga	Radtke	GDR 62	7.21	1.6	2		Dresden	26 Jul 84
Vali	Ionescu	RUM 60	7.20	-0.5	1	NC	Bucuresti	1 Aug 82
	Daute		7.18	0.0	1		Potsdam	25 May 84
	Daute		7.18	0.3	1		Berlin	15 Jul 84
	Cusmir		7.15	0.3	2	NC	Bucuresti	1 Aug 82
	Drechsler		7.15	-0.3	1	DRZ	Praha	17 Aug 84
	Daute		7.14	1.1	1	PTS	Bratislava	4 Jun 83
	Stanciu		7.14		1	NC	Bucuresti	12 Jul 84
Sabine	Mobius-PAETZ	GDR 57	7.12	1.6	2		Dresden	19 May 84
	Ionescu		7.11	1.6	1		Madrid	21 Jun 84
	Radtke		7.11	0.6	2	DRZ	Praha	17 Aug 84
	Chistyakova(21/6)		7.11	-0.5	3	DRZ	Praha	17 Aug 84
Vilma	Augustinaviciute-BARDAUSKIENE	SU 53	7.09	0.0	Q	EC	Praha	29 Aug 78
Yelena	Kokonova	SU 63	7.09	0.1	1	NC	Donetsk	9 Sep 84
Tatyana	Kolpakova	SU 59	7.06	0.4	1	OG	Moskva	31 Jul 80
Brigitte	Kunzel-WUJAK	GDR 55	7.04	0.5	2	OG	Moskva	31 Jul 80
(10)								
Svetlana	Vanyushina-ZORINA	SU 60	7.04	2.0	1	Spart	Moskva	20 Jun 83
Tatyana	Proskuryakova	SU 56	7.04	0.9	1		Kiev	25 Aug 83
Niole	Bluskite-MEDVEDYEVA	SU 60	7.02	0.5	4	DRZ	Praha	17 Aug 84
Tatyana	Pakhovskaya-SKACHKO	SU 54	7.01	-0.4	3	OG	Moskva	31 Jul 80
Eva	Murkova	CS 62	7.01	-0.3	1	PTS	Bratislava	26 May 84
Yelena	Ivanova	SU 61	7.01		2		Moskva	9 Jul 84
Jodi	Anderson	USA 57	7.00	2.0	1	FOT	Eugene	28 Jun 80
Margarita	Treinite-BUTKIENE	SU 49	7.00		1		Vilnius	25 May 83
Birgit	Grosshennig	GDR 65	7.00	-0.2	2		Berlin	9 Jun 84
Siegrun	Thon-SIEGL	GDR 54	6.99	2.0	1	OD	Dresden	19 May 76
(20)								
Carol	Lewis	USA 63	6.97	0.0	1		Luxembourg	20 Jul 83
Anna	Wlodarczyk	POL 51	6.96	2.0	1	NC	Lublin	22 Jun 84
Christine	Schima	GDR 62	6.96	1.8	3		Dresden	26 Jul 84
Irina	Valyukevich	SU 59	6.95	0.2	1	NC	Donetsk	9 Sep 84
Yelena	Dubinina-CHICHEROVA	SU 58	6.94	1.3	2		Kiev	23 Jun 84
Angela	Schmalfeld-VOIGT	GDR 51	6.92	1.6	1		Dresden	9 May 76
Heike	DUWE-Gielow	GDR 60	6.91	1.8	3		Berlin	9 Jun 84
Ramona	Gohler-NEUBERT	GDR 58	6.90	1.8	–	v UK	Dresden	14 Jun 81
Tatyana	Turulina	SU 58	6.90		1		Krasnodar	26 May 83
Bev	Kinch	UK 64	6.90	1.4	–	WC	Helsinki	14 Aug 83
(30)								
Sigrid	Heimann-ULBRICHT	GDR 58	6.89	-0.3	2	NC	Jena	9 Aug 81
Jarmila	Nygrynova-STREJCKOVA	CS 53	6.89	1.8	1		Praha	18 Sep 82
Natalya	Shevchenko	SU 66	6.88	0.6	2		Sochi	26 May 84
Yelena	Mityayeva	SU 63	6.88		2		Riga	6 Jul 84
Heidemarie	ROSENDAHL-Ecker	FRG 47	6.84	0.0	1	WUG	Torino	3 Sep 70
Lidia	Alfeyeva	SU 46	6.84	0.0	2		Moskva	12 Jun 80
Natalya	Alyoshina	SU 56	6.84	-0.6	2	Spart	Moskva	20 Jun 83
Larisa	Baluta	SU 65	6.84		2		Krasnodar	6 Aug 83
Natalya	Chemidronova	SU 59	6.84		1		Kazan	14 Jul 84
Galina	Salo	SU 59	6.84	0.2	Q	NC	Donetsk	8 Sep 84
(40/4)								
Sue	HEARNSHAW-Telfer	UK 61	6.83	0.2	1		Cleckheaton	6 May 84
Yolanda	Chen	SU 61	6.83	1.0	2	Znam	Sochi	9 Jun 84
Viorica	Belmega-						‹F799	

All-time Lists – Women

	VISCOPOLEANU	RUM 39	A6.82	0.0	1	OG	Mexico, D.F.	14 Oct 68
Jennifer	Inniss	GUY 59	6.82		1	Nik	Nice	14 Aug 82
Olga	Anufriyeva	SU 55	6.82	0.6	6		Kiev	23 Jun 84
Margrit	HERBST-Olfert	GDR 47	6.81	−0.4	P	NC	Leipzig	26 Jun 71
Zsuzsa	Vanyek	HUN 60	6.81	1.4	6	WC	Helsinki	14 Aug 83
Angela	Thacker	USA 64	6.81		1		Lincoln	11 May 84
Jackie	Joyner	USA 62	6.81	−0.2	H	FOT	Los Angeles	17 Jun 84
Nadezhda	Sokolova	SU 59	6.81		4		Riga	6 Jul 84

(50)
Marks made with assisting wind greater than 2 m/s:

	Daute		7.27	2.2	1	WC	Helsinki	14 Aug 83
Eva	Murkova	CS 62	7.17	3.6	1		Nitra	26 Aug 84
	Cusmir		7.15	3.4	2	WC	Helsinki	14 Aug 83

(3/3)

Carol	Lewis	USA 63	7.04	4.3	3	WC	Helsinki	14 Aug 83
Ramona	Gohler-NEUBERT	GDR 58	7.00	3.8	1	v UK	Dresden	14 Jun 81
Sue	HEARNSHAW-Telfer	UK 61	7.00	4.2	1	NC	Cwmbran	27 May 84
Bev	Kinch	UK 64	6.99	4.6	5	WC	Helsinki	14 Aug 83
Ines	Geipel-SCHMIDT	GDR 60	6.98	3.4	2		Nitra	26 Aug 84
Anna	Wlodarczyk	POL 51	6.97	2.7	1	v Bul,FRG,Hun	Warszawa	15 Jul 84
Tatyana	Shchelkanova	SU 37	6.96		P	NC	Dnepropetrovsk	14 Aug 66

(10)

Kathy	McMILLAN-Ray	USA 57	6.91				Houston	3 May 80
Shonel	Ferguson	BAH 57	6.91	2.7	1	CG	Brisbane	8 Oct 82
Robyne	Strong-LORRAWAY	AUS 61	6.90	2.6	1		Adelaide	4 Feb 84
Heidemarie	Rabiger-WYCISK	GDR 49	6.86	5.6	2		Dresden	9 May 76
Jennifer	Inniss	GUY 59	6.85	2.4	2	TAC	Indianapolis	18 Jun 83
Gwen	Loud	USA 61	6.85		1	NCAA	Eugene	2 Jun 84
Susan	Scott-REEVE	UK 51	6.84	3.2	1		Edinburgh	25 Jun 77
Ilona	BRUZSENYAK-Gresa	HUN 50	6.83		P	EP-sf	Innsbruck	11 Aug 73
Isabella	Keller-Lusti	SWZ 53	6.82	2.2	1		Winterthur	7 Jun 75
Maryna	Meyer-VAN NIEKERK	RSA 54	A6.82		1		Johannesburg	10 Nov 82

(20)

SHOT PUT

Natalya	Lisovskaya	SU 62	22.53		1		Sochi	27 May 84
Helena	Fibingerova	CS 49	22.50		i1		Jablonec	19 Feb 77
Ilona	Schoknecht-SLUPIANEK-Briesenick	GDR 56	22.45		1	OT	Potsdam	11 May 80
	Slupianek		22.41		1	OG	Moskva	24 Jul 80
	Slupianek		22.40		1		Berlin	3 Jun 83
	Slupianek		22.38		1	OT	Karl-Marx-Stadt	25 May 80
	Slupianek		22.36		1	Skok	Celje	2 May 80
	Slupianek		22.34		1		Berlin	7 May 80
	Slupianek		22.34		1	NC	Cottbus	18 Jul 80
	Fibingerova		22.32		1		Nitra	20 Aug 77
	Slupianek		22.22		1		Potsdam	13 Jul 80
	Slupianek		22.13		1		Split	29 Apr 80
	Slupianek		22.06		1		Berlin	15 Aug 78
	Slupianek		22.05		1	OD	Berlin	28 May 80
	Slupianek		22.05		1	OT	Potsdam	31 May 80
	Slupianek		22.04		1		Potsdam	4 Jul 79
	Slupianek		22.04		1		Potsdam	29 Jul 79
	Fibingerova		21.99		1		Opava	26 Sep 76
	Slupianek		21.98		1		Berlin	17 Jul 79
	Fibingerova		21.96		1	GS	Ostrava	8 Jun 77
	Lisovskaya		21.96		1	DRZ	Praha	16 Aug 84

(21/3)

Ivanka	Khristova-TODOROVA	BUL 41	21.89		1		Belmeken	4 Jul 76
Marianne	Adam	GDR 51	21.86		1	v SU	Leipzig	23 Jun 79
Verzhinia	Veselinova-IGNATOVA	BUL 57	21.61		1		Sofia	21 Aug 82

349

All-time Lists – Women

Margitta	DROESE-Pufe	GDR 52	21.58	1		Erfurt	28 May 78	
Nunu	Abashidze	SU 55	21.53	2		Kiev	22 Jun 84	
Nadezhda	Chizhova	SU 45	21.45	1		Varna	29 Sep 73	
Eva	Wilms	FRG 52	21.43	2		Munchen	17 Jun 77	
(10)								
Svetlana	Dolzhenko-KRACHEVSKAYA	SU 46	21.42	2	OG	Moskva	24 Jul 80	
Ines	Reichenbach-MULLER	GDR 59	21.32	2	Skok	Celje	5 May 84	
Liane	Schmuhl	GDR 61	21.27	1		Cottbus	26 Jun 82	
Helma	Knorscheidt	GDR 56	21.19	1		Berlin	24 May 84	
Zdenka	Kusa-Bartonova-SILHAVA	CS 54	21.05	2	NC	Praha	23 Jul 83	
Ivanka	PETROVA-Stoicheva	BUL 51	21.01	1	NC	Sofia	28 Jul 79	
Mihaela	Loghin	RUM 52	21.00	1		Formia	30 Jun 84	
Cordula	Schulze	GDR 59	21.00	4	OD	Potsdam	21 Jul 84	
Elena	Stoyanova-SIMEONOVA	BUL 52	20.95	2	Balk	Sofia	14 Jun 80	
Maria Elena	Sarria	CUB 54	20.61	1		Habana	22 Jul 82	
(20)								
Claudia	Losch	FRG 60	20.55	1	v CS,Fra,Pol	Hannover	15 Jun 84	
Heidi	Krieger	GDR 65	20.51	i2		Budapest	8 Feb 84	
Nina	Isayeva	SU 50	20.47	1		Bryansk	28 Aug 82	
Natalya	Petrova-AKHRIMENKO	SU 55	20.44	3	Znam	Moskva	4 Jul 80	
Tatyana	Orlova	SU 55	20.44	1		Staiki	28 May 83	
Heike	DITTRICH-Hartwig	GDR 62	20.28	4		Dresden	27 Jul 84	
Lyudmila	Voyevudskaya	SU 58	20.24	1		Dnepropetrovsk	5 Aug 84	
Margitta	Helmbold-GUMMEL	GDR 41	20.22	2	OG	Munchen	7 Sep 72	
Svetlana	Orlova-MELNIKOVA	SU 51	20.21	1		Riga	5 Jun 82	
Lyudmila	Limina-SAVINA	SU 55	20.21	2	Znam	Sochi	9 Jun 84	
(30)								
Marina	Antonyuk	SU 62	20.19	3		Kiev	22 Jun 84	
Vera	TSAPKALENKO-Bokova	SU 54	20.12	2	Prav	Sochi	29 May 77	
Rimma	Makauskaite-MUZIKAVICIENE	SU 52	20.12	1		Vilnius	16 Aug 80	
Tatyana	Shcherbanos	SU 60	20.07	4	NC	Donetsk	7 Sep 84	
Raisa	Taranda	SU 47	20.06	2	NC	Kiev	23 Jun 76	
Gabriele	Retzlaff	GDR 54	20.04	5	NC	Cottbus	18 Jul 80	
Faina	MELNIK-Veleva	SU 45	20.03	2	PTS	Bratislava	2 Jun 76	
Simone	Rudrich	GDR 61	19.96	i2	NC	Senftenberg	20 Feb 83	
Natalya	Zubekhina	SU 51	19.94	1		Tula	14 Jul 84	
Yelena	Kozlova	SU 62	19.94	2		Kiev	14 Aug 84	
(40)								
Tamara	Bufetova	SU 51	19.92	1	Prav	Tbilisi	17 Jun 78	
Nina	Samsonova	SU 51	19.91	2	NC	Kiev	20 Aug 82	
Natalya	Vinogradova-NOSENKO	SU 51	19.90	2	v UK	Kiev	23 May 76	
Aleksandra	Abashidze	SU 58	19.81	3	NC	Kiev	20 Aug 82	
Konstanze	Simm	GDR 64	19.78	1		Karl-Marx-Stadt	11 Jul 84	
Danguole	Bimbaite	SU 62	19.77	1		Vilnius	8 May 84	
Gael	Mulhall-MARTIN	AUS 56	19.74	1		Berkeley	14 Jul 84	
Brunhilde	LOEWE-Martin	GDR 51	19.73	1		Potsdam	17 Aug 75	
Lyubov	Vasilyeva	SU 57	19.68	1		Gorlovka	28 Aug 83	
Carmen	Niesche	GDR 64	19.66	1e2	OD	Potsdam	21 Jul 84	
(50)								

DISCUS THROW

Zdenka	Kusa-Bartonova-SILHAVA	CS 54	74.56	1		Nitra	26 Aug 84	
Irina	Meszynski	GDR 62	73.36	1	DRZ	Praha	17 Aug 84	
Galina	Savinkova	SU 53	73.28	1	NC	Donetsk	8 Sep 84	
	Savinkova		73.26			Leselidze	21 May 83	
Gisela	Beyer	GDR 60	73.10	1	OD	Berlin	20 Jul 84	
Martina	Opitz	GDR 60	72.32	1		Leipzig	13 Jul 84	
	Beyer		72.28	1		Berlin	15 Jul 84	

All-time Lists – Women

Galina	Murashova	SU 55	72.14		2	DRZ	Praha	17 Aug 84
	Meszynski		72.02		2	OD	Berlin	20 Jul 84
	Silhava		72.00		1		Litomysl	28 Jul 84
Maria	Vergova-PETKOVA	BUL 50	71.80		1		Sofia	13 Jul 80
	Opitz		71.60		3	OD	Berlin	20 Jul 84
Evelin	Schlaak-JAHL-Herberg	GDR 56	71.50		1	OT	Potsdam	10 May 80
	Jahl		71.46		1	OD	Berlin	10 Jun 81
	Meszynski		71.40		1	v USA	Karl-Marx-Stadt	10 Jul 82
	Petkova		71.30		1		Sofia	1 Aug 81
Ria	Stalman	HOL 52	71.22		1		Walnut, CA	15 Jul 84
	Petkova		71.22		1		Sofia	28 Jul 84
	Petkova		71.20		1		Sofia	28 Aug 82
	Savinkova		71.18		1	v Rum	Bucuresti	16 Sep 84
(20/9)								
Tsvetanka	Khristova	BUL 62	70.64		1		Sofia	21 Aug 82
(10)								
Faina	MELNIK-Veleva	SU 45	70.50		1	Znam	Sochi	24 Apr 76
Valentina	Stepanenko-KHARCHENKO	SU 49	69.86		1		Fyodosiya	16 May 81
Carmen	Ferrer-ROMERO	CUB 50	69.08		1	NC	Habana	17 Apr 76
Florenta	Tacu-CRACIUNESCU	RUM 55	68.98		1	PTS	Bratislava	6 Jun 81
Sabine	Engel	GDR 54	68.92		1	v Pol,SU	Karl-Marx-Stadt	25 Jun 77
Margitta	Droese-PUFE	GDR 52	68.64		1	ISTAF	W Berlin	17 Aug 79
Nadezhda	Kugayevskikh	SU 60	68.60		1		Orel	30 Aug 83
Lyubov	Urakova-ZVERKOVA	SU 55	68.58		1		Kiev	22 Jun 84
Ellina	Zvereva-KISHEYEVA	SU 60	68.56		2		Moskva	6 Jul 84
Silvia	Madetzky	GDR 62	68.24		1		Potsdam	27 Aug 82
(20)								
Tatyana	Starodubtseva-LESOVAYA	SU 56	68.18				Alma Ata	23 Sep 82
Argentina	Menis	RUM 48	67.96		1	RumIC	Bucuresti	15 May 76
Petra	Wendlandt-SZIEGAUD	GDR 58	67.90		1		Berlin	19 May 82
Maritza	Marten	CUB 63	67.76		1		Habana	8 Jul 84
Hilda	Ramos	CUB 64	67.56		2		Habana	8 Jul 84
Svetlana	Videneyeva-PETROVA	SU 51	67.54		1		Brest	20 Sep 78
Meg	Ritchie	UK 52	67.48		1	MSR	Walnut, CA	26 Apr 81
Brigitte	Sander-MICHEL	GDR 56	67.40		2		Halle	14 Jun 79
Natalya	Baranova-GORBACHOVA	SU 47	67.32		1		Leningrad	4 Jun 83
Svetla	Bozhkova	BUL 51	67.26		2		Sofia	5 Jul 80
(30)								
Ingra-Anne	Manecke	FRG 56	67.06		1		Furth	29 May 82
Gabriele	Trepschek-HINZMANN	GDR 47	67.02		1		Potsdam	1 Sep 73
Ulla	Lundholm	FIN 57	67.02		1		Helsinki	23 Aug 83
Nadezhda	YEROKHA-Sobolyova	SU 52	66.94		1		Leselidze	23 Mar 80
Svetla	Mitkova	BUL 64	66.80		1		Sofia	2 Aug 83
Maria Cristina	Betancourt	CUB 47	66.54		1		Habana	13 Feb 81
Diana	Sachse	GDR 63	66.36		3		Berlin	15 Jul 84
Lyudmila	Isayeva	SU 49	66.30		1	Znam	Kaunas	11 Aug 79
Svetlana	Orlova-MELNIKOVA	SU 51	66.06		2	EP	Torino	4 Aug 79
Grit	Haupt	GDR 66	65.96		3		Leipzig	13 Jul 84
Tatyana	Dorozhenko-BEREZHNAYA	SU 56	65.94		3	NC	Donetsk	9 Sep 80
Tatyana	Stepanova	SU 51	65.58		1		Tula	6 Aug 82
Irina	Ivannikova	SU 50	65.50		1		Leningrad	17 Jun 82
Valentina	Stepushina	SU 50	65.38		Q	NC	Kiev	23 Jun 76
Irina	Dmitriyeva	SU 59	65.30		1		Leselidze	8 Sep 84
Olga	Koryagina-ANDRIANOVA	SU 49	65.26					76
Agnes	Herczeg	HUN 50	65.22		1		Debrecen	30 May 82
Daniela	Costian	RUM 65	65.22		3		Nitra	26 Aug 84
Vera	Agromakova-SAFONOVA	SU 48	65.20		1		Kaluga	23 Aug 77
Leslie	Deniz	USA 62	65.20		1		Tempe	7 Apr 84
(50)								

All-time Lists – Women

JAVELIN THROW

Tiina	Lillak	FIN 61	74.76	1			Tampere	13 Jun 83
Petra	Felke	GDR 59	74.72	1		Skok	Celje	5 May 84
	Lillak		74.24	1			Fresno	7 Apr 84
	Felke		74.24	1		OD	Potsdam	21 Jul 84
Sofia	SAKORAFA-Kostaveli	GRE 57	74.20	1		NC	Hania	26 Sep 82
	Lillak		74.14	1		NC	Pori	3 Jul 83
	Lillak		73.92	1		v UK	Lappeenranta	18 Jun 83
	Lillak		73.80	1			Thessaloniki	23 Sep 83
	Felke		73.74	1			Praha	28 Aug 84
Tessa	Sanderson	UK 56	73.58	1			Edinburgh	26 Jun 83
	Felke		73.30	1		DRZ	Praha	16 Aug 84
	Felke		72.86	1		8N	Tokyo	14 Sep 84
Anna	Verouli	GRE 56	72.70	1			Hania	20 May 84
	Lillak		72.66	1		v Swe	Stockholm	4 Sep 83
	Verouli		72.64	1		NC	Thessaloniki	1 Jun 84
	Lillak		72.58	1			Myyrmaki	9 Jun 83
	Lillak		72.40	1		WG	Helsinki	29 Jul 82
	Lillak		72.38	1			Kauklahti	7 Jun 83
	Lillak		72.36	1		ISTAF	W Berlin	17 Aug 83
	Sakorafa		72.28	1			Oslo	9 Jul 83
(20/5)								
Antje	KEMPE-Zollkau	GDR 63	72.16	2		Skok	Celje	5 May 84
Antoaneta	Todorova	BUL 63	71.88	1		EP	Zagreb	15 Aug 81
Fatima	Whitbread	UK 61	71.86	1			Limassol	29 Apr 84
Tatyana	Biryulina	SU 55	70.08	1			Podolsk	12 Jul 80
Ruth	Gamm-FUCHS	GDR 46	69.96	1			Split	29 Apr 80
(10)								
Maria	Colon-SALCEDO	CUB 58	69.96	1			Sofia	17 Jun 84
Kate	Schmidt	USA 53	69.32	1			Furth	11 Sep 77
Petra	Rivers	AUS 52	69.28	1		NC	Brisbane	20 Mar 82
Eva	Zorgo-RADULY	RUM 54	68.80	1		Znam	Moskva	5 Jul 80
Mayra	Vila	CUB 60	68.76	1		PTS	Bratislava	3 Jun 83
Saida	GUNBA-Kikidze	SU 59	68.28	2		Znam	Moskva	5 Jul 80
Ingrid	Thyssen	FRG 56	68.10	1			Dormagen	5 Jun 82
Jadviga	Dunaiskaite-PUTINIENE	SU 45	67.84	3		Znam	Moskva	5 Jul 80
Tuula	Laaksalo	FIN 53	67.40	2			Pihtipudas	24 Jul 83
Ute	Hommola	GDR 52	67.24	1		v UK	Dresden	13 Jun 81
(20)								
Corina	Girbea	RUM 59	67.00	1		v Hun	Debrecen	13 Jun 82
Zinaida	Gavrilina	SU 60	67.00	1		NC	Donetsk	9 Sep 84
Ute	Richter	GDR 58	66.96	1			Neubrandenburg	21 May 83
Beate	Peters	FRG 59	66.86	1		WUG	Edmonton	9 Jul 83
Elena	Kubanova-BURGAROVA	CS 52	66.56	2			Nitra	26 Aug 84
Eva	Helmschmidt	FRG 57	66.48	1		v Hol,Pol	Bielefeld	4 Jun 83
Rositha	Potreck	GDR 59	66.08	1		NC	Jena	9 Aug 81
Pam	Matthews	AUS 58	65.74	1			Brisbane	16 Dec 79
Sue	Howland	AUS 60	65.74	1			Melbourne	19 Sep 82
(30)								
Genowefa	Olejarz	POL 62	65.52	1			Zabrze	20 May 84
Sabine	Kargel-SEBROWSKI	GDR 51	65.46	1		OT	Karl-Marx-Stadt	30 May 76
Ivanka	Vancheva	BUL 53	65.38	5		OG	Moskva	25 Jul 80
Olga	Chistyakova	SU 50	65.26	2		Znam	Sochi	10 Jun 84
Marion	Steiner-BECKER	FRG 50	65.14	Q		OG	Montreal	23 Jul 76
Nina	Marakina-NIKANOROVA	SU 47	65.02	1			Sochi	23 May 80
Trine	Solberg	NOR 66	65.02	1		PTS	Bratislava	26 May 84
Leolita	Blodniece	SU 59	64.90	1		NC	Donetsk	7 Sep 80
Iris	de Grasse	CUB 64	64.90	1			Zinnowitz	13 May 84
Galina	Kondrina	SU 53	64.82	1		SU P	Tashkent	18 Sep 82

All-time Lists – Women

(40)
Karin	Smith	USA 55	64.78		1		Koln	10 Aug 80
Sandra	Leiskalne	SU 58	64.38		1		Koblenz	26 Aug 81
Jacqueline	TODTEN-Hein	GDR 54	64.34		1	NC	Leipzig	4 Jul 74
Natalya	Kalenchukova	SU 64	64.26		1		Moskva	20 Jul 84
Helena	Ekbom-LAINE	FIN 55	64.00		1		Salo	26 May 83
Elvira	Ozolina-LUSIS	SU 39	63.96		1	v USA	Minsk	23 Jul 73
Lyudmila	Pasternakevich	SU 59	63.86		1		Lvov	19 Jul 76
Svetlana	Korolyova-BABICH	SU 47	63.74		1	NC	Kiev	23 Jun 76
Valentina	Shapovalova	SU 57	63.70		1		Dnepropetrovsk	6 Oct 83
Nadezhda	Yakubovich-PARAKHINA	SU 54	63.68		1		Moskva	30 May 83

(50)

HEPTATHLON

Sabine	Mobius-PAETZ	GDR 57	6867		1	NC	Potsdam	5/ 6 May 84
12.64 180 15.37 23.37 / 686 44.62 2:08.93								
Ramona	Gohler-NEUBERT	GDR 58	6836		1	Spart	Moskva	18/19 Jun 83
13.42 182 15.25 23.49 / 679 49.94 2:07.51								
Natalya	Shubenkova	SU 57	6799		1	NC	Kiev	20/21 Jun 84
12.93 183 13.66 23.57 / 673 46.26 2:04.60								
	Paetz		6785		1	OD	Potsdam	20/21 Jul 84
12.71 174 16.16 23.23w/ 658 41.94 2:07.03								
	Neubert		6773		1	v SU	Halle	19/20 Jun 82
13.58 183 15.10 23.14 / 684w 42.54 2:06.16								
	Neubert		6740		2	OD	Potsdam	20/21 Jul 84
13.48 174 15.03 23.47w/ 671 47.88 2:04.73								
	Neubert		6722		1	EP	Sofia	10/11 Sep 83
13.39 178 15.21 23.52 / 669 45.30 2:06.70								
Anke	Vater	GDR 61	6722		3	OD	Potsdam	20/21 Jul 84
13.30 186 14.86 23.20w/ 684 34.04 2:03.76								
	Neubert		6716		1	v SU	Kiev	27/28 Jun 81
13.70 186 15.41 23.58 / 682 40.62 2:06.72								
	Neubert		6714		1	WC	Helsinki	8/ 9 Aug 83
13.29 180 15.38 23.27 / 667 45.12 2:11.34								
Jane	Frederick	USA 52	6714		1		Talence	15/16 Sep 84
13.27 187 15.49 24.15 / 643 51.74 2:13.55								
	Paetz		6662		2	WC	Helsinki	8/ 9 Aug 83
13.11 183 14.23 23.60 / 668 44.52 2:11.59								
	Neubert		6622		1	EC	Athinai	9/10 Sep 82
13.61 183 15.02 23.40 / 663 42.48 2:11.06								
	Neubert		6621		1	NC	Halle	23/24 May 81
13.58 180 14.75 23.70 / 682 40.98 2:07.55								
Natalya	Prokopchenko-GRACHOVA	SU 52	6611		1	NC	Moskva	1/ 2 Aug 82
13.80 180 16.18 23.86 / 665w 39.42 2:06.59								
	Frederick		6611		4	OD	Potsdam	20/21 Jul 84
13.76 186 15.91 24.86 / 621 52.74 2:10.25								
	Mobius		6594		2	EC	Athinai	9/10 Sep 82
12.89 183 13.51 23.71 / 668 41.30 2:11.55								
	Vater		6566		1	v SU	Neubrandenburg	2/ 3 Jun 84
13.37 177 13.95 23.26 / 671w 37.82 2:06.40								
	Grachova		6563		1	v FRG	Ahlen	8/ 9 Sep 84
13.45 181 16.11 24.23w/ 647w 39.96 2:08.83								
	Neubert		6551		1	EP-sf	Zug	11/12 Jul 81
13.64 181 14.64 24.00 / 674 41.66 2:09.30								

(20/6)
Nadezhda	Vinogradova	SU 59	6532		2	NC	Kiev	20/21 Jun 84
2:06.80								
Jackie	Joyner	USA 62	6520		1	FOT	Los Angeles	16/17 Jun 84
13.61 183 13.06 23.77 / 681 45.38 2:13.41								
Yekaterina	Smirnova	SU 56	6493		3	Spart	Moskva	18/19 Jun 83
13.41 182 14.82 24.84 / 656 45.66 2:13.38								
Mila	Kolyadina	SU 60	6485		4	Spart	Moskva	18/19 Jun 83
2:15.26								

353

All-time Lists – Women

(10)
Sabine	Everts	FRG 61	6484	1	v SU	Mannheim	9/10 Jun 82	
13.45 189 12.39 23.73 / 675 36.02 2:07.73								
Sabine	Braun	FRG 65	6442	1	v Bul	Mannheim	8/ 9 Jun 84	
13.68 178 13.09 23.88 / 603 52.14 2:09.41								
Valentina	Dimitrova	BUL 56	6440	2		Gotzis	28/29 May 83	
14.31 186 16.07 24.78 / 626 42.26 2:08.74								
Olga	Yakovleva	SU 57	6424	1	SU P	Tashkent	26/27 Sep 82	
13.53 179 15.14 24.26 / 613 41.42 2:09.20								
Sibylle	Thiele	GDR 65	6421	1	EC-j	Schwechat	27/28 Aug 83	
13.49 190 14.63 24.07 / 665 36.22 2:18.36								
Valentina	Kurochkina	SU 59	6418	1		Tallinn	10/11 Aug 83	
13.89 185 14.40 24.51 / 663 43.98 2:15.94								
Jodi	Anderson	USA 57	6413	2	FOT	Los Angeles	16/17 Jun 84	
13.52 180 13.40 24.49 / 636 48.52 2:13.20								
Glynis	Saunders-NUNN	AUS 60	6390	1	OG	Los Angeles	3/ 4 Aug 84	
13.02 180 12.82 24.06 / 666 35.58 2:10.57								
Marianna	Maslennikova	SU 61	6383	3	NC	Kiev	20/21 Jun 84	
13.47 186 12.83 24.43 / 638 38.10 2:06.99								
Heike	Tischler	GDR 64	6381	5	OD	Potsdam	20/21 Jul 84	
14.41 177 14.18 24.34w/ 612 50.18 2:07.67								

(20)
Kristine	Nitzsche	GDR 59	6364	4	EP	Sofia	10/11 Sep 83	
13.96 190 16.10 24.28 / 610 41.54 2:20.16								
Judy	LIVERMORE-Simpson	UK 60	6353	5	EP	Sofia	10/11 Sep 83	
13.23 187 13.54 24.75 / 632 38.60 2:12.50								
Antonina	Sukhova	SU 59	6351	5	NC	Kiev	20/21 Jun 84	
13.32 183 14.33 24.47 / 603 32.40 2:13.98								
Malgorzata	Guzowska-NOWAK	POL 59	6346	1	NC	Lublin	3/ 4 Jul 82	
13.64w 187 14.14 24.53 / 645 43.70 2:20.86								
Svetlana	Filatyeva	SU 64	6322	6	NC	Kiev	20/21 Jun 84	
13.60 180 13.14 24.96 / 638 45.30 2:11.69								
Yekaterina	Zaslavets-GORDIYENKO	SU 51	6321	1	v USA/NC	Leningrad	1/ 2 Aug 81	
13.58 174 15.37 24.44 / 645 34.80 2:09.67								
Olga Kuragina	–NEMOGAYEVA	SU 59	6299	7	Spart	Moskva	18/19 Jun 83	
13.53 182 13.15 24.56 / 634 37.40 2:08.79								
Tatyana	Shpak	SU 60	6297	8	Spart	Moskva	18/19 Jun 83	
14.03 179 14.47 24.00 / 643 32.32 2:06.87								
Cindy	Greiner	USA 57	6281	4	OG	Los Angeles	3/ 4 Aug 84	
13.71 183 13.36 24.40 / 615 40.86 2:11.75								
Lyudmila	Serbul	SU 60	6279	7	NC	Kiev	20/21 Jun 84	
14.02 174 14.37 24.77 / 600 43.38 2:05.60								

(30)
Jana	Sobotka	GDR 65	6266	6	OD	Potsdam	20/21 Jul 84	
14.40 174 13.28 24.19 / 627 43.64 2:06.83								
Lyubov	Ratsu	SU 61	6260	1	SU P	Baku	14/15 Sep 84	
13.74 180 13.54 24.91 / 632 42.56 2:12.86								
Larisa	Nikitina	SU 65	6255	8	NC	Kiev	20/21 Jun 84	
13.87 186 14.04 25.26 / 631 48.62 2:22.76								
Nina	Aldatova-VASHCHENKO	SU 60	6254	2	SU P	Tashkent	26/27 Sep 82	
13.74 182 13.02 24.68 / 650 40.02 2:13.88								
Natalya	Alyoshina	SU 56	6253	3	SU P	Tashkent	26/27 Sep 82	
13.65 179 12.91 23.80 / 669 36.20 2:16.68								
Daniela	Nenova	BUL 61	6250	3		Gotzis	28/29 May 83	
13.93 183 13.93 23.67 / 608 30.70 2:06.50								
Yordanka	Donkova	BUL 61	6240	7	EP	Sofia	10/11 Sep 83	
12.65 178 12.80 23.25 / 637 29.40 2:17.51								
Marina	Spirina	SU 55	6234	1	SU P	Kiev	3/ 4 Sep 83	
13.64 168 13.15 24.67 / 636 40.08 2:05.66								
Valentina	Savchenko	SU 68	6226	1	DRZ–j	Plovdiv	4/ 5 Aug 84	
13.88 159 15.10 24.15 / 607 48.16 2:12.42								
Heidrun	Geissler	GDR 61	6223	2	EP	Birmingham	29/30 Aug 81	

(40)
Svetlana	Ovchinnikova	SU 56	6217	4	NC	Moskva	1/ 2 Aug 82	
13.52 171 16.78 24.19 / 641w 37.12 2:25.94								

354

All-time Lists – Women

Iris	Kunstner	FRG 60	6216	3	v SU	Mannheim	9/10 Jun 82
13.90 189 13.38 24.78 / 624 35.32 2:11.30
Anke	Troger	GDR 63	6203	5	NC	Neubrandenburg	21/22 May 83
14.14 183 13.68 24.45 / 609 41.20 2:13.99
Svetlana	Korolkova	SU 60	6184	1		Moskva	4/ 5 Aug 84
14.18 183 13.99 24.45 / 633 35.52 2:13.43
Ute	Rompf	FRG 59	6172	2	NC	Lage	8/ 9 Aug 81
14.41 165 15.15 23.78 / 602 44.42 2:14.11
Aleksandra	Konstantinova	SU 53	6172	4	SU P	Tashkent	26/27 Sep 82
14.16 176 13.20 24.82 / 597 45.10 2:09.24
Birgit	Dressel	FRG 60	6172	2	v Bul	Mannheim	8/ 9 Jun 84
13.84 190 13.15 25.37 / 593 42.54 2:14.30
Marcela	Koblasova	CS 56	6164	1		Praha	11/12 Jun 83
13.89 171 14.47 24.40 / 608 43.70 2:17.06
Liliana	Alexandru–NASTASE	RUM 62	6160	1	NC	Bucuresti	10/11 Jul 84
6161 = 13.20 172 12.63 23.50 / 627 33.46 2:14.14
Tineke	Hidding	HOL 59	6155	8	WC	Helsinki	8/ 9 Aug 83
13.77 177 12.22 24.19 / 630 38.52 2:12.46
(50)
Assisting wind in 200m greater than 4 m/s
Marlene	Harmon	USA 62	A6266	1	NSF	AF Academy,CO	1/ 2 Jul 83
13.10w 173 12.40 23.32W/ 647 34.20 2:12.60

Hand timing

Heptathlon point totals made with hand timing have an estimated of 55 points advantage over totals made with automatic timing

Lyubov	Ratsu	SU 61	6467 M	1		Kishinyov	27/28 Aug 83
13.6 180 14.75 24.2 / 653 41.86 2:11.3
Antonina	Sukhova	SU 59	6467 M	1		Tula	25/26 Aug 84
13.0 182 13.79 24.8 / 641 45.88 2:13.5
Vera	Kulbatskaya–YURCHENKO	SU 59	6308 M	1		Kiev	14/15 Aug 84
13.1 170 14.96 23.6 / 576 40.06 2:12.0
Galina	Safronenko	SU 55	6283 M	1		Alma Ata	28/29 Jul 84
13.6 174 14.50 25.0 / 631 45.92 2:15.4
Irina	Ivadko–PESTRIKOVA	SU 56	6271 M	2		Tashkent	24/25 May 83
13.1 181 14.48 24.4 / 598 39.48 2:17.3
Tatyana	Shlapakova–GUDENKO	SU 53	6227 M	1		Kharkov	29/30 Sep 81
13.6 174 16.06 25.5 / 644 36.84 2:14.5

4 x 100 METRES RELAY

GDR		41.53	1		Berlin	31 Jul 83
(Gladisch, Koch, Auerswald, Gohr)
GDR		41.60	1	OG	Moskva	1 Aug 80
(Muller, Wockel, Auerswald, Gohr)
USA		A41.61	1	NSF	AF Academy, CO	3 Jul 83
(Brown, Williams, Cheeseborough, Ashford)
USA		41.63	1	v GDR	Los Angeles	25 Jun 83
(Brown, Williams, Cheeseborough, Ashford)
USA		41.65	1	OG	Los Angeles	11 Aug 84
(Brown, Bolden, Cheeseborough, Ashford)
GDR		41.69	1	OD	Potsdam	21 Jul 84
(Gladisch, Koch, Auerswald, Gohr)
GDR		41.76	1	WC	Helsinki	10 Aug 83
(Gladisch, Koch, Auerswald, Gohr)
GDR		41.85	1		Potsdam	13 Jul 80
(Muller, Wockel, Auerswald, Gohr)
GDR		41.85	1	WK	Zurich	22 Aug 84
(Gladisch, Koch, Auerswald, Gohr)
GDR		41.94	1		Cottbus	17 Jul 80
(Muller, Wockel, Auerswald, Gohr)
(10)
GDR		41.97	1		Potsdam	28 Aug 82
(G.Walther, Wockel, Scholzel, Gohr)

All-time Lists – Women

GDR	41.97	1		Leipzig	27 Jul 83
(Gladisch, Koch, Auerswald, Gohr)					
GDR	41.99	1	v USA	Karl-Marx-Stadt	9 Jul 82
(G.Walther, Wockel, Scholzel, Gohr)					
GDR	42.09	1	EP	Torino	4 Aug 79
(Brehmer, Schneider, Auerswald, Gohr)					
GDR	42.09	1		Berlin	9 Jul 80
(Muller, Wockel, Auerswald, Gohr)					
GDR	42.09	2	vUSA	Angeles	25 Jun 83
(Koch, Wockel, Gladisch, Gohr)					
GDR	42.10	1	v Can	Karl-Marx-Stadt	10 Jun 79
(Koch, Schneider, Auerswald, Gohr)					
SU	42.10	2	OG	Moskva	1 Aug 80
(Komisova, Maslakova, V.Anisimova, Bochina)					
USA	42.15	1		Walnut, CA	25 Jul 84
(Brown, Griffith, Cheeseborough, Ashford)					
GDR	42.15	1		Dresden	27 Jul 84
(G.Walther, Wockel, Auerswald, Gohr)					
(20)					
GDR	42.16	1		Karl-Marx-Stadt	17 Jun 83
(Koch, Wockel, Gladisch, Gohr)					
GDR	42.18	1		Berlin	26 Jul 79
(Brehmer, Schneider, Auerswald, Gohr)					
Europe	42.19	1	WP	Montreal	26 Aug 79
(Haglund/Swe, Rega/Fra, Richter/FRG, Hunte/UK)					
GDR	42.19	1	EC	Athinai	11 Sep 82
(G.Walther, Wockel, Rieger, Gohr)					
SC Motor Jen a GDR	42.20	1	NC	Erfurt	2 Jun 84
(Schmidt, Wockel, Auerswald, Gohr)					
GDR	42.21	1		Karl-Marx-Stadt	20 May 84
(G.Walther, Koch, Auerswald, Gohr)					
GDR	42.22	1	WP	Roma	6 Sep 81
(Siemon, Wockel, G.Walther, Gohr)					
GDR	42.23	1		Berlin	15 Jul 84
(Gladisch, Koch, Auerswald, Gohr)					
GDR	42.25	1		Cottbus	22 Aug 82
(G.Walther, Wockel, Rieger, Gohr)					
GDR	42.27	1		Potsdam	19 Aug 78
(Klier, Hamann, Bodendorf, Gohr)					
(30/3)					

4 x 400 METRES RELAY

GDR	3:15.92	1		Erfurt	3 Jun 84
(G.Walther, Busch, Rubsam, Koch)					
USA	3:18.29	1	OG	Los Angeles	11 Aug 84
(Leatherwood, S.Howard, Hooks, Cheeseborough)					
GDR	3:19.04	1	EC	Athinai	11 Sep 82
(Siemon, Busch, Rubsam, Koch)					
SU	3:19.12	1	DRZ	Praha	18 Aug 84
(Baskakova, Nazarova, Pinigina, Vladykina)					
GDR	3:19.23	1	OG	Montreal	31 Jul 76
(Maletzki, Rohde, Streidt, Brehmer)					
USA	3:19.60	1		Walnut, CA	25 Jul 84
(Leatherwood, S.Howard, Hooks, Cheeseborough)					
GDR	3:19.62	1	EP	Torino	5 Aug 79
(Kotte, Brehmer, Kohn, Koch)					
GDR	3:19.73	1	WC	Helsinki	14 Aug 83
(K.Walther, Busch, Koch, Rubsam)					
GDR	3:19.83	1	EP	Zagreb	16 Aug 81
(Rubsam, Steuk, Wockel, Koch)					
SU	3:20.12	1	OG	Moskva	1 Aug 80
(Prorochenko, Goyshchik, Zyuskova, Nazarova)					
(10)					
GDR	3:20.23	1	v USA	Karl-Marx-Stadt	10 Jul 82
(Siemon, Busch, Rubsam, Koch)					

All-time Lists – Women

CS		3:20.32	2	WC	Helsinki	14 Aug 83	
(Kocembova, Moravcikova, Matejkovicova, Kratochvilova)							
GDR		3:20.35	2	OG	Moskva	1 Aug 80	
(Lowe, Krug, Lathan, Koch)							
GDR		3:20.37	1	WP	Montreal	24 Aug 79	
(Kotte, Brehmer, Kohn, Koch)							
SU		3:20.39	2	EP	Torino	5 Aug 79	
(Bagryantseva, Zyuskova, Prorochenko, Kulchunova)							
GDR		3:20.62	1	WP	Roma	4 Sep 81	
(Rubsam, Steuk, Wockel, Koch)							
CS		3:20.79	1	EP	London	21 Aug 8	
(Moravcikova, Kocembova, Matejkovicova, Kratochvilova)							
SU		3:21.16	3	WC	Helsinki	14 Aug 83	
(Korban, Ivanova, Baskakova, Pinigina)							
GDR		3:21.20	1	EC	Praha	3 Sep 78	
(Marquardt, Krug, Brehmer, Koch)							
CAN		3:21.21	2	OG	Los Angeles	11 Aug 84	
(Crooks, Richardson, Killingbeck, Payne)							
(20)							
SU		3:21.71	2	EP	London	21 Aug 83	
(Korban, Ivanova, Baskakova, Pinigina)							
CS		3:21.89	2	DRZ	Praha	18 Aug 84	
(Bulirova, Moravcikova, Kratochvilova, Kocembova)							
CS		3:22.17	2	EC	Athinai	11 Sep 82	
(Tylova, Matejkovicova, Kocembova, Kratochvilova)							
SU		3:22.53	2	EC	Praha	3 Sep 78	
(Prorochenko, Mushta, Providokhina, Kulchunova)							
GDR		3:22.70	3	EP	London	21 Aug 83	
(K.Walther, Busch, Bremer, Rubsam)							
SU		3:22.73	1	v GDR	Tbilisi	27 Jun 81	
(Goyshchik, Litvinova, Bochina, Nazarova)							
SU		3:22.79	3	EC	Athinai	11 Sep 82	
(Korban, Olkhovnikova, Mineyeva, Baskakova)SU							
SU		3:22.8	1	v GDR	Leipzig	24 Jun 79	
(Kulchunova, Bagryantseva, Prorochenko, Zyuskova)							
USA		3:22.81	2	OG	Montreal	31 Jul 76	
(Sapenter, Ingram, Jiles, Bryant)							
USA		3:22.82	1h1	OG	Los Angeles	10 Aug 84	
(Leatherwood, S.Howard, Dixon, D.Howard)							
(30/5)							

5000 METRES WALK (TRACK)

Olga	Krishtop	SU 57	21:36.2	(1)	RCh	Penza	4 Aug 84
Hong	Yan	Chn 66	21:40.3	(1)	SGP	Fana	5 May 84
Hongju	Xu	Chn 64	21:41.0	(2)	SGP	Fana	5 May 84
Olga	Yarutkina	SU 60	21:42.2	(2)	RCh	Penza	4 Aug 84
Giuliana	Salce	Ita 55	21:51.85	(1)		L'Aquila	1 Oct 83
Natalya	Serbinenko *	SU 59	21:59.0	(3)	SGP	Fana	5 May 84
Sue	Cook	Aus 58	22:04.42	(1)	NCh	Melbourne	1 Apr 84
Aleksandra	Deverinskaya	SU 60	22:14.01	(1)		Oryol	9 Jul 82
Ann	Peel	Can 61	22:17.5	(4)	SGP	Fana	5 May 84
Galina	Bildina	SU 60	22:18.8	(1)		Krasnodar	22 Sep 84
Vera	Osipova	SU 57	22:22.0	(2)		Krasnodar	22 Sep 84
Roza	Undyerova	SU 57	22:22.0	(5)	SGP	Fana	5 May 84
Sally	Pierson	Aus 63	22:24.0	(1)		Leicester	14 Sep 83
Lyudmila	Khrushchova	SU 55	22:25.2	(3)	RCh	Penza	4 Aug 84
Guan	Ping	Chn 66	22:30.7	(3)		Fuxin	25 Sep 84
Vera	Lyuzhanova	SU 61	22:38.6	(2)		Krasnodar	22 Sep 84
Ann	Jansson	Swe 58	22:41.1	(4)	IM	Varnamo	19 May 84
Lorraine	Young	Aus 59	22:52.0	(2)		Canberra	17 Feb 84
Yan	Wang	Chn 71	22:53.9	(4)		Fuxin	25 Sep 84
Heping	Yu	Chn 67	22:56.0	(6)	IM	Varnamo	19 May 84

All-time Lists – Women

Polina	Biznya	SU 55	22:56.2	(2)		Shelkovo	27 Mar 83
Sujie	Lie	Chn 66	22:58.7	(6)		Fuxin	25 Sep 84
Monica	Gunnarsson	Swe 65	23:01.1	(1)		Boras	27 Sep 84
Vera	Prudnikova	SU 53	23:01.7	(3)		Shelkovo	27 Mar 83
Yulian	Yan	Chn 66	23:02.7	(7)		Fuxin	25 Sep 84
Galina	Yezhova	SU 62	23:03.0	(2)	Army	Moskva	7 Jul 84
Olga	Tsugunova	SU 61	23:03.02	(3)		Leningrad	24 Jul 83
Valentina	Antonova	SU 61	23:03.44	(4)		Leningrad	24 Jul 83
Svetlana	Vasilyeva	SU 65	23:06.2	(4)	RCh	Penza	4 Aug 84
Yongju	Xu	Chn 62	23:07.2	(2)		Shanghai	14 Mar 83
Regina	Balkovskaya	SU 61	23:09.4	(3)		Kislovodsk	28 Feb 83
Carol	Tyson	UK 57	23:11.2	(1)		Ostersund	30 Jun 79
Marina	Shupilo	SU 58	23:12.3	(4)		Shelkovo	27 Mar 83
Yelena	Lisnik	SU 66	23:13.0	(3)	Army	Moskva	7 Jul 84
Hong	Xiao	Chn 66	23:13.9	(8)		Fuxin	25 Sep 84
Rachel	Thompson	Aus 62	23:15.82	(3)	NCh	Melbourne	1 Apr 84
Suzanne	Griesbach	Fra 45	23:16.0	(1)		Epinay/Seine	25 Apr 82
Tatyana	Kobzar	SU 54	23:16.0	(1)		Tiraspol	24 Apr 83
Thorill	Gylder	Nor 58	23:17.5	(1)		Oslo	4 Aug 78
Fengyun	Song	Chn 65	23:17.8	(5)	NCh	Jiading	12 Mar 84
Sirkka	Oikarinen	Fin 59	23:18.1	(1)		Lahti	1 Jul 84
Siw	Gustavsson *	Swe 57	23:18.6	(1)		Goteborg	16 Jun 81
Sue	Brodock	USA 56	23:19.1	(1)		Walnut	13 Jun 80
Marion	Fawkes	UK 48	23:19.2	(2)		Ostersund	30 Jun 79
Elisabeth	Olsson	Swe 54	23:19.7	(2)		Fana	3 May 80
Natalya	Spiridonova	SU 63	23:20.0	(1)		Leningrad	7 Jul 84
Anne	Miller	Aus 63	23:23.0	(2)		Melbourne	22 Mar 84
Xiaoling	Shi	Chn 60	23:23.8	(9)		Fuxin	25 Sep 84
Aleksandra	Grigoryeva	SU 60	23:25.5	(5)	RCh	Penza	4 Aug 84
Froydis	Hilsen	Nor 59	23:25.6	(1)		Sant Celoni	3 Apr 83

Road performances

	Undyerova		21:49.8	(2)		Cheboksary	13 May 84
	Gustavsson		22:04	(1)		Boras	1 Oct 83

*Note: Serbinenko formerly Sharypova; Gustavson now Vera-Ybanez

10000 METRES WALK (TRACK)

Hong	Yan	Chn 66	45:39.5	(1)	IM	Kobenhavn	13 May 84
Sue	Cook	Aus 58	45:47.0	(1)		Leicester	14 Sep 83
Roza	Undyerova	SU 57	46:15.6	(1)		Oryol	28 Aug 83
Vera	Osipova	SU 58	46:52.8	(1)		Novosibirsk	28 Aug 82
Natalya	Sharypova*	SU 59	46:59.4	(2)		Novosibirsk	28 Aug 82
Aleksandr	Deverinskaya	SU 60	47:08.8	(1)		Cheboksary	13 Jun 82
Ann	Jansson	Swe 58	47:24.0	(1)		Goteborg	24 Apr 83
Siw	Vera-Ybanez*	Swe 57	47:35.6	(1)	NCh	Norrkoping	28 Apr 84
Valentina	Filina	SU 64	47:42.6	(3)		Novosibirsk	28 Aug 82
Giuliana	Salce	Ita 55	47:45.3	(1)		Roma	23 Apr 83
Monica	Gunnarsson	Swe 65	47:58.0	(2)	NCh	Norrkoping	28 Apr 84
Olga	Yarutkina	SU 60	48:00.4	(3)		Togliatti	28 Aug 82
Marion	Fawkes	UK 48	48:11.4	(1)		Harnosand	8 Jul 79
Suzanne	Griesbach	Fra 45	48:21.4	(1)	NCh	Epinay/Seine	13 May 84
Valentina	Antonova	SU 59	48:32.6	(1)		Oryol	29 Aug 81
Elisabeth	Olsson	Swe 54	48:33.2	(1)		Vaxjo	14 Oct 79
Carol	Tyson	UK 57	48:34.5	(1)		Stretford	22 Aug 81
Rachel	Thompson	Aus 61	48:34.9	(3)	IM	Kobenhavn	13 May 84
Irene	Bateman	UK 47	48:52.5	(1)	WAAA	Kirkby	19 Mar 83
Heping	Yu	Chn 67	48:52.6	(4)	IM	Kobenhavn	13 May 84
Margareta	Simu	Swe 53	48:59.0	(1)		Vasteras	17 Apr 77

All-time Lists – Women

Lilya	Grigoryeva	SU 60	49:04.0	(5)		Togliatti	28 Aug 82
Teresa	Vaill	USA 62	49:06.0	(1)		Lexington	5 May 84
Vera	Lyuzhanova	SU 61	49:11.6	(6)		Togliatti	28 Aug 82
Galina	Zakharova	SU 60	49:16.1	(5)		Novosibirsk	28 Aug 82
Thorill	Gylder	Nor 58	49:19.7	(1)		Bergen	9 Jun 78
Galina	Bildina	SU 61	49:21.4	(7)		Togliatti	28 Aug 82
Britt-Marie	Carlsson	Swe 62	49:30.4	(3)		Stockholm	23 Sep 78
Britt	Holmquist	Swe 48	49:35.6	(2)		Nalden	20 Sep 80
Monika	Karlsson	Swe 59	49:41.5	(3)		Nalden	20 Sep 80
Sally	Pierson	Aus 63	49:45.2	(2)		Leicester	14 Sep 83
Ann	Peel	Can 61	49:46.0	(1)		Niagara Falls	16 Jul 83
Froydis	Hilsen	Nor 60	49:49.0	(2)		Vasteras	19 Jun 82
Lorraine	Young	Aus 59	49:49.8	(5)	IM	Kobenhavn	13 May 84
Tatyana	Pulkina	SU 50	49:51.5	(1)		Chelyabinsk	3 Sep 82
Tatyana	Bukharinova	SU 58	49:52.2	(2)		Chelyabinsk	3 Sep 82
Helen	Elleker	UK 56	49:52.3	(1)	WAAA	Birmingham	17 Mar 84
Lyudmila	Khrushchova	SU 55	49:54.8	(1)		Kirov	28 Aug 82
Ginny	Birch	UK 55	49:55.0	(1)		Brighton	5 Feb 84
Natalya	Spiridonova	SU 63	50:03.4	(2)		Dnipropetrovdsk	24 Sep 83
Brenda	Lupton	UK 52	50:10.2	(2)	WAAA	Birmingham	17 Mar 84
Joan	Bender	Can 63	50:10.2	(6)	IM	Kobenhavn	13 May 84
Micheline	Daneau	Can 60	50:11.1	(1)		Montreal	10 May 83
Jill	Barrett	UK 64	50:11.2	(2)	WAAA	Kirkby	19 Mar 83
Zoya	Baurdinova	SU 54	50:12.4	(3)		Chelyabinsk	3 Sep 82
Marica	Onos-Zethof	Hol 56	50:14.9	(1)		Zoonhoven	5 Jun 83
Lilian	Harpur	Aus 48	50:19.0	(2)		Adelaide	23 May 82
Ann	Ryan	Aus 62	50:24.0	(2)		Canberra	31 Jul 83
Sue	Brodock	USA 56	50:32.8	(1)		Walnut	16 Jun 79

Road performances

	Krishtop		44:51.6	(1)	RCh	Penza	5 Aug 84
	Yarutkina		45:03.2	(2)	RCh	Penza	5 Aug 84
Yongju	Xu	Chn 62	45:13.4	(1)	LT	Bergen	24 Sep 83
	Sharypova		45:25.2	(2)	LT	Bergen	24 Sep 83
	Cook		45:26.4	(3)	LT	Bergen	24 Sep 83
	Osipova		45:28.1	(3)	RCh	Penza	5 Aug 84
	Pierson		45:39.4	(4)	LT	Bergen	24 Sep 84
	Khrushchova		45:51.0	(4)	RCh	Penza	5 Aug 84

*Note: Sharypova now Serbinenko; Vera-Ybanez formerly Gustavsson

1984 WORLD LISTS

100 METRES

Evelyn	Ashford	USA 57	10.76	1.7	1	WK	Zurich	22 Aug
Marlies	Gohr	GDR 58	10.84	1.7	2	WK	Zurich	22 Aug
	Gohr		10.86	0.4	1		Potsdam	5 May
	Gohr		10.87	1.9	1		Dresden	26 Jul
	Gohr		10.89	0.7	1	NC	Erfurt	1 Jun
	Gohr		10.91	-0.5	1	OD	Berlin	20 Jul
	Ashford		10.92	1.3	1h2	ISTAF	W Berlin	17 Aug
	Ashford		10.93	1.6	1	GGala	Roma	31 Aug
	Ashford		10.94	-0.1	1	ISTAF	W Berlin	17 Aug
	Gohr		10.95	-0.2	1	DRZ	Praha	16 Aug
	Gohr		10.96	0.9	1		Erfurt	12 May
	Ashford		10.97	-1.2	1	OG	Los Angeles	5 Aug
	Gohr		10.97	-0.8	1	8N	Tokyo	14 Sep
	Gohr		10.99	0.1	1		Berlin	15 Jul
Florence	Griffith	USA 59	10.99	-0.1	2	ISTAF	W Berlin	17 Aug
Merlene	Ottey	JAM 60	11.01	0.0	1r2		Walnut, CA	25 Jul
Lyudmila	Kondratyeva	SU 58	11.02	-0.2	2	DRZ	Praha	16 Aug
	Griffith		11.02	1.3	1h1	ISTAF	W Berlin	17 Aug
	Ashford		11.03	-0.3	1s1	OG	Los Angeles	5 Aug
Barbel	Wockel	GDR 55	11.04	1.9	2		Dresden	26 Jul
Diane	Williams	USA 61	11.04	1.7	3	WK	Zurich	22 Aug
Ingrid	Auerswald	GDR 57	11.04	1.7	4	WK	Zurich	22 Aug
	Ashford		11.06	1.4	1h3	OG	Los Angeles	4 Aug
	Kondratyeva		11.06	-0.8	2	8N	Tokyo	14 Sep
	Gohr		11.07		1h		Potsdam	5 May
	Williams		11.08	1.6	1h2	WK	Zurich	22 Aug
Valerie	Brisco	USA 60	11.08	0.9	1		Koblenz	29 Aug
	Kondratyeva		11.09	1.1	1		Kiev	21 Jun
	Kondratyeva		11.09	1.6	2	GGala	Roma	31 Aug
Anelia	Nuneva	BUL 62	11.10	-0.2	3	DRZ	Praha	16 Aug
(10)								
Silke	Gladisch	GDR 64	11.10	-0.2	4	DRZ	Praha	16 Aug
	Auerswald		11.10	-0.2	5	DRZ	Praha	16 Aug
	Williams		11.10	-0.1	3	ISTAF	W Berlin	17 Aug
(33/11)								
Marita	Koch	GDR 57	11.13	0.4	2		Potsdam	5 May
Gesine	Walther	GDR 62	11.13	1.9	3		Dresden	26 Jul
Alice	Brown	USA 60	11.13	-1.2	2	OG	Los Angeles	5 Aug
Chandra	Cheeseborough	USA 59	11.13	-0.1	4	ISTAF	W Berlin	17 Aug
Jeanette	Bolden	USA 60	11.15	1.5	1	Pepsi	Westwood	13 May
Tatyana	Alekseyeva	SU 63	11.16	0.0	1		Sochi	19 May
Angella	Taylor	CAN 58	A11.16	0.1	1		Provo	19 May
Elzbieta	Tomczak	POL 61	11.18	1.7	1	NC	Lublin	22 Jun
Nadezhda	Georgieva	BUL 61	11.21	0.5	1	v GDR,Rum	Sofia	16 Jun
(20)								
Ewa	Kasprzyk	POL 57	11.22	1.7	2	NC	Lublin	22 Jun
Zelda	Johnson	USA 64	11.23	1.4	1		Bakersfield	26 May
Ines	Schmidt	GDR 60	11.23	1.9	5		Dresden	26 Jul
Sherri	Howard	USA 62	11.24	1.7	1	MSR	Walnut, CA	28 Apr
Marina	Zhirova	SU 63	11.24	0.0	1h2		Sochi	19 May
Heide-Elke	Gaugel	FRG 59	11.24	0.0	1		Munchen	20 Jul
Grace	Jackson	JAM 61	11.24	1.4	2h3	OG	Los Angeles	4 Aug
Kathy	Cook	UK 60	11.24	0.9	3		Koblenz	29 Aug
Angela	Bailey	CAN 62	11.25	1.6	2h1	WK	Zurich	22 Aug
Marina	Molokova	SU 62	11.26	0.0	h		Sochi	19 May
(30)								

361

1984 Lists – Women

Jennifer	Inniss	GUY 59	11.26	1.1	1		Walnut, CA	15 Jul
Randy	Givens	USA 62	11.27	1.7	1		Tallahassee	21 Apr
Heather	Oakes	UK 59	11.27	1.9	1s2	NC	Cwmbran	27 May
Irina	Slyusar	SU 63	11.27	0.0	1		Kiev	3 Jul
Els	Vader	HOL 59	11.28	2.0	1h2		Furth	9 Jun
Olga	Zolotaryova	SU 61	11.29	0.0	2		Sochi	19 May
Svetlana	Zuyeva	SU 63	11.30	0.1	1r2		Sochi	19 May
Liliane	Gaschet	FRA 62	11.31	1.1	1		Fort-de-France	24 Mar
Kathrene	Wallace	USA 63	11.31	0.3	1h4		Baton Rouge	4 May
Antonina	Nastoburko	SU 59	11.31	−1.3	1		Moskva	19 Jul
(40)								
Pepa	Pavlova	BUL 61	11.31	0.5	3		Sofia	8 Aug
Esmeralda	Garcia	BRA 59	11.32	0.3	1		Sao Paulo	17 Jun
Wendy	Vereen	USA 66	11.32	0.0	1r1		Walnut, CA	25 Jul
Olga	Antonova	SU 60	11.32	−0.6	3h3	DRZ	Praha	16 Aug
Helina	Marjamaa	FIN 56	11.33	0.0	1	WG	Helsinki	4 Jul
Jackie	Washington	USA 62	11.33	0.0	2r1		Walnut, CA	25 Jul
Mary	Bolden	USA 64	11.34	0.5	1		Baton Rouge	13 May
Rose-Aimee	Bacoul	FRA 52	11.34	1.7	7	WK	Zurich	22 Aug
Michele	Glover	USA 63	11.36	1.7	2		Houston	6 May
Iwona	Pakula	POL 62	11.36	1.7	3	NC	Lublin	22 Jun
(50)								
Tatana	Kocembova	CS 62	11.36	1.6	5	GGala	Roma	31 Aug
Lisa	Hopkins	USA 58	11.37		2		Los Angeles	14 Apr
Marina	Babenko	SU 60	11.37	0.1	1q3		Kiev	20 Jun
Stepanka	Sokolova	CS 58	11.38	0.5	1		Praha	2 Jun
Debbie	Wells	AUS 61	11.39	1.5	1		Sydney	11 Mar
Marie France	Loval	FRA 64	11.39	1.1	2		Fort-de-France	24 Mar
Angela	Thacker	USA 64	11.39		1h1		Baton Rouge	13 Apr
Elvira	Barbashina	SU 63	11.39	0.0	h		Sochi	19 May
Nelli	Cooman	HOL 64	11.39	0.0	2	PTS	Bratislava	25 May
Shirley	Thomas	UK 63	11.39	1.9	1s1	NC	Cwmbran	27 May
(60)								
Raymonde	Naigre	FRA 60	11.39	1.4	3		Brest	6 Jun
Gwen	Torrence	USA 65	11.41	−0.2	1		Athens, GA	5 May
Inger	Peterson	USA 64	11.41	1.5	4	Pepsi	Westwood	13 May
Atanaska	Georgieva	BUL 60	11.41	−0.3	5	NarMl	Sofia	19 May
Svetlana	Zhizdrikova	SU 60	11.41	0.0	h		Sochi	26 May
Jayne	Andrews	UK 63	11.41	1.9	2s1	NC	Cwmbran	27 May
Marisa	Masullo	ITA 59	11.41	0.5	1		Firenze	13 Jun
Elzbieta	Wozniak	POL 59	11.41	1.7	4	NC	Lublin	22 Jun
Mari Lise	Furstenberg	RSA 66	A11.42		1	NC-j	Pretoria	31 Mar
Juliet	Cuthbert	JAM 64	11.42	2.0	2h1		Austin	11 May

Natalya	Pomoshchnikova	SU 65	11.42	0.0	h		Sochi	26 May
Heike	Morgenstern	GDR 62	11.42	1.9	7		Dresden	26 Jul
Evette	de Klerk	RSA 65	A11.43		1		Sasolburg	21 Apr
Pam	Marshall	USA 60	11.43	0.6	3		Irvine, CA	5 May
Michelle	Finn	USA 65	11.43	1.8	1h3	NCAA	Eugene	30 May
Sabine	Rieger	GDR 63	11.43	1.9	8		Dresden	26 Jul
Barbel	Scholzel	GDR 59	11.44		3r2	OD	Berlin	20 Jul
Simone	Jacobs	UK 66	11.45	1.0	3		Gateshead	6 Jul
Sabine	Paetz	GDR 57	11.46		1		Leipzig	13 Jul
Ginka	Zagorcheva	BUL 58	11.47	0.5	4		Sofia	8 Aug
(80)								
Teresa	Rione	SPA 65	11.48	0.9	1		Madrid	29 May
Janet	Burke	JAM 62	11.48	1.1	2		Walnut, CA	15 Jul
Lucyna	Kalek	POL 56	11.48	0.8	1r2		Koblenz	29 Aug
Rufina	Ubah	NIG 60	11.49	1.5	1h1		Cape Girardeau	6 Apr
Sheila	de Oliveira	BRA 59	11.49	0.3	2		Sao Paulo	17 Jun
Yelena	Vinogradova	SU 64	11.49	−1.3	2h1		Moskva	19 Jul
Diane	Dixon	USA 64	11.50		3		Los Angeles	14 Apr
Jarmila	Kratochvilova	CS 51	11.50	0.0	3	PTS	Bratislava	25 May
Bev	Kinch	UK 64	11.50	0.5	1		Belfast	19 Jun
Carla	Mercurio	ITA 60	11.50	0.4	2	NC	Roma	10 Jul

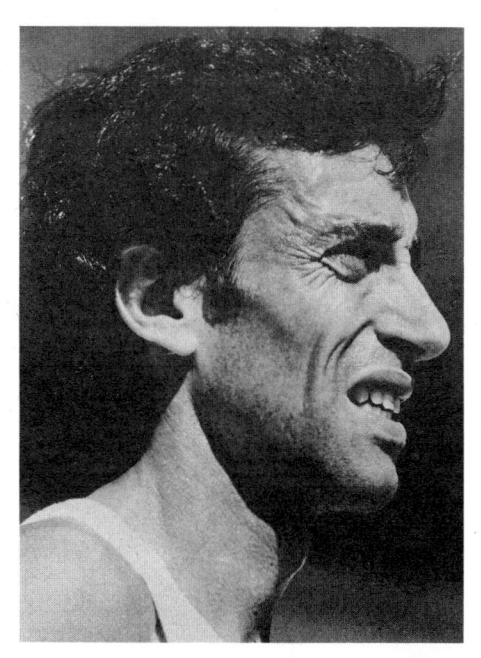

Fernando Mamede – a world record at 10000 metres, yet again failure in the major championships.

Rosa Mota was a reluctant participant in the 1982 European Championships marathon, but after that win has compiled a splendidly consistent marathon record.

Julius Korir on his way to Olympic steeplechase victory. 919 is Henry Marsh and Colin Reitz is between them.

Tatyana Kazankina passed drugs tests taken in the USSR after her world records at 2000m and 3000m, but was banned after refusing a test in Paris.

Ricky Bruch – the controversial Swede again took part in a series of 'mini-meets' in late season, and smashed his Swedish discus record.

Jarmila Kratochvilova (l) and Tatana Kocembova (r).

John Treacy leads in a heat of the Olympic 5000m in 1980 from Miruts Yifter and Dave Moorcroft. Four years later he won the Olympic silver medal in his first marathon.

Rob De Castella wins the Commonwealth marathon in Brisbane in 1982.

Harald Schmid – Europe's best 400m hurdler (2).

Glynis Nunn added Olympic to her Commonwealth gold at heptathlon.

Zhu Jianhua has set three world records but has yet to win a major championship.

Greg Foster – gold in Helsinki, silver in Los Angeles.

1984 Lists – Women

(90)								
Vroni	Werthmuller	SWZ 59	11.50	0.9	1s2	NC	Zofingen	20 Jul
Silvia	Heinrich	GDR 64	11.51		h		Potsdam	5 May
Sharon	Danville	UK 55	11.51	0.1	1		Toledo, OH	12 May
Tatyana	Vilisova	SU 59	11.51	0.1	2h1		Sochi	19 May
Galina	Mikheyeva	SU 62	11.51	0.2	h		Sochi	26 May
Radislava	Soborova	CS 59	11.51	0.5	2		Praha	2 Jun
Gail	Devers	USA 66	11.51	0.1	1		Los Angeles	2 Jun
LaShon	Nedd	USA 63	11.51	0.6	5s2	FOT	Los Angeles	18 Jun
Pauline	Davis	BAH 66	11.51	−0.2	1h2	OG	Los Angeles	4 Aug
Joan	Baptiste	UK 59	11.51	1.6	5h2	WK	Zurich	22 Aug
(100)								
Kirsten	Emmelmann	GDR 61	11.52	− i	3		Berlin	15 Jan
Sharon	Ware	USA 63	11.52	1.8	2h1	NCAA	Eugene	30 May
Barbara	Bell	USA 63	11.52	1.8	3h1	NCAA	Eugene	30 May
Ute	Thimm	FRG 58	11.52	0.4	2h1		Furth	9 Jun
Edith	Oker	FRG 61	11.52	2.0	2h2		Furth	9 Jun
Valentina	Bozhina	SU 66	11.52	−2.0	1	NC-j	Riga	13 Jul
(106)								

Donna	Dennis	USA 64	11.53	1.0	14 Apr
Eva	Murkova	CS 62	11.53	−0.4	22 Sep
Marita	Payne	CAN 60	11.54		13 Apr
Monica	Taylor	USA 65	11.54	1.7	28 Apr
(110)					
Rhonda	Blanford	USA 63	11.54	0.2	12 May
Angela	Williams	TRI 65	11.54		19 May
Veronica	Findley	JAM 64	11.55	0.5	13 May
Gillian	Forde	TRI 67	11.55		19 May
Luisa	Ferrer	CUB 62	11.55	0.5	16 Jun
Marie Francoise	Lubeth	FRA 62	11.55	2.0	30 Jul
Natalya	Bochina	SU 62	11.55		6 Jul
Susan	Shurr	USA 63	11.56		13 Apr
Lilyana	Ivanova	BUL 56	11.56	1.8	2 Jun
Christelle	Bulteau	FRA 63	11.56	1.4	6 Jun
(120)					
Francoise	Philippe	FRA 61	11.56		16 Jun
Fabienne	Ficher	FRA 66	11.56	2.0	10 Jul
Oralee	Fowler	BAH 61	11.57	1.6	22 Apr
Tammy	Henderson	USA	11.57	0.4	13 May
Olga	Mnukhina	SU 60	11.57	0.3	21 Jun
Alice	Jackson	USA 58	11.57		14 Jul
Michelle	Scutt	UK 60	11.57	−0.4	2 Sep
Natalya	Kovtun	SU 64	11.58	0.1	19 May
Svetlana	Morar	SU 63	11.58	0.1	19 May
Roberta	Rabaioli	ITA 63	11.58	1.9	20 May
(130)					
Michaela	Schabinger	FRG 61	11.58	2.0	9 Jun
Dijana	Istvanovic	YUG 57	11.58		16 Jun
Sonia	Lannaman	UK 56	11.58	0.5	19 Jun
Lucia	Militaru	RUM 62	11.58	0.6	10 Jul
Irina	Shkarina	SU 65	11.58	−2.0	13 Jul
Andralette	Gill	USA 62	11.59		14 Apr
Molly	Killingbeck	CAN 59	A11.59	−0.2	22 May
Kim	Jamison	USA 62	11.59	1.8	25 May
Susana	Armenteros	CUB 61	11.59	0.5	16 Jun
Yelena	Fyodorova	SU 66	11.59	−2.0	13 Jul
(140)					
Xenia	Siska	HUN 57	11.60	−0.3	5 May
Ingrid	Verbruggen	BEL 64	11.60		26 May
Sigrid	Ulbricht	GDR 58	11.60	0.0	15 Jul
Christiane	Prajet	FRA 57	11.61	1.8	10 Jul
Teri	Smajstrla	USA 64	11.62		13 Apr
Romy	Muller	GDR 58	11.62	0.7	1 Jun

Elke	Vollmer	FRG 61	11.62	1.6	3 Jun
Yordanka	Donkova	BUL 61	11.62	−0.4	9 Jun
Marie-France	Mollex	FRA 60	11.62	2.0	30 Jun
Brenda	Cliette	USA 63	11.62	0.0	25 Jul
(150)					
Deirdre	Jackson	USA	11.63	0.3	4 May
Anna	Catalano	ITA 65	11.63	1.9	20 May
Pam	Qualls	USA 66	11.63	0.1	2 Jun
Sandra	Whittaker	UK 63	11.63	0.5	19 Jun
Tatyana	Papilina	SU 67	11.63	0.2	18 Aug
Sandra	Terblanche	RSA 63	A11.63		24 Nov
Clotee	Cowans	USA 62	11.64	1.2	31 Mar
Pat	Dunlap	USA 60	11.64	1.7	5 May
Genowefa	Blaszak	POL 57	11.64	−1.4	19 May
Vivien	McKenzie	USA 64	11.64	1.4	19 May
(160)					
Anke	Koninger	FRG 61	11.64		2 Sep
Madele	Naude	RSA 63	A11.64		24 Nov
Eunice	Jones	USA 64	11.65		31 Mar
Vivian	Riley	USA 64	11.65	1.4	26 May
Patrice	Carpenter	USA 65	11.65	1.4	26 May
Christiane	Wage	FRG 63	11.65	2.0	9 Jun
Martina	Frank	FRG 65	11.65	2.0	9 Jun
Esmie	Lawrence	CAN 61	11.65	1.5	29 Jun
Natalia	Karaiosifoglu	RUM 61	11.65	0.6	10 Jul
Roberta	Belle	USA 58	11.65	1.1	15 Jul
(170)					
Marina	Krivosheina	SU 67	11.66		26 May
Sandra	Howard	USA 56	11.66	1.9	7 Jun
Laurence	Labrousse	FRA 61	11.66		16 Jun
Sue	Telfer	UK 61	11.66	1.6	16 Jun
Elvira	Kotoviene	SU 58	11.66		28 Jun
Bev	Callender	UK 56	11.66	1.0	6 Jul
France	Gareau	CAN 67	11.66	1.4	4 Aug
Katura	Anderson	CAN 68	11.66	0.1	25 Aug
Liping	Wu	CHN 60	11.66	1.4	22 Sep
Karen	Kruger	RSA 67	A11.67		1 Mar
(180)					
Danette	Young	USA 64	11.67		23 Mar
Lori	Smith	USA 61	11.67	0.0	22 Apr
Ethlyn	Tate	JAM 66	11.67	0.9	26 May
Odessa	Smalls	USA 64	11.67	1.8	30 May
Resi	Marz	FRG 60	11.67	−0.2	9 Jun
Helen	Barnett	UK 58	11.67	1.6	16 Jun

363

1984 Lists – Women

Aleksandra	Majewska	POL 64	11.67	1.7	22 Jun	Marie-					
Doreen	Antemann	GDR 66	11.67		30 Jun	Christine	Cazier	FRA 63	11.70	0.6	13 May
Cecile	Ngambi	CAM 60	11.67	1.0	4 Aug	Natalya	Potapova	SU 65	11.70	0.1	19 May
Elinda	Rademeyer	RSA 65	A11.68		14 Jan	(200)					
(190)						Georgina	Oladapo	UK 67	11.70	1.9	27 May
Michelle	King	USA 64	11.68	−0.7	27 Apr	Marita	Payne	CAN 60	11.70	−0.2	17 Jun
Donna	King	USA 63	11.68	−0.8	20 May	Christine	Wahl	FRG 67	11.70	1.7	20 Jul
Christine	Elsner	FRG 63	11.68	0.4	9 Jun	(203)					
Laura	Miano	ITA 59	11.68		30 Jun	**Best outdoor mark**					
Doina	Jinga	RUM 59	11.68	0.6	10 Jul		Emmelmann		11.55	0.9	12 May
Sona	Tomova	CS 65	11.69	0.5	2 Jun						
Larisa	Sivokon	SU 59	11.69	−0.1	7 Sep						
Renee	Jones	USA 65	11.70		23 Mar						

Best low-altitude mark

	Taylor		11.23	0.2	1h5	OG	Los Angeles	4 Aug
Carla	Mercurio	ITA 60	11.39	1.8	2		Rieti	4 Jul
Rossella	Tarolo	ITA 64	11.53	1.8				4 Jul
Daniela	Ferrian	ITA 61	11.68	1.8				4 Jul

	1	10	20	30	50	100	Under 11.50	Under 11.60
1980	10.93	11.20	11.28	11.34	11.43	11.65	63	92
1981	10.90	11.21	11.29	11.36	11.51	11.66	47	74
1982	10.88	11.14	11.28	11.33	11.43	11.58	67	106
1983	10.79	11.09	11.22	11.30	11.41	11.54	79	122
1984	10.76	11.10	11.21	11.26	11.36	11.51	86	140

Marks made with assisting wind greater than 2 m/s

	Ashford		10.78	3.1	1		Modesto, CA	12 May
	Ashford		10.88	3.0	1r2	MSR	Walnut, CA	29 Apr
Valerie	Brisco	USA 60	11.02	2.3	1		Walnut, CA	3 Jun
	Ottey		11.03	3.0	2r2	MSR	Walnut, CA	29 Apr
Randy	Givens	USA 62	11.06	3.7	1	NCAA	Eugene	1 Jun
Alice	Brown	USA 60	11.07	2.2	1s1	TAC	San Jose	8 Jun
	Ottey		11.07	3.4	1s2	TAC	San Jose	8 Jun
Heather	Oakes	UK 59	11.08	3.8	1	NC	Cwmbran	27 May
Angela	Williams	TRI 65	11.09		1		Nashville	14 Apr
Wanda	Fort	USA 63	11.09		2		Nashville	14 Apr
Angella	Taylor	CAN 58	A11.09	4.4	1		Provo	26 May
	Brisco		11.10	3.1	2		Modesto, CA	12 May
(12/9)								
Shirley	Thomas	UK 63	11.13	3.8	2	NC	Cwmbran	27 May
(10)								
Brenda	Cliette	USA 63	11.14	3.7	2	NCAA	Eugene	1 Jun
Jackie	Washington	USA 62	11.17	3.7	3	NCAA	Eugene	1 Jun
Michelle	Finn	USA 65	11.20	3.7	4	NCAA	Eugene	1 Jun
Michele	Glover	USA 63	11.21	3.8	1	TexR	Austin	6 Apr
Mary	Bolden	USA 64	11.23	4.3	1		Knoxville	14 Apr
Jayne	Andrews	UK 63	11.23	4.2	1		Edinburgh	17 Jul
Barbara	Frazier	USA 63	11.24		3		Nashville	14 Apr
Jennifer	Inniss	GUY 59	11.24	2.3	2		Walnut, CA	3 Jun
Els	Vader	HOL 59	11.25	2.4	1	NC	Sittard	24 Jun
Marie France	Loval	FRA 64	11.25	3.3	1		Lille	30 Jun
(20)								
Andrea	Bush	USA 66	A11.25	2.8	1		Provo	14 Jul
Simone	Jacobs	UK 66	11.26	3.8	3	NC	Cwmbran	27 May
Nelli	Cooman	HOL 64	11.26	2.4	2	NC	Sittard	24 Jun
Helina	Marjamaa	FIN 56	11.27	2.4	1	v Swe	Helsinki	1 Sep
Liliane	Gaschet	FRA 62	11.29	3.3	2	NC	Lille	30 Jun
Rose-Aimee	Bacoul	FRA 52	11.30	3.3	3	NC	Lille	30 Jun
Gail	Devers	USA 66	11.34	2.4	1h2		Norwalk, CA	25 May
Donna	Dennis	USA 64	11.35	3.9	1h1	TexR	Austin	6 Apr
Tammy	Henderson	USA	11.36	6.0	1h3		Univ Park, PA	12 May
Gwen	Torrence	USA 65	11.37	2.9	1		Athens, GA	31 Mar

1984 Lists – Women

(30)								
Rufina	Ubah	NIG 60	11.37	3.8	3		Knoxville	19 May
Angela	Thacker	USA 64	11.37	3.7	7	NCAA	Eugene	1 Jun
Christelle	Bulteau	FRA 63	11.37	3.3	4	NC	Lille	30 Jun
Sandra	Whittaker	UK 63	11.38	4.2	2		Edinburgh	17 Jul
France	Gareau	CAN 67	11.38	6.9	1r1		Sacramento	21 Jul
Bev	Callender	UK 56	11.39	5.5	1		Birmingham	23 Jun
Vroni	Werthmuller	SWZ 59	11.39	2.4	1	NC	Zofingen	21 Jul
Ruth	Enang	CAM 58	11.41	8.5	1		Atlanta	20 Jul
Cecile	Ngambi	CAM 60	11.41	8.5	2		Atlanta	20 Jul
Lillie	Leatherwood	USA 64	11.42	2.9	3		Athens, GA	31 Mar
(40)								
Barbara	Bell	USA 63	11.42	3.0	1r1	MSR	Walnut, CA	29 Apr
Sandra	Howard	USA 56	11.42	3.0	4r2	MSR	Walnut, CA	29 Apr
Sonia	Lannaman	UK 56	11.42	5.5	2		Birmingham	23 Jun
Marie Francoise	Lubeth	FRA 62	11.43	3.3	5t	NC	Lille	30 Jun
Francoise	Philippe	FRA 61	11.43	3.3	5t	NC	Lille	30 Jun
Donna	Carley	USA 59	11.45	3.1	5		Modesto, CA	12 May
Sharon	Ware	USA 63	11.46	6.1	1		Las Vegas	31 Mar
Odessa	Smalls	USA 64	11.46		4		Nashville	14 Apr
Paula	Ready	USA 66	11.46	4.8	1		Norwalk, CA	19 May
Joan	Baptiste	UK 59	11.46	4.2	3		Edinburgh	17 Jul
(50)								
Monica	Taylor	USA 65	11.47	3.1	1s1		San Angelo	18 May
Teri	Smajstrla	USA 64	11.50	3.6	1h4	TexR	Austin	6 Apr
Vivien	McKenzie	USA 64	11.50	2.9	1		Columbus	20 May
Danette	Young	USA 64	11.50	6.2	1h2		Cape Girardeau	25 May
Chewuakii	Knighten	USA 67	11.50	2.4	2h2		Norwalk, CA	25 May
Davera	Taylor	USA 65	11.51	2.7	1h2		Columbus	19 May
Clotee	Cowans	USA 62	11.52	3.8	3	TexR	Austin	6 Apr
Marie-France	Mollex	FRA 60	11.52	3.3	7	NC	Lille	30 Jun
(58)								

Helen	Barnett	UK 58	11.53	3.8	27 May	Eldece	Clarke	BAH 65	11.61	2.4	4 Aug
Jacqueline	Pusey	JAM 59	11.54	3.1	12 May	Fawn	Young	USA 64	11.62	4.3	14 Apr
(60)						Janet	Dodson	USA 61	11.62		19 May
Tara	Mastin	USA 62	11.56	3.2	12 May	Linda	Haglund	SWE 56	11.62	3.7	19 Jun
Andralette	Gill	USA 62	11.56	2.2	23 May	Denise	Liles	USA 68	11.62		25 Aug
Sue	Telfer	UK 61	11.56	5.5	23 Jun	Sara	Parros	USA	11.63	4.8	19 May
Bridgette	Tate	USA 66	11.57	3.8	19 May	Laurence	Bily	FRA 63	11.63	3.3	30 Jun
Lisa	Ford	USA 66	11.58		20 Apr	(80)					
Katura	Anderson	CAN 68	11.58	6.0	30 Jun	Maria	Fernstrom	SWE 67	11.63	2.4	1 Sep
Angela	Phipps	CAN 64	11.58	5.8		Maicel	Malone	USA	11.64		2 Jun
Cathy	Roberts	USA	11.60	4.8	19 May	Esmie	Lawrence	CAN 61	11.64	6.9	21 Jul
Klavdia	Salyga	SU 61	11.60	2.1	20 Jun	Robin	Simmons	USA 65	11.65	3.0	3 Jun
Ute	Beck	GDR 65	11.60	2.1	26 Jul	Urszula	Jaros	POL 56	11.66	4.8	12 Aug
(70)						Nzaeli	Kyomo	TAN 57	11.67		5 May
Patrice	Carpenter	USA 65	11.61	2.7	14 Apr	Kris	Eiring	USA 63	11.68	2.9	20 May
Stephanie	Hightower	USA 58	11.61	4.3	14 Apr	Renee	Jones	USA 65	11.68	2.9	20 May
Jeri	Domes	USA	11.61	6.2	23 May	(80)					

Hand timing

Antonina	Nastoburko	SU 59	10.9	0.6	1		Kiev	14 Aug
Pauline	Davis	BAH 66	11.1		1		Nassau	24 Aug
Marina	Babenko	SU 60	11.1	0.1	1		Gorkiy	11 Aug
Natalya	Bochina	SU 62	11.2	– i	1h		Gomel	25 Feb
Eunice	Jones	USA 64	11.2	0.2	1h2		Baton Rouge	4 May
Jackie	Jones	USA	11.2	0.2	2h2		Baton	
Velisa	Harris	USA 65	11.2	0.2	3h2		Baton Rouge	4 May
Marina	Zhirova	SU 63	11.2	0.0	2		Sochi	26 May
Els	Vader	HOL 59	11.2	–0.5	1		Aachen	30 May
Andrea	Bush	USA 66	A11.2	2.0	1		Aurora, CO	30 Jun
(10)								
Sigrid	Ulbricht	GDR 58	11.2		1		Wolmirstedt	1 Jul
Natalya	Kovtun	SU 64	11.2		1		Tula	14 Jul

1984 Lists – Women

Bev	Kinch	UK 64	11.2	1.0	4		Berkeley	14 Jul
Irina	Slyusar	SU 63	11.2					
Svetlana	Zuyeva	SU 63	11.2	0.1	2		Gorkiy	11 Aug
Yelena	Fyodorova	SU 66	11.2	0.1	3		Gorkiy	11 Aug
Larisa	Sivokon	SU 59	11.2	0.6	2		Kiev	14 Aug
Natalya	Pomoshchnikova	SU 65	11.2		1		Tula	31 Aug
(18)								
Valentina	Gusseinova	SU 60	11.3		18 Apr	Galina	Sorokina	SU 60	11.3		6 Jul
Eldece	Clarke	BAH 65	11.3		24 Apr	Olga	Mnukhina	SU 60	11.3		6 Jul
(20)						Yelena	Kelchevskaya	SU 55	11.3		6 Jul
Teresa	Rione	SPA 65	11.3	1.5	1 May	(30)				
Svetlana	Zhizdrikova	SU 60	11.3		11 May	Inger	Peterson	USA 64	11.3	1.0	14 Jul
Elvira	Barbashina	SU 63	11.3	0.0	26 May	Vera	Sevalnikova	SU 62	11.3		7 Aug
Svetlana	Morar	SU 63	11.3	0.0	26 May	Margarita	Butkiene	SU 49	11.3		18 Aug
Irina	Romanova	SU 60	11.3		16 Jun	Elvira	Kotoviene	SU 58	11.3		18 Aug
Yelena	Zaitseva	SU 65	11.3		29 Jun	Carla	McLaughlin	USA 67	11.3		19 Aug
Tatyana	Vilisova	SU 59	11.3		5 Jul	(35)					

Mark made in mixed race with men

| Debbie | Wells | AUS 61 | 11.1 | 1.3 | 1 | | Sydney | 29 Feb |

Marks made with assisting wind greater than 2 m/s

Cornelia	Riefstahl	GDR 61	11.1		1		Split	30 Apr
Vivien	McKenzie	USA 64	11.2		1		Ames	5 May
Nawal	El Moutawakil	MOR 62	11.2		2		Ames	5 May
Ines	Schmidt	GDR 60	11.2		1		Nitra	26 Aug

200 METRES

Marita	Koch	GDR 57	21.71	0.3	1	OD	Potsdam	21 Jul
Marlies	Gohr	GDR 58	21.74	0.4	1	NC	Erfurt	3 Jun
Valerie	Brisco	USA 60	21.81	−0.1	1	OG	Los Angeles	9 Aug
Barbel	Wockel	GDR 55	21.85	0.3	2	OD	Potsdam	21 Jul
	Koch		21.87	0.0	1	WK	Zurich	22 Aug
Florence	Griffith	USA 59	22.04	−0.1	1	OG	Los Angeles	9 Aug
Merlene	Ottey	JAM 60	22.09	−0.1	3	OG	Los Angeles	9 Aug
Kathy	Cook	UK 60	22.10	−0.1	4	OG	Los Angeles	9 Aug
	Wockel		22.10	0.0	2	WK	Zurich	22 Aug
	Koch		22.13	−2.0	1		Karl-Marx-Stadt	20 May
	Brisco		22.14	1.5	1	VD	Bruxelles	24 Aug
	Wockel		22.15	0.4	1	DRZ	Praha	17 Aug
	Brisco		22.16	−0.2	1	FOT	Los Angeles	22 Jun
	Koch		22.17	0.0	1		Jena	13 May
	Wockel		22.19	0.4	2	NC	Erfurt	3 Jun
	Ottey		22.20	0.6 •	1	TAC	San Jose	9 Jun
Grace	Jackson	JAM 61	22.20	−0.1	5	OG	Los Angeles	9 Aug
	Cook		22.21	0.0	1	Nik	Nice	20 Aug
	Gohr		22.22	0.3	3	OD	Potsdam	21 Jul
	Koch		22.22	0.8	1	8N	Tokyo	14 Sep
	Cook		22.25	0.0	3	WK	Zurich	22 Aug
	Brisco		22.26	0.0	4	WK	Zurich	22 Aug
	Griffith		22.27	1.0	1s1	OG	Los Angeles	9 Aug
	Brisco		22.28	1.4	1s2	OG	Los Angeles	9 Aug
Gesine	Walther	GDR 62	22.32	0.5	1r2	OD	Potsdam	21 Jul
	Jackson		22.32	1.4	2s2	OG	Los Angeles	9 Aug
	Jackson		22.33	0.6	2	TAC	San Jose	9 Jun
	Griffith		22.33	1.4	1q4	OG	Los Angeles	8 Aug
	Walther		22.34	0.4	3	NC	Erfurt	3 Jun
	Gohr		22.35	−2.0	2		Karl-Marx-Stadt	20 May
	Ottey		22.35	−0.4	1		Burnaby	16 Jul

1984 Lists – Women

Randy	Ottey	USA 62	22.35	1.5	2	VD	Bruxelles	24 Aug
	Givens		22.36	−0.1	6	OG	Los Angeles	9 Aug
	Cook		22.38	1.4	3s2	OG	Los Angeles	9 Aug
	Jackson		22.38	0.0	2	Nik	Nice	20 Aug
(35/10)								
Ewa	Kasprzyk	POL 57	22.42	1.4	1		Sopot	5 Aug
Natalya	Bochina	SU 62	22.45	0.1	1		Kiev	23 Jun
Tatana	Kocembova	CS 62	22.47	0.2	1		Barcelona	8 Jul
Chandra	Cheeseborough	USA 59	22.47	0.0	5	WK	Zurich	22 Aug
Nadezhda	Georgieva	BUL 61	22.51	−1.0	1	NC	Sofia	3 Jun
Rose-Aimee	Bacoul	FRA 52	22.53	1.4	4s2	OG	Los Angeles	9 Aug
Jarmila	Kratochvilova	CS 51	22.57	−0.7	1	v FRG,Fra,Pol	Hannover	16 Jun
Angella	Taylor	CAN 58	A22.61	0.0	1		Provo	29 May
Maya	Azarashvili	SU 64	22.63	0.1	2		Kiev	23 Jun
Sabine	Rieger	GDR 63	22.65	0.5	2r2	OD	Potsdam	21 Jul
(20)								
Pam	Marshall	USA 60	22.67	0.6	3	TAC	San Jose	9 Jun
Anelia	Nuneva	BUL 62	22.67	−2.0	2	Balk	Athinai	9 Sep
Svetlana	Zhizdrikova	SU 60	22.69	0.1	3		Kiev	23 Jun
Silke	Gladisch	GDR 64	22.70	0.0	2		Jena	13 May
Heide-Elke	Gaugel	FRG 59	22.72	0.4	1		Munchen	20 Jul
Marita	Payne	CAN 60	22.72	0.0	2r2	WK	Zurich	22 Aug
Liliane	Gaschet	FRA 62	22.73	1.0	4s1	OG	Los Angeles	9 Aug
Galina	Mikheyeva	SU 62	22.74	0.1	4		Kiev	23 Jun
Evelyn	Ashford	USA 57	22.75	2.0	1		Santa Monica	14 Apr
Angela	Bailey	CAN 62	22.75	1.4	5s2	OG	Los Angeles	9 Aug
(30)								
Evette	de Klerk	RSA 65	A22.76		1		Sasolburg	21 Apr
Irina	Slyusar	SU 63	22.76	1.8	1		Moskva	20 Jul
Tatyana	Alekseyeva	SU 63	22.77	0.1	1		Sochi	20 May
Kirsteni	Emmelmann	GDR 61	22.80		1r2		Split	30 Apr
Olga	Zolotaryova	SU 61	22.80	0.1	2		Sochi	20 May
Brenda	Cliette	USA 63	22.81	−0.2	4	FOT	Los Angeles	22 Jun
Sabine	Busch	GDR 62	22.86	0.9	2		Rehlingen	11 Jun
Joan	Baptiste	UK 59	22.86	1.0	5s1	OG	Los Angeles	9 Aug
Ines	Schmidt	GDR 60	22.87	0.4	4	NC	Erfurt	3 Jun
Dagmar	Rubsam	GDR 62	22.87	0.2	1		Praha	28 Aug
(40)								
Yelena	Vinogradova	SU 62	22.87	0.0	1	NC	Donetsk	9 Sep
Marisa	Masullo	ITA 59	22.88	0.0	1	v Hun,Pol,SU	Verona	1 Jun
Els	Vader	HOL 59	22.90	1.0	1	NC	Sittard	23 Jun
Lilyana	Ivanova	BUL 56	22.93	−1.0	2	NC	Sofia	3 Jun
Ingrid	Auerswald	GDR 57	22.94	−2.0	4		Karl-Marx-Stadt	20 May
Ute	Thimm	FRG 58	22.95	1.3	1		San Diego	30 Jul
Sherri	Howard	USA 62	22.97	1.8	1		Los Angeles	21 Jun
Marina	Molokova	SU 62	22.97	0.1	5		Kiev	23 Jun
Pauline	Davis	BAH 66	22.97	1.1	4q1	OG	Los Angeles	8 Aug
Debbie	Wells	AUS 61	22.98	0.0	1		Sydney	11 Mar
(50)								
Sandra	Whittaker	UK 63	22.98	1.1	5q1	OG	Los Angeles	8 Aug
Mary	Bolden	USA 64	23.00	1.7	1h1	NCAA	Eugene	31 May
Pepa	Pavlova	BUL 61	23.00	0.3	2	v GDR,Rum	Sofia	17 Jun
Lilia	Novoseltsova	SU 62	23.06	0.1	4		Sochi	20 May
Atanaska	Georgieva	BUL 60	23.07	−0.5	3	NarMl	Sofia	20 May
Diane	Williams	USA 61	23.08	0.6	4	TAC	San Jose	9 Jun
Alice	Brown	USA 60	23.08	0.0	1r3	WK	Zurich	22 Aug
Jackie	Washington	USA 62	23.10	1.3	1		Austin	12 May
Molly	Killingbeck	CAN 59	A23.12	1.0	1		Provo	22 May
Zelda	Johnson	USA 64	23.12	0.3	1		Bakersfield	26 May
(60)								
Helina	Marjamaa	FIN 56	23.12	1.0	6s1	OG	Los Angeles	9 Aug
Janet	Davis	USA 65	23.13	1.7	2h1	NCAA	Eugene	31 May
Lori	Smith	USA 61	23.14	0.6	5	TAC	San Jose	9 Jun
Angela	Thacker	USA 64	23.15	1.7	3h1	NCAA	Eugene	31 May
Cornelia	Riefstahl	GDR 61	23.15	0.4	5	NC	Erfurt	3 Jun

1984 Lists – Women

LaShon	Nedd	USA 63	23.16	1.8	1r2		Walnut, CA	3 Jun
Ana	Quirot	CUB 63	23.16	0.3	3		Sofia	17 Jun
Elzbieta	Tomczak	POL 61	23.17	0.8	2		Molfetta	1 Jul
Bev	Callender	UK 56	23.18	1.8	2	WAAA	London	16 Jun
Heike	Morgenstern	GDR 62	23.19	0.5	4r2	OD	Potsdam	21 Jul
(70)								
Marina	Zhirova	SU 63	23.20	0.1	6		Sochi	20 May
Mari-Lise	Furstenberg	RSA 66	A23.21		2	NC-j	Pretoria	30 Mar
Elzbieta	Wozniak	POL 59	23.21	1.4	2		Sopot	5 Aug
Genowefa	Blaszak	POL 57	23.22	−1.9	1		Sevilla	19 May
Elvira	Barbashina	SU 63	23.23	0.7	2		Kiev	4 Jul
Wendy	Vereen	USA 66	23.24	1.2	1h5	TAC	San Jose	7 Jun
Maria	Pinigina	SU 58	23.25	1.8	1h1	NarMl	Sofia	20 May
Helen	Barnett	UK 58	23.25	1.8	3	WAAA	London	16 Jun
Anke	Vater	GDR 63	23.26		H	NC	Potsdam	5 May
Roberta	Belle	USA 58	23.28	1.6	1		Walnut, CA	15 Jul
(80)								
Galina	Penkova	BUL 58	23.29		h	NarMl	Sofia	20 May
Lisa	Hopkins	USA 58	23.32	1.8	2r2		Walnut, CA	3 Jun
Diane	Dixon	USA 64	23.32	−0.2	6	FOT	Los Angeles	22 Jun
Simone	Jacobs	UK 66	23.33	0.9	3	OT	Gateshead	10 Jun
Michele	Glover	USA 63	23.34	1.3	2		Austin	12 May
Merry	Johnson	USA 59	23.34	0.6	6	TAC	San Jose	9 Jun
Malinka	Girova	BUL 66	23.34		1	v Hun,Rum,SU-j	Debrecen	19 Aug
Galina	Sorokina	SU 60	23.35	0.0	3	NC	Donetsk	9 Sep
Shirley	Thomas	UK 63	23.36	0.4	1h1	OT	Gateshead	10 Jun
Sabine	Paetz	GDR 57	23.37		H	NC	Potsdam	5 May
(90)								
Michaela	Schabinger	FRG 61	23.37	0.4	4		Munchen	20 Jul
Ruth	Waithera	KEN 58	23.37	0.5	4q3	OG	Los Angeles	8 Aug
Undine	Bremer	GDR 61	23.38		2r2		Split	30 Apr
Tara	Mastin	USA 62	23.38	1.3	3		Austin	12 May
Danette	Young	USA 64	23.38	0.3	1		Cape Girardeau	26 May
Ulrike	Sommer	FRG 59	23.38	1.4	1h3	NC	Dusseldorf	24 Jun
Angela	Williams	TRI 65	23.38	0.9	4h4	OG	Los Angeles	8 Aug
Valentina	Bozhina	SU 66	23.38	0.0	4	NC	Donetsk	9 Sep
Yordanka	Donkova	BUL 61	23.39	−1.0	4	NC	Sofia	3 Jun
Alice	Jackson	USA 58	23.39		1		Atlanta	29 Jun
(100)								
Janet	Burke	JAM 62	23.39	1.6	2		Walnut, CA	15 Jul
(101)								

Elinda	Rademeyer	RSA 65	A23.41		30 Mar	Michelle	Scutt	UK 60	23.50	−0.8	2 Sep
Sheila	de Oliveira	BRA 59	23.41	−0.2	15 Jun	Clotee	Cowans	USA 62	23.52	1.4	26 May
Edith	Otterman	RSA 66	A23.42		30 Mar	Olga	Mnukhina	SU 60	23.52	0.1	23 Jun
Christina	Lathan	GDR 58	23.42	−0.2	6 May	Michele	Morris	USA 64	23.53	1.4	13 May
Antonina	Nastoburko	SU 59	23.42	1.8	20 Jul	Susan	Shurr	USA 63	23.53	1.3	12 May
Renata	Cernochova	CS 65	23.43	1.8	2 Jun	Judi	Brown	USA 61	23.53	1.2	12 May
Sue	Telfer	UK 61	23.43	1.8	16 Jun	Luisa	Ferrer	CUB 62	23.53	0.3	17 Jun
Malgorzata	Dunecka	POL 56	23.43	−0.1	10 Jul	Svetlana	Zuyeva	SU 63	23.53	0.0	9 Sep
Maria	Samungi	RUM 50	23.44	−1.0	12 Jul	(130)					
(110)						Gwen	Torrence	USA 65	23.54		24 Mar
Donna	Dennis	USA 64	23.45	0.6	9 Jun	Tammy	Henderson	USA	23.54	−0.1	13 May
Raymonde	Naigre	FRA 60	23.47	−2.4	1 Jul	Paulette	Blalock	USA 67	23.54	−2.5	19 May
Wendy	Addison	UK 60	23.49	1.8	16 Jun	Irina	Baskakova	SU 56	23.54	0.0	1 Jun
Teresa	Rione	SPA 65	23.49	−0.6	17 Jun	Kim	Robertson	NZ 57	23.56		18 Feb
Gervaise	McCraw	USA 64	23.49	0.9	21 Jun	Natalya	Shubenkova	SU 57	23.57	−0.4	20 Jun
Karoline	Kafer	AUT 54	23.49	1.5	26 Aug	Gaby	Bussmann	FRG 59	23.58	1.3	30 Jul
Marie-Christine	Cazier	FRA 63	23.50	1.0	28 Apr	Janet	Dodson	USA 61	23.59	1.0	6 May
Dawn	Sowell	USA 66	23.50		26 May	Cathy	Roberts	USA	23.59	−2.5	19 May
Liliana	Nastase	RUM 62	23.50		10 Jul	Teri	Smajstrla	USA 64	23.60	1.3	12 May
Lucia	Militaru	RUM 62	23.50	−1.0	12 Jul	(140)					
(120)						Radislava	Soborova	CS 59	23.60	1.8	2 Jun
Vroni	Werthmuller	SWZ 59	23.50	1.0	22 Jul	Annett	Hesselbarth	GDR 66	23.60		1 Jul
Jeanette	Bolden	USA 60	23.50	−0.2	2 Sep	Charmaine	Crooks	CAN 61	23.60	0.0	22 Aug

1984 Lists – Women

Name		Nat	Mark	Wind	Date
Michelle	Finn	USA 65	23.61		13 May
Inger	Peterson	USA 64	23.61	1.9	19 May
Donna	King	USA 63	23.61	0.6	20 May
Jillian	Richardson	CAN 65	A23.61	1.0	22 May
Heike	Schulte-Mattler	FRG 58	23.61	1.5	24 Jun
Fransie	Pieterse	RSA 61	A23.64		21 Apr
Leslie	Maxie	USA 67	23.64		7 Jul
(150)					
Cynthia Marie	Green	JAM 60	23.65	2.0	4 May
Francoise	Lubeth	FRA 62	23.65	1.3	1 Jul
Mona	Evjen	NOR 55	23.65	1.5	24 Aug
Lillie	Leatherwood	USA 64	23.66		24 Mar
Tatyana	Papilina	SU 67	23.66		19 Aug
Christelle	Bulteau	FRA 63	23.68	0.4	20 Jul
Galina	Chereshneva	SU 62	23.68	0.0	9 Sep
Martina	Frank	FRG 65	23.69	0.0	19 Aug
Patricia	Beckford	UK 65	23.70	0.9	10 Jun
Rhonda	Blanford	USA 63	23.71	-2.3	12 May
(160)					
Dawn	Flockhart	UK 67	23.71	0.9	10 Jun
Laurence	Labrousse	FRA 61	23.71	1.3	1 Jul
Irina	Nazarova	SU 57	23.72	0.4	5 Aug
Karin	Verguts	BEL 61	23.73		8 Jul
Christine	Wahl	FRG 67	23.73	0.0	22 Jul
Elzbieta	Kapusta	POL 60	23.73	1.4	5 Aug
Darlene	Jefferson	USA 62	23.74		13 May
Vera	Tylova	CS 60	23.74	1.8	2 Jun
Katya	Ilieva	BUL 63	23.74	-1.0	3 Jun
Heike	Terpe	GDR 64	23.74	0.4	3 Jun
(170)					
Sasa	Kranjc	YUG 63	23.74	-2.0	9 Sep
Svetlana	Morar	SU 63	23.75	0.1	20 May
Heather	Oakes	UK 59	23.75		20 May
Stepanka	Sokolova	CS 58	23.76	-0.3	26 May
Angela	Bridgeman	UK 63	A23.77		14 Apr
Sharon	Ware	USA 63	23.77		14 Apr
Ellen	Fiedler	GDR 58	23.77		30 Apr
Debbie	Greene	BAH 64	23.77	1.4	26 May
Pam	Qualls	USA 66	23.77	-0.1	2 Jun
Jackie	Joyner	USA 62	23.77	1.9	16 Jun
(180)					
Veronica	Findley	JAM 64	23.78	1.4	13 May
Esmie	Lawrence	CAN 61	A23.78	0.9	19 May
Rositsa	Stamenova	BUL 55	23.78		9 Jun
Susan	Armenteros	CUB 61	23.78		21 Jun
Natalia	Karaiosifoglu	RUM 61	23.78	-1.0	12 Jul
Iwona	Pakula	POL 62	23.79		12 May
Yelena	Biserova	SU 62	23.79	0.1	20 May
Fabienne	Ficher	FRA 66	23.79	1.8	15 Jul
Elvira	Kotoviene	SU 58	23.79		9 Sep
Helen	Davey	AUS 58	23.80	-2.7	1 Apr
(190)					
Oralee	Fowler	BAH 61	23.80		26 May
Gillian	Forde	TRI 67	23.80		Jun
Aelita	Yurchenko	SU 65	23.80	0.7	4 Jul
Marina	Krivosheina	SU 67	23.80		19 Aug
Natasa	Seliskar	YUG 60	23.80		26 Aug
(195)					

Indoor marks

Marie-Christine	Cazier	FRA 63	23.48		18 Feb
Olga	Antonova	SU 60	23.66		3 Mar
Raisa	Makhova	SU 57	23.70		20 Feb

Best low altitude marks

| | Taylor | | 22.75 | 1.0 | 1 | | Fort-de-France | 28 Apr |
| | de Klerk | | 23.36 | | 1 | NC | Durban | 14 Apr |

| | Furstenberg | 23.60 | | | 14 Apr |
| | Killingbeck | 23.62 | 1.0 | | 28 Apr |

	1	10	20	30	50	100	Under 23.00	Under 23.50
1980	22.01	22.47	22.82	22.97	23.28	23.64	30	78
1981	21.84	22.72	22.98	23.11	23.43	23.71	20	60
1982	21.76	22.39	22.91	22.96	23.23	23.56	31	95
1983	21.82	22.42	22.79	22.97	23.15	23.54	32	94
1984	21.71	22.36	22.65	22.75	22.98	23.39	51	116

Marks made with assisting wind greater than 2 m/s

	Brisco		22.13		1r2	MSR	Walnut, CA	29 Apr
	Brisco		22.15	2.5	1		San Jose	26 May
	Griffith		22.16	2.5	2		San Jose	26 May
	Ottey		22.24	2.1	1h2	TAC	San Jose	7 Jun
	Brisco		22.25	2.8	1		Walnut, CA	3 Jun
	Griffith		22.31	2.1	1s1	FOT	Los Angeles	22 Jun
(6/3)								
Angella	Taylor	CAN 58	A22.44	3.1	1		Provo	26 May
Pam	Marshall	USA 60	22.59	2.4	1s2	TAC	San Jose	9 Jun
Marita	Payne	CAN 60	22.64	4.2	2	NC	Winnipeg	1 Jul
Wendy	Vereen	USA 66	22.75	2.5	1		Los Angeles	14 Apr

1984 Lists – Women

Sherri	Howard	USA 62	22.78	2.6	1	MSR	Walnut, CA		28 Apr
Gervaise	McCraw	USA 64	22.98		2r2	MSR	Walnut, CA		29 Apr
Heather	Oakes	UK 59	23.00	2.1	1	NC	Cwmbran		28 May
(10)									
Simone	Jacobs	UK 66	23.01	2.1	2	NC	Cwmbran		28 May
Jeanette	Bolden	USA 60	23.02	4.0	2		Modesto, CA		12 May
Heike	Morgenstern	GDR 62	23.06	2.8	3		Dresden		27 Jul
Shirley	Thomas	UK 63	23.14	2.1	3	NC	Cwmbran		28 May
Alice	Jackson	USA 58	23.16	2.5	3		San Jose		26 May
Merry	Johnson	USA 59	23.20	2.4	3s2	TAC	San Jose		9 Jun
Anke	Vater	GDR 61	23.20		H	OD	Potsdam		20 Jul
Sabine	Paetz	GDR 57	23.23		H	OD	Potsdam		20 Jul
Tammy	Henderson	USA	23.26	3.6	1h1		Univ Park, PA		12 May
Raymonde	Naigre	FRA 60	23.30	2.5	2		Les Abymes		13 May
(20)									
Diane	Dixon	USA 64	23.31	2.1	3s1	FOT	Los Angeles		22 Jun
Danette	Young	USA 64	23.32	2.1	4s1	FOT	Los Angeles		22 Jun
Michelle	Scutt	UK 60	23.33	2.1	4	NC	Cwmbran		28 May
Christelle	Bulteau	FRA 63	23.39	2.5	3s1	NC	Lille		1 Jul
(24)									

Urszula	Jaros	POL 56	23.43	3.1	15 Jun	Jackie	Joyner	USA 62	23.72		26 Apr
Iwona	Pakula	POL 62	23.44	2.1	23 Jun	Marcella	Kendall	GUY 64	23.72	3.4	20 May
Odessa	Smalls	USA 64	23.46	3.3	19 May	(40)					
Michelle	Finn	USA 65	23.47	2.1	31 May	Arlene	Van Warmerdam	USA 59	23.73	4.0	12 May
Ramona	Neubert	GDR 58	23.47		20 Jul		Forde	TRI 67	23.73		Jun
Cathy	Roberts	USA 66	23.52	3.0	28 Apr	Gilliani	Antemann	GDR 66	23.74	3.0	22 Jul
(30)						Doreen	Georges	FRA 66	23.75	2.7	30 Jun
Sonia	Lannaman	UK 56	23.52	5.5	15 Jul	Annick	Petrika	HUN 57	23.75	2.8	27 Jul
France	Gareau	FRA 67	23.54	4.2	1 Jul	Ibolya	Davey	AUS 58	23.78	4.2	12 Feb
Davera	Taylor	USA 65	23.59	3.3	19 May	Helen	Boothe	UK 54	23.78		18 Mar
Tami	Stiles	USA 68	23.60	3.0	28 Apr	Lorna	Sowunmi	NIG 64	23.78	2.3	4 May
Gwen	Gardner	USA 60	23.64	2.6	28 Apr	Sadia	Fort	USA 63	23.79		14 Apr
Angela	Phipps	CAN 64	A23.64	3.1	26 May	Wanda	Clachet	FRA 68	23.79	3.8	15 Jul
Natalie	Dillon	AUS 67	23.65	3.0	28 Apr	Veronique					
Dorothy	Scott	JAM 57	23.66		5 May	(50)					

Hand timing

Natalya	Bochina		SU 62	22.1	1		Moskva	7 Jul
Galina	Mikheyeva		SU 62	22.5	1		Tula	15 Jul
Kirsten	Emmelmann		GDR 61	22.7	1		Split	30 Apr
Petra	Pfaff		GDR 60	22.8	2		Split	30 Apr
Svetlana	Zuyeva		SU 63	22.9	1		Krasnodar	8 Apr
Ana	Quirot		CUB 63	22.9	1r2		Verona	1 Jun
Galina	Sorokina		SU 60	22.9	1		Leningrad	6 Jul
Irina	Baskakova		SU 56	22.9	2		Moskva	7 Jul
Natalya	Pomoshchnikova		SU 65	23.1	1		Tula	1 Sep
(9)								

Olga	Mnukhina		SU 60	23.2	11 May	Alejandra	Flores	MEX 61	A23.4	6 May
Elinda	Rademeyer	RSA 65	A23.3		25 Feb	Alma	Vazquez	MEX 63	A23.4	20 May
Leanne	Lynch	AUS 60	23.3	-0.5	18 Mar	Irina	Parfenkova	SU 58	23.4	17 Jun
Luisa	Ferrer	CUB 62	23.3		1 Jun	Tatyana	Ledovskaya	SU 66	23.4	1 Jul
Antonina	Nastoburko	SU 59	23.3		6 Jul	Natalya	Miljauskiene	SU 64	23.4	6 Jul
Elvira	Kotoviev	SU 58	23.3		7 Jul	Vera	Akchurina	SU 57	23.4	15 Jul
Jacqueline	Pusey	JAM 59	23.4		4 Feb	Sonia	Lannaman	UK 56	23.4	29 Jul
Edith	Otterman	RSA 66	A23.4		19 Mar	Carla	McLaughlin	USA 67	23.4	19 Aug
Dawn	Sowell	USA 66	23.4		14 Apr	Olga	Kozlova	SU 64	23.4	22 Sep
Ellen	Fiedler	GDR 58	23.4		30 Apr					
(20)						Sylvia	Kirchner	GDR 63	23.4 i	22 Jan
						(30)				

1984 Lists – Women

Svetlana	Zuyeva	SU 63	22.7		1		Chelyabinsk	29 Jul
Jackie	Washington	USA 62	22.8	3.5	1h1		Austin	11 May
Diane	Williams	USA 61	22.9	2.8	2		Walnut, CA	3 Jun
Leanne	Lynch	AUS 60	23.0	4.8	1		Perth	24 Mar
Inger	Peterson	USA 64	23.0	4.8	1		Las Vegas	31 Mar
Mari-Lise	Furstenberg	RSA 66	A23.2				9 Mar	
Barbara	Bell	USA 63	23.2				29 Apr	

400 METRES

Marita	Koch	GDR 57	48.16		1	DRZ	Praha	16 Aug
	Koch		48.26		1		Dresden	27 Jul
Tatana	Kocembova	CS 62	48.73		2	DRZ	Praha	16 Aug
Valerie	Brisco	USA 60	48.83		1	OG	Los Angeles	6 Aug
	Koch		48.86		1	NC	Erfurt	2 Jun
	Koch		48.89		1		Berlin	15 Jul
Olga	Vladykina	SU 63	48.98		1		Kiev	22 Jun
Jarmila	Kratochvilova	CS 51	49.02		1		Rieti	2 Sep
Chandra	Cheeseborough	USA 59	49.05		2	OG	Los Angeles	6 Aug
	Kocembova		49.23		1	BGP	Budapest	20 Aug
Sabine	Busch	GDR 62	49.24		2	NC	Erfurt	2 Jun
	Kratochvilova		49.25		1		Luxembourg	8 Jul
	Cheeseborough		49.28		1	FOT	Los Angeles	19 Jun
	Kocembova		49.30		1		Paris	4 Sep
	Kratochvilova		49.33		1	v FRG,Fra,Pol	Hannover	15 Jun
	Kratochvilova		49.35		2	BGP	Budapest	20 Aug
	Kocembova		49.36		1	OD	Berlin	20 Jul
Kathy	Cook	UK 60	49.42		3	OG	Los Angeles	6 Aug
	Koch		49.44		1		Potsdam	25 May
	Kratochvilova		49.47		1	NC	Praha	22 Jul
	Kratochvilova		49.47		2		Paris	4 Sep
	Vladykina		49.52		3	DRZ	Praha	16 Aug
	Kratochvilova		49.56		1		Koln	26 Aug
Dagmar	Rubsam	GDR 62	49.58		3	NC	Erfurt	2 Jun
	Kratochvilova		49.58		1	VD	Bruxelles	24 Aug
	Busch		49.60		1		Karl-Marx-Stadt	20 May
	Busch		49.62		1		Jena	13 May
	Rubsam		49.65		1	Nik	Nice	20 Aug
	Kocembova		49.72		1	GS	Ostrava	23 May
	Kratochvilova		49.73		1	Ros	Praha	9 Jun
Maria	Pinigina	SU 58	49.74		2		Kiev	22 Jun
	Busch		49.74		1	OD	Potsdam	21 Jul

(32/10)

Marita	Payne	CAN 60	49.91		4	OG	Los Angeles	6 Aug
Gesine	Walther	GDR 62	50.03		2		Jena	13 May
Lillie	Leatherwood	USA 64	50.19		3	FOT	Los Angeles	19 Jun
Lilia	Novoseltsova	SU 62	50.28		2		Moskva	20 Jul
Barbel	Wockel	GDR 55	50.35		4		Jena	13 May
Ute	Thimm	FRG 58	50.37		6	OG	Los Angeles	6 Aug
Sherri	Howard	USA 62	50.40		4	FOT	Los Angeles	19 Jun
Irina	Baskakova	SU 56	50.45		1		Moskva	4 Aug
Charmaine	Crooks	CAN 61	50.45		7	OG	Los Angeles	6 Aug
Irina	Nazarova	SU 57	50.56		2		Moskva	4 Aug

(20)

| Kirsten | Emmelmann | GDR 61 | 50.62 | | 3 | BGP | Budapest | 20 Aug |

1984 Lists – Women

Lyudmila	Belova	SU 58	50.63	3		Moskva	4 Aug
Rositsa	Stamenova	BUL 55	50.82	4h1	DRZ	Praha	16 Aug
Ana	Quirot	CUB 63	50.87	5h1	DRZ	Praha	16 Aug
Gaby	Bussmann	FRG 59	50.98	2		Munchen	20 Jul
Denean	Howard	USA 64	51.05	5	FOT	Los Angeles	19 Jun
Evelyn	Ashford	USA 57	51.08	1h3	TAC	San Jose	7 Jun
Florence	Griffith	USA 59	51.11	6	FOT	Los Angeles	19 Jun
Dalia	Matuseviciene	SU 62	51.12	7		Kiev	22 Jun
Diane	Dixon	USA 64	51.19	3		Rieti	2 Sep

(30)

Genowefa	Blaszak	POL 57	51.21	1		Rieti	4 Jul
Nadezhda	Olizarenko	SU 53	51.22	5		Moskva	4 Aug
Roberta	Belle	USA 58	51.26	8	FOT	Los Angeles	19 Jun
Petra	Muller	GDR 65	51.38	2r2	DRZ	Praha	16 Aug
Tatyana	Alekseyeva	SU 63	51.39	2		Sochi	28 Apr
Kerstin	Walther	GDR 61	51.41	4		Karl-Marx-Stadt	20 May
Ruth	Waithera	KEN 58	51.56	8	OG	Los Angeles	6 Aug
Marina	Stepanova	SU 50	51.60	2h3		Sochi	19 May
Irina	Podyalovskaya	SU 59	51.67	5		Moskva	20 Jul
Niculina	Lazarciuc	RUM 57	51.68	1	NC	Bucuresti	10 Jul

(40)

Molly	Killingbeck	CAN 59	51.72	5s2	OG	Los Angeles	5 Aug
Nadezhda	Zvyagintseva	SU 61	51.77	6		Moskva	20 Jul
Lyudmila	Borisova	SU 59	51.79	1		Kiev	5 Jul
Undine	Bremer	GDR 61	51.81	1	Skok	Celje	5 May
Nina	Kravchenko	SU 59	51.81	h	NC	Donetsk	7 Sep
Nawal	El Moutawakil	MOR 62	51.84	2	DrakeR	Des Moines	28 Apr
Judit	Forgacs	HUN 59	51.85	1	PTS	Bratislava	25 May
Jillian	Richardson	CAN 65	51.85	1		Walnut, CA	25 Jul
Inna	Yevseyeva	SU 64	51.88	h	NC	Donetsk	7 Sep
Michelle	Scutt	UK 60	51.89	2	Bisl	Oslo	28 Jun

(50)

Alice	Jackson	USA 58	51.90	5s1	FOT	Los Angeles	18 Jun
Brenda	Cliette	USA 63	51.92	3q1	FOT	Los Angeles	17 Jun
Maria	Samungi	RUM 50	51.92	2	NC	Bucuresti	10 Jul
Katya	Ilieva	BUL 63	51.92	2	v Pol,FRG,Hun	Warszawa	15 Jul
Joslyn	Hoyte-Smith	UK 54	51.93	1		Oslo	21 Jul
Malgorzata	Dunecka	POL 56	51.97	2		Hengelo	6 Jul
Margarita	Ponomaryova	SU 63	52.05	5		Rieti	2 Sep
Larisa	Dzhigalova	SU 62	52.06	h	NC	Donetsk	7 Sep
Svetlana	Korchagina	SU 57	52.09	h	SU P	Baku	15 Sep
Helen	Barnett	UK 58	52.13	3	Bisl	Oslo	28 Jun

(60)

Ilrey	Oliver	JAM 62	52.14	7s2	OG	Los Angeles	5 Aug
Mercy	Akinyemi	NIG 54	52.15	1		Houston	26 May
Ibolya	Korodi	RUM 57	52.15	3	NC	Bucuresti	10 Jul
Elzbieta	Kapusta	POL 60	52.16	1		Lublin	21 May
Karoline	Kafer	AUT 54	52.18	1		Wien	2 Sep
Cathy	Rattray	JAM 63	52.19	2	King	Atlanta	22 Apr
Christine	Wachtel	GDR 65	52.19	5		Karl-Marx-Stadt	20 May
June	Griffith	GUY 57	52.19	1r2		Koln	26 Aug
Elena	Lina	RUM 54	52.20	4	NC	Bucuresti	10 Jul
Alena	Bulirova	CS 61	52.21	6h1	DRZ	Praha	16 Aug

(70)

Yelena	Korban	SU 61	52.27	s		Kiev	21 Jun
Aelita	Yurchenko	SU 65	52.27			Kiev	5 Jul

1984 Lists – Women

Chewuakii	Knighten	USA 67	52.31		3	Pepsi	Westwood	13 May
Christina	Lathan	GDR 58	52.31		2		Potsdam	25 May
Gwen	Gardner	USA 60	52.32		6s2	FOT	Los Angeles	18 Jun
Merry	Johnson	USA 59	52.35		6s1	FOT	Los Angeles	18 Jun
Heike	Schulte-Mattler	FRG 58	52.37		3	NC	Dusseldorf	23 Jun
Kelia	Bolton	USA 60	52.38		7s1	FOT	Los Angeles	18 Jun
Birgit	Uibel	GDR 61	52.39		1r2		Karl-Marx-Stadt	20 May
Regine	Berg	BEL 58	52.41		1	NC	Bruxelles	8 Jul

(80)

Gladys	Taylor	UK 53	52.43		2		Birmingham	2 Sep
Marina	Ivanova	SU 62	52.45		2r2	NC	Donetsk	7 Sep
Galina	Penkova	BUL 58	52.46		1		Sofia	12 May
Myrtle	Simpson	RSA 64	A52.47		1		Germiston	3 Apr
Easter	Gabriel	USA 60	52.47		4q2	FOT	Los Angeles	17 Jun
Malena	Andonova	BUL 57	52.51		3	NC	Sofia	2 Jun
Svobodka	Damyanova	BUL 55	52.51		4	v GDR,Rum	Sofia	16 Jun
Tatyana	Smeyan	SU 59	52.51		s		Kiev	21 Jun
Kim	Robertson	NZ 57	52.54		1	Aus C	Melbourne	31 Mar
Cynthia	Green	JAM 60	52.54		1h	NC	Kingston	15 Jun

(90)

Edith	Otterman	RSA 66	A52.55		1		Pretoria	10 Mar
Natalya	Bochina	SU 62	52.55		h	Znam	Sochi	9 Jun
Andrea	Thomas	JAM 68	52.57		1	PA-j	Nassau	24 Aug
Gail	Emmanuel	TRI 62	52.59		1		Baton Rouge	5 May
Ibolya	Petrika	HUN 57	52.60		1	NC	Budapest	26 Jul
Raymonde	Naigre	FRA 60	52.61		1	NC	Lille	30 Jun
Ann-Louise	Skoglund	SWE 62	52.61		1	v Fin	Helsinki	1 Sep
Aldona	Mendzorite	SU 61	52.61		h	NC	Donetsk	7 Sep
Annett	Hesselbarth	GDR 66	52.62		1	NC-j	Potsdam	30 Jun
Judi	Brown	USA 61	52.63		3	MSR	Walnut, CA	29 Apr

(100)

| Rosalyn | Bryant | USA 56 | 52.63 | | 5q3 | FOT | Los Angeles | 17 Jun |
| Tanya | McIntosh | USA 66 | 52.64 | | 1 | TAC-j | Los Angeles | 24 Jun |

(102)   (120)

Christine	Nathler	GDR 66	52.65	30 Jun		Nicole	Leistenschneider	FRG 67	52.89	20 Jul
Zuzana	Moravcikova	CS 56	52.66	2 Jun		P.T.	Usha	IND 64	52.90	14 Sep
Tracey	Lawton	UK 62	52.67	8 Jul		Daniela	Gamalie	RUM 67	52.91	16 Sep
Jane	Parry	UK 64	52.69	10 Jun		Christine	Wahl	FRG 67	52.92	3 Jun
Christiane	Brinkmann	FRG 62	52.71	26 May		Cristina	Cojocaru	RUM 62	52.92	16 Jun
Vera	Tylova	CS 60	52.72	2 Jun		Christina	Sussiek	FRG 60	52.94	15 Jun
Renee	Ross	USA 63	52.72	16 Jun		Tania	Miranda	BRA 58	52.96	17 Jun
Rosalyn	Dunlap	USA 61	52.73	12 May		Margarita	Volskite	SU 61	52.96	19 Jul
						Sigrun	Ludwigs	GDR 65	52.97	13 May
						Maree	Holland	AUS 63	52.99	31 Mar

(110)

Malinka	Girova	BUL 66	52.78	28 Jul
Michele	Morris	USA 64	52.79	13 May
Robbin	Bell	USA 60	52.79	17 Jun
Vera	Akchurina	SU 57	52.79	15 Sep
Randy	Givens	USA 62	52.80	18 May
Angela	Wright	USA 61	52.80	29 Aug
Erika	Rossi	ITA 55	52.81	4 Jul
Janet	Davis	USA 65	52.85	5 May
Elke	Decker	FRG 57	52.85	23 Jun
Arlise	Emerson	USA 61	52.88	17 Jun

(130)

Marcia	Tate	JAM 61	53.01	13 Apr
Claudia	Steger	FRG 59	53.01	31 May
Pam	Oliver	USA	53.02	5 May
Gisela	Kinzel	FRG 61	53.02	23 Jun
Natasa	Seliskar	YUG 60	53.05	8 Sep
Yanka	Dimova	BUL 59		
Terri	Turner	USA 63	53.07	28 Apr
Bonka	Dimova	BUL 56	53.08	16 Jun
Loreen	Hall	UK 67	53.08	29 Jul
Larisa	Lesnykh	SU 64	53.09	9 Jun

373

1984 Lists – Women

(140)

Sharon	Dabney	USA 57	53.09		16 Jun
Iulia	Radu	RUM 59	53.09		10 Jul
Debbie	Flintoff	AUS 60	53.09		16 Jul
Christine	Slythe	CAN 61	A53.11		22 May
Kerstin	Jahn	GDR 65	53.11		18 Aug
Linda	Forsyth	UK 60	53.12		5 May
Leanne	Cassidy	AUS 60	53.13		3 Mar
Petra	Pfaff	GDR 60	53.14		15 Jul
Sadia	Sowunmi	NIG 64	53.16		21 Apr
Paulette	Blalock	USA 67	53.20		19 May

(150)

Marcella	Kendall	GUY 64	53.20		20 May
Lyudmila	Gaman	SU 60	53.20		7 Sep
Joyce	Wilson	USA 64	53.22		5 May
Joy	Hutchings	USA	53.22		26 May
Martina	Steuk	GDR 59	53.23		5 May
Mary	Wagner	FRG 61	53.24		2 Jun
Janice	Carter	JAM 66	53.24		24 Aug
Delisa	Walton	USA 61	53.25		6 May
Mary	Jones	USA	53.26		5 May
Yordanka	Krumova	BUL 59	53.26		2 Jun

(150)

Antoaneta	Yancheva	BUL 64	53.26		2 Jun
Erika	Szopori	HUN 63	53.27		26 Jul
Marie Lande	Mathieu	PR 56	53.27		4 Aug
Ulrike	Sommer	FRG 59	53.30		23 Jun
Elisabeth	Hofstetter	SWZ 55	53.32		16 Jun
Annette	Campbell	USA 62	53.33		20 Apr
Nathalie	Simon	FRA 62	53.34		29 Jun
Erzsebet	Szabo	HUN 63	53.35		23 Jun
Yelena	Vinogradova	SU 64	53.36		4 Aug
Loretta	Edwards	USA 59	53.38		6 May

(170)

Kaylene	Coster	AUS 61	53.40		3 Mar
Tatyana	Grebenchuk	SU 60	53.40		5 Jul

Indoor marks

Christina	Lathan	GDR 58	51.75	i	
Erika	Rossi	ITA 55	52.37	i	

Christina	Sussiek	FRG 60	52.66	i	11 Feb
Milena	Matejkovicova	CS 61	52.74	i	1 Feb
Natalya	Denisko	SU 55	52.91	i	19 Feb
Larisa	Krylova	SU 55	52.97	i	19 Feb
Sabine	Everts	FRG 61	53.00	i	15 Jan
Ellen	Fiedler	GDR 58	53.28	i	15 Jan
Sylvia	Kirchner	GDR 63	53.32	i	15 Jan
Helga	Arendt	FRG 64	53.41	i	11 Feb

Carlon	Blackman	BAR 65	53.42		12 May
Heather	Barralet	AUS 54	53.42		1 Jul
Ella	Kovacs	RUM 64	53.44		2 Sep
Michelle	Collins	USA	53.45		19 May
Tudorita	Chidu	RUM 67	53.45		4 Aug
Renata	Cernochova	CS 65	53.46		9 Jun
Marita	Arente	SU 57	53.46		27 Aug
Linda	Keough	UK 63	53.46		7 Sep

(180)

Ellen	Fiedler	GDR 58	53.47		27 Jul
Nicole	Ali	CAN 64	53.48		12 May
Svetlana	Andreyeva	SU 65	53.48		13 Jul
Desiree	de Leeuw	HOL 59	53.49		24 Jun
Nadezhda	Sudarova	SU 54	53.50		20 Jun
Ann	Lariviere	CAN 60	A53.53		22 May
Sally	Oakley	AUS 61	53.54		31 Mar
Patrizia	Lombardo	ITA 58	53.54		20 May
Svetlana	Romanovskaya	SU 66	53.54		23 Jun
Zhivka	Petkova	BUL 67	53.56		4 Jun

(190)

Rose	Jackson	NIG	53.57		11 May
Irina	Zhdanova	SU 63	53.57		21 Jun
Marina	Pereskokova	SU 63	53.57		4 Aug
Karen	Bakewell	USA	53.58		19 May
Durten	Behrendt	GDR 62	53.60		13 May
Andrea	Erdelyi	HUN 67	53.60		19 Jul
Karin	Lix	FRG 65	53.60		18 Aug
Giuseppina	Cirulli	ITA 59	53.60		2 Sep
Michelle	Maxey	USA	53.61		12 May
Sylvia	Sam	GDR 65	53.61		25 May

(200)

Katica	Matakovic	YUG 63	53.61		15 Sep
Caroline	O'Shea	IRL 60	53.62		14 Jul

(202)

3				Berlin	15 Jan
2			EC	Goteborg	4 Mar

Ruth	Patten	UK 57	53.47	i	14 Jan
Yvette	Wray	UK 58	53.49	i	14 Jan

(12)

(10)

	1	10	20	30	50	100	Under 52.00	Under 53.00
1980	48.88	51.00	51.31	51.60	52.12	53.00	44	99
1981	48.61	51.43	51.77	52.02	52.52	53.28	28	80
1982	48.16	50.63	51.18	51.79	52.08	52.95	42 1	08
1983	47.99	50.63	50.99	51.37	51.89	52.77	56	116
1984	48.16	49.74	50.56	51.19	51.89	52.63	56	130

1984 Lists – Women

Hand timing

Irina	Baskakova	SU 56	50.4		1		Moskva	8 Jul	
Marina	Ivanova	SU 62	51.5		1		Gorkiy	12 Aug	
Nina	Ruchayeva	SU 56	51.8		2		Gorkiy	12 Aug	
Marie Lande	Mathieu	PR 56	52.0		1		San Juan	2 Jun	
Edith	Otterman	RSA 66	A52.2		1		Pretoria	19 Mar	
Cristina	Cojocaru	RUM 62	52.2		1		Bucuresti	3 Jun	
Margarita	Navickaite	SU 61	52.2		2		Klaipeda	19 Aug	
Margarita	Volskite	SU 61	52.3		2		Moskva	8 Jul	
Vera	Akchurina	SU 57	52.3				Gorkiy	12 Aug	
Tatyana	Smeyan	SU 59	52.4		3		Moskva	8 Jul	
Marita	Arente	SU 57	52.4		4		Moskva	8 Jul	
Irina	Zaitseva	SU 63	52.5	16 Jun	Jennie	Badami	USA 61	53.0	12 May
Yelena	Vinogradova	SU 64	52.5	14 Jul	Lyudmila	Rybalko	SU 59	53.0	14 Jul
Aldona	Mendzorite	SU 61	52.5	19 Aug	Rita	Paulaviciene	SU 60	53.0	4 Aug
P.T.	Usha	IND 64	52.6	30 Apr	Nadezhda	Rumyantseva	SU 55	53.1	14 Jul
Kaylene	Coster	AUS 61	52.8	11 Feb	Olga	Mineyeva	SU 52	53.1	14 Jul
Bonka	Dimova	BUL 56	52.8		Irina	Zakharova	SU 64	53.1	14 Jul
Leanne	Cassidy	AUS 60	52.9	11 Feb	Galina	Reznikova	SU 60	53.1	7 Aug
Debbie	Flintoff	AUS 60	52.9	4 Mar	Olga	Airopetyan	SU 57	53.1	12 Aug
Larisa	Abramova	SU 61	53.0	7 Apr	Oralee	Fowler	BAH 61	53.2	26 May
					Madele	Naude	RSA 63	A53.2	29 Oct
Petra	Pfaff	GDR 60	52.1	i	2	NC	Senftenberg	22 Jan	

800 METRES

Irina	Podyalovskaya	SU 59	1:55.69		1		Kiev	22 Jun
Nadezhda	Olizarenko	SU 53	1:56.09		2		Kiev	22 Jun
Lyubov	Gurina	SU 57	1:56.26		1r1		Moskva	19 Jul
	Olizarenko		1:56.37		1	OD	Potsdam	21 Jul
Doina	Melinte	RUM 56	1:56.53		1	NC	Bucuresti	11 Jul
Lyudmila	Borisova	SU 59	1:56.78		3		Kiev	22 Jun
	Gurina		1:56.82		4		Kiev	22 Jun
Nina	Ruchayeva	SU 56	1:56.84		2r1		Moskva	19 Jul
Valentina	Zhukova	SU 59	1:56.97		5		Kiev	22 Jun
Yekaterina	Podkopayeva	SU 52	1:57.07		2	OD	Potsdam	21 Jul
Galina	Zakharova	SU 56	1:57.08		1	SU P	Baku	16 Sep
Tatyana	Kazankina (10)	SU 51	1:57.20		1h1	NC	Donetsk	7 Sep
	Podyalovskaya		1:57.24		1		Sochi	27 May
	Podyalovskaya		1:57.31		1	DRZ	Praha	17 Aug
	Melinte		1:57.36		1	Bisl	Oslo	28 Jun
Nadezhda	Zvyagintseva	SU 61	1:57.47		6		Kiev	22 Jun
	Borisova		1:57.53		3	OD	Potsdam	21 Jul
	Melinte		1:57.60		1	OG	Los Angeles	6 Aug
	Gurina		1:57.67		1r2	NC	Donetsk	8 Sep
Jarmila	Kratochvilova	CS 51	1:57.68		01	WK	Zurich	22 Aug
	Zvyagintseva		1:57.72		1h		Sochi	26 May
Hildegard	Ullrich	GDR 59	1:57.77		4	OD	Potsdam	21 Jul
	Podyalovskaya		1:57.84		1s		Kiev	21 Jun
Katrin	Wuhn	GDR 65	1:57.86		1	Skok	Celje	5 May
	Zhukova		1:57.87		3r1		Moskva	19 Jul
	Ullrich		1:57.89		1		Potsdam	25 May
Yelena	Medvedyeva	SU 59	1:57.90		1h	Znam	Sochi	9 Jun
	Podyalovskaya		1:57.93		1r1	Znam	Sochi	10 Jun
	Gurina		1:57.93		1	v Rum	Bucuresti	16 Sep
	Melinte		1:57.97		1		Firenze	13 Jun
	Olizarenko		1:57.97		1h		Kiev	20 Jun
	Gurina		1:57.98		s		Kiev	21 Jun
(32/15)								
Fita	Lovin	RUM 51	1:58.0		1h	NC	Bucuresti	10 Jul
Zuzana	Moravcikova	CS 56	1:58.06		2	DRZ	Praha	17 Aug
Antje	Schroder	GDR 63	1:58.08		1		Erfurt	12 May
Ravilya	Agletdinova	SU 60	1:58.08		1r2	Znam	Sochi	10 Jun
Svetlana	Kitova	SU 60	1:58.08		2s		Kiev	21 Jun

375

1984 Lists – Women

(20)

Maricica	Puica	RUM 50	1:58.12	2	NC	Bucuresti	11 Jul
Christine	Wachtel	GDR 65	1:58.24	3		Potsdam	25 May
Dagmar	Rubsam	GDR 62	1:58.36	4		Potsdam	25 May
Galina	Reznikova	SU 61	1:58.4	1		Alma Ata	8 Aug
Ella	Kovacs	RUM 64	1:58.42	3	NC	Bucuresti	11 Jul
Kim	Gallagher	USA 64	1:58.50	1	FOT	Los Angeles	19 Jun
Natalya	Artemova	SU 63	1:58.5	1		Leningrad	3 Jun
Ulrike	Bruns	GDR 53	1:58.60	5		Potsdam	25 May
Marita	Arente	SU 57	1:58.64	4r1		Moskva	19 Jul
Ruth	Wysocki	USA 57	1:58.65	2		Paris	4 Sep

(30)

Dalia	Matuseviciene	SU 62	1:58.7	1		Klaipeda	18 Aug
Vera	Chuvasheva	SU 58	1:58.8	1		Ustinovsk	15 Jul
Zamira	Zaitseva	SU 53	1:58.83	4h1	NC	Donetsk	7 Sep
Lyubov	Kiryukhina	SU 63	1:58.87	5r1		Moskva	19 Jul
Roswitha	Gerdes	FRG 61	1:58.88	4	WK	Zurich	22 Aug
Lyudmila	Veselkova	SU 50	1:58.9	2		Leningrad	3 Jun
Olga	Mineyeva	SU 52	1:58.92	1h2	NC	Donetsk	7 Sep
Lyubov	Kremleva	SU 61	1:58.95	3s		Kiev	21 Jun
Valentina	Lastovka	SU 58	1:59.0	2		Ryazan	11 Aug
Nina	Vershinina	SU 58	1:59.04	5s		Kiev	21 Jun

(40)

Gabriella	Dorio	ITA 57	1:59.05	4	OG	Los Angeles	6 Aug
Olga	Zhuravleva	SU 56	1:59.1	3		Ryazan	11 Aug
Olga	Dogadina	SU 59	1:59.2	2		Ustinovsk	15 Jul
Lyudmila	Medvedyeva	SU 57	1:59.30	4h2	NC	Donetsk	7 Sep
Vera	Dodika	SU 59	1:59.33	5r2	Znam	Sochi	10 Jun
Tatyana	Pozdnyakova	SU 56	1:59.4	3		Moskva	6 Jul
Lyubov	Lapina	SU 54	1:59.4	4		Ustinovsk	15 Jul
Andzhela	Romanova	SU 61	1:59.5	4		Moskva	6 Jul
Sigrun	Ludwigs	GDR 65	1:59.53	1		Potsdam	5 May
Natalya	Boborova	SU 59	1:59.6	1		Leningrad	11 Aug

(50)

Olga	Parlyuk	SU 63	1:59.7	2		Leningrad	11 Aug
Robin	Campbell	USA 59	1:59.77	3	FOT	Los Angeles	19 Jun
Christiane	Wartenberg	GDR 56	1:59.84	3		Dresden	27 Jul
Claudette	Groenendaal	USA 63	1:59.98	1		Oslo	21 Jul
Margrit	Klinger	FRG 60	2:00.00	3s2	OG	Los Angeles	4 Aug
Cristina	Cojocaru	RUM 62	2:00.0				
Lidia	Volodina	SU 53	2:00.0			Moskva	15 Jul
Durten	Behrendt	GDR 62	2:00.02	2		Potsdam	5 May
Lorraine	Baker	UK 64	2:00.03	5	OG	Los Angeles	6 Aug
Valentina	Furletova	SU 66	2:00.04	h	Znam	Sochi	9 Jun

(60)

Galina	Afonina	SU 62	2:00.04	s		Kiev	21 Jun
Chris	Gregorek	USA 59	2:00.06	1		Gavle	9 Jul
Nadezhda	Raldugina	SU 57	2:00.10	h		Sochi	26 May
Yanka	Dimova	BUL 59	2:00.12	6	OD	Potsdam	21 Jul
Jolanta	Januchta	POL 55	2:00.12	7	OD	Potsdam	21 Jul
Vanya	Stoyanova	BUL 58	2:00.2	1		Stara Zagora	23 Jun
Mariana	Simianu	RUM 64	2:00.27	2	RumIC	Bucuresti	10 Jun
Ellen	Schulz	GDR 62	2:00.29	4	NC	Erfurt	2 Jun
Nina	Gritskevich	SU 58	2:00.31	7h2	NC	Donetsk	7 Sep
Paula	Ilie	RUM 63	2:00.33	4	NC	Bucuresti	11 Jul

1984 Lists – Women

(70)

Essie	Washington	USA 57	2:00.35		3s1	FOT	Los Angeles	17 Jun
Tatyana	Khamitova	SU 61	2:00.4		1		Leningrad	7 Jul
Shireen	Bailey	UK 59	2:00.44		3		Oslo	21 Jul
Cynthia	Warner	USA 60	2:00.48		4s1	FOT	Los Angeles	17 Jun
Heather	Barralet	AUS 54	2:00.50		1		Adelaide	14 Mar
Julia	Noskova	SU 60	2:00.51		5r2	NC	Donetsk	8 Sep
Aurica	Mitrea	RUM 59	2:00.6		2		Bucuresti	16 Jun
Caroline	O'Shea	IRL 60	2:00.70		3		Cork	3 Jul
Jill	McCabe	SWE 62	2:00.71		3	BisI	Oslo	28 Jun
Lidia	Svechikhina	SU 52	2:00.83		3		Moskva	5 Aug

(80)

Zola	Budd	RSA 66	2:00.9		1		Kroonstad	16 Mar
Elly	van Hulst	HOL 59	2:00.92		1	DNG	Stockholm	2 Jul
Delisa	Walton	USA 61	2:00.94		5s1	FOT	Los Angeles	17 Jun
Sue	Addison	USA 56	2:00.98		6s1	FOT	Los Angeles	17 Jun
Aldona	Mendzorite	SU 61	2:01.0		2		Klaipeda	19 Aug
Brit	McRoberts	CAN 57	2:01.06		4	Nik	Nice	20 Aug
Katalin	Szalai	HUN 61	2:01.07		2		Koblenz	29 Aug
Lynne	MacDougall	UK 65	2:01.11		2		London	18 Aug
Diana	Richburg	USA 63	2:01.12		1	Pepsi	Westwood	13 May
Joetta	Clark	USA 62	2:01.15		1		Baton Rouge	13 May

(90)

Jane	Finch	UK 59	2:01.15		3		London	18 Aug
Angelita	Lind	PR 59	2:01.31		2		Walnut, CA	25 Jul
Svetlana	Sofina	SU 62	2:01.33		4r2		Moskva	19 Jul
Ivana	Kleinova	CS 62	2:01.36		2		Praha	28 Aug
Sylvia	Schierjott	GDR 63	2:01.40		5	BGP	Budapest	20 Aug
Lyudmila	Lagutenko	SU 62	2:01.4				Tula	15 Jul
Svetlana	Guskova	SU 59	2:01.4		1		Kishinyov	11 Aug
Astrid	Pfeiffer	GDR 64	2:01.43		4		Potsdam	5 May
Galina	Rakova	SU 59	2:01.48		5r2		Moskva	19 Jul
Kaylene	Coster	AUS 61	2:01.50		2		Adelaide	14 Mar

(100)

Nadezhda	Gizatulina	SU 59	2:01.5		6		Ustinovsk	15 Jul
Gabriele	Wagner	GDR 59	2:01.53		5		Potsdam	5 May
Louise	Romo	USA 63	2:01.59		7s1	FOT	Los Angeles	17 Jun

(103)

Christina	Boxer	UK 57	2:01.64	28 May	Nathalie	Thoumas	FRA 62	2:02.33	26 May
Teena	Colebrook	UK 56	2:01.65	21 Jul	Kirsty	McDermott	UK 62	2:02.34	3 Jul
Olga	Snitsar	SU 63	2:01.67	20 Jun					
Gail	Conway	USA 62	2:01.70	16 Jun	(120)				
Ranza	Clark	CAN 61	2:01.76	16 Jul					
Christine	Benning	UK 55	2:01.77	21 Jul	Mirela	Sket	YUG 65	2:02.35	16 Sep
Nina	Vasilkiv	SU 63	2:01.84	7 Sep	Cornelia	Burki	SWZ 53	2:02.37	29 Aug
					Yelena	Zhemchugova	SU 60	2:02.4	14 Jul
(110)					Kaisa	Ylimaki	FIN 60	2:02.42	28 Jun
					Agnese	Possamai	ITA 53	2:02.42	22 Aug
Helga	van Wermeskerken	RSA 60	2:01.92	14 Apr	Milena	Matejkovicova	CS 61	2:02.43	21 Jul
Yelena	Lesnikova	SU 61	2:01.97	9 Jun	Monika	Bens	FRG 66	2:02.45	9 Jun
Lenuta	Rata	RUM 66	2:01.98	10 Jul	Maria	Radu	RUM 59	2:02.49	13 Jun
Michelle	Baumgartner	AUS 63	2:02.10	14 Mar	Nery	Mc Keen	CUB 57	2:02.5	19 May
Karoline	Kafer	AUT 54	2:02.11	29 Aug	Irina	Solomatina	SU 60	2:02.5	11 Aug
Elize	Fouche	RSA 60	2:02.18	14 Apr					
Anne	Purvis	UK 59	2:02.32	2 Jul	(130)				
Martina	Steuk	GDR 59	2:02.32	15 Jul					

377

1984 Lists – Women

Grace	Verbeek	CAN 58	2:02.53	14 Jul	(160)					
Aurora	Miu	RUM 63	2:02.57	11 Jul						
Martina	van Dam	FRG 58	2:02.6	3 Aug	Lyudmila	Pavlova	SU 59	2:03.2	23 Sep	
Brygida	Bak	POL 61	2:02.61	24 Jun	Rose	Monday	USA 59	2:03.21	16 Jun	
Petra	Kleinbrahm	FRG 59	2:02.62	24 Jun	Maria	Caba	RUM 66	2:03.24	29 Jul	
Laima	Baikauskaite	SU 56	2:02.65	7 Sep	Birgit	Brudel	GDR 61	2:03.25	25 May	
Isabelle	De Bruycker	BEL 63	2:02.68	7 Sep	Larisa	Zavarukhina	SU 64	2:03.27		
Eranee	van Zyl	RSA 62	2:02.69	14 Apr	Ilze	Venter	RSA 59	A2:03.29	20 Feb	
Natalya	Betekhtina	SU 61	2:02.7	23 Sep	Annette	Campbell	USA 62	2:03.30	12 May	
Kornelija	Matesic	YUG 66	2:02.73	16 Sep	Tatyana	Veremeyeva	SU 59	2:03.3	15 Aug	
(140)					Sandra	Gasser	SWZ 62	2:03.38	17 Aug	
					Svetlana	Barybina	SU 60	2:03.39		
Diane	Edwards	UK 66	2:02.75	16 Sep	(170)					
Terri-Anne	Cater	AUS 56	2:02.80	14 Mar						
Tatyana	Arefyeva	SU 62	2:02.8	6 Jul	Yelena	Skiba	SU 64	2:03.4		
Tina	Krebs	DEN 63	2:02.81	21 Apr	Mitica	Junghiatu	RUM 62	2:03.52		
Lee	Arbogast	USA 58	2:02.82	13 May	Elena	Lina	RUM 54	2:03.59	26 May	
Georgia	Troubouki	GRE 60	2:02.87	4 Jul	Patty	Bradley	USA 62	2:03.59	2 Jun	
Vera	Michallek	FRG 58	2:02.9	3 Aug	Heike	Huneke	FRG 66	2:03.59	29 Aug	
Brigitte	Kraus	FRG 56	2:02.93	20 Jul						
Margarita	Volskite	SU 61	2:02.94	19 Jul						
Mihaela	Rachieru	RUM 62	2:02.99	19 Aug						

Matuseviciene (1:58.7) also did 1:58.83 h NC Donetsk 7 Sep;

(150)

Chuvasheva (1:58.8) also did 1:59.01 6r1 Moskva 19 Jul;

Slobodanka	Colovic	YUG 65	2:03.0	3 Jun
Rimma	Batalova	SU 64	2:03.0	21 Jun
Tatyana	Sychova	SU 64	2:03.0	14 Jul
Irina	Nikitina	SU 61	2:03.1	29 Apr
Christine	Slythe	CAN 61	2:03.1	
Nikolina	Shtereva	BUL 55	2:03.11	17 Jun
Margit	Schultheiss	FRG 56	2:03.14	9 Jun
Rommy	Stade	GDR 59	2:03.15	5 May
Galina	Bochkayeva	SU 63	2:03.17	19 Jul
Lyubov	Smolka	SU 52	2:03.2	3 May

Stoyanova (2:00.2) also did 2:00.35 4 v GDR,Rum Sofia 17 Jun;

Zhemchugova (2:02.4) also did 2:02.48 19 Jul;

Colovic (2:03.0) also did 2:03.04 17 Jun.

Marks made in mixed race with men

Jolanta	Januchta	POL 55	1:59.57		Sopot	2 Aug
Kaylene	Coster	AUS 61	2:00.2		Sydney	24 Mar
Heather	Barralet	AUS 54	2:00.23		Melbourne	6 Mar
Christine	Slythe	CAN 61	2:00.4		Sherbrooke	11 Jul
Terri-Anne	Cater	AUS 56	2:00.5		Melbourne	11 Feb
Michelle	Baumgartner	AUS 63	2:01.2		Melbourne	25 Feb
Grace	Verbeek	CAN 58	2:01.2		North York	16 Jul
Maxine	Corcoran	AUS 54	2:02.9			14 Feb
Camille	Cato	CAN 63	2:03.4			16 Jul

Indoor marks

Milena	Matejkovicova	CS 61	1:59.43	i	1		Stuttgart	3 Feb
Svetlana	Popova	SU 59	2:01.65	i		10 Feb	Brigitte	Bruckner	FRG 56	2:02.49	i	11 Feb
Petra	Kleinbrahm	FRG 59	2:01.67	i		11 Feb	Tina	Krebs	DEN 63	2:02.64	i	10 Feb
Martina	van Dam	FRG 58	2:02.17	i		11 Feb	Jana	Cervenkova	CS 55	2:03.05	i	4 Feb
Maria	Radu	RUM 59	2:02.47	i		4 Feb	Ellen	Fiedler	GDR 58	2:03.1	i	7 Jan

(9)

1984 Lists – Women

	1	10	20	30	50	100	Under 2:00.0	Under 2:02.0
1980	1:53.43	1:57.0	1:58.51	1:59.20	2:00.5	2:02.5	41	84
1981	1:56.98	1:58.22	1:59.22	2:00.2	2:01.00	2:02.82	26	78
1982	1:55.05	1:57.3	1:59.0	1:59.93	2:00.9	2:02.8	30	83
1983	1:53.28	1:57.4	1:58.5	1:59.28	2:00.1	2:01.91	45	101
1984	1:55.69	1:57.20	1:58.08	1:58.65	1:59.6	2:01.50	54	113

1000 METRES

Ulrike	Bruns	GDR 53	2:34.2		1		Potsdam	12 Jul
Hildegard	Ullrich	GDR 59	2:34.8		2		Potsdam	12 Jul
Gabriella	Dorio	ITA 57	2:34.86		1		Riccione	26 Aug
Katrin	Wuhn	GDR 65	2:35.4		3		Potsdam	12 Jul
Christiane	Wartenberg	GDR 56	2:35.5		4		Potsdam	12 Jul
Maricica	Puica	RUM 50	2:35.7		1		Poiana Brasov	1 Jun
Yanka	Dimova	BUL 59	2:36.58		1		Sofia	8 Aug
Galina	Kireyeva	SU 56	2:36.9		1		Leningrad	4 Aug
Roswitha	Gerdes	FRG 61	2:37.68		1		Hannover	19 Aug
Diana	Richburg	USA 63	2:37.92		2		Riccione	26 Aug
(10)
Irina	Solomatina	SU 60	2:38.6		2		Leningrad	4 Aug
Lynn	Williams	CAN 60	2:39.23		2		San Diego	30 Jul
Marita	Arente	SU 57	2:39.3		1		Riga	12 Aug
Agnese	Possamai	ITA 53	2:39.36		3		Riccione	26 Aug
Debbie	Scott	CAN 58	2:39.76		3		San Diego	30 Jul
(15)

Indoor marks

Nadezhda	Raldugina	SU 57	2:36.07	i	1		Moskva	11 Feb
Yekaterina	Podkopayeva	SU 52	2:36.35	i	2		Moskva	11 Feb
Ravilya	Agletdinova	SU 60	2:37.18	i	3		Moskva	11 Feb
Natalya	Artemova	SU 63	2:37.45	i	4		Moskva	11 Feb
Tamara	Koba	SU 57	2:37.51	i	5		Moskva	11 Feb
Natalya	Boborova	SU 59	2:38.15	i	6		Moskva	11 Feb
Svetlana	Guskova	SU 59	2:38.69	i	7		Moskva	11 Feb
Astrid	Pfeiffer	GDR 64	2:39.24	i	3		Berlin	14 Jan
Tatyana	Khamitova	SU 61	2:39.4	i	1		Donetsk	29 Jan
Irina	Nikitina	SU 61	2:39.67	i	8		Moskva	11 Feb
(10)

1500 METRES

Nadezhda	Raldugina	SU 57	3:56.63		1	DRZ	Praha	18 Aug
Yekaterina	Podkopayeva	SU 52	3:56.65		1		Rieti	2 Sep
Maricica	Puica	RUM 50	3:57.22		1		Bucuresti	1 Jul
Tatyana	Pozdnyakova	SU 56	3:57.70		2		Rieti	2 Sep
Galina	Zakharova	SU 56	3:57.72		1	SU P	Baku	14 Sep
Doina	Melinte	RUM 56	3:58.1		1	RumIC	Bucuresti	9 Jun
	Melinte		3:58.26		1	NC	Bucuresti	12 Jul
Tatyana	Kazankina	SU 51	3:58.63		2	SU P	Baku	14 Sep
Ravilya	Agletdinova	SU 60	3:58.70		2	DRZ	Praha	18 Aug
	Pozdnyakova		3:58.9		1		Ryazan	12 Aug

379

1984 Lists – Women

Mary	Decker	USA 58	3:59.19		1		Eugene	4 Jun
	Podkopayeva		3:59.83		1		Moskva	3 Aug
	Agletdinova		3:59.84		1		Kiev	24 Jun
Ruth	Wysocki	USA 57	4:00.18		1	FOT	Los Angeles	24 Jun
	Zakharova		4:00.19		2		Moskva	3 Aug
	Decker		4:00.40		2	FOT	Los Angeles	24 Jun
Lyudmila	Medvedyeva	SU 57	4:00.42		3	SU P	Baku	14 Sep
Zamira	Zaitseva	SU 53	4:00.50		1		Moskva	20 Jul
	Podkopayeva		4:00.56		2		Kiev	24 Jun
	Raldugina		4:00.57		3		Kiev	24 Jun
Christina	Boxer	UK 57	4:00.57		1		Gateshead	6 Jul
Natalya	Boborova	SU 59	4:00.62		2		Moskva	20 Jul
	Boborova		4:00.63		3		Moskva	3 Aug
Natalya	Artemova	SU 63	4:00.68		3		Rieti	2 Sep
	Pozdnyakova		4:01.17		4		Kiev	24 Jun
Ulrike	Bruns	GDR 53	4:01.38		1	NC	Erfurt	3 Jun
Fita	Lovin	RUM 51	4:01.43		2	NC	Bucuresti	12 Jul
	Zaitseva		4:01.43		4		Moskva	3 Aug
	Artemova		4:01.57		5		Kiev	24 Jun
	Bruns		4:01.6		1		Potsdam	31 May
	Podkopayeva		4:01.61		3	DRZ	Praha	18 Aug
Alla	Yushina	SU 58	4:01.80		5		Moskva	3 Aug
Zola	Budd	RSA 66	4:01.81		1		Port Elizabeth	21 Mar
Christine	Benning	UK 55	4:01.83		2		Gateshead	6 Jul
(20)								
Gabriella	Dorio	ITA 57	4:01.96	4			Rieti	2 Sep
Lyubov	Kremleva	SU 61	4:02.04	6			Kiev	24 Jun
Lidia	Volodina	SU 53	4:02.25	8			Kiev	24 Jun
Olga	Zhuravleva	SU 56	4:02.33	h			Kiev	22 Jun
Lyudmila	Veselkova	SU 50	4:02.37	h			Kiev	22 Jun
Tatyana	Khamitova	SU 61	4:02.41	3			Moskva	20 Jul
Svetlana	Guskova	SU 59	4:03.05	1		BGP	Budapest	20 Aug
Maria	Radu	RUM 59	4:03.08	3		NC	Bucuresti	12 Jul
Vanya	Stoyanova	BUL 58	4:03.14	h		Znam	Sochi	9 Jun
Irina	Nikitina	SU 61	4:03.2	2			Ryazan	12 Aug
(30)								
Katalin	Szalai	HUN 61	4:03.51	3		BGP	Budapest	20 Aug
Andzhela	Romanova	SU 61	4:03.70	h			Kiev	22 Jun
Diana	Richburg	USA 63	4:04.07	3		FOT	Los Angeles	24 Jun
Olga	Parlyuk	SU 63	4:04.16	h			Kiev	22 Jun
Olga	Dvirna	SU 53	4:04.35	h			Kiev	22 Jun
Roswitha	Gerdes	FRG 61	4:04.41	4		OG	Los Angeles	11 Aug
Yelena	Zhupiyeva	SU 60	4:04.44	h			Kiev	22 Jun
Nadezhda	Olizarenko	SU 53	4:04.94	6			Rieti	2 Sep
Lidia	Svechikhina	SU 52	4:05.13	6			Moskva	3 Aug
Agnese	Possamai	ITA 53	4:05.14	4		BGP	Budapest	20 Aug
(40)								
Brit	McRoberts	CAN 57	4:05.23	4			Koln	26 Aug
Elly	van Hulst	HOL 59	4:05.44	1			Hengelo	6 Jul
Margrit	Klinger	FRG 60	4:05.50	1		v CS,Fra,Pol	Hannover	16 Jun
Ivana	Kleinova	CS 62	4:05.52	5		BGP	Budapest	20 Aug
Christiane	Wartenberg	GDR 56	4:05.53	1			Karl-Marx-Stadt	20 May
Cornelia	Burki	SWZ 53	4:05.67	7			Rieti	2 Sep
Irina	Lebedinskaya	SU 61	4:05.7	2			Dnepropetrovsk	4 Aug
Lynne	MacDougall	UK 65	4:05.96	6		BGP	Budapest	20 Aug
Brigitte	Kraus	FRG 56	4:06.00	2		v CS,Fra,Pol	Hannover	16 Jun
Francie	Larrieu	USA 52	4:06.09	1			Burnaby	16 Jul
(50)								
Lynn	Williams	CAN 60	4:06.09	6			Koln	26 Aug
Darlene	Beckford	USA 61	4:06.17	2			Hengelo	6 Jul
Mariana	Simianu	RUM 64	4:06.2	3		RumIC	Bucuresti	9 Jun
Olga	Bondarenko	SU 60	4:06.2	2			Chelyabinsk	28 Jul
Tatyana	Leonova	SU 56	4:06.21	h			Kiev	22 Jun

1984 Lists – Women

Vera	Michallek	FRG 58	4:06.25	7		Koln	26 Aug
Ella	Kovacs	RUM 64	4:06.38	2		Bucuresti	18 Aug
Missy	Kane	USA 55	4:06.47	4	FOT	Los Angeles	24 Jun
Pavlina	Evro	ALB 65	4:06.62	1	Nik	Nice	20 Aug
Hildegard	Ullrich	GDR 59	4:06.65	2	NC	Erfurt	3 Jun
(60)							
Lyudmila	Baranova	SU 50	4:06.7	2		Ryazan	2 Jul
Sue	Addison	USA 56	4:06.91	5	FOT	Los Angeles	24 Jun
Galina	Kireyeva	SU 56	4:06.94	h	Znam	Sochi	9 Jun
Lyudmila	Legotnikova	SU 60	4:06.97	h		Kiev	22 Jun
Marina	Rodchenkova	SU 61	4:07.27			Moskva	3 Aug
Valentina	Zhukova	SU 59	4:07.39	8		Moskva	20 Jul
Tatyana	Lunegova	SU 57	4:07.41	h		Kiev	22 Jun
Ranza	Clark	CAN 61	4:07.50	8		Koln	26 Aug
Gillian	Green	UK 58	4:07.90	2	WAAA	London	16 Jun
Kim	Gallagher	USA 64	4:08.08	1	TAC	San Jose	9 Jun
(70)							
Claudette	Groenendaal	USA 63	4:08.13	2		Lausanne	10 Jul
Tatyana	Sychova	SU 57	4:08.2	4		Ryazan	12 Aug
Lyubov	Smolka	SU 52	4:08.3	2		Kiev	14 Aug
Joan	Hansen	USA 58	4:08.4	2		Berkeley	14 Jul
Laima	Baikauskaite	SU 56	4:08.4	2		Vilnius	4 Aug
Julia	Noskova	SU 60	4:08.4	6		Ryazan	12 Aug
Galina	Rakova	SU 59	4:08.57	h	Znam	Sochi	9 Jun
Wendy	Sly	UK 59	4:08.69	3	Pre	Eugene	21 Jul
Sylvia	Schierjott	GDR 63	4:08.82	3		Berlin	24 May
Nina	Vasilkiv	SU 63	4:09.0	3		Kiev	14 Aug
(80)							
Jill	Haworth	USA 61	4:09.01	4		Lausanne	10 Jul
Corine	De Baets	BEL 63	4:09.02	4	VD	Bruxelles	24 Aug
Debbie	Scott	CAN 58	4:09.16	6h2	OG	Los Angeles	9 Aug
Louise	Romo	USA 63	4:09.29	7	FOT	Los Angeles	24 Jun
Nina	Gritskevich	SU 58	4:09.30	11	NC	Donetsk	9 Sep
Olga	Politova	SU 64	4:09.33	10r2		Sochi	26 May
Cleopatra	Palaceanu	RUM 68	4:09.37	5	NC	Bucuresti	12 Jul
Chris	Gregorek	USA 59	4:09.42	3		Gateshead	6 Jul
Donna	Gould	AUS 66	4:09.54	4		Burnaby	16 Jul
Olga	Dogadina	SU 59	4:09.7	7		Ryazan	12 Aug
(90)							
Galina	Kuimova	SU 54	4:09.71	h	Znam	Sochi	9 Jun
Margarita	Zhupikova	SU 65	4:09.71	h		Kiev	22 Jun
Tatyana	Mamayeva	SU 62	4:09.8	2		Riga	5 Jul
Rasa	Virsilovaite	SU 62	4:09.91			Kiev	22 Jun
Cindy	Bremser	USA 53	4:09.94	3	TAC	San Jose	9 Jun
Isabelle	De Bruycker	BEL 63	4:09.98	7	VD	Bruxelles	24 Aug
Sandra	Gasser	SWZ 62	4:10.04	5		Lausanne	10 Jul
Maggie	Keyes	USA 58	4:10.19	6		Lausanne	10 Jul
Nadezhda	Stepanova	SU 59	4:10.2	3		Riga	5 Jul
Katrin	Wuhn	GDR 65	4:10.22	2		Rijeka	2 May
(100)							
Birgit	Schmidt	FRG 63	4:10.38	26 Aug			
Lyubov	Konyukhova	SU 56	4:10.40	27 Apr			
Lyudmila	Matveyeva	SU 57	4:10.4	15 Jul			
Jo	White	UK 60	4:10.41	10 Jun			
Cathie	Twomey	USA 56	4:10.50	9 Jul			
Irina	Karbolina	SU 60	4:10.5	15 Jul			
Valentina	Lastovka	SU 58	4:10.5	12 Aug			
Diane	Rodger	NZ 56	4:10.62	16 Jul			
Natalya	Sorokiyevskaya	SU 61	4:10.67	14 Sep			
Tamara	Koba	SU 57	4:10.7	12 May			
(110)							
Astrid	Pfeiffer	GDR 64	4:10.71	24 May			
Ruth	Smeeth	UK 60	4:10.76	16 Jun			
Gabriele	Wagner	GDR 59	4:10.78	24 May			
Rositsa	Ekova	BUL 61	4:10.78	2 Jun			
Svetlana	Barybina	SU 60	4:10.90	6 Jul			
Jana	Cervenkova	CS 55	4:10.97	20 Aug			
Lee	Arbogast	USA 58	4:11.15	22 Jun			
Irina	Mozharova	SU 58	4:11.2	22 Sep			
Suzanne	Morley	UK 57	4:11.21	6 Jul			
Annette	Sergent	FRA 62	4:11.27	1 Jul			
(120)							
Jan	Merrill	USA 56	4:11.3 +	13 May			
Cindy	Grant	CAN 63	4:11.31	16 Jul			
Regina	Jacobs	USA 63	4:11.33	22 Jun			
Antje	Schroder	GDR 63	4:11.36	2 May			
PattiSue	Plumer	USA 62	4:11.36	10 Jul			
Olga	Savoshko	SU 61	4:11.4	4 Aug			
Birgit	Brudel	GDR 61	4:11.43	16 Jun			

1984 Lists – Women

Mary	Knisely	USA 59	4:11.43	21 Jul
Lenuta	Rata	RUM 66	4:11.45	12 Jul
Ines	Deselaers	FRG 63	4:11.47	9 Jun
(130)				
Marina	Belyayeva	SU 58	4:11.48	20 May
Yvonne	Murray	UK 64	4:11.5 +	18 Aug
Radka	Naplatanova	BUL 57	4:11.51	19 May
Janet	Marlow	UK 58	4:11.51	16 Jun
Elena	Fidatov	RUM 60	4:11.6	9 Jun
Yelena	Medvedyeva	SU 59	4:11.65	9 Sep
Tatyana	Veremeyeva	SU 59	4:11.7	14 Aug
Tatyana	Rubachova	SU 60	4:11.71	22 Jun
Cathy	Branta	USA 63	4:11.72	9 Jun
Yelena	Zhemchugova	SU 60	4:11.8	12 Aug
(140)				
Marina	Pluzhnikova	SU 63	4:11.8	22 Sep
Iulia	Ionescu	RUM 65	4:11.90	12 Jul
Jurate	Urbonaviciute	SU 62	4:11.91	6 Jul
Iva	Jurkova	CS 66	4:11.99	28 Aug
Vera	Burdina	SU 54	4:12.1	28 Jul
Aurora	Cunha	POR 59	4:12.14	16 Jun
Gabriele	Martins	GDR 62	4:12.19	26 Jul
Nadezhda	Gizatulina	SU 59	4:12.2	12 Aug
Eranee	van Zyl	RSA 62	4:12.3	21 Mar
Grete	Waitz	NOR 53	4:12.38	22 May
(150)				
Yelizaveta	Bradu	SU 54	4:12.38	9 Sep

Albina	Mefodyeva	SU 61	4:12.5	6 Jul
Carole	Bradford	UK 61	4:12.58	10 Jun
Kathy	Carter	UK 59	4:12.58	6 Jul
Mariana	Stanescu	RUM 64	4:12.63	18 Aug
Suzanne	Girard	USA 62	4:12.7	28 Apr
Stefa	Statkuviene	SU 63	4:12.7	4 Aug
Julie-Ann	Laughton	UK 59	4:12.79	10 Jun
Deborah	Pihl	USA 61	4:12.94	9 Jun
Galina	Kholod	SU 58	4:13.0	12 Aug
(160)				
Veronique	Rusch	FRA 59	4:13.26	1 Jul
Ingrid	Kristiansen	NOR 56	4:13.27	1 Jul
Monica	Joyce	IRL 58	4:13.3	14 Jul
Valentina	Yeltsova	SU 60	4:13.4	6 Jul
Ines	Bibernell	GDR 65	4:13.49	21 Jul
Zhanna	Tursunova	SU 57	4:13.6	7 Jul
Geri	Fitch	CAN 54	4:13.6	
Anna	Bukis	POL 53	4:13.69	1 Jun
Svetlana	Zhelnova	SU 59	4:13.8	14 Jul
Isabelle	Matthys	FRA 61	4:13.83	1 Jul
(170)				
Renata	Kokowska	POL 58	4:13.91	5 Aug
Irina	Matrosova	SU 62	4:13.95	22 Jun
Mirela	Sket	YUG 65	4:13.95	15 Sep
Christine	Hughes	NZ 59	4:13.98	
(174)				

Marks made in mixed race with men

Debbie	Scott	CAN 58	4:07.0				Burnaby	11 Jul

Geri	Fitch	CAN 54	4:11.8	11 Jul
Michelle	Baumgartner	AUS 63	4:12.0	18 Feb

Indoor marks

Svetlana	Popova	SU 59	4:09.22i
Alla	Libutina	SU 53	4:09.43i
Tamara	Koba	SU 57	4:10.49i	17 Feb
Monika	Schafer	FRG 59	4:12.24i	11 Feb

	1	10	20	30	50	100	Under 4:05.0	Under 4:10.0
1980	3:52.47	3:59.82	4:02.98	4:04.6	4:07.3	4:13.2	33	69
1981	3:57.78	4:01.44	4:03.88	4:05.5	4:08.78	4:13.60	25	64
1982	3:54.23	3:59.24	4:03.05	4:05.33	4:07.72	4:13.25	28	65
1983	3:57.12	4:01.4	4:03.36	4:04.77	4:08.32	4:12.2	32	63
1984	3:56.63	4:00.18	4:01.83	4:03.2	4:06.09	4:10.22	38	96

ONE MILE

Natalya	Artemova	SU 63	4:15.8		1		Leningrad	5 Aug
Ruth	Wysocki	USA 57	4:21.78		1	Coke	London	7 Sep
Christina	Boxer	UK 57	4:22.64		2	Coke	London	7 Sep
Mary	Decker	USA 58	4:22.92		1	Pepsi	Westwood	13 May
Christine	Benning	UK 55	4:24.57		3	Coke	London	7 Sep
Wendy	Sly	UK 59	4:28.07		1		London	18 Aug
	Decker		4:28.5 +		1		Eugene	3 Aug
Suzanne	Morley	UK 57	4:29.15		2		London	18 Aug
Francie	Larrieu	USA 52	4:29.79		2	Pepsi	Westwood	13 May
Lynne	MacDougall	UK 65	4:30.08		4	Coke	London	7 Sep

1984 Lists – Women

(10/9)

| Jan | Merrill | USA 56 | 4:30.12 | | 3 | Pepsi | Westwood | 13 May |

(10)

Yvonne	Murray	UK 64	4:30.25		3		London	18 Aug
Zola	Budd	UK 66	4:30.7 +		1		London	13 Jul
Cindy	Bremser	USA 53	4:30.78		4	Pepsi	Westwood	13 May
Ruth	Smeeth	UK 60	4:30.89		4		London	18 Aug
Jane	Furniss	UK 60	4:30.95		5		London	18 Aug
Brigitte	Kraus	FRG 56	4:31.34		1		Nelson	Feb
melia	Burki	SWZ 53	4:31.75		5	Coke	London	7 Sep
Carole	Bradford	UK 61	4:32.00		6		London	18 Aug
Jill	Haworth	USA 61	4:32.60		1		Edinburgh	17 Jul
Janet	Marlow	UK 58	4:33.53		7		London	18 Aug

(20)

Maggie	Keyes	USA 58	4:34.30		5	Pepsi	Westwood	13 May
Debbie	Peel	UK 58	4:34.70		8		London	18 Aug
Darlene	Beckford	USA 61	4:36.32		6	Pepsi	Westwood	13 May
Michele	Bush	USA 61	4:36.47		7	Pepsi	Westwood	13 May
Mary	Knisely	USA 59	4:37.5		1		Villanova	14 Jul
Diana	Richburg	USA 63	4:37.6		1		Boston	8 Jul
Monica	Joyce	IRL 58	4:37.74		8	Pepsi	Westwood	13 May
Sue	Addison	USA 56	4:37.99		9	Pepsi	Westwood	13 May

(28)

Indoor marks

Monica	Joyce	IRL 58	4:33.4	i	1		Inglewood, CA	10 Feb
Brit	McRoberts	CAN 57	4:33.91	i	1	TAC	New York	24 Feb
Angela	Chalmers	CAN 63	4:35.0	i	2		San Diego	17 Feb

2000 METRES

Tatyana	Kazankina	SU 51	5:28.72		1		Moskva	4 Aug
Tatyana	Pozdnyakova	SU 56	5:29.64		2		Moskva	4 Aug
Galina	Zakharova	SU 56	5:30.92		3		Moskva	4 Aug
Mary	Decker	USA 58	5:32.7		1		Eugene	3 Aug
Zola	Budd	UK 66	5:33.15		1		London	13 Jul
Christina	Boxer	UK 57	5:33.85		2		London	13 Jul
Christine	Benning	UK 55	5:37.00		3		London	13 Jul
Zamira	Zaitseva	SU 53	5:37.55		4		Moskva	4 Aug

(8)

3000 METRES

Tatyana	Kazankina	SU 51	8:22.62		1		Leningrad	26 Aug
Svetlana	Guskova	SU 59	8:29.59		1		Moskva	6 Aug
Tatyana	Pozdnyakova	SU 56	8:32.0		1		Ryazan	11 Aug
	Kazankina		8:33.01		1	DRZ	Praha	16 Aug
Maricica	Puica	RUM 50	8:33.57		1	NC	Bucuresti	10 Jul
	Pozdnyakova		8:34.35		1	Znam	Sochi	9 Jun
Mary	Decker	USA 58	8:34.91		1	FOT	Los Angeles	23 Jun
	Puica		8:35.05		1		Bucuresti	30 Jun
	Pozdnyakova		8:35.45		1	GGala	Roma	31 Aug
	Puica		8:35.96		1	OG	Los Angeles	10 Aug

383

1984 Lists – Women

Olga	Bondarenko	SU 60	8:36.20		2	Znam	Sochi	9 Jun
Ulrike	Bruns	GDR 53	8:36.38		1	OD	Berlin	20 Jul
	Puica		8:37.04		1		Firenze	13 Jun
Galina	Zakharova	SU 56	8:37.07		1	NC	Donetsk	8 Sep
Zola	Budd	RSA 66	8:37.5		1		Stellenbosch	29 Feb
	Guskova		8:37.63		2	NC	Donetsk	8 Sep
Alla	Yushina	SU 58	8:37.76		2	OD	Berlin	20 Jul
	Pozdnyakova		8:37.98		1	v Rum	Bucuresti	16 Sep
	Bruns		8:38.40		1	WK	Zurich	22 Aug
Cindy	Bremser	USA 53	8:38.60		2	WK	Zurich	22 Aug
Natalya	Artemova	SU 63	8:38.84		1		Kiev	20 Jun
	Pozdnyakova		8:39.02		3	NC	Donetsk	8 Sep
	Bondarenko		8:39.28		2		Kiev	20 Jun
Wendy	Sly	UK 59	8:39.47		2	OG	Los Angeles	10 Aug
Yelena	Zhupiyeva	SU 60	8:39.52		3		Kiev	20 Jun
Ingrid	Kristiansen	NOR 56	8:39.56		1		Oslo	21 Jul
	Kazankina		8:39.71		4		Kiev	20 Jun
	Zakharova		8:40.20		5		Kiev	20 Jun
	Budd	UK	8:40.22		1	OT	London	6 Jun
	Guskova		8:40.50		1		Moskva	19 Jul
	Artemova		8:40.53		2	DRZ	Praha	16 Aug
	Puica		8:40.89		2	GGala	Roma	31 Aug
Brigitte	Kraus	FRG 56	8:40.90		2		Firenze	13 Jun
(33/16)								
Zhanna	Tursunova	SU 57	8:41.07		6		Kiev	20 Jun
Joan	Hansen	USA 58	8:41.43		3	FOT	Los Angeles	23 Jun
Lyubov	Smolka	SU 52	8:41.72		4	NC	Donetsk	8 Sep
Lynn	Williams	CAN 60	8:42.14		3	OG	Los Angeles	10 Aug
(20)								
Christine	Benning	UK 55	8:44.46		3	WK	Zurich	22 Aug
Cornelia	Burki	SWZ 53	8:45.20		5	OG	Los Angeles	10 Aug
Agnese	Possamai	ITA 53	8:45.84		3h1	OG	Los Angeles	8 Aug
Lyubov	Konyukhova	SU 56	8:45.88		2		Moskva	19 Jul
Irina	Nikitina	SU 61	8:46.0		2		Ryazan	11 Aug
Tatyana	Lunegova	SU 57	8:46.32		6	Znam	Sochi	9 Jun
Aurora	Cunha	POR 59	8:46.37		4h1	OG	Los Angeles	8 Aug
Marina	Rodchenkova	SU 61	8:47.06		3		Moskva	6 Aug
Diane	Rodger	NZ 56	8:47.90		5h1	OG	Los Angeles	8 Aug
Rositsa	Ekova	BUL 61	8:47.94		5	OD	Berlin	20 Jul
(30)								
Jane	Furniss	UK 60	8:48.00		6h1	OG	Los Angeles	8 Aug
Natalya	Boborova	SU 59	8:48.31		7	Znam	Sochi	9 Jun
Gabriele	Martins	GDR 62	8:48.46		1		Dresden	19 May
Andzhela	Romanova	SU 61	8:48.54		5	NC	Donetsk	8 Sep
Cathie	Twomey	USA 56	8:48.55		2		Oslo	21 Jul
Lidia	Svechikhina	SU 52	8:48.81		4		Moskva	6 Aug
Olga	Dvirna	SU 53	8:49.16		4		Sochi	26 May
Natalya	Sorokiyevskaya	SU 61	8:49.28		4		Moskva	19 Jul
Tatyana	Leonova	SU 56	8:49.29		8	Znam	Sochi	9 Jun
Monica	Joyce	IRL 58	8:49.51		1		San Diego	25 May
(40)								
Cathy	Branta	USA 63	8:49.94		4	FOT	Los Angeles	23 Jun
Anna	Domoradskaya	SU 53	8:50.66		5		Moskva	19 Jul
Tatyana	Sychova	SU 57	8:50.76		8	NC	Donetsk	8 Sep
Francie	Larrieu	USA 52	8:50.85		5	FOT	Los Angeles	23 Jun
Marina	Belyayeva	SU 58	8:50.98		10	Znam	Sochi	9 Jun
Katalin	Szalai	HUN 61	8:51.50		2	DNG	Stockholm	2 Jul
Mary	Knisely	USA 59	8:51.9		2		Walnut, CA	25 Jul
Olga	Zhuravleva	SU 56	8:52.20		2		Sochi	28 Apr
Irina	Mozharova	SU 58	8:52.42		3		Sochi	28 Apr
Lyudmila	Matveyeva	SU 57	8:52.49		11	Znam	Sochi	9 Jun
(50)								
Angela	Tooby	UK 60	8:52.59		2	OT	London	6 Jun

1984 Lists – Women

Zamira	Zaitseva	SU 53*	8:53.2	2		Moskva	8 Jul
Rosa	Mota	POR 58	8:53.84	4	DNG	Stockholm	2 Jul
Valentina	Yeltsova	SU 60	8:53.96	11		Kiev	20 Jun
Arina	Zinurova	SU 56	8:54.0	1		Ustinovsk	15 Jul
Elena	Fidatov	RUM 60	8:54.32	2	NC	Bucuresti	10 Jul
Ruth	Smeeth	UK 60	8:54.47	3		Oslo	21 Jul
Roswitha	Gerdes	FRG 61	8:54.60	1		Koblenz	29 Aug
Vera	Michallek	FRG 58	8:54.62	2		Koblenz	29 Aug
Tatyana	Nikanorova	SU 59	8:54.70	7		Moskva	19 Jul

(60)
PattiSue	Plumer	USA 62	8:54.91	4s1	FOT	Los Angeles	21 Jun
Brenda	Webb	USA 54	8:55.15	5s1	FOT	Los Angeles	21 Jun
Olga	Kuzyukova	SU 53	8:55.45	8		Moskva	19 Jul
Ille	Kukk	SU 57	8:55.75	1r2	NC	Donetsk	8 Sep
Albina	Lozhnova	SU 61	8:56.0	1		Orel	22 Jun
Suzanne	Morley	UK 57	8:56.39	4		Oslo	21 Jul
Radka	Naplatanova	BUL 57	8:56.62	3	RumIC	Bucuresti	10 Jun
Rasa	Virsilovaite	SU 62	8:56.79	13		Kiev	20 Jun
Galina	Kireyeva	SU 56	8:56.9	1		Leningrad	13 Aug
Susan	Tooby	UK 60	8:57.17	4	OT	London	6 Jun

Kathy	Carter	UK 59	8:57.2	1		Stretford	7 Apr
Helen	Kimaiyo	KEN 68	8:57.21	7h1	OG	Los Angeles	8 Aug
Margarita	Zhupikova	SU 65	8:57.54	15	Znam	Sochi	9 Jun
Corine	De Baets	BEL 63	8:57.76	4		Koblenz	29 Aug
Roisin	Smyth	IRL 63	8:57.94	2		Cork	3 Jul
Eva	Ernstrom	SWE 61	8:57.95	5	DNG	Stockholm	2 Jul
Maria	Bystrykh	SU 56	8:58.18	14		Kiev	20 Jun
Iulia	Ionescu	RUM 65	8:58.23	4	RumIC	Bucuresti	10 Jun
Sandra	Gasser	SWZ 62	8:58.31	6		Koblenz	29 Aug
Anna	Pedan	SU 61	8:58.38	2		Kiev	3 Jul

(80)
Yvonne	Murray	UK 64	8:58.54	7		Koblenz	29 Aug
Maggie	Keyes	USA 58	8:58.70	6	DNG	Stockholm	2 Jul
Yelizaveta	Bradu	SU 54	8:59.17	1		Tartu	28 Aug
Sabrina	Dornhoefer	USA 63	8:59.25	4s2	FOT	Los Angeles	21 Jun
Svetlana	Poltorak	SU 60	8:59.3	7		Moskva	8 Jul
Eleanor	Simonsick	USA 58	8:59.48	5s2	FOT	Los Angeles	21 Jun
Albina	Mefodyeva	SU 61	8:59.5	2		Leningrad	7 Jul
Debbie	Peel	UK 58	8:59.74	3		Cork	3 Jul
Mariana	Stanescu	RUM 64	9:00.10	2		Bucuresti	19 Aug
Albertina	Machado	POR 61	9:00.1	1		Lisboa	14 Jul

(90)
Christine	Hughes	NZ 59	9:00.17			Auckland	3 Mar
Eva	Kadas	RUM 59	9:00.40				
Vera	Burdina	SU 54	9:00.7	8		Ryazan	11 Aug
Nadezhda	Stepanova	SU 59	9:00.76	10		Moskva	19 Jul
Marie-Louise	Hamrin	SWE 57	9:00.84	8	DNG	Stockholm	2 Jul
Geri	Fitch	CAN 54	9:01.02	5		Eugene	4 Jun
Betty	Springs	USA 61	9:01.28	7s1	FOT	Los Angeles	21 Jun
Birgit	Schmidt	FRG 63	9:01.30	10		Koblenz	29 Aug
Jan	Merrill	USA 56	9:01.31	1	TAC	San Jose	9 Jun
Lyudmila	Baranova	SU 50	9:01.5	1		Khabarovsk	17 Jun

(100)
Lyudmila	Legotkina	SU 60	9:01.78		Znam	Sochi	9 Jun
Karolin	Szabo	HUN 61	9:01.78	5	RumIC	Bucuresti	10 Jun
Galina	Kholod	SU 58	9:01.9	9		Ryazan	11 Aug

(103)

Annette	Sergent	FRA 62	9:02.05	29 Jun	Shelly	Steely	USA 62	9:03.86	1 Jun
Betty	van Steenbroeck	BEL 63	9:02.43	2 Jul	(110) Katrin	Dorre	GDR 61	9:04.01	5 May
Olga	Kryshnya	SU 61	9:02.8	7 Jul	Donna	Gould	AUS 66	9:04.02	14 Mar
Irina	Matrosova	SU 62	9:03.24	9 Jun	Francine	Peeters	BEL 57	9:04.29	22 Jun
Irina	Karbolina	SU 60	9:03.73	3 Jul	Tatyana	Zuyeva	SU 62	9:04.70	20 Jun
Sue	French	CAN 60	9:03.81	1 Jul	Svetlana	Zhelnova	SU 57	9:04.9	8 Jul

1984 Lists – Women

Mary	Cotton	UK 56	9:05.4	29 Jul
Raisa	Smekhnova	SU 50	9:05.48	19 Jul
Xiuyun	Zhang	CHN 64	9:05.57	18 Sep
Debbie	Scott	CAN 58	9:05.58	
Becky	Cotta	USA 62	9:05.87	5 May
(120)				
Sue	Bruce	NZ	9:05.95	28 Jan
Paivi	Tikkanen	FIN 60	9:05.98	1 Sep
Suzanne	Girard	USA 62	9:06.0	26 Apr
Ivana	Kleinova	CS 62	9:06.08	16 Aug
Kathy	Hayes	USA 62	9:06.14	21 Jun
Alison	Quelch	AUS 63	9:06.58	1 Jun
Cleopatra	Palaceanu	RUM 68	9:06.75	10 Jun
Tuija	Toivonen	FIN 58	9:06.75	1 Sep
Linden	Wilde	NZ	9:07.2	
Julie	Brown	USA 55	9:07.35	28 Apr
(130)				
Jody	Eder	USA 63	9:07.46	1 Jun
Daniela	Vieru	RUM 64	9:07.92	10 Jul
Nadezhda	Vazhenina	SU 63	9:08.0	4 Jun
Mary	O'Connor	NZ 55	9:08.21	28 Jan
Nina	Konyakhina	SU 53	9:08.31	9 Jun
Sylvia	Schierjott	GDR 63	9:08.40	5 May
Shireen	Samy	UK 60	9:08.4	4 Aug
Vanya	Stoyanova	BUL 58	9:08.41	30 May
Tatyana	Sokolova	SU 58	9:08.43	20 Jun
Sue	Foster	USA 61	9:08.44	13 Apr
(140)				

Renata	Kokowska	POL 58	9:08.70	29 Jul
Tatyana	Yevstigeyeva	SU 62		
Kim	Lock	UK 59	9:09.0	7 Apr
Deborah	Pihl	USA 61	9:09.01	1 Jun
Nina	Anikiyenko	SU 58	9:09.09	3 Jul
Renee	Odom	USA 56	9:09.25	28 Apr
Valentina	Gudinauskaite	SU 62	9:09.32	3 Jul
Louise	McGrillen	IRL	9:09.34	
Alison	Wiley	CAN 63	9:09.4	26 Apr
Zita	Agoston	HUN 65	9:09.74	26 Jul
(150)				
Lynn	Nelson	USA	9:09.76	21 Jun
Svetlana	Kuznetsova	SU 62	9:09.77	3 Jul
Sigrid	Wulsch	FRG 53	9:09.91	29 Aug
Christiane	Finke	FRG 62	9:10.13	16 May
Svetlana	Markova	SU	9:10.15	19 Jul
Tanya	Peckham	RSA 67	9:10.8	14 Apr
Julie	Holland	UK 66	9:10.9	7 Apr
Anni	Muller	AUT 56	9:10.92	30 May
Elly	van Hulst	HOL 59	9:11.13	31 Aug
Brit	McRoberts	CAN 57	9:11.20	28 Jan
(160)				

Marks made in mixed race with men

Donna	Gould	AUS 66	8:44.1	
Sue	French	CAN 60	8:57.5	
Debbie	Scott	CAN 58	8:58.5	
Geri	Fitch	CAN 54	8:58.7	
Wanda	Panfil	POL 59	9:01.30	
Kathy	Hayes	USA 62	9:01.7	

Indoor marks

Galina	Kireyeva	SU 56	8:55.86i	
Alla	Libutina	SU 53	9:00.96i	
Yelena	Malykhina	SU 63	9:01.34i	
Lesley	Welch	USA 63	9:01.6i	
Joan	Benoit	USA 57	9:06.99i	11 Feb
Annika	Lewin	SWE 66	9:10.78i	19 Feb

							Eugene	13 Jul
							Tillsonburg	7 Jul
							Burnaby	20 Jun
							Burnaby	20 Jun
							Sopot	2 Aug
							Eugene	13 Jul

				3		NC	Moskva	19 Feb
						NC	Moskva	19 Feb
						NC	Moskva	19 Feb
				2			Boston	10 Feb

	1	10	20	30	50	100	Under 8:55.0	Under 9:05.0
1980	8:33.53	8:44.7	8:52.2	8:57.30	9:00.6	9:16.21	27	64
1981	8:34.30	8:49.61	8:53.10	8:56.13	9:01.55	9:11.74	25	65
1982	8:26.78	8:36.54	8:46.01	8:51.79	8:55.98	9:08.02	42	88
1983	8:32.08	8:37.40	8:47.36	8:50.36	8:55.09	9:05.7	49	97
1984	8:22.62	8:37.76	8:42.14	8:47.94	8:52.49	9:01.5	61	115

5000 METRES

Ingrid	Kristiansen	NOR 56	14:58.89	1		Bisl	Oslo	28 Jun
Zola	Budd	RSA 66	15:01.83	1			Stellenbosch	5 Jan
Aurora	Cunha	POR 59	15:09.07	2		Bisl	Oslo	28 Jun
	Budd		15:09.86	1			Port Elizabeth	7 Mar
	Cunha		15:21.0	1		NC	Lisboa	21 Apr
Angela	Tooby	UK 60	15:22.50	3		Bisl	Oslo	28 Jun

1984 Lists – Women

Brenda	Webb	USA 54	15:22.76		1		Knoxville	13 Apr
Tatyana	Kazankina	SU 51	15:23.12		1		Paris	4 Sep
	Kristiansen		15:25.16		1		Trondheim	13 Sep
	Tooby		15:27.56		1	NC	Cwmbran	28 May
Marie-Louise	Hamrin	SWE 57	15:27.96		4	Bisl	Oslo	28 Jun
PattiSue	Plumer	USA 62	15:29.0		1	PennR	Philadelphia	26 Apr
	Hamrin		15:29.85		1	TexR	Austin	6 Apr
Cathie	Twomey	USA 56	15:30.50		5	Bisl	Oslo	28 Jun
Rosa	Mota	POR 58	15:30.63		6	Bisl	Oslo	28 Jun

(10)

Susan	Tooby	UK 60	15:35.40		2	NC	Cwmbran	28 May
	Cunha		15:37.66		2		Paris	4 Sep
Joan	Hansen	USA 58	15:39.08		3		Paris	4 Sep
Dorthe	Rasmussen	DEN 60	15:39.3		1		Glostrup	26 Sep
	Plumer		15:39.38		1	NCAA	Eugene	2 Jun

(20/13)

Julie	Brown	USA 55	15:39.50		1	FOT	Los Angeles	24 Jun
Betty	Springs	USA 61	15:39.72		2	FOT	Los Angeles	24 Jun
Donna	Gould	AUS 66	15:40.6		1		Adelaide	15 Feb
Shelly	Steely	USA 62	15:40.97		3	FOT	Los Angeles	24 Jun
Helen	Kimaiyo	KEN 68	15:41.09		1		Tokyo	6 May
Cindy	Bremser	USA 53	15:41.82		2		Knoxville	13 Apr
Monica	Joyce	IRL 58	15:42.03		4	FOT	Los Angeles	24 Jun

(20)

Lisa	Martin	AUS 60	15:43.21		5	FOT	Los Angeles	24 Jun
Katie	Ishmael	USA 64	15:45.08		6	FOT	Los Angeles	24 Jun
Carol	Urish	USA 51	15:45.28		7	FOT	Los Angeles	24 Jun
Regina	Joyce	IRL 57	15:45.45		3	Pre	Eugene	21 Jul
Alison	Wiley	CAN 63	15:45.52		2	NCAA	Eugene	2 Jun
Suzanne	Girard	USA 62	15:45.86		1		Villanova	6 May
Eva	Ernstrom	SWE 61	15:46.00		8	Bisl	Oslo	28 Jun
Nan	Doak	USA 62	15:47.64		8	FOT	Los Angeles	24 Jun
Kathy	Hayes	USA 62	15:48.43		1		Eugene	5 May
Cathy	Branta	USA 63	15:48.44		1		Baton Rouge	13 Apr

(30)

Mary	O'Connor	NZ 55	15:49.3		1		Christchurch	21 Jan
Elly	van Hulst	HOL 59	15:50.11		1	NC	Lisse	5 May
Yvonne	Murray	UK 64	15:50.54		3	NC	Cwmbran	28 May
Debbie	Peel	UK 58	15:50.9		1		Bracknell	30 Sep
Vera	Michallek	FRG 58	15:52.15		4		Paris	4 Sep
Joan	Benoit	USA 57	15:52.7	+	1	FOT	Los Angeles	17 Jun
Joan	Nesbit	USA 62	15:52.9		1		Durham	7 Apr
Lynn	Williams	CAN 60	15:53.78		2		Eugene	5 May
Marty	Cooksey	USA 54	15:56.09		5	Pre	Eugene	21 Jul
Sonja	Laxton	RSA 48	15:57.01		2		Port Elizabeth	7 Mar

(40)

Lynn	Nelson	USA	15:58.57		3	NCAA	Eugene	2 Jun
Tuija	Toivonen	FIN 58	15:59.3		1		Valkeakoski	5 Jun
Christine	McMiken	NZ	16:00.49		2	TexR	Austin	6 Apr
Ludmila	Melicherova	CS 64	16:01.43		5		Paris	4 Sep
Edel	Hackett	IRL	16:01.93		4	NCAA	Eugene	2 Jun
Kim	Bird	CAN 61	16:02.27		5	NCAA	Eugene	2 Jun
Sue	Bruce	NZ 64	16:02.3		2		Christchurch	21 Jan
Elana	van Zyl	RSA 66	16:02.55		3		Port Elizabeth	7 Mar

387

1984 Lists – Women

| Christina | Mai | FRG 61 | 16:02.9 | | 1 | | Dortmund | 15 Sep |
| Shireen | Samy | UK 60 | 16:02.95 | | 4 | NC | Cwmbran | 28 May |

(50)

Joelle	Debrouwer	FRA 50	16:03.40				4 Sep
Tatyana	Nikanorova	SU 59	16:03.4				3 Jun
Margaret	Groos	USA 59	16:04.01				24 Jun
Paula	Renzi	USA 63	16:04.05				2 Jun
Ellen	Lyons	USA 62	16:04.63				24 Jun
Glenys	Quick	NZ 57	16:04.77				24 Jun
Yuxiu	Luo	CHN 59	16:05.38				8 Sep
Rosemarie	Schonfeld	GDR 62	16:07.0				7 Jul
Beth	Farmer	USA 63	16:07.8				23 Mar
Evy	Palm	SWE 42	16:08.13				29 Sep

(60)

Hisano	Yokosuka	JAP 65	16:09.0				28 Oct
Esther	Kiplagat	KEN 66	16:09.46				6 May
Suxian	Zhang	CHN 66	16:09.87				8 Sep
Marina	Rodchenkova	SU 61	16:09.9				9 May

(64)

Marks made in mixed race with men

Donna   Gould   AUS 66   15:27.3   Adelaide   6 Jun

Sally   Pierson   AUS 63   16:09.0   20 Oct

Indoor mark

Judi   St. Hilaire   USA 59   16:04.63 i   7 Jan

10000 METRES

Olga	Bondarenko	SU 60	31:13.78	1		Kiev	24 Jun
Galina	Zakharova	SU 56	31:15.00	2		Kiev	24 Jun
Zhanna	Tursunova	SU 57	31:53.53	3		Kiev	24 Jun
Lyubov	Konyukhova	SU 56	31:56.01	4		Kiev	24 Jun
Anna	Domoradskaya	SU 53	31:56.02	5		Kiev	24 Jun
Raisa	Smekhnova	SU 50	31:59.70	6		Kiev	24 Jun
Joan	Benoit	USA 57	32:07.41	1	FOT	Los Angeles	17 Jun
Lyudmila	Matveyeva	SU 57	32:25.99	7		Kiev	24 Jun
Tuija	Toivonen	FIN 58	32:29.25	1	NC	Kajaani	6 Jul
Aurora	Cunha	POR 59	32:30.91	1		Rovereto	29 Aug

(10)

Regina	Joyce	IRL 57	32:35.7	1	MSR	Walnut, CA	28 Apr
Katie	Ishmael	USA 64	32:37.37	2	FOT	Los Angeles	17 Jun
Karolin	Szabo	HUN 61	32:38.5	1	NC	Budapest	24 May
Margarita	Zhupikova	SU 65	32:40.85	8		Kiev	24 Jun
	Joyce		32:41.78	3	FOT	Los Angeles	17 Jun
Kathy	Hayes	USA 62	32:43.81	1	NCAA	Eugene	30 May
Ulrike	Bruns	GDR 53	32:46.08	1	8N	Tokyo	14 Sep
	Ishmael		32:48.18	2	NCAA	Eugene	30 May
Albina	Mefodyeva	SU 61	32:48.33	9		Kiev	24 Jun
	Bondarenko		32:48.50	2	8N	Tokyo	14 Sep

Nadezhda	Gumerova	SU 49	32:50.04	10		Kiev	24 Jun
Esther	Kiplagat	KEN 66	32:50.25			Kobe	30 Apr
Lisa	Martin	AUS 60	32:50.5	1		Melbourne	14 Feb

(20)

| Carey | May | IRL 59 | 32:51.23 | 3 | NCAA | Eugene | 30 May |
| Marty | Cooksey | USA 54 | 32:52.91 | 4 | FOT | Los Angeles | 17 Jun |

1984 Lists – Women

	Martin		32:53.53	5	FOT	Los Angeles	17 Jun
Joan	Nesbit	USA 62	32:54.19	4	NCAA	Eugene	30 May
Nanae	Sasaki	JAP 56	32:54.90	2		Kobe	30 Apr
Margaret	Groos	USA 59	32:55.15	6	FOT	Los Angeles	17 Jun
Valentina	Yeltsova	SU 60	32:57.25	11		Kiev	24 Jun
Angela	Tooby	UK 60	32:58.07	3	8N	Tokyo	14 Sep
(31/27)							
Katrin	Dorre	GDR 61	33:00.0	1		Leipzig	30 May
Sinikka	Keskitalo	FIN 51	33:01.27	2	NC	Kajaani	6 Jul
Galina	Ikonnikova	SU 62	33:02.61	12		Kiev	24 Jun
(30)							
Carol	Urish	USA 51	33:03.06	7	FOT	Los Angeles	17 Jun
Ellen	Lyons	USA 62	33:03.7	2	MSR	Walnut, CA	28 Apr
Glenys	Quick	NZ 57	33:04.96	8	FOT	Los Angeles	17 Jun
Christine	McMiken	NZ	33:05.7	5	NCAA	Eugene	30 May
Linda	King	USA 64	33:05.96	6	NCAA	Eugene	30 May
Tatyana	Sokolova	SU 58	33:06.04	13		Kiev	24 Jun
Irina	Bondarchuk	SU 52	33:10.7	1		Leningrad	10 Aug
Lucia	Belyayeva	SU 57	33:11.17	14		Kiev	24 Jun
Tatyana	Orlova	SU 53	33:17.5	1		Moskva	2 May
Nadezhda	Yerokhina	SU 59	33:18.18	15		Kiev	24 Jun
(40)							
Beth	Farmer	USA 63	33:22.58	7	NCAA	Eugene	30 May
Tatyana	Zuyeva	SU 57	33:23.51	16		Kiev	24 Jun
Debbie	Eide	USA 56	33:24.33	10	FOT	Los Angeles	17 Jun
Tori	Neubauer	USA 62	33:25.80	8	NCAA	Eugene	30 May
Cathy	Schiro	USA 67	33:26.53	11	FOT	Los Angeles	17 Jun
Albina	Lozhnova	SU 61	33:27.51	17		Kiev	24 Jun
Sally	Pierson	AUS 63	33:28.1	2		Melbourne	14 Feb
Rita	Marchisio	ITA 50	33:29.68	2	NC	Rovereto	29 Aug
Charlotte	Teske	FRG 49	33:29.76	1	NC	Dusseldorf	22 Jun
Priscilla	Welch	UK 44	33:34.7	1		Birmingham	2 Jun
(50)							
Susanne	Riermeier	FRG 60	33:36.2	1		Wetter	4 Feb
Jill	Molen	USA 60	33:37.0	9	NCAA	Eugene	30 May
Laura	Fogli	ITA 59	33:39.04	3	NC	Rovereto	29 Aug
Ria	van Landeghem	BEL 57	33:40.30	1	NC	Woluwe	1 Jul
Birgit	Weinhold	GDR 64	33:41.5	2		Leipzig	30 May
Kellie	Cathey	USA 61	33:42.8	4	MSR	Walnut, CA	28 Apr
Janell	Neeley	USA 63	33:44.1	10	NCAA	Eugene	30 May
Magda	Ilands	BEL 50	33:45.40	2	NC	Woluwe	1 Jul
Karen	Campbell	USA 62	33:47.9	11	NCAA	Eugene	30 May
Patsy	Sharples	RSA 61	33:49.8	12	NCAA	Eugene	30 May
(60)							
Christina	Mai	FRG 61	33:50.26	2	NC	Dusseldorf	22 Jun
Emma	Scaunich	ITA 54	33:51.09	4	NC	Rovereto	29 Aug
Eryn	Forbes	USA 61	33:52.7	13	NCAA	Eugene	30 May
Yuxiu	Luo	CHN 59	33:52.84	1		Nanjing	5 Sep
Sirkku	Kumpulainen	FIN 56	33:53.8	3		Helsinki	24 May
Ilona	Janko	HUN 57	33:56.3	2	NC	Budapest	24 May
Erika	Vereb	HUN 63	33:57.0	3	NC	Budapest	24 May
Lyubov	Svirskaya	SU 60	33:57.58	18		Kiev	24 Jun
Hisano	Yokosuka	JAP 65	33:58.04	1	NC	Tokyo	21 Oct
Tatyana	Nikanorova	SU 59	33:58.2	2		Leningrad	10 Aug
(70)							

Renata	Kokowska	POL 58	34:04.66	19 Sep	Maria	Klyukina	SU 50	34:13.07	24 Jun
Bonnie	Sons	USA 65	34:05.72	11 May	(80)				
Huabi	Wang	CHN 66	34:06.53	5 Sep	Renee	Wyckoff	USA 62	34:13.4	30 May
Kathy	Pfiefer	USA 59	34:06.9	30 May	Conceicao	Ferreira	POR 62	34:13.89	29 Aug
Ludmila	Melicherova	CS 64	34:06.99	21 Jul	Zita	Agoston	HUN 65	34:14.5	24 May
Maria	Curatolo	ITA 63	34:07.99	20 May	Susan	Berenda	USA	34:14.7	28 Apr
Pat	Story	USA 49	34:08.1	28 Apr	Tatyana	Gridneva	SU 60	34:14.8	8 Jul
Kim	Schnurpfeil	USA 61	34:08.72	17 Jun	Kate	Wiley	CAN 62	34:15.99	29 Apr
Tuula	Konttinen	FIN 63	34:09.6	24 May	Christa	Vahlensieck	FRG 49	34:17.97	22 Jun

389

1984 Lists – Women

Aleksandra	Tarasova	SU 58	34:18.6	12 Aug		Mika	Kawai	JAP 67	34:25.7	9 Sep
Ellen	Wessinghage	FRG 48	34:18.7	29 May	(100)					
Jenni	Peters	USA	34:18.82	17 Jun		Denise	Verhaert	BEL 59	34:26.36	1 Jul
(90)						Yasuko	Hashimoto	SU 65	34:26.5	9 Sep
Carol	Gleason	USA 63	34:20.47	23 May		Brenda	Gray	USA	34:27.6	28 Apr
Valentina	Ustinova	SU 57	34:20.6	12 Aug		Rosanna	Munerotto	ITA 62	34:27.65	20 May
Agnes	Komjaty	HUN 50	34:20.9	24 May		Sari	Ruottinen	FIN 65	34:28.76	6 Jul
Yelizaveta	Bradu	SU 54	34:21.6	17 Jun		Natalie	Updegrove	USA 61	34:28.8	18 May
Marina	Sany	UK 60	34:22.7	7 Jul		Julie	Bowers	USA	34:29.98	23 May
Yoko	Higuchi	JAP 63	34:22.9	9 Sep	(107)					
Lynn	Nelson	USA	34:24.9	11 May	**Mark amd in mixed race with men**					
Nadezhda	Likhacheva	SU 59	34:25.0	2 May		Julie	Bowers	USA	34:07.0	31 Mar
Ann	Foley	AUS	34:25.6	10 Mar						

100 METRES HURDLES

Lucyna	Kalek	POL 56	12.43	−0.9	1		Hannover	19 Aug
	Kalek		12.49	0.8	1	GGala	Roma	31 Aug
Vera	Akimova	SU 59	12.50	0.0	1		Sochi	19 May
Yordanka	Donkova	BUL 61	12.50	0.7	1		Sofia	8 Aug
	Akimova		12.51	−0.5	1		Kiev	22 Jun
Bettine	Jahn	GDR 58	12.53	0.5	1	OD	Berlin	20 Jul
	Kalek		12.53	0.0	1	WK	Zurich	22 Aug
Sabine	Paetz	GDR 57	12.54	0.9	1		Berlin	15 Jul
	Donkova		12.54	1.7	1	BGP	Budapest	20 Aug
	Kalek		12.54	−0.8	1		Paris	4 Sep
	Donkova		12.55	−0.2	1	DRZ	Praha	16 Aug
Cornelia	Riefstahl	GDR 61	12.57	0.5	2	OD	Berlin	20 Jul
	Kalek		12.58	−0.4	1h2	DRZ	Praha	16 Aug
	Paetz		12.60	−0.2	2	DRZ	Praha	16 Aug
	Donkova		12.61	0.8	1		Barcelona	8 Jul
	Kalek		12.61	−0.2	3	DRZ	Praha	16 Aug
	Donkova		12.62	−0.4	1	NC	Sofia	2 Jun
	Kalek		12.62	0.7	1		Munchen	20 Jul
Ginka	Zagorcheva	BUL 58	12.62	0.7	2		Sofia	8 Aug
	Akimova		12.62	−0.2	4	DRZ	Praha	16 Aug
	Donkova		12.63	0.5	1		Sofia	4 Jul
	Paetz		12.64	0.3	H	NC	Potsdam	5 May
	Riefstahl		12.64	1.5	1	NC	Erfurt	1 Jun
	Akimova		12.64	0.0	1s1		Kiev	22 Jun
	Kalek		12.64	0.7	1		Koln	26 Aug
	Riefstahl		12.65	−0.8	1	Skok	Celje	5 May
Nadezhda	Korshunova	SU 61	12.65	0.0	2		Sochi	19 May
	Riefstahl		12.65	0.9	2		Berlin	15 Jul
	Donkova		12.65	0.5	3	OD	Berlin	20 Jul
	Kalek		12.65		1		Warszawa	25 Jul
(30/8)								
Yelena	Biserova	SU 62	12.66	0.0	3		Sochi	19 May
Svetlana	Gusarova	SU 59	12.74	−0.5	3		Kiev	22 Jun
(10)								
Xenia	Siska	HUN 57	12.76	1.7	3	BGP	Budapest	20 Aug
Gloria	Kovarik	GDR 64	12.79	0.9	4		Berlin	15 Jul
Benita	Fitzgerald	USA 61	12.84	−0.7	1	OG	Los Angeles	10 Aug
Shirley	Strong	UK 58	12.88	−0.7	2	OG	Los Angeles	10 Aug
Stephanie	Hightower	USA 58	12.90	0.6	2	Nik	Nice	20 Aug
Natalya	Shubenkova	SU 57	12.93	1.0	H	NC	Kiev	20 Jun
Laurence	Elloy	FRA 59	12.94	0.8	3	GGala	Roma	31 Aug
Kerstin	Knabe	GDR 59	12.98	0.3	1		Jena	13 May
Ulrike	Denk	FRG 64	12.98	1.3	2		Furth	9 Jun
Kim	Turner	USA 61	13.01	0.8	3s2	FOT	Los Angeles	23 Jun

1984 Lists – Women

(20)								
Heike	Terpe	GDR 64	13.02	1.5	4	NC	Erfurt	1 Jun
Glynis	Nunn	AUS 60	13.02	−1.5	H	OG	Los Angeles	3 Aug
Cornelia	Feuerbach	GDR 63	13.04	1.5	5	NC	Erfurt	1 Jun
Maria	Merchuk	SU 59	13.05	−0.1	1	NC	Donetsk	7 Sep
Michele	Chardonnet	FRA 56	13.06	−0.7	3t	OG	Los Angeles	10 Aug
Pam	Page	USA 58	13.07	1.5	1h3	FOT	Los Angeles	22 Jun
Judy	Simpson	UK 60	13.07	−1.5	H	OG	Los Angeles	3 Aug
Edith	Oker	FRG 61	13.09	1.3	4		Furth	9 Jun
Lyudmila	Oliyar	SU 58	13.11	0.1	3s2		Kiev	22 Jun
Marie-Noelle	Savigny	FRA 57	13.13	1.7	1r2	WK	Zurich	22 Aug
(30)								
Candy	Young	USA 62	13.14	0.6	3	TAC	San Jose	8 Jun
Vera	Komisova	SU 53	13.14	0.1	4s2		Kiev	22 Jun
Lyubov	Stolyar	SU 61	13.18	0.6	1h4		Kiev	3 Jul
Marjan	Olijslager	HOL 62	13.20	1.3	5		Furth	9 Jun
Liliana	Nastase	RUM 62	13.20		H	NC	Bucuresti	10 Jul
Natalya	Grigoryeva	SU 62	13.20	−0.1	2	NC	Donetsk	7 Sep
Yelena	Kudinova	SU 64	13.21	0.0	3s1		Kiev	22 Jun
Ina	van Rensburg	RSA 56	A13.26		1		Sasolburg	21 Apr
Elida	Aveille	CUB 61	13.27	1.3	1	Bar	Habana	19 May
Sharon	Danville	UK 55	13.27	1.9	2	Kuso	Warszawa	9 Jun
(40)								
Jane	Frederick	USA 52	13.27	1.2	H		Talence	15 Sep
Irina	Svetonosova	SU 58	13.29	0.9	3h1		Moskva	19 Jul
Sally	Gunnell	UK 66	13.30	1.9	2	WAAA	London	16 Jun
Anke	Vater	GDR 61	13.30	0.4	H	OD	Potsdam	20 Jul
Anke	Koninger	FRG 61	13.30				Nurtingen	2 Sep
Lorna	Boothe	UK 54	13.31	1.9	3	WAAA	London	16 Jun
Antonina	Sukhova	SU 59	13.32	0.7	H	NC	Kiev	20 Jun
Marina	Kibakina	SU 60	13.32	0.0	4s1		Kiev	22 Jun
Yelizaveta	Chernyshova	SU 58	13.32	−0.1	5	NC	Donetsk	7 Sep
Grisel	Machado	CUB 59	13.33	1.9	3	Kuso	Warszawa	9 Jun
(50)								
Yelena	Meshkova	SU 59	13.33	0.0	1	SU P	Baku	16 Sep
Rhonda	Scott	USA	13.34	1.9	1		Baton Rouge	21 Apr
Sue	Kameli	CAN 56	A13.34	2.0	1		Provo	19 May
Angela	Weiss	SWZ 53	13.34	0.8	3		Barcelona	8 Jul
Jackie	Washington	USA 61	13.34	1.8	2		Walnut, CA	15 Jul
Tonya	Lowe	USA 62	13.35	1.8	1		Baton Rouge	13 May
Karen	Nelson	CAN 63	A13.35	2.0	2		Provo	19 May
Deby	Smith	USA 53	13.35	1.3	2		Walnut, CA	3 Jun
Natalya	Dolgaya	SU 64	13.35	1.6	H	SU P	Baku	14 Sep
Maria	Usifo	NIG 64	13.36	1.9	2		Baton Rouge	21 Apr
(60)								
Faye	Blackwood	CAN 57	A13.36	2.0	3		Provo	19 May
Pat	Rollo	UK 61	13.36	1.9	4	WAAA	London	16 Jun
Wendy	Jeal	UK 60	13.36	1.3	1		Birmingham	1 Sep
Elisabet	Pantazi	GRE 56	13.36	−1.1	3	Balk	Athinai	9 Sep
Ramona	Neubert	GDR 58	13.37	−0.6	3		Potsdam	6 May
Valentina	Kurochkina	SU 59	13.37	0.7	H	NC	Kiev	20 Jun
Sabine	Everts	FRG 61	13.37	0.1	5	ISTAF	W Berlin	17 Aug
Nina	Derbina	SU 56	13.38	0.0	5s1		Kiev	22 Jun
Hilsa	van den Heever	RSA 61	A13.38		1		Germiston	14 Nov
Anne	Piquereau	FRA 64	13.39	1.8	2s1	NC	Lille	1 Jul
(70)								
Kim	Hagger	UK 61	13.39	−0.4	H	OG	Los Angeles	3 Aug
Heike	Tillack	GDR 68	13.39		1	DRZ	Plovdiv	4 Aug
Svetlana	Chistyakova	SU 61	13.40	− i	1		Tashkent	25 Feb
Patricia	Davis	USA 65	13.40	−0.9	6	FOT	Los Angeles	23 Jun
Lilyana	Ivanova	BUL 56	13.41		1		Sofia	5 May
Natalya	Gorbunova	SU 64	13.41	0.3	2h2		Sochi	19 May
Gudrun	Lattner	FRG 59	13.41	−1.2	3	NC	Dusseldorf	22 Jun
Galina	Kazakova	SU 61	13.41	0.9	5h3		Moskva	19 Jul
Huajin	Liu	CHN 60	13.41	1.0	5	8N	Tokyo	14 Sep
Isabelle	Kaftandjian	FRA 64	13.42	0.0	1		Paris	2 Jun

1984 Lists – Women

(80)
Sylwia	Bednarska	POL 66	13.42	0.5	1		Sopot	29 Jul
Sylwia	Forgrave	CAN 57	13.42	-0.2	6s1	OG	Los Angeles	10 Aug
Marina	Sukhareva	SU 62	13.42	-0.1	6	NC	Donetsk	7 Sep
Svetlana	Ovchinnikova	SU 56	13.43	0.7	H	NC	Kiev	20 Jun
Linda	Weekly	USA 58	13.44	-0.8	3s1	FOT	Los Angeles	23 Jun
Birgit	Engel	FRG 62	13.44	1.3	1r2		Stuttgart	21 Jul
Sophia	Hunter	JAM 64	13.44	1.0	1		Walnut, CA	25 Jul
Claudia	Reidick	FRG 62	13.45	1.3	8		Furth	9 Jun
Dorthe	Rasmussen	DEN 58	13.45		1	NC	Frederiksberg	18 Aug
Natalya	Grachova	SU 52	13.45		H	v FRG	Ahlen	8 Sep

(90)
Beatriz	Capotosto	ARG 62	13.45		1		Santiago de Chile	28 Oct
Gayle	Watkins	USA 58	13.46	1.3	3		Walnut, CA	3 Jun
Rhonda	Blanford	USA 63	13.47	1.2	1		Lincoln	12 May
Heather	Ross	UK 62	13.47	1.9	7	WAAA	London	16 Jun
Marianna	Maslennikova	SU 61	13.47	1.6	H	NC	Kiev	20 Jun
Arnita	Epps	USA 64	13.47	1.5	3h3	FOT	Los Angeles	22 Jun
Riana	Raath	RSA 61	A13.48		2		Sasolburg	21 Apr
Galina	Bakhchevanova	BUL 62	13.48		2		Sofia	5 May
Elzbieta	Szulc	POL 59	13.48	-0.6	5	v FRG,CS,Fra	Hannover	16 Jun
Ildiko	Baranyai	HUN 58	13.48	1.6	1		Budapest	23 Jun

(100)
Natalya	Belenkova	SU 65	13.48	1.0	1h7		Kiev	3 Jul
Brigitte	Gerstenmaier	FRG 60	13.48	1.3	2r2		Stuttgart	21 Jul

(102)

Natalya	Alyoshina	SU 56	13.49	0.4	20 Jun	Maria	Vlasceanu	RUM 62	13.61		18 Aug
Florence	Picaut	FRA 52	13.49	1.3	30 Jul	Milena	Tebichova	CS 62	13.63	0.0	2 Jun
Rita	Heggli	SWZ 62	13.50	0.5	22 Jul	Julieta	Rousseaux	CUB 66	A13.63		16 Jun
Jana	Petrikova	CS 67	13.50	0.6	28 Aug	(140)					
Lori	Smith	USA 61	13.51	0.6	7 Apr	Odalys	Adams	CUB 67	A13.63		16 Jun
Jodi	Anderson	USA 57	13.52	-0.3	16 Jun	Lyudmila	Orinyanskaya	SU 56	13.63	0.0	22 Jun
Chantal	Beaugeant	FRA 61	13.52	1.8	1 Jul	Angelika	Kuhmann	FRG 57	13.63	-0.7	22 Jun
Irina	Dobrenko	SU 60	13.52			Elize	van Huyssteen	RSA 58	A13.64		21 Mar

(110)
Florence	Colle	FRA 65	13.52	1.2	21 Jul	Kathy	Freeman	USA 62	13.64	1.9	21 Apr
Malgorzata	Nowak	POL 59	13.52		25 Jul	Helena	Otahalova	CS 59	13.64	0.0	2 Jun
Natalya	Pozdina	SU 58	13.52	-0.1	7 Sep	Margita	Papic	YUG 61	13.64	-0.1	10 Jun
Elzbieta	Schmid	FRG 56	13.53	1.3	14 Jul	Irina	Gritsenko	SU 65	13.65	1.8	14 Jul
Jianjing	Zhang	CHN 57	13.53		8 Sep	Cindy	Greiner	USA 57	13.65	1.1	25 Jul
Jackie	Joyner	USA 62	13.53	1.2	15 Sep	Daniela	Bizbac	RUM 67	13.65	0.6	19 Aug
Rhonda	Brady	USA 59	13.54	0.1	12 May	(150)					
Cecile	Ngambi	CAM 60	13.54	1.5	23 Jun	Agnieszka	Muszynska	POL 65	13.65		19 Aug
Sherifa	Sanders	USA 63	13.55	1.2	12 May	Margit	Palombi	HUN 65	13.65	1.7	20 Aug
Cece	Chandler	USA 64	13.55	0.6	26 May	Lillian	Cole	USA 61	13.66	-0.1	31 Mar

(120)
						Rosalind	Pendergraft	USA 65	13.66	-0.1	31 Mar
Missy	Jerald	USA 61	13.55	1.3	3 Jun	Laura	Rosati	ITA 60	13.66	0.8	11 Jul
Beatrice	Pluss	SWZ 61	13.55	0.5	22 Jul	Annie	le Roux	RSA 65	A13.67		7 Apr
LaVonna	Martin	USA 66	13.55	0.1	24 Aug	Karen	Wilkenson	RSA 66	A13.68		18 Feb
Marina	Spirina	SU 55	13.55		14 Sep	Tineke	Hidding	HOL 59	13.68	2.0	28 Apr
Pat	Lavallias	USA 62	13.56	1.4	20 May	Berit	Meyer	GDR 67	13.68		1 Jul
Christine	Sallaz	FRA 61	13.56	1.7	1 Jul	Kemei	Chen	CHN 63	13.68		8 Sep
Coculeana	Oltean	RUM 56	13.56		12 Jul	(160)					
Yekaterina	Smirnova	SU 56	13.58	-0.2	19 May	Silva	Oja	SU 61	13.69	0.4	20 Jun
Dagmar	Schenten	FRG 58	13.58	-0.7	22 Jun	Radostina	Dimitrova	BUL 66	13.69		14 Jul
Sibylle	Thiele	GDR 58	13.58	0.6		Svetlana	Kurdyuk	SU 60	13.69	1.5	19 Jul
						Clara	Hairston	USA 63	13.70	0.4	31 Mar

(130)
						Edit	Molnar	HUN 65	13.70	0.8	20 Jun
Natalya	Mikheyeva	SU 60	13.59	0.1	22 Jun	Tatyana	Susuyeva	SU 64	13.70	0.2	3 Jul
Sabine	Braun	FRG 65	13.59	0.5	22 Jun	Yinghua	Feng	CHN 66	13.70		6 Oct
Nadezhda	Asenova	BUL 62	13.60	-0.4	2 Jun	Juraciara	Silva	BRA 61	13.71	0.1	17 Jun
Svetlana	Filatyeva	SU 64	13.60	1.0	20 Jun	Laura	Lim	USA 62	13.72		24 Mar
Oksana	Lomot	SU 63	13.60	-0.8	19 Jul	Isabel	Campher	RSA 58	13.72		13 Apr
Ilse	Ras	RSA 65	A13.61		21 Mar	(170)					
Patsy	Walker	USA 59	13.61	1.8	15 Jul						

1984 Lists – Women

Conceicao	Geremias	BRA 56	13.72	0.1	17 Jun	Sylvia	Dethier	BEL 65	13.76	-2.3	14 Jul
Olga	Litvinova	SU 64	13.72	0.6	21 Jun	Viktoria	Marushchak	SU 66	13.77		5 May
Jill	Giffen	CAN 58	13.72	-0.4	3 Aug	Vera	Yurchenko	SU 59	13.77	1.6	20 Jun
Svetlana	Gerevich	SU 66	13.72		8 Sep	(190)					
Naomi	Jyojima	JAP 68	13.72	1.6	13 Oct	Natalya	Martynova	SU	13.77	0.2	3 Jul
Thomasina	Busch	USA 62	13.73		25 May	Sabine	Seitl	AUT 65	13.77	1.9	22 Jul
Mila	Kolyadina	SU 60	13.73	1.0	20 Jun	Kay	Garnett	USA 61	13.78	1.0	14 Apr
Donna	Smellie	CAN 64	13.73	1.1	30 Jun	Tatyana	Kirichenko	SU 65	13.78		19 May
Lidia	Okolo-Kulak	SU 67	13.73		4 Aug	Monique	Ewanje-Epee	FRA 67	13.78	1.8	1 Jul
Marlene	Harmon	USA 62	13.73	1.2	15 Sep	(195)					
(180)											
Cecilia	Branch	CAN 57	A13.74	2.0	19 May	**Best outdoor mark**					
Jitka	Tesarkova	CS 65	13.74	0.0	2 Jun		Chistyakova		13.77		26 May
Lyubov	Ratsu	SU 61	13.74	1.8	14 Sep						
Maureen	Prendergast	UK 59	13.75	1.8	5 May	**Best low-altitude mark**					
Corina	Tifrea	RUM 58	13.75				Nelson		13.52	1.2	22 Apr
Jocelyne	Junod	SWZ 65	13.75	0.4	22 Jul		Kameli		13.54	0.0	25 Jul
Emi	Sasaki	JAP 56	13.76	-1.1	6 May						

	1	10	20	30	50	100	Under 13.30	Under 13.70
1980	12.36	12.80	13.10	13.21	13.42	13.77	37	83
1981	12.68	13.14	13.25	13.36	13.51	13.75	23	83
1982	12.44	12.88	13.09	13.17	13.42	13.68	37	102
1983	12.42	12.86	13.00	13.13	13.25	13.55	55	145
1984	12.43	12.74	13.01	13.13	13.33	13.48	42	163

Marks made with assisting wind greater than 2 m/s

Sabine	Paetz	GDR 57	12.51	3.6	1		Dresden	27 Jul
	Paetz		12.58	4.1	1h1		Dresden	27 Jul
	Riefstahl		12.65	4.1	2h1		Dresden	27 Jul
(3/2)								
Laurence	Elloy	FRA 59	12.72	2.9	1	NC	Lille	1 Jul
Stephanie	Hightower	USA 58	12.78	4.6	1		Modesto, CA	12 May
Shirley	Strong	UK 58	12.86	2.8	1h2	OG	Los Angeles	9 Aug
Michele	Chardonnet	FRA 56	12.91	2.9	2	NC	Lille	1 Jul
Kim	Turner	USA 61	12.96	4.6	2		Modesto, CA	12 May
Heike	Terpe	GDR 64	12.99	4.1	3h1		Dresden	27 Jul
Pam	Page	USA 58	13.01	4.2	1h4	TAC	San Jose	7 Jun
Candy	Young	USA 62	13.05	3.7	2	NCAA	Eugene	2 Jun
(10)								
Sharon	Danville	UK 55	13.06	2.8	1h2		Montreal	14 Jul
Edith	Oker	FRG 61	13.08	3.5	1		Ludenscheid	26 May
Pat	Rollo	UK 61	13.12	4.5	1	NC	Cwmbran	27 May
Rhonda	Brady	USA 59	13.18	4.2	2h4	TAC	San Jose	7 Jun
Wendy	Jeal	UK 60	13.18	4.1	1		Birmingham	15 Jul
Deby	Smith	USA 53	13.18	4.1	3		Birmingham	15 Jul
Rhonda	Scott	USA	13.20	3.2	1	TexR	Austin	7 Apr
Arnita	Epps	USA 64	13.20	3.7	3	NCAA	Eugene	2 Jun
Heather	Ross	UK 62	13.22	4.5	2	NC	Cwmbran	27 May
Sue	Kameli	CAN 56	A13.24	3.4	1		Provo	23 May
(20)								
Sylvia	Forgrave	CAN 57	13.29	3.9	1	NC	Winnipeg	30 Jun
Anne	Piquereau	FRA 64	13.30	2.9	4	NC	Lille	1 Jul
Rhonda	Blanford	USA 63	13.34	2.1	2h3	NCAA	Eugene	31 May
Karen	Nelson	CAN 63	13.34	3.9	2	NC	Winnipeg	30 Jun
Gayle	Watkins	USA 58	13.35	4.6	6		Modesto, CA	12 May
Maria	Usifo	NIG 64	13.35	3.7	4	NCAA	Eugene	2 Jun
Clara	Hairston	USA 63	13.37	3.4	3h2	NCAA	Eugene	31 May
Margit	Palombi	HUN 61	13.38	2.8	H		Budapest	26 Jul ii
Isabelle	Kaftandjian	FRA 64	13.39	3.9	1h4	NC	Lille	30 Jun
Lillian	Cole	USA 61	13.40	2.2	1		Athens, GA	31 Mar
(30)								
Jana	Petrikova	CS 57	13.40	3.5	1	v Hun,GDR-j	Miskolc	7 Jul
Huajin	Liu	CHN 60	13.41		2		Eugene	21 Jul
Ann-Louise	Skoglund	SWE 62	13.41	3.0	1		Sollentuna	12 Jun

1984 Lists – Women

Florence	Picaut	FRA 52	13.41	3.9	2h4	NC		Lille	30 Jun
Elzbieta	Szulc	POL 59	13.43	2.6	2	NC		Lublin	23 Jun
Christine	Sallaz	FRA 61	13.43	2.9	5	NC		Lille	1 Jul
Kerry	Robin-Millerchip	UK 61	13.44	4.5	4	NC		Cwmbran	27 May
Sherifa	Sanders	USA 63	13.45		1			Waco	20 Apr
Laura	Lim	USA 62	13.46	3.2	2	TexR		Austin	7 Apr
Carol	Lewis	USA 63	13.47	3.2	3	TexR		Austin	7 Apr
Pat	Lavallias	USA 62	13.48	2.9	1			Austin	12 May
Malgorzata	Nowak	POL 59	13.48	3.2	2h1	Kuso		Warszawa	9 Jun
Missy	Jerald	USA 61	13.51	4.2	7 Jun	Val	Flemmings	USA	13.65	4.4	12 May
Florence	Colle	FRA 65	13.51	2.9	1 Jul	Maria Jose	Martinez	SPA 61	13.68	2.2	1 Jul
Cecilia	Branch	CAN 57	13.52	3.9	30 Jun	Irina	Malykh	SU 58	13.69	2.5	20 Jun
Sabine	Braun	FRG 65	13.55	3.5	26 May	Jane	Flemming	AUS 65	13.71	4.5	14 Jan
Ann	Girvan	UK 65	13.56	4.1	15 Jul	Joann	Brown	USA 65	13.71	2.1	31 May
Yolanda	Jones	CAN 67	13.58	3.9	30 Jun	Connie	Polman-Tuin	CAN 63	13.71	3.5	14 Jul
Delores	Gibbs	USA 61	13.61	3.3	7 Jun	Karen	Cannon	USA 58	13.72		29 Apr
Berit	Meyer	GDR 67	13.61	3.5	7 Jul	Elaine	McMaster	UK 57	13.72	4.5	27 May
Shirley	Walker	USA 65	13.62		29 Apr	Julie	Rocheleau	CAN 64	13.72	3.9	30 Jun
Brenda	Calhoun	USA 59	13.62	3.3	7 Jun	Yolanda	Johnson	USA 68	13.73	2.2	22 Jun
Tineke	Hidding	HOL 59	13.63	2.1	22 Apr	Cindy	Stewart	USA 61	13.74		20 Apr
Heather	Platt	UK 59	13.63	3.6	1 Jul	Lynne	Roper	UK 64	13.76	4.5	27 May
Jeanette	Bolden	USA 60	13.64	3.3	7 Jun	Patricia	Lutherean	FRA 59	13.76	3.9	30 Jun

Hand timing

Maria	Merchuk	SU 59	12.6		1		Kishinyov		11 Aug
Natalya	Grigoryeva	SU 62	12.7	0.6	1		Kiev		14 Aug
Yelena	Kudinova	SU 64	12.8	0.6	2		Kiev		14 Aug
Natalya	Bordyugova	SU 61	12.8	0.6	3		Kiev		14 Aug
Ulrike	Denk	FRG 64	12.9	−0.8	1		Aachen		30 May
Yelena	Meshkova	SU 59	12.9		1		Alma Ata		7 Aug
Kim	Turner	USA 61	13.0	0.1	1s1	TAC	San Jose		8 Jun
Irina	Svetonosova	SU 58	13.0		1		Leningrad		6 Jul
Vera	Komisova	SU 53	13.0		1		Vilnius		4 Aug
Yelizaveta	Chernyshova	SU 58	13.0		1s		Gorkiy		11 Aug
(10)									
Antonina	Sukhova	SU 59	13.0		H		Tula		25 Aug
Ina	van Rensburg	RSA 56	13.1		1		Stellenbosch		23 Apr
Brigitte	Gerstenmaier	FRG 60	13.1	1.5	1		Recklinghausen		11 Jun
Sabine	Everts	FRG 61	13.1		H		Arnsberg		6 Jul
Galina	Kazakova	SU 61	13.1		1		Alma Ata		28 Jul
Vera	Yurchenko	SU 59	13.1		1		Kiev		14 Aug
Elida	Aveille	CUB 61	13.2		1		Habana		11 May
Marina	Kuznetsova	SU 63	13.2		1		Irpinsk		12 May
Oksana	Lomot	SU 63	13.2		1		Minsk		8 Jun
Natalya	Gorbunova	SU 64	13.2		1		Leningrad		15 Jun
(20)									
Galina	Gorbunova	SU 60	13.2		3		Leningrad		6 Jul
Sharon	Danville	UK 55	13.2	1.2	2		Tillsonburg		7 Jul
Marina	Spirina	SU 55	13.2		H		Tula		25 Aug
Lidia	Okolo-Kulak	SU 67	13.2		1		Minsk		26 Aug
Svetlana	Gerevich	SU 66	13.2		1		Vinnitsa		29 Sep
(25)									
Odalys	Adams	CUB 67	13.3		2 Mar	Natalya	Belenkova	SU 65	13.4		6 Jul
Maria	Usifo	NIG 64	13.3		31 Mar	Irina	Zaitseva	SU 60	13.4	0.0	14 Jul
Pauline	Calhoun	USA	13.3		31 Mar	LaVonna	Martin	USA 66	13.4		14 Jul
Hilsa	van den Heever	RSA 61	13.3		23 Apr	Valda	Ruskite	SU 62	13.4		4 Aug
Marina	Morozova	SU 60	13.3		6 Jul	Olga	Litvinova	SU 64	13.4	0.1	11 Aug
(30)						Svetlana	Ovchinnikova	SU 56	13.4		11 Aug
Kathy	Freeman	USA 62	13.4		31 Mar	(40)					
Marina	Yachnyuk	SU 60	13.4		12 May	Lyudmila	Orinyanskaya	SU 56	13.4	0.9	14 Aug
Lyudmila	Palamarenko	SU 50	13.4		12 May	Natalya	Tochilova	SU 64	13.4		25 Aug
Irina	Malykh	SU 58	13.4		5 Jul	Riana	Raath	RSA 61	A13.4		3 Nov

1984 Lists – Women

Marks made with assisting wind greater than 2 m/s

Liliana	Nastase	RUM 62	12.8		1		Bucuresti	20 May
Sally	Gunnell	UK 66	13.1	4.0	H	v Nor	Nadderud	7 Jul
Lillian	Cole	USA 61	13.2		1		Tuskegee	21 Apr
Florence	Colle	FRA 65	13.2		1		Poitiers	27 May
Karen	Nelson	CAN 63	13.2	5.0	1		Sacramento	21 Jul
Isabelle	Kaftandjian	FRA 64	13.3		27 May			
Heidi	Benserud	NOR 58	13.3	4.0	7 Jul			
Sophia	Hunter	JAM 64	13.3	5.0	21 Jul			
Heather	Ross	UK 62	13.4		7 May			
Patsy	Walker	USA 59	13.4	5.0	21 Jul			

400 METRES HURDLES

Margarita	Ponomaryova	SU 63	53.58	1		Kiev	22 Jun
Marina	Stepanova	SU 50	53.67	1	DRZ	Praha	17 Aug
	Stepanova		54.34	2		Kiev	22 Jun
Yekaterina	Grun	SU 58	54.34	1		Moskva	20 Jul
	Ponomaryova		54.36	1	OD	Potsdam	21 Jul
	Stepanova		54.40	2	OD	Potsdam	21 Jul
	Grun		54.42	2	DRZ	Praha	17 Aug
Tatyana	Zubova	SU 58	54.43	3		Kiev	22 Jun
Yelena	Filipishina	SU 62	54.56	2		Moskva	20 Jul
	Ponomaryova		54.61	1s2		Kiev	21 Jun
Nawal	El Moutawakil	MOR 62	54.61	1	OG	Los Angeles	8 Aug
	Ponomaryova		54.65	3	DRZ	Praha	17 Aug
Birgit	Uibel	GDR 61	54.68	1		Dresden	19 May
	Stepanova		54.68	1		Moskva	4 Aug
	Stepanova		54.78	1	Znam	Sochi	10 Jun
Genowefa	Blaszak	POL 57	54.78	1	DNG	Stockholm	2 Jul
Anna	Ambraziene	SU 55	54.81	1	NarMl	Sofia	20 May
	Stepanova		54.83	1h2	DRZ	Praha	16 Aug
	Filipishina		54.84	4		Kiev	22 Jun
	Grun		54.85	5		Kiev	22 Jun
	Uibel		54.90	1	NC	Erfurt	2 Jun
	Ponomaryova		54.93	1		Sochi	20 May
Judi	Brown	USA 61	54.93	1	FOT	Los Angeles	21 Jun

(10)

	Zubova		54.98	1s1		Kiev	21 Jun
	Brown		54.99	1	TAC	San Jose	9 Jun
Margarita	Navickaite	SU 61	55.02	6		Kiev	22 Jun
	Filipishina		55.02	1	NC	Donetsk	8 Sep
	Blaszak		55.04	1	v Ita,Hun,SU	Verona	1 Jun
	Ponomaryova		55.09	2	Znam	Sochi	10 Jun
Ann-Louise	Skoglund	SWE 62	55.17	1s1	OG	Los Angeles	6 Aug
	Filipishina		55.18	2		Sochi	20 May
	Stepanova		55.19	2s1		Kiev	21 Jun
	Zubova		55.19	3		Moskva	20 Jul
Leslie	Maxie	USA 67	55.20	2	TAC	San Jose	9 Jun
	Brown		55.20	2	OG	Los Angeles	8 Aug

(35/13)

Cristina	Cojocaru	RUM 62	55.24	2s1	OG	Los Angeles	6 Aug
Angela	Wright	USA 61	55.33	2	FOT	Los Angeles	21 Jun
Ellen	Fiedler	GDR 58	55.40	2		Dresden	19 May
P.T.	Usha	IND 64	55.42	4	OG	Los Angeles	8 Aug
Radostina	Dimitrova	BUL 66	55.53	3	OD	Potsdam	21 Jul

395

1984 Lists – Women

Sharieffa	Barksdale	USA 61	55.58		3	FOT	Los Angeles	21 Jun	
Lori	McCauley	USA 61	55.60		4	FOT	Los Angeles	21 Jun	

(20)

Petra	Pfaff	GDR 60	55.63		2	NC	Erfurt	2 Jun	
Marina	Kotenyova	SU 64	55.64		7		Kiev	22 Jun	
Nicoleta	Vornicu	RUM 64	55.67		2	NC	Bucuresti	12 Jul	
Yelena	Goncharova	SU 63	55.76		2	v Rum	Bucuresti	16 Sep	
Valentina	Grishkina	SU 56	55.79		5		Moskva	20 Jul	
Petra	Krug	GDR 63	55.95		3	Skok	Celje	5 May	
Latanya	Sheffield	USA 63	56.02		1	Pepsi	Westwood	13 May	
Debbie	Flintoff	AUS 60	56.02		1	ISTAF	W Berlin	17 Aug	
Sandra	Farmer	JAM 62	56.05		4s1	OG	Los Angeles	6 Aug	
Charmaine	Fick	RSA 59	A56.08		1		Bloemfontein	6 Feb	

(30)

Tatyana	Vasilenko	SU 57	56.10		6		Moskva	20 Jul	
Larisa	Abramova	SU 61	56.11		3		Sochi	20 May	
Myrtle	Simpson	RSA 64	56.25		1	NC	Durban	14 Apr	
Patty	Bradley								
		USA 62	56.26		1	King	Atlanta	22 Apr	
Christine	Slythe	CAN 61	A56.32		1		Provo	19 May	
Sylvia	Kirchner	GDR 63	56.36		2		Jena	13 May	
Edna	Brown	USA 60	56.42		1		Tempe	7 Apr	
Robin	Marks	USA 62	56.42		3s2	FOT	Los Angeles	19 Jun	
Yelena	Yefimova	SU 61	56.42		h		Moskva	19 Jul	
Giuseppina	Cirulli	ITA 59	56.44		1	v CS	Catania	7 Sep	

(40)

Piper	Bressant	USA 63	56.48		4s1	FOT	Los Angeles	19 Jun	
Olga	Commandeur	HOL 58	56.51		1		Hengelo	6 Jul	
Tuija	Helander	FIN 61	56.55		7	OG	Los Angeles	8 Aug	
Nadezhda	Asenova	BUL 62	56.59		1	NC	Sofia	3 Jun	
Sue	Morley	UK 60	56.67		7s1	OG	Los Angeles	6 Aug	
Jeanette	Kreisch	GDR 65	56.70		2		Berlin	15 Jul	
Gladys	Taylor	UK 53	56.72		5s2	OG	Los Angeles	6 Aug	
Natalya	Baranova	SU 60	56.77		h		Sochi	26 May	
Irina	Dorofeyeva	SU 62	56.82		5s2		Kiev	21 Jun	
Iris	Radisch	GDR 63	56.86		4h1	NC	Erfurt	1 Jun	

(50)

Olga	Gerasimova	SU 56	56.88		1r2	Znam	Sochi	10 Jun	
Colleen	Cozzetto	USA 60	56.96		3h4	FOT	Los Angeles	18 Jun	
Ruth	Kyalisima	UGA 55	57.02		7s2	OG	Los Angeles	6 Aug	
Jolanta	Stalmach	POL 60	57.04		2	v Bul,FRG,Hun	Warszawa	15 Jul	
Emilia	Pencheva	BUL 60	57.06		2	NC	Sofia	3 Jun	
Svetlana	Korchagina	SU 57	57.12		1r2	NC	Donetsk	8 Sep	
Cornelia	Mangelow	GDR 62	57.18		5h1	NC	Erfurt	1 Jun	
Erika	Szopori	HUN 63	57.18		7	DRZ	Praha	17 Aug	
Marlies	Harnes	FRG 53	57.20		1		Stuttgart	21 Jul	
Sybil	Perry	USA 63	57.22		7s1	FOT	Los Angeles	19 Jun	

(60)

Andrea	Page	CAN 56	57.26		1	NC	Winnipeg	1 Jul	
Gwen	Wall	CAN 63	57.28		1		Saskatoon	27 May	
Caroline	Pluss	SWZ 59	57.36		2		Riehen	11 Jun	
Lexie	Beck	USA 61	57.36		6s2	FOT	Los Angeles	19 Jun	
Leanna	Stojanowski	CAN 65	57.36		2	NC	Winnipeg	1 Jul	
Maria	Usifo	NIG 64	57.39		1		Baton Rouge	4 May	
Frauke	Jurgens	GDR 66	57.40		1		Leipzig	13 Jun	
Lynnette	Grime	NZ 62	57.42		2	Aus C	Melbourne	1 Apr	

1984 Lists – Women

| Natalya | Sukhorukova | SU 64 | 57.42 | | /s1 | | Kiev | 21 Jun |
| Lyubov | Shelomkova | SU 56 | 57.44 | | h | | Moskva | 19 Jul |

(70)

Dana	Wright	CAN 59	57.45		1		Montreal	14 Jul
Bonka	Dimova	BUL 56	57.48		3		Sofia	4 Jul
Ovrill	Brown	JAM 61	57.49		2		Tallahassee	21 Apr
Maureen	Prendergast	UK 59	57.49		2	WAAA	London	16 Jun
Debbie	Tomsett	AUS 60	57.51		3	NC	Melbourne	1 Apr
Leisa	Davis	USA 63	57.51		3h1	FOT	Los Angeles	18 Jun
Irina	Petrova	SU 61	57.55		h		Leningrad	15 Jul
Anna	Filickova	CS 62	57.55		1	NC	Praha	22 Jul
Kathy	Freeman	USA 62	57.57		2		Baton Rouge	4 May
Elina	Babich	SU 64	57.60		3r2	NC	Donetsk	8 Sep

(80)

Dominique	Le Disses	FRA 57	57.65		1	NC	Lille	1 Jul
Helle	Sichlau	DEN 57	57.65		2		Stockholm	17 Jul
Stella	Edwinson	USA 57	57.72		1		Los Gatos	19 May
Sigrun	Ludwigs	GDR 65	57.80		1		Praha	28 Aug
Gisela	Kinzel	FRG 61	57.81		2	v CS,Fra,Pol	Hannover	15 Jun
Justine	Craig	NZ	57.83		2	TexR	Austin	6 Apr
Gudrun	Abt	FRG 62	57.85		1		Friedrichshafen	24 Aug
Olga	Veikshina	SU 61	57.88		h	NC	Donetsk	8 Sep
Evalene	Hatcher	USA 59	57.91		4h2	FOT	Los Angeles	18 Jun
Gayle	Kellon	USA 65	57.94		2	MSR	Walnut, CA	29 Apr

(90)

Teresa	Hoyle	UK 63	57.96		1		Dallas	19 May
Alla	Bolshakova	SU 61	57.98		h	NC	Donetsk	8 Sep
Shannon	Vessup	USA 60	A57.99		1		Provo	12 May
Terry	Genge	NZ 57	58.01		4	Aus C	Melbourne	1 Apr
Yelena	Ryazanova	SU 62	58.04		1		Kiev	4 Jul
Kristina	Jauch	GDR 65	58.05		5		Erfurt	12 May
Michelle	Taylor	USA 67	58.06		1s2	TAC-j	Los Angeles	23 Jun
Gerda	Haas	AUT 65	58.06		1		Schwechat	30 Jun
Eva	Eibnerova	CS 62	58.06		2	v Ita	Catania	7 Sep
Margaret	Southerden	UK 56	58.07		3	WAAA	London	16 Jun

(100)

Sylvia	Sam	GDR 65	58.09		3		Potsdam	6 May
Diana	Ivanova	BUL 66	58.10		5		Sofia	4 Jul
Beate	Holzapfel	FRG 66	58.10		1	NC-y	Fulda	21 Jul
Xenia	Siska	HUN 57	58.12		2		Miskolc	17 Jun
Sametra	King	USA 66	58.13		2s2	TAC-j	Los Angeles	23 Jun
Rachel	Clary	USA 62	58.14		1		Austin	12 May

(106)   (110)

Lynnette	Kay	NZ	58.21	15 Dec	Mojca	Pertot	YUG 59	58.28	8 Sep
Olga	Rovnyagina	SU 65	58.24	4 Jul	Maria	Shoup	USA 63	58.29	19 May
Heike	Tillack	GDR 68	58.24	5 Aug	Wendy	Griffiths	UK 60	58.34	10 Jun
Gaby	Pruter	FRG 63	58.28	19 Aug	Elmarie	Vogel	RSA 60	A58.35	5 Mar

1984 Lists – Women

Sally	Andersen	USA 61	58.35	7 Jun	Chantal	Beaugeant	FRA 61	59.04		30 Sep
Debbie	Grant	USA 65	58.37	13 May	Nicole	Ali	CAN 64	59.06		5 May
Martine	Mathiot	FRA 57	58.37	1 Jul	Jinhua	Liu	CHN 61	59.07		6 Sep
Bermien	Conradie	RSA 62	A58.38	5 Mar	Cathy	Wilson	AUS 67	59.10		30 Mar
Elsbeth	Helbling	SWZ 55	58.38	1 Jun	Yvette	Cash	USA 65	59.11		12 May
Malgorzata	Gasior	POL 63	58.39	18 Aug	Selina	Christian	USA 64	59.11		25 May

(120) (170)

Sabine	Nolte	FRG 68	58.47	1 Jul	Svetla	Bankova	BUL 67	59.12		5 Aug
Angela	Wilhelm	FRG 59	58.48	24 Jun	Eszter	Tarjanyi	HUN 62	59.15		27 Jul
Yelena	Klimova	SU 66	58.50	23 Jun	Annie	le Roux	RSA 65	59.16		10 Dec
Clare	Sugden	UK 64	58.53	16 Jun	Tracy	Nelson	USA 63	59.18		18 May
Lih-jiau	Lai	TAI 55	58.54	5 Aug	Marina	Kogut	SU 66	59.19		13 Jul
Lyudmila	Komarova	SU 61	58.58	4 Jul	Tatyana	Ivanova	SU 64	59.22		9 Jun
Cristina	Moretti	SWZ 63	58.59	11 Jun	Chris	McKay	CAN 62	59.23		26 May
Chris	Crowther	USA 63	58.60	14 Apr	April	Cook	USA 65	59.24		12 May
Ingrid	Stoot	HOL 64	58.62	23 Jun	Susan	Cluney	UK 59	59.24		15 Jun
Helene	Huart	FRA 65	58.63	1 Jul	Irmgard	Trojer	ITA 64	59.25		11 Jul

(130) (180)

Tonja	Brown	USA 60	58.66	28 Apr	Jennifer	Seamon	UK 62	59.26		16 Jun
Suzi	Shreckhise	USA 61	58.66	19 May	Yolanda	Dolz	SPA 61	59.26		1 Jul
Rose	Tata-Muya	KEN 60	58.66	20 May	Kerstin	Goransson	SWE 65	59.27		18 Aug
Christina	Wennberg	SWE 63	58.66	26 Aug	Christa	Vandercruyssen	BEL 61	59.28		1 Jun
Leonie	Louwrens	RSA 59	58.70	14 Apr	Dagmar	Karck	FRG 53	59.29		21 Jul
Jacqueline	Hautenauve	BEL 62	58.71	8 Jul	Angela	Williams	USA 63	59.30		28 Apr
Lynn	Gamble	USA 61	58.72	7 Jun	Almetha	Rowland	USA 63	59.30		26 May
Sabine	Zwiener	FRG 67	58.72	20 Jul	Florence	Barbarit	FRA 61	59.30		3 Jun
Cynthia	Green	JAM 60	58.73	22 Apr	Kim	Duke	USA 66	59.33		24 Jun
Elaine	McLaughlin	UK 63	58.73	2 Sep	Cheryl	Blackman	BAR 57	59.35		8 Jul

(140) (190)

Mary	Parr	IRL 61	58.74	8 Jul	Mia	Gabbedy	AUS 66	59.39		30 Mar
Anne	Gundersen	NOR 66	58.75	17 Jun	Marinela	Docea	RUM 68	59.39		1 Sep
Simone	Gandy	UK 65	58.76	28 May	Corne	Harmse	RSA 65	59.42		14 Apr
Rosa	Colorado	SPA 54	58.76	14 Jul	Judit	Szekeres	HUN 66	59.42		20 May
Lyubov	Kovalenko	SU 63	58.76	5 Aug	Svetlana	Kovazhenkova	SU 64	59.43		5 Aug
Glynis	Nunn	AUS 60	58.82	11 Mar	Camelia	Jianu	RUM 67	59.44		
Yoko	Satoh	JAP 66	58.82	30 Aug	Olesya	Ilmovskaya	SU 62	59.45		27 May
Dongmei	Chen	CHN 60	58.83	6 Sep	Annika	Sjolen	SWE 63	59.45		26 Aug
Joanne	Finkbeiner	CAN 58	A58.84	1 Jun	Christine	Karcher	FRG 61	59.48		7 Jul
LaVonna	Martin	USA 66	58.84	22 Jul	Francoise	Dethier	BEL 65	59.48		8 Jul

(150) (200)

Carol	Dawkins	UK 60	58.84	2 Sep	Grace	Jackson	JAM 61	59.49		21 Apr
Galina	Levchenko	SU 63	58.86	16 Sep	Dana	Tesarova	CS 65	59.49		8 Jul
Cristina	Vlasceanu	RUM 67	58.89	1 Sep						
Natalya	Kalinnikova	SU 62	58.89	8 Sep	(202)					
Karin	Wiesel	FRG 64	58.90	19 Aug						
Birgit	Wolf	FRG 60	58.92	24 Jun	**Best low altitude marks**					
Konnie	Mackey	USA 62	A58.93	12 May						
Claudia	Schittenhelm	FRG 65	58.94	19 Aug	Slythe		57.93	2	Montreal	14 Jul
Margaret	Hemmans	USA	58.96	26 May						
Donalda	Duprey	CAN 67	58.99	23 Aug	Vogel			58.47		14 Apr
					Conradie			58.61		

(160)

Debbie	Carson	USA 58	59.00	19 May	Vessup			59.34	18 Jun
Heike	Huneke	FRG 66	59.00	1 Jul	Mackey			59.44	21 Apr
Karen	Wilkenson	RSA 66	59.02	7 Dec					
Elke	Krammel	FRG 66	59.03	19 Aug					

1984 Lists – Women

Marks made in mixed race with men

| Evalene | Hatcher | USA 59 | 57.69 | | | | Knoxville | 25 May |

| | | | | | | | Under | Under |
	1	10	20	30	50	100	57.00	59.00
1980	54.28	56.16	56.96	57.79	58.48	59.69	20	63
1981	54.79	56.36	56.93	57.45	58.10	59.24	20	84
1982	54.57	55.76	56.48	57.00	57.86	58.79	29	109
1983	54.02	55.49	56.03	56.26	57.00	58.20	49	147
1984	53.58	54.93	55.60	56.08	56.86	58.07	52	160

Hand timing

	Ponomaryova		54.7		1h		Kiev	20 Jun
	Zubova		54.7		1		Moskva	9 Jul
	Filipishina		54.9		1		Gorkiy	12 Aug
	Ponomaryova		55.0		1		Tashkent	22 Apr

(4/3)

Olga	Veikshina	SU 61	55.5		1		Leningrad	3 Jun
Yelena	Yefimova	SU 61	55.9		1		Kirov	15 Jul
Natalya	Baranova	SU 60	56.0		2		Tula	15 Jul
Larisa	Abramova	SU 61	56.1		1		Krasnodar	7 Apr
Olga	Gerasimova	SU 56	56.2		2		Tashkent	22 Apr
Lyubov	Shelomkova	SU 56	56.4		2		Vilnius	5 Aug
A	Strezkite	SU	56.4		1		Klaipeda	19 Aug

(10)

Galina	Yepanova	SU 60	56.7		4		Gorkiy	12 Aug
Irina	Petrova	SU 61	56.8		1		Riga	5 Jul
Audra	Racaite	SU 64	57.1		5		Vilnius	5 Aug
Svetlana	Azhel	SU 63	57.2		h		Gorkiy	12 Aug
Lexie	Beck	USA 61	57.3		1		San Diego	25 May
Galina	Levchenko	SU 63	57.4		3		Alma Ata	29 Jul
Yekaterina	Bezborodova	SU 62	57.5		4		Leningrad	7 Jul
M.D.	Valsamma	IND 60	57.7		2		New Delhi	15 Jun
Lyubov	Kovalenko	SU 63	57.7		5		Leningrad	7 Jul
Alla	Bolshakova	SU 61	57.9				Yaroslav	30 May

(20)

Tonja	Brown	USA 60	58.0	25 May	Olga	Kosovskaya	SU 64	58.6	20 Jun
Rose	Tata-Muya	KEN 60	58.0	16 Jun	Marina	Volokhova	SU 64	58.6	8 Aug
Maria	Fialho	BRA 60	58.0	17 Jun	Lyudmila	Rybalko	SU 59	58.7	9 Jul
Wendy	Griffiths	UK 60	58.2	28 May	Galina	Kotova	SU 60	58.7	15 Jul
Andzhela	Smantser	SU 63	58.2	29 Jul	Galina	Govdun	SU 63	58.7	5 Aug
Olga	Velikanova	SU 68	58.2	21 Sep	Ina	van Rensburg	RSA 56	58.8	29 Feb
Chris	Crowther	USA 63	58.3	13 May	Olesya	Ilmovskaya	SU 62	58.8	3 Jun
Simone	Gandy	UK 65	58.3	14 Jul	Rositsa	Petkova	BUL 65	58.8	
Mary	Parr	IRL 61	58.3	14 Jul					
Yelena	Merzlyakova	SU 62	58.5	12 Aug	(40)				

(30)

					Yelena	Naumova	SU 60	58.8	13 Aug
					Lyudmila	Myachikova	SU 64	58.9	16 Jun
Elaine	McLaughlin	UK 63	58.5	25 Aug	Yelena	Bushuyeva	SU 60	58.9	9 Jul
Aurica	Mitrea	RUM 59	58.6	3 Jun	Yelena	Timishenko	SU 67	59.0	May

399

1984 Lists – Women

Marina	Kogut	SU 66	59.0	1 Jul	(50)					
Aileen	Mills	UK 62	59.0	26 Aug						
Svetlana	Opushanskaya	SU 63	59.1	12 Aug	Maureen	Barnes	UK 63	59.2		
Jane	Finch	UK 57	59.2	5 May	Rimma	Klimantaite	SU 66	59.2		20 Sep
Yelena	Lukyanova	SU 64	59.2	24 Jun						
Yekaterina	Gaponova	SU 60	59.2	7 Jul	(52)					

HIGH JUMP

Lyudmila	Andonova	BUL 60	2.07		1	OD	Berlin	20 Jul	
Tamara	Bykova	SU 58	2.05		1		Kiev	22 Jun	
	Bykova		2.03		1		Moskva	6 Aug	
	Andonova		2.03		1		Rieti	2 Sep	
Ulrike	Meyfarth	FRG 56	2.02		1	OG	Los Angeles	10 Aug	
	Andonova		2.02		1	GGala	Roma	31 Aug	
	Bykova		2.00	i	1	TAC	New York	24 Feb	
	Bykova		2.00		1	Znam	Sochi	10 Jun	
	Andonova		2.00		1		Sofia	8 Aug	
Sara	Simeoni	ITA 53	2.00		2	OG	Los Angeles	10 Aug	
Stefka	Kostadinova	BUL 65	2.00		1		Sofia	25 Aug	
	Andonova		2.00		1		Rovereto	29 Aug	
Silvia	Costa	CUB 64	1.99		1		Verona	1 Jun	
	Andonova		1.99		1		Worrstadt	9 Jun	
	Bykova		1.98	i	1	v Ita,Spa	Milano	1 Feb	
Lyudmila	Butuzova	SU 57	1.98		2	Znam	Sochi	10 Jun	
	Bykova		1.98		2	OD	Berlin	20 Jul	
	Kostadinova		1.98		2		Sofia	8 Aug	
	Bykova		1.98		2	GGala	Roma	31 Aug	
Debbie	Brill	CAN 53	1.98		2		Rieti	2 Sep	
	Andonova		1.98		1		Paris	4 Sep	
Marina	Doronina	SU 61	1.97	i	1		Vilnius	14 Jan	
Danuta	Bulkowska	POL 59	1.97		2		Worrstadt	9 Jun	
(10)									
Olga	Belkova	SU 56	1.97		2		Kiev	22 Jun	
	Butuzova		1.97		2		Moskva	6 Aug	
Joni	Huntley	USA 56	1.97		3	OG	Los Angeles	10 Aug	
	Andonova		1.97		1	Balk	Athinai	9 Sep	
	Kostadinova		1.97		2	Balk	Athinai	9 Sep	
Louise	Ritter	USA 58	1.96	i	1		Ottawa	13 Jan	
Susanne	Helm	GDR 61	1.96	i	1	NC	Senftenberg	22 Jan	
	Andonova		1.96		1	NarMl	Sofia	19 May	
Andrea	Bienias	GDR 59	1.96		1		Potsdam	25 May	
	Bykova		1.96		1		Saint Denis	2 Jun	
	Helm		1.96		3	OD	Berlin	20 Jul	
	Bienias		1.96		4	OD	Berlin	20 Jul	
	Kostadinova		1.96		5	OD	Berlin	20 Jul	
	Butuzova		1.96		6	OD	Berlin	20 Jul	
	Andonova		1.96		1	DRZ	Praha	17 Aug	
	Butuzova		1.96		2	DRZ	Praha	17 Aug	
	Bykova		1.96		3	DRZ	Praha	17 Aug	
	Brill		1.96		1	Nik	Nice	20 Aug	
	Brill		1.96		1	WK	Zurich	22 Aug	
	Bulkowska		1.96		1		Koln	26 Aug	
	Brill		1.96		2		Koln	26 Aug	
	Kostadinova		1.96		2		Paris	4 Sep	
Olga	Turchak	SU 67	1.96		1	NC	Donetsk	7 Sep	
	Doronina		1.96		2	NC	Donetsk	7 Sep	
(47/16)									
Maryse	Ewanje-Epee	FRA 64	1.95	i	2	EC	Goteborg	4 Mar	
Niculina	Vasile	RUM 58	1.95		1		Bucuresti	20 May	
Larisa	Petrus	SU 63	1.95		3		Kiev	22 Jun	
Jolanta	Komsa	POL 58	1.95		1		Zabrze	14 Sep	

1984 Lists – Women

Christine	Soetewey	BEL 57	1.94	i	1		Hoboken	5 Feb
Chris	Stanton	AUS 59	1.94		1		Adelaide	14 Mar
Albina	Kazakova	SU 62	1.94		2		Chelyabinsk	29 Jul
Vanessa	Browne	AUS 63	1.94		6	OG	Los Angeles	10 Aug
Svetlana	Nikolayeva	SU 59	1.93	i	2	NC	Moskva	19 Feb
Galina	Brigadnaya	SU 58	1.93	i	3	NC	Moskva	19 Feb
Brigitte	Holzapfel	FRG 58	1.93	i	2		W Berlin	24 Feb
Pam	Spencer	USA 57	1.93		1	Pepsi	Westwood	13 May
Susanne	Lorentzon	SWE 61	1.93		1	NC	Vaxjo	26 Aug
Heike	Grabe	GDR 62	1.92	i	2	NC	Senftenberg	22 Jan
Tamara	Malesev	YUG 67	1.92	i	5	EC	Goteborg	4 Mar
Brigitte	Rougeron	FRA 61	1.92		1		Haguenau	27 May
Olga	Juha	HUN 62	1.92		2		Formia	30 Jun
Gabriela	Mihalcea	RUM 64	1.92		2	NC	Bucuresti	12 Jul
Wenqing	Yang	CHN 60	1.92		1		Eugene	18 Jul
Diana	Davies	UK 61	1.92		2	8N	Tokyo	14 Sep
Yelena	Duginets	SU 59	1.91	i	1		Klaipeda	28 Jan
Heike	Redetzky	FRG 64	1.91	i	1		Nordlingen	26 Feb
Ping	Ge	CHN 61	1.91		2		Perth	18 Mar
Marina	Serkova	SU 61	1.91		1		Yaroslavl	30 May
Dazhen	Zheng	CHN 59	1.91		7	OG	Los Angeles	10 Aug
Vesna	Lukovic	YUG 59	1.91		1	v UK	Karlovac	16 Sep
Lisa	Bernhagen	USA 66	1.905		1		Pocatello	18 Feb
Nina	Serbina	SU 52	1.90	i	2		Minsk	15 Jan
Svetlana	Mokrak	SU 67	1.90		1		Chelyabinsk	5 Feb
Yelena	Chaykovskaya	SU 63	1.90		1		Minsk	5 Feb
Larisa	Kositsyna	SU 63	1.90		1		Moskva	10 Feb
Gaby	Lindenthal	SWZ 59	1.90		1	NC	Magglingen	19 Feb
Petra	Wziontek	FRG 60	1.90	i	4t		W Berlin	24 Feb
Liliana	Arigoni	ARG 63	1.90		1		Santa Fe	5 May
Birgit	Dressel	FRG 60	1.90		H	v Bul	Mannheim	8 Jun
Judy	Simpson	UK 60	1.90		H		Mannheim	8 Jun
Natalya	Kravchinskaya	SU 57	1.90		1		Poltava	16 Jun
Ivana	Jobbova	CS 65	1.90		1		Bratislava	8 Jul
Valentina	Andryushchenko	SU 59	1.90		1		Yalta	29 Sep
Hisayo	Fukumitsu	JAP 60	1.90		1	NC	Tokyo	21 Oct
Kristine	Nitzsche	GDR 59	1.89	i	P	v SU	Senftenberg	26 Jan
Andrea	Breder	FRG 64	1.89	i	2		Sindelfingen	1 Feb
Wendy	Brown	USA 66	1.89		1		San Jose	21 Apr
Ana Maria	Marcon	BRA 59	1.89		1		Sao Paulo	5 May
Debora	Marti	UK 68	1.89		1		Hendon	2 Jun
Lidija	Lapajne	YUG 59	1.89		6		Worrstadt	9 Jun
Xiuling	Ni	CHN 62	1.89				Nanjing	10 Jun
Alla	Fedorchuk	SU 57	1.89		2		Minsk	27 Jun
Sabine	Everts	FRG 61	1.89		H	OG	Los Angeles	3 Aug
Galina	Nazaurova	SU 58	1.89		1		Jablonec	5 Aug
Svetlana	Dvornik	SU 62	1.89		1		Minsk	10 Aug
Raisa	Zemshchikova	SU 57	1.89		1		Minsk	10 Aug
Thordis	Gisladottir	ICE 61	1.88	i	3		Ottawa	13 Jan
Lilia	Zablotskaya	SU 65	1.88	i	5		Vilnius	14 Jan
Alessandra	Fossati	ITA 63	1.88	i	1		Genova	25 Jan
Zhanna	Nekrasova	SU 55	1.88	i	2		Klaipeda	28 Jan
Katrina	Morrow	AUS 59	1.88		1		Sydney	11 Feb
Marina	Sysoyeva	SU 59	1.88	i		NC	Moskva	19 Feb
Charmaine	Gale	RSA 64	1.88		1		Pretoria	7 Apr
Irina	Barinova	SU 61	1.88		2		Moskva	11 May
Carina	Westover	USA 61	1.88		1		Pullman	12 May
Jane	Frederick	USA 52	1.88		2	Pepsi	Westwood	13 May
Malgorzata	Nowak	POL 59	1.88		H		Bydgoszcz	19 May
Phyllis	Bluntson	USA 59	1.88		1		San Jose	26 May
Kim	Hagger	UK 61	1.88		H	NC	Cwmbran	27 May
Svetlana	Gorbunova	SU 62	1.88		1		Riga	2 Jun

1984 Lists – Women

Name	Surname	Nat/Yr	Mark		Rd	Meet	Venue	Date
Ute	Kuhn	GDR 65	1.88		2		Berlin	9 Jun
Sylvia	Sittner	GDR 61	1.88		5		Berlin	9 Jun
Latrese	Johnson	USA 66	1.88		1	TAC–j	Los Angeles	24 Jun
Niina	Vihanto	FIN 62	1.88		1	NC	Kajaani	6 Jul
Svetlana	Isaeva	BUL 67	1.88		1		Pleven	7 Jul
Irina	Kharkova	SU 65	1.88		1	NC–j	Riga	13 Jul
Nadezhda	Sharpilova	SU 59	1.88		3		Leningrad	14 Jul
Ortensia	Iancu	RUM 67	1.88		1	Balk–j	Maribor	29 Jun
Beate	Holzapfel	FRG 66	1.88		H	NC–y	Ulm	25 Aug
Yelena	Topchina	SU 66	1.88		2		Tashkent	22 Sep
Desiree	du Plessis	RSA 65	1.87		1	NC	Durban	14 Apr
Sue	McNeal	USA 62	1.87		1		Berkeley	14 Apr
Liliane	Menissier	FRA 60	1.87		H		Arles	28 Apr
Yolanda	Jones	USA 65	1.87		1		Austin	5 May
Louise	Manning	UK 67	1.87		1		Crawley	6 May
Astrid	Tveit	NOR 57	1.87		1		Oslo	22 May
Iris	Kunstner	FRG 60	1.87		H	v Bul	Mannheim	8 Jun
Katrena	Johnson	USA 64	1.87		3	TAC	San Jose	8 Jun
Elzbieta	Rosiak	POL 57	1.87		1		Zabrze	30 Jun
Sigrid	Kirchmann	AUT 66	1.87		1	NC	Wien	20 Jul
Ivana	Gerzova	CS 63	1.87		2	NC	Praha	21 Jul
Daniela	Reiska	CS 61	1.87		2		Praha	28 Aug
Natalya	Golodnova	SU 67	1.87		1		Frunze	8 Sep
Megumi	Satoh	JAP 66	1.87		2	NC	Tokyo	21 Oct
(106)								

Name	Surname	Nat/Yr	Mark	Date		Name	Surname	Nat/Yr	Mark	Date
Natalya	Sokolova	SU 60	1.86i	17 Jan		Ann	Bair	USA 61	1.85i	13 Jan
Sibylle	Thiele	GDR 65	1.86i	26 Jan		Yvona	Tichopadova	CS 64	1.85i	22 Jan
Ringa	Ropo	FIN 66	1.86i	29 Jan		Yevgenia	Peremetina	SU 59	1.85i	28 Jan
Agata	Jaroszek	POL 63	1.86i	11 Feb		Asta	Pociute	SU 62	1.85i	19 Feb
Jan	Chesbro	USA 58	1.86i	11 Feb		Irina	Grachova	SU 62	1.85i	19 Feb
Bonnie	Harrington	USA 62	1.86i	12 Feb		Lola	Butakhanova	SU 64	1.85i	19 Feb
Jana	Brenkusova	CS 64	1.86i	23 Feb		Christiane	Mergemann	FRG 65	1.85i	26 Feb
Deann	Bopf	AUS 62	1.86	11 Mar		Heidi	de Kock	RSA 59	1.85	17 Mar
Orlane	Santos	BRA 66	1.86	31 Mar		Galina	Gudileva	SU 65	1.85i	18 Mar
Debra	Larsen	USA 64	1.86	29 Apr		Annalize	Blignaut	RSA 67	1.85	31 Mar
Katalin	Vajda	HUN 65	1.86	6 May		Madelein	Otto	RSA 67	1.85	14 Apr
Judit	Kovacs	HUN 69	1.86	19 May		Lyudmila	Sachava	SU 63	1.85	27 Apr
Yekaterina	Smirnova	SU 56	1.86	19 May		Asuncion	Morte	SPA 59	1.85	1 May
Urszula	Kielan	POL 60	1.86	20 May		Petra	Zech	GDR 62	1.85	25 May
Tonya	Alston	USA 60	1.86	2 Jun		Annette	Hausner	GDR 64	1.85	25 May
Gillian	Evans	UK 56	1.86	5 Jun		Svetlana	Musatkina	SU 66	1.85	2 Jun
Peisu	Ye	CHN 58	1.86	10 Jun		Yekaterina	Ryzhikh	SU 59	1.85	2 Jun
Svetlana	Ivshina	SU 62	1.86	20 Jun		Juliana	Tsvetanova	BUL 61	1.85	2 Jun
Marianna	Maslennikova	SU 61	1.86	20 Jun		Sylvie	Prenveille	FRA 58	1.85	3 Jun
Larisa	Nikitina	SU 65	1.86	20 Jun		Andreina	Antonini	ITA 62	1.85	9 Jun
Yelena	Bondar	SU 62	1.86	21 Jun		Natalya	Sergiyevich	SU 63	1.85	10 Jun
Mary	Moore	USA 65	1.86	22 Jun		Andrea	Matay	HUN 55	1.85	10 Jun
Frances	Calcutt	USA 61	1.86	22 Jun		Galina	Denisova	SU 60	1.85	16 Jun
Sandra	Dini	ITA 58	1.86	28 Jun		Anja	Barelkowski	FRG 65	1.85	16 Jun
Isabel	Mozun	SPA 60	1.86	1 Jul		May	Verheyen	BEL 63	1.85	
Christina	Nordstrom	SWE 61	1.86	9 Jul		Monica	Matei	RUM 63	1.85	12 Jul
Petra	Riehmann	GDR 68	1.86	11 Jul		Dorota	Kobedza	POL 65	1.85	13 Jul
Anke	Vater	GDR 61	1.86	20 Jul		Isabelle	Chevallier	FRA 67	1.85	13 Jul
Inese	Peterhofa	SU 62	1.86	28 Jul		Mirja	Jarvenpaa	FIN 62	1.85	15 Jul
Corinne	Schneider	SWZ 62	1.86	3 Aug		Svetlana	Filatyeva	SU 64	1.85	19 Jul
Maria	Danisova	CS 68	1.86	4 Aug		Angela	Palinske	GDR 65	1.85	21 Jul
Sabine	Bramhoff	FRG 64	1.86	29 Sep		Jayne	Barnetson	UK 68	1.85	21 Jul
Iris	Sonneborn	FRG 63	1.86	29 Sep		Brigitte	Kristoffersen	NOR 67	1.85	29 Jul
Peggy	Beer	GDR 69	1.86i	15 Dec		Minna	Vehmasto	FIN 62	1.85	7 Aug
Shelley	Fehrman	USA 65	1.855	17 Mar		Galina	Shatun	SU 63	1.85	11 Aug
Heather	Smith	JAM 64	1.855	14 Apr		Marianne	Vikne	NOR 67	1.85	11 Aug
						Marina	Degtyar	SU 62	1.85	15 Aug

1984 Lists – Women

Jackie	Joyner	USA 62	1.85	2 Sep
Yongjun	Liu	CHN 65	1.85	22 Sep
Inna	Naumova	SU 68	1.85	29 Sep

Best outdoor mark

Ewanje-Epee	1.94	4	OG	Los Angeles	10 Aug
Ritter	1.93	1		Philadelphia	27 Apr
Holzapfel	1.93	3		Worrstadt	9 Jun
Grabe	1.91	3		Karl-Marx-Stadt	20 May
Redetzky	1.91	1	NC	Dusseldorf	24 Jun
Soetewey	1.90	1		Bruxelles	30 Apr
Lindenthal	1.90	1		Riehen	11 Jun
Brigadnaya	1.90	3t	NC	Donetsk	7 Sep
Breder	1.89	7		Worrstadt	9 Jun
Bernhagen	1.89	1	PA-j	Nassau	24 Aug
Mokrak	1.88	1		Simferopol	27 May
Zablotskaya	1.88	6		Kiev	22 Jun
Duginets	1.88	1		Leningrad	14 Jul
Nekrasova	1.88	2		Leningrad	14 Jul

Thiele	1.86	5 May	Fossati	1.85	27 May
Malesev	1.86	9 Jun	Sokolova	1.85	2 Jun
Wziontek	1.86	9 Jun	Jaroszek	1.85	9 Jun
Chesbro	1.85	18 Mar	Brenkusova	1.85	30 Aug
Nikolayeva	1.85	19 May	Butakhanova	1.85	30 Sep
Gisladottir	1.85	19 May			

Extra trial

| Chris | Stanton | AUS 59 | 1.96 | | | Perth | 4 Feb |

Mark made with in mixed competition with men

| Chris | Stanton | AUS 59 | 1.95 | | | Perth | 22 Apr |

Additional jumps in series

Bykova	2.02	22 Jun	Andonova	2.00	2 Sep
Andonova	2.02	20 Jul	Bykova	1.99	22 Jun
Andonova	2.00	20 Jul	Andonova	1.98	20 Jul
Bykova	2.00	6 Aug	Andonova	1.98	31 Aug
Meyfarth	2.00	10 Aug	Andonova	1.98	2 Sep

	1	10	20	30	50	100	Over 1.90	Over 1.85
1980	1.98	1.94	1.92	1.90	1.88	1.85	35	110
1981	1.97	1.94	1.92	1.90	1.88	1.85	35	114
1982	2.02	1.97	1.93	1.91	1.89	1.86	48	135
1983	2.04	1.97	1.93	1.91	1.90	1.87	56	165
1984	2.07	1.97	1.95	1.92	1.90	1.87	56	182

LONG JUMP

Heike	Daute	GDR 64	7.40	1.8	1		Dresden	26 Jul
	Daute		7.34	1.6	1		Dresden	19 May
	Daute		7.32	−0.2	1	OD	Berlin	20 Jul
	Daute		7.29	0.0	1		Jena	13 May
Galina	Chistyakova	SU 62	7.29	−0.5	1		Moskva	6 Aug
Anisoara	Stanciu	RUM 62	7.27	1.0	1	v Bul,GDR	Sofia	17 Jun
	Chistyakova		7.21	1.6	1		Moskva	14 Jul
Helga	Radtke	GDR 62	7.21	1.6	2		Dresden	26 Jul
	Daute		7.18	0.0	1		Potsdam	25 May
	Daute		7.18	0.3	1		Berlin	15 Jul
	Daute		7.15	−0.3	1	DRZ	Praha	17 Aug
	Stanciu		7.14		1	NC	Bucuresti	12 Jul

403

1984 Lists – Women

Sabine	Paetz	GDR 57	7.12	1.6	2		Dresden	19 May
Vali	Ionescu	RUM 60	7.11	1.6	1		Madrid	21 Jun
	Radtke		7.11	0.6	2	DRZ	Praha	17 Aug
	Chistyakova		7.11	-0.5	3	DRZ	Praha	17 Aug
	Ionescu		7.09	0.5	1	RumIC	Bucuresti	9 Jun
	Daute		7.09	1.2	1		Berlin	9 Jun
Yelena	Kokonova	SU 63	7.09	0.1	1	NC	Donetsk	9 Sep
	Stanciu		7.08	1.6	2	RumIC	Bucuresti	9 Jun
	Radtke		7.07	0.8	2	OD	Berlin	20 Jul
	Radtke		7.07		1		Thessaloniki	29 Aug
	Ionescu		7.06		2	NC	Bucuresti	12 Jul
	Stanciu		7.03	1.6	1		Saint Denis	2 Jun
Tatyana	Proskuryakova	SU 56	7.02		1		Moskva	9 Jul
Niole	Medvedyeva	SU 60	7.02	0.5	4	DRZ	Praha	17 Aug
Eva	Murkova	CS 62	7.01	-0.3	1	PTS	Bratislava	26 May
	Ionescu		7.01	2.0	2	v Bul,GDR	Sofia	17 Jun
	Stanciu		7.01	1.8	–		Byrkjelo	1 Jul
Yelena	Ivanova	SU 61	7.01		2		Moskva	9 Jul
	Medvedyeva		7.01	0.8	2		Moskva	19 Jul
	Murkova		7.00	0.1	1	GS	Ostrava	23 May
	Daute		7.00	-0.9	1	NC	Erfurt	2 Jun
Birgit	Grosshennig	GDR 65	7.00	-0.2	2		Berlin	9 Jun
	Kokonova		7.00		1		Riga	6 Jul
(35/12)								
Carol	Lewis	USA 63	6.97	0.1	1	MSR	Walnut, CA	29 Apr
Anna	Wlodarczyk	POL 51	6.96	2.0	1	NC	Lublin	22 Jun
Christine	Schima	GDR 62	6.96	1.8	3		Dresden	26 Jul
Irina	Valyukevich	SU 59	6.95	0.2	2	NC	Donetsk	9 Sep
Yelena	Chicherova	SU 58	6.94	1.3	2		Kiev	23 Jun
Brigitte	Wujak	GDR 55	6.93	1.8	4		Dresden	19 May
Heike	Duwe	GDR 60	6.91	1.8	3		Berlin	9 Jun
Natalya	Shevchenko	SU 66	6.88	0.6	2		Sochi	26 May
Yelena	Mityayeva	SU 63	6.88		2		Riga	6 Jul
Sigrid	Ulbricht	GDR 58	6.84	0.2	2	NC	Erfurt	2 Jun
Natalya	Chemidronova	SU 59	6.84		1		Kazan	14 Jul
Anke	Vater	GDR 61	6.84	0.5	H	OD	Potsdam	21 Jul
Galina	Salo	SU 59	6.84	0.2	Q	NC	Donetsk	8 Sep
Sue	Telfer	UK 61	6.83	0.2	1		Cleckheaton	6 May
Yolanda	Chen	SU 61	6.83	1.0	2	Znam	Sochi	9 Jun
Olga	Anufriyeva	SU 55	6.82	0.6	6		Kiev	23 Jun
Angela	Thacker	USA 64	6.81	1.8	1		Lincoln	11 May
Jackie	Joyner	USA 62	6.81	-0.2	H	FOT	Los Angeles	17 Jun
Nadezhda	Sokolova	SU 59	6.81		4		Riga	6 Jul
Lyudmila	Ninova	BUL 60	6.80	1.5	1		Sofia	27 May
Vera	Olenchenko	SU 59	6.79		5		Riga	6 Jul
Bev	Kinch	UK 64	6.79		1		San Diego	7 Jul
Natalya	Pozdina	SU 58	6.78		2		Kazan	14 Jul
Sabine	Everts	FRG 61	6.77	1.6	1		Stuttgart	21 Jul
Natalya	Grachova	SU 52	6.77	0.6	1	DRZ	Praha	17 Aug
Klara	Novobaczky	HUN 58	6.76	1.8	1		Budapest	23 Jun
Ines	Schmidt	GDR 60	6.76	-0.6	1		Praha	18 Aug
Robyne	Lorraway	AUS 61	6.75		1		Canberra	28 Jan
Jennifer	Inniss	GUY 59	6.74		1		Los Angeles	21 Apr
Natalya	Shubenkova	SU 57	6.73	0.4	H	NC	Kiev	21 Jun
Larisa	Baluta	SU 65	6.71	– i	Q	NC	Moskva	17 Feb
Shonel	Ferguson	BAH 57	6.71	-0.4	1	TAC	San Jose	8 Jun
Tsetska	Kancheva	BUL 63	6.71	1.6	1		Pleven	7 Jul
Ramona	Neubert	GDR 58	6.71		H	OD	Potsdam	21 Jul
Nadezhda	Vinogradova	SU 59	6.70	1.8	H	v GDR	Neubrandenburg	3 Jun
Sibylle	Thiele	GDR 65	6.69	-0.5	H		Gotzis	20 May
Irina	Oreshkina	SU 64	6.69		1		Tula	15 Jul
Marieta	Ilcu	RUM 62	6.69		1		Deva	28 Jul

404

1984 Lists – Women

Gina	Ghioroaie	RUM 58	6.68		4	v Bul,GD	R Sofia	17 Jun
Siegrun	Siegl	GDR 54	6.67	0.0	3		Jena	13 May
Valentina	Kovalyova	SU 60	6.67		2		Tula	15 Jul
Marion	Weser	GDR 62	6.66	– i	1		Berlin	25 Jan
Glynis	Nunn	AUS 60	6.66	–0.8	H	OG	Los Angeles	4 Aug
Svetlana	Bazukiene	SU 57	6.66		1		Klaipeda	18 Aug
Margarita	Butkiene	SU 49	6.65	– i	1		Donetsk	4 Mar
Elzbieta	Klimaszewska	POL 59	6.64	0.0	1		Warszawa	6 May
Silvia	Khristova	BUL 65	6.64	1.6	2	NC	Sofia	3 Jun
Jodi	Anderson	USA 57	6.64	1.1	Q	TAC	San Jose	7 Jun
Nadezhda	Klishina	SU 60	6.64		1		Novokuznetsk	15 Jul
Larisa	Berezhnaya	SU 61	6.63	0.3	Q		Kiev	22 Jun
Anna	Buballa	FRG 54	6.63	2.0	1		Nicosia	15 Sep
Zsuzsa	Vanyek	HUN 60	6.62	1.6	4	BGP	Budapest	20 Aug
Lilyana	Ivanova	BUL 56	6.61		7	OD	Berlin	20 Jul
Yelena	Yatsuk	SU 61	6.60	0.1	7	NC	Donetsk	9 Sep
Tatyana	Lepota	SU 60	6.59	1.2	1		Kiev	5 Jul
Nevena	Ignatova	BUL 62	6.59	1.4	2		Pleven	7 Jul
Gwen	Loud	USA 61	6.58		1		Honolulu	5 Apr
Eloina	Echevarria	CUB 61	6.58	0.9	2	Bar	Habana	20 May
Sofia	Gladyr	SU 62	6.58		4		Moskva	9 Jul
Maryna	van Niekerk	RSA 54	A6.58		1		Johannesburg	24 Oct
Wenfen	Liao	CHN 63	6.57		1		Nanjing	7 Jun
Lyudmila	Khaustova	SU 56	6.57				Tula	15 Jul
Marina	Kibakina	SU 60	6.57	0.6	5		Gorkiy	12 Aug
Snezana	Dancetovic	YUG 57	6.57	0.7	1	v UK	Karlovac	16 Sep
Tatyana	Shpak	SU 60	6.55	– i	S	NC	Zaporozhe	11 Feb
Kathy	Rankins	USA 62	6.55		1		Athens, GA	5 May
Antonina	Sergeyeva	SU 57	6.55	1.9	10		Kiev	23 Jun
Jarmila	Strejckova	CS 53	6.54		1		Plzen	18 Sep
Kathy	McMillan	USA 57	6.53	1.2	1	Pepsi	Westwood	13 May
Irina	Osipova	SU 63	6.52	– i	4		Chelyabinsk	5 Feb
Tatyana	Kolpakova	SU 59	6.52	– i		NC	Moskva	18 Feb
Sabrina	Douglas	USA 60	6.52		Q		Cape Girardeau	24 May
Georgina	Oladapo	UK 67	6.52	0.8	2	WAAA	London	16 Jun
Nadezhda	Zheludkova	SU 59	6.52		1		Leningrad	5 Aug
Petra	Ernst	GDR 63	6.51	– i	2		Berlin	25 Jan
Ludmila	Jimramovska	CS 58	6.51		1		Praha	2 Jun
Neringa	Untonaite	SU 63	6.50	– i	2		Vilnius	15 Jan
Marina	Spirina	SU 55	6.50	– i	1		Bryansk	29 Jan
Galina	Yegorova	SU 63	6.50	– i	1		Karaganda	6 Feb
Linda	Garden	AUS 55	6.50	0.4	2		Adelaide	14 Mar
Pat	Johnson	USA 60	6.50		1		San Jose	21 Apr
Yelena	Obizhayeva	SU 60	6.50		1		Riga	11 Aug
Anke	Weigt	FRG 57	6.49	– i	1		Dusseldorf	29 Jan
Conceicao	Geremias	BRA 56	6.49	0.0	1		Sao Paulo	17 Jun
Olga	Nemogayeva	SU 59	6.49		H		Dnepropetrovsk	5 Aug
Natalya	Alyoshina	SU 56	6.48	– i		NC	Moskva	18 Feb
Donna	Thomas	USA 62	6.48	0.2	1		Arlington	5 May
Vangelia	Ilieva	BUL 63	6.48	0.5	8	v GDR,Rum	Sofia	17 Jun
Kim	Hagger	UK 61	6.48		2	v Yug	Karlovac	16 Sep
Nadezhda	Shaprinskaya	SU 68	6.48		2		Tashkent	21 Sep

Brenda	Bailey	USA 64	6.47		24 Mar	Daiva	Valentinaite	SU 64	6.45	– i	21 Jan
Nadine	Fourcade	FRA 63	6.47		26 Apr	Carla	Seldon	USA 63	6.45	0.2	26 May
Tineke	Hidding	HOL 59	6.47	0.9	24 Jun	Irina	Privalova	SU 68	6.45		23 Jun
Ruta	Gudaviciene	SU 63	6.47	1.2	5 Jul	Sofia	Bozhanova	BUL 67	6.45	0.8	5 Aug
Dorothy	Scott	JAM 57	6.47	0.5	8 Aug	Margaret	Cheetham	UK 68	6.45	1.0	18 Aug
Anna	Derevyankina	SU 67	6.47		21 Sep	Ilona	Redanz	GDR 66	6.44	– i	25 Feb
Sabrina	Williams	USA 63	6.46		2 Jun	Larisa	Nikitina	SU 65	6.44		4 Jul
Tatyana	Shchapova	SU 63	6.46		3 Jun	Inesa	Shulyak	SU 66	6.44	–1.9	13 Jul

405

1984 Lists – Women

Marianna	Maslennikova	SU 61	6.44	0.3	20 Jul	Judy	Simpson	UK 60	6.40		26 Aug
Heidrun	Geissler	GDR 61	6.44		26 Jul	Jasmin	Feige	FRG 59	6.39	– i	1 Feb
Liliana	Nastase	RUM 62	6.43		10 May	Svetlana	Filatyeva	SU 64	6.39	1.5	3 Jun
Gaby	Ehlert	GDR 65	6.43		25 May	Dalia	Kutelite	SU 60	6.38	– i	15 Jan
Marina	Karapetova	SU 62	6.43		15 Jul	Irina	Shugayeva	SU 67	6.38		8 Apr
Yelena	Pershina	SU 63	6.43	–0.9	15 Aug	Ildiko	Fekete	HUN 66	6.38	0.8	17 May
Galina	Podleshchuk	SU 60	6.43	0.1	8 Sep	Lidia	Bierka	POL 60	6.38	0.6	29 May
Jane	Frederick	USA 52	6.43	0.2	16 Sep	Larisa	Zolotaya	SU 52	6.38		9 Jul
Nicole	Boegman	AUS 67	6.43		17 Sep	Agata	Jaroszek	POL 63	6.38	1.6	2 Sep
Olga	Molodtsova	SU 70	6.43		17 Oct	Monika	Staubli	SWZ 60	6.38	–0.5	15 Sep
Monika	Lorenz	GDR 64	6.42	0.6	20 May	Cynthia	Henry	JAM 62	6.37	– i	17 Jan
Hildelisa	Despaigne	CUB 57	6.42		19 Jun	Eva	Szabo	HUN 60	6.37	1.3	11 Jul
Tatyana	Kirichenko	SU 65	6.42		6 Jul	Sabine	Seitl	AUT 65	6.37		21 Jul
Natalya	Yaskova	SU 57	6.42	0.1	8 Sep	Stefanie	Huhn	FRG 66	6.37	0.3	19 Aug
Elida	Aveille	CUB 61	6.41		1 Feb	Oksana	Kubyshkina	SU 68	6.37		22 Sep
Irina	Koyunkova	SU 59	6.41		16 Jun	Olimpia	Constantea	RUM 68	6.37		30 Sep
Esmeralda	Garcia	BRA 59	6.41	0.0	17 Jun	Jana	Sobotka	GDR 65	6.36	– i	15 Jan
Irina	Malykh	SU 58	6.41		6 Jul	Sheila	Nicks	USA 63	6.36	1.6	5 May
Geraldine	Bonnin	FRA 64	6.41	1.0	14 Jul	Silke	Harms	FRG 67	6.36	1.5	9 Jun
Lyudmila	Serbul	SU 60	6.41		10 Aug	Lyubov	Lizogub	SU 61	6.36	1.6	5 Jul
Antonina	Sukhova	SU 59	6.41		26 Aug	Marcela	Koblasova	CS 56	6.36		11 Jul
Adelina	Polledo	CUB 66	6.40		2 Mar	Lena	Wallin	SWE 58	6.36	0.6	21 Jul
Meledy	Smith	USA 64	6.40		24 Mar	Teresa	Allen	USA 65	6.35		24 Mar
Evalene	Hatcher	USA 59	6.40		5 May	Lyubov	Pavlovskaya	SU 56	6.35		4 Jun
Janet	Yarbrough	USA 61	6.40	1.9	5 May	Anette	Hellig	FRG 64	6.35	0.9	23 Jun
Veronica	Bell	USA 61	6.40		12 May	Mila	Kolyadina	SU 60	6.35	0.4	20 Jul
Ulrike	Keller	FRG 64	6.40	0.0	19 May	Emilia	Lenk	MEX 61	A6.35		21 Jul
Joyce	Oladapo	UK 64	6.40	0.2	16 Jun						

Best outdoor mark

	Weser		6.66	1.3	7			Dresden	19 May
	Butkiene		6.57		2			Klaipeda	18 Jul
	Shpak		6.52	0.2	H		NC	Kiev	21 Jun
	Spirina		6.48		H			Tula	26 Aug
	Weigt		6.45		17 Jun				
	Redanz		6.40		16 May				
	Valentinaite		6.36		26 May				
	Feige		6.36		27 May				

Best low-altitude mark

van Niekerk 6.42 23 Apr

Additional jumps in series

Daute	7.23	1.5	19 May	
Daute	7.22	0.9	19 May	
Daute	7.21	1.7	19 May	
Stanciu	7.18		17 Jun	
Daute	7.17		26 Jul	
Daute	7.13	0.5	15 Jul	
Daute	7.12	0.9	19 May	
Stanciu	7.12		17 Jun	
Daute	7.10	0.6	20 Jul	
Daute	7.09		9 Jun	

Daute	7.09	0.5	15 Jul
Daute	7.07		13 May
Daute	7.07		20 Jul
Radtke	7.07	1.0	17 Aug
Daute	7.07	0.6	17 Aug
Daute	7.06	0.9	26 Jul
Daute	7.04		13 May
Ionescu	7.04		21 Jun
Chistyakova	7.04		14 Jul

	1	10	20	30	50	100	Over 6.60	Over 6.40
1980	7.06	6.81	6.72	6.64	6.54	6.34	38	81
1981	6.96	6.78	6.66	6.61	6.51	6.39	34	97
1982	7.20	6.86	6.79	6.72	6.57	6.44	45	121
1983	7.43	6.90	6.79	6.73	6.59	6.47	48	126
1984	7.40	7.01	6.88	6.81	6.69	6.48	66	147

1984 Lists – Women

Marks made with assisting wind greater than 2 m/s

Eva	Murkova	CS 62	7.17	3.6	1		Nitra	26 Aug
	Stanciu		7.08	2.7	1		Byrkjelo	1 Jul
Carol	Lewis	USA 63	7.03		1		San Jose	26 May
Sue	Telfer	UK 61	7.00	4.2	1	NC	Cwmbran	27 May
(4/4)								
Ines	Schmidt	GDR 60	6.98	3.4	2		Nitra	26 Aug
Anna	Wlodarczyk	POL 51	6.97	2.7	1	v Bul,FRG,Hun	Warszawa	15 Jul
Robyne	Lorraway	AUS 61	6.90	2.6	1		Adelaide	4 Feb
Gwen	Loud	USA 61	6.85		1	NCAA	Eugene	2 Jun
Evalene	Hatcher	USA 59	6.77		1		Modesto	12 May
Carla	Seldon	USA 63	6.62	5.9	1		San Angelo	14 Apr
Anna	Van	USA 62	6.58		1		Las Vegas	31 Mar
Joyce	Oladapo	UK 64	6.54	2.2	2	NC	Cwmbran	27 May
Carol	Galloway	CAN 64	6.54	3.3	1	NC	Winnipeg	1 Jul
Meledy	Smith	USA 64	6.52		3	NCAA	Eugene	2 Jun
Kim	Hagger	UK 61	6.51	3.3	H	NC	Cwmbran	28 May
Margaret	Cheetham	UK 68	6.49		1		Birmingham	23 Sep
Noeline	Hodgins	NZ 56	6.48	3.7	1		Auckland	7 Jan
Carla	Jackson	USA 64	6.47				14 Apr	
Ildiko	Fekete	HUN 66	6.47	3.1			30 Jun	
Lena	Wallin	SWE 58	6.46	2.7			25 Aug	
Teresa	Allen	USA 65	6.44				13 May	
Jasmin	Feige	FRG 59	6.43				23 Jun	
Agata	Jaroszek	POL 63	6.43	2.4			2 Sep	
Chris	Stanton	AUS 59	6.42	3.7			4 Mar	
Christina	Sundberg	SWE 60	6.42	2.9			5 Jun	
Ulrike	Keller	FRG 64	6.42	2.2			19 Aug	
Megan	Clarken	NZ	6.40				15 Dec	
Shiri	Milton	USA 62	6.38				12 May	
Olga	Dalmau	SPA 59	6.38				10 Jun	
Anna-Leena	Tirronen	FIN 63	6.38				8 Sep	
Dorothea	Brown	USA 64	6.37				19 May	
Olga	Godunova	SU 62	6.37	3.7			4 Jul	

Additional jump in series

Murkova   7.13   4.6   26 Aug

SHOT PUT

Natalya	Lisovskaya	SU 62	22.53	1		Sochi	27 May
	Lisovskaya		21.96	1	DRZ	Praha	16 Aug
	Lisovskaya		21.86	1	Ros	Praha	9 Jun
Ilona	Briesenick	GDR 56	21.85	1		Berlin	15 Jul
	Lisovskaya		21.75	1		Sochi	20 May
	Lisovskaya		21.72	1		Kiev	22 Jun
	Briesenick		21.61	1	OD	Potsdam	21 Jul
Helena	Fibingerova	CS 49	21.60	1		Zaragoza	3 Jun
	Lisovskaya		21.59	2	OD	Potsdam	21 Jul
	Lisovskaya		21.56	1		Moskva	4 Aug
Nunu	Abashidze	SU 55	21.53	2		Kiev	22 Jun
	Briesenick		21.49	1	Skok	Celje	5 May
	Briesenick		21.41	1		Berlin	16 May
	Lisovskaya		21.40	1		Tallinn	28 Jun
	Fibingerova		21.38	1		Linz	22 Aug
	Briesenick		21.35	1		Berlin	25 Jul
	Fibingerova		21.33	2	DRZ	Praha	16 Aug

407

1984 Lists – Women

Ines	Briesenick Muller Abashidze	GDR 59	21.32 21.32 21.30		1 2 1	Skok Znam	Split Celje Sochi	30 Apr 5 May 9 Jun
Helma	Abashidze Briesenick Lisovskaya Briesenick Knorscheidt Knorscheidt Abashidze Muller Abashidze Briesenick	GDR 56	21.28 21.24 21.21 21.20 21.19 21.18 21.18 21.15 21.13 21.12		1 1 2 1 1 2 3 2 1 2	v Ita,Hun,Pol v Ita,Hun,Pol NC DRZ NC NC	Verona Jena Verona Erfurt Berlin Split Praha Erfurt Donetsk Berlin	1 Jun 13 May 1 Jun 3 Jun 24 May 30 Apr 16 Aug 3 Jun 7 Sep 24 May
(31/6) Margitta Mihaela Cordula Claudia	Knorscheidt Pufe Loghin Schulze Losch	GDR 52 RUM 52 GDR 59 FRG 60	21.10 21.01 21.00 21.00 20.55		3 3 1 4 1	OD Skok OD v CS,Fra,Pol	Potsdam Celje Formia Potsdam Hannover	21 Jul 5 May 30 Jun 21 Jul 15 Jun
Heidi Liane Heike Maria Elena Lyudmila Lyudmila Marina Zdenka Tatyana Natalya	Krieger Schmuhl Dittrich Sarria Voyevudskaya Savina Antonyuk Silhava Shcherbanos Zubekhina	GDR 65 GDR 61 GDR 62 CUB 54 SU 59 SU 55 SU 62 CS 54 SU 60 SU 51	20.51 20.37 20.28 20.25 20.24 20.21 20.19 20.12 20.07 19.94		2 3 4 2 1 2 3 2 4 1	 RumIC Znam v Ita NC	Budapest Jena Dresden Bucuresti Dnepropetrovsk Sochi Kiev Catania Donetsk Tula	8 Feb 13 May 27 Jul 10 Jun 5 Aug 9 Jun 22 Jun 7 Sep 7 Sep 14 Jul
Yelena Konstanze Danguole Gael Carmen Tatyana Grit Natalya Lyubov Verzhinia	Kozlova Simm Bimbaite Martin Niesche Orlova Haupt Akhrimenko Kovtunova Veselinova	SU 62 GDR 64 SU 62 AUS 56 GDR 64 SU 55 GDR 66 SU 55 SU 59 BUL 57	19.94 19.78 19.77 19.74 19.66 19.58 19.57 19.52 19.46 19.42		2 1 1 1 1e2 2 1 1 3 1	 OD v Rum	Kiev Karl-Marx-Stadt Vilnius Berkeley Potsdam Moskva Gera Leningrad Bucuresti Sofia	14 Aug 11 Jul 8 May 14 Jul 21 Jul 7 Jul 7 Jul 16 Jun 16 Sep 13 May
Svetlana Lyubov Larisa Aleksandra Aleksandra Svetla Venissa Tamara Skaidrite Olga	Melnikova Vasilyeva Agapova Abashidze Mititelu Mitkova Head Bufetova Baikova Miticheva	SU 51 SU 57 SU 64 SU 58 SU 59 BUL 64 UK 56 SU 51 SU 50 SU 62	19.41 19.34 19.30 19.30 19.26 19.11 19.06 18.91 18.75 18.70	 i i	2 1 4 4 1 1 1 1 3 1	 Znam SU P	Gorkiy Riga Sochi Sochi Kishinyov Hengelo St. Athan Baku Riga Bryansk	12 Aug 2 Jun 20 May 9 Jun 21 Jul 6 Jul 7 Apr 15 Sep 2 Jun 22 Jan
Natalya Irina Astrid Olga Tatyana Meisu Margarita Gabriele Vera Nina	Shlyakhtich Bogomolova Wagner Turta Belova Li Chuguyevskaya Naumann Yevko Samsonova	SU 62 SU 59 GDR 65 SU 57 SU 61 CHN 59 SU 62 GDR 63 SU 59 SU 51	18.69 18.68 18.64 18.52 18.48 18.47 18.46 18.42 18.42 18.42	 i	4 7 3 5 1 1 Q 1 5	 NC SU P NC	Kiev Moskva Berlin Moskva Baku Beijing Leningrad Erfurt Gorkiy Moskva	14 Aug 19 Feb 24 May 2 May 15 Sep 7 Apr 22 Jan 2 Jun 24 Jun 7 Jul
Judith Viktoria Lorna	Oakes Szelinger Griffin	UK 58 HUN 56 USA 56	18.35 18.34 18.16	i	1 1 1	v GDR	Cosford Papa Walnut, CA	1 Feb 6 Oct 15 Jul

1984 Lists – Women

Valentina	Fedyushina	SU 65	18.15		1		Riga	5 Jul
Vera	Schmidt	FRG 61	18.14		1		Regensburg	16 Jun
Yanqin	Yang	CHN 66	18.08		1		Eugene	18 Jul
Simona	Andrusca	RUM 62	18.05		3	PTS	Bratislava	25 May
Galina	Kuzhel	SU 59	18.04		2		Riga	5 Jul
Ria	Stalman	HOL 52	18.02		1	TAC	San Jose	9 Jun
Biyun	Peng	CHN 63	17.98				Guangzhou	28 Mar
Alena	Vitoulova	CS 60	17.96		3		Nitra	26 Aug
Simone	Rudrich	GDR 61	17.95	i	9	NC	Senftenberg	22 Jan
Ramona	Pagel	USA 61	17.89		1		Los Angeles	29 Dec
Bonnie	Dasse	USA 59	17.87		1		Long Beach	15 Dec
Meg	Ritchie	UK 52	17.85	i	1	TAC	Princeton	24 Feb
Mechthild	Schonleber	FRG 63	17.81		1		Thannhausen	2 Sep
Yuzhen	Cong	CHN 63	17.80				Nanjing	6 Sep
Nina	Isayeva	SU 50	17.78		1		Stavropol	18 Apr
Galina	Kalinina	SU 62	17.76				Omsk	19 May
Marcelina	Rodriguez	CUB 60	17.76		1		Boras	19 Jun
Irina	Fedchenko	SU 66	17.75				Kiev	27 Aug
Birgit	Petsch	FRG 63	17.73	i	2	NC	Stuttgart	11 Feb
Mariana	Lengyel	RUM 53	17.73		2		Bucuresti	19 Aug
Nadezhda	Frantseva	SU 62	17.71		3		Moskva	20 Aug
Irina	Vidosova	SU 61	17.70		4		Chelyabinsk	29 Jul
Iris	Plotzitzka	FRG 66	17.67		2		Cannes	29 Dec
Larisa	Baranova	SU 61	17.58		2		Stavropol	18 Apr
Yelena	Selivanova	SU 62	17.56		1		Odessa	6 Jun
Nadezhda	Kugayevskikh	SU 60	17.56		2		Omsk	17 Jun
Simone	Thamm	GDR 65	17.54	i	6		Berlin	25 Jan
Yelena	Trush	SU 63	17.51		3		Riga	5 Jul
Svetlana	Tatichek	SU 62	17.46		4		Riga	5 Jul
Liquan	Shen	CHN 58	17.45				Beijing	24 Mar
Simone	Creantor	FRA 48	17.45		1		Creteil	23 Jun
Lyudmila	Lisovskaya	SU 60	17.44	i	12	NC	Moskva	18 Feb
Snezhana	Vasileva	BUL 64	17.43		2	NarMI	Sofia	20 May
Rimma	Juskiene	SU 52	17.42		1		Klaipeda	18 Aug
Zhanna	Shcherbach	SU 60	17.40		1		Minsk	4 Jul
Carol	Cady	USA 62	17.40		2		Sacramento	21 Jul
Inessa	Sedachova	SU 64	17.38		2		Sochi	1 Apr
Yelena	Belovolova	SU 65	17.32				Vilnius	3 Jul
Galina	Yeshkova	SU 63	17.30 *	i	1		Rostov/Don	9 Mar
Yelena	Plastinina	SU 60	17.25		3		Stavropol	18 Apr
Nina	Korsunskaya	SU 54	17.23	i	2		Leningrad	15 Jan
Florenta	Craciunescu	RUM 55	17.23		8	OG	Los Angeles	3 Aug
Lyudmila	Ostapenko	SU 59	17.22		6		Kiev	14 Aug
Nina	Kuritsyna	SU 59	17.20		1		Kazan	14 Jul
Natalya	Didenko	SU 62	17.19		4		Stavropol	18 Apr
Astra	Etienne	AUS 60	17.19		1		Canberra	19 Dec
Soultana	Saroudi	GRE 58	17.18		1		Athinai	20 Jul

Veronika	Czorny	FRG 54	17.16	20 May	Jana	Naujoks	GDR 65	16.94	19 May
Tatyana	Rybalko	SU 60	17.13		Galina	Kurochkina	SU 65	16.89	20 Aug
Natalya	Andreyeva	SU 62	17.13	6 Jul	Leone	Bertimon	FRA 54	16.87	1 Jul
Hajnal	Voros	HUN 58	17.11	12 Aug	Anna	Vnukova	SU 63	16.86	20 Aug
Myrtle	Augee	UK 65	17.10	16 Jun	Petra	Leidinger	FRG 66	16.81	3 Jun
Lisette	Martinez	CUB 66	17.10	16 Jun	Natalie	Kaaiawahia	USA 65	16.80i	11 Feb
Tatyana	Zakharkina	SU 63	17.09	23 Aug	Bettina	Beetz	GDR 67	16.80	23 Jun
Lidia	Davidyuk	SU 56	17.05	18 Apr	Elaine	Sobansky	USA 61	16.77	25 May
Zhihong	Huang	CHN 65	17.04	7 May	Yelena	Ortina	SU 62	16.77	7 Aug
Tamara	Posmetyukh	SU 49	17.02i	18 Feb	Denise	Wood	USA 50	16.76i	27 Jan
Larisa	Yurchenko	SU 63	17.02	14 Jul	Yelena	Drigota	SU 62	16.75	14 Aug
Regina	Cavanaugh	USA 64	17.01	16 Jun	Peggy	Pollock	USA 60	16.74	7 Apr
Rose	Hauch	CAN 57	16.97	12 Jul	Sandy	Burke	USA 59	16.74	21 Apr
Leslie	Deniz	USA 62	16.96i	11 Feb	Cheng	Lu	CHN 56	16.74	7 Jun
Yelena	Kukushkina	SU 63	16.95	4 Jul	Sona	Vasickova	CS 62	16.73i	19 Feb

409

1984 Lists – Women

Svetlana	Ovchinnikova	SU 56	16.69i	11 Feb	Alla	Kurillo	SU 65	16.46	4 Jul
Lyubov	Khvostikova	SU 66	16.68	9 Jun	Monika	Andris	SU 65	16.46	5 Jul
Mihaela	Samoila	RUM 66	16.67		Marta	Kripli	HUN 60	16.46	25 Jul
Asta	Hovi	FIN 63	16.66	2 Sep	Ilke	Wyludda	GDR 69	16.42	4 Aug
Carmen	Ionesco	CAN 51	16.58	19 May	Glenda	Hughes	NZ 50	16.37	28 Jan
Marita	Walton	IRL 60	16.52	14 Apr	Lyudmila	Shalugina	SU 61	16.37i	9 Mar
Eha	Runne	SU 63	16.50i	21 Jan	Mila	Kolyadina	SU 60	16.37	2 Jun
Gabriela	Hanulakova	CS 57	16.50	26 Aug	Antoaneta	Koci	ALB	16.36	Apr
Dace	Linare	SU 61	16.49	16 Jun	Melody	Torcolacci	CAN 60	16.34	4 Aug
Assunta	Chiumarello	ITA 58	16.48	30 Jun	Xiuying	Li	CHN 59	16.33	7 Jul
Sharen	Hamilton	USA 62	16.47	29 Apr					

Best outdoor mark

Krieger	20.24	5		Split	30 Apr
Head	18.93	1		Haverfordwest	13 May
Bogomolova	18.53	2		Moskva	2 May
Oakes	18.28	2	OT	London	6 Jun
Chuguyevskaya	17.78	10		Sochi	27 May
Ritchie	17.69	2		Hamilton	26 Jan
Petsch	17.66	2		Alttotting	5 May
Miticheva	17.44	1		Frankfurt/	1 May
Thamm	17.44			Berlin	24 May

Kaaiawahia	16.79	16 Jun
Wood	16.55	14 Apr
Ovchinnikova	16.48	19 Jul

Additional marks in series

Lisovskaya	21.89	16 Aug
Lisovskaya	21.83	16 Aug
Lisovskaya	21.83	16 Aug
Lisovskaya	21.80	27 May
Lisovskaya	21.75	16 Aug
Lisovskaya	21.74	27 May
Briesenick	21.42	5 May
Briesenick	21.40	15 Jul
Lisovskaya	21.40	16 Aug
Briesenick	21.35	5 May
Lisovskaya	21.26	27 May
Fibingerova	21.26	16 Aug
Abashidze	21.24	1 Jun

	1	10	20	30	50	100	Over 18.00	Over 17.00
1980	22.45	20.54	19.36	18.74	17.58	16.33	39	71
1981	21.61	19.54	18.75	18.06	17.41	16.47	32	71
1982	21.80	20.55	19.62	18.85	17.96	16.82	49	96
1983	22.40	20.54	19.61	19.01	18.19	17.00	52	100
1984	22.53	20.55	19.94	19.42	18.42	17.18	59	112

DISCUS THROW

Zdenka	Silhava	CS 54	74.56		1			Nitra	26 Aug
Irina	Meszynski	GDR 62	73.36		1		DRZ	Praha	17 Aug
Galina	Savinkova	SU 53	73.28		1		NC	Donetsk	8 Sep
Gisela	Beyer	GDR 60	73.10		1		OD	Berlin	20 Jul
Martina	Opitz	GDR 60	72.32		1			Leipzig	13 Jul
	Beyer		72.28		1			Berlin	15 Jul
Galina	Murashova	SU 55	72.14		2		DRZ	Praha	17 Aug
	Meszynski		72.02		2		OD	Berlin	20 Jul
	Silhava		72.00		1			Litomysl	28 Jul
	Opitz		71.60	*	3		OD	Berlin	20 Jul

1984 Lists – Women

Ria	Stalman	HOL 52	71.22	1		Walnut, CA	15 Jul
Maria	Petkova	BUL 50	71.22	1		Sofia	28 Jul
	Savinkova		71.18	1	v Rum	Bucuresti	16 Sep
	Beyer		71.02	1		Split	30 Apr
	Beyer		70.88	1		Rijeka	2 May
	Murashova		70.86	1		Sochi	19 May
	Beyer		70.80	1		Berlin	9 Jun
	Silhava		70.76	1	Nik	Nice	20 Aug
	Petkova		70.70	1		Sofia	8 Aug
	Petkova		70.56	1		Petrich	21 Apr
	Beyer		70.52	2	Nik	Nice	20 Aug
	Petkova		70.42	1	NarMl	Sofia	19 May
	Murashova		70.36	1		Sochi	26 May
	Petkova		70.34	1		Sofia	12 May
	Beyer		70.32	1	NC	Erfurt	3 Jun
	Opitz		70.30	1		Dresden	19 May
	Beyer		70.24	1	Skok	Celje	5 May
	Silhava		70.14	3	DRZ	Praha	17 Aug
	Savinkova		70.10	1		Moskva	6 Aug
	Petkova		69.98	1		Sofia	5 May
(30/8)							
Lyubov	Zverkova	SU 55	68.58	1		Kiev	22 Jun
Ellina	Kisheyeva	SU 60	68.56	2		Moskva	6 Jul
Tsvetanka	Khristova	BUL 62	68.34	1		Barcelona	8 Jul
Maritza	Marten	CUB 63	67.76	1		Habana	8 Jul
Hilda	Ramos	CUB 64	67.56	2		Habana	8 Jul
Svetla	Bozhkova	BUL 51	67.10	2		Petrich	21 Apr
Nadezhda	Kugayevskikh	SU 60	67.04	1		Gorkiy	11 Aug
Ingra-Anne	Manecke	FRG 56	66.68	2	MSR	Walnut, CA	29 Apr
Tatyana	Lesovaya	SU 56	66.50	1		Riga	6 Jul
Diana	Sachse	GDR 63	66.36	3		Berlin	15 Jul
Florenta	Craciunescu	RUM 55	66.08	2		Nitra	26 Aug
Ulla	Lundholm	FIN 57	66.02	1		Pertteli	2 Jun
Grit	Haupt	GDR 66	65.96	3		Leipzig	13 Jul
Irina	Dmitriyeva	SU 59	65.30	1		Leselidze	8 Sep
Daniela	Costian	RUM 65	65.22	3		Nitra	26 Aug
Leslie	Deniz	USA 62	65.20	1		Tempe	7 Apr
Silvia	Madetzky	GDR 62	65.20	4		Berlin	9 Jun
Irina	Pozharitskaya	SU 58	65.10	1	SU P	Baku	14 Sep
Meg	Ritchie	UK 52	65.02	1		Eugene	5 May
Svetla	Mitkova	BUL 64	64.84	5	v GDR,Rum	Sofia	16 Jun
Svetlana	Motusenko	SU 54	64.74	1		Rovno	5 May
Yelena	Kovaleva	SU 61	64.36	1		Orel	20 Jun
Gabriela	Hanulakova	CS 57	64.00	4		Nitra	26 Aug
Elju	Kubi	SU 51	63.98	1		Rapla	14 Jul
Andrea	Thieme	GDR 64	63.96	4		Leipzig	13 Jul
Valentina	Korsak	SU 56	63.92	1		Irpinsk	12 May
Larisa	Baranova	SU 61	63.46	3		Sochi	27 Apr
Valentina	Zolotykh	SU 49	63.38	1		Ustinovsk	15 Jul
Margitta	Pufe	GDR 52	63.32	5		Nitra	26 Aug
Carol	Cady	USA 62	62.96	Q	NCAA	Eugene	31 May
Simone	Rudrich	GDR 61	62.96	1		Rostock	4 Jul
Larisa	Kuleshina	SU 63	62.84			Sochi	13 May
Lorna	Griffin	USA 56	62.80	2		Walnut, CA	15 Jul
Vera	Melentyeva	SU 55	62.80	8	NC	Donetsk	8 Sep
Nina	Samsonova	SU 51	62.66	2		Moskva	19 Aug
Tatyana	Belova	SU 61	62.56	2		Orel	20 Jun
Jitka	Prouzova	CS 50	62.56	6		Nitra	26 Aug
Antonina	Patoka	SU 64	62.52	1		Chimkent	15 Jun
Skaidrite	Baikova	SU 50	62.32	Q	NC	Donetsk	7 Sep
Ines	Muller	GDR 59	62.26	3		Berlin	16 May
Venissa	Head	UK 56	62.14	1		San Diego	30 Jul
Zsuzsa	Pallay	HUN 48	62.10	1		Miskolc	27 Sep

411

1984 Lists – Women

Simona	Andrusca	RUM 62	62.00		3		Bucuresti	19 Aug
Nadezhda	Zhitkova	SU 52	61.94		1		Rovno	15 Jul
Natalya	Akhrimenko	SU 55	61.80		1		Leningrad	12 May
Heike	Dittrich	GDR 62	61.72		1		Berlin	5 Jul
Agnes	Herczeg	HUN 50	61.72		1		Szeged	23 Aug
Mariana	Lengyel	RUM 53	61.70		7	v Bul,GDR	Sofia	16 Jun
Gabriele	Reinsch	GDR 63	61.68		5		Dresden	19 May
Lyudmila	Platonova	SU 64	61.66		5		Moskva	19 Jul
Tatyana	Pishchalnikova	SU 59	61.62		3		Orel	20 Jun
Galina	Kudryavtseva	SU 61	61.62		2		Rovno	15 Jul
Gael	Martin	AUS 56	61.52		2		Sacramento	21 Jul
Lyubov	Yelizarova	SU 56	61.34		1		Frunze	8 Apr
Marta	Kripli	HUN 60	61.00		2	v Pol,Bul,FRG	Warszawa	15 Jul
Simone	Thamm	GDR 65	60.94		4		Berlin	16 May
Natalya	Gorbachova	SU 47	60.92		1		Kharkov	7 Jul
Irina	Ivannikova	SU 50	60.70		1		Leningrad	13 Aug
Irina	Shabanova	SU 64	60.68		2		Adler	31 Mar
Galina	Vasilyeva	SU 60	60.68		1		Gorkiy	24 Jun
Renata	Katewicz	POL 65	60.60		1	v FRG-j	Bochum	15 Jun
Kadi	Bebber	GDR 65	60.50		2		Rostock	11 Jul
Heidi	Krieger	GDR 65	60.48		2		Berlin	5 Jul
Anne	Paavolainen	FIN 60	60.40		1		Alavieska	23 Aug
Claudia	Losch	FRG 60	60.34		1		Munchen	19 Jun
Svetlana	Melnikova	SU 51	60.26		2		Adler	10 Feb
Tatyana	Kaptyukh	SU 56	60.26		3		Irpinsk	12 May
Marja-Leena	Larpi	FIN 59	60.12		1		Humppila	24 Jul
Elisabeta	Neamtu	RUM 60	59.94		3	NC	Bucuresti	11 Jul
Carmen	Ionesco	CAN 51	59.88		1		Montreal	18 Jul
Anna	Salak	SU 59	59.86		3		Moskva	19 Aug
Laura	DeSnoo	USA 62	59.84		7	MSR	Walnut, CA	29 Apr
Stefenia	Simova	BUL 63	59.72		5		Sofia	12 May
Irina	Yatchenko	SU 65	59.54		1		Staiki	Apr
Bea	Wiarda	HOL 59	59.36		1		Sneek	10 Jul
Irina	Khval	SU 62	59.26		3		Stavropol	18 Apr
Kathy	Picknell	USA 58	59.22		3	TAC	San Jose	8 Jun
Ewa	Siepsiak	POL 57	59.20		1		Sopot	8 Aug
Nadezhda	Zvezdina	SU 62	59.18		1		Stavropol	9 Aug
Irina	Vasyutina	SU 59	59.16		8	SU P	Baku	14 Sep
Doris	Gutewort	FRG 54	59.08		2		Schweinfurt	3 Jun
Julie	Hansen	USA 57	59.06		1		Seattle	20 Apr
Jana	Harter	GDR 66	59.06		2		Cottbus	26 May
Patricia	Katona	FRA 60	59.04		1		Szentes	21 Apr
Maria	Badea	RUM 60	58.94		7	RumIC	Bucuresti	9 Jun
Marina	Zubenko	SU 62	58.88		4		Stavropol	18 Apr
Jianhua	Xie	CHN 56	58.82		1		Nanjing	9 Jun
Natalya	Sindyanova	SU 59	58.68		9		Sochi	19 May
Penny	Neer	USA 60	58.64		1		Lexington	20 Apr
Eva	Saskoi	HUN 61	58.62		1		Budapest	12 Aug
Helgi	Parts	SU 37	58.58		1		Tbilisi	29 Sep
Tatyana	Simashova	SU 58	58.50		2		Dnepropetrovsk	4 Aug
Larisa	Mikhalchenko	SU 63	58.22		21 May			
Barbara	Beuge	FRG 60	58.20		26 May			
Alla	Yakovleva	SU 59	58.14		31 Mar			
Tatyana	Berezhnaya	SU 56	58.12		19 Aug			
Valentina	Zhudina	SU 63	58.00		7 May			
Nadezhda	Martynchuk	SU 46	57.90		12 May			
Tatyana	Fedorenkova	SU 58	57.78		8 Jun			
Olga	Cinibulkova	CS 60	57.76		1 Sep			
Ilke	Wyludda	GDR 69	57.74		26 Jul			
Aleksandra	Mititelu	SU 59	57.74		10 Aug			
Patricia	Walsh	IRL 60	57.60		7 Jul			

Dagmar	Galler	FRG 61	57.60	21 Jul				
Nadezhda	Frantseva	SU 61	57.58	19 Aug				
Larisa	Platonova	SU 66	57.42	15 Jun				
Lynda	Whiteley	UK 63	57.32	16 Jun				
Yunxiang	Jiao	CHN 57	57.18	31 Mar				
Tatyana	Kibitova	SU 62	57.16	4 Sep				
Irina	Yevsiyevich	SU 62	57.08	7 Jul				
Svetlana	Savchenko	SU 65	57.04	12 Aug				
Quenna	Beasley	USA 62	56.92	21 Apr				
Juliana	Georgieva	BUL 64	56.90	26 May				
Yelena	Yurova	SU 64	56.90	13 Jun				

1984 Lists – Women

Olga	Davydova	SU 63	56.88	6 Jul	Galina	Veremchuk	SU 62	56.10	5 May
Christine	Lohofener	GDR 66	56.86	2 May	Yelena	Belovolova	SU 65	56.02	4 Jul
Ramona	Pagel	USA 61	56.84	31 Mar	Xiaohui	Li	CHN 56	56.00	8 Sep
Larisa	Korotkevich	SU 67	56.70	8 Jun	Vilma	Zubaityte	SU	55.90	19 Aug
Andrea	Roddecke	FRG 58	56.58	3 Jun	Ursula	Weber	AUT 60	55.86	17 Jul
Agnes	Elek	HUN 57	56.58	30 Jun	Catherine	Beauvais	FRA 65	55.76	30 Jun
Valentina	Seroshtan	SU 58	56.44	10 Feb	Margarita	Yavicha	SU 64	55.74	19 May
Svetlana	Dorokhova	SU 64	56.40	15 Apr	Lynne	Anderson	USA 53	55.70	26 May
Pia	Iacovo	USA 61	56.30	2 Jun	Mariette	van Heerden	ZIM 52	55.70	
Xiaoyan	Xin	CHN 60	56.26	16 May	Yelena	Yefrosinina	SU 65	55.68	19 Aug
Iveta	Garancha	SU 64	56.20	22 Aug	Denise	Wood	USA 50	55.52	24 Mar
Mette	Bergmann	NOR 62	56.18	19 Aug	Becky	Fettig	USA 63	55.32	21 Apr
Natalya	Yakovleva	SU 63	56.16	3 Jun	Irina	Grachova	SU 62	55.30	16 Jun
Galina	Kvacheva	SU 65	56.16	19 Jul	Katalin	Toth	HUN 57	55.18	27 Jul
Eha	Runne	SU 63	56.14	1 Jun	Yelena	Koshikova	SU 61	55.08	30 Sep

Additional marks in series

	Savinkova		72.70	8 Sep	Opitz	70.64	13 Jul
	Savinkova		72.68	8 Sep	Silhava	70.58	28 Jul
	Silhava		72.54	26 Aug	Murashova	70.46	17 Aug
	Silhava		71.78	26 Aug	Meszynski	70.46	17 Aug
	Silhava		71.62	28 Jul	Silhava	70.28	26 Aug
	Meszynski		71.34	17 Aug	Opitz	70.26	13 Jul
	Murashova		71.32	17 Aug	Beyer	70.16	30 Apr
	Meszynski		71.10	17 Aug	Petkova	70.00	19 May

	1	10	20	30	50	100	Over 60.00	Over 57.00
1980	71.80	66.02	65.26	64.20	61.80	56.46	59	89
1981	71.46	66.80	64.20	62.70	60.82	56.42	56	91
1982	71.40	68.18	65.04	63.44	60.90	57.04	63	103
1983	73.26	67.32	65.10	64.16	61.98	58.52	75	130
1984	74.56	68.56	66.02	64.36	62.10	58.50	76	119

JAVELIN THROW

Petra	Felke	GDR 59	74.72	1		Skok	Celje	5 May
Tiina	Lillak	FIN 61	74.24	1			Fresno	7 Apr
	Felke		74.24	1		OD	Potsdam	21 Jul
	Felke		73.74	1			Praha	28 Aug
	Felke		73.30	1		DRZ	Praha	16 Aug
	Felke		72.86	1		8N	Tokyo	14 Sep
Anna	Verouli	GRE 56	72.70	1			Hania	20 May
	Verouli		72.64	1		NC	Thessaloniki	1 Jun
Antje	Kempe	GDR 63	72.16	2		Skok	Celje	5 May
	Felke		72.02	1			Berlin	15 Jul
Fatima	Whitbread	UK 61	71.86	1			Limassol	29 Apr
	Kempe		71.74	2		OD	Potsdam	21 Jul
	Felke		70.60	1			Karl-Marx-Stadt	20 May
	Kempe		70.58	1			Erfurt	12 May
	Felke		70.40	1			Dresden	26 Jul
	Verouli		70.36	1			Athinai	27 Jun
	Kempe		70.28	1			Split	30 Apr
Maria	Colon	CUB 58	69.96	1			Sofia	17 Jun
Tessa	Sanderson	UK 56	69.56	1		OG	Los Angeles	6 Aug
	Kempe		69.16	1		BGP	Budapest	20 Aug
	Lillak		69.00	2		OG	Los Angeles	6 Aug
	Lillak		68.90	1			Lahti	19 May
	Sanderson		68.88	1			Belfast	19 Jun
	Kempe		68.88	2			Berlin	15 Jul
	Sanderson		68.58	1			Bolzano	20 May

1984 Lists – Women

	Felke		68.24	1		Rijeka	2 May
	Whitbread		67.96	1		London	13 Jul
	Sanderson		67.92	3	OD	Potsdam	21 Jul
	Sanderson		67.88	2		London	13 Jul
	Felke		67.82	2		Erfurt	12 May
(30/7)							
Tuula	Laaksalo	FIN 53	67.38	1		Saarijarvi	23 Jun
Zinaida	Gavrilina	SU 60	67.00	1	NC	Donetsk	9 Sep
Elena	Burgarova	CS 52	66.56	2		Nitra	26 Aug
Ingrid	Thyssen	FRG 56	66.12	1		Stuttgart	21 Jul
Mayra	Vila	CUB 60	66.02	1	Bar	Habana	20 May
Genowefa	Olejarz	POL 62	65.52	1		Zabrze	20 May
Antoaneta	Todorova	BUL 63	65.40	2	DRZ	Praha	16 Aug
Rositha	Potreck	GDR 59	65.26	3	Skok	Celje	5 May
Olga	Chistyakova	SU 50	65.26	2	Znam	Sochi	10 Jun
Trine	Solberg	NOR 66	65.02	1	PTS	Bratislava	26 May
Iris	de Grasse	CUB 64	64.90	1		Zinnowitz	13 May
Karin	Smith	USA 55	64.68	2	8N	Tokyo	14 Sep
Natalya	Kalenchukova	SU 64	64.26	1		Moskva	20 Jul
Natalya	Shikolenko	SU 64	63.64	1		Minsk	17 Aug
Olga	Gavrilova	SU 57	63.52	2		Adler	25 Feb
Helena	Laine	FIN 55	63.08	1		Tampere	14 Jun
Beate	Peters	FRG 59	63.02	2	NC	Dusseldorf	23 Jun
Fausta	Quintavalla	ITA 59	62.92	2		Madrid	27 May
Natalya	Cherniyenko	SU 65	62.90	1	NC–j	Riga	13 Jul
Ute	Hommola	GDR 52	62.82	1		Potsdam	5 May
Petra	Rivers	AUS 52	62.66	1	NC	Melbourne	1 Apr
Lyudmila	Medvedyeva	SU 54	62.50	Q		Adler	25 Feb
Eva	Raduly	RUM 54	62.28	2	RumIC	Bucuresti	10 Jun
Saida	Gunba	SU 59	62.18	2		Sochi	19 May
Regula	Egger	SWZ 58	62.12	1	v Fra	Luzern	9 Jun
Zsuzsa	Malovecz	HUN 62	62.10	1		Budapest	5 May
Diane	Royle	UK 59	61.94	2		Birmingham	2 Sep
Katalin	Hartai	HUN 63	61.88	3		Nitra	26 Aug
Terese	Nekrosaite	SU 61	61.60	1		Klaipeda	18 Aug
Sandra	Leiskalne	SU 58	61.54	1		Riga	3 Jun
Lyudmila	Zadko	SU 56	61.48	1		Sochi	28 Apr
Karin	Bergdahl	SWE 64	61.42	1		Boden	12 May
Hongyang	Zhu	CHN 64	61.30	1		Beijing	25 Mar
Galina	Isayeva	SU 54	61.12	4	NC	Donetsk	9 Sep
Cathy	Sulinski	USA 58	61.10	1		Berkeley	14 Jul
Kerstin	Brauer	GDR 63	61.06	2	NC	Erfurt	3 Jun
Carola	Furst	GDR 61	61.00	1		Berlin	16 May
Jana	Kopping	GDR 66	60.88	2		Potsdam	5 May
Sharon	Gibson	UK 61	60.88	Q	OG	Los Angeles	5 Aug
Elena	Revayova	CS 58	60.86	3	v Ita	Catania	7 Sep
Eva	Budavari	HUN 53	60.86	1		Szolnok	25 Sep
Maria	Janak	HUN 58	60.74	1		Miskolc	26 Aug
Andrea	Schramm	GDR 62	60.68	5	OD	Potsdam	21 Jul
Nadezhda	Parakhina	SU 54	60.58	2		Bolzano	20 May
Manuela	Alizadeh	FRG 63	60.50	3		Stuttgart	21 Jul
Emi	Matsui	JAP 63	60.40	1		Walnut, CA	25 Jul
Lynda	Sutfin	USA 62	60.30	1		Austin	20 May
Brigitte	Graune	FRG 61	60.28	4	v Fin	Stuttgart	21 Jul
Elisabet	Nagy	SWE 60	60.26	2		Helsinki	2 Sep
Natalya	Gnutova	SU 54	59.90	9		Adler	25 Feb
Xueqing	Yu	CHN 63	59.90	1		Beijing	31 Aug
Ibolya	Torma	HUN 55	59.74	1		Osijek	13 May
Ivanka	Vancheva	BUL 53	59.74	2	NC	Sofia	3 Jun
Jing	Wang	CHN 62	59.68			Guiyang	15 Oct
Fenghua	Ding	CHN 64	59.60			Nanjing	6 Jun
Minori	Mori	JAP 57	59.58	1		Fuse	27 May

414

1984 Lists – Women

First Name	Last Name	Nat/Year	Mark	Pos	Meet	Venue	Date
Mihaela	Stanescu	RUM 59	59.52	1		Pitesti	1 Jul
Hilde	Bratvold	NOR 60	59.48	2	NC	Ovre Ardal	26 Aug
Tatyana	Shikolenko	SU 68	59.40	1		Moskva	6 Aug
Yelena	Kucherenko	SU 66	59.36	1		Tashkent	22 Sep
Yelena	Medvedyeva	SU 65	59.34	2		Moskva	8 Jul
Xia	Li	CHN 58	59.32			Shanghai	20 May
Marina	Terenchenko	)SU 61	59.26	3		Gorkiy	11 Aug
Mariann	Kispal	HUN 60	59.24	1		Miskolc	13 Oct
Shuhua	Qui	CHN 62	59.08			Beijing	15 Mar
Marie	Fukalova	CS 52	59.08	2	Ros	Praha	9 Jun
Galya	Nikolova	BUL 65	58.90	2		Sofia	7 May
Herminia	Bouza	CUB 65	58.86	4	Bar	Habana	20 May
Ute	Richter	GDR 58	58.80	4	Skok	Celje	5 May
Simone	Grafe	GDR 64	58.80	3		Berlin	15 Jul
Zhiying	Gao	CHN 60	58.78			Zhengzhou	8 Apr
Kate	Schmidt	USA 53	58.70	2	Pepsi	Westwood	13 May
Paivi	Alafrantti	FIN 64	58.66	3		Pihtipudas	1 Jul
Ivonne	Leal	CUB 66	58.54	6		Habana	6 Feb
Lyudmila	Chaynikova	SU 60	58.54	4		Gorkiy	11 Aug
Anna	Bondarenko	SU 60	58.50	1		Klaipeda	26 May
Yuan	Chi	CHN 63	58.46			Jinan	18 May
Helena	Uusitalo	FIN 62	58.44	4		Pihtipudas	1 Jul
Sirpa	Vepsalainen	FIN 60	58.38	3		Lahti	19 May
Nadine	Schoellkopf	FRA 64	58.34	1		Joinville	3 Jun
Xiaoli	Xin	CHN 66	58.32			Beijing	31 May
Yelena	Zhilichkina	SU 63	58.30	2	SU P	Baku	16 Sep
Larisa	Avdeyeva	SU 62	58.12	2		Krasnodar	7 Apr
Solvi	Nybu	NOR 66	58.12	2	v Nord–j	Sollentuna	11 Aug
Raili	Kadarik	SU 57	58.04	2		Klaipeda	26 May
Zoya	Karepina	SU 61	57.98			Adler	25 Feb
Guoli	Tang	CHN 62	57.96	1t		Nanjing	17 Sep
Rili	Cui	CHN 61	57.96	1t		Nanjing	17 Sep
Galina	Zaliskaya	SU 65	57.90	3		Sochi	28 Apr
Susan	Lion-Cachet	RSA 62	57.82	1		Pretoria	14 Mar
Lihua	Huo	CHN 57	57.82			Zhengzhou	18 Apr
Shufeng	Li	CHN 63	57.80			Zhengzhou	13 Apr
Danica	Zivanov)	YUG 67	57.74	1		Zagreb	17 Jun
Svetlana	Pestretsova	SU 61	57.74	1		Moskva	15 Jul
Dulce M	Garcia	CUB 65	57.64	2		Habana	9 Jul
Leolita	Blodniece	SU 59	57.62	1		Klaipeda	20 May
Veronika	Langle	AUT 65	57.52	1	NC	Wien	21 Jul
Nellie	Basson	RSA 59	57.46	18 Feb	Weiping	Tian	CHN 58	56.42	Sep
Maria	Dzhaleva	BUL 64	57.46	3 Jun	Lorna	Martinson	USA 61	56.16	21 Apr
Baolian	Li	CHN 63	57.34	16 May	Iris	Gronfeldt	ICE 63	56.14	1 Jun
Celine	Chartrand	CAN 62	57.26	13 Jun	Gusti	Hoss	FRG 55	56.10	18 Jul
Agnes	Tchuinte	CAM 59	57.24	24 Jun	Asa	Westman	SWE 53	56.00	10 Jun
Denise	Thiemard	SWZ 60	57.10	9 Jun	Simone	Frandsen	DEN 61	56.00	29 Jul
Ruiling	Song	CHN 66	57.08	8 Apr	Ansie	Rogers	RSA 64	55.98	23 Feb
Vera	Shapina	SU 62	57.06	27 Apr	Sonya	Smith	BER 62	55.98	25 May
Eva	Kruze	SU 64	56.98	26 May	Valentina	Shapovalova	SU 57	55.84	6 Jul
Susie	Ray	USA 62	56.72	7 Jun	Irina	Gumovskaya	SU 62	55.72	31 May
Maria	Jablonska	POL 55	56.66	9 Jun	Marina	Kochneva	SU 63	55.68	9 Sep
Galina	Medvedyeva	SU 61	56.64	25 Feb	Ankica	Sumaher	YUG 62	55.64	9 Sep
Regine	Kempter	GDR 67	56.60	22 Jul	Tatyana	Silayeva	SU 67	55.60	8 Aug
Tatyana	Yermolayeva	SU 62	56.56	25 Feb	Evelyne	Giardino	FRA 61	55.56	3 Jun
Valentina	Ivanova	SU 52	56.54	26 Aug	Susanne	Hoffmann	GDR 65	55.56	14 Aug
Guohua	Liu	CHN 61	56.52	6 Jun	Mihaela	Popescu	RUM 66	55.54	29 Jul
Yingyi	Xia	CHN 63	56.52	6 Jun	Danute	Montrimaite	SU 59	55.52	12 Feb
Liangying	Feng	CHN 62	56.46	6 Jun	Laila	Kublicka	SU 65	55.48	13 May
Heike	Galle	GDR 67	56.44	2 Feb	Ambra	Giacchetti	ITA 79	55.46	26 May
Marina	Kozoderova	SU 64	56.42	11 Aug	Kathy	Calo	USA 60	55.42	12 May

1984 Lists – Women

Catherine	Garside	UK 67	55.38		19 May		Jeannette	Kieboom		AUS 59	55.14		1 Apr
Margit	Lazar	HUN 53	55.34		14 Jul		Laurie	Schultz		CAN 57	55.14		14 Jul
Irina	Kostyuchenkova	SU 61	55.22		26 May		Huiching	Lee		TAI 67	55.04		20 May
Natividad	Vizcaino	SPA 54	55.22		29 May								

Additional marks in series

	Felke		72.94	5 May		Felke		69.92	16 Aug
	Felke		72.64	5 May		Felke		69.32	14 Sep
	Felke		72.12	16 Aug		Kempe		69.28	30 Apr
	Kempe		71.56	21 Jul		Felke		69.20	15 Jul

	1	10	20	30	50	100	Over 60.00	Over 56.00
1980	70.08	66.40	62.92	61.50	58.42	55.08	36	86
1981	71.88	64.62	63.10	61.34	59.00	55.30	41	82
1982	74.20	66.64	64.00	61.88	59.70	56.20	48	108
1983	74.76	67.20	64.60	63.12	60.70	56.82	57	122
1984	74.72	66.56	64.26	62.28	60.68	57.74	56	130

HEPTATHLON (1971 scoring table)

Sabine	Paetz	GDR 57	6867	1	NC	Potsdam	5/6 May
12.64 180 15.37 23.37/686 44.62 2:08.93							
Natalya	Shubenkova	SU 57	6799	1	NC	Kiev	20/21 Jun
12.93 183 13.66 23.57/673 46.26 2:04.60							
	Paetz		6785	1	OD	Potsdam	20/21 Jul
12.71 174 16.16 23.23w/658 41.94 2:07.03							
Ramona	Neubert	GDR 58	6740	2	OD	Potsdam	20/21 Jul
13.48 174 15.03 23.47w/671 47.88 2:04.73							
Anke	Vater	GDR 61	6722	3	OD	Potsdam	20/21 Jul
13.30 186 14.86 23.20w/684 34.04 2:03.76							
Jane	Frederick	USA 52	6714	1		Talence	15/16 Sep
13.27 187 15.49 24.15/643 51.74 2:13.35							
	Frederick		6611	4	OD	Potsdam	20/21 Jul
13.76 186 15.91 24.86/621 52.74 2:10.25							
	Vater		6566	1	v SU	Neubrandenburg	2/3 Jun
13.37 177 13.95 23.26/671w 37.82 2:06.40							
Natalya	Grachova	SU 52	6563	1	v FRG	Ahlen	8/9 Sep
13.45 181 16.11 24.23w/647w 39.96 2:08.83							
Nadezhda	Vinogradova	SU 59	6532	2	NC	Kiev	20/21 Jun
13.92 180 15.19 23.84/667 38.60 2:06.80							
Jackie	Joyner	USA 62	6520	1	FOT	Los Angeles	16/17 Jun
13.61 183 13.06 23.77/681 45.38 2:13.41							
	Grachova		6512	1		Moskva	19/20 Jul
13.74 182 15.23 24.21/651 39.56 2:07.48							
	Vater		6485	2	NC	Potsdam	5/6 May
13.67 183 15.11 23.26/628 35.08 2:08.11							
	Grachova		6477	1	DRZ	Praha	16/17 Aug
13.61 176 15.31 24.13/677 35.84 2:07.55							
	Shubenkova		6475	2	v GDR	Neubrandenburg	2/3 Jun
13.13 174 13.42 24.05/617 46.98 2:07.22							
Sabine	Braun	FRG 65	6442	1	v Bul	Mannheim	8/9 Jun
13.68 178 13.09 23.88/603 52.14 2:09.41							
Jodi	Anderson	USA 57	6413	2	FOT	Los Angeles	16/17 Jun
13.52 180 13.40 24.49/636 48.52 2:13.20							
Mila	Kolyadina	SU 60	6402	3	v GDR	Neubrandenburg	2/3 Jun
13.87 183 16.37 24.62/618 43.32 2:15.33							
Glynis	Nunn	AUS 60	6390	1	OG	Los Angeles	3/4 Aug
13.02 180 12.82 24.06/666 35.58 2:10.57							
	Joyner		6385	2	OG	Los Angeles	3/4 Aug
13.63 180 14.39 24.05/611 44.52 2:13.03							

1984 Lists – Women

Marianna	Maslennikova	SU 61	6383	3	NC	Kiev	20/21 Jun
13.47 186 12.83 24.43/638 38.10 2:06.99							
Heike	Tischler	GDR 64	6381	5	OD	Potsdam	20/21 Jul
14.41 177 14.18 24.34w/612 50.18 2:07.67							
	Kolyadina		6373	4	NC	Kiev	20/21 Jun
13.73 177 16.05 24.52/615 44.32 2:14.72							
Sabine	Everts	FRG 61	6363	3	OG	Los Angeles	3/4 Aug
13.54 189 12.49 24.05/671 32.62 2:09.05							
Sibylle	Thiele	GDR 65	6359	3	NC	Potsdam	5/6 May
13.84 186 14.53 24.31/668 36.46 2:15.49							
	Vinogradova		6357	2	DRZ	Praha	16/17 Aug
14.14 170 14.36 23.94/659 43.72 2:10.70							
Antonina	Sukhova	SU 59	6351	5	NC	Kiev	20/21 Jun
13.32 183 14.33 24.47/603 42.40 2:13.98							
	Grachova		6334	4	v GDR	Neubrandenburg	2/3 Jun
14.00 177 15.77 24.66/644 41.12 2:14.05							
	Vinogradova		6330	5	v GDR	Neubrandenburg	2/3 Jun
14.09 165 14.90 23.91/670 39.82 2:09.27							
	Joyner		6329	1	MSR	Walnut, CA	26/27 Apr
13.69 175 13.13 23.72w/670w 40.22 2:14.45							

(30/17)

Malgorzata	Nowak	POL 59	6322	1		Bydgoszcz	19/20 May
13.93 188 15.04 24.66/617 44.54 2:19.88							
Svetlana	Filatyeva	SU 64	6322	6	NC	Kiev	20/21 Jun
13.60 180 13.14 24.96/638 45.30 2:11.69							
Cindy	Greiner	USA 57	6281	4	OG	Los Angeles	3/4 Aug
13.71 183 13.36 24.40/615 40.86 2:11.75							
Judy	Simpson	UK 60	6280	5	OG	Los Angeles	3/4 Aug
13.07 186 13.86 24.95/633 33.64 2:13.01							
Lyudmila	Serbul	SU 60	6279	7	NC	Kiev	20/21 Jun
14.02 174 14.37 24.77/600 43.38 2:05.60							
Jana	Sobotka	GDR 65	6266	6	OD	Potsdam	20/21 Jul
14.40 174 13.28 24.19/627 43.64 2:06.83							
Lyubov	Ratsu	SU 61	6260	1	SU P	Baku	14/15 Sep
13.74 180 13.54 24.91/632 42.56 2:12.86							
Larisa	Nikitina	SU 65	6255	8	NC	Kiev	20/21 Jun
13.87 186 14.04 25.26/631 48.62 2:22.76							
Valentina	Savchenko	SU 68	6226	1	DRZ–j	Plovdiv	4/5 Aug
13.88 159 15.10 24.15/607 48.16 2:12.42							
Svetlana	Ovchinnikova	SU 56	6201	1		Kiev	5/6 May
13.79 170 16.12 25.16/618 39.82 2:13.39							
Svetlana	Korotkova	SU 60	6184	1		Moskva	4/5 Aug
14.18 183 13.99 24.45/633 35.52 2:13.43							
Yekaterina	Smirnova	SU 56	6173	3		Gotzis	19/20 May
13.58 186 14.91 26.22/606 48.76 2:25.99							
Birgit	Dressel	FRG 60	6172	2	v Bul	Mannheim	8/9 Jun
13.84 190 13.15 25.37/593 42.54 2:14.30							
Liliana	Nastase	RUM 62	6161	1	NC	Bucuresti	10/11 Jul
13.20 172 12.63 23.50/627 33.46 2:14.14							
Patsy	Walker	USA 59	6153	4	FOT	Los Angeles	16/17 Jun
13.81 171 14.04 24.68/620 39.86 2:12.57							
Vera	Yurchenko	SU 59	6148	9	NC	Kiev	20/21 Jun
13.77 171 14.71 24.12/624 34.82 2:14.39							
Tineke	Hidding	HOL 59	6147	7	OG	Los Angeles	3/4 Aug
13.70 174 13.48 24.12/635 33.94 2:12.84							
Tatyana	Shpak	SU 60	6139	10	NC	Kiev	20/21 Jun
13.92 177 14.29 24.21/652 33.48 2:18.38							
Kim	Hagger	UK 61	6127	8	OG	Los Angeles	3/4 Aug
13.39 186 12.29 24.72/637 35.42 2:18.44							
Galina	Safronenko	SU 55	6114	11	NC	Kiev	20/21 Jun
13.91w 171 14.19 25.23/604 44.48 2:14.08							

1984 Lists – Women

Corinne	Schneider	SWZ 62	6110	1	Aut C	Innsbruck	7/8 Jul
13.99 183 12.74 24.84/607 47.82 2:22.65								
Helena	Otahalova	CS 59	6099	4		Talence	15/16 Sep
13.80 175 13.66 24.69/592 44.20 2:18.04								
Kristine	Nitzsche	GDR 59	6092	4	NC	Potsdam	5/6 May
14.35 183 15.43 24.90/596 39.94 2:21.25								
Nina	Vashchenko	SU 60	6092	5		Moskva	19/20 Jul
13.97 179 13.86 25.43/607 38.80 2:12.13								
Chantal	Beaugeant	FRA 61	6089	1	NC	Lons-le-Saunier	23/24 Jun
13.69 169 12.83 24.48/585 42.46 2:10.45								
Marcela	Koblasova	CS 56	6078	1		Praha	9/10 Jun
13.90 178 14.15 25.18/617 39.38 2:18.36								
Corina	Tifrea	RUM 58	6062	1	Balk	Athinai	7/8 Sep
13.96 170 12.64 24.86625 42.40 2:13.46								
Emilia	Pencheva	BUL 60	6050	1	NC	Sofia	15/16 Jun
14.22 179 12.44 24.88624 38.48 2:12.62								
Svetlana	Ivshina	SU 62	6048	12	NC	Kiev	20/21 Jun
14.60 186 12.41 25.36615 39.20 2:10.58								
Yelena	Martsenyuk	SU 61	6044	2		Kiev	5/6 May
14.44 176 14.00 24.75598 38.64 2:12.77								
Birgit	Clarius	FRG 65	6044	4	v Bul	Mannheim	8/9 Jun
14.14 175 12.29 25.00586 44.14 2:09.98								
Sabine	Kertz	GDR 64	6031	7	OD	Potsdam	20/21 Jul
14.05 165 13.80 24.63633 38.10 2:14.19								
Marjon	Wijnsma	HOL 65	6015	11	OG	Los Angeles	3/4 Aug
13.93 183 12.57 24.91606 34.12 2:12.91								
Florence	Picaut	FRA 52	6002	2	NC	Lons-le-Saunier	23/24 Jun
13.51 175 13.00 25.35606 36.70 2:14.59								
Ines	Schulz	GDR 65	5990	8	OD	Potsdam	20/21 Jul
14.28 168 12.97 25.05615 37.62 2:07.89								
Kristine	Tannander	SWE 55	5985	12	OG	Los Angeles	3/4 Aug
14.01 180 12.74 25.03557 42.34 2:13.93								
Ilona	Dietze	GDR 63	5980	7	NC	Potsdam	5/6 May
14.65 177 13.96 25.12571 44.12 2:15.55								
Hildelisa	Despaigne	CUB 57	5973	7	DRZ	Praha	16/17 Aug
14.21 182 12.02 25.44636 40.04 2:18.86								
Marina	Spirina	SU 55	5972	13	NC	Kiev	20/21 Jun
13.97 165 12.73 25.24626 37.98 2:09.68								
Annette	Tannander	SWE 58	5972	1	NC	Stockholm	7/8 Jul
14.14 180 12.75 25.92w577 49.88 2:19.73								
Iris	Kunstner	FRG 60	5968	7	v Bul	Mannheim	8/9 Jun
13.91 187 12.50 25.22596 35.86 2:17.50								
Zsuzsa	Vanyek	HUN 60	5948	1	NC	Budapest	26/27 Jul
13.79w 175 12.59 25.51634 38.34 2:19.69								
Svetlana	Chistyakova	SU 61	5944	14	NC	Kiev	20/21 Jun
13.78 177 12.30 25.88600 41.12 2:15.47								
Silva	Oja	SU 55	5944	1	v Ita,Swz	Tallinn	8/9 Sep
13.81 173 14.69 26.38613 43.44 2:25.11								
Yelena	Davydova	SU 67	5921	2	DRZ–j	Plovdiv	4/5 Aug
14.48 183 11.55 25.14625 38.42 2:16.92								
Vera	Polyakova	SU 66	5920	1	NC–y	Simferopol	26/27 May
14.35 175 12.65 24.35593 35.62 2:14.33								
Mirja	Jarvenpaa	FIN 62	5919	1		Turku	23 Jun
14.18w 183 12.70 25.71580 44.60 2:21.49								
Olga	Permyakova	SU 63	5917	4	SU P	Baku	14/15 Sep
14.60 177 13.38 24.59582w 39.56 2:18.26								
Jill	Giffen	CAN 58	5913	1	NC	Winnipeg	30 Jun/1 Jul
13.78 175 11.95 25.54594w 39.30 2:13.78								
Lyubov	Pavlovskaya	SU 56	5907	5	SU P	Baku	14/15 Sep
14.64 183 12.08 26.39609w 41.04 2:12.02								

1984 Lists – Women

Name			Score			Meet	Location	Date
Heidrun	Geissler	GDR 61	5904		10	OD	Potsdam	20/21 Jul
14.99 180 13.68 25.47633 34.76 2:16.16								
Olga	Tokareva	SU 66	5902		2	NC–j	Riga	14/15 Jul
14.40 179 12.04 24.90605 38.30 2:16.75								
Zuzana	Lajbnerova	CS 63	5895		8	DRZ	Praha	16/17 Aug
14.79 179 14.67 26.64599 44.80 2:21.46								
Irina	Oleynik	SU 61	5876		1		Kiev	3/4 Jul
14.43 171 13.63 25.25603 37.76 2:16.62								
Liliane	Menissier	FRA 60	5875		1		Arles	28/29 Apr
14.16w 187 10.80 25.73605w 42.06 2:19.72								
Lidia	Bierka	POL 60	5866		2	Ger	Sopot	14/15 Jul
14.43 175 12.70 25.37611 43.16 2:23.24								
Valda	Ruskite	SU 62	5859		8	SU P	Baku	14/15 Sep
13.88 171 13.08 25.62593 44.56 2:24.91								
Debra	Larsen	USA 64	5856		3	TAC	Westwood	19/20 May
15.14 181 13.66 25.05571 44.20 2:23.13								
Sheila	Tarr	USA 64	5856		1	NCAA	Eugene	28/29 May
14.02 174 14.07 25.78584 45.60 2:29.67								
Anke	Koninger	FRG 61	5850		1		Bad Rappenau	21/22 Jul
13.68 172 12.01 24.01590 31.34 2:17.23								
Beate	Holzapfel	FRG 66	5846		1	NC–y	Ulm	25/26 Aug
14.63 188 11.33 25.07590 39.40 2:19.64								
Joan	Russell	USA 55	5841		5	FOT	Los Angeles	16/17 Jun
14.76 177 12.65 25.75566 38.72 2:08.55								
Irina	Malykh	SU 58	5840		16	NC	Kiev	20/21 Jun
13.69w 174 13.10 25.78628 31.16 2:18.57								
Yelena	Kirgizova	SU 61	5839		17	NC	Kiev	20/21 Jun
14.40w 160 13.99 25.38609 37.54 2:12.95								
Margit	Palombi	HUN 61	5822		2	NC	Budapest	26/27 Jul
13.38w 163 12.04 25.28572 39.10 2:13.92								
Marlene	Harmon	USA 62	5818		6	FOT	Los Angeles	16/17 Jun
14.07 174 11.67 25.20601 37.46 2:17.19								
Esther	Suter	SWZ 62	5817		1	NC	Winterthur	15/16 Jun
14.03 180 11.51 25.26579 38.28 2:18.20								
Christiane	van Landschoot	BEL 56	5810		1	NC	Hechtel	21/22 Jul
14.18 175 11.79 25.25566 39.94 2:14.72								
Tatyana	Susuyeva	SU 64	5797		3		Kiev	3/4 Jul
13.70 160 13.45 24.88593 34.32 2:16.81								
Myrtle	Chester	USA 62	5793		2	NCAA	Eugene	28/29 May
13.98 177 11.19 24.64576 33.26 2:14.08								
Inna	Ivanova	SU 58	5790		20	NC	Kiev	20/21 Jun
14.30 171 12.60 24.57573 33.66 2:14.17								
Yelena	Oskirko	SU 65	5786		2		Frunze	8/9 Sep
14.48 172 12.77 25.01610 31.36 2:14.31								
Alla	Yeremina	SU 56	5786		9	SU P	Baku	14/15 Sep
14.48 174 12.82 25.22w596 34.52 2:16.37								
Elisavet	Pantazi	GRE 56	5773		1		Athinai	15/16 Sep
13.68 165 12.13 24.79595 41.96 2:27.66								
Malgorzata	Lisowska	POL 62	5755		3	Ger	Sopot	14/15 Jul
14.88 172 12.98 25.86576 45.82 2:20.75								
Jocelyn	Millar	AUS 62	5753		2	NC	Canberra	14/15 Apr
14.39 183 9.63 24.66573 37.46 2:14.40								
Beate	Osterer	AUT 60	5752		2	NC	Innsbruck	7/8 Jul
14.87 174 12.76 25.57541 47.48 2:19.03								
Melitta	Aigner	AUT 61	5742		3	NC	Innsbruck	7/8 Jul
15.10 171 14.43 25.61559 41.64 2:19.35								
Isabelle	Kaftandjian	FRA 64	5741		1	NC–j	Lons-le-Saunier	21/22 Jul
13.59 163 10.70 24.97607 39.88 2:20.18								

1984 Lists – Women

Name		Nat	Score				Venue	Date
Renate	Pfeil	FRG 63	5729		9	v Bul	Mannheim	89 Jun
14.17 172 13.43 25.24567 33.70 2:18.93								
Connie	Polman-Tuin	CAN 63	5728		5	TAC	Westwood	19/20 May
14.15 163 12.85 24.46611 33.92 2:22.93								
Christine	Dalage	FRA 58	5727		2		Nice	19/20 May
14.20 178 12.46 25.74588 31.20 2:15.73								
Irina	Kushenko	SU 65	5727		3	NC–j	Riga	14/15 Jul
14.18 176 12.35 25.33592 27.40 2:12.29								
Viktoria	Marushchak	SU 66	5718		2	v GDR–j	Tallinn	23/24 Jun
14.15 182 11.82 25.89605 29.92 2:16.99								
Annie	Moelo	FRA 62	5716		3	NC	Lons-le-Saunier	23/24 Jun
14.03 166 10.03 25.14598 37.06 2:10.88								
Jacqueline	Hautenauve	BEL 62	5712		2		Bosvoorde	9/10 Jun
14.16 173 11.23 25.75595 37.92 2:17.57								
Svetlana	Degtyareva	SU 60	5704		21	NC	Kiev	20/21 Jun
14.33 168 12.61 25.47563 42.62 2:21.37								
Heidrun	Wellhofer	FRG 64	5700		1		Immenstadt	28/29 Jul
14.29 170 13.84 24.68581 34.06 2:27.74								

Kerry	Bell	USA 61	5698	16/17 Jun	Esmeralda	Pecchio	ITA 63	5606	9/10 Jun
Rita	Heggli	SWZ 62	5690	15/16 Jun	Lesley	Richards	AUS 63	5599	14/15 Apr
Mary	Harrington	USA 56	5688	16/17 Jun	Tonya	Alston	USA 60	5597	16/17 Jun
Valya	Vasileva	BUL 61	5679	14/15 Jul	Linda	Spenst	CAN 62	5594	28/29 May
Tatyana	Dremina	SU 57	5678	14/15 Sep	Lilia	Fastivets	SU 64	5585	20/21 Jun
Yelena	Shalamova	SU 66	5676	26/27 May	Sharon	Hatfield	USA 64	5582	28/29 May
Katrin	Hochrein	GDR 66	5675	1/ 2 Jun	Yelena	Patyukova	SU 60	5576	5/ 6 May
Heidi	de Kock	RSA 59	5674	13/14 Apr	Camelia	Cornateanu	RUM 67	5569	4/ 5 Aug
Stefanie	Huhn	FRG 66	5672	25/26 Aug	Eleonora	Teglasi	HUN 64	5567	26/27 Jul
Natalya	Bagreyeva	SU 61	5659	20/21 Jun	Ann	Turnbull	AUS 62	5565	14/15 Apr
Bettina	Beinhauer	FRG 65	5657	8/ 9 Sep	Tracy	Hanlon	USA 62	5560	28/29 May
Renate	Stanova	CS 67	5653	7/ 8 Jul	Maria	Khomitskaya	SU 64	5558	3/ 4 Jul
Sally	Gunnell	UK 66	5647	27/28 May	Naomi	Yagata	JAP 62	5551	19/20 May
Joanne	Mulliner	UK 66	5644	18/19 Aug	Lijiau	Tsai	TAI 62	5549	26/27 Apr
Donna	Smellie	CAN 64	5638	3/ 4 Aug	Yelena	Babikova	SU 67	5548	26/27 May
Yelena	Zaitseva	SU 66	5636	26/27 May	Mariana	Nakova	BUL 63	5548	15/16 Jun
Taimi	Konn	SU 61	5634	8/ 9 Sep	Kimiko	Tatsumi	JAP 62	5546	26/27 May
Lilyana	Ivanova	BUL 56	5628	8/ 9 Jun	Helle	Saadlo	SU 60	5546	8/ 9 Sep
Peggy	Beer	GDR 69	5626	7/ 8 Jul	Florence	Colle	FRA 65	5545	21/22 Jul
Kathy	Warren	UK 58	5617	27/28 May	Grit	Colditz	GDR 66	5544	30 Jun/1 Jul
Janet	Nicolls	USA 63	5613	20/21 Apr	Deb	Clark	USA 65	5541	16/17 Jun
Susan	Brownell	USA 60	5613	19/20 May	Sylvie	Levecq	FRA 62	5541	23/24 Jun
Kirsten	Schallau	FRG 62	5611	8/ 9 Sep					

Assisting wind in 200m greater than 4 m/s

Donna	Smellie	CAN 64	5814		1		Saskatoon	14/15 Jul
13.76w 169 12.44 25.34W/ 624 37.34 2:23.42								
Connie	Polman-Tuin	CAN 63	5787		2		Saskatoon	14/15 Jul
13.71w 160 13.18 24.48W/ 599w 33.82 2:19.42								
Alison	Eades	CAN 65	5587				14/15	Jul

Assisting wind in 100mH greater than 4 m/s

Alison	Armstrong	CAN 61	5601			9/10	Jun

Hand timing

Heptathlon point totals made with hand timing have an estimated of 55 points advantage over totals made with automatic timing

Antonina	Sukhova	SU 59	6467 M	1		Tula	25/26 Aug
13.0 182 13.79 24.8/641 45.88 2:13.5							

1984 Lists – Women

Vera	Yurchenko	SU 59	6308 M	1	Kiev	14/15 Aug	
13.1 170 14.96 23.6/576 40.06 2:12.0							
Galina	Safronenko	SU 55	6283 M	1	Alma Ata	28/29 Jul	
13.6 174 14.50 25.0/631 45.92 2:15.4							
Svetlana	Ovchinnikova	SU 56	6265 M	1	Leningrad	11/12 Aug	
13.4 175 16.42 24.7/603 35.06 2:12.3							
Marina	Spirina	SU 55	6235 M	2	Tula	25/26 Aug	
13.2 165 12.20 24.3/648 40.18 2:07.8							
Nina	Vashchenko	SU 60	6212 M	2	Leningrad	11/12 Aug	
13.6 178 13.83 25.1/618 41.62 2:13.3							
Liliana	Nastase	RUM 62	6175 M	1	Bucuresti	26/27 May	
6179 = 13.3 176 11.55 23.6/630 36.18 2:12.9							
Valda	Ruskite	SU 62	6120 M	1	Vilnius	4/ 5 Aug	
13.4 171 14.67 25.3/615 42.20 2:19.6							
Lyubov	Pavlovskaya	SU 56	6106 M	1	Cheboksary	3/ 4 Jun	
14.0 183 12.80 25.7/635 39.20 2:12.5							
Olga	Permyakova	SU 64	6102 M	1	Chelyabinsk	28/29 Jul	
14.1 176 13.20 24.1/596 42.68 2:16.7							
Olga	Nemogayeva	SU 59	6092 M	3	Dnepropetrovsk	4/ 5 Aug	
14.3 179 12.86 24.2/649 39.90 2:21.2							
Svetlana	Ivshina	SU 62	6064 M	1	Kharkov	7/ 8 Jul	
14.2 170 13.07 25.3/631 43.10 2:12.0							
Olga	Commandeur	HOL 58	6027 M	1	Zwolle	29/30 Sep	
14.2 172 10.91 24.4/622 40.68 2:08.3							
Tatyana	Potapova	SU 54	6021 M	1	Rostov/Don	23/24 Jun	
13.9 165 13.17 24.4/628 35.22 2:11.0							
Irina	Rusakova	SU 62	5966 M	1	Tula	14/15 Jul	
14.2 176 13.03 25.3/618 41.22 2:19.2							
Yelena	Kirgizova	SU 61	5964 M	2	Kiev	14/15 Aug	
14.2 160 14.31 24.3/606 36.54 2:12.2							
Olga	Makovets	SU 63	5941 M	2	Krivoy Rog	14/15 Jul	
13.9 160 13.68 24.6/592 41.78 2:15.8							
Aleksandra	Konstantinova	SU 53	5933 M	3	Kiev	14/15 Aug	
14.0 178 12.65 25.3/547 42.58 2:13.0							
Alla	Sekach	SU 59	5929 M	1	Staiki	9/10 Aug	
14.4 174 13.60 25.4/612 39.88 2:18.0							
Alla	Yeremina	SU 56	5901 M	4	Moskva	6/ 7 Jul	
14.2 165 13.69 24.8/605 37.16 2:15.2							
Irina	Dudkova	SU 59	5893 M	2	Staiki	9/10 Aug	
13.8 160 13.62 24.8/595 37.78 2:14.5							
Irina	Malykh	SU 58	5883 M	1	Riga	5/ 6 Jul	
13.4 170 13.35 25.3/641 30.12 2:20.3							
Natalya	Tochilova	SU 64	5849 M	6	Tula	25/26 Aug	
13.4 165 12.60 24.1/606 32.90 2:21.9							
Irina	Kushenko	SU 65	5832 M	4	Kiev	14/15 Aug	
14.1 175 12.23 25.1/580 33.70 2:11.8							
Yelena	Yesina	SU 65	5816 M	7	Tula	25/26 Aug	
14.5 165 12.52 26.3/598 42.98 2:10.2							
Tatyana	Dremina	SU 57	5815 M	8	Tula	25/26 Aug	
14.1 173 12.00 24.5/544 38.66 2:14.4							
Renate	Pfeil	FRG 63	5813 M	1	Wetzlar	11/12 Aug	
14.3 169 14.09 25.0/579 36.36 2:19.1							
Marina	Prokopenko	SU 64	5798 M	1	Shakhty	14/15 Jul	
14.7 166 12.25 25.2/600 40.10 2:12.9							
Nadezhda	Zakharova	SU 63	5795 M	2	Cheboksary	3/ 4 Jun	
14.3 168 12.20 25.9/606 43.56 2:18.4							
Galina	Ivanova	SU 60	5782 M	1	Orel	20/21 Jun	
14.3 155 14.23 26.0/520 41.36 2:18.8							
Natalya	Zolotukhina	SU 54	5777 M	9	Tula	25/26 Aug	
14.0 170 13.22 25.7/600 32.96 2:16.2							
Yelena	Patyukova	SU 60	5776 M	2	Kharkov	7/ 8 Jul	
14.7 175 13.76 25.4/618 31.38 2:18.7							

1984 Lists – Women

Svetlana	Degtyareva	SU 60	5766 M		Svetlana	Besprozvannaya	SU 65	5670 M	27/28 Aug
Yelena	Shalamova	SU 66	5757 M	12/13 May	Galina	Odnodvorkina	SU 55	5663 M	25/26 Aug
Conceicao	Geremias	BRA 56	5751 M	31 Mar/1 Apr	Aleksandra	Bogdanova	SU 54	5661 M	25/26 Aug
Natalya	Skobina	SU 66	5739 M	4/5 Aug	Tonya	Alston	USA 60	5659 M	11/12 May
Monika	Krolkiewicz	FRG 57	5727 M	11/12 Aug	Sylvie	Levecq	FRA 62	5654 M	28/29 Apr
Tatyana	Bobretsova	SU 60	5718 M	28/29 Jul	Janet	Nicolls	USA 63	5652 M	4/5 May
Virginia	Jokubauskaite	SU 61	5716 M	2/3 Jun	Lilia	Fastivets	SU 64	5631 M	14/15 Aug
Stefanie	Huhn	FRG 66	5707 M	26/27 May	Nadezhda	Boldovskaya	SU 59	5626 M	9/10 Aug
Natalya	Shcherbakova	SU 63	5706 M	29/30 Sep	Juanita	Alston	USA 61	5618 M	26/27 May
Kirsten	Schallau	FRG 62	5699 M	11/12 Aug	Lyubov	Polyakova	SU	5617 M	
Deb	Clark	USA 65	5697 M	18/19 Apr	Natalya	Ganchenko	SU 58	5615 M	28/29 Jul
Cornelia	Eckl	FRG 63	5692 M	7/8 Jul	Lyudmila	Rybakova	SU 58	5610 M	9/10 Aug
Tamara	Afanasyeva	SU 63	5689 M	9/10 Aug	Lana	Zimmerman	USA 62	5608 M	2/3 Jun
Bettina	Beinhauer	FRG 65	5681 M		Vera	Suvorova	SU 59	5607 M	
Sally	Gunnell	UK 66	5680 M	7/8 Jul	Vera	Shchapova	SU	5603 M	29/30 Sep

(1971 scoring table/scores converted from manual timing included)

	1	10	20	30	50	100	Over 6000	Over 5600
1980	6144	5871+	5686	5522	–	–	3	23
1981	6716	6212	6040	5949	5825	5563	26	88
1982	6773	6359	6189	6114	5938	5652	41	118
1983	6836	6418	6250	6152	6030	5773	55	144
1984	6867	6413	6281	6184	6048	5773	56	158

4 x 100 METRES RELAY

USA	41.65	1	OG	Los Angeles	11 Aug
(Brown, Bolden, Cheeseborough, Ashford)					
GDR	41.69	1	OD	Potsdam	21 Jul
(Gladisch, Koch, Auerswald, Gohr)					
GDR	41.85	1	WK	Zurich	22 Aug
(Gladisch, Koch, Auerswald, Gohr)					
USA	42.15	1		Walnut, CA	25 Jul
(Brown, Griffith, Cheeseborough, Ashford)					
GDR	42.15	1		Dresden	27 Jul
(G.Walther, Wockel, Auerswald, Gohr)					
SC Motor Jena GDR	42.20	1	NC	Erfurt	2 Jun
(Schmidt, Wockel, Auerswald, Gohr)					
GDR	42.21	1		Karl-Marx-Stadt	20 May
(G.Walther, Koch, Auerswald, Gohr)					
GDR	42.23	1		Berlin	15 Jul
(Gladisch, Koch, Auerswald, Gohr)					
Bulgaria	42.44	1	OD	Berlin	20 Jul
(Pavlova, Nuneva, Georgieva, Ivanova)					
GDR	42.44	1	8N	Tokyo	14 Sep
(Gladisch, Wockel, Auerswald, Gohr)					
USA	42.59	1h2	OG	Los Angeles	11 Aug
(Brown, Bolden, Cheeseborough, Ashford)					
Bulgaria	42.61	2	OD	Potsdam	21 Jul
(Pavlova, Nuneva, Georgieva, Ivanova)					
GDR	42.62	1		Berlin	9 Jun
(Gladisch, Koch, Wockel, Gohr)					
Bulgaria	42.62	1	DRZ	Praha	18 Aug
(Pavlova, Nuneva, Georgieva, Ivanova)					
GDR – B	42.64	2	OD	Berlin	20 Jul
(Riefstahl, Wockel, G.Walther, Scholzel)					
Bulgaria	42.69	1	NarMl	Sofia	19 May
(A.Georgieva, Nuneva, N.Georgieva, Donkova)					
Bulgaria	42.69	1	v Pol,FRG,Hun	Warszawa	15 Jul
(Pavlova, Nuneva, Georgieva, Ivanova)					
SU	42.71	2	DRZ	Praha	18 Aug
(Kondratyeva, Azarashvili, Zhizdrikova, Antonova)					

1984 Lists – Women

GDR	42.74	1		Potsdam	25 May
(Schmidt, Wockel, Auerswald, Gohr)					
Canada	42.77	2	OG	Los Angeles	11 Aug
(Bailey, Payne, Taylor, Gareau)					
Jamaica	42.80	2		Walnut, CA	25 Jul
(Burke, Jackson, Findley, Ottey)					
USA – 1	42.88	1		Berkeley	14 Jul
(Cheeseborough, Washington, Cliette,)					
USA – B	42.92	3		Walnut, CA	25 Jul
(Williams, Washington, Cliette, Givens)					
Bulgaria	42.98	1	v GDR,Rum	Sofia	16 Jun
(Pavlova, Ivanova, Georgieva, Donkova)					
USA – 2	42.98	2		Berkeley	14 Jul
(Bolden, Brown, Williams, Griffith)					
GDR – B	43.03	3	OD	Potsdam	21 Jul
(Riefstahl, G.Walther, Wockel, Scholzel)					
GDR – B	43.04	2		Berlin	15 Jul
(Schmidt, Wockel, G.Walther, Rieger)					
Jamaica	43.05	1h1	OG	Los Angeles	11 Aug
(Burke, Jackson, Findley, Ottey)					
UK	43.11	3	OG	Los Angeles	11 Aug
(Jacobs, Cook, Callender, Oakes)					
GDR – B	43.12	2		Berlin	9 Jun
(30/7)					
(Schmidt, Morgenstern, Rieger, Scholzel)					
France	43.15	4	OG	Los Angeles	11 Aug
(Bacoul, Gaschet, Loval, Naigre)					
FRG	43.17	1		Munchen	20 Jul
(Oker, Schabinger, Gaugel, Thimm)					
Czechoslovakia	43.21	3	DRZ	Praha	18 Aug
(10)					
(Murkova, Kocembova, Cernochova, Kratochvilova)					
Poland	43.41	1	v FRG,CS,FRA	Hannover	15 Jun
(Pakula, Wozniak, Tomczak, Kasprzyk)					
Bahamas	44.15	4h1	OG	Los Angeles	11 Aug
(Clarke, Davis, Greene, Fowler)					
Trinidad	44.23	7	OG	Los Angeles	11 Aug
(Bernard, Forde, Hope, Williams)					
Holland	44.28	1	WA	Lisboa	16 Jun
(Cooman, Derby, Olijslager, Vader)					
Italy	44.31	2	v Hun,Pol,SU	Verona	1 Jun
(Mercurio, Ferrian, Rabaioli, Masullo)					
Steaua Bucuresti RUM	44.41	1	NC	Bucuresti	11 Jul
(Voinea, Militaru, Grecescu, Stanciu)					
Brazil	45.03	1		Sao Paulo	16 Jun
(Miranda, J.Silva, C.C.Silva, de Oliveira)					
New South Wales AUS	45.04	1	NC	Melbourne	31 Mar
(Meres, Goodrope, Armstrong, Schmidt)					
Ghana	45.20	5h2	OG	Los Angeles	11 Aug
(Armah, Mensah, Quartey, Wiredu)					
Yugoslavia (20)	45.28	1	v UK	Karlovac	15 Sep
(Puskas, Istvanovic, Kranjc, Seliskar)					
Cuba	45.29	1	Bar	Habana	20 May
(Ferrer, Armenteros, Petiton, Aveille)					
Auckland NZ	45.34	1	NC	Auckland	10 Mar
Finland	45.36	1	WG	Helsinki	4 Jul
(Markkanen, Marjamaa, Palonen, Honkaharju)					
Hungary	45.46	5	8N	Tokyo	14 Sep
(Siska, Forgacs, Novobaczky, Szopori)					
Switzerland	45.50	1		Luzern	9 Jun
(Blaser, Aebi, T.Schweizer, Frattini)					
Thailand	45.62	5h1	OG	Los Angeles	11 Aug
(Sripet, Tangjitnusorn, Patarach, Panyapuek)					
Noord-Transvaal RSA	45.71	1	NC	Durban	14 Apr

1984 Lists – Women

Sweden	45.72	1	v Nor	Malmo	16 Jun
(Fernstrom, Haglund, Engstrom, Wallin)					
Barbados – South Carolina St	45.74	7	NCAA	Eugene	2 Jun
(Hinkson, Austin, Clarke, Coulthrust)					
China	45.76	1		Shanghai	22 Sep
(30)					

Mark made in mixed race with men

Bulgaria	42.08			Sofia	8 Aug
(Pavlova, Nuneva, Georgieva, Ivanova)					

4 X 400 METRES RELAY

GDR	3:15.92	1		Erfurt	3 Jun
(G.Walther, Busch, Rubsam, Koch)					
USA	3:18.29	1	OG	Los Angeles	11 Aug
(Leatherwood, S.Howard, Brisco, Cheeseborough)					
SU	3:19.12	1	DRZ	Praha	18 Aug
(Baskakova, Nazarova, Pinigina, Vladykina)					
USA	3:19.60	1		Walnut, CA	25 Jul
(Leatherwood, S.Howard, Brisco, Cheeseborough)					
Canada	3:21.21	2	OG	Los Angeles	11 Aug
(Crooks, Killingbeck, Richardson, Payne)					
Czechoslovakia	3:21.89	2	DRZ	Praha	18 Aug
(Bulirova, Moravcikova, Kratochvilova, Kocembova)					
USA	3:22.82	1h1	OG	Los Angeles	10 Aug
(Leatherwood, S.Howard, Dixon, D.Howard)					
FRG	3:22.98	3	OG	Los Angeles	11 Aug
(Schulte-Mattler, Thimm, Gaugel, Bussmann)					
SU	3:25.16	1	v Ita,Hun,Pol	Verona	1 Jun
(Pinigina, Baskakova, Vladykina, Nazarova)					
UK	3:25.51	4	OG	Los Angeles	11 Aug
(Scutt, Barnett, Taylor, Hoyte-Smith)					
Dinamo SU	3:25.95	1		Kiev	24 Jun
(Vladykina, Nazarova, Smeyan, Abramova)					
USA	3:25.99	1		Berkeley	14 Jul
(Leatherwood, S.Howard, Brisco, Cheeseborough)					
Ukraina SU	3:26.02	1	NC	Donetsk	9 Sep
(Yevseyeva, Dzhigalova, Vladykina, Pinigina)					
Soviet Army SU	3:26.28	2		Kiev	24 Jun
(Zubova, Olizarenko, Volskite, Baskakova)					
Jamaica	3:26.56	2h1	OG	Los Angeles	10 Aug
(Thomas, Green, Rattray, Oliver)					
USA – B	3:27.03	2		Berkeley	14 Jul
(D.Howard, Cliette, Dixon, Belle)					
Moskva SU	3:27.10	2	NC	Donetsk	9 Sep
(Babich, Nazarova, Korchagina, Belova)					
Trud SU	3:27.32	3		Kiev	24 Jun
(Korban, Novoseltsova, M.Grishina, Podyalovskaya)					
Jamaica	3:27.41	3		Berkeley	14 Jul
(Thomas, Green, Oliver, Rattray)					
Spartak SU	3:27.42	4		Kiev	24 Jun
(Zhdanova, I.Zakharova, Zvyagintseva, Y.Yefimova)					
Jamaica	3:27.51	5	OG	Los Angeles	11 Aug
(Oliver, Green, Rattray, Jackson)					
UK	3:27.68	3h1	OG	Los Angeles	10 Aug
(Scutt, Barnett, Taylor, Hoyte-Smith)					
Florida State USA	3:27.72	1	NCAA	Eugene 3:28.93y	1 Jun
(J.Davis, Cliette, Givens, Payne/CAN)					
Bulgaria	3:28.34	3	DRZ	Praha	18 Aug
(Penkova, Ilieva, Dimitrova, Stamenova)					
Lithuania SU	3:28.45	3	NC	Donetsk	9 Sep
(Navickaite, Paulaviciene, Mendzorite, Matusiviciene)					

1984 Lists – Women

RSFSR	SU	3:28.75	1	v Rum	Bucuresti	16 Sep	
(Ivanova, Novoseltsova, Gurina, Ruchayeva)							
USA – B		3:28.81	2		Walnut, CA	25 Jul	
(D.Howard, Maxie, Dixon, Belle)							
Czechoslovakia		3:29.00	1	v FRG,Fra,Pol	Hannover	16 Jun	
(Cernochova, Tylova, Moravcikova, Kratochvilova)							
Poland		3:29.09	4	DRZ	Praha	18 Aug	
(Kapusta, Dunecka, Januchta, Blaszak)							
(10)							
RSFSR		3:29.49	4	NC	Donetsk	9 Sep	
(Akchurina, Ruchayeva, Gurina, Ivanova)							
(30/10)							
Rumania		3:30.23	2	v RSFSR	Bucuresti	16 Sep	
(Korodi, Vornicu, Lina, Samungi)							
Italy		3:30.82	6	OG	Los Angeles	11 Aug	
(Lombardo, Campana, Masullo, Rossi)							
Cuba		3:31.17	3		Sofia	17 Jun	
(, Mc Keen, Alvarez, Quirot)							
Hungary		3:32.42	3	v Ita,Pol,SU	Verona	1 Jun	
(Szopori, Petrika, Szabo, Forgacs)							
India		3:32.49	7	OG	Los Angeles	11 Aug	
(Valsamma, Rao, Abraham, Usha)							
Holland		3:34.47	1	v Nor,Swz	Romedal	9 Sep	
(v Agt, Stoot, de Leeuw, Commandeur)							
Yugoslavia		3:35.21	3	Balk	Athinai	9 Sep	
(Matakovic, Colovic, Bozinovska, Seliskar)							
Victoria	AUS	3:35.47	1	NC	Melbourne	1 Apr	
(Flintoff, Tomsett, Cater, Corcoran)							
France		3:36.52	5	v FRG,CS,Pol	Hannover	16 Jun	
(Naigre, Champenois, Simon, Lise)							
Noord-Transvaal	RSA	3:36.84	1	NC	Durban	14 Apr	
(20)							
Puerto Rico		3:37.39	5h1	OG	Los Angeles	10 Aug	
(E.Mathieu, de Jesus, Lind, M.Mathieu)							
Kenya		3:37.76	1	AfrC	Rabat	15 Jul	
(Esendi, Wanjiru, Chepchirchir, Atuti)							
Norway		3:37.76	2	v Hol,Swz	Romedal	9 Sep	
(Systad, Evjen, Gundersen, Brun)							
Switzerland		3:38.44	2	WA	Lisboa	17 Jun	
(Duboux, C.Pluss, Hofstetter, T.Schweizer)							
Sweden		3:38.77	1	v Fin	Helsinki	2 Sep	
(Strand, Bergman, Halldin, Fernstrom)							
Finland		3:39.08	2	v Swe	Helsinki	2 Sep	
(Vesanen, Pakkala, Helander, Ylimaki)							
Ireland		3:39.31	1	v Bel, Eng	Dublin	14 Jul	
(,O'Shea)							
Antigua		3:39.32	4h2	OG	Los Angeles	10 Aug	
(Joseph, Charles, Stevens, Bryan)							
Ghana		3:40.38	5h2	OG	Los Angeles	10 Aug	
(Appiah, Addy, Mensah, Bakari)							
Auckland	NZ	3:41.07	1	NC	Auckland	11 Mar	
(30)							

5000 METRES WALK (TRACK)

Olga	Krishtop	SU 57	21:36.2	(1)	RCh	Penza	4 Aug
Hong	Yan	Chn 66	21:40.3	(1)	SGP	Fana	5 May
Hongju	Xu	Chn 64	21:41.0	(2)	SGP	Fana	5 May
Olga	Yarutkina	SU 60	21:42.2	(2)	RCh	Penza	4 Aug
	Krishtop		21:52.8	(1)		Krasnodar	8 Apr
Natalya	Serbinenko	SU 59	21:59.0	(3)	SGP	Fana	5 May
Sue	Cook	Aus 58	22:04.42	(1)	NCh	Melbourne	1 Apr
	Cook		22:06.34	(1)		Melbourne	3 Mar
	Xu		22:06.8	(1)	NCh	Jiading	12 Mar
	Yan		22:07.0	(2)	NCh	Jiading	12 Mar

1984 Lists – Women

	Cook		22:16.3	(1)		Canberra	17 Feb
	Yan		22:17.0	(1)	IM	Varnamo	19 May
Ann	Peel	Can 61	22:17.5	(4)	SGP	Fana	5 May
	Yan		22:18.2	(1)		Fuxin	25 Sep
	Xu		22:18.4	(2)		Fuxin	25 Sep
Galina	Bildina	SU 60	22:18.8	(1)		Krasnodar	22 Sep
Vera	Osipova	SU 57	22:22.0	(2)		Krasnodar	8 Apr
Roza	Undyerova	SU 57	22:22.0	(5)	SGP	Fana	5 May
Lyudmila	Khrushchova	SU 55	22:25.2	(3)	RCh	Penza	4 Aug
	Peel		22:27.0	(2)	IM	Varnamo	19 May
Giuliana	Salce	Ita 55	22:28.3	(1)		Roma	21 Jun
	Salce		22:29.0	(6)	SGP	Fana	5 May
Guan	Ping	Chn 66	22:30.7	(3)		Fuxin	25 Sep
Vera	Lyuzhanova	SU 61	22:38.6	(2)		Krasnodar	22 Sep
	Ping		22:39.0	(3)	IM	Varnamo	19 May
Sally	Pierson	Aus 63	22:39.5	(1)		Melbourne	22 Mar
	Ping		22:41.0	(3)	NCh	Jiading	12 Mar
Ann	Jansson	Swe 58	22:41.1	(4)	IM	Varnamo	19 May
	Yan		22:43.2	(1)	IM	Kobenhavn	13 May
	Salce		22:46.3	(1)		Roma	14 Apr
	Xu		22:48.0	(5)	IM	Varnamo	19 May
	Cook		22:49.8	(2)	IM	Kobenhavn	13 May
	Pierson		22:50.39	(2)	NCh	Melbourne	1 Apr
Lorraine	Young	Aus 59	22:52.0	(2)		Canberra	17 Feb
	Ping		22:52.0	(7)	SGP	Fana	5 May
	Pierson		22:53.06	(2)		Melbourne	3 Mar
	Peel		22:53.8	(3)	IM	Kobenhavn	13 May
Yan	Wang	Chn 71	22:53.9	(4)		Fuxin	25 Sep
	Pierson		22:55.0	(5)		Fuxin	25 Sep
Heping	Yu	Chn 67	22:56.0	(6)	IM	Varnamo	19 May
	Cook		22:58.0	(7)	IM	Varnamo	19 May
Polina	Biznya	SU 55	22:58.0	(1)	Army	Moskva	7 Jul
Sujie	Lie	Chn 66	22:58.7	(6)		Fuxin	25 Sep
	Wang		22:59.0	(6)	IM	Varnamo	19 May
	Cook		22:59.6	(1)		Canberra	11 Jan
Monica	Gunnarsson	Swe 65	23:01.1	(1)		Boras	27 Sep
Yulian	Yan	Chn 66	23:02.7	(7)		Fuxin	25 Sep
Galina	Yezhova	SU 62	23:03.0	(2)	Army	Moskva	7 Jul
Svetlana	Vasilyeva	SU 65	23:06.2	(4)	RCh	Penza	4 Aug
	Salce		23:09.8	(1)		Lanuvio	5 Jul
Yelena	Lisnik	SU 66	23:13.0	(3)	Army	Moskva	7 Jul
Hong	Xiao	Chn 66	23:13.9	(8)		Fuxin	25 Sep
Rachel	Thompson	Aus 62	23:15.82	(3)	NCh	Melbourne	1 Apr
Fengyun	Song	Chn 65	23:17.8	(5)	NCh	Jiading	12 Mar
Sirkka	Oikarinen	Fin 59	23:18.1	(1)		Lahti	1 Jul
Natalya	Spiridonova	SU 63	23:20.0	(1)		Leningrad	7 Jul
Anne	Miller	Aus 63	23:23.0	(2)		Melbourne	22 Mar
Xiaoling	Shi	Chn 60	23:23.8	(9)		Fuxin	25 Sep
Aleksandra	Grigoryeva	SU 60	23:25.5	(5)	RCh	Penza	4 Aug
Marina	Shupilo	SU 58	23:26.0	(4)	Army	Moskva	7 Jul
Maria	Diaz	Spa 69	23:30.3	(10)	SGP	Fana	5 May
Siw	Vera-Ybanez	Swe 57	23:32.0	(1)	NCh	Norrkoping	28 Apr
Tamara	Kovalenko	SU 64	23:33.2	(6)	RCh	Penza	4 Aug
Joan	Bender	Can 63	23:34.0	(10)	IM	Varnamo	19 May
Vera	Prudnikova	SU 54	23:34.0	(1)		Kharkiw	7 Jul
Raisa	Tsupyrka	SU 66	23:38.0	(5)	Army	Moskva	7 Jul
Karin	Jensen	Den 61	23:38.0	(1)	NCh	Odense	15 Sep
Xiong	Yan	Chn 67	23:38.3	(10)		Fuxin	25 Sep
Olympiada	Ivanova	SU 67	23:39.4	(2)		Tashkent	22 Sep
Liliana	Dragan	Rom 63	23:40.8	(1)	NCh	Bucuresti	10 Jun
Maria	Reyes	Spa 67	23:44.8	(11)	SGP	Fana	5 May
Svetlana	Kashina	SU 62	23:45.0	(6)	Army	Moskva	7 Jul

1984 Lists – Women

Tamara	Klimova	SU 64	23:45.0	(7)	RCh	Penza	4 Aug
Fenyun	Song	Chn 65	23:45.0	(11)		Fuxin	25 Sep
Irina	Shubina	SU 61	23:47.2	(1)		Leningrad	12 Aug
Rimma	Makarova	SU 63	23:47.8	(2)		Leningrad	12 Aug
Mia	Kjolberg	Nor 60	23:48.5	(13)	SGP	Fana	5 May
Nadyezhda	Prudnikova	SU 54	23:49.9	(2)		Kharkiw	7 Jul
Jill	Barrett	UK 64	23:51.1	(14)	SGP	Fana	5 May
Vida	Salciute	SU 60	23:52.0	(1)		Klaipeda	27 May
Teresa	Palacios	Spa 58	23:52.2	(15)	SGP	Fana	5 May
Tatyana	Kobzar	SU 50	23:53.0	(8)	Army	Moskva	7 Jul
Haifong	Hu	Chn 68	23:54.0	(9)	NCh	Jiading	12 Mar
Froydis	Hilsen	Nor 59	23:54.4	(1)		Trondheim	12 Aug
Helena	Astrom	Fin 64	23:54.6	(1)		Helsinki	17 May
Dana	Vakrasova	CS 54	i23:54.83	(1)		Jablonec	21 Jan
Natalya	Dmitroshenko	SU 60	23:55.2	(2)		Klaipeda	27 May
Beverley	Wilkins	Aus 61	23:55.69	(2)		Sydney	3 Mar
Suzanne	Griesbach	Fra 45	23:55.60	(1)		Villeneuve d'Asq	30 Jun
Antonella	Marangoni	Ita 63	23:56.1	(1)		Siena	4 Jul
Natalya	Yaroshenko	SU 60	23:56.99	(1)		Kiyev	6 Jul
Alison	Baker	Can 64	23:57.8	(2)			
Svetlana	Kirpichonok	SU 64	23:59.0	(9)	Army	Moskva	7 Jul
Maria Grazia	Cogoli	Ita 62	23:59.71	(1)		Roma	11 Jul
Lenura	Ignat	Rom ..	24:01.0	(2)		Bucuresti	10 Jun
Zhimin	Chen	Chn 67	24:01.5	(12)		Fuxin	25 Sep
Nicola	Jackson	UK 65	24:02.15	(2)	NCh	Cwmbran	27 May
Natalya	Gavazdina	SU 61	24:02.2	(1)		Alma-Ata	8 Aug
Helen	Elleker	UK 56	24:04.34	(3)	NCh	Cwmbran	27 May
Lingcheng	Wu	Chn 67	24:04.5	(13)		Fuxin	25 Sep
Kerry	Saxby	Aus ..	24:05.15	(5)	NCh	Melbourne	1 Apr
Maria	Sehlin	Swe 67	24:05.7	(1)		Ornskoldsvik	7 Jul
Larisa	Lobach	SU 65	24:09.5	(1)		Minsk	11 Jun
Ginny	Birch	UK 55	24:09.96	(2)	WAAA	London	15 Jun
Marta	Hrubanova	CS 51	i24:10.26	(2)		Jablonec	21 Jan
Gunhild	Kristiansen	Den 63	24:12.0	(18)	SGP	Fana	5 May
Valentina	Antonova	SU 59	24:13.0	(10)	Army	Moskva	7 Jul
Mirva	Hamalainen	Fin 62	24:14.2	(1)		Vantaa	12 Aug
Lan	Yu	Chn 66	24:14.2	(14)		Fuxin	25 Sep
Huanfeng	Qiu	Chn 66	24:16.9	(15)		Fuxin	25 Sep
Irina	Tolstik	SU 60	24:17.10	(3)		Klaipeda	27 May
Lene	Cassidy	Den 51	24:18.07	(3)	IM	Lyngby	21 Jul
Irina	Prisekina	SU 65	i24:18.2	(3)		Moskva	7 Jan
Brenda	Lupton	UK 52	24:18.6	(19)	SGP	Fana	5 May
Sari	Essayah	Fin 67	24:18.90	(1)		Turku	20 Jul
Yevgeniya	Mikheyeva	SU 69	24:19.1	(4)		Tashkent	21 Sep
Kazmiera	Mroz	Pol 64	24:19.45	(1)		Poznan	13 Jul
Guihua	Xiang	Chn 68	24:19.7	(10)	NCh	Jiading	12 Mar
Beata	Baczyk	Pol 65	24:21.02	(1)		Lublin	24 Jun
Lillian	Millen	UK 45	24:21.47	(4)	NCh	Cwmbran	27 May
Zhanna	Zhuravlyova	SU 66	24:24.3	(6)		Tashkent	21 Sep
Lifeng	Wang	Chn 66	24:24.4	(16)		Fuxin	25 Sep
Galina	Verzun	SU 67	24:26.4	(7)		Tashkent	21 Sep
Lyubov	Teleman	SU 62	24:26.70	(2)		Kiyev	5 Jul
Mei	Weng	Chn 67	24:26.7	(17)		Fuxin	25 Sep

Indoor performances

Polina	Biznya	SU 55	23:13.0	(1)		Minsk	2 Feb
Ann	Peel	Can 61	23:14.44	(1)		Toronto	25 Feb
Nadyezhda	Prudnikova	SU 54	24:01.0	(2)		Moskva	7 Jan

Road performances

	Krishtop		21:45.4	(1)		Cheboksary	13 May
	Undyerova		21:49.8	(2)		Cheboksary	13 May
	Yarutkina		21:58.8	(3)		Cheboksary	13 May

427

1984 Lists – Women

10000 METRES WALK (TRACK)

Hong	Yan	Chn 66	45:39.5	(1)	IM	Kobenhavn	13 May
Sue	Cook	Aus 58	47:34.2	(2)	IM	Kobenhavn	13 May
Siw	Vera-Ybanez	Swe 57	47:35.6	(1)	NCh	Norrkoping	28 Apr
Monica	Gunnarsson	Swe 65	47:58.0	(2)	NCh	Norrkoping	28 Apr
Ann	Jansson	Swe 58	48:18.0	(3)	NCh	Norrkoping	28 Apr
Suzanne	Griesbach	Fra 45	48:21.4	(1)		Epinay-sur-Seine	13 May
Giuliana	Salce	Ita 55	48:28.4	(1)		Aprilia	9 Sep
Rachel	Thompson	Aus 62	48:34.9	(3)	IM	Kobenhavn	13 May
Heping	Yu	Chn 67	48:52.6	(4)	IM	Kobenhavn	13 May
	Griesbach		48:52.9	(1)	IM	Ahlen	23 Sep
Teresa	Vaill	USA 62	49:06.0	(1)		Lexington	5 May
Lorraine	Young	Aus 59	49:49.8	(5)	IM	Kobenhavn	13 May
Helen	Elleker	UK 56	49:52.3	(1)	WAAAA	Birmingham	17 Mar
Ginny	Birch	UK 55	49:55.0	(1)		Brighton	5 Feb
Brenda	Lupton	UK 52	50:10.2	(2)	WAAA	Birmingham	17 Mar
Joan	Bender	Can 63	50:10.2	(6)	IM	Kobenhavn	13 May
Helena	Astrom	Fin 64	50:38.1	(1)		Helsinki	24 May
Ester	Lopez/Marques	USA 56	50:41.18	(1)	FOT	Los Angeles	23 Jun
Deborah	Spino						
Mirva	Hamalainen	Fin 62	51:04.8	(1)		Naantali	24 Jul
	Lopez		51:16.1	(2)		San Jose	8 Jun
	Vaill		51:16.67	(2)	FOT	Los Angeles	23 Jun
Karin	Jensen	Den 61	51:17.1	(1)		Greve	18 Aug
Ingrid	Adam	FRG 45	51:22.4	(2)	IM	Ahlen	23 Sep
Helen	Ringshaw	UK 66	51:31.2	(3)	WAAA	Birmingham	17 Mar
	Jensen		51:45.0	(1)		Odense	9 Aug
Jeannine	Gosselin	Fra 58	51:46.6	(2)	NCh	Epinay-sur-Seine	13 May
Gunhild	Kristiansen	Den 63	i51:47.0	(1)		Odense	17 Mar
Alyson	Baker	Can 64	51:56.4	(1)	IM	Quebec	12 May
Jutta	Schwoche	FRG 55	52:01.2	(1)		Hildesheim	31 Aug
Lene	Cassidy	Den 51	52:03.8	(7)	IM	Kobenhavn	13 May
Viviane	Humbert	Fra 63	52:03.9	(3)	NCh	Epinay-sur-Seine	13 May
Jana	Zarubova	CS 58	52:04.1	(1)		Praha	7 Oct
Monique	Boueroux	Fra 63	52:06.1	(3)	IM	Ahlen	23 Sep
Carol	Brown	USA 63	52:08.6	(2)	IM	Quebec	12 May
Raija	Kuusivuori	Fin ..	52:17.6	(1)		Myryla	15 Sep
Karen	Nipper	UK 64	52:31.5	(4)	WAAA	Birmingham	17 Mar
Vieno	Heikkila	Fin 38	52:48.9	(2)		Naantali	24 Jul
Monica	Robertson	Fin 51	52:56.4	(1)		Helsinki	19 Sep
Sue	Westerfield	USA 58	53:00.40	(3)	FOT	Los Angeles	23 Jun
Anna	Bak	Pol 61	53:02.0	(1)		Zabrze	13 Oct
Ulla	Kristiansen	Den 60	i53:13.0	(3)		Odense	17 Mar
Chris	Andersson	USA 53	53:17.03	(4)	FOT	Los Angeles	23 Jun
Sue	Miller	USA 52	53:26.0	(1)		Seattle	1 Apr
Sari	Essayah	Fin 67	53:26.8	(2)		Helsinki	24 May
Norma	Arnesen	USA 59	53:45.0	(1)		Piscataway	21 Apr
Lucyna	Rokitowska	Pol 56	i53:52.0	(1)		Zabrze	15 Mar
Helle	Jorgensen	Den 66	53:56.0	(4)	NCh	Odense	9 Sep
Agnieszka	Wyszynska	Pol 55	54:07.0	(2)		Zabrze	13 Oct
Kwona	Dadzibog	Pol 66	54:12.0	(3)		Zabrze	13 Oct
Lillian	Millen	UK 45	54:13.5	(5)	WAAA	Birmingham	17 Mar
Elisabeth	Creuze	Fra 58	54:15.0	(5)	IM	Ahlen	23 Sep
Maria	Sehlin	Swe 67	54:16.0	(4)	NCh	Norrkoping	28 Apr
Micheline	Daneau	Can 60	54:19.5	(3)	IM	Quebec	12 May

Outdoor performances for those listed with indoor marks
| Gunhild | Kristiansen | | 52:55.0 | (2) | | Greve | 18 Aug |
| Ulla | Kristiansen | | 53:35.0 | (8) | IM | Kobenhavn | 13 May |

1984 Lists – Women

Other outdoor performances
| | Cassidy | | i52:53.0 | (2) | | Odense | 17 Mar |

Road performances
Olga	Krishtop	SU 57	44:51.6	(1)	RCh	Penza	5 Aug
Olga	Yarutkina	SU 60	45:03.2	(2)	RCh	Penza	5 Aug
Vera	Osipova	SU 58	45:28.1	(3)	RCh	Penza	5 Aug
Lyudmila	Khrushchova	SU 55	45:51.0	(4)	RCh	Penza	5 Aug

429

Tiina Lillak – world champion and Olympic silver medallist.

Luis Delis – world's No.1 discus thrower in 1984.

Roger Kingdom – Olympic gold at 110 hurdles.

Natalya Lisovskaya – regained the women's shot record for the Soviet Union in 1984.

JUNIOR ALL-TIME LISTS

100 METRES

Chandra	Cheeseborough	USA 59	11.13	2.0	(2)	FOT	Eugene	21 Jun 76
Marlies	Oelsner	GDR 58	11.17	1.3	(2)		Karl-Marx-Stadt	29 May 76
Wendy	Vereen	USA 66	A11.17	0.6	(4)	USOCF	Colorado Springs	3 Jul 83
Silvia	Chivas	CUB 54	11.18	−0.3	(1)H1	OG	Munchen	2 Sep 72
Raelene	Boyle	AUS 51	A11.20	1.2	(4)	OG	Mexico, D.F.	15 Oct 68
	Chivas		11.22	0.9	(1)Q1	OG	Munchen	1 Sep 72
Romy	Schneider	GDR 58	11.22	1.3	(5)		Karl-Marx-Stadt	29 May 76
Natalya	Bochina	SU 62	11.22	0.2	(2)	ZNAM	Moskva	4 Jul 80
	Chivas		11.24	−0.2	(3)	OG	Munchen	2 Sep 72
Gesine	Walther	GDR 62	11.28	2.0	(3)		Berlin	9 Jul 80
Margaret	Bailes	USA 51	A11.29	1.3	(1)H2	OG	Mexico, D.F.	14 Oct 68
Sharon	Ware	USA 63	11.34	0.0	(1)	TAC-J	Knoxville	16 Jun 80
Kathrin	Bohme	GDR 63	11.36	0.8	(1)S2	EC-J	Utrecht	20 Aug 81
Evette	de Klerk	RSA 65	A11.36	1.6	(1)	NC	Bloemfontein	15 Apr 83
Marie-France	Loval	FRA 64	11.38	0.8	(2)S2	EC-J	Utrecht	20 Aug 81
Diane	Holden	AUS 63	11.39	1.9	(1)		Sydney	13 Dec 80
Mari-Lise	Furstenberg	RSA 66	A11.42		(1)	NC-J	Pretoria	31 Mar 84
Michele	Glover	USA 63	11.42	−0.9	(1)	TAC-J	Westwood	1 Jul 81
Michelle	Walsh	IRL 61	11.43	1.4	(1)	EP/SF	Sittard	17 Jun 78
Angela	Bailey	CAN 62	11.44	0.5	(4)	LB	Philadelphia	17 Jul 80
Sonia	Lannaman	UK 56	11.45	−1.3	(4)H6	OG	Munchen	1 Sep 72
Simone	Jacobs	UK 66	11.45	1.0	(3)		Gateshead	6 Jul 84

Marks made with assisting wind

Gesine	Walther	GDR 62	10.97	3.3	(4)	NC	Cottbus	16 Jul 80
	Walther		11.07	3.8	(3)S2	NC	Cottbus	16 Jul 80
Shirley	Thomas	UK 63	11.25	3.7	(1)S1	EC-J	Utrecht	20 Aug 81
Simone	Jacobs	UK 66	11.26	3.8	(3)	NC	Cwmbran	27 May 84
Angela	Bailey	CAN 62	11.27	3.1	(2)	NC	Sherbrooke	14 Jun 80
Carola	Beuster	GDR 63	11.31	3.7	(2)S1	EC-J	Utrecht	20 Aug 81
Kathrin	Bohme	GDR 63	11.33	2.4	(1)	EC-J	Utrecht	20 Aug 81
Silke	Gladisch	GDR 64	11.33	1.5	(3)H1		Cottbus	21 Aug 82
Petra	Koppetsch	GDR 58	11.34	4.9	(1)	EC-J	Athinai	22 Aug 75
Gail	Devers	USA 66	11.34	2.2	(1)H2		Norwalk	25 May 84
France	Gareau	CAN 67	11.38	6.9	(1)		Sacramento	21 Jul 84
Debbie	Jones	BER 59	11.39	2.5	(1)S2	AAU	Westwood	11 Jun 77
Barbel	Lockhoff	GDR 59	11.44	2.6	(1)	NC-J	Erfurt	9 Jun 77

200 METRES

Natalya	Bochina	SU 62	22.19	1.5	(2)	OG	Moskva	30 Jul 80
	Bochina		22.26	−0.9	(1)q3	OG	Moskva	28 Jul 80
	Bochina		22.26	0.0	(1)	NIK	Nice	17 Aug 80
	Bochina		22.45	0.1	(1)	ZNAM	Moskva	5 Jul 80
Gesine	Walther	GDR 62	22.55	0.6	(2)	NC	Cottbus	18 Jul 80
	Bochina		22.57	0.1	(2)		Moskva	12 Jun 80
Raelene	Boyle	AUS 51	A22.74	2.0	(2)	OG	Mexico, D.F.	18 Oct 68
	Bochina		22.75	1.0	(2)S2	OG	Moskva	30 Jul 80
Chandra	Cheeseborough	USA 59	A22.77	0.0	(1)	PAG	Mexico, D.F.	16 Oct 75
	Walther		22.79	−1.2	(2)		Potsdam	13 Jul 80
Margit	Sinzel	GDR 58	22.81	1.5	(2)		Halle	15 May 76
Barbel	Eckert	GDR 55	22.85	0.6	(1)	EC-J	Duisburg	26 Aug 73
Margaret	Bailes	USA 51	A22.95	1.7	(3)S2	OG	Mexico, D.F.	17 Oct 68
Pauline	Davis	BAH 66	22.97	1.1	(4)Q1	OG	Los Angeles	8 Aug 84
Kathy	Smallwood	UK 60	22.99	1.0	(1)S1	CG	Edmonton	8 Aug 78

Junior All-time Lists Women

Wendy	Vereen	USA 66	22.99	1.1	(2)		Villanova	12 Jun 83
Dagmar	Rubsam	GDR 62	23.02	1.4	(1)R2	OT	Potsdam	11 May 80
Simone	Schumann	GDR 65	23.04	1.1	(1)	EC-J	Schwechat	28 Aug 83
Maria	Kulchunova	SU 58	23.08	0.6	(1)	vGDR-J	Erfurt	11 Sep 76
Kerstin	Walther	GDR 61	23.11	−0.4	(1)	EC-J	Bydgoszcz	19 Aug 79
Sabine	Rieger	GDR 63	23.11	1.9	(1)H3	NC-J	Halle	5 Jul 81
Irena	Kirszenstein	POL 46	23.12	0.8	(2)	OG	Tokyo	19 Oct 64
Barbel	Lockhoff	GDR 59	23.12	0.0	(1)	EC-J	Donyetsk	21 Aug 77
Evette	de Klerk	RSA 65	A23.13		(1)	NC	Bloemfontein	16 Apr 83
Valentina	Bozhina	SU 66	23.14	1.1	(2)	EC-J	Schwechat	28 Aug 83
Diane	Holden	AUS 63	23.14		(1)		Sydney	8 Feb 81

Marks made with assisting wind

Chandra	Cheeseborough	USA 59	22.64	2.3	(2)	OT	Eugene	24 Jun 76
Kathy	Smallwood	UK 60	22.73	4.3	(1)H2	CG	Edmonton	8 Aug 78
Wendy	Vereen	USA 66	22.75	2.5	(1)		Los Angeles	14 Apr 84
Sabine	Rieger	GDR 63	22.91	2.2	(1)	EC-J	Utrecht	23 Aug 81
Gwen	Loud	USA 61	23.00	2.5	(2)H1	AAU	Walnut	15 Jun 79
Linsey	Macdonald	UK 64	23.11	6.0	(1)	vFRG-J	Grangemouth	5 Jul 80

400 METRES

Christina	Brehmer	GDR 58	49.77		(1)		Dresden	9 May 76
	Brehmer		50.02		(1)	OT	Berlin	10 Jul 76
	Brehmer		50.13		(1)H		Dresden	19 May 76
	Brehmer		50.17		(1)		Dresden	19 May 76
	Brehmer		50.28		(1)H		Dresden	8 May 76
	Brehmer		50.39		(1)	vYUG-UK	Split	1 May 76
	Brehmer		50.51		(2)	OG	Montreal	29 Jul 76
	Brehmer		50.84		(2)S2	OG	Montreal	28 Jul 76
Denean	Howard	USA 64	50.87		(1)	TAC	Knoxville	20 Jun 82
Margit	Sinzel	GDR 58	50.92		(4)	OT	Berlin	10 Jul 76
Dagmar	Rubsam	GDR 62	51.01		(3)	OT	Erfurt	18 May 80
Marilyn	Neufville	JAM 52	51.02		(1)	CG	Edinburgh	23 Jul 70
Sherri	Howard	USA 62	A51.09		(1)	USOCF	Colorado Springs	28 Jul 79
Linsey	Macdonald	UK 64	51.16		(1)	OT	London	15 Jun 80
Sabine	Busch	GDR 62	51.41		(4)		Potsdam	13 Jul 80
Ericka	Harris	USA 64	51.45		(1)		Lincoln	2 Aug 81
Marita	Koch	GDR 57	51.60		(2)	EC-J	Athinai	23 Aug 75
Lilya	Tuznikova	SU 62	51.68		(2)	EC-J	Bydgoszcz	18 Aug 79
Diane	Dixon	USA 64	51.75		(1)	PEPSI	Westwood	16 May 82
Petra	Muller	GDR 65	51.79		(1)	EC-J	Schwechat	27 Aug 83
Maria	Kulchunova	SU 58	51.80		(5)	NC	Kiev	24 Jun 76
Mable	Fergerson	USA 55	51.91		(4)S2	OG	Munchen	4 Sep 72
Jillian	Richardson	CAN 65	51.91		(4)		Munchen	26 Jul 83
Jennie	Gorham	USA 61	A51.94		(2)	USOCF	Colorado Springs	28 Jul 79
Marion	Heilmann	GDR 61	52.08		(3)	EC-J	Bydgoszcz	18 Aug 79
Sigrun	Ludwigs	GDR 65	52.09		(1)	NC-J	Jena	2 Jul 83
Ann-Louise	Skoglund	SWE 62	52.25		(1)		Varberg	12 Jul 80

Hand timing

	Brehmer		50.1		(1)		Sochi	25 Apr 76
	Brehmer		50.5		(1)H		Sochi	24 Apr 76
Sabine	Busch	GDR 62	51.0		(1)	NC-J	Karl-Marx-Stadt	3 Aug 80
Kathy	Hammond	USA 51	52.1		(1)	vPOL	Warszawa	29 Aug 68
Brigitte	Rohde	GDR 54	52.1		(3)		Berlin	13 Aug 72
Sharon	Dabney	USA 57	52.1		(1)		Los Angeles	31 Aug 75

800 METRES

Christine	Wachtel	GDR 65	1:59.40		(2)	vUSA	Los Angeles	26 Jun 83
Yelena	Kozenkova	SU 65	1:59.6		(3)		Leningrad	18 Jul 83

Junior All-time Lists Women

Marion	Hubner	GDR 62	1:59.65	(3)	NC	Karl-Marx-Stadt	11 Aug 79
	Wachtel		1:59.72	(1)		Jena	28 May 83
	Wachtel		1:59.77	(1)		Neubrandenburg	22 May 83
	Wachtel		1:59.89	(1)	NC	Karl-Marx-Stadt	17 Jun 83
Valentina	Furletova	SU 66	2:00.04	( )H	ZNAM	Sochi	9 Jun 84
Kim	Gallagher	USA 64	2:00.07	(1)	USOCF	Indianapolis	24 Jul 82
	Wachtel		2:00.07	(1)	OD	Berlin	8 Jun 83
Anna	Rybicka	POL 63	2:00.17	(1)	NC	Zabrze	8 Aug 81
Katrin	Wuhn	GDR 65	2:00.18	(2)		Berlin	3 Jun 83
Irina	Nikitina	SU 61	2:00.5	(1)		Donyetsk	14 Sep 79
Kathy	Weston	USA 58	2:00.73	(3)	FOT	Eugene	22 Jun 76
Zola	Budd	RSA/UK 66	2:00.9	(1)		Kroonstad	16 Mar 84
Tatyana	Petrova	SU 64	2:01.01	(4)		Leningrad	16 Jul 82
Astrid	Pfeiffer	GDR 64	2:01.15	(2)		Karl-Marx-Stadt	9 Jul 82
Monika	Bens	FRG 66	2:01.29	(3)	EC-J	Schwechat	27 Aug 83
Lyubov	Kiryukhina	SU 63	2:01.36	(7)		Moskva	7 Aug 81
Olga	Commandeur	HOL 58	2:01.6	(1)		Aalst	7 Sep 75
Lorraine	Baker	UK 64	2:01.66	(3)	BISL	Oslo	26 Jun 82
Martina	Kampfert	GDR 59	2:01.7	(1)	NC-J	Erfurt	10 Jul 77
Mary	Decker	USA 58	2:01.8 I	(1)		San Diego	17 Feb 74
Birgit	Brudel	GDR 61	2:01.90	(2)	EC-J	Bydgoszcz	18 Aug 79
Hildegard	Ullrich	GDR 59	2:01.9	(2)	NC-J	Erfurt	10 Jul 77
Eranee	van Zyl	RSA 62	2:01.9	(2)		Stellenbosch	21 Apr 80

1500 METRES

Zola	Budd	RSA/UK 66	4:01.81	(1)		Port Elizabeth	21 Mar 84
	Budd		4:04.39	(1)	NC	Cwmbran	28 May 84
	Budd		A4:05.81	(1)		Bloemfontein	20 Feb 84
Birgit	Friedmann	FRG 60	4:06.02	(7)	vSU	Dortmund	1 Jul 78
Glenda	Reiser	CAN 55	4:06.71	(2)H1	OG	Munchen	4 Sep 72
	Budd		A4:06.87	(1)		Bloemfontein	28 Oct 83
Inger	Knutsson	SWE 55	4:07.47	(1)	EC-J	Duisburg	26 Aug 73
	Budd		4:08.96	(1)		Sasolburg	26 Mar 83
Gabriella	Dorio	ITA 57	4:09.1	(2)		Milano	2 Jul 75
	Budd		A4:09.1	(1)		Bloemfontein	19 Feb 82
Tatyana	Petrova	SU 64	4:09.19	(5)		Leningrad	19 Jul 82
Irina	Nikitina	SU 61	4:09.2	(1)		Tbilisi	10 Sep 79
Kleopatra	Palaceanu	RUM 68	4:09.37	(5)	NC	Bucuresti	12 Jul 84
Donna	Gould	AUS 66	4:09.54	(4)		Burnaby	16 Jul 84
Betty	van Steenbroek	BEL 63	4:09.72	(2)	VD	Bruxelles	28 Aug 81
Olga	Politova	SU 64	4:11.09	(8)		Leningrad	19 Jul 82
Gunvor	Hilde	NOR 63	4:11.17	(7)		Basel	26 May 80
Lenuta	Rata	RUM 66	4:11.45	(6)	NC	Bucuresti	12 Jul 84
Nadyezhda	Ivanova	SU 59	4:11.8	(6)	WUG	Sofia	23 Aug 77
Lyudmila	Sudak	SU 65	4:11.93	(1)		Moskva	7 Aug 81
Iva	Jurkova	CS 66	4:11.99	(2)		Praha	28 Aug 81
Christina	Cojocaru	RUM 62	4:12.14	(3)	EC-J	Bydgoszcz	19 Aug 79
Valentina	Furletova	SU 66	4:13.03	(1)	vGDR-J	Halle	25 Jun 83
Yvonne	Grabner	GDR 65	4:13.06	(2)	vSU-J	Halle	25 Jun 83
Carsta	Mehnert	GDR 62	4:13.12	(4)	EC-J	Bydgoszcz	19 Aug 79

3000 METRES

Zola	Budd	RSA/UK 66	8:37.5	(1)		Stellenbosch	29 Feb 84
	Budd		8:39.00	(1)		Durban	2 Apr 83
	Budd		8:40.22	(1)	OT	London	6 Jun 84
Donna	Gould	AUS 66	8:44.1	(M)		Eugene	13 Jul 84
	Budd		8:44.62	(3)H3	OG	Los Angeles	8 Aug 84
	Budd		8:46.41	(1)		Stellenbosch	22 Feb 83

433

Junior All-time Lists Women

	Budd		8:48.80	(7)	OG	Los Angeles	10 Aug 84
	Budd		8:51.99	(1)		Belfast	19 Jun 84
	Budd		A8:52.84	(1)		Germiston	5 Mar 84
	Gould		8:53.7	(M)		Adelaide	30 May 84
Yelena	Malykhina	SU 63	8:56.03	(1)	vGDR-J	Cottbus	25 Jun 81
Lyudmila	Sudak	SU 65	8:56.13	(2)	vGDR-J	Cottbus	25 Jun 81
Helen	Kimaiyo	KEN 68	8:57.21	(7)H1	OG	Los Angeles	8 Aug 84
Inger	Knutsson	SWE 55	8:58.38	(1)	vFIN	Stockholm	1 Sep 73
Birgit	Friedmann	FRG 60	9:02.9	(1)	NC	W. Berlin	28 May 78
Vera	Kuznyetsova	SU 64	9:04.5	(1)		Cheboksary	1 Aug 81
Carolyn	Schuwallow	AUS 65	9:04.96	(1)		Melbourne	20 Feb 83
Kleopatra	Palaceanu	RUM 68	9:06.75	(1)		Bucuresti	10 Jun 84
Elvira	Hofmann	FRG 61	9:07.4	(2)		Ingelheim	15 Jul 78
Yvonne	Murray	UK 64	9:07.77	(1)		Edinburgh	10 Jul 82
Jeanette	Hain	GDR 66	9:07.77	(2)	NC	Jena	28 May 83
Lynn	Bjorklund	USA 57	9:08.6	(3)	vSU	Kiev	5 Jul 75
Elana	Van Zyl	RSA 66	9:09.32	(2)		Stellenbosch	22 Feb 83
Annika	Lewin	SWE 66	9:10.78i	(2)		Solna	19 Feb 84
Tanya	Peckham	RSA 66	9:10.8	(1)	NC	Durban	14 Apr 84
Julie	Holland	UK 66	9:10.9	(4)		Stretford	7 Apr 84
Fernanda	Ribeiro	POR 69	9:11.62	(2)		Lisboa	7 Jul 84
Justina	Chepchirchir	KEN 68	9:11.74	(1)		Tokyo	9 May 81

100 HURDLES

Candy	Young	USA 62	12.95	1.5	(2)	AAU	Walnut	16 Jun 79
	Young		13.13	1.8	(1)S2	AAU	Walnut	15 Jun 79
Heike	Terpe	GDR 64	13.17	1.1	(1)H3	NC-J	Erfurt	18 Jul 82
	Young		13.20	2.0	(1)H2	AAU	Walnut	15 Jun 79
Kathrin	Bohme	GDR 63	13.20	0.8	(1)	EC-J	Utrecht	21 Aug 81
	Terpe		13.20	1.2	(1)	NC-J	Erfurt	18 Jul 82
	Bohme		13.21		(1)	NC-J	Halle	5 Jul 81
Susanne	Losch	GDR 66	13.22	0.0	(1)	EC-J	Schwechat	26 Aug 83
Grisel	Machado	CUB 60	A13.24		(1)H1	CAC	Medellin	17 Jul 78
Lena	Spoof	FIN 61	13.24	-0.7	(1)	EC-J	Bydgoszcz	17 Aug 79
	Losch		13.24	0.9	(1)S1	EC-J	Schwechat	26 Aug 83
Regina	Beyer	GDR 59	13.25		(1)	NC-J	Erfurt	10 Jul 77
Gloria	Kovarik	GDR 64	13.26	-1.1	(2)H2	NC	Jena	8 Aug 81
Jeanette	Kreisch	GDR 65	13.26	0.0	(2)	EC-J	Schwechat	26 Aug 83
Sally	Gunnell	UK 66	13.30	1.9	(2)	WAAA	London	16 Jun 84
Kerstin	Claus	GDR 59	13.32	0.2	(1)	EC-J	Donyetsk	20 Aug 77
Benita	Fitzgerald	USA 61	A13.24	0.0	(4)H3	WUG	Mexico, D.F.	9 Sep 79
Heike	Tillack	GDR 68	13.39		(1)	DRUZHBA	Plovdiv	4 Aug 84
Edith	Oker	FRG 61	13.41	0.0	(2)	NC	Koln	13 Aug 78
Sylvia	Bednarska	POL 66	13.42	0.5	(1)	NC-J	Sopot	29 Jul 84
Veronique	Truwant	FRA 65	13.46	1.1	(1)	NC-J	Fontainbleau	10 Jul 83
Nathalie	Byer	UK 65	13.46	0.0	(3)	EC-J	Schwechat	26 Aug 83
Patricia	Davis	USA 65	13.48	-1.9	(1)	vCAN-J	New Britain	30 Jul 83
Bozena	Nowakowska	POL 55	13.49	1.6	(1)H2	EC-J	Duisburg	24 Aug 73
Carola	Stock	GDR 59	13.49		(3)	NC-J	Erfurt	10 Jul 77
Sybille	Thiele	GDR 65	13.49	1.3	(H)	EC-J	Schwechat	27 Aug 83

Marks made with assisting wind

Barbel	Eckert	GDR 55	13.14	2.6	(1)	EC-J	Duisburg	25 Aug 73
Rhonda	Brady	USA 59	13.25	2.3	(1)	FOT	Eugene	27 Jun 76
Barbel	Muller	GDR 56	13.29		(P)	EC-J	Duisburg	25 Aug 73
Chantal	Rega	FRA 55	13.38	2.6	(2)	EC-J	Duisburg	25 Aug 73
Maria	Usifo	NIG 64	13.39	4.5	(8)	CG	Brisbane	8 Oct 82
Jana	Petrikova	CS 67	13.40	3.5	(1)		Miskolc	7 Jul 84
Gudrun	Berend	GDR 55	13.43	2.6	(3)	EC-J	Duisburg	25 Aug 73

Junior All-time Lists Women

400 METRES HURDLES

Name	Surname	Nat/Yr	Time		Pos	Meet	Venue	Date
Leslie	Maxie	USA 67	55.20		(2)	NC	San Jose	9 Jun 84
Radostina	Dimitrova	BUL 66	55.53		(3)	OD	Potsdam	21 Jul 84
	Dimitrova		55.61		(3)	NAR	Sofia	20 May 84
	Dimitrova		55.63		(5)	FRI	Praha	17 Aug 84
	Maxie		55.66		(5)	OT	Los Angeles	21 Jun 84
	Maxie		55.92		(2)S2	OT	Los Angeles	19 Jun 84
	Dimitrova		56.01		(1)	EC-J	Schwechat	28 Aug 83
	Maxie		56.08		(1)S1	NC	San Jose	8 Jun 84
	Maxie		56.12		(3)		Walnut	25 Jul 84
Sylvia	Kirchner	GDR 63	56.41		(1)	EC-J	Utrecht	23 Aug 81
Ann-Louise	Skoglund	SWE 62	56.68		(1)	vFIN	Helsinki	31 Aug 80
Anita	Lauvensteine	SU 63	56.93		(2)	EC-J	Utrecht	23 Aug 81
Frauke	Jurgens	GDR 66	57.40		(1)		Leipzig	13 Jun 84
Margarita	Ponomaryova	SU 63	57.45		(3)	EC-J	Utrecht	23 Aug 81
Sigrun	Ludwigs	GDR 65	57.56		(4)	EC-J	Utrecht	23 Aug 81
Kritsina	Jauch	GDR 65	57.56		(2)	EC-J	Schwechat	28 Aug 83
Andrea	Kiefer	GDR 64	57.60		(4)	NC	Dresden	1 Jul 82
Gayle	Kellon	USA 65	57.60		(5)	PO	Los Angeles	26 Jun 83
Sylvia	Nagel	FRG 63	57.68		(5)	EC-J	Utrecht	23 Aug 81
Sally	Hamilton	AUS 61	57.86		(1)	NC-J	Perth	23 Mar 79
Marina	Mironova	SU 66	57.93		(2)	DRUZHBA	Leningrad	12 Aug 83
Montserrat	Pujol	SPA 61	57.94		(1)	EP/SF	Sittard	17 Jun 78
Simone	Bungener	FRG 62	57.97		(2)	vRUM,UK	Stuttgart	5 Jun 80
Michelle	Taylor	USA 67	58.06		(1)S2	NC-Y	Los Angeles	23 Jun 84
Christine	Wachtel	GDR 65	58.08		(1)	NC-Y	Erfurt	17 Jul 82
Diana	Ivanova	BUL 66	58.10		(5)		Sofia	4 Jul 84
Beate	Holzapfel	FRG 66	58.10		(1)	NC-Y	Fulda	21 Jul 84

Hand timing

| Debbie | Esser | USA 57 | 57.3 | | (1) | AAU | White Plains | 28 Jun 75 |
| Inna | Yevseyeva | SU 64 | 57.9 | | ( )H | | Kiev | 25 Jun 82 |

HIGH JUMP

Name	Surname	Nat/Yr	Height		Pos	Meet	Venue	Date
Charmaine	Gale	RSA 64	A1.96		(1)		Bloemfontein	4 Apr 81
Olga	Turchak	SU 67	1.96		(1)	NC	Donyetsk	7 Sep 84
Silvia	Costa	CUB 64	1.95		(1)		Rhede	1 Sep 82
	Costa		1.94		(1)		Santiago de Cuba	6 Mar 82
Yelena	Topchina	SU 66	1.94		(1)	EC-J	Schwechat	28 Aug 83
Marina	Serkova	SU 61	1.93i		(1)	NC	Minsk	12 Feb 79
Kerstin	Dedner	GDR 61	1.93		(1)	NC-J	Erfurt	24 Jun 79
	Gale		1.93		(1)		Durban	25 Apr 81
Andrea	Breder	FRG 64	1.93		(1)	NC-J	Koblenz	30 Aug 81
	Costa		1.93		(1)		Caorle	3 Jul 82
Nina	Baranova	SU 64	1.93		(1)		Togliatti	30 Aug 82
	Turchak		1.93		(1)	DRUZHBA	Plovdiv	4 Aug 84
	Turchak		1.93		(1)		Tashkent	22 Sep 84
Ulrike	Meyfarth	FRG 56	1.92		(1)	OG	Munchen	4 Sep 72
Tamara	Malesev	YUG 67	1.92i		(5)	EC	Goteborg	4 Mar 84
Brigitte	Holzapfel	FRG 58	1.91		(1)		Dusseldorf	8 Jun 76
Manuela	Schroder	GDR 63	1.91		(3)	NC	Jena	8 Aug 81
Lisa	Bernhagen	USA 66	1.905i		(1)		Pocatello	18 Feb 84
Urszula	Kielan	POL 60	1.90i		(1)		Trinec	3 Mar 77
Kristine	Nitzsche	GDR 59	1.90		(1)	NC-J	Erfurt	10 Jul 77
Andrea	Reichstein	GDR 59	1.90		(1)		Halle	27 Aug 77
Stefka	Kostadinova	BUL 65	1.90		(1)		Budapest	24 Jul 82
Desiree	Du Plessis	RSA 65	1.90		(1)	NC	Bloemfontein	16 Apr 83
Megumi	Satoh	JAP 66	1.90		(1)		Niigata	10 Jul 83
Sybille	Thiele	GDR 65	1.90		(H)	EC-J	Schwechat	27 Aug 83
Babara	Fiammengo	ITA 67	1.90		(1)		Riccione	17 Sep 83

435

Junior All-time Lists Women

LONG JUMP

Heike	Daute	GDR 64	6.98	1.1	(1)		Potsdam	18 Aug 82
	Daute		6.91	1.0	(1)	NC	Jena	9 Aug 81
Natalya	Shevchenko	SU 66	6.88	0.6	(2)		Sochi	26 May 84
Larisa	Baluta	SU 65	6.85		(2)		Krasnodar	6 Aug 83
	Shevchenko		6.82		(1)		Novokuzneck	17 Jul 83
	Daute		6.79	0.3	(2)		Potsdam	28 Aug 82
	Shevchenko		6.78	1.2	(2)		Sochi	19 May 84
Marianne	Voelzke	GDR 56	6.77		(2)		Berlin	24 Aug 74
	Daute		6.77	0.9	(q)	EC	Athinai	6 Sep 82
	Shevchenko		6.74	0.0	(4)	ZNAM	Sochi	9 Jun 84
Helga	Radtke	GDR 62	6.71	2.0	(3)	OD	Berlin	28 May 80
Susan	Hearnshaw	UK 61	6.68	1.7	(1)	vRSFSR	London	22 Sep 79
Sybille	Thiele	GDR 65	6.65	1.1	(H)	EC-J	Schwechat	28 Aug 83
Jana	Sobotka	GDR 65	6.65	1.5	(H)	EC-J	Schwechat	28 Aug 83
Svetlana	Krotova	SU 65	6.62		(2)		Angarsk	13 Jul 83
Yelena	Lugovaya	SU 64	6.61		(1)		Moskva	28 May 81
Irena	Kirszenstein	POL 46	6.60	-1.8	(2)	OG	Tokyo	14 Oct 64
Carol	Lewis	USA 63	6.60	0.3	(2)	LB	Philadelphia	17 Jul 80
Eloina	Echevarria	CUB 61	6.59		(1)		Habana	4 Feb 79
Kathy	McMillan	USA 57	6.58		(1)		Praha	8 Jul 75
Sabine	Everts	FRG 61	6.57		(1)	NC-Y	Munchen	29 Jul 79
Nicole	Boegman	AUS 67	6.55	1.9	(1)		Sydney	15 Oct 83
Eva	Kuchtova	CS 65	6.54i		(1)		Praha	19 Feb 83
Anisoara	Cusmir	RUM 62	6.53		(-)vHUN	,POL-J	Budapest	5 Sep 80
Monika	Beyer	GDR 65	6.53	-1.1	(2)	EC-J	Schwechat	25 Aug 83
Georgina	Oladapo	UK 67	6.52	0.8	(2)	WAAA	London	16 Jun 84

Marks made with assisting wind

Heike	Daute	GDR 64	7.02	4.0	(1)	EC-J	Utrecht	20 Aug 81
Beverley	Kinch	UK 64	6.78	3.3	(3)	CG	Brisbane	8 Oct 82
Nicole	Boegman	AUS 67	6.71	4.0	(1)		Sydney	15 Sep 83
Sabine	Everts	FRG 61	6.69		(P)		Wilhelmshaven	14 Jul 79
Sylvia	Fuchs	GDR 63	6.65	4.8	(1)		Dresden	13 Jun 81
Dorothea	Brown	USA 64	6.59		(1)		Charleston	22 May 82
Anisoara	Cusmir	RUM 62	6.55	2.1	(1)vHUN	,POL-J	Budapest	5 Sep 80

SHOT PUTT

Grit	Haupt	GDR 66	19.57		(1)		Gera	7 Jul 84
	Haupt		19.44		(1)	NC-J	Potsdam	1 Jul 84
Ilona	Schoknecht	GDR 56	19.23		(3)		Berlin	15 Sep 74
Simone	Michel	GDR 60	19.22		(3)		Potsdam	19 Aug 78
	Michel		19.06		(1)		Potsdam	25 Aug 78
	Michel		19.05		(1)	NC	Leipzig	23 Jul 78
Heidi	Krieger	GDR 65	19.03i		(2)		Senftenburg	29 Dec 83
	Krieger		19.01		(9)	OD	Berlin	8 Jun 83
	Michel		19.00		(1)		Halle	16 Aug 78
	Krieger		18.89		(2)		Berlin	17 Aug 83
Liane	Schmuhl	GDR 61	18.63		(2)		Leipzig	4 Aug 79
Cordula	Schulze	GDR 59	18.36		(2)		Potsdam	10 Aug 77
Silvia	Madetzky	GDR 62	18.28		(1)		Karl-Marx-Stadt	11 Jun 80
Carmen	Niesche	GDR 64	18.24		(1)	NC-J	Cottbus	25 Jul 82
Galina	Kurochkina	SU 65	18.19		(1)	NC-J	Simferopol	5 Jun 83
Brigitte	Griessing	GDR 56	18.18		(3)	NC	Leipzig	5 Jul 74
Yang	Yan Qin	CHN 66	18.08		(1)		Eugene	18 Jul 84
Svetla	Mitkova	BUL 64	18.03		(1)	vRUM,HUN,POL3N-J	Pitesti	22 Aug 82
Simone	Rudrich	GDR 61	17.99		(7)		Karl-Marx-Stadt	26 May 79
Tatyana	Prishchep	SU 66	17.83		(1)		Bryansk	3 Jul 83
Karin	Kracik	GDR 58	17.79		(2)		Potsdam	17 Aug 75
Irina	Fedchenko	SU 66	17.75		(1)		Kiev	28 Aug 84

Junior All-time Lists Women

Mechtild	Schonleber	FRG 63	17.65	(1)		Koln	27 Sep 81
Iris	Plotzitzka	FRG 66	17.65i	(2)		Cannes	29 Dec 84
Birgit	Schimmel	GDR 60	17.52	(1)		Neubrandenburg	4 Jun 78
Livia	Simon	RUM 66	17.35i	(4)		Bucuresti	19 Feb 83

DISCUS THROW

Grit	Haupt	GDR 66	65.96	(3)		Leipzig	13 Jul 84
Irina	Meszynski	GDR 62	64.86	(1)		Potsdam	15 Jun 80
	Meszynski		64.32	(1)		Berlin	10 Feb 80
	Meszynski		64.02	(1)		Potsdam	11 Jun 80
	Meszynski		63.42	(4)	PTS	Bratislava	7 Jun 80
Evelyn	Schlaak	GDR 56	63.26	(2)		Potsdam	28 Aug 74
	Haupt		63.06	(6)	NC	Erfurt	3 Jun 84
	Haupt		62.58	(1)	vSU-J	Tallinn	24 Jun 84
Silvia	Madetsky	GDR 62	62.54	(1)	NC-Y	Jena	16 Jul 80
	Meszynski		62.42	(1)	NC-J	Erfurt	23 Jun 79
Heidi	Krieger	GDR 65	61.98	(1)		Berlin	19 May 83
Larisa	Platonova	SU 66	61.96	(2)	vUK	Birmingham	5 Jun 83
Svetla	Mitkova	BUL 62	60.58	(1)	vRUM,HUN,POL3N-P	Pitesti	21 Aug 82
Daniela	Costian	RUM 65	60.50	(1)		Bucuresti	7 Aug 83
Galina	Kvacheva	SU 65	60.04	(1)		Chelyabinsk	16 Jul 83
Sieglinde	Bludau	GDR 58	59.88	(1)		Erfurt	12 Sep 76
Jana	Harter	GDR 66	59.06	(2)		Cottbus	26 May 84
Diana	Sachse	GDR 63	59.00	(1)	vSU-J	Cottbus	25 Jun 81
Renata	Katewicz	POL 65	58.52	(1)		Zielona Gora	20 Jul 83
Tsvetana	Khristova	BUL 62	58.44	(4)		Sofia	13 Jul 80
Simone	Thamm	GDR 65	57.98	(6)		Berlin	31 Jul 83
Martina	Opitz	GDR 60	57.82	(6)	NC	Leipzig	2 Jul 78
Ilke	Wyludda	GDR 69	57.74	(1)		Cottbus	26 Jul 84
Brigite	Sander	GDR 56	57.52	(1)		Berlin	26 Jun 74
Catherine	Beauvais	FRA 65	57.50	(1)		Thonon-Les-Bains	18 Aug 83
Irina	Efrosina	SU 65	57.40	(3)	EC-J	Schwechat	27 Aug 83

JAVELIN

Antoaneta	Todorova	BUL 63	71.88	(1)	EP	Zagreb	15 Aug 81
	Todorova		70.08	(1)	WP	Roma	6 Sep 81
	Todorova		69.66	(1)		Sofia	7 Jun 81
	Todorova		67.52	(1)	vFRA	St Etienne	20 Jun 81
	Todorova		67.04	(1)	NC	Sofia	30 Aug 81
	Todorova		66.72	(1)	vFRG	Bielefeld	13 Jun 81
	Todorova		66.70	(1)	NC-J	Sofia	9 Aug 81
	Todorova		66.40	(1)		Sofia	25 May 80
	Todorova		65.10	(1)	BALK-J	Pleven	26 Jul 81
Trine	Solberg	NOR 66	65.02	(1)	PTS	Bratislava	26 May 84
Antje	Kempe	GDR 63	64.62	(1)		Potsdam	29 Aug 81
Lyudmila	Pasternakevich	SU 59	63.86	(1)		Lvov	19 Jul 76
Jacqueline	Todten	GDR 54	62.54	(2)	OG	Munchen	1 Sep 72
Jana	Kopping	GDR 66	62.54	(4)	NC	Karl-Marx-Stadt	18 Jun 83
Natalya	Chernienko	SU 65	62.04	(1)	EC-J	Schwechat	27 Aug 83
Heidi	Repser	FRG 60	61.96	(1)	EC-J	Donyetsk	20 Aug 77
Petra	Rivers	AUS 52	61.76	(1)		Melbourne	17 Oct 70
Karin	Bergdahl	SWE 64	61.30	(2)	vFIN	Stockholm	30 Aug 81
Petra	Felke	GDR 59	61.24	(1)		Halle	27 Aug 77
Leolita	Blodniece	SU 59	61.14	(1)		Praha	25 Sep 75
Barbara	Friedrich	USA 49	60.56	(1)		Long Beach	4 Jun 67
Mihaela	Penes	RUM 47	60.54	(1)	OG	Tokyo	16 Oct 64
Natalya	Sipova	SU 61	60.32	(1)	vUSA-J	Boston	5 Jul 79
Yelena	Medvedyeva	SU 65	60.00	(1)		Kiev	30 Jul 83
Cathy	Sulinski	USA 58	59.76	(1)		Saratoga	6 Jun 76

Junior All-time Lists Women

Tatyana	Shikolenko		59.40	( )		Moskva	6 Aug 84
Yelena	Kucherenko	SU 66	59.36	(1)		Tashkent	22 Sep 84
Katrin	Strobel	GDR 61	59.28	(1)		Halle	30 Jun 79

HEPTATHLON

| Sybille | Thiele | GDR 65 | 6421 | (1) | EC-J | Schwechat | 28 Aug 83 |
13.49 1.90 14.63 24.07 6.65 36.22 2:18.36
| | Thiele | | 6301 | (3) | NC | Neubrandenburg | 22 May 83 |
13.68 1.89 14.10 24.42 6.46 34.20 2:14.47
| Sabine | Braun | FRG 65 | 6273 | (2) | EC-J | Schwechat | 28 Aug 83 |
13.55 1.81 12.35 24.06 6.24 44.96 2:16.31
| Valentina | Savchenko | SU 68 | 6226 | (1) | DRUZHBA | Plovdiv | 5 Aug 84 |
13.88 1.59 15.10 24.15 6.07 48.16 2:12.42
| Jana | Sobotka | GDR 65 | 6222 | (3) | EC-J | Schwechat | 28 Aug 83 |
14.36 1.69 12.74 23.86 6.65 44.36 2:12.98
| | Thiele | | 6156 | (9) | EP | Sofia | 11 Sep 83 |
14.11 1.81 14.31 24.67 6.64 36.32 2:20.52
| | Braun | | 6154 | (1) | | Lage | 4 Sep 83 |
13.91 1.76 12.42 24.70 6.18 48.74 2:17.21
| | Savchenko | | 6175H | (1) | | Tashkent | 20 Sep 84 |
13.8 1.65 14.55 24.4 6.11 46.72 2:16.7
| | Braun | | 6088 | (1) | NC-J | Munchen | 17 Jul 83 |
13.99 1.76 12.42 24.70 6.01 43.66 2:17.50
| | Thiele | | 6063 | (7) | vSU | Halle | 20 Jun 82 |
13.83 1.83 12.98 25.41 6.59w 34.58 2:17.96
| Anke | Troger | GDR 63 | 6032 | (1) | EC-J | Utrecht | 23 Aug 81 |
14.40w 1.81 13.31 24.70 5.66 44.62 2:16.28
| Ilona | Dietze | GDR 63 | 5991 | (2) | EC-J | Utrecht | 23 Aug 81 |
14.75 1.78 13.27 24.88w 6.14w 38.86 2:14.30
| Heike | Tischler | GDR 64 | 5978 | (9) | vSU | Halle | 20 Jun 82 |
14.92 1.74 12.48 25.55 6.30w 45.02 2:12.80
| Tatyana | Georgieva | BUL 65 | 5961 | (1) | | Sofia | 10 Jul 83 |
13.85 1.67 11.98 24.23 6.10 37.26 2:12.80
| Helga | Nüsko | FRG 65 | 5937 | (4) | EC-J | Schwechat | 28 Aug 83 |
14.17 1.75 13.54 25.41 6.19 41.92 2:23.72
| Yelena | Davidova | SU 67 | 5921 | (2) | DRUZHBA | Plovdiv | 5 Aug 84 |
14.48 1.83 11.55 25.14 6.25 38.42 2:16.92
| Vera | Polyakova | SU 66 | 5920 | (1) | NC-Y | Simferopol | 27 May 84 |
14.35 1.75 12.65 24.35 5.93 35.62 2:14.33
| Olga | Tokareva | SU 66 | 5902 | (2) | NC-J | Riga | 15 Jul 84 |
14.40 1.79 12.04 24.90 6.05 38.30 2:16.75
| Heike | Daute | GDR 64 | 5891 | (5) | NC | Halle | 24 May 81 |
14.81 1.80 11.97 25.41 6.30 33.14 2:17.07
| Tatyana | Stoicheva | BUL 63 | 5887 | (3) | NC | Sofia | 2 Aug 81 |
14.02 1.55 13.02 25.63 6.39 43.92 2:15.12
| Petra | Mihalache | RUM 65 | 5847 | (1) | BALK-J | Bucuresti | 31 Jul 83 |
14.37 1.74 13.37 25.84 6.05 36.02 2:14.93
| Beate | Holzapfel | FRG 66 | 5846 | (1) | NC-Y | Ulm | 26 Aug 84 |
14.63 1.88 11.33 25.07/ 5.90 39.40 2:19.64
| Bettina | Beinhauer | FRG 65 | 5832 | (1) | NC-Y | Hannover | 29 Aug 82 |
14.22 1.60 13.75 24.98 5.62 48.62 2:21.4
| Olga | Abramova | SU 64 | 5778 | (8) | | Tashkent | 27 Sep 82 |
15.38 1.70 12.94 25.41 6.19 41.46 2:18.16
| Meike | Neumann | GDR 65 | 5776 | (1) | NC-J | Jena | 3 Jul 83 |
14.57 1.69 11.78 25.90 5.73 47.32 2:14.84
| Marjon | Wignsma | HOL 65 | 5773 | (6) | EC-J | Schwechat | 28 Aug 83 |
13.93 1.84 10.89 25.12 5.87 30.86 2:14.71

1984 WORLD JUNIOR LISTS

100 METRES

Wendy	Vereen	USA 66	11.32	0.0	(1)R2		Walnut	25 Jul
Mari-Lise	Furstenberg	RSA 66	A11.42		(1)	NC-J	Pretoria	31 Mar
Simone	Jacobs	UK 66	11.45	1.0	(3)		Gateshead	6 Jul
Gail	Devers	USA 66	11.51	0.1	(1)		Los Angeles	2 Jun
Pauline	Davis	BAH 66	11.51	−0.2	(1)H2	OG	Los Angeles	4 Aug
Valentina	Bozina	SU 66	11.52	−2.0	(1)	NC-J	Riga	13 Jul
Gillian	Forde	TRI 67	11.55		(2)		Port of Spain	20 May
Fabienne	Ficher	FRA 66	11.56	2.0	(1)		Colombes	10 Jul
Yelena	Fedorova	SU 66	11.59	−2.0	(3)	NC-J	Riga	13 Jul
Pam	Wualls	USA 66	11.63	0.1	(2)		Los Angeles	2 Jun
Tatyana	Papilina	SU 67	11.63	0.2	(1)		Debrecen	18 Aug
Marina	Krivoshina	SU 67	11.66		(1)H	NC-Y	Simferopol	26 May
France	Gareau	CAN 67	11.66	1.4	(5)H3	OG	Los Angeles	4 Aug
Katurah	Anderson	CAN 68	11.66	0.1	(1)H1	PAG-J	Nassau	25 Aug
Karen	Kruger	RSA 67	A11.67		(1)		Pretoria	1 Mar
Ethlyn	Tate	JAM 66	11.67	0.9	(1)		Houston	26 May
Doreen	Antemann	GDR 66	11.67		(1)	NC-J	Potsdam	30 Jun
Georgina	Oladapo	UK 67	11.70	1.9	(5)S1	NC	Cwmbran	27 May
Christine	Wahl	FRG 67	11.70	1.7	(1)S2	NC-Y	Fulda	20 Jul
Maria	Fernstrom	SWE 67	11.71	0.3	(1)	NC	Vaxjo	24 Aug
Dawn	Sowell	USA 66	11.71		(1)		Charlottesville	26 May

Marks made with assisting wind

Andrea	Bush	USA 66	A11.25	2.8	(1)		Provo	14 Jul
Simone	Jacobs	UK 66	11.26	3.8	(3)	NC	Cwmbran	27 May
Gail	Devers	USA 66	11.34	2.2	(1)H2		Norwalk	22 May
France	Gareau	CAN 67	11.38	6.9	(1)		Sacramento	21 Jul
Paula	Ready	USA 66	11.46	4.8	(1)		Norwalk	19 May
Chewukaii	Knighten	USA 67	11.50	2,4	(2)H2		Norwalk	25 May
Lisa	Ford	USA 66	11.58		(1)		Denton	20 Apr
Katurah	Anderson	CAN 68	11.58	6.0	(4)	NC	Winnipeg	30 Jun
Cathy	Roberts	USA 66	11.60	4.8	(2)		Norwalk	19 May
Denise	Liles	USA 68	11.62	2.5	(2)	PAG-J	Nassau	25 Aug
Maria	Fernstrom	SWE 67	11.63	2.4	(2)	vFIN	Helsinki	1 Sep
Sara	Parros	USA 66	11.63	4.8	(3)		Norwalk	19 May
Maicel	Malone	USA 69	11.64		(1)		Indianapolis	2 Jun

Hand timing

Pauline	Davis	BAH 66	11.1		(1)		Nassau	24 Apr
Andrea	Bush	USA 66	A11.2	2.0	(1)		Aurora	30 Jun
Yelena	Fedorova	SU 66	11.2		(1)		Gomel	11 Aug
Carla	McLaughlin	USA 67	11.3		(1)		Jacksonville	19 Aug
Dawn	Sowell	USA 66	11.4		(1)		Charlottesville	14 Apr
Gillian	Forde	TRI 67	11.4		(1)		Paolo Seco	15 Apr
Tatyana	Ledovskaya	SU 66	11.4		( )		Vilnius	1 Jul

200 METRES

Pauline	Davis	BAH 66	22.97	1.1	(4)Q1	OG	Los Angeles	8 Aug
Mari-Lise	Furstenburg	RSA 66	A23.21		(2)		Pretoria	30 Mar
Wendy	Vereen	USA 66	23.24	1.2	(1)H5	TAC	San Jose	7 Jun
Simone	Jacobs	UK 66	23.33	0.9	(3)	OT	Gateshead	10 Jun
Malinka	Girova	BUL 66	23.34		(1)		Debrecen	19 Aug
Valentina	Bozina	SU 66	23.38	0.0	(4)	NC	Donyetsk	9 Sep
Edith	Otterman	RSA 66	A23.42		(4)		Pretoria	30 Mar
Dawn	Sowell	USA 66	23.50		(1)		Charlottesville	26 May
Paulette	Blalock	USA 67	23.54	−2.5	(1)		Norwalk	19 May
Cathy	Roberts	USA 66	23.59	−2.5	(2)		Norwalk	19 May

439

Junior 1984 Lists – Women

Annett	Hesselbarth	GDR 66	23.60		(1)		NC-J	Potsdam	1 Jul
Leslie	Maxie	USA 67	23.64		(1)			Los Gatos	7 Jul
Tatyana	Palina	SU 67	23.66		(1)R2			Debrecen	19 Aug
Dawn	Flockhart	UK 67	23.71	0.9	(7)		OT	Gateshead	10 Jun
Christiane	Wahl	FRG 67	23.73	0.0	(1)		NC-Y	Fulda	22 Jul
Pam	Qualls	USA 66	23.77	−0.1	(2)			Los Angeles	2 Jun
Fabienne	Ficher	FRA 66	23.79	1.8	(1)		NC-J	Fontainbleau	15 Jul
Gillian	Forde	TRI 67	23.80		(1)S			San Juan	Jun
Marina	Krivoshina	SU 67	23.80		(2)R2			Debrecen	19 Aug
Rosey	Edeh	CAN 66	23.85	1.0	(3)			Montreal	14 Jul
Yelena	Fedorova	SU 66	23.85		(2)			Frunze	8 Sep

Marks made with assisting wind

Wendy	Vereen	USA 66	22.75	2.5	(1)			Los Angeles	4 Apr
Simone	Jacobs	UK 66	23.01	2.1	(2)		NC	Cwmbran	28 May
Cathy	Roberts	USA 66	23.52	3.0	(1)			Walnut	28 Apr
France	Gareau	CAN 67	23.54	4.2	(3)		NC	Winnipeg	1 Jul
Tami	Stiles	USA 68	23.60	3.0	(2)			Walnut	28 Apr
Natalie	Dillon	AUS 66	23.65	3.0	(3)			Walnut	28 Apr
Gillian	Forde	TRI 67	23.73		(1)			San Juan	Jun
Doreen	Antemann	GDR 66	23.74	3.0	(2)		NC-Y	Magdeburg	22 Jul
Annick	Georges	FRA 66	23.75	2.7	(2)Q2		NC	Villeneuve	30 Jun
Veronique	Clachet	FRA 68	23.79	3.8	(1)		NC-C	Fontainbleau	15 Jul

Hand timing

Tatyana	Ledovskaya	SU 66	23.4		(1)			Vilnius	1 Jul
Dawn	Sowell	USA 66	23.4		(1)			Charlottesville	14 Apr
Carla	McLaughlin	USA 67	23.4		(1)			Jacksonville	19 Aug
Irina	Kot	SU 67	23.6		( )			Kiev	5 Sep
Marina	Krivoshina	SU 67	23.6	0.9	(1)			Tashkent	21 Sep
Tatyana	Paplina	SU 67	23.6	0.9	(2)			Tashkent	21 Sep

Marks made with assisting wind

Mari-Lise	Furstenberg	RSA 66	A23.2		(1)			Pretoria	9 Mar
Lisa	Ford	USA 66	23.5		(2)			Denton	20 Apr
Annick	Georges	FRA 66	23.6	5.2	(1)			Marignane	27 May

400 METRES

Chewuakii	Knighten	USA 67	52.31		(3)			Los Angeles	13 May
Edith	Otterman	RSA 66	A52.55		(1)			Germiston	8 Mar
Andrea	Thomas	JAM 68	52.57		(1)		PAG-J	Nassau	24 Aug
Annett	Hesselbarth	GDR 66	52.62		(1)		NC-J	Potsdam	30 Jun
Tanya	McIntosh	USA 66	52.64		(1)		TAC-J	Los Angeles	24 Jun
Christine	Nathler	GDR 66	52.65		(2)		NC-J	Potsdam	30 Jun
Malinka	Girova	BUL 66	52.78		(1)		BALK-J	Maribor	28 Jul
Nicole	Leistenschneider	FRG 67	52.89		(4)			Munchen	20 Jul
Daniela	Gamalie	RUM 67	52.91		(4)			Bucuresti	16 Sep
Christiane	Wahl	FRG 67	52.92		(1)			Waiblingen	3 Jun
Leslie	Maxie	USA 67	53.07		(M)			Los Gatos	7 Jul
Loreen	Hall	UK 67	53.08		(1)			Haugesund	29 Jul
Paulette	Blalock	USA 67	53.20		(1)			Norwalk	19 May
Janice	Carter	JAM 66	53.24		(4)		PAG-J	Nassau	24 Aug
Todorica	Chidu	RUM 67	53.45		(2)		DRUZHBA	Plovdiv	4 Aug
Svetlana	Romanovskaya	SU 66	53.54		(1)		vGDR-J	Tallinn	23 Jun
Schiva	Petkova	BUL 67	53.56		(3)		DRUZHBA	Plovdiv	4 Aug
Heike	Huneke	FRG 66	53.60		(2)		NC-J	Munchengladbach	18 Aug
Andrea	Erdelyi	HUN 67	53.60		(1)			Budapest	19 Jul
Rosey	Edeh	CAN 66	53.65		(1)			Edmonton	21 Jul

Hand timing

Edith	Otterman	RSA 66	A52.2		(1)			Pretoria	19 Mar

Junior 1984 Lists – Women

800 METRES

Valentina	Furletova	SU 66	2:00.04	( )H	ZNAM	Sochi	9 Jun
Zola	Budd	RSA 66	2:00.9	(1)		Kroonstad	16 Mar
Lenuta	Rata	RUM 66	2:01.98	(2)H2	NC	Bucuresti	10 Jul
Monika	Bens	FRG 66	2:02.45	(2)		Furth	9 Jun
Kornelia	Matesic	YUG 66	2:02.73	(4)	vUK	Karlovac	16 Sep
Diane	Edwards	UK 66	2:02.75	(5)	vYUG	Karlovac	16 Sep
Maria	Kaba	RUM 67	2:03.24	(1)	BALK-J	Maribor	29 Jul
Heike	Huneke	FRG 66	2:03.59	(1)R2		Koblenz	29 Aug
Carmen	Bohme	GDR 66	2:03.70	(4)	OD	Berlin	20 Jul
Tatyana	Varfolomeyeva	SU 66	2:03.9	( )		Riga	5 Jul
Lyudmila	Rogatsova	SU 66	2:03.7	( )		Yekabpils	1 Jul
Ermyntrude	Vermeulen	RSA 68	A2:03.8	(1)		Bloemfontein	29 Oct
Iva	Jurkova	CS 66	2:03.87	(10)	BGP	Budapest	20 Aug
Tatyana	Varfolomeyeva	SU 66	2:03.9	( )		Riga	5 Jul
Florence	Giolitti	FRA 66	2:03.98	(1)	NC	Villeneuve	1 Jul
Gabriella	Sedlakova	CS 68	2:04.01	(1)	DRUZHBA	Plovdiv	5 Aug
Maria	Pantis	RUM 67	2:04.14	(2)H1	NC	Bucuresti	9 Jul
Jeanette	Henkel	GDR 66	2:04.37	(1)	NC-Y	Magdeburg	22 Jul
Tatyana	Vochminzeva	SU 67	2:04.45	(3)	DRUZHBA	Plovdiv	5 Aug
Justina	Chepcherchir	KEN 68	2:04.52	(1)	AFR	Rabat	14 Jul
Svetlana	Masterkova	SU 68	2:04.59	(1)		Debrecen	19 Aug

1500 METRES

Zola	Budd	RSA 66	4:01.81	(1)		Port Elizabeth	21 Mar
Kleopatra	Palaceanu	RUM 68	4:09.37	(5)	NC	Bucuresti	12 Jul
Donna	Gould	AUS 66	4:09.54	(4)		Burnaby	16 Jul
Lenuta	Rata	RUM 66	4:11.45	(6)	NC	Bucuresti	12 Jul
Iva	Jurkova	CS 66	4:11.99	(2)		Praha	28 Aug
Elana	Van Zyl	RSA 66	4:14.5	(1)		Stellenbosch	22 Feb
Tatyana	Gurinova	SU 66	4:14.8	( )		Riga	5 Jul
Bridget	Smyth	UK 67	4:15.20	(1)	vNOR-J	Haugesund	29 Jul
Lyudmila	Rogatsova	SU 66	4:15.8	( )		Yekabpils	30 Jun
Tatyana	Vochminceva	SU 67	4:15.87	(1)	DRUZHBA	Plovdiv	4 Aug
Tanya	Peckham	RSA 66	4:16.20	(1)		Stellenbosch	26 Apr
Julie	Holland	UK 66	4:16.4	(2)		Stretford	15 May
Mariana	Sulescu	RUM 67	4:16.73	( )			
Annika	Lewin	SWE 66	4:16.84	(3)		Galve	9 Jul
Elise	Lyon	UK 66	4:16.85	(6)	WAAA	London	16 Jun
Ana	Padurean	RUM 69	4:17.12	( )			
Andriana	Dumitru	RUM 68	4:17.57	(3)H1	NC	Bucuresti	11 Jul
Mia	Marcu	RUM 68	4:17.9	(1)		Bacau	1 Jul
Mary	Chepkemboi	KEN 68	4:18.2	(1)	OT	Kisumu	30 Jun
Justina	Chepcherchir	KEN 68	4:18.45	(1)	AFR-C	Rabat	12 Jul
Jodie	Nykvist	AUS 66	4:18.52	(2)	NC	Melbourne	31 Mar

3000 METRES

Zola	Budd	RSA 66	8:37.5	(1)		Stellenbosch	29 Feb
Donna	Gould	AUS 66	8:44.1	(M)		Eugene	13 Jul
Helen	Kimaiyo	KEN 68	8:57.21	(7)H1	OG	Los Angeles	8 Aug
Kleopatra	Palaceanu	RUM 68	9:06.75	(1)		Bucuresti	10 Jun
Annika	Lewin	SWE 66	9:10.78i	(2)		Solna	19 Feb
	Lewin		9:16.97	(12)	DNG	Stockholm	4 Jul
Tanya	Peckham	RSA 66	9:10.8	(1)	NC	Durban	14 Apr
Julie	Holland	UK 66	9:10.9	(4)		Stretford	7 Apr
Fernanda	Ribeiro	POR 69	9:11.62	(2)	NC	Lisboa	8 Jul

441

Junior 1984 Lists – Women

Carol	Haigh	UK 66	9:12.1i		(1)		Cosford	7 Jan
Elano	Van Zyl	RSA 66	9:12.20		(1)		Port Elizabeth	10 Dec
Catarina	Gheorghiu	RUM 69	9:13.28		( )			
Sharon	Dalton	AUS 67	9:14.5		(2)	NC	Melbourne	13 Dec
Kathrin	Ulrich	GDR 67	9:15.8i		(1)		Senftenburg	12 Feb
	Ulrich		9:17.04		(1)		Miskolc	8 Jul
Marion	Josefsen	NOR 67	9:16.28		(4)		Stavanger	26 Jun
Anneli	Edling	SWE 68	9:16.50		(3)	NC	Vaxjo	24 Aug
Eva	Jurkova	CS 66	9:16.57		(1)	PTS	Bratislava	25 May
Li	Xiu Xia	CHN 67	9:16.71		( )		Nanjing	7 Jun
Mara	Micanovic	YUG 66	9:18.77		(4)	BALK	Athinai	8 Sep
Olga	Ceryvakova	SU 66	9:18.9		( )		Ryazan	11 Aug
Kathrin	Kley	GDR 68	9:20.25		(2)	NC-J	Potsdam	1 Jul

100 METRES HURDLES

Sally	Gunnell	UK 66	13.30	1.9	(2)	WAAA	London	16 Jun
Heike	Tillack	GDR 68	13.39		(1)	DRUZHBA	Plovdiv	4 Aug
Sylvia	Bednarska	POL 66	13.42	0.5	(1)		Sopot	29 Jul
Jana	Petrickova	CS 67	13.50	0.6	(2)		Praha	28 Aug
Lavonna	Martin	USA 66	13.55	−0.1	(1)	PAG-J	Nassau	24 Aug
Julieta	Rousseaux	CUB 66	A13.63		(1)		Mexico, D.F.	16 Jun
Odalys	Adams	CUB 67	A13.63		(2)		Mexico, D.F.	16 Jun
Daniela	Bizbac	RUM 67	13.65	0.6	(1)		Debrecen	19 Aug
Karen	Wilkinson	RSA 66	A13.68		(1)		Pretoria	18 Feb
Berit	Meyer	GDR 67	13.68		(1)	NC-J	Potsdam	1 Jul
Radostina	Dimitrova	BUL 66	13.69		(1)		Plovdiv	17 Jul
Feng	Yinghua	CHN 66	13.70		( )		Shanghai	6 Oct
Svetlana	Gerevits	SU 66	13.72		(1)		Frunze	8 Sep
Naomi	Jyojima	JAP 68	13.72		(1)		Nara	13 Oct
Natalia	Schwandt	FRG 67	13.73		(1)		Kevelaer	11 Jun
Viktoriya	Maruscak	SU 66	13.77		( )		Kiev	5 Jun
Monique	Ewanje-Epee	FRA 67	13.78	1.8	(5)S1	NC	Villeneuve	1 Jul
Gabi	Lippe	FRG 67	13.80		(1)		Schutterwald	2 Jun
Yolanda	Johnson	USA 68	A13.81		(1)		Provo	14 Jul
Annette	Kersten	GDR 68	13.83		(2)	NC-Y	Magdeburg	22 Jul

Marks made with assisting wind

Jana	Petrickova	CS 67	13.40	3.5	(1)		Miskolc	7 Jul
Yolanda	Jon	CAN 67	13.58	3.9	(6)	NC	Winnipeg	30 Jun
Berit	Meyer	GDR 67	13.61	3.5	(2)		Miskolc	7 Jul
Yolanda	Johnson	USA 68	13.73	2.2	(1)S1	TAC-J	Los Angeles	23 Jun

Hand timing

Lilya	Okolo-Kulak	SU 67	13.2		(1)		Minsk	26 Aug
Svetlana	Gerevits	SU 66	13.2		(1)		Vinnitsa	29 Sep
Odalys	Adams	CUB 67	13.3		(1)S		Santiago	2 Mar
Irina	Tyukhay	SU 67	13.3		(2)		Kharkov	7 Jul
Lavonna	Martin	USA 66	13.4		(1)H		Towson	14 Jul
Daniela	Bizbac	RUM 67	13.5		(2)		Bucuresti	30 May
Yolanda	Johnson	USA 68	A13.6	0.2	(1)		Aurora	30 Jun
Yolanda	Jones	CAN 67	13.6		(2)		Miami	20 Aug

400 METRES HURDLES

Leslie	Maxie	USA 67	55.20		(2)	TAC	San Jose	9 Jun
Radostina	Dimitrova	BUL 66	55.53		(3)	OD	Potsdam	21 Jul
Frauke	Jurgens	GDR 66	57.40		(1)		Leipzig	13 Jun
Michelle	Taylor	USA 67	58.06		(1)S2	TAC-J	Los Angeles	23 Jun
Diana	Ivanova	BUL 66	58.10		(5)		Sofia	4 Jul
Beate	Holzapfel	FRG 66	58.10		(1)	NC-Y	Fulda	21 Jul
Sametra	King	USA 67	58.13		(2)S2	TAC-J	Los Angeles	23 Jun

Junior 1984 Lists – Women

Heike	Tillack	GDR 68	58.24		(1)	DRUZHBA	Plovdiv	5 Aug
Sabine	Nolte	FRG 68	58.47		(1)		Oldenburg	1 Jul
Yelena	Klimova	SU 66	58.50		(1)	vGDR-J	Tallinn	23 Jun
Sabine	Zweiner	FRG 67	58.72		(1)H3	NC-Y	Fulda	20 Jul
Anne	Gundersen	NOR 66	58.75		(1)	vSWE	Malmo	17 Jun
Yoko	Satoh	JAP 66	58.82		( )		Shanghai	30 Aug
Lavonna	Martin	USA 66	58.84		(1)	NC-Y	Baton Rouge	21 Jul
Cristina	Vlasceanu	RUM 67	58.89		(1)		Bucuresti	1 Sep
Karin	Wiesel	FRG 69	58.90		(2)	NC-J	Munchengladbach	19 Aug
Donelda	Duprey	CAN 67	58.99		(2)	PAG-J	Nassau	23 Aug
Heike	Huneke	FRG 66	59.00		(2)		Oldenburg	1 Jul
Karen	Wilkinson	RSA 66	59.02		(1)		Port Elizabeth	7 Dec
Elke	Krammel	FRG 66	59.03		(4)	NC-J	Munchengladbach	19 Aug
Hand timing								
Olga	Velikanova	SU 68	58.2		(1)		Tashkent	21 Sep

HIGH JUMP

Olga	Turchak	SU 67	1.96		(1)	NC	Donyetsk	7 Sep
Tamara	Malesev	YUG 67	1.92i		(5)	E-I	Goteburg	4 Mar
			1.86		(8)		Worstadt	9 Jun
Lisa	Bernhagen	USA 66	1.905i		(1)		Pocatello	18 Feb
			1.89		(1)	PAG-J	Nassau	24 Aug
Svetlana	Mokarjak	SU 67	1.90i		(1)		Chelyabinsk	5 Feb
			1.88		(1)	NC-Y	Simferopol	27 May
Wendy	Brown	USA 66	1.89		(1)		San Jose	21 Apr
Debbie	Marti	UK 68	1.89		(1)		Hendon	2 Jun
Latrese	Johnson	USA 66	1.88		(1)	TAC-J	Los Angeles	24 Jun
Svetlana	Isayeva	BUL 67	1.88		(1)		Pleven	7 Jul
Hortensia	Jancu	ROM 67	1.88		(1)	BALK-J	Maribor	29 Jul
Beate	Holzapfel	FRG 66	1.88		(H)		Ulm	25 Aug
Yelena	Topchina	SU 66	1.88		(2)		Tashkent	22 Sep
Louise	Manning	UK 67	1.87		(1)		Crawley	7 May
Sigrid	Kirchmann	AUT 66	1.87		(1)	NC	Wien	20 Jul
Natalya	Golodnova	SU 67	1.87		(1)		Frunze	8 Sep
Megumu	Satoh	JAP 66	1.87		(1)		Tokyo	21 Oct
Ringa	Ropo	FIN 66	1.86i		(1)		Laukaa	29 Jan
Orlane	Dos Santos	BRA 66	1.86		(H)		Sao Paulo	31 Mar
Judit	Kovacs	HUN 69	1.86		(1)		Nyiregyhaza	15 May
Petra	Riehmann	GDR 68	1.86		(1)		Cottbus	11 Jul
Maria	Danisova	CS 68	1.86		(3)	DRUZHBA	Plovdiv	4 Aug
Peggy	Beer	GDR 69	1.86i		(1)		Senftenburg	15 Dec

LONG JUMP

Natalya	Shevchenko	SU 66	6.88	0.6	(1)		Sochi	26 May
Georgina	Oladapo	UK 67	6.52	0.8	(2)	WAAA	London	16 Jun
Natalya	Shaprinskaya	SU 68	6.48		(2)		Tashkent	21 Sep
Anna	Dyerevyankina	SU 67	6.47		(3)		Tashkent	21 Sep
Irina	Privalova	SU 68	6.45		(1)	vGDR-J	Tallinn	23 Jun
Sofia	Bozhanova	BUL 67	6.45	0.8	(1)	DRUZHBA	Plovdiv	5 Aug
Margaret	Cheetham	UK 68	6.45	1.0	(1)		Middlesbrough	18 Aug
Ilona	Redanz	GDR 66	6.44i		(2)		Leningrad	25 Feb
Inessa	Sulyak	SU 66	6.44	−1.9	(1)	NC-J	Riga	13 Jul
Nicole	Boegman	AUS 67	6.43		(1)		Nanjing	17 Sep
Olga	Molodtsova	SU 70	6.43		(1)		Odessa	17 Oct
Adelina	Polledo	CUB 66	6.40		(1)		Santiago	2 Mar
Venera	Kirkova	BUL 66	6.39i		(3)		Sofia	11 Feb
Irina	Sugaveya	SU 67	6.38		( )		Krasnodar	8 Apr

443

Junior 1984 Lists – Women

Ildiko	Fekete	HUN 66	6.38		(2)	NC-J	Budapest	17 May
Stefanie	Huhn	FRG 66	6.37		(2)		Munchengladbach	19 Aug
Oksana	Kubiskina	SU 68	6.37		(1)		Angarsk	22 Sep
Olimpia	Constantiu	RUM 68	6.37		(2)		Vinnitsa	30 Sep
Silke	Harms	FRG 67	6.36	1.5	(3)		Furth	9 Jun
Wendy	Brown	USA 66	6.34		(1)		Los Angeles	2 Jun

Marks made with assisting wind

Margaret	Cheetham	UK 68	6.49		(1)		Birmingham	23 Sep
Ildiko	Fekete	HUN 66	6.47	3.1	(1)		Budapest	30 Jun

SHOT PUT

Grit	Haupt	GDR 66	19.57		(1)		Gera	7 Jul
Yang	Yanqin	CHN 66	18.08		(1)		Eugene	18 Jul
Irina	Fedchenko	SU 66	17.75		(1)		Kiev	28 Aug
Iris	Plozitzka	FRG 66	17.67i		(2)		Cannes	29 Dec
			17.28		(1)		Bad Mergestheim	14 Oct
Lisette	Martinez	CUB 66	17.10		(1)		Mexico, D.F.	16 Jun
Petra	Leidinger	FRG 66	16.81		(1)		Ingelheim	3 Jun
Bettina	Beetz	GDR 67	16.80		(2)	vSU-J	Tallinn	23 Jun
Lyubov	Kostikova	SU 66	16.68		( )		Leningrad	9 Jun
Alla	Kurillo	SU 66	16.46		(1)		Riga	4 Jul
Ilke	Wyludda	GDR 69	16.42		(1)	DRUZHBA	Plovdiv	4 Aug
Mihaela	Samolia	ROM 66	16.30		(2)		Vinnitsa	29 Sep
Kathrin	Niemke	GDR 66	16.09		(3)		Leipzig	13 Jun
Bepsis	Laza	CUB 67	16.09		(2)		Mexico, D.F.	16 Jun
Yelena	Stupakova	SU 67	16.05		(2)		Tashkent	19 Sep
Deborah	Dunant	HOL 66	15.87		(1)		Sittard	29 Jun
Aina	Romanova	SU 68	15.67		(2)	NC-Y	Simferopol	27 May
Edith	Haider	FRG 66	15.59		(2)		Bad Reichenhall	30 Jun
Svetlana	Stepanenko	SU 67	15.50		( )		Mogilev	19 Jul
Tatyana	Prishchep	SU 66	15.47i		(4)		Leningrad	25 Feb
Jezno	Mosinova	BUL 66	15.38		(2)		Ruse	6 May

DISCUS

Grit	Haupt	GDR 66	65.96		(3)		Leipzig	13 Jul
Jana	Harter	GDR 66	59.06		(2)		Cottbus	26 May
Ilke	Wyludda	GDR 69	57.74		(1)		Cottbus	26 Jul
Larisa	Platonova	SU 66	57.42		(1)		Tallinn	15 Jun
Christine	Lohofener	GDR 66	56.86		(1)		Schwerin	2 May
Larissa	Korotkovich	SU 67	56.70		(1)		Staiki	8 Jun
Sonja	Rust	GDR 66	54.48		(2)		Berlin	24 Jun
Kathrin	Niemke	GDR 66	53.84		(3)	NC-Y	Magdeburg	21 Jul
Vladmira	Palyzova	CS 67	53.64		(5)		Praha	13 May
Viktoria	Kotschetova	SU 67	53.58		(2)		Debrecen	18 Aug
Tatyana	Bevzyuk	SU 66	53.46					
Wen	Chunfeng	CHN 69	53.14		( )		Nanjing	8 Sep
Vikoriya	Popova	SU 69	53.04		( )		Omsk	19 May
Rita	Alvarez	CUB 66	53.00		(2)	BARR	Habana	12 May
Deborah	Dunant	HOL 66	52.86		(2)		Hoorn	8 Jul
Dazina	Boveva	BUL 66	52.44		(1)		Pleven	7 Jul
Tanja	Yaneva	BUL 66	52.36		(1)		Stara Zagora	23 Jun
Carla	Garrett	USA 67	52.28		(1)		Tuscon	8 Dec
Olga	Buryak	SU 67	52.04					
Ines	Ardilles	CUB 66	51.70		(3)		Habana	12 May

Junior 1984 Lists – Women

JAVELIN

Trine	Solberg	NOR 66	65.02	(1)	PTS	Bratislava	26 May
Jana	Kopping	GDR 66	60.88	(2)		Potsdam	2 May
Tatyana	Shikolenko	SU 68	59.40	( )		Moskva	6 Aug
Yelena	Kucherenko	SU 66	59.36	(1)		Tashkent	22 Sep
Ivonne	Leal	CUB 66	58.54	(6)		Habana	6 Feb
Xin	Xiaoli	CHI 66	58.32	( )		Beijing	31 May
Solvi	Nybu	NOR 66	58.12	(2)		Sollentuna	11 Aug
Danica	Zivanov	YUG 67	57.74	(1)		Beograd	17 Jun
Song	Ruiling	CHN 66	57.08	( )		Zhengzhou	8 Apr
Regine	Kempter	GDR 67	56.60	(1)	NC-Y	Magdeburg	22 Jul
Heike	Galle	GDR 67	56.44	(1)		Berlin	2 Feb
Tatyana	Silaveya	SU 67	55.60	( )		Dnepropetrovsk	8 Aug
Mihalea	Popescu	ROM 66	55.54	(2)	BALK-J	Maribor	29 Jul
Layla	Kublicka	SU 66	55.48	( )		Yekabpils	13 May
Catherine	Garside	UK 67	55.38	(1)		Cleckheaton	19 May
Lee	Hui-Ching	CHN 67	55.04				20 May
Mari	Nakayamo	JAP 66	54.28	( )		Odaware	28 Oct
Michelle	Oliveira	USA 66	54.12	(1)	PAG-J	Nassau	25 Aug
Svetlana	Budischan	SU 67	54.04	(2)		Tashkent	22 Sep
Yelena	Petrova	SU 66	53.50	(3)		Adler	26 Feb

HEPTATHLON

Valentina	Savchenko	SU 68	6226	(1)	DRUZHBA	Plovdiv	5 Aug
13.88 1.59 15.10 24.15/ 6.07 48.16 2:12.42							
Yelena	Davidova	SU 67	5921	(2)	DRUZHBA	Plovdiv	5 Aug
14.48 1.83 11.55 25.14/ 6.25 38.42 2:16.92							
Vera	Polyakova	SU 66	5920	(1)	NC-Y	Simferopol	27 May
14.35 1.75 12.65 24.35/ 5.93 35.62 2:14.33							
Olga	Tokareva	SU 66	5902	(2)	NC-J	Riga	15 Jul
14.40 1.79 12.04 24.90/ 6.05 38.30 2:16.75							
Beate	Holzapfel	FRG 66	5846	(1)		Ulm	26 Aug
14.63 1.88 11.33 25.07/ 5.90 39.40 2:19.64							
Viktoria	Maruscak	vGDR 66	5718	(3)	vGDR-J	Tallinn	24 Jun
14.15 1.82 11.82 25.89/ 6.05 29.92 2:16.99							
Yelena	Salamova	SU 66	5757H	(1)		Sachty	13 May
14.2 1.75 10.97 24.9 / 5.75 39.38 2:17.9							
Natalya	Skobina	SU 66	5739H	(5)		Dnepropetrovsk	5 Aug
14.7 1.76 12.86 25.4/ 5.76 35.70 2:16.8							
Katrin	Hochrein	GDR 66	5675	(12)	NC	Neubrandenburg	2 Jun
14.27 1.79 11.95 24.84/ 5.88 34.94 2:29.10							
Stefanie	Huhn	FRG 66	5672			Ulm	26 Aug
14.28 1.84 11.01 25.5/ 6.23 29.22 2:20.99							
Renata	Stanova	CS 67	5653	(1)		Miskolc	8 Jul
15.01 1.68 12.80 25.30/ 6.10 43.50 2:31.51							
Sally	Gunnell	UK 66	5647	(2)	NC	Cwmbran	28 May
13.40w 1.61 10.20 24.09/ 5.76 29.72 2:13.22							
Joanne	Mulliner	UK 66	5644	(1)	vFRA-J	Dombasle	19 Aug
14.22 1.78 11.52 24.99/ 5.98 31.26 2:24.60							
Yelena	Zaitseva	SU 67	5636	(5)	NC-Y	Simferopol	27 May
15.05 1.81 11.53 25.53/ 5.87 33.08 2:16.66							
Peggy	Beer	GDR 69	5618	(4)	DRUZHBA	Plovdiv	5 Aug
14.50 1.77 10.42 25.11/ 5.64 32.32 2:12.50							
Camelia	Carnateanu	RUM 67	5569	(5)	DRUZHBA	Plovdiv	5 Aug
14.61 1.77 12.25 25.88/ 5.35 31.76 2:13.13							
Yelena	Bankova	SU 67	5548	(6)	NC-Y	Simferopol	27 May
15.19 1.78 11.94 26.26/ 5.70 35.50 2:17.67							
Grit	Colditz	GDR 66	5544	(1)	NC-J	Potsdam	1 Jul
14.93 1.72 12.28 26.72/ 5.83w 40.68 2:23.53							
Teodora	Palosanu	RUM 66	5581H				
Sharon	Jaklofsky-Smith	AUS 68	5580H	(1)		Brisbane	8 Dec
14.1 1.71 11.89 25.8 / 5.82 42.26 2:34.4							

445

INTERNATIONAL MARATHON WINNERS 1984

ROGER GYNN

Men

Date	Location	Winner	Time
7 Jan	Miami	Tommy Persson (Swe)	2.13.27
14 Jan	Houston	Charlie Spedding (UK)	2.11.54
21 Jan	Hong Kong	Graeme Kennedy (Aus)	2:17:27
22 Jan	Manila	Kjell-Erik Stahl (Swe)	2:19:24
29 Jan	Hamilton, Ber	Bud Coates (USA)	2:18:25
29 Jan	New Orleans	Alan Dehlinger (USA)	2:18:24
29 Jan	Osaka		
5 Feb	Beppu	Cor Vriend (Hol)	2:12:05
5 Feb	Oakland	Fraser Clyne (UK)	2:15:21
12 Feb	Tokyo	Juma Ikangaa (Tan)	2:10:49
12 Feb	Kuala Lumpur	Tommy Persson (Swe)	2:23:08
19 Feb	Los Angeles	Gidamis Shahanga (Tan)	2:10:19
4 Mar	Nagoya		
11 Mar	Otsu	Tetsuharu Iwase (Jap)	2:14:24
18 Mar	Barcelona	Werner Meier (Swz)	2:14:50
18 Mar	Essonne	Marc Agosta (Lux)	2:18:22
25 Mar	Vienna	Anton Niemczak (Pol)	2:12:17
7 Apr	Maassluis	Cor Vriend (Hol)	2:11:41
8 Apr	Lyon	Robleh Djama (Djibouti)	2:11:25
8 Apr	Rome	Bernie Ford (UK)	2:17:01
14 Apr	Rotterdam	Gidamis Shananga (Tan)	2:11:12
16 Apr	Boston	Geoff Smith (UK)	2:10:34
28 Apr	Karl Marx Stadt	Frank Konzack (GDR)	2:16:31
6 May	Bremen	Kjell-Erik Stahl (Swe)	2:13:47
6 May	Debno	Wojciech Ratkowski (Pol)	2:12:49
6 May	Munich	Karel Lismont (Bel)	2:12:50
12 May	Paris	Ahmed Saleh (Djibouti)	2:11:58
13 May	London	Charlie Spedding (UK)	2:09:57
13 May	Frankfurt	Dereje Nedi (Eth)	2:11:18
20 May	Cleveland	Demetrio Cabanillas (Mex)	2:16:13
27 May	Geneva	Svend-Erik Kristensen (Den)	2:14:55
2 Jun	Stockholm	Agapius Masong (Tan)	2:13:47
10 Jun	Sydney	Jon Anderson (USA)	2:13:18
17 Jun	Duluth	Derek Stevens (UK)	2:12:41
24 Jun	Otwock	Anastassios Psathas (Gre)	2:17:45
21 Jul	Helsinki	Niilo Kempe (Fin)	2:20:41
5 Aug	Olympic Games		
12 Aug	Olympic Games	Carlos Lopes (Por)	2:09:21
17 Aug	Prague (Friendship G)		
18 Aug	Moscow (Friendship G)	Dereje Nedi (Eth)	2:10:32
19 Aug	San Francisco	Simeon Kigen (Ken)	2:10:18
26 Aug	Reykjavik	Sigurdur Sigmundsson (Ice)	2:28:57
1 Sep	Oslo	Kjell-Erik Stahl (Swe)	2:13:01
1 Sep	Penang	Bud Coates (USA)	2:29:56
2 Sep	East Berlin	Stanislaw Zdunek (Pol)	2:20:58
23 Sep	Montreal	Jorge Gonzalez (Pur)	2:12:48
24 Sep	Paris (Avon)		
30 Sep	Seoul	Kjell-Erik Stahl (Swe)	2:13:57
30 Sep	St Paul	Fred Torneden (USA)	2:11:35
30 Sep	Toronto	Kevin Forster (UK)	2:12:32
30 Sep	West Berlin	John Skovbjerg (Den)	2:13:35
7 Oct	Columbus	Gerard Nijboer (Hol)	2:13:39
7 Oct	Kosice	Li Dong Meng (PRK)	2:18:59
14 Oct	Beijing	Hideki Kita (Jap)	2:12:16

Women

Winner	Time
Joëlle Debrouwer (Fra)	2:44:41
Ingrid Kristiansen (Nor)	2:27:51
Yuko Gordon (Hong Kong)	2:42:35
Denise Verhaert (Bel)	2:45:27
Tracy Robinson (Can)	2:46:25
Sally Hales (UK)	2:44:45
Katrin Dörre (GDR)	2:31:41
Leslie McMullin (USA)	2:42:19
Lone Dybdal (Den)	2:48.03
Jacqueline Gareau (Can)	2:31:57
Glenys Quick (NZ)	2:34:25
Margaret Lockley (UK)	2:41:42
Chantal Langlace (Fra)	2:38:46
Renate Kieninger (GFR)	2:47:40
Jarmila Urbanova (CS)	2:40:07
Solveig Harrysson (Swe)	2:47:01
Daniela Tiberti (Ita)	2:41:40
Carla Beurskens (Hol)	2:34:56
Lorraine Moller (NZ)	2:29:28
Brigitte Weinhold (GDR)	2:36:55
Ursula Koether (GFR)	2:47:32
Ludmila Melicharova (CS)	2:36:31
Christa Vahlensieck (GFR)	2:38:50
Sylviane Levesque (Fra)	2:38:20
Ingrid Kristiansen (Nor)	2:24:26
Charlotte Teske (GFR)	2:31:16
Maricarmen Cardenas (Mex)	2:41:13
Valentina Kerimova (USSR)	2:41:43
Ria van Landeghem (Bel)	2:34:13
Ngaire Drake (NZ)	2:41:36
Anne Hird (USA)	2:37:31
Alexandra Tarasova (USSR)	2:41:45
Diane Palmason (Can)	2:48:21
Joan Benoit (USA)	2:24:52
Zoya Ivanova (USSR)	2:33:44
Katie Schilly (USA)	2:35:56
Leslie Watson (UK)	2:53:47
Marit Groendalen (Nor)	3:02:13
Leslie Watson (UK)	3:02:43
Tatyana Orlova (USSR)	2:46:02
Lisa Larsen (USA)	2:36:26
Lorraine Moller (NZ)	2:32:44
Brigitte Lennartz (GFR)	2:40:46
Debbie Mueller (USA)	2:34:50
Anne Hird (USA)	2:41:45
Agnes Sipka (Hun)	2:39:32
Priscilla Welch (UK)	2:34:04
Christa Vahlensieck (GFR)	2:37:19
Margaret Reddan (Aus)	2:43:40

International Marathon Winners 1984

14 Oct	Melbourne	Juma Ikangaa (Tan)	2:15:31
21 Oct	Chicago	Steve Jones (UK)	2:08:05
28 Oct	New York	Orlando Pizzolato (Ita)	2:14:53
29 Oct	Dublin	Svend-Erik Kristensen (Den)	2:18:25
4 Nov	Lisbon (41.07 km)	Cidalio Caetano (Por)	2:08:05
18 Nov	Tokyo		
2 Dec	Fukuoka	Takeyuki Nakayama (Jap)	2:10:00
2 Dec	Florence	Andy Robertson (UK)	2:15:23
2 Dec	Sacramento	Ken Martin (USA)	2:11:24
9 Dec	Honolulu	Jorge Gonzalez (Pur)	2:16:25
9 Dec	Singapore	Tommy Persson (Swe)	2:18:30
21 Dec	Galilee	Lindsay Robertson (UK)	2:16:28

Rosa Mota (Por)	2:26:01
Grete Waitz (Nor)	2:29:30
Ailish Smyth (Ire)	2:47:30
Ines Deselaers (Bel)	2:45:50
Katrin Dörre (GDR)	2:33:23
Gillian Burley (UK)	2:32:53
Katie Schilly (USA)	2:32:40
Patti Grey (USA)	2:42:50
Kersti Jacobsen (Den)	2:41:34

1984 WORLD MARATHON RANKINGS – MEN

Name	Nat/Yr	Time	(Pos)	Venue	Date	Meet
Steve Jones	GBR 55	2:08:05	(1)	Chicago	21 Oct	Int
Carlos Lopes	POR 47	2:09:06	(2)	Chicago	21 Oct	Int
Rob de Castella	AUS 57	2:09:09	(3)	Chicago	21 Oct	Int
Jörg Peter	GDR 55	2:09:14	(1)	Grunau	21 Jul	
Lopes		2:09:21	(1)	Los Angeles	12 Aug	OG
Michael Heilmann	GDR 61	2:09:30	(2)	Grunau	21 Jul	
Ernest Seleke	RSA 59	2:09:41	(1)	Port Elizabeth	31 Mar	NC
John Treacy	IRE 57	2:09:56	(2)	Los Angeles	12 Aug	OG
Charlie Spedding	GBR 52	2:09:57	(1)	London	13 May	NC/Int
Spedding		2:09:58	(3)	Los Angeles	12 Aug	OG
Takeyuki Nakayama	JAP 59	2:10:00	(1)	Fukuoka	2 Dec	Int
Gabriel Kamau	KEN 57	2:10:05	(4)	Chicago	21 Oct	Int
Geoff Smith	GBR 53	2:10:08	(5)	Chicago	21 Oct	Int
Simeon Kigen	KEN 61	2:10:18	(1)	San Francisco	19 Aug	Int
Gidamis Shahanga	TAN 57	2:10:19	(1)	Los Angeles	19 Feb	Int
Martin Pitayo	MEX 60	2:10:29	(6)	Chicago	21 Oct	Int
Dereje Nedi	ETH 55	2:10:32	(1)	Moscow	18 Aug	DRZ
Smith		2:10:34	(1)	Boston	16 Apr	Int
Taisuke Kodama	JAP 58	2:10:36	(2)	Fukuoka	2 Dec	Int
Joseph Nzau	KEN 50	2:10:40	(2)	Los Angeles	19 Feb	Int
Yakov Tolstikov	SOV 59	2:10:48	(1)	Moscow	18 Aug	Pop
Juma Ikangaa	TAN 57	2:10:49	(1)	Tokyo	12 Feb	Int
Gerard Nijboer	HOL 55	2:10:53	(3)	Los Angeles	19 Feb	Int
Takeshi Soh	JAP 53	2:10:55	(4)	Los Angeles	12 Aug	OG
Peter		2:10:57	(2)	Tokyo	12 Feb	Int
Heilmann		2:10:59	(3)	Fukuoka	2 Dec	Int
Jesus Herrera	MEX 62	2:11:00	(4)	Los Angeles	19 Feb	Int
Gianni Poli	ITA 57	2:11:05	(1)	Milan	28 Apr	NC
de Castella		2:11:09	(5)	Los Angeles	12 Aug	OG
Santiago de la Parte	SPA 48	2:11:10	(3)	Tokyo	19 Feb	Int
Ikangaa		2:11:10	(6)	Los Angeles	12 Aug	OG
31 performances to 2:11:10						
Ralf Salzmann	GFR 55	2:11:21	(4)	Tokyo	12 Feb	Int
Ken Martin	USA 58	2:11:24	(1)	Sacramento	2 Dec	Int/TAC
Robleh Djama	DJI 58	2:11:25	(1)	Lyon	8 Apr	Int
Abebe Mekonnen	ETH 64	2:11:30	(2)	Moscow	18 Aug	DRZ
Henrik Jorgensen	DEN 61	2:11:31	(5)	Tokyo	12 Feb	Int
Li Jong Hyong	PRK 56	2:11:34	(4)	Fukuoka	2 Dec	Int
Fred Torneden	USA 59	2:11:35	(1)	St Paul	30 Sep	Int
Kebede Balcha	ETH 51	2:11:40	(2)	Frankfurt	13 May	Int
Cor Vriend	HOL 49	2:11:41	(1)	Maassluis	7 Apr	Int
Kevin Forster	GBR 58	2:11:41	(2)	London	13 May	NC/Int
Cidalio Caetano	POR 52	2:11:42	(3)	Frankfurt	13 May	Int

447

International Marathon Winners 1984

Name	Nat/Age	Time	(Pl)	Location	Date	Type
Pete Pfitzinger	USA 57	2:11:43	(1)	Niagara Falls	26 May	OT
Alberto Salazar	USA 58	2:11:44	(2)	Niagara Falls	26 May	OT
Lee Chang Chen	PRK 56	2:11:44	(3)	Moscow	18 Aug	DRZ
Zacharia Barie	TAN 53	2:11:47	(2)	Rotterdam	14 Apr	Int
Ryszard Kopijasz	POL 52	2:11:50	(2)	Maassluis	7 Apr	Int
Fraser Clyne	GBR 55	2:11:50	(2)	Sacramento	2 Dec	Int/TAC
John Tuttle	USA 58	2:11:50	(3)	Niagara Falls	26 May	OT
Massimo Magnani	ITA 51	2:11:54	(2)	Houston	15 Jan	Int
Hugh Jones	GBR 55	2:11:54	(5)	Los Angeles	19 Feb	Int
Mark Finucane	USA 56	2:11:55	(3)	Houston	15 Jan	Int
Ahmed Saleh	DJI 56	2:11:58	(1)	Paris	12 May	Int
Alain Lazare	FRA 52	2:11:59	(7)	Tokyo	12 Feb	Int
Jacky Boxberger	FRA 49	2:11:59	(2)	Paris	12 May	Int
David Gordon	USA 59	2:11:59	(4)	Niagara Falls	26 May	OT
Waldemar Cierpinski	GDR 50	2:12:00	(8)	Tokyo	12 Feb	Int
Kjell-Erik Stahl	SWE 46	2:12:00	(3)	Sacramento	2 Dec	Int
Don Janicki	USA 60	2:12:01	(2)	St Paul	30 Sep	Int
Koshiro Kawaguchi	JAP 54	2:12:04	(9)	Tokyo	12 Feb	Int
Kunimitsu Itoh	JAP 55	2:12:04	(5)	Fukuoka	2 Dec	Int
Jim Wellerding	USA 54	2:12:06	(4)	Houston	15 Jan	Int
Kaneo Hikima	JAP 54	2:12:08	(6)	Fukuoka	2 Dec	Int
Freddy Vandervennet	BEL 52	2:12:09	(10)	Tokyo	12 Feb	Int
Dennis Fowles	GBR 51	2:12:12	(3)	London	13 May	Int/NC
Allan Zachariassen	DEN 55	2:12:16	(11)	Tokyo	12 Feb	Int
Johan Geinaert	BEL 51	2:12:16	(1)	Peer	1 May	NC
Hideki Kita	JAP 52	2:12:16	(1)	Beijing	14 Oct	Int
Anton Niemczak	POL 55	2:12:17	(1)	Vienna	25 Mar	Int
Oyvind Dahl	NOR 51	2:12:19	(4)	London	13 May	Int/NC
Jerry Kiernan	IRE 53	2:12:20	(9)	Los Angeles	12 Aug	OG
Isamu Sennai	JAP 60	2:12:20	(7)	Fukuoka	2 Dec	Int
Dirk Vanderherten	BEL 57	2:12:21	(2)	Peer	1 May	NC
Jorn Lauenborg	DEN 44	2:12:21	(5)	London	13 May	Int/NC
Dean Matthews	USA 55	2:12:25	(5)	Niagara Falls	26 May	OT
Yoshihiro Nishimura	JAP 57	2:12:26	(2)	Beppu	5 Feb	Int
Teruo Chiba	JAP 57	2:12:33	(3)	Beppu	5 Feb	Int
Patrick Joannes	FRA 56	2:12:36	(1)	Chatelleraut	10 Jul	NC
Jerzy Skarzynski	POL 56	2:12:37	(2)	Vienna	25 Mar	Int
Rudi Verriet	HOL 56	2:12:41	(3)	Maassluis	7 Apr	Int
Tony Sandoval	USA 54	2:12:41	(6)	Niagara Falls	26 May	OT
Derek Stevens	GBR 54	2:12:41	(1)	Duluth	17 Jun	Int
Fumiaki Abe	JAP 58	2:12:41	(8)	Fukuoka	2 Dec	Int
Jose Gomez	MEX 56	2:12:47	(12)	Tokyo	12 Feb	Int
Hiroji Hayashi	JAP	2:12:47	(9)	Fukuoka	2 Dec	Int
Cor Lambregts	HOL 58	2:12:48	(13)	Tokyo	12 Feb	Int
Jorge Gonzalez	PUR 52	2:12:48	(1)	Montreal	23 Sep	Int
Henryk Lupa	POL 56	2:12:49	(4)	Maassluis	7 Apr	Int
Wojciech Ratkowski	POL 54	2:12:49	(1)	Debno	6 May	NC
Karel Lismont	BEL 49	2:12:50	(1)	Munich	6 May	Int
John Makanya	TAN 60	2:12:52	(3)	Vienna	25 Mar	Int
Michael Spottel	GFR 56	2:12:53	(7)	Houston	15 Jan	Int
Willy van Huylenbroek	BEL 56	2:12:53	(3)	Peer	1 May	NC
Derrick May	RSA 53	2:12:53	(4)	Sacramento	2 Dec	Int/TAC
Zbigniew Pierzynka	POL 51	2:12:53	(2)	Debno	6 May	NC
Frans Ntoale	RSA 50	2:12:57	(2)	Port Elizabeth	31 Mar	NC
Bruno Lafranchi	SWZ 55	2:12:57	(4)	Frankfurt	13 May	Int
Rod Dixon	NZL 50	2:12:57	(10)	Los Angeles	12 Aug	OG
Martti Vainio	FIN 50	2:13:04	(3)	Rotterdam	14 Apr	Int
Andreas Weniger	GFR 58	2:13:06	(8)	Houston	15 Jan	Int
Ahmet Altun	TUR 58	2:13:07	(5)	Frankfurt	13 May	Int
Tetsuhara Iwase	JAP 54	2:13:07	(10)	Fukuoka	2 Dec	Int
Gian-Paolo Messina	ITA 57	2:13:14	(9)	Houston	15 Jan	Int
Ryszard Misiewicz	POL 57	2:13:15	(3)	Debno	6 May	NC

International Marathon Winners 1984

Jon Andersen	USA 49	2:13:18	(1)	Sydney	10 Jun	Int
Dave Edge	CAN 54	2:13:20	(1)	Ottawa	13 May	NC
Gelindo Bordin	ITA 59	2:13:20	(1)	Milan	7 Oct	
41.4 km						
Kimurger Ng'eny	KEN 51	2:10:56	(1)	Kisumu	20 May	Int
Joseph Otieno	KEN	2:10:57	(2)	Kisumu	20 May	Int
Daniel Nzioka	KEN 58	2:11:00	(3)	Kisumu	20 May	Int
41.07 km						
Cidalio Caetano	POR 52	2:08:05	(1)	Lisbon	4 Nov	Int
Zbigniew Pierzynka	POL 51	2:09:41	(2)	Lisbon	4 Nov	Int
41 km						
Stanislav Tomanek	CZE 54	2:12:34	(1)	Brezno	2 May	Int/NC
Gyula Poczos	HUN 55	2:12:41	(2)	Brezno	2 May	
ca. 41 km						
Alejandro Silva	CHL 58	2:10:50	(1)	Santiago	6 May	NC

Hiroshi Noda (Jap)60	2:13:22	2 Dec
Martin McCarthy (GB)57	2:13:24	15 Jan
Emiel Puttemans (Bel)47	2:13:24	1 May
Tommy Persson (Swe)54	2:13:25	7 Apr
Hideki Yamaoka (Jap)55	2:13:28	5 Feb
Eleuterio Anton (Spa)50	2:13:28	20 May
Gideon Moshaba (RSA)56	2:13:29	31 Mar
Greg Meyer (USA)55	2:13:29	26 May
Martti Kiiholma (Fin)50	2:13:30	15 Jan
Bill Rodgers (USA)47	2:13:30	26 May
Petr Salikov (Sov)59	2:13:31	18 Aug
Peter Lyrenmann (Swz)57	2:13:34	13 May
Wiktor Sawicki (Pol)55	2:13:35	6 May
John Skovbjerg (Den)56	2:13:35	30 Sep
Aldo Fantoni (Ita)60	2:13:35	25 Nov
Delfim Moreira (Por)55	2:13:36	13 May
Vladimir Nikityuk (Sov)56	2:13:36	13 May
Richard Umber (Swz)50	2:13:37	7 Apr
Vicente Anton (Spa)59	2:13:38	20 May
Frank Plasso (USA)60	2:13:38	30 Sep
Yoshihira Nishimura (Jap)57	2:13:41	2 Dec
Wolfgang Kruger (GFR)47	2:13:43	30 Sep
Jacques Valentin (Hol)55	2:13:45	7 Apr
Hiroshi Yuge (Jap)56	2:13:46	12 Feb
Agapius Masong (Tan)60	2:13:47	2 Jun
Jimmy Ashworth (GB)57	2:13:49	13 May
Jean-Yves Madelon (Fra)57	2:13:50	7 Oct
Jean Michel Charbonnel (Fra)52	2:13:51	7 Oct
John Offord (GB)47	2:13:52	7 Apr
Ewald Bonzet (RSA)51	2:13:54	30 Jun
Hiroshi Munakata (Jap)59	2:13:57	12 Feb
Yevgeniy Okorokov (Sov)59	2:13:59	13 May
Jean-Jacques Padel (Fra)54	2:14:00	7 Oct
Malcolm East (GB)56	2:14:01	13 May
Mike Pinocci (USA)54	2:14:02	17 Jun
Mark Plaatjies (RSA)62	2:14:03	31 Mar
Chris Bunyan (GB)58	2:14:03	13 May
Martin Brewer (GB)56	2:14:07	19 Aug
Luc Waegeman (Bel)58	2:14:07	14 Sep
Fumiaki Asada (Jap)60	2:14:09	5 Feb
Daniel Grimes (USA)59	2:14:10	2 Dec
Miguel Cruz (Mex)51	2:14:12	19 Feb
Leodigard Martin (Tan)60	2:14:13	12 Feb
Toshihiko Seko (Jap)56	2:14:13	12 Aug
Dennis Rinde (USA)58	2:14:13	2 Dec
Frantisek Visnicky (Cze)58	2:14:14	7 Apr

Armand Parmentier (Bel)54	2:14:16	14 Apr
Svend-Erik Kristensen (Den)56	2:14:17	30 Jun
Alain Bordeleau (Can)56	2:14:18	13 May
Silverio Vega (USA)57	2:14:18	26 May
John Moreno (USA)55	2:14:20	18 Mar
Mehmet Terzi (Tur)55	2:14:20	12 Aug
Doug Avrit (USA)59	2:14:21	19 Aug
Igor Yefimov (Sov)58	2:14:22	7 Oct
Pertti Tiainen (Fin)54	2:14:24	12 Feb
Katsumitsu Sakai (Jap)60	2:14:24	2 Dec
Rudy Dirickx (Bel)55	2:14:26	13 May
Viktor Semyenov (Sov)58	2:14:28	13 May
Herbert Steffny (GFR)53	2:14:30	15 Apr
Marc de Blander (Bel)59	2:14:32	14 Apr
Zoltan Koszegi (Hun)63	2:14:32	28 Oct
Vlad. Byeloborodov (Sov)51	2:14:34	13 May
Shigemasu Ikeda (Jap)57	2:14:36	11 Mar
Dmitriy Fioktiskov (Sov)60	2:14:36	25 Apr
Sergey Rudenko (Sov)58	2:14:36	13 May
Andy Lloyd (Aus)59	2:14:36	10 Jun
Don Norman (USA)58	2:14:36	19 Aug
Art Boileau (Can)57	2:14:37	13 May
Shigeru Soh (Jap)53	2:14:38	12 Aug
Dick Hooper (Ire)56	2:14:39	23 Apr
John Graham (GB)56	2:14:40	13 May
Harry Servaanck (Bel)58	2:14:41	25 Mar
Vito Basiliana (Ita)53	2:14:43	7 Oct
Mike Longthorn (GB)46	2:14:45	13 May
Hiroshi Sunaga (Jap)61	2:14:48	11 Mar
Paul Campbell (GB)58	2:14:48	7 Apr
Yasunori Hameda (Jap)46	2:14:49	5 Feb
Gerald Vanesse (USA)60	2:14:49	16 Apr
Gary Siriano (USA)57	2:14:49	30 Sep
Gerald Dravitski (NZ)43	2:14:50	3 Mar
Werner Meier (Swz)49	2:14:50	18 Mar
Jerzy Kowol (Pol)51	2:14:50	6 May
Richard Kaitany (Ken)56	2:14:50	21 Oct
Adrian Leek (GB)58	2:14:51	7 Oct
Andras Jenkei (Hun)58	2:14:51	28 Oct
Pawel Lorens (Pol)58	2:14:53	30 Sep
Orlando Pizzolato (Ita)58	2:14:53	28 Oct
John Boyes (GB)58	2:14:54	30 Sep
Rich Sayre (USA)53	2:14:55	30 Sep
Aleksandr Baza (Sov)53	2:14:55	7 Oct
Hong-Yul Lee (Kor)61	2:14:59	18 Mar

International Marathon Winners 1984

1984 WORLD MARATHON RANKINGS – WOMEN

Name	Nat/Yr	Time	(n)	Venue	Date	Type
Ingrid Kristiansen	NOR 56	2:24:26	(1)	London	13 May	Int
Joan Benoit	USA 57	2:24:52	(1)	Los Angeles	5 Aug	OG
Rosa Mota	POR 58	2:26:01	(1)	Chicago	21 Oct	Int
Grete Waitz	NOR 53	2:26:18	(2)	Los Angeles	5 Aug	OG
Katrin Dörre	GDR 61	2:26:52	(1)	Grunau	21 Jul	
Mota		2:26:57	(3)	Los Angeles	5 Aug	OG
Kristiansen		2:27:34	(4)	Los Angeles	5 Aug	OG
Lisa Martin	AUS 60	2:27:40	(2)	Chicago	21 Oct	Int
Kristiansen		2:27:51	(1)	Houston	15 Jan	Int
Lorraine Moller	NZL 55	2:28:34	(5)	Los Angeles	5 Aug	OG
Priscilla Welch	GBR 44	2:28:54	(6)	Los Angeles	5 Aug	OG
Martin		2:29:03	(7)	Los Angeles	5 Aug	OG
Sylvia Ruegger	CAN 61	2:29:09	(8)	Los Angeles	5 Aug	OG
Raissa Smekhnova	SOV 50	2:29:10	(1)	Vilnius	7 Oct	
Moller		2:29:28	(1)	Boston	16 Apr	Int
Laura Fogli	ITA 59	2:29:28	(9)	Los Angeles	5 Aug	OG
Waitz		2:29:30	(1)	New York	28 Oct	Int
Welch		2:30:06	(2)	London	13 May	Int/NC
Kristiansen		2:30:21	(3)	Chicago	21 Oct	Int
Nadyezhda Usmanova	SOV 52	2:30:36	(2)	Vilnius	7 Oct	
Ruegger		2:30:37	(1)	Ottawa	13 May	NC
Dorthe Rasmussen	DEN 60	2:30:42	(4)	Chicago	21 Oct	Int
Natalya Bardina	SOV 61	2:30:50	(1)	Krasnodar	28 Oct	
Benoit		2:31:04	(1)	Olympia	12 May	OT
Zoya Ivanova	SOV 52	2:31:11	(1)	Baku	13 May	NC
Charlotte Teske	GFR 49	2:31:16	(1)	Frankfurt	13 May	Int
Sarah Rowell	GBR 62	2:31:28	(3)	London	13 May	Int/NC
Lisa Larsen	USA 61	2:31:31	(5)	Chicago	21 Oct	Int
Dörre		2:31:41	(1)	Osaka	29 Jan	Int
Julie Brown	USA 55	2:31:41	(2)	Olympia	12 May	OT
Jacqueline Gareau	CAN 53	2:31:57	(1)	Los Angeles	19 Feb	Int

31 performances to 2:32.00

Akemi Masuda	JAP 64	2:32:05	(2)	Osaka	29 Jan	Int
Anne Audain	NZL 55	2:32:07	(2)	Los Angeles	19 Feb	Int
Tuija Toivonen	FIN 58	2:32:07	(10)	Los Angeles	5 Aug	OG
Julie Isphording	USA 61	2:32:26	(3)	Olympia	12 May	OT
Christine-Marie Deurbroeck	BEL 57	2:32:32	(1)	Peer	1 May	NC
Kate Schilly	USA 56	2:32:40	(1)	Sacramento	2 Dec	Int
Joyce Smith	GBR 37	2:32:48	(11)	Los Angeles	5 Aug	OG
Carla Beurskens	HOL 52	2:32:53	(2)	Paris	23 Sep	Avon
Gillian Burley	GBR 56	2:32:53	(1)	Florence	2 Dec	Int
Glenys Quick	NZL 57	2:32:53	(6)	Chicago	21 Oct	Int
Anne-Marie Malone	CAN 60	2:33:00	(2)	Ottawa	13 May	NC
Alba Milana	ITA 59	2:33:01	(12)	Los Angeles	5 Aug	OG
Paolo Moro	ITA 52	2:33:03	(1)	Milan	28 Apr	NC
Margaret Groos	USA 59	2:33:38	(5)	Olympia	12 May	OT
Janice Ettle	USA 58	2:33:41	(6)	Olympia	12 May	OT
Karolina Szabo	HUN 61	2:33:43	(1)	Budapest	28 Oct	
Eriko Asai	JAP 59	2:33:43	(2)	Tokyo	18 Nov	Int
Mary O'Connor	NZL 55	2:33:44	(3)	Los Angeles	19 Feb	Int
Nancy Ditz	USA 54	2:33:52	(7)	Olympia	12 May	OT
Veronique Marot	GBR 55	2:33:52	(4)	London	13 May	Int/NC
Midde Hamrin	SWE 57	2:33:53	(2)	Boston	16 Apr	Int
Lucia Belyayeva	SOV 57	2:33:54	(2)	Prague	18 Aug	DRZ
Martha White	USA 59	2:34:09	(8)	Olympia	12 May	OT
Gail Kingma	USA	2:34:09	(2)	Sacramento	2 Dec	Int
Yelena Tsukhlo	SOV 54	2:34:10	(3)	Vilnius	7 Oct	
Ria van Landeghem	BEL 57	2:34:13	(1)	Stockholm	2 Jun	Int
Cathy Schiro	USA 67	2:34:24	(9)	Olympia	12 May	OT

International Marathon Winners 1984

Name	Nat/Yr	Time	(Pos)	Venue	Date	Type
Christa Vahlensieck	GFR 49	2:34:28	(4)	Paris	23 Sep	Avon
Sue King	USA 58	2:34:29	(10)	Olympia	12 May	OT
Monica Joyce	USA	2:34:49	(2)	Sacramento	2 Dec	Int
Debbie Mueller	USA 59	2:34:50	(1)	St Paul	30 Sep	Int
Chantal Langlacé	FRA 55	2:34:51	(1)	Creil	7 Apr	
Francine Peeters	BEL 57	2:34:53	(2)	Peer	1 May	NC
Kersti Jakobsen	DEN 56	2:34:53	(5)	London	13 May	Int
Lyubov Svirskaya	SOV 62	2:34:53	(4)	Vilnius	7 Oct	
Ellen Hart	USA 58	2:35:04	(11)	Olympia	12 May	OT
Regina Joyce	IRE 57	2:35:05	(7)	Chicago	21 Oct	Int
Carol McLatchie	USA 51	2:35:09	(12)	Olympia	12 May	OT
Sinikka Keskitalo	FIN 51	2:35:15	(15)	Los Angeles	5 Aug	OG
Irina Bondarchuk	SOV 52	2:35:17	(2)	Baku	13 May	NC
Brigitte Weinhold	GDR 64	2:35:17	(3)	Tokyo	18 Nov	Int
Tatyana Sokolova	SOV 58	2:35:20	(5)	Vilnius	7 Oct	
Dorothy Goertzen	CAN 55	2:35:24	(5)	Paris	23 Sep	Avon
Bente Moe	NOR 60	2:35:28	(6)	London	13 May	Int
Magda Ilands	BEL 50	2:35:36	(6)	Paris	23 Sep	Avon
Gaby Wolf	GFR 60	2:35:41	(2)	Frankfurt	13 May	Int
Martha Cooksey	USA 54	2:35:42	(13)	Olympia	12 May	OT
Doris Schlosser	GFR 44	2:35:43	(3)	Frankfurt	13 May	Int
Rita Borralho	POR 54	2:35:43	(9)	Chicago	21 Oct	Int
Weng Xinnin	CHN	2:35:50	(1)	Jinan	28 Oct	
Jane Welzel	USA 55	2:35:53	(14)	Olympia	12 May	OT
Julie Barleycorn	GBR 55	2:35:53	(7)	London	13 May	Int/NC
Liz Bussieres	CAN 61	2:35:53	(3)	Ottawa	13 May	NC
Maria Curatolo	ITA 63	2:36:05	(1)	Cesano Boscone	25 Nov	
Debbie Eide	USA 56	2:36:06	(15)	Olympia	12 May	OT
Margaret Lockley	GBR 47	2:36:06	(8)	London	13 May	Int/NC
Sissel Grottenberg	NOR 56	2:36:07	(3)	Boston	16 Apr	Int
Patti Catalano	USA 53	2:36:13	(16)	Olympia	12 May	OT
Elisabeth Oberli-Schuh	VEN 52	2:36:17	(4)	Frankfurt	13 May	Int
Beth Farmer	USA 53	2:36:22	(18)	Olympia	12 May	OT
Kate Wiley	CAN 62	2:36:22	(4)	Ottawa	13 May	NC
Janis Klecker	USA 60	2:36:27	(4)	St Paul	30 Sep	Int
Ludmila Melicharova	CZE 64	2:36:31	(1)	Debno	6 May	Int
Ford Madeira	USA 44	2:36:35	(19)	Olympia	12 May	OT
Anna Domoradskaya	SOV 53	2:36:37	(4)	Baku	13 May	NC
Svetlana Khramenikova	SOV	2:36:39	(6)	Vilnius	7 Oct	
Sonja Laxton	RSA 48	2:36:44	(1)	Cape Town	30 Jun	
Galina Ikannikova	SOV 62	2:36:45	(7)	Vilnius	7 Oct	
Sarah Quinn	USA 58	2:36:54	(20)	Olympia	12 May	OT
Ngaire Drake	NZL 49	2:36:54	(7)	Paris	23 Sep	Avon
Lyubov Putilova	SOV 53	2:37:00	(1)	Moscow	18 Aug	Pop
Jenny Spangler	USA 63	2:37:01	(2)	Houston	15 Jan	Int
Laurie Crisp	USA 61	2:37:01	(5)	Osaka	29 Jan	Int
Nanae Sasaki	JAP 56	2:37:04	(19)	Los Angeles	5 Aug	OG
Gillian Horowitz	GBR 55	2:37:10	(9)	London	13 May	Int/NC
Anne Hird	USA 59	2:37:11	(4)	Boston	16 Apr	Int
Jane Wipf	USA 58	2:37:16	(1)	Seattle	18 Mar	
Lorna Irving	GBR 47	2:37:19	(1)	Glasgow	30 Sep	
Jane Buch	USA 48	2:37:23	(21)	Olympia	12 May	OT
Irina Ruban	SOV 62	2:37:29	(8)	Vilnius	7 Oct	

Karen Dunn (USA)62	2:37:30	18 Nov	
Sylviane Levesque (Fra)53	2:37:41	23 Sep	
Arina Zinurova (Sov)56	2:37:42	7 Oct	
Emma Scaunich (Ita)61	2:37:43	7 Oct	
Nadyezhda Yerokhina (Sov)56	2:37:46	13 May	
Judi St Hilaire (USA)59	2:37:49	28 Oct	
Susan Schneider (USA)56	2:37:58	12 May	
Tatyana Vasilyeva (Sov)62	2:37:58	7 Oct	
Nancy Conz (USA)57	2:38:00	18 Nov	
Laura Albers (USA)57	2:38:03	17 Jun	
Carey May (Ire)59	2:38:11	28 Oct	
Susi Riemeier (GFR)60	2:38:13	15 Apr	
Ramilya Gareyeva (Sov)61	2:38:21	13 May	
Ilona Zsilak (Hun)42	2:38:27	13 May	

International Marathon Winners 1984

Zinaide Gavrilyuk (Sov)59	2:38:32	7 Oct		Linda Korman (USA)51	2:39:21	18 Aug
Allison Roe (NZ)56	2:38:36	29 Jan		Susan Kainulainen (Can)62	2:39:21	30 Sep
Polina Grigorenko (Sov)58	2:38:41	19 Feb		Ann Peisch (USA)56	2:39:25	12 May
Debbie Butterfield (USA)52	2:38:44	12 May		Gabriele Andersen (Swz)45	2:39:28	16 Apr
Kelly Spatz (USA)59	2:38:45	12 May		Stefania Colombo (Ita)	2:39:31	25 Nov
Kim Burns (USA)59	2:38:45	12 May		Agnes Sipka (Hun)54	2:39:32	30 Sep
Kyungja Choi (Kor)62	2:38:47	29 Jan		Lone Dybdal (Den)55	2:39:39	13 May
Maria Trujillo (Mex)59	2:38:50	5 Aug		Brigitte Lennartz (GFR)65	2:39:41	13 May
Chie Matsuda (Jap)48	2:38:51	18 Nov		Jenni Peters (USA)55	2:39:43	15 Jan
Tatyana Lunegova (Sov)57	2:38:58	18 Aug		Karen Cosgrove (USA)56	2:39:45	12 May
Maria Lelut (Fra)56	2:38:58	23 Sep		Kim Burns (USA)56	2:39:45	23 Sep
Evy Palm (Swe)42	2:38:59	14 Apr		Meeri Bodelid (Swe)43	2:39:47	30 Jun
Denise Verhaert (Bel)59	2:39:02	1 May		Solveig Harrysson (Swe)59	2:39:48	30 Sep
Donna Roark (USA)53	2:39:11	12 May		Debbie Raunig (USA)55	2:39:51	12 May
Cathie Twomey (USA)56	2:39:15	30 Sep		Heide Jacobsen (Nor)57	2:39:54	13 May
Eunjoo Lim (Kor)61	2:39:17	29 Jan		Marilyn Hudak (USA)58	2:39:55	12 May
Gabriele Schmidt (GDR)60	2:39:17	29 Apr		Ngaire Drake (NZ)49	2:39:56	4 Mar
Sylvie Bornet (Fra)	2:39:18	23 Sep		Wilma Rusman (Hol)58	2:39:59	23 Sep
Annick Loir (Fra)58	2:39:21	29 Jan		(153)		
Gabriela Gorzynska (Pol)56	2:39:21	6 May				

Ingrid Kristiansen & Grete Waitz the great Norwegian marathon duo had to give best to Joan Benoit in Los Angeles.

INDEX

Name	First	Nat	DOB	Ht/Wt	Event	Best	Season	Year
Abada	Patrick	FRA	20Mar54	189/80	PV	5.53i,5.50	5.70	−83
Abascal	Jose Manuel	SPA	17Mar58	182/67	1500	3:33.69	3:33.12	−82
					Mile	3:55.69i	3:51.71	−83
					2k	5:01.1	5:01.4	−83
Abbyasov	Shamil	SU	16Apr57	185/74	TJ	16.66i,	17.27	−83
						16.53	17.30i	−81
Abdulin	Ilyas	SU	16Nov58	183/80	Dec	7760, 7852m	8000m	−83
Abe	Fumiaki	JAP	31Jul58	167/49	Mar	2:12:41	2:13:41	−83
Abramov	Sergey	SU	6May58	183/70	TJ	16.71	16.59	−81
Abramov	Valeriy	SU	22Aug56	173/61	1500	3:38.2m	3:36.80	−81
					5k	13:34.24	13:11.99	−81
					10k	27:55.17	28:02.87	−83
Adamec	Zdenek	CS	9Jan56	180/93	JT	91.12	85.66	−83
Adamski	Marek	POL	30Jan61	176/64	1500	3:38.28	3:43.09	−83
Adebanji	Moses	NIG	56		100	10.1	10.43	−77
Aebischer	Daniel	SWZ	17Mar57	185/75	PV	5.40	5.40	−82
Afteni	Aleksandr	SU	58	173/64	100	10.30	10.1,10.41	−83
Agbebaku	Ajayi	NIG	6Dec55	185/80	TJ	16.96	17.26	−83
Aguilar	Omar	CHL	1Dec59	175/64	10k	28:29.06	28:43.47	−83
Aho	Aimo	FIN	31May51	185/89	JT	83.38	89.42	−77
Akabusi	Kriss	UK	28Nov58	187/80	400	45.37	46.10	−83
Akhapkin	Konstantin	SU	19Jan56	185/86	Dec	8327	8458	−82
Akhundov	Mahmed	SU	64		TJ	16.96	16.25	−83
Akins	Kevin	USA	27Jan60	196/136	SP	20.70i,20.13	21.61	−83
Akonniemi	Aulis	FIN	16Dec58	184/105	SP	20.18	20.12	−82
Alcala	Gerardo	MEX	28Jun61	170/57	5k	13:33.4	13:36.1	−83
Aldridge	Dan	USA	13Sep56	170/57	2k	5:06.15	5:04.41	−83
					10k	28:28.7	28:36.78	−83
Aleksandrov	Igor	SU	57		LJ	7.88	7.64	−81
Alexander	Ricky	USA	31Jul60	190/82	110h	13.83		
Alfaro	Jorge	CUB	10Jun62	198/82	HJ	2.28	2.25	−83
Allen	Tony	USA	21Jun67	183/72	100	10.1w		
Alli	Yussuf	NIG	28Jul60	185/80	LJ	7.93	8.21	−83
							8.25	−82
Alonso	Jose	SPA	12Feb57	183/75	400h	49.94	49.7,49.75	−83
Alouini	Mohamed	TUN	19Oct57	183/70	800	1:45.78	1:46.75	−83
Altun	Ahmet	TUR	25Jan58	168/57	Mar	2:13:07	2:12:41	−83
Alvarez	Martin	CUB	60		JT	83.80	79.70	−83
Alves	Guilherme	POR	19Dec61	175/59	St	8:32.21	8:28.99	−82
Amboree	Troy	USA	12Feb62	178/69	LJ	8.04	7.94,8.09w	−83
Amike	Henry	NIG	4Oct61	185/71	400h	49.33	50.9−81,51.34	−83
Amimo	Reuben	KEN	63		400	46.0A	46.6A,47.44	−82
Anderson	Colin	USA	20Nov51	188/120	SP	20.01	21.08	−80
Anderson	Jon	USA	12Oct49	187/73	Mar	2:13:18	2:12:03	−80
Anderson	Mark	USA	3Nov58	190/90	JT	82.68	78.72	−83
Andonov	Atanas	BUL	16Jul55	190/85	Dec	7823	8220	−81
Andrade	Henry	USA	17Apr62	180/73	110h	13.45,	13.66A	−82
						13.28w	13.75,13.58w	−83
Andrei	Alessandro	ITA	3Jan59	191/118	SP	21.50	20.35	−82
Andrianov	Aleksandr	SU	5Feb58	196/117	DT	60.96	63.22	−80
Andryushchenko	Sergey	SU	60		DT	60.62	59.94	−83
Angel	Wendel	USA	16Aug52	183/73	400h	50.25	49.93A	−80
							50.53,50.5	−81
Anikin	Yevgeniy	SU	13Mar58	188/73	TJ	16.73	17.07	−80
Annys	Eddy	BEL	15Dec58	187/73	HJ	2.32	2.34	−83
Ansberry	Tom	USA	22Aug63	172/57	10k	28:14.8	28:52.4	−83
Antibo	Salvatore	ITA	7Feb62	163/55	5k	13:33.65	13:31.84	−82
					10k	27:48.02	28:16.25	−82
Anton	Abel	SPA	24Oct62	179/63	5k	13:27.95	14:06.04	−83
Anzrah	John	KEN	27Oct54	176/70	400	45.67,	46.3A	−80

453

Men's Index

Aouita	Said	MOR	2Nov60	175/58	800 1k 1500 Mile 2k 3k 5k	45.3A 1:46.81 2:19.17 3:31.54 3:49.54 5:03.0 7:33.3 13:04.78	46.80 1:44.38 2:15.75 3:32.54 3:52.97 5:02.44 8:01.59 13:48.5	−82 −83 −83 −83 −83 −82 −82 −79
Apaychev	Aleksandr	SU	6May61	187/90	110h Dec	13.93 8642	13.96 8260	−83 −83
Apostolovski	Sasa	YUG	20Jan63	189/65	HJ	2.28i,2.24	2.22	−83
Aragon	Chuck	USA	29Mar59	183/67	800 1500 Mile	1:46.34 3:34.7 3:51.62	1:47.00 3:35.35 3:56.59	−82 −82 −83
Arendar	Aleksandr	SU	5Feb58	175/66	PV	5.50	5.55	−82
Areshin	Aleksandr	SU	9Mar61	188/83	Dec	7945	8016,8204m	−83
Arkhipenko	Vasiliy	SU	28Jan57	178/65	400h	48.81	48.34	−79
Arnold	Marcel	SWZ	17Jan62	183/78	400	45.37	46.44	−83
Armstead	Ray	USA	27May60	187/76	400	44.83	46.13	−82
Armstrong	Ainsley	TRI	27Dec52	180/70	100	10.29	10.2−73,10.46	
Asadov	Vasil	SU	27Aug65	180/69	TJ	16.68	10.1w 16.11	−76 −83
Ashford	David	USA	24Jan64	185/82	110h	13.82,13.7 13.7,13.5w	2w 13.8	−82
Assmann	Matthias	FRG	2Feb57	191/84	800 1k	1:44.93 2:18.61	1:45.05 2:21.33	−82 −83
Astapkovich	Igor	SU	63		HT	79.98	75.02	−83
Atanasov	Atanas	BUL	7Oct56	185/76	LJ	8.31	8.16	−83
Atanasov	Valentin	BUL	7May61	188/84	100	10.32	10.15,10.1	−82
Atkinson	John	AUS	29Oct63	184/71	HJ	2.28	2.15	−82
Atuti	James	KEN	19Mar54	188/80	400	45.9A	45.21A−79,45.82	−80
Atwood	Duncan	USA	11Oct55	186/93	JT	93.44	87.00	−80
Austel	Jens-Uwe	GDR	28Oct61	192/82	HJ	2.24	2.25	−82
Austin	Darrell	USA	11May63	175/77	100	10.32w	10.38w−83,10.3	−83
Avdeyenko	Gennadiy	SU	4Nov63	202/82	HJ	2.31	2.32	−83
Avrunin	Igor	SU	16Jun57	193/124	SP DT	20.50 67.14	20.68 62.02	−83 −83
Azizmuradov	Oleg	SU	26Jan62	193/74	HJ	2.26	2.24	−83
Babaly	Laszlo	HUN	14Mar57	168/62	200	20.82w	20.83	−83
Babers	Alonzo	USA	31Oct61	188/70	400	44.27	45.07	−83
Babits	Laslo	CAN	17Apr58	183/100	JT	86.90	86.08	−83
Babits	Paul	USA	59		PV	5.51	5.18	−82
Babiy	Ivan	SU	22Jul63	186/83	Dec	7781	7088m	−82
Backes	Ron	USA			SP	19.58		
Baccouche	Fethi	TUN	16Nov60	171/59	5k St	13:27.1 8:18.70	13:38.08 8:32.34	−83 −81
Badinelli	Dario	ITA	10Aug60	185/68	TJ	17.00	16.64	−83
Badra	Hassan	EGY	19May59	191/72	TJ	16.48w	15.80	−83
Baginski	Adam	POL	30Mar59	190/85	Dec	7855	7936	−82
Baker	Ken	UK	9Jul63	193/80	St	8:34.83	8:44.91	−82
Baker	Mel-II	USA	16May60	195/79	HJ	2.25	2.20	−81
Baker	Stefan	USA	12Jan61	185/71	110h	13.63, 13.57w	13.84 13.82w	−82 −83
Bakhta	Ali	ALG	13Aug61		200	20.6	20.7,21.11, 20.95w	−83
Bakirov	Ravil	SU	58		TJ	16.67	16.82	−83
Bakos	Gyorgy	HUN	6Jul60	188/77	110h	13.45	13.49	−83

454

Men's Index

Name								
Bakosi	Bela	HUN	18Jun57	180/67	TJ	17.15i, 16.85	17.20, 17.29w	−82
Balashov	Andrey	SU	62		LJ	8.06	7.75	−82
Balcha	Kassa	ETH	5Dec55	182/66	5k	13:32.01	13:35.00	−83
Balcha	Kebede	ETH	7Sep51	165/51	Mar	2:11:40	2:10:03	−83
Balcindes	Lazaro	CUB	8Feb63	177/73	TJ	16.93	16.61	−83
Balkin	Lee	USA	7Jun61	192/75	HJ	2.27	2.24	−81
Balogh	Gyula	HUN	15Feb61	186/68	St	8:33.7	8:30.57	−82
Banks	Willie	USA	11Mar56	190/77	TJ	17.39	17.56	−81
Bankston	Bobby	USA			100	10.31,10.24w	10.30w	−83
Baptiste	Kirk	USA	20Jun63	184/79	100	10.16,10.13w	10.34	−83
					200	19.96	20.38	−83
Barbosa	Jose Luis	BRA	27May61	184/68	800	1:44.98	1:44.3	−83
Barbu	Augustin	RUM	21Apr63	165/60	St	8:32.83	8:42.03	−83
Barella	Mauro	ITA	12Dec56	178/70	PV	5.50	5.41i −82, 5.40	−80
Barie	Zakariah	TAN	29May53	174/56	3k	7:51.46i	7:52.0	−81
					10k	28:03.17	27:38.6	−82
					Mar	2:11:47	2:18:24	−79
Barksdale	Rod	USA	8Sep62	185/86	200	20.35	20.68,20.58A	−82
Barnett	Mike	USA	21May61	185/102	JT	83.34	90.34	−83
Barney	David	USA	18Jan60	175/58	St	8:34.12	8:39.50	−83
Baroni	Fernando	ITA	3Sep57		SP	19.67	18.83	−83
Barr	Oslen	GUY	3Apr61	165/67	800	1:46.42	1:47.39	−83
Barre	Patrick	FRA	12Apr59	172/63	200	20.74, 20.67w	20.60 20.55w	−81 −82
Barrineau	James	USA	25Jun55	190/70	HJ	2.25	2.30	−83
Baryshnikov	Aleksandr	SU	11Nov48	199/122	SP	21.35	22.00	−76
Bastians	Werner	FRG	2Feb57	178/74	100	10.36	10.40−75,10.2	−81
Batrachenko	Viktor	SU	6Jan63	186/78	110h	13.93	13.92,13.6	−82
Bayi	Filbert	TAN	23Jun53	183/59	5k	13:32.11	13:18.2	−80
					St	8:30.97	8:12.48	−80
Beattie	Phil	UK	8Sep63	178/74	400h	50.43	51.05	−83
Beck	Volker	GDR	30Jun56	191/82	400h	49.46	48.58	−79
Becker	Uwe	FRG	10Dec55	188/70	1500	3:35.51	3:34.84	−83
					Mile	3:54.95	3:52.36	−82
					2k	5:02.00	5:02.56	−83
Bednar	Zdenek	CS	1Mar57	196/110	HT	73.10	74.12	−83
Bednarski	Zbigniew	POL	4Jun60	173/81	JT	85.88	79.54	−82
Bedrosian	Bedros	RUM	21May55	176/64	TJ	17.27	17.07	−82
Beer	Ron	GDR	29Aug65	182/80	LJ	8.06	7.93	−83
Begouin	Didier	FRA	27Dec56	185/73	1500	3:38.06	3:38.9	−79
Behmer	Bodo	GDR	4Aug61	187/73	TJ	16.60	16.61	−83
Behrendt	Ulf	GDR	31Oct62	196/96	Dec	8045	7735	−83
Belevskiy	Sergey	SU	4Nov59	190/81	TJ	17.03	16.75	−83
Belkov	Gennadiy	SU	24Jun56	191/84	HJ	2.28i,2.24	2.32	−82
Belkov	Sergey	SU	61		SP	20.03		
Bell	Earl	USA	25Aug55	191/75	PV	5.80	5.67	−76
Bell	Kipper	USA			100	10.35,	10.44,10.42w	−83
Bello	Jorge	SPA	28Mar63	187/70	St	8:32.35	8:50.68	−82
Belskiy	Viktor	SU	22Feb55	184/72	LJ	8.12	8.20	−82
Bender	Jason	USA	13Nov60	188/90	JT	81.38	77.96	−83
Bender	Paul	USA	29Nov61	190/116	DT	63.64	54.82	−83
Bennett	Todd	UK	6Jul62	171/66	200	20.36	21.02,20.86w	−83
					400	45.45	45.58	−83
Benjamin	Lester	ANT	14Sep63	178/69	100	10.33	10.62−82,10.34w	−83
					LJ	8.02	7.89	−83
Benjamin	Mike	USA	17May61	185/82	110h	13.84w	14.00−82,13.8	−81
Bereczki	Jozsef	HUN	7Jan62	176/54	1500	3:38.6	3:38.7	−82
Bereglazov	Vladimir	SU	59		TJ	16.75i,16.69	17.03	−83
Bergmann	Uwe	GDR	20Dec61	181/66	1500	3:38.65	3:39.12	−83
Berqvist	Goran	SWE	9Aug60		DT	60.52	59.26	−83
Bertimon	Charlus-Mi.	FRA	1Jan57	186/85	JT	83.50	86.00	−83

455

Men's Index

Bertocchi	Luigi	ITA	10Jun65		110h	13.6	14.63	−83
Beskrovniy	Aleksandr	SU	5Apr60	189/83	TJ	16.92	17.53	−83
Betancourt	Lazaro	CUB	18Mar63	189/81	TJ	17.45	17.40,17.50w	−83
Bethel	Kerry	USA	10Oct57	188/82	110h	13.65	A13.45,13.3w	−78
							13.54−79,13.4	−81
Bezruchko	Mikhail	SU	62		TJ	16.55	16.40	−83
Beyer	Olaf	GDR	4Aug57	186/69	800	1:46.60	1:43.84	−78
					2k	5:02.6	5:05.7i	−81
Beyer	Udo	GDR	9Aug55	194/135	SP	22.04	22.22	−83
Bianchini	Orlando	ITA	4Jun55	193/130	HT	77.94	77.02	−80
Bichea	Vasile	RUM	18Nov50	183/70	St	8:26.56	8:22.51	−80
Bickford	Bruce	USA	12Mar57	180/60	3k	7:51.34	7:54.18	−82
					5k	13:33.78	13:38.08	−81
							13:30.5i	−83
					10k	27:47.91	28:48.2	−83
					St	8:30.43	8:25.36	−82
Biczysko	Dariusz	POL	25Jun62	190/78	HJ	2.26	2.28i,2.28	−83
Bieber	Bernd	FRG	13Jul59		LJ	7.92,7.94w	7.49	−82
Bile	Abdi	SOM	63	185/75	800	1:46.1	1:50.0	−81
					1k	2:18.32		
					1500	3:36.0dq	3:51.6	−82
					Mile	3:57.43		
Billy	Ikem	UK	25Jan64	181/62	800	1:44.65	1:47.0	−83
Binley	Judd	USA	4Jan55	186/102	DT	63.62	58.12	−83
Bishop	Paul	USA	20Dec57	193/127	DT	62.86	64.50	−83
Bitok	Sosthenes	KEN	23Mar57	188/68	5k	13:34.06i	13:29.02i	−83
							13:43.47	−83
					10k	27:50.0	28:29.12	−83
Bjorbaek	Oystein	NOR	3Sep53	192/104	DT	60.54	66.32	−83
Bjorklund	Garry	USA	22Apr51	178/62	10k	27:46.9	27:49.77	−76
Blackledge	John	UK	4May61	175/64	1k	2:19.65	2:25.4	−79
Blake	Arthur	USA	19Aug66	183/66	110h	13.84	−0−	
Blalock	Stanley	USA	18Mar64	175/71	100	10.30,	10.31,10.09w	−83
						10.24w	10.3	−82
					200	20.54,20.4	20.50,	
						20.3w	20.4w	−83
Blank	Peter	FRG	10Apr62	194/81	JT	81.98	78.22	−83
Block	Richard	USA	21Mar60	190/77	1k	2:19.23		
Block	Peter	GDR	28May	200/120	SP	20.38	21.04	−82
Blom	Jyrki	FIN	11May62	183/82	JT	83.94	79.40	−83
Blomstrand	Staffan	SWE	3Aug60	185/	Dec	7709	7336	−83
Bly	Donald	USA	25May62	178/68	100	10.34	10.32A,10.24w,	
							10.42,10.1	−82
					200	20.37	20.84,20.49A	−82
					400	45.87		
Bobryshev	Viktor	SU	28May57	187/120	HT	75.48	78.28	−83
Bochin	Viktor	SU	60		JT	83.08	79.90	−83
Bodo	Bela	HUN	19Jan58	185/80	110h	13.90,13.69w	13.68	−83
Bohni	Felix	SWZ	14Feb58	189/82	PV	5.61	5.71	−83
Bottcher	Holger	FRG	27Jul63	183/73	800	1:46.94	1:48.0	−83
Boffi	Franco	ITA	2Nov58	186/70	2k	5:06.65	5:11.2	−82
					5k	13:31.27	13:46.4	−83
					St	8:27.66	−0−	
Bogatyryov	Pavel	SU	19Mar61	194/84	PV	5.75	5.74	−83
Boileau	Art	CAN	9Oct57	176/67	10k	28:29.91	29:05.07	−80
Boit	Mike	KEN	6Jan49	180/68	1500	3:37.29	3:33.67	−81
					Mile	3:57.44	3:49.45	−81
Bojars	Janis	SU	12May56	185/127	SP	21.74	21.40	−83
Bolgar	Tamas	HUN	24Aug55	184/102	JT	84.32	84.86	−80
Booker	Angelo	USA	30Nov59	187/80	110h	13.93,13.7	13.80,13.6	−83
Booker	Frank	USA			100	10.1		

Men's Index

Name	First	Nat	DOB	Ht/Wt	Event	Mark1	Mark2	Yr
Booker	Martin	USA	8Mar63	185/82	110h	13.81	14.02	−83
					400h	50.52	51.0	−83
Bordeleau	Alain	CAN	7Oct56	177/63	10k	28:08.87	28:46.79	−82
Bordin	Gelindo	ITA	2Apr59	180/68	Mar	2:13:20		
Bordukov	Vyacheslav	SU	1Jan59	184/69	TJ	17.37	17.30	−83
Boreham	Colin	UK	26Mar54	188/87	Dec	7884	7935	−82
Boreyko	Aleksandr	SU	10Mar56	185/118	SP	20.23	20.20	−83
Borghi	Paolo	ITA	27Nov61	189/76	HJ	2.25	2.28	−80
Borglund	Peter	SWE	29Jan64	182/80	JT	81.34	82.26	−83
Borodkin	Nikolay	SU	4Apr55	190/127	SP	21.00	20.78	−83
Borra	Marc	BEL	6Jan57	190/82	HJ	2.26	2.22	−79
Bounour	Abderazzak	ALG	11Jan57	176/60	5k	13:25.26	13:43.4	−82
Bourke	Peter	AUS	23Apr58	182/73	800	1:46.8	1:44.78	−82
Bouschen	Peter	FRG	16May60	181/78	TJ	17.20	17.33	−83
Boussemart	J-Jacques	FRA	11Apr63	180/68	100	10.33	10.40,10.3,10.2w	−83
					200	20.41	20.54,20.41w	−83
Boxberger	Jacques	FRA	16Apr49	183/70	Mar	2:11:59	2:12:38	−83
Bradford	Colin	JAM	30May55	188/80	100	10.36	10.15−81, 10.0w	−83
					200	20.66	20.67−83, 20.43w	−78
Bradley	Vesco	USA	22May53	183/66	LJ	8.02,8.08w	8.13	−83
Bradstock	Roald	UK	24Apr62	180/95	JT	88.26	85.34	−83
Brahm	Terry	USA	21Nov62	180/65	1500	3:38.0		
					Mile	3:54.56	4:12.27	−81
Bran	Mihai	RUM	12Jan62	190/84	TJ	16.59	16.25	−83
Brantley	Dennis	USA	13Jul61	183/71	110h	13.75	13.79,13.60w	−81
							13.7	−83
Brauer	Eckbert	GDR	11Sep59	187/110	HT	75.86	73.32	−83
Braun	Peter	FRG	1Aug62	183/64	800	1:45.62	1:47.10	−83
Brecka	Frantisek	CS	21Jun58	178/68	200	20.61	20.87	−82
Brenner	John	USA	4Jan61	192/130	SP	21.92	20.80	−83
					DT	63.44	62.16	−83
Bridges	Oliver	USA	30Jun62	192/86	400	45.45	45.58−83,45.35A	−82
Bridges	Steve	USA	17Mar60	183/77	100	10.35,	10.49,10.2	−80
						10.0w	10.35w	−83
Brige	Norbert	FRA	9Jan64	185/75	LJ	7.97	7.86i,7.83	−83
Briggs	Martin	UK	4Jan64	180/75	400h	49.86	50.22	−83
Bright	Tim	USA	28Jul60	188/79	PV	5.50i,5.40	5.51	−82
					Dec	8098	7743	−83
Bringmann	Steffen	GDR	11Mar64	183/72	100	10.30w	10.27,10.25w	−83
Britz	Kelly	CAN	29May58		Mile	3:58.46	3:58.86	−83
Broadway	Marshall	USA	12Aug62	193/79	HJ	2.25	2.26	−82
Brodeur	Michel	CAN	62		110h	13.84w	14.71	−83
Brotzmann	Norbert	GDR	4Jun61	188/70	St	8:34.02	8:21.08	−83
Brooks	Calvin	USA	8Apr63	175/66	400	45.69	45.72	−83
Brooks	Kelly	USA	30Sep58	183/110	SP	20.09	20.13	−83
Brown	Courtney	CAN	21Apr65	176/70	200	20.81	20.93	−82
Brown	Ed	USA	2Jun61	196/86	400h	49.89	49.52	−82
Brown	Gareth	UK	29Dec61	185/73	800	1:46.16	1:48.1	−83
					1k	2:17.43	2:19.89	−82
Brown	Garry	AUS	27Oct54	190/83	400h	50.52,50.4	49.37	−82
Brown	Laron	USA	10Nov63	185/76	400	45.94	45.45	−83
Brown	Mike	USA	8May57	196/94	Dec	7785e	7970m	−82
Brown	Phil	UK	6Jan62	180/73	400	45.76	45.45	−82
Brown	Ron	USA	31Mar61	180/84	100	10.12,	10.06,	
						10.05w	10.01w	−83
Bruch	Ricky	SWE	2Jul46	199/130	DT	71.26	68.58	−72
Bruin	Erik de	HOL	25May63	186/110	SP	20.58i,	19.49i,	
						20.20	18.95	−83
					DT	63.66	57.87	−82
Brummer	Deon	RSA	59		1k	2:19.00A	2:22.27	−83
					1500	3:37.7	3:46.33	−83
					Mile	3:55.62	4:00.7	−83

457

Men's Index

Brunel	Gerard	FRA	17Aug57	188/73	2k 400h	5:06.3 50.11	50.31	−83
Brunner	Wulf	FRG	20Mar62	187/104	DT	60.72	58.40	−83
Bruziks	Maris	SU	25Aug62	186/70	LJ TJ	7.91 17.15	7.31 16.55	−82 −82
Bryggare	Arto	FIN	26May58	194/82	110h	13.35	13.44	−83
Bryzgin	Viktor	SU	22Aug62	180/72	100	10.18,10.0	10.20	−83
Bubka	Sergey	SU	4Dec63	183/80	PV	5.94	5.70	−83
Bubka	Vasiliy	SU	26Nov60	184/76	PV	5.70i, 5.50	5.50 5.60i	−82 −83
Bucci	Marco	ITA	29Nov60	190/108	DT	66.96	64.56	−83
Buckingham	Jeff	USA	14Jun60	172/68	PV	5.65i,5.42	5.76	−83
Buckley	Owen	USA	3Nov59	183/80	Dec	7837m	7567	−83
Buckner	Jack	UK	22Sep61	173/62	1500	3:37.32	3:37.25	−83
					Mile	3:51.57	3:53.44	−82
					2k	5:02.6	5:01.90	−83
					3k	7:45.19	7:57.77i	−83
Budnik	Scott	USA	16Jun62	180/66	HJ	2.25i	8:02.2 2.18,2.20i	−82 −83
Budko	Vladimir	SU	4Feb65	186/79	400h	48.74	50.05	−83
Bueno	Angel	CUB	2Mar63	177/73	110h	13.89w	13.81−83, 13.7w	−82
Burkle	Thomas	FRG	11Sep58		400h	50.53	51.37	−83
Bugar	Imrich	CS	14Apr55	195/120	DT	70.26	70.72	−83
Buliga	Ion	RUM	19Mar63	185/82	Dec	7788	7667	−82
Bulti	Wodajo	ETH	11Mar57	185/60	5k 10k	13:1 08 27:58.24	13:07.39	−82
Buncic	Mike	USA	25Jul62	193/111	SP	19.50i		
					DT	64.74	59.68	−83
Bunney	Elliot	UK	11Dec66	183/76	100	10.29w	10.75,10.62w	−83
Burger	Kobus	RSA	7Nov62		400h	50.04,50.0	49.98A,50.4	−83
Burke	Ed	USA	4Mar40	185/112	HT	74.34	74.10	−83
Burns	Art	USA	19Jul54	185/118	DT	70.98	71.18	−83
Burton	Darren	USA	26Feb63	188/84	HJ	2.24	2.21	−83
Busse	Andreas	GDR	6May59	185/69	1k 1500	2:16.3 3:34.10	2:15.25 3:37.09	−83 −80
Busse	Joachim	FRG	10Mar54	189/81	LJ	8.01	8.12	−81
Butler	James	USA	21Jun60	175/66	200	20.31,	20.32,20.23A	−82
Butler	Peter	CAN	15Feb58	185/65	10k	20.3w 28:28.7	20.07Aw 28:12.0	−82 −81
Bychkov	Vitaliy	SU	12Apr60	182/107	HT	74.68	76.48	−82
Byers	Tom	USA	12May55	185/71	1500 Mile	3:37.95 3:55.7i	3:35.75 3:50.84	−82 −82
Bystedt	Kjell	SWE	24May60	189/112	HT	74.62	72.84	−83
Cabral	Carlos	POR	20Jun52	177/62	2k	5:06.4		
Cado	Jan	CS	7May63	181/76	LJ	8.09	7.72	−82
					TJ	17.34	17.06	−83
Caetano	Cidalio	POR	22Jan52	173/67	Mar	2:11:42	2:14:49	−83
Cai	Shu	CHN	14Jun62	176/68	HJ	2.27	2.29	−82
Caire	Anthony	USA	16Dec63	190/82	HJ	2.25	2.235	−83
Calderon	Raul	CUB	27Nov62	183/92	DT	63.18	60.48	−83
Caldwell	Greg	USA	28Jul57	188/82	TJ	16.70	16.86,17.03w	−81
Caldwell	Willie	USA	25Sep63	186/75	400	45.36	45.96	−83
Callan	Richard	UK	15Nov55	180/64	5k	13:27.67	13:27.14	−82
Cameron	Bert	JAM	16Nov59	188/79	400	45.07	44.58	−81
Campbell	Tonie	USA	14Jun60	188/77	110h	13.23,13.1	13.32,13.1	−83
Campos	Joao	POR	22Sep58	173/55	2k 5k	5:00.8 13:19.10	13:36.5	−82
Canario	Ezequiel	POR	10Apr60	181/60	3k 5k	7:49.8 13:26.50	13:30.43	−83
Cannon	Mike	USA	26Nov64	175/64	400	45.85	45.48A,45.72	−83
Cannon	Robert	USA	9Jul58	186/74	TJ	17.04	17.18	−82

Men's Index

Name	First	Nat	DOB	Ht/Wt	Event	Mark1	Mark2	Year
Cano	Alfonso	SPA	14Mar60	182/68	PV	5.50	5.20	−83
Canovic	Novica	YUG	29Nov61	192/77	HJ	2.27	2.23	−83
Canti	Aldo	FRA	9Mar61	185/80	200	20.69	20.99−83,20.79w	−82
					400	45.09	45.29	−83
Carey	Eddie	USA	11May60	180/73	400	45.74	44.94A,45.20	−83
Caristan	Stephane	FRA	31Mar64	187/75	110h	13.43	13.86	−83
Carlowitz	Jens	GDR	8Aug64	185/75	400	44.95	45.72	−83
Carreira	Jose-Luis	SPA	30Mar62	169/63	1500	3:38.79		
Carter	Carl	USA	7Mar64	180/82	100	10.12w	10.39w	−83
					200	20.80,20.69w	20.9w	−83
Carter	Dannie	USA	27Dec60	178/66	100	10.33,	10.45,10.28w	−82
					200	20.53, 20.45w	20.66A, 20.49w	−82
Carter	Jerome	USA	25Mar63	185/66	HJ	2.30	2.31i,2.27	−83
Carter	Mike	USA	29Oct60	189/127	SP	21.76	21.25i,21.20	−81
Cartlidge	Perry	USA	29Mar63	175/75	400	45.86	47.59	−83
Casanas	Alejandro	CUB	29Jan54	188/79	110h	13.53, 13.40w	13.21 13.2	−77 −75
Cassuto	David	USA	3Feb66	196/84	100	10.1w		
Castello	Jorge	SPA	30Sep60	180/67	St	8:35.35	8:37.70	−82
Castro	Eduardo	MEX	1May54	173/63	5k	13:30.59	13:30.99	−83
Cecchini	Stefano	ITA	22Oct61	172/52	800	1:46.60	1:47.0	−83
					1500	3:38.67	3:42.99	−83
Centelles	J.Francisco	CUB	26Jan61	196/81	HJ	2.30	2.32	−83
Chaliy	Valentin	SU	3Jul58	185/99	HT	73.70	72.40	−83
Chashchin	Yuriy	SU	63		400h	50.34	50.26	−83
Chatta	Ahmed Kh.	EGY	23Jan61	190/115	SP	19.58	18.41	−82
Chekmaryov	Igor	SU	58		TJ	16.46i,16.44	16.92	−83
Chernikov	Vladimir	SU	3Aug59	188/74	TJ	17.19	17.10	−83
Chernyayev	Aleksandr	SU	19May60	177/68	PV	5.70	5.71	−83
Chernyetskiy	Nikolay	SU	29Nov59	186/78	400	45.9	45.12A−79,45.51	−83
					400h	49.78	−0−	
Cheruiyot	Charles	KEN	2Dec64	165/54	5k	13:18.41	13:25.33	−83
Cheruiyot	Kipkoech	KEN	2Dec64	164/55	1500	3:37.0	3:34.92	−83
Chesire	Joseph	KEN	12Nov57	167/57	1500 3k	3:34.52 7:49.4	3:49.0	−83
Chevallier	Franck	FRA	3Jan64	185/71	110h	13.85,13.84w	14.12	−83
Chiba	Teruo	JAP	3Aug57		Mar	2:12:33	2:15:25	−83
Chorlton	Mike	UK	19Jan63	173/60	5k	13:32.71	13:38.71	−83
Chouri	Mohamed A.	TUN	7May62	170/60	10k	28:07.24	29:08.1	−83
Christie	Linford	UK	2Apr60	184/77	100	10.31w	10.46,10.4	−83
Chumakov	Viktor	SU	31May57	176/59	3k	7:49.47		
					5k	13:29.68	13:30.56	−83
Chuntunov	Sergey	SU	59		Dec	7821m		
Churilin	Yuriy	SU	59		LJ	7.94i,7.92	7.85i,7.76	−83
Chyuzhas	Anatoliy	SU	18Apr56	180/103	HT	80.16	80.00	−83
Cierpinski	Waldemar	GDR	3Aug50	170/59	Mar	2:12:00	2:09:55	−76
Ciofani	Walter	FRA	17Feb62	185/105	HT	76.38	72.08	−83
Clark	Belfred	USA	19Aug65	183/79	400h	49.45	52.37	−82
Clark	Cletus	USA	20Jan62	193/86	110h	13.41,13.39w	13.56	−83
Clark	Darren	AUS	6Sep65	179/76	200	20.76	20.49	−83
					400	44.75	45.05	−83
Clark	Oki	USA	14Nov60	180/69	800	1:46.90	1:48.21	−83
Clary	Don	USA	29Jul57	175/74	5k	13:28.62	13:28.88	−83
					10k	28:07.01	28:13.98	−82
Cleary	Fred	USA	13Oct62	183/70	400h	50.34	51.45	−83
Cleveland	Johnny	USA	10May66	183/75	LJ	7.92	7.48	−83
Clyne	Fraser	UK	23Aug55	180/64	Mar	2:11:49	2:14:29	−83
Coe	Sebastian	UK	29Sep56	175/54	800	1:43.64	1:41.73	−81
					1500	3:32.39	3:31.95	−81
					Mile	3:54.6	3:47.33	−81
Collet	Philippe	FRA	13Dec63	176/70	PV	5.60	5.60	−83

Men's Index

Collins	Bill	USA	20Nov50	183/67	200	20.69	20.52–77,20.2	−76
Conley	Mike	USA	5Oct62	185/78	200	20.37,20.0	21.09,20.73w	−83
					LJ	8.22,8.23w	8.28,8.38w	−83
					TJ	17.50	17.23i,	
							17.21,17.37w	−83
Connolly	Jim	USA	24Mar63	185/88	Dec	7746	7768	−83
Connor	Keith	UK	16Sep57	186/78	TJ	16.87 I	7.57A,17.81w,	
							17.30	−82
Cook	Darwin	USA	16Jul62	178/75	100	10.26,10.19w	10.20	−82
					200	20.73	20.87,20.66w	−83
Cook	Garry	UK	10Jan58	185/72	800	1:44.55	1:44.71	−82
Cooper	Brad	BAH	30Jun57	188/132	DT	64.08	66.72	−82
Cooper	Brian	USA	21Aug65	180/79	LJ	7.97		
Cooper	Dedy	USA	22May56	191/77	110h	13.85w	13.34–80,13.2w	−81
Cooper	Ed	USA	4Sep63	185/68	400h	50.09,49.8	50.78	−83
Cooper	Fabian	USA	14Jan64		200	20.73	21.27,20.88w,	
							21.0	−82
Cooper	Jim	USA	6Oct59	180/65	St	8:30.10	8:28.77	−83
Cooper	Todd	USA	4Mar63	178/64	PV	5.49	5.32	−83
Cooper	William	USA	23Nov62	193/84	110h	13.87	13.82–82,13.6	−83
Corgos	Antonio	SPA	10Mar60	183/76	LJ	8.02i,8.02	8.23	−80
Council	Daron	USA	26Dec64	188/73	200	20.68	20.9–82,21.15	−83
Cova	Alberto	ITA	1Dec58	176/58	3k	7:51.18	7:46.40	−83
					5k	13:18.24	13:13.71	−82
					10k	27:47.54	27:37.59	−83
Cowling	Larry	USA	6Jul60	191/76	110h	13.43	13.39	−82
Crabb	Steve	UK	30Nov63	179/64	800	1:45.80	1:47.85	−83
					1k	2:18.13		
					1500	3:35.16	3:48.6	−82
					Mile	3:54.36	4:08.4	−83
Crain	Brady	USA	8Aug56	168/62	200	20.57,20.08w	20.37	−83
Cram	Steve	UK	14Oct60	186/69	800	1:46.0m,	1:43.61	−83
						1:46.05		
					1k	2:15.98	2:15.12	−82
					1500	3:33.13	3:31.66	−83
					Mile	3:49.65	3:49.90	−82
Crawford	Hasely	TRI	16Aug50	187/90	100	10.25	10.06,10.0	−76
							9.8w	−75
Criddle	Byron	USA	21Feb62	179/74	TJ	16.58,17.08w	16.86,16.96Aw	−83
Crist	John	USA	28Aug54	188/84	Dec	8130	8149	−79
Crouser	Brian	USA	9Jul62	188/102	JT	89.20	86.24	−82
Crouser	Mitch	USA	30Dec57	192/118	DT	65.62	63.62	−82
Crunkleton	George	USA	5Feb56	192/84	200	20.74A	20.82	−83
Cruz	Joaquim C.	BRA	12Mar63	187/73	800	1:41.77	1:44.04	−83
					1k	2:14.09	2:15.28	−83
					1500	3:36.46	3:39.5	−83
					Mile	3:53.00		
Culp	Greg	USA	26Aug60	188/79	Dec	7837	7797w,7891m	−83
Cummings	Paul	USA	5Sep53	177/63	10k	27:43.7	30:58.96A	−83
Cunningham	James	USA	4Jun62	185/79	HJ	2.24i	2.21	−83
Curp	Mark	USA	5Jan59	174/52	10k	28:01.02	28:42.35	−82
Curran	Anthony	USA	27Jun59	183/75	PV	5.40	5.55	−82
Cutler	Mickey	USA	16Jan59	185/109	JT	81.20	75.36	−82
Dabulskis	Algis	SU	15Dec61		10k	28:24.13		
					5k	13:31.65		−83
Daenens	Peter	BEL	23Nov60	175/60	5k	13:35.4	13:48.0	−82
					St	8:20.7m	8:23.11	−83
Dahl	Oyvind	NOR	12May51	181/64	Mar	2:12:19	2:11:40	−80

Men's Index

D'Aleo	Giovanni	ITA	1Jul59	178/65	10k	28:14.62	28:40.03	−83
Dalhauser	Roland	SWZ	12Apr58	191/86	HJ	2.30i,	2.31	−81
						2.30	2.32i	−82
Daniel	Clarence	USA	11Jun61	183/79	400	45.39	45.81	−83
Daniels	Dave	USA	28Oct58	188/73	St	8:24.77	8:24.32	−83
Daniels	Sansiski	USA	31May64	183/73	110h	13.66,13.65w,	13.95	−83
						13.6		
Daniels	Scott	USA	23Apr60	187/88	Dec	7922m	7501	−81
Danneberg	Rolf	FRG	1Mar53	198/112	DT	67.40	63.74	−82
Da Silva	Joao B.	BRA	22Aug63	178/74	200	20.30	20.51A,20.65,	
							20.5	−83
Da Silva	Jose Joao	BRA	5May54	178/62	10k	28:09.59	28:37.3	−81
Da Silva	Robson C.	BRA	4Sep64	187/64	200	20.71	20.95	−82
Davies-Hale	Paul	UK	2Jun62	176/60	3k	7:45.45	7:51.18	−83
					5k	13:24.59	13:35.95	−81
					St	8:20.83	8:29.85	−81
Davis	Bruce	USA	25Feb63	173/70	100	10.16w,	10.22	−82
						10.1	10.21w	−83
Davis	Dale	USA	16Jul60	193/84	HJ	2.24	2.20i−83,2.19	−82
Davis	Del	USA	3May60	188/73	HJ	2.29	2.32	−82
Davis	Mike	USA	5Jan64	187/72	LJ	7.90,8.11w	7.56	−83
Davis	Reggie	USA			400h	50.10		
Davis	Sylvester	USA	11Sep62	185/73	400	46.0	47.3*i	−83
					400h	50.23	50.85	−83
Davito	Gianni	ITA	19Aug57	193/78	HJ	2.25i	2.27i−82,2.27	−83
Davydov	Vadim	SU	60		100	10.1	10.2,10.45	−82
Deal	Lance	USA	21Aug61	188/108	DT	61.62	60.84	−83
Debacker	Pascal	FRA	8Apr60	170/58	St	8:20.34	8:26.86	−83
de Beer	Chris	RSA	18Aug61		JT	83.44	82.44	−83
Debele	Bekele	ETH	12Mar63	170/55	5k	13:33.74	13:49.19	−83
					10k	28:03.06	27:49.30	−83
de Castella	Robert	AUS	27Feb57	180/65	Mar	2:09:09	2:08:18	−81
Dedukhov	Sergey	SU	4May63	194/90	400h	50.1	50.6 −82, 51.06	−83
Dees	Tony	USA	6Aug63	193/91	200	20.54	20.64,20.37w,	
							20.2w	−83
					110h	13.65	13.68,13.6	−83
Degtyar	Oleg	SU	64		110h	13.7	14.3	−83
Degtyaryev	Grigoriy	SU	16Aug58	190/90	Dec	8652	8538	−83
de la Garza	Juan	MEX	20Sep61	180/83	JT	82.44	80.08	−83
de la Parte	Santiago	SPA	18Aug48	166/58	Mar	2:11:10	2:12:54	−83
Deleze	Pierre	SWZ	25Sep58	175/62	1500	3:33.64	3:32.97	−83
					Mile	3:56.81	3:50.38	−82
					2k	4:57.27	4:56.51	−83
Delis	Luis M.	CUB	6Dec57	185/106	DT	69.74	71.06	−83
DeLoach	Joe	USA	5Jun67	182/76	100	10.34w,10.0w	10.5	−83
					200	20.79w	21.33	−83
Delonge	Marco	GDR	16Jun66	194/77	LJ	7.96w	7.16	−83
del Prado	Isidro	PHI	15May59	176/73	400	45.57	46.24	−83
De Madonna	Gianni	ITA	14Jun54	178/65	10k	28:04.60	28:32.4	−83
Demirev	Krasimir	BUL	28Aug62	180/70	400h	50.51	50.00	−83
Demyanyuk	Aleksey	SU	30Jul58	188/80	HJ	2.33	2.33	−81
Dennis	Ronnie	USA	65	175/64	200	20.80w,20.3w	21.2*21.38*	−83
de Oliveira	Arnaldo S.	BRA	26Mar64	172/71	200	20.62	22.1	−83
de Raad	Detlef	FRG	10May60	183/71	PV	5.40	5.45i−83,5.40	−82
Desruelles	Patrick	BEL	24Apr57	188/78	PV	5.50i	5.60i,5.60	−81
Desruelles	Ronald	BEL	14Feb55	186/80	100	10.25,	10.42	−79
						10.0	9.9	−78
					200	20.66	20.96	−79
					LJ	7.94	8.08	−79
de Waal	Arend	RSA	3Jan63		400h	50.53A,	A50.86,	
						50.2A	50.5A,50.7	−83
De Wijngaert	Rudi	BEL	23Jun59		1500	3:37.94	3:39.80	−83

461

Men's Index

Dexter	Mike	USA	31Dec64		200	20.5	20.78,20.56w	−83
Dia Ba	Amadou	SEN	22Sep58	188/72	400	46.04	45.8−82,46.33	−83
					400h	48.73	49.03	−83
Dial	Joe	USA	26Oct62	174/59	PV	5.66	5.62i−83,5.60	−82
Diallo	Boubacar	SEN	22Nov60	176/65	400	46.07	45.86	−83
Diallo	Mamadou	SEN	16Nov54	180/70	TJ	16.68	16.70	−83
Diaz Ferreira	Antonio E.	BRA	2Mar60	173/62	400h	49.65˙	50.04	−81
Diemer	Brian	USA	10Oct61	178/64	St	8:13.16	8:22.13	−83
Dima	Vasile	RUM	3Jan58	186/74	TJ	16.60	16.57	−83
Dimitrov	Kamen	BUL	18Jan62	194/90	DT	64.56	61.72	−83
Dimitrov	Raicho	BUL	22May55	173/77	JT	82.42	80.28	−82
Dixon	Adam	USA	12Mar60	187/79	1500	3:36.71	3:43.02	−83
					Mile	3:57.2i	3:59.39	−83
Dixon	Fred	USA	5Nov49	192/88	Dec	8067*	8390	−77
Dixon	Malcolm	USA	11Oct59	188/84	110h	13.89,	13.75,	
						13.86w	13.54w	−83
Dixon	Rod	NZ	13Jul50	186/70	Mar	2:12:57	2:08:59	−83
Djedjemel	Rene M.	IVC	5Jun58	186/80	400h	50.27,50.2	52.3	−82
Dmitriyev	Dmitriy	SU	3Mar56	175/65	1500	3:36.50	3:39.05	−81
					3k	7:42.05	7:44.5	−82
					5k	13:17.37	13:19.18	−82
Dmitriyev	Pavel	SU	57		HT	76.66	73.02	−82
DoDoo	Francis	GHA	13Apr60	179/75	TJ	16.45i	16.34−83,16.59w	−82
Doehring	Jim	USA	27Jan62	183/114	SP	19.97	18.30	−83
Doherty	John	UK	22Jul61	175/62	5k	13:26.23	13:47.52	−81
Dolegiewicz	Bishop	CAN	8Jul53	198/145	SP	19.74	20.85	−78
Dombrowski	Lutz	GDR	25Jun59	187/87	LJ	8.50	8.54	−80
Domorosov	Mikhail	SU	3May55	178/107	SP	20.38	20.62	−82
Donakowski	Bill	USA	21Jun56	168/59	10k	28:20.1	28:13.9	−79
Donakowski	Gerard	USA	20Feb60	172/58	10k	28:03.92	28:53.7	−83
Donias	Alain	FRA	15Jan60	184/75	PV	5.50	5.50	−81
Donoghue	Ross	USA	19Jul59	183/61	1500	3:36.95	3:37.89	−83
					Mile	3:55.26	3:57.3	−83
					5k	13:33.37	13:39.9	−82
Donovan	Paul	IRL	11Jul63	179/63	1500	3:38.31	3:42.87	−83
					Mile	3:55.82	4:01.18	−83
Donskikh	Sergey	SU	25Jan56	196/128	SP	21.09	20.58i,20.27	−83
Dorozhon	Sergey	SU	17Feb64	184/110	HT	76.54	78.00	−83
Doshev	Valentin	BUL	12Apr63	180/110	HT	73.02	70.74	−83
Draddy	Vince	USA	19Apr61	184/66	3k	7:49.55		
					5k	13:32.6		
Dragoescu	Petru	RUM	22Jul62	183/69	800	1:46.81	1:46.43	−83
Druppers	Rob	HOL	29Apr62	186/70	800	1:44.60	1:44.20	−83
					1k	2:17.07	2:17.20	−83
Duany	Ubaldo	CUB	16May60	183/73	LJ	8.14	8.10	−81
Dubinin	Vladimir	SU	7Oct63	180/118	HT	74.64	77.12	−83
Duckett	Terrence	USA	7Mar62	188/70	200	20.5	21.1	−82
Duginyets	Igor	SU	20May56	196/100	DT	66.56	68.52	−82
Duhaime	Greg	CAN	11Aug53	180/64	5k	13:34.7	13:40.6	−82
					St	8:26.32	8:19.05	−82
Dumchev	Yuriy	SU	5Aug58	200/128	DT	67.42	71.86	−83
Dunecki	Leszek	POL	2Oct56	180/72	100	10.26	10.31−78,10.28A	−79
					200	20.62	20.24A,20.50	−79
Duplantis	Greg	USA	22Jan62	173/61	PV	5.40	5.48	−81
Dupont	Philippe	FRA	31May58	180/64	800	1:46.51	1:45.55	−83
Dupree	Rayfield	USA	2Apr53	186/80	TJ	16.58	16.76,17.01w	−76
Dupuis	John	USA	22Mar54	188/117	SP	19.85	19.77	−80
Durham	Nat	USA	27Apr54	190/84	PV	5.60i,5.55	5.41	−79
Durr	Kris	USA	21May64	180/70	400	45.84	47.10	−83
Dvoretskiy	Sergey	SU	30Apr57	191/108	HT	78.62	75.76	−82
Dyatlov	Oleg	SU	22Apr49	177/108	HT	75.46	77.08	−83

Men's Index

Dyer	Wayne	AUS	18Feb58	175/66	St	8:35.02		
Dyulgherov	Emanuil	BUL	7Feb55	178/95	HT	80.64	77.98	−83
Dzienisik	Miroslaw	POL	5Jun59	176/61	10k	28:28.03		
Easker	John	USA	30May63	178/67	10k	28:29.2	30:23.09	−83
Easley	Craig	USA			110h	13.7w		
Eddings	Trent	USA			SP	19.53		
Edge	Dave	CAN	11Nov54	170/55	Mar	2:13:20	2:11:04	−83
Edwards	Clancy	USA	9Aug55	175/76	200	20.61w	20.03,20.0	−78
Edwards	Dothel	USA	9Sep66	193/72	HJ	2.27	2.285	−83
Edwards	Norman	JAM	24Sep62	185/82	100	10.21	10.3	−82
Egbunike	Innocent	NIG	30Nov61	174/68	100	10.15,10.12w	10.26	−83
					200	20.59,20.23w	20.42,20.4	−83
					400	44.81		
Einarsson	Sigurdur	ICE	28Sep62	190/102	JT	82.76	79.64	−83
Einspahr	Kregg	USA	19Apr60	180/68	St	8:33.46	8:25.05	−83
Ekblom	Tommy	FIN	20Sep59	176/62	St	8:20.54	8:19.40	−83
Elbe	Jorg	GDR	11Apr64	187/71	TJ	16.72	16.20	−83
Eldebrink	Kenth	SWE	14May55	190/95	JT	87.08	91.14	−83
Elliott	Peter	UK	9Oct62	181/67	800	1:45.49	1:43.98	−83
					1500	3:36.97	3:49.1	−82
					Mile	3:55.71	4:07.4	−81
Emmelmann	Frank	GDR	15Sep61	185/76	100	10.19,	10.18	−83
						10.1	10.11w	−82
					200	20.46	20.33,20.23w	−81
Emmiyan	Robert	SU	19Feb65	178/69	LJ	8.13	8.01	−83
Emordi	Paul	NIG	25Dec65	189/80	LJ	7.90	7.78	−82
					TJ	16.78	15.85−82,15.86w	−83
Ene	Mihai	RUM	24Jul60	183/69	TJ	16.73	16.74	−83
Enekes	Bela	HUN	22Jul63	175/57	2k	5:06.05		
Engels	Hawie	RSA	27Dec62		400h	A50.4	51.27	−83
Epps	Sammy	USA	6Jan62	185/79	400	46.06	46.9*	−81
Erickson	Steve	USA	13Jan61	190/86	Dec	7767	7791	−83
Eriksson	Thomas	SWE	1May63	183/74	HJ	2.28	2.27	−82
					TJ	16.43,	15.12	−82
						16.51w	16.06w	−83
Erixon	Mats	SWE	19Mar58	175/61	5k	13:26.96	13:28.08	−82
					10k	28:07.49	27:56.56	−82
Evangelisti	Giovanni	ITA	11Sep61	179/60	LJ	8.24	8.09	−83
							8.10i,8.21w	−82
Evans	Dwayne	USA	13Oct58	187/75	100	10.34,10.16w	10.20,10.07w	−81
					200	20.38,	20.22	−76
						20.21w	20.20w	−81
Ewaliko	Rod	USA	18Apr54	188/109	JT	90.66	88.70	−80
Eyestone	Ed	USA	15Jun61	185/66	5k	13:32.52	13:51.0	−83
					10k	27:56.06	28:46.1	−83
Fall	Moussa	SEN	28Aug63	178/67	800	1:45.03	1:49.0	−83
Farmer	Peter	USA	25Jun52	184/130	HT	75.88	75.90	−79
Fedotkin	Aleksandr	SU	3Nov55	168/57	5k	13:31.08	13:17.66	−79
Fehringer	Hermann	AUT	8Dec62	180/82	PV	5.45	5.40	−83
Fell	Graeme	UK	19Mar59	184/73	St	8:17.71	8:15.16	−83
Ferner	Hans-Peter	FRG	6Jun56	176/72	800	1:45.11	1:44.93	−83
					1k	2:17.83	2:17.3	−81
Fernholm	Stefan	SWE	2Jul59	186/114	DT	66.30,67.00ex	62.08	−83
Ferreira	Serge	FRA	11Aug59	183/72	PV	5.71	5.70	−80
Filippou	Filippos	CYP	25Sep56	168/56	St	8:30.09	8:24.01	−83

463

Men's Index

Finucane	Mark	USA	25Nov56		Mar	2:11:55		
Fishman	Gennadiy	SU	7Sep59	182/68	5k	13:18.46	13:28.74	−81
Fitzpatrick	Enda	IRL	28Apr65	183/66	2k	5:09.73		
Fizuleto	Hrvoje	YUG	15Jan63	190/69	HJ	2.26	2.22	−83
Fleschen	Karl	FRG	28Jun55	177/60	5k	13:30.08	13:13.88	−77
Flynn	Ray	IRL	22Jan57	182/65	1500	3:35.06	3:33.5	−82
					Mile	3:52.79	3:49.77	−82
					3k	7:41.60	7:50.16	−81
					5k	13:19.52	13:34.7	−82
Fomochkin	Andrey	SU	24May63	182/81	Dec	7840,7912m	7511m	−82
Fontecchio	Daniele	ITA	29Dec60	188/80	110h	13.71	13.83−81,13.63w	−83
Forde	Elvis	BAR	18Nov59	180/74	400	45.32	45.5,45.57	−82
Forney	Eric	USA	12Jan62	178/74	PV	5.43	5.38	−83
Forster	Kevin	UK	16May58		Mar	2:11:41	2:14:19	−83
Foster	Charles	USA	2Jul53	183/77	110h	13.90	13.41	−76
							13.38*w	−74
Foster	Greg	USA	4Aug58	190/84	100	10.30	10.28−79,10.1w	−78
					200	20.47w	20.20	−79
					110h	13.15	13.03,13.0	−81
Fouche	Francois	RSA	5Jun63	183/71	LJ	8.00A,7.90	7.95A,7.69	−83
Fourie	Johan	RSA	2Dec59	180/70	1k	2:17.34A	2:18.25	−79
					1500	3:34.3	3:35.2	−83
					Mile	3:51.23	3:52.31	−83
					2k	4:56.5	4:57.2	−83
Fowles	Dennis	UK	18Apr51	176/67	Mar	2:12:12	2:13:21	−83
Fox	Chris	USA	22Oct58	185/57	2k	5:04.68		
					3k	7:47.18	7:49.82	−83
					5k	13:25.78	13:21.60	−83
Fraley	Doug	USA	7Mar65	185/76	PV	5.41	5.19	−83
Frank	Georg	AUT	13Jun51	192/117	DT	60.78	63.32	−81
Franks	Michael	USA	23Sep63	180/70	100	10.25	10.45	−82
					200	20.62,20.58w	20.77	−83
					400	45.20	44.96A,45.22	−83
Frayne	Bruce	AUS	24Jan58	179/66	400	45.21	46.37	−82
Frazier	Ed	USA	31Mar64	180/79	400	45.77	47.8	−82
Frazier	James	USA	16Sep59	183/70	HJ	2.24	2.29	−80
Frazier	Ken	USA	25Feb63	178/75	LJ	8.14	7.92	−83
Freimuth	Uwe	GDR	10Sep61	191/90	Dec	8704	8501	−83
Friedrich	Lutz	GDR	8Aug61	196/110	DT	62.40	59.38	−82
Frombold	Wolfgang	FRG	11Jan59	173/65	1k	2:18.22	2:20.30	−80
Frommeyer	Paul	FRG	28Jun57	193/74	HJ	2.24i,2.24	2.34	−83
Fulop	Laszlo	HUN/FRA	2Jan57	178/72	PV	5.40	5.40	−82
Fuzesi	Sandor	HUN	15Dec59	186/120	HT	74.62	72.94	−82
Furdylo	Vladimir	SU	6Apr58		JT	85.42	82.70	−82
Futterknecht	Thomas	AUT	24Dec62	177/68	400h	49.92	50.11	−83
Fuwa	Hiroki	JAP	9Jul66	170/60	100	10.34	10.46	−83
Fye	Oumar	GAM	13Sep60	183/80	100	10.1	10.64−81,10.4	−83
Gaffney	George	USA	25Jul60	185/79	LJ	8.02	8.18Ai,8.06	−83
Gambke	Wolfram	FRG	2Nov59	180/80	JT	85.80	85.64	−81
Gamlin	Dirk	GDR	26Oct63	191/84	TJ	16.64i,16.42	16.17,16.37w	−83
Garcia	Jorge	SPA	2May61	170/54	5k	13:32.17	13:28.20	−83
Garcia	Richard	USA	22Mar61	180/70	St	8:34.13	8:37.91	−83
Garner	Doug	USA	8Jun54	183/75	TJ	16.59	16.94w−80,16.64	−82
Garrett	James	USA	15Feb64	178/60	800	1:46.77	1:48.02	−83
Gartung	Viktor	SU	18May60	189/85	Dec	8017	7793,8109m	−83
Gasparoni	Marc	FRA	15Jul59	170/75	100	10.35w	10.36−83,10.2	−80
					200	20.67	20.89	−83
Gassowski	Janusz	POL	1Mar58	189/118	SP	20.85	20.68	−83
Gataullin	Rodion	SU	23Nov65	191/78	PV	5.65	5.55	−83
Gavras	Sergey	SU	16Apr57	185/95	JT	86.18	85.52	−83
Gavrilyuk	Vladimir	SU	17Jun60	182/78	JT	81.42	79.92	−83
Gavryushin	Sergey	SU	27Jun59	192/125	SP	21.60	21.03	−82

Men's Index

Gecsek	Tibor	HUN	22Sep64	182/84	HT	73.66	67.90	−83
Gees	Jef	BEL	10Dec56		5k	13:26.13	13:26.61	−83
					10k	28:22.13	28:34.2	−80
Gefre	Gary	USA	15Mar57	190/91	Dec	7718,	7562	−83
						7819m	7758m	−80
Geinaert	Johan	BEL	9Jan51	174/64	Mar	2:12:16	2:14:40	−83
Gelhausen	Udo	FRG	5Jul56	188/127	SP	20.00	19.74	−82
Gellens	Patrick	FRA	8Feb59	184/74	Dec	7829	7680	−83
Gemizhev	Nikolay	BUL	4Aug56	188/110	SP	20.20	20.01	−82
Georgakopoulos	Konstanti.	GRE	14Jul63	186/102	DT	62.14	62.58	−83
George	Vernon	USA	6Oct64	190/75	LJ	8.07w	7.72	−83
Gerasimenya	Viktor	SU	30Jan60	187/78	TJ	17.10	17.01	−82
Gerber	Farley	USA	25Apr60	178/68	St	8:19.27	8:27.66	−83
Gericke	Henning	RSA	23Jun60	180/71	1k	2:18.38A		
					1500	3:38.0	3:41.1	−82
					Mile	3:56.17	3:58.7	−83
					2k	5:06.3	5:07.6	−83
Gerloff	Maco	GDR	19Jul64	189/105	HT	74.26	72.64	−83
Gerson	Dmitriy	SU	60		DT	60.74	58.74	−83
Gerstenberg	Detlef	GDR	5Mar57	186/115	HT	80.50	78.94	−80
Ghesini	Agostino	ITA	4Aug58	190/96	JT	85.68	89.12	−83
Gibicsar	Istvan	HUN	13Jan57	190/72	HJ	2.26	2.24,2.26i	−80
Giegiel	Romuald	POL	8May57	186/78	110h	13.69,	13.57	−82
						13.64w	13.54w	−83
Gilbert	Paul	AUS	29Dec60	175/60	800	1:45.6	1:45.90	−83
Gilchrist	John	USA	17Apr63		100	10.36		
					200	20.74		
Gilchrist	Mike	NZ	9Aug60	178/69	1500	3:38.42	3:38.4	−83
Gilkes	Eugene	UK	5Mar62	193/90	Dec	7718,7930mw	7476	−83
Gillingham	Martin	UK	9Sep63	182/72	400h	50.24	53.2	−82
Girma	Berhanu	ETH	60	158/50	10k	27:57.89	28:16.60	−83
Girvan	Martin	UK	17Apr60	194/118	HT	77.54	74.18	−82
Gjovaag	Roger	NOR	7Sep56	192/83	St	8:34.70	8:38.63	−83
Gladwin	John	UK	7May63	190/70	800	1:46.48	1:46.46	−82
					1k	2:19.14	2:23.18	−83
Glance	Harvey	USA	28Mar57	171/67	100	10.09,10.07w	10.11	−76
						10.0	9.8−77,10.07w	−78
					200	20.42,	20.39	−79
						20.3	20.1	−76
Glass	Jeff	CAN	21Apr62	185/82	110h	13.73A,13.79	13.98,13.96w	−83
Gloor	Rene	SWZ	3Nov56	179/72	LJ	8.06,8.11w	8.07	−82
Goater	Julian	UK	12Jan53	183/66	5k	13:30.13	13:15.59	−81
					10k	28:13.02	27:34.58	−82
Golanko	Waldemar	POL	15Jul61	179/70	TJ	16.57,16.60w	16.39	−83
Golda	Ireneusz	POL	23Jan55	189/115	HT	77.00	77.96	−82
Gomez	Jose	MEX	19Mar56	165/55	5k	13:34.1	13:29.4	−80
					10k	28:28.50	27:56.74	−83
					Mar	2:12:47	2:12:27	−83
Gonsalves	Greg	USA	3Aug63	188/70	HJ	2.26i	2.20	−82
Gonzales	Mike	USA	13Mar64	185/84	Dec	7960	7097	−83
Gonzalez	Alex	FRA	16Mar51	183/71	1500	3:37.58	3:35.07	−79
Gonzalez	Benjamin	SPA	12Apr58	177/67	800	1:46.58	1:46.6	−82
Gonzalez	Francis	FRA	6Feb52	171/59	5k	13:26.22	13:20.24	−79
					10k	28:26.04		
Gonzalez	Jorge	PR	20Dec52	177/57	Mar	2:12:48	2:12:43	−83
Gonzalez	Jose Luis	SPA	8Dec57	180/61	1500	3:34.61	3:33.44	−83
					Mile	3:56.41	3:49.67	−81
					3k	7:45.44	7:46.57	−81
Gonzalez	Juan A.	SPA	24Jun60	171/57	TJ	16.64	16.22	−83
Gonzalez	Ramon	CUB	24Aug65	182/83	JT	86.82	87.90	−83
Gonzalez	Tomas	CUB	11Jun59	178/75	100	10.33w	10.37,10.1	−83
							10.26w	−81
					200	20.68	20.85	−83

465

Men's Index

						20.55w	20.5A	−79
Goode	Milton	USA	16Feb60	183/73	HJ	2.28	2.27−81, 2.31i	−82
Gorak	Stanislaw	POL	24Feb59	182/90	JT	88.10	87.40	−83
Gordien	Marcus	USA	29Apr55	194/116	DT	65.28	63.72	−83
Gordon	Dave	USA	30Aug59	175/58	Mar	2:11:59	2:11:41	−83
Gordon	Lee	USA	10Oct63	172/70	100	10.29,10.21w	10.51	−83
Gotovskiy	Yuriy	SU	31May61	194/74	HJ	2.25i	2.24	−83
Grabowski	Stanislaw	POL	26Apr55	190/109	DT	63.50	64.38	−83
Graddy	Sam	USA	10Feb64	178/70	100	10.09,	10.18,	
						10.08w	10.16w	−83
					200	20.62	21.21	−83
Granyenkov	Vladimir	SU	1Jun59	194/78	HJ	2.33	2.30	−81
Gray	Johnny	USA	19Jun60	190/76	800	1:42.96	1:45.41	−82
					1k	2:17.27		
Gray	Ken	JAM	9Dec60	188/76	400h	49.91	50.11	−83
Gray	Rob	CAN	5Oct56	188/120	DT	67.32	62.94	−83
Greaves	Wilbert	UK	23Dec56	187/77	110h	13.86,13.82w	13.66	−82
Grebenstein	Matthias	GDR	12Jan64	186/70	HJ	2.27	2.21	−83
Green	Bill	USA	1May61	178/73	400	45.65	45.07,45.0A	−81
Green	Bill	USA	28Apr60	186/109	HT	76.52	71.80	−83
Greer	Victor	USA	29May62	183/82	200	20.77	21.50	−83
Gregorek	John	USA	15Apr60	185/75	3k	7:49.12i	7:56.4i	−80
					St	8:18.45	8:21.26	−81
Griffiths	Steve	JAM	30Jun64	175/65	400	46.08	46.37	−83
Grigorash	Igor	SU	18Aug59	184/104	HT	81.20	76.00	−83
Grimes	Jason	USA	10Sep59	178/56	LJ	8.32,	8.39	−83
						8.40w	8.57w	−82
Grimes	Malcolm	USA	12Aug57	186/77	LJ	7.92A		
Grishchenkov	Vasiliy	SU	23Jan58	181/78	TJ	16.69	17.55	−83
Gritskevich	Aleksey	SU	12Nov62		JT	82.18	84.68	−83
Gromov	Ivan	SU	13Mar56	180/80	JT	81.36	83.56	−77
Groshev	Vyacheslav	SU	58		St	8:34.2	8:32.0,8:32.07	−83
Gross	Axel	GDR	20Sep60	193/81	TJ	16.68	16.64,16.84w	−83
Gross	Jeff	USA	4Mar63	183/70	400	45.54	47.02	−82
Grothe	Jurgen	FRG	14Apr60	182/69	1k	2:19.69	2:17.93	−82
Grummt	Steffen	GDR	15Sep59	191/94	Dec	8186	8274	−82
Grushnik	Aleksandr	SU	4May59	183/73	TJ	16.42	16.41	−83
Gruzenkin	Viktor	SU	19Dec51	175/78	Dec	8337	8320	−83
Gryaznov	Valeriy	SU	3Jan61	170/59	St	8:26.43	8:29.61	−81
Gudilin	Vladimir	SU	28Aug52	185/107	HT	76.94	74.68	−81
Gunthor	Werner	SWZ	1Jun61	200/124	SP	20.80	20.01	−83
Guimaraes	Agberto	BRA	18Aug57	175/57	800	1:43.63	1:45.13	−82
					1k	2:17.52	2:15.81	−83
Guss	Lloyd	CAN	22Jan59	188/81	400h	50.01	50.31,49.98A	−82
Gutteridge	Jeff	UK	28Oct56	183/76	PV	5.40	5.40	−80
Gyori	Lajos	HUN	4Jan56	189/100	DT	62.24	62.04	−83
Haas	Christian	FRG	22Aug58	181/76	100	10.20	10.16−83,10.12w	−80
					200	20.61	20.46	−83
Haber	Ralf	GDR	18Aug62	189/110	HT	79.38	79.02	−83
Hacker	Tim	USA	27Dec62	172/64	1500	3:37.78	3:45.08	−82
Hackett	Robert	USA	3Aug64	172/68	200	20.62	20.77	−83
Hackney	Roger	UK	2Sep57	183/74	3k	7:49.47	7:53.39i	−83
							7:55.9	−80
					St	8:20.16	8:19.38	−83
Hadfield	Peter	AUS	21Jan55	188/87	Dec	8089m	7886−81, 7931m	−79
Haberle	Hans-Joachim	FRG	7Apr59	185/80	Dec	8053	7967−81, 8018m	−83
Hafsteinsson	Vesteinn	ICE	12Dec60	190/112	DT	63.60	65.60	−83
Hagelbrand	Jan	SWE	8Jul54	175/62	St	8:28.28	8:26.51	−82

Hagelsteens	Alex	BEL	15Jul56	178/60	5k	13:35.1	13:28.56	−81
					10k	28:17.00	27:26.95	−82
Haley	Roddie	USA	6Dec65	178/64	400	45.66		
Hall	Randy	USA	1Apr59	183/73	PV	5.41	5.54	−80
Hall	Steven	USA	20Feb63	172/70	100	10.33w	10.34,10.29w	−83
					200	20.66	20.75w	−82
Hamilton	Owen	JAM	21Apr59	178/64	800	1:46.02	1:46.9	−80
Hanacek	Zdenek	CS	11Jan62	183/72	LJ	8.02	7.80i−83, 7.74	−82
Handelsman	Mark	ISR	9Jun61	183/70	800	1:46.53	1:45.3	−81
Hannecker	Alois	FRG	10Jul61	190/110	DT	64.82	63.86	−83
Hansen	Ray	USA	7Mar61	185/98	JT	86.26	81.58	−81
Harbour	Todd	USA	24Mar59	175/61	1500	3:38.22	3:33.99	−82
					Mile	3:55.29	3:50.34	−81
					5k	13:30.57	13:38.5	−82
Hargrove	Andri	USA	5Feb58	187/77	400h	50.12	50.24	−83
Harken	Brent	USA	1Dec61	192/79	HJ	2.31	2.30	−83
Harkness	Jack	CAN	11Mar59	188/113	DT	61.58dh	61.98	−82
Harkonen	Arto	FIN	31Jan59	190/95	JT	92.40	91.04	−81
Harlin	Tony	USA	4Sep59	190/120	SP	20.57	20.44	−83
Harper	Derek	USA	25Dec61	170/61	LJ	7.89i	7.78	−82
Harries	Axel	FRG	19Sep64	186/76	800	1:46.04	1:47.3	−83
Harris	Danny	USA	7Sep65	183/77	400	45.79,45.3		
					400h	48.02	−0−	
Harris	Doug	USA	16Oct62	170/66	100	10.36	10.46,10.29w	−83
Harris	Jackie	USA	31Mar61	180/86	400	45.74	45.89	−83
Harris	Rich	USA	4Mar59	175/61	1500	3:36.05	3:37.97	−81
					Mile	3:51.39	3:53.99	−82
					2k	4:59.04	4:59.33	−82
					3k	7:47.87	7:48.08	−82
Harris	Tom	USA	3May57	185/84	Dec	7768	7660m	−80
Harris	Steve	UK	17Nov61	175/60	5k	13:31.45	13:30.79	−83
Harrison	Ken	USA	13Feb65	175/68	TJ	16.50	15.96	−83
Harrison	Rob	UK	5Jun59	180/70	800	1:45.31	1:45.50	−83
					1k	2:17.20	2:17.78	−83
					Mile	3:56.76	4:10.2	−81
Hartmann	Werner	FRG	20Apr59	189/115	DT	65.60	67.54	−82
Hartnett	Joe	IRL	3Oct56	172/62	St	8:34.52	8:44.72	−83
Hassan	El Kashief	SUD	26Mar56	175/68	400	45.19	44.76A−82,45.18	−79
Hauck	Andreas	GDR	19Jun60	185/70	800	1:45.78	1:46.03	−81
					1k	2:16.3	2:19.2	−81
Haugom	Ole	NOR	23Feb57	192/100	DT	64.02	61.22	−82
Hawkins	Tranel	USA	17Sep62	196/80	400h	48.28	50.35	−83
Hayashi	Kiyoshi	JAP	61	166/54	Mar	2:12:47		
Hays	Ken	USA	5Oct56	198/84	TJ	16.67	16.23	−80
Heard	Floyd	USA	24Mar66		100	10.1w	10.5	−83
Heber-Suffrin	Dominique	FRA	7Jan55	188/77	PV	5.50i,5.40	5.50	−83
							5.50i	−82
Hegarty	Declan	IRL	12Oct60	183/102	HT	76.34	73.50	−83
Heilmann	Michael	GDR	26Oct61	175/54	Mar	2:09:30	2:11:49	−83
Heinrich	Gerald	FRG	13Dec56	192/83	PV	5.40	5.50	−81
Heisler	Randy	USA	7Aug61	192/107	DT	62.22	60.20	−83
Hejret	Daniel	CS	4Mar62	186/76	400h	50.52	51.28	−83
Helan	Serge	FRA	24Feb64	175/67	TJ	16.66	16.12	−83
Hemmila	Jari	FIN	18Nov59	178/65	10k	28:21.74	28:46.27	−83
Henderson	Chappelle	USA	19Mar61	183/75	110h	13.86w	14.00−83,13.9	−82
					400h	49.92	50.7,50.86	−83
Henderson	Dan	USA	26Jun58	183/66	5k	13:24.75	13:30.44	−83
					10k	28:02.41		
Henderson	Kevin	USA	4Feb65	183/73	400h	49.94	52.53	−83
Henderson	Reggie	USA	18May60	189/81	400	45.80	46.1	−83
Henley	Howard	USA	14Aug61	178/75	100	10.30	10.35	−81
							10.30w	−82

467

Men's Index

					200	20.80w	20.58,20.43w	−82
							20.3w	−83
Henry	Garry	AUS	17May55	178/62	10k	28:22.5	28:18.2	−80
Heras	Angel	SPA	18Sep58	177/67	400	45.54	45.98	−83
Herbert	John	UK	20Apr62	188/76	TJ	16.79i,16.77	17.05	−83
Herbst	Wes	USA	30Jun56	190/91	Dec	7701	7903	−79
Herle	Christoph	FRG	19Nov55	183/68	2k	5:05.14	5:03.9	−80
					5k	13:28.73	13:21.31	−83
					10k	28:05.0	28:03.25	−82
Herrera	Jesus	MEX	22Mar62	174/56	Mar	2:11:00		
Hertner	Roland	SWZ	21Mar57	170/63	St	8:34.25	8:32.1	−79
Hess	Jeff	USA	16Dec60	180/64	St	8:25.48	8:33.23	−82
Hikima	Kaneo	JAP	11Sep54	166/54	Mar	2:12:20	2:14:00	−83
Hill	Jim	USA	1Jul61	180/63	3k	7:48.82	7:51.63	−83
					5k	13:34.5	13:19.73	−83
Hillardt	Mike	AUS	22Jan61	180/70	800	1:46.06	1:45.74	−83
					1k	2:17.49	2:18.1	−83
					1500	3:34.20	3:38.04	−82
					Mile	3:52.34	3:53.33	−82
Hingsen	Jurgen	FRG	15Apr58	200/100	110h	13.84w	14.10	−83
					Dec	8798	8779	−83
Hintnaus	Tom	BRA	15Feb58	180/78	PV	5.56	5.60	−80
Hjeltnes	Knut	NOR	8Dec51	191/110	SP	19.91	20.55	−80
					DT	67.30	69.50	−79
Hjort	Niels Kim	DEN	29Jun59	182/62	5k	13:34.63	13:45.0	−83
Hodge	David	USA	1Oct62	183/73	PV	5.55	5.18	−83
Hodge	Robert	USA	3Aug55	174/56	10k	28:24.6	28:44.3	−82
Hoffer	Ales	CS	9Dec62	182/75	110h	13.6	14.39	−82
Hoff	Narve	NOR	10Jul57	194/99	JT	83.64	76.16	−83
Hoffmann	Zdzislaw	POL	27Aug59	190/85	TJ	17.34,17.55w	17.42	−80
Hogan	Deon	USA	21Mar60	183/82	200	20.68	20.68	−79
Hohn	Uwe	GDR	16Jul62	198/112	JT	104.80	91.34	−82
Hollender	Frank	GDR	19Nov59	189/86	100	10.35w	10.39−81,10.35w	−83
					200	20.81	21.13	−80
Hollo	Csaba	HUN	6Jul58	190/110	DT	62.40	60.00	−81
Holloway	Bernie	USA	20Nov61	180/73	400h	49.78	49.35−83,49.10A	−82
Holmes	Stan	USA	3Aug57	191/77	LJ	7.89	7.96	−80
Holopainen	Hannu	FIN	25Jan58	185/88	JT	83.66	82.84	−83
Holtom	Mark	UK	6Feb58	188/84	110h	13.82,13.60w	13.43	−82
Honey	Gary	AUS	26Jul59	183/70	LJ	8.27,8.39w	8.13	−82
Hoogewerf	Simon	CAN	11May63	175/66	800	1:46.73	1:48.01	−83
							1:48.0	−82
					1k	2:19.05		
Hooper	Brian	UK	18May53	174/72	PV	5.41	5.59	−80
Hopson	Bob	USA	20Jun61	198/86	HJ	2.25	2.26i,2.24	−83
Horta	Luis	POR	14Jan58	176/52	10k	28:18.13	28:41.36	−83
Hossfeld	Hilmar	GDR	18Jan54	195/117	DT	65.32	67.54	−80
Houvion	Philippe	FRA	5Oct57	180/80	PV	5.60i,5.40	5.77	−80
Howard	Jim	USA	11Sep59	196/80	HJ	2.33	2.30	−83
Hrabal	Josef	CS	18Oct58	193/73	HJ	2.27i,2.25	2.26	−82
							2.28i	−81
Hubbard	Zane	USA	3Jul58	192/114	SP	20.30	19.64	−82
Hudec	Jiri	CS	15Aug64	184/78	110h	13.78,13.6	13.85,13.78w	−83
Hudson	Willie	USA	21Mar61		200	20.69w	20.51*w	−83
					400	46.08*i	45.92,45.6*	
Hubler	Jens	GDR	28Aug61	176/72	200	20.63	20.83	−83
Huff	Ivan	USA	31Jul59	178/70	5k	13:34.8	13:53.6	−82
					St	8:22.80	8:29.88	−83
Huhtala	Harri	FIN	13Aug52	187/110	HT	78.74	78.68	−83
Hunt	Thom	USA	17Mar58	173/55	10k	28:18.8	27:59.1	−82
Hunter	Gary	USA	26Feb56	180/74	PV	5.40	5.36	−80
Hurd	Lamar	USA	28Feb62	188/77	110h	13.81	13.85	−83

Men's Index

Name	First	Country	DOB	Ht/Wt	Event	Mark1	Mark2	Year
Husby	Stig Roar	NOR	12Sep54	179/63	5k	13:27.53	13:42.71	−82
Hussein	Ibrahim	KEN	59		3k	7:51.19		
Hutchings	Tim	UK	4Dec58	183/72	St	8:35.4	8:37.77	−83
					1500	3:38.06	3:39.3	−82
					Mile	3:56.88	3:54.53	−83
					3k	7:44.55	7:49.13	−83
					5k	13:11.50	13:24.10	−83
Huumonen	Ari	FIN	5Mar56	196/120	DT	63.66	65.44	−83
Hyde	Bret	USA	3Jul59	193/81	St	8:25.39	8:32.74	−83
Ignatov	Evgeni	BUL	25Jun59	183/66	2k	5:04.2	5:07.7	−82
					3k	7:47.74	7:54.6	−80
					5k	13:26.35	13:27.78	−82
					10k	28:24.73		
Ihalainen	Kari	FIN	24Jul54	181/95	JT	85.84	87.04	−83
Ikangaa	Juma	TAN	19Jul57	163/58	10k	28:23.29	29:27.2	−81
					Mar	2:10:49	2:08:55	−83
Ikaunieks	Aivars	SU	19Sep59	181/74	110h	13.4	14.34,13.9	−83
Ikegami	Masao	JAP	4Sep57	175/61	TJ	16.46w	16.45	−81
Ilg	Patriz	FRG	5Dec57	173/63	2k	5:05.84i		
Iliev	Stoitsa	BUL	16Jan60	184/73	TJ	17.09	16.53,16.69w	−83
Ilnitskiy	Sergey	SU	62		HJ	2.26i,2.25	2.21	−82
Imo	Chidi	NIG	27Aug65	188/77	100	10.30,	10.23	−83
						10.25w	10.2	−82
Ingraham	Allen	BAH	7Mar62	183/73	400	45.26	46.5	−83
Inaoka	Atsushi	JAP	4Jul62		HJ	2.26	2.25	−83
Ingram	Bob	USA	28Jun62	190/73	St	8:35.43	8:55.7	−82
Inozemtsev	Vladimir	SU	25May64		TJ	16.68	16.40	−83
Isakin	Oleg	SU	10Aug60	174/60	PV	5.40	5.30i−80,5.30	−83
Isayev	Anton	SU	25Jun62		110h	13.4	13.75,13.6,13.5w	−83
Isayev	Vasiliy	SU	1Feb59	188/78	TJ	17.22	17.16	−81
Ishchenko	Sergey	SU	25May54	186/101	HT	74.88	76.94	−83
Ishutin	Valeriy	SU	5Dec65		PV	5.40	5.30	−83
Itoh	Kunimitsu	JAP	6Jan55	163/53	Mar	2:12:04	2:09:35	−83
Ivancic	Ivan	YUG	6Dec37	190/128	SP	20.17	20.77	−83
Ivanov	Sergey	SU	3Jan62	182/120	HT	74.86	73.32	−82
Ivanushkin	Leonid	SU	61		PV	5.55i	5.55	−82
Iwancin	Vern	CAN	3Aug60	183/68	St	8:34.9	8:37.81	−82
Iwase	Tetsuhara	JAP	18Sep54	173/56	Mar	2:13:07	2:18:21	−83
Jackson	Bernie	USA	22Oct61	185/75	200	20.63w	20.26	−83
Jackson	Dannie	USA	11May58	187/83	Dec	7937m	7861−81,7872m	−80
Jackson	Jeff	USA	19Jun63		400	45.84	46.32	−82
Jackson	Randy	USA	8Feb58	183/67	St	8:29.95	8:22.81	−80
Jacobs	Franklin	USA	31Dec57	173/70	HJ	2.25i	2.28,2.32i	−78
Jacoby	Jake	USA	24Sep61	198/82	HJ	2.285	2.21	−83
Jacques	Kevin	UK	17Sep58		3k	7:51.88	8:15.5	−82
Jadwin	Tom	USA	12Apr58	183/93	JT	83.20	81.50	−83
Jakobsson	Oskar	ICE	29Jan55	196/120	SP	19.80	20.61	−82
					DT	60.68	63.24	−80
Jakstis	Jonas	SU	2Oct59	182/74	110h	13.85,13.7	13.8,14.03	−83
James	Charles	USA	19Jul64	180/77	110h	13.67	14.23	−83
James	Steve	USA	28Jul60	178/66	St	8:35.5	8:36.72	−81
Janiak	Arkadiusz	POL	3Oct63	173/68	100	10.29,10.24w	10.44	−82
					200	20.75	21.53	−82
Janicki	Don	USA	23Apr60	178/72	Mar	2:12:01	−0−	
Jansa	Frantisek	CS	12Sep62	180/76	PV	5.55	5.62	−83

469

Men's Index

Jaros	Ralf	FRG	13Dec65	193/83	TJ	16.81	16.51i,16.14	−83
Jasinski	Bill	USA	13Feb64	190/77	HJ	2.27i,2.26	2.21	−82
Jaskulka	Stanislaw	POL	25Aug58	182/73	LJ	8.06	8.13	−80
Jaspers	Stijn	HOL	3Jun61	188/74	3k	7:47.4	7:53.86	−82
					5k	13:24.46	13:24.64	−83
Jefferson	Jai	CUB	17Jan62	189/78	LJ	8.37	8.05	−83
Jefferson	Thomas	USA	8Jun62	183/75	100	10.25,	10.50	−83
						10.17w,9.9w		
					200	20.26,20.21w	20.90	−83
Jelstrom	Jorgen	DEN	22Apr63	186/87	JT	82.04	81.74	−82
Jenkins	Dale	USA	27Feb63	178/66	PV	5.54	5.59	−83
Jenner	Kyle	USA	7Feb59	193/120	DT	61.90	57.68	−82
Jensen	Kelly	USA	1Jul54	182/70	5k	13:32.47	13:36.0	−83
					St	8:25.13	8:22.54	−83
Jessee	Larry	USA	31Mar52	178/79	PV	5.73	5.71	−82
Jessie	Neal	USA	23Feb64	172/70	100	10.30	10.37,10.29w	−83
Ji	Zebiao	CHN	3Aug64	172/62	PV	5.46	5.25	−83
Joannes	Patrick	FRA	17Oct56	173/62	Mar	2:12:36	2:14:08	−83
Johansson	Jan-Olov	SWE	9Sep62	184/90	JT	82.10	82.58	−83
Johnsen	Tore	NOR	5May61	197/115	HT	73.86	71.58	−83
Johnson	Ashley	RSA	31Dec61		1500	3:38.66	3:43.3	−82
Johnson	Ben	CAN	30Dec61	180/75	100	10.12,	10.19	−83
						10.01w	10.05w	−82
Johnson	Dave	USA	7Apr63	189/86	Dec	8043m		
Johnson	Floyd	USA	23May59	175/70	400h	50.32	50.15	−81
Johnson	Fred	USA	10May62	168/55	100	10.24w	10.3	−82
					200	20.81	20.99	−81
Johnson	John	USA	20Jan60	188/82	110h	13.47	13.65,13.64w	−83
Johnson	Kevin	USA	3Dec60	180/66	1k	2:18.93		
					1500	3:36.04	3:41.0	−83
					Mile	3:54.06	3:58.57	−83
Johnson	Mario	USA	10Nov61	170/68	100	10.33,10.31w	10.47−81,10.29w	−82
Johnson	Nat	USA	25Oct63	188/88	100	10.1	10.62,10.48w	−82
							10.2	−83
					200	20.66	21.2,21.34w	−82
Johnson	Vance	USA	13Mar63	180/82	LJ	8.13,	8.21A	−82
						8.18w	7.97	−83
Jones	Albert	USA	8Oct62	183/81	110h	13.80,	13.78,	
						13.60w	13.6w	−83
Jones	Aubrey	USA	26Dec63	183/76	200	20.50	21.56,20.88w	−83
					400	45.99		
Jones	Earl	USA	17Jul64	180/73	800	1:43.74	1:48.6	−83
Jones	Hugh	UK	1Nov55	180/64	Mar	2:11:54	2:09:24	−82
Jones	Jerald	USA	20Jun53	180/70	5k	13:32.5	13:33.3	−80
Jones	Rod	USA	31Mar64	178/73	400	44.94	46.57	−82
Jones	Ron	USA	1Jan62	178/70	HJ	2.24i	2.20,2.23i	−83
Jones	Steve	UK	4Aug55	178/61	3k	7:49.80	7:51.69	−80
					5k	13:27.84	13:18.6	−82
					10k	27:58.64	27:39.14	−83
					Mar	2:08:05	−0−	
Jonot	Franck	FRA	1Apr61	187/75	400h	50.31	51.09	−83
Jordan	Paul	USA	17Jun56	185/80	TJ	17.19	17.00i,16.94	−82
Jorgensen	Henrik	DEN	10Oct61	178/59	Mar	2:11:31	2:10:47	−83
Joyner	Al	USA	19Jan60	186/77	110h	13.83,	13.89,13.6w	−83
						13.6	13.7,13.81w	−80
					TJ	17.19,17.26w	17.12,17.14Aw	−83
Juantorena	Alberto	CUB	21Nov50	190/84	400	45.69	44.26	−76
					800	1:44.88	1:43.44	−77
Juda	Ahmed Musa	SUD	1Jan57	180/58	10k	28:20.26	28:38.03	−83
Jurjevicius	Rimantas	SU	64		400h	50.1	52.2−82,53.53	−83
Juszczak	Ryszard	POL	3Apr58	179/69	TJ	16.43h	15.78,16.11w	−83

Men's Index

Kachanov	Valeriy	SU	12Jul54	188/84	Dec	7918	8306	−80
Kaduskiewicz	Jerzy	POL	24May52	176/72	TJ	16.42	16.33	−82
Kahkola	Vesa	FIN	30Jan59	173/58	10k	28:29.54	28:38.02	−82
Kalb	Werner	FRG	30Jul60	181/82	JT	82.50	81.64	−83
Kaleta	Marek	SU	17Dec61	180/70	JT	83.30	75.50	−83
Kalinkin	Viktor	SU	23Feb60	180/70	800	1:44.73	1:45.6	−83
					1k	2:19.89i		
					1500	3:37.1	3:40.9	−83
Kalliomaki	Antti	FIN	8Jan47	184/78	PV	5.40	5.66	−80
Kalogiannis	Athanassios	GRE	10Sep65	193/80	400	45.90	47.07	−82
					400h	50.22	51.67	−83
Kalsin	Vladimir	SU	15Oct58		1500	3:37.54	3:39.4	−79
Kalutskiy	Anatoliy	SU	60		1500	3:36.36	3:39.29	−81
Kamau	Gabriel	KEN	20Mar57	172/64	Mar	2:10:05	2:14:54	−83
Kanai	Yutaka	JAP	16Oct59	178/64	10k	27:59.59	28:14.4	−83
Karczmarek	Piotr	POL	21Jul57	190/80	400h	50.58	50.99	−81
Kariuki	Julius	KEN	12Apr61	181/62	St	8:17.47	9:34.5	−81
Karna	Jarmo	FIN	4Aug58	180/80	LJ	7.90,8.02w	7.84,7.88w	−82
Karpov	Yuriy	SU	10Jan57	191/84	Dec	7946m		
Kashanov	Panayot	BUL	19Jun57	176/62	St	8:28.02	8:26.91	−83
Kasnauskas	Sergey	SU	4Apr61	192/126	SP	21.64,22.09ls	21.17	−83
Kasten	Olaf	GDR	20Jan62	182/76	PV	5.40	5.30	−83
Katamine	Takashi	JAP	3Apr58	173/63	HJ	2.25	2.27	−83
Katkov	Aleksandr	SU	11Sep59	183/77	LJ	7.97	7.90	−82
Kattis	Dimitrios	GRE	7Feb56	194/80	HJ	2.24	2.20	−81
Kaulin	Matthias	FRG	3Feb63	187/76	400h	50.24	50.66	−83
Kavanaugh	Bubba	USA	24Feb60	180/73	PV	5.41	5.29	−83
Kawaguchi	Koshiro	JAP	15Aug54	165/53	Mar	2:12:04	2:13:22	−83
Kayukov	Andrey	SU	64		TJ	16.43	15.57	−83
Kazanov	Igor	SU	24Sep63	186/81	110h	13.59	13.7,14.08	−83
Kedir	Mohamed	ETH	18Sep54	166/45	10k	27:57.09	27:39.44	−81
Keiss	Andris	SU	20Dec58	186/83	JT	81.74	80.30	−82
Kelly	Reggie	USA	30Sep62	183/79	LJ	7.95i	8.33i,8.07,8.10w	−83
Kenworthy	Dave	USA	27Jun60	183/75	PV	5.61	5.56	−82
Kerho	Steve	USA	24Mar64	188/75	110h	13.68	13.94,13.83w	−83
Kessler	Markus	FRG	28Jan62	181/74	LJ	7.92	7.71−81,7.78w	−80
Khalifa	Omer	SUD	1Jan56	174/64	800	1:44.87	1:45.30	−81
					1500	3:34.59	3:34.11	−80
					Mile	3:53.74	3:55.46	−80
					2k	5:05.78		
Kharitonov	Yuriy	SU	59		LJ	8.22	8.04i−83,7.83	−77
Kharlov	Aleksandr	SU	18Mar58	194/80	400h	49.15	48.78	−83
Khokhlov	Boris	SU	20Dec58	186/69	TJ	16.59	17.02	−82
Khrishchuk	Viktor	SU	58		200	20.6	20.7−82,21.24	−83
Khristov	Ventsislav	BUL	18May62	188/110	SP	19.68	19.25	−83
Khudyakov	Aleksandr	SU	60		5k	13:34.19		
					10k	28:07.30		
Kiernan	Gerry	IRL	31May53	183/66	Mar	2:12:20	2:13:20	
Kigen	Simeon	KEN	7Jun61	170/63	10k	27:57.68		
					Mar	2:10:18	2:10:52	−83
Kiilunen	Matti	FIN	17Mar62	180/77	JT	86.20	82.38	−82
Kim	Anatoliy	SU	58		LJ	7.93	7.84	−83
Kim	Yong Il	KOR	11Sep62	178/77	LJ	8.09w	7.94−82,7.98A	−81
Kimble	Ray	USA	19Apr53	183/84	TJ	16.99	16.97,17.21w	−83
King	Emmit	USA	24Mar59	175/78	100	10.18, 10.17w	10.06,10.05w 10.0	−83 −79
King	James	USA	9May49	180/74	400h	49.72	49.00	−79
King	Kevin	USA	11Aug63	180/68	1500	3:39.19	3:41.15	−83
Kingdom	Roger	USA	27Oct62	185/84	110h	13.16,13.1, 13.00w	13.44	−83
Kio	Joshua	NIG	7Sep57	176/72	TJ	16.56	16.69	−82
Kipkemboi	Joshua	KEN	22Feb60	165/60	St	8:27.88	8:28.41	−83

471

Men's Index

Kipkoech	Paul	KEN	6Jan62	173/58	5k	13:14.40	13:24.02	-83
					10k	28:05.4	28:36.05	-83
Kipsang	Joseph	KEN	25Sep62	162/57	10k	28:15.35	28:48.85	-83
Kiptum	Joseph	KEN	56		10k	28:06.5	29:29.4	-82
Kirilov	Sergey	SU	62		LJ	7.88		
Kisheyev	Vladimir	SU	58	193/108	SP	20.07		
Kiselyov	Vladimir	SU	1Jan57	186/125	SP	21.58	21.35	-80
Kiss	Ferenc	HUN	10Nov55	180/69	200	20.54w	20.85	-81
Kiss	Tibor	HUN	21Oct55	178/73	TJ	16.56	16.56,16.62w	-83
Kissin	Roy	USA	4Feb57	178/62	10k	28:19.5	28:47.6	-83
Kistner	Rolf	FRG	4Oct62	179/75	100	10.34w	10.39,10.27w	-81
Kita	Hideki	JAP	28Sep52	172/60	Mar	2:12:16	2:10:30	-83
Kitur	David	KEN	12Oct62	183/72	400	45.62,	46.42	-83
						A45.1	46.2	-82
Kitur	Simon	KEN	12Jun59	182/74	400h	49.70	51.1A	-83
Kivina (Juma)	Ibrahim	TAN	25Feb58	165/57	10k	28:06.00	28:52.0	-76
Kiyai	Moses	KEN	60	185/75	LJ	8.08	7.50A-82,7.49	-83
Klee	Mark	USA	24Feb62	178/70	PV	5.40	5.50	-83
Klepsch	Winfried	FRG	22Jun56	190/74	LJ	8.00	7.93-77,8.21i	-81
Klimczyk	Mariusz	POL	16Sep56	185/77	PV	5.50i,5.40	5.60	-80
Klimes	Pavel	CS	27Oct58	177/60	2k	5:05.3		
					3k	7:50.37	8:03.8	-81
					10k	28:23.16		
Klimes	Petr	CS	27Oct58	177/60	2k	5:04.8	5:24.3	-81
Kneissler	Bernd	FRG	13Sep62	198/130	DT	61.62	58.56	-83
Knipl	Istvan	HUN	11Jul61	183/66	1500	3:36.74	3:40.90	-83
					Mile	3:55.13		
Kobylyanskiy	Vadim	SU	8Aug61	180/73	LJ	8.28	8.17	-83
Kobza	Marty	USA	6Mar62	194/118	SP	19.84	18.86	-83
Koch	Mathias	GDR	3Sep62	188/75	LJ	8.09i,8.08	7.79,8.05w	-83
Kodama	Taisuke	JAP	26Jul58	165/49	Mar	2:10:36	2:12:51	-83
Koduah	Sam	GHA			400	45.9	48.36	-81
Koech	Edwin	KEN	23Jul61	174/64	800	1:44.12	1:47.2	-82
Koech	Peter	KEN	18Feb58	180/67	5k	13:30.59	13:09.50	-82
					St	8:29.09		
Koeleman	Hans	HOL	5Oct57	181/67	St	8:23.73	8:21.72	-81
Koivuniemi	Kauko	FIN	22Dec59	192/95	JT	84.78	77.26	-83
Konig	Markus	FRG	8Sep62	183/73	400h	50.11	51.00	-83
Kolasa	Marian	POL	12Aug59	195/88	PV	5.60	5.50	-81
Kolasa	Ryszard	POL	17Apr64	184/77	PV	5.50	5.45	-83
Kolehmainen	Olavi	SWE	4Feb57	195/92	JT	82.20	81.74	-81
Kolnootchenko	Georgiy	SU	7May59	197/115	DT	66.52	69.44	-82
Kolovanov	Igor	SU	1Dec58	187/83	Dec	8065	8018,8308m	-83
Komarov	Viktor	SU	66		PV	5.40	5.10	-83
Konchellah	Billy	KEN	20Oct61	188/74	800	1:44.03	1:46.79	-80
Koncicky	Vladislav	CS	14Feb58	198/102	SP	19.79	19.24	-82
Konow	Manfred	GDR	22Feb58	186/79	400h	49.78	49.69	-79
Konovalov	Ivan	SU	59		St	8:25.81	8:28.34	-83
Konovalov	Yuriy	SU	57		St	8:35.6	8:37.68	-82
Konrad	Wolfgang	AUT	22Dec58	184/65	3k	7:50.07i	7:52.5	-80
Konstantinov	Bozhidar	BUL	1Sep63	188/70	400h	50.03	50.99	-83
Kopijasz	Ryszard	POL	8Feb52	170/60	Mar	2:11:50	2:14:49	-82
Koptilov	Sergey	SU	2Jun60	183/85	HT	74.06	73.16	-83
Korir	Julius	KEN	21Apr60	172/64	St	8:11.80	8:20.02	-83
Korjus	Tapio	FIN	10Feb61	195/102	JT	87.24	81.12	-83
Korobenko	Anatoliy	SU	12Aug57	183/71	HJ	2.28	2.23i-83,2.20	-82
Korolyov	Vladislav	SU	27May60	183/84	JT	85.80	81.92	-83
Koroso	Harrison	KEN	15Jan56	183/68	St	8:33.29	8:28.93	-81
Korovin	Vyacheslav	SU	8Sep62		HT	77.32	75.32	-83
Korte	Matti	FIN	20Aug56	188/82	JT	84.80	80.00	-81
Koskei	Kipsubai	KEN	51	172/57	10k	28:11.7	28:07.40	-80

Men's Index

Koskei	Sam	KEN	14May61	183/68	800	1:42.28	1:44.40	−83
					1k	2:19.26i	2:16.58	−83
Kostetskiy	Aleksandr	SU	14Jan60	186/69	800	1:45.17	1:45.66	−82
					1500	3:38.59	3:39.40	−82
Kostin	Mikhail	SU	59		SP	20.96	19.74	−83
Kostrzewski	Daniel	POL	9Jul54	190/113	DT	61.92	60.02	−81
Kotovich	Aleksandr	SU	6Nov61	180/76	HJ	2.33	2.26	−83
Kottke	Torsten	GDR	5Feb65	194/89	LJ	7.88i,7.88	7.75	−83
Kotze	Hennie	RSA	15Jan60	181/75	400h	49.66A	49.26A,49.56	−83
Kotze	Izak	RSA	14Nov56	186/100	DT	62.12	62.06	−81
Koutsoukis	Dimitrios	GRE	8Dec62	193/120	SP	20.51	18.79i,18.68	−83
Kovacs	Attila	HUN	2Sep60	182/72	100	10.18	10.41	−81
					200	20.60,20.51w	20.81	−82
Kovar	Jay	USA	15May60	193/114	DT	61.26		
Kovtsun	Dmitriy	SU	29Sep55	191/116	DT	68.64	67.84	−80
Kozakiewicz	Wladyslaw	POL	8Dec53	187/86	PV	5.75	5.78	−80
Kozlov	Vladimir	SU	60		HT	73.66		
Krakhmalyuk	Anatoliy	SU	6Sep60	182/65	5k	13:30.95	13:21.2	−83
Kramss	Andreas	GDR	12Jun62	184/76	PV	5.55	5.30	−83
Krasovskiy	Sergey	SU	18May63	192/85	110h	13.6	14.20−83,13.8	−82
Krastev	Plamen	BUL	18Nov58	187/76	110h	13.46,13.4	13.68,13.5	−81
Kratschmer	Guido	FRG	10Jan53	186/94	Dec	8420	8649	−80
Krawczyk	Krzysztof	POL	28Jan62	187/73	HJ	2.27i	2.26	−81
Kraychir	Hank	USA	10Apr60	186/127	SP	20.00	20.13	−83
					DT	60.52	62.06	−83
Krdzalic	Sead	YUG	5Jan60	186/98	JT	83.70	80.86	−83
Kreider	Steve	USA	10Apr58	185/92	JT	82.02	80.50	−79
Krieger	Helmut	POL	17Jul58	196/139	SP	21.03	20.28	−83
Krippschock	Axel	GDR	5Feb62	188/62	3k	7:48.38i	7:53.2i	−83
Krolak	Henryk	POL	15Jan60	187/109	HT	78.60	76.70	−83
Krulee	Marty	USA	4Nov56	170/68	100	10.31,10.29w	10.19,10.0,10.16w	−83
					200	20.78	20.4−81,20.51	−83
Krupskiy	Aleksandr	SU	4Jan60	185/77	PV	5.82	5.74	−83
Krylov	Vladimir	SU	64		400	46.05	48.52	−83
Kubes	Josef	CS	2Sep57	190/110	SP	20.64	21.20	−83
					DT	62.00	63.14	−83
Kubiszewski	Marek	POL	7Oct55	180/82	Dec	7979	7989	−81
Kucherenko	Igor	SU	60		HT	74.94	77.36	−83
Kuchmenko	Vladimir	SU	21May58	187/87	Dec	8054m	7992	−83
Kulske	Frank-Pet.	GDR	8Jul60	189/77	LJ	8.10i	7.99i−83,7.96	−81
Kula	Dainis	SU	28Apr59	190/98	JT	88.80	92.06	−80
Kulak	Paul	USA	12Nov59	190/90	JT	82.48	78.50	−83
Kulesh	Viktor	SU	18Sep60	187/89	Dec	7907m	8025,8092m	−83
Kulikov	Mikhail	SU	61		100	10.36		
Kulinkovich	Nikolay	SU	8Dec60	186/82	Dec	7918m	7755m	−82
Kulyasha	Nikolay	SU	17May59	191/84	110h	13.91,	14.00	−83
						13.7	13.8	−80
Kunze	Hansjorg	GDR	28Dec59	179/63	3k	7:47.5i	7:44.05	−83
					5k	13:33.90i	13:10.40	−81
					10k		27:30.69	
Kuphaldt	Harold	USA	24Aug64	183/68	St	27:33.10	8:58.99	−83
Kuprishenkov	Igor	SU	60		HT	8:34.86	70.02	−83
Kuprovskiy	Vladimir	SU	18Oct57	186/96	HT	75.68	73.56	−81
Kurochkin	Aleksandr	SU	23Jul61	187/79	400	73.08	45.90	−83
Kus	Bogumil	POL	10Jun57	173/62	10k	45.52,45.3	28:44.5	−83
Kutsebo	Sergey	SU	7Feb61	181/74	400h	28:26.92	49.92	−81
Kutsenko	Yuriy	SU	5Mar52	190/93	Dec	50.25	8331	−82
Kuusela	Kimmo	FIN	7Oct62	181/74	PV	8512	5.25	−80
Kuusisto	Timo	FIN	28Jun59	181/68	PV	5.51	5.55	−83
						5.50,5.52i		−82
Kuyumdzhan	Yuriy	SU	61		SP	19.65i,19.49	19.90i,19.83	−83
Kuzmenko	Aleksandr	SU	5Mar55	182/75	110h	13.7	14.20−82,13.9	−83
Kuznetsov	Aleksandr	SU	4Nov57	185/82	110h	13.5	14.10,13.6w	−83
							13.9	−82

Men's Index

Kwasny	Zdzislaw	POL	6Nov60	194/104	HT	73.76	80.18	−83
Lacika	Jozef	CS	8Jun61	191/110	SP	20.02	18.39	−82
Lacy	Jerry	USA	23Dec62	168/62	100	10.22w,	10.51,	
						10.1,10.0w	10.2w	−83
Lacy	Steve	USA	17Jan56	185/70	5k	13:27.72	13:33.26	−79
Ladanyi	Zsigmond	HUN	4Aug61	191/110	SP	19.60	18.90	−82
Lafranchi	Bruno	SWZ	19Jul55	178/59	Mar	2:12:57	2:11:12	−82
Lahbi	Faouzi	MOR	2Mar58	176/60	800	1:45.67	1:45.82	−83
Laheurte	Phil	CAN	4Jun57	180/64	St	8:30.39	8:35.89	−82
Laine	Gordon	USA	24Feb58	183/69	LJ	7.88	7.90	−80
						8.24w	7.96w	−83
Lakafia	Jean-Paul	FRA	29Jun61	192/103	JT	85.08	84.74	−83
Lambert	Craig	RSA	8Sep57		IM	3:58.41	4:0001	−81
Lambregts	Cor	HOL	4Aug58	178/66	10k	28:09.5	28:38.20	−83
					Mar	2:12:48	2:12:40	−83
Lane	Al	USA	27Apr62	184/88	110h	13.60,13.38w	13.57	−83
						13.5		
Lang	Anatoliy	SU	18Feb55	186/93	DT	61.32	66.36	−82
Lange	Joachim	GDR	25Jan60	188/96	JT	87.42	85.30	−80
Lange	Uwe	GDR	13Dec54	184/80	LJ	8.22	8.12,8.21w	−81
Lapshin	Igor	SU	63		TJ	16.56	15.68	−81
Laptyev	Yevgeniy	SU	5Jun62	183/70	PV	5.50	5.40	−83
Lara	Osvaldo	CUB	13Jul55	171/72	100	10.14,	10.11A−78,10.0	−76
						10.0	10.21−80,9.7w	−82
Larkins	Paul	UK	19May63	183/67	1500	3:38.44	3:44.38	−82
Last	Detlef	GDR	7Jun60	192/110	SP	19.90i	20.06	−83
Lattany	Mel	USA	10Aug59	175/72	100	9.96	10.03,9.95w	
							9.8w−83, 9.9	−82
					200	20.73,	20.21	−81
						20.41w	19.9	−79
Lauenborg	Jorn	DEN	14Sep44	185/65	Mar	2:12:21	2:12:58	−83
Laut	Dave	USA	21Dec56	193/114	SP	21.64	22.02	−82
Lauterbach	Henry	GDR	22Oct57	190/79	LJ	7.95w	8.35	−81
Laventure	Cyrille	FRA	29Mar64	187/62	1500	3:38.82	3:43.85	−83
Lavie	Andre	FRA	28Jun59	180/68	800	1:46.92	1:46.90	−83
Lavrenyev	Mikhail	SU	64		HT	76.36		
Lawrence	Albert	JAM	26Apr61	175/76	100	10.34w	10.34	−81
Layevskiy	Sergey	SU	23May59	178/69	LJ	8.32	8.13	−82
Lazare	Alain	FRA	23Mar52	169/53	Mar	2:11:59	2:12:51	−83
Lazarevic	Jovan	YUG	3May52	194/114	SP	20.29i	20.49	−81
Lazdins	Ray	CAN	25Sep64		DT	61.02dh	50.88	−83
Leach	Jason	USA	11Mar66	175/64	100	10.26w,10.1w	10.5	−83
Leach	Tim	USA	25Jun64		LJ	7.88,8.06w	7.76	−83
Leavy	Brett	AUS	8Feb65	178/79	200	20.6w		
Lebedyev	Igor	SU	30Apr55	184/115	HT	74.26	75.94	−82
Lee	Chang Chen	NKO	3Jan56	163/54	Mar	2:11:44	2:14:44	−82
Lee	David	USA	23Apr59	190/80	400h	49.49	48.42	−83
Lega	Mario	ITA	13Jan57		LJ	7.89w	7.95	−80
Legeda	Anatoliy	SU	27Oct62	172/61	1500	3:37.17	3:39.8	−83
Lehmann	Mike	USA	11Mar60	185/122	SP	21.27	21.43	−83
Lehtinen	Jouko	FIN	18Dec58	183/76	200	20.6w	21.40	−83
Lehto	Timo	FIN	2Mar56	179/66	1500	3:38.92	3:40.96	−83
Leitao	Antonio	POR	22Jul60	176/68	3k	7:51.94	7:39.69	−83
					5k	13:09.20	13:07.70	−82
					St	8:26.19	8:34.5	−81
Leitner	Jan	CS	14Sep53	186/87	LJ	8.10	8.10	−82
Lemme	Armin	GDR	28Oct55	199/115	DT	65.76	68.50	−82

474

Men's Index

Name	First	Country	DOB	Ht/Wt	Event	Best	2nd	Year
Lenstrohm	John	USA	27Feb61	185/77	110h	13.80,13.6w	13.59	−82
					400h	49.9	49.69A,50.27	−82
Leonard	Iosif	SU	29May60		1500	3:39.15	3:43.0	−83
Leonard	Silvio	CUB	20Sep55	173/64	100	10.28,	9.98A,10.03	−77
						10.1	9.9	−75
Lesniewicz	Janusz	POL	14Apr55	185/79	Dec	8051	7672	−83
Levchenko	Leonid	SU	6Jan58	183/74	TJ	16.45	16.61	−82
Leveille	Pierre	CAN	19Feb62	184/73	400h	50.32A	51.69	−83
Leveur	Serge	FRA	17Jun57	182/76	PV	5.50i,	5.50	−81
						5.50	5.60ex	−82
Levisse	Pierre	FRA	21Feb52	176/60	10k	28:08.11	27:58.05	−78
Levola	Mikko	FIN	7Mar59	186/72	HJ	2.26	2.24	−83
Lewis	Carl	USA	1Jul61	188/80	100	9.99	9.97,9.93w	−83
							9.9	−82
					200	19.80	19.75	−83
					LJ	8.79i,8.71	8.79	−83
Lewis	David	UK	15Oct61	180/68	3k	7:49.77	7:42.47	−83
					5k	13:27.03	13:30.55	−83
Lewis	Dennis	USA	20Mar59	193/81	HJ	2.31i,	2.21i	−78
						2.28	2.20−82,2.32iex	−83
Liang	Xuereng	CHN	7Mar65	186/60	PV	5.40	5.15	−83
Li	Jong Hyong	NKO	15Mar61	170/56	Mar	2:11:34	2:16:15	−83
Li	Jieqiang	CHN	29May59	187/68	110h	13.92w	14.20	−82
Lieske	Guido	GDR	23Jul64	183/72	200	20.63	21.14	−83
					400	45.91		
Lindner	Johann	AUT	3May59	187/104	HT	76.12	72.70	−83
Lindsay	Herb	USA	12Nov54	175/68	2k	5:09.12		
					10k	28:05.07	28:16.3	−82
Link	Kenny	USA	28Jun61	188/87	110h	13.76,13.71w	14.05w	−83
Lipscomb	Ed	USA	11Jan51	188/77	PV	5.40	5.33	−76
Lis	Czeslaw	POL	26Apr56	187/100	DT	61.32	60.92	−83
Lishebo	Davison	ZAM	1Oct55	184/73	400	45.57	46.8−81, 47.11	−82
Lisichonok	Aleksandr	SU	22Dec58	178/80	TJ	16.95	17.03	−81
Lismont	Karel	BEL	8Mar49	168/62	Mar	2:12:50	2:11:13	−76
Little	Danny	USA	29Oct60	188/73	LJ	7.91	7.72w	−82
Litvinenko	Dmitriy	SU	12Aug63	184/72	TJ	16.55i	16.78i−83, 16.36	−80
Litvinenko	Viktor	SU	22Dec57	188/105	HT	80.68	76.68	−83
Litvinov	Aleksey	SU	31May59	179/60	1500	3:39.14	3:40.6	−83
Litvinov	Sergey	SU	23Jan58	180/100	HT	85.20	84.14	−83
Liu	Yuhuang	CHN	25Jul59	176/67	LJ	7.99	8.14−82,8.22w	−81
Liu	Yunpeng	CHN	24Oct62	192/85	HJ	2.29	2.26	−83
Liuttu	Seppo	FIN	29Dec56	182/60	10k	28:06.58	28:55.69	−82
Li	Weinan	CHN	17Apr57	182/110	DT	60.64	60.00	−83
Lloyd	Andrew	AUS	14Feb59	172/59	10k	28:18.6	28:16.7	−82
Lofquist	Scott	USA	20Mar60	201/133	SP	19.92	20.35i,19.76	−83
					DT	61.44	62.58	−81
Logan	Jud	USA	19Jul59	193/122	HT	74.56	67.66	−83
Lohre	Gunther	FRG	12May53	191/80	PV	5.55i,5.53	5.65	−82
Loikkanen	Antti	FIN	15Apr55	177/64	1500	3:37.63	3:36.3	−80
					3k	7:50.77	7:46.87	−82
					5k	13:27.76	13:41.2	−83
Lomtyev	Yevgeniy	SU	20Oct61	184/73	400	45.05	45.69	−83
Lonergan	Rob	CAN	8Oct59	175/61	3k	7:50.44	7:58.54	−83
					5k	13:35.76	13:40.57	−83
Looks	Burkhardt	GDR	8Jul58	180/85	JT	82.26	85.96	−82
Loontjer	Glen	USA	7Mar61	185/77	PV	5.41i,5.40	5.28	−83
Lopes	Carlos	POR	18Feb47	167/55	5k	13:16.38	13:17.28	−82
					10k	27:17.48	27:23.44	−83
					Mar	2:09:06	2:08:39	−83
Lopez-Egea	Jaime	SPA	5Apr59	169/60	1500	3:37.64	3:39.02	−83
Lorentzen	Reidar	NOR	22Sep56	180/85	JT	88.46	87.32	−79
Loris	Ainars	SU	7Jul61	184/72	110h	13.6	14.1	−83

Men's Index

Lorraway	Ken	AUS	6Feb56	181/78	TJ	16.81i,16.59 17.07w	17.46, 17.54w	−82
Lotarev	Igor	SU	30Aug64	181/66	800 1500	1:46.34 3:34.88	1:46.37 3:38.3	−83 −83
Lott	James	USA	13Oct65	186/83	HJ	2.27	2.255	−83
Lovachev	Sergey	SU	18May59	178/69	400	45.37	45.62	−83
Lucero	Ben	USA	22Jun62	186/70	HJ	2.25	2.25	−82
Ludick	Edwin	RSA	15Jul64		HJ	2.24	2.22	−83
Lubke	Ralf	FRG	17Jun65	192/80	200	20.51	20.50	−83
Lundmark	Leif	SWE	7Sep53	178/90	JT	83.76	89.92	−79
Lupa	Henryk	POL	16Jul56	177/68	Mar	2:12:49	2:15:11	−82
Luxenburger	Richard	FRG	2Nov58	185/80	100	10.33	10.34	−82
Lyakh	Aleksey	SU	4May62	187/83	Dec	7845	7817,7960m	−83
Lysenko	Aleksandr	SU	5Apr55	181/70	1500	3:38.55	3:40.4	−83
Lytle	Doug	USA	7Aug62	185/80	PV	5.71	5.61	−83
McArdle	John	USA	13Jun57	193/125	HT	73.70	73.58	−83
McAlexander	Ross	USA	6Jan60	180/75	PV	5.45	5.38	−82
McCalla	Eric	UK	18Aug60	175/80	TJ	17.01	16.54	−82
McCants	Tom	USA	27Nov62	185/79	HJ	2.26i	2.21	−83
McClain	Barry	USA	23Jan62	183/68	110h	13.77	13.97,13.7w	−83
McCloy	Paul	CAN	6Nov63	187/70	10k	28:11.72	29:59.0	−83
McCoy	Keith	USA			100	10.35w		
McCoy	Ronnie	USA	20May63	184/74	110h	13.84w	13.72,13.66w	−83
McCoy	Walter	USA	15Nov58	178/75	400	44.76	44.97	−82
McCraney	James	USA	28Mar55	188/82	110h	13.55, 13.43w,13.4	13.74−81,13.6w 13.70w	−78 −78
McCulla	Pat	USA	29Nov58	186/109	DT	62.74	62.18	−83
McDaniel	Eugene	USA	8Aug63	175/75	400	45.82		
McDermott	Art	USA	7Nov61	183/111	SP DT	19.76i,19.68 64.04	19.25i,18.97 58.08	−82 −83
McDougald	Forika	USA	12Sep62	185/81	400h	50.11	50.87	−83
McFadgen	David	USA	22Sep60	187/78	TJ	16.58	16.64−82,17.21w	−83
McFarlane	Mike	UK	2May60	178/75	100	10.27, 10.08w	10.32 10.11w	−78 −82
McGeorge	Chris	UK	13Jan62	176/65	800 1k	1:45.85 2:17.45	1:45.14 2:22.3	−83 −81
McGoldrick	Jim	USA	1Jun53	188/114	DT	64.14	65.58	−77
McGuirk	Matt	USA	15Aug64	185/70	St	8:33.03	8:52.14	−83
McIntosh	Jack	USA	22Jun59	180/68	800 1k	1:46.16 2:19.57	1:46.58	−82
McKay	Antonio	USA	9Feb64	183/77	400	44.71	46.22*,45.9	−82
McKenzie	Dave	USA	10May49	188/111	HT	74.98	74.50	−83
McKenzie	Leander	USA	27Jan63	180/73	110h	13.81, 13.7w 400h	14.19 13.9 50.96,50.5	−83 −82 −82
McKoy	Mark	CAN	10Dec61	181/70	110h	49.51 13.27,13.16w	13.37	−82
McLaughlin	Willie	USA	13Dec63	190/78	400	45.4,45.70	45.30	−83
McLeod	Mike	UK	25Jan52	180/63	3k 5k 10k	7:49.59 13:26.14 28:06.22	7:48.18 13:23.26 27:39.76	−78 −80 −79
McNair	Alvin	USA	22Oct62	182/79	100 200	10.31 20.67,20.66w 20.4	10.41A 20.47	−83 −83
McNeil	Mark	USA	25Aug61	183/86	100 200	10.23 20.77	10.19A−82,10.34 21.0*	−83 −79
McRae	Mike	USA	9Jul55	185/82	100	10.34w		
					LJ	8.27, 8.34w	8.19 8.32w	−83 −81
McSeveney	Greg	USA	29May59	190/118	DT	63.16	61.56	−83

Men's Index

McStravick	Brad	UK	25May56	183/85	Dec	7975,8018m	7704	−80
MacDonald	Brad	USA	6Sep58	178/75	200	20.47w,	20.61	−80
						20.2	20.6	−83
					400	45.38	46.3	−83
Machura	Remigius	CS	3Jul60	187/111	SP	21.52	21.74	−82
Maestretti	Lane	USA	28Apr59	185/84	Dec	7891e	7700e−83,7703m	−82
Mafe	Ade	UK	12Nov66	185/79	200	20.57,20.55w	20.92	−83
Magee	Claude	USA	7Apr62	178/77	100	10.16w	10.25	−82
					200	20.68,20.6		
Magnani	Massimo	ITA	4Oct51	173/60	Mar	2:11:54	2:11:28	−82
Mahmoud	Joseph	FRA	13Dec55	174/65	1500	3:38.39	3:40.1	−83
					3k	7:47.58	7:57.33	−83
					St	8:07.62	8:15.59	−83
Mahorn	Atlee	CAN	27Oct65	187/77	200	20.69	20.65A,20.95	−83
Mahovlich	Mike	CAN	27Aug60	188/110	JT	83.22	79.26	−81
Mai	Volker	GDR	3May66	193/71	TJ	17.12	16.20,16.22w	−83
Maina Boi	James	KEN	4Apr54	168/63	800	1:46.39	1:44.24	−79
Makanya	John	TAN	60		Mar	2:12:52	2:25:26	−83
Makarov	Sergey	SU	15Mar58	179/76	Dec	7804m	7703	−81
Makin	Michael	UK	1Mar62	185/73	TJ	16.47	16.22,16.43w	−81
Makhotkin	Boris	SU	60		400	45.9	47.0	−82
Makovskiy	Fyodor	SU	65		HT	73.34	68.10	−83
Malchenko	Sergey	SU	63		HJ	2.25	2.29	−83
Malchugin	Viktor	SU	16Apr62	190/75	HJ	2.28	2.28	−83
Malekwa	Zakayo	TAN	2Feb51	183/84	JT	87.68	80.22	−82
Malts	Olavi	SU	3Mar59		JT	81.36	77.54	−83
Mamayev	Oleg	SU	29Aug58	189/74	LJ	8.08	8.08	−81
Mamede	Fernando	POR	1Nov51	175/59	2k	5:00.8		
					5k	13:12.83	13:08.54	−83
					10k	27:13.81	27:22.95	−82
Maminski	Boguslaw	POL	18Dec55	181/68	5k	13:32.26	13:26.09	−82
					St	8:09.18	8:12.62	−83
Maness	James	USA	10May63	185/77	200	20.77	20.86	−83
Mangan	Larry	USA	24Mar59	188/70	1500	3:38.44	3:39.25	−80
					Mile	3:58.36	3:56.9	−83
Mann	Patrick	USA	24Apr66	180/77	400h	50.06	51.56	−83
Manninen	Raimo	FIN	17Sep55	179/84	JT	93.42	87.86,92.26uns	−83
Marajo	Jose	FRA	10Aug54	177/64	800	1:46.18	1:43.9	−79
					1500	3:36.23	3:34.93	−83
					Mile	3:58.35	3:50.98	−83
Mardle	Paul	UK	10Nov62	192/110	DT	61.86	58.62	−83
Maree	Sydney	USA	9Sep56	180/66	1500	3:37.02	3:31.24	−83
Marie-Rose	Bruno	FRA	20May65	193/83	100	10.29	10.43,10.33w	−83
Marinec	Vlastimil	CS	9Jan57	184/76	TJ	17.16i,17.06	17.21	−83
Markin	Aleksandr	SU	62		110h	13.93	14.18,14.0	−83
Markin	Viktor	SU	23Feb57	183/73	400	44.78	44.60	−80
Marko	Gabor	HUN	7Feb60	184/63	St	8:17.97	8:26.13	−83
Markov	Khristo	BUL	27Jan65	185/76	LJ	7.95	7.51	−83
					TJ	17.42	16.88	−83
Markus	Jorma	FIN	28Nov52	178/78	JT	86.90	90.18	−82
Marlow	Mike	USA	31Jul56	183/76	TJ	16.58,16.60w	17.17,17.21w	−81
Marquant	Didier	FRA	9Jul58	176/69	800	1:46.46	1:46.54	−81
Marsh	Henry	USA	15Mar54	178/72	St	8:14.25	8:12.37	−83
Marshall	John	USA	5Nov63	190/74	800	1:43.92	1:46.65	−83
Marshall	LaNoris	USA	6Oct60	183/82	100	10.30w	10.31	−83
Martin	Eamonn	UK	9Oct58	182/68	2k	5:01.09		
					3k	7:47.8	7:40.94	−83
					5k	13:23.33	13:20.94	−83
Martin	Fred	AUS	4Oct66	181/76	200	20.71,20.6	21.11	−83
Martin	Ken	USA	10Sep58	178/67	St	8:20.40	8:20.97	−80
					Mar	2:11:24	−0−	
Martin	Roy	USA	25Dec66	185/79	100	10.32,	10.58,10.3	−83

477

Men's Index

Martin	Steve	UK	16Jul59	192/75	200 Mile 2k	10.14w,10.1w 20.28,20.25*w 3:56.71 5:02.61	21.00,20.28*w 4:04.8	−83 −83
Martinez	Juan	CUB	17May58	186/122	DT	67.32	70.00	−83
Martinez	Lazaro	CUB	11Dec62	180/75	400	45.97	45.37	−83
Martino	Marco	ITA	21Feb60	190/108	DT	66.90	63.70	−83
Martsepp	Kalev	SU	1Feb59	188/80	HJ	2.24	2.18	−83
Maryin	Igor	SU	65		Dec	7844	7021m	−83
Marzouk	Faraj	QAT		175/70	100	10.1	10.2,10.66	−83
Masunov	Leonid	SU	62	177/61	800 1500	1:45.08 3:38.11	1:46.64	−83
Mateï	Sorin	RUM	6Jul63	184/67	HJ	2.34	2.30	−83
Materazzi	Riccardo	ITA	15Jun63	176/63	800	1:46.03	1:47.13	−83
					1k 1500	2:17.14 3:35.79	3:38.34	−83
Matsubara	Kaoru	JAP	22Feb60	174/62	100	10.28w	10.54,10.2	−83
Matthews	Dean	USA	19Apr55	175/54	Mar	2:12:25	2:14:00	−82
Matveyev	Vasiliy	SU	4Feb62	174/60	800 1500	1:44.25 3:38.1	1:46.6 3:42.7	−83 −83
Mavrin	Aleksandr	SU	58		St	8:35.62	8:41.0	−83
May	Derrick	RSA	2Jul55		Mar	2:12:53	2:19:13	−79
Mayr	Marco	SWZ	19Jul60	178/59	800	1:45.75	1:47.87	−83
Mays	James	USA	15Aug59	188/73	800	1:44.62	1:45.23	−83
					1k	2:17.67	2:19.34	−83
Medved	Mikhail	SU	30Jan64	199/89	Dec	7881m	7572	−83
Meghoo	Greg	JAM	11Aug65	180/74	100	10.36		
Mehl	Fritz	FRG	18Sep55	190/90	Dec	8042	8099m−83, 7917	−79
Mei	Stefano	ITA	3Feb63	181/62	1500 2k 5k	3:36.62 4:58.65 13:29.61	3:36.72 5:13.0 13:32.06	−83 −81 −83
Meier	Franz	SWZ	16Sep56	176/67	400h	49.42	49.53	−83
Meintjies	Nollie	RSA	9May57	176/62	St	8:34.3	8:21.72	−83
Mekonnene	Abebe	ETH	64	158/59	Mar	2:11:30		
Melnikov	Sergey	SU	26Jan60	190/82	400h	49.45	49.35	−83
Melzer	Hagen	GDR	16Jun59	178/62	St	8:21.32	8:20.28	−83
Menczer	Gusztav	HUN	15Oct59	185/72	200	20.65w	21.16 20.73w	−82 −83
					400	46.07	46.85	−83
Menefee	Terry	USA	24Aug62	178/62	400h	50.10	49.88	−83
Mennea	Pietro	ITA	28Jun52	178/68	100	10.28	10.01A,10.15 10.0−72, 9.99w	−79 −78
					200	20.07	19.72A−79,19.96	−80
Mersal	Nafi	EGY	27Jul60	180/68	400	46.0	46.08	−83
Messina	Gian Paolo	ITA	10Sep57	179/61	Mar	2:13:14	2:12:42	−82
Metellus	Alain	CAN	8Apr65	190/72	HJ	2.28i,2.25	2.26,2.26i	−83
Michel	Detlef	GDR	13Oct55	188/97	JT	93.68	96.72	−83
Mihas	Dimitrios	GRE	6Mar58	175/71	TJ	16.79	17.04	−81
Mikisch	Sven	FRG	6Jan65	184/70	400h	50.11	50.78	−83
Milburn	Rod	USA	18May50	18/180	110h	13.79	13.24−72, 13.0*	−71
Mileham	Matt	UK	27Dec56	188/109	HT	77.02	75.02	−83
Milic	Vladimir	YUG	23Oct55	190/115	SP	20.66	21.19	−82
					DT	61.44	59.32	−79
Militaru	Constantin	RUM	17Feb63	188/65	HJ	2.31, 2.26	2.26i 2.22	−83 −82
Miller	Eugene	USA	8Jan59	175/69	110h	13.68	13.67,13.59w 13.6	−80 −81
Millin	Anatoliy	SU	59		800	1:46.50	1:47.30	−82
Millonig	Dietmar	AUT	1Jun55	169/56	3k 5k	7:44.10 13:27.13	7:43.66 13:15.31	−80 −82
Milovsorov	Tony	UK	4Nov58	178/66	5k	13:30.88	13:36.05	−81

Men's Index

Name	First	Country	DOB	Ht/Wt	Event	Mark1	Mark2	Year
Minev	Plamen	BUL	28Apr65	190/107	HT	73.08	65.40	−83
Minihan	Gary	AUS	24Jan62	173/70	400	45.87	45.65	−83
Mironov	Yevgeniy	SU	1Nov49	194/124	SP	20.43	21.53	−76
Misiewicz	Ryszard	POL	10Mar57	170/61	Mar	2:13:15	2:15:24	−83
Mitchell	Dennis	USA	20Feb66	175/67	400	46.02	46.30	−83
Mitchell	Rick	AUS	24Mar55	182/75	400	46.09	44.84	−80
Mitchell	Russell	USA	30Aug60	187/75	LJ	7.88	7.77−82, 7.84w	−81
Mitrakyev	Tsetsko	BUL	2Apr56	188/80	Dec	7829	7949	−82
Mizoguchi	Kazuhiro	JAP	11Jul61	182/84	JT	82.74	82.70	−83
Moder	Matthias	GDR	17Jun63	184/110	HT	79.38	74.78	−82
Modibede	Edwin	RSA	14Jun64	188/77	400	45.51A,45.57	46.49A	−83
Mogenburg	Dietmar	FRG	15Aug61	201/78	HJ	2.36	2.35	−80
Moller	Frank	GDR	16Feb60	182/78	100	10.29	10.34	−83
					200	20.73	20.90	−83
Monkemeyer	Uwe	FRG	22Sep59	183/70	1500	3:36.95	3:38.71	−83
					Mile	3:56.84		
					2k	5:02.37	5:06.6	−83
					3k	7:49.86	7:51.84	−83
					5k	13:27.05	13:38.79	−83
Mojzysz	Czeslaw	POL	3Aug58	179/62	3k	7:50.67	7:55.17	−83
					St	8:27.58	8:26.21	−83
Monien	Mario	GDR	15Jun61	185/71	800	1:46.97	1:47.46	−83
Monoco	Mark	USA			200	20.49w		
Monroe	Walter	USA	13Sep62	175/68	100	10.33	10.40,10.32w	−80
					200	20.80	21.14*	−80
Montelatici	Marco	ITA	25Aug53	188/126	SP	20.59	20.13	−78
Moody	Craig	USA	8May62	188/73	110h	13.91w	14.00,13.92w, 13.7w	
					400h	50.52	50.53	−83
Moorcroft	David	UK	10Apr53	180/68	1500	3:34.2	3:33.79	−82
					Mile	3:50.95	3:49.34	−82
					3k	7:48.88	7:32.79	−82
					5k	13:28.44	13:00.41	−82
Moore	Aston	UK	5Feb56	180/80	TJ	16.80	16.86,17.02w	−81
Moore	Greg	USA	8Nov59	178/73	100	10.26w	10.37	−83
							10.24w	−78
					200	20.57, dq20.41w	20.84	−80
							20.76Aw	−78
Moore	Neil	USA	22Oct57		800	1:46.9	1:48.1	−83
Moore	Victor	USA	19May64	183/77	110h	13.91,13.7w		
Moracho	Javier	SPA	19Aug57	180/74	110h	13.57	13.52−81,13.5	−80
Morales	Luis	PR/USA	4Mar64	168/64	100	10.30	10.21,10.18w	−83
					200	20.67,20.42w	20.82	−82
Moran	Jim	USA	13Nov62	203/93	HJ	2.24	2.17	−82
Morceli	Abderrahmane	ALG	1Jan57	174/67	1500	3:37.03	3:36.26	−77
Moreno	John	USA	30Mar55	180/63	10k	28:25.6	28:42.2	−83
Moriniere	Max	FRA	16Feb64	183/78	100	10.32w	10.44,10.36w	−83
Morkovkin	Yuriy	SU	20May57	185/80	LJ	7.99i	7.93	−82
Morozov	Andrey	SU	14Jun60	185/78	HJ	2.25i	2.28	−83
Morris	Devon	JAM	22Jan61	180/75	400	45.80		
Morris	John	USA	20Jan64	187/81	HJ	2.27	2.22	−83
Morris	Mike	USA	7May63	173/74	100	10.28,10.20w	10.36,10.34w	−81
Morrison	Walter	USA	25Sep59	173/70	400h	50.47	51.19	−83
Moses	Edwin	USA	31Aug55	188/77	400h	47.32	47.02	−83
Motti	William	FRA	25Jul64	199/92	Dec	8266	7745	−82
Moutsanas	Sotirios	GRE	2Jan58	178/54	800	1:46.34	1:46.66	−79
Mowatt	Andrew	CAN	24May64	178/75	100	10.34w	10.80,10.45w	−83
Muders	Wolfgang	FRG	5Nov57	194/91	Dec	7701	8114m−83, 8100	−80
Muir	Brian	USA	18Dec60	190/110	SP	20.58	19.02	−83
Muir	Nat	UK	12Mar58	175/59	5k	13:32.06	13:17.9	−80
Muller	Rolf	FRG	4Aug61	183/80	Dec	7708	7726m	−83
Mulligan	Jerry	USA	9Apr58	183/77	PV	5.50	5.35	−83

479

Men's Index

Mullins	Billy	USA	1Feb58	186/84	400	46.03	44.84	−80
Munkelt	Thomas	GDR	3Aug52	185/78	110h	13.51	13.37	−77
Munyoro	Meshak	KEN	24Aug58	172/65	400h	49.9A	49.93	−83
Muravyev	Vladimir	SU	30Sep59	178/75	100	10.23	10.34−80,10.26w	−83
					200	20.34	20.46−83,20.37w	−82
Murawa	Jorg	GDR	5Jun64	191/90	JT	81.84	77.30	−83
Murofushi	Shigenobu	JAP	2Oct45	181/93	HT	75.94	75.20	−82
Musiyenko	Nikolay	SU	16Dec59	183/79	TJ	17.24	17.16i−82,17.00	−83
Musonik	Wilson	KEN	56		St	8:30.5A	8:52.7	−83
Muster	Jean-Marc	SWZ	1Nov61	188/75	110h	13.78	14.01	−83
Musyoki	Mike	KEN	28May56	168/54	10k	27:46.0	27:41.92	−77
Muzzio	Rob	USA	25Jun64	188/86	Dec	8227	7664mw	−83
Myburgh	Ludwig	RSA	26Apr62	180/74	200	20.6A	20.89A	−83
					400	45.66A,45.78	45.32A,45.62	−83
Myers	Dub	USA	4Apr64	183/69	1500	3:37.89	3:41.92	−83
					Mile	3:58.24	3:57.06	−83
Myricks	Larry	USA	10Mar56	186/82	200	20.50,20.34w	20.03	−83
					LJ	8.59	8.64Aw−83,8.56	−82
Myshkin	Yuriy	SU	63		110h	13.7i,13.6w	13.9,14.28	−82
							14.27w	−83
Nabein	Klaus-Peter	FRG	10May60	186/75	1500	3:38.42	3:36.24	−83
Naduda	Aleksandr	SU	61		100	10.1	10.63,10.2,10.1w	−83
Nagao	Takashi	JAP	31Aug57	175/68	400h	50.21	49.59	−78
Nagel	Gerd	FRG	22Oct57	188/74	HJ	2.30	2.31	−81
Naguib	Mohamed	EGY	15Aug53	195/102	DT	63.30	61.52	−82
Nagurniy	Vladimir	SU	28Sep58		HT	76.94	72.18	−78
Nagy	Iosif	RUM	20Nov46	193/116	DT	65.20	68.12	−83
Nakayama	Takeyuki	JAP	20Dec59	179/56	Mar	2:10:00	2:14:15	−83
Nandapi	Paul	AUS	21Dec61	185/109	DT	61.28	57.02	−83
Narracott	Paul	AUS	8Oct59	182/72	100	10.26, 9.9	10.31,10.09w 10.0	−82 −78
					200	20.3w	20.65−82,20.4	−79
Nazarov	Igor	SU	27May62	187/76	PV	5.40i	5.45i−82,5.40	−83
Nazhimov	Aleksandr	SU	16Feb52	203/125	DT	64.16	65.24	−80
Ncube	Zephaniah	ZIM	10Jan57	175/55	5k	13:24.07	13:50.94	−82
					10k	28:28.53	28:38.85	−82
N'diwa	Juma	KEN	28Nov60	186/70	800	1:45.59	1:44.20	−83
Nechayev	Yevgeniy	SU	59		1500	3:38.32	3:38.88	−82
Nedi	Dereje	ETH	13Jan54	174/55	Mar	2:10:32	2:10:39	−83
Nedosekov	Yuriy	SU	58		110h	13.6	13.8	−83
Negoita	Dumitru	RUM	8Feb60	182/83	JT	84.58	80.78	−83
Nemeth	Robert	AUT	5Jun58	189/70	1500	3:35.80	3:35.8	−81
					2k	4:59.56	5:02.08	−81
					3k	7:44.08	7:45.36	−83
					5k	13:35.90	13:36.73	−81
Nenow	Mark	USA	16Nov57	172/57	5k	13:18.54	13:33.90	−83
					10k	27:40.56	27:36.7	−82
Neugebauer	Michael	FRG	7Apr62	188/77	Dec	7922	7763m	−83
Nevskiy	Aleksandr	SU	21Feb58	190/88	Dec	8476	8412	−83
Ngatia	Sam	KEN	57	168/59	St	8:35.47	8:33.19	−83
Ngobeni	Peter	RSA	62		100 200	A10.0,9.9ds A20.5		
Niang	Babacar	SEN	9Sep58	178/63	800	1:45.71	1:45.30	−83
Nicholas	George	USA	28Mar63	175/75	100	10.30	10.5	−83
Nichols	Jeff	USA			110h	13.86w	13.99	−83
Nicosia	Salvatore	ITA	8Mar63		10k	28:05.35	28:35.02	−82
Niederhaus	Grant	USA	29Dec54	188/84	Dec	8021m	7646−83,7723m	−81
Niemczak	Antoni	POL	17Nov55	176/67	10k	28:22.24	28:43.13	−82

480

Men's Index

Niemi	Erkki	FIN	18Apr62	201/80	Mar	2:12:17	2:14:15	−83
Niestaedt	Carlo	GDR	4Apr63	191/81	HJ	2.28	2.20	−82
Nijboer	Gerard	HOL	18Aug55	182/70	400	46.07	47.3i−83,47.40	−82
Nikitin	Yevgeniy	SU	14Jun58	189/78	Mar	2:10:53	2:09:01	−80
Niklaus	Stephan	SWZ	17Apr58	189/90	HJ	2.24	2.22	−83
Nikolaidis	Angelos	GRE	56		Dec	8036	8337	−83
Nikolic	Mladen	YUG	1May59	176/69	DT	60.84	58.98	−83
					100	10.34,	10.49	−83
						10.33w	10.2	−82
					200		20.74,20.5	
Nikulin	Boris	SU	60		100	10.32,	10.37	−83
						10.0	10.2	−82
Nikulin	Igor	SU	14Aug60	191/105	HT	82.56	83.54	−82
Nilsson	Lars-Erik	SWE	1Feb61	175/59	10k	28:09.22	28:58.55	−82
Nishimura	Yoshihiro	JAP	24Apr57	172/56	Mar	2:12:26	2:13:55	−83
Nix	Sunder	USA	2Dec61	175/65	400	44.75	44.68	−82
Nnakwe	Thomas	NIG	23Sep68	190/82	110h	13.78	13.87,13.79w	−81
Noji	Rick	USA	22Oct67	173/54	HJ	2.25	2.11	−83
Nordquist	Doug	USA	20Dec58	193/79	HJ	2.31	2.25	−81
Norman	Eugene	USA	21Sep61	185/84	110h	13.74,	13.64,	
						13.62w	13.2w	−83
Novacek	Jay	USA	24Oct62	193/95	Dec	7762		
Novikov	Vladimir	SU	17Dec60	184/78	Dec	8061m		
Novikov	Yuriy	SU	58		JT	84.72	82.66	−81
Ntoale	Franse	LES/RSA	8Aug50	167/63	Mar	2:12:57	2:15:23	−83
Nyambane	Alfred	KEN	15Jun56	167/63	200	20.6A	20.98	−83
Nyberg	Thomas	SWE	17Apr62	195/86	400h	50.47	50.34	−82
Nylander	Sven	SWE	1Jan62	192/80	400h	48.97	48.88	−83
Nzau	Joseph	KEN	14Apr50	173/64	10k	28:06.63	28:20.62	−79
					Mar	2:10:40	2:09:45	−83
Oakes	Gary	UK	21Sep58	178/69	400h	50.24	49.11	−80
Obeng	Ernest	GHA	8Apr56	167/60	100	10.25	10.21	−80
							10.1,10.20w	−79
Obikwu	Fidelis	UK	12Jun60	193/90	Dec	7763	7726	−82
Obizhayev	Aleksandr	SU	16Sep59	185/85	PV	5.70	5.74i−83,5.62	−81
O'Brien	Liam	IRL	11Oct54	179/66	St	8:27.24	8:39.65	−83
Odenthal	Marc	FRG	19Feb63	194/110	HT	73.80	74.82	−83
O'Donoghue	Peter	NZ	1Oct61	177/64	1500	3:37.08	3:39.84	−82
					Mile	3:57.69	3:58.20	−82
Oerter	Al	USA	19Sep36	193/125	DT	63.92	69.46	−80
Oganyan	Vadim	SU	9Apr63	185/74	HJ	2.30	2.28	−83
Ogidi	Daniel	NIG	9Aug63	175/72	400h	50.58	49.51	−83
Ohmori	Shigenobu	JAP	9Jul60	184/72	400h	50.12	49.74	−82
Ojastu	Aivar	SU	21Sep61	186/77	400	46.03	46.5,46.79	−83
Okkola	Hannu	FIN	23Jan54	176/64	3k	7:51.82	7:58.20	−83
Okot	Mike	UGA	25Dec58	170/62	400	45.99	46.12	−82
Okoye	Christian	NIG	61		DT	61.92	59.18	−83
Oldfield	Brian	USA	1Jun45	196/125	SP	22.19	22.86	−75
Olsen	Per Erling	NOR	30Mar58	186/75	JT	84.76	90.30	−83
Olson	Billy	USA	19Jul58	188/73	PV	5.80i,	5.80i	−83
						5.54	5.72	−82
Olsson	Ronny	SWE	1Oct61	184/69	800	1:46.28	1:46.43	−83
O'Mara	Frank	IRL	17Jul61	176/61	1500	3:37.91	3:37.7	−83
					3k	7:46.54		
Oosthuizen	Johan	RSA	26Jun61	182/75	400	46.06	45.42A−83,45.72	−82
Oosthuizen	Wessel	RSA	23Feb61	184/75	200	20.62A,	20.41A,20.68,	
						20.5A	20.1A	−83
Orlov	Aleksandr	SU	21Apr58	185/70	TJ	16.80	16.51i−83,16.41	−82
Oschkenat	Andreas	GDR	9Jun62	190/75	110h	13.89	13.50	−83

Men's Index

Osipenko	Valeriy	SU	30Aug57	185/73	PV	5.40	5.40	−82
Osipov	Andrey	SU	58		DT	63.24	58.16	−82
Ostrowski	Ryszard	POL	6Feb61	176/62	800	1:45.68	1:45.90	−83
					1k	2:18.0nc	2:18.56	−82
O'Sullivan	Marcus	IRL	22Dec61	175/60	800	1:46.21	1:48.5	−82
					1500	3:37.40	3:42.7	−82
					Mile	3:55.82	3:56.65	−83
Otrando	Bob	USA	17Apr56		SP	19.91	18.91	−80
Ottey	Milton	CAN	29Dec59	178/66	HJ	2.29	2.32	−82
Ottley	David	UK	5Aug55	188/95	JT	85.86	85.52	−80
Ovett	Steve	UK	9Oct55	183/70	800	1:44.81	1:44.09	−78
					1500	3:34.50	3:30.77	−83
Ovsyannikov	Yevgeniy	SU	10Jul63	183/85	Dec	8075	8053	−83
Pachecho	Francisco	MEX	10Oct61	168/51	10k	28:21.8	29:30.50	−83
Padilla	Doug	USA	4Oct56	176/60	1500	3:38.39	3:37.95	−83
					3k	7:47.09	7:35.84	−83
						7:46.87i		
					5k	13:23.56	13:17.69	−83
Paetow	Thomas	GDR	3Oct63	184/90	JT	84.00	83.56	−83
Page	Nat	USA	26Jan57	193/81	110h	13.71,13.6w	14.09	−79
Paige	Don	USA	13Oct56	186/70	800	1:45.17	1:44.29	−83
					1k	2:18.18	2:18.06	−83
Paklin	Igor	SU	15Jul63	191/72	HJ	2.36i,2.30	2.33	−83
Palachevskiy	Oleg	SU	62		HJ	2.28i,2.24		
Palchikov	Igor	SU	61		SP	20.25	19.04	−83
Palles	Lee	GRE/USA	8Mar56	193/95	Dec	7721	8159	−80
Pallonen	Kimmo	FIN	17Jan59	190/81	PV	5.50	5.56	−82
Palmer	Sam	USA	29Jul63	180/82	100	10.29	10.48w	−83
Paloczi	Gyula	HUN	13Sep62	185/67	LJ	8.22	8.07,8.09w	−83
Panasiuk	Zdzislaw	POL	9Feb58	187/81	PV	5.55	5.35	−83
Panetta	Francesco	ITA	10Jan63	171/58	5k	13:35.32	13:42.54	−83
					10k	28:03.99	28:41.2	−83
					St	8:26.90	8:33.24	−82
Pang	Yan	CHN	15Jan63	185/70	LJ	7.99	7.66	−83
Pannier	Raymond	FRA	12Feb61	174/63	St	8:34.47	8:28.61	−82
Panych	Viktor	SU	60		TJ	16.66	17.07	−83
Papadimitrou	Antonios	GRE	20Feb65	187/89	JT	83.56	81.34	−83
Parakhnenko	Aleksandr	SU	61		DT	62.10	58.52	−81
Parakhovskiy	Nikolay	SU	1Jan57	184/90	Dec	8001m	7962,8300m	−83
Parker	Dudley	BAH	5Jun62	177/59	200	20.6		
Parker	John	USA	19Mar64	189/84	LJ	8.01i	7.32	−82
Parnov	Aleksandr	SU	10May59	187/69	PV	5.60i,5.60	5.60	−83
Parsons	Geoff	UK	14Aug64	203/75	HJ	2.26	2.25	−83
Pascuzzo	Mike	USA	8Nov61	193/83	HJ	2.24i	2.24i−82,2.21	−83
Paskalev	Anton	BUL	6Nov58	185/74	PV	5.60	5.45	−81
Patek	Vaclav	CS	21Jun59	176/65	St	8:33.11	8:50.01	−83
Paton	Stuart	UK	24May63		1k	2:19.36	2:21.41	−83
Patrick	David	USA	12Jun60	183/72	400h	48.80	48.05	−83
Patrignani	Claudio	ITA	9Jan59	179/65	1500	3:36.68	3:36.08	−83
Patrone	Joe	USA	7Dec62	193/75	HJ	2.26i	2.19 −82, 2.21	−83
Patterson	John	USA	6May65	175/68	400	45.96	46.06,46.0	−83
Patterson	Reinaldo	CUB	7Feb56	178/84	JT	84.64	84.38	−81
Paul	Mike	TRI	28Mar57	185/77	400	45.42	44.88	−82
Pavlov	Igor	SU	60		St	8:34.2m,	8:38.08	−82
						8:34.25		
Pavlyuk	Yuriy	SU	7Jan60		Dec	7821m	7783	−83
Peacock	Tyke	USA	24Feb61	188/78	HJ	2.28	2.33	−83
Pearless	Peter	NZ	4Jun57	188/73	800	1:45.9	1:46.57	−83
Pearson	Steve	UK	13Sep59	184/105	JT	84.96	82.46	−83
Pekkala	Ilkka	FIN	18Feb55	177/74	PV	5.45	5.45	−81
Peltier	David	BAR	26Sep63	180/70	400	45.94	46.9	−83

482

Men's Index

Peltoniemi	Arto	FIN	26Feb66	174/66	PV	5.42	5.40	−83
Peltoniemi	Asko	FIN	7Feb63	182/70	PV	5.50	5.45	−83
Pelzer	Torsten	GDR	26Jun63	198/115	SP	20.39	19.59	−83
Penalver	Leandro	CUB	23May61	175/71	100	10.14	10.06	−83
					200	20.65	20.42,20.3	−82
Penchev	Stanimir	BUL	19Feb59	181/72	PV	5.50	5.55	−82
Pendergrass	Boris	USA	22Dec63	185/79	110h	13.75	13.96,13.5w	−83
Perevedentsev	Igor	SU	64		110h	13.87,13.6	14.25,14.24w	−83
Perkins	Robbie	USA	14Oct55	185/68	2k	5:09.71		
					10k	28:20.4	28:11.3	−79
Perry	Chuck	USA	29May61	203/93	HJ	2.24i	2.23	−82
Pesavento	Sergio	ITA	16Jan58		10k	28:11.99	28:54.9	−83
Pesonen	Harri	FIN	17Mar62	191/76	TJ	16.42,	15.32	−83
						16.43w	15.62w	−82
Peter	Herbert	FRG	24Jun57	187/84	Dec	8009	8160w−83, 8078	−82
Peter	Jorg	GDR	23Oct55	176/66	10k	28:17.95	27:55.50	−77
					Mar	2:09:14	2:12:56	−80
Petersen	Pat	USA	3Dec59	183/67	10k	28:19.3	28:38.2	−82
Peterson	Orville	USA	19Apr61	185/88	Dec	8018e	7743	−83
Petersson	Jens	GDR	8Sep64	195/88	Dec	7708	7313	−83
Petkov	Ivan	BUL	15Feb60	182/95	HT	75.38	73.22	−83
Petranoff	Tom	USA	8Apr58	186/98	JT	89.50	99.72	−83
Petrosyan	Grigoriy	SU	58		LJ	7.99	7.93i,7.91	−83
Petunin	Boris	SU	58		St	8:34.9	8:31.3	−83
Pfeffer	Kirk	USA	20Jul56	190/64	10k	28:27:8	28:19.1	−82
Pfitzinger	Pete	USA	29Aug57	174/60	Mar	2:11:43	2:12:19	−83
Phillips	Andre	USA	5Sep59	188/81	400	45.94	46.48	−82
					400h	48.42	47.78	−83
Phillips	Bob	USA	10Feb59	183/73	PV	5.50i	5.42i,5.33	−82
Pichugin	Nikolay	SU	60		HT	77.00	73.40	−83
Pienaar	Hannes	RSA	23Aug60	183/79	400h	49.63A,	49.32A,	
						50.1	49.7,49.96	−83
Pienaar	Jaco	RSA	28Mar58	179/73	400h	50.0A	50.6	−83
							50.74,50.41A	−81
Pierce	Jack	USA	23Sep62	185/75	110h	13.60	13.61A,13.62,	
							13.44w,13.6	−83
Pierzynka	Zbigniew	POL	21Oct51	168/65	Mar	2:12:53	2:13:30	−80
Pinchuk	Vladimir	SU	54		JT	82.16	79.10	−83
Piochi	Marco	ITA	1Jan57	176/65	LJ	7.93i	8.09	−83
Pishchalnikov	Vitaliy	SU	1Apr58	198/110	DT	67.76	64.84	−83
Pitaiyo	Martin	MEX	10Jan60	173/55	10k	28:11.4		
					Mar	2:10:29		
Pittman	Ricky	USA	4Oct61	175/61	St	8:26.03	8:23.66	−83
Piwinski	Paul	USA	3Nov61	196/80	HJ	2.24i,2.24	2.26i,2.21	−83
Plasencia	Steve	USA	28Oct56	178/64	5k	13:31.28	13:25.96	−81
Platek	Krzysztof	POL	13Jan62	186/85	110h	13.91,13.83w	14.00,13.7w	−83
Plekhanov	Vladimir	SU	58	174/70	TJ	17.09i	16.79	−83
Ploghaus	Klaus	FRG	31Jan56	186/110	HT	79.36	80.56	−81
Plucknett	Ben	USA	13Apr54	201/136	DT	63.16	72.34	−81
Podmaryov	Igor	SU	8Dec61	182/74	110h	13.7	14.0	−83
Podmaryov	Vadim	SU	5Sep58	181/81	Dec	8121	8031	−82
Podsiadlo	Wojciech	POL	22Apr58	188/83	Dec	8017	7960	−82
Pogoreliy	Andrey	SU	59		PV	5.40i	5.50	−83
Pohland	Holger	GDR	5Apr63	182/75	110h	13.73	13.47	−82
Polevoy	Sergey	SU	27Feb57		100	10.0		
Poli	Giovanni	ITA	5Nov57	180/68	Mar	2:11:05	2:11:05	−83
Polk	Damon	USA			110h	13.72w		
Pollari	Urpo	FIN	31Jan53	170/85	JT	82.82	82.94	−80
Polvi	Hannu	FIN	29Nov48	186/105	HT	73.64	74.74	−81
Polyakov	Vladimir	SU	17Apr60	190/75	PV	5.80	5.81	−81
Pomashki	Georgi	BUL	10Jan60	190/80	TJ	16.55i,16.54	16.91	−83
Popelyayev	Andrey	SU	63		St	8:21.75	8:33.0	−83

Men's Index

Popescu	Eugen	RUM	12Aug62	194/71	HJ	2.25	2.24i,2.24	−83
Popov	Sergey	SU	2Dec57		Dec	8201e	7945−83,8137m	−82
Poptsov	Nikolay	SU	5Feb57	190/84	Dec	7943	8104	−83
Porter	Pat	USA	31May59	183/60	10k	27:49.5	28:04.31	−83
Potapenko	Vasiliy	SU	64		Dec	7858m	7465	−83
Potapenko	Vladimir	SU	7Mar6	190/78	LJ	7.94	7.94	−83
Potapov	Sergey	SU	15Jul62	173/90	Dec	7814m	7649	−83
Potgieter	Herman	RSA	31Oct53	195/113	JT	82.22	88.62	−78
Powell	Jeff	USA	27May63	178/79	110h	13.90	14.04−82,13.97w	−83
Powell	John	USA	25Jun47	188/110	DT	71.26	69.98	−81
Powell	Mike	USA	10Nov63	190/75	LJ	7.98,8.14w	8.06	−83
Poyser	Delroy	JAM	5Jan62	198/77	100	10.30w		
					TJ	16.42i	16.34i	−83
Prado	Julio	CUB	27Jul60	191/71	400h	49.61	50.5,50.86	−83
Pradzynski	Czeslaw	POL	24Aug60	178/75	100	10.32w	10.71,10.38w	−83
							10.3	−82
					200	20.70	20.5−82,20.78	−83
Pradzynski	Krzysztof	POL	6Apr58	181/66	1500	3:38.85	3:40.90	−83
Prenzler	Olaf	GDR	24Aug58	182/78	200	20.57	20.46−82,20.39w	−79
Prianon	J-Louis	FRA	22Feb60	176/58	3k	7:49.58	7:58.6	−83
					5k	13:35.95	13:42.42	−83
Pringle	Jim	USA	3Oct58	196/86	HJ	2.26i	2.27i−80,2.25	−82
Priscak	Jaroslav	CS	28Aug56	179/72	TJ	17.23	16.73	−83
Priymak	Boris	SU	30Jan57	190/105	DT	61.42	61.64	−83
Prokhaska	Velislav	BUL	29Dec53	193/115	DT	63.28	66.04	−81
Prokofyev	Andrey	SU	6Jun59	187/83	110h	13.57	13.3−79,13.46	−82
Prosin	Vladimir	SU	9Jan59	186/75	400	45.47	45.97	−81
Protsenko	Oleg	SU	11Aug63	190/81	TJ	17.52	17.27	−83
Pruss	Boris	SU	9Feb58	182/72	St	8:32.07	8:24.8	−82
Ptacnik	Frantisek	CS	27Feb62	183/80	100	10.35	10.78,10.4	−79
Puccetti	Perry	USA	5Jan61	188/95	JT	82.52	80.26	−83
Puchkov	Aleksandr	SU	30Apr60	177/100	HT	77.28	76.30	−83
Pugh	Joe	USA	28Jun63	180/77	110h	13.79w	14.34	−83
Pukownik	Eligiusz	POL	30Jun62	196/105	DT	61.04	60.48	−83
Purnomo		INA	21Apr61	167/60	100	10.34	10.60	−82
Pursley	Brad	USA	24May60	185/77	PV	5.65	5.75	−83
Pusinaitis	Algis	SU	15Feb57	195/110	SP	20.71	20.25	−83
Puuste	Heino	SU	7Sep55	188/90	JT	91.86	94.20	−83
Puvogel	Dave	USA	6May62	186/70	HJ	2.25i	2.25	−82
Puzyrev	Vladimir	SU	62		LJ	7.91i	7.85	−83
Pyka	Ian	USA	24May56	186/116	SP	20.11	20.36	−80
Pyshkin	Sergey	SU	11May55	185/110	HT	73.38	74.36	−78
Quarrie	Don	JAM	25Feb51	175/70	100	10.31w	9.9,10.07	−76
							10.03w	−78
					200	20.48,20.2	19.86A−71,20.06	−74
						20.41w	19.8	−75
Quinn	James	USA	30Sep63	187/86	110h	13.53	13.85	−83
Quinon	Pierre	FRA	20Feb62	180/74	PV	5.80	5.82	−83
Quow	Elliot	USA	3Mar62	188/79	100	10.30w	10.35	−83
					200	20.47,20.40w	20.16	−83
						20.4		
Radan	Joe	USA	24Jul57	183/76	HJ	2.28	2.26	−83
Radev	Venzislav	BUL	9Jan61	187/70	110h	13.66,13.5	13.59,13.5	−83
Radzikowski	Zbigniew	POL	29Feb60	180/74	PV	5.40i	5.55	−82
Radzius	Jurdanas	SU	24May61	185/77	Dec	7954m	7693	−83

Men's Index

Rahal	Nick	USA	28Jul63	189/73	LJ	7.92,7.96w	7.60	−83
Rambo	Tony	USA	30May60	175/78	400h	48.16	48.90	−82
Ramon	Domingo	SPA	10Mar58	162/57	St	8:17.27	8:15.74	−80
Ramos	Mike	USA	1Nov62	183/86	Dec	7995	7838w	−83
Rangelov	Dimitar	BUL	14Nov63	181/68	400	46.08	46.20	−83
Ransby	Mike	USA			200	20.79		
Ransford	Curt	USA	28Oct58	188/107	JT	84.40	84.28	−80
Rappe	Grey	USA	14Jun59	180/73	PV	5.51i,5.41	5.50	−83
Rashchupkin	Viktor	SU	16Oct50	188/107	DT	63.14	66.64	−80
Ratkowski	Jacek	POL	29Oct54	173/61	Mar	2:12:49	2:17:21	−83
Raty	Seppo	FIN	27Apr62	186/81	JT	82.60	75.42	−81
Reardon	Jim	USA	31Aug47	190/120	DT	61.60	61.38	−82
Redman	Tim	UK	5Jul60		3k	7:48.81	7:58.7	−83
Redwine	Stanley	USA	10Apr61	186/73	800	1:44.87	1:46.13	−83
Reed	Kelly	USA	21Sep65	175/69	100	10.32w	10.53	−83
Reichelt	Andre	GDR	9Oct62	185/76	LJ	8.13	7.94	−82
Reichnach	Ferenc	HUN	5Jun64	186/75	800	1:46.72	1:48.57	−83
Reid	Donovan	UK	31Aug63	177/73	100	10.32, 10.45,10.4,		
						10.17w	10.10w	−83
					200	20.62,20.6	20.87−82,20.69w	−83
Reid	Leroy	JAM	3Aug63	187/77	200	20.62,20.53w 20.4	20.73	−83
Reintak	Sven	SU	17Jun63	195/83	Dec	8132	7715	−83
Reitz	Colin	UK	6Apr60	186/73	1500	3:38.86	3:40.75	−80
					St	8:13.78	8:17.75	−83
Rene-Corail	Alain	FRA	21Apr62	186/70	TJ	16.49,16.52w	16.42	−83
Renner	Peter	NZ	27Oct59	186/75	St	8:14.05	8:23.38	−83
Reshetnikov	Valeriy	SU	59		HT	76.10	74.80	−83
Reyna	Jorge	CUB	10Jan63	179/68	TJ	16.87	17.05	−83
Reynolds	Harry	USA	8Aug64	193/84	400	45.47		
Reyte	Carlos	CUB	12Jan56	172/66	400	45.63	45.78	−83
Richard	Antoine	FRA	8Sep60	174/63	100	10.35	10.26	−83
Richards	Jon	UK	19May64	173/67	5k	13:35.50	13:48.74	−83
Richardson	Joe	USA	24Jan66	192/79	LJ	7.94	7.23−82, 7.31w	−83
Richardson	Pete	USA	19Apr63	188/73	800	1:46.62	1:47.17	−83
Richardson	Rod	USA	17Sep62	178/76	100	10.30	10.17	−83
							10.09w−82,10.0w	−81
Ricks	Charles	USA	4Nov63	175/82	200	20.55w	21.38,21.3	−83
Ricks	Mike	USA	16Jun59	180/77	400	45.9A	46.20	−80
Ridgeon	Jonathon	UK	14Feb67	186/77	110h	13.92	−0−	
Riecke	Hans-Ulrich	GDR	3Oct63	192/91	Dec	8212	7997	−83
Riehm	Karl-Hans	FRG	31May51	187/107	HT	79.44	80.80	−80
Rios	Carmelo	PR	11Oct59	172/62	10k	28:27.1	28:51.9	−83
					St	8:31.88	8:28.89	−83
Ripley	Dan	USA	7Oct53	180/81	PV	5.60i,5.60	5.72	−82
Roata	Nicu	RUM	6Jul61	188/83	JT	85.86	80.20	−83
Roberson	Gary	USA	7Dec61	178/74	200	20.52	20.97,20.74w	−83
Roberson	Mike	USA	25Mar56	173/60	110h	13.88	13.5−76,13.85	−77
Roberts	Bruce	CAN	3Nov57	190/70	800	1:46.53	1:49.9	−80
Roberts	Mark	UK	12Feb59		5k	13:29.93	14:16.9	−83
Robinson	Albert	USA	28Nov64	187/84	100	10.24, 10.23w	10.3,10.39w 10.57	−82 −83
					200	20.07	20.78	−83
Robinson	Darrell	USA	23Dec63	186/66	400	45.40	44.69	−82
Robinson	James	USA	27Aug54	178/65	800	1:43.92	1:44.32	−83
Robinson	Ken	USA	15Jul63	176/70	100	10.28, 10.24w	10.27 10.24w	−82 −81
Robinson	Len	USA	15Sep62	185/82	400h	49.83	49.55,49.5	−83
Robinzine	Kevin	USA	12Apr66	178/64	400	46.04,45.8	47.4	−83
Robleh	Djama	DJI	58	169/52	Mar	2:11:25	2:16:49	−83
Robson	John	UK	31Jan57	175/61	1500	3:38.89	3:33.83	−79
					Mile	3:58.38	3:52.44	−81
					3k	7:45.81	7:51.08	−81

Men's Index

Roby	Wayne	USA	10Jan62	188/82	110h	13.64	13.94,13.92w	−83
Rockett	Bob	USA	21Apr64	190/86	JT	81.38	81.36	−83
Rodehau	Gunther	GDR	6Jul59	179/116	HT	80.20	78.14	−83
Rodin	Sergey	SU	28May63	188/80	LJ	7.90,8.37w	8.33	−83
Rodrigues	Abcelvio	BRA	26May57	181/76	TJ	16.76	16.02	−82
Rogers	Tony	NZ	30Apr57	182/66	1500	3:36.48	3:39.76	−82
					Mile	3:55.18	3:57.19	−83
Roggy	Bob	USA	6Aug56	194/109	JT	90.80	95.80	−82
Rolle	Greg	BAH	14Oct59	188/79	400h	49.66	49.46	−83
Rolle	James	USA	2Feb64	187/74	400	45.34	44.73A,45.30	−83
Roller	Steve	USA	20Feb54	181/95	JT	83.94	78.84	−83
Romanov	Mikhail	SU	59		St	8:32.94	8:36.3	−80
Romanov	Vladimir	SU	25Sep81	183/82	Dec	7930m		
Romanyuk	Mikhail	SU	6Feb62	182/82	Dec	7949,8310m	7931,8171m	−83
Rono	George Kip	KEN	4Jan58	178/54	St	8:29.4A	8:12.0	−80
Rose	Nick	UK	30Dec51	174/60	3k	7:48.39	7:40.4	−78
					5k	13:18.91	13:20.35	−77
					10k	28:00.70	27:31.19	−83
Ross	Desmond	USA	30Dec61	193/77	100	10.34w	10.48	−83
					200	20.77w	21.04	−83
Ross	Ed	USA	28Dec61	188/77	110h	13.83,13.82w	13.89	−83
Ross	Nick	USA	27Mar60	180/73	400h	50.58	51.07	−82
Rossland	Frank	GDR	17Jul60	188/83	110h	13.92w	13.84	−80
Rousseau	Vincent	BEL	29Jul62	176/60	3k	7:50.3	7:51.5	−83
					5k	13:24.81	13:33.2	−83
Rowe	Mark	USA	28Jul60	192/79	400	45.30	45.39	−81
Royer	J-Bernard	FRA	17Oct62	179/75	Dec	7717	7423e	−83
Rucli	Giorgio	ITA	11May63	183/75	400h	50.51	51.23	−83
Rudd	Dwayne	USA	17Apr61	190/79	TJ	16.68w	16.55	−83
Rufenacht	Michele	SWZ	15Sep59	186/86	Dec	7924	7896	−83
Ruter	Eckhard	FRG	24Oct63	177/68	800	1:46.85	1:48.06	−83
Ruhkieck	Frank	GDR	23Nov61	176/60	St	8:29.93	8:41.06	−82
Ruiz	Alberto	SPA	22Dec61	178/76	PV	5.55	5.45	−83
Rutkowski	Jacek	POL	31Aug60	193/80	110h	13.64,13.59w	13.60,13.59w	−83
Rwamuhanda	Peter	UGA	11Dec53	175/65	400h	50.46	49.78	−78
Ryan	Kevin	USA	1Feb57	180/68	Mile	3:58.4	3:55.9	−83
					5k	13:32.50	13:42.15	−83
Rybin	Valeriy	SU	18Aug54	187/77	PV	5.40	5.50	−83
Ryffel	Markus	SWZ	5Feb55	167/55	Mile	3:58.05	4:05.3	−79
					2k	4:59.54	4:59.54	−78
					3k	7:50.59,	7:41.00	−79
						7:49.27i		
					5k	13:07.54	13:13.32	−79
Ryzhkov	Aleksandr	SU	56		100	10.1	10.73	−83
							10.2,10.1w	−82
Ryzhkov	Sergey	SU	56		110h	13.7w	13.6,14.09	−83
Sabia	Donato	ITA	11Sep63	178/65	400	45.73	46.22	−83
					800	1:43.88	1:46.22	−83
Sacco	Frederic	FRA	22Aug61	185/88	Dec	7751	7509	−82
Sahner	Christoph	FRG	23Sep63	179/97	HT	78.04	77.88	−83
Sakamoto	Takao	JAP	19Dec58	183/73	HJ	2.30	2.27	−82
Sala	Carlos	SPA	20Mar60	186/76	110h	13.56	13.64,13.55w	−83
Salazar	Alberto	USA	7Aug58	181/64	10k	27:45.5	27:25.61	−82
					Mar	2:11:44	2:08:13	−81
Salazar	Jose	VEN	12Sep57	182/67	TJ	16.43Ai	16.41	−79
							16.46w	−83
Salbert	Ferenc	HUN	5Aug60	190/80	PV	5.50	5.55	−82
Saleh	Ahmed	DJI	56	180/54	10k	28:17.4	30:15.9	−82
					Mar		2:11:58	2:17:29	−83
Salzmann	Ralf	FRG	6Feb55	172/58	10k	28:15.3	28:23.57	−82
					Mar	2:11:21	2:12:57	−83

Men's Index

Surname	Given	Nat	DOB	Ht/Wt	Event	Mark	Prev	Yr
Sam	Andreas	GDR	5Feb60	186/84	HJ	2.31	2.26	−83
Samarin	Gennadiy	SU	55		DT	66.16	60.30	−78
Samarin	Yuriy	SU	27Dec60	179/74	LJ	8.23	8.18	−83
Samoylenko	Vladimir	SU	25Oct61	178/68	800	1:46.7	1:48.1	−83
Samylov	Igor	SU	22Feb62	193/80	HJ	2.26i	2.24i−82,2.23	−83
Sanchez	Antonio	SPA	22Sep63	181/72	200	20.67	21.22,21.20w, 21.0	−83
					400	45.76	46.72	−83
Sanders	Eugene	USA	25Mar60	188/81	800	1:46.77	1:46.03	−83
Sandoval	Tony	USA	19May54	173/52	10k	27:47.0	28:29.94	−80
					Mar	2:12:41	2:10:19	−80
Sands	Lyndon	BAH	6Feb64	178/62	LJ	7.93	7.42	−83
Sanford	James	USA	27Dec57	180/75	100	10.29, 10.22w	10.02,9.88w, 10.0	−80
					200	20.79	20.19	−79
Sanford	Mike	USA	6Mar60	178/75	100	10.33w	19.7A,19.94w 10.26 10.24w	−80 −82 −81
Sang	Patrick	KEN		173/62	St	8:22.45	8:41.00	−83
Santos	Francisco	BRA	24Apr60	188/80	TJ	16.83	16.33	−82
Saracevic	Zlatan	YUG	27Jul56	196/145	SP	21.11	20.31,20.57i	−80
Sargalski	Janusz	POL	26May58	186/105	DT	60.54	57.28	−83
Sarul	Edward	POL	16Nov58	195/117	SP	20.89	21.68	−83
Saskoi	Alfonz	HUN	12Jun58	184/86	DT	63.24	61.28	−78
Saulite	Janis	SU	18Feb58	190/84	110h	13.82,13.4	13.74	−83
Saunders	Nick	BER	14Sep63	188/75	HJ	2.28	2.30i,2.27	−83
Saviniemi	Tero	FIN	8Jul63	182/82	JT	86.78	85.14	−83
Saye	David	USA	14Mar59	186/84	Dec	7803m	7732w−83,7781m	−81
Sayre	John	USA	25Mar61	190/88	PV	5.49i	5.24	−81
					Dec	7891	7703,7927m	−83
Scammell	Pat	AUS	15Apr61	189/67	800	1:45.74	1:45.86	−82
					1500	3:37.86	3:38.11	−82
Scanella	Jim	USA	11Aug61	187/73	400h	50.09	50.71,50.3	−83
Schafer	Lutz	GDR	6Aug61	188/107	HT	73.34	72.36	−83
Schaeffer	Jorg	FRG	17Jul59	197/111	HT	76.58	76.32	−82
Schaffner	Thomas	GDR	3Aug63	192/85	JT	82.68	79.74	−83
Schaffer	Frank	GDR	23Oct58	188/80	400	46.07	44.87	−80
Schenk	Christian	GDR	9Feb65	201/88	Dec	8053	7614	−83
Schersing	Mathias	GDR	7Oct64	184/69	400	44.86	47.06	−83
Schildhauer	Werner	GDR	5Jun59	182/65	5k	13:26.23	13:12.54	−82
					10k	28:09.05	27:24.95	−83
Schlisske	Andreas	GDR	5Jun57	188/80	110h	13.68	13.60	−83
Schmid	Harald	FRG	29Feb57	187/82	400	45.36	44.92	−79
					400h	47.69	47.48	−82
Schmidt	Gerhard	FRG	12Jan61	183/70	PV	5.55i,5.52	5.55i,5.50	−83
Schmidt	Holger	FRG	11Jan57	188/93	Dec	7829	8079	−79
Schmidt	Matthias	GDR	22Nov56	189/110	SP	20.19i,19.82	20.92	−81
Schmitt	Uwe	FRG	17Aug61	184/74	400	45.9	46.69	−82
					400h	49.48	50.36	−83
Schnabel	Stefan	FRG	15May63		400h	50.56	51.80	−83
Schneider	Joe	USA	30Jun57	188/86	Dec	7806m	7688	−80
Schneider	Robert	FRG	1Oct60		5k	13:35.15	13:48.00	−83
Schneider	Roberto	SWZ	26May57	184/67	110h	13.83	13.5−76, 13.75	−78
Schneider-Laub	Andre	FRG	12Aug58	194/76	HJ	2.25	2.30	−79
Schoch	Jurgen	FRG	10Apr62	181/69	110h	13.87	13.84,13.83w	−83
Schoeman	Kobus	RSA	16Nov65		110h	13.7A		
Schonlebe	Thomas	GDR	6Aug65	185/72	400	45.01	45.29e	−83
Schnur	Jim	USA	29Dec54	188/83	Dec	7867m	7850	−82
Scholz	Peter	FRG	31Oct59	184/75	400h	49.45	50.8−82, 51.08	−83
Schreiber	Helmut	FRG	26Jun55	182/87	JT	81.52	92.72	−79
Schroder	Thomas	GDR	23Aug62	178/73	100	10.27	10.22−83,10.14w	−81
					200	20.56	20.68	−82

487

Men's Index

Schult	Jurgen	GDR	11May60	193/110	DT	68.82	66.78	−83
Schulting	Harry	HOL	11Feb56	192/79	400h	50.26	48.44A,48.71	−79
Schulze	Jens	FRG	6Apr56	183/76	Dec	8302	8216	−83
Schwarz	Rainer	FRG	5Jun59	181/63	St	8:31.8	8:19.64	−83
Scott	Steve	USA	5May56	186/73	800	1:46.73	1:45.05	−82
					1500	3:33.46	3:31.96	−81
					Mile	3:52.99	3:47.69	−82
Scott	Terry	USA	23Jun64	190/86	100	10.34,10.31w	10.21	−83
Scott	Vince	USA	7Dec62	188/77	100	10.1w	10.4	−82
Scruton	Mark	UK	24Oct58		1k	2:17.95	2:22.96	−79
					1500	3:38.78	3:43.50	−80
Scrutton	Mark	UK	14Apr60	185/69	10k	28:25.6	28:44.2	−82
Seck	Charles	SEN	11May65	167/70	100	10.36	10.5	−82
Seck	Karl-Heinz	FRG	18Sep54	190/68	St	8:32.06	8:31.61	−82
Seck	Saliou	SEN	15Dec55	185/78	100	10.0w		
Sedykh	Yuriy	SU	11Jun55	185/106	HT	86.34	81.80	−80
Seko	Toshihiko	JAP	15Jul56	169/64	10k	28.11.25	27:43.44	−80
Sekulic	Dragan	YUG	26May57	184/69	2k	5:05.91		
					3k	7:49.85		
Seleke	Ernest	RSA	12Jun59		Mar	2:09:41		
Seleznyev	Aleksandr	SU	64	180/100	HT	75.80	74.28	−83
Selivanov	Nikolay	SU	25Jun58	191/82	PV	5.60i,5.50	5.70	−83
Selmon	Thomas	USA	1Feb62	173/68	LJ	8.17w	7.63,7.85w	−82
Selvaggio	Antonio	ITA	1Jan58	176/56	2k	5:06.80		
					3k	7:48.14	7:50.7	−79
					5k	13:25.63	13:40.93	−81
Selvaggio	Piero	ITA	1Jan58	176/56	5k	13:27.08	13:32.09	−81
Semiraz	Oleg	SU	61		LJ	8.07,8.10w	8.03	−83
Semyonov	Aleksandr	SU	62		100	10.34	10.35−83,10.3	−82
Semykin	Konstantin	SU	26May60	180/76	LJ	8.38	8.10	−83
Sena	Jose	POR	13Jul55	171/62	10k	28:17.83	28:02.8	−81
Senior	Mark	JAM	13Dec63	170/67	400	45.75		
Sennai	Isamu	JAP	11Aug60	171/58	Mar	2:12:20	2:17:43	−83
Sereda	Valeriy	SU	30Jun59	186/76	HJ	2.37	2.35	−83
Sergiyenko	Yuriy	SU	19Mar65	190/73	HJ	2.26i,2.24	2.29	−83
Serrani	Lucio	ITA	11Mar61	190/120	HT	75.76	70.04	−83
Serrano	Guillermo	MEX	15Nov60	170/60	St	8:35.64		
Sevinskas	Vidmantas	SU	60		HT	73.30	70.80	−81
Shabanov	Georgiy	SU	26Apr60	187/80	110h	13.7	13.71−82,13.5	−81
Shahanga	Gidamis	TAN	4Sep57	180/57	10k	28:03.24	27:38.1	−82
					Mar	2:10:19	2:11:05	−83
Shannon	Dan	USA	24Oct63	183/66	400	46.09	47.50	−83
Sharp	Cameron	UK	3Jun58	182/77	100	10.30w	10.20	−83
							10.07w	−82
Sharpe	Tony	CAN	28Jun61	178/73	100	10.33,	10.30	−82
						10.09w	A10.19,10.11w	−82
					200	20.64A,	20.77,20.22A	−82
						20.56w		
Shchegolev	Igor	SU	60	186/95	HT	76.18	71.26	−82
Shenkerman	Yakov	SU	14Nov60	182/64	800	1:46.16	1:46.7	−83
Sheppard	Darryl	USA			110h	13.5w		
Shesterov	Vladimir	SU	16Jan54	176/65	10k	28:26.31	28:07.0	−80
Shevchenko	Yuriy	SU	18Apr60	190/78	HJ	2.25	2.28i−82,2.26	−83
Shilev	Nikolay	BUL	18Jul63	186/76	110h	13.54	13.84	−83
Shintaku	Masanari	JAP	21Dec57	175/60	10k	27:59.79	27:44.5	−83
Shkvira	Arkadiy	SU	18Oct60	188/73	PV	5.60	5.50	−82
Shmakov	Vladimir	SU	20Nov58	190/83	Dec	7947,7958m	7852,8119m	−83
Sholars	Greg	USA	8Feb66	172/66	100	10.16w	10.30w	−83
Shopin	Vladimir	SU	63		JT	81.40	78.42	−83
Shulgin	Vladimir	SU	22Apr61	182/80	PV	5.60	5.60	−83
Shumilin	Aleksandr	SU	53		TJ	16.43	16.41	−83
Siaudinis	Jonas	SU	24Feb58	188/110	DT	61.80	63.34	−83

Men's Index

Sidorenko	Vasiliy	SU	61	186/100	HT	76.80	74.10	−83
Sidorov	Ivan	SU	8May62		Dec	7715	7793m	−83
Sidorov	Nikolay	SU	26Nov56	190/84	100	10.32	10.32−82,10.1	−81
					200	20.65w,20.4	20.79	−82
Sidorov	Vladimir	SU	31Dec58	178/80	LJ	8.11w	7.92	−82
Sigurdsson	Oddur	ICE	28Apr59	181/70	400	45.36	46.49	−83
Siitonen	Reijo	FIN	15Nov61	185/74	PV	5.40	5.40	−83
Silanchenko	Aleksandr	SU	57		HT	73.06	72.92	−82
Siler	David	USA	15May61	190/82	TJ	16.53	16.68,16.85i,	
							16.02w−83,16.68A	−82
Silfver	Conny	SWE	18Oct57	186/85	Dec	7877	7736,7809m	−82
							7758w	−83
Silva	Alejandro	CHL	28Jul58		Mar	2:10:50dm		
Simionato	Carlo	ITA	7Jan61	178/66	200	20.76	20.53	−83
Simon	Andres	CUB	61		100	10.25		
Simon Balla	Istvan	HUN	9Feb58	186/69	400h	50.26	50.14	−82
Simpkins	Charles	USA	19Oct63	185/70	TJ	16.76,17.18w	16.64	−83
Sinclair	Jon	USA	4Sep57	169/57	5k	13:35.3	13:44.5	−81
Sinitsyn	Viktor	SU	59		DT	62.64	61.54	−82
Sinka	Albert	HUN	22Nov62	187/95	HT	73.30	71.62	−82
Sivillon	Philippe	FRA	25May58	182/76	PV	5.50i,5.50	5.52	−82
Sjoberg	Patrik	SWE	5Jan65	200/78	HJ	2.33	2.33	−83
Skalidas	Galvidas	SU	21Nov60	183/83	Dec	8045m		
Skamrahl	Erwin	FRG	8Mar58	178/67	200	20.80w	20.44	−83
							20.25w	−81
					400	45.74	44.50	−83
Skarzynski	Jerzy	POL	13Jan56	176/62	Mar	2:12:37	2:15:31	−83
Sklyarov	Vitaliy	SU	31Jan60	187/75	110h	13.88,	13.87,13.3w	−83
						13.5	13.7	−82
Skramstad	Trond	NOR	6Dec60	184/85	Dec	8132	7999e	−83
Sladinov	Vyacheslav	SU	21Jan59	180/73	TJ	16.42	16.51	−82
Slaney	Richard	UK	16May56	201/130	DT	64.66	64.64	−82
Slater	Elton	USA	10Mar64	178/84	LJ	7.95	7.47,7.68w	−82
Slusarski	Tadeusz	POL	19May50	178/76	PV	5.55i,5.50	5.70,5.71ex	−83
Smirnov	Sergey	SU	23Sep60	192/126	SP	21.63	21.00	−83
Smirnov	Yuriy	SU	6Apr61	191/90	JT	87.10	80.54	−81
Smith	Calvin	USA	8Jan61	178/64	100	10.11,	9.93A,9.97	−83
						9.94w	9.91w	−82
					200	20.33	19.99	−83
Smith	Charles	USA	24May66	180/74	LJ	8.06	7.94	−83
Smith	Dave	JAM			100	10.27w	10.46	−83
					200	20.79,20.22w	20.95	−83
						20.5		
Smith	Dave	UK	21Jun62	190/110	HT	74.62	71.60	−83
Smith	Fred	USA			110h	13.7	13.8	−83
Smith	Geoff	UK	24Oct53	173/61	10k	28:14.87	27:43.76	−81
					Mar	2:10:08	2:09:08	−83
Smith	Karl	JAM	15Sep59	180/73	400h	49.58	49.17	−82
Smith	Kenny	USA	22Nov62	186/70	HJ	2.24	2.21	−83
Smith	Lamar	USA	5Jan64	178/76	400	45.90	46.25	−83
Smith	Mike	USA	4Jun58	183/118	SP	20.90	19.99	−83
Smith	Ray	USA	16Apr57	196/80	400h	49.18	51.07,50.5	−83
Smith	Tom	USA	9Oct57	180/60	1500	3:38.8	3:38.87	−81
					Mile	3:54.65	3:57.64	−81
					5k	13:30.93	13:45.54	−81
Smith	Willie	USA	28Feb56	173/73	400	45.07	44.73	−78
Smolyakov	Sergey	SU	12Oct62		PV	5.70	5.55i,5.50	−83
Snoddy	William	USA	6Dec57	180/76	200	20.64A,20.77	20.27A,20.28	−78
Sobolev	Viktor	SU	23Jul60	186/78	PV	5.50	5.60	−81
Sobolevskiy	Igor	SU	6May62	180/85	LJ	7.98	7.84	−83
					Dec	8530	8234	−83
Sorensen	Lars	FIN	13Feb59	181/65	St	8:27.27	8:34.6	−82

489

Men's Index

Sogomo	Elijah	KEN	9Mar54		400	45.8A	46.84,46.8	−81
Solanas	Alberto	SPA	6Nov55	188/75	LJ	7.92w	8.00	−80
Soh	Takeshi	JAP	9Jan53	178/58	Mar	2:10:55	2:08:55	−83
Sokolov	Sergey	SU	29Mar62	187/85	200	20.52	20.54,20.48w	−82
Sokolov	Vitaliy	SU	1Aug55	183/115	DT	64.40	62.50	−83
Solly	Jon	UK	28Jun63	183/66	5k	13:30.91	14:15.7	−83
Solomko	Sergey	SU	28May58	192/110	SP	21.02	20.62	−83
Solomon	Mike	TRI	29Sep54	171/60	800	1:46.88	1:46.17	−82
Sommerfeld	Burkhard	GDR	22Jul62	187/105	HT	73.10	67.24	−83
Sosnin	Viktor	SU	54		SP	20.44	19.84	−83
Sotomayor	Javier	CUB	13Oct67	195/82	HJ	2.33	2.17	−83
Souza	Gerson Andrade	BRA	2Jan59	176/74	400	45.44, 45.4	45.21 45.2	−82 −83
Spasov	Viktor	SU	19Jul59	185/75	PV	5.60	5.65,5.70i	−82
Spearmon	Wallace	USA	3Sep62	188/76	100	10.25w	10.3−82,10.41 10.0w,10.38Aw	−83 −81
					200	20.36	20.89	−81
Spedding	Charles	UK	9May52	173/63	Mar	2:09:57	−0−	
Speer	Brad	USA	28Nov65	193/82	HJ	2.25		
Spivey	Jim	USA	7Mar60	178/61	1k	2:16.54	2:19.03	−81
					1500	3:34.19	3:36.4	−83
					Mile	3:53.88	3:50.59	−83
Spottel	Michael	FRG	30Jan56	180/63	Mar	2:12:53	2:13:35	−83
Spry	Ralph	USA	16Jun60	173/70	LJ	8.16	8.18,8.36w	−83
Stahl	Kjell-Erik	SWE	17Feb46	188/71	Mar	2:12:00	2:10:38	−83
Stan	Tudor	RUM	4Jan53	182/102	HT	73.02	72.92	−83
Stanley	Leotha	USA	25Jul56		LJ	7.90,7.91w	7.65,7.87w	−83
Stapylton-Smith	John	NZ	12Aug61	191/85	JT	83.10		
Stark	Siegfried	GDR	12Jun55	186/86	Dec	7783	8480	−80
Starodubtsev	Valeriy	SU	62		800	1:46.24	1:48.3	−83
Stavro	Aleksandr	SU	5Jan63	186/82	Dec	7842m	7643m	−82
Steen	Dave	CAN	14Nov59	185/80	Dec	8242	8205w	−83
Steinbrecher	Jorg	GDR	6Dec63	181/70	400h	50.53	51.00	−83
Stekic	Nenad	YUG	7Mar51	181/73	LJ	8.10	8.45	−75
Stepankov	Aleksandr	SU	13May58	188/124	SP	20.11	19.72	−81
Stepanskiy	Viktor	SU	25Apr59	184/118	SP	20.05	20.08	−83
Stepanyan	Oganes	SU	1Jan56	175/76	LJ	8.10	8.09	−83
Stephan	Herbert	FRG	6Oct59	179/65	2k	5:05.23	5:14.0	−83
Stepnicki	Marek	POL	11Nov55	188/77	St	8:35.18	8:35.36	−83
Steuk	Roland	GDR	5Mar59	190/117	HT	79.90	78.72	−81
Stevens	Derek	UK	19May54	174/60	Mar	2:12:41	2:15:18	−83
Stevens	Tom	USA	23Jun61	183/70	St	8:25.21	8:29.89	−83
Stewart	Craig	USA			LJ	7.92w		
Stewart	Milan	USA	31Oct60	183/79	110h	13.48,13.4	13.46,13.44w	−82
Stewart	Ray	JAM	18Mar65	178/73	100	10.19	10.22	−83
Stinson	Elliston	USA	3Oct62	175/72	100	10.23,10.16w	10.20	−83
					200	20.68	21.10,20.80w, A20.86	−82
Stoch	Ryszard	POL	24Mar62	181/74	400h	50.50	50.87	−83
Stock	Keith	UK	18Mar57	176/73	PV	5.42i,5.40	5.65	−81
Stolz	Karsten	FRG	23Jul64	208/130	SP	19.73	18.73	−81
Stones	Dwight	USA	6Dec53	196/82	HJ	2.34	2.32	−76
Strawderman	Mark	USA	28Jun60	183/73	PV	5.50	5.43i,5.34	−82
Strebkov	Sergey	SU	55		200	20.6		
Strelchenko	Sergey	SU	61		110h	13.6i,13.6	13.8	−83
Strizhakov	Oleg	SU	63		5k	13:30.88	13:57.7	−83
					10k	28:23.80		
Stroud	Byron	USA			200	20.6w		
Stuart	Jesse	USA	18Mar51	190/120	SP	19.71	20.84	−83
Stubblefield	Keith	USA	11Feb65	165/66	100	10.29w	10.57,10.37w	−83
Stubblefield	Steve	USA	30Dec61	183/77	PV	5.60i,5.50	5.36	−82
Stukonis	Donatas	SU	19Nov57	192/108	SP	20.14	20.82	−82

Men's Index

Styopochkin	Vladimir	SU	64		HT	73.64	69.52	−83
Suelflohn	Rob	USA	15Feb59	190/118	SP	20.46	19.75	−82
Suey	Chuck	USA	7Dec60	185/82	PV	5.42	5.24	−83
Sukharev	Gennadiy	SU	65		PV	5.53i	4.90i	−82
Sula	Karel	CS	30Jun59	189/104	SP	19.69i	19.15	−83
Suliman	Jamal	QAT		170/65	100	10.1	10.58,10.33w	−83
					200	20.6	21.16	−83
Sullivan	Shannon	USA	15Oct59	183/86	Dec	7777	−0−	
Sulyok	Attila	HUN	17Feb59	173/54	2k	5:08.98	5:06.94	−83
Surguchev	Aleksey	SU	58		PV	5.40i,5.40	5.30	−83
Sutton	Kenneth	USA	10Oct62	175/64	100	10.20w	10.2,10.39w	−83
					200	20.44w,20.4w	21.23	−81
Swarts	Art	USA	14Feb45	193/116	DT	64.66	69.40	−79
Swezey	David	USA	10Feb59	185/82	PV	5.50	5.36	−82
Szabo	Gabor K.	HUN	19Jun62	182/66	3k	7:48.93i	7:47.4	−83
Szabo	Laszlo	HUN	6Jan55	192/120	SP	19.87	19.80	−83
Szabo	Zsolt	HUN	12Nov64	183/68	LJ	7.93w	7.75	−83
Szalai	Istvan	HUN	25May62	181/63	800	1:46.54	1:46.94	−81
Szalai	Jozsef	HUN	8Mar61	180/75	400h	50.05	49.64	−80
Szalma	Laszlo	HUN	21Oct57	190/80	LJ	8.27	8.24−83,8.25w	−80
Szegletes	Ferenc	HUN	14Apr48	186/106	DT	62.26	63.46	−83
Szitas	Imre	HUN	4Sep61	185/105	HT	78.84	74.08	−82
Szpak	Mieczyslaw	POL	10Jul61	188/110	DT	61.10	57.96	−83
Szparak	Ryszard	POL	2Jul51	178/66	400h	49.81	49.17	−83
Szybowski	Miroslaw	POL	15Sep60	178/90	JT	81.18	82.86	−83
Taavitsainen	Ari	FIN	12Apr58	181/100	HT	75.62	72.40	−83
Tafelmeier	Klaus	FRG	12Apr58	190/87	JT	91.04	91.44	−83
Tafralis	Greg	USA	9Apr58	183/120	SP	21.25	20.20	−83
Taft	Tim	USA	27Apr58	188/84	Dec	7927m	6838m	−80
Taiwo	Joseph	NIG	24Aug59	183/74	TJ	17.19	16.91	−82
Takacs	Istvan	HUN	20Jan59	183/69	400h	50.23	50.31	−83
Takahashi	Tomomi	JAP	29Jan56	171/62	PV	5.53	5.52	−83
Takano	Susumu	JAP	21May61	178/67	400	45.69	45.86	−83
Talley	Keith	USA	28Jan64	193/88	110h	13.69,13.50w		
					LJ	7.95,7.97w		
Tallhem	Soren	SWE	16Feb64	192/108	SP	20.60i,20.26	17.40	−83
Tamm	Juri	SU	5Feb57	193/120	HT	84.40	80.46	−80
Tanczi	Tibor	HUN	6Oct58	176/90	HT	76.80	75.48	−82
Tanev	Ivan	BUL	1May57	187/95	HT	76.50	72.14	−83
Tarasov	Sergey	SU	62		TJ	16.85	16.72	−83
Tarasyuk	Yuriy	SU	11Apr57	188/101	HT	81.44	81.18	−83
Tarev	Atanas	BUL	31Jan58	180/75	PV	5.72	5.70−82, 5.71ex	−83
Tarnavetskiy	Pavel	SU	22Feb61	182/76	Dec	8233	7878,8072m	−83
Tarpenning	Kory	USA	27Feb62	180/75	PV	5.50	5.28	−83
Tatum	Roscoe	USA	13Feb66	183/91	100	10.26w	10.65−82,10.49w	−83
Taushanski	Georgi	BUL	26Dec57	192/108	DT	65.78	63.94	−82
Tave	Ed	USA	27Jun63	190/75	LJ	7.97,8.07w	7.88,8.16w	−83
Taylor	Keith	USA	11Nov56	180/73	LJ	8.08	7.78−79, 7.94w	−78
Tegla	Ferenc	HUN	15Jul47	185/98	DT	62.44	67.38	−77
Temane	Matthew	RSA	14Dec60	174/62	1500	3:38.3	3:40.6	−83
					Mile	3:56.58	3:55.4	−83
Temesi	Andras	HUN	14Nov50	184/95	JT	83.62	85.36	−79
Tesacek	Lubomir	CS	9Feb57	171/54	2k	5:08.46	5:23.3	−77
					3k	7:49.20i	7:46.99	−83
					5k	13:30.88	13:30.42	−83
Tesitel	Jan	CS	29May58	189/77	110h	13.93	14.01−83, 14.0w	−80
Thaxton	Steve	USA	29Jul64	187/82	PV	5.41	5.11	−83
Theriot	Brian	USA	15Feb57	183/69	800	1:46.50	1:45.79	−81
					1k	2:18.91	2:22.14	−83
					1500	3:37.0	3:38.74	−83
					Mile	3:56.10	4:00.70	−83
Therwanger	Kerry	USA			LJ	7.95w	7.66	−83

491

Men's Index

Thiebaut	Pascal	FRA	6Jun59	175/61	1k	2:18.7		
					1500	3:35.8	3:36.07	−83
					Mile	3:52.02		
					3k	7:46.89	7:51.02	−83
Thomas	Curtis	USA	13Jan62	193/89	200	20.65,	21.01	−83
						20.53w	20.4	−81
Thomas	Henry	USA	10Jul67	188/77	100	10.27	10.46,10.2w	−83
					200	20.73	21.02	−83
					400	45.82	48.57−82,48.5	−83
Thomas	Johnny	USA	3Aug63	175/80	100	10.28w	10.66−83,10.3	−82
					200	20.56,	21.47	−83
						20.4w	21.26w	−82
Thomas	Jon	USA	1Feb63	190/81	400h	49.63	49.04	−83
Thomas	Larnell	USA	28Feb64		100	10.34,10.26w	10.65	−83
					200	20.6	21.3	−83
Thomas	Robert	USA	25Jul60	178/70	110h	13.80	13.86−82,13.7	−83
							13.6w	−81
Thomas	Robin	USA	19Aug62	178/70	400	45.95		
Thompson	Daley	UK	30Jul58	185/86	100	10.36,	10.45	−79
						10.28w	10.32w	−81
					LJ	8.01	8.00−80,8.11w	−78
					Dec	8798	8743	−82
Thompson	Reyna	USA	28Aug63	185/82	110h	13.91,13.64w	13.80	−82
Thranhardt	Carlo	FRG	5Jul57	199/85	HJ	2.37	2.34	−83
Tiacoh	Gabriel	IVC	10Sep63	180/75	200	20.71	21.23	−82
					400	44.54	45.86	−83
Tiainen	Juha	FIN	5Dec55	182/107	HT	81.52	81.02	−83
Tietjens	Brian	USA	21Sep62	196/77	HJ	2.27	2.285i,2.285	−83
Tiller	Torsten	FRG	27Feb62	183/64	St	8:28.95	8:33.94	−83
Tilli	Stefano	ITA	22Aug62	175/65	100	10.16	10.28,10.06w	−83
					200	20.40	20.54	−83
Tillman	John	USA	11Feb65	183/75	TJ	16.61	15.44	−83
Timmermann	Ulf	GDR	1Nov62	194/118	SP	21.75	21.36	−83
Timpson	John	USA	28Dec62	183/72	110h	13.48	13.83,13.59w	−83
Tishchenko	Vitaliy	SU	28Jul57	174/60	1500	3:36.91	3:35.8	−80
Titov	Anatoliy	SU	3Mar56		110h	13.72,	13.70	−82
						13.6i	13.6	−81
Titov	Vladimir	SU	24Apr59	186/76	400h	50.12,50.0	49.90	−83
Tkachev	Sergey	SU	7Oct58		TJ	17.02	16.58	−82
Toboc	Horia	RUM	7Feb55	184/71	400h	50.02	49.64	−80
Todorov	Georgi	BUL	7Mar60	193/112	SP	20.30	19.99	−83
Tokarev	Nikolay	SU	18Nov60	188/89	Dec	7880m	7983m	−83
Toyryla	Kari	FIN	17Aug56	195/120	SP	19.70	19.52	−83
Toivonen	Antero	FIN	13Oct48	182/88	JT	81.38	88.62	−81
Tolstikov	Yakov	SU	20May59		Mar	2:10:48	2:13:35	−83
Tomaszewski	Mariusz	POL	23Apr56	190/115	HT	79.46,81.46ex	78.40	−82
Tomko	Jan	CS	27Aug62	175/68	400	45.76	45.64	−83
Tommelein	Rik	BEL	1Nov62	178/66	400h	49.64	49.94	−83
Tomov	Toma	BUL	6May58	179/68	400	45.86	46.42	−83
					400h	48.99	49.24	−83
Toon	Albert	USA	30Apr63	193/89	110h	13.90w	14.03w	−82
Torneden	Fred	USA	2Jul59	183/60	Mar	2:11:34	2:14:44	−83
Torres	Juan	SPA	26Nov57	173/62	St	8:16.25	8:20.7	−83
Toska	Ajet	ALB	61		HT	73.62	67.76	−83
Toth	Laszlo	HUN	31Aug55	177/61	1500	3:38.8	3:38.40	−81
Towns	Reggie	USA	27Sep61	193/86	110h	13.92,	13.63,13.56w	−83
						13.80w	13.5	−80
Tozzi	Gianni	ITA	6May62		110h	13.84	13.81w,13.85	−83
Tozzi	Roberto	ITA	17Dec58	180/72	400	46.03	46.28A,46.31	−79
Trabado	Coloman	SPA	2Jan58	182/71	800	1:45.15	1:45.90	−82
Treacy	John	IRL	4Jun57	175/59	5k	13:16.81	13:21.93	−80
					10k	28:01.3	27:48.7	−80
					Mar	2:09:56		

Men's Index

Trinks	Uwe	GDR	19Feb62	182/92	JT	81.44	76.16	−82
Trofimenko	Vasiliy	SU	28Jan62	195/80	PV	5.40i,5.40	5.30	−82
Troshchilo	Aleksandr	SU	16Jan60	183/73	400	45.51	45.66	−83
Tsepelyov	Vladimir	SU	10Oct56	194/84	LJ	8.05	8.13	−82
Tsvetikov	Aleksey	SU	62		HT	73.78	70.96	−83
Tsyplyakov	Vladimir	SU	56		HJ	2.24i	2.22	−81
Tully	Mike	USA	21Oct56	190/86	PV	5.82	5.71	−78
Tuomola	Juhani	FIN	3Jun42	188/115	DT	62.48	63.68	−76
Tuparov	Ivan	BUL	15Nov59	175/64	LJ	8.07	8.03	−80
Tura	Eshetu	ETH	19Jan5	179/66	St	8:32.08	8:13.57	−80
Turanok	Vladimir	SU	5Jun57	185/100	DT	61.86	60.64	−80
Turb	Toomas	SU	31Jan57	178/65	10k	28:20.35	27:54.18	−81
Turnbull	Geoff	UK	15Apr61	173/60	3k	7:47.88	8:07.6	−82
					5k	13:33.86	13:47.18	−83
Turner	Sam	USA	17Jun57	191/80	200	20.52	21.15	−83
					110h	13.49,13.38w	13.17	−83
Tuttle	Gary	USA	12Oct47	176/60	10k	28:26.4	28:35.2	−74
Tuttle	John	USA	16Oct58	185/70	Mar	2:11:50	2:10:51	−83
Tyler	Cary	USA	19Sep59	177/76	TJ	16.42	16.46−83,16.66w	−81
Ubartas	Romas	SU	26May60	202/120	DT	66.92	66.64	−83
Ujino	Shuji	JAP	15Jan60		HJ	2.28	2.24	−83
Ueta	Yasushi	JAP	13Nov55	181/72	TJ	16.71	16.49	−78
Ugbisie	Moses	NIG	11Dec64	182/76	400	46.09	46.9	−82
Ullo	Antonio	ITA	7Jan63	180/80	100	10.36,	10.52,10.3	−83
						10.1	10.50w	−82
Ulloa	Emilio	CHL	22Oct54	184/72	St	8:28.99	8:37.36	−83
Ulmer	Christoph	SWZ	29Jun61	181/65	800	1:46.82	1:46.82	−83
Urlando	Giampaolo	ITA	7Jan45	178/100	HT	78.16	77.92	−82
Uryadnikov	Mikhail	SU	23Oct59	175/74	100	10.34		
Usov	Igor	SU	28Mar61	181/75	TJ	16.76	17.02	−82
Usov	Sergey	SU	14Jan64	188/87	110h	13.74,	13.96	−83
						13.7	13.8i	−82
Ustinov	Vyacheslav	SU	10May57	190/86	110h	13.57	13.73,13.5	−83
Usui	Junichi	JAP	6Oct57	178/70	LJ	8.02,8.03w	8.10	−79
Uti	Sunday	NIG	23Oct62	175/68	200	20.6	21.1−83,21.50	−82
					400	44.83	44.96	−83
Uusmaa	Mati	SU	16Sep59	182/74	St	8:34.20	8:31.19	−83
Vago	Bela	HUN	3Oct63	176/63	St	8:34.90	8:45.19	−83
Vainio	Martti	FIN	30Dec50	190/74	3k	7:44.42	7:46.24	−82
					5k	13:16.02	13:20.07	−83
					10k	27:41.75	27:30.99	−78
					Mar	2:13:04dq		
Valakhanovich	Nikolay	SU	19May57	187/103	SP	19.77	20.65	−83
Valentine	Tony	USA	6Sep64	190/77	400h	49.66	51.34	−83
Valent	Gejza	CS	3Oct53	196/120	DT	69.70	67.56	−82
Valmon	Andrew	USA	1Jan65	185/75	400	45.99	46.81	−83
Valvik	Svein-Inge	NOR	20Sep56	190/112	DT	63.82	68.00	−82
Valyukevich	Gennadiy	SU	1Jun58	182/74	TJ	17.42	17.42	−82
Vamvakas	Georgios	GRE	1Jan60	185/76	400h	50.30	50.67	−79
Vanags	Aldis	SU	31Oct60	190/80	HJ	2.24	2.15	−83
Vanatta	Mike	USA	18Oct61	175/63	St	8:31.14	8:37.7	−83
van den Abeele	Theo	BEL	15Aug60		10k	28:18.65	28:53.59	−83
van der Herten	Dirk	BEL	9Mar57		Mar	2:12:21		
van der Vennet	Freddy	BEL	18Dec52	170/62	Mar	2:12:09	2:13:01	−83

493

Men's Index

van Dijck	William	BEL	24Jan61	180/59	3k	7:49.7	7:57.6	−83
					5k	13:32.77	13:53.47	−82
					St	8:18.75	8:21.73	−83
van Huylenbroek	Willy	BEL	21Jun56		Mar	2:12:53	2:14:00	−83
Vanichkin	Aleksandr	SU	55		TJ	16.55i	16.55i,16.54	−83
van Miltenberg	Peter	AUS	16Aug57	174/73	100	10.1w	10.71,10.3	−83
					200	20.69,	21.06,	
						20.6,20.5w	20.8	−83
Vannesluoma	Veijo	FIN	29Jul58	184/77	PV	5.50	5.55	−83
van Paemel	Raymond	BEL	24Oct56		5k	13:31.93	13:44.6	−80
Vashchenko	Sergey	SU	58		HT	76.96	70.42	−82
Vashchenko	Viktor	SU	19Mar58	192/88	Dec	7978	8124	−82
Vasilyev	Aleksandr	SU	26Jul61	191/83	400h	48.45	49.07	−83
Vaughans	Cedric	USA	13Oct61	188/79	400	45.78,45.6	45.78A,45.99	−82
Vaughn	Pat	USA	7Oct59	175/60	10k	28:21.7	28:31.9	−82
Vedra	Josef	CS	1Feb56	172/60	2k	5:07.83		
Velev	Velko	BUL	4Jan48	189/118	DT	65.70	67.82	−78
Vera	Andres	SPA	31Dec60	186/72	800	1:46.85	1:46.86	−83
					1k	2:19.83		
					1500	3:36.55	3:40.2	−82
					Mile	3:55.33		
Verbeeck	Bob	BEL	5Aug60	176/60	1500	3:36.96	3:39.55	−83
					Mile	3:58.34	3:57.98	−83
					3k	7:47.22	7:52.09	−82
					5k	13:24.73	13:39.10	−83
Verriet	Rudi	HOL	29Dec56		Mar	2:12:41	2:13:48	−82
Verzy	Franck	FRA	13May61	181/66	HJ	2.26	2.32	−83
Vetterli	Patrick	SWZ	6Oct61	198/100	Dec	7864	7660	−83
Vida	Jozsef	HUN	9Jan63	192/108	HT	79.06	74.92	−83
Videv	Valentin	BUL	20Jan63	184/70	PV	5.40	5.30	−82
Vigneron	Thierry	FRA	9Mar60	181/73	PV	5.91	5.83	−83
Viitasalo	Esa	FIN	19May60	184/76	TJ	16.53w	16.52,16.74w	−83
Vikhrov	Valeriy	SU	61		400h	49.40	49.95	−83
Vilhjalmsson	Einar	ICE	1Jun60	188/97	JT	92.42	90.66	−83
Viluckis	Benjaminas	SU	20Mar61	187/118	HT	78.20	77.50	−83
Vinci	Baker	USA	19Oct62	183/73	PV	5.40	4.99	−83
Virgin	Craig	USA	2Aug55	179/59	10k	28:02.27	27:29.16	−80
Vitshel	Aleksandr	SU	4Sep63	179/50	St	8:30.76	8:31.0	−79
Vogel	Uwe	GDR	6Jul58	189/75	LJ	8.05	7.69	−82
Volkey	Don	USA	14May62	175/64	1500	3:38.59	3:49.0	−83
Volkov	Konstantin	SU	28Feb60	185/79	PV	5.85	5.75,5.84ex	−81
Volmer	Peter	FRG	14Jan58	180/69	PV	5.65i,5.50	5.55	−83
Volz	Dave	USA	2May62	180/82	PV	5.50	5.75	−82
Voronin	Mikhail	SU	2Oct60	187/79	PV	5.50i,5.50	5.58	−82
Voronkov	Pavel	SU	58	193/85	110h	13.87	14.06,13.5w	−83
							13.8	−80
Voss	Torsten	GDR	24Mar63	186/88	LJ	8.02	7.70	−82
					Dec	8535	8387	−82
Vostrikov	Nikolay	SU	2Jan60	190/110	DT	61.24	62.86	−83
Voykin	Valeriy	SU	14Oct45	192/123	SP	19.59	20.78	−79
Vrabel	Martin	CS	21Sep55	165/55	10k	28:19.66	28:37.41	−81
Vrbka	Frantisek	CS	23Jul58	187/102	HT	78.84	77.30	−83
Vriend	Cor	HOL	8Nov49	173/65	Mar	2:11:41	2:12:15	−82
Vukicevic	Petar	YUG	17Aug56	184/70	110h	13.87,	13.92	−80
						13.6	13.7	−82
Waddell	Clark	USA	12Jun65	178/73	200	20.79	21.11	−83
Wagenknecht	Detlef	GDR	3Jan59	193/74	800	1:45.44	1:44.81	−81
Wagner	Alwin	FRG	11Aug50	196/122	DT	66.58	67.10	−82
Wahlander	Yngve	SWE	15Sep58	186/105	SP	20.35	20.00	−83
Waigwa	Wilson	KEN	15Feb49	172/64	5k	13:27.34	13:20.36	−80
Walker	Greg	USA	5Aug63	184/77	100	10.33		
Walker	James	USA	25Oct57	178/67	400h	49.40	48.84	−79

494

Men's Index

Walker	John	NZ	12Jan52	183/74	800	1:46.83	1:44.94	−74
					1k	2:19.37	2:16.57	−80
					1500	3:35.93	3:32.4	−75
					Mile	3:49.73	3:49.08	−82
					5k	13:24.46	13:20.89	−81
Walker	Johnny	USA	25Aug63	183/70	800	1:46.86	1:47.22	−83
Walker	Nigel	UK	15Jun63	180/72	110h	13.78	14.19	−83
Wallow	Detlef	FRG	21Jan63		1k	2:18.86	2:22.51	−82
Walsh	Stephen	NZ	17Dec60	184/72	LJ	7.96,	7.80	−83
						8.10w	7.96w	−82
Ward	Don	USA	20Feb62	180/73	400h	50.19	50.99	−81
Warnemunde	Wolfgang	GDR	8May53	202/117	DT	67.30	67.56	−80
Washington	Alex	USA	28Dec62	187/77	110h	13.83,	13.82,	
						13.64w	13.77w,13.7w	−83
Washington	James	USA	15Apr62	183/82	LJ	7.98	7.64w	−81
Washington	Lester	USA	5Sep55	178/73	100	10.33,	10.36	−82
						10.24w	10.1,10.25w	−80
					200	20.75,	20.58	−79
						20.65w	20.54w	−83
Watkins	Rick	USA	25Dec60	188/77	HJ	2.25	2.16	−83
Watrice	Thierry	FRA	23Jan57	180/69	3k	7:49.56	7:54.06	−83
					5k	13:34.62	13:27.58	−83
					10k	28:04.61	28:09.41	−82
Watson	Luke	UK	19Nov57	191/84	100	10.12w	10.32,10.16w	−83
					200	20.80,20.5w	20.62	−83
Waynes	Ron	USA	2Sep60	183/73	LJ	7.90i	8.03	−83
Weber	Hartmut	FRG	17Oct60	186/70	400	45.97i,45.99	44.72	−82
Webster	Rob	USA	15May60	178/68	800	1:46.35	1:46.5	−83
Wedderburn	Eddie	UK	6Dec60	183/66	St	8:27.17	8:30.02	−83
Weeks	Mike	USA	6Feb54	196/125	SP	19.57	20.32	−81
Weil	Gert	CHL	3Jan60	197/105	SP	19.94	18.29	−83
Weir	Robert	UK	4Feb61	187/116	DT	62.50	60.48	−83
					HT	73.70	75.08	−82
Weiss	Gerald	GDR	8Jan60	191/100	JT	90.06	89.56	−81
Weitzl	Erwin	AUT	17Jul60	194/120	SP	19.86	19.44	−83
Wellerding	Jim	USA	17May54		Mar	2:12:06		
Wells	Allan	UK	3May52	183/83	100	10.18	10.11	−80
							10.02w−82,10.0w	−79
					200	20.62,20.55w	20.21,20.11w	−80
Wells	Joey	BAH	22Dec65	170/64	LJ	7.97	8.04	−83
Weniger	Andreas	FRG	19Jan58	188/68	Mar	2:13:06	2:16:09	−83
Wennlund	Dag	SWE	9Oct63	188/92	JT	82.34	81.06	−83
Wenta	Edmund	POL	26Dec53	202/130	SP	19.57	19.54	−81
Wentz	Siegfried	FRG	7Mar60	192/87	Dec	8482	8718	−83
Weppler	Martin	FRG	21Feb58	186/76	400	46.08	45.74	−83
Werner	Bernard	POL	17Apr51	175/87	JT	82.20	83.80	−80
Werthner	Georg	AUT	7Apr56	190/87	Dec	8061	8229	−82
Wesolowski	Krzysztof	POL	9Dec56	179/64	St	8:15.28	8:19.53	−78
Wessig	Gerd	GDR	16Jul59	201/84	HJ	2.30	2.36	−80
Wessinghage	Thomas	FRG	22Feb52	183/69	1500	3:38.61	3:31.58	−80
					2k	5:08.34	4:52.20	−82
					3k	7:49.49,	7:36.75	−81
						7:49.13i		
West	Jeff	USA	2Dec61	190/75	800	1:46.57	1:47.00	−81
					1k	2:19.49		
Wheeler	Jere	USA	29Jan64	168/64	100	10.26,10.17w	10.52,10.36w	−83
					200	20.81	20.85	−83
White	Craig	USA	25Jan64	190/86	110h	13.83	13.93	−83
White	Elliott	USA	17Apr63	179/74	110h	13.85,13.82w	14.23	−82
White	Jeff	USA	27Oct61	173/75	400	45.75	45.93	−82
White	William	USA			400	46.0A		
Whitehead	Brian	USA	24Feb62	180/70	HJ	2.24	2.21	−83

495

Men's Index

Whitlock	Chris	USA	18May59	190/84	400	45.19	44.80A,45.04	−83
Wijns	Raf	BEL	7Jan64	180/67	1500	3:38.96	3:41.19	−83
					10k	28:28.1	29:03.3	−82
Wilcher	Thomas	USA	11Apr64	180/84	110h	13.80		
Wiley	Cliff	USA	21May55	173/61	400	45.86	44.70	−81
Wilkins	Mac	USA	15Nov50	193/115	DT	70.44	70.98	−80
Willbanks	Charles	USA	11Dec63	193/70	HJ	2.24	2.21i,2.21	−83
Williams	Art	USA	11May63	175/72	200	20.80,	20.95,20.5Aw	−83
						20.54w	20.6A	−82
Williams	Bart	USA	20Sep56	179/73	400h	48.63	48.81	−81
Williams	Carter	USA			400	46.0		
Williams	Desai	USA	12Jun56	175/72	100	10.27,	10.17A,10.22	−83
						10.19w	10.12w	−80
					200	20.45,	20.29A,20.39	−83
						20.40w	20.35w	−80
					400	45.92A	46.50	−82
Williams	Dwight	USA	7Sep60	180/77	200	20.36		
Williams	Fred	RSA	24Feb62	170/62	800	1:46.85	1:46.65,1:46.6	−83
Williams	Leo	USA	28Apr60	193/83	HJ	2.28	2.29	−82
Williams	Miguel	USA	30Jun60	183/75	110h	13.81w	13.69	−83
Williams	Milton	USA	1Dec56	186/122	SP	19.86	19.20	−83
Williams	Paul	CAN	7Aug56	178/63	5k	13:29.18	13:33.15	−83
					10k	27:55.92	28:26.82	−83
Williams	Randy	USA	23Aug53	175/69	LJ	7.95A	8.34−72,8.46w	−73
Williams	Steve	USA	13Nov53	192/80	100	10.34,10.26w	10.07	−78
						10.1w	9.9−74,9.8w	−75
Williamson	Frank	USA	18May62	185/77	110h	13.89	14.01	−83
Williamson	Graham	UK	15Jun60	183/64	1k	2:16.82	2:18.72	−82
					1500	3:34.13	3:34.01	−83
					Mile	3:51.60	3:50.64	−82
Williky	Gary	USA	16Jul59	188/111	SP	20.22	20.78	−82
Wilson	Kevin	USA	4Dec57	180/73	LJ	8.00w	7.88	−83
Wilson	Jerome	USA	24Apr62	178/70	110h	13.84	14.01	−83
							13.8−81,13.85w	−82
Wilson	Randy	USA	7Sep55	188/73	Mile	3:58.74	4:00.64	−81
Wilson	Rex	NZ			10k	28:26.1	28:40.52	−82
Wilson	Rod	USA	24Sep61	183/76	110h	13.66	13.65−82,13.46w	−83
Winkler	Jurgen	FRG	1Mar59	188/78	PV	5.43i,5.40	5.66	−83
Wirz	Peter	SWZ	29Jul60	181/68	1500	3:35.83	3:36.81	−83
					2k	4:58.29	5:06.82	−82
Witek	Stanislaw	POL	24Apr60	180/87	JT	85.10	84.80	−83
Witherspoon	Mark	USA	3Sep63	190/85	100	10.27w	10.57,	
							10.3,10.32w	−83
					200	20.63,20.55w	20.59	−83
					400	45.37	46.29	−83
Wlodarczyk	Miroslaw	POL	24Feb59	190/72	HJ	2.24i,2.24	2.27i,2.26	−83
Wlodarczyk	Wlodzimierz	POL	23Aug57	184/74	LJ	8.06,	7.93,	
						8.18w	8.11w	−83
Woderski	Leszek	POL	4Apr58	188/110	HT	76.88	76.30	−83
Woepse	Greg	USA	4Mar57	186/82	PV	5.60	5.53	−81
Worner	Jurgen	FRG	6Jul59	184/77	LJ	7.99	7.79	−83
Wolf	Augie	USA	3Sep61	199/125	SP	21.73	20.47	−83
Wolodko	Stanislaw	POL	20Mar50	185/110	DT	62.82	64.80	−78
Wooding	Jim	USA	6Feb54	193/91	Dec	8091	7819e−83,8055m	−82
Woods	Jay	USA	24Aug57	183/71	Mile	3:58.36i,	3:54.40i	−83
						3:58.3i		
Woodson	Rod	USA	10Mar65		110h	13.71	−0−	
Word	Barry	USA	17Jul64	188/97	110h	13.89,13.88w		
Woronin	Marian	POL	13Aug56	186/82	100	10.00	10.16−79,10.10w	−83
					200	20.78	20.49−80,20.43w	−79
Wournell	Doug	CAN	13Jan61	183/79	800	1:46.87	1:48.5	−82
Wright	Don	AUS	26Apr59	183/76	110h	13.72,	13.58	−82

496

Men's Index

						13.7	13.5	−83
Wszola	Jacek	POL	30Dec56	194/75	HJ	2.31	2.35	−80
Wu	ChingChin	TAI	15May58	181/75	110h	13.91	13.90–83, 13.6A	−80
Wuycke	William	VEN	21May58	173/63	800	1.43.93	1:45.07	−83
Wynn	Ken	USA	18Jun61	193/82	800	1:46.97	1:46.82	−83
Wyzykowski	Andrzej	POL	7Nov60	190/78	Dec	7881	7633	−83
Yakovlev	Aleksandr	SU	9Sep57	182/74	LJ	8.10i	7.85	−83
					TJ	17.50	17.05i,16.97	−82
Yakovlev	Pavel	SU	16Jan58	183/70	1500	3:36.99	3:36.4	−80
Yamashita	Norifumi	JAP	10Sep62	177/63	TJ	16.50	15.89	−83
Yanchev	Ivo	BUL	5Sep60	186/78	PV	5.65,5.70ex	5.65	−83
Yanev	Yordan	BUL	29Jul54	180/74	LJ	7.95	8.02	−80
Yang	Weimin	CHN	16May58	185/72	PV	5.46i	5.36	−83
Yaryshkin	Vladimir	SU	63		SP	19.67	17.54	−82
Yates	Peter	UK	15Jun57	181/84	JT	85.92	85.28	−83
Yearwood	Ed	USA	23Apr59	186/77	400	45.66	45.51–81, 45.5	−83
Yefimov	Anatoliy	SU	18Jun56	185/108	HT	78.86	79.56	−83
Yegorov	Grigoriy	SU	67		PV	5.45	5.00	−83
Yemelyanov	Vyacheslav	SU	58		SP	19.94	20.02	−83
Yemets	Grigoriy	SU	8Oct57	192/80	TJ	17.33i,17.30	17.27	−83
Yepishin	Sergey	SU	22Jan58	173/64	St	8:26.92	8:22.49	−81
Yershov	Vasiliy	SU	15Aug49	184/112	JT	81.86	89.02	−83
Yevgenyev	Aleksandr	SU	20Jul61	174/70	100	10.22	10.43–82, 10.2	−83
					200	20.41	20.72	−83
Yevsyukov	Viktor	SU	6Oct56	190/100	JT	90.94	88.10	−83
Yoneshige	Shuichi	JAP	24Jun61		10k	28:17.0	28:19.4	−83
Yoshida	Masami	JAP	14Jun58	179/85	JT	85.52	87.18	−83
Yoshida	Ryoichi	JAP	2Mar65	174/63	400h	49.75	50.20	−83
Young	Carlton	USA	20May61	180/73	200	20.73	21.02	−80
							20.68w–82,20.7*	−78
Young	Donnie	USA	62	185/75	100	10.1w	10.43–82,10.0w	−83
					200	20.64		
Young	Gus	JAM	19Sep61	173/74	100	10.34	10.45,10.1w	−83
					200	20.47	20.5	−81
Young	Verril	USA	28Aug60	180/73	100	10.27w	10.37,10.14w,9.9w	−83
Yushmanov	Nikolay	SU	18Dec61	180/70	100	10.25	10.42,10.29w,10.1	−83
Zachariassen	Allan	DEN	4Nov55	170/58	Mar	2:12:16	2:11:05	−83
Zachery	Ken	USA	19Nov63	183/93	100	10.35w	10.67	−82
Zadok	Yehuda	ISR	29Dec58	173/65	St	8:35.41	8:41.3	−81
Zagoruyko	Aleksandr	SU	4Nov55	175/64	St	8:32.94	8:26.73	−83
Zalar	Kasimir	SWE	24Mar57	180/76	PV	5.60	5.61	−83
Zalutskiy	Mikhail	SU	57		100	10.26,	10.36	−83
						10.1	10.1	−82
Zamfirache	Ion	RUM	23Aug53	190/120	DT	66.84	65.90	−82
Zanello	Giuliano	ITA	22May63	184/110	HT	73.06	71.72	−83
Zasimovich	Sergey	SU	6Sep62	188/73	HJ	2.36	2.29	−82
Zasypkin	Aleksey	SU	15Apr59	170/65	100	10.1	10.3	−82
Zawila	Wojciech	POL	18Mar61	187/75	110h	13.86,13.70w	13.93,13.8,13.7w	−83
Zayka	Vladimir	SU	3Aug57	190/82	110h	13.88,13.6	14.14,13.7	−82
Zaytsev	Aleksandr	SU	16Apr57	191/100	JT	81.30	88.18	−81
Zdravkovic	Dragan	YUG	16Dec59	175/56	2k	5:04.61	5:01.0	−82
Zelenov	Nikolay	SU	22Aug60	200/110	DT	60.54	59.20	−83
Zelezniak	Joe	USA	29Aug51	190/120	SP	19.48	19.75	−82
Zemskov	Tagir	SU	4Aug62	182/67	400h	50.05,49.7	49.53	−83
Zerbini	Luciano	ITA	12Feb60	194/110	DT	64.00	61.02	−83
Zerkowski	Miroslaw	POL	20Aug56	176/60	1500	3:38.00	3:36.19	−80

Men's Index

Zeuner	Gary	AUS	29Aug53	189/70	St	8:34.52	8:31.18	−82
Zhao	Ming	CHN	24Nov63	177/80	JT	84.38	78.52	−83
Zhelanov	Sergey	SU	14Jun57	190/82	Dec	8376	8306	−82
Zhirov	Yuriy	SU	60	177/80	JT	81.94	83.98	−80
Zhu	Jianhua	CHN	29May63	193/70	HJ	2.39	2.38	−83
Zichichi	Gian Maria	ITA	8Jan64		HT	75.02	68.92	−83
Zielke	Dariusz	POL	21Oct60	193/78	HJ	2.31	2.26i,2.26	−83
Ziembicki	Wieslaw	POL	17Jan60	173/62	St	8:30.50	8:29.91	−83
Zimmerman	Kerry	USA	10Dec60	180/76	LJ	7.90	7.88A−82, 7.77	−83
							7.83i,7.99w	−83
Zimmerman	Michel	BEL	1Jan60	186/70	400h	49.64	50.2−82,50.29	−81
Zinchenko	Vladimir	SU	25Jul59	192/115	DT	66.16	66.70	−83
Zirnis	Janis	SU	28Nov47	190/100	JT	84.84	89.48	−81
Zivko	Romeo	YUG	62		St	8:34.01	9:10.2	−83
Zou	Zhenxian	CHN	10Nov55	184/72	TJ	16.83	17.34	−81
Zubrilin	Vladimir	SU	63		TJ	16.58	16.65	−83

WOMEN'S INDEX

Abashidze	Alexandra	SU	14Dec58	176/105	SP	19.30	19.81	−82
Abashidze	Nunu	SU	27Mar55	168/90	SP	21.53	21.37	−80
Abramova	Larisa	SU	61		400h	56.11	56.89 56.5	−83
Abt	Gudrun	FRG	3Aug62	178/61	400h	57.85	57.93	−83
Addison	Sue	USA	28Jul56	163/52	800	2:00.98	2:01.76	−82
(Latter)					1500	4:06.91	4:09.03	−82
					Mile	4:37.99	4:34.11	−82
Afonina	Galina	SU	62		800	2:00.04		
Agapova	Larisa	SU	29Feb64	184/80	SP	19.30	18.23	−83
Agletdinova	Ravilya	SU	10Feb60	168/57	800	1:58.08	1:56.1	−82
					1k	2:37.18i	2:37.91i	−83
					1500	3:58.70	3:59.31	−82
Aigner	Melitta	AUT	5Dec61	185/74	Hept	5742	5876	−83
Akchurina	Vera	SU	57		400	52.3 52.79	53.68 53.4	−80
Akhrimenko	Natalya	SU	12May55	181/84	SP	20.10	20.44	−80
					DT	61.80	64.60	−80
Akimova	Vera	SU	5Jun59	168/58	100h	12.50	13.03	−83
(Yeremeyeva-Tinkova)							12.88w 12.7	−83
Akinyemi	Mercy	NIG	28Aug54	165/50	400	52.15	51.92	−80
Alafranti	Paivi	FIN	8May64	176/72	JT	58.66	51.24	−82
Alexeyeva	Tatyana	SU	7Oct63	173/58	100	11.16	11.45 11.2	−83
					200	22.77	23.28	−83
					400	51.39		
Alizadeh	Manuela	FRG	29Jan63	172/75	JT	60.50	58.26	−83
Alyoshina	Natalya	SU	5Apr56	175/63	100h	13.49	13.65	−82
Ambraziene	Anna	SU	14Apr55	173/61	400h	54.81	54.02	−83
(Kastetskaya)								
Anderson	Jodi	USA	10Nov57	168/57	LJ	6.64	7.00	−80
					Hept	6413	p 4651	−80
Andonova	Lyudmila	BUL	6May60	177/58	HJ	2.07	1.95	−82
(Zhecheva)								
Andonova	Malena	BUL	6Jul57	169/57	400	52.51	51.87	−80
Andrews	Jayne	UK	29Mar63	174/60	100	11.41	12.13–79 11.8	−83
(Christian)						11.23w	12.04w	−81
Andrusca	Simona	RUM	24Mar62	178/93	SP	18.05	16.02i	−83
(Sapunaru)					DT	62.00	64.24	−83
Andryushchenko	Valentina	SU	59		HJ	1.90	1.86	−83
Antonova	Olga	SU	16Feb60	165/55	100	11.32	11.24–82 11:09w	−83
(Nasonova)								
Antonyuk	Marina	SU	12May62	182/91	SP	20.19	19.38	−83
Anufriyeva	Olga	SU	25Jun56	176/62	LJ	6.82	6.80	−82
Arente	Marita	SU	5Dec57	171/58	400	52.4 53.46	53.92 53.2	−79
(Ruzgaite)					800	1:58.64	1:59.31	−83
					1k	2:39.3		
Arigoni	Liliana	ARG	6Mar63	183/68	HJ	1.90	1.82	−80
Artyemova	Natalya	SU	5Jan63	166/49	800	1:58.6	1:59.0	−83
					1k	2:37.45i	2:38.95i	−83
					1500	4:00.68	4:02.63	−83
					Mile	4:15.8	4:35.2i	−83
					3000	8:38.84	8:47.98	−83
Asai	Eriko	JAP	20Oct59		Mar	2:33:43	2:39:47	−83
Asenova	Nadyezhda	BUL	28Mar62	171/53	400h	56.59	55.94	−82
Ashford	Evelyn	USA	15Apr57	165/54	100	10.76	A10.79–83 10.93	−82
					200	22.75	21.83	−79
					400	51.08	51.57	−79
Audain	Anne	NZ	1Nov55	165/51	Mar	2:32:07	2:32:14	−83
Auerswald	Ingrid	GDR	2Sep57	168/59	100	11.04	11.08 10.93w	−80
					200	22.94	22.60	−80

499

Women's Index

Avdyeyeva	Larisa	SU	62		JT	58.12	54.58	−83
Aveille	Elida	CUB	21Dec61	170/65	100h	13.27	13.26 13.17w	−83
Azarashvili	Maya	SU	6Apr64	169/57	200	22.63	23.67	−83
Azhel	Svetlana	SU	15May63	172/68	400h	57.2	59.87 57.4	−83
Babenko (Starlychanova)	Marina	SU	60		100	11.37 11.1	11.47 11.1	−83
Babich	Elina	SU	64		400h	57.60	58.15	−83
Bacoul	Rose-Aimee	FRA	9Jan52	160/56	100	11.34 11.30w	11.16	−83
					200	22.53	22.59	−83
Badea	Maria	RUM	15Jan60	171/73	DT	58.94	62.92	−83
Baikauskaite	Laimaute	SU	10Jun56	162/54	1500	4:08.4	4:03.6	−83
Baikova	Skaidrite	SU	26Apr50	174/80	SP	18.75	18.33	−83
					DT	62.32	64.92	−81
Bailey	Angela	CAN	28Feb62	157/50	100	11.25	11.17	−83
					200	22.75	A22.64 22.82	−83
Bailey (Hassan)	Shireen	UK	27Sep59	173/60	800	2:00.44	1:59.54	−83
Baker	Lorraine	UK	9Apr64	160/46	800	2:00.03	2:01.66	−82
Bakhchevanova (Simeonova)	Galina	BUL	9Jul62	165/60	100h	13.48	13.64	−83
Baluta	Larisa	SU	13Aug65	176/74	LJ	6:71i 6.34	6.84	−83
Baptiste	Joan	UK	12Oct59	171/57	100	11.51,11.46w	11.32,11.23w	−83
					200	22.86	22.96	−83
Baranova	Larisa	SU	61		SP	17.58	17.56	−82
					DT	63.46	60.62	−82
Baranova	Lydumila	SU	50		1500	4:06.7	4:04.36	−83
					3000	9:01.5	8:50.63	−83
Baranova	Natalya	SU	60		400h	56.77 56.0	55.67	−83
Baranyai	Ildiko	HUN	14May58	170/56	100h	13.48	13.37	−83
Barbarshina (Ismiyanova)	Elvira	SU	25Dec63	166/57	100	11.39	11.61 11.3 11.37w	−83
					200	23.23	23.66	−83
Bardina	Natalya	SU	61		Mar	2:30:50		
Barinova	Irina	SU	61		HJ	1:88		
Barksdale	Sharieffa	USA	16Feb61	162/54	400h	55.58	55.78	
Barleycorn	Julie	UK	5Nov55		Mar	2:35:53	2:42:57	−83
Barnett	Helen	UK	13May58	170/62	200	23.25	23.14	−82
					400	52.13	52.90	−83
Barralet (Wright)	Heather	AUS	16Sep54	167/51	800	2:00.57	2:00.23& 2:01.50	−83
Baskakova	Irina	SU	25Aug56	176/67	200	22.9 23.54	22.96 22.80w	−83
					400	50.45	50.19	−83
Baumgartner	Michelle	AUS	27May63	169/58	800	2:01.2& 2:02.10	2:01.1	−82
Bazukiene	Svetlana	SU	20Apr57	172/66	LJ	6.66	6.47	−83
Beaugeant	Chantal	FRA	16Feb61	170/58	Hept	6089	5710 5818wH	−83
Bebber	Kadi	GDR	27Sep65	176/68	DT	60.50	55.84	−83
Beck (Miller)	Lexie	USA	26May61	178/54	400h	57.30	57.08	−83
Beckford	Darlene	USA	9Oct61	162/50	1500	4:06.17	4:12.85	−83
					Mile	4:36.32	4:30.12i	−83
Bednarska	Sylwia	POL	23Feb66	174/58	100h	13.42	13.71	−83
Behrendt	Durten	GDR	12Jan62	165/51	800	2:00.02	2:00.37	−83
Bell	Barbara	USA	5May63	163/56	100	11.42w,11.52	A11.66 A11.49w	−83 −83
Belle	Roberta	USA	29Sep58	178/56	200	23.28	23.60−83 23.3	−79
					400	51.26	51.72	−83
Benning	Christine	UK	30Mar55	160/49	1500	4:01.83	4:01.53	−79
					Mile	4:24.57	4:42.3	−80
					3000	8:44.46	8:49.71	−83
Benoit Samuelson	Joan	USA	16May57	157/46	5000	15:52.7+	15:40.42	−82
					10k	32:07.41	32:30.8	−82
					Mar	2:24:52	2:22:43	−83

Women's Index

Berenda	Susan	USA			10k	34:14.7		
Berezhnaya	Larisa	SU	61		LJ	6.63	6.68	−83
Berg	Regine	BEL	5Oct58	172/58	400	52.41	52.72	−83
Bergdahl	Karin	SWE	6Jan64	177/70	JT	61.42	63.52	−83
Bernhagen	Lisa	USA	22Jan66	177/57	HJ	1:905i 1.89	1.90	−83
Beurskens	Carla	HOL	15Feb52	165/45	Mar	2:32:53	2:34:14	−82
Beyer	Gisela	GDR	16Jul60	180/94	DT	73:10	70.96	−83
Bezborodova	Yekaterina	SU	62		400h	57.5	58.8	−83
Bienias (Reichstein)	Andrea	GDR	11Nov59	180/68	HJ	1.96	1.99i−82 1.97	−83
Bierka	Lidia	POL	13Aug60	178/68	Hept	5866	5550	−83
Bimbaite	Danguole	SU	62		SP	19.77	19.06	−83
Bird	Kim	CAN	61		5000	16:02.27	16:32.8	−83
Biserova	Yelena	SU	24Mar62	177/67	100h	12.66	12.87	−83
Blackwood	Faye	CAN	19Jan57	170/62	100h	A13.36	13.68−82 13.65w	−83
Blanford	Rhonda	USA	15Dec63	174/50	100h	13.47 13.34w	13.45	−83
Blaszak	Genowefa	POL	2Aug57	167/62	200	23.22	24.25−76 24.15w	−81
							23.9	−78
					400	51.21	52.33	−82
					400h	54.78	55.76	−82
Blodniece	Leolita	SU	23Mar59	177/79	JT	57.62	64.90	−80
Blunston	Phyllis	USA	24Apr59	188/65	HJ	1.88	1.92	−82
Boborova	Natalya	SU	12Feb59	168/53	800	1:59.6	2:00.4	−83
					1k	2:38.15i		
					1500	4:00.62	4:00.99	−81
					3000	8:48.31	8:57.22	−83
Bochina	Natalya	SU	4Jan62	173/56	100	11.2i 11.3	11.22, 11.0	−80
					200	22.45 22.1	22.19	−80
Bogmolova	Irina	SU	3Oct59	172/92	SP	18.68i 18.53	19.40	−83
Bolden	Jeanette	USA	26Jan60	174/65	100	11.15	A11.16 A11.12w	−82
							11.18	−81
					200	23.02w 23.50	23.49	−82
Bolden	Mary	USA	11Nov64	165/51	100	11.34 11.23w	11.5w	−82
					200	23.00	23.98	−83
Bolshakova	Alla	SU	61		400h	57.98	56.77 57.16	−83
Bolton	Kelia	USA	28Apr60	160/52	400	52.38	51.93	−83
Bondarchuk	Irina	SU	17Sep52	163/46	10k	33:10.7		
					Mar	2:35:17	2:37:38	−82
Bondarenko	Anna	SU	60		JT	58.50	55.46	−82
Bondarenko (Krentser)	Olga	SU	2Jun60	153/41	1500	4:06.2	4:08.20	−81
					3000	8:36.20	8:47.02	−83
					10k	31:13.78	31:35.61	−83
Boothe	Lorna	UK	5Dec54	163/51	100h	13.31	13.07 12.90w	−82
Bordyuga	Natalya	SU	61		100h	12.8 13.96	13.57 13.2	−79
Borisova (Ashikhmina)	Lyudmila	SU	59		400	51.79	52.07 51.9	−82
					800	1:56.78	1:57.4	−83
Borralho	Rita	POR	21Mar54	163/55	Mar	2:35:43	2:44:09	−83
Bouza	Herminia	CUB	25Sep65		JT	58.86	51.40	−83
Bowers	Julie	USA			10k	34:07.0		
Boxer	Christina	UK	25Mar57	164/51	1500	4:00.57	4:04.48	−82
					Mile	4:22.64	4:30.20	−79
Bozhina	Valentina	SU	1Jan66		200	23.38	23.14 23.13w	−83
Bozhkova	Svetla	BUL	13Mar51	174/85	DT	67.10	67.26	−80
Bradford	Carole	UK	30Nov61		Mile	4:32.00	4:41.8	−82
Bradley	Patty	USA	16Jul62	168/52	400h	56.26	A56.66 56.76	−83
Bradu	Elizabeth	SU	27Oct54	157/44	3000	8:59.13	9:17.0	−81
Brady	Rhonda	USA	16Jul59	160/58	100h	13.18w 13.54	13.53 13.2	−76
Branta	Cathy	USA	6Jan63	165/51	3000	8:49.94	9:18.0	−82
					5000	15:48.44	16:02.35	−83
Bratvold	Hilde	NOR	29Feb60	177/70	JT	59.48	60.88	−82
Brauer (Figiel)	Kerstin	GDR	29Jul63	170/63	JT	61.06	59.14	−83
Braun	Sabine	FRG	19Jun65	172/60	Hept	6442	6273	−83

501

Women's Index

Name	First	Country	DOB	Ht/Wt	Event	Mark	Mark	Year
Breder	Andrea	FRG	7Dec64	167/49	HJ	1.89i 1.89	1.93	-81
Bremer	Undine	GDR	30Jun61	168/58	200	23.38	23.06	-82
(Hartmann)					400	51.81	51.40	-83
Bremser	Cindy	USA	5May53	162/54	1500	4:09.94	4:05.76	-82
					Mile	4:30.78	4:29.21	-82
					3000	8:38.60	8:51.11	-82
					5000	15:41.82	15:47.7	-79
Bressant	Piper	USA	8Jul63	161/50	400h	56.48	56.78	-83
Briesenick (Schoknecht-	Ilona Slupianek)	GDR	24Sep56	180/94	SP	21.85	22.45	-80
Brigadnaya (Zhilo)	Galina	SU	30Oct58	174/58	HJ	1.93i 1.90	1.91i 1.88	-83 -82
Brill	Debbie	CAN	10Mar53	177/60	HJ	1.98	1.99i-82 1.97	-80
Brisco-Hooks	Valerie	USA	6Jul60	169/50	100	11.08 11.02w	11.39	-83
					200	21.81	23.10-83 22.53w	-79
					400	48.83	52.08	-79
Brown	Alice	USA	20Sep60	157/59	100	11.13 11.07w	11.08	-83
					200	23.08	22.41	-83
Brown	Edna	USA	22Feb60	168/52	400h	56.42	A56.46 56.74	-82
Brown	Judi	USA	14Jul61	178/67	400	52.63		
					400h	54.93	56.03 56.02dq	-83
Brown	Julie	USA	4Feb55	168/49	5000	15:39.50	15.55.5	-79
					Mar	2:31:41	2:26:26	-83
Brown	Ovril	JAM	4Jan61	171/59	400h	57.49	56.94	-83
Brown	Wendy	USA	28Jan66	178/68	HJ	1.89	1.75	-82
Browne	Vanessa	AUS	5Jan63	170/53	HJ	1.94	1.94	-83
Bruce	Sue	NZ	25Jul64		5000	16:02.3		
Brudel	Birgit	GDR	4Nov61	176/59	1k	2:39.8i		
Bruns	Ulrike	GDR	17Nov53	170/58	800	1:58.60	1:57.06	-76
					1k	2:34.2	2:31.95	-78
					1500	4:01.38	3:59.9	-76
					3000	8:36.38	8:44.88	-83
					10k	32:46.08		
Bryant	Rosalyn	USA	7Jan56	168/58	400	52.63	50.62	-76
Buballa	Anna	FRG	27Jul54	169/57	LJ	6.63	6.51	-83
Buch	Jane	USA	27Jul48	155/44	Mar	2:37:23	2:36:54	-83
Budavari	Eva	HUN	30Jul53	166/61	JT	60.86	60.32	-82
Budd	Zola	RSA/UK	26May66	158/38	800	2:00.9	2:05.4	-83
					1500	4:01.81	4:08.96	-83
					Mile	4:30.7+		
					3000	8:37.5	8:39.00	-83
					5k	15:01.83	15:10.65	-83
Bufetova	Tamara	SU	2Sep51	178/96	SP	18.91	19.92	-78
Bulirova	Alena	CS	24Dec61	168/57	400	52.21	52.28	-83
Bulkowska	Danuta	POL	31Jan59	178/58	HJ	1.97	1.91	-83
Bulteau	Christelle	FRA	23Jul63	159/52	100	11.37w 11.55	11.55	-83
					200	23.39w 23.68	23.93	-83
Burdina	Vera	SU		54	3000	9:00.7	8:53.93	-83
Burgarova	Elena	CS	13Nov52	168/65	JT	66.56	65.56	-83
Burke	Janet	JAM	11Nov62	162/61	100	11.48	11.58 11.42w	-83
					200	23.39	23.65 23.33w	-83
Burki	Cornelia	SWI	3Oct53	160/53	1500	4:05.67	4:04.39	-80
					Mile	4:31.75		
					3000	8:45.20	8:46.13	-78
Burley	Gillian	UK	24Sep56		Mar	2:32:53	2:38:27	-83
Busch	Sabine	GDR	21Nov62	175/65	200	22.86	22.83	-83
					400	49.24	50.26	-83
Bush	Andrea	USA	30Dec66	155/52	100	A11.25w A11.2		
Bush	Michele	USA	30Oct61	157/50	Mile	4:36.47	4:36.3	-81
Bussieres	Lizanne	CAN	20Aug61		Mar	2:35:53	2:36:02	-83
Bussmann	Gabriele	FRG	8Oct59	170/55	400	50.98	49.75	-83

Women's Index

Butkiene	Margarita	SU	19Aug49	163/54	LJ	6.65i 6.57	7.00	-83
Butuzova	Lyudmila	SU	28Feb57	184/71	HJ	1.98	1.91	-83
Byelenkova	Natalya	SU	65		100h	13.48	14.49 13.7	-83
Byelkova (Barinova)	Olga	SU	21Feb55		HJ	1.97	1.96	-83
Byelova	Lyudmila	SU	23Nov58	168/56	400	50.63	50.67	-83
Byelova	Tatyana	SU	12May61	182/88	SP	18.48	18.12	-82
					DT	62.56	63.26	-83
Byelovolova	Yelena	SU	6Feb65		SP	17.32	16.54i 16.34	-83
Byelyayeva (Rizvanova)	Lutsya	SU	22Jun57	160/47	10k	33:11.17	34:28.83	-81
					Mar	2:33:54	2:34:44	-83
Byelyayeva	Marina	SU	58		3000	8:50.98	8:54.52	-83
Bykova	Tamara	SU	21Dec58	179/62	HJ	2.05	2.04	-83
Bystrykh	Maria	SU	55		3000	8:58.18	9:19.6	-80
Cady	Carol	USA	6Jun62	169/79	SP	17.40	17.24	-83
					DT	62.96	63.30	-83
Callender	Beverley	UK	28Aug56	170/58	100	11.39w	A11.22-79 11.35	-81
							11.19w	-80
					200	23.18	22.72-80 22.69w	-81
Campbell	Karen	USA	11Aug62	165/52	10k	33:47.9	34:54.73	-83
Campbell	Robin	USA	25Jan59	172/58	800	1:59.77	1:59.00	-83
Capotosto	Beatriz	ARG	16May62	170/62	100h	13.45	13.52 13.2	-83
Carley	Donna	USA	14Jul59	167/60	100	11.45w	11.68 11.45w	-83
						11.74	11.4	-82
Carter (Pilling)	Kathryn	UK	24Feb59		3000	8:57.2	9:14.8	-82
Catalano	Patti	USA	6Apr53	165/50	Mar	2:36:13	2:27:52	-81
(DelaTorra-Lyons)								
Cater	Terri-Anne	AUS	25Sep56	169/58	800	2:00.5& 2:0	2.80 2:00.56	-81
Cathey	Kellie	USA	24Nov61	157/44	10k	33:42.8	32:22.5	-82
Chalmers	Angella	CAN	9Jun63	170/56	Mile	4:35.0i		
Chardonnet	Michele	FRA	27Oct56	170/60	100h	13:06 12.91w	12.97	-82
Chaykovskaya	Yelena	SU	63		HJ	1.90i		
Chaynikova	Lyudmila	SU	60		JT	58.54	55.30	-83
Cheeseborough	Chandra	USA	10Jan59	165/61	100	11.13	11.13-76 10.99w	-83
					200	22.47	21.99	-83
					400	49.05	51.00	-83
Cheetham	Margaret	UK	19Oct68	170/57	LJ	6.49w 6.45	6.34 6.49w	-83
Chemidronova	Natalya	SU	59		LJ	6.84	6.47	-83
Chen	Yolanda	SU	26Jul61	169/54	LJ	6.83	6.77	-83
Cherniyenko	Natalya	SU	65		JT	62.90	62.04	-83
Chernysheva (Kvashnina)	Yelizaveta	SU	26Jan58	169/56	100h	13.32 13.0	13.64-81 13.2	-82
Chester	Myrtle	USA	18Oct62	163/50	Hept	5793	5591 A5659w	-83
Chi	Yuan	CHN	63		JT	58.46		
Chicherova (Dubinina-Drebezova)	Yelena	SU	9Aug58	172/58	LJ	6.94	6.87	-83
Chistyakova	Galina	SU	26Jul62	174/62	LJ	7.29	6.54	-81
Chistyakova	Olga	SU	50		JT	65.26	62.14	-83
Chistyakova	Svetlana	SU	9Aug61		100h	13.40	14.34	-83
					Hept	5944	5750H	-83
Chuguyevskaya	Margarita	SU	16Feb62	180/90	SP	18.46i 17.78	18.85	-83
Chuvasheva	Vera	SU	58		800	1:58.8	2:01.8	-82
Cirulli	Giuseppina	ITA	19Mar59	163/58	400h	56.44	56.87	-82
Clarius	Birgit	FRG	18Mar65	175/60	Hept	6044	5669	-82
Clark	Joetta	USA	1Aug62	173/52	800	2:01.14	2:01.32	-82
Clark	Ranza	CAN	13Dec61	175/57	1500	4:07.50	4:15.09	-83
Cliette	Brenda	USA	5Sep63	175/76	100	11.14w	11.30	-83
						11.62	11.23w	-83
					200	22.81	22.86	-83
					400	51.92	53.49	-81
Cojocaru	Cristina	RUM	2Jan62	172/59	400	52.2	52.11	-83
					800	2:00.76	2:03.5	-79

503

Women's Index

Cole	Lillian	USA	31Jul61	165/51	400h	55.24	56.26	−83
Colle	Florence	FRA	4Dec65	169/55	100h	13.40w 13.66	13.60	−83
Colon	Maria Caridad	CUB	25Mar58	175/70	100h	13.2w 13.52	13.66	−83
					JT	69.96	68.40	−80
Commandeur	Olga	HOL	3Oct58	171/64	400h	56.51	57.40	−83
					Hept	6027H	5820	−81
Cong	Yuzhen	CHN	22Jan63	175/85	SP	17.80	17.25	−83
Conz	Nancy	USA	1May57	173/53	Mar	2:38:00	2:33:23	−82
Cook	Kathryn	UK	3May60	180/64	100	11.24	11.10−81 11.08w	−83
					200	22.10	22.13	−83
					400	49.42	50.46	−82
Cooksey	Marty	USA	18Jul54	165/50	5000	15:56.09	16:01.88	−82
					10k	32:52.91	34:24.8	−82
					Mar	2:35:42	2:35:44	−83
Cooman	Nelli	HOL	6Jun64	168/62	100	11.39 11.26w	11.54	−82
Costa	Silvia	CUB	4May64	179/60	HJ	1.99	1.98	−83
Coster	Kaylene	AUS	24Jul61	175/56	800	2:01.50 2:00.2&	2:06.61	−83
Costian	Daniela	RUM	30Apr65	182/91	DT	65.22	60.50	−83
Cozzetto (Williams)	Colleen	USA	10May60	162/50	400h	56.96	A57.99 58.32 57.7	−82
Craciunescu	Florenta	RUM	7May55	184/84	SP	17.23	17.71i−80 17.42	−79
					DT	66.08	68.98	−81
Craig	Justine	NZ			400h	57.83	59.06	−83
Creantor	Simone	FRA	2Jun48	169/74	SP	17.45	17.45i 17.28	−83
Crisp	Laurie	USA			Mar	2:37:01		
Crooks	Charmaine	CAN	8Aug61	170/60	400	50.45	51.49	−83
Cui	Rili	CH	61		JT	57.96	57.12	−83
Cunha	Aurora	POR	31May59	155/48	3000	8:46.37	8:50.20	−83
					5000	15:09.07	15:31.7	−83
					10k	32:30.91	31:52.85	−83
Curatolo	Maria	ITA	16Oct63	145/39	10k	34:07.99	35:03.99	−83
					Mar	2:37:29	2:55:50	−83
Cuthbert	Juliet	JAM	14Sep64	157/52	100	11.42	11.63 11.39w	−83
Czorny	Veronika	FRG	6Mar54	174/98	SP	17.16	16.87	−83
Dalage	Christine	FRA	21Jun58	180/61	Hept	5727	P 4139	−80
Damyanova	Svobodka	BUL	31Jul55	165/51	400	52.51	51.63	−80
Dancetovic	Snezana	YUG	4Dec57	179/61	LJ	6.57	6.47	−83
Danville	Sharon	UK	22Apr55	169/58	100	11.51	11.35−77 11.1w	−76
					100h	13.27 13.06w	13.11	−76
Dasse	Bonnie	USA	22Jul59	176/80	SP	17.87	16.98	−83
Daute-Drechsler	Heike	GDR	16Dec64	181/70	LJ	7.40	7.14 7.27w	−83
Davis	Janet	USA	11Feb65	155/50	200	23.13	23.76−83 23.21w	−82
Davis	Leisa	USA	17Mar63	165/59	400h	57.51	58.74	−83
Davis	Patricia	USA	24Feb65	163/56	100h	13.40	13.48	−83
Davis	Pauline	BAH	9Jul66	168/57	100	11.51 11.1	11.56 11.3	−83
					200	22.97	23.57	−83
Davydova	Yelena	SU	16Nov67	180/61	Hept	5921		
De Bruycker	Isabelle	BEL	22Mar63	177/55	1500	4:09.98		
de Grasse	Iris	CUB	18Aug64	172/72	JT	64.90	63.16	−83
de Jesus	Madeline	PR	4Nov57	167/57	LJ	6.49	6.49	−83
de Klerk	Evette	RSA	21Aug65	165/47	100 A	11.43	A11.36 11.60	−83
					200 A	22.76	A23.13	−83
						23.36 23.0	23.34	−83
de Oliveira	Sheila	BRA	18Feb59	169/59	100	11.49	11.61	−81
Debaets	Corine	BEL	2Dec63		1500	4:09.02	4:19.8	−82
					3000	8:57.76	9:13.31	−83
Debrouwer	Joelle	FRA	18Oct50	163/48	5000	16:03.40	15:52.60	−83
Decker-Slaney	Mary	USA	4Aug58	168/51	1500	3:59.19	3:57.12	−83
					Mile	4:22.92	4:18.08	−82
					3000	8:34.91	8:29.71	−82
Deniz	Leslie	USA	25May62	170/86	DT	65.20	64.96	−83
Denk	Ulrike	FRG	10May64	170/53	100h	12.98	13.09	−83

Women's Index

Dennis	Donna	USA	6Jun64	170/57	100	11.35w 11.52	11.52 11.42w	−82 −83
Derbina	Nina	SU	5Dec56	169/62	100h	13.38	12.76	−80
DeSnoo	Laura	USA	21Sep62	181/98	DT	59.84	53.22	−83
Despaigne	Hildelisa	CUB	23Dec57	167/62	Hept	5973	5667	−83
Deurbroeck	Marie-Christine	BEL	1Feb57	162/56	Mar	2:32:32	2:38:39	−83
Devers	Gail	USA	19Nov66	163/50	100	11.51 11.34w	11.69	−83
DeWald-Aalbers	Laura	USA	27Jul57	168/54	Mar	2:38:01	2:34:59	−82
Didenko	Natalya	SU	62		SP	17.19	14.37	−81
Dietze	Ilona	GDR	25Sep63	182/72	Hept	5980	5991	−81
Dimitrova	Radostina	BUL	1Jun66	163/48	400h	55.53	56.01	−83
Dimova	Bonka	BUL	15Mar56	173/60	400h	57.48	56.96	−80
(Peneva) Ding	Fenghua	CHN	64		JT	59.60	58.66	−82
Dittrich	Heike	GDR	30Dec62	180/95	SP	20.28	19.50	−83
-Hartwig					DT	61.72	60.52	−83
Ditz	Nancy	USA	25Jun54	165/51	Mar	2:33:52	2:35:31	−83
Dixon	Diane	USA	23Sep64	165/52	100	11.50	11.64	−83
					200	23.32 23.31w	23.49,23.24w	−83
					400	51.19	51.60	−83
Dmitriyeva	Irina	SU	59		DT	65.30	58.66	−83
Doak	Nan	USA	3Jul62	150/41	5000	15:47.64	16:08.69	−83
Dogadina	Olga	SU	59		800	1:59.2		
					1500	4:09.7		
Dodika	Vera	SU	59		800	1:59.33	2:01.0	−83
Dolgaya	Natalya	SU	64		100h	13.35	14.34	−83
Domoratska	Anna	SU	17Nov53	168/53	3000	8:50.66	8:48.67	−82
					10k	31:56.02	31:48.23	−82
					Mar	2:36:37	2:36:20	−83
Donkova	Yordanka	BUL	28Sep61	175/67	200	23.39	22.95	−82
					100h	12.50	12.44	−82
Dorio	Gabriella	ITA	26Jun57	167/55	800	1:59.05	1:57.66	−80
					1k	2:34.86	2:33.18	−82
					1500	4:01.96	3:59.82	−80
Dornhoefer	Sabrina	USA	2Dec63	165/52	3000	8:59.25		
Dorofeyeva	Irina	SU	63		400h	56.82	57.9	−83
Doronina	Marina	SU	29Jan61	181/60	HJ	1.97i 1.96	1.91i 1.90	−83
Dorre	Katrin	GDR	6Oct61	170/55	10k	33:00.0		
					Mar	2:26:52	2:37:41	−83
Douglas	Sabrina	USA	5Sep60	176/68	LJ	6.52	6.32	−83
Drake	Ngaire	NZ	11May49	163/48	Mar	2:36:54	2:42:15	−82
Dremina	Tatyana	SU	57		Hept	5678 5815H	5509H	−83
Dressel	Birgit	FRG	4May60	171/56	HJ	1.90	1.90	−82
					Hept	6172	6025	−83
du Plessis	Desiree	RSA	20May65	179/58	HJ	1.87	1.90	−83
Dudkova	Irina	SU	59		Hept	5893H		
Duginyets	Yelena	SU	4Dec59	176/66	HJ	1.91i 1.88	1.89i 1.89	−82
(Ponikarovskikh Dunecka	Malgorzata	POL	21Dec56	175/65	400	51.97	51.81	−80
(Gajewska) Dunn	Karen	USA	21Nov62	170/52	Mar	2:37:35	2:33:36	−83
Duwe-Gielow	Heike	GDR	4Jul60	168/57	LJ	6.91	6.69	−82
Dvirna	Olga	SU	11Feb53	164/50	1500	4:04.35	3:54.23	−82
					3000	8:49.16	8:36.40	−82
Dvornik	Svetlana	SU	62		HJ	1.89	1.84i−82 1.80	−81
Dzhigalova	Larisa	SU	22Oct62	176/61	400	52.06	51.60	−83
Echevarria	Eloina	CUB	25Aug61	168/63	LJ	6.58	6.67−83 6.71w	−82
Edwinson	Stella	USA	24Jan57	173/61	400h	57.72	59.28	−82
Egger	Regula	SWI	10Jan58	178/70	JT	62.12	60.04	−81
Eibnerova	Eva	CS	1Jun62	167/56	400h	58.06	61.29	−80
(Sulekova) Eide	Debbie	USA	31Jan56	165/48	10k	33:24.33	33:14.6	−82

Women's Index

Surname	Given	Nat	DOB	Ht/Wt	Event	Mark	Mark2	Yr
					Mar	2:36:06	2:35:16	−83
Ekova	Rositsa	BUL	30Jun61	164/50	3000	8:47.94	9:29:25	−83
el Moutawakil	Nawal	MOR	15Apr62	162/50	100	11.2w	11.86−81 11.4	−83
					400	51.84	54.9	−83
					400h	54.61	56.23	−83
Elliott-Davies	Diana	UK	7May61	173/60	HJ	1.92	1.95	−82
Elloy	Laurence	FRA	3Dec59	168/57	100h	12.94	12.90	−82
(Machabey)						12.72w	12.81w	−82
Emmanuel	Gail	TRI	29Aug62	175/58	400	52.59	53.38	−83
Emmelmann	Kirsten	GDR	19Apr61	173/63	200	22.78	22.50	−81
(Siemon)					400	50.62	51.14	−82
Enang Mesode	Ruth	CMR	24Feb58		100	11.41w	12.12−80 11.4	−81
Engel	Birgit	FRG	8May62	168/55	100h	13.44	13.42	−81
Epps	Arnita	USA	6Jun64	170/57	100h	13.47 13.20w	13.68	−83
Ernst	Petra	GDR	12Aug63		LJ	6.51i 6.34	6.51i−83 6.32	−82
Ernstrom	Eva	SWE	2Sep61	170/50	3000	8:57.95	8:51.91	−83
					5k	15:46.00	15:34.76	−83
Etienne	Astra	AUS	19Jul60	171/79	SP	17.19	15.93	−83
(Vitols)								
Ettle	Janice	USA	3Dec58		Mar	2:33:41	2:40:18	−83
Everts	Sabine	FRG	4Mar61	168/55	400	53.00i	52.35i	−81
					100h	13.37 13.1	13.17	−82
					HJ	1.89	1.89	−81
					LJ	6.77	6.77	−82
					Hept	6363	6484	−82
Evro	Pavlina	ALB	22Feb65		1500	4:06.62	4:13.77	−83
Ewanje-Epee	Maryse	FRA	4Sep64	172/62	HJ	1.95i 1.94	1.95	−83
Farmer	Beth	USA	29May63	170/49	5k	16:07.8	16:17.08	−83
					10k	33:22.58	32:49.1	−83
					Mar	2:36:22	2:37:47	−83
Farmer	Sandra	JAM	18Aug62	173/63	400h	56.05	56.43	−83
Fedchenko	Irina	SU	15Jan66	184/95	SP	17.75	16.96i 15.90	−83
Fedorchuk	Alla	SU	11Jun57	170/55	HJ	1.89	1.88	−75
Fedyushina	Valentina	SU	65		SP	18.15	17.31	−83
Felke	Petra	GDR	30Jul59	172/64	JT	74.72	69.02	−83
Ferguson	Shonel	BAH	6Nov57	170/54	LJ	6.71	6.80 6.91w	−82
Ferreira	Conceicao	POR	13Mar62	148/40	10k	34:13.89		
Fesenko-Grun	Yekaterina	SU	10Aug58	168/57	400h	54.34	54.14	−83
Feuerbach	Cornelia	GDR	26Apr63	172/59	100	11.48 11.31w	11.75	−82
					100h	13.04	12.86	−83
Fibingerova	Helena	CS	13Jul49	179/95	SP	21.60	22.50i 22.32	−77
Fick	Charmaine	RSA	3Jun59	169/58	400hA	56.08	A55.49 56.03	−83
Fidatov	Elena	RUM	24Jul60	168/53	3000	8:54.32	9:29.10	−81
Fiedler	Ellen	GDR	26Nov58	174/65	400h	55.40	54.20	−83
Filatova	Svetlana	SU	64		Hept	6322	6116	−83
Filickova	Anna	CS	10Jun62	167/59	400h	57.55	56.18	−83
Filipishina	Yelena	SU	18Jun62	176/63	400h	54.56	54.72	−83
Finch	Jane	UK	8Nov57	162/51	800	2:01.15	2:00.6	−77
Finn	Michelle	USA	8May65	165/52	100	11.43 11.20w	11.56	−83
Fitch	Geri	CAN	7Apr54	170/51	3000	9:01.02 8:58.7	8:57.3	−82
Fitzgerald-Brown	Benita	USA	6Jul61	178/65	100h	12.84	12.84	−83
Flintoff	Debbie	AUS	20Apr60	171/53	400h	56.02	55.89	−82
Fogli	Laura	ITA	5Oct59	168/50	10k	33:39.04		
					Mar	2:29:28	2:31:49	−83
Forbes	Eryn	USA	29Apr61	170/51	10k	33:52.7	33:31.7	−82
Forgacs	Judith	HUN	15May59	165/53	400	51.85	51.55	−83
Forgrave	Sylvia	CAN	22May57	172/60	100	13.42 13.29w	13.38	−82
(Malgadey)							13.1 13.35w	−83
Fort	Wanda	USA	63		100	11.09w	11.61	−82
Fossatti	Alessandra	ITA	21Oct63	170/55	HJ	1.88i 1.85	1.89	−81
Frantseva	Nadyezhda	SU	61		SP	17.71	17.46	−83
Frazier	Barbara	USA	19Jul63		100	11.24w	11.66	−82

506

Women's Index

Name	First	Nat	DOB	Ht/Wt	Event	Mark 1	Mark 2	Yr
Frederick	Jane	USA	7Apr52	182/72	100h	13.27	13.25	−78
					HJ	1.88	1.89	−83
					Hept	6714	6458	−82
Freeman	Kathy	USA	13Jan62	172/54	400h	57.57	58.20	−83
French	Sue	CAN	7May60	157/48	3000	8:57.5 & 9:03.81	9:17.92	−83
Fukalova	Marie	CS	27Feb52	176/70	JT	59.08	56.64	−83
(Labanova)								
Fukumitsu	Hisayo	JAP	19Feb60	167/49	HJ	1.87	1.93	−81
Furletova	Valentina	SU	23Feb66	176/55	800	2:00.04	2:04.0	−83
Furniss-Shields	Jane	UK	23Aug60	162/45	Mile	4:30.95	4:30.29	−83
					3000	8:48.00	8:45.69	−83
Furst	Carola	GDR	2Jun61	176/74	JT	61.00	58.50	−80
Furstenberg	Mari-Lise	RSA	17Jun66	166/54	100 A	11.42	A11.54	−83
							11.77 A11.49w	−82
					200 A	23.21 23.60	A23.37 23.65	−83
Fyodorova	Yelena	SU	20Feb66	161/56	100	11.2 11.59	11.56 11.2	−83
Gabriel	Easter	USA	15Jun60	169/53	400	52.47	50.99	−83
Gale	Charmaine	RSA	27Feb64	176/60	HJ	1.88	1.96	−81
Gallagher	Kim	USA	11Jun64	165/46	800	1:58.50	2:00.07	−82
					1500	4:08.08	4:16.6	−82
Galloway	Carol	CAN	27Aug64	171/62	LJ	6.54w 6.27	6.26 6.47w	−83
Gao	Zhiying	CHN	60		JT	58.78	57.60	−82
Garcia	Dulce-Maria	CUB	2Jul65		JT	57.64	52.40	−83
Garcia Silami	Esmeralda	BRA	16Feb59	163/57	100	11.32	11.31−83 11.29w	−81
Garden	Linda	AUS	17Oct55	178/63	LJ	6.50	6.62−81 6.80w	−82
Gardner	Gwen	USA	7Sep60	170/59	400	52.32	51.59	−80
Gareau	France	CAN	15Apr67	167/59	100	11.38w 11.66	11.97	−83
Gareau	Jacqueline	CAN	10Mar53	157/45	Mar	2:31:57	2:29:28	−83
Gareyeva	Ravilya	SU	61		Mar	2:38:21	2:42:21	−83
Gaschet	Liliane	FRA	16Mar62	165/56	100	11.31 11.29w	11.16	−83
					200	22.73	22.95	−82
Gasser	Sandra	SWI	27Jul62	168/53	1500	4:10.04	4:19.92	−83
					3000	8:58.31	9:15.93	−83
Gavrilina	Zinaida	SU	15Apr60	170/62	JT	67.00	63.10	−81
Gavrilova	Olga	SU	8Feb57	176/75	JT	63.52	63.10	−83
Gaugel	Heidi-Elke	FRG	11Jul59	167/54	100	11.24	11.39−82 11.35w	−81
					200	22.72	23.02	−81
Ge	Ping	CHN	11Jan61	169/56	HJ	1.91	1.92	−83
Geissler	Heidrun	GDR	16Nov61	180/68	Hept	5904	6223	−81
Genge (Yaxley)	Terry	NZ	27Jul57	174/61	400h	58.01	58.66	−83
Georgieva	Atanaska	BUL	18Oct60	166/63	100	11.41	11.42	−83
					200	23.07	23.25	−83
Georgieva	Nadezhda	BUL	2Sep61	158/48	100	11.21	11.09	−83
					200	22.51	22.42	−83
Gerasimova	Olga	SU	56		400h	56.88 56.2	56.68	−83
Gerdes	Roswitha	FRG	28Jun61	177/59	800	1:58.68	2:01.79	−82
					1k	2:37.68	2:38.94	−82
					1500	4:04.41	4:10.41	−83
					3000	8:54.60		
Geremias	Conceicao	BRA	23Jul56	172/64	LJ	6.49	6.47	−81
Gerevich	Svetlana	SU	66		100h	13.2 13.72	14.74 14.2	−83
Gerstenmaier	Brigitte	FRG	9Jun60	172/58	100h	13.48 13.1	13.40 13.36w	−83
Gerzova	Ivana	CS	29Jan63	172/54	HJ	1.87	1.86	−83
Ghioroaie	Gina	RUM	18Nov58	162/56	LJ	6.68	6.76	−82
Gibson	Sharon	UK	31Dec61	167/	JT	60.88	59.88	−83
Giffen (Ross)	Jill	CAN	23Feb58	176/65	Hept	5913	6110	−82
Girard	Suzanne	USA	30Nov62	169/43	5000	15:45.86	16:10.90	−83
Girova	Malinka	BUL	18Feb66	166/52	200	23.34	23.93	−82
Gisladottir	Thordis	ICE	5Mar61	170/56	HJ	1.88i 1.85	1.905i 1.87	−83
Givens	Randy	USA	27Mar62	165/54	100	11.27,11.06w	11.28,11.16w	−83
					200	22.36	22.31	−83
Gizatullina	Nadezhda	SU	59		800	2:01.5		

507

Women's Index

Gladisch	Silke	GDR	20Jun64	168/59	100	11.0	11.03	-83
					200	22.70	22.72	-83
Gladyr	Sofia	SU	62		LJ	6.58		
Glover	Michele	USA	18Jul63	170/63	100	11.36 11.21w	11.42	-82
							11.41w 11.1w	-83
					200	23.34	23.93 23.56w	-80
Gnutova	Natalya	SU	4Mar54	163/58	JT	59.90	61.58	-82
(Nevgad)								
Goertzen	Dorothy	CAN	11Aug55	169/59	Mar	2:35:24	2:41:41	-83
Gohr	Marlies	GDR	21Mar58	165/55	100	10.84	10.81-83 10.79w	-80
					200	21.74	22.36	-79
Golodnova	Natalya	SU	67		HJ	1.87	1.82	-83
Goncharova	Yelena	SU	21Mar61	169/56	400h	55.76	56.83	-83
Gorbacheva	Natalya	SU	24Jul47	181/96	DT	60.92	67.32	-83
Gorbunova	Galina	SU	60		100h	13.2 13.90	13.80	-83
Gorbunova	Natalya	SU	64		100h	13.41	13.83 13.5	-82
Gorbunova	Svetlana	SU	62		HJ	1.88	1.86	-83
Gould	Donna	AUS	10Jun66	182/53	1500	4:09.54	4:26.4	-83
					3000	8:44.1&	9:25.6	-83
					5000	15:40.6	15:27.3&	
Grabe	Heike	GDR	11Mar62	189/67	HJ	1.92i 1.91	1.88i 1.88	-83
Grachova	Natalya	SU	21Feb52	178/79	100h	13.45	13.80	-82
(Prokopchenko)					LJ	6.77	6.11 6.65w	-82
					Hept	6563	6611	-82
Grafe	Simone	GDR	18Nov64	171/68	JT	58.80	57.78	-83
Graune	Brigitte	FRG	14Mar61	180/70	JT	60.28	59.16	-83
Green	Cynthia	JAM	10Sep60	173/58	400	52.54	56.3	-80
Green	Gillian	UK	24Nov58	160/48	1500	4:07.90	4:08.32	-83
(Dainty)								
Gregorek	Chris	USA	9Jul59	170/57	800	2:00.06	2:01.23	-83
(Mullen)					1500	4:09.42	4:18.1	-80
Greiner	Cindy	USA	15Feb57	175/63	Hept	6281	6069	-83
Gridneva	Tatyana	SU	60		10k	34:14.8		
Griffin	Lorna	USA	9Jun56	181/82	SP	18.16	17.81	-83
					DT	62.80	63.22 80	-83
Griffith	Florence	USA	100	DT		10.99	11.06 10.96w	-83
					200	22.04	22.23	-83
					400	51.11	50.94	-83
Griffith	June	GUY	16Jun57	183/52	400	52.19	51.37	-79
Grigoryeva	Natalya	SU	62		100h	13.20 12.7	13.26	-83
(Dorofeyeva)								
Grime (Massey)	Lynnette	NZ	10Sep62	174/60	400h	57.42		
Grishkina	Valentina	SU	56		400h	55.79	56.82 56.3	-83
Gritskevich	Nina	SU	58		800	2:00.31	2:02.8	-83
					1500	4:09.30	4:13.22	-82
Groenendaal	Claudette	USA	1Nov63	175/67	800	1:59.98		
					1500	4:08.13	4:18.4	-83
Groos	Margaret	USA	21Feb59	167/54	5000	16:04.01	15:51.64	-80
					10k	32:55.15		
					Mar	2:33:38	2:37:04	-83
Grosshennig	Birgit	GDR	21Feb65	177/67	LJ	7.00	6.25	-82
Grottenborg	Sissel	NOR	17Aug56	171/54	Mar	2:36:07	2:33:02	-81
Gumerova	Nadezhda	SU	1Jan49	160/47	10k	32:50.04	32:54.45	-82
Gunba	Saida	SU	30Aug59	168/85	JT	62.18	68.28	-80
Gunnell	Sally	UK	29Jul66	170/58	100h	13.30	13.71	-83
Gurina	Lyubov	SU	6Aug57	166/54	800	1:56.26	1:56.11	-83
Gusarova	Svetlana	SU	29May59	164/54	100h	12.74	12.86	-83
Guskova	Svetlana	SU	19Aug59	163/49	800	2:01.4	1:59.5	-78
					1k	2:38.69i		
					1500	4:03.05	3:57.05	-82
					3000	8:29.59	8:29.36	-82
Gutewort	Doris	FRG	3Dec54	178/75	DT	59.08	63.60	-82

Women's Index

Name								
Haas	Gerda	AUT	19May65	180/60	400h	58.06	62.62	−83
Hackett	Edel	IRL			5000	16:01.93		
Hagger	Kim	UK	2Dec61	171/58	100h	13.39	13.61	−83
					HJ	1.88	1.84	−83
					LJ	6.48 6.51w	6.38	−83
					Hept	6127	5842	−83
Hairston	Clara	USA	30Jan63	169/58	100h	13.37w 13.70	13.67	−83
Hamrin	Marie-Louise	SWE	19Apr57	166/53	3000	9:00.84	8:59.11	−83
					5000	15:27.96	15:36.41	−82
					Mar	2:33:53	2:34:29	−82
Hansen	Joan	USA	18Jul58	164/45	1500	4:08.4	4:10.99	−83
					3000	8:41.43	8:53.74	−83
					5000	15:39.08	16:02.6	−82
Hansen	Julie	USA	2Nov57	183/78	DT	59.06	56.16	−83
Hanulakova	Gabriela	CS	6Mar57	180/98	DT	64.00	58.54	−83
Hamon	Marlene	USA	11Oct62	174/59	Hept	5818	6266Aw 6152	−83
Hames (Gutewort-Schwalbe)	Marlies	FRG	13Sep53	179/62	400h	57.20	56.79	−82
Harns	Velisa	USA	11May65		100	11.2		
Hart	Ellen	USA	19May58	165/51	Mar	2:35.04	2:35.18	−82
Hartai	Katalin	HUN	24Mar63	177/65	JT	61.88	56.26	−82
Harter	Jana	GDR	16Jun66	181/73	DT	59.06	56.10	−83
Hatcher	Evalene	USA	19Nov59	165/54	400h	57.69		
					LJ	6.77w 6.40	6.36i	−82
							6.34 6.38w	−81
Haupt	Grit	GDR	4Jun66	180/90	SP	19.57	16.68	−83
					DT	65.96	56.64	−83
Haworth	Jill	USA	13Apr61	178/55	1500	4:09.01	4:16.06	−83
					Mile	4:32.60	4:34.32	−82
Hayes	Kathy	USA	27Jan62	165/48	3000	9:01.7&9:06.14	8:50.79	−83
					5000	15:48.43	15:33.51	−83
					10k	32:43.81		
Head	Venissa	UK	1Sep56	185/87	SP	19:06i 18.93	18.41	−83
					DT	62.14	64.68	−83
Heamshaw-Telfer	Susan	UK	26May61	178/66	LJ	6:83 7.00w	6.68	−79
Heinrich	Silvia	GDR	22Dec64		100	11.51	11.81	−83
Helander	Tuijia	FIN	23May61	171/61	400h	56.55	57.84	−80
Helm	Susanne	GDR	24Jun61	178/58	HJ	1.96i 1.96	1.97	−83
Henderson	Tammy	USA			100	11.36w 11.57		
					200	23.26w 23.54		
Herczeg	Agnes	HUN	28Aug50	180/82	DT	61.72	65.22	−82
Hesselbarth	Anett	GDR	4Jun66	177/62	400	52.62		
Hidding	Tineke	HOL	28Jul59	174/62	Hept	6147	6155	−83
Hightower	Stephanie	USA	19Jul58	164/54	100h	12.90 12.78w	12.79	−82
Hird (Sullivan)	Anne	USA	18Apr59	165/54	Mar	2:37.11	2:39.40	−83
Hodgkins	Noeline	NZ	25Dec56		LJ	6.48w	6.47 6.56w	−82
Holzapfel	Beate	FRG	9Apr66	176/61	HJ	1.88	1.88	−82
					Hept	5846	5419	−82
Holzapfel	Brigitte	FRG	10Apr58	HJ	1.93i 1.93	1.95	−78	
Hommola	Ute	GDR	20Jan52	174/78	JT	62.82	67.24	−81
Hopkins	Lisa	USA	5Jun58	157/55	100	11.37	11.30-80 11.0w	−76
					200	23.32	23.13	−80
Horowitz	Gillian	UK	7Jun55	170/54	Mar	2:37.10	2:37.56	−80
Howard	Denean	USA	5Oct64	168/53	400	51.87	50.87	−82
Howard	Sandra	USA	26May56	173/62	100	11.42w 11.66	11.51	−77
							11.29w	−81
Howard	Sherri	USA	1Jun62	162/52	100	11.24	11.61	−80
					200	22.97 22.78w	23.19	−80
					400	50.40	A51.09−79 51.48	−80
Hoyle	Teresa	UK	4Aug63		400h	57.96	57.86	−83

Women's Index

Hoyte-Smith	Joslyn	UK	16Dec54	162/51	400	51.93	50.75	−82
Hughes	Christine	NZ	24Jan59		3000	9:00.17		
Hunter	Sophia	JAM	9Dec64	162/50	100h	13.44	14.45 14.2	−82
Huntley	Joni	USA	4Aug56	173/60	HJ	1.97	1.95i−81 1.90	−75
Huo	Lihua	CHN	57		JT	57.82	55.76	−82
Lancu	Ortensia	RUM	21Aug67	175/56	HJ	1.88	1.79	−83
Ignatova	Nevena	BUL	1Jan62	172/59	L	6.59	6.39	−83
Ikonnikova	Galina	SU	62		10k	33:02.61	34:22.0	−82
					Mar	2:36.50	2:44.46	−83
Ilands (Moons)	Magda	BEL	16Jan50	159/53	10k	33:45.40	33:12.17	−83
					Mar	2:35.36	2:37.51	−83
Ilcu	Marieta	RUM	16FOct62	170/56	LJ	6.69	6.34	−80
Ilie	Paula	RUM	20Jul63	169/57	800	2:00.63	2:02.31	−83
Ilieva	Katya	BUL	3Jan63	165/58	400	51.92	51.27	−83
Ilieva	Vangelia	BUL	15Jan63	176/58	LJ	6.48	6.37	−83
Innis	Jennifer	GUY	21Nov59	175/61	100	11.26 11.24w	11.47	−83
							11.1 11.17w	−83
					LJ	6.74	6.82−82 6.85w	−83
Ionesco	Carmen	CAN	28Jul51	177/84	DT	59.88	64.78	−76
Ionescu	Iulia	RUM	3Jul65	169/51	3000	8:58.23	9:24.86	−83
Ionescu	Vali	RUM	2Aug60	173/58	LJ	7.11	7.20	−83
Irving	Lorna	UK	23Mar47		Mar	2:37.19	2:52.08	−83
Isaeva	Svetlana	BUL	18Mar67	176/60	HJ	1.88	1.87	−83
Isayeva	Galina	SU	21Feb54	166/72	JT	61.12	63.00	−82
(Borkovskaya)								
Isayeva	Nina	SU	6Jul50	180/105	SP	17.78	20.47	−82
Ishmael	Katie	USA	17Aug64	160/44	5000	15:45.08	16:07.06	−83
					10k	32:37.37	33:07.46	−83
Isphording	Julie	USA	5Dec61	165/47	Mar	2:32.26	2:34.24	−82
Ivannikova	Irina	SU	25Feb50	177/90	DT	60.70	65.50	−82
Ivanova	Galina	SU	60		Hept	5782H	5535H	−83
Ivanova	Inna	SU	58		Hept	5790	6104 6196H	−83
(Romanchenkova)								
Ivanova	Lilyana	BUL	17Mar56	174/62	200	22.93	22.73	−79
(Panayotova)					100h	13.41	14.54−76 13.5	−79
					LJ	6.61	6.71	−76
Ivanova	Marina	SU	24May62	177/62	400	52.45 51.5	50.63	−83
Ivanova	Yelena	SU	23Jan61	173/66	LJ	7.01	6.81	−82
Ivanova	Zoya	SU	14Mar52	164/51	Mar	2:31.11	2:34.26	−82
Ivshina	Svetlana	SU	8Feb62	171/62	Hept	6048 6064H	5930 6151H	−83
Jackson	Alice	USA	28Dec58	157/54	200	23.39 23.16w	23.59	−81
							23.44w	−82
					400	51.90	52.41	−82
Jackson	Grace	JAM	14Jun61	181/59	100	11.24	11.27 11.22w	−83
					200	22.20	22.46	−83
Jacobs	Simone	UK	5Sep66	157/50	100	11.45 11.26w	11.59	−83
					200	23.33 23.01w	23.28	−83
Jahn	Bettina	GDR	3Aug58	170/60	100h	12.53	12.42−83 12.35w	−83
Jakobsen	Kersti	HUN	15Feb56	170/56	Mar	2:34:53	2:38:31	−83
Janak	Maria	HUN	9Feb58	180/70	JT	60.74	62.10	−82
Janko	Ilona	HUN	18Aug57	160/50	10k	33:56.3	34:04.8	−83
Januchta	Jolanta	POL	16Jan55	163/51	800	2:00.12	1:56.95	−80
						1:59.57&		
Jarvenpaa	Mirja-Liisa	FIN	13Mar62	175/62	Hept	5919	5680	−83
Jauch	Kristina	GDR	9May65	170/55	400h	58.05	57.56	−83
Jeal	Wendy	UK	21Nov60	169/59	100h	13.36 13.18w	13.45	−83
(McDonnell)								
Jimramovska	Ludmila	CS	5Jun58	168/54	LJ	6.51	6.62	−82
Jobbova	Ivana	CS	16Dec65	172/53	HJ	1.90	1.88	−83
Johnson	Katrena	USA	17Feb64	183/61	HJ	1.87	1.87	−83
Johnson	Latrese	USA	24Dec66	178/54	HJ	1.88	1.75	−82

Women's Index

Johnson	Merry	USA	25Dec59	170/57	200	23.34 23.20w	23.57	−82
					400	52.35	52.34	−82
Johnson	Pat	USA	19Nov60	173/55	LJ	6.50	6.56	−80
Johnson	Zelda	USA	5Jul64	162/47	100	11.23	11.59–83 11.58w	−81
					200	23.12	23.55	−83
Jones	Eunice	USA	7Jan64		100	11.2 11.65		
Jones	Jackie	...			100	11.2		
Jones	Yolanda	USA	6Nov65	178/63	HJ	1.87		
Joyce	Monica	IRL	16Jul58	164/49	Mile	4:37.74 4:33.4i	4:30.4	−82
					3000	8:49.51	8:53.24	−82
					5000	15:42.03	15:27.5	−83
Joyce	Regina	IRL	7Feb57	163/48	5000	15:45.45	15.35.60	−82
					10k	32:35.7	33:14.45	−83
					Mar	2:34:38	2:32:57	−83
Joyner	Jackie	USA	3Mar62	178/66	LJ	6.81	6.74 6.77w	−83
					Hept	6520	6372	−83
Juha	Olga	HUN	22Mar62	171/53	HJ	1.92	1.97	−83
Jurgens	Frauke	GDR	5Oct66	173/61	400h	57.40		
Juskiene (Makauskaite-Kadarik)	Rimma Muzikeviciene)	SU	1Mar52	180/90	SP	17.42	20.12	−80
	Raili	SU	20Dec57	171/69	JT	58.04	60.80	−83
Kafer	Karoline	AUT	31Oct54	168/60	400	52.18	50.62	−77
Kaftandjian	Isabelle	FRA	27Mar64	166/57	100h	13.42 13.39w	13.80 13.70w	−83
					Hept	5741	5445H–82 5445	−83
Kalek	Lucyna	POL	9Jan56	167/54	100	11.48	11.44	−82
					100h	12.43	12.44	−80
Kalinina	Galina	SU	62		SP	17.76	17.27	−83
Kameli	Sue	CAN	17Sep56	169/53	100hA	13.34 A13.27	A13.20 13.27	−83
							13.10w	−82
Kancheva	Tsetska	BUL	7Aug63	176/66	LJ	6.71	6.52	−83
Kane	Missy	USA	21Jun55	164/51	1500	4:06.47	4:10.92	−83
Kaptyukh	Tatyana	SU	56		DT	60.26	58.80	−80
Kapusta	Elzbieta	POL	21Nov60	170/57	400	52.16	52.71	−83
Karepina	Zoya	SU	3Jan61	176/72	JT	57.98	55.98	−83
Kasprzyk (Witkowska)	Ewa	POL	7Sep57	164/54	100	11.22	11.53	−83
					200	22.42	22.79	−83
Katewicz	Renata	POL	2Jun65	179/80	DT	60.60	58.52	−83
Katona (Guillaume)	Patricia	FRA	7Aug80	177/77	DT	59.04	56.08	−83
Kazakova	Albina	SU	62		HJ	1.94	1.85	−82
Kazakova	Galina	SU	61		100h	13.44 13.1	13.64–83 13.2	−83
(Rotach) Kazankina	Tatyana	SU	17Dec51	162/47	800	1:57.20	1:54.94	−76
					1500	3:58.63	3:52.47	−80
					3000	8:22.62	8:32.08	−83
					5000	15:23.12		
Kellon	Gayle	USA	29Mar65	178/57	400h	57.94	57.60	−83
Kempe-Zollkau	Antje	GDR	23Jun63	172/69	JT	72.16	71.00	−83
Kertz	Sabine	GDR	11Sep64	173/62	Hept	6031	5985	−83
Keskitalo	Sinikka	FIN	29Jan51	153/46	10k	33:01.27	33:41.15	−83
					Mar	2:35:15	2:37:07	−83
Keyes	Maggie	USA	28Jun58	167/57	1500	4:10.19	4:10.44	−83
					Mile	4:34.30	4:31.52	−82
					3000	8:58.70	8:49.96	−83
Khamitova	Tatyana	SU	61		800	2:00.4	2:01.0	−83
					1k	2:39.4i		
					1500	4:02.41	4:10.85	−83
Kharkova	Irina	SU	65		HJ	1.88	1.80	−81
Khristova	Silvia	BUL	15Aug65	165/59	LJ	6.64	6.29	−83
Khristova	Tsvetanka	BUL	14Mar62	175/80	DT	68.34	70.64	−82
Khromenkova	Yelena	SU	56		Mar	2:36:36		
Khval	Irina	SU	62		DT	59.26	63.96	−83

511

Women's Index

Name	First	Country	DOB	Ht/Wt	Event	Mark1	Mark2	Year
Kibakina	Marina	SU	22Oct60	169/61	100h	13.32	13.1	−83
					LJ	6.57	6.66	−83
Killingbeck	Molly	CAN	3Feb59	170/56	200 A	23.12	A22.79 23.07	−83
						23.62	A22.69w	−83
					400	51.72	51.08	−83
Kimaiyo	Helen	KEN	8Sep68	163/50	3000	8:57.21	9:15.9	−83
					5000	15:41.09		
Kinch	Beverly	UK	14Jan64	169/55	100	11.50 11.2	11.30 11.13w	−83
					LJ	6.79	6.90 6.93w	−83
King	Linda	USA	13Aug64		10k	33:05.96		
King	Sue	USA	9Jun58	176/55	Mar	2:34:29	2:33:53	−83
Kinzel (Gottwald)	Gisela	FRG	17May61	172/55	400h	57.81	57.55	−83
Kigplagat	Esther	KEN	8Dec66	168/50	5000	16:09.46		
					10k	32:50.25		
Kirchmann	Sigrid	AUT	29Mar66	180/61	HJ	1.87	1.86	−83
Kirchner	Sylvia	GDR	7May63	168/53	400h	56.36	56.41	−81
Kireyeva	Galina	SU	1Mar56	169/52	1k	2:36.9		
					1500	4:06.94	4:01.2	−82
					3000	8:55.86i 8:56.9	8:55.17	−82
Kirgizova	Yelena	SU	61		Hept	5964H 5839	5505H	−83
Kiryukhina	Lyubov	SU	19May63	164/54	800	1:58.87	1:59.46	−83
Kispal	Marianna	HUN	7May60	173/72	JT	59.24	55.26	−83
Kisheyeva (Zvereva)	Ellina	SU	16Nov60		DT	68.56	65.18	−83
Kitova	Svetlana	SU	25Jun60	168/60	800	1:58.08	1:58.82	−83
Klecker	Janis	USA	18Jul60	168/48	Mar	2:36:27	2:35:44	−83
Kleinova -Walterova	Ivana	CS	26May62	174/61	800	2:01.36	2:02.98	−83
					1500	4:05.52	4:10.82	−83
Klimaszewska	Elzbieta	POL	3Jan59	172/53	LJ	6.64	6.47	−81
Klinger	Margrit	FRG	22Jun60	166/55	800	2:00.00	1:57.22	−82
					1500	4:05.50	4:02.66	−82
Klishina	Nadezhda	SU	60		LJ	6.64		
Klyukina	Maria	SU	13Sep50	160/49	10k	34:13.07	32:37.40	−81
Knabe	Kerstin	GDR	7Jul59	180/68	100h	12.98	12.54−82 12.42w	−83
Knighten	Chewuakii	USA	6Aug67	167/49	100	11.50w 11.75	11.80w	−82
					400	52.31	53.27	−83
Knisely (Schilly)	Mary	USA	29May59	162/49	Mile	4:37.5		
					3000	8:51.9	9:07.65	−83
Knorscheidt	Helma	GDR	31Dec56	176/90	SP	21.19	21.12	−82
Koba	Tamara	SU	24Feb57	164/50	1k	2:37.51i		
Koblasova	Marcela	CS	15Jun56	180/73	Hept	6078	6164	−83
Kocembova	Tatana	CS	2May62	169/55	100	11.36	11.31	−83
					200	22.47	22.50	−83
					400	48.73	48.59	−83
Koch	Marita	GDR	18Feb57	171/65	100	11.13	10.83	−83
					200	21.71	21.71	−79
					400	48.16	48.15	−82
Kokonova	Yelena	SU	4Aug63	171/64	LJ	7.09	6.83	−83
(Stetsura) Kokowska	Renata	POL	4Dec58	170/59	10k	34:04.66		
Kolenchukova	Natalya	SU	29Apr64		JT	64.26	61.62	−83
Kolyadina (Kubyshkina)	Mila	SU	31Dec60	181/78	Hept	6402	6485	−83
Komisova	Vera	SU	11Jun53	168/58	100h	13.14 12.6	12.39	−80
Komsa	Jolanta	POL	20Dec58	183/52	HJ	1.95	1.88	−83
Kondratyeva -Sedykh	Lyudmila	SU	11Apr58	168/57	100	11.02	11.06	−80
Konttinen	Tuula	FIN	10May63	164/48	10k	34:09.6	36:02.8	−83
Koninger	Anke	FRG	22Mar61	170/60	100h	13.30	13.49−80 13.48w	−81
					Hept	5850	5831	−81
Konstantinova	Alexandra	SU	9Jul53		Hept	5933H 5505	6172−82 6205H	−83

512

Women's Index

Konyukhova	Lyubov	SU	56		1500	4:10.40		
					3000	8:45.88	8:48.64	−83
					10k	31:56.01		
Kopping	Jana	GDR	12Apr66	172/65	JT	60.88	62.54	−83
Korban	Yelena	SU	10Apr61	176/51	400	52.27	50.77	−83
Korchagina	Svetlana	SU	57		400	52:09		
					400h	57.12	58.95	−83
Korodi	Ibolya	RUM	18Jul57	161/49	400	52.15	51.90	−82
Korolkova	Svetlana	SU	23May60	175/63	Hept	6184	5778H	−83
Korsak	Valentina	SU	13May56	168/72	DT	63.92	63.44	−83
Korshunova	Nadezhda	SU	18May61	167/56	100h	12.65	12.99 12.97w	−83
Korsunskaya	Nina	SU	26May54	176/94	SP	17.23i 16.22	17.05	−79
Kositsyna	Larisa	SU	14Dec63	181/58	HJ	1.90i	1.98	−83
Kostadinova	Stefka	BUL	25Mar65	180/60	HJ	2.00	1.90	−82
Kotenyeva	Marina	SU	12Apr64	172/63	400h	55.64	56.87 56.5	−83
Kovacs	Ella	RUM	11Dec64	170/52	800	1:58.42	2:04.55	−82
					1500	4:06.38		
Kovalenko	Lyubov	SU	63		400h	57.7 58.76		
Kovalyeva	Valentina	SU	60	179/65	LJ	6.67	6.46	−82
Kovalyeva	Yelena	SU	61		DT	64.36	60.08	−83
Kovtun	Natalya	SU	27May64		100	11.2 11.58	11.51	−81
Kovtunova (Volkova)	Ltubov	SU	59		SP	19.46	18.82	−83
Kowarik	Gloria	GDR	13Jan64	172/54	100	11.46w 11.60	11.70	−81
					100h	12.79	13.00	−83
Kozlova	Yelena	SU	13Feb62	172/79	SP	19.94	19.41	−83
Kratochvilova	Jarmila	CS	26Jan51	170/64	100	11.50	11.09	−81
					200	22.57	21.97	−81
					400	49.02	47.99	−83
					800	1:57.68	1:53.28	−83
Kraus	Brigitte	FRG	12Aug56	180/56	1500	4:06.00	4:01.54	−78
					Mile	8:40.90	8:35.11	−83
Kravchenko	Nina	SU	23May59	165/53	400	51.81	51.00	−83
Kravchinskaya	Natalya	SU	57		HJ	1.90		
Kreish-During	Jeanette	GDR	1Feb65	165/52	400h	56.70		
Kremleva	Lyubov	SU	61		800	1:58.95	2:00.05	−83
					1500	4:02.04	4:05.67	−83
Krieger	Heidi	GDR	20Jul65	187/100	SP	20.51i 20.24	19.03i 19.01	−83
					DT	60.48	61.98	−83
Kripli	Marta	HUN	1Oct60	178/86	DT	61.00	60.06	−83
Kristiansen	Ingrid	NOR	21Mar56	169/50	3000	8:39.56	8:51.79	−82
					5000	14:58.89	15:21.81	−82
					Mar	2:24:26	2:30:09	−81
Krug	Petra	GDR	9Nov63	181/70	400h	55.95	54.76	−83
Kubi	Elju	SU	25Mar51	179/79	DT	63.98	64.44	−83
Kucherenko	Yelena	SU	66		JT	59.36	51.56	−83
Kudinova	Yelena	SU	24Aug64	170/65	100h	13.21 12.8	13.47	−83
Kudryavtseva	Galina	SU	11Apr61	170/85	DT	61.62	58.04	−83
Kugayevskikh	Nadezhda	SU	19Apr60	170/85	SP	17.56	18.08	−82
					DT	67.04	68.60	−83
Kuhn	Ute	GDR	23Jul65	180/63	HJ	1.88	1.87	−83
Kuimova	Galina	SU	54		1500	4:09.71	4:06.0	−83
Kukk	Ille	SU	6May57	169/49	3000	8:55.75	9:00.57	−83
Kuleshina	Larisa	SU	4Jan63	175/80	DT	62.84	62.38	−83
Kumpulainen	Sirkku	FIN	12Jan56	163/55	10k	33:53.8	33:58.81	−83
Kunster	Iris	FRG	5Jan60	173/64	HJ	1.87	1.89	−82
					Hept	5968	6216	−82
Kuritsina	Natalya	SU	60		SP	17.20	17.37	−82
Kurochkina	Valentina	SU	13Dec59	177/70	100h	13.37	13.50	−83
Kushenko	Irina	SU	6Jun65		Hept	5727 5832H	5039	−82
Kuzhel	Galina	SU	4Oct59	181/86	SP	18.04	18.22	−83
Kuznetsova	Marina	SU	5May63		100h	13.2	13.90 13.3	−83

513

Women's Index

Kuzyukova	Olga	SU	17Mar53	170/60	3000	8:55.45	8:38.22	−83
Kyalisima	Ruth	UGA	21Nov55	157/52	400h	57.02	57.10	−82
Laaksalo	Tuula	FIN	21Apr53	171/70	JT	67.38	67.40	−83
Laglace	Chantal	FRA	6Jan55	155/48	Mar	2:34:51	2:35:16	−77
Lagutenko	Lyudmila	SU	62		800	2:01.4		
Laine	Helena	FIN	30Mar55	178/76	JT	63.08	64.00	−83
Lajbnerova	Zuzana	CS	20May63	177/74	Hept	5895	5975	−83
Lannaman	Sonia	UK	24Mar56	162/61	100	11.42w 11.58	11.20	−80
							10.93w	−77
Lapajne (Benedetic)	Lidia	YUG	1Apr59	175/62	HJ	1.89	1.91	−83
Lapina	Lyubov	SU	54		800	1:59.4	2:01.4	−82
Larpi	Marja-Leena	FIN	28Apr59	176/82	DT	60.12	62.00	−81
Larrieu	Francie	USA	23Nov52	163/48	1500	4:06.09	4:05.09	−76
					Mile	4:29.79	4:27.52	−79
					3000	8:50.85	8:51.03	−79
Larsen	Debra	USA	7Jun64	178/65	Hept	5856	5612	−83
Larsen	Lisa	USA	13Dec61	175/57	Mar	2:31:31	2:34:56	−83
Lastovka	Valentina	SU	53		800	1:59.0	1:58.7	−83
Lathan (Brehmer)	Christina	GDR	28Feb58	169/65	400	52.31 51.75i	49.66	−80
Lattner	Gudrun	FRG	30Apr59	173/58	100h	13.41	13.62 13.54w	−83
Lavallias	Pat	USA	20Apr62	165/55	100h	13.48w 13.56	13.65 13.53w 13.53w	−83
Laxton	Sonja	RSA	6Aug48	170/50	5000	15:57.01	16:12.87	−83
					Mar	2:36:44	2:43:49	−80
Lazarciuc	Niculina	RUM	6Dec57	171/54	400	51.68	51.70	−81
Leal	Ivonne	CUB	27Feb66	164/64	JT	58.54	56.82	−83
Leatherwood	Lillie	USA	6Jul64	168/56	100	11.42w 11.74		
					400	50.19	53.76 53.2	−83
Lebedinskaya	Irina	SU	61		1500	4:05.7		
LeDisses (Laval)	Dominique	FRA	29Aug57	166/53	400h	57.65	57.87	−83
Legotnikova	Lyudmila	SU	60		1500	4:06.97	4:09.2	−83
					3000	9:01.78		
Leiskalne	Sandra	SU	15Apr58	162/58	JT	61.54	64.38	−81
Lengyel (Ionescu)	Mariana	RUM	14Apr53	179/85	SP	17.73	17.10i 16.75	−82
					DT	61.70	64.92	−82
Leonova (Vakhmyanina)	Tatyana	SU	26Jul56		1500	4:06.21	4:03.05	−82
					3000	8:49.29	8:47.35	−83
Lepota	Tatyana	SU	60		LJ	6.59	6.47	−83
Lesovaya	Tatyana	SU	1Jan56	174/87	DT	66.50	68.18	−82
Levchenko	Galina	SU	63		400h	57.4 58.86	57.91 57.6	−82
Levesque (Fouache)	Sylviane	FRA	6Apr53	159/46	Mar	2:37:41	2:37:55	−83
Lewis	Carol	USA	8Aug63	178/68	100h	13.47w	13.46 13.45w	−83
					LJ	6.97 7.03w	6.97 7.04w	−83
Li	Meisu	CHN	17Apr59	176/80	SP	18.47	17.97	−83
Li	Shufeng	CHN	63		JT	57.80	61.64	−82
Li	Xia	CHN	24Jan57	168/61	JT	59.32	58.52	−78
Liao	Wenfen	CHN	30Apr63	169/53	LJ	6.57	6.41	−82
Lillak	Tiina	FIN	15Apr61	181/74	JT	74.24	74.76	−83
Lim (Cole)	Laura	USA	3Mar62	169/57	100h	13.46w 13.72	13.61 13.41w	−83
Lina (Tarita)	Elen	RUM	18Nov54	170/57	400	52.20	52.04	−80
Lind	Angelita	PR	13Jan59	165/51	800	2:01:31	2:03.9	−81
Lindenthal	Gaby	SWI	15Apr59	179/60	HJ	1.90i 1.90	1.94	−82
(Meier) Lindeque	Collen	RSA	13Mar64		5k	15:52.72		
Lion-Cachet	Susan	RSA	8May62		JT	57.82	58.12	−83
Lisovskaya	Lyudmila	SU	60		SP	17.44i	18.10	−83

Women's Index

Lisovskaya	Natalya	SU	16Jul62	188/94	SP	22.53	20.85	−83
Lisowska	Malgorzata	POL	18Apr62	178/66	Hept	5755	5711	−83
Liu	Huajin	CHN	2Aug60	174/65	100h	13.41 13.40w	13.75	−83
Lockley	Margaret	UK	15May47		Mar	2:36:06	2:42:08	−83
Loghin	Mihaela	RUM	1Jun52	169/74	SP	21.00	20.95	−83
Lomot	Oksana	SU	63		100h	13.2 13.60	14.60 13.8	−81
Lorentzon	Susanne	SWE	11Jun61	175/59	HJ	1.93	1.91	−81
Lorraway (Strong)	Robyn	AUS	20Jul61	168/54	LJ	6.75 6.90w	6.74−83 6.88w	−82
Losch	Claudia	FRG	10Jan60	181/84	SP	20.55	20.08	−83
					DT	60.34	55.22	−83
Loud	Gwen	USA	6Sep61	165/56	LJ	6.58 6.85w	6.64 6.65w	−83
Loval	Marie-France	FRA	12Aug64	164/50	100	11.39 11.25w	11.38	−81
Lovin	Fita	RUM	14Jan51	166/57	800	1:58.47	1:56.67	−80
					1500	4:01.43	4:00.12	−83
Lowe	Tonya	USA	28Jun62	168/54	100h	13.35	13.56	−83
Lozhnova	Albina	SU	61		3000	8:56.0		
					10k	33:27.51		
Lubeth	Marie-Francoise	FR	A20Nov62	168/52	100	11.43w 11.55	12.23 11.8	−83
Ludwigs	Sigrun	GDR	7Nov65	166/55	800	1:59.53	2:03.40	−83
					400h	57.80	57.56	−81
Lukovic	Vesna	YUG	10Mar59	180/60	HJ	1.91	1.80−83 1.80i	−82
Lundholm	Ulla	FIN	20Jan57	175/72	DT	66.02	67.02	−83
Lunegova	Tatyana	SU	57		1500	4:07.41		
					3000	8:46.32	9:08.2	−83
Luo	Yuxiu	CHN	59		5000	16:05.38		
					10k	33:52.84		
Lynch	Leanne	AUS	1Dec60	170/54	200	23.0w 23.3	23.8 23.3w	−83
Lyons	Ellen	USA	11Jul62	173/59	5000	16:04.63	16:23.8	−81
					10k	33:03.7	34:09.4	−82
MacDougall	Lynne	UK	18Feb65	158/47	800	2:01.11	2:05.67	−83
					1500	4:05.96	4:15.39	−83
					Mile	4:30.08	4:49.60	−83
McCabe	Jill	SWE	5Sep62	174/56	800	2:00.71	2:01.10	−83
McCauley	Lori	USA	27Oct61	173/57	400h	55.60	A55.69 56.32	−83
McCraw	Gervaise	USA	10Dec64	167/54	200	22.98w 23.49	23.16 23.11w	−83
McIntosh	Tanya	USA	27Dec66	165/54	400	52.64	53.8	−83
McKenzie	Vivien	USA	27Apr64	168/62	100	11.50w 11.2 11.64	11.90 11.74w	−83 −82
McMiken	Christine	NZ			5000	16:00.49		
					10k	33:05.7		
McMillan	Kathy	USA	7Nov57	173/57	LJ	6.53	6.78−76 6.91w	−80
McNeal	Sue	USA	15May62	175/65	HJ	1.87	1.88	−82
McRoberts (Lind-Petersen)	Brit	CAN	10Feb57	178/56	800	2:01.06	2:00.02	−83
					1500	4:05.23	4:03.36	−83
					Mile	4:33.91i	4:29.90	−83
Machado	Grisel	CUB	25Oct59	174/63	100h	13.33	13.18	−82
Machado	Albertina	POR	25Dec61	167/56	3000	9:00.1	9:17.4	−83
Madeira	Fordie	USA	44		Mar	2:36:35	2:48:56	−81
Madetzky	Silvia	GDR	24Jun62	185/105	DT	65.20	68.24	−82
Mai	Christina	FRG	3Sep61	159/49	5000	16:02.9		
					10k	33:50.26	33:50.1	−83
Makovets	Olga	SU	63		Hept	5941H 5497		
Malesev	Tamara	YUG	8Jan67	181/55	HJ	1.92i 1.86	1.88	−83
Malone	Anne Marie	CAN	28Jul60	165/42	Mar	2:33:00	2:36:23	−82
Malovecz	Zsuzsa	HUN	21May62	176/60	JT	62.10	59.60	−83
Malykh (Zhidova)	Irina	SU	8Feb58	170/66	Hept	5840 5883H	5874−83 6013H	−82
Mamayeva	Tatyana	SU	62		1500	4:09.8		
Manecke	Ingra	FRG	31Mar56	184/80	DT	66.68	67.06	−82
Mangelow	Cornelia	GDR	28Sep62	180/62	400h	57.18	60.62	−82
Manning	Louise	UK	21Jan67	183/64	HJ	1.87	1.85	−82
Marchisio	Rita	ITA	13Feb50	170/53	10k	33:29.68	33:39.79	−83

Women's Index

Marcon	Ana Maria	BRA	10Sep59	185/63	HJ	1.89	1.85	−83
Marjamaa	Helina	FIN	5Jun56	168/58	100	11.33 11.27w	11.13	−83
(Laihorinne)					200	23.12	22.86	−83
Marks	Robin	USA	28Feb62	178/60	400h	56.42	57.24	−81
Marlow	Janet	UK	9Dec58	165/55	Mile	4:33.53	4:33.2	−79
Marot	Veronique	UK	16Sep55	168/52	Mar	2:33:52	2:36:24	−83
Marshall	Pam	USA	16Aug60	175/64	100	11.43	11.44	−82
					200	22.67 22.59w	23.34	−82
							23.32w	−80
Marten	Maritza	CUB	17Aug63	177/83	DT	67.76	63.94	−83
Marti	Debora	UK	14May68	170/52	HJ	1.89	1.88	−83
Martin	Gael	AUS	27Aug56	175/98	SP	19.74	18.98	−83
(Mulhall)					DT	61.52	63.08	−79
Martin	Lisa	AUS	12May60	165/54	5000	15:43.21	16:06.15	−83
(O'Dea)					10k	32:50.6	33:12.1	−83
					Mar	2:27.40	2:32:22	−83
Martins	Gabriele	GDR	1Jun62	170/53	3000	8:48.46	8:54.27	−82
(Riemann)								
Martsenyuk	Yelena	SU	61		Hept	6044	5943	−83
Maslennikova	Marianna	SU	17May61	173/66	100h	13.47	13.66	−82
					Hept	6383	6134	−82
Mastin	Tara	USA	29May62	162/59	200	23.38	24.05 23.55w	−81
Masuda	Akemi	JAP	1Jan64	150/41	Mar	2:32:05	2:30:30	−83
Masullo	Marisa	ITA	8May59	170/56	100	11.41	11.29	−80j
					200	22.88	23.00	−83
Mathieu	Marielande	PR	28Nov56	161/55	400	52.0 53.27	55.5	−81
Matejkovicova	Milena	CS	23May61	161/53	800	1:59.43i 2:02.43	1:57.28	−83
-Strnadova								
Matsui	Emi	JAP	20Feb63	159/57	JT	60.40	60.52	−82
Matuseviciene	Dalia	SU	62		400	51.12		
(Zauraite)					800	1:58.7	2:03.65	−83
Matveyeva	Lyudmila	SU	57		1500	4:10.4		
					3000	8:52.49	8:55.44	−83
					10k	32:25.99	32:28.28	−83
Maxie	Leslie	USA	4Jan67	178/59	400h	55.20		
May	Carey	IRL	19Jul59	163/48	10k	32:51.23	33:04.23	−83
					Mar	2:38:11	2:29:23	−83
Medvedyeva	Lyudmila	SU	18Jan57		800	1:59.30	2:01.18	−83
(Farnosova)					1500	4:00.42	4:10.19	−83
Medvedyeva	Lyudmila	SU	54		JT	62.50	63.12	−83
Medvedyeva	Niole	SU	20Oct60	175/61	LJ	7.02	6.71i−82 6.50	−80
(Bluskite)								
Medvedyeva	Yelena	SU	14Jul59	165/51	800	1:57.90	2:02.3	−83
Medvedyeva	Yelena	SU	65		JT	59.34	60.00	−83
Mefodyeva	Albina	SU	28Mar61		3000	8:59.5	8:53.93	−83
					10k	32:48.33		
Melentyeva	Vera	SU	55		DT	62.80	64.92	−83
Melicherova	Ludmila	CS	6Jun64	155/43	5000	16:01.43		
					10k	33:06.99		
					Mar	2:36:31	2:42:39	−83
Melinte	Doina	RUM	27Dec56	172/59	800	1:56.53	1:55.05	−82
					1500	3:58.1	4:01.49	−83
Melnikova	Svetlana	SU	29Jan51	189/94	SP	19.41	20.21	−82
					DT	60.26	66.06	−79
Mendzorite	Aldona	SU	23Jan61		400	52.61	52.99 52.5	−82
					800	2:01.0	2:02.9	−82
Menissier	Liliane	FRA	12Nov60	171/63	HJ	1.87	1.78	−83
					Hept	5875	5866	−83
Merchuk	Maria	SU	28Oct59	167/59	100h	13.05 12.6	12.81	−82
(Kemenchezhi)							12.5w	−81
Mercurio	Carla	ITA	26Oct60	164/56	100	11.50	11.70	−80
Merrill	Jan	USA	18Jun56	169/51	Mile	4:30.12	4:28.23	−79

Women's Index

					3000	9:01.31	8:42.6	−78
Meshkova	Yelena	SU	19Jan59		100h	13.33 12.9	13.65−82 13.2	−83
Meszynski	Irina	GDR	24Mar62	175/97	DT	73.36	71.40	−82
Meyfarth	Ulrike	FRG	4May56	188/70	HJ	2.02	2.03	−83
Michallek (Steiert)	Vera	FRG	6Nov58	170/52	1500 3000 5000	4:06.25 8:54.62 15:52.15	4:09.32 8:52.57	−81 −81
Mihalcea	Gabriela	RUM	27Jan64	173/66	HJ	1.92	1.89	−83
Mikheyeva	Galina	SU	17Dec62	168/59	100 200	11.51 22.74	11.58 23.16	−81 −81
Milana	Alba	ITA	17Mar59	171/50	Mar	2:33:01	2:32:57	−83
Millar	Jocelyn	AUS	23Mar62	167/57	Hept	5753	5670	−83
Robin-Millerchip	Kerry	UK	27Sep61		100h	13.44w 14.22	14.08 13.8 13.97w	−83 −83
Mineyeva	Olga	SU	1Sep52	178/60	800	1:58.92	1:54.81	−80
Mitishcheva	Olga	SU	62		SP	18.62i 17.44	17.97	−83
Mititelu	Alexandra	SU	27Jun59	183/92	SP	19.26	18.25	−82
Mitkova	Svetla	BUL	17Jun64	178/96	SP DT	19.11 64.84	18.83 66.80	−83 −83
Mitrea	Aurica	RUM	19Nov59	170/60	800	2:00.6		
Mityayeva	Yelena	SU	11Oct63	177/57	LJ	6.88	6.76	−83
Moe	Bente	NOR	2Dec60	171/58	Mar	2:35:28	2:41:52	−83
Mokryak	Svetlana	SU	2Jun67	175/60	HJ	1.90i 1.88	1.85	−83
Molen-Koeven	Jill	USA	26Sep60	170/52	10k	33:37.0	33:35.19	−83
Moller	Lorraine	NZ	1Jun55	172/54	Mar	2:28:34	2:29:36	−81
Molokova	Marina	SU	24Aug62	171/61	100 200	11.26 11.58 22.97	11.3 11.40w 23.33	−83 −83
Moneva	Yanka	BUL	27Jan59	171/62	800 1k	2:00.12 2:36.58	2:02.37	−83
Moravcikova	Zuzana	CS	30Dec56	166/52	800	1:58.06	1:56.96	−83
Morgenstern	Heike	GDR	13Dec62	173/56	100 200	11.42 23.19 23.06w	11.71 23.81	−82 −82
Mori	Minori	JAP	9Dec57	161/68	JT	59.58	56.14	−82
Morley	Susan	UK	6Jan60	168/57	400h	56.67	56.04	−83
Morley	Suzanne	UK	11Oct57		Mile 3000	4:29.15 8:56.39	9:30.8	−83
Moro	Paola	ITA	14Aug52	160/50	Mar	2:33:03	2:37:46	−83
Morrow (Gibbs)	Katrina	AUS	7Apr59	176/55	HJ	1.88	1.93	−78
Mota	Rosa	POR	29Jun58	157/45	3000 5000 Mar	8:53.84 15:30.63 2:26:01	9:04.24 16:05.8 2:31:12	−83 −81 −83
Motusenko (Sukhova)	Svetlana	SU	25Dec54	177/81	DT	64.74	64.42	−79
Mozharova	Irina	SU	58		3000	8:52.42	9:05.0	−83
Mueller	Debbie	USA	28Jan59	155/42	Mar	2:34:50	2:36:55	−83
Muller	Ines	GDR	2Jan59	182/94	SP DT	21.32 62.26	21.14 65.04	−81 −82
Muller	Petra	GDR	18Jul65	180/64	400	51.38	51.79	−83
Murashova	Galina	SU	22Dec55	180/92	DT	72.14	69.06	−82
Murkova	Eva	CS	29May62	168/56	LJ	7.01 7.17w	6.92	−83
Murray	Yvonne	UK	4Oct64	166/42	Mile 3000 5000	4:30.25 8:58.54 15:50.54	4:43.78 9:04.14 15:52.55	−83 −83 −83
Nagy	Elisabet	SWE	14Mar60	165/62	JT	60.26	58.58	−81
Naigre	Raymonde	FRA	23Jan60	161/57	100 200 400	11.39 23.33w 23.47 52.61	11.36−79 11.30w 22.97 52.78	−81 −80 −83
Naplatanova	Radka	BUL	11Jul57	163/57	3000	8:56.62	9:16.11	−83
Nastase (Alexandru)	Liliana	RUM	1Aug62	169/60	100h Hept	13.20 12.8w 6160	13.47 5861	−83 −83
Nastoburko (Strategopulo)	Antonina	SU	59		100	11.31 10.9	11.52 11.1 11.50w	−83 −83

517

Women's Index

Naumann	Gabriele	GDR	4Jul63	180/73	SP	18.42	17.63i 17.52	−83
Navickaite	Margarita	SU	10Dec61	166/59	400	52.2	52.8	−83
					400h	55.02	55.20	−80
Nazarova	Irina	SU	31Jul57	170/54	400	50.56	50.07	−80
Nazaurova	Galina	SU	58		HJ	1.89		
Neamtu	Elisabeta	RUM	16Oct60	178/78	DT	59.94	59.10	−83
Nedd	LaShon	USA	8Jun63	165/57	100	11.51	11.35−83 A11.27w	−82
					200	23.16	22.89	−83
Neeley	Janell	USA	27May63	179/53	10k	33:44.1	34:23.7	−83
Neer	Penny	USA	7Nov60	183/75	DT	58.64	57.98	−83
Nekrasova	Zhanna	SU	4Dec55	176/53	HJ	1.88i 1.88	1.97i 1.91	−82
Nekrosaite	Terese	SU	61		JT	61.60	60.52	−83
Nelson	Karen	CAN	3Dec63	164/52	100hA	13.35 13.34w	13.30	−83
						13.52	13.10w	−82
Nelson	Lynn	USA	8Jan62		5000	15:58.57		
Nemogayeva (Kugarina)	Olga	SU	21Apr59	170/58	LJ	6.49	6.77	−80
					Hept	6092H	6299	−83
Nesbit	Joan	USA	20Jan62	152/43	5000	15:52.9		
					10k	32:54.19		
Neubauer	Tori	USA	7Jan62	168/48	10k	33:25.80		
Neubert	Ramona	GDR	26Jul58	174/65	100h	13.37	13.13	−83
					LJ	6.71	6.90 7.00w	−81
					Hept	6740	6836	−83
Ngambi	Cecile	CMR	15Nov60		100	11.41w 11.67	11.5	−83
Ni	Xiulin	CHN	62	173/58	HJ	1.89	1.85	−82
Niesche	Carmen	GDR	1Jun64	171/78	SP	19.66	18.40	−83
Nikanorova	Tatyana	SU	59		3000	8:54.70	9:04.63	−83
					5000	16:03.4	16:07.1	−83
					10k	33:58.2		
Nikitina	Irina	SU	10Jun61	169/57	1k	2:39.67i	2:35.4	−79
					1500	4:03.2	4:00.18	−82
					3000	8:46.0	8:45.70	−82
Nikitina	Larisa	SU	29Apr65		Hept	6255	5767	−83
Nikolayeva	Svetlana	SU	29Oct59	180/65	HJ	1.93i 1.85	1.88	−80
Nikolova	Galya	BUL	14Nov65	174/65	JT	58.90	57.68	−83
Ninova	Ludmila	BUL	30Jun60	171/56	LJ	6.80	6.23	−83
Nitzsche	Kristine	GDR	1Jun59	187/75	HJ	1.89i 1.83	1.95	−79
					Hept	6092	6364	−83
Noskova	Yulia	SU	60		800	2:00.51	2:03.0	−82
					1500	4:08.4	4:10.4	−83
Novobaczky (Lajer)	Klara	HUN	30May58	168/60	LJ	6.76	6.59	−83
Novoseltsova (Tuznikova)	Lilia	SU	5Sep62	169/57	200	23.06	23.86−80 23.6	−81
					400	50.28	51.68	−79
Nowak (Guzowska)	Malgorzata	POL	9Feb59	180/70	100h	13.48w 13.52	13.47	−80
					HJ	1.88	1.87	−82
					Hept	6321	6346	−82
Nuneva	Anelia	BUL	3Jan62	167/57	100	11.10	11.07	−83
					200	22.67	22.58	−83
Nunn (Saunders)	Glynis	AUS	4Dec60	168/58	100h	13.02	13.17	−83
					LJ	6.66	6.55	−83
Nybu	Solvi	NOR	3Jun66	166/58	JT	58.12	52.88	−82
Oakes (Hunte)	Heather	UK	14Aug59	163/64	100	11.27 11.08w	11.20 11.01w	−80
					200	23.00w	23.06 22.9	−80
Oakes	Judith	UK	14Feb58	164/76	SP	18.35i 18.28	18.28	−83
Oberli-Schuh	Elizabeth	VEN	28Dec52	175/56	Mar	2:16:17	2:45:34	−83
Obizhayeva (Freimane)	Yelena	SU	9Oct60	178/61	LJ	6.50	6.79	−83
O'Connor	Mary	NZ	19Jun55	155/43	5000	15:49.3		
					Mar	2:33:54	2:28:20	−83
Oja	Silva	SU	17Jan61	182/79	Hept	5944	5975 6156H	−83
Oker	Edith	FRG	1Feb61	168/56	100h	13.09 13.08w	13.29	−80

Women's Index

Okolo-Kulak	Lidiya	SU	15Jan67		100h	13.2 13.73	13.27w 13.84	−81 −83
Oladapo	Georgina	UK	15May67	167/61	LJ	6.52	6.32	−83
Oladapo	Joyce	UK	11Feb64	175/57	LJ	6.54w 6.40	6.55	−83
Olejarz	Genowefa	POL	17Oct62	174/78	JT	65.52	63.12	−83
Olenchenko	Vera	SU	59		LJ	6.79	6.75	−83
Oleynik	Irina	SU	61		Hept	5876	5321	−83
Olijar	Ludmila	SU	58		100h	13.11	13.29 12.9 12.89w	−83
Olijslager	Marjan	HOL	8Mar62	172/58	100h	13.20	13.52	−82
							13:26w 13.0	−83
Oliver	Ilrey	JAM	2Sep62	170/57	400	52.14	52.93	−83
Olizarenko	Nadezhda	SU	28Nov53	165/57	400	51.22	50.96	−80
					800	1:56.09	1:53.43	−80
					1500	4:04.94	3:56.8	−80
Opitz	Martina	GDR	12Dec60	178/85	DT	72.32	70.26	−83
Oreshkina	Irina	SU	64		LJ	6.69	6.34	−83
Orlova (Chernova)	Tatyana	SU	53		10k	33:17.5	33:02.0	−82
Orlova	Tatyana	SU	55		SP	19.58	20.44	−83
O'Shea	Caroline	IRL	30Dec60	168/56	800	2:00.70	2:07.5	−82
Osipova	Irina	SU	63		LJ	6.52i	6.48	−83
Oskirko	Yelena	SU	65		Hept	5786	5556	−83
Ostapenko	Lyudmila	SU	26Nov60		SP	17.22	17.29	−83
Osterer	Beate	AUT	13Aug60	170/59	Hept	5754	5527	−83
Otahalova	Helena	CS	1Jan59	178/65	Hept	6099	5961	−83
Otterman	Edith	RSA	8Jul66		400 A	52.55 A52.2	A54.03	−83
Ottey-Page	Merlene	JAM	10May60	174/57	100	11.01	11.03−82 10.97w	−81
					200	22.09	22.17−82 22.11w	−83
Ovchinnikova	Svetlana	SU	31Oct56	177/67	100h	13.43	13.52	−82
(Yakimovich)					Hept	6201 6265H	6217 6227H	−82
Paavolainen	Anne	FIN	21Jun60	173/76	DT	60.40	64.24	−83
Paetz	Sabine	GDR	16Oct57	174/67	100	11.46	12.25−77 11.5	−82
(Mobius)					200	23.37 23.23w	23.60	−83
					100h	12.54 12.51w	12.83	−82
					LJ	7.12	6.90	−82
					Hept	6867	6662	−83
Page	Andrea	CAN	4Sep56	162/52	400h	57.26	A57.19 57.70	−82
Page	Pam	USA	12Feb58	268/59	100h	13.07 13.01w	13.00	−83
Pagel	Ramona	USA	10Nov61	183/86	SP	17.89	16.72	−83
Pakula-Kolodziejak	Iwona	POL	17May62	163/53	100	11.36	11.54	−82
Palacean	Cleopatra	RUM	3Jan68	160/47	1500	4:09.37	4:13.85	−83
Pallay	Zsuzsa	HUN	28Sep48	173/71	DT	62.10	62.36	−81
Palm	Evy	SWE	31Jan42	166/52	5000	16:08.13	16:37.22	−83
Palombi	Margit	HUN	5Mar61	165/58	Hept	5822	5451	−83
Panfil	Wanda	POL	26Jan59	166/56	3000	9:01.30& 9:12.61	9:09.38	−82
Pantazi	Elisavet	GRE	21May56	174/62	100h	13.36	13.42 13.30w	−83
					Hept	5773	5441	−82
Parakhina	Nadezhda	SU	24Feb54	169/66	JT	60.58	63.68	−83
Parlyuk	Olga	SU	63		800	1:59.7	2:01.39	−83
					1500	4:04.16		
Parts	Helgi	SU	15Sep37	182/80	DT	58.58	63.70	−80
Patoka	Antonina	SU	12Jan64	180/85	DT	62.52	58.16	−83
Pavlova	Pepa	BUL	1Jan61	162/55	100	11.31	11.48	−83
					200	23.00	23.30	−83
Pavlovskaya	Lyubov	SU	9Jan56	170/60	Hept	6106H 5907	5491 5828H	−83
Payne	Marita	CAN	7Oct60	172/57	200	22.72 22.64w	22.62	−83
					400	49.91	50.06	−83
Pedan	Anna	SU	61		3000	8:58.38	9:16.4i	−83
Peel	Deborah	UK	19Aug58	163/45	Mile	4:34.70	4:50.66	−83
					3000	8:59.74	8:50.52	−82
					5000	15:50.9		
Peeters	Francine	BEL	23Feb57	159/55	Mar	2:34:53		

519

Women's Index

Pencheva (Kunova)	Emilia	BUL	14Feb60	175/60	400h Hept	57.06 6050	59.14 6030	−83 −81
Peng	Biyun	CHN	63		SP	17.98	16.63	−81
Penkova	Galina	BUL	18May58	178/60	200	23.29	23.10	−81
					400	52.46	51.66	−83
Permyakova	Olga	SU	64		Hept	5917 6102H	5580H	−83
Perry	Sybil	USA	9Sep63	155/52	400h	57.22	58.70	−83
Pestretsova	Svetlana	SU	61	173/72	JT	57.74	61.68	−83
Peters	Beate	FRG	12Oct59	178/80	JT	63.02	66.86	−83
Peters	Jenni	USA			10k	34:18.82		
Peterson	Inger	USA	14Apr64	172/59	100	11.41	11.62	−81
					200	23.0w 23.61	24.04 23.84w	−81
Petkova (Vergova)	Maria	BUL	3Nov50	182/105	DT	71.22	71.80	−80
Petrika-Kiss	Ibolya	HUN	27May57	171/56	400	52.60	52.41	−81
Petrikova	Jana	CS	12Jan67	174/56	100h	13.40w 13.50	13.82 13.67w	−82 −83
Petrova	Irina	SU	2Nov58		400h	57.55 56.8	59.17 58.8	−83
Petruss	Larisa	SU	63		HJ	1.95	1.88	−83
Petsch	Birgit	FRG	20Feb63	175/78	SP	17.73i 17.66	17.03	−82
Pfaff	Petra	GDR	16Oct60	172/58	200 400 400h	23.11 52.1i 53.14 55.63	24.36−80 24.0 52.45 54.64	−79 −81 −83
Pfeiffer	Astrid	GDR	6Dec64	173/56	800	2:01.43	1:59.93	−83
					1k Hept	2:39.24i 5813H 5729	2:39.6i 5745	−83 −83
Pfeil	Renate	FRG	4Feb63		10k	34:06.9		
Pfeifer	Kathy	USA	59		100	11.43w 11.56	11.63	−83
Philippe	Francoise	FRA	4Oct61	160/49	100h	13.49 13.41w	13.40	−80
Picaut	Florence	FRA	25Oct52	167/58	Hept DT	6002 59.22	6012H−83 5899 58.16	−82 −82
Picknell	Kathy	USA	22Jan58	185/85	5000	16:09.0&		
Pierson	Sally	AUS	10Mar63	160/39	10k	33.28.1	33:31.4	−83
Pinigina	Maria	SU	9Feb58	172/59	200	23.25	22.80	−83
(Kulchunova)					400	49.74	49.19	−83
Piquereau	Anne	FRA	15Jun64	170/67	100h	13.39 13.30w	13.22	−83
Pishchalnikova	Tatyana	SU	59		DT	61.62	56.18	−83
Plastinina	Yelena	SU	60	190/100	SP	17.25	17.11	−82
Platonova	Lyudmila	SU	17Nov64	186/100	DT	61.66	56.44	−83
Plotzitzka	Iris	FRG	7Jan66	181/	SP	17.67	14.15	−83
Plumer	PattiSue	USA	27Apr62	162/49	3000 5000	8:54.91 15:29.0	8:53.81 15:49.4	−83 −83
Pluss	Caroline	SWI	8Jun59		400h	57.36	60.16	−83
Podkopayeva	Yekaterina	SU	11Jun52	168/57	800	1:57.07	1:55.96	−83
(Poryvkina)					1k 1500	2:36.35i 3:56.65	2:38.03i 3:57.4	−83 −80
Podyalovskaya	Irina	SU	19Oct59	165/55	400 800	51.67 1:55.69	52.61 1:57.99	−83 −83
Politova	Olga	SU	25Nov64		1500	4:09.33	4:11.09	−83
Polman-Tuin	Connie	CAN	10Jan63	181/66	Hept	5728 5787w	5751H 5609	−83
Poltorak	Svetlana	SU	60		3000	8:59.3		
Polyakova	Vera	SU	66		Hept	5920	5828	
Pomoshchnikova	Natalya	SU	9Jul65		100 200	11.42 23.1	11.48 23.26	−83 −83
Ponomaryeva (Khromova)	Margarita	SU	19Jun63	178/58	400 400h	52.05 53.58	52.87 57.45−81 56.9	−83 −83
Possamai	Agnese	ITA	17Jan53	164/52	1k 1500 3000	2:39.36 4:05.14 8:45.84	4:05.45 8:46.68	−80 −83
Potapova	Tatyana	SU	23Apr54	170/61	Hept	6021H	6076	−81
Potreck	Rositha	GDR	11Mar59	176/80	JT	65.26	66.08	−81
Pozdina	Natalya	SU	19Mar58	164/56	LJ	6.78	6.54	−83

Women's Index

Name	First	Nat	DOB	Ht/Wt	Event	Best	Prev	Year
Pozdnyakova	Tatyana	SU	4Mar56	164/52	800	1:59.4	1:57.5	−82
					1500	3:57.70	3:56.50	−82
					3000	8:32.0	8:34.80	−81
Pozharitskaya	Irina	SU	58		DT	65.10	62.52	−83
Prendergast	Maureen	UK	27Nov59		400h	57.49	58.95–83 58.6	−82
Prokopenko	Marina	SU	64		Hept	5798H	5479H	−82
Proskuryakova-Rodionova	Tatyana	SU	13Jan56	174/65	LJ	7.02	7.04	−83
Prouzova	Jitka	CS	5Dec50	176/81	DT	62.56	64.04	−78
Pufe	Margitta	GDR	10Sep52	180/90	SP	21.01	21.58	−78
					DT	63.32	68.64	−79
Puica	Maricica	RUM	29Jul50	179/52	800	1:58.12	1:57.8	−79
					1k	2:35.7		
					1500	3:57.22	3:58.29	−81
					3000	8:33.57	8:31.67	−82
Putilova	Lyubov	SU	53		Mar	2:37:00	2:39:01	−80
Qui	Shuhua	CHN	12Oct62	168/65	JT	59.08	57.26	−83
Quick	Glenys	NZ	29Nov57	168/52	5000	16:04.77		
					10k	33:04.96	33:57.82	−81
					Mar	2:32:53	2:35:25	−81
Quinn	Sarah	USA	14May58		Mar	2:36:54	2:39:40	−82
Quintavalla	Fausta	ITA	4May59	175/74	JT	62.92	67.20	−83
Quirot	Ana Fidelia	CUB	23Mar63	165/59	200	23.16 22.9	24.18 23.9	−83
					400	50.87	51.83	−83
Raath (Swart)	Riana	RSA	23Mar61		100hA	13.48	A13.21–83 13.38	−82
Racaite	Audra	SU	64		400h	57.1	59.18–83 59.0	−82
Racu	Lyubov	SU	61		Hept	6260	6467H 6077	−83
Radisch	Iris	GDR	7Jun63	177/63	400h	56.86	56.58	−83
Radtke	Helga	GDR	16May62	171/65	LJ	7.21	6.83	−82
Radu	Maria	RUM	25May59	164/53	1500	4:03.08	4:00.62	−83
Raduly-Zorgo	Eva	RUM	23Oct54	178/71	JT	62.28	68.80	−80
Rakova	Galina	SU	7Nov59	170/58	800	2:01.48		
					1500	4:08.57	4:08.96	−82
Ralldugina	Nadezhda	SU	15Nov57	166/54	800	2:00.10	2:00.94	−82
					1k	2:36.07i		
					1500	3:56.63	3:58.17	−82
Ramos	Hilda	CUB	1Sep64	176/80	DT	67.56	63.60	−83
Rankins	Kathy	USA	24Apr62	168/52	LJ	6.55	6.39	−82
Rasmussen	Dorthe	DEN	27Jan60	180/62	Mar	2:30:42	2:31:45	−83
Rasmussen	Dòrthe	DEN	2Dec58	171/55	100h	13.45	13.60–80 13.2	−81
Rattray	Cathy	JAM	19Aug63	162/50	400	52.19	51.71	−82
Ready	Paula	USA	17Mar66	168/55	100	11.46w 11.78		
Redetzky	Heike	FRG	5May64	181/62	HJ	1.91i 1.91	1.89	−82
Reidick	Claudia	FRG	4Jul62	169/56	100h	13.45	13.67 13.52w	−83
Reinsch	Gabriele	GDR	23Sep63	185/78	DT	61.68	60.02	−83
Reiska	Daniela	CS	14May61	166/50	HJ	1.87	1.86	−82
Renzi	Paula	USA	14Jul63		5000	16:04.05	16:18.71	−83
Revayova	Elena	CS	10Jul58	165/62	JT	60.86	59.18	−82
Reznikova	Galina	SU	17Apr61	157/49	800	1:58.4	2:00.42	−83
Richardson	Jill	CAN	10Mar65	172/59	400	51.58	51.91	−83
Richburg	Diana	USA	2Jul63	179/54	800	2:01.12	2:00.82	−83
					1k	2:37.92		
					1500	4:04.07	4:23.8	−82
					Mile	4:37.6		
Richter	Ute	GDR	14Jul68	180/85	JT	58.80	66.96	−83
Riefstahl-Oschkenat	Cornelia	GDR	29Oct61	178/65	100	11.1w	11.66	−82
					200	23.15	24.35	−81
					100h	12.57	12.72	−83
Rieger	Sabine	GDR	6Nov63	170/60	100	11.43	11.32 11.29w	−82
					200	22.65	22.37	−82
Riermeier	Susanne	FRG	23Dec60	172/54	10k	33:36.2	33:54.03	−80
					Mar	2:38:13	2:36:29	−83

Women's Index

Rione	Teresa	SPA	23Mar65	163/49	100	11.48	12.01 11.6	−83
Ritchie	Margaret	UK	6Jul52	178/87	SP	17.85i 17.69	18.99	−83
					DT	65.02	67.48	−81
Ritter	Louise	USA	18Feb58	178/59	HJ	1.96i 1.93	2.01	−83
Rivers	Petra	AUS	11Dec52	174/75	JT	62.66	69.28	−82
Robertson	Kim	NZ	10Mar57	171/55	400	52.54	51.60	−80
Rodchenkova	Marina	SU	30Jul61		1500	4:07.27	4:11.0	−83
					3000	8:47.06	8:53.85	−83
					5000	16:09.9		
Rodger	Diane	NZ	9Nov56	170/62	3000	8:47.90	8:59.48	−82
Rodriguez	Marcelina	CUB	26Apr60	170/90	SP	17.76	17.95	−83
Rollo	Patricia	UK	12Nov61		100h	13.36 13.12w	13.35	−83
Romanova	Anzhela	SU	6May61	168/47	800	1:59.5	2:01.76	−83
					1500	4:03.70	4:04.92	−83
					3000	8:48.54		
Romo	Louise	USA	11Oct63	167/54	1500	4:09.29	4:16.24	−83
Rosiak	Elzbieta	POL	3Mar57	169/54	HJ	1.87	1.86	−80
Ross	Heather	UK	14Feb62	170/59	100h	13.47 13.22w	13.90	−79
							13.71w	−83
Rossi	Erika	ITA	20Nov55	178/61	400	52.37i	52.01	−82
Rougeron	Brigitte	FRA	14Jun61	183/69	HJ	1.92	1.88	−83
Rowell	Sarah	UK	19Nov62	162/47	Mar	2:31:28	2:39.11	−83
Royle (Williams)	Diane	UK	24Nov59	176/72	JT	61.94	56.68	−83
Ruban	Irina	SU	62		Mar	2:37:39		
Rubsam-Neubauer	Dagmar	GDR	3Jun62	172/58	200	22.87	22.93 22.89w	−82
					400	49.58	50.48	−83
					800	1:58.36		
Ruchayeva	Nina	SU	17Apr56	169/54	400	51.8	52.6	−80
					800	1:56.84	1:57.0	−80
Rudrich	Simone	GDR	21Nov61	188/91	SP	17.95i	19.96i 19.83	−83
					DT	62.96	61.40	−83
Ruegger	Sylvie	CAN	23Feb61	166/54	Mar	2:29:09		
Rusakova	Irina	SU	62		Hept	5966H	5788 5811H	−82
Ruskite	Valda	SU	62		Hept	6120H 5859	6096	−83
Russell	Joan	USA	10Jul57	175/64	Hept	5841	5705H 5622	−83
Ryazanova	Yelena	SU	62		400h	58.04		
St. Hillaire	Judi	USA	5Sep59	173/52	5000	16:04.63i	16:02.16	−83
					Mar	2:37:49		
Sachse	Diana	GDR	14Dec63	180/87	DT	66.36	61.88	−83
Safronenko	Galina	SU	12May55	174/63	Hept	6114 6283H	5977 6172H	−82
Salak	Anne	SU	2Aug59		DT	59.86	57.60	−83
Sallaz	Christine	FRA	17Feb61	173/62	100h	13.43w 13.56	13.55	−83
Salo	Galina	SU	14Jun59	170/62	LJ	6.84	6.52i 6.50	−83
Sam	Sylvia	GDR	14Mar65		400h	58.09	60.58	−83
Samsonova	Nina	SU	7Dec51	182/89	SP	18.42	19.91	−82
					DT	62.66	64.90	−82
Samungi	Maria	RUM	28Aug50	168/58	400	51.92	51.76–81 51.6	−80
Samy	Shireen	UK	4Sep60		5000	16:02.95		
Sanders	Sherifa	USA	25Apr63	160/57	100h	13.45w 13.75	13.84	−82
Sanderson	Tessa	UK	14Mar56	170/71	JT	69.56	13.70w	−83
							73.58	−83
Saroudi	Sultana	GRE	19Aug58	167/83	SP	17.18	18.19	−83
Sarria	Maria Elena	CUB	14Sep54	183/110	SP	20.25	20.61	−82
Sasaki	Nanae	JAP	8Feb56	162/53	10k	32:54.90	32:58.94	−82
					Mar	2:37:04	2:35:00	−82
Saskoi (Szucs)	Eva	HUN	25Jul61	174/78	DT	58.62	56.02	−83
Savchenko	Valentina	SU	68		Hept	6226		
Savigny	Marie-Noelle	FRA	11Oct57	167/55	100h	13.13	13.19	−83
Savina (Limina)	Lyudmila	SU	15Jul55	179/94	SP	20.21	19.61	−83
Savinkova	Galina	SU	15Jul53	182/98	DT	73.28	73.26	−83
Scaunich	Emma	ITA	1Mar54		10k	33:51.09		

522

Women's Index

Schabinger	Michaela	FRG	23Mar61	172/58	Mar 200	2:37:43 23.37	2:40:48 23.28	−83 −83
Schierjott (Koitzsch)	Sylvia	GDR	6Dec64	174/60	800 1500	2:01.40 4:08.82	2:02.68 4:11.01	−83 −83
Schilly	Katy	USA	19Oct56	162/51	Mar	2:32:40	2:39:44	−83
Schima	Christine	GDR	6Sep62	180/67	LJ	6.96	6.85	−82
Schiro	Cathy	USA	19Jul67	157/44	10k Mar	33:26.53 2:34:24	34:01.1&	−83
Schlosser	Doris	FRG	29Sep44		Mar	2:35:43	2:36:31	−83
Schmidt	Birgit	FRG	12Sep63	172/57	1500 3000	4:10.38 9:01.30	4:13.23 9:23.0	−83 −83
Schmidt	Ines	GDR	7Jul60	166/62	100 200 LJ	11.23 22.87 6.76 6.98w	11.21 22.97 6.55	−83 −83 −83
Schmidt	Kate	USA	29Dec53	186/80	JT	58.70	69.32	−77
Schmidt	Vera	FRG	1Mar61	180/80	SP	18.14	15.78	−83
Schmuhl	Liane	GDR	29Jun61	184/90	SP	20.37	21.27	−82
Schneider	Corine	SWI	28Jul62	177/62	Hept	6110	5937	−83
Schneider	Sue	USA	3Aug56	173/57	Mar	2:37:58		
Schnurpfeil	Kim	USA	23Sep61	165/48	10k	34:08.72	33:06.09	−82
Schoellkopf	Nadine	FRA	19Aug64	176/64	JT	58.34	62.46	−83
Scholzel (Lockhoff)	Barbel	GDR	9Oct59	170/54	100	11.44	11.11	−83
Schonfeld	Rosemarie	GDR	1Jan62		5000	16:07.0		
Schonleber	Mechthild	FRG	10Jul63	175/82	SP	17.81	18.61i 18.08	−83
Schramm (Junghans)	Andrea	GDR	17Nov62	169/71	JT	60.68	59.66	−83
Schroder	Antje	GDR	2Sep63	175/58	800	1:58.08	1:57.57	−83
Schulte-Mattler (Schmidt)	Heike	FRG	27May58	170/54	400	52.37	52.26	−82
Schulz	Ellen	GDR	13Apr62	176/61	800	2:00.29	2:01.01	−83
Schulz	Ines	GDR	10Jul65	176/62	Hept	5990	5307	−83
Schulze	Cordula	GDR	11Sep59	189/92	SP	21.00	20.58	−83
Scott	Debbie	CAN	16Dec58	163/52	1k 1500 3000	2:39.76 4:09.16 4:07.0& 8:58.5& 9:11.6	4:06.89 8:48.85	−83 −83
Scott	Rhonda	USA			100h	13.34 13.20w	13.74 13.4	−83 −82
Scutt	Michelle	UK	17Jun60	170/56	200 400	23.33w 23.50 51.89	22.80 22.48w 50.63	−82 −82
Sedachova	Inesa	SU	64		SP	17.38	15.66	−83
Sekach	Alla	SU	59		Hept	5929H	5740H	−82
Seldon	Carla	USA	14Aug63	170/58	LJ	6.62w 6.45		
Selivanova	Yelena	SU	62		SP	17.56	17.34	−83
Serbina	Nina	SU	21Jul52	177/60	HJ	1.90i	1.96	−80
Serbul	Lyudmila	SU	60		Hept	6279	6073	−83
Sergeyeva	Antonina	SU	57		LJ	6.62	6.34i−82 6.28	−79
Serkova	Marina	SU	12Sep61	176/55	HJ	1.91	1.93i−79 1.92	−80
Shabanova	Irina	SU	64		DT	60.68	57.18	−83
Shaprinskaya	Nadezhda	SU	68		LJ	6.48	6.13	−83
Sharpilova	Nadezhda	SU	2Jan59	178/66	HJ	1.88	1.88	−83
Sharples	Patsy	RSA	13Dec61	168/54	10k	33:49.8	33:34.85	−82
Shcherbach	Zhanna	SU	61		SP	17.40	17.38	−83
Shcherbanos	Tatyana	SU	16Feb60	182/100	SP	20.07	19.41	−83
Sheffield	Lattanya	USA	63		400h	56.02	59.68	−83
Shelomkova	Lyubov	SU	56		400h	57.44 56.4	57.49 56.8	−83
Shen	Liquan	CHN	4Jul58	170/85	SP	17.45	18.15	−81
Shevchenko	Natalya	SU	28Dec66	178/60	LJ	6.88	6.82	−83
Shikolenko	Natalya	SU	64	179/83	JT	63.64	60.48	−83
Shikolenko	Natalya	SU	68		JT	59.40		
Shlyakhtich	Natalya	SU	62	180/84	SP	18.69	17.72	−83
Shpak	Tatyana	SU	17Jan60	174/72	LJ	6.55i 6.52	6.48	−82

523

Women's Index

Shubenkova	Natalya	SU	25Sep57	175/65	Hept 100h LJ	6139 12.93 6.73	6297 6320H 13.25 6.52	−83 −83 −83
Sichlau	Helle	DEN	25Oct57	180/70	Hept 400h	6799 57.65	6526 57.90	−83 −83
Siegl	Siegrun	GDR	29Oct54	178/60	LJ	6.67	6.99	−76
Siepsiak	Ewa	POL	1Jan57	174/79	DT	59.20	60.60	−83
Silhava	Zdenka	CS	15Jun54	178/84	SP DT	20.12 74.56	21.05 70.00	−83 −83
Simashova	Tatyana	SU	58		DT	58.50	63.80	−81
Simeoni	Sara	ITA	19Apr53	178/61	HJ	2.00	2.01	−78
Simianu	Mariana	RUM	15Aug64	160/47	800 1500	2:00.27 4:06.2	2:02.63 4:21.2	−83 −82
Simm	Konstanze	GDR	14May64	170/94	SP	19.78	18.46	−83
Simonsick	Eleanor	USA	30Apr58	176/54	3000	8:59.48	9:03.9	−83
Simova	Stefania	BUL	5Jun63	172/79	DT	59.72	59.32	−83
Simpson (Livermore)	Judy	UK	14Nov60	184/72	100h HJ Hept	13.07 1.90 6280	13.22 1.92 6353	−82 −83 −83
Simpson	Myrtle	RSA	18Feb64	175/55	400 400h	A52.47 52.0 53.30 56.25	A51.89 52.4 A55.74	−83 −82 −83
Siska	Xenia	HUN	3Nov57	174/57	100h	12.76	13.16−83 13.05w	−82
Sittner (Hirschke)	Sylvia	GDR	19Aug61	177/64	HJ	1.88	1.91	−82
Sivokon	Larisa	SU	4Dec59	162/55	100	11.2 11.69	11.75−79 11.3	−82
Skoglund	Ann-Louise	SWE	28Jun62	174/58	400 100h 400h	52.61 13.41w 13.88 55.17	51.78 13.46 13.26w 54.57	−83 −81 −82
Sly (Smith)	Wendy	UK	5Nov59	169/47	1500 Mile 3000	4:08.69 4:28.07 8:39.47	4:04.14 4:30.09i 8:37.06	−83 −83 −83
Slythe	Christine	CAN	10Aug61	165/53	800 400h	2:00.4& 2:03.1 A56.32	2:03.0 A57.04 57.40	−83 −83
Slyusar	Irina	SU	19Mar63	160/49	100 200	11.27 11.62 22.76	11.2 11.52w 23.85 23.1	−83 −83
Smajstrla	Terri	USA	11Sep64	160/53	100	11.50w 11.62	11.72	−81
Smalls	Odessa	USA	8Jul64	175/61	100	11.46w 11.67	11.5	−83
Smeeth	Ruth	UK	19Jun60	162/52	1500 Mile 3000	4:10.76 4:30.89 8:54.47	4:12.71 4:36.65 8:51.40	−81 −79 −82
Smekhnova	Raisa	SU	16Sep50	166/53	10k Mar	31:59.70 2:29:10	32:36.05 2:31:13	−82 −83
Smellie	Donna	CAN	2Sep64	175/61	Hept	5814w 5638	5263H	−83
Smeyan	Tatyana	SU	59		400	52.51	52.94 52.5	−83
Smirnova	Yekaterina	SU	22Oct56	169/62	Hept	6173	6493	−83
Smith (LaPlante-Lansky)	Deby	USA	3Apr53	168/57	100h	13.35 13.18w	12.86	−79
Smith	Joyce	UK	26Oct37	168/50	Mar	2:32:48	2:29:43	−82
Smith	Karin	USA	4Aug55	167/61	JT	64.68	64.78	−80
Smith	Lori	USA	4Dec61	183/66	200	23.14	23.40	−83
Smith	Meledy	USA	11Dec64	168/53	LJ	6.52w 6.40	6.43	−82
Smolka	Lyubov	SU	29Nov52	170/59	1500 3000	4:08.3 8:41.72	3:56.7 8:36.0	−80 −80
Smyth	Roisin	IRL	26Oct63	160/50	3000	8:57.94		
Soborova	Radislava	CS	16Apr59	166/58	100	11.51	11.59	−83
Sobotka	Jana	GDR	3Oct65	176/66	Hept	6266	6222	−83
Soetewey	Chris	BEL	19Aug57	170/56	HJ	1.94 1.90	1.94	−83
Sofina	Svetlana	SU	62		800	2:01.33	2:03.0	−82
Sokolova	Nadezhda	SU	31Mar59		LJ	6.81	6.39	−83
Sokolova	Stepanka	CS	30Jul58	168/62	100	11.38	11.48 11.41w	−82
Sokolova	Tatyana	SU	58		10k	33:06.04	34:26.80	−83

Women's Index

Name	First	Country	DOB	Ht/Wt	Event	Mark1	Mark2	Yr
(Shadrina)					Mar	2:35:20	2:45:15	−83
Solberg	Trine	NOR	18Apr66	172/65	JT	65.02	61.58	−83
Solomatina	Irina	SU	5Mar60		1k	2:38.6		
Sommer	Ulrike	FRG	11Apr59	168/51	200	23.38	23.00	−81
Sons	Bonnie	USA			10k	34:05.72		
Sorokina	Galina	SU	60		200	23.35 22.9	23.5	−83
Sorokiyevskaya	Natalya	SU	61		3000	8:49.28	8:53.72	−83
Southerden	Margaret	UK	14Jan56		400h	58.07	57.81	−82
Spangler	Jenny	USA	20Jul53	157/45	Mar	2:37:01	2:33:52	−83
Spencer	Pam	USA	8Oct57	184/68	HJ	1.93	1.97	−81
Spirina	Marina	SU	19Feb55	168/60	100h	13.2 13.55	13.64	−83
					LJ	6.50i 6.48	6.52	−82
					Hept	6235M 5972	6234	−83
Springs	Betty	USA	12Jun61	157/46	3000	9:01.28	8:59.79	−83
					5000	15:39.72	15:33.43	−83
Stalmach	Jolanta	POL	3Aug60	170/51	400h	57.04	57.97	−83
Stalman	Ria	HOL	11Dec52	179/82	SP	18.02	17.66	−83
					DT	71.22	67.20	−83
Stamenova	Rositsa	BUL	6Mar52	167/53	400	50.82	51.31	−83
Stanciu	Anisoara	RUM	28Jun62	172/63	LJ	7.27	7.48	−83
(Cusmir)								
Stanescu	Mariana	RUM	7Sep64	168/47	3000	9:00.10	9:23.6	−83
Stanescu	Mihaela	RUM	15Apr59	171/68	JT	59.52	60.12	−83
Stanton	Chris	AUS	12Dec59	183/66	HJ	1.94 1.95&	1.92	−81
(Annison)						1.96ex		
Steely	Shelly	USA	23Oct62	168/53	5000	15:40.97		
Stepanova	Marina	SU	1May50	170/58	400	51.60	51.25	−80
(Makeyeva)					400h	53.67	54.78	−79
Stepanova	Nadezhda	SU	59		1500	4:10.2	4:13.8	−83
					3000	9:00.76		
Stojanowski	Leanna	CAN	29Jun65	167/54	400h	57.36	61.24	−83
Stolyar	Lyubov	SU	61		100h	13.18		
(Lyakisheva)								
Story	Pat	USA	6Mar49		10k	34:08.1		
Stoyanova	Vanya	BUL	12Dec58	160/54	800	2:00.2	1:58.78	−82
					1500	4:03.14	4:04.53	−80
Strejckova	Jarmila	CS	15Feb53	167/57	LJ	6.54	6.89	−82
(Nygrynova)								
Strong	Shirley	UK	18Nov58	173/63	100h	12.88 12.86w	12.87	−83
							12.78w	−82
Sukhareva	Marina	SU	62		100h	13.42	13.06	−83
Sukhorukova	Zhanna	SU	64		400h	57.42	59.05	−83
Sukhova	Antonina	SU	1Jan59	178/67	100h	13.32 13.0	14.14	−83
(Filippova)					Hept	6467M 6351	5667−81 5682H	−83
Sulinski	Cathy	USA	3Apr58	175/76	JT	61.10	59.76	−76
Susuyeva	Tatyana	SU	64		Hept	5797	5417H	−82
Suter	Esther	SWI	25Feb62	179/55	Hept	5817	5571	−83
Sutfin (Hughes)	Lynda	USA	6Oct47	171/68	JT	60.30	61.66	−82
Svechikhina	Lidiya	SU	26Dec52		800	2:00.83		
					1500	4:05.13	4:07.0	−83
					3000	8:48.81	8:53.6	−83
Svetonosova	Irina	SU	58		100h	13.29 13.0	13.85−81 13.5	−83
Svirskaya	Lyubov	SU	60		10k	33:57.58		
					Mar	2:34:53	2:43:43	−82
Sycheva	Tatyana	SU	29Nov57	155/47	1500	4:08.2	4:04.13	−81
					3000	8:50.76	8:33.9	−80
Syemshchikova	Raisa	SU	57		HJ	1.89	1.90i−83 1.86	−82
Szabo	Karolin	HUN	17Nov61	149/36	3000	9:01.78	9:11.93	−82
					10k	32:38.5	33:17.8	−82
					Mar	2:33:43	2:36:22	−83
Szalai	Katalin	HUN	4Mar61	165/52	800	2:01.07	2:01.69	−81
(Weninger)					1500	4:03.51	4:08.69	−81

525

Women's Index

Name	First	Nat	DOB	Ht/Wt	Event	Mark1	Mark2	Yr
Szelinger	Viktoria	HUN	18Aug56	182/87	3000 SP	8:51.50 18.34	9:18.64 18.04	−81 −81
(Horvath) Szopori	Erika	HUN	1Dec63	170/55	400h	57.18	57.97	−83
Szulc	Elzbieta	POL	23May59	165/53	100h	13.48 13.43w	13.31	−78
Tang	Guoli	CHN	61	171/75	JT	57.96	61.64	−81
Tannander	Annette	SWE	13Feb58	179/66	Hept	5972	5977	−83
Tannander	Kristine	SWE	21Nov55	179/61	Hept	5985	5984	−82
Tarasova	Alexandra	SU	58		10k	34:18.6	34:32.8	−82
Tarr	Sheila	USA	14Jun64	178/66	Hept	5856		
Tatichek	Svetlana	SU	62		SP	17.46	16.89	−83
Taylor	Angella	CAN	28Sep58	167/61	100	A11.16 11.23	11.00	−82
					200	A11.09w A22.61 22.75 A22.44w	10.92w A22.25 22.3 A22.19w	−82 −82 −82
Taylor	Davera	USA	12May65		100	11.51w	11.94 11.5w	−83
Taylor	Gladys	UK	5May53	175/62	400 400h	52.43 56.72	52.50 57.31	−82 −83
Taylor	Michelle	USA	10Apr67	181/64	400h	58.06		
Taylor	Monica	USA	3Mar65	175/53	100	11.47w 11.54	11.59	−83
Terenchenko	Marina	SU	61		JT	59.26	62.12	−82
Terpe	Heike	GDR	4Oct64	172/62	100h	13.02 12.99w	13.05	−83
Teske	Charlotte	FRG	23Nov49	167/55	10k Mar	33:29.76 2:31:16	32:00.26 2:28:32	−83 −83
Thacker	Angela	USA	27Jun64	168/60	100 200 LJ	11.39 11.37w 23.15 6.81	11.43 11.20w 23.34 23.07w 6.53 6.54w	−83 −83 −83
Thamm	Simone	GDR	8Apr65	180/70	SP DT	17.45i17.44 60.94	17.33i 17.32 59.78	−83 −83
Thiele	Sybille	GDR	6Mar65	178/72	LJ Hept	6.69 6359	6.65 6421	−83 −83
Thieme	Andrea	GDR	8Jun64	285/85	DT	63.96	58.56	−83
Thimm (Finger)	Ute	FRG	10Jul58	168/52	200 400	22.95 50.37	23.15 50.78	−83 −83
Thomas	Andrea	JAM	3Aug68	175/60	400	52.57	55.61	−82
Thomas	Donna	USA	3May62	165/61	LJ	6.48	6.40 A6.46w	−82
Thomas	Shirley	UK	15Jun63	160/48	100 200	11.39 11.13w 23.36 23.14w	11.31 11.22w 23.46	−83 −82
Thyssen	Ingrid	FRG	9Jan56	171/72	JT	66.12	68.10	−82
Tifrea	Corina	RUM	11Feb58	169/61	Hept	6066	6130	−82
Tillack	Heike	GDR	6Jan68	171/59	100h	13.39		
Tischler	Heike	GDR	4Feb64	174/63	Hept	6381	6105	−82
Tochilova	Natalya	SU	64		Hept	5849H	5477	−83
Todorova	Antoaneta	BUL	8Jun63	170/74	JT	65.40	71.88	−81
Toivonen	Tuija	FIN	22Sep58	171/55	5000 10k Mar	15:59.3 32:29.25 2:32:07	15:42.28 32:23.1 2:34:14	−82 −83 −83
Tokareva	Olga	SU	66		Hept	5902	5709	−83
Tomczak	Elzbieta	POL	7Jan61	172/56	100 200	11.18 23.17	11.85−79 11.6 23.95	−78 −82
Tomsett (Cooper)	Debbie	AUS	9Apr60	160/51	400h	57.51	58.60−83 58.1	−82
Tooby	Angela	UK	24Oct60	166/51	3000	8:52.59	9:23.3	−83
Tooby	Susan	UK	24Oct60	161/50	5000 10k 3000 5000	15:22.50 32:58.07 8:57.17 15:35.40	9:17.56	−83
Topchina	Yelena	SU	21Oct66	174/52	HJ	1.88	1.94	−83
Torma	Ibolya	HUN	22Sep55	164/62	JT	59.74	61.34	−81
Torrence	Gwen	USA	12Jun65	170/52	100	11.41 11.37w	11.92	−83
Trus	Yelena	SU	63		SP	17.51		
Tsukhlo	Yelena	SU	13May54	165/54	Mar	2:34:10	2:37:44	−81
Turchak	Olga	SU	5Mar67	188/58	HJ	1.96	1.84	−83

526

Women's Index

Turner	Kim	USA	21Mar61	165/57	100h	13.01 12.96w	12.95	−83
Tursunova	Zhanna	SU	23Oct57	157/46	3000	8:41.07	8:48.14	−83
					10k	31:53.53	33:53.91	−82
Turta	Olga	SU	13Feb57	176/91	SP	18.52	19.10	−80
(Khoroshilova)								
Tveit	Astrid	NOR	26Jun57	178/66	HJ	1.87	1.90	−82
Twomey	Cathie	USA	24Oct56	162/50	3000	8:48.55	8:58.0	−82
					5000	15:30.50	15:39.49	−81
Ubah	Rufina	NIG	4Apr60	166/62	100	11.49 11.37w	11.31 11.18w	−82
Uibel	Birgit	GDR	30Oct61	166/54	400	52.39 51.27i	52.87 52.65i	−82
(Sonntag)					400h	54.68	55.70	−82
Ulbricht	Siegrid	GDR	25Jul58	174/66	LJ	6.84	6.89	−81
Ullrich-Korner	Hildegard	GDR	20Dec59	170/54	800	1:57.77	1:57.20	−80
					1k	2:34.8		
					1500	4:06.63	4:06.5	−80
Untonaite	Neringa	SU	18Oct63		LJ	6.50i	6.49	−83
Urish	Carol	USA	28Oct51	173/55	5000	15:45.28	16:00.1	−82
-McLatchie					10k	33:03.06	33:33.08	−80
					Mar	2:35:09	2:37:58	−83
Usha	P.T.	IND	20May64	170/57	400h	55.42		
					200	23.0	23.9−83 24.28	−82
Usifo	Maria	NIG	1Aug64	174/63	100h	13.36 13.35w	13.71 13.39w	−82
					400h	57.39	61.8	−82
Usmanova	Nadezhda	SU	16Dec56	160/52	Mar	2:30:36	2:35:02	−83
Uusitalo	Helena	FIN	7Nov62	167/56	JT	58.44	58.90	−82
van den Heerden	Hilsa	RSA	23Mar61		100h	A13.38	A13.56−83 13.71	−82
van Hulst	Elly	HOL	9Jun59	178/57	800	2:00.92	1:59.62	−81
					1500	4:05.44	4:08.86	−81
					5000	15:50.11	15:50.6	−83
van Landeghem	Rita	BEL	19Jul57	164/58	10k	33:40.30	35:14.5	−83
					Mar	2:34:13	2:40:39	−83
van Landschoot	Christiane	BEL	8Aug56		Hept	5810	5633	−83
van Niekerk	Marvna	RSA	14May54	168/55	LJ	A6.58	A6.77−80 A6.82w	−82
							6.64	−82
van Rensburg	Ina	RSA	29Oct56	169/56	100h	A13.26	A13.14 13.19	−82
							A13.11w	−82
van Zyl	Eranee	RSA	10Oct66	172/55	5000	16:02.55	15:59.62	−83
Vader	Els	HOL	24Sep59	164/53	100	11.28 11.25w	11.25 11.0	−81
					200	22.90	22.81	−81
Vahlensieck	Christa	FRG	27May49	160/51	10k	34:17.97		
					Mar	2:34:28	2:33:24	−83
Valsamma	M.D.	IND	20Oct60	157/47	400h	57.7 60.03	58.47	−82
Valyukevich	Irina	SU	59		LJ	6.95	6.46	−83
(Apollonova)								
Van	Anna	USA	62		LJ	6.58w 6.32	6.00−81 6.18w	−83
Vancheva	Ivanka	BUL	31Oct53	170/65	JT	59.74	65.38	−80
Vanyek	Zsuzsanna	HUN	18Jan60	168/59	LJ	6.62	6.81	−83
					Hept	5948	6114	−82
Vashchenko	Nina	SU	31May60	170/60	Hept	6092 6212H	6254−82 6280	−83
(Aldatova)								
Vasile	Niculina	RUM	13Feb58	175/58	HJ	1.95	1.97	−83
Vasilenko	Tatyana	SU	21Jul57	170/62	400h	56.10	55.78	−82
Vasileva	Snezhana	BUL	1Jul64	173/80	SP	17.43	18.57	−83
(Shileva)								
Vasilkiv	Nina	SU	2May63	159/50	1500	4:09.0	4:16.59	−81
(Gorbatyuk)								
Vasilyeva	Galina	SU	60		DT	60.68	57.80	−82
Vasilyeva	Lyubov	SU	24May57	174/76	SP	19.34	19.68	−83
(Kharitonchik)								
Vasilyeva	Tatyana	SU	61		Mar	2:37:58	2:48:17	−83
Vasyutina	Irina	SU	13Jan59	184/88	DT	59.16	63.46	−83
Vater	Anke	GDR	5Jun61	174/63	200	23.26 23.20w	23.44	−83

527

Women's Index

					100h	13.30	13.38	−83
					LJ	6.84	6.76	−83
					Hept	6722	6532	−83
Veikshina	Olga	SU	21Jan61	168/65	400h	57.88 55.5	57.11	−83
Vepsalainen	Sirpa	FIN	7Sep60	175/66	JT	58.38	56.02	−83
Vereb	Grace	CAN	10Aug58	170/51	800	2:01.2& 2:02.53	2:02.77	−82
Verbe (Fazekas)	Erszebet	HUN	23Oct63	160/54	10k	33:57.0	35:34.8	−83
Vereen	Wendy	USA	23Apr66	160/54	100	11.32	A11.17 11.45	−83
					200	23.24 22.75w	22.99	−83
Verouli	Anna	GRE	13Nov56	165/84	JT	72.70	70.90	−83
Vershinina	Nina	SU	58		800	1:59.04	1:58.5	−79
(Kovylina)								
Veselinova	Verzhinia	BUL	18Nov57	170/95	SP	19.42	21.62	−82
Veselkova	Lyudmila	SU	25Oct50	170/56	800	1:58.9	1:55.96	−82
					1500	4:02.37	4:02.96	−81
Vessup	Shannon	USA	13May60	181/58	400h	A57.99 59.34	58.94	−83
Vidosova	Irina	SU	61		SP	17.70		
Vihanto (Ranta)	Niina	FIN	8Jul62	174/58	HJ	1.88	1.86	−83
Vila	Mayra	CUB	5Jun60	167/64	JT	66.02	68.76	−83
Vilisova	Tatyana	SU	30May59	168/56	100	11.51	11.60−81 11.3	−82
Vinogradova	Nadezhda	SU	1May59	170/64	LJ	6.70	6.54	−83
					Hept	6532	6228−82 6443H	−83
Vinogradova	Yelena	SU	28Mar64	170/58	100	11.49	11.53 11.23w	−83
					200	22.87	23.11 23.01w	−83
					400	52.5 53.36	55.38	−83
Virsilovaite	Rasa	SU	62		1500	4:09.01	4:10.6	−83
					3000	8:56.79	9:09.50	−83
Vitoulova	Alena	CS	6May60	176/89	SP	17.96	18.23	−83
Vladykina	Olga	SU	30Jun63	170/62	400	48.98	50.48	−83
Volodina	Lidia	SU	53		800	2:00.0	1:59.9	−83
					1500	4:02.25	4:05.19	−83
Volskite	Margarita	SU	61		400	52.3 52.96	53.13	−83
Vornicu	Nicoleta	RUM	14Feb64	173/62	400h	55.67	59.55	−83
Voyevudskaya	Lyudmila	SU	22Jun58	175/90	SP	20.24	19.82	−83
(Dyevitskaya)								
Wachtel	Christine	GDR	6Jan65	166/56	400	52.19	52.54	−83
					800	1:58.24	1:59.40	−83
Wagner	Astrid	GDR	3Nov65	175/60	SP	18.64	17.22	−83
Waithera	Ruth	KEN	17Aug58	168/61	200	23.37	23.88−83 23.4	−80
					400	51.56	52.70	−79
Waitz	Grete	NOR	1Oct53	172/52	Mar	2:26:18	2:25:29	−83
Walker	Patsy	USA	6Jul59	155/60	Hept	6153	5985	−83
Wall	Gwen	CAN	16Jan63	175/56	400h	57.28	56.10	−83
Wallace	Kathrene	USA	14Nov63	155/52	100	11.31	11.33	−82
Walther	Gesine	GDR	6Oct62	176/65	100	11.13	11.13−82 10.97w	−80
					200	22.32	22.24	−82
					400	50.03	51.10	−82
Walther	Kerstin	GDR	15Apr61	175/65	400	51.41	51.12	−83
Walton-Floyd	Delisa	USA	28Jul61	173/58	800	2:00.94	2:00.67	−82
Wang	Huabi	CHN	66		10k	34:06.53		
Wang	Jing	CHN	62		JT	59.68	55.84	−80
Ware	Sharon	USA	27Sep63	152/48	100	11.46w 11.52	11.34	−80
							A11.31w	−82
Warner	Cynthia	USA	17Dec60	177/59	800	2:00.48	2:02.75	−83
Wartenberg	Christiane	GDR	27Oct56	170/53	800	1:59.84	1:57.6	−76
					1k	2:35.5	2:32.29	−80
					1500	4:05.53	3:57.71	−80
Washington	Essie	USA	12Jan57	179/52	800	2:00.35	2:01.0	−78
(Kelley)								
Washington	Jackie	USA	17Jun62	168/61	100	11.33 11.17w	A11.11 11.33	−83
					200	23.10 22.8w	23.35	−83
							22.9w	−81

Women's Index

Name	First	Country	DOB	Ht/Wt	Event	Mark	Mark2	Yr
Washington-Brown	Jackie	USA	20Aug61	175/55	100h	13.34	13.18	−81
Watkins	Gayle	USA	5Nov58	167/54	100h	13.46 13.35w	A13.40 13.57	−82 −83
Webb	Brenda	USA	30May54	175/56	3000 5000	8:55.15 15:22.76	8:48.09 15:33.64	−83 −83
Weekly	Linda	USA	16Dec58	173/58	100h	13.44	13.35−80 13.1	−81
Weigt	Anke	FRG	13Jun57	178/67	LJ	6.49i 6.45	6.80	−80
Weinhold	Birgit	GDR	27Sep64	164/48	10k Mar	33:41.5 2:35:17		
Weiss	Angela	SWI	13Nov53	166/60	100h	13.34	13.60	−82
Welch	Lesley	USA	12Mar63	175/56	3000	9:01.6i	9:09.54	−82
Welch	Priscilla	UK	22Nov44	165/50	10k Mar	33:34.7 2:28:54	2:32:31	−83
Wells	Debbie	AUS	29May61	180/70	100	11.39 11.1&	11.47 11.1w 11.2	−76 −79
Welzel	Jane	USA	24Apr55	168/54	200 Mar	22.98 2:35:53	23.06 2:36:18	−80 −83
Werthmuller	Vroni	SWI	5May59	170/54	100	11.50 11.39w	11.54	−83
Weser	Marion	GDR	23Dec62	171/49	LJ	6.66i 6.66	6.50i−82 6.39	−81
Wessinghage	Ellen	FRG	28Jun48	159/48	10k	34:18.7	34:03.9	−83
Westover	Carina	USA	5Jul61	179/64	HJ	1.88	1.83	−83
Whitbread	Fatima	UK	3Mar63	166/67	JT	71.86	69.54	−83
White	Josephine	UK	7Dec60	175/58	1500	4:10.41	4:10.57	−80
White	Martha	USA	31Oct59	157/43	Mar	2:34:09	2:39:41	−83
Whittaker	Sandra	UK	29Jan63	168/	100	11.38w 11.63	11.63 11.34w	−83
Wiarda	Bea	HOL	24Feb59	172/65	200 DT	22.98 59.36	23.13 57.88	−83 −80
Wijnsma	Marion	HOL	18Jul65	168/66	Hept	6015	5773	−83
Wiley	Alison	CAN	11Oct63	164/45	5000	15:36.55	15:41.5	−83
Wiley	Kate	CAN	28Feb62	172/	10k Mar	34:15.99 2:36:22	34:34.24 2:43:00	−83 −83
Williams	Angela	TRI	15May65	175/61	100	11.09w 11.54	11.1w 11.70	−83 −82
Williams	Diane	USA	14Dec61	1 /54	200 100 200	23.38 11.04 23.08	23.49 A10.94 11.00 23.04 22.65w	−83 −83 −83
Williams (Kanuka)	Lynn	CAN	11Jul60	155/49	1k 1500 3000 5000	2:39.23 4:06.09 8:42.14 15:53.78	4:08.64 8:50.20 15:55.04	−83 −83 −83
Wipf	Jane	USA	10Apr58	165/50	Mar	2:37:16	2:37:19	−83
Wlodarczyk	Anna	POL	24Mar51	174/63	LJ	6.96 6.97w	6.95	−80
Wockel	Barbel	GDR	21Mar55	174/62	100	11.04	10.95−82 10.92w	−80
Wolf	Gabriele	FRG	28Oct60		200 400 Mar	21.85 50.35 2:35:41	22.01 21.85w 49.56 2:38:56	−82 −82 −83
Wozniak (Stachurska)	Elzbieta	POL	24Mar59	171/59	100 200	11.41 23.21	1.36 11.1 23.11	−80 −80
Wright-Scott	Angela	USA	10Nov61	165/54	400h	55.33	56.74	−83
Wright	Dana	CAN	20Sep59	163/56	400	57.45	A57.35 58.09	−83
Wuhn	Katrin	GDR	19Nov65	173/57	800 1k 1500	1:57.86 2:35.4 4:10.22	2:00.18 4:28.10	−83 −82
Wujak	Brigitte	GDR	6Mar55	169/58	LJ	6.93	7.04	−80
Wyckoff	Renee	USA	28Jan62	165/50	10k	34:13.4		
Wysocki (Kleinsasser-Caldwell)	Ruth	USA	8Mar57	176/61	800 1500 Mile	1:58.65 4:00.18 4:21.78	2:01.99 4:16.0	−78 −76
Wziontek	Petra	FRG	30Aug60	182/60	HJ	1.90i 1.86	1.91	−79
Xie	Jiahua	CHN	1Mar56	164/72	DT	58.82	59.26	−80
Xin	Xiaoli	CHN	22Sep66	165/60	JT	58.32	58.56	−83

529

Women's Index

Yelizarova (Skoropistseva)	Lyubov	SU	56		DT	61.34	62.22	−83
Yeltsova	Valentina	SU	60		3000	8:53.96	9:10.5	−83
					10k	32:57.25		
Yepanova	Galina	SU	60		400h	56.7	56.16	−83
Yeremina	Alla	SU	16Nov56	168/59	Hept	5901H 5786	6088	−83
Yerokhina	Nadezhda	SU	59		10k	33:18.18	33:46.19	−83
					Mar	2:37:46	2:48:39	−83
Yeshkova	Galina	SU	18Nov63	180/80	SP	17.30i	17.30i−83 16.19	−82
Yesina	Yelena	SU	65		Hept	5816H		
Yevko	Vera	SU	59		SP	18.42	18.46	−83
Yevseyeva	Inna	SU	14Aug64	181/57	400	51.88	53.2	−83
Young	Candy	USA	21May62	168/58	100h	13.14 13.05w	12.89	−82
Young	Danette	USA	6Oct64	165/57	100	11.50w 11.67		
					200	23.38 23.32w	23.76	−83
Yu	Xuequing	CHN	63		JT	59.90	56.54	−83
Yurchenko	Aelita	SU	65		400	52.27	55.19 54.8	−83
Yurchenko (Kulbatskaya)	Vera	SU	9Aug59	174/70	100h	13.1 13.77	13.86 13.4	−83
					Hept	6148 6308H	6088 6167H	−83
Yushina	Alla	SU	20Aug58	171/60	1500	4:01.80	4:00.26	−81
					3000	8:37.76	8:34.02	−83
Zablotskaya	Liliya	SU	65		HJ	1.88i 1.88	1.89	−83
Zadko	Lyudmila	SU	15Feb56	176/80	JT	61.48	58.26	−82
Zagorcheva	Ginka	BUL	12Apr58	171/53	100	11.47	11.38	−83
					100h	12.62	12.49	−83
Zakharova	Galina	SU	7Sep56	162/50	800	1:57.08	2:00.0	−82
					1500	3:57.72	4:00.25	−82
					3000	8:37.07	8:33.40	−82
					10k	31:15.00	31:57.0	−82
Zakharova	Nadezhda	SU	63		Hept	5795H		
Zaliskaya	Galina	SU	65		JT	57.90	54.96	−82
Zaytseva	Zamira	SU	16Feb53	163/51	800	1:58.83	1:56.21	−83
					1500	4:00.50	3:56.14	−82
					3000	8:53.2	8:56.14	−82
Zhang	Suxian	CHN	66		5000	16:09.87		
Zheludkova (Zuyeva)	Nadezhda	SU	13Aug59	169/58	LJ	6.52	6.68	−80
Zheng	Dazhen	CHN	22Sep59	175/61	HJ	1.91	1.93	−82
Zhilitskaya	Yelena	SU	17Aug63	179/66	JT	58.30	54.58	−83
Zhirova (Titova)	Marina	SU	6Jun63	170/53	100	11.24	11.97 11.72w	−79
							11.4	−82
					200	23.20	23.71−83 23.4	−81
Zhitkova	Nadezhda	SU	10Mar52	168/72	DT	61.94	60.38	−83
Zhizdrikova	Svetlana	SU	27Aug60	164/54	100	11.41	11.83 11.1	−82
					200	22.69	23.60	−82
Zhu	Hongyang	CHN	11Feb64	174/78	JT	61.30	57.16	−83
Zhukova (Parkhuta)	Valentina	SU	59		800	1:56.97	1:58.6	−83
					1500	4:07.39	4:11.1	−83
Zhupikova	Margarita	SU	65		1500	4:09.71	4:15.2	−83
					3000	8:57.54	9:15.58	−83
					10k	32:40.85		
Zhupiyeva (Dershan-Skachkova)	Yelena	SU	18Apr60		1500	4:04.44	4:12.23	−82
					3000	8:39.52	8:55.8	−81
Zhuravleva	Olga	SU	56		800	1:59.1	2:00.3	−83
					1500	4:02.33	4:02.58	−83
					3000	8:52.20		
Zimdyanova	Natalya	SU	59		DT	58.68	54.82	−83
Zinurova	Arina	SU	56		3000	8:54.0	9:04.8	−83
					Mar	2:37:42	3:11:37	−81
Zivanov	Danica	YUG	8Feb67	178/74	JT	57.74	54.08	−83
Zolotaryeva	Olga	SU	1Nov61	165/50	100	11.29	11.36−81 11.1	−82

Early 1985 Results

Yakovleva	Alla	SU	59		DT	57.56		
Yang	Wenqin	CHN	30Apr60	175/60	HJ	1.92	1.90	−82
Yang	Yanqin	CHN	28Aug66	168/110	SP	18.08	17.36	−83
Yatchenko	Irina	SU	65		DT	59.54	57.04	−83
Yatsuk	Yelena	SU	16Mar61	170/64	LJ	6.60	6.70	−82
Yefimova	Yelena	SU	61		400h	56.42 55.9	58.45 57.2	−83
Yegorova	Galina	SU	63		LJ	6.50i	6.56i−82 6.54	−83
(Kolganova	)				200	22.80	23.24	−81
Zolotykh	Valentina	SU	49		DT	63.38	69.86	−81
(Kharchenko)								
Zubekhina	Natalya	SU	4Mar51	172/95	SP	19.94	19.50	−82
Zubenko	Marina	SU	62		DT	58.88	57.56	−82
Zubova	Tatyana	SU	12Dec58	165/55	400h	54.43	55.58 55.4	−81
Zuyeva	Svetlana	SU	16Mar63		100	11.30	11.62−82 11.49w	−81
					200	22.9 23.53	23.65 23.3	−83
Zuyeva	Tatyana	SU	57		10k	33:23.51	33:14.72	−83
Zverkova	Lyubov	SU	14Jun55	180/101	DT	68.58	64.68	−83
(Urakova)								
Zvezdina	Nadezhda	SU	62		DT	59.18	51.64	−81
Zvyagintseva	Nadezhda	SU	61		400	51.77	52.24	−83
					800	1:57.47	1:58.70	−83

EARLY 1985 RESULTS

Note that World Indoor Games results are included in biographies in this annual, but later events are not.

AFRICAN CROSS-COUNTRY CHAMPIONSHIPS

Nairobi, Kenya 16 Feb 1985
MEN: 1. Paul Kipkoech (Ken) 35:34.0, 2. Andrew Masai (Ken) 36:02.0, 3. Joshua Kipkemboi (Ken) 36:18.6, 4. Jackson Ruto (Ken) 36:36.0, 5. James Kipngetich (Ken) 36:58.8. Team: 1. Kenya 21, 2. Uganda 83, 3. Tanzania 141.
WOMEN: Helen Kemaiyo (Ken) 16:57.1, 2. Marcelina Cheboi (Ken) 17:40.6. Team: 1. Kenya 10, 2. Tanzania 40, 3. Uganda 44.

EUROPEAN INDOOR CHAMPIONSHIPS

Athens, Greece 2–3 March 1985
Results of Finals – MEN
60 METRES
1. Mike McFarlane (UK)   6.61
2. Antoine Richard (Fra)   6.63
3. Ronald Desruelles (Bel)   6.64
4. Antonio Ullo (Ita)   6.66
5. Attila Kovacs (Hun)   6.69
6. Frantisek Platcnik (CS)   6.71

200 METRES
1. Stefano Tilli (Ita)   20.77
2. Olaf Prenzler (GDR)   20.83
3. Aleksandr Yevgenyev (USSR)   20.95
4. Daniel Sangouma (Fra)   21.13
5. Istvan Nagy (Hun)   21.53

400 METRES
1. Tood Bennett (UK)   45.56
2. Klaus Just (GFR)   45.90
3. Jose Alonso (Spa)   46.52
4. Roberto Tozzi (Ita)   46.66
5. Angel Heras (Spa)   46.68

800 METRES
1. Robert Harrison (UK)   1:49.09
2. Petru Dragoescu (Rom)   1:49.38
3. Leonid Masunov (USSR)   1:49.59
4. Viktor Kalinkin (USSR)   1:49.92
5. Axel Harries (GFR)   1:50.00
6. Benjamin Gonzalez (Spa)   1:50.05

1500 METRES
1. Jose-Luis Gonzalez (Spa)   3:39.26
2. Marcus O'Sullivan (Irl)   3:39.75
3. Jose-Luis Carreira (Spa)   3:40.43
4. Andres Vera (Spa)   3:40.56
5. Riccardo Materazzi (Ita)   3:40.85
6. Anti Loikkanen (Fin)   3:41.19

3000 METRES
1. Bob Verbeeck (Bel)   8:10.84

Early 1985 Results

2. Thomas Wessinghage (GFR) 8:10.88
3. Vitaliy Tishchenko (USSR) 8:10.91
4. Frank O'Mara (Irl) 8:11.11
5. Dietmar Millonig (Aut) 8:11.21
6. Robert Nemeth (Aut) 8:11.24

60m HURDLES
1. György Bakos (Hun) 7.60
2. Jiri Hudec (Cs) 7.68
3. Vyacheslav Ustinov (USSR) 7.70
4. Daniele Fontecchio (Ita) 7.71
5. Nigel Walker (UK) 7.72
6. Jonathan Ridgeon (UK) 7.77

HIGH JUMP
1. Patrik Sjöberg (Swe) 2.35
2. Aleksandr Kotovich (USSR) 2.30
3. Dariusz Biczsyko (Pol) 2.30
4. Eddy Annijs (Bel) 2.24
5. Gennadiy Avdeyenko (USSR) 2.24
6. Dariusz Zielke (Pol) 2.24

POLE VAULT
1. Sergey Bubka (USSR) 5.70
2. Aleksandr Krupskiy (USSR) 5.70
3. Atanas Tarev (Bul) 5.60
4. Valeriy Bubka (USSR) 5.60
5. Ryszard Kolosa (Pol) 5.50
6. Alberto Ruiz (Spa) 5.50

LONG JUMP
1. Gyula Paloczi (Hun) 8.15
2. Laszlo Szalma (Hun) 8.15
3. Sergey Layevskiy (USSR) 8.14
4. Jan Leitner (Cs) 8.13
5. Giovanni Evangelisti (Ita) 8.01
6. Antonio Corgos (Spa) 7.94

TRIPLE JUMP
1. Khristo Markov (Bul) 17.29
2. Jan Cado (Cs) 17.23
3. Volker Mai (GDR) 17.14
4. Ralf Jaros (FRG) 16.78
5. Gennadiy Valyukevich (USSR) 16.75
6. Dario Badinelli (Ita) 16.42

SHOT
1. Remigius Machura (Cs) 21.74
2. Ulf Timmermann (GDR) 21.44
3. Werner Günthor (Swi) 21.23
4. Janis Bojars (USSR) 20.03
5. Marco Montelatici (Ita) 19.64
6. Knut Hjeltnes (Nor) 19.54

WOMEN

60 METRES
1. Nellie Cooman (Hol) 7.10
2. Marlies Göhr (GDR) 7.13
3. Heather Oakes (UK) 7.22
4. Silke Gladisch (GDR) 7.24
5. Els Vader (Hol) 7.25
6. Elzbieta Tomczak (Pol) 7.30

200 METRES
1. Marita Koch (GDR) 22.82
2. Kirsten Emmelmann (GDR) 23.06
3. Els Vader (Hol) 23.64
4. Joan Baptiste (UK) 23.67
5. Ann-Louise Skoglund (Swe) 24.00

400 METRES
1. Sabine Busch (GDR) 51.35
2. Dagmar Neubauer (GDR) 51.40
3. Alina Bulirova (Cs) 52.54
4. Erika Rossi (Ita) 52.59
5. Regine Berg (Bel) 53.15

800 METRES
1. Ella Kovacs (Rom) 2:00.51
2. Nadezhda Olizarenko (SU) 2:00.90
3. Cristina Cojocaru (Rom) 2:01.01
4. Rosa Colorado (Spa) 2:04.53
5. Slobodanka Colovic (Yug) 2:06.38
6. Kirsty McDermott (UK) 2:07.98

1500 METRES
1. Doina Melinte (Rom) 4:02.54
2. Fita Lovin (Rom) 4:03.46
3. Brigitte Kraus (GFR) 4:03.64
4. Nikolina Shtereva (Bul) 4:05.34
5. Yekaterina Podkopayeva (SU) 4:06.79
6. Elly Van Hulst (Hol) 4:08.30

3000 METRES
1. Agnese Possamai (Ita) 8:55.25
2. Olga Bondarenko (USSR) 8:58.03
3. Yvonne Murray (UK) 9:00.94
4. Birgit Schmidt (GFR) 9:06.85
5. Iva Jurkova (Cs) 9:14.17
6. Ludmila Melicherova (Cs) 9:19.17

60m HURDLES
1. Cornelia Oschkenat (GDR) 7.90
2. Ginka Zagorcheva (Bul) 8.02
3. Anne Piquereau (Fra) 8.03

Early 1985 Results

4. Laurence Elloy (Fra)   8.09
5. Ulrike Denk (GFR)   8.09
5. Nadezhda Korshunova (USSR)   8.11

HIGH JUMP
1. Stefka Kostadinova (Bul)   1.97
2. Susanne Helm (GDR)   1.94
3. Danuta Bulkowska (Pol)   1.90
4. Susanne Lorentzon (Swe)   1.90
5. Brigitte Rougeron (Fra)   1.90
6. Andrea Matay (Hun)   1.85

LONG JUMP
1. Galina Chistyakova (USSR)   7.02
2. Eva Murkova (Cs)   6.99
3. Heike Drechsler (GDR)   6.97
4. Helga Radtke (GDR)   6.89
5. Jasmin Feige (GFR)   6.58
6. Vali Ionescu (Rom)   6.49

SHOT
1. Helena Fibingerova (Cs)   20.84
2. Claudia Losch (GFR)   20.59
3. Heike Hartwig (GDR)   19.93
4. Mihaela Loghin (Rom)   19.59
5. Natalia Lisovskaya (USSR)   18.85
6. Judith Oakes (UK)   17.83

WORLD CROSS-COUNTRY CHAMPIONSHIPS
Lisbon, Portugal 24 March 1985.
Men: 1. Carlos Lopes (Por) 33:33, 2. Paul Kipkoech (Ken) 33:37, 3. Wodajo Bulti (Eth) 33:38, 4. Bekele Debele (Eth) 33:45, 5. John Treacy (Ire) 33:48, 6. Kassa Balcha (Eth) 33:51, 7. Christoph Herle (GFR) 33:53, 8. Abderrezak Bounour (Alg) 33:54, 9. Pierre Levisse (Fra) 33:56, 10. Bruce Bickford (USA) 33:57, 11. Fernando Mamede (Por) 33:59, 12. Pat Porter (USA) 34:02, 13. Antonio Leitao (Por) 34:04, 14. Andrew Masai (Ken) 34:06, 15. Viktor Chumakov (USSR) 34:08, 16. Ed Eyestone (USA) 34:09, 17. Boniface Merande (Ken) 34:10, 18. David Lewis (Eng) 34:12, 19. Craig Virgin (USA) 34:12, 20. Rob de Castella (Aus) 34:17. Team: 1. Ethiopia 130, 2. Kenya 141, 3. USA 154, 4. Italy 259, 5. Spain 321, 6. Ireland 361, 7. Portugal 365, 8. England 434, 9. Australia 436, 10. France 437... a record 33 nations completed teams.

WOMEN: Zola Budd (Eng) 15:01, 2. Cathy Branta (USA) 15:24, 3. Ingrid Kristiansen (Nor) 15:27, 4. Fita Lovin (Rom) 15:35, 5. Cornelia Burki (Swi) 15:38, 6. Angela Tooby (Wal) 15:40, 7. Olga Bondarenko (USSR) 15:40, 8. Sue Bruce (NZ) 15:42, 9. Betty Jo Springs (USA) 15:44, 10. Elene Fidatof (Rom) 15:47, 11. Debbie Scott (Can) 15:49, 12. Monica Joyce (Ire) 15:49, 13. Rosa Mota (Por) 15:50, 14. Agnese Possamai (Ita) 15:50, 15. Shelly Steely (USA) 15:51, 16. Kathy Hayes (USA) 15:54, 17. Annette Sergent (Fra) 15:55, 18. Sue French/Lee (Can) 15:56, 19. Tatyana Pozdnyakova (USSR) 15:56, 20. Marina Rodchenkova (USSR) 15:56. Team: 1. USA 42, 2. USSR 77, 3. Romania 96, 4. France 109, 5. Canada 113, 6. Portugal 134, 7. New Zealand 144, 8. England 153, 9. Norway 159, 10. Italy 185... 23 nations completed teams.

JUNIOR MEN: 1. Kimeli Kipkemboi (Ken) 22:18, 2. Habte Negash (Eth) 22:37, 3. Milkesa Woldsilasse (Eth) 22:37, 4. Rafera Workench (Eth) 22:45, 5. Ngotho Musyoki (Ken) 22:48, 6. Lawrence Gatogo (Ken) 23:04, 7. Ebba Tilahun (Eth) 23:07, 8. Demisse Debeb (Eth) 23:11, 9. Manuel Garcia (Spa) 23:15, 10. Brahin Boutayeb Moulay (Mor) 23:19. Team: 1. Ethiopia 16, 2. Kenya 25, 3. Spain 64, 4. USA 95, 5. England 122, 6. Italy 127, 7. Hungary 197, 8. Tunisia 216, 9. France 216, 10. Wales 223... 22 nations completed teams.

WORLD MARATHON CUP
Hiroshima, Japan 13/14 April 1985
A very high standard men's race resulted in the first international success for Djibouti, both in the team race and individual, in which Ahmed Saleh missed Steve Jones's world best by just four seconds.

MEN: 1. Ahmed Saleh (Dji) 2:08:09, 2. Takeyuki Nakeyama (Jap) 2:08:15, 3. Djama Robleh (Dji) 2:09:03, 4. Michael Heilmann (GDR) 2:09:03, 5. Mekome Abede (Eth) 2:09:05, 6. Orlando Pizzolato (Ita) 2:10:23, 7. Charmarke Abdilahi (Dji) 2:10:33, 8. Takeshi Soh (Jap) 2:11:01, 9. Massimo Magnani (Ita) 2:11:02, 10. Juma Ikangaa (Tan) 2:11:06. Team: 1. Djibouti, 2. Japan, 3. Ethiopia.

WOMEN: 1. Katrin Dörre (GDR) 2:33:30, 2. Zoya Ivanova (USSR) 2:34:17, 3. Karolin Szabo (Hun) 2:34:57, 4. Laura Fogli (Ita) 2:35:45, 5. Kersti Jacobsen (Den) 2:35:57, 6. Rita Marchisio (Ita) 2:36:00, 7. Ludmilla Melicherova (Cs) 2:36:27, 8. Veronique Marot (UK) 2:37:05, 9. Eriko Asai (Jap) 2:37:19, 10. Raissa Smekhnova (USSR) 2:37:32. Team: 1. Italy, 2. USSR, 3. GDR.

Early 1985 Results

INDOOR WORLD BESTS SET IN 1985

MEN

200m:	20.52	Stefano Tilli (Ita)	21 Feb	Torino
400m:	45.60	Thomas Schönlebe (GDR)	19 Jan	Paris
	45.56	Todd Bennett (UK)	3 Mar	Athens
500m:	1:01.26	Mike Armour (USA)	13 Jan	Gainesville
	1:01.24	Willie Caldwell (USA)	9 Mar	Syracuse
50mh:	6.35	Greg Foster (USA)	27 Jan	Chicago
HJ:	2.38	Patrik Sjöberg (Swe)	22 Feb	Berlin
	2.39	Dietmar Mögenburg (GFR)	24 Feb	Koln

WOMEN

SP:	22.15	Ulf Timmermann (GDR)	16 Feb	Senftenberg
60m:	7.04	Marita Koch (GDR)	16 Feb	Senftenberg
2000m:	5:34.52	Mary Slaney (USA)	18 Jan	Los Angeles
LJ:	6.99	Heike Drechsler (GDR)	2 Feb	Senftenberg
	7.25	Galina Chistyakova (USSR)	16 Feb	Kishinev
3kmW:	12:31.57	Giulliana Salce (Ita)	6 Feb	Firenze
5kmW:	21:44.52	Giulliana Salce (Ita)	20 Feb	Torino

WORLD INDOOR GAMES

BERCY, PARIS, FRANCE 19–20 JANUARY 1985

These Games, the forerunners of intended World Indoor Championships were contested by representatives of 70 nations, each of whom had been allocated by the IAAF a number of places based on their athletics strengths.

While many top athletes took part, the overall standard in depth was rather disappointing. The Games were held at the start of the indoor season and clashed with events in North America. One world indoor best was achieved, by Thomas Schönlebe in the 400 metres.

RESULTS – MEN – First four in each event

60 Metres
1. Ben Johnson (UK) 6.62
2. Sam Graddy (USA) 6.63
3. Ronald Desruelles (Bel) 6.68
4. Lincoln Asquith (UK) 6.69

200 Metres
1. Aleksandr Yevgenyev (USSR) 20.95
2. Ade Mafe (UK) 20.96
3. Joao Batista da Silva (Bra) 21.19
4. Daniel Sangouma (Fra) 21.36

400 Metres
1. Thomas Schönlebe (GDR) 45.60

2. Todd Bennett (UK) 45.97
3. Mark Rowe (USA) 46.31
4. Amadou Dia Ba (Sen) 46.94

800 Metres
1. Coloman Trabado (Spa) 1:47.42
2. Benjamin Gonzalez 1:47.94
3. Ikem Billy (UK) 1:48.28
4. Petru Dragoescu (Rom) 1:48.34

1500 Metres
1. Mike Hillardt (Aus) 3:40.27
2. José-Luis Gonzales (Spa) 3:41.36
3. Joseph Cheshire (Ken) 3:41.38
4. Miroslaw Zerkowski (Pol) 3:42.21

3000 Metres
1. Joao Campos (Por) 7:57.63
2. Don Clary (USA) 7:57.76
3. Ivan Uvizl (Cs) 7:57.92
4. Antonio Leitao (Por) 7:58.14

60m Hurdles
1. Stéphane Caristan (Fra) 7.67
2. Javier Moracho (Spa) 7.69
3. Jonathan Ridgeon (UK) 7.70
4. Cletus Clark (USA) 7.74

Early 1985 Results

High Jump
1. Patrik Sjöberg (Swe) 2.32
2. Javier Sotomayor (Cuba) 2.30
3. Othmane Belfaa (Alg) 2.27
4. Valeriy Sereda (USSR) 2.24

Pole Vault
1. Sergey Bubka (USSR) 5.75
2. Thierry Vigneron (Fra) 5.70
3. Vasiliy Bubka (USSR) 5.60
4= Marian Kolasa (Pol) 5.50
4= Patrick Abada (Fra) 5.50

Long Jump
1. Jan Leitner (Cs) 7.96
2. Gyula Paloczi (Hun) 7.94
3. Giovanni Evangelisti (Ita) 7.88
4. Laszlo Szalma (Hun) 7.85

Triple Jump
1. Khristo Markov (Bul) 17.22
2. Lazaro Betancourt (Cuba) 17.15
3. Lazaro Balcindes (Cub) 16.83
4. Oleg Protsenko (USSR) 16.80

Shot
1. Remigius Machura (Cs) 21.22
2. Udo Beyer (GDR) 21.10
3. Janis Bojars (USSR) 19.94
4. Jozef Lacika (Cs) 19.75

5000 Metres Walk
1. Gérard Lélièvre (Fra) 19:06.22
2. Maurizio Damilano (Ita) 19:11.41
3. David Smith (Aus) 19:16.04
4. Roman Mrazek (CS) 19:39.73

WOMEN

60 Metres
1. Silke Gladisch (GDR) 7.20
2. Heather Oakes (UK) 7.21
3. Christelle Bulteau (Fra) 7.34
4. Lyudmila Kondratyeva (USSR) 7.36

200 Metres
1. Marita Koch (GDR) 23.09
2. Marie-Christine Cazier (Fra) 23.33
3. Kim Robertson (NZ) 23.69
4. Fabrienne Ficher (Fra) 23.75

400 Metres
1. Diane Dixon (USA) 53.35
2. Regine Berg (Bel) 53.81
3. Charmaine Crooks (Can) 54.08
4. Antonella Ratti (Ita) 55.30

800 Metres
1. Cristina Cojocaru (Rom) 2:04.22
2. Jane Finch (UK) 2:04.71
3. Maria Simeanu (Rom) 2:05.51
3. Nathalie Thoumas (Fra) 2:07.63

1500 Metres
1. Elly Van Hulst (Hol) 4:11.41
2. Fita Lovin (Rom) 4:11.42
3. Brit McRoberts (Can) 4:11.83
4. Natalya Artyemova (USSR) 4:14.11

3000 Metres
1. Debbie Scott (Can) 9:04.99
2. Agnese Possamai (Ita) 9:09.66
3. Patti Sue Plumer (USA) 9:12.12
4. Dianne Rodger (NZ) 9:12.68

60m Hurdles
1. Xenia Siska (Hun) 8.03
2. Laurence Elloy (Fra) 8.08
3. Anne Piquereau (Fra) 8.10
4. Stephanie Hightower (USA) 8.12

High Jump
1. Stefka Kostadinova (Bul) 1.97
2. Suzanne Lorentzon (Swe) 1.94
3. Danuta Bulkowska (Pol) 1.90
4= Silvia Costa (Cub) 1.90
4= Debbie Brill (Can) 1.90

Long Jump
1. Helga Radtke (GDR) 6.86
2. Tatyana Rodionova (USSR) 6.72
3. Niole Medvedyeyeva (USSR) 6.44
4. Lene Demsitz (Den) 6.38

Shot
1. Natalya Lissovskaya (USSR) 20.07
2. Ines Muller (GDR) 19.68
   Nuna Abashidze (USSR) 18.82
4. Li Meisu (Chn) 17.67

3000 Metres Walk
1. Giulliana Salce (Ita) 12:53.42
2. Yan Hong (Chn) 13:05.56
3. Ann Peel (Can) 13:06.97
4. Dan Vavracova (Cs) 13:29.06

535